Preface

Since the last edition was published considerable developments in case law have taken place, and the Insurance Companies Act 1982 has consolidated the Insurance Companies Acts 1974 and 1981.

The Act of 1982 forms the subject of Chapter 6, which has had to be completely re-written.

In Chapter 11 ('The Formation of a Contract for a Lloyd's Policy') *General Reinsurance Corpn v Forsakringsaktiebolaget Fennia Patria* [1983] 2 Lloyd's Rep 287, CA (reinsurance) lays down the principle that the underwriter is bound by his line subject only to the contingency that it may fall to be written down on 'closing' to some extent if the 'slip' turns out to have been overscribed.

In Chapter 13 ('Non-disclosure') *Container Transport International Inc v Oceanus Mutual Underwriting Association (Bermuda) Ltd* [1984] 1 Lloyd's Rep 476, CA (marine insurance) and *Johns v Kelly* [1986] 1 Lloyd's Rep 468 (professional indemnity insurance) consider the test for determining what is a material fact. In *Allden v Raven, The Kylie* [1983] 2 Lloyd's Rep 444 (marine insurance) it was held that there had been no waiver of the assured's duty to disclose previous convictions.

In Chapter 14 ('Misrepresentation') *Highland Insurance Co v Continental Insurance Co* (1986) Times, 6 May (reinsurance) shows what is meant by a material fact. *Irish National Insurance Co Ltd v Oman Insurance Co Ltd* [1983] 2 Lloyd's Rep 453 (reinsurance) is a decision in which a statement made by the brokers that the business was written on a 'first loss basis' and not on an 'excess of loss basis' was held to be one of opinion.

Balfour v Beaumont [1984] 1 Lloyd's Rep 272, CA (reinsurance) and *Silver Dolphin Products Ltd v Parcels and General Assurance Association Ltd* [1984] 2 Lloyd's Rep 404 (marine insurance) in Chapter 21 ('The Commencement and Duration of the Policy') establish the date when the particular policies concerned came into effect.

Chapter 24 ('The Rectification of the Policy') now contains *Mint Security Ltd v Blair* [1982] 1 Lloyd's Rep 188 (cash in transit insurance), *Excess Life Assurance Co Ltd v Firemen's Insurance Co of Newark New Jersey* [1982] 2 Lloyd's Rep 599 (fidelity insurance), *Pindos Shipping Corpn v Raven, The Mata Hari* [1983] 2 Lloyd's Rep 449 (marine insurance) and *Black King Shipping Corpn and Wayang (Panama) SA v Massie, The Litsion Pride* [1985] 1 Lloyd's Rep 437 (marine insurance).

In Chapter 28 ('The Exceptions in the Policy') *Spinney's (1948) Ltd v Royal Insurance Co Ltd* [1980] 1 Lloyd's Rep 406 (fire insurance) discusses the meaning of civil war, hostilities, rebellion and usurped power, whilst in *Athens Maritime Enterprises Corpn v Hellenic Mutual War Risks Association (Bermuda) Ltd, The Andreos Lemos* [1982] 2 Lloyd's Rep 483 (marine insurance) the word 'riot' had to be construed.

In Chapter 30 ('The Conditions of the Policy') *HTV Ltd v Lintner* [1984] 2 Lloyd's Rep 125 (entertainment risk insurance) shows whether or not a stipulation in a policy should or should not be interpreted as a condition. There are many new decisions on breach of condition: *Victor Melik & Co Ltd v Norwich Union Fire Insurance Society Ltd and Kemp* [1980] 1 Lloyd's Rep 523 (burglary insurance), *Cox v Orion Insurance Co Ltd* [1982] RTR 1 (motor insurance), *Mint Security Ltd v Blair* (supra) (cash in transit insurance), *Berliner Motor Corpn and Steiers Lawn and Sports Inc v Sun Alliance and London Insurance Ltd* [1983] 1 Lloyd's Rep 320 (products and public liability insurance), *Linden Alimak Ltd v British Engine Insurance Ltd* [1984] 1 Lloyd's Rep 416 (extraneous damage insurance), *Pioneer Concrete (UK) Ltd v National Employers Mutual General Insurance Association Ltd* [1985] 1 Lloyd's Rep 274 (public liability insurance), *Insurance Co of Africa v Scor (UK) Reinsurance Co Ltd* [1985] 1 Lloyd's Rep 312 (reinsurance), *Aluminium Wire and Cable Co Ltd v Allstate Insurance Co Ltd* [1985] 2 Lloyd's Rep 280 (public liability insurance) and *Port-Rose v Phoenix Assurance Co Ltd* (1986) Times 21 February (all risks insurance).

In Chapter 31 ('The Alteration of the Risk under the Policy') *Linden Alimak Ltd v British Engine Insurance Ltd* [1984] 1 Lloyd's Rep 416 (extraneous damage insurance) and *Hadenfayre Ltd v British National Insurance Society Ltd* [1984] 2 Lloyd's Rep 393 (contingency insurance) are the latest examples of material alterations of the risk, whereas in *Exchange Theatre Ltd v Iron Trades Mutual Insurance Co Ltd* [1984] 1 Lloyd's Rep 149, CA (fire insurance) no material alteration was proved.

In Chapter 35 ('The Construction of the Policy') *Victor Melik & Co Ltd v Norwich Union Fire Insurance Society Ltd and Kemp* (supra) (burglary insurance) illustrates the principle that the intention of the parties must prevail. *Balfour v Beaumont* [1984] 1 Lloyd's Rep 272, CA (reinsurance) shows that the grammatical meaning of the words used in the policy will be adopted. The rule that the words are to be construed in their ordinary meaning is exemplified by *Oei v Foster (formerly Crawford) and Eagle Star Insurance Co Ltd* [1982] 2 Lloyd's Rep 170 (householder's insurance) ('custody and control of house'), *Stolos Compania SA v Ajax Insurance Co Ltd, 'The Admiral C'* [1981] 1 Lloyd's Rep 9, CA (marine insurance) ('claims to be collected'), *Commonwealth Smelting Ltd v Guardian Royal Exchange Assurance Ltd* [1984] 2 Lloyd's Rep 608 (property insurance) ('explosion'), *Mint Security Ltd v Blair* (supra) (cash in transit insurance) ('pavement limit'), *Rigby v Sun Alliance and London Insurance Ltd* [1980] 1 Lloyd's Rep 359 (householder's comprehensive insurance) ('liability at law only as owner'), and *Grundy (Teddington) Ltd v Fulton* [1983] 1 Lloyd's Rep 16, CA (property insurance) ('theft'). *Rowlinson Construction Ltd v Insurance Co of North America (UK) Ltd* [1981] 1 Lloyd's Rep 332 (contractors' public liability policy) concerns the principle that the meaning of the words of the policy may be limited by the context. *Nittan (UK) Ltd v Solent Steel Fabrication Ltd trading as Sargrove Automation and Cornhill Insurance Co Ltd* [1981] 1 Lloyd's Rep 633, CA (product liability insurance) relates to the rule that the *contra proferentem* rule will be applied only where the wording of the policy is ambiguous.

Chapter 39 ('The Making of a Claim') now contains a section on the Insurance Ombudsman Bureau. *Pioneer Concrete (UK) Ltd v National Mutual General Insurance Association Ltd* [1985] 1 Lloyd's Rep 274 (public liability insurance) indicates that the notice of a claim must be made by the time prescribed by a condition in the policy, and that the insurers are entitled to rely on a breach of the condition whether or not it has caused prejudice to them.

General Principles of Insurance Law

Butterworths Insurance Library

First edition	1966
Second edition	1970
Third edition	1975
Fourth edition	1979
Fifth edition	1986

General Principles of Insurance Law

Fifth edition

E R Hardy Ivamy LLB, PhD, LLD
of the Middle Temple, Barrister,
Professor of Law in the University of London

London
Butterworths
1986

Butterworths Insurance Library

United Kingdom — Butterworth & Co (Publishers) Ltd, 88 Kingsway, LONDON WC2B 6AB and 61A North Castle Street, EDINBURGH EH2 3LJ

Australia — Butterworths Pty Ltd, SYDNEY, MELBOURNE, BRISBANE, ADELAIDE, PERTH, CANBERRA and HOBART

Canada — Butterworths. A division of Reed Inc., TORONTO and VANCOUVER

New Zealand — Butterworths of New Zealand Ltd, WELLINGTON and AUCKLAND

Singapore — Butterworth & Co (Asia) Pte Ltd, SINGAPORE

South Africa — Butterworth Publishers (Pty) Ltd, DURBAN and PRETORIA

USA — Butterworth Legal Publishers, ST PAUL, Minnesota, SEATTLE, Washington, BOSTON, Massachusetts, AUSTIN, Texas and D & S Publishers, CLEARWATER, Florida

British Library Cataloguing in Publication Data

Ivamy, E. R. Hardy
General Principles of insurance law.—
5th ed.
1. Insurance law—England
I. Title
344.206'86 KD1859

ISBN 0 406 25280 7

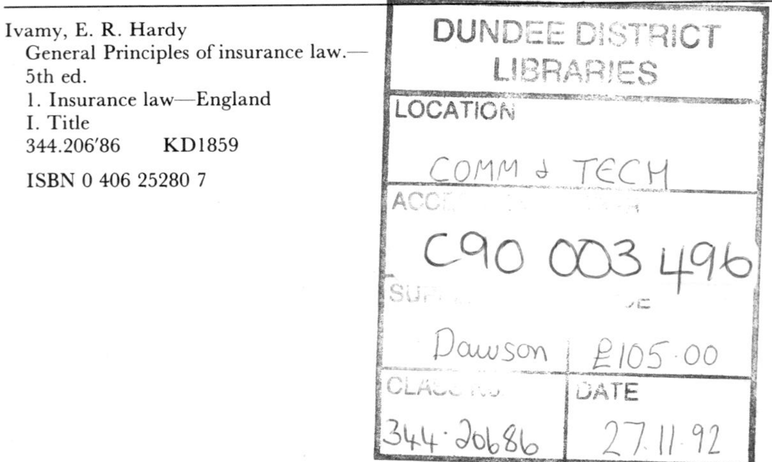

Typeset by Cotswold Typesetting Ltd, Gloucester
Printed and bound in Great Britain by Billing & Sons Ltd, Worcester

Black King Shipping Corporation and Wayang (Panama) SA v Massie, The 'Litsion Pride' [1985] 1 Lloyd's Rep 437 (marine insurance) holds that the duty not to make fraudulent claims is an implied term of the contract. The claim in *Watkins & Davis Ltd v Legal and General Assurance Co Ltd* [1981] 1 Lloyd's Rep 674 (fire insurance) was held to be fraudulent as the fire had been deliberately started by the assured. In *S & M Carpets (London) Ltd v Cornhill Insurance Co Ltd* [1982] 1 Lloyd's Rep 423, CA (fire insurance) a fire was deliberately started by the assured's managing director.

In Chapter 40 ('Burden of Proof') *Rhesa Shipping Co SA v Edmunds, The Popi M* [1985] 2 Lloyd's Rep 1, HL (marine insurance) and *Courtaulds plc and Courtaulds (Belgium) SA v Lissenden* [1986] 1 Lloyd's Rep 368 (contingency insurance) emphasise the necessity for the assured to prove a loss by a peril insured against.

In Chapter 42 ('Payment of the Loss') *Excess Life Assurance Co Ltd v Firemen's Insurance Co of Newark New Jersey* [1982] 2 Lloyd's Rep 599 (fidelity insurance) and *Avandero (UK) Ltd v National Transit Insurance Co Ltd* [1984] 2 Lloyd's Rep 613 (goods in transit insurance) are cases in which a clause in the policy imposed a limit on the amount recoverable. *Pleasurama Ltd v Sun Alliance and London Insurance Ltd* [1979] 1 Lloyd's Rep 389 (fire insurance) relates to the measure of indemnity. *National Employers Mutual General Insurance Association Ltd v Haydon* [1980] 2 Lloyd's Rep 149, CA (professional indemnity insurance) is an authority on the effect of a contribution clause.

In Chapter 45 ('Reinstatement') *Davidson v Guardian Royal Exchange Assurance* [1979] 1 Lloyd's Rep 406 (motor insurance) is a case on the effect of the insurers' election to reinstate.

To Chapter 46 ('Subrogation') have been added *Mark Rowlands Ltd v Berni Inns Ltd* [1985] 2 Lloyd's Rep 437, CA (fire insurance) and *MH Smith (Plant Hire) Ltd v Mainwaring (trading as Inshore)* (1986) Times, 10 June (marine insurance).

Chapter 50 ('The Relationship between the Principal and the Agent') now includes *Woolcott v Excess Insurance Co Ltd and Miles, Smith, Anderson and Game Ltd (No 2)* [1979] 2 Lloyd's Rep 210 (fire insurance), *Commonwealth Insurance Co of Vancouver v Groupe Sprinks SA, Compagnie Française d'Assurances Européenes, J H Minet & Co and C E Heath & Co (Marine) Ltd* [1983] 1 Lloyd's Rep 67 (reinsurance), and *Dunbar v A and B Painters Ltd and Economic Insurance Co Ltd and Whitehouse & Co* [1985] 2 Lloyd's Rep 616 (employers' liability insurance) with regard to the duty of an insurance broker to show proper skill.

In Chapter 54 ('Registration of Insurance Brokers') *Pickles v Insurance Brokers Registration Council* [1984] 1 All ER 1073 is the latest case on the Insurance Brokers (Registration) Act 1977.

In Chapter 55 ('Conflict of Laws') *Amin Rasheed Shipping Corpn v Kuwait Insurance Co Ltd* [1983] 2 Lloyd's Rep 365, HL (marine insurance) shows how the 'proper law' of the policy is found.

Chapter 58 ('Compulsory Insurance') is a new Chapter.

I should like to thank the staff of Butterworths for undertaking the arduous job of preparing the Index and the Tables of Cases and Statutes and for seeing the book through the press.

University College London
July 1986

E R HARDY IVAMY

Contents

PART V—THE SETTLEMENT OF THE CLAIM

PART VII—MISCELLANEOUS

Table of statutes

Page references printed in **bold** type indicate where the section of the Act is set out in part or in full.

Table of cases

PAGE

A

B

D

PAGE

E

F

H

J

K

L

M

N

O

Q

PAGE

R

S

U

X

Y

Z

PART I

Introductory

CHAPTER 1

The definition of insurance

A contract of insurance in the widest sense of the term may be defined as a contract[1] whereby one person, called the 'Insurer', undertakes, in return for the agreed consideration, called the 'Premium', to pay to another person, called the 'Assured', a sum of money, or its equivalent, on the happening of a specified event.[2]

The specified event must have some element of uncertainty about it;[3] the uncertainty may be either (*a*) as in the case of life insurance, in the fact that, although the event is bound to happen in the ordinary course of nature, the time

---

1 An agreement binding in honour only is not enforceable: *Home Insurance Co and St Paul Fire and Marine Insurance Co v Administratia Asigurarilor de Stat* [1983] 2 Lloyd's Rep 674 (reinsurance), where a clause in a reinsurance treaty stated: 'Arbitration . . . The award of the arbitrators or the umpire shall be final and binding upon all parties without appeal. This treaty shall be interpreted as an honourable engagement rather than as a legal obligation and the award shall be made with a view to effecting the general purpose of this treaty rather than in accordance with a literal interpretation of its language . . .', and it was held that, on the true construction of the agreement it was the parties' intention that there should be an enforceable obligation to arbitrate and abide by the award. All that was intended by the clause was to free the arbitrators to some extent from strict rules, and that was permissible. (See the judgment of Parker J, ibid, at 677.) As to reinsurance treaties, see Ivamy, *Personal Accident, Life and Other Insurances* (2nd Edn 1980) pp 326–329.

2 *Prudential Insurance Co v IRC* [1904] 2 KB 658 at 663 (life insurance) per Channell J 'Where you insure a ship or a house, you cannot insure that the ship shall not be lost or the house burned, but what you do insure is that a sum of money shall be paid on the happening of a certain event. That I think is the first requirement in a contract of insurance. It must be a contract whereby, for some consideration, usually, but not necessarily, for periodical payment called premiums, you secure to yourself some benefit, usually, but not necessarily the payment of a sum of money upon the happening of some event'; *Department of Trade and Industry v St Christopher Motorists Association Ltd* [1974] 1 All ER 395, [1974] 1 WLR 99 where it was held that a contract to provide a motorist, who was disqualified or prevented by injury from driving, with a chauffeur was a contract of insurance. (See the judgment of Templeman J, ibid, at 400–401); *Medical Defence Union Ltd v Department of Trade* [1980] Ch 82, [1979] 2 All ER 421 where it was held that the right of a member of the Medical Defence Union, on a claim being made against him, to have his application for help with that claim considered by the Union did not suffice to constitute the contract between him and the Union a contract of insurance, for it was merely a right to a benefit other than money or money's worth. In that case Megarry V-C said (ibid, at 429); 'I am quite unable to see any justification for replacing "money" or its equivalent by "benefit" as a constituent part of the definition of a contract of insurance. I can see nothing in the authorities which gives any real support for so wide and extensive a generalisation, especially as the term "money or money's worth" seems to be adequate for all normal circumstances. It may be that in view of *Department of Trade and Industry v St Christopher Motorists Association Ltd* (supra) some further addition should be made so as to cover explicitly the provision of services.'

3 *Prudential Insurance Co v IRC* (supra), per Channell J, at 663: 'Then the next thing that is necessary is that the event should be one which involves some amount of uncertainty. There must be either some uncertainty whether the event will ever happen or not, or if the event is one which must happen at some time or another, there must be uncertainty as to the time at which it will happen.'

of its happening is uncertain; or (*b*) in the fact that the happening of the event depends upon accidental causes, and the event, therefore, may never happen at all. In the latter case, the event is called an 'accident'.

The specified event must further be of a character more or less adverse to the interest of the assured, or in other words, the accident must be calculated, if it happens, to result in loss to the assured.[4]

Where the payment of the money or other benefit is discretionary and not obligatory, the contract is not one of insurance.[5]

---

4 Ibid, per Channell J, at 664: 'A contract of insurance then must be a contract for the payment of a sum of money, or for some corresponding benefit such as the rebuilding of a house or the repairing of a ship, to become due on the happening of an event, which event must have some amount of uncertainty about it, and must be of a character more or less adverse to the interest of the person effecting the insurance.' But this statement has been criticised in *Gould v Curtis* [1913] 3 KB 84 (life insurance) per Buckley LJ, at 95, where he pointed out that whilst it is true of fire and marine insurance, it is not necessarily so in the case of life insurance, particularly if the life policy also contains endowment provisions. *Scottish Amicable Heritable Securities Association Ltd v Northern Assurance Co* 1883 11 R (Ct of Sess) 287, per Lord Justice Clerk (Moncrieff), at 303: 'It is a contract belonging to a very ordinary class by which the insurer undertakes, in consideration of the payment of an estimated equivalent beforehand, to make up to the assured any loss he may sustain by the occurrence of an uncertain contingency. It is a direct, not an accessory obligation like that of a surety, and is fulfilled and terminated by payment of the loss.' See also *Law v London Indisputable Life Policy Co* (1855) 1 K & J 223 (life insurance) per Wood V-C, at 228; *Daff v Midland Colliery Owners' Mutual Indemnity Co* (1913) 6 BWCC 799, HL (employer's liability insurance) per Lord Moulton, at 820.

5 *Medical Defence Union Ltd v Department of Trade* [1980] Ch 82, [1979] 2 All ER 421, where a member of the Union against whom a claim had been made could merely require the Union to consider whether to conduct the proceedings on his behalf and whether to provide him with an indemnity, and had no right to require the Union to assist him in this way, and it was held that the contract was not a contract of insurance; *C V G Siderurficia del Orinoco SA v London SS Owners Mutual Insurance Association Ltd: The Vainqueur José* [1979] 1 Lloyd's Rep 557 (marine insurance), where a shipowner who was insured with a mutual insurance association merely had the possibility of an ex gratia payment in respect of forwarding expenses, but not a right to payment. (See the judgment of Mocatta J, ibid, at 580). As to mutual insurance associations, see Ivamy, *Marine Insurance* (4th Edn 1985), pp 475–479.

CHAPTER 2

The parties to the contract

The parties to a contract of insurance are the 'Assured' (or 'Insured') and the 'Insurers'.

1 The assured (or insured)

Any person who is capable of contracting may be the assured under a contract of insurance. Thus, a minor may enter into a contract of insurance if it is for his benefit;[1] otherwise, the contract will not be binding upon him.[2] Similarly, a contract of insurance made by a person of unsound mind or drunken person is, in certain circumstances, voidable.[3]

2 The insurers

Two classes of persons carry on insurance business, insurance companies[4] and underwriters.

(a) Insurance companies

The power of an insurance company to enter into insurances of any particular kind depends upon the terms of its memorandum of association or other instrument constituting it.[5]

---

1 *Clements v London and North Western Rly Co* [1894] 2 QB 482, CA.

2 *Imperial Life Insurance Co v Charlebois* (1902) 22 CLT 417 (life insurance), where a minor whose health was not good insured his life for a large sum at a premium which absorbed nearly the whole of his income, and it was held that he was entitled to avoid the policy.

3 *Imperial Life Assurance of Canada v Audett* (1912) 20 WLR 372 (life insurance), where a proposal form signed when the proposed assured was drunk, to the knowledge of the insurers' agent, was held not to be binding.

4 An association of more than 20 members (other than solicitors, accountants or members of a stock exchange) formed for the purpose of carrying on business, having for its object the acquisition of gain, is unlawful, unless incorporated: Companies Act 1985, s 716(1), (2). The Secretary of State may by regulations in a statutory instrument provide that subs 1 is not to apply to the formation, for a purpose specified in the regulations, of a partnership of a description so specified: ibid, s 716(3). See *Great Britain 100 A1 SS Insurance Association v Wyllie* (1889) 22 QBD 710, CA (marine insurance), approving *Ocean Iron SS Insurance Association Ltd v Leslie* (1887) 22 QBD 722n (marine insurance) and distinguishing *United Kingdom Mutual SS Assurance Association Ltd v Nevill* (1887) 19 QBD 110, CA (marine insurance). If, however, there is no association for the purpose of carrying on business, and all that is done is that certain persons receive subscriptions out of which they pay certain benefits and at the end of the year distribute the balance among the members, the association is not illegal: *Re One and All Sickness and Accident Assurance Association* (1909) 25 TLR 674.

5 The memorandum of association may be altered: Companies Act 1985, s 4, *Re National Boiler Insurance Co* [1892] 1 Ch 306. See generally R R Pennington, *Company Law* (5th Edn), pp 78–84.

Any insurance policy not authorised by the terms of its memorandum is *ultra vires* and cannot be enforced by the company against the assured.[6]

But the assured, provided that he has acted in good faith, can enforce an *ultra vires* insurance policy against the company in a case where the issue of the policy was decided on by the directors.[7] It is presumed that the assured has acted in good faith unless the contrary is proved.[8]

Where it is proved that the assured has not acted in good faith, he cannot claim the sum payable under the policy,[9] though he may be entitled to a return of premium.

When the memorandum specifies the kinds of insurance to be undertaken[10] or expressly prohibits certain kinds of insurance business,[11] insurances falling outside the specified kinds or within the prohibited kinds, as the case may be, are clearly *ultra vires* and void.

Where, however, the memorandum is framed in general terms, sufficiently wide to include the insurance in question, such insurance is not to be regarded as invalid because the company has not previously effected insurances of the particular kind, but has confined its business to insurances belonging to a different kind;[12] and the company, though it has previously restricted itself to life insurance, may issue policies of fire insurance or fidelity insurance.[13]

(b) Underwriters

In the case of an underwriter, such as an underwriting member of Lloyd's, the question of incapacity to enter into a contract belonging to a particular kind of insurance does not arise.

Since, however, it is the practice for a Lloyd's policy to be underwritten by one underwriter on behalf of a group of underwriters who are known as his 'names', the authority of the underwriter who actually signs the policy, to bind the 'names' by underwriting a policy of that kind, is a material element to be taken into consideration.[14]

---

6 *Joseph v Law Integrity Insurance Co Ltd* [1912] 2 Ch 581, CA (life insurance), following *Flood v Irish Provident Assurance Co Ltd and Hibernian Bank Ltd* [1912] 2 Ch 597n (life insurance).

7 Companies Act 1985, s 35(1). See generally Pennington, op cit, pp 113–115.

8 Companies Act 1985, s 35(2).

9 *Re Phoenix Life Assurance Co, Burgess and Stock's Case* (1862) 2 John & H 441 (marine insurance), where a life insurance company had issued marine policies.

10 See *Maunsell v Midland Great Western (Ireland) Rly Co* (1863) 1 Hem & M 130 (company) per Wood V-C, at 148.

11 *Joseph v Law Integrity Insurance Co Ltd* (supra); *Flood v Irish Provident Assurance Co Ltd and Hibernian Bank Ltd* (supra).

12 *Re Norwich Provident Insurance Society, Bath's Case* (1878) 8 ChD 334, CA (fire insurance), where the deed of settlement of a life insurance company referred to insurances 'against all and every kind of risk special and general, which may be effected according to law'.

13 Ibid, per Jessel, MR, at 341.

14 *Hambro v Burnand* [1904] 2 KB 10 CA; cf *Anglo-Californian Bank Ltd v London and Provincial Marine and General Insurance Co Ltd* (1904) 10 Com Cas 1.

CHAPTER 3

Classification of contracts of insurance

Contracts of insurance may be classified in three different ways:

1 According to the nature of the event on which the sum insured becomes payable.
2 According to the nature of the interest affected.
3 According to the nature of the insurance.

1 According to the nature of the event

Four main classes of insurance are to be distinguished:

a *Marine Insurance*—in which the sum insured becomes payable on the happening of a marine peril.
b *Fire Insurance*—in which the sum insured becomes payable on the happening of a fire.
c *Life Insurance*—in which the sum insured becomes payable on death.
d *Accident Insurance*[1]—in which the sum insured becomes payable on the happening of any other event.

The distinction between the various kinds of insurance recognised in ordinary practice and designated by separate names is largely conventional. Both the scope and the name of any particular kind of insurance may vary according to the practice of different insurers. The distinction is not necessarily due to any legal difference between particular kinds of insurance. It may arise from the varying needs of the public which it is advisable for insurers, as a matter of business, to attempt to meet. It may be convenient to offer protection against a particular peril; hence, burglary insurance is distinguished from fire insurance. In other cases, it may be convenient to offer protection in respect of a particular kind of property against the dangers to which it is specially exposed, e g in the case of livestock insurance or licence insurance; or against all the consequences entailed upon its owner by virtue of his ownership, e g in the case of motor insurance.

2 According to the nature of the interest affected

The different classes of insurance are distinguished according to the manner in which the assured is prejudiced by the happening of the specified event. He may

---

1 This term is used for convenience only. It is intended to comprehend insurances against personal accident, against accidental loss of, or damage to, property, and against liability for accident.

die or suffer personal injury, his property may be lost or damaged, or he may be involved in liability.

(a) Personal insurance

In this type of insurance the specified event operates on the person of the assured or on that of a third party. This class of insurance comprises life insurance, personal accident insurance, and sickness insurance.

(b) Property insurance

In this type of insurance the specified event operates on the property of the assured. It comprises marine insurance, fire insurance, burglary insurance, fidelity insurance, solvency insurance, and insurance against loss of property by other accidental causes, e g plate glass insurance, livestock insurance, licence insurance, and insurance against war risks.

(c) Liability insurance

Here, the specified event imposes upon the assured a liability towards third persons. This class comprises the following:

- i Public liability insurance, e g insurance in respect of liabilities connected with particular buildings, motor vehicles, or machinery.
- ii Employers' liability insurance.

The same policy may combine several insurances belonging to different classes. The combination may be based simply upon convenience, e g in the case of a householder's comprehensive policy which combines insurances against fire and burglary with an insurance against employer's liability. In other cases, the combination is necessary if the assured is to be fully protected, seeing that it is possible for the same event to affect his interests in more ways than one. Thus, a motor accident may cause damage to the vehicle and personal injury to its owner, and may at the same time involve him in liability to third persons. A boiler explosion may destroy the boiler and wreck the building containing it. It may cause death or injury to workmen in the employment of its owner, and may, in addition, damage adjoining buildings and injure members of the public. Hence, a motor policy or a steam-boiler policy is usually framed to apply to all or most of the cases mentioned.

3 According to the nature of the insurance

Some contracts of insurance merely secure the payment of money on the happening of the specified event. Other types of contract, however, are contracts of indemnity.

(a) Where the contract is not one of indemnity

In this class of insurance the amount recoverable is not measured by the extent of the assured's loss, but is payable whenever the specified event happens, irrespective of whether the assured in fact sustains a pecuniary loss or not.[2] Thus, contracts of life insurance,[3] personal accident insurance[4] and sickness insurance are not contracts of indemnity.

(b) Contracts of indemnity

In this class of insurance the amount recoverable is measured by the extent of the assured's pecuniary loss. It includes all contracts of insurance except life insurance, personal accident insurance and sickness insurance.

Thus, the contract of marine insurance is an example of this type. The Marine Insurance Act 1906, s 1, provides:

> 'A contract of marine insurance is a contract whereby the insurer undertakes to indemnify the assured, in manner and to the extent thereby agreed, against marine losses, that is to say, the losses incident to marine adventure.'

So also is a policy of fire insurance.[5]

Even where by the terms of the contract, as is usually the case, the insurers expressly undertake, in the event of loss or damage by fire to the property insured, to pay or make good the loss or damage up to a specified sum, the contract is nevertheless one of indemnity,[6] and of indemnity only.[7]

A contract of insurance, which is otherwise a contract of indemnity, does not cease to be a contract of indemnity because it is contained in a 'valued' policy, providing for payment of a specified sum on the happening of the event.[8] The effect of the valuation is to dispense with proof of the extent of the loss. The assured must still prove that he has, in fact, sustained a loss.

Where an action is brought against an insurer for wrongful repudiation of an indemnity insurance policy, the action sounds in unliquidated damages rather than in debt.[9] The measure of damages is the loss actually suffered by the

---

[2] *Dalby v India and London Life Assurance Co* (1854) 15 CB 365 (life insurance) per Parke B, at 387; *Law v London Indisputable Life Policy Co* (1855) 1 K & J 223 (life insurance); *Gould v Curtis* [1913] 3 KB 84, CA (life insurance) per Buckley LJ, at 95.

[3] *Dalby v India and London Life Assurance Co* (supra).

[4] *Theobald v Railway Passengers Assurance Co* (1854) 10 Exch 45 (personal accident insurance) per Alderson B, at 53.

[5] *North British and Mercantile Insurance Co v London, Liverpool and Globe Insurance Co* (1877) 5 ChD 569, CA (fire insurance).

[6] *Dane v Mortgage Insurance Corpn Ltd* [1894] 1 QB 54, CA (insurance of securities) per Lord Esher MR, at 61: 'By the law of insurance, though the underwriter directly promises to pay on a certain event, the contract is treated as one of indemnity.'

[7] *Dalby v India and London Life Assurance Co* (1854) 15 CB 365 (life insurance) per Parke B, at 387: 'Policies of assurance against fire and against marine risks are both properly contracts of indemnity, the insurer engaging to make good, within certain limited amounts, the losses sustained by the assured in their buildings, ships, and effects.'; *Castellain v Preston* (1883) 11 QBD 380, CA (fire insurance) per Brett LJ, at 386: 'The very foundation, in my opinion, of every rule which has been applied to insurance law is this, namely, that the contract of insurance contained in a marine or fire policy is a contract of indemnity, and of indemnity only.' See also *Darrell v Tibbitts* (1880) 5 QBD 560, CA (fire insurance); *Chapman v Pole* (1870) 22 LT 306 (fire insurance); *West of England Fire Insurance Co v Isaacs* [1897] 1 QB 226, CA (fire insurance); *Britton v Royal Insurance Co* (1886) 4 F & F 905 (fire insurance) per Willes J, at 908; *Mason v Sainsbury* (1782), 3 Doug KB 61 (fire insurance) per Lord Mansfield, at 64; *London Assurance Co v Sainsbury* (1783) 3 Doug KB 245 (fire insurance) per Lord Mansfield, at 253.

[8] As to 'valued' policies, see pp 212–213, post.

[9] *Jabbour v Custodian of Israeli Absentee Property* [1954] 1 WLR 139, at 143 et seq, and the cases there cited.

insured in so far as it is not too remote. In the majority of cases the only loss suffered is that the insurer failed to pay the sum due and the result is the same as if the claim had been in debt.[10] But sometimes the loss is greater, e g where the insured incurs costs in defending an action brought against him by a third party, and such costs would not have been incurred if the insurer had not repudiated liability under the policy.[11]

10 *Forney v Dominion Insurance Co Ltd* [1969] 3 All ER 831, [1969] 1 Lloyd's Rep 502 (solicitor's indemnity insurance) per Donaldson J, at 509.

11 Ibid.

CHAPTER 4

The nature of the contract of insurance

In considering the nature of the contract of insurance it is necessary to distinguish between the subject-matter of the contract of insurance and the subject-matter of insurance. In all contracts of insurance the subject-matter must be adequately described.

A THE SUBJECT-MATTER OF THE CONTRACT OF INSURANCE

The protection given by a contract of insurance is not a protection against accident in that the contract can prevent an accident from happening. It merely secures for the assured, when the accident happens, the payment of a sum of money.[1] The subject-matter of the contract of insurance is, therefore, money, and it must be distinguished from the subject-matter of insurance, which exists independently of the contract.

Thus, in the words of Brett LJ:

> 'Now, in my judgment, the subject-matter of the contract of insurance is money, and money only. The subject-matter of insurance is a different thing from the subject-matter of the contract of insurance . . . The only result in the policy, if an accident which is within the insurance happens, is a payment of money. It is true that under certain circumstances in a fire policy there may be an option to spend the money in rebuilding the premises, but that does not alter the fact that the only liability of the insurance company is to pay money.'[2]

Similarly, in another case Bowen LJ, said:

> 'What is it that is insured in a fire policy? Not the bricks and the materials used in building the house, but the interest of the assured in the subject-matter of insurance.'[3]

B THE SUBJECT-MATTER OF INSURANCE

A contract of insurance necessarily contemplates the existence of something to which an accident may happen, and anything, to which an accident may happen, may, therefore, be the subject-matter of insurance. Strictly speaking, an accident can only happen to a physical object. There are, however, certain kinds of insurance intended to protect the assured in cases where he requires

---

1 *Prudential Insurance Co v IRC* [1904] 2 KB 658 (life insurance) per Channell J, at 663.

2 *Rayner v Preston* (1881) 18 ChD 1 at 9, CA (fire insurance).

3 *Castellain v Preston* (1883) 11 QBD 380 at 397, CA (fire insurance).

protection not against accidents to physical objects, but against the consequences to himself of such accidents. In these kinds of insurance, the interest of the assured which will be adversely affected by the happening of the accident insured against, and not the physical object to which the accident actually happens, is to be regarded as the subject-matter of insurance.

The subject-matter of insurance may be one or other of the following:

1 A physical object.
2 A chose-in-action.
3 A liability imposed on the assured.

1 A physical object

Thus, the subject-matter of insurance in personal accident insurance is the body of the assured. In burglary insurance it is the property exposed to the peril.[4] Similarly, in fire insurance the building insured is the subject-matter of insurance.

The insurance of certain kinds of property, however, may be void on the ground of public policy,[5] e g an insurance on enemy property.[6]

2 A chose-in-action

In solvency insurance, in which the assured insures against the non-payment of a debt, the debt or chose-in-action, against the loss of which the assured seeks to protect himself, appears to be the subject-matter of insurance. The subject-matter of insurance cannot be the property of the debtor, since, in the absence of a charge, a creditor, as such, has no insurable interest in the property of his debtor and therefore cannot insure it.[7]

The same principle applies to licence insurance and patent insurance, in which the assured insures against the loss of a licence or the invalidity of a patent. In these cases, the subject-matter of insurance is the monopoly, and not the physical object or class of objects to which the monopoly attaches.

3 A liability imposed on the assured

In liability insurance, in which the assured insures against liability to third parties arising otherwise than from contract, the liability insured against is the real subject-matter of insurance. The assured has no direct interest in the safety of third persons or in the preservation of their property from harm. The loss against which he seeks protection is not the injury or damage caused by the

---

4 But in *Re George and Goldsmiths and General Burglary Insurance Association Ltd* [1899] 1 QB 595, CA (burglary insurance) Lord Russell CJ, at 601, referred to the perils insured against as the subject-matter of the insurance. See also *Maurice v Goldsbrough Mort & Co Ltd* [1939] AC 452, [1939] 3 All ER 63, PC per Lord Wright, at 460.

5 *King v Glover* (1806) 2 Bos & P NR 206 (marine insurance) per Rooke J, at 209.

6 *Janson v Driefontein Consolidated Mines Ltd* [1902] AC 484 (marine insurance) per Lord Davey, at 499. But an insurance on goods purchased from an alien enemy (*Bell v Gilson* (1798) 1 Bos & P 345 (marine insurance) or purchased with the proceeds of a robbery (*Bird v Appleton* (1800) 8 Term Rep 562 (marine insurance) per Lawrence J, at 569) is not invalid.

7 *Wolff v Horncastle* (1798) 1 Bos & P 316 (marine insurance) per Buller J, at 323; *Macaura v Northern Assurance Co Ltd* [1925] AC 619 at 626 (fire insurance), approving *Moran, Galloway & Co v Uzielli* [1905] 2 KB 555 (marine insurance) per Walton J, at 560.

accident. It is the consequence of the fact that he happens to be responsible for the accident in the circumstances in which it takes place.

C THE DESCRIPTION OF THE SUBJECT-MATTER

A description of the subject-matter of insurance is necessary for three purposes:

1 To identify the subject-matter.
2 To show the nature of the risk.
3 To define the risk.

1 To identify the subject-matter

A description of the subject-matter of insurance necessarily forms part of every policy,[8] and this description must be framed in terms sufficiently adequate to enable the subject-matter to be identified with precision.[9]

If the subject-matter does not answer the description at all, an action on the policy would clearly fail, since the assured will be unable to show that the subject-matter in respect of which he has suffered loss is the subject-matter which is, in fact, insured by the policy. Thus, Blackburn J, said in a case concerning marine insurance:[10]

> 'A description of the subject-matter of the insurance is required both from the nature of the contract and from the universal practice of insurers . . . If no property which answers the description in the policy be at risk, the policy will not attach, though the assured may have other property at risk of equal or greater value. The reason being that the assurers have not entered into a contract to indemnify the assured from any loss on that property.'

If, on the other hand, the subject-matter answers the description, but the description is ambiguous, being equally capable of being applied to a different subject-matter, the policy may be void for uncertainty.

The kinds of description

There are two kinds of description:

a specific descriptions.
b general descriptions.

(a) Specific descriptions

The description of the subject-matter of insurance may be expressed in terms so specific as to be capable of being applied only to one particular object.[11] In this case, there is one possible subject-matter to which the accident insured against can happen, i e the actual object described in the policy, and the assured must,

---

8 *Griffiths v Bramley-Moore* (1878) 4 QBD 70, CA (marine insurance) per Brett LJ, at 73.

9 *Palmer v Pratt* (1824) 2 Bing 185 (marine insurance), where a policy on 'bills of exchange' was held not to cover conditional orders for payment.

10 *Mackenzie v Whitworth* (1875) 1 ExD 36, CA (marine insurance), at 40. See also *Joel v Harvey* (1857) 5 WR 488 (fire insurance).

11 *Gorman v Hand-in-Hand Insurance Co* (1877) IR 11 CL 224 (fire insurance), where two ricks of hay were specifically insured.

therefore, before he can recover, prove the identity of the object to which the accident has happened with the object described in the policy.[12]

For this purpose he must show that the object to which the accident has happened answers the description in the policy. An object which does not answer the description is not within the terms of the policy. It is immaterial that it is, in fact, the object which the assured intended to insure. Thus, an insurance company has been held not liable where the pedigree of the horse insured was wrongly described,[13] where a policy insuring a warehouse failed to include the machinery situated in it although the assured intended to insure it,[14] and also where a factory at New Southgate was described as being at Newington Green.[15] The fact that the object which did answer the description has been replaced by the object to which the accident has happened is also immaterial.[16]

(b) General descriptions

The description of the subject-matter may be framed in general terms capable of being applied to any object belonging to a particular class. In this case the subject-matter of insurance is the class designated by the description.

The question of identity, therefore, only affects the class, and, so far as the object to which the accident has happened is concerned, it is sufficient to show that it belongs to a class which answers the description.[17] Hence, it is not necessary to establish a specific intention to insure the particular object, since the policy is intended to apply to any object belonging to the class. If the terms of the policy permit,[18] the assured may recover, although the object to which the accident happens was not in his possession or even in existence at the date of the policy.

Thus, where 'stock-in-trade' is insured against burglary, the assured must prove that the articles stolen formed part of his stock-in-trade.[19] He need not, however, show that they formed part of his stock-in-trade at the time of insuring.[20] The insurance is not an insurance on the articles which constitute

---

12 *Palmer v Pratt* (1824) 2 Bing 185 (marine insurance); cf *Newcastle Fire Insurance Co v Macmorran & Co* (1815) 3 Dow 255, HL (fire insurance).

13 *Yorkshire Insurance Co v Campbell* [1917] AC 218, PC (marine insurance).

14 *Hare v Barstow* (1844) 8 Jur 928 (fire insurance).

15 *Grover and Grover Ltd v Mathews* [1910] 2 KB 401 (fire insurance).

16 *Law Guarantee Trust and Accident Society Ltd v Munich Reinsurance Co* (1915) 31 TLR 572, where a mortgage which replaced the insured mortgage was held not to be covered, since, though the mortgagees and the mortgaged property were the same, the mortgagors were different; *Gorman v Hand-in-Hand Insurance Co* (1877) IR 11 CL 224 (fire insurance); cf *Rogerson v Scottish Automobile and General Insurance Co Ltd* (1931) 48 TLR 17, HL, where the policy was held not to apply to a new car of similar make.

17 *Gorman v Hand-in-Hand Insurance Co* (supra) per Palles CB, at 235: 'I assume that it was within the contemplation of both parties that farmers must from year to year consume portions of their then present stock of hay and replace it with the produce of later years. These considerations would, in my mind, be most coercive to lead to construe the words describing the hay as pointing to hay which should from time to time answer the description in the policy, provided they were susceptible of that construction.' See also *Hill v Patten* (1807) 8 East 373 (marine insurance) per Lord Ellenborough CJ, at 377; *Tobin v Harford* (1864) 17 CBNS 528, ExCh (marine insurance) per Blackburn J, at 537.

18 In *Gorman v Hand-in-Hand Insurance Co* (supra) (fire insurance) the terms of the policy were specific to apply to any risks except those existing at the time when the insurance was effected.

19 *Watchorn v Langford* (1813) 3 Camp 422 (fire insurance); *Joel v Harvey* (1857) 5 WR 488 (fire insurance).

20 *Gorman v Hand-in-Hand Insurance Co* (1877) IR 11 CL 224 (fire insurance) per Palles CB, at 58.

the stock-in-trade at any particular date, but is an insurance on a fluctuating class.[1] The substitution, therefore, of other articles for those disposed of in the ordinary course of dealing with stock-in-trade or the acquisition of additional articles does not affect the identity of the class.

On the other hand, objects which do not belong to the class described are not within the policy, since they do not fall within the description of the subject-matter. Thus, 'stock-in-trade' does not include a stock of linen drapery, if the assured is not a linen draper.[2] Similarly, 'fixtures' do not include furniture, nor does the term 'goods' include wearing apparel[3] or personal effects.[4]

I DESCRIPTION OF THE LOCALITY OF THE SUBJECT-MATTER

The description of the subject-matter, whether expressed in general[5] or specific[6] terms, may include a statement as to locality. Where the insurance is connected with a building, such a statement is a necessary part of the description for the purpose of identification. The building must be in the described locality if an accident happening there is to be covered.[7]

In other cases a statement as to locality is not essential. But, if it is included in the description, the accident must take place in the described locality.

Thus, if a personal accident insurance is limited to the United Kingdom, the accident must take place in the United Kingdom.[8] Further, if goods are described as being on certain premises, they are not covered elsewhere.[9] Similarly, a policy against liability for accidents to third persons caused by the negligence of the assured's workmen whilst at work at a particular place applies to accidents happening at that place only.[10] In accordance with the same

1 *Joel v Harvey* (supra) per Crompton J, at 489.

2 *Watchorn v Langford* (supra) (fire insurance). If the stock-in-trade is expressed to be of a particular kind, it does not include stock-in-trade of a different kind: *Joel v Harvey* (supra) (fire insurance), where an insurance on 'stock-in-trade, consisting of corn, seed, hay, straw, fixtures and utensils in business', did not cover other articles such as crops, or malting, though equally forming part of the assured's stock-in-trade.

3 *Ross v Thwaites* (1776) Park's Marine Insces, 8th ed, p 23 (marine insurance).

4 *Brown v Stapyleton* (1827) 4 Bing 119 (marine insurance).

5 *Gorman v Hand-in-Hand Insurance Co* (1877) IR 11 CL 224 (fire insurance).

6 *Pearson v Commercial Union Assurance Co* (1876) 1 App Cas 498 (fire insurance).

7 *Grover and Grover Ltd v Mathews* (1910) 15 Com Cas 249, at 260 (fire insurance) per Hamilton J.

8 *Stoneham v Ocean Railway and General Accident Insurance Co* (1887) 19 QBD 237.

9 *Re Calf and Sun Insurance Office* [1920] 2 KB 366, CA, per Younger LJ, at 385; *Pasquali & Co v Traders' and General Insurance Association Ltd* (1921) 9 LlL Rep 514, where the goods insured were placed in a warehouse outside the specified locality; *Dia v County Fire Office* (1930) 37 LlL Rep 24, where the place from which the insured property was stolen was not the assured's 'private dwelling-house'; *Bonney v Cornhill Insurance Co Ltd* (1931) 40 LlL Rep 39, where the opinion was expressed that a motor vehicle insured for use in London and Wales would not be covered on journeys between London and Wales; *Pearson v Commercial Union Assurance Co* (1876) 1 App Cas 498 (fire insurance); cf *Australian Agricultural Co v Saunders* (1875) LR 10 CP 668, ExCh (fire insurance) per Bramwell B, at 675; *Lilley v Doubleday* (1881) 7 QBD 510 (agency), where the plaintiff had lost the benefit of his fire insurance by reason of the defendant placing his goods in a different warehouse; *Allom v Property Insurance* (1911) Times, 10 February (fire insurance), where the goods were described as being in a stone and brick building; *Gorman v Hand-in-Hand Insurance Co* (supra), where the policy was held to cover horses and agricultural implements only whilst in the specified locality.

10 *Smellie v British General Insurance Co* [1918] WC & Ins Rep 233; cf *Pigott v Employers' Liability Assurance Corpn* (1900) 31 OR 666.

principle, goods insured in transit 'per land conveyance until on board' are not covered whilst in barges.[11] An insurance on securities in transit 'between houses or places' contemplates a transit between different houses or places, and does not cover a mere removal from one room to another in the same building.[12]

II DESCRIPTION OF OTHER CIRCUMSTANCES

The description of the subject-matter may further include statements relating to other circumstances, e g the business carried on by the assured,[13] or the use which is made of the insured property.[14] These statements may be necessary for the purpose of identification; more usually they serve to define the risk.

---

11 *Ewing & Co v Sicklemore* (1918) 35 TLR 55.

12 *Pennsylvania Co for Insurances on Lives and Granting Annuities v Mumford* [1920] 2 KB 537, 2 LlL Rep 351, CA; cf *Baring Bros & Co v Marine Insurance Co* (1894) 10 TLR 276, CA.

13 *Biggar v Rock Life Assurance Co* [1902] 1 KB 516; *Holdsworth v Lancashire and Yorkshire Insurance Co* (1907) 23 TLR 521; cf *Wembley UDC v Poor Law and Local Government Officers' Mutual Guarantee Association Ltd* (1901) 17 TLR 516; *Cosford Union v Poor Law and Local Government Officers' Mutual Guarantee Association Ltd* (1910) 103 LT 463.

14 *Farr v Motor Traders' Mutual Insurance Society* [1920] 3 KB 669, CA, followed in *Roberts v Anglo-Saxon Insurance Association* (1927) 137 LT 243; *Murray v Scottish Automobile and General Insurance Co Ltd* [1929] WC & Ins Rep 73; *Pailor v Co-operative Insurance Society* (1930) 38 LlL Rep 237, CA, where the insured car was to be used for 'personal calls', and this was held to be limited to personal business calls of the assured, and did not extend to calls personal to the friend using the car at the time of the accident; *Alliance Aeroplane Co v Union Insurance Society of Canton Ltd* (1920) 5 LlL Rep 406, where the insurance of an aeroplane was limited to trial flights; cf *Dawsons Ltd v Bonnin* [1922] 2 AC 413, 12 LlL Rep 237, HL, where the insured car was described as garaged in a particular place; *Piddington v Co-operative Insurance Society Ltd* [1934] 2 KB 236, 48 LlL Rep 235 (motor insurance), where Lawrence J held that a car was not being used for other than private purposes when the assured had tied to the vehicle two laths which he intended to use in connection with his garden; *Gray v Blackmore* [1934] 1 KB 95, 47 LlL Rep 69, where the insured, a garage proprietor, towed with the insured car a vehicle which had broken down, and it was held that he had done so 'for a purpose in connection with the motor trade', and consequently could not claim an indemnity for damages caused to a third party, for the policy only covered him whilst the car was being used for 'private purposes'; *Wood v General Accident Fire and Life Assurance Corpn Ltd* (1948) 82 LlL Rep 77 (motor insurance), where the insured was riding as a passenger in a car being driven on business by one of his employees, and it was held that the car was not being used 'for social, domestic and pleasure purposes', although the insured had only travelled in it in order to make the journey more comfortable, pleasurable and restful than it would have been if he had used alternative means of transport; *McCarthy v British Oak Insurance Co* [1938] 3 All ER 1, 61 LlL Rep 194, where the car was found to be used 'for social, domestic and pleasure purposes' although the person driving with the insured's consent had paid for the petrol and oil put into it; *Browning v Phoenix Assurance Co Ltd* [1960] 2 Lloyd's Rep 360 (motor insurance), where the policy covered 'use for social domestic and pleasure purposes and use for the business of the insured . . . excluding use for any purpose connected with the motor trade', and also covered 'any person driving with the permission of the insured'; *Tattersall v Drysdale* [1935] 2 KB 174, 52 LlL Rep 21 (motor insurance), where the insurance cover extended to any person driving with the assured's consent; *Digby v General Accident Fire and Life Assurance Corpn* [1943] AC 121, [1942] 2 All ER 319, 73 LlL Rep 175, HL (motor insurance), where the insurance policy covered any person driving with the permission of the assured; *Herbert v Railway Passengers Assurance Co Ltd* [1938] 1 All ER 650, 60 LlL Rep 143 (motor insurance), where the policy excluded the liability of the insurers where the motor-cycle was being ridden by any person other than the insured; *Izzard v Universal Insurance Co Ltd* [1937] AC 773, [1937] 3 All ER 79, 58 LlL Rep 121, HL (motor insurance), where the company was not to be liable 'in respect of the death of any person (other than a passenger carried by reason of

2 To show the nature of the risk

The insurers are necessarily guided in deciding whether to accept the risk by

---

a contract of employment)'; *Peters v General Accident, Fire and Life Assurance Corpn Ltd* [1938] 2 All ER 267, 60 LlL Rep 311, CA (motor insurance), where the policy extended to cover any person driving with the permission of the assured; *Jones v Welsh Insurance Corpn Ltd* [1937] 4 All ER 149, 59 LlL Rep 13 (motor insurance), where the policy excluded liability if the vehicle were used for the 'carriage of goods or samples in connection with any trade or business'; *Passmore v Vulcan Boiler and General Insurance Co Ltd* (1936) 54 LlL Rep 92 (motor insurance), where a clause in the policy excluded liability when the car was used 'otherwise than for the business' of the assured, and it was used in fact for the business purposes of the assured and another employee of the same firm; *Orr v Trafalgar Insurance Co Ltd* (1948) 82 LlL Rep 1, CA (motor insurance), where the indemnity was limited to the use of the vehicle 'for private purposes only'; *Lester Bros (Coal Merchants) Ltd v Avon Insurance Co Ltd* (1942) 72 LlL Rep 109 (motor insurance), where the insurers were not to be liable if the driver did not hold a driving licence; *Burton v Road Transport and General Insurance Co Ltd* (1939) 63 LlL Rep 253 (motor insurance), where the insurance policy extended to any person driving with the consent of the insured; *Weldrick v Essex and Suffolk Equitable Insurance Society Ltd* (1949) 83 LlL Rep 91 (motor insurance), where the policy excluded liability for passengers 'other than a passenger carried by reason of or in pursuance of a contract of employment'; *Wyatt v Guildhall Insurance Co* [1937] 1 KB 653, [1937] 1 All ER 792, 57 LlL Rep 90 (motor insurance), where the policy covered 'use for social, domestic and pleasure purposes'; *Baker v Provident Accident and White Cross Insurance Co Ltd* [1939] 2 All ER 690, (1939) 64 LlL Rep 14 (motor insurance), where the insurance policy covered liability in respect of passengers carried 'by reason of or in pursuance of a contract of employment'; *Bonham v Zurich General Accident and Liability Insurance Co Ltd* [1945] KB 292, [1945] 1 All ER 427, 78 LlL Rep 245, CA (motor insurance), where the use of the vehicle was limited 'to social, domestic and pleasure purposes . . . excluding use for hiring . . .'; *Spraggon v Dominion Insurance Co Ltd* (1941) 69 LlL Rep 1 (motor insurance), where the policy provided an indemnity to persons hiring cars from the insured who did not come 'within the category of excluded drivers'; *Provincial Insurance Co Ltd v Morgan* [1933] AC 240 (motor insurance), where the statements in the proposal form that the lorry was to be used for the delivery of coal were merely descriptive of the risk insured; *Paget v Poland* (1947) 80 LlL Rep 283 (motor insurance), where the policy extended to cover any person 'driving with the insured's consent'; *Haworth v Dawson* (1946) 80 LlL Rep 19 (motor insurance), where the policy extended to persons other than 'excluded hirers'; *Kelly v Cornhill Insurance Co Ltd* [1964] 1 All ER 321, [1964] 1 Lloyd's Rep 1, HL (motor insurance), where it was held by a majority of three to two that where the policy contained a clause extending cover to any driver who was driving with the permission of the assured, the permission, if not already withdrawn, continued even after the death of the assured; *McGoona v Motor Insurers' Bureau and Marsh* [1969] 2 Lloyd's Rep 34 (motor insurance), where the indemnity was limited to the use of the vehicle 'for social, domestic and pleasure purposes and use by the policy holder in person in connection with his business or profession . . .'; *D H R Moody (Chemists) Ltd v Iron Trades Mutual Insurance Co Ltd* [1971] 1 Lloyd's Rep 386, QB (motor insurance), where the 'description of use' clause in the policy confined its cover to the use of the vehicle 'for social, domestic and pleasure purposes . . .', and was held to apply when the car was being used to bring back from the airport persons who had seen off French visitors to an English town which was twinned with a French town. (See the judgment of Wrangham J, ibid, at 388); *Seddon v Binions (Zurich Insurance Co Ltd, Third Party)* [1978] 1 Lloyd's Rep 381, CA (motor insurance), where the policy covered use for 'social, domestic and pleasure purposes', and it was held that when a father used his son's car to take the son's employee home, such use was a business use and fell outside the terms of the policy; *Sands v O'Connell* [1981] RTR 42 (motor insurance), where the policy covered a hirer and a person driving with the permission of the hire-car company, and it was held that it did not extend to a person who was allowed by the hirer to drive for such authority had not been given by the company; *Samuelson v National Insurance and Guarantee Corpn* [1985] 2 Lloyd's Rep 541, CA (motor insurance), where an exception stated that the insurers would not be liable for the loss of the vehicle 'occurring whilst it is being used otherwise than in accordance with the limitation as to use except that the exclusion of use for any purpose in connection with the motor trade shall not prejudice the indemnity to the insured whilst the motor car . . . is in the custody or control of a member of the motor trade for the purpose of its overhaul, upkeep or repair.'

the description of the subject-matter given by the assured.[15] Accuracy of description is, therefore, required from the assured in discharge of the duty of good faith. An inaccuracy which does not prevent the subject-matter of insurance from being identified may, nevertheless, preclude the assured from recovering, inasmuch as he has failed to discharge this duty.[16]

3 To define the risk

The subject-matter of insurance, whatever its nature, is liable to undergo alteration during the currency of the policy, and, in case of its alteration, the question may arise as to whether the insurers remain responsible for its safety as altered. Their responsibility clearly ceases where the alteration destroys the identity of the subject-matter since it no longer answers the description in the policy.[17]

More usually, no question of identity arises, but the effect of the alteration renders the subject-matter more susceptible to the peril insured against. An alteration of this kind may be prohibited, either by the general law or by the express terms of the policy. But, unless prohibited, the alteration may take place without affecting the validity of the policy or of the claim. For the purpose of determining whether any particular alteration is a prohibited alteration or not, reference must be made to the description in the policy, which defines the subject-matter as at the inception of the insurance and furnishes the standard by which any subsequent alteration is to be measured.[18]

---

15 *Sillem v Thornton* (1854) 3 E & B 868 (fire insurance) per Campbell CJ, at 884, approved in *Thompson v Hopper* (1858) EB & E 1038, ExCh (marine insurance) per Willes J, at 1049. If the description emanates from the agent of the insurers, the assured is not responsible for its inaccuracy: *Re Universal Non-Tariff Fire Insurance Co, Forbes & Co's Claim* (1875) LR 19 Eq 485 (fire insurance); cf *Newcastle Fire Insurance Co v Macmorran & Co* (1815) 3 Dow 255, HL (fire insurance) per Lord Eldon C, at 263; *de Maurier (Jewels) Ltd v Bastion Insurance Co Ltd and Coronet Insurance Co Ltd* [1967] 2 Lloyd's Rep 550 (jewellers' all risks insurance) where it was held that a warranty stating: '[Warranted] road vehicles . . . fitted with locks and alarm system (approved by underwriters) and in operation' delimited and was part of the description of the risk, and was not of a promissory character. (See the judgment of Donaldson J, ibid, at 558–559.)

16 See pp 119–121, post.

17 *Thompson v Hopper* (supra) (marine insurance) per Willes J, at 1049.

18 See p 300, post.

CHAPTER 5

Insurable interest

The subject of insurable interest is of great importance in the three leading branches of insurance, i e marine insurance,[1] fire insurance[2] and life insurance,[3] and gives rise to many difficult questions.

Similar questions no doubt, may, in theory, arise in the different branches of accident insurance. But, in practice, they rarely do so, either because of the nature of the insurance,[4] or because the language of the policy prevents them from arising.[5]

A WHAT CONSTITUTES AN INSURABLE INTEREST

The classical definition of insurable interest was given by Lawrence J in *Lucena v Craufurd*:[6]

> 'A man is interested in a thing to whom advantage may arise or prejudice happen from the circumstances which may attend it . . . and whom it importeth that its condition as to safety or other quality should continue: interest does not necessarily imply a right to the whole or a part of a thing, nor necessarily and exclusively that which may be the subject of privation, but the having some relation to, or concern in the subject of the insurance, which relation or concern by the happening of the perils insured against may be so affected as to produce a damage, detriment, or prejudice to the person insuring; and where a man is so circumstanced with respect to matters exposed to certain risks or damages, or to have a moral certainty of advantage or benefit, but for those risks or dangers, he may be said to be interested in the safety of the thing. To be interested in the preservation of a thing, is to be so circumstanced with respect to it as to have benefit from its existence, prejudice from its destruction. The property of a thing and the interest devisable from it may be very different; of the first the price is generally the measure, but by interest in a thing every benefit or advantage arising out of or depending on such thing may be considered as being comprehended.'

---

1 Marine Insurance Act 1906, ss 4–15. See generally Ivamy, *Marine Insurance* (4th Edn 1985), pp 16–29.

2 See generally Ivamy, *Fire and Motor Insurance* (4th Edn 1984), pp 17–18.

3 See generally Ivamy, *Personal Accident, Life and Other Insurances* (2nd Edn 1980), pp 91–97. In life insurance, the question of insurable interest is only of importance where the insurance is on the life of a third person; see, e g *Dalby v India and London Life Assurance Co* (1854) 15 CB 365 (life insurance); *Hebdon v West* (1863) 3 B & S 579 (life insurance); *Howard v Refuge Friendly Society* (1886) 54 LT 644 (life insurance); *Anctil v Manufacturers Life Insurance Co* [1899] AC 604, PC (life insurance); *Griffiths v Fleming* [1909] 1 KB 805, CA (life insurance).

4 E g in the case of liability insurance, where the assured insures against his own liability, or of personal accident insurance, where the assured insures himself against accident.

5 E g in the case of insurances on goods, which are expressly described as the assured's own.

6 (1806) 2 Bos & PNR 269, HL (marine insurance) at 302. In *Macaura v Northern Assurance Co Ltd* [1925] AC 619 at 627 (fire insurance) Lord Buckmaster pointed out the difficulty of defining a moral certainty so as to render it an essential part of a definite legal proposition.

This definition forms the basis of s 5(2) of the Marine Insurance Act 1906, which provides:

> 'In particular, a person is interested in a marine adventure where he stands in any legal or equitable relation to the adventure or to any insurable property at risk therein, in consequence of which he may benefit by the safety or due arrival of insurable property, or may be prejudiced by its loss or by damage thereto, or by the detention thereof, or may incur liability in respect thereof.'

Where, as in the case of personal accident insurance and most branches of property insurance, the subject-matter of insurance is a physical object exposed to certain perils, an insurable interest is constituted by the fact that the assured, from his relation to the subject-matter, will suffer prejudice if the subject-matter is lost or damaged by such perils. Thus, the assured is clearly prejudiced by the loss of life or limb, or by the theft of his own goods, and has, therefore, an insurable interest for the purposes of a personal accident or burglary insurance.

In the case of liability insurance, in which the subject-matter of insurance is not, strictly speaking, a physical object, the definition of insurable interest must be broadened. It is sufficient if the assured has an insurable interest in the event insured against, i e the event must be one by the happening of which he would suffer prejudice.[7] Thus, it is clear that the assured will suffer prejudice by the happening of an accident for which he is responsible to third persons, or by the insolvency of his debtor; and he has, therefore, an insurable interest for the purposes of a liability or solvency insurance policy.

In the case of goods, or other property, insurable interest may be based on ownership, and this ownership may be either sole[8] or joint;[9] absolute or limited;[10] legal[11] or equitable.[12]

Ownership is not, however, necessary; insurable interest may be founded upon contract.[13]

---

7 *Prudential Insurance Co v IRC* [1904] 2 KB 658 (life insurance) per Channell J, at 664.

8 *Inglis v Stock* (1885) 10 App Cas 263 (marine insurance) per Blackburn J, at 270.

9 *Page v Fry* (1800) 2 Bos & P 240 (marine insurance) per Heath J, at 243; *Robertson v Hamilton* (1811) 14 East 522 (marine insurance); *Robinson v Gleadow* (1835) 2 Bing NC 156 (marine insurance).

10 *Castellain v Preston* (1883) 11 QBD 380, CA (fire insurance) per Bowen LJ, at 401; *Warwicker v Bretnall* (1882) 23 ChD 188 (fire insurance).

11 Whether as trustee (*Payne v Payne* (1908) Times, 6 November; *Lucena v Craufurd* (1806) 2 Bos & PNR 269, HL (marine insurance) per Lord Eldon, at 324; *Ex p Yallop* (1808) 15 Ves 60 (fire insurance); *Ex p Houghton* (1810) 17 Ves 251 (fire insurance)); executor (*Stirling v Vaughan* (1809) 11 East 619 (marine insurance) per Lord Ellenborough CJ, at 629; *Fry v Fry* (1859) 27 Beav 144 (fire insurance); *Re Betty, Betty v A-G* [1899] 1 Ch 821 (fire insurance)); administrator; or mortgagee (*Dobson v Land* (1850) 8 Hare 216 (fire insurance); *North British and Mercantile Insurance Co v London, Liverpool and Globe Insurance Co* (1877) 5 ChD 569, CA (fire insurance) per Mellish LJ, at 583; *Castellain v Preston* (supra) (fire insurance) per Bowen LJ, at 398). As far as marine insurance is concerned, s 14(1) of the Marine Insurance Act 1906, provides that: 'Where the subject-matter insured is mortgaged, . . . the mortgagee has an insurable interest in respect of any sum due or to become due under the mortgage.'

12 Whether as *cestui que trust* (*Lucena v Craufurd* (1802) 3 Bos & P 75, ExCh (marine insurance) per Chambre J, at 103; *Ex p Yallop* (supra) (fire insurance); *Ex p Houghton* (supra) (fire insurance); or mortgagor (*Provincial Insurance Co of Canada v Leduc* (1874) LR 6 PC 224 (marine insurance)). As far as marine insurance is concerned, s 14(1) of the Marine Insurance Act 1906, provides that 'where the subject-matter insured is mortgaged, the mortgagor has an insurable interest in the full value thereof . . .'.

13 *Lucena v Craufurd* (supra) (marine insurance) per Lord Eldon, at 321. An insurer has therefore an insurable interest sufficient to support a reinsurance: *Re Law Guarantee Trust and Accident Society,*

Thus, a bailee who has contracted, expressly or impliedly, to be responsible for the safety of goods belonging to another,[14] or who has contracted to insure them,[15] has an insurable interest in them. Apart from any question of contract, the mere fact of possession, if lawful,[16] is sufficient to give an insurable interest.[17]

An interest, to be insurable must have a pecuniary value.[18] Its nature, however, is broadly speaking, immaterial.

An insurable interest need not be a permanent or continuing interest; it is nonetheless insurable because it is defeasible, since it is a valid interest until it is defeated.[19]

The fact that the interest of the assured is precarious, and that other persons are entitled at any moment to call on him to hand over the object insured to them, does not therefore prevent his interest from being sufficient to support a contract of insurance.[20]

The interest must, however, be a real interest, since the mere expectation of acquiring an interest, however probable, does not give the right to insure the property out of which the expectation arises.[21]

So long as there is a real interest, it is not necessary that the assured should be entitled to a present enjoyment. A right to future possession, or a future interest, however remote, is equally insurable, since the assured's prospect of benefit is clear, and the prejudice, which he suffers by reason of the object insured being

---

Liverpool Mortgage Insurance Co's Case [1914] 2 Ch 617, CA (debenture insurance) per Buckley LJ, at 631; *Uzielli v Boston Marine Insurance Co* (1884) 15 QBD 11, CA (marine insurance) per Brett MR, at 16.

14 *Crowley v Cohen* (1832) 3 B & Ad 478 (transit insurance); *Joyce v Kennard* (1871) LR 7 QB 78 (transit insurance); *Stephens v Australasian Insurance Co* (1872) LR 8 CP 18 (marine insurance); *Hill v Scott* [1895] 2 QB 713, CA (marine insurance); *Marks v Hamilton* (1852) 7 Exch 323 (fire insurance) per Pollock CB, at 324.

15 Cf *McNeill v Millen & Co* [1907] 2 IR 328, CA; *Joyce v Swann* (1864) 17 CBNS 84 (marine insurance) per Willes J, at 104; *Heckman v Isaac* (1862) 6 LT 383 (fire insurance) per Crompton J, at 385.

16 Thus, a finder has an insurable interest: *Marks v Hamilton* (fire insurance) as reported 21 LJ Ex 109 per Pollock CB, at 110; but a trespasser has not.

17 *Lucena v Craufurd* (supra) (marine insurance), followed in *Stirling v Vaughan* (supra) (marine insurance); cf *Martineau v Kitching* (1872) LR 7 QB 436 (fire insurance) per Blackburn J, at 457. Thus, a bankrupt has an insurable interest in goods which he is fraudulently concealing from his creditors: *Goulstone v Royal Insurance Co* (1858) 1 F & F 276 (fire insurance); or which he purchased after a discharge which is subsequently set aside: *Marks v Hamilton* (supra) (fire insurance).

18 *Halford v Kymer* (1830) 10 B & C 724 (life insurance).

19 *Goulstone v Royal Insurance Co* (1858) 1 F & F 276 (fire insurance); *Lucena v Craufurd* (1806) 2 Bos & PNR 269, HL (marine insurance) per Chambre J, at 299; *Colonial Insurance Co of New Zealand v Adelaide Marine Insurance Co* (1886) 12 App Cas 128 at 140, PC (marine insurance); *Geismar v Sun Alliance and London Insurance Ltd* [1978] QB 383, [1977] 3 All ER 570 (theft insurance), where the insured had an insurable interest in smuggled jewellery although such interest was subject to defeasance in that the jewellery might be confiscated by the Customs and Excise authorities. (See the judgment of Talbot J, ibid, at 69.)

20 *Goulstone v Royal Insurance Co* (supra) (fire insurance), where the assured was an insolvent debtor; *Anderson v Commercial Union Assurance Co* (1885) 55 LJQB 146, CA (fire insurance) where the assured was a tenant on sufferance.

21 *Devaux v Steele* (1840) 6 Bing NC 358 (marine insurance); *Knox v Wood* (1808) 1 Camp 543 (marine insurance); *Routh v Thompson* (1809) 11 East 428 (marine insurance); *Buchanan & Co v Faber* (1899) 4 Com Cas 223 (marine insurance).

destroyed by the peril insured against, cannot be attributed with absolute certainty to any other cause than such peril.[1]

Where the assured has, in fact, an interest, it is immaterial how such interest has been acquired.[2]

The inclination of the Courts is to find in favour of an insurable interest, whenever the facts of the case and the law applicable permit.[3]

B THE NECESSITY FOR AN INSURABLE INTEREST

Every contract of insurance requires an insurable interest to support it;[4] otherwise, it is invalid.[5]

In certain kinds of insurance, e g liability insurance and fidelity or solvency insurance, the very nature of the insurance implies the existence of an insurable interest,[6] whilst other kinds of insurance, e g personal accident insurance and

---

1 *Lucena v Craufurd* (1806) 2 Bos & PNR 269, HL (marine insurance) per Lord Eldon, at 324, 325: 'Suppose A to be possessed of a ship limited to B in case A dies without issue; that A has twenty children, the eldest of whom is twenty years of age; and B ninety years of age; it is a moral certainty that B will never come into possession, yet this is a clear interest. On the other hand, suppose the case of the heir at law of a man who has an estate worth £20,000 a year who is ninety years of age; upon his death-bed intestate, and incapable from incurable lunacy of making a will, there is no man who will deny that such an heir at law has a moral certainty of succeeding to the estate, yet the law will not allow that he has any interest, or anything more than a mere expectation.' Likewise a guarantor, who, if called upon to implement his guarantee, would be entitled to take over the security held by the creditor, has an insurable interest in that security: *General Accident, Fire and Life Assurance Corpn Ltd v Midland Bank Ltd* [1940] 2 KB 388, [1940] 3 All ER 252, CA per Greene MR, at 401.

2 *Bell v Gilson* (1798) 1 Bos & P 345 (marine insurance), where the goods insured had been purchased from an enemy alien; *Goulstone v Royal Insurance Co* (1858) 1 F & F 276 (fire insurance), where it was held that an insolvent debtor had an insurable interest in property concealed from his creditors, and was entitled to recover upon his policy to the extent of his interest; *Marks v Hamilton* (1852) 7 Exch 323 (fire insurance), where also the assured was an insolvent debtor; cf *Stevenson v London and Lancashire Fire Assurance Co* (1866) 26 UCR 148, where it was doubted whether an insurance company with whom the actual owner of a house, without fraud or wilful misrepresentation, effected an insurance thereon could set up the legal title of a stranger to the land on which the house stood as a defence against the claim of the assured; *Lucena v Craufurd* (1806) 2 Bos & PNR 269, HL (marine insurance) per Chambre J, at 309.

3 *Stock v Inglis* (1884) 12 QBD 564, CA (marine insurance) (affirmed without reference to this point, *Inglis v Stock* (1885) 10 App Cas 263) per Brett MR, at 571; *Cousins v Nantes* (1811) 3 Taunt 513 (marine insurance) per Mansfield CJ, at 522; *Re London County Commercial Reinsurance Office Ltd* [1922] 2 Ch 67 (peace insurance) per Lawrence J, at 79; and cf *Brady v Irish Land Commission* [1921] 1 IR 56.

4 A provision in a policy that it is to be incontestable does not override the rule as to insurable interest: *Anctil v Manufacturers Life Insurance Co* [1899] AC 604 PC (life insurance).

5 *Cosford Union v Poor Law and Local Government Officers' Mutual Guarantee Association Ltd* (1910) 103 LT 463 per Phillimore J, at 465: 'Anybody who sues on a policy can only sue in respect of his own interest unless by special provisions, the law allowing it, the policy is made for the sake of another, or unless some statute says the policy shall enure for the benefit of somebody else.' See also, *Rogerson v Scottish Automobile and General Insurance Co Ltd* (1930) 47 TLR 46, CA (motor insurance) per Scrutton LJ, at 47; *Castellain v Preston* (1883) 11 QBD 380, CA (fire insurance) per Bowen LJ, at 379; *Prudential Insurance Co v IRC* [1904] 2 KB 658 (life insurance) per Channell J, at 663, speaking, inter alia, of fire insurance.

6 But, in the case of fidelity insurance, where the same person is employed in two different capacities, by two different employers, a policy effected by one employer covering his acts in that employment does not entitle his other employer to recover the amount of his defalcations in the other employment, since the first employer has no insurable interest in the losses of the

burglary or livestock insurance, are, in practice, effected by the assured, for the most part, in respect of his own person or property. Occasionally, however, the assured may, for his own benefit, effect an insurance on the person or property of another, and then the question of insurable interest becomes important.

Thus, a personal accident policy may be effected by the assured against the loss which he may suffer by reason of an accident to a third person. To render such an insurance valid, the assured must have an insurable interest in such person's safety;[7] and this interest must be of a pecuniary nature.[8] A son, therefore, whose father is a pauper and dependent on him, has not a sufficient insurable interest to support an insurance on his father against personal accident.[9]

Again, the assured cannot recover on a contract of fire insurance unless he shows that he has an insurable interest in the subject-matter of insurance. For it is clear that if he has no insurable interest in a particular object, he cannot be prejudiced by its destruction, nor is there anything to which the right of indemnity given by the contract can attach. The contract will be nothing more than a contract to pay a sum of money on an uncertain event, in the determination of which neither of the contracting parties has any interest, and which, apart from the contract itself, cannot, therefore, by any possibility be adverse to the interest of the assured, i e it will be a mere wager.

As far as marine insurance is concerned, the Marine Insurance Act 1906, s 4, provides that:

> (1) Every contract of marine insurance by way of gaming or wagering is void.
> (2) A contract of marine insurance is deemed to be a gaming or wagering contract—
> (a) Where the assured has not an insurable interest as defined by the Act, and the contract is entered into with no expectation of acquiring such an interest; or
> (b) Where the policy is made 'interest or no interest', or 'without further proof of interest than the policy itself', or 'without benefit of salvage to the insurer', or subject to any other like term:
>
> provided that where there is no possibility of salvage a policy may be effected without benefit of salvage to the insurer.'[10]

By the Life Assurance Act 1774, s 1, insurances without interest are prohibited.[11] The Act, notwithstanding its title, is not confined to life

---

second employer: *Cosford Union v Poor Law and Local Government Officers' Mutual Guarantee Association Ltd* (supra).

7 *Shilling v Accidental Death Insurance Co* (1857) 2 H & N 42. Thus, an employee has an insurable interest in the life of his employer: *Hebdon v West* (1863) 3 B & S 579; and an employer in the life of his employee; *Turnbull & Co v Scottish Provident Institution* 1896 34 ScLR 146 (life insurance).

8 *Halford v Kymer* (1830) 10 B & C 724 (life insurance), followed in *Hebdon v West* (supra), where the assured, who had a seven years' engagement at a salary of £600 per annum, was held, on effecting an insurance when his engagement had five years to run, to have a pecuniary interest to the amount of £3,000.

9 *Shilling v Accidental Death Insurance Co* (supra).

10 See further, Ivamy, *Marine Insurance* (4th Edn 1985), pp 11–15.

11 Section 1 provides: 'From and after the passing of this Act no insurance shall be made by any person or persons bodies politick or corporate, on the life or lives of any person or persons, or any other event or events whatsoever, wherein the person or persons for whose use, benefit, or on whose account such policy or policies shall be made, shall have no interest, or by way of gaming or wagering; and that every assurance made contrary to the true intent and meaning hereof shall be null and void to all intents and purposes whatsoever.' The objection as to want of interest can only be taken by the insurers; if the insurers waive it, it cannot be raised between persons claiming the proceeds of the policy; *Hadden v Bryden* 1899 1 F (Ct of Sess) 710 (life insurance) per Lord Robertson, at 715. The text of the Act is set out in Appendix I, p 627, post.

insurance,[12] for it expressly refers to insurances on any other event or events whatsoever.[13] Hence, it has been held to apply to policies of personal accident insurance,[14] and to instruments in the form of policies[15] on the rise or fall in the price of shares,[16] on the determination of the sex of a particular person,[17] and on the date of the conclusion of peace.[18] On the other hand, the Act does not apply to insurances on ships, goods or merchandise,[19] or to mere wagers not expressed in the form of a policy.[20] The Act further provides that no greater amount shall be recoverable from the insurers than the amount or value of the assured's interest.[21]

C DESCRIPTION OF INTEREST

1 The general rule

Although the assured must have some interest in the subject-matter to entitle him to effect an insurance in respect of it, it is not, as a general rule, necessary that he should specify in the contract, or even disclose to the insurers, either the nature or the extent of his interest.[22]

---

12 *Paterson v Powell* (1832) 9 Bing 320 (wager on shares) per Tindal CJ, at 328.

13 Section 1 (supra).

14 *Shilling v Accidental Death Insurance Co* (1857) 2 H & N 42.

15 It is to be observed that the Act expressly refers to policies, and unless the contract is embodied in a policy, the Act has no application: *Good v Elliott* (1790) 3 Term Rep 693 (wager) per Lord Kenyon CJ, at 706; *Paterson v Powell* (supra), where importance was attached to the fact that the instrument was in the form of a policy; *Morgan v Pebrer* (1837) 3 Bing NC 457 (wager on shares) per Tindal CJ, at 466; *Cook v Field* (1850) 15 QB 460 (sale of expectancy) per Lord Campbell CJ, at 475; *Carlill v Carbolic Smoke Ball Co* [1892] 2 QB 484 (affd [1893] 1 QB 256, CA) per Hawkins J, at 493.

16 *Paterson v Powell* (supra).

17 *Roebuck v Hammerton* (1778) 2 Cowp 737 (wager).

18 *Mollison v Staples* (1778) Park 909 (wager); *Re London County Commercial Reinsurance Office Ltd* [1922] 2 Ch 67.

19 Section 4, which states: 'Provided always, that nothing herein contained shall extend or be construed to extend to insurances bona fide made by any person or persons on ships, goods, or merchandises, but every such insurance shall be as valid and effectual in the law as if this Act had not been made'.

20 *Good v Elliott* (supra).

21 Section 3, which states: 'And . . . in all cases where the insured hath interest in such life or lives, event or events, no greater sum shall be recovered or received from the insurer or insurers than the amount of value of the interest of the insured in such life or lives, or other event or events'; *Hebdon v West* (1863) 3 B & S 579 (life insurance), where the assured, having effected two policies, recovered under one policy the full amount of his interest, and this was held to be a bar to a claim on the second policy.

22 *MacKenzie v Whitworth* (1875) LR 10 Exch 142 (marine insurance) per Bramwell B, at 148: 'The rule is that you must specify the subject-matter of insurance, not your interest in it.' See also *Crowley v Cohen* (1832) 3 B & Ad 478 (insurance on canal boats) per Lord Tenterden CJ, at 485; *Glover v Black* (1763) 3 Burr 1394 (marine insurance) per Lord Mansfield CJ, at 1401; *Palmer v Pratt* (1824) 2 Bing 185 (marine insurance); *London and North-Western Rly Co v Glyn* (1859) 1 E & E 652 (fire insurance) per Crompton J, at 664; *Inglis v Stock* (1885) 10 App Cas 263 (marine insurance) per Lord Blackburn, at 270, 274; *Ogden v Montreal Insurance Co* (1853) 3 C & P 497, where it was held that a mortgagor insuring in the name of the mortgagee need not specify the amount of the mortgage; *Keefer v Phoenix Insurance Co* (1903) 1 Com LR (Can) 1, where it was held that a person insuring need not disclose the fact that he was not sole owner.

As far as marine insurance is concerned, the Marine Insurance Act 1906, s 26(2) provides:

> 'The nature and extent of the interest of the assured in the subject-matter insured need not be specified in the policy.'[1]

All that is required is an adequate description of the subject-matter, and such description is sufficient to cover any interest which the assured may have in the subject-matter, whether as owner or otherwise.[2] This equally applies where the assured has several interests, differing as regards both nature and extent, in respect of the same subject-matter.[3]

2 Exceptions to the general rule

A specific description of the assured's interest is, however, required in the following cases:

a Where there is an express condition to this effect.
b Where the insurance is prospective profits or is against consequential loss.
c Where the interest is, from its precarious nature, material to the risk.

(a) Express condition

Sometimes the insurers make it an express condition that the policy shall not extend to cover certain kinds of interest, unless the assured shall specify them, e g in the case of goods held in trust or on commission.

The assured is occasionally required by an express condition to disclose to the insurers at the time of effecting the insurance, or to specify in the contract, the extent of his interest in the subject-matter of insurance. In any case, however, he cannot recover after loss in an action brought on the policy, unless he proves the extent of his interest,[4] or, where he has intended to cover by the insurance more interests than his own, their extent and his intention to cover them.

(b) Prospective profits or consequential loss

Where the peculiar nature of his interest is such that the risk may be affected thereby, and it may, therefore, be properly said that such interest is itself the subject-matter of insurance, the interest must be specified.[5]

---

1 See further, Ivamy, *Marine Insurance* (4th Edn 1985), p 111.

2 *London and North-Western Rly Co v Glyn* (supra) (fire insurance) per Crompton J, at 664: 'I think that, notwithstanding the condition [i e as to the declaration of goods in trust] an insurance simply on "goods" would have covered the plaintiffs' interest as carriers in the goods.' See also *Mackenzie v Whitworth* (supra) (marine insurance); *Allison v Bristol Marine Insurance Co* (1876) 1 App Cas 209 (marine insurance) per Brett J, at 216. Hence, if the assured failed to prove that he is owner, he may recover as mortgagee: *Scatcherd v Equitable Fire Insurance Co* (1858) 8 CP 415.

3 *Carruthers v Sheddon* (1815) 6 Taunt 14 (marine insurance), where the assured, who was interested as a partner in a portion of the cargo and as consignee in the whole, and had also a lien on the whole for advances, was held entitled to cover all his interests in one insurance without specifying their number or nature; *Irving v Richardson* (1831) 2 B & Ad 193 (marine insurance); *South Australian Insurance Co v Randell* (1869) LR 3 PC 101, 112 (fire insurance).

4 *Hodgson v Glover* (1805) 6 East 316 (marine insurance); *Mackenzie v Whitworth* (1875) LR 10 Exch 142 (marine insurance) per Pollock B, at 149.

5 *Mackenzie v Whitworth* (1875) LR 10 Exch 142 (affd on appeal (1875) 1 Ex D 36 (marine

In this case the interest is not a direct interest in the safety of the subject-matter, but only a collateral interest, i e a prospective advantage to be derived from its continued safety.[6]

Thus, profit, or remuneration,[7] which has already been ascertained at the date of the insurance, or which must necessarily be earned in the ordinary course of events before the loss, need not be separately specified, since either is recoverable under an insurance on the property out of which it is earned, as being a direct interest in such property.

Prospective or anticipated profit to be derived from the use of property is, on the other hand, in a different category. It is not ascertainable at the date of the insurance, nor is there at that date any certainty that it will ever be earned. The destruction of the property out of which profit is expected to be earned cannot be said to carry with it as a necessary consequence the loss of such profit, for the profit might never be earned, even though the property were not destroyed. Under an insurance on the property, therefore, prospective profit cannot be recovered. To enable it to be recovered it must be specifically insured as such.

Such an insurance is an anomaly, since prospective profit is in the nature of an expectancy.[8] But the insurability of such profit is well recognized.

Similarly, where the insurance is against consequential loss, a specific description of the assured's interest is necessary.[9]

(c) Precarious nature of the interest

Even when the interest of the assured in the subject-matter is a direct interest, it is necessary for him to disclose it, if it is of so precarious or unusual a nature as materially to affect the risk.[10]

D THE TIME FOR INSURABLE INTEREST

1 Interest at the time of the loss sometimes essential

(a) Insurances other than life insurance

Where the assured seeks, in the event of loss by fire, to recover from the insurers

---

insurance) per Blackburn J, at 42), followed in *Dixon v Whitworth* (1879) 4 CPD 371 (marine insurance) per Lindley J, at 375.

6 *Mackenzie v Whitworth* (supra) (marine insurance) per Blackburn J, at 41, 42; *Maurice v Goldsbrough Mort & Co Ltd* [1939] AC 452, [1939] 3 All ER 63, 64 LlL Rep 1, PC.

7 Hence, a carrier's remuneration, being capable of being ascertained, is covered by an ordinary insurance, and it is therefore unnecessary for a carrier to specify the nature of his interest: *London and North-Western Rly Co v Glyn* (1859) 1 E & E 652 (fire insurance) per Crompton J, at 664.

8 *Lucena v Craufurd* (1806) 2 Bos & PNR 269, HL (marine insurance) per Lawrence J, at 312: ibid, per Lord Eldon, at 326; *Barclay v Cousins* (1802) 2 East 544 (marine insurance); *King v Glover* (1806) 2 Bos & PNR 206 (marine insurance); *Re Wright and Pole* (1834) 1 Ad & El 621 (fire insurance), followed in *Menzies v North British Insurance Co* 1847 9 Dunl (Ct of Sess) 694 (fire insurance).

9 See *Inman SS Co v Bischoff* (1882) 7 App Cas 670 (marine insurance) per Lord Selborne LC, at 676. For consequential loss insurance, see Ivamy, *Fire and Motor Insurance* (4th Edn 1984), pp 75–79.

10 *Anderson v Commercial Union Assurance Co* (1885) 55 LJQB 146, CA (fire insurance), where the assured was tenant on sufferance of the premises where the insured machinery was situated, and the Court below thought that the fact ought to have been disclosed; *Steyn v Malmesbury Board of Executors and Trust and Assurance Co* [1921] CPD 96.

sums payable under the policy, it is essential for him to show that at the time of the loss he had an insurable interest in the object destroyed.[11] This is the crucial date; for if he had then no interest, he can have suffered no loss, and is therefore entitled to no indemnity.

The possession of an interest, or of its acquisition at any particular date, so long as it is acquired before loss, appears to be of less importance.

In the case of marine insurance, the Marine Insurance Act 1906, s 6(1) provides that:

> 'The assured must be interested in the subject-matter insured at the time of the loss though he need not be interested when the insurance is effected.'[12]

The view, however, has been expressed that, in the case of fire insurance, the assured must have an insurable interest at the date of effecting the insurance, and that otherwise he cannot recover.[13]

Where the policy contemplates the possible substitution of other property in place of that possessed by the assured at the date of effecting the insurance, e g in the case of a tradesman insuring his stock-in-trade, the assured will be entitled to recover notwithstanding that the property actually destroyed was not acquired by him until after the date of the policy. As in this case, however, the insurance is not an insurance on specific objects, but only on a class of objects, it may be said that the class, and, therefore, his interest in it, existed at the date of the contract.

In the case of policies effected by carriers, warehousemen and bailees of a similar type, it is clear that the policies must apply to such goods as may, from time to time, come into their hands, and not merely to those goods which happened, in fact, to be in their possession at the date of effecting the policy.

There, however, the insurance is equally an insurance on a class of objects, and not on the specific object; the assured's interest is an interest in the permanent subject-matter, i e the class, and exists throughout the duration of the contract, unaffected by any change in the individual objects composing the class.

The same reasoning does not, however, apply to insurances on specific objects, in which the assured has no interest at the time of insuring. In the case of specific goods, there appears to be no reason for drawing a distinction between fire insurance and marine insurance, and, accordingly, the insurance of the future interest is valid, provided that the interest is, in fact, acquired before loss.[14]

The position, however, may be different in the case of insurances upon houses, buildings, and similar property, and under the Life Assurance Act 1774, if, as may be the case, it applies to such insurances, it may perhaps be necessary for the interest to subsist at the time of insuring. Apart from this possible statutory prohibition, there is no reason why future interests in such property should not be insurable in the same way as future interests in specific goods.

In any case, if the assured expressly represents that he has an interest at the

---

11 *Sadlers' Co v Badcock* (1743) 2 Atk 554 (fire insurance); *Lynch v Dalzell* (1729) 4 Bro Parl Cas 431.

12 See further, Ivamy, *Marine Insurance* (4th Edn 1985), pp 27–29.

13 *Sadlers' Co v Badcock* (supra) per Lord Hardwicke C, at 556; *Howard v Lancashire Insurance Co* (1885) 11 SCR 92.

14 *Williams v Baltic Insurance Association of London Ltd* [1924] 2 KB 282, 19 LlL Rep 126 (accident insurance); *Tattersall v Drysdale* [1935] 2 KB 174, 52 LlL Rep 21 (accident insurance).

time of insuring, he must, in fact, have an insurable interest at the time of insuring. The acquisition of an interest subsequently, before the loss, will not be sufficient.[15]

(b) Life insurance

The insured must have an insurable interest at the time at which the policy is effected.[16] It is immaterial whether or not he later ceases to have such an interest, e g where before the debtor, whose life is insured, dies, he pays the creditor the amount of the debt.[17]

2 Retrospective insurance

Although the subject-matter may, in fact, have been destroyed by fire at the date of effecting the insurance, the contract may, nevertheless, in some cases be valid, and operate to indemnify the assured notwithstanding such destruction; for there is no objection, in principle, to a retrospective insurance, provided that the assured had, in fact, at the date of the loss, an insurable interest.[18]

Such an insurance, in the case of houses, buildings, or similar property, does not appear to be prohibited by the Life Assurance Act 1774, ss 1 and 3,[19] even if that Act applies to fire insurance, since the assured is, in fact, prejudiced by reason of the happening of the peril insured against, and he has therefore an insurable interest existing at the date of effecting the insurance. To render a contract of this kind valid, it is necessary to establish

a that both the assured and the insurers were ignorant of the loss at the time of making the contract;[20] and
b that they both intended the contract to apply to such a loss.[21]

Their intention need not necessarily be shown by express words.[22] It must, however, be clear from the language used that such was the intention of the parties;[1] if this cannot be shown, the policy is void, and the premium must be

---

15 *Howard v Lancashire Insurance Co* (1885) 11 SCR 92, as explained in *Williams v Baltic Insurance Association of London Ltd* (supra) (accident insurance).
16 *Dalby v India and London Life Assurance Co* (1854) 15 CB 365 (life insurance).
17 Ibid.
18 *Bradford v Symondson* (1881) 7 QBD 456, CA (marine insurance) per Brett LJ, at 462: 'The fact that the question of whether there was a loss or not was determined before the making of the policy is no objection to the policy'. Such an insurance may perhaps be explained as equivalent to the contract, 'if my goods are in fact now destroyed, you contract to pay'. See also, *Earl March v Pigot* (1771) 5 Burr 2802 (wager) per Lord Mansfield CJ, at 2805, followed in *Mead v Davison* (1835) 3 Ad & El 303 (marine insurance).
19 In *Bufe v Turner* (1815) 6 Taunt 338, which appears from the facts to have been a retrospective insurance upon a warehouse, and in *Sillem v Thornton* (1854) 3 E & B 868, where the policy was ante-dated, no objection was taken on this ground.
20 *Mead v Davison* (1835) 3 Ad & El 303 (marine insurance) per Lord Denman CJ, at 307; *Lishman v Northern Maritime Insurance Co* (1873) LR 8 CP 216; affd (1875) LR 10 CP 179 (marine insurance).
21 *Giffard v Queen Insurance Co* (1869) 12 NBR 433, where property covered by an ante-dated policy was held to be insured 'burnt or not burnt'.
22 *Earl March v Pigot* (1771) 5 Burr 2802 (wager); *Giffard v Queen Insurance Co* (supra).
1 *Bradford v Symondson* (supra) per Brett LJ, at 46.

returned.[2] It would further appear that where the fact of a loss is known to both parties, but its amount is unascertained, a contract indemnifying the assured against such loss would be equally valid;[3] for, in this case the contract is still a contract upon a contingency.

As far as marine insurance is concerned, the Marine Insurance Act 1906, s 6(1) provides that:

> 'The assured must be interested in the subject-matter insured at the time of the loss though he need not be interested when the insurance is effected: provided that where the subject-matter is insured "lost or not lost", the assured may recover although he may have acquired his interest until after the loss, unless at the time of effecting the contract of insurance the assured was aware of the loss, and the insurer was not.'

Section 6(2) of the Act goes on to state:

> 'Where the assured has no interest at the time of the loss, he cannot acquire interest by any act or election after he is aware of the loss.'[4]

---

2 *Pritchard v Merchants' and Tradesman's Life Assurance Society* (1858) 3 CBNS 622 (life insurance), where a payment of premium after the assured's death by a policy holder was held not to revive the policy, the contract referring to the future event of the assured's death; see ibid, per Byles J, at 644, 645.

3 *Bradford v Symondson* (supra) (marine insurance) per Brett LJ, at 461, who, after referring to policies on ships, 'lost or not lost', continued: 'Indeed the decisions, or at all events the dicta of Lord Mansfield and others of the greatest insurance Judges in England, have gone as far as this, that if both parties knew that the subject-matter was lost at the time when they entered into the policy, and the policy in terms covers that loss, the policy is good'. See also *Mead v Davison* (supra) (marine insurance) per Lord Denman CJ, at 308; *Gledstanes v Royal Exchange Assurance* (1864) 5 B & S 797 (marine insurance) per Cockburn CJ, at 809.

4 See further, Ivamy, *Marine Insurance* (4th Edn 1985), p 29.

CHAPTER 6

The Insurance Companies Act 1982

Insurance companies are governed by the Companies Act 1985. In addition, they are affected by the Insurance Companies Act 1982.

Part I of the Insurance Companies Act 1982 imposes restrictions on the carrying on of certain classes of insurance business.[1] Part II, which applies to all insurance companies whether established within or outside the United Kingdom carrying on insurance business in the United Kingdom, regulates insurance companies with regard to e g accounts, transfer of long term business, insolvency and winding up, and gives wide powers of intervention to the Secretary of State.[2] Part III concerns the conduct of insurance business.[3] Part IV deals with special classes of insurers.[4] Supplementary provisions are contained in Part V.[5]

RESTRICTION ON CARRYING ON INSURANCE BUSINESS

1 Preliminary

Classification

For the purposes of the Insurance Companies Act 1982 insurance business is divided into:

---

1 See pp 30–40, infra. For the purposes of the Insurance Companies Act 1982 'insurance business' includes:

a the effecting and carrying out, by a person not carrying on a banking business, of contracts for fidelity bonds, performance bonds, administration bonds, bail bonds or customs bonds or similar contracts of guarantee, being contracts effected by way of business (and not merely incidentally to some other business carried out by the person effecting them) in return for the payment of one or more premiums;

b the effecting and carrying out of tontines;

c the effecting and carrying out, by a body (not being a body carrying on a banking business) that carries on business which is insurance business apart from this paragraph, of

i capital redemption contracts;

ii contracts to manage the investments of pension funds (other than funds solely for the benefit of its own officers or employees and their dependants) or, in the case of a company, partly for the benefit of those persons and partly for the benefit of officers or employees and their dependants of its subsidiary or holding company or a subsidiary of its holding company;

d the effecting and carrying out of contracts to pay annuities on human life: Insurance Companies Act 1982, s 95.

2 See pp 40–78, post.

3 See pp 78–83, post.

4 See pp 83–85, post.

5 See pp 85–87, post.

a 'long term business' i e insurance business of any of the classes specified in Schedule 1[6] to the Act of 1982; and
b 'general business' i e insurance business of any of the classes specified in Part I of the Schedule 2[7] to that Act.[8]

The effecting and carrying out of a contract whose principal object is within one class of insurance but which contains related and subsidiary provisions within another class or classes is taken to constitute the carrying on of insurance business of the first-mentioned class and no other[9] if:

i the contract is one whose principal object is within any class of long term business[10] but which contains subsidiary provisions relating to accident and sickness insurance if the insurer is authorised to carry on life and annuity insurance business; or
ii the contract is one whose principal object is within one of the classes of general business[11] but which contains subsidiary provisions within another of those classes, not being credit or suretyship insurance business.

Restriction on carrying on insurance business

No person can carry on insurance business in the United Kingdom unless authorised to do so.[12]

But this rule does not apply to:

i insurance business (other than industrial assurance business) carried on:

a by a member of Lloyd's; or
b by a body registered under the enactments relating to friendly societies; or
c by a trade union[13] or employers' association[14] where the insurance

---

6 I life and annuity; II marriage and birth; III linked long term; IV permanent health; V tontines; VI capital redemption; and VII pension fund management.

7 I e (1) accident; (2) sickness; (3) land vehicles; (4) railway rolling stock; (5) aircraft; (6) ships; (7) goods in transit; (8) fire and natural forces; (9) damage to property; (10) motor vehicle liability; (11) aircraft liability; (12) liability for ships; (13) general liability; (14) credit; (15) suretyship; (16) miscellaneous financial loss; and (17) legal expenses.

8 Insurance Companies Act 1982, s 1(1).

9 Ibid, s 1(2).

10 For 'long term business', see footnote 6, supra.

11 For 'general business', see footnote 7, supra.

12 Insurance Companies Act 1982, s 2(1).

13 'Trade union' means an organisation (whether permanent or temporary) which either:
a consists wholly or mainly of workers of one or more descriptions and is an organisation whose principal purposes include the regulation of relations between workers of that description or those descriptions and employers or employers' associations; or
b consists wholly or mainly of
i constituent or affiliated organisations which fulfil the conditions specified in paragraph (a) above (or themselves consist wholly or mainly of constituent or affiliated organisations which fulfil those conditions), or
ii representatives of such constituent or affiliated organisations; and in either case is an organisation whose principal purposes include the regulation of relations between workers and employers or between workers' and employers' associations, or include the regulation of relations between its constituent or affiliated organisations: ibid, s 2(2).

14 'Employers' association' means an organisation (whether permanent or temporary) which

business carried on by the union or association is limited to the provision for its members of provident benefits or strike benefits.[15]

ii to industrial assurance business carried on by a friendly society registered under the enactments relating to such societies.[16]

iii credit, suretyship, miscellaneous financial loss and legal expenses insurance if it is carried on solely in the course of carrying on, and for the purposes of, banking business.[17]

iv general business consisting in the effecting and carrying out, by an insurance company that carries on no other insurance business, of contracts of such descriptions as may be prescribed, being contracts under which the benefits provided by the insurer are exclusively or primarily benefits in kind.[18]

Where authorisation is required but not obtained, an innocent insured to whom a policy has been issued is entitled to enforce it.[19] Whether it can be enforced by the insurer is unsettled.[20]

2 Authorised insurance companies

Authorisation by Secretary of State

The Secretary of State may authorise a body to carry on in the United Kingdom such of the classes of insurance business specified in Schedules 1[1] or 2[2] to the Insurance Companies Act 1982, or such parts of those classes, as may be specified in the authorisation.[3]

An authorisation may be restricted to industrial assurance business or to

---

either:

a consists wholly or mainly of employers or individual proprietors of one or more descriptions and is an organisation whose principal purposes include the regulation of relations between employers of that description or those descriptions and workers or trade unions; or

b consists wholly or mainly of:

i constituent or affiliated organisations which fulfil the conditions specified in paragraph (a) above (or themselves consist wholly or mainly of constituent or affiliated organisations which fulfil those conditions), or

ii representatives of such constituent or affiliated organisations; and in either case is an organisation whose principal purposes include the regulation of relations between employers and workers or between employers and trade unions, or include the regulation of relations between its constituent or affiliated organisations: ibid, s 2(2).

15 Ibid, s 2(2).

16 Ibid, s 2(3).

17 Ibid, s 2(4).

18 Ibid, s 2(5). For the regulations prescribing the contracts referred to in this subsection, see the Insurance Companies Regulations 1981 (SI 1981 No 1654) reg 23. See Appendix II, post.

19 *Stewart v Oriental Fire & Marine Insurance Co Ltd* [1985] QB 985, [1984] 3 All ER 777, [1984] 2 Lloyd's Rep 109 (see the judgment of Leggatt J, ibid, at 119–120), not following *Bedford Insurance Co Ltd v Institutio de Ressaguros do Brasil* [1985] QB 966, [1984] 3 All ER 706, [1984] 1 Lloyd's Rep 210; *Phoenix General Insurance Co of Greece SA v Halvanon Insurance Co Ltd* [1985] 2 Lloyd's Rep 599 at 609 (per Hobhouse J).

20 *Stewart v Oriental Fire & Marine Insurance Co Ltd* (supra), at 120 (per Leggatt J).

1 See p 31, ante.

2 See p 31, ante.

3 Insurance Companies Act 1982, s 3(1).

reinsurance business.[4] A body may not carry on industrial assurance business unless the authorisation expressly extends to such business.[5]

An authorisation may identify classes or parts of general business by referring to the appropriate groups specified in Part II of Schedule 2 to the Insurance Companies Act 1982.[6]

On the issue to a body of an authorisation under the above provisions, any previous authorisation[7] of that body lapses.

Existing insurance companies

A body which was immediately before 1 January 1982 authorised[8] to carry on in the United Kingdom insurance business of a class specified in Schedules 1 or 2 to the Insurance Companies Act 1981 (or part of such class) is authorised to carry on there business of the corresponding class specified in Schedules 1 or 2 to the Insurance Companies Act 1982 (or that part of such a class).[9]

A body may not carry on industrial assurance business unless:

i it was carrying on such business immediately before 1 January 1982; or
ii it was immediately before 28 January 1982 authorised to carry on such business under the Insurance Companies Act 1981, s 3.[10]

3 Application for authorisation

Submission of proposals

The Secretary of State must not issue an authorisation unless:

a the applicant has submitted to him such proposals as to the manner in which it proposes to carry on business, such financial forecasts and such other information as may be required or in accordance with regulations under the Insurance Companies Act 1982[11] and
b he is satisfied on the basis of that and any other information received by him that the application ought to be granted.[12]

He must decide an application for an authorisation within 6 months of receiving the information referred to above.[13] If he refuses to issue the authorisation, he must inform the applicant in writing of the reasons for the refusal.[14]

Combination of long term and general business

The Secretary of State must not authorise a body to carry on both long term business and general business unless:

---

4 Ibid, s 3(2).
5 Ibid, s 3(2).
6 Ibid, s 3(3).
7 Ibid, s 3(4).
8 Under the Insurance Companies Act 1981, s 3 or s 4.
9 Insurance Companies Act 1982, s 4(1).
10 Ibid, s 4(2).
11 The regulations at present in force are the Insurance Companies Regulations 1981 (SI 1981 No 1654), regs 29 and 30. See Appendix II, post.
12 Insurance Companies Act 1982, s 5(1).
13 Ibid, s 5(2).
14 Ibid, s 5(2).

a the long term insurance business is restricted to reinsurance; or
b the body is at the time the authorisation is issued lawfully carrying on in the United Kingdom both long term business and general business (in neither case restricted to reinsurance).[15]

United Kingdom applicants

The Secretary of State must not issue an authorisation to an applicant whose head office is in the United Kingdom unless the applicant is:

a a company;[16] or
b a registered society; or
c a body corporate established by royal charter or Act of Parliament and already authorised[17] to carry on insurance business (though not to the extent proposed in the application).[18]

He must not issue an authorisation to an applicant whose head office is in the United Kingdom if it has an issued share capital any part of which was issued after 28 January 1983 but is not fully paid up.[19]

He must not issue an authorisation to an applicant whose head office is in the United Kingdom if it appears to him that any director, controller,[20] manager[1]

---

15 Ibid, s 6.
16 As defined in the Companies Act 1985, s 735(1).
17 Under the Insurance Companies Act 1982, s 3 or s 4. See pp 32–33, ante.
18 Insurance Companies Act 1982, s 7(1).
19 Ibid, s 7(2).
20 'Controller', in relation to the applicant, means:
a a managing director of the applicant or of a body corporate of which the applicant is a subsidiary;
b a chief executive of the applicant or of a body corporate, being an insurance company, of which the applicant is a subsidiary;
c a person—
i in accordance with whose directions or instructions the directors of the applicant or of a body corporate of which it is a subsidiary are accustomed to act, or
ii who either alone or with any associate or associates is entitled to exercise, or control the exercise of, one-third or more of the voting power at any general meeting of the applicant or of a body corporate of which it is a subsidiary: ibid, s 7(4).

'Chief executive', in relation to the applicant or a body corporate of which it is a subsidiary, means an employee of the applicant or that body corporate, who, either alone or jointly with others, is responsible under the immediate authority of the directors for the conduct of the whole of the insurance business of the applicant or that body corporate: ibid, s 7(7). 'Associate' in relation to any person means:
a the wife or husband or minor son or daughter of that person;
b any company of which that person is a director;
c any person who is an employee or partner of that person;
d if that person is a company—
i any director of that company;
ii any subsidiary of that company;
iii any director or employee of any such subsidiary: ibid, s 7(8).

The word 'son' includes step-son, and 'daughter' includes step-daughter: ibid, s 7(8).

1 'Manager', in relation to the applicant, means an employee of the applicant (other than a chief executive) who, under the immediate authority of a director or chief executive of the applicant—
a exercises managerial functions, or
b is responsible for maintaining accounts or other records of the applicant,
not being a person whose functions relate exclusively to business conducted from a place of business outside the United Kingdom: ibid, s 7(5).

or main agent[2] of the applicant is not a fit and proper person to hold the position held by him.[3]

Applicants from other member States of the European Communities

The Secretary of State must not issue an authorisation to an applicant whose head office is in a member State other than the United Kingdom unless the applicant has a representative who:

i is a person[4] resident in the United Kingdom who has been designated as the applicant's representative; and
ii is authorised to act generally and to accept service of any document on behalf of the applicant; and
iii is not an auditor, or a partner or employee of an auditor, of the accounts of any business carried on by the applicant.[5]

The Secretary of State must not issue an authorisation to an applicant whose head office is in a member State other than the United Kingdom if it appears to the Secretary of State that any relevant executive[6] or main agent[7] of the applicant is not a fit and proper person to hold the position held by him.[8]

Where an applicant whose head office is in a member State other than the United Kingdom seeks an authorisation restricted to reinsurance business:

---

2 'Main agent', in relation to the applicant means, subject to such exceptions as may be prescribed, a person appointed by the applicant to be its agent in respect of general business in the United Kingdom, with authority to enter into contracts on behalf of the applicant in any financial year—
a without limit on the aggregate amount of premiums; or
b with a limit in excess of 10 per cent of the premium limit as determined in accordance with Sch 3 to the Insurance Companies Act 1981: ibid, s 7(6).
For the exceptions prescribed, see the Insurance Companies Regulations 1981 (SI 1981 No 1654), reg 24. See Appendix II, post.

3 Insurance Companies Act 1982, s 7(3).

4 If the representative is not an individual, it must be a company as defined in the Companies Act 1985, s 735(1), with its head office in the United Kingdom and must itself have an individual representative resident in the United Kingdom who is authorised to act generally, and to accept service of any document, on behalf of the company in its capacity as representative of the applicant: ibid, s 10(5).

5 Ibid, s 8(1).

6 'Relevant executive' in relation to the applicant means a person who is:
a the representative referred to in the Insurance Companies Act 1982, s 8(1), or the individual representative referred to in s 10(5);
b an officer or employee of the applicant who, either alone or jointly with others, is responsible for the conduct of the whole of the insurance business carried on by the applicant in the United Kingdom, not being a person who—
i is also responsible for the conduct of insurance business carried on by the applicant elsewhere, and
ii has a subordinate who is responsible for the whole of the insurance business carried on by the applicant in the United Kingdom; or
c an employee of the applicant who, under the immediate authority of a director or of an officer or employee within paragraph b above,—
i exercises managerial functions, or
ii is responsible for maintaining accounts or other records of the applicant,
not being a person whose functions relate exclusively to business conducted from a place of business outside the United Kingdom: ibid, s 8(4).

7 'Main agent' has the same meaning as in s 7: ibid, s 8(4). See footnote 2, supra.

8 Insurance Companies Act 1982, s 8(4).

a the Secretary of State must not issue the authorisation unless he is satisfied that the applicant is a body corporate entitled under the law of that State to carry on insurance business there; and
b he must not issue the authorisation if it appears to him that any person who is a director, controller[9] or manager[10] or a person within the Insurance Companies Act 1981, s 8(4)(a) or (b), or main agent of the applicant is not a fit and proper person to hold the position held by him.[11]

Applicants from outside the Community

The Secretary of State must not issue an authorisation in respect of long term[12] or general business[13] to an applicant whose head office is not in a member State unless he is satisfied:

a that the applicant is a body corporate entitled, under the law of the place where its head office is, to carry on long term or, as the case may be, general business there;
b that the applicant has in the United Kingdom assets of such value as may be prescribed; and
c that the applicant has made a deposit of such amount and with such person as may be prescribed.[14]

Where the applicant seeks to carry on business in the United Kingdom and one or more other member States, and the Secretary of State and the supervisory authority in the other State or States agree, the Secretary of State must not issue an authorisation in respect of long term or general business unless he is satisfied:

i that the applicant has in the member States concerned taken together assets of such value as may be prescribed; and
ii that the applicant has made a deposit of such amount and with such person as may be agreed between the Secretary of State and the other supervisory authority or authorities concerned.[15]

The Secretary of State must not issue an authorisation to an applicant whose head office is not in a member State unless the applicant has a representative who:

i is a person[16] resident in the United Kingdom who has been designated as the applicant's representative; and

---

9 'Controller' has the same meaning as in s 7: ibid, s 10(4). See p 34, footnote 20, ante.
10 'Manager' has the same meaning as in s 7: Insurance Companies Act 1982, s 10(4). See p 34, footnote 1, ante.
11 Insurance Companies Act 1982, s 8(2).
12 For the meaning of 'long term business', see p 31, ante.
13 For the meaning of 'general business', see p 31, ante.
14 Insurance Companies Act 1982, s 9(1). Para (c) of the subsection does not apply where the authorisation sought is one restricted to reinsurance: ibid, s 9(3).
15 Ibid, s 9(2). 'Supervisory authority', in relation to a member State other than the United Kingdom, means the authority responsible in that State for supervising insurance companies: ibid, s 96(1).
16 If the representative is not an individual, it must be a company as defined in the Companies Act

ii is authorised to act generally, and to accept service of any document, on behalf of the applicant; and
iii is not an auditor, or a partner or employee of an auditor, of the accounts of any business carried on by the applicant.[17]

The Secretary of State must not issue an authorisation to an applicant whose head office is not in a member State if it appears to him that:

a the representative of the applicant or the individual representative, or
b any director, controller or manager of the applicant, or
c a main agent of the applicant

is not a fit and proper person to hold the position held by him.[18]

Regulations may make such provision as to deposits as appears to the Secretary of State to be necessary or expedient,[19] including provision for the deposit of securities instead of money,[20] and in relation to deposits with the Accountant General of the Supreme Court, provision applying (with or without modification) any of the provisions of the rules for the time being in force under the Administration of Justice Act 1982, s 38(7).[1]

4 Withdrawal of authorisation

Withdrawal in respect of new business

The Secretary of State may, at the request of the company or on the ground:

i that it appears to him that the company has failed to satisfy an obligation to which it is subject by virtue of the Insurance Companies Act 1982; or
ii that there exists a ground on which he would be prohibited[2] from issuing an authorisation to the company; or
iii that the company has ceased to be authorised to effect contracts of insurance, or contracts of a particular description, in a member State where it has its head office or where it has made a deposit,[3]

1985, s 735(1) with its head office in the United Kingdom and must itself have an individual representative resident in the United Kingdom who is authorised to act generally, and to accept service of any document, on behalf of the company in its capacity as representative of the applicant: ibid, s 10(5).

17 Ibid, s 9(4).

18 Ibid, s 9(5). 'Controller', 'manager' and 'main agent' have the same meanings as in s 7, except that the controllers of the applicant are to be taken to include any officer or employee who, either alone or jointly with others, is responsible for the conduct of the whole of the insurance business carried on by the applicant in the United Kingdom, not being a person who:
a is also responsible for the conduct of business carried on by it elsewhere; and
b has a subordinate who is responsible for the whole of the insurance business carried on by the applicant in the United Kingdom: ibid, s 9(6).
For s 7, see pp 34–35, ante.

19 Insurance Companies Act 1982, s 9(7). See the Insurance Companies Regulations 1981 (SI 1981 No 1654), regs 14 to 22. See Appendix II, post.

20 See the Insurance Companies Regulations 1981 (SI 1981 No 1654), reg 17.

1 See ibid, reg 22.

2 By the Insurance Companies Act 1982, s 7 (United Kingdom applicants), s 8 (applicants from other member States of the European Communities) or s 9 (applicants from outside the Community). See pp 34–37, ante.

3 In accordance with the Insurance Companies Act 1982, s 9(2). See p 36, ante.

direct that an insurance company authorised to carry on business shall cease to be authorised to effect contracts of any description specified in the direction.[4]

After giving a direction otherwise than at the request of the company concerned the Secretary of State must inform the company in writing of his reasons for giving the direction.[5]

A direction does not prevent a company from effecting a contract of insurance in pursuance of a term of a subsisting contract of insurance.[6]

Where a direction has been given in respect of a company which has its head office, or has made a deposit,[7] in a member State other than the United Kingdom, the Secretary of State may revoke or vary the direction if after consultation with the supervisory authority[8] in that member State he considers it appropriate to do so.[9]

Except in the above case a direction of any insurance company may not be revoked or varied.[10] But if the Secretary of State subsequently issues to the company an authorisation to carry on insurance business of a class to which the direction relates, the direction ceases to have effect in relation to such business.[11]

Notices of withdrawal

Before giving a direction otherwise than at the request of the company concerned the Secretary of State must serve on the company a written notice stating:

- i that he is considering giving a direction and the ground on which he is considering it; and
- ii that the company may, within the period of 1 month from the date of service of the notice make written representations to him and, if the company so requests, oral representations to an officer of the Department of Trade appointed for the purpose by him.[12]

Before giving a direction in respect of a company on the ground that he would be prohibited by the Insurance Companies Act 1982, s 7(3),[13] s 8(2)[14] or s 9(5)[15] from issuing an authorisation to the company the Secretary of State must serve on the person whose fitness is in question a written notice stating:

---

4 Insurance Companies Act 1982, s 11(1), (2).
5 Ibid, s 11(3).
6 Ibid, s 11(4).
7 In accordance with the Insurance Companies Act 1982, s 9(2). See p 36, ante.
8 'Supervisory authority', in relation to a member State other than the United Kingdom, means the authority responsible in that State for supervising insurance companies: Insurance Companies Act 1982, s 96(1).
9 Ibid, s 11(5).
10 Ibid, s 11(6).
11 Ibid, s 11(6).
12 Ibid, s 12(1).
13 Which concerns the unfitness of a director, controller, manager or main agent of the applicant to hold the position held by him. See p 35, ante.
14 Which concerns the unfitness of any relevant executive or main agent of the applicant to hold the position held by him. See p 35, ante.
15 Which concerns the unfitness of the representative, individual representative, director, controller, manager or main agent of the applicant to hold the position held by him. See p 37, ante.

i that he is considering giving a direction on that ground; and
ii that the person on whom the notice is served may, within the period of 1 month from the date of the service of the notice, make written representations to him and, if that person so requests, oral representations to an officer of the Department of Trade appointed for the purpose by the Secretary of State.[16]

Except where the person whose fitness for the position concerned is in question is a controller, the Secretary of State must consider any representations made in response to a notice under s 12(2) before serving a notice under s 12(1).[17]

A notice under s 12(1) or s 12(2) must give particulars of the ground on which the Secretary of State is considering giving a direction.[18]

Where representations are made in response to a notice, the Secretary of State must take them into consideration before giving a direction.[19]

Any notice to be served on a person may be served by post, and a letter containing the notice is deemed to be properly addressed if it is addressed to that person at his last known residence or last known place of business in the United Kingdom.[20]

After giving a direction the Secretary of State must publish notice of it in the *London Gazette* and in such other ways as appear to him to be expedient for notifying the public.[1]

Final withdrawal of authorisation

Where an insurance company ceases to carry on in the United Kingdom any insurance business, or insurance business of any class, the Secretary of State may direct that it shall cease to be authorised to carry on insurance business, or insurance business of that class.[2]

If a body authorised to carry on insurance business of any class has not at any time carried on business of that class, and at least 12 months have elapsed since the issue of the authorisation, the Secretary of State may direct that it shall cease to be authorised to carry on business of that class.[3]

A direction is without prejudice to the subsequent issue of an authorisation to carry on business of a class to which the direction relates.[4]

5 Offences

A person who carries on business in contravention of Part I of the Insurance Companies Act 1982 is guilty of an offence.[5]

A person who for the purpose of obtaining the issue of an authorisation

---

16 Insurance Companies Act 1982, s 12(2).
17 Ibid, s 12(3)(4).
18 Ibid, s 12(5).
19 Ibid, s 12(6).
20 Ibid, s 12(7).
1 Ibid, s 12(8).
2 Ibid, s 13(1).
3 Ibid, s 13(2).
4 Ibid, s 13(3).
5 Ibid, s 14(1).

furnishes information which he knows to be false in a material particular or recklessly furnishes information which is false in a material particular is guilty of an offence.[6]

A person guilty of an offence is liable:[7]

i on conviction on indictment, to imprisonment for a term not exceeding 2 years or to a fine, or to both;
ii on summary conviction, to a fine not exceeding £1,000, or if it is greater, the prescribed sum within the meaning of the Magistrates' Courts Act 1980, s 32.

REGULATION OF INSURANCE COMPANIES

In general, Part II of the Insurance Companies Act 1982 applies to all insurance companies, whether established within or outside the United Kingdom, which carry on business within the United Kingdom.[8]

But Part II does not apply to:

i any insurance company which is registered under the Acts relating to friendly societies,[9]
ii a trade union[10] or an employers' association[11] carrying on insurance business if the insurance business is limited to the provision for its members of provident benefits or strike benefits;[12]
iii a member of Lloyd's who carries on business of any class provided that he complies with the requirements set out in the Insurance Companies Act 1982, s 83 and applicable to business of that class;[13]

---

6 Ibid, s 14(2).
7 Ibid, s 14(3).
8 Ibid, s 15(1).
9 Ibid, s 15(2).
10 For the meaning of 'trade union', see p 31, ante.
11 For the meaning of 'employers' association', see p 31, ante.
12 Insurance Companies Act 1982, s 15(3).
13 Ibid, s 15(4). The requirements of s 83 are that (i) every underwriter must, in accordance with the provisions of a trust deed approved by the Secretary of State, carry to a trust fund all premiums received by him or on his behalf in respect of any insurance business; (ii) premiums in respect of long term business must in no case be carried to the same trust fund as premiums received in respect of general business, but the trust deed may provide for carrying the premiums received in respect of all or any classes of long term business and all or any classes of general business either to a common fund or to any number of separate funds; (iii) the accounts of every underwriter must be audited annually by an accountant approved by the Committee of Lloyd's, and the auditor must furnish a certificate in the prescribed form to the Committee and the Secretary of State; (iv) the certificate must in particular state whether in the opinion of the auditor the value of the assets available to meet the underwriter's liabilities in respect of insurance business is correctly shown in the accounts, and whether or not that value is sufficient to meet the liabilities calculated: (a) in the case of liabilities in respect of long term business, by an actuary; and (b) in the case of other liabilities, by the auditor on a basis approved by the Secretary of State; (v) where any liabilities of an underwriter are calculated by an actuary, he must furnish a certificate of the amount to the Committee of Lloyd's, and must state in the certificate on what basis the calculation is made; (vi) a copy of the certificate must be annexed to the auditor's certificate; and (vii) the underwriter must, when required by the Committee of Lloyd's furnish to them such information as they may require for the purpose of preparing the statement of business which is to be deposited with the Secretary of State under s 86 of the Act. By s 86(1) the statement of business must be in the prescribed form summarising the extent and

iv a person by reason only that he carries on general business of class 14, 15, 16 or 17[14] in the course of carrying on, and for the purposes of, banking business;[15]

v an insurance company whose insurance business is restricted to general business consisting in the effecting and carrying out of contracts of such descriptions as may be prescribed, being contracts under which the benefits provided by the insurer are exclusively or primarily benefits in kind.[16]

Part II contains provisions relating to:

a restriction of business to insurance;[17]
b accounts and statements;[18]
c assets and liabilities attributable to long term business;[19]
d financial resources;[20]
e liabilities of unlimited amount;[1]
f powers of intervention;[2]
g transfers of long term business;[3]
h transfers of general business;[4]
i insolvency and winding up;[5]
j changes of director, controller or manager;[6]
k change of main agent;[7] and
l miscellaneous matters.[8]

A *Restriction of business to insurance*

An insurance company to which Part II of the Insurance Companies Act 1982 applies[9] must not carry on any activities, in the United Kingdom or elsewhere, otherwise than in connection with or for the purposes of its insurance business.[10]

---

character of the insurance business done by the members of Lloyd's in the twelve months to which the statement relates. By s 86(2) regulations may require the statement to deal separately with such classes or descriptions of business as may be specified in the regulations. See pp 85–86, post.

14 As to these classes, see p 31, ante.
15 Insurance Companies Act 1982, s 15(5).
16 Ibid, s 15(6). The regulations at present in force are the Insurance Companies Regulations 1981 (SI 1981 No 1654), reg 23. See Appendix II, post.
17 See infra.
18 See pp 42–47, post.
19 See pp 47–52, post.
20 See pp 52–54, post.
1 See p 54, post.
2 See pp 54–64, post.
3 See pp 64–66, post.
4 See pp 66–67, post.
5 See pp 67–72, post.
6 See pp 72–76, post.
7 See p 76, post.
8 See pp 76–78, post.
9 See pp 40–41, ante.
10 Insurance Companies Act 1982, s 16(1). For the purpose of this subsection any activities of an insurance company that are excluded from the definition of s 95(c)(iii) are to be treated as carried on in connection with its insurance business: ibid, s 16(2).

B Accounts and statements

1 Annual accounts and balance sheets

Every insurance company to which Part II of the Insurance Companies Act 1982 applies[11] must, with respect to each financial year of the company, prepare a revenue account for the year, a balance sheet as at the end of the year and a profit and loss account for the year or, in the case of a company not trading for profit, an income and expenditure account for the year.[12]

The contents of the documents are such as may be prescribed, but regulations may provide for enabling information required to be given by such documents to be given instead in a note thereon or statement or report annexed thereto or may require there to be given in such a note, statement or report such information in addition to that given in the documents as may be prescribed.[13]

Regulations may, as respects such matters stated in such documents or in statements or reports annexed thereto as may be prescribed, require there to be given by such persons as may be prescribed and to be annexed to the documents certificates of such matters as may be prescribed.[14]

If a form is prescribed for any such document or as that in which information authorised or required to be given in a statement or report annexed to any such document is to be given or for a certificate to be so annexed, the document must be prepared, the information must be given or, as the case may be, the certificate must be framed, in that form.[15]

2 Periodic actuarial investigation of company with long term business

Every insurance company to which Part II of the Insurance Companies Act 1982 applies[16] which carries on long term business:

a must, once in every period of 12 months, cause an investigation to be made into its financial condition in respect of that business by the person who for the time being is its actuary;[17] and
b when such an investigation has been made, or when at any other time an investigation into the financial condition of the company in respect of its long term business has been made with a view to the distribution of profits, or the results of which are made public, must cause an abstract of the actuary's report of the investigation to be made.[18]

---

11 See pp 40–41, ante.
12 Insurance Companies Act 1982, s 17(1).
13 Ibid, s 17(2). The regulations at present in force are the Insurance Companies (Accounts and Statements) Regulations 1983 (SI 1983 No 1811) regs 2, 4–22, 26, Schs 1–3, Sch 6, Pts I and II. See Appendix II, post.
14 Insurance Companies Act 1982, s 17(3).
15 Ibid, s 17(4).
16 See pp 40–41, ante.
17 Insurance Companies Act 1982, s 18(1)(a). At least once in every period of 5 years an insurance company must prepare a statement of its long term business at the date to which the accounts of the company are made up for the purpose of an investigation in pursuance of an investigation under this subsection: ibid, s 18(3).
18 Ibid, s 18(1)(b). An investigation to which this paragraph relates must include:
a a valuation of the liabilities of the company attributable to its long term business; and
b a determination of any excess over those liabilities of the assets representing the fund or funds maintained by the company in respect of that business and where any rights of any long term

For the purposes of any investigation the value of any assets and the amount of any liabilities must be determined in accordance with any applicable valuation regulations.[19]

The regulations may provide that for any specified purpose, assets or liabilities of any specified class or description must be left out of account or must be taken into account only to a specified extent.[20] They may make different provision in relation to different cases or circumstances.[1]

The form and contents of any abstract or statement are such as may be prescribed.[2]

3 Appointment of actuary by company with long term business

Every company to which Part II of the Insurance Companies Act 1982 applies[3] must within one month of beginning to carry on long term business appoint an actuary as actuary to the company.[4] When the actuary's appointment comes to an end, the company must as soon as practicable make a fresh appointment.[5]

A company must within 14 days of appointing an actuary serve on the Secretary of State a written notice stating that it has done so and giving the name and qualifications of the person appointed.[6] If an appointment comes to an end, the company must within 14 days serve on the Secretary of State a written notice stating that fact and the name of the person concerned.[7]

4 Annual statements

Classes of insurance business may be prescribed and every insurance company to which Part II of the Insurance Companies Act 1982 applies[8] which carries on such business of a prescribed class must annually prepare the prescribed statement of business of that class.[9] If a form is prescribed for the statement, the statement must be in that form.[10]

---

policy holders to participate in profits relate to particular parts of such a fund, a determination of any excess of assets over liabilities in respect of each of those parts: ibid, s 18(2).

19 Ibid, s 18(4). The regulations at present in force are the Insurance Companies Regulations 1981 (SI 1981 No 1654), regs 37 to 64. See Appendix II, post.

20 Insurance Companies Act 1982, s 90(2).

1 Ibid, s 90(3).

2 Ibid, s 18(5). The regulations at present are the Insurance Companies (Accounts and Statements) regulations 1983 (SI 1983 No 1811), regs 2, 9, Sch 2. See Appendix II, post.

3 See pp 40–41, ante.

4 Insurance Companies Act 1982, s 19(1). An actuary means an actuary possessing the prescribed qualifications: ibid, s 96(1). For the prescribed qualifications see Insurance Companies (Accounts and Statements) Regulations 1983 (SI 1983 No 1811), reg 28. See Appendix II, post.

5 Insurance Companies Act 1982, s 19(1).

6 Ibid, s 19(2). If an insurance company fails to comply with this requirement, it is guilty of an offence, and is liable, on summary conviction, to a fine not exceeding level 5 on the standard scale: ibid, s 71(3).

7 Ibid, s 19(2). If an insurance company fails to comply with this requirement, it is guilty of an offence, and is liable, on summary conviction, to a fine not exceeding level 5 on the standard scale: ibid, s 71(3).

8 See pp 40–41, ante.

9 Insurance Companies Act 1982, s 20. The regulations at present in force are the Insurance Companies (Accounts and Statements) Regulations 1983 (SI 1983, No 1811), regs 2, 23, Sch 2. See Appendix II, post.

10 Insurance Companies Act 1982, s 20.

5 Audit of accounts

The accounts and balance sheets of every insurance company to which Part II of the Insurance Companies Act 1982 applies[11] must be audited in the prescribed manner by a person of the prescribed description.[12] Regulations may apply to such companies the provisions of the Companies Act 1985 relating to audit, subject to such adaptations and modifications as may appear necessary or expedient.[13]

6 Deposit of accounts with Secretary of State

Every account, balance sheet, abstract or statement, and any report of the auditor of the company must be printed.[14] Five copies must be deposited with the Secretary of State within six months after the close of the period to which the account, balance sheet, abstract, statement or report relates.[15]

But if in any case it is made to appear to the Secretary of State that a longer period than six months should be allowed, he may extend that period by such period not exceeding three months as he thinks fit.[16]

At the same time as the accounts, balance sheet, abstract or statement are deposited, there must also be deposited with the Secretary of State five printed copies of a statement of the names and connection with the company of any persons who, during the period to which those documents relate:

a were authorised by the company to issue, or to the knowledge of the company have issued, any invitation to another person to make an offer or proposal or to take any other step with a view to entering into a contract of insurance with the company; and
b were connected with the company as provided by regulations.[17]

One of the copies of any document which is deposited except an auditor's report must be a copy signed by such persons as may be prescribed.[18]

One of the copies of an auditor's report must be a copy signed by him.[19]

The Secretary of State must consider the documents deposited with him, and

---

11 See pp 40–41, ante.

12 Insurance Companies Act 1982, s 21(1). The reference in this subsection to accounts and balance sheets includes a reference to any statement or report annexed to them giving information authorised or required by s 17(2) to be given in a statement or report so annexed: ibid, s 21(2). As to s 17(2), see p 42, ante. The regulations at present in force are the Insurance Companies (Accounts and Statements) Regulations 1983 (SI 1983, No 1811), regs 2, 27, 28, Sch 6, Pt III. See Appendix II, post.

13 Insurance Companies Act 1982, s 21(1).

14 Ibid, s 22(1). When documents are deposited under this subsection, the company must pay to the Secretary of State such fee as may be prescribed: ibid, s 94A(1). The regulations at present in force are the Insurance (Fees) Regulations 1986 (SI 1986/446).

15 Insurance Companies Act 1982.

16 Ibid, s 22(1). If any insurance company makes default in complying with this requirement, it is guilty of an offence and liable on summary conviction to a fine not exceeding level 5 on the standard scale: ibid, s 71(3). Where a person continues to make default in complying with s 22(1) after being convicted of that default he is guilty of a further offence and liable on summary conviction to a fine not exceeding £40 for each day on which the default continues: ibid, s 71(4).

17 Ibid, s 22(2).

18 Ibid, s 22(3). The regulations at present in force are the Insurance Companies (Accounts and Statements) Regulations 1983 (SI 1983 No 1811), regs 2, 25. See Appendix II, post.

19 Insurance Companies Act 1982, s 22(4).

if any document appears to him to be inaccurate or incomplete, he must communicate with the company with a view to the correction of any such inaccuracies and the supply of deficiencies.[20]

With every revenue account and balance sheet of a company there must be deposited any report on the affairs of the company submitted to the shareholders or policy holders in respect of the financial year to which the account and balance sheet relate.[1]

Any person who causes or permits to be included in any document copies of which are required[2] to be deposited with the Secretary of State a statement which he knows to be false in a material particular or recklessly causes or permits to be so included any statement which is false in a material particular, is guilty of an offence.[3]

7 Right of shareholders and policy holders to receive copies of deposited documents

An insurance company must forward by post or otherwise to any shareholder or policy holder who applies for one:

- a a printed copy of any account, balance sheet, abstract or statement, and of any report of the auditor of the company;
- b a copy of any document supplied to the Secretary of State where it appears to him that the document originally submitted is inaccurate or incomplete;
- c a copy of any report on the affairs of the company submitted to the shareholders or policy holders in respect of the financial year to which the account and balance sheet relate.[4]

If, in the opinion of the Secretary of State, the disclosure of information contained in:

- a a statement or report annexed to a revenue account, a balance sheet and profit and loss account (or, in the case of a company not trading for profit, an income and expenditure account); or
- b a statement by a company in connection with a prescribed class of business;

would be harmful to the business of the company or of any of its subsidiaries, the Secretary of State may dispense the company from complying with its obligation to forward a copy of the document containing the information to a shareholder or policy holder who applies for it.[5]

---

[20] Ibid, s 22(5).
[1] Ibid, s 22(6).
[2] Under the Insurance Companies Act 1982, s 22.
[3] Insurance Companies Act 1982, s 71(1)(c). He is liable on conviction on indictment, to imprisonment for a term not exceeding 2 years, or to a fine, or to both; and on summary conviction, to a fine not exceeding £1,000 or, if it is greater, the prescribed sum within the meaning of the Magistrates' Courts Act 1980, s 32: ibid, s 71(2). Where a person continues to make default in complying with s 22(1), after being convicted of that default, he is guilty of a further offence and liable on summary conviction to a fine not exceeding £40 for each day on which the default continues: ibid, s 71(4).
[4] Ibid, s 23(1). Any insurance company which makes default in complying with this subsection is guilty of an offence and liable, on summary conviction, to a fine not exceeding level 5 on the standard scale: ibid, s 71(3)(a).
[5] Ibid, s 23(2).

8 Periodic statements by company with prescribed class of business

Every insurance company to which Part II of the Insurance Companies Act 1982 applies[6] which carries on business of a prescribed class or description must prepare at such intervals and for such periods as may be prescribed, a statement of its business of that class or description.[7]

The form and contents of any statement must be such as may be prescribed.[8]

Regulations may, as respects such matters contained in a statement as may be prescribed, require there to be given by such persons as may be prescribed and to be annexed to the statement certificates of such matters and in such form as may be prescribed.[9]

Five copies of any statement together with any certificate, where required, must be deposited by the company with the Secretary of State within such period as may be prescribed. One of the copies must be a copy signed:

i where there are more than two directors of the company, by at least two of those directors and where there are not more than two directors, by all the directors;
ii by a chief executive, if any, of the company, or (if there is no chief executive) by the secretary.[10]

The whole or any part of any document deposited may be deposited by the Secretary of State with the Registrar of Companies, and may be published by the Secretary of State in such ways as he thinks appropriate.[11]

Any person who causes or permits to be included in any document deposited with the Secretary of State a statement which he knows to be false in a material particular or recklessly causes or permits to be so included any statement which is false in a material particular, is guilty of an offence.[12]

9 Statements of transactions of prescribed class or description

Classes or descriptions of agreements or arrangements appearing to the Secretary of State as likely to be undesirable in the interests of policy holders may be prescribed, and every insurance company to which Part II of the Insurance Companies Act 1982 applies[13] or any 'subordinate company'[14] of

---

6 See pp 40–41, ante.
7 Insurance Companies Act 1982, s 25(1).
8 Ibid, s 25(2).
9 Ibid, s 25(3).
10 Ibid, s 25(4). Any insurance company which makes default in complying with this subsection is guilty of an offence and liable on summary conviction to a fine not exceeding level 5 on the standard scale: ibid, s 71(3). Where a person continues to make default in complying with s 22(1) after being convicted of that default, he is guilty of a further offence and liable on summary conviction to a fine not exceeding £40 for every day on which the default continues: ibid, s 71(4).
11 Ibid, s 25(5).
12 Ibid, s 71(1)(c)(iii). A person guilty of an offence under this subsection is liable on conviction on indictment, to imprisonment for a term not exceeding 2 years, or to a fine or to both; and on summary conviction, to a fine not exceeding £1,000 or, if it is greater, the prescribed sum within the meaning of the Magistrates' Courts Act 1980, s 32: ibid, s 71(2).
13 See pp 40–41, ante.
14 Within the meaning of s 31. As to s 31, see p 50, post.

any such company which enters into an agreement or arrangement of a class or description so prescribed must, within such period as may be prescribed, furnish the Secretary of State with a statement containing such particulars of that agreement or arrangement as may be prescribed.[15]

Different classes or descriptions of agreements or arrangements may be prescribed in relation to companies of different classes or descriptions.[16]

The whole or any part of any statement furnished to the Secretary of State may be deposited by him with the Registrar of Companies and may be published by the Secretary of State in such ways as he thinks appropriate.[17]

Any person who causes or permits to be included in any statement which he knows to be false in a material particular or recklessly causes or permits to be so included any statement which is false in a material particular, is guilty of an offence.[18]

10 Companies from outside the Community

An insurance company to which Part II of the Insurance Companies Act 1982 applies[19] whose head office is not in a member State must keep in the United Kingdom proper accounts and records in respect of insurance business carried on in the United Kingdom.[20]

C Assets and liabilities attributable to long term business

1 Separation of assets and liabilities

Where an insurance company to which Part II of the Insurance Companies Act 1982 applies[1] carries on ordinary long term insurance business[2] or industrial assurance business or both of those kinds of insurance business,

a the company must maintain an account in respect of that business or, as the case may be, each of those kinds of business, and

b the receipts of that business or, as the case may be, of each of those kinds of business must be entered in the account maintained for that business, and must be carried to and form a separate insurance fund with an appropriate name.[3]

---

15 Insurance Companies Act 1982, s 26(1). Any insurance company or any other person who makes default in complying with s 26 is guilty of an offence and liable, on summary conviction to a fine not exceeding level 5 on the standard scale: ibid, s 71(3).

16 Ibid, s 26(2).

17 Ibid, s 26(3).

18 Ibid, s 71(1). Any person guilty of an offence under this subsection is liable, on conviction on indictment, to imprisonment for a term not exceeding 2 years, or to a fine, or to both, and on summary conviction, to a fine not exceeding £1,000 or, if it is greater, the prescribed sum within the meaning of the Magistrates' Courts Act 1980, s 32: ibid, s 71(2).

19 See pp 40–41, ante.

20 Insurance Companies Act 1982, s 27.

1 See pp 40–41, ante.

2 As to 'long term insurance business', see p 31, ante.

3 Insurance Companies Act 1982, s 28(1). If a person makes default in complying with s 28, he is guilty of an offence, and is liable: i on conviction on indictment, to imprisonment for a term not exceeding 2 years, or to a fine, or to both; ii on summary conviction, to a fine not exceeding £1,000, or, if it is greater, the prescribed sum within the meaning of the Magistrates' Courts Act 1980, s 32: ibid, s 71(1)(2).

An insurance company to which Part II of the Insurance Companies Act 1982 applies,[4] which carries on ordinary long term insurance business or industrial assurance business or both of those kinds of business must maintain such accounting and other records as are necessary for identifying:

a the assets representing the fund or funds maintained by the company (but without necessarily distinguishing between the funds if more than one); and
b the liabilities attributable to that business or, as the case may be, each of those kinds of business.[5]

2 Application of assets of company with long term business

In general, the assets representing the fund or funds maintained by an insurance company in respect of its long term business:

a are applicable only for the purposes of that business; and
b must not be transferred so as to be available for other purposes of the company except where the transfer constitutes reimbursement of expenditure borne by other assets (in the same or the last preceding financial year) in discharging liabilities wholly or partially attributable to long term business.[6]

But where the value of such assets is shown by the periodic actuarial investigations of a company[7] or by an investigation made in pursuance of a requirement of an actuarial investigation required by the Secretary of State,[8] to exceed the amount of the liabilities attributable to the company's long term business, so much of the assets as represents the excess need not be applied for the purposes of its long term business.[9]

Again, nothing precludes an insurance company from exchanging, at fair market value, assets representing a fund maintained by the company in respect of its long term business for other assets of the company.[10]

Any mortgage or charge (including a charge imposed by a court on the application of a judgment creditor) is void to the extent that it contravenes the rule that the assets representing the fund or funds maintained in respect of the company's long term business are applicable only for the purposes of that business.[11]

Money from a fund maintained by a company in respect of its long term business must not be used for the purposes of any other business of the company notwithstanding any arrangement for its subsequent repayment out of receipts of that other business.[12]

No insurance company to which Part II of the Insurance Companies Act

---

4 See pp 40–41, ante.
5 Insurance Companies Act 1982, s 28(2).
6 Ibid, s 29(1).
7 Under the Insurance Companies Act 1982, s 18. See pp 42–43, ante.
8 Under the Insurance Companies Act 1982, s 42. See p 59, post.
9 Insurance Companies Act 1982, s 29(2). This subsection does not authorise a transfer or other application of assets by reference to an actuarial investigation at any time after the date when the abstract of the actuary's report has been deposited with the Secretary of State in accordance with s 22(1) or s 42(4): ibid, s 29(3). For 22(1) see p 44, ante, and s 42(4), p 59, post.
10 Insurance Companies Act 1982, s 29(4).
11 Ibid, s 29(5).
12 Ibid, s 29(6).

1982 applies,[13] and no company of which any such insurance company is a subsidiary, must declare a dividend at any time when the value of the assets representing the fund or funds maintained by the insurance company in respect of its long term business, as determined in accordance with any applicable valuation regulations, is less than the amount of the liabilities attributable to that business as so determined.[14]

3 Allocations to policy holders

Where in the case of an insurance company to which Part II of the Insurance Companies Act 1982 applies:[15]

a there is an established surplus[16] in which long term policy holders of any category are eligible to participate, and
b an amount has been allocated[17] to policy holders of that category in respect of a previously established surplus in which policy holders of that category were eligible to participate,

the company cannot[18] transfer or otherwise apply assets representing any part of the surplus unless the company has either allocated to policy holders of that category in respect of that surplus an amount not less than the relevant minimum[19] or complied with the 'requirements' mentioned below and made to those policy holders any allocation of which notice is given.[20]

---

13 See pp 40–41, ante.

14 Insurance Companies Act 1982, s 29(7). Any person who makes default in complying with s 29 is guilty of an offence and liable on conviction on indictment, to imprisonment for a term not exceeding 2 years or to a fine or to both, and, on summary conviction, to a fine not exceeding £1,000, or if it is greater, the prescribed sum within the meaning of the Magistrates' Courts Act 1980, s 32: ibid, s 71(1)(2). Any person who makes default in complying with s 29(7) is guilty of an offence and liable, on summary conviction, to a fine not exceeding level 5 on the standard scale: ibid, s 71(3).

15 See pp 40–41, ante.

16 'Established surplus' means an excess of assets representing the whole or a particular part of the fund or funds maintained by the company in respect of its long term business over the liabilities, or a particular part of the liabilities, of the company attributable to that business as shown by a periodic actuarial investigation under s 18 or by an actuarial investigation required by the Secretary of State under s 42: Insurance Companies Act 1982, s 30(4). For a periodic actuarial investigation, see pp 42–43, ante, and for an actuarial investigation required by the Secretary of State, see p 59, post.

17 An amount is allocated to policy holders if, and only if,
a bonus payments are made to them; or
b reversionary bonuses are declared in their favour or a reduction is made in the premiums payable by them;
and the amount of the allocation is, in a case within para a, the amount of the payments and, in a case within para b the amount of the liabilities assumed by the company in consequence of the declaration or reduction: Insurance Companies Act 1982, s 30(5). For the purposes of s 30 the amount of any bonus payments made in anticipation of an established surplus must be treated as an amount allocated in respect of the next established surplus in respect of which an amount is allocated to eligible policy holders generally: ibid, s 30(6). For the purposes of s 30(2) the amount of any surplus is treated as increased by the amount of any such payments in respect of which such an allocation is made: ibid, s 30(6).

18 By virtue of the Insurance Companies Act 1982, s 29(2). See p 48, ante.

19 The 'relevant minimum' is the amount represented by the formula $\frac{b \times c}{a} - \frac{c}{200}$ where:
a is the last previously established surplus in respect of which an amount was allocated to policy holders of the category in question;
b is the amount so allocated; and
c is the surplus referred to in s 30(1)(a): Insurance Companies Act 1982, s 30(2).

20 Ibid, s 30(1). For the purposes of this subsection policy holders are taken to be eligible to

The 'requirements' are that the company:

a has served on the Secretary of State a written notice that it proposes to make no allocation or an allocation of a specified amount which is smaller than the relevant minimum; and
b has published a statement approved by the Secretary of State in the *London Gazette* and in such other ways as he may have directed,

and that a period of not less than 56 days has elapsed since the date, or the last date, on which the company has published the statement mentioned above.[1]

4 Restrictions on transactions with connected persons

Neither an insurance company to which Part II of the Insurance Companies Act 1982 applies[2] which carries on long term business nor a subordinate company[3] must enter into certain transactions mentioned below:

a at a time when the aggregate of the value of the assets and the amount of the liabilities[4] attributable to such transactions already entered into by the insurance company and its subordinate companies exceeds the prescribed percentage[5] of the total amount standing to the credit of the insurance company's long term funds;[6] or

---

participate in an established surplus in any case where they would be eligible to participate in a later established surplus representing it if it were carried forward unappropriated: ibid, s 30(2). Any person who makes default in complying with s 30 is guilty of an offence and liable on conviction on indictment, to imprisonment for a term not exceeding 2 years or to a fine or to both, and, on summary conviction, to a fine not exceeding £1,000, or, if it is greater, the prescribed sum within the meaning of the Magistrates' Courts Act 1980, s 32: ibid, s 71(1)(2).

1 Ibid, s 30(3).

2 See pp 40–41, ante.

3 'Subordinate company' means:

a a company having equity share capital some or all of which is held by the insurance company:
  i amounts to more than half in nominal value of that share capital; and
  ii confers on the insurance company the power to appoint or remove the holders of all or a majority of the directorships of the company whose share capital is held and more than half of the voting power at any general meeting of that company;
b a company having equity share capital some or all of which is held by another company which is itself a subordinate company of the insurance company where the share capital held by that other company:
  i amounts to more than half in nominal value of that share capital; and
  ii confers on that other company the power to appoint or remove the holders of all or a majority of the directorships of the company whose share capital is held and more than one half of the voting power at any general meeting of that company: Insurance Companies Act 1982.

Share capital held for any person by a nominee must (except where that person is concerned only in a fiduciary capacity) be treated as held by that person, and share capital held by a person in a fiduciary capacity or by way of security must be treated as not held by that person: ibid, s 31(4). 'Long term assets' mean assets representing the fund or funds maintained by the company in respect of its long term business: ibid, s 31(7). 'Long term funds' mean the fund or funds maintained by the company in respect of its long term business: ibid, s 31(7).
'Equity share capital' means share capital excluding any part thereof which, neither as respects dividends nor as respects capital, carries any right to participate beyond a specified amount in a distribution: ibid, s 31(7).

4 'Liability' includes a contingent liability: ibid, s 31(7).

5 'Prescribed percentage' means 5 per cent or such greater percentage as may from time to time be prescribed by regulations: ibid, s 31(7).

6 For the meaning of 'long term funds', see footnote 3, supra.

b at any other time when the aggregate of the value of those assets and the amount of those liabilities would exceed that percentage if the transaction were entered into.[7]

The transactions referred to above into which the insurance company (whether or not itself a subordinate company) must not enter are those in which:

a a person connected with the insurance company will owe it money; or
b the insurance company acquires shares in a company which is a person connected with it; or
c the insurance company undertakes a liability to meet an obligation of a person connected with it or to help such a person to meet an obligation,

if the right to receive the money would constitute a long term asset[8] of the insurance company, the acquisition is made out of its long term funds[9] or the liability would fall to be discharged out of those funds, as the case may be.[10]

The transactions referred to above into which a subordinate company of any insurance company must not enter are where:

a the insurance company or a person connected with it will owe money to the subordinate company (not being money owed by the insurance company which can properly be paid out of its long term funds); or
b the subordinate company acquires shares in the insurance company or in a company which is a person connected with the insurance company; or
c the subordinate company undertakes a liability to meet an obligation of the insurance company or of a person connected with that company or to help the insurance company or such a person to meet an obligation.[11]

A person is 'connected with' an insurance company if that person is not a subordinate company of the insurance company but:

a controls, or is a partner of a person who controls, the insurance company; or
b being a company, is controlled by the insurance company or by another person who also controls the insurance company; or
c is a director of the insurance company or the wife or husband or a minor son or daughter of such a director.[12]

---

7 Insurance Companies Act 1982, s 31(1). Any insurance which makes default in complying with s 31 and any other person who does so is guilty of an offence and liable, on summary conviction, to a fine not exceeding level 5 on the standard scale: ibid, s 71(3).
8 For the meaning of 'long term assets', see p 50, footnote 3, ante.
9 For the meaning of 'long term funds', see p 50, footnote 3, ante.
10 Insurance Companies Act 1982, s 31(2).
11 Ibid, s 31(3). But where the subordinate company is itself such an insurance company as is mentioned in s 31(1), s 31 does not apply to any such transaction if the right to receive the money would constitute a long term asset of the subordinate company, the acquisition is made out of its long term funds or the liability would fall to be discharged out of those funds, as the case may be: ibid, s 31(3).
12 Ibid, s 31(5). A person 'controls' a company if he is a 'controller' of it within the meaning of s 7(4)(c): ibid, s 31(5). For s 7(4)(c), see p 34, ante. 'Son' includes step-son and adopted son, and 'daughter' includes step-daughter and adopted daughter: Insurance Companies Act 1982, s 31(7).

The value of any assets and the amount of any liabilities must be determined in accordance with any applicable valuation regulations.[13]

Non-compliance by the company or subordinate company with any of the above provisions does not make any transaction unenforceable as between the parties to it or make unenforceable any rights or liabilities in respect of property.[14]

D Financial resources

Margins of solvency

Every insurance company to which Part II of the Insurance Companies Act 1982 applies:[15]

a whose head office is in the United Kingdom; or
b whose business in the United Kingdom is restricted to reinsurance,

must maintain a margin of solvency[16] of such amount as may be prescribed by or determined in accordance with regulations.[17]

Every insurance company to which Part II of the Insurance Companies Act 1982 applies[18] whose head office is not in a member State must maintain:

a a margin of solvency, and
b a United Kingdom margin of solvency,[19]

of such amounts as may be prescribed by or determined in accordance with regulations made for the purpose.[20]

An insurance company which has made a deposit in the United Kingdom[1] must maintain:

a a margin of solvency, and
b a Community margin of solvency,[2]

---

13 Ibid, s 31(6). The regulations at present in force are the Insurance Companies Regulations 1981 (SI 1981 No 1654), regs 37 to 64. See Appendix II, post.

14 Insurance Companies Act 1982, s 31(8).

15 See pp 40–41, ante.

16 The 'margin of solvency' of an insurance company is the excess of the value of its assets over the amount of its liabilities, that value and amount being determined in accordance with any applicable valuation regulations: Insurance Companies Act 1982, s 32(5)(a). The valuation regulations at present in force are the Insurance Companies Regulations 1981 (SI 1981 No 1654), regs 37 to 64. See Appendix II, post.

17 Insurance Companies Act 1982, s 32(1). The regulations at present in force are the Insurance Companies Regulations 1981 (SI 1981 No 1654), regs 3 to 13. See Appendix II, post.

18 See p 40, ante.

19 The 'United Kingdom margin of solvency' of an insurance company is its margin of solvency computed by reference to the assets and liabilities of the business carried on by the company in the United Kingdom: Insurance Companies Act 1982, s 32(5)(b).

20 Ibid, s 32(2). This subsection does not apply to an insurance company if its business in the United Kingdom is restricted to reinsurance or if s 9(2), applies to it: ibid, s 32(3). As to s 9(2), see p 36, ante. The regulations at present in force are the Insurance Companies Regulations 1981 (SI 1981 No 1654), regs 3 to 13. See Appendix II, post.

1 In accordance with s 9(2)(b). For the provisions of that subsection, see p 36, ante.

2 The 'Community margin of solvency' of an insurance company is its margin of solvency computed by reference to the assets and liabilities of the business carried on by the company in member States (taken together): Insurance Companies Act 1982, s 32(5)(c).

of such amounts as may be prescribed by or determined in accordance with regulations made for the purpose.[3]

An insurance company which fails to comply with the above provisions:

a must, at the request of the Secretary of State, submit to him a plan for the restoration of a sound financial position;
b must propose modifications to the plan (or the plan as previously modified) if he considers it inadequate;
c must give effect to any plan accepted by him as adequate.[4]

In the case of an insurance company which carries on both long term and general business it must maintain a separate margin of solvency, a separate United Kingdom margin of solvency and a Community margin of solvency in respect of the two kinds of business.[5]

Failure to maintain minimum margin

If the margin of solvency, the United Kingdom margin of solvency or the Community margin of solvency falls below such amount as may be prescribed by or determined in accordance with regulations made for the purpose, the company must at the request of the Secretary of State submit to him a short-term financial scheme.[6]

An insurance company which has submitted a scheme to the Secretary of State must propose modifications to the scheme (or the scheme as previously modified) if he considers it inadequate, and must give effect to any scheme accepted by him as adequate.[7]

Companies supervised in other member States

An insurance company to which Part II of the Insurance Companies Act 1982 applies:[8]

a whose head office is in a member State other than the United Kingdom, or
b which has made a deposit in such a member State

must secure that the value of the assets of the business carried on by it in the United Kingdom does not fall below the amount of the liabilities of that business, that value and amount being determined in accordance with any applicable valuation regulations.[9]

---

[3] Ibid, s 32(3). The regulations at present in force are the Insurance Companies Regulations 1981 (SI 1981 No 1654), regs 3 to 13. See Appendix II, post.
[4] Insurance Companies Act 1982, s 32(4).
[5] Ibid, s 32(6).
[6] Ibid, s 33(1).
[7] Ibid, s 33(2). Where a company is required by s 32(6) (supra) to maintain separate margins in respect of long term and general business, s 33(2) has effect as if any reference to the margin of solvency, the United Kingdom margin of solvency or the Community margin of solvency were a reference to the margin in respect of either of the two kinds of business: ibid, s 33(3).
[8] See pp 40–41, ante.
[9] Insurance Companies Act 1982, s 34(1).

Form and situation of assets

Regulations may make provision for securing that, in such circumstances and to such extent as may be prescribed, the assets of an insurance company to which Part II of the Insurance Companies Act 1982 applies[10] must be maintained in such places as may be prescribed and the nature of the assets must be appropriate in relation to the currency in which the liabilities of the company are or may be required to be met.[11]

Regulations made for the purposes specified above do not have effect in relation to the assets of an insurance company whose head office is in a member State so far as their value exceeds the amount of the liabilities of the business carried on by the company in the United Kingdom, that value being determined in accordance with any applicable valuation regulations.[12]

E Liabilities of unlimited amount

A contract entered into by an insurance company to which Part II of the Insurance Companies Act 1982 applies[13] is void if:

- a it is a contract under which the company undertakes a liability, the amount, or the maximum amount, of which is uncertain at the time when the contract is entered into; and
- b it is not a contract of insurance or a contract of a class or description exempted by regulations to be made for the purpose.[14]

F Powers of intervention

The Secretary of State has power to impose the following requirements in relation to an insurance company to which Part II of the Insurance Companies Act 1982 applies:[15]

- a requirements about investments;
- b maintenance of assets in the United Kingdom;
- c custody of assets;
- d limitation of premium income;
- e actuarial investigations;
- f acceleration of information required by accounting provisions;
- g information and production of documents;
- h protection of policy holders.

1 Grounds on which powers are exercisable

Any of the above powers are exercisable in relation to any insurance company to which Part II of the Insurance Companies Act 1982 applies[16] on the following grounds:[17]

---

[10] See pp 40–41, ante.
[11] Insurance Companies Act 1982, s 35(1). The regulations at present in force are the Insurance Companies Regulations 1981 (SI 1981 No 1654), regs 25 to 28. See Appendix II, post.
[12] Insurance Companies Act 1982, s 35(2).
[13] See pp 40–41, ante.
[14] Insurance Companies Act 1982, s 36.
[15] See pp 40–41, ante.
[16] See pp 40–41, ante.
[17] Insurance Companies Act 1982, s 37(1).

a that the Secretary of State considers the exercise of the power to be desirable for protecting policy holders or potential policy holders of the company against the risk that the company may be unable to meet its liabilities, or, in the case of long term business[18] to fulfil the reasonable expectations of policy holders or potential policy holders; or

b that it appears to him:

  i that the company has failed to satisfy an obligation to which it is subject by virtue of the Act;

  ii that a company of which it is a subsidiary has failed to satisfy an obligation not to declare a dividend in certain circumstances[19]; or

  iii that a subordinate company[20] has failed to satisfy an obligation not to declare a dividend in certain circumstances or an obligation to furnish the Secretary of State with a statement concerning particulars of transactions of a prescribed class or description;[1]

c that it appears to him that the company has furnished misleading or inaccurate information to him or for the purposes of any provision of the Act;

d that he is not satisfied that adequate arrangements are in force or will be made for the reinsurance of risks against which persons are insured by the company in the course of carrying on business, being risks of a class in the case of which he considers that such arrangements are required;

e that there exists a ground on which he would be prohibited[2] from issuing an authorisation with respect to the company if it were applied for;

f that it appears to him that there has been a substantial departure from any proposal submitted to him by the company in accordance with s 5.[3]

g that the company has ceased to be authorised to effect contracts of insurance, or contracts of a particular description, in a member State where it has its head office or has made a deposit.[4]

The powers conferred on the Secretary of State in relation to the maintenance of assets in the United Kingdom and the custody of assets are not exercisable in relation to an insurance company except:[5]

a where the Secretary of State has given (and not revoked) a direction in respect of the company under s 11[6]; or

b on the ground that it appears to the Secretary of State that the company has failed to satisfy an obligation to which it is subject by virtue of ss 33[7], 34[8] or 35[9]; or

---

18 As to 'long term business', see p 31, ante.
19 See Insurance Companies Act 1982, s 29. See p 48, ante.
20 For the meaning of 'subordinate company', see p 50, ante.
1 See pp 46–47, ante.
2 Under the Insurance Companies Act 1982, ss 7, 8 or 9. See pp 34–37, ante.
3 See p 33, ante.
4 In accordance with the Insurance Companies Act 1982, s 9(2). See p 36, ante.
5 Insurance Companies Act 1982, s 37(3).
6 Which concerns the withdrawal of authorisation in respect of new business. See pp 37–38, ante.
7 Which concerns the failure to maintain the minimum margin of solvency. See p 53, ante.
8 Which concerns companies supervised in other member States. See p 53, ante.
9 Which concerns the form and situation of assets. See p 54, ante.

c on the ground that a submission by the company to the Secretary of State of an account or statement specifies, as the amount of any liabilities of the company, an amount appearing to the Secretary of State to have been determined otherwise than in accordance with valuation regulations or, where no such regulations are applicable, generally accepted accounting concepts, bases and policies or other generally accepted methods appropriate for insurance companies.

The power conferred on the Secretary of State to require the production of documents is also exercisable[10] on the ground that he considers the exercise of that power to be desirable in the general interests of persons who are or may become policy holders of insurance companies to which Part II of the Insurance Companies Act applies.[11]

Any power relating to:

i requirements about investments;
ii limitation of premium income;
iii actuarial investigations;
iv obtaining of information;
v protection of policy holders;

is also exercisable[12] in relation to:

a any body in respect of which the Secretary of State has issued an authorisation;
b any insurance company to which Part II of the Insurance Companies Act applies[13] in the case of which a person has become a controller,[14]

if that power is exercised before the expiration of the period of 5 years beginning with the date on which the authorisation was issued or that person became such a controller.[15]

The power to impose requirements for the protection of policy holders is not exercisable in a case in which he considers that such protection cannot be appropriately achieved by the exercise of his other powers of intervention or by the exercise of those powers alone.[16]

The Secretary of State must, when exercising any of his powers of intervention, state the ground on which he is exercising it.[17]

(a) Requirements about investments

The Secretary of State may require a company:

a not to make investments of a specified class or description;
b to realise, before the expiration of a specified period (or such longer period as the Secretary of State may allow), the whole or a specified

---

10 Insurance Companies Act 1982, s 37(4).
11 See pp 40–41, ante.
12 Insurance Companies Act 1982, s 37(5).
13 See pp 40–41, ante.
14 For the meaning of 'controller', see p 34, ante.
15 But no requirement imposed under s 37(5) may continue in force after the expiration of 10 years beginning with that date: Insurance Companies Act 1982, s 37(5).
16 Ibid, s 37(6).
17 Ibid, s 37(7).

proportion of investments of a specified class or description held by the company when the requirement is imposed.[18]

A requirement imposed by the Secretary of State may be framed so as to apply only to investments which are (or, if made, would be) assets representing a fund or funds maintained by the company in respect of its long term business[19] or so as to apply only to other investments.[20]

A requirement does not apply to the assets of a company so far as their value exceeds:

a in the case of a company whose head office is in a member State other than the United Kingdom or which has made a deposit[21] in such a member State, the amount of the liabilities of the business carried on by the company in the United Kingdom;

b in any other case, the amount of the liabilities of the company;

that value and amount being determined in accordance with any applicable valuation regulations.[22]

(b) Maintenance of assets in the United Kingdom

The Secretary of State may require that assets of a company of a value which at any time is equal to the whole or a specified proportion of the amount of its domestic liabilities must be maintained in the United Kingdom.[23]

He may direct that for the purposes of any such requirement assets of a specified class or description must or must not be treated as assets maintained in the United Kingdom.[24]

He may also direct that the domestic liabilities of a company, or such liabilities of any class or description, must be taken to be the net liabilities after deducting any part of them which is reinsured.[25]

A requirement may be framed so as to come into effect immediately after the date on which it is imposed or so as to come into effect after the expiration of a specified period (or such longer period as the Secretary of State may allow).[1]

In computing the amount of any liabilities all contingent and prospective liabilities must be taken into account, but not liabilities in respect of share capital.[2]

---

18 Insurance Companies Act 1982, s 38(1). Any insurance company and any other person who makes default in complying with, or with a requirement imposed under, s 38 are guilty of an offence and liable, on summary conviction, to a fine not exceeding level 5 on the standard scale: ibid, s 71(3).

19 As to 'long term business', see p 34, ante.

20 Insurance Companies Act 1982, s 38(2).

21 Under the Insurance Companies Act 1982, s 9(2). See p 36, ante.

22 Insurance Companies Act 1982, s 38(3).

23 Ibid, s 39(1). A 'domestic liability' means a liability of the business carried on by the company in the United Kingdom: ibid, s 39(5). Any insurance company and any other person who makes default in complying with a requirement under s 39 are guilty of an offence and liable, on summary conviction, to a fine not exceeding level 5 on the standard scale: ibid, s 71(3).

24 Ibid, s 39(2).

25 Ibid, s 39(3).

1 Ibid, s 39(4).

2 Ibid, s 39(6).

The value of any assets and the amount of any liabilities are to be determined in accordance with any applicable valuation regulations.[3]

(c) Custody of assets

The Secretary of State may, in the case of a company on which a requirement[4] to maintain assets of a value equal to the whole or a specified proportion of the amount of its domestic liabilities in the United Kingdom has been imposed, impose an additional requirement that the whole or a specified proportion of the assets must be held by a person approved by him for the purposes of the requirement as trustee for the company.[5]

Such a requirement may be framed so as to come into effect immediately after the day on which it is imposed or so as to come into effect after the expiration of a specified period (or such longer period as the Secretary of State may allow).[6]

Assets of a company held by a person as trustee for a company are to be taken to be held by him in compliance with a requirement if, and only if, they are assets in whose case the company has given him written notice that they are to be held by him in compliance with such a requirement or they are assets into which assets in whose case the company has given him such written notice have, by any transaction or series of transactions, been transposed by him on the instructions of the company.[7]

No assets held by a person as trustee for a company in compliance with a requirement must, so long as the requirement is in force, be released except with the consent of the Secretary of State.[8]

If a mortgage or charge is created by a company at a time where there is in force a requirement imposed on the company, being a mortgage or charge conferring a security on any assets which are held by a person as trustee for the company in compliance with the requirement, the mortgage or charge, to the extent that it confers such a security, is void against the liquidator and any creditor of the company.[9]

(d) Limitation of premium income

The Secretary of State may require a company to take all such steps as are requisite to secure that the aggregate of the premiums:

a to be received by the company in consideration of the undertaking by it during a specified period of liabilities in the course of carrying on general business or any specified part of such business; or

b to be received by it in a specified period in consideration of the undertaking by the company during that period of liabilities in the

---

3 Ibid, s 39(7).

4 Under the Insurance Companies Act 1982, s 39. See pp 57–58, ante.

5 Insurance Companies Act 1982, s 40(1). Any insurance company and any other person who makes default in complying with, or with a requirement imposed under, s 40 are guilty of an offence and liable, on summary conviction, to a fine not exceeding level 5 on the standard scale: ibid, s 71(3).

6 Ibid, s 40(2).

7 Ibid, s 40(3).

8 Ibid, s 40(4).

9 Ibid, s 40(5).

course of carrying on long term business or any specified part of such business,

does not exceed a specified amount.[10]

Such requirement may apply either to the aggregate premiums to be received or to the aggregate of those premiums after deducting any premiums payable by the company for reinsuring the liabilities in consideration of which the first-mentioned premiums are receivable.[11]

(e) Actuarial investigations

The Secretary of State may require a company which carries on long term business:[12]

a to cause the person who for the time being is its actuary to make an investigation into its financial condition in respect of that business, or any specified part of that business, as at a specified date;

b to cause an abstract of that person's report of the investigation to be made; and

c to prepare a statement of its long term business or of that part of it as at that date.[13]

For the purposes of any investigation made in pursuance of such a requirement the value of any assets and the amount of any liabilities must be determined in accordance with any applicable valuation regulations.[14]

The form and contents of any abstract or statement made in pursuance of such a requirement must be the same as for an abstract or statement which is made in connection with the periodic actuarial investigation of the company.[15]

Five copies of any abstract or statement made in pursuance of the requirement must be deposited by the company with the Secretary of State on or before such date as he may specify, and one of the copies must be a copy signed by the actuary who made the investigation to which the abstract relates or by reference to which the statement was prepared.[16]

Any person who causes or permits to be included in any abstract or abstract deposited with the Secretary of State a statement which he knows to be false in a material particular or recklessly causes or permits to be so included any statement which is false in a material particular is guilty of an offence.[17]

---

[10] Ibid, s 41(1). Any insurance company and any other person who makes default in complying with, or with a requirement imposed under, s 41 are guilty of an offence and liable, on summary conviction, to a fine not exceeding level 5 on the standard scale: ibid, s 71(3).

[11] Ibid, s 41(2).

[12] As to 'long term business', see p 34, ante.

[13] Insurance Companies Act 1982, s 42(1). Any insurance company which makes default in complying with, or with a requirement imposed under s 42 is guilty of an offence and is liable, on summary conviction, to a fine not exceeding level 5 on the standard scale: ibid, s 71(3).

[14] Ibid, s 42(2).

[15] Ibid, s 42(3). For the periodic actuarial investigation of a company, see ibid, s 18, and pp 42–43, ante.

[16] Insurance Companies Act 1982, s 42(4). Where a person continues to make default in complying with s 42(4) after being convicted of that default, he is guilty of a further offence and is liable, on summary conviction, to a fine not exceeding £40 for each day on which the default continues: ibid, s 71(4).

[17] Ibid, 71(1). Any person guilty of such an offence is liable on conviction on indictment to imprisonment for a term not exceeding 2 years, or to a fine, or to both, and on summary

(f) Acceleration of information required by accounting provisions

The Secretary of State may require that the account, balance sheet, abstract or statement required by an actuary, and any report of the auditor of the company which are required to be deposited with him within the required period, to be deposited with him on or before a specified date before the end of that period, being a date not earlier than three months before the end of that period and not earlier than one month after the date on which the requirement is imposed.[18]

The Secretary of State may require any periodic statement by a company with the prescribed class of business required to be deposited with him by a company within a prescribed period to be deposited with him on or before a specified date before the end of that period.[19]

(g) Power to obtain information and require production of documents

The Secretary of State may require a company to furnish him, at specified times or intervals, with information about specified matters being, if he so requires, information verified in a specified manner.[20]

He may:

a require a company to produce, at such time and place as he may specify, such books or papers as he may specify; or

b authorise any person, on producing (if required so to do) evidence of his authority, to require a company to produce to him forthwith any books or papers which that person may specify.[1]

The Secretary of State or a person authorised by him has a similar power to require production of those books or papers from any person who appears to him to be in possession of them; but where any person from whom such production is required claims a lien on books or papers produced by him, the production shall be without prejudice to the lien.[2]

The power conferred on the Secretary of State or a person authorised by him to require a company or other person to produce books or papers includes power:

---

conviction, to a fine not exceeding £1,000 or, if it is greater, the prescribed sum within the meaning of the Magistrates' Courts Act 1980, s 32: ibid, s 71(2).

18 Ibid, s 43(1). Any insurance company which makes default in complying with, or with a requirement imposed under, s 43 is guilty of an offence and liable, on summary conviction, to a fine not exceeding level 5 on the standard scale: ibid, s 71(3). Where a person continues to make default in complying with a requirement imposed under s 43(1), he is guilty of a further offence and liable, on summary conviction, to a fine not exceeding £40 for every day on which the default continues: ibid, s 71(4).

19 Ibid, s 43(2). For periodic statements by a company with a prescribed class of business, see ibid, s 25 and p 46, ante.

20 Insurance Companies Act 1982, s 44(1). Any insurance company and any other person who makes default in complying with, or with a requirement imposed under, s 44 are guilty of an offence and liable, on summary conviction, to a fine not exceeding level 5 on the standard scale: ibid, s 71(3). Where a person continues to make default in complying with a requirement imposed under s 44(1) after being convicted of that default, he is guilty of a further offence and liable, on summary conviction, to a fine not exceeding £40 for each day on which the default continues: ibid, s 71(4).

1 Ibid, s 44(2). 'Books and papers' include accounts, deeds, writing and documents: ibid, s 44(6).

2 Ibid, s 44(3).

a if the books or papers are produced:

i to take copies of them or extracts from them; and
ii to require that person, or any other person who is a present or past director, controller or auditor of, or is or was at any time employed by the company in question, to provide an explanation of any of them;

b if the books or papers are not produced, to require the person who was required to produce them to state, to the best of his knowledge and belief, where they are.[3]

A statement made by a person in compliance with such a requirement may be used in evidence against him.[4]

Any person who in purported compliance with a requirement furnishes information which he knows to be false in a material particular or recklessly furnishes information which is false in a material particular, is guilty of an offence.[5]

(h) Residual power to impose requirements for protection of policy holders

The Secretary of State may require a company to take such action as appears to him to be appropriate for the purpose of protecting policy holders or potential policy holders of the company against the risk that the company may be unable to meet its liabilities or, in the case of long term business, to fulfil the reasonable expectations of policy holders or potential policy holders.[6]

The above power must not be exercised in such a way as to restrict the company's freedom to dispose of its assets except where it is exercised:[7]

a after the Secretary of State has given a direction under s 11;[8]
b on the ground that it appears to him that the company has failed to satisfy an obligation to which it is subject by virtue of ss 33[9], 34[10] or 35[11]; or
c where the ground for intervention arises out of the submission to him of an account or statement specifying, as the amount of any liabilities of the company, an amount appearing to him to have been determined otherwise than in accordance with valuation regulations or, where no such regulations are applicable, generally accepted accounting concepts, bases and policies or other generally accepted methods appropriate for insurance companies.

---

3 Ibid, s 44(4).
4 Ibid, s 44(5).
5 Ibid, s 71(1). A person guilty of an offence under this subsection is liable on conviction on indictment to imprisonment for a term not exceeding 2 years, or to a fine, or to both, and, on summary conviction, to a fine not exceeding £1,000 or, if it is greater, the prescribed sum within the meaning of the Magistrates' Courts Act 1980, s 32: ibid, s 71(2).
6 Ibid, s 45(1). Any insurance company and any other person who makes default in complying with, or with a requirement under, s 45 is guilty of an offence and liable, on summary conviction, to a fine not exceeding level 5 on the standard scale: ibid, s 71(3).
7 Ibid, s 45(2).
8 Which concerns the withdrawal of authorisation in respect of new business. See pp 37–38, ante.
9 Which concerns the failure to maintain the minimum margin of solvency. See p 53, ante.
10 Which concerns companies supervised in other member States. See p 53, ante.
11 Which concerns the form and situation of assets. See p 54, ante.

2 Notice of proposed exercise of powers on ground of unfitness of director or manager

Before exercising with respect to a company any of his powers of intervention[12] on the ground that he would be prohibited from issuing an authorisation to the company because of the unfitness of a person for the position held by him (not being that of controller[13] of the company) the Secretary of State must serve on him a written notice stating:

a that the Secretary of State is considering exercising a power or powers of intervention and the ground on which he is considering the exercise of the power or powers; and
b that the person on whom the notice is served may, within the period of one month from the date of the service of the notice, make written representations to the Secretary of State and, if that person so requests, oral representations to an officer of the Department of Trade appointed for the purpose by the Secretary of State.[14]

Unless the Secretary of State, after considering any such representations by the person served with a notice, decides not to exercise the power or powers in relation to which the notice was served, he must before exercising the power or powers serve on the company a written notice:

a containing the matters mentioned above; and
b specifying the power or powers which he proposes to exercise and, if the power or one of them concerns his residual power to impose requirements for the protection of policy holders,[15] specifying the manner of its proposed exercise.[16]

A notice must give particulars of the ground on which the Secretary of State is considering the exercise of the power or powers in question.[17]

Where representations are made to him, the Secretary of State must take them into consideration before exercising the power or powers in question.[18]

A requirement imposed on a company in the exercise of any power or powers of intervention may be framed so as to come into effect after the expiration of a specified period (or such longer period as the Secretary of State may allow) unless before the expiration of that period the person whose fitness is in question has ceased to hold the position concerned.[19]

3 Rescission, variation and publication of requirements

The Secretary of State may rescind a requirement which he has imposed[20] if it

---

[12] Under the Insurance Companies Act 1982, ss 38 to 45. See pp 37–61, ante.
[13] For the meaning of 'controller', see p 34, ante.
[14] Insurance Companies Act 1982, s 46(1).
[15] Under the Insurance Companies Act 1982, s 45. See p 61, ante.
[16] Insurance Companies Act 1982, s 46(2).
[17] Ibid, s 46(3).
[18] Ibid, s 46(4).
[19] Ibid, s 46(5).
[20] Under the Insurance Companies Act 1982, ss 38 to 45. See pp 37–61, ante.

appears to him that it is no longer necessary for the requirement to continue in force, and may from time to time vary any such requirement.[1]

Where a requirement as to the custody of assets[2] is imposed or any such requirement is rescinded or varied, the Secretary of State must forthwith serve on the Registrar of Companies a written notice stating that fact, and:

i in the case of a notice of the imposition of a requirement, setting out the terms of the requirement;
ii in the case of a notice of the rescission of a requirement, identifying the requirement; and
iii in the case of a notice of a variation of a requirement, identifying the requirement and setting out the terms of the variation.[3]

A notice served on the Registrar of Companies is open to inspection, and a copy of it may be procured by any person on payment of such fee as the Secretary of State may direct.[4]

Every document purporting to be certified by the Registrar of Companies to be a copy of such a notice is deemed to be a copy of such a notice and must be received in evidence as if it were the original notice unless some variation between it and the original is proved.[5]

4 Security of information

No information or document relating to a body which has been obtained under s 44(2) to (4)[6] may, without the previous consent of that body, be published or disclosed except to a competent authority,[7] unless the publication or disclosure is required for the purposes specified in the Companies Act 1985, s 449(1)(a) to (e).[8]

5 Privilege from disclosure

A requirement imposed under s 44(2) to (4)[9] must not compel the production by any person of a document which he would in an action in the High Court be entitled to refuse to produce on grounds of legal professional privilege or authorise the taking of possession of any such document which is in his possession.[10]

6 Power of Secretary of State to bring civil proceedings

If from any information or document obtained under the Insurance Companies

---

1 Insurance Companies Act 1982, s 47(1). No requirement imposed under s 37(5) must be varied after the expiration of 5 years mentioned in that subsection except in a manner which relaxes that requirement: ibid, s 47(2). As to s 37(5), see p 56, ante.
2 As to the custody of assets, see p 58, ante.
3 Insurance Companies Act 1982, s 47(3).
4 Ibid, s 47(4).
5 Ibid, s 47(4).
6 See pp 60–61, ante.
7 The 'competent authorities' are the same as those specified in the Companies Act 1985: Insurance Companies Act 1982, s 47A(2).
8 Ibid, s 47A(1).
9 See pp 60–61, ante.
10 Insurance Companies Act 1982, s 47B(1).

Act 1982 it appears to the Secretary of State that any civil proceedings ought in the public interest to be brought by an insurance company to which Part II of the Act applies,[11] he may bring such proceedings in the name and on behalf of the company.[12]

Where under a judgment given in such proceedings a sum is recovered in respect of a loss of assets representing a fund or funds maintained by the company in respect of its long term business, the Court must direct that the sum shall be treated for the purposes of the Act as assets of the fund or funds.[13]

G Transfers of long term business

Where it is proposed to carry out a scheme under which the whole or part of the long term business[14] carried on in the United Kingdom by an insurance company to which Part II of the Insurance Companies Act 1982 applies[15] is to be transferred to another body (whether incorporated or not), the transferor company or transferee company may apply to the Court, by petition, for an order sanctioning the scheme.[16]

The Court must not determine an application unless the petition is accompanied by a report on the terms of the scheme by an independent actuary and the Court is satisfied that the following requirements have been complied with:

a a notice has been published in the *London Gazette* and, except where the Court has otherwise directed, in two national newspapers stating that the application has been made and giving the address of the offices at which, and the period for which, copies of the documents mentioned in para d below will be available;

b except where the Court has otherwise directed, a statement:

  i setting out the terms of the scheme; and

  ii containing a summary of the report mentioned above sufficient to indicate the opinion of the actuary on the likely effects of the scheme on the long term policy holders of the companies concerned,

  has been sent to each of those policy holders and to every member of those companies;

c a copy of the petition, of the report mentioned above and of any statement sent out has been served on the Secretary of State and a period of not less than 21 days has elapsed since the date of service;

d copies of the petition and of the report mentioned above have been open to inspection at offices in the United Kingdom of the companies concerned for a period of not less than 21 days beginning with the date of the first publication of the notice.[17]

Each of the companies concerned must, on payment of such fee as may be

---

[11] See pp 40–41, ante.
[12] Insurance Companies Act 1982, s 48(1), (2).
[13] Ibid, s 48(3).
[14] As to 'long term business', see p 34, ante.
[15] See pp 40–41, ante.
[16] Insurance Companies Act 1982, s 49(1).
[17] Ibid, s 49(2), (3).

prescribed by rules of Court, furnish a copy of the petition and of the report mentioned above to any person who asks for one at any time before the order sanctioning the scheme is made on the petition.[18]

On any such petition, the Secretary of State and any person (including any employee of the transferor company or the transferee company) who alleges that he would be adversely affected by the carrying out of the scheme, are entitled to be heard.[19]

The Court must not make an order sanctioning the scheme unless it is satisfied that the transferee company is, or immediately after the making of the order will be, authorised[20] to carry on long term business of the class or classes to be transferred under the scheme.[1]

No transfer must be carried out unless the scheme relating to it has been sanctioned by the Court.[2]

Where the Court makes an order sanctioning a scheme, it may, either by that order or by any subsequent order, make provision for all or any of the following matters:[3]

a the transfer to the transferee company of the whole or any part of the undertaking and of the property[4] or liabilities[5] of the transferor company;
b the allotting or appropriation by the transferee company of any shares, debentures, policies or other like interests in that company which under the scheme are to be allotted or appropriated by the company to or for any person;
c the continuation by or against the transferee company of any legal proceedings pending by or against the transferor company;
d the dissolution, without winding up, of the transferor company;
e such incidental, consequential and supplementary matters as are necessary to secure that the scheme is fully and effectively carried out.

Where any such order provides for the transfer of property or liabilities, the property must be transferred to and vest in, and those liabilities must be transferred to and become the liabilities of, the transferee company.[6] In the case of any property, if the order so directs, it must be freed from any mortgage or charge which is by virtue of the scheme to cease to have effect.[7]

Where a scheme is sanctioned by an order of the Court, the transferee company must, within ten days from the date on which the order is made or

---

18 Ibid, s 49(4). Any insurance company which makes default in complying with this requirement and any other person who does so is guilty of an offence and liable, on summary conviction, to a fine not exceeding level 5 on the standard scale: ibid, s 71(3).
19 Ibid, s 49(5).
20 Under the Insurance Companies Act 1982, s 3 or s 4. As to authorisation, see pp 33–37, ante.
1 Insurance Companies Act 1982, s 49(6).
2 Ibid, s 49(7). Further, no order must be made under the Companies Act 1985, s 425 or s 427 in respect of so much of any compromise or arrangement as involves any such transfer: ibid, s 49(7).
3 Ibid, s 50(1).
4 'Property' includes property, rights and powers of every description: ibid, s 50(5).
5 'Liabilities' include duties: ibid, s 50(5).
6 Ibid, s 50(2).
7 Ibid, s 50(2).

such longer period as the Secretary of State may allow, deposit two office copies of the order with him.[8]

H Transfers of general business

Approval of transfer

Where it is proposed to execute an instrument by which an insurance company to which Part II of the Insurance Companies Act 1982 applies[9] (the 'transferor') is to transfer to another body (the 'transferee') all its rights and obligations under such general policies,[10] or general policies of such descriptions as may be specified in the instrument, the transferor may apply to the Secretary of State for his approval of the transfer.[11]

The Secretary of State must not determine an application for approval of the transfer unless he is satisfied that:

a a notice approved by him has been published in the *London Gazette*, and, if he thinks fit, in two national newspapers which have been so approved; and
b except in so far as he has otherwise directed a copy of the notice has been sent to every affected policy holder[12] and every person who claims an interest in a policy included in the transfer and has given written notice of his claim to the transferor; and
c copies of a statement setting out particulars of the transfer and approved by him have been available for inspection at one or more places in the United Kingdom for a period of not less than 30 days beginning with the date of the first publication of the notice.[13]

The notice must include a statement that written representations concerning the transfer may be sent to the Secretary of State before a specified day, which must not be earlier than 60 days after the day of the first publication of the notice. The Secretary of State must not determine the application until after considering any representations made to him before the specified day.[14]

The Secretary of State must not approve a transfer unless he is satisfied that:

a every policy included in the transfer evidences a contract which

i was entered into before the date of the application; and
ii imposes on the insurer obligations the performance of which will constitute the carrying on of insurance business in the United Kingdom; and

---

8 Ibid, s 50(4). Any insurance company which makes default in complying with this requirement and any other person who does so is guilty of an offence and liable, on summary conviction, to a fine not exceeding level 5 on the standard scale; ibid, s 71(3).
9 See pp 40–41, ante.
10 'General policy' means a policy evidencing a contract the effecting of which constituted the carrying on of general business: Insurance Companies Act 1982, s 51(7).
11 Ibid, s 51(1).
12 A policy holder is an 'affected policy holder' in relation to a proposed transfer if:
a his policy is included in the transfer; or
b his policy is with the transferor and the Secretary of State has certified, after consulting the transferor, that in the opinion of the Secretary of State the policy holder's obligations under the policy will or may be materially affected by the transfer: ibid, s 51(7).
13 Ibid, s 51(2).
14 Ibid, s 51(3).

b the transferee is, or immediately after the approval, will be authorised[15] to carry on in the United Kingdom insurance business of the appropriate class or classes;

and unless in his opinion the transferee's financial resources and the other circumstances of the case justify the giving of his approval.[16]

On determining an application the Secretary of State must:

a publish a notice of his decision in the *London, Edinburgh* and *Belfast Gazettes* and in such other manner as he may think fit, and
b send a copy of the notice to the transferor, the transferee and every person who made representations;

and if he refuses the application, he must inform the transferor and the transferee in writing of the reasons for his refusal.[17]

Any notice or other document authorised or required to be given or served[18] may, without prejudice to any other method of service, be served by post.[19] A letter containing the notice or other document is deemed to be properly addressed if it is addressed to that person at his last known address or last known place of business in the United Kingdom.[20]

Effect of approval

An instrument giving effect to a transfer approved by the Secretary of State is effectual in law:

a to transfer to the transferee all the transferor's rights and obligations under the policies included in the instrument, and
b if the instrument so provides, the continuation by or against the transferee of any legal proceedings by or against the transferor which relate to those rights or obligations,

notwithstanding the absence of any agreements or consents which would otherwise be necessary for it to be effectual in law for those purposes.[1]

Except in so far as the Secretary of State may otherwise direct, a policy holder whose policy is included in such an instrument is not bound by it unless he has been given written notice of its execution by the transferor or the transferee.[2]

I Insolvency and winding up

1 Winding up of insurance companies under Companies Act 1985

The Court may order[3] the winding up, in accordance with the Companies Act 1985, of an insurance company to which Part II of the Insurance Companies Act 1982 applies.[4]

---

15 Under the Insurance Companies Act 1982, s 3 or s 4. As to authorisation, see pp 33–37, ante.
16 Insurance Companies Act 1982, s 51(4).
17 Ibid, s 51(5).
18 Under the Insurance Companies Act 1982, s 51 or s 52.
19 Insurance Companies Act 1982, s 51(6).
20 Ibid, s 51(6).
1 Ibid, s 52(1).
2 Ibid, s 52(2).
3 Insurance Companies Act 1982, s 53.
4 See pp 40–41, ante.

The provisions of the Companies Act 1985 apply accordingly subject to the modification that the company may be ordered to be wound up on the petition of ten or more policy holders owning policies of an aggregate value of not less than £10,000.[5]

Such a petition, however, must not be presented except by leave of the Court. Leave must not be granted until a prima facie case has been established to the satisfaction of the Court and until security for costs for such amount as the Court may think reasonable has been given.[6]

2 Winding up on petition of Secretary of State

The Secretary of State may present a petition for the winding up,[7] in accordance with the Companies Act 1985, of an insurance company to which Part II of the Insurance Companies Act 1982 applies[8] on the ground that:

- a the company is unable to pay its debts;[9]
- b the company has failed to satisfy an obligation to which it is subject by virtue of the Insurance Companies Act 1982; or
- c the company, being under an obligation imposed by the Companies Act 1985, s 221, with respect to the keeping of accounting records, has failed to satisfy that obligation or to produce records kept in satisfaction of that obligation and that the Secretary of State is unable to ascertain its financial position.

In any proceedings on a petition to wind up an insurance company presented by the Secretary of State, evidence that the company was insolvent:[10]

- a at the close of the period which:
  - i the accounts and balance sheet of the company last deposited;[11] or
  - ii any statement of the company last deposited,[12] relate; or
- b at any date or time specified in a requirement as to actuarial investigations[13] or as to the production of documents,[14]

is evidence that the company continues to be unable to pay its debts, unless the contrary is proved.[15]

If, in the case of an insurance company to which Part II of the Act applies,[16] it appears to the Secretary of State that it is expedient in the public interest that the company should be wound up, he may, unless the company is already being

---

5 Insurance Companies Act 1982, s 53.
6 Ibid, s 53.
7 Ibid, s 54(1).
8 See pp 40–41, ante.
9 Within the meaning of ss 517 and 518 or ss 666–669 of the Companies Act 1985.
10 'Insolvent' means, in relation to an insurance company at any relevant date, that if proceedings had been taken for the winding up of the company, the Court could, in accordance with the provisions of ss 517 and 518 or ss 666–669 hold or have held that the company was at that date unable to pay its debts: Insurance Companies Act 1982, s 96(1).
11 Under s 22. See pp 44–45, ante.
12 Under s 25. See p 46, ante.
13 Under s 42. See p 59, ante.
14 Under s 44. See pp 60–61, ante.
15 Insurance Companies Act 1982, s 54(3).
16 See pp 40–41, ante.

wound up by the Court, present a petition for it to be so wound up if the Court thinks it just and equitable for it to be so wound up.[17]

Where a petition for the winding up of an insurance company to which Part II of the Act applies[18] is presented by a person other than the Secretary of State, a copy of the petition must be served on him, and he is entitled to be heard on the petition.[19]

3 Winding up of insurance companies with long term business

No insurance company to which Part II of the Insurance Companies Act 1982 applies[20] carrying on long term business must be wound up voluntarily.[1]

In any winding up of such a company:

a the assets representing the fund or funds maintained by the company in respect of its long term business are only available for meeting the liabilities of the company attributable to that business;
b the other assets of the company are available only for meeting the liabilities of the company attributable to its other business.[2]

Where under the Companies Act 1985, s 631(2)[3] a Court orders any money or property to be repaid or restored to a company or any sum to be contributed to its assets, then, if and so far as the wrongful act which is the reason for the making of the order related to assets representing a fund or funds maintained by the company in respect of its long term business, the Court must include in the order a direction that the money, property or contribution must be treated for the purposes of the Insurance Companies Act 1982 as assets of that fund or those funds.[4]

4 Continuation of long term business of insurance company in liquidation

The liquidator must, unless the Court otherwise orders, carry on the long term business of an insurance company to which Part II of the Act applies[5] with a view to its being transferred as a going concern to another insurance company, whether an existing company or a company formed for that purpose.[6] In carrying on that business the liquidator can agree to the variation of any

---

17 Insurance Companies Act 1982, s 54(4).
18 See pp 40–41, ante.
19 Insurance Companies Act 1982, s 54(5).
20 See pp 40–41, ante.
1 Insurance Companies Act 1982, s 55(2).
2 Ibid, s 55(3). Where the value of the assets mentioned in either paragraph of s 55(3) exceeds the amount of the liabilities mentioned in that paragraph, the restriction imposed by that subsection does not apply to so much of the assets as represents the excess; ibid, s 55(4). In relation to the assets falling within either paragraph of s 47(3) the creditors mentioned in the Companies Act 1985, s 540(1), (2) are only those who are creditors falling within that paragraph, and any general meetings of creditors summoned for the purpose of the Companies Act 1985, s 540 are general meetings of the creditors in respect of the liabilities falling within each paragraph: ibid, s 55(5).
3 Which concerns defalcations of directors and other persons disclosed in the course of winding up a company.
4 Insurance Companies Act 1982, s 55(6).
5 See pp 40–41, ante.
6 Insurance Companies Act 1982, s 56(2).

contracts of insurance in existence when the winding up order is made, but he must not effect any new contracts of insurance.[7]

If he is satisfied that the interests of the creditors in respect of liabilities of the company attributable to its long term business require the appointment of a special manager of the company's long term business, he may apply to the Court.[8]

The Court may on such application appoint a special manager of that business to act during such time as the Court may direct, with such powers, including any of the powers of a receiver or manager, as may be entrusted to him by the Court.[9]

The Court may, if it thinks fit and subject to such conditions (if any) as it may determine, reduce the amount of the contracts made by the company in the course of carrying on its long term business.[10]

The Court may, on the application of the liquidator, a special manager appointed under the above provisions, or the Secretary of State, appoint an independent actuary to investigate the long term business of the company, and to report to the liquidator, the special manager or the Secretary of State, as the case may be, on the desirability or otherwise of that business being continued and on any reduction in the contracts made in the course of carrying on that business that may be necessary for its successful continuation.[11]

5 Subsidiary companies

Where the insurance business or any part of the insurance business of an insurance company has been transferred to an insurance company to which Part II of the Act applies[12] under an arrangement in pursuance of which the 'subsidiary company'[13] or its creditors has or have claims against the 'principal company',[14] then if the principal company is being wound up by or under the supervision of the Court, the Court must order the subsidiary company to be wound up in conjunction with the principal company.[15]

Further, the Court may by the same or subsequent order appoint the same person to be liquidator for the two companies, and make provision for such other matters as may seem to the Court necessary, with a view to the companies being wound up as if they were one company.[16]

The commencement of the winding up of the 'principal company' is, except as otherwise ordered by the Court, the commencement of the winding up of the 'subsidiary company'.[17]

In adjusting the rights and liabilities of the members of the several companies

---

7 Ibid, s 56(2).
8 Ibid, s 56(3). The Companies Act 1985, s 556(3) (which relates to the special manager giving security and receiving remuneration) applies to a special manager appointed under the Insurance Companies Act 1982: ibid, s 56(4).
9 Ibid, s 56(3).
10 Ibid, s 56(5).
11 Ibid, s 56(6).
12 See pp 40–41, ante.
13 I e the company transferring the business.
14 I e the company to which the business is transferred.
15 Insurance Companies Act 1982, s 57(1).
16 Ibid, s 57(1).
17 Ibid, s 57(2).

between themselves, the Court must have regard to the constitution of the companies, and to the arrangements entered into between them, in the same manner as it has regard to the rights and liabilities of different classes of contributories in the case of the winding up of a single company, or as near thereto as circumstances admit.[18]

Where any company alleged to be 'subsidiary' is not in process of being wound up at the same time as the 'principal company' to which it is subsidiary, the Court must not direct the 'subsidiary company' to be wound up unless, after hearing all objections (if any) that may be urged by or on behalf of the company against its being wound up, the Court is of opinion that the company is subsidiary to the 'principal company', and that the winding up of the company in conjunction with the 'principal company' is just and equitable.[19]

An application may be made in relation to the winding up of any 'subsidiary company' in conjunction with a 'principal company' by any creditor, of, or person interested, in the 'principal' or 'subsidiary company'.[20] Where a company stands in the relation of a principal to one company, and in the relation of a 'subsidiary company' to some other company, or where there are several companies standing in the relation of subsidiary companies to one principal company, the Court may deal with any number of such companies together or in separate groups, as it thinks most expedient, upon the principles mentioned above.[1]

6 Reduction of contracts as alternative to winding up

In the case of an insurance company which has been proved to be unable to pay its debts, the Court may, if it thinks fit, reduce the amount of the contracts of the company on such terms and subject to such conditions as it thinks just, in place of making a winding up order.[2]

The words 'unable to pay its debts' have the same meaning as they have in the Companies Act 1985, ss 517 and 518.[3] The mere evidence that a company has for the time being insufficient liquid assets to pay all its presently owing debts, whether or not repayment of such debts has been demanded, does not by itself prove inability on its part to pay its debts.[4]

The word 'contracts' means insurance contracts and no others.[5] The phrase 'the amount of the contracts' means 'the sum or sums payable under the contracts', i e the sums prospectively payable under the company's current insurance contracts.[6]

But the Court has power to reduce the amount of any insurance contracts which have ripened into presently payable debts at a date later than the date of the presentation of the winding up petition.[7]

---

18 Ibid, s 57(3).
19 Ibid, s 57(4).
20 Ibid, s 57(5).
1 Ibid, s 57(6).
2 Ibid, s 58.
3 *Re Capital Annuities Ltd* [1978] 3 All ER 704 at 717 (per Slade J).
4 Ibid, at 718 (per Slade J).
5 *Re Fidelity Life Assurance Ltd* (23 July 1976, unreported); *Re Capital Annuities Ltd* (supra), at 719 (per Slade J).
6 *Re Capital Annuities Ltd* (supra), at 719, 724 (per Slade J).
7 Ibid, at 725 (per Slade J).

The fact that a scheme of reduction does not provide for strict equality between the various policy holders and, in particular, special provisions for reduction of excessive benefits, does not deprive the Court of jurisdiction to approve it.[8]

The Court has jurisdiction to order a proposed reduction without directing meetings of policy holders or any further advertisements or communications with them.[9]

7 Winding up rules

Rules may be made[10] for determining the amount of the liabilities of an insurance company to policy holders of any class or description for the purpose of proof in a winding up and generally for carrying into effect the provisions of Part II of the Insurance Companies Act 1982 with respect to the winding up of insurance companies.[11]

The rules may also make provision[12] for:

- i the identification of the assets and liabilities falling within either paragraph of s 55(3) of the Insurance Companies Act 1982;[13]
- ii the apportionment between the assets falling within paragraphs (a) and (b) of s 55(3) of the Insurance Companies Act 1982 of the costs, charges and expenses of the winding up and of any debts of the company having priority under the Companies Act 1985, s 614;
- iii the determination of the amount of liabilities of any description falling within either paragraph of the Insurance Companies Act 1982, s 55(3) for the purpose of establishing whether or not there is any such excess in respect of that paragraph as is mentioned in s 55(4) of the Act.[14]
- iv the application of assets within paragraph (a) of s 55(3) for meeting the liabilities within that paragraph;
- v the application of assets representing any such excess as is mentioned in s 55(4).

J Changes of director, controller or manager

1 Approval of proposed managing director, chief executive or principal United Kingdom executive of insurance company

No insurance company to which Part II of the Insurance Companies Act 1982 applies[15] must appoint[16] a person as managing director or chief executive[17] of the company unless:

---

[8] Ibid, at 726 (per Slade J).

[9] Ibid, at 728 (per Slade J). In *Re Fidelity Life Assurance Ltd* (supra) an order for reduction of contracts was made without directing meetings of policy holders to be called.

[10] Under the Companies Act 1985, s 663.

[11] Insurance Companies Act 1982, s 59(1). The rules at present in force are the Insurance Companies (Winding-Up) Rules 1985 (SI 1985 No 95). See Appendix II, post.

[12] Insurance Companies Act 1982, s 59(2).

[13] See p 69, ante.

[14] See p 69, ante.

[15] See pp 40–41, ante.

[16] Insurance Companies Act 1982, s 60(1).

[17] For the meaning of 'chief executive', see p 34, ante.

a the company has served on the Secretary of State a written notice stating that it proposes to appoint that person to that position and containing such particulars as may be prescribed.[18]

b either the Secretary of State has, before the expiration of the period of three months beginning with the date of service of that notice, notified the company in writing that there is no objection to that person being appointed to that position or that period has elapsed without the Secretary of State having served on the company a written notice of objection.

A notice served by a company must contain a statement signed by the person proposed to be appointed that it is served with his knowledge and consent.[19]

The Secretary of State may serve a notice of objection on the ground that it appears to him that the person proposed to be appointed is not a fit and proper person to be appointed to the position in question.[20]

Before serving such a notice the Secretary of State must serve on the company and on that person a preliminary written notice stating:

a that the Secretary of State is considering the service on the company of a notice of objection on that ground; and

b that the company and that person may, within the period of one month from the date of service of the preliminary notice, make written representations to the Secretary of State and, if the company or that person so requests, oral representations to an officer of the Department of Trade appointed for the purpose by the Secretary of State.[1]

The Secretary of State is not obliged to disclose to the company or to the person proposed to be appointed any particulars of the ground on which he is considering the service on the company of a notice of objection.[2]

Where representations have been made, the Secretary of State must take them into consideration before serving the notice of objection.[3]

In relation to an insurance company whose head office is in a member State other than the United Kingdom, excluding a company whose business in the United Kingdom is restricted to reinsurance, the above provisions have effect as if the references to a managing director or chief executive were references to a principal United Kingdom executive.[4]

In relation to any other company whose head office is outside the United Kingdom the above provisions have effect as if the references to a chief executive included references to a principal United Kingdom executive.[5]

---

18 The regulations at present in force are the Insurance Companies Regulations 1981 (SI 1981 No 1654), reg 31. See Appendix II, post.

19 Insurance Companies Act 1982, s 60(2).

20 Ibid, s 60(3).

1 Ibid, s 60(3).

2 Ibid, s 60(4).

3 Ibid, s 60(5).

4 Ibid, s 63(1)(a). 'Principal United Kingdom executive' means an officer or employee within s 8(4)(b) or s 9(6): ibid, s 63(3).

5 Ibid, s 63(2).

2 Approval of person proposing to become controller of insurance company where s 60 does not apply

No person can become a controller[6] of an insurance company to which Part II of the Insurance Companies Act 1982 applies[7] otherwise than by virtue of an appointment in relation to which s 60 has effect unless:

a he has served on the Secretary of State a written notice stating that he intends to become a controller of that company and containing such particulars as may be prescribed;[8] and
b either the Secretary of State has, before the expiration of the period of three months beginning with the date of service of that notice, notified him in writing that there is no objection to his becoming a controller of the company or that period has elapsed without the Secretary of State having served on him a written notice of objection.[9]

The Secretary of State may serve a notice of objection on the ground that it appears to him that the person concerned is not a fit and proper person to be a controller of the company.[10]

But before serving such a notice the Secretary of State must serve on that person a preliminary written notice stating:

a that the Secretary of State is considering the service on him of a notice of objection on that ground; and
b that that person may, within the period of one month from the date of service of the preliminary notice, make written representations to the Secretary of State, and if that person so requests, oral representations to an officer of the Department of Trade appointed for the purpose by the Secretary of State.[11]

The Secretary of State is not obliged to disclose to any person any particulars of the ground on which he is considering the service on him of a notice of objection.[12]

Where representations are made, the Secretary of State must take them into consideration before serving the notice of objection.[13]

In relation to an insurance company whose head office is in a member State other than the United Kingdom, excluding a company whose business in the

---

6 As to the meaning of 'controller', see p 34, ante.
7 See pp 40–41, ante.
8 The regulations at present in force are the Insurance Companies Regulations 1981 (SI 1981 No 1654), reg 32. See Appendix II, post.
9 Insurance Companies Act 1982, s 61(1). A person who makes default in complying with s 61(1) is guilty of an offence and liable, on summary conviction, to a fine not exceeding level 5 on the standard scale: ibid, s 71(3). A person is not guilty of an offence by reason of his default in complying with s 61 if he proves that he did not know that the acts or circumstances by virtue of which he became or ceased to be a controller of the body in question were such as to have that effect: ibid, s 71(5). As to the service of a notice, see p 78, post.
10 Insurance Companies Act 1982, s 61(2).
11 Ibid, s 61(2).
12 Ibid, s 61(3).
13 Ibid, s 61(4).

United Kingdom is restricted to reinsurance, the above provisions do not apply.[14]

3 Duty to notify change of director, controller or manager

A person who becomes or ceases to be a controller of an insurance company to which Part II of the Insurance Companies Act 1982 applies[15] must, before the expiration of the period of seven days beginning with the day next following that on which he does so, notify the insurance company in writing of that fact and of such other matters as may be prescribed.[16]

A person who becomes a director or manager of any such insurance company must, before the expiration of seven days beginning with the day next following that on which he does so, notify the insurance company in writing of such matters as may be prescribed.[17]

An insurance company to which Part II of the Insurance Companies Act 1982 applies[18] must give written notice to the Secretary of State of the fact that any person has become or has ceased to be a director, controller or manager of the company and of any matter of which any such person is required to notify the company.[19]

The notice must be given before the expiration of fourteen days beginning with the day next following that on which that fact or matter comes to the company's knowledge.[20]

In relation to an insurance company whose head office is in a member State other than the United Kingdom, excluding a company whose business in the United Kingdom is restricted to reinsurance, the above provisions have effect as if the references to a director or manager were references to a principal United Kingdom executive, an employee within the Insurance Companies Act 1982, s 8(4)(c) or an authorised United Kingdom representative.[1]

In relation to any other insurance company whose head office is outside the United Kingdom the above provisions have effect as if the references to a

---

14 Ibid, s 63(1)(b).

15 See pp 40–41, ante.

16 Insurance Companies Act 1982, s 62(1). Any person who makes default in complying with s 62(1) is guilty of an offence and liable (a) on conviction on indictment, to imprisonment for a term not exceeding 2 years, or to a fine, or to both; (b) on summary conviction, to a fine not exceeding £1,000 or, if it is greater, the prescribed sum within the meaning of the Magistrates' Courts Act 1980, s 32: ibid, s 71(1), (2). A person is not guilty of an offence by reason of his default in complying with s 62(1) if he proves that he did not know that the acts or circumstances by virtue of which he became or ceased to be a controller of the body in question were such as to have that effect: ibid, s 71(5). The regulations at present in force are the Insurance Companies Regulations 1981 (SI 1981 No 1654) regs 33 and 35. See Appendix II, post.

17 Insurance Companies Act 1982, s 62(1). For failure to comply with this subsection, see footnote 16, supra.

18 See pp 40–41, ante.

19 Insurance Companies Act 1982, s 62(2). A company which fails to comply with this provision is guilty of an offence and liable, on summary conviction, to a fine not exceeding level 5 on the standard scale: ibid, s 71(3).

20 Ibid, s 62(2).

1 Ibid, s 63(1)(c). 'Principal United Kingdom executive' means an officer or employee within s 8(4)(b) or s 9(6): ibid, s 63(3). See p 35, ante. 'Authorised United Kingdom representative' means a representative fulfilling the requirements of s 10 or an individual representative of the kind described in s 10: Insurance Companies Act 1982, s 63(3).

director included references to a principal United Kingdom executive and to an authorised United Kingdom executive.[2]

K Change of main agent

An insurance company to which Part II of the Insurance Companies Act 1982 applies[3] must give written notice of the fact that any person has become or ceased to be a main agent[4] of the company and, if a main agent is a body corporate or a firm, of the fact that any person has become or ceased to be a director of the body or partner of the firm.[5]

The notice must be given before the expiration of the period of fourteen days beginning with the day next following that on which the change comes to the knowledge of the insurance company.[6]

L Miscellaneous

1 Documents deposited with Secretary of State

The Secretary of State must deposit with the Registrar of Companies one copy of:[7]

a any document deposited with the Secretary of State under s 22,[8] including any document obtained under s 22(5);[9]
b any document deposited with him under s 42(4)[10] or s 50(4).[11]

Any document deposited under the above provisions or under s 25(5)[12] or s 26(3)[13] with the Registrar of Companies is open to inspection and copies of it may be procured by any person on payment of such fees as the Secretary of State may direct.[14]

Every document deposited with the Secretary of State and certified by the Registrar of Companies to be a document so deposited is to be deemed to be a document so deposited.[15]

---

2 Ibid, s 63(2)(b).
3 See pp 40–41, ante.
4 'Main agent' has the meaning given in the Insurance Companies Act 1982, s 96(1). See p 35, ante.
5 Insurance Companies Act 1982, s 64(1). A company which fails to comply with this provision is guilty of an offence and liable, on summary conviction, to a fine not exceeding level 5 on the standard scale: ibid, s 71(3).
6 Ibid, s 64(2).
7 Insurance Companies Act 1982, s 65(1).
8 This section concerns the deposit of accounts, balance sheet etc. See pp 44–45, ante.
9 See p 45, ante.
10 This subsection concerns the deposit of an abstract of an actuary's report. See p 59, ante.
11 This subsection concerns the deposit of a copy of an order of the Court sanctioning a scheme for the transfer of long term business. See p 66, ante.
12 This subsection concerns the deposit of a periodic statement by a company with a prescribed class of business. See p 46, ante.
13 This subsection concerns the deposit of a statement of transactions of a prescribed class or description. See p 47, ante.
14 Insurance Companies Act 1982, s 65(2). This subsection does not apply to any document if it is a copy of a document in respect of which a dispensation has been given under s 23(2): ibid, s 65(3). For dispensation under s 23(2), see p 45, ante.
15 Insurance Companies Act 1982, s 65(4).

Every document purporting to be certified by the Registrar of Companies to be a copy of a document so deposited is to be deemed to be a copy of that document and shall be received in evidence as if it were the original document unless some variation between it and the original is proved.[16]

2 Power to treat certain business as or as not being ordinary long term insurance business

The Secretary of State may,[17] on the application of or with the consent of an insurance company to which Part II of the Insurance Companies Act 1982 applies,[18] by order direct that for the purpose of certain provisions[19] of the Act:

a business of a kind specified in the order, not being ordinary long term insurance business, shall be treated as being such business; or
b ordinary long term insurance business of a kind so specified shall be treated as not being such business.[20]

An order may be subject to conditions and may be varied or revoked at any time by the Secretary of State.[1]

3 Power to modify Part II of the Insurance Companies Act 1982 in relation to particular companies

The Secretary of State may,[2] on the application or with the consent of an insurance company to which Part II of the Insurance Companies Act 1982 applies,[3] by order direct that certain provisions[4] of the Act shall not apply to the company or shall apply to it with such modifications as may be specified in the order.

An order may be subject to conditions.[5] It may be revoked at any time by the Secretary of State.[6] He may at any time vary it on the application or with the consent of the company to which it applies.[7]

4 Power to alter insurance company's financial year

The Secretary of State may[8] extend or shorten the duration of any financial

---

16 Ibid, s 65(4).
17 Ibid, s 67(1).
18 See pp 40–41, ante.
19 The provisions are ss 17 to 20, 25, 28 to 31, 42, 55, 56 and 50(2) of the Insurance Companies Act 1982, and the Policyholders Protection Act 1975, s 22 and Sch 3.
20 An order under s 67(1)(b) may direct that the business specified in the order is to be treated as falling within a specified class of business: Insurance Companies Act 1982, s 67(2).
1 Ibid, s 67(3).
2 Ibid, s 68(1).
3 See pp 40–41, ante.
4 The provisions are ss 16 to 22, 23(1) and 25 to 36 of the Insurance Companies Act 1982, the provisions of regulations made for the purposes of any of those sections and the provisions of any valuation regulations: Insurance Companies Act 1982, s 68(4).
5 Ibid, s 68(2).
6 Ibid, s 68(3).
7 Ibid, s 68(3).
8 Ibid, s 69.

year[9] of any insurance company to which Part II of the Insurance Companies Act 1982 applies.[10]

5 Service of notices

Any notice which is required to be sent to a policy holder may be addressed and sent to the person to whom notices respecting that policy are usually sent.[11] Any notice so addressed and sent is deemed to be notice to the policy holder.[12]

Where any person claiming to be interested in a policy has given to the company notice of his interest, any notice which is required to be sent to policy holders must also be sent to that person at the address specified by him in his notice.[13]

Any notice to be served by the Secretary of State under the Insurance Companies Act 1982, ss 46[14], 60[15] or 61,[16] may be served by post, and a letter containing that notice is deemed to be properly addressed if it is addressed to that person at his last known residence or last known place of business in the United Kingdom.[17]

6 Offences under Part II of the Insurance Companies Act 1982

Various offences under Part II of the Act are set out in s 71.

CONDUCT OF INSURANCE BUSINESS

In connection with the conduct of insurance business, Part III of the Insurance Companies Act 1982 contains various provisions relating to: (1) insurance advertisements; (2) misleading statements inducing persons to enter into contracts of insurance; (3) intermediaries in insurance transactions; (4) statutory notices in relation to ordinary long-term policies, and the right to withdraw from a transaction in respect of such policies; (5) linked long-term policies; and (6) capital redemption business.

1 Insurance advertisements

Regulations may be made as to the form and contents of insurance

---

9 'Financial year' means each period of 12 months at the end of which the balance of accounts of the insurance company is struck or, if no such balance is struck, the calendar year: ibid, s 96(1).
10 See pp 40–41, ante.
11 Insurance Companies Act 1982, s 70(1).
12 Ibid, s 70(1).
13 Ibid, s 70(2).
14 See p 62, ante.
15 See pp 72–73, ante.
16 See p 74, ante.
17 Insurance Companies Act 1982, s 70(3).

advertisements.[18] They may make different provisions in relation to insurance advertisements of different classes or descriptions.[19]

Any person who issues an insurance advertisement which contravenes the regulations is guilty of an offence.[20] But a person who in the ordinary course of his business issues to the order of another person an advertisement which contravenes the regulations is not himself guilty of an offence if he proves that the matters contained in it were not, wholly or in part, devised or selected by him or by any person under his direction or control.[1]

An advertisement issued by any person on behalf of or to the order of another person is to be treated as an advertisement by that other person.[2] Further, an advertisement inviting persons to enter into or to offer to enter into contracts with a person specified in the advertisement is presumed, unless the contrary is proved, to have been issued by that person.[3]

2 Misleading statements

Any person who by any statement, promise or forecast which he knows to be misleading, false or deceptive, or by any dishonest concealment of material facts or by the reckless making (dishonestly or otherwise) of any statement, promise or forecast which is misleading, false or deceptive, induces or attempts to induce another person to enter into or offer to enter into any contract insurance with an insurance company, is guilty of an offence.[4]

3 Intermediaries in insurance transactions

Regulations may be made for requiring any person who:

- a invites another person to make an offer or proposal or to take any other step with a view to entering into a contract of insurance with an insurance company; and
- b is connected with that company as provided in the regulations,

---

18 Insurance Companies Act 1982, s 72(1). 'Insurance advertisement' means an advertisement inviting persons to enter into or to offer to enter into contracts of insurance, and an advertisement which contains information calculated to lead directly or indirectly to persons entering into such contracts is to be treated as an advertisement inviting them to so do: ibid, s 72(5). 'Advertisement' includes every form of advertising, whether in a publication or by the display of notices or by means of circulars or other documents or by an exhibition of photographs or cinematograph films or by way of sound broadcasting or television, and references to the issue of an advertisement are to be construed accordingly: ibid, s 72(6). The regulations at present in force are the Insurance Companies Regulations 1981 (SI 1981 No 1654) regs 65, 65A, 65B, 65C and 66. See Appendix II, post.

19 Insurance Companies Act 1982, s 72(2).

20 Ibid, s 72(3). Any person who is guilty of an offence under this section is liable (a) on conviction on indictment, to imprisonment for a term not exceeding 2 years or to a fine, or to both; (b) on summary conviction, to a fine not exceeding £1,000 or, if it is greater, the prescribed sum within the meaning of the Magistrates' Courts Act 1980, s 32: ibid, s 81(1).

1 Ibid, s 72(4).

2 Ibid, s 72(7).

3 Ibid, s 72(7).

4 Ibid, s 73. Any person who is guilty of an offence under this section is liable (a) on conviction on indictment, to imprisonment for a term not exceeding 2 years or to a fine, or to both; (b) on summary conviction, to a fine not exceeding £1,000 or, if it is greater, the prescribed sum within the meaning of the Magistrates' Courts Act 1980, s 32: ibid, s 81(1).

to give the prescribed information with respect to his connection with the company to the person to whom the invitation is issued.[5]

Regulations may be made for requiring any person who, in the course of carrying on any business or profession, issues any such invitation in relation to an insurance company which is not an authorised insurer[6] in respect of the contract in question, to inform the person to whom the invitation is issued that the company is not such an insurer.[7]

Any person who contravenes the regulations is guilty of an offence.[8]

4 Ordinary long-term insurance policies

(a) Statutory notice

No insurance company, whether established within or outside the United Kingdom, which carries on insurance business within the United Kingdom, and no member of Lloyd's must enter into a contract the effecting of which constitutes the carrying on of ordinary long-term insurance business[9] unless that company or member, as the case may be, either:

- a has sent by post to the other party to the contract a statutory notice in relation to that contract; or
- b does so at the time when the contract is entered into.[10]

A 'statutory notice' is one which:

- a contains such matters (and no others) and is in such form as may be prescribed and complies with such requirements (whether as to type, size, colour or disposition of lettering, quality or colour of paper, or otherwise) as may be prescribed for securing that the notice is easily legible; and
- b has annexed to it a form of notice of cancellation of the prescribed description.[11]

The Secretary of State may, on the application of any insurer, alter the requirements of any regulations so as to adapt them to the circumstances of the insurer or to any particular kind of contract proposed to be entered into by that insurer.[12]

---

5 Ibid, s 74(1). The regulations at present in force are the Insurance Companies Regulations 1981 (SI 1981 No 1654), regs 67 to 69. See Appendix II, post.

6 'Authorised insurer', in relation to a contract of any description, means a person entitled to carry on in the United Kingdom insurance business of a class comprising the effecting of contracts of that description: Insurance Companies Act 1982, s 74(2).

7 Ibid, s 74(2).

8 Ibid, s 74(3). Any person who is guilty of an offence under this section is liable (a) on conviction on indictment, to imprisonment for a term not exceeding 2 years or to a fine or to both; (b) on summary conviction, to a fine not exceeding £1,000 or, if it is greater, the prescribed sum within the meaning of the Magistrates' Courts Act 1980, s 32: ibid, s 81(1).

9 'Ordinary long-term insurance business' means long term business that is not industrial assurance business: ibid, s 96(1).

10 Ibid, s 75(1). This subsection does not apply to a contract for the effecting of which by the insurer constitutes the carrying on of industrial assurance business; and regulations may exempt from that subsection contracts of any other class or decription: ibid, s 75(5).

11 Ibid, s 75(2). The regulations at present in force are the Insurance Companies Regulations 1981 (SI 1981 No 1654), regs 70 to 71. See Appendix II, post.

12 Insurance Companies Act 1982, s 75(3).

Any insurer who contravenes any of the provisions relating to a statutory notice is guilty of an offence.[13] But no contract is invalidated by reason of the fact that the insurer has contravened the provisions relating to the statutory notice in relation to that contract.[14]

(b) Right to withdraw from transaction

A person who has received a statutory notice in relation to a long term insurance policy may before the expiration of:

a the tenth day after that on which he received the notice; or
b the earliest day on which he knows both that the contract has been entered into and that the first or only premium has been paid,

whichever is the later, serve a notice of cancellation on the insurer.[15]

A person to whom an insurer ought to have, but has not, sent a statutory notice may serve a notice of cancellation on the insurer.[16] But if the insurer sends him a statutory notice before he has served a notice of cancellation, then his right to do so ceases.[17]

A notice of cancellation may, but need not, be in the form annexed to the statutory notice and has effect if, however expressed, it indicates the intention of the person serving it to withdraw from the transaction in relation to which the statutory notice was or ought to have been sent.[18]

Where a person serves a notice of cancellation, then if at the time when the notice is served the contract has been entered into, the notice operates so as to rescind the contract.[19] In any other case the service of the notice operates as a withdrawal of any offer to enter into the contract which is contained in, or implied by, any proposal made to the insurer by the person serving the notice of cancellation and as notice to the insurer that any such offer is withdrawn.[20]

Where a notice of cancellation operates to rescind a contract or as the withdrawal of an offer to enter into a contract:

a any sum which the person serving the notice has paid in connection with the contract (whether by way of premium or otherwise and whether to the insurer or to any person who is the agent of the insurer for the purpose of receiving that sum) is recoverable from the person serving the notice;
b any sum which the insurer has paid under the contract is recoverable by him from the person serving the notice.[1]

---

13 Ibid, s 75(4). Any person who makes default in complying with, or with a requirement imposed under s 75 is liable on summary conviction to a fine not exceeding level 5 on the standard scale: ibid, s 81(2).
14 Ibid, s 75(4).
15 Ibid, s 76(1).
16 Ibid, s 76(2).
17 Ibid, s 76(2).
18 Ibid, s 76(3).
19 Ibid, s 76(4)(a).
20 Ibid, s 76(4)(b).
1 Ibid, s 76(5). Any such sum is recoverable as a simple contract debt in any court of competent jurisdiction: ibid, s 76(6).

(c) Service of notice of cancellation

A notice of cancellation is deemed to be served on the insurer if it is sent by post to any person specified in the statutory notice as a person to whom a notice of cancellation may be sent and is addressed to that person at an address so specified.[2] Further, the notice of cancellation is deemed to be served on the insurer at the time when it is posted.[3]

A notice of cancellation may, however, be served in any other way (whether by post or not) whether the notice is served on the insurer or on a person who is the agent of the insurer for the purpose of receiving such a notice.[4]

Again, a notice which is sent by post to a person at his proper address is deemed to be served on him at the time when it is posted.[5]

5 Linked long term policies

Regulations may be made[6] in relation to ordinary long term policies which:

a are entered into by insurance companies, whether established within or outside the United Kingdom which carry on insurance business within the United Kingdom, or by members of Lloyd's; and

b are contracts under which the benefits payable to the policy holder are wholly or partly to be determined by reference to the value of, or the income from, property of any description (whether or not specified in the contract) or by reference to fluctuations in, or in an index of, the value of property of any description (whether or not so specified).[7]

The regulations may make provision for:

a restricting the descriptions of property or the indices of the value of property by reference to which benefits under the contract may be determined;

b regulating the manner in which and the frequency with which property of any description is to be valued for the purpose of determining such benefits and the times at which reference is to be made for that purpose to the index of the value of property;

c requiring the insurers under the contracts to appoint valuers for carrying out valuations of property of any description for the purpose of determining such benefits (being valuers who comply with the prescribed requirements as to qualifications and independence from the insurer) and to furnish the Secretary of State with the prescribed information in relation to such appointments;

---

2 Ibid, s 77(1)(a).

3 Ibid, s 77(1)(b).

4 Ibid, s 77(2).

5 Ibid, s 77(3).

6 The regulations at present in force are the Insurance Companies Regulations 1981 (SI 1981 No 1654), reg 72. See Appendix II, post.

7 Insurance Companies Act 1982, s 78(1). Regulations under this section do not apply in relation to any contract the effecting of which by the insurer constitutes the carrying on of industrial assurance business or to any contract entered into by an insurance company, whether established within or outside the United Kingdom which carries on insurance business within the United Kingdom, by reason only that the policy holder is eligible to participate in any established surplus as defined in s 30(4) of the Act: ibid, s 78(6). As to the meaning of the words 'established surplus', see p 49, ante.

d requiring insurers under the contracts to furnish, in such manner and at such times or intervals as may be prescribed, such information relating to the value of the benefits under the contracts as may be prescribed, whether by sending notices to policy holders, depositing statements with the Secretary of State or the Registrar of Companies, publication in the press or otherwise;

e requiring insurers under the contracts to furnish to the Secretary of State, in such manner and at such times or intervals as may be prescribed, such information certified in such manner as may be prescribed with respect to so much of their business as is concerned with the contracts or with any class or description of the contracts, and enabling the Secretary of State to publish such information in such ways as he thinks appropriate.[8]

The regulations may, in relation to notices required to be sent to policy holders, impose requirements as to type, size, colour or disposition of lettering, quality or colour of paper, or otherwise for securing that such notices are easily legible.[9]

6 Capital redemption business

Where an insurance company, whether established within or outside the United Kingdom, carries on in the United Kingdom capital redemption business in the case of which premiums in return for which a contract is effected are payable at intervals of less than six months, the company must not give the holder of any policy issued after 2 December 1909, any advantage dependent on lot or chance.[10]

SPECIAL CLASSES OF INSURERS

Part IV of the Insurance Companies Act 1982 concerns special classes of insurers including:[11]

1 Industrial assurance companies; and
2 Lloyd's underwriters.

1 Industrial assurance companies

The provisions of the Insurance Companies Act 1982 are modified[12] in their application to companies carrying on industrial assurance business.[13]

---

8 Insurance Companies Act 1982, s 78(2).

9 Ibid, s 78(3). The Secretary of State may, on the application of any insurer, alter requirements of any regulations so as to adapt them to the circumstances of that insurer or to any particular kind of contract entered into or proposed to be entered into by that insurer: ibid, s 78(4).

10 Ibid, s 80. But this section is not to be construed as in any way prejudicing any question as to the application to any such transaction, whether in respect of a policy issued before, on or after that date, of the law relating to lotteries.

11 There are also provisions relating to companies established outside the United Kingdom (Insurance Companies Act 1982, s 87), unregistered companies (ibid, s 88) and insurance companies formed before 1967 in contravention of the Companies Act 1948, s 434 (ibid, s 89).

12 See the Insurance Companies Act 1982, s 82.

13 'Industrial assurance business' means 'the business of effecting assurances upon human life

2 Lloyd's underwriters

(a) Requirements to be complied with

Certain requirements must be fulfilled by Lloyd's underwriters with respect to the carrying to a trust fund all premiums and the audit of their accounts.[14]

(b) Financial resources

Subject to such modifications as may be prescribed and to any determination made by the Secretary of State in accordance with regulations, ss 32,[15] 33[16] and 35[17] apply to the members of Lloyd's taken together as they apply to an insurance company to which Part II of the Insurance Companies Act 1982 applies[18] and whose head office is in the United Kingdom.[19]

The powers conferred on the Secretary of State by ss 38 to 41,[20] 44[21] and 45[1] are exercisable in relation to the members of Lloyd's if there is a breach of an obligation imposed by virtue of the above provisions.[2]

(c) Transfer of business

Sections 49 to 52[3] apply in relation to transfers to and from members of Lloyd's if, and only if, the following conditions are satisfied:

- a the transfer is not one where both the transferor and the transferee are members of Lloyd's;
- b the Committee of Lloyd's have by resolution authorised one person to act in connection with the transfer for the members concerned as transferor or transferee; and
- c a copy of the resolution has been given to the Secretary of State.[4]

(d) Statement of business by Committee of Lloyd's

The Committee of Lloyd's must deposit every year with the Secretary of State a statement in the prescribed form summarising the extent and character of the

---

premiums in respect of which are received by means of collectors': ibid, s 96(1). For industrial assurance business, see generally Ivamy *Personal Accident, Life and Other Insurances* (2nd Edn, 1980) pp 123–137.

14 Insurance Companies Act 1982, s 83. For these requirements, see p 40, footnote 13, ante.

15 Which concerns the margin of solvency. See pp 52–53, ante.

16 Which concerns the failure to maintain the minimum margin of solvency. See p 53, ante.

17 Which concerns the form and situation of assets. See p 54, ante.

18 See pp 40–41, ante.

19 Insurance Companies Act 1982, a 84(1). The regulations at present in force are the Insurance (Lloyd's) Regulations 1983 (SI 1983 No 224) reg 3, Sch 1. See Appendix II, post.

20 These sections concern requirements about investments, the maintenance of assets in the United Kingdom, the custody of assets and the limitation of premium income. See pp 56–59, ante.

21 Which concerns the Secretary of State's power to obtain information and require the production of documents. See pp 60–61, ante.

1 Which concerns the Secretary of State's residual power to impose requirements for the protection of policy holders. See p 61, ante.

2 Insurance Companies Act 1982, s 84(2).

3 Which concern the sanction of the Court for the transfer of long term business, supplementary provisions, the approval of transfers of general business and the effect of an instrument giving effect to a transfer approved by the Secretary of State. See pp 64–67, ante.

4 Insurance Companies Act 1982, s 85(1), (2).

insurance business done by the members of Lloyd's in the 12 months to which the statement relates.[5]

Regulations may require the statement to deal separately with such classes or descriptions of business as may be specified.[6]

When the statement is deposited such fee as may be prescribed must be paid to the Secretary of State.[7]

SUPPLEMENTARY PROVISIONS

Part V of the Insurance Companies Act 1982 contains a number of supplementary provisions including those relating to:

1 valuation regulations;
2 criminal proceedings;
3 interpretation;
4 miscellaneous matters.

1 Valuation regulations

Regulations may be made with respect to the determination of the value of assets and the amount of liabilities in which the value or amount is required by any provision of the Insurance Companies Act 1982 to be determined in accordance with valuation regulations.[8]

The regulations may provide that, for any specified purpose, assets or liabilities of any specified class or description must be left out of account or must be taken into account only to a specified extent.[9]

Regulations may make different provision in relation to different cases or circumstances and for the purpose of different enactments.[10]

2 Criminal proceedings

(a) Criminal liability of directors

Where an offence under the Insurance Companies Act 1982 committed by a body corporate is proved to have been committed with the consent or connivance of, or to be attributable to any neglect on the part of any director,[11] chief executive,[12] manager,[13] secretary or other similar officer of the body corporate or any person who was purporting to act in any such capacity, he, as well as the body corporate, is guilty of that offence and liable to be proceeded against and punished accordingly.[14]

---

5 Ibid, s 86(1). The regulations at present in force are the Insurance (Lloyd's) Regulations 1983 (SI 1983 No 224) reg 5, Sch 3. See Appendix II, post.

6 Insurance Companies Act 1982, s 86(2).

7 Ibid, s 94A(3). The regulations at present in force are the Insurance (Fees) Regulations 1986 (SI 1986/446).

8 Insurance Companies Act 1982, s 90(1). The regulations at present in force are the Insurance Companies Regulations 1981 (SI 1981 No 1654), regs 37 to 64. See Appendix II, post.

9 Insurance Companies Act 1982, s 90(2).

10 Ibid, s 90(3).

11 'Director' includes any person occupying the position of director by whatever name called: ibid, s 96(1).

12 'Chief executive' has the meaning given in s 7: ibid, s 96(1). See p 34, ante.

13 'Manager' has the meaning given in s 7: Insurance Companies Act 1982, s 96(1). See p 34, ante.

14 Insurance Companies Act 1982, s 91(1). For the purposes of s 91 a person is deemed to be a director of a body corporate if he is a person in accordance with whose directions or instructions the directors of the body corporate or any of them act: ibid, s 91(2).

(b) Criminal proceedings against unincorporated bodies

Proceedings for an offence alleged to have been committed under the Insurance Companies Act 1982 by an unincorporated body must be brought in the name of that body and not in that of any of its members.[15] For the purposes of any such proceedings any rules of court relating to the service of documents have effect as if that body were a corporation.[16] A fine imposed on an unincorporated body on its conviction of an offence under the Act must be paid out of the funds of that body.[17]

(c) Restriction on institution of proceedings

Proceedings in respect of an offence under the Insurance Companies Act 1982 must not be instituted except by or with the consent of the Secretary of State, the Industrial Assurance Commissioner or the Director of Public Prosecutions.[18]

(d) Summary proceedings

Summary proceedings for any offence under the Insurance Companies Act 1982 may be taken against any body corporate at any place at which it has a place of business, and against any other person at any place at which he is for the time being.[19]

Any information relating to an offence under the Act which is triable by a magistrates' court may so be tried if it is laid at any time within three years after the commission of the offence and within 12 months after the date on which evidence sufficient, in the opinion of the Director of Public Prosecutions, the Secretary of State or the Industrial Assurance Commissioner, as the case may be, to justify the proceedings comes to his knowledge.[20]

3 Interpretation

A long list of words used in the Insurance Companies Act 1982 is given in s 96(1).[1]

4 Miscellaneous matters

(a) Regulations and orders

The Secretary of State may make regulations under the Insurance Companies Act 1982 for any purpose for which regulations are authorised or required to be

---

15 Ibid, s 92(1).

16 Ibid, s 92(1).

17 Ibid, s 92(2).

18 Ibid, s 93.

19 Ibid, s 94(1). This subsection is without prejudice to any jurisdiction exercisable apart from it: ibid, s 94(1).

20 Ibid, s 94(2). For the purposes of s 94 a certificate of the Director of Public Prosecutions, the Secretary of State or the Industrial Assurance Commissioner, as the case may be, as to the date on which such evidence came to his knowledge is conclusive evidence: ibid, s 94(7).

1 E g 'actuary', 'annuities on human life', etc.

made under it.[2] Regulations may make different provision for cases of different descriptions.[3]

Any power conferred by the Act to make regulations is exercisable by statutory instrument.[4]

(b) Annual report by Secretary of State

The Secretary of State must cause a general annual report of matters within the Insurance Companies Act 1982 to be laid before Parliament.[5]

---

2 Insurance Companies Act 1982, s 97(1).

3 Ibid, s 97(2).

4 Ibid, s 97(3). Any statutory instrument containing regulations under the Act is subject to annulment in pursuance of a resolution of either House of Parliament: ibid, s 97(4).

5 Ibid, s 98.

PART II

The making of the contract

CHAPTER 7

Introduction

To establish the existence of the contract it is not necessary that all its terms should have been separately agreed. As the contract is in common form, there is, as a rule no real negotiation of terms, the agreement being, on the part of the insurers, to issue, and, on the part of the proposer, to take, a policy in the ordinary form issued by the insurers.[1]

There must, however, be a clear agreement as to the distinctive features of the particular contract.[2] The parties, therefore, must be ascertained; the insurers must have agreed to insure the particular assured, and the assured must have agreed to the particular insurers.[3] They must be ad idem as regards the subject-matter of the insurance. The period of insurance must be fixed, and there must be agreement as to the sum to be insured and the premium to be paid. Finally, it must be clear that there was, in fact, an offer[4] to enter into the

---

1 *Acme Wood Flooring Co Ltd v Marten* (1904) 9 Com Cas 157 per Bruce J, at 162: 'Where a person insures with Lloyd's and obtains from Lloyd's a policy in the form ordinarily granted by Lloyd's, he must be taken to accept the terms expressed in the policy and to agree to the meaning which the words ordinarily bear.' See also, *Adie & Sons v Insurance Corpn Ltd* (1898) 14 TLR 544 per Bigham J; *General Accident Insurance Corpn v Cronk* (1901) 17 TLR 233 (accident insurance), where it was held that when the proposer applied for the ordinary form of policy issued by the insurers, it was not necessary that he should approve of all the terms of the policy before the contract became complete, and he must therefore be taken to have agreed to be bound by them; *Sanderson v Cunningham* [1919] 2 IR 234. If the form is altered by deletion of one of its clauses, the proposer is not bound; *South-East Lancashire Insurance Co Ltd v Croisdale* (1931) 40 LlL Rep 22 (motor insurance), where a clause providing for rebate of premium was struck out.

2 *Allis-Chalmers Co v Maryland Fidelity and Deposit Co* (1916) 114 LT 433, HL (fidelity insurance); *Rust v Abbey Life Assurance Co Ltd* [1978] 2 Lloyd's Rep 386 (property bond insurance), where C M Clothier QC said (ibid, at 392): 'One thing is perfectly clear from authorities old and new, and that is that a binding contract of this kind can be made even though the parties have neither discussed nor expressly agreed upon every individual term of a policy. The commonest such agreement, made daily in hundreds, is the policy of motor insurance, where the initial agreement may even be made by telephone between parties unknown to each other. In such cases the function of the policy is to state the terms already agree upon, knowledge of which is imputed to the insured.' The decision was subsequently affd [1979] 2 Lloyd's Rep 334, CA. Cf *Murfitt v Royal Insurance Co Ltd* (1922) 38 TLR 334, 10 LlL Rep 191 per McCardie J, at 336.

3 *Mackie v European Assurance Society* (1869) 21 LT 102 (fire insurance). In this case the proposed assured, on discovering that the cover note was issued by different insurers, reserved the right to be satisfied as to their standing, and, when the fire happened, took steps to enforce the cover note. This cover note was, in effect, an offer by such insurers. It purported on the face of it to be in force for a month, and the insurers had not withdrawn it. The conduct of the assured in taking steps to enforce the cover note may be regarded as an acceptance of the offer. If, however, there had been no fire, and the proposed assured had done nothing to indicate acceptance, it seems clear that the insurers could not have maintained an action for the premium. See further, *Giffard v Queen Insurance Co* (1869) 12 NBR 433.

4 See Chapter 8.

contract on the one side, followed by an acceptance[5] of the offer on the other, and that thus a complete contract resulted.

Usually the acceptance of the offer will not take place at once, and before it does so, it is the practice for a 'cover note'[6] to be issued.

Before acceptance, neither party is bound, and either may withdraw at pleasure.[7] After acceptance, there is a contract from which neither party can withdraw, binding the assured to pay the premium, and the insurers to accept the premium when tendered, to issue a policy, and to pay any sum that may become payable under the terms of the contract.

The various steps in the negotiations leading up to a contract of insurance are usually recorded in certain formal documents, i e the proposal, the cover note, and, finally, the policy. The absence, however, of any such document does not necessarily lead to the inference that there is no contract of insurance between the parties.

As far as Lloyd's policies are concerned, a 'slip' is sometimes used instead of a proposal form, and the contract is concluded as soon as the 'slip' has been initialled by the insurer.[8]

The position of the parties during the preliminary negotiations leading up to the completion of a contract of insurance is much the same as in the case of any other contract, except that, the contract being a contract uberrimae fidei, the utmost good faith is required on both sides.[9]

The proposer is under a duty to disclose[10] to the insurer all material facts relating to the proposed insurance and not to make any misrepresentations.[11]

In due course the assured will become liable to pay the premium to the insurer.[12]

---

[5] See Chapter 9.

[6] See Chapter 10.

[7] *Allis-Chalmers Co v Maryland Fidelity and Deposit Co* (1916) 114 LT 433, HL, per Lord Loreburn at 434; *Re Yager and Guardian Assurance Co Ltd* (1912) 108 LT 38 (fire insurance); *Canning v Farquhar* (1886) 16 QBD 727, CA (life insurance) per Lord Esher MR, at 731.

[8] See Chapter 11.

[9] See Chapter 12.

[10] See Chapter 13.

[11] See Chapter 14.

[12] See Chapter 15.

CHAPTER 8

The offer

Since the contract of insurance is constituted by the acceptance of an offer, it is necessary in the first instance to make certain that an offer has, in fact, been made which is capable of being accepted.[1]

A WHAT CONSTITUTES AN OFFER

To constitute an offer capable of being accepted, the following conditions must be fulfilled:

1 The alleged offer must be intended by the party making it to be an offer.

The party who begins the negotiations does not necessarily make an offer thereby; he may merely indicate his readiness to consider an offer.

2 The alleged offer must be complete.

It must show with precision the contract into which the party making it is prepared to enter.[2]

3 The alleged offer must be communicated to the other party.[3]

4 The alleged offer must be in force at the time when the other party purports to accept it.

Any offer may be revoked before acceptance;[4] and an offer once refused ceases to be in force and cannot afterwards be accepted unless it is repeated.[5]

---

1 *Canning v Farquhar* (1886) 16 QBD 727 (life insurance) per Lord Esher MR, at 730: 'At the beginning . . . I was much taken with the ordinary proposition that a proposal and an acceptance of that proposal make a contract. Whether that is so or not, depends on whether the one was meant to be a proposal and the other an acceptance by way of contract.'

2 *Christie v North British Insurance Co* 1825 3 Sh (Ct of Sess) 519 (fire insurance), where the premium had not been arranged; *Canning v Farquhar* (supra), where the proposal contained no reference to the premium. Cf *Murfitt v Royal Insurance Co* (1922) 38 TLR 334, 10 LlL Rep 191 (fire insurance) per McCardie J, at 336; *Allis-Chalmers Co v Maryland Fidelity Deposit Co* (1916) 114 LT 433, HL (fidelity insurance); *General Accident Insurance Corpn v Cronk* (1901) 17 TLR 233, where the proposal included an undertaking to pay the premium on acceptance.

3 *Rose v Medical Invalid Life Assurance Society* 1848 11 Dunl (Ct of Sess) 151 (life insurance), where the insurers stated in a letter handed to their own agent the premium at which they were willing to accept the proposal, but the agent never handed over the letter to the proposed assured.

4 *Mackie v European Assurance Society* (1869) 21 LT 102 (fire insurance) per Malins V-C, at 104; *Canning v Farquhar* (1886) 16 QBD 727 (life insurance) per Lord Esher MR, at 732; *Henderson v State Life Insurance Co* (1905) 9 OLR 540 (life insurance), where the proposed assured was held entitled to withdraw although he had paid the premium and received a cover note.

5 Cf *Hyde v Wrench* (1840) 3 Beav 334 (sale of land).

B BY WHOM THE OFFER IS MADE

The offer to enter into a contract of insurance may, as a general rule, be considered as addressed to the insurers by the person who is seeking to protect himself by insurance against loss. He may have been invited by the insurers to put himself into communication with them; but, whether the invitation comes to him from the insurers direct, or through the medium of an agent, or whether it is given to him personally, or only as a member of the public through an advertisement, the position remains unchanged, and he must submit his proposal, which they may accept or decline at their pleasure. The offer therefore proceeds from the proposed assured when he has filled up the proposal and forwarded it to the insurers.[6]

The terms of an ordinary contract of insurance are not specially arranged between the parties; the insurers have their own terms on which they are prepared to contract and from which, as a rule, they are not willing to depart. There is no real negotiation between the parties, the assured being compelled to contract with the insurers on their own terms. There is, therefore, no difficulty, in an ordinary case[7], in ascertaining from whom the offer proceeds.[8] Sometimes, however, the wording of the documents issued by the insurers may, however, show that the offer proceeds from them, as, for instance, in the case of coupon insurance.[9]

Where the terms of the proposed contract are really a matter of negotiation, as in the case of special insurances falling outside the ordinary business of the insurers, greater difficulty arises, and each case must be judged by its own circumstances. During the course of the negotiations, the parties may repeatedly change places, each party in turn putting forward an offer to be met by a refusal and a counter-offer from the other. The facts may show that it is the insurers who have made an offer, from which they cannot recede, and which the proposer may turn at his option into a binding contract.[10]

This may take place, even in an ordinary case where a proposal form is used,

---

6 *Linford v Provincial Horse and Cattle Insurance Co* (1864) 34 Beav 291 per Lord Romilly MR, at 293; *General Accident Insurance Corpn v Cronk* (supra); *Adie & Sons v Insurance Corpn Ltd* (1898) 14 TLR 544 (fire insurance) per Bigham J, at 544.

7 But see *Rust v Abbey Life Assurance Co Ltd* [1978] 2 Lloyd's Rep 386 (property bond insurance), where C M Clothier QC said (ibid, at 392): 'The traditional analysis of business activity into invitations to treat, offers and acceptances, or counter-offers and acceptances, presupposes an orderliness of thought among busy people which is seldom encountered in practice. Contracts involving very large sums are often drawn by lawyers and examined by company secretaries and the proper steps towards agreement can be readily discerned. But in hundreds of everyday transactions conducted by parties with no legal qualifications, the analysis is not always helpful because the distinct stages of formation of contract may be blurred by inartistic use of language and untrained habits of thought.' The decision was subsequently affd [1979] 2 Lloyd's Rep 334, CA.

8 *Rust v Abbey Life Assurance Co Ltd* (supra) (property bond insurance), where the application form was held to be an offer to invest a sum which accompanied it on a policy in the insurers' ordinary form, as amended. (See the judgment of C M Clothier QC, ibid, at 392.) The decision was subsequently affd [1979] 2 Lloyd's Rep 334, CA.

9 *General Accident, Fire and Life Assurance Corpn v Robertson* [1909] AC 404. For coupon insurance see p 113, post. See further, Ivamy *Personal Accident, Life and Other Insurances* (2nd Edn, 1980), pp 65–70.

10 *Re Yager and Guardian Assurance Co* (1912) 108 LT 38; *Bhugwandass v Netherlands India Sea and Fire Insurance Co of Batavia* (1888) 14 App Cas 83 PC (marine insurance).

if the insurers, in their acceptance, introduce terms[11] or impose conditions which did not appear in the proposal. In this case what purports to be an acceptance is not in reality an acceptance, but a new offer to contract on new terms and conditions. Thus, where the premium to be charged has to be settled by the insurers after consideration of the particulars furnished by the proposed, the offer to enter into a contract of insurance is made by the insurers when they settle the premium and inform the proposer of this fact, whilst the proposer, by tendering the premium, accepts their offer and does not merely offer to contract with them on their terms.[12]

C THE PROPOSAL FORM

1 The usual contents of proposal forms

Proposal forms necessarily vary in their content according to the nature of the proposed insurance; they also vary according to the practice of different insurers. All proposal forms, however, contain questions which the proposed assured is required to answer, and these questions, whatever the nature of the insurance, are framed on the same general lines.

The matters to which the questions relate may be classified as follows:

a The description of the proposed assured.
b The description of the risk proposed to be insured.
c The description of circumstances affecting the risk.
d The previous history of the proposed assured.

(a) Description of the proposed assured

The description of the proposed assured will include his name, address,[13] and occupation.[14] Where the proposed assured has more than one occupation or profession, it is not a misrepresentation or non-disclosure entitling the insurers to avoid the policy to state one of them only and to omit the rest, provided that the rate of premium for the different occupations is the same.[15] The policy is,

---

[11] *Star Fire and Burglary Insurance Co v Davidson* 1902 5 F (Ct of Sess) 83 (fire insurance), where the policy recited untruly that the assured had agreed to become a member of the company issuing the policy.

[12] *Canning v Farquhar* (1886) 16 QBD 727, CA (life insurance) per Lindley LJ, at 732, 733.

[13] This means the place where he is living or residing at the time of making the proposal, and not the place where he has been residing before, or where he is going to reside afterwards: *Grogan v London and Manchester Industrial Assurance Co* (1885) 53 LT 761 (life insurance) per Smith LJ, at 763. In *Huguenin v Rayley* (1815) 6 Taunt 186 (life insurance) it was held to be for the jury to say whether it was material that the assured's place of residence was the county jail, the name of the town only having been given.

[14] In considering whether the description of occupation is accurate, it must be construed as understood in the assured's district: *Woodall v Pearl Assurance Co* [1919] 1 KB 593, CA (accident insurance).

[15] *Perrins v Marine and General Travellers' Insurance Society* (1859) 2 E & E 317 Ex Ch (accident insurance), distinguishing *Anderson v Fitzgerald* (1853) 4 HL Cas 484 (life insurance). Thus, an ironmonger and esquire may describe himself as an esquire (*Perrins v Marine and General Travellers' Insurance Society* (supra)), a wine merchant and banker as a banker; a wine merchant, banker and Justice of the Peace as a banker and Justice of the Peace (ibid per Hill J, at 323), or a peer carrying on business as a brewer, banker or ironmaster as a peer only. (Ibid per Williams J, at 324).

however, voidable when the rates of premium differ and the omission is, therefore, material,[16] unless the insurers are precluded from denying that they did not know the proposed assured's various occupations.[17]

(b) Description of the risk

This necessarily varies according to the nature of the insurance. Thus, in the case of personal accident insurance, the assured is usually required to state his age, weight and height. In the case of insurance on property, a full description of the property proposed to be insured must be given. Further, in the case of liability insurance, the circumstances out of which the liability may arise must be stated.

(c) Description of circumstances affecting the risk

Questions falling under this head are directed to ascertain whether there are any special circumstances connected with the proposed insurance tending to show that the risk is greater than usual. These also must necessarily vary according to the nature of the insurance.

Thus, in the case of personal accident insurance, the proposed assured is usually asked for details as to his present and past state of health, and as to any existing physical defects. In the case of property insurance, a description of the nature and situation of any building containing the property proposed to be insured and of any measures taken to prevent or minimise loss may be needed. In the case of liability insurance, a description of the state of the proposed assured's premises, the nature of his business, or the machinery and appliances used, or a statement as to the number of persons employed by him, may be required, according to the nature of the proposed insurance.

The proposed assured may further be required by a general question to state whether there are any other circumstances material to the risk. Unless the question permits the proposed assured to use his own judgment,[18] the circumstances to be stated include all circumstances which any reasonable man would think material.[19]

(d) Previous history of the proposed assured

Questions relating to the previous history of the proposed assured so far as it affects the risk[20] fall under two heads:

---

[16] *Biggar v Rock Life Assurance Co* [1902] 1 KB 516 (accident insurance), where a person described as a tea traveller was also a publican; *Equitable Life Assurance Society v General Accident Assurance Corpn* 1904 12 SLT 348, where, in a reinsurance against motor accidents, the assured, who described himself in the original proposal as a motor car driver, was described as a gentleman.

[17] *Holdsworth v Lancashire and Yorkshire Insurance Co* (1907) 23 TLR 521 (employers' liability insurance), where a person described as a builder was also a joiner, and where the rates of premium were not altered until after the insurance was effected; *Ayrey v British Legal and United Provident Assurance Co* [1918] 1 KB 136 (life insurance); cf *Equitable Life Assurance Society v General Accident Assurance Corpn* (supra), where the knowledge of the brokers who acted for both parties was not imputed to the reinsurers.

[18] *Jones v Provincial Insurance Co* (1857) 3 CBNS 65 (life insurance) per Cresswell J, at 86.

[19] *Lindenau v Desborough* (1828) 8 B & C 586 (life insurance) per Lord Tenterden CJ, at 592; cf *Shilling v Accidental Death Insurance Co* (1858) 1 F & F 116 (accident insurance), where the omitted circumstances were held not to be material.

[20] In the case of an insurance by a firm, it is a question of construction whether the questions relate

i the experience of the proposed assured.
ii the relations of the proposed assured with other insurers.

(i) Experience of the proposed assured

The proposed assured is required to state whether he has, in the past,[1] suffered loss by the peril proposed to be insured against, or whether he has ever been exposed to the danger of loss.[2]

(ii) Relations with other insurers

The proposed assured is required to state whether he has ever made a similar proposal to other insurers,[3] whether such proposal was declined,[4] or accepted at a higher premium, whether any previous policy has been cancelled,[5] or its renewal refused,[6] or whether he has ever claimed under a similar policy.[7] He may also be required to state whether he is already insured[8] or intending to be

---

only to the previous history of the firm or whether they extend to the individual partners. Thus, in *Davies v National Fire and Marine Insurance Co of New Zealand* [1891] AC 485, PC (fire insurance) a question as to previous claims was held to be limited to claims made by the firm, and did not cover claims made by a member of the firm before becoming a partner. On the other hand, in *Glicksman v Lancashire and General Assurance Co Ltd* [1925] 2 KB 593, 22 LlL Rep 179, CA (burglary insurance) two members of the Court took the view that the questions covered the previous history of both the firm and the individual partners. The House of Lords, however, [1927] AC 139, declined to express any opinion on the point, but held that there had been a breach of the general duty of disclosure.

1 The proposal form may specify the period to which the questions relate.

2 As to the limitation to be put upon questions of this kind, see *Connecticut Mutual Life Insurance Co of Hertford v Moore* (1881) 6 App Cas 644, at 648, PC (life insurance); *Joel v Law Union and Crown Insurance Co* [1908] 2 KB 863, CA (life insurance) per Fletcher Moulton LJ, at 884; *IOF v Turmelle* (1910) QR 19 KB 261 (life insurance); *Yorke v Yorkshire Insurance Co* [1918] 1 KB 662 (life insurance).

3 *Hambrough v Mutual Life Insurance Co of New York* (1895) 72 LT 140, CA (life insurance); *Scottish Provident Institution v Boddam* (1893) 9 TLR 385 (life insurance).

4 *Holt's Motors Ltd v South East Lancashire Insurance Co Ltd* (1930) 35 Com Cas 281, CA (motor insurance), where the insurers had written refusing to renew although the assured had made no application for renewal; *Taylor v Yorkshire Insurance Co* [1913] 2 IR 1; *Anderson v Fitzgerald* (1853) 4 HL Cas 484 (life insurance); *Fowkes v Manchester and London Life Insurance Co* (1862) 3 F & F 440 (life insurance); *Re General Provincial Life Assurance Co Ltd ex p Daintree* (1870) 18 WR 396 (life insurance); *London Assurance v Mansel* (1879) 11 ChD 363 (life insurance).

5 This does not mean determined by mutual consent: *Smith v Dominion of Canada Accident Insurance Co* (1902) 36 NBR 300.

6 *Biggar v Rock Life Assurance Co* [1902] 1 KB 516 (accident insurance) per Wright J, at 523; *Re Yager and Guardian Assurance Co* (1912) 108 LT 38 (fire insurance). But a refusal to transfer to the proposed assured an existing policy issued to another assured is not a refusal to accept or renew an insurance within the meaning of the question: *Golding v Royal London Auxiliary Insurance Co* (1914) 30 TLR 350 (fire insurance). On the other hand, a refusal to renew except upon restrictive conditions must be disclosed: *Dent v Blackmore* (1927) 29 LlL Rep 9 (motor insurance).

7 *Biggar v Rock Life Assurance Co* (supra) (accident insurance); *Reid & Co v Employers' Accident and Live Stock Insurance Co* (1899) 1 F (Ct of Sess) 1031 (accident insurance); *Condogianis v Guardian Assurance Co* [1921] 2 AC 125, 3 LlL Rep 40, PC (fire insurance).

8 *Biggar v Rock Life Assurance Co* (supra) (accident insurance); *Citizens Insurance Co of Canada v Parsons* (1881) 7 App Cas 96, PC (fire insurance); *Wainwright v Bland* (1836) 1 M & W 32 (life insurance), where the question was asked verbally; *Marcovitch v Liverpool Victoria Friendly Society* (1912) 28 TLR 188 (life insurance).

insured[9] with other insurers,[10] and whether the proposed insurance is intended to be in substitution for other insurances or as an additional protection.

The proposal form concludes with a declaration that the statements made in the answers to questions are true,[11] and that the proposed assured agrees that they are to be the basis of the contract.

2 The questions asked in various types of insurance

As has been pointed out above, the contents of proposal forms vary according to the nature of the subject-matter insured. In the pages which follow a brief survey will be made of the questions found in the proposal forms used in the principal branches of non-marine insurance—life, personal accident, fire, burglary and motor.

(a) Life insurance

The proposer is required to give his name, his present address and occupation and to state whether he is married or single, and also the date and place of birth. An important question relates to previous proposals for life insurance which may have been made to the company concerned or to another insurance company. The proposer has to say whether such a proposal has ever been declined, delayed, withdrawn, or accepted at an extra premium. The insurance company sometimes asks whether he has ever resided abroad, and, if so, when and for how long, and whether his health was in any way affected. He may be asked whether he has any intention of going abroad, and if so, where and for what purpose and for how long. A question of particular importance which he is required to answer is whether he has suffered from any disease or incurred any accident requiring medical attention. Usually this question is limited to a period, e g of five years immediately before the submission of the proposal. The proposer will have to supply the insurance company with the names and addresses of the medical men whom he has consulted. Another question refers to the possibility of the proposer engaging in aviation or other hazardous pursuits. If he intends to travel on any regular air route, he will usually have to state to what part of the world he intends to travel.

The proposer has to state whether there are any circumstances not referred to in the previous questions which bear on the suitability of his life for insurance. The proposer, after he has completed his answers to the questions, then has to sign the declaration whereby he declares that he is at present in good health and not afflicted with any disease or disorder tending to shorten life, and that his answers to the questions are true. He further agrees to answer any questions put to him by a doctor appointed on behalf of the insurance company regarding his health. Further, he has to state that he will not withhold any circumstance tending to render an assurance on his life more than usually hazardous. Finally, he agrees that the answers to the questions and the declaration and the answers given to the doctor, who is acting on behalf of the insurance company, are to be

---

9 *Re Marshall and Scottish Employers' Liability and General Insurance Co Ltd* (1901) 85 LT 757 (accident insurance).

10 It is unnecessary to name the other insurers unless their names are asked for: *National Protector Fire Insurance Co Ltd v Nivert* [1913] AC 507, PC (fire insurance).

11 See pp 161–164, post.

the basis of the contract, and that if any untrue statement has been, or will be made, or any information necessary to be made known to the company has been or will be withheld, all sums which have been paid to the company will be forfeited and the insurance policy will be null and void.

(b) Personal accident insurance

The proposer must state his name in full, his address and business address, his occupation, his age, his height, and his weight. He must state whether he is at present in good health and whether he ordinarily enjoys good health. He must disclose whether he has ever had any physical defect and infirmity, whether his sight or hearing has in any way been impaired, or whether he has suffered from any disease of the eye or ear. A question also asks him whether he has ever had any fit of any kind, or paralysis, or whether he has suffered from certain diseases, e g pneumonia, erysipelas. Another question asks him whether he has had smallpox or ever been vaccinated.

He will have to say whether he has at any time or times in the recent past, e g the last five years, been incapacitated by accident or illness from following his occupation for more than a week at a time. If he has been away from work, he has to give the particulars. He has to state the name and address of his usual medical attendant. The insurance company will want to know whether he is of sober and temperate habits, whether he plays football, engages in mountaineering, aviation or gliding. The proposer will have to say whether there are any circumstances connected with his occupation which render him especially liable to accident or disease. He will have to say whether any previous proposal in respect of accidents has been declined or not proceeded with, and whether he has ever had any insurance cancelled or discontinued or its renewal refused. He must supply the insurance company with full particulars of any claim made under any accident insurance policy.

The proposal form usually ends with a declaration in the form similar to that described above in the case of life insurance, which has to be signed by the proposer.

(c) Fire insurance

In the case of fire insurance the proposer has to state his name and address, and, in the case of a firm, the name and addresses of all the partners, or, in the case of a limited company, the names and addresses of all the directors. The business or profession must be given together with the situation of the property to be insured. The proposer has to describe the property to be insured with the amount in respect of each item. He has to say how the building proposed to be insured is lighted, heated, and protected against fire. He must disclose whether any manufacturing process or any hazardous trade is carried on in the building or near it. If the property or any part of it is already covered by insurance against fire, the details of such insurance must be given. There is always a question whether a previous proposal for fire insurance has ever been made by or on behalf of the proposer or ever been declined or accepted at an increased rate of premium. Sometimes the proposer is asked whether a proposal in respect of any type of insurance policy has ever been declined, and whether any insurance policy which has been effected by him has ever been cancelled or discontinued. He is also required to state whether any property belonging to him has ever been destroyed by fire. The proposer is also asked whether there are any other facts within his knowledge which are material to the insurance proposed. If so, he must give particulars of them.

The proposal form ends with a declaration, which has to be completed by the proposer, and is similar to those mentioned above in other types of insurance.

(d) Burglary insurance

The proposer will have to give his name and address in full, and his occupation. He must give a full description of the premises which are to be insured, together with their rental and a statement as to how long the premises have been occupied by him, whether he is the sole occupier, and whether the premises are left unoccupied at any time. An important question relates to the security of the premises, e g how are the outer doors secured, and whether the windows on the ground floor are protected. In the case of insurance of business premises, the proposer will have to say whether he keeps a stock book and where it is left at night, and whether all valuables are put in a safe when the premises are closed. The insurance company will want to know whether the premises have ever been entered by thieves, and what precautions have been taken to prevent a recurrence. As in the case of other types of insurance, the proposer will have to give details of previous proposals being declined, and the details of any claims which he has made. A declaration which he has to sign says that he declares that all the answers and particulars which he has given are true, and that the amount proposed for insurance represents to the best of his knowledge and belief the full value of the articles to be insured, and he undertakes to exercise all ordinary and reasonable precautions for the safety of the property. He agrees that the declaration shall be the basis of the contract between him and the company.

(e) Motor insurance

The proposer will have to give his name and address and occupation in full. The particulars of the car to be insured, e g the maker's name, the registration letters, the number of seats, the date of manufacture, the date of purchase, the original cost, the estimated present value, the chassis and engine numbers. He must say whether the car is to be used solely for private purposes, and whether he will be the sole driver. His age must be given, and any details of any physical defects from which he suffers. The insurance company will want to know whether he has ever been involved in an accident in the car to be insured, and whether he has ever made any claims in connection with any other car. The proposer will be asked whether he has ever been convicted in respect of any offence in relation to the driving of cars, or had his licence endorsed. Sometimes this question is extended in its scope so that the proposer will have to give the details of any previous convictions of those persons who he expects will drive the vehicle. He is also asked whether any insurance company has declined his proposal or required an increased premium or imposed special conditions, or cancelled or refused to renew his policy. He then has to sign a declaration stating that the answers he has given are true, and that he agrees that the declaration shall be the basis of the contract.

3 The effect of the proposal form

The proposal form, when duly filled in and signed by the proposed assured[12] and forwarded to the insurers, operates as a formal offer by the proposed assured to the insurers to enter into a contract of insurance. The proposal form shows the terms on which he is willing to contract,[13] and if the offer is accepted, he cannot insist on having an insurance differing in its terms from those specified in the proposal.[14]

Since the proposal form, in practice, proceeds from the insurers, it further shows the terms upon which they too are willing to contract. They are bound, therefore, after acceptance, to issue a policy in accordance with the proposal.[15]

4 Statement by BIA and Lloyd's

In 1977 The British Insurance Association[16] and Lloyd's drew up a statement of non-life insurance practice which they recommended to their members.[17] The statement applies only to non-life policyholders domiciled in the United Kingdom and insured in their private capacity only, and so far as proposal forms are concerned, provides:

> 'a The declaration at the foot of the proposal form should be restricted to completion according to the proposer's knowledge and belief.
>
> b If not included in the declaration, prominently displayed on the proposal form should be a statement:
>
> i drawing the attention of the proposer to the consequences of the failure to disclose all material facts, explained as those facts an insurer would regard as likely to influence the acceptance and assessment of the proposal;
>
> ii warning that if the proposer is in any doubt about facts considered material, he should disclose them.
>
> c Those matters which insurers have found generally to be material will be the subject of clear questions in proposal forms.
>
> d So far as is practicable, insurers will avoid asking questions which would require expert

---

[12] As to the place of signature, see *Foster v Mentor Life Assurance Co* (1854) 3 E & B 48 (life insurance) per Coleridge J, at 71: 'I apprehend it cannot be laid down, simply and without qualification, that it is immaterial in what part of a paper you find the signature of the party to be bound by it; it is rather true to say that, if you find it at the foot of the matter written, it is to be taken conclusively to apply to the whole, unless there be something expressly to rebut that presumption; and that, if you find it anywhere else, it *may* apply to the whole, if upon the evidence you find that the party signing so intended. Where the intention to sign is found and the signature is so placed as apparently to apply no more to one part than to another, there can be no reason prima facie to consider it otherwise than as intended to apply to the whole; but when the contents of the paper are divisible, and the signature is placed under or opposite one portion only, the question whether it applies to all or only that one portion is still purely one of intention. Now, wherever that question arises, it must be for the jury.'

[13] *General Accident Insurance Corpn v Cronk* (1901) 17 TLR 233 (accident insurance), where it was held that the assured must be taken to have applied for a policy in the ordinary form issued by the insurers; *Rust v Abbey Life Assurance Co Ltd* [1978] 2 Lloyd's Rep 386 (property bond insurance), where it was held that the proposer's application form was an offer to invest the sum which accompanied it on a policy in the insurers' ordinary printed form as amended. (See the judgment of C M Clothier QC ibid, at 392); cf *Allis-Chalmers Co v Maryland Fidelity and Deposit Co* (1916) 114 LT 433, HL (fidelity insurance) per Lord Loreburn, at 434.

[14] *General Accident Insurance Corpn v Cronk* (supra) (accident insurance). Nor is he relieved, if the wrong form of policy is tendered, from the obligation to accept the correct one: ibid.

[15] *General Accident Insurance Corpn v Cronk* (supra) (accident insurance) per Wills J, at 233.

[16] Now the Association of British Insurers.

[17] See 931 House of Commons, Official Report, May 4, 1977, Written Answers, cols 218–220.

knowledge beyond that which the proposer could reasonably be expected to possess or obtain or which would require a value judgment on the part of the proposer.

e Unless the prospectus or the proposal form contains full details of the standard cover offered and whether or not it contains an outline of that cover, the proposal form shall include a statement that a copy of the policy form is available on request.

f Unless the completed form or a copy of it has been sent to a policyholder a copy will be made available when an insurer raises an issue under the proposal form.'

5 Statement by Life Offices' Association

A similar statement has been issued by the Life Offices' Association in relation to long-term insurance practice. It applies to such insurance effected by individuals resident in the United Kingdom in a private capacity. In so far as proposal forms are concerned it says:

'a If the proposal form calls for the disclosure of material facts a statement should be included in the declaration, or prominently displayed elsewhere on the form or in the document of which it forms part:

i drawing attention to the consequences of failure to disclose all material facts and explaining that these are facts that an insurer would regard as likely to influence the assessment and acceptance of a proposal;

ii warning that if the signatory is in any doubt about whether certain facts are material, these facts should be disclosed.

b Those matters which insurers have commonly found to be material should be the subject of clear questions in proposal forms.

c Insurers should avoid asking questions which would require knowledge beyond that which the signatory could reasonably be expected to possess.

d The proposal form or a supporting document should include a statement that a copy of the policy form or of the policy conditions is available on request.

e A copy of the proposal should be made available to the policyholder when an insurer raises an issue under that proposal—information not relevant to that issue being deleted where necessary to preserve confidentiality.'

CHAPTER 9

The cover note

1 The purpose of the cover note

A proposal is not necessarily accepted at once, since the insurance company may take time to consider it. If the proposal is submitted through an agent, the agent usually has no authority to accept it himself,[1] but must forward it to the insurers in order that they may decide whether to accept it or not. There is, therefore, as a rule an interval of time between the making of the proposal and the final decision, so it is the practice of insurance companies in the case of some types of insurance especially motor, burglary and fire insurance to give the proposer protection by the issue of a 'cover note'. Cover notes are not issued in life insurance.

The purpose of a cover note in motor insurance is well explained by Pearson J, in *Julien Praet et Cie, S/A v H G Poland Ltd*,[2] where he pointed out that a number of developments or adaptations of the traditional Lloyd's practice or pattern of business had taken place in response to the requirements of foreign insurance business, motor insurance business, and especially foreign motor insurance business. He said that traditionally the underwriter of a syndicate sat in his box in the underwriting room at Lloyd's, and a Lloyd's broker, who had prepared the proposed policy, presented a 'slip' giving details of the proposed risk to the underwriter, and the underwriter, if he found the risk acceptable, insured it by initialling the slip. A policy was then prepared and issued. The Lloyd's broker was the agent of the assured. The underwriter dealt only with the Lloyd's broker and not with any outside broker, nor with the assured. This procedure, if it had to be maintained in its full rigour without relaxation or modification, would impede foreign insurance business, and would make motor insurance business impossible. He went on to say:[3]

> 'The typical motorist is an impatient person in the sense that, having bought a car, he wishes to take delivery and drive off in it at once, and he would not be willing to wait for the traditional steps to be taken at Lloyd's before he could obtain cover. Therefore, even in the United Kingdom, there has to be the familiar system of the cover note, which is issued at once on receipt of a proposal, and covers the assured and puts the underwriters on risk for the period while the proposal is being considered and until a policy is either granted or refused.'

He then said that great care was taken, however, to comply with the requirements of Lloyd's. The authority to issue cover notes was applied for and granted through a Lloyd's broker, and the proposals were sent to him and

[1] If the agent has authority to accept the proposal without referring it to the insurance company, his acceptance completes the contract and his issue of a receipt for the premium will cover the proposer until the formal policy is prepared: cf *Hancock v Macnamara* (1868) IR 2 Eq 486 (life assurance). As to the authority of agents, see further, pp 524–532, post.

[2] [1960] 1 Lloyd's Rep 420.

[3] Ibid, at 428.

presented by him to the underwriter, and he received the policy from the underwriter and sent it to the assured as his agent. The underwriter looked to the Lloyd's broker for the premium, and had his account with a Lloyd's broker. The main insurance was duly granted at Lloyd's and the preliminary cover note, which was inevitably granted outside Lloyd's by a person acting as agent for the underwriter, was regarded as merely an incidental or ancillary matter.

He continued:[4]

> 'In the case of foreign motor insurance business, the practice is similar in principle, but the 'coverholder', as he is called, has to have a more extensive range of duties and therefore a wider authority from the underwriters to act on their behalf. The coverholder is the person authorised to grant temporary cover so as to bind the underwriters, and the agreement by which he is so authorised is sometimes called a 'binder'. The coverholder has to do the 'servicing' of the policies, and that includes collecting premiums, adjusting premiums, issuing indorsements, receiving claims, settling the smaller claims and referring larger claims to assessors.'

2 The form of the cover note and its issue

The cover note is, in practice, printed in common form; it is usually signed on behalf of the insurance company by the agent through whom the proposal was submitted, and issued by him to the proposer.

If the agent is entrusted with a number of cover notes in blank, to be filled up and issued by him when required, he has authority to give cover and the issue of a cover note binds the company.[5] In this case the company may be bound, even though the cover note is not in the precise form required by the agent's instructions,[6] provided that the variance is technical only,[7] and does not relate to matters of substance.[8]

In many cases the agent is not entrusted with cover notes in blank; but on each occasion when a proposal form is received from him, the company sends him a cover note with instructions to sign it and issue it to the proposer. The agent's authority is then limited to the particular cover note; he has then no general authority to grant cover.[9]

No formal document is, however, necessary to bind the company. Cover may be given informally, as, for instance, by letter from the head office. Even verbal cover is sufficient, and the verbal cover may be given by the agent submitting the proposal, if his authority extends thus far.[10]

---

4 [1960] 1 Lloyd's Rep 420 at 428.

5 *Mackie v European Assurance Society* (1869) 21 LT 102; *Home Insurance Co and St Paul Fire and Marine Insurance Co v Administratia Asigurarilor de Stat* [1983] 2 Lloyd's Rep 674 (reinsurance).

6 See *Marshall v Western Canada Fire Insurance Co* (1911) 18 WLR 68, where the assured had no knowledge of the variation. Cf *Towle v National Guardian Assurance Society* (1861) 30 LJ Ch 900 at 916 (per Turner LJ), where it was held that the assured, in taking a receipt from the agent varying from the printed form of receipt for guarantee insurance, of the existence of which he was aware, trusted the agent and not the insurance company.

7 *Rossiter v Trafalgar Life Assurance Association* (1859) 27 Beav 377 (life assurance), where the agent's signature was printed instead of being written.

8 *Levy v Scottish Employers' Insurance Co* (1901) 17 TLR 229 (accident insurance); *Richards v Port of Manchester Insurance Co Ltd* (1934) 152 LT 261 (affd 152 LT 413, 50 LlL Rep 132, CA) (accident insurance), where the point was not raised.

9 Cf *Linford v Provincial Horse and Cattle Insurance Co* (1864) 34 Beav 291 (livestock insurance).

10 *Stockton v Mason and the Vehicle and General Insurance Co Ltd and Arthur Edward (Insurance) Ltd* [1978] 2 Lloyd's Rep 430, CA (motor insurance) per Lord Diplock, at 432: 'There must be every day thousands of cases, not only in motor insurance but in other forms of non-marine insurance,

There may be a further interval of time between the acceptance of the proposal and the issue of the policy. By the terms of the acceptance, the proposer may be given cover in express words pending the issue of the policy.[11] This does not affect the legal position, since, on intimating the acceptance to the proposer, the insurance company becomes finally bound.

3 The duration of the cover note

The question of the duration of the cover note is of little importance where the proposal is accepted, since the cover note comes to an end when the policy is issued.[12] It is only where the proposal is not accepted that the question becomes important.

Where the cover note provides that it is to remain in force until the insurers intimate that they have rejected the proposal, no difficulty arises as to the period during which it is current, since it remains in force until the rejection is brought to the knowledge of the proposer.[13]

Where, however, as is usually the case, the cover note is expressly stated to be in force for a fixed period, it does not follow, as a matter of course, that it remains in force during the whole of that period, since the insurers may reserve the right to determine it at an earlier date by intimating their rejection of the proposal.[14]

---

where persons wishing to become insured or wishing to transfer an insurance ring up their brokers and ask for cover or ask for fresh cover or ask to transfer the cover from an existing vehicle to another. In every case they rely upon the brokers' statement that they are covered as constituting a contract binding upon the insurance company . . . A contract of this kind can be made orally, it can be made in informal, colloquial language . . .'; *Murfitt v Royal Insurance Co Ltd* (1922) 38 TLR 334, 10 LlL Rep 191; *Parker & Co (Sandbank) Ltd v Western Asurance Co* [1925] WC & Ins Rep 82; *Hochbaum v Pioneer Insurance Co* [1933] 1 WWR 403; cf *James v Ocean Accident and Guarantee Co* [1921] 1 WWR 551, where the authority was limited as to value.

11 *South Staffordshire Tramways Co v Sickneess and Accident Assurance Association* [1891] 1 QB 402, CA; *Sickness and Accident Assurance Association v General Accident Assurance Corpn* 1892 19 R (Ct of Sess) 977.

12 *Roberts v Security Co* [1897] 1 QB 111, CA (burglary insurance) per Lopes LJ, at 115; cf *Davies v National Fire and Marine Insurance Co of New Zealand* [1891] AC 485, at 486, PC (fire insurance). Until acceptance, the proposer may withdraw, notwithstanding the issue of the cover note: *Mackie v European Assurance Society* (1869) 21 LT 102 (fire insurance) per Malins V-C, at 104.

13 *Rossiter v Trafalgar Life Assurance Association* (1859) 27 Beav 377 (life insurance); *Mackie v European Assurance Society* (supra) (fire insurance); *Queen Insurance Co v Parsons* (1881) 7 App Cas 96, PC (fire insurance); *Goodwin v Lancashire Fire and Life Insurance Co* (1873) 18 LCJ 1; *Bruce v Gore District Mutual Insurance Co* (1869) 20 CP 207. Cf *Connecticut Fire Insurance Co v Kavanagh* [1892] AC 473, PC (fire insurance), where the agent disobeyed instructions to reject the proposal, but transferred the insurance to the books of another company of which he was also an agent.

14 *Stockton v Mason, Vehicle and General Insurance Co Ltd and Arthur Edward (Insurance) Ltd* [1978] 2 Lloyd's Rep 430, CA (motor insurance) per Lord Diplock, at 431: 'The essential nature of the contract of interim insurance is that it is for a temporary period, generally a maximum of 30 days or so, but is terminable by notice by the insurer at any time during that period.'; *Mackie v European Assurance Society* (1869) 21 LT 102, per Malins V-C, at 104: 'It was competent for the office by return of post to decline the proposal without giving a reason, but until such notice was received, the insurance would continue, and if a fire happened in the interval, this office would have been answerable.' In this case the cover note provided that 'the property shall be held insured for one month from this date, unless the proposal be previously declined'; *Levy v Scottish Employers' Insurance Co* (1901) 17 TLR 229 (accident insurance), where the cover note stated 'Held covered for 14 days from date hereof, subject to the conditions of the policy, unless the proposal be previously declined'; *Goodfellow v Times and Beacon Assurance Co* (1859) 17 UCR 411,

Nor does it necessarily cease to be in force when the specified period has expired, since the effect of its issue may have been to impose on the insurers certain duties towards the proposer, which they must discharge before they are exonerated from further liability. It is therefore necessary to consider the terms in which the particular cover note is framed.

Where the cover note imposes upon the insurers the obligation of intimating their rejection of the proposal, it remains in force until they have done so.[15] It is not sufficient that they have decided to reject the proposal, nor, in the absence of an express condition to that effect, that they have posted a letter intimating their rejection.[16] They must bring home to the proposer the knowledge of the rejection, and unless they can do this, they remain liable for any loss sustained by him.[17] It is immaterial that the proposal never came to their knowledge, owing to the failure of their agent to transmit it to them,[18] or that their agent failed to transmit the rejection to the proposer.[19]

Where the cover note provides not only that the insurers are to intimate their rejection of the proposal, but also that any deposit paid by the proposer is to be returned to him, subject to a deduction in respect of the days during which the cover note has been operative, the insurers remain liable until they have fully discharged their obligation.[20] Even where they have intimated their rejection of his proposal, they remain bound to the proposer, unless and until they have repaid him the balance of his deposit, in accordance with the terms of the cover note.[1]

Where the cover note expressly provides that the insurers are to intimate their acceptance of the proposal, or that the proposed insurance is not to bind them until a policy is issued, the cover note will cease to have any force at the expiration of the specified period, unless such acceptance has been intimated, or unless the policy has been issued, as the case may be.[2]

---

where the cover note provided that the proposer should be considered insured for 21 days from its date, 'within which time the determination of the Board will be notified', and it was held that this was not an absolute insurance for 21 days, but that the insurers might, within that time, reject the risk and give notice, after which their liability would cease; *Roberts v Security Co Ltd* [1897] 1 QB 111, CA (burglary insurance), where the cover note stated that it was to be 'in force for 7 days from the date hereof, or until the proposal in the meantime be rejected.'

15 *Hawke v Niagara District Mutual Fire Insurance Co* (1876) 23 Gr 139.

16 *Tough v Provincial Insurance Co of Canada* (1875) 20 LCJ 168, where the fire took place after the posting of the letter, but before its receipt, and it was held that the notice of rejection was insufficient.

17 *Rossiter v Trafalgar Life Assurance Association* (1859) 27 Beav 377 (life insurance); *Mackie v European Assurance Society* (1869) 21 LT 102 (fire insurance).

18 *Patterson v Royal Insurance Co* (1867) 14 Gr 169, followed in *Hawke v Niagara District Mutual Fire Insurance Co* (supra).

19 *Connecticut Fire Insurance Co v Kavanagh* [1892] AC 473, PC (fire insurance).

20 *Mackie v European Assurance Society* (supra) (fire insurance).

1 *Grant v Reliance Mutual Insurance Co* (1879) 44 UCR 229 where, by the terms of the cover note, the insurers had to give 10 days' notice of their intention to terminate the insurance before the expiration of the cover note, and also to repay the premium, and it was held that the insurance was not terminated unless they gave both 10 days' notice and repaid the premium.

2 *Levy v Scottish Employers' Insurance Co* (1901) 17 TLR 229 (accident insurance); cf *General Accident, Fire and Life Assurance Corpn v Robertson* [1909] AC 404 (accident insurance), where the acceptance had to be intimated by the assured, and Lord Loreburn LC at 411, refused to decide whether the acceptance was complete when the letter containing it was posted, or when the letter was delivered at the office of the insurers, or when it was actually opened by a person in their employment; *Penley v Beacon Assurance Co* (1859) 7 Gr 130, where the Court held that the proposal had in fact been accepted, though no policy had been issued.

Usually a cover note expressly states the period for which it is to be in force, eg 'the insurance is provisionally held in force for 14 days from noon, January 1, 1986'. But where the period is not expressly so defined, difficulties may arise.

Thus, in *Cartwright v MacCormack (Trafalgar Insurance Co Ltd, Third Party)*:[3]

> The insurance company had issued a temporary cover note granting the insured comprehensive motor insurance. He was involved in a road accident at 5.45 pm on December 17, 1959, and the question was whether the company was bound to indemnify him in respect of the damages which he had had to pay to a motor-cyclist who had been injured. The cover note contained a column entitled 'Effective Time and Date of Commencement of Risk'. Under the column 'Time' was written '11.45 am', and under the column 'Date' was written '2.12.59'. Another part of the note contained the words 'This cover note is only valid for 15 days from the commencement of risk'. Also included in the note was a statement that 'Under no circumstances is the time and commencement of risk to be prior to the actual time of issue of this cover note.' The insurance company contended that it was not liable because the period for which the note had been issued had expired, i e that the period started at 11.45 am on December 2, and expired at 11.45 am on December 17, six hours before the accident happened.
>
> *Held,* by the Court of Appeal, that the time did not begin to run until midnight of December 2, and that consequently, the insured was entitled to be indemnified.

Harman LJ, said that the time of 11.45 am was inserted to protect the company until that hour of the day, showing that it was not at risk until that time. The duration of the company's liability was expressed as 15 days from the commencement date. It was not 15 days from the commencement of the risk. The risk ran from 11.45 am, but the date of commencement was December 2. The note therefore expired 15 days from December 2, and those words excluded the first date and began at midnight.[4]

4 The effect of the cover note

The cover note is in itself a contract of insurance,[5] governing the rights and liabilities of the parties in the event of a loss taking place during its currency.[6] The assured is, therefore, entitled to enforce the contract contained in the cover note, provided that he has complied with its conditions, e g as to payment of the premium.[7]

5 The incorporation of the terms of the policy

The cover note itself may contain no terms at all, but usually it incorporates the conditions of the company's policy, e g as in *Queen Insurance Co v Parsons,*[8] where

---

3 [1963] 1 All ER 11, CA (motor insurance).

4 On this point, see generally *Lester v Garland* (1808), 15 Ves 248; *Mercer v Ogilvie* (1796), cited in 15 Ves 254; *Young v Higgon* (1840) 6 M & W 49; *Stewart v Chapman* [1951] 2 KB 792, [1951] 2 All ER 613.

5 *Mackie v European Assurance Society* (1869) 21 LT 102 at 104 (per Malins V-C).

6 *Re Coleman's Depositories Ltd and Life and Health Assurance Association* [1907] 2 KB 798, CA.

7 The issue of a policy may amount to a waiver of such a condition: *Roberts v Security Co Ltd* [1897] 1 QB 111 at 116 (per Rigby LJ).

8 (1881) 7 App Cas 96, PC. See also *Nicholson v Southern Star Fire Insurance Co Ltd* (1927) 28 SRNSW 124. Where during the currency of the risk the amount of insurance is increased and a cover note is issued for the increased amount pending the preparation of a new policy, the conditions of the original policy apply: *Burton and Watts v Batavia Sea and Fire Insurance Co* [1922] SASR 466.

the cover note stated that the proposer 'had proposed to effect an insurance against fire, subject to all the usual terms and conditions of this company'.[9]

Sometimes the cover note incorporates the terms of the policy not by referring to them directly but by referring to the proposal form which itself alludes to them.[10]

The insurance company may also rely on the terms and conditions of the policy if it can be shown that the assured knew of them, or to have had the opportunity of knowing them, and to have agreed to be bound by them.[11]

On the other hand, as against the insurers, the cover note is to be construed with reference to the common form of policy issued by them, and they cannot rely upon a construction of the cover note inconsistent therewith.[12]

6 Replacement of the cover note by a policy

Normally the cover note will be replaced in due course by a policy, but the insurance company is not bound to issue one, unless there is an agreement to that effect.

The assured, too, is not bound to accept the policy. 'During that month it was open to the [company] on further inquiry to refuse to grant the policy and to terminate the contract at the end of the month. It was equally open to the assured to say that he did not like the [company], not thinking the capital sufficient, or for other reasons.'[13]

7 Broker's cover note

Where the insurance is effected through a broker, the broker, pending the preparation of the policy, issues a broker's cover note, certifying that the insurance has been effected and setting out its terms.

By issuing the cover note, the broker does not incur liability on the insurance, since he does not purport to be an insurer. But he is to be presumed to warrant to the proposer that his instructions have been properly carried out, and that the insurance has been effected. If, therefore, there is no insurance in fact, he will be liable for breach of the warranty. Such a cover note is not binding on the insurers.[14]

---

[9] See also, *General Accident, Fire and Life Assurance Corpn Ltd v Shuttleworth* (1938) 60 LlL Rep 301, where a motor car cover note stated that the risk was covered 'in terms of the [company's] usual form of policy applicable thereto.'

[10] *Wyndham, Rather Ltd v Eagle Star and British Dominions Insurance Co Ltd* (1925) 21 LlL Rep 214, CA: *Neil v South-Eastern Lancashire Insurance Co* 1932 SC 35; *Houghton v Trafalgar Insurance Co Ltd* [1953] 2 Lloyd's Rep 18 (motor insurance), where Gorman J held that the cover note was a provisional cover which had its origin in the proposal form, and that the marginal words in the proposal form stating 'All policies exclude legal liability to passengers' were part of the proposal form, and therefore the assured in completing the form had agreed to accept a policy containing a clause excluding liability in respect of passengers. This case was affirmed on another point: [1954] 1 QB 247, [1953] 2 All ER 1409, [1953] 2 Lloyd's Rep 503, CA.

[11] *Re Coleman's Depositories Ltd and Life and Health Assurance Association* [1907] 2 KB 798 at 805, CA (per Vaughan Williams LJ); *Irving v Sun Insurance Office* [1906] ORC 24. In *Golding v Royal London Auxiliary Insurance Co Ltd* (1914) 30 TLR 350, where the fire took place during the currency of the cover note, the claim was referred under the arbitration clause in the company's ordinary form of policy, no question having been raised as to whether it applied or not.

[12] *Browning v Provincial Insurance Co of Canada* (1873) LR 5 PC 263 at 273 (marine insurance).

[13] *Mackie v European Assurance Society* (1869) 21 LT 102 at 104 (per Malins V-C).

[14] *Broit v S Cohen & Son (NSW) Ltd* (1926) 27 SRNSW 29.

CHAPTER 10

The acceptance

It is necessary to consider what constitutes an acceptance, the methods of acceptance, the effect of acceptance, and the prohibition of discrimination on the grounds of sex or race.

A WHAT CONSTITUTES AN ACCEPTANCE

There cannot be an acceptance so long as the terms of the contract of insurance are still under discussion[1] and the premium remains to be fixed,[2] since there is no contract until complete agreement has been reached,[3] and nothing remains to be done by either party except to perform what has been agreed.

The offer, therefore, must be complete on the face of it, and the acceptance must be in the very terms of the offer. If the acceptance departs from the offer by introducing a fresh term,[4] or if it comes from insurers other than those to whom the offer was made,[5] there is no contract between the parties, even though a policy may have been issued.

Such an acceptance is equivalent to a counter-offer, which must in its turn be accepted before the parties are bound. In the absence of acceptance, the assured cannot be sued under the policy for the premium,[6] nor can he enforce the policy

1 *Sickness and Accident Assurance Association v General Accident Assurance Corpn* 1892 19 R (Ct of Sess) 977, where, notwithstanding the issue of a policy, the negotiations continued; *Re Yager and Guardian Assurance Co* (1912) 108 LT 38 (fire insurance); *Canning v Farquhar* (1886) 16 QBD 727. CA (life insurance).

2 *Allis-Chalmers Co v Maryland Fidelity and Deposit Co* (1916) 114 LT 433, HL (fidelity insurance); *Christie v North British Insurance Co* 1825 3 Shaw (Ct of Sess) 519 (fire insurance); *Canning v Farquhar* (supra) (life insurance). But the premium may be subject to adjustment, see p 183, post.

3 *Murfitt v Royal Insurance Co Ltd* (1922) 38 TLR 334, 10 LlL Rep 191 (fire insurance) per McCardie J, at 336.

4 *Star Fire and Burglary Insurance Co v Davidson* 1902 5 F (Ct of Sess) 83 (fire insurance), where the policy recited untruly that the assured had agreed to become a member of the company issuing the policy; *Canning v Farquhar* (supra) (life insurance), where the insurance was conditional on pre-payment of the premium; *Canning v Hoare* (1885) 1 TLR 526 (life insurance).

5 In *Mackie v European Assurance Society* (1869) 21 LT 102 (fire insurance) the proposed assured, on discovering that the cover note was issued by different insurers, reserved the right to be satisfied as to their standing, and, when the fire happened, took steps to enforce the cover note. This cover note was, in effect, an offer by such insurers; it purported on the face of it to be in force for a month, and the insurers had not withdrawn it. The conduct of the assured in taking steps to enforce the cover note may be regarded as an acceptance of the offer. If, however, there had been no fire, and the proposed assured had done nothing to indicate acceptance, it seems clear that the insurers could not have maintained an action for the premium; see *Boulton v Jones* (1857) 2 H & N 564 (sale of goods).

6 *Star Fire and Burglary Insurance Co v Davidson* (supra) (fire insurance).

against the insurers.[7] Thus, if the policy introduces a condition requiring pre-payment of the premium, there may be no contract until he accepts the offer contained in the policy and pays the premium.[8]

On the other hand, the insurers may have finally accepted the offer of the assured before the policy is issued, in which case a departure in the policy from the terms of the offer does not affect the contract which has already come into existence.[9]

B THE METHODS OF ACCEPTANCE

The methods of accepting the offer will depend on whether the offer is made by the proposer as it normally will be, or whether it is made by the insurers as in the case of coupon insurance.[10]

A Where the offer is made by the proposer

The acceptance of a proposal may be signified by the insurers in one or other of the following ways:

1 By a formal acceptance.
2 By the issue of a policy.
3 By acceptance of the premium.
4 By the conduct of the insurers.

1 By formal acceptance[11]

If, however, the acceptance is subject to a condition, there is no contract until the condition is fulfilled.[12]

2 By the issue of a policy

The issue of the policy is a conclusive intimation that the insurers have accepted the proposal.[13] They are, therefore, bound by their acceptance, and from it they cannot recede.[14] In the case of a policy under seal, the acceptance is completed

---

[7] *Linford v Provincial Horse and Cattle Insurance Co* (1864) 34 Beav 291 (livestock insurance) per Lord Romilly MR, at 293; *Canning v Farquhar* (supra) (life insurance), followed in *Sickness and Accident Assurance Association v General Accident Assurance Corpn* 1892 19 R (Ct of Sess) 977 (accident insurance), and in *Re Yager and Guardian Assurance Co* (supra) (fire insurance).

[8] *Canning v Farquhar* (supra) (life insurance).

[9] *General Accident Insurance Corpn v Cronk* (1901) 17 TLR 233, *Re Bradley and Essex and Suffolk Accident Indemnity Society* [1912] 1 KB 415, CA, per Farwell LJ, at 430; *Xenos v Wickham* (1867) LR 2 HL 296 (marine insurance) per Lord Cranworth at 324.

[10] For coupon insurance, see p 113, post. See further, Ivamy *Personal Accident, Life and Other Insurances* (2nd Edn 1980), pp 65–70.

[11] *Adie & Sons v Insurance Corpn Ltd* (1898) 14 TLR 544 (fire insurance), where the fire took place before a policy was issued.

[12] *Canning v Hoare* (1885) 1 TLR 526 (life insurance), where a letter formally accepting the proposal contained a notice that no insurance was to be effective until the premium had been paid.

[13] Where an insurance company is by its constitution bound to issue its policies under seal, a policy issued without a seal may be effective as a valid contract to issue a policy under seal: *Wright v Sun Mutual Life Insurance Co* (1878) 5 AR 218 (life insurance).

[14] *McElroy v London Assurance Corpn* 1897 24 R (Ct of Sess) 287 per Lord Maclaren at 290: *Pearl Life Assurance Co v Johnson* [1909] 2 KB 288 (life insurance), where the insurers were estopped by the issue of a policy and the receipt of premiums from alleging that there was no contract on the ground that no proposal had ever been signed.

by the execution of the policy.[15] It is, therefore, immaterial that the policy is retained by the insurers in their possession, and never handed over to the proposer, inasmuch as no formal acceptance is required from him, nor need he take away the policy in order to complete the delivery.[16]

The policy, as an enforceable contract of insurance, is complete as from the date of its issue, even though no premium has been paid at the time of the loss in respect of which the proposer seeks to enforce it. By the terms of the policy, however, he may be, in some cases, precluded from enforcing it in respect of any loss happening before he has complied with its conditions.[17]

At the same time the insurers cannot refuse to allow him to comply with such conditions, and thereby discharge themselves from liability under the policy. The issue of the policy binds them to carry out their part, even though by their conduct they may have released him from the necessity of performing the conditions in question.[18]

The issue of a policy is not, however, an acceptance in the following cases:

i Where the assured does not treat the policy as an acceptance, but continues the negotiations for the purpose of obtaining an alteration in its terms;[19]

ii Where the policy, as issued, departs from the proposal by introducing a fresh term, and thus constitutes not an acceptance but a counter-offer.[20] The introduction of the fresh term shows that the agreement is not yet complete, since something remains to be done by the proposer to declare his adoption of it.[1]

3 By acceptance of the premium

Where no policy has been issued to the proposer before the loss, the receipt[2] of

---

15 *Roberts v Security Co* [1897] 1 QB 111 (burglary insurance) per Lopes LJ, at 115: 'The question we have to consider is whether there was a concluded agreement for insurance, or the matter had not gone beyond the stage of negotiation. In my opinion the policy, being duly executed as it was by the sealing and signature by the directors and secretary of the company, constituted a concluded agreement . . . in my opinion if the day after its being so executed, the plaintiff had tendered the premium and demanded the policy, there would have been no answer to the demand.' See also the judgment of Rigby LJ, ibid, at 116–7: *Xenos v Wickham* (1867) LR 2 HL 296 (marine insurance), where a subsequent cancellation with the consent of the assured's broker was held inoperative; *McFarlane v Andes Insurance Co* (1873) 20 Gr 486. Cf *Allis-Chalmers Co v Maryland Fidelity and Deposit Co* (1916) 114 LT 433, HL, where there was no evidence that the assured had ever agreed to or knew the terms of the policy.

16 *Xenos v Wickham* (supra). Unless, perhaps, the execution is conditional: *Roberts v Security Co Ltd* (supra).

17 E g by paying the premium.

18 See pp 292–299, post.

19 *Sickness and Accident Assurance Association v General Accident Asurance Corpn* 1892 19 R (Ct of Sess) 977.

20 *Allis-Chalmers Co v Maryland Fidelity and Deposit Co* (supra) per Lord Loreburn LC, at 434; *Sickness and Accident Assurance Association v General Accident Assurance Corpn* (supra), following *Canning v Farquhar* (1886) 16 QBD 727, CA (life insurance). As to the effect of a stipulation that the policy is not to be in force until the premium is paid, see p 229, post.

1 This must be distinguished from the case in which the agreement is complete, but the policy which is issued does not correctly embody the terms of the agreement: *Xenos v Wickham* (supra) per Lord Cranworth at 324.

2 In some cases the insurers may be estopped from denying the receipt, e g where a receipt was given to the employee insured for the purpose of being shown to his employer: *Re Economic Fire Office Ltd* (1896) 12 TLR 142.

the premium and its retention[3] by the insurers, though by no means conclusive, may raise the presumption, in the absence of any circumstances leading to a contrary conclusion,[4] that the insurers have definitely accepted his proposal.[5]

In such a case they are not entitled to refuse to issue a policy to him,[6] and they are, therefore, liable to him in the event of a loss.

4 By the conduct of the insurers

Even where the premium has not been paid,[7] nor the policy issued,[8] the facts may clearly show that the insurers have accepted the proposal, and that there is a binding contract between the parties, on the part of the proposer to pay the premium, and on the part of the insurers to issue a policy.[9] Where this is the case, the insurers cannot refuse to accept the premium when tendered,[10] or otherwise repudiate their contract,[11] and will be liable for a loss happening even before a policy is issued or the premium is paid.[12]

---

3 It is otherwise where the insurers repudiate the contract on a valid ground and tender the amount of the premium, but the assured refuses it: *Hancock v Macnamara* (1868) IR 2 Eq 486 (life insurance).

4 *Harrington v Pearl Life Assurance Co Ltd* (1913) 30 TLR 24 (life insurance), where it was held, notwithstanding the payment of the premium, that the matter had not passed beyond negotiations which might have ripened into a contract if the circumstances had been favourable: affd (1914) 30 TLR 613. Cf *Linford v Provincial Horse and Cattle Insurance Co* (1864) 34 Beav 291, where the agent misappropriated the premium and never forwarded the proposal to the insurers.

5 *McElroy v London Assurance Corpn* (supra) per Lord MacLaren at 291: 'The company are not bound to deliver a policy without payment of the premium. If they accept a premium before delivering a policy, I should be disposed to hold that the acceptance of the premium and the delivery of the receipt therefor was sufficient to create the obligation to issue a policy.'; *Canning v Farquhar* (supra) (life insurance) per Lord Esher MR, at 731: 'If the premium is offered and accepted, there is at once an insurance.' See also, *Mead v Davison* (1835) 3 Ad & El 303 (marine insurance) per Denman CJ, at 308; *Re Norwich Equitable Fire Assurance Society, Royal Insurance Co's Claim* (1887) 57 LT 241 (fire insurance) per Kay LJ, at 243. *Queen Insurance Co v Parsons* (1881) 7 App Cas 96 at 125, PC (fire insurance) where, however, a cover note had been issued. Cf *Solvency Mutual Guarantee Co v Froane* (1861) 7 H & N 5 per Bramwell B, at 15.

6 Hence, specific performance of the contract to issue a policy will be decreed: *Bhugwandass v Netherlands India Sea and Fire Insurance Co of Batavia* (1888) 14 App Cas 83, PC (marine insurance); *Queen Insurance Co of America v British Traders Insurance Co* [1927] 1 WWR 508.

7 *Christie v North British Insurance Co* 1825 3 Sh (Ct of Sess) 519 (fire insurance) per Lord Boyle at 522: 'If the premium in this case had been agreed on, the insurance would have been effected, although no policy was delivered.'

8 *Bhugwandass v Netherlands India Sea and Fire Insurance Co of Batavia* (supra) (marine insurance): *Royal Exchange Assurance Corpn v Tod* (1892) 8 TLR 669 (marine insurance).

9 *Adie and Sons v Insurance Corpn Ltd* (1898) 14 TLR 544; *Re Yager and Guardian Assurance Co* (1912) 108 LT 38 per Channell J at 44; *Rust v Abbey Life Assurance Co Ltd* [1978] 2 Lloyd's Rep 386 (property bond insurance), where the insurers allocating units in their property bond fund to the proposer at the unit offer price prevailing on the date on which they received his cheque was held to constitute an acceptance of the offer, and the sending of the policy was no more than a record of an antecedent agreement on the terms contained in it. (See the judgment of C M Clothier QC, ibid, at 392). The decision was subsequently affd [1979] 2 Lloyd's Rep 334, CA.

10 *Thompson v Adams* (1889) 23 QBD 361; *Canning v Farquhar* (supra).

11 *Cornelissen v Equitable Fire Insurance Co* (1861) 4 Searle's R (Cape) 35, where a subsequent cancellation of the policy by the insurers without the knowledge of the assured was held to have no effect.

12 *Adie & Sons v Insurance Corpn Ltd* (supra), where both parties for some time after the loss acted on the mistaken assumption that there was no contract.

What facts constitute an acceptance on the part of the insurers will depend on the circumstances of the particular case. A mere demand for the premium is sufficient.[13] But mere delay in dealing with an application for insurance does not constitute an acceptance, unless it is the duty of the insurers to intimate their rejection promptly.[14]

B Where the offer is made by the insurers

In the case of coupon insurance the offer proceeds from the insurers, and the terms of the offer must be considered to ascertain what constitutes a sufficient acceptance. When the offer has been accepted, there is a contract binding on the insurers, the contract being, according to the form of the coupon, either a contract of insurance or a contract to issue a policy of insurance.

The offer contained in the coupon is accepted when the requirements of the coupon have been complied with. The acceptance usually takes one of two forms:

1. Signing the coupon or purchasing the coupon or the article to which it is attached
2. Notifying the insurers that their offer has been accepted.

1 Mere signature of coupon or purchase of an article

The holder of the coupon may not be required to do any act to bring the fact of his acceptance to the knowledge of the insurers. All that he has to do is to purchase[15] the article to which the coupon is attached, and carry it on his person, or sign and fill in the coupon with the details asked for, or do any other act which the terms of the coupon may prescribe. In this case the acceptance is complete when the holder has done whatever acts may be prescribed.[16]

2 Notification to the insurers

The holder may be required to register himself with the insurers as the holder of the coupon, or to exchange the coupon for a policy, at the same time paying a prescribed registration fee. In this case, the acceptance is, perhaps, complete when the holder has posted a letter addressed to the insurers applying for registration or for a policy in accordance with the terms of the coupon;[17] but it is, at any rate, complete when the letter is actually received by the insurers.[18]

---

[13] *Xenos v Wickham* (1867) LR 2 HL 296 (marine insurance) per Pigott B, at 308.

[14] *Sickness and Accident Assurance Association v General Accident Assurance Corpn* 1892 19 R (Ct of Sess) 977, per Lord Robertson at 985; *Mackie v European Assurance Society* (1869) 21 LT 102 (fire insurance) per Malins V-C, at 104.

[15] The fact that he has not paid for it is immaterial: *Shanks v Sun Life Assurance Co of India* 1896 4 SLT 65.

[16] Cf *Carlill v Carbolic Smoke Ball Co* [1893] 1 QB 256, CA.

[17] See *Household Fire and Carriage Accident Insurance Co v Grant* (1879) 4 ExD 216, CA (contract).

[18] In *General Accident, Fire and Life Assurance Corpn v Robertson* [1909] AC 404, where the letter of acceptance from the holder was posted on December 25, delivered at the insurance company's office on December 26, and actually received by one of the company's employees on December 27, Lord Loreburn LC, at 411, declined to enter upon the nice point when a contract was concluded by correspondence, but held that at any rate there was a contract by December 27.

C THE EFFECT OF ACCEPTANCE

On the acceptance of the proposal the negotiations come to an end and the duty of disclosure ceases. The assured, therefore, is under no obligation either to disclose any material facts which only come to his knowledge, or to correct any misrepresentation the inaccuracy in which is only discovered, after acceptance.[19]

An acceptance once given binds the parties and cannot be withdrawn except by mutual consent;[20] it is immaterial that the parties have misapprehended their position and have cancelled the policy on the assumption that no contract exists between them.[1]

The parties are bound to each other as from the date of the acceptance, the assured to take the policy[2] and to pay the premium,[3] the insurers to issue the policy,[4] to accept the premium when tendered,[5] and to pay a loss when it happens.[6]

After a final acceptance the insurers cannot depart from it by attempting to introduce fresh terms into the policy;[7] the assured is entitled to insist upon a

---

19 See pp 151–155, post.

20 See pp 231–232, post.

1 *Adie & Sons v Insurance Corpn Ltd* (1898) 14 TLR 544 (fire insurance).

2 *Solvency Mutual Guarantee Co v Freeman* (1861) 7 H & N 17: *General Accident Insurance Corpn v Cronk* (1901) 17 TLR 233.

3 *General Accident Insurance Corpn v Cronk* (supra); *Adie & Sons v Insurance Corpn Ltd* (supra) per Bigham J, at 544. Cf *Star Fire and Burglary Insurance Co v Davidson* 1902 5 F (Ct of Sess) 83 (fire insurance), where an action for the premium failed because there was no acceptance.

4 *Roberts v Security Co Ltd* [1897] 1 QB 111, CA; *Royal Exchange Assurance Corpn v Tod* (1892) 8 TLR 669 (marine insurance): *Bhugwandass v Netherlands India Sea and Fire Insurance Co of Batavia* (1888) 14 App Cas 83, PC (marine insurance); *Adie & Sons v Insurance Corpn Ltd* (supra) (fire insurance).

5 *Honour v Equitable Life Asssurance Society of the United States* [1900] 1 Ch 852 (life insurance) per Buckley J, at 855. Cf *Adie & Sons v Insurance Corpn Ltd* (supra), where the premium was tendered and refused. In *Canning v Farquhar* (1886) 16 QBD 727, CA (life insurance), where it was held that there was no acceptance of the proposal by the insurers but a counter-offer (see p 94, ante), Lord Esher MR said at 731: 'It follows that after the insurance company have said that they accept the proposal and that if the premium is paid, they will issue a policy, although there is no change in the circumstances, and all that has happened is that they alter their mind, yet they are not bound to accept the premium. I do not shrink from saying that in my view of insurance law there is no contract in such a case binding them to accept the premium.' It is, of course, clear that an offer may be withdrawn at any time before acceptance, and that an acceptance after the withdrawal is of no effect; but, as pointed out by Lindley LJ, at 733, the counter-offer would be a continuing offer, and a tender of the premium would be an acceptance of it. If, therefore, the insurers never in fact withdrew their counter-offer and the premium was duly tendered, it is difficult to see on what grounds it can be contended that a binding contract had not been concluded. It is submitted that the above-mentioned dictum of Lord Esher, in so far as it suggests the contrary, is inconsistent with the authorities and cannot be regarded as correctly stating the law. It is more probable, however, that Lord Esher's dictum must be considered in connection with the special facts of the case, and that in his opinion there was no counter-offer by the insurers, but a mere continuance of the negotiations which did not bind either party.

6 *Roberts v Security Co Ltd* (supra); *Adie & Sons v Insurance Corpn Ltd* (supra). Cf *Sickness and Accident Assurance Association v General Accident Assurance Corpn* 1892 19 R (Ct of Sess) 977 per Lord Maclaren at 987.

7 *Canadian Casualty and Boiler Insurance Co v Boulter Davies & Co* and *Hawthorne & Co* (1907) 39 SCR 558; *Motteux v Governor & Co of London Assurance* (1739) 1 Atk 545 (marine insurance) followed in *Collett v Morrison* (1851) 9 Hare 162 (life insurance); *Griffiths v Fleming* [1909] 1 KB 805, CA (life insurance) per Farwell LJ, at 818.

policy in the exact terms of the proposal.[8] Moreover, any such attempt on the part of the insurers does not relieve the assured from the obligation of performing the contract into which he has, in fact, entered.[9]

D DISCRIMINATION

It is unlawful for any person concerned with the provision of insurance facilities to the public or section of the public to discriminate against a woman who seeks to obtain or use those facilities:

a by refusing or deliberately omitting to provide her with them; or
b by refusing or deliberately omitting to provide her with facilities of the like quality, in the like manner and on the like terms as are normal in his case in relation to male members of the public or other members of that section of the public.[10]

But nothing renders unlawful the treatment of a woman in relation to an annuity, life assurance policy, accident insurance policy or similar matter involving the assessment of risk, where the treatment:

a was effected by reference to actuarial or other data from a source on which it was reasonable to rely, and
b was reasonable having regard to the data and any other relevant factors.[11]

It is unlawful for any person concerned with the provision of insurance facilities to discriminate against a person who seeks to obtain or use those facilities:

a by refusing or deliberately omitting to provide him with any of them; or
b by refusing or deliberately omitting to provide him with facilities of the like quality, in the like manner and on the like terms as are normal in relation to other members of the public.[12]

---

8 *General Accident Insurance Corpn v Cronk* (supra) per Wills J, at 233. Cf *Newman v Belstein* (1884) 28 Sol Jo 301, CA (life insurance); *Rust v Abbey Life Assurance Co Ltd* [1979] 2 Lloyd's Rep 334, CA (property bond insurance). As to rectification, see pp 239–243, post.

9 *Solvency Mutual Guarantee Co v Freeman* (supra); *General Accident Insurance Corpn v Cronk* (supra).

10 Sex Discrimination Act 1975, s 29(1), (2)(c).

11 Ibid, s 45.

12 Race Relations Act 1976, s 20(1), (2)(c). A person discriminates against another if:
a on racial grounds he treats that person less favourably than he treats or would treat other persons; or
b he applies to that other a requirement or condition which he applies or would apply to persons not of the same racial group as that other but:
i which is such that the proportion of persons of the same racial group as that other who can comply with it is considerably smaller than the proportion of persons not of that racial group who can comply with it; and
ii which he cannot show to be justifiable irrespective of the colour, race, nationality or ethnic or national origins of the person to whom it is applied; and
iii which is to the detriment of that other because he cannot comply with it: ibid, s 1(1).
'Racial grounds' means any of the following grounds: colour, race, nationality or ethnic or nationality origins: ibid, s 3(1). 'Racial group' means a group of persons defined by reference to colour, race, nationality or ethnic or national origins, and references to a person's racial group refer to any racial group into which he falls: ibid, s 3(1). As to the enforcement of s 20, see ibid, s 57.

CHAPTER 11

The formation of a contract for a Lloyd's policy

In some classes of insurance at Lloyd's proposal forms[1] are used. But in others, a broker who is instructed to effect a Lloyd's policy must prepare a 'slip', which is a document taking the place both of the proposal and of the cover note in other insurances.

A THE NATURE OF THE 'SLIP'

On a slip of paper he writes down the essential features of the proposed insurance for the purpose of enabling the policy to be adapted to the particular insurance proposed by the insertion of the necessary details, and for the purpose of disclosing to the underwriter the risk which he is being invited to run, and to enable him to fix the premium to be charged.

The 'slip' must, therefore, contain a description not only of the assured, and of the amount proposed to be insured, but also of the subject-matter of insurance, including in the case of fire insurance a statement as to the location of the building concerned. In addition, it contains a statement as to the peril insured against, and as to the commencement and duration of the contract.[2]

As the ordinary terms of a Lloyd's policy are familiar to both broker and underwriter, it is unnecessary to refer to them in the 'slip'. But any proposed variation from the ordinary terms must be specified.[3]

The 'slip', as prepared by the broker, is submitted by him to the various underwriters with whom he is in the habit of doing business. Each underwriter, as it is submitted to him, initials it, if he accepts the proposed insurance, for himself and the 'names' of the other members of the syndicate, adding opposite his initials the amount for which he is willing to accept liability.[4]

It is the duty of the broker, as representing the proposed assured, to disclose every material fact to the underwriter, on submitting the 'slip'; and if he fails to

---

1 As to the statement made by The British Insurance Association and Lloyd's concerning non-life insurance practice relating to various matters including proposal forms, see pp 101–102, ante.

2 See *Grover and Grover Ltd v Mathews* [1910] 2 KB 401 (fire insurance) where the form of the 'slip' was as follows: 'Fire, 12 months at March 26, 1909, Building (Pianoforte Factory), £1,000, Grover & Grover Ltd, The Bank House, Newington Green, N.'

3 See *Allom v Property Insurance Co* (1911) Times, 10 February (fire insurance), where Scrutton J attached importance to the fact that an alleged warranty was not inserted in the 'slip'.

4 *Seaton v Burnand* [1899] 1 QB 782, CA (reversed without affecting this point, [1900] AC 135) per Smith LJ, at 790.

do so, the policy is liable to be avoided.[5] In this connection, it is important to consider the order in which the initials of the different underwriters to whom the 'slip' has been submitted, appear on the 'slip'.[6] Each underwriter following the first is necessarily influenced by the fact that the proposal has already been accepted by the first underwriter,[7] and any fraud, misrepresentation, or non-disclosure committed against the first underwriter is equally a breach of duty against the subsequent underwriters.[8] On the other hand, a breach of duty against any other underwriter than the first affects such underwriter only, and cannot be relied upon by the others whether they precede or follow him upon the 'slip'.[9]

B THE EFFECT OF INITIALLING THE 'SLIP'

The initialling of the 'slip' by the underwriter is the acceptance of the assured's proposal,[10] and the underwriter is bound by his line subject only to the contingency that it may fall to be written down on 'closing' to some extent if the 'slip' turns out to have been oversubscribed.[11] He thereby binds himself to sign a policy in accordance with the 'slip', when tendered to him for signature, and he cannot refuse to do so except upon grounds which call in question the validity of the acceptance.[12] The signing of a policy is, however, a mere formality; it may take place even after loss, and the underwriter cannot refuse to sign the policy on the ground that the broker failed to tender it within a reasonable time after the initialling of the 'slip'.[13]

The contract is complete on the initialling of the 'slip', and, if there is no formal policy in existence, the underwriter may be sued on the 'slip'.[14] The 'slip' is not a mere undertaking in honour to issue a policy; it constitutes in itself a

---

5 This rule applies to all kinds of insurance: *Seaton v Burnand* (supra) per Smith LJ, at 790. The statements in the 'slip' may, however, put the underwriter on inquiry: *British and Foreign Marine Insurance Co v Sturge* (1897) 2 Com Cas 43 (marine insurance). For the duty of disclosure generally, see Chapter 13, and the Marine Insurance Act 1906, ss 18 and 19. See further, Ivamy *Marine Insurance* (4th Edn 1985), pp 39–70.

6 *Pawson v Watson* (1778) 2 Cowp 785 (marine insurance).

7 Hence, if the first underwriter is a decoy duck, the policy is voidable for fraud: *Wilson v Ducket* (1762) 3 Burr 1361 (marine insurance).

8 *Barber v Fletcher* (1779) 1 Doug KB 305 (marine insurance); *Marsden v Reid* (1803) 3 East 572 (marine insurance); *Brine v Featherstone* (1813) 4 Taunt 869 (marine insurance). But see *Forrester v Pigou* (1813) 1 M & S 9 (marine insurance) per Lord Ellenborough CJ, at 13.

9 *Bell v Carstairs* (1810) 2 Camp 543 (marine insurance).

10 *Grover and Grover Ltd v Mathews* (1910) 15 Com Cas 249 (fire insurance) per Hamilton J, at 256; *General Reinsurance Corpn v Forsakringsaktiebolaget Fennia Patria* [1983] QB 856, [1983] 3 WLR 318, [1983] 2 Lloyd's Rep 287, CA (reinsurance), at pp 290–291 (per Kerr LJ). As to the meaning of the letters 'NE', i e 'not entered', if inserted after the initials of the underwriters, see *Thompson v Adams* (1889) 23 QBD 361 (fire insurance) per Mathew J, at 364.

11 Ibid, at 291 (per Kerr LJ).

12 *Thompson v Adams* (supra) (fire insurance) per Mathew J, at 364–5; cf *Ionides v Pacific Fire Insurance Co* (1871) LR 6 QB 674 (marine insurance) (affd (1872) LR 7 QB 517 ExCh) per Blackburn J, at 684.

13 *Thompson v Adams* (supra).

14 *Thompson v Adams* (supra); *Grover and Grover Ltd v Mathews* (supra); *Eagle Star Insurance Co Ltd v Spratt* [1971] 2 Lloyd's Rep 116, CA (reinsurance) at 127 (per Lord Denning MR). It is immaterial that the premium is not paid until after the loss: *Thompson v Adams* (supra).

binding contract of insurance.[15] No objection can be taken to its form on the ground that it does not completely express the intended contract of insurance; it contains the essential terms of the contract, since it must be read in connection with the common form of Lloyd's policy to which it is intended to relate.[16]

In the absence of a custom to that effect, an assured (or reassured) is bound to the same extent as the insurer by the initialling of the 'slip' and has no option to rescind the contract thereafter.[17] Further, no term to that effect arises by implication of law as a matter of necessary business efficacy.[18]

The duty of disclosure ceases on the 'slip' being initialled and does not continue until the actual signature of the policy.[19] It is, therefore, immaterial that the assured, after the initialling of the 'slip', makes a statement to the underwriters which is inaccurate,[20] or discovers a material fact which he fails to disclose.[1]

As far as marine insurance is concerned, the Marine Insurance Act 1906, s 21[2] states:

> 'A contract of marine insurance is deemed to be concluded when the proposal of the assured is accepted by the insurer, whether the policy be then issued or not; and for the purpose of showing when the proposal was accepted, reference may be made to the slip or covering note or other customary memorandum of the contract, . . .'

As to the duration of the duty of disclosure, s 18(1) provides:

> 'Subject to the provisions of this section, the assured must disclose to the insurer, before the contract is concluded, every material circumstance which is known to the assured . . .'[3]

---

15 *Thompson v Adams* (supra).

16 *Grover and Grover Ltd v Mathews* (supra) per Hamilton J, at 256.

17 *General Reinsurance Corpn v Forsakringsaktiebolaget Fennia Patria* [1983] QB 856, [1983] 3 WLR 318, [1983] 2 Lloyd's Rep 287, CA (reinsurance), where no such custom was established. (See the judgment of Kerr LJ, at 295, that of Slade LJ, ibid, at 296, and that of Oliver LJ, ibid, at 297.)

18 Ibid, at 295 (per Kerr LJ).

19 *Cory v Patton* (1874) LR 9 QB 577, ExCh (marine insurance) followed in *Lishman v Northern Maritime Insurance Co* (1875) LR 10 CP 179, ExCh (marine insurance).

20 *Ionides v Pacific Fire and Marine Insurance Co* (1872) LR 7 QB 517, ExCh (marine insurance).

1 *Cory v Patton* (supra) (marine insurance); *Lishman v Northern Maritime Insurance Co* (supra) (marine insurance).

2 As amended by the Finance Act 1959, Sch 8, Pt II.

3 See further, Ivamy *Marine Insurance* (4th Edn 1985), pp 66–68.

CHAPTER 12

The principle of good faith

It is a fundamental principle of insurance law that the utmost good faith must be observed by each party. This rule was clearly stated by Lord Mansfield as long ago as 1766, when he said:[1]

> 'Insurance is a contract upon speculation. The special facts, upon which the contingent chance is to be computed, lie more commonly in the knowledge of the insured only: the underwriter trusts to his representation, and proceeds upon confidence that he does not keep back any circumstance in his knowledge, to mislead the underwriter into a belief that the circumstance does not exist, and to induce him to estimate the risque as if it did not exist. The keeping back such a circumstance is a fraud, and, therefore, the policy is void.[2] Although the suppression should happen through mistake, without any fraudulent intention; yet still the underwriter is deceived, and the policy is void; because the risque run is really different from the risque understood and intended to be run at the time of the agreement . . . The governing principle is applicable to all contracts and dealings. Good faith forbids either party by concealing what he privately knows, to draw the other into a bargain, from his ignorance of that fact, and his believing the contrary . . .'

This case concerned a policy which had effected against the taking of a fort by a foreign enemy. But the same principle was applied in a case concerning life insurance in which Jessel MR observed:[3]

> 'The first question to be decided is, what is the principle on which the Court acts in setting aside contracts of assurance? As regards the general principle I am not prepared to lay down the law as making any difference in substance between one contract of assurance and another. Whether it is life, or fire, or marine assurance, I take it good faith is required in all cases, and though there may be certain circumstances from the peculiar nature of marine insurance which require to be disclosed, and which do not apply to other contracts of insurance, that is rather, in my opinion, an illustration of the application of the principle than a distinction in principle.'

Further examples can be found in other judgments, 'In policies of insurance, whether marine insurance or life insurance, there is an understanding that the contract is uberrima fides,[4] that, if you know any circumstance at all that may influence the underwriter's opinion as to the risk he is incurring, and consequently as to whether he will take it, or what premium he will charge, if he does take it, you will state what you know. There is an obligation there to disclose what you know, and the concealment of a material circumstance known to you, whether you thought it material or not, avoids the policy.'[5]

'It has been for centuries in England the law in connection with insurance of all sorts, marine, fire, life, guarantee and every kind of policy, that, as the

---

1 *Carter v Boehm* (1766) 3 Burr 1905 at 1909.

2 This, of course, means voidable.

3 *London Assurance v Mansel* (1879) 11 ChD 363 at 367.

4 Sic.

5 *Brownlie v Campbell* (1880) 5 App Cas 925 at 954 (per Lord Blackburn); see also *Joel v Law Union and Crown Insurance Co* [1908] 2 KB 863 at 883 (per Fletcher Moulton LJ).

underwriter knows nothing and the man who comes to him to ask him to insure knows everything, it is the duty of the assured, the man who desires to have a policy, to make a full disclosure to the underwriters without being asked of all the material circumstances, because the underwriter knows nothing and the assured knows everything. That is expressed by saying that it is a contract of the utmost good faith—uberrima fides.'[6]

'Now, insurance is a contract of the utmost good faith, and it is of the gravest importance to commerce that that position should be observed. The underwriter knows nothing of the particular circumstances of the voyage to be insured. The assured knows a great deal, and it is the duty of the assured to inform the underwriter of everything that he has not taken as knowing, so that the contract may be entered into on an equal footing.[7]

As far as marine insurance is concerned, the Marine Insurance Act 1906, s 17, provides:[8]

> 'A contract of marine insurance is a contract based upon the utmost good faith, and, if the utmost good faith be not observed by either party, the contract may be avoided[9] by the other party.'

It is the duty of the parties to help each other to come to a right conclusion, and not to hold each other at arm's length in defence of their conflicting interest.[10]

It is the duty of the assured not only to be honest and straightforward, but also to make a full disclosure of all material facts.[11] Further, all statements made by him during the negotiations must be accurate.[12]

---

6 *Rozanes v Bowen* (1928) 32 LlL Rep 98 at 102.

7 *Greenhill v Federal Insurance Co Ltd* [1927] 1 KB 65 at 76 (per Scrutton LJ).

8 This section appears under the general heading of 'Disclosure and Representations'. It would seem therefore that the application of the principle of good faith in contracts of marine insurance is limited to the period before the contract is concluded, and not afterwards though, of course, this does not mean that the assured is entitled to succeed if the claim is a fraudulent one, for such a matter is governed by a different rule. As to which, see pp 407–411, post. But in *Black King Shipping Corpn and Wayang (Panama) SA v Massie, The 'Litsion Pride'* [1985] 1 Lloyd's Rep 437 (marine insurance) both parties accepted the approach that s 17 was equally applicable to events after as well as before the conclusion of the contract of insurance. (See the judgment of Hirst J ibid, at 512.)

9 'Avoidance' means 'avoidance ab initio', and not avoidance as far as, but no further back than, the loss in relation to which the breach was committed: ibid, at 515 (per Hirst J).

10 *Joel v Law Union and Crown Insurance Co* [1908] 2 KB 863, CA (life insurance) per Fletcher-Moulton LJ, at 890.

11 *Lindeneau v Desborough* (1828) 8 B & C 586 (life insurance) per Bayley J, at 592: 'I think that in all cases of insurance, whether on ships, houses, or lives, the underwriter should be informed of every material circumstance within the knowledge of the assured; and that the proper question is, Whether any particular circumstance was in fact material? and not whether the party believed it to be so'; *Laing v Union Marine Insurance Co Ltd* (1895) 1 Com Cas 11 (marine insurance) per Mathew J, at 14; *Re Yager and Guardian Assurance Co Ltd* (1912) 108 LT 38 (fire insurance) per Channell J, at 44; *Dalglish v Jarvie* (1850) 2 Mac & G 231 (injunction) per Rolfe B, at 243: '. . . the application for a special injunction is very much governed by the same principles which govern insurances, matters which are said to require the utmost degree of good faith, "uberrima fides". In cases of insurance a party is required not only to state all matters within his knowledge, which he believes to be material to the question of the insurance, but all which in point of fact are so. If he conceals anything he knows to be material, it is a fraud; but besides that, if he conceals anything that may influence the rate of premium which the underwriter may require, although he does not know it would have that effect, such concealment entirely vitiates the policy'; *Lee v British Law Insurance Co Ltd* [1972] 2 Lloyd's Rep 49, CA (personal accident insurance) per Karminski LJ, at 57: 'Full disclosure is of the very essence of the contract.'

12 *Everett v Desborough* (1829) 5 Bing 503 (life insurance) per Park J, at 518: 'It is absolutely

Similarly, it is the duty of the insurers and their agents to disclose all material facts within their knowledge, since the obligation of good faith applies to them equally with the assured.[13] All representations made by them during the negotiations with a view of inducing the assured to accept a policy must be true.[14]

necessary that there should be the purest good faith between the parties and the most accurate representation of all material particulars.'

13 *Carter v Boehm* (1766) 3 Burr 1905 (marine insurance) per Lord Mansfield CJ, at 1909: 'The policy would be equally void, against the underwriter, if he concealed; as, if he insured a ship on her voyage which he privately knew to be arrived; and an action would lie to recover the premium'; *Re Bradley and Essex and Suffolk Accident Indemnity Society* [1912] 1 KB 415, CA, per Farwell LJ, at 430: 'Contracts of insurance are contracts in which uberrima fides is required, not only from the assured, but also from the company assuring.'

14 *Duffel v Wilson* (1808) 1 Camp 401, where the insurance was against being drawn for the militia, and there was a misrepresentation as to the period during which the assured was liable to be drawn for service; *Pontifex v Bignold* (1841) 3 Man & G 63 (life insurance).

CHAPTER 13

Non-disclosure

The assured is under a duty to disclose all material facts relating to the insurance which he proposes to effect. In addition, he must make no misrepresentation regarding such facts.[1] Usually, however, these duties are modified by the terms of the contract. The burden of proving that there has been a breach of duty on the part of the assured rests on the insurers.

A THE EXTENT OF THE ASSURED'S DUTY

The assured must disclose all material facts which are within his actual or presumed knowledge. The absence of a proposal form[2] does not modify the assured's duty of disclosure.[3]

1 Actual knowledge

It is the duty of the proposed assured to disclose to the insurers all material facts within his actual knowledge. The special facts distinguishing the proposed insurance are, as a general rule, unknown to the insurers who are not in a position to ascertain them. They lie, for the most part, solely within the knowledge of the proposed assured.

Thus, Kennedy LJ said in one case:[4]

> 'No class of case occurs to my mind in which our law regards mere non-disclosure as invalidating the contract, except in the case of insurance. That is an exception which the law has wisely made in deference to the plain exigencies of this particular and most important class of transactions. The person seeking to insure may fairly be presumed to know all the circumstances which materially affect the risk, and, generally, is, as to some of them, the only person who has the knowledge; the underwriter, whom he asks to take the risk, cannot, as a rule, know and but rarely has either the time or the opportunity to learn by inquiry, circumstances which are, or may be, most material to the formation of his judgment as to his acceptance or rejection of the risk, and as to the premium which he ought to require.'

Further, in another case, Fletcher Moulton LJ remarked:[5]

---

1 See Chapter 14.

2 See Chapter 8.

3 *Woolcott v Sun Alliance and London Insurance Ltd* [1978] 1 All ER 1253, [1978] 1 Lloyd's Rep 629 (fire insurance) at 633 (per Caulfield J). In this case a building society had a block policy of insurance and the names of the insured were expressed to be the society as mortgagees and the mortgagors mentioned in the record sheets, and it was held that the mortgagor, when he completed his application for a loan, was under a duty to disclose his criminal record for by that application he was accepting that the society would effect the insurance of his property on his behalf as well as their own behalf: ibid, at 632.

4 *London General Omnibus Co Ltd v Holloway* [1912] 2 KB 72, CA (guarantee) at 85.

5 *Joel v Law Union and Crown Insurance Co* [1908] 2 KB 863, CA (life insurance), at 885.

'Insurers are thus in the highly favourable position that they are entitled not only to bona fides on the part of the applicant, but also to full disclosure of all knowledge possessed by the applicant that is material to the risk.'[6]

Good faith, therefore, requires that he should not, by his silence, mislead the insurers into believing that the risk, as proposed, differs to their detriment from the risk which they will actually run.[7] On the contrary, he should help them by every means in his power to estimate the risk at its proper value.[8]

A failure on the part of the assured to disclose a material fact is sometimes called 'concealment'.[9] Strictly speaking, however, the word implies the keeping back or suppression[10] of something which it is the duty of the assured to bring specifically to the notice of the insurers,[11] and not merely an inadvertent omission to disclose it. Hence, where the failure to disclose is not due to design and the assured has no intention to deal otherwise than frankly and fairly with the insurers, the term 'non-disclosure' may perhaps be more appropriate.

Every contract of insurance proceeds on the basis that the duty of disclosure has been discharged by the proposed assured,[12] and the failure to discharge it renders the contract voidable at the instance of the insurer.

2 Presumed knowledge

The duty of making disclosure is not confined to such facts as are within the actual knowledge of the assured. It extends to all material facts which he ought in the ordinary course of business to have known, and he cannot escape the consequences of not disclosing them on the ground that he did not know them.[13]

There is, however, no duty to disclose facts which the assured did not know, and which he could not be reasonably expected to know at any material time.

Thus, Fletcher Moulton LJ stated the principle in a case concerning life insurance[14] in these words:[15]

'But the question always is: Was the knowledge you possess such that you ought to have disclosed it? Let me take an example. I will suppose that a man, as is the case with most of us, occasionally had a headache. It may be that a particular one of these headaches would have told a brain specialist of hidden mischief. But to the man it was an ordinary headache indistinguishable from the rest. Now, no reasonable man would deem it material to tell an insurance company of all the casual headaches he had had in his life, and, if he knew no more as

---

6 See also, *Dalglish v Jarvie* (1850) 2 Mac & G 231 (injunction).

7 *Carter v Boehm* (1766) 3 Burr 1905 (marine insurance) per Lord Mansfield CJ, at 1909. See also *Seaton v Burnand* [1899] 1 QB 782, CA (solvency insurance) per Romer LJ, at 793; revsd without affecting this point [1900] AC 135; *Re Denton's Estate, Licenses Insurance Corpn and Guarantee Fund Ltd v Denton* [1904] 2 Ch 178, CA (guarantee) per Vaughan Williams LJ, at 188.

8 *Joel v Law Union and Crown Insurance Co* [1908] 2 KB 863, CA (life insurance) per Fletcher Moulton LJ, at 890.

9 *London Assurance v Mansel* (1879) 11 ChD 363 (life insurance) per Jessel MR, at 370: 'Concealment, properly so called, means non-disclosure of a fact which it is a man's duty to disclose, and it is his duty to disclose the fact if it is a material fact.' See also *Asfar & Co v Blundell* [1896] 1 QB 123, CA (marine insurance) per Lord Esher MR, at 129.

10 *Carter v Boehm* (1766) 3 Burr 1905 (marine insurance) per Lord Mansfield CJ, at 1909.

11 *Asfar & Co v Blundell* (supra) (marine insurance) per Kay LJ, at 133.

12 *Joel v Law Union and Crown Insurance Co* (supra) (life insurance) per Vaughan Williams LJ, at 878.

13 *Proudfoot v Montefiore* (1867) LR 2 QB 511 (marine insurance) per Cockburn CJ, at 521, approved in *Blackburn, Low & Co v Vigors* (1887) 12 App Cas 531 (marine insurance) per Lord Halsbury LC, at 537; cf *Pimm v Lewis* (1862) 2 F & F 778 (fire insurance).

14 *Joel v Law Union and Crown Insurance Co* (supra).

15 Ibid, at 884.

> to this particular headache than that it was an ordinary casual headache, there would be no breach of his duty towards the insurance company in not disclosing it. He possessed no knowledge that it was incumbent on him to disclose, because he knew of nothing which a reasonable man would deem material, or of a character to influence the insurers in their action. It was what he did not know which would have been of that character, but he cannot be held liable for non-disclosure in respect of facts which he did not know.'[16]

Where the fact could have been discovered by the assured if he had made reasonable enquiries, he is guilty of a breach of duty towards the insurers. This is clearly the case where, although the fact in question was never within his actual knowledge, his ignorance was due to his intentional failure to make such inquiries as he might reasonably have been expected to make in the circumstances; and the policy is, therefore, voidable at the instance of the insurers since his failure to make them is evidence of fraud and lack of uberrima fides.[17]

Where the fact could have been discovered by the assured if he had made reasonable inquiries, he is guilty of a breach of duty towards the insurers. This is clearly the case where, although the fact in question was never within his actual knowledge, his ignorance was due to his intentional failure to make such inquiries as he might reasonably have been expected to make in the circumstances; and the policy is, therefore, voidable at the instance of the insurers since his failure to make them is evidence of fraud and lack of uberrima fides.[17]
had made such inquiries as to its system of supervision as a reasonable prudent board of directors of such a company would have made in the ordinary course of business. McNair J said that he had been referred to no authority to suggest that the board of a company proposing to insure owed any duty to carry out a detailed investigation as to the manner in which the company's operations were performed, and he knew of no principle in law which led to that result. He went on to say:[20]

> 'If a company is proposing to insure wages in transit, I cannot believe that they owe a duty to the insurers to find out exactly how the weekly wages are, in fact, carried from the bank to their premises, though clearly they must not deliberately close their eyes to defects in the system and

---

16 See *Jones v Provincial Insurance Co* (1857) 3 CBNS 65 (life insurance), where the assured, who had had two bilious attacks two years before insuring, had not been informed that two medical men, who had examined him, had taken a serious view of the effect of the attacks upon his health.

17 *Blackburn, Low & Co v Vigors* (1887) 12 App Cas 531 (marine insurance) per Lord Halsbury LC, at 537.

18 *London General Insurance Co v General Marine Underwriters' Association* [1921] 1 KB 104: 4 LlL Rep 382, CA (marine insurance), where a casualty slip was in the possession of the plaintiffs, although they had not read it before reinsuring the risk; *Wake v Atty* (1812) 4 Taunt 493 (marine insurance), where a letter stating that the ship was lost did not come to the knowledge of the broker until after the policy was effected, owing to his failure to call at his office before obtaining the signature of the insurers, and it was held that, as, in the circumstances, he had no reason to believe that his information was not complete or that the letter was on its way, the policy could not be avoided on the ground of non-disclosure; *Cantiere Meccanico Brindisino v Janson* [1912] 3 KB 452, CA (marine insurance); *Swete v Fairlie* (1833) 6 C & P 1 (life insurance), where the person whose life was insured had suffered from a disorder of such a character as to prevent him from knowing that he had suffered from it; *Fowkes v Manchester and London Life Insurance Co* (1862) 3 F & F 440 (life insurance), where the proposed assured had had some symptoms which a medical man could not detect as denoting the presence of gout in the system, but did not know that he had had an attack of gout.

19 [1960] 2 Lloyd's Rep 241.

20 Ibid, at 252.

must disclose any suspicions or misgivings they have. To impose such an obligation upon the proposer is tantamount to holding that insurers only insure persons who conduct their business prudently, whereas it is a commonplace that one of the purposes of insurance is to cover yourself against your own negligence or the negligence of your servant.'

The ignorance of a material fact does not excuse the proposed assured from the consequences of failing to disclose it where his ignorance is due to the failure of his agent to communicate to him material facts within his knowledge. It must, however, be the duty of the agent in question to communicate such facts to his principal.[21]

B IS THE DUTY OF DISCLOSURE AN IMPLIED TERM?

In considering whether the duty of disclosure is an implied term of the contract of insurance,[1] Scott LJ said that he realised that there were several reported cases[2] in which learned Judges had, in the course of their judgments, expressed an opinion that the duty of disclosure might be regarded as resting on an implied term, but he did not know of any case where the point had come up for actual decision. On principle it seemed plain that the equitable jurisdiction to avoid a contract for misrepresentation could not rest on such a foundation. Even the Common Law duty of disclosure he found difficult to explain fully on the theory of its resting only on an implied term of the contract. If it did, it would not arise until the contract had been made; and then its sole operation would be to unmake the contract. Although the question had not been decided judicially, it was worthy of note that ss 17 and 18 of the Marine Insurance Act 1906, seemed to treat the twin duties of disclosing all the material facts, and of misrepresenting none, as existing outside the contract, and not as mere implications inside the contract; for that Act was intended to be declaratory of the Common Law; and he saw nothing in the language of those particular sections to justify interpreting them as being anything but declaratory.

In the same case Luxmore LJ said that counsel had maintained that the right of an insurer to avoid a policy of insurance for misrepresentation or non-disclosure with regard to a material fact was based in law on implied contract. But he himself thought that, whatever might be the position with regard to non-disclosure, as to which he said nothing, he was satisfied that in a case of positive misrepresentation the right to avoid a contract, whether of insurance or not, depended not on any implied term of the contract but arose by reason of the jurisdiction originally exercised by the Courts of Equity to prevent imposition.

In *March Cabaret Club and Casino Ltd v London Assurance*,[3] May J considered that the duty to disclose was not based upon an implied term of the contract at all, and arose outside the contract. It applied to all contracts uberrimae fidei and was not limited to insurance contracts.

---

21 See pp 541–542, post.

1 *Merchants' and Manufacturers' Insurance Co Ltd v Hunt and Thorne and Thorne* [1941] 1 KB 295 at 313.

2 E g *Blackburn, Low & Co v Vigors* (1887) 12 App Cas 531 (marine insurance) per Lord Watson at 539; *Joel v Law Union and Crown Insurance Co* [1908] 2 KB 863, CA (life insurance) per Fletcher Moulton LJ, at 886.

3 [1975] 1 Lloyd's Rep 169 (trader's combined insurance) at 175. See also, *Claude R Ogden & Co Pty Ltd v Reliance Fire Sprinkler Co Pty Ltd* [1975] 1 Lloyd's Rep 52, Supreme Court of Australia (public and products liability insurance) per MacFarlan J, at 62.

C THE TESTS OF MATERIALITY

Various tests have been adopted by the Courts in order to ascertain what facts are to be regarded as material.

The test which is usually adopted is whether the non-disclosure of the facts would influence a 'prudent' insurer (though in some cases the term 'reasonable' has been substituted for 'prudent'). Another test is whether a 'reasonable' assured would consider them material.

In no case is it relevant to consider whether the non-disclosure would influence the particular insurer concerned or whether the assured himself thought that the facts were material.

1 The test of the 'prudent insurer'

As far as marine insurance is concerned, the question as to what facts are material is settled by the Marine Insurance Act 1906, s 18(2), which provides that:

> 'Every circumstance is material which would influence the judgment of a prudent insurer in fixing the premium or determining whether he will take the risk.'[4]

This test was adopted in a motor insurance case by the Supreme Court of Victoria, Court of Appeal, in *Babatsikos v Car Owners' Mutual Insurance Co Ltd,*[5] by the Court of Appeal in an 'all risks' insurance policy[6] and by the Judicial Committee of the Privy Council and by the High Court in fire policies,[7] and by the High Court in a professional indemnity insurance policy.[8]

The meaning of the term 'prudent insurer' was considered by Atkin J (as he then was) in *Associated Oil Carriers Ltd v Union Insurance Society of Canton Ltd,*[9] where the question was whether it was material on July 31, 1914 to disclose that the charterers of a vessel were of German nationality. His Lordship pointed out that this fact had been held material in *British and Foreign Marine Co Ltd v Samuel Sanday & Co,*[10] which had been decided by the House of Lords in 1916, and then went on to say:[11]

> '[Counsel] said that a prudent insurer within the meaning of the section must be taken to know the law as laid down in *Sanday's* case. Knowing so much, he would clearly have been influenced. I think that this standard of prudence indicates an insurer much too bright and good for human nature's daily food. There seems no reason to impute to the insurer a higher

---

[4] See generally *Container Transport International Inc v Oceanus Mutual Underwriting Association (Bermuda) Ltd* [1984] 1 Lloyd's Rep 476, CA; (marine insurance), at 501 (per Kerr LJ) and at 511 (per Parker LJ), and Ivamy *Marine Insurance* (4th Edn 1985), pp 44–45. See also Road Traffic Act 1972, s 149(5): 'In this section "material" means of such a nature as to influence the judgment of a prudent insurer in determining whether he will take the risk, and, if so, at what premium and on what conditions', and Ivamy *Fire and Motor Insurance* (4th Edn 1984), p 343.

[5] [1970] 2 Lloyd's Rep 314, where Pape J said (ibid, at 325): 'S 18(2) of the [English] Marine Insurance Act 1906 (s 24(2) of the [Australian] Commonwealth Insurance Act 1909) adopts the test of the judgment of a prudent insurer, and since marine and non-marine insurance law is identical in this respect, this test may be regarded as the proper one.'

[6] *Lambert v Co-operative Insurance Society Ltd* [1975] 2 Lloyd's Rep 485, CA (all risks insurance).

[7] *Marene Knitting Mills Pty Ltd v Greater Pacific General Insurance Ltd* [1976] 2 Lloyd's Rep 631, PC (fire insurance); *Reynolds and Anderson v Phoenix Assurance Co Ltd* [1978] 2 Lloyd's Rep 440, QB (fire insurance).

[8] *Johns v Kelly* [1986] 1 Lloyd's Rep 468.

[9] [1917] 2 KB 184.

[10] [1916] 1 AC 650.

[11] [1917] 2 KB 184 at 192.

> degree of knowledge and foresight than that reasonably possessed by the more experienced and intelligent insurers carrying on business in that market at that time. The evidence satisfies me that if the standard of prudence is the ideal one contended for by [Counsel], there were in July, 1914, no prudent insurers in London, or if there were, they were not to be found in the usual places where one would seek for them.'

In some cases, however, the test adopted has been that of a 'reasonable' insurer. But it is submitted that the words 'reasonable' and 'prudent' are interchangeable.

For instance, Lord Salvesen in delivering the judgment of the Judicial Committee of the Privy Council in a case of life insurance[12] said:[13] 'It is a question of fact in each case whether, if the matters concealed or misrepresented had been truly disclosed, they would, on a fair consideration of the evidence, have influenced a reasonable insurer to decline the risk or to have stipulated for a higher premium.' This same test was applied by Lord Greene MR, in a case relating to a motor policy,[14] and by May J, in the case of a trader's combined insurance policy.[15]

2 The 'reasonable assured' test

Another test which is sometimes applied is, 'What would a reasonable assured consider material?' Thus, in one case Fletcher Moulton LJ, said:[16] 'If a reasonable man would have recognised that it was material to disclose the knowledge in question, it is no excuse that you did not recognise it to be so.' In another case Lush J, stated:[17] 'If a reasonable person would know that underwriters would naturally be influenced, in deciding whether to accept the risk and what premiums to charge, by [the] circumstances [if disclosed] the fact that they were kept in ignorance of them and indeed were misled, is fatal to the plaintiff's claim. The plaintiff was making a contract of insurance, and if he failed to disclose what a reasonable man would disclose, he must suffer the same consequences as any other person who makes a similar contract.'

This test may not necessarily be the same as that of the 'prudent insurer', for although a reasonable assured might think it material to disclose that another company had refused to insure him, this is not regarded as material.[18]

Hence, it is suggested that the 'prudent insurer' test is the one that should always be adopted. In the words of Scrutton LJ:[19]

> 'In my view it is very important to maintain the obligation on the assured of communicating to the underwriter every material fact, and I understand, and have always understood the definition of material fact to be that contained in the Marine Insurance Act:—"Every circumstance is material which would influence the judgment of a prudent insurer in fixing the premium or determining whether he will take the risk."'

Again, in a later case relating to life insurance Roskill J, said that 'It is well established that every circumstance is material which would influence the

---

12 *Mutual Life Insurance Co of New York v Ontario Metal Products Co Ltd* [1925] AC 344, PC.
13 Ibid, at 351.
14 *Zurich General Accident and Liability Insurance Co Ltd v Morrison* [1942] 2 KB 53 at 58. But the 'prudent' test was adopted by MacKinnon LJ, in the same case: ibid, at 60.
15 *March Cabaret Club and Casino Ltd v London Assurance* [1975] 1 Lloyd's Rep 169, at 176.
16 *Joel v Law Union and Crown Insurance Co* [1908] 2 KB 863, CA at 884.
17 *Horne v Poland* [1922] 2 KB 364 at 367.
18 *Glasgow Assurance Corpn Ltd v William Symondson & Co* (1911) 16 Com Cas 109.
19 *Becker v Marshall* (1922) 12 LlL Rep 413 at 414.

judgment of a prudent underwriter in fixing the premium or in determining whether he will take the risk'.[20]

3 Whether the non-disclosure would influence the particular insurer is irrelevant

Whether the non-disclosure would influence the particular insurer concerned is irrelevant.

> 'What is material is that which would influence the mind of a prudent insurer in deciding whether to accept the risk or fix the premium, and if this be proved it is not necessary further to prove that the mind of the actual insurer was so affected. In other words, the assured could not rebut the claim to avoid the policy because of a material representation by a plea that the particular insurer concerned was so stupid, ignorant, or reckless, that he could not exercise the judgment of a prudent insurer and was, in fact, unaffected by anything the assured has represented or concealed.'[1]

Further, in a case concerning a treaty of marine insurance Scrutton J said that although the underwriter would have agreed to it even if he had known of the material fact alleged not to have been disclosed, he would on its disclosure in effect have said: 'Yes, I must think about this, and I am glad you told me.' But the test which had to be applied was *not* materiality to the underwriter.[2]

4 Assured's opinion as to whether the fact is material is irrelevant

So, too, the assured's opinion as to whether the fact not disclosed is material is irrelevant.

'It is also well established law, that it is immaterial whether the omission to communicate a material fact arises from . . . it not being present to the mind of the assured that the fact was one which it was material to make known.'[3]

'The proper question is "whether any particular circumstance was in fact material?" and not whether the party believed it to be so. The contrary doctrine would lead to frequent suppression of information, and it would often

---

20 *Godfrey v Britannic Assurance Co Ltd* [1963] 2 Lloyd's Rep 515 at 529.

1 *Zurich General Accident and Liability Insurance Co Ltd v Morrison* [1942] 2 KB 53 at 60, CA (per MacKinnon LJ).

2 *Glasgow Assurance Corpn Ltd v William Symondson & Co* (1911) 16 Com Cas 109, at 119. The view expressed by Kerr J in *Berger and Light Diffusers Pty Ltd v Pollock* [1973] 2 Lloyd's Rep 442 (marine insurance) would appear to be out of line with the authorities. In that case his Lordship observed (ibid, at 463): 'It seems to me, as a matter of principle, that the Court's task in deciding whether or not the defendant insurer can avoid the policy for non-disclosure must be to determine as a question of fact whether by applying the standard of the judgment of a prudent insurer, the insurer in question would have been influenced in fixing the premium or determining whether to take the risk if he had been informed of the undisclosed circumstances before entering into the contract. Otherwise one could in theory reach the absurd position where the Court might be satisfied that the insurer in question would in fact not have been so influenced but that other insurers would have been. It would then be a very odd result if the defendant underwriter could nevertheless avoid the policy. I do not think that this is the correct interpretation of s 18 [of the Marine Insurance Act 1906] despite the generality of the language. The effect of the non-disclosure may, of course, be so clear that the Court will require no evidence, or only little evidence, to decide in favour of the insurer. In doubtful cases, on the other hand, the Court may require evidence from the insurers themselves before being able to hold that the right to avoid the policy has been established.'

3 *Bates v Hewitt* (1867) LR 2 QB 595 at 607 (per Cockburn CJ).

be extremely difficult to show that the party neglecting to give the information thought it material.'[4]

'The question on such a policy is not whether a certain individual thought a particular fact material, but whether it was in truth material.'[5]

'The obligation to disclose, therefore necessarily depends upon the knowledge you possess . . . your opinion of the materiality of that knowledge is of no moment.'[6]

'I cannot help thinking that to enable a person proposing an insurance to speculate upon the maximum or minimum of information he is bound to communicate, would be introducing a most dangerous principle into the law of insurance.'[7]

'A policy is not binding if any material fact is not disclosed, and that . . . is so whether or not the person who does not disclose it knows that it is material, which is sometimes rather hard upon the assured . . . The question depends upon whether the fact is material or not, and not upon whether the person supposed it to be material.'[8]

'It is also well established that the opinion of the assured whether or not a material fact is material is irrelevant. Even if the assured fails to disclose a fact because he does not think it is material when in fact it is, does not avail him.'[9]

Thus, in *Godfrey v Britannic Assurance Co Ltd:*[10]

> The assured under a life policy had been told that he might have minor kidney trouble and should take care. Later he was told that the kidney condition was unchanged and that an X-ray showed lung infection which would probably clear up with treatment. He also suffered from attacks of pharyngitis. None of these facts was disclosed to the insurance company when the proposal was signed.
> *Held,* that these were material facts, and the company could avoid liability under the policy, for the assured as a reasonable man without any specialist knowledge, should have appreciated that he possessed knowledge of his health which was of materiality to the company.

5 Fifth Report of Law Reform Committee

In January 1957 the Law Reform Committee stated in their Fifth Report[11] that the practical effect of the law relating to non-disclosure was that insurers were

---

4 *Lindenau v Desborough* (1828) 8 B & C 586 at 592 (per Bayley J).

5 Ibid.

6 *Joel v Law Union and Crown Insurance Co* [1908] 2 KB 863 at 884, CA (per Fletcher Moulton LJ).

7 *Bates v Hewitt* (1867) LR 2 QB 595 at 608 (per Mellor J). See further, *Dalglish v Jarvie* (1850) 2 Mac & G 231 at 243 (per Rolfe B) (a case on the granting of an injunction); *Brownlie v Campbell* (1880) 5 App Cas 925 at 954 (per Lord Blackburn) (a case on the sale of land).

8 *Re Yager and Guardian Assurance Co* (1913) 108 LT 38 at 44 (per Channell J).

9 *Godfrey v Britannic Assurance Co Ltd* [1963] 2 Lloyd's Rep 515, QB (life insurance) at 529 (per Roskill J). The passage in the judgment of Megaw J in *Anglo-African Merchants Ltd v Bayley* [1970] 1 QB 311, [1969] 1 Lloyd's Rep 268, QBD (Commercial Court) (all risks insurance) where his Lordship said (ibid at 277): 'If however, the assured knew of facts, and if as a reasonable man he should have realized that knowledge of those facts might be—not necessarily would be, but might be—regarded as material by a normal prudent underwriter, then, if those facts are not disclosed and if they would have been material, the defence of non-disclosure prevails. The proposition may be more favourable to insurers than is indicated in that proposition. I am satisfied that it is no less favourable. It is an a fortiori case if the assured not merely ought as a reasonable man to have realized, but actually did realize, that the facts of which he had knowledge might be regarded as material.' would appear to be inconsistent with the principles set out in the text above.

10 [1963] 2 Lloyd's Rep 515, QB.

11 *Conditions and Exceptions in Insurance Policies,* 1957, Cmnd 62.

entitled to repudiate liability whenever they could show that a fact within the knowledge of the insured was not disclosed which, according to current insurance practice, would have affected the judgment of the risk.[12]

The Report then continued: 'Whether the insuring public at large is aware of this it is difficult to say; but it seems to us to follow from the accepted definition of materiality that a fact may be material to insurers, in the light of the great volume of experience of claims available to them, which would not appear to a proposer for insurance, however honest and careful, to be one which he ought to disclose.'[13]

The Committee recommended 'that for the purpose of any contract of insurance no fact should be deemed material unless it would be considered material by a reasonable insured'.[14]

6 Law Commission's proposals

In 1981 the Law Commission proposed that the assured's duty was to disclose a material fact which was known to him or which he could be assumed to know and which a reasonable man in his position would disclose to the insurers. The same duty would apply in the case of renewal of a policy. The Commission's proposals do not relate to marine, aviation and transport contracts nor to contracts of reinsurance.[15]

D MATERIALITY IS A QUESTION OF FACT

Whether a particular fact is material depends on the particular circumstances of the particular case. It does not necessarily follow that because a fact has been held to be immaterial in one case, a similar fact is not material in another. At the same time, similar circumstances may be assumed to be equally material or immaterial, whatever the nature of the insurance.

The question is one of fact[16] to be decided, if necessary, by a jury,[17] as representing reasonable men.[18]

---

12 *Conditions and Exceptions in Insurance Policies*, 1957, Cmnd 62, para 4.

13 Para 4.

14 Para 14. In *Lambert v Co-operative Insurance Society Ltd* [1975] 2 Lloyd's Rep 485, CA (all risks insurance) MacKenna J said (ibid, at 491): 'I would only add . . . the expression of my personal regret that the Committee's recommendation has not been implemented. The present case shows the unsatisfactory state of the law.'

15 See 'Insurance Law: Non-disclosure and Breach of Warranty'. (Cmnd 8064: Law Commission No 104).

16 *Yorkshire Insurance Co Ltd v Campbell* [1917] AC 218 (marine insurance) per Lord Sumner, at 221; *Scottish Shire Line Ltd v London and Provincial Marine and General Insurance Co Ltd* [1912] 3 KB 51 (marine insurance) per Hamilton J, at 70. As far as marine insurance is concerned, the Marine Insurance Act 1906, s 18(4), provides that: 'Whether any particular circumstance, which is not disclosed, be material or not is, in each, a question of fact.' But sometimes questions of law are involved on the facts as found: *Vance v Lowther* (1876) 1 ExD 176 (cheque) per Kelly CB, at 178, speaking of insurance.

17 *Hoare v Bremridge* (1872) 8 Ch App 22 (life insurance) per Lord Selborne LC, at 28: 'It has been also suggested in the course of the argument that in questions like this [i e concealment] on policies of insurance, the assured prefers a jury, and the office prefers a Judge . . . We are bound to take notice that, according to the ordinary course of law in this country, and having regard to the principles on which trial by jury is established, the jury is not only the most usual, but the most suitable and proper forum for the trial of questions of this description.' See also *Quin v*

E THE TIME WHEN MATERIALITY IS TO BE JUDGED

The materiality of a fact is determined by reference to the date at which it should, if at all, have been communicated to the insurers.[19]

If at that date the fact was material, its non-disclosure is a ground for avoiding the contract, notwithstanding that it afterwards turns out to be immaterial, or indeed untrue.[20] Thus, a fact such as a rumour[1] or suspicion[2] which proves unfounded, may be material for the purpose of the duty of disclosure.

On the other hand, the non-disclosure of a fact which was not at that date material, and which was, therefore, not a fact to which the duty of disclosure then attached, does not affect the validity of the policy, even though the fact afterwards becomes material and actually brings about the loss.[3]

F THE CLASSIFICATION OF MATERIAL FACTS

A Facts normally material

In general, it can be said that the following facts will usually be held to be material:

1 All facts suggesting that the subject-matter of insurance is exposed to more than ordinary danger from the peril insured against.
2 All facts suggesting that the proposed assured is actuated by some special motive.
3 All facts showing that the liability of the insurers might be greater than would normally be expected.
4 All facts relating to the 'moral hazard'.
5 All facts which to the knowledge of the proposed assured are regarded by the insurers as material.

1 Exposure to more than ordinary danger

All facts are material which suggest that the subject-matter of insurance, by

---

National Assurance Co (1839) Jo & Car 316 ExCh (fire insurance) per Joy CB, at 328. But the modern practice in insurance cases is to dispense with trial by jury except in a case of fraud.

18 *Joel v Law Union and Crown Insurance Co* [1908] 2 KB 863, CA (life insurance) per Fletcher Moulton LJ, at 884.

19 *Seaton v Burnand* [1900] AC 135 (solvency insurance) per Lord Halsbury LC, at 140; *Fracis, Times & Co v Sea Insurance Co Ltd* (1898) 3 Com Cas 229 (marine insurance) per Bigham J, at 235; *Lynch v Dunsford* (1811) 14 East 494, ExCh (marine insurance).

20 *De Costa v Scandret* (1723) 2 P Wms 170 (marine insurance); *Lynch v Dunsford* (supra) (marine insurance).

1 *Lynch v Dunsford* (supra) (marine insurance).

2 *Seaman v Fonereau* (1743) 2 Stra 1183 (marine insurance); *Leigh v Adams* (1871) 25 LT 566 (marine insurance). But if the facts are disclosed, apprehensions based on the facts need not be disclosed: *Bell v Bell* (1810) 2 Camp 475 (marine insurance).

3 *Watson v Mainwaring* (1813) 4 Taunt 763 (life insurance), where the proposed assured was suffering and ultimately died of a disease which was not generally a 'disorder tending to shorten life' within the meaning of the proposal; *Associated Oil Carriers Ltd v Union Insurance Society of Canton Ltd* [1917] 2 KB 184 (marine insurance).

reason of its nature,[4] condition,[5] user,[6] surroundings,[7] or other circumstances,[8] is exposed to more than ordinary danger from the peril insured against.

Thus, where a car is insured against fire, the structure and locality of the garage may be material as affecting the chances of fire or the chance of fire being extinguished.[9] Further, in the case of merchandise insured against fire, it may be material that a portion of the building, in which it is stored, is used as a kitchen.[10]

In particular, the following facts have been held to be material in the case of a

---

4 Contrast, for instance, *Biggar v Rock Life Assurance Co* [1902] 1 KB 516 (accident insurance), where the proposed assured was described as a tea-traveller, and the omission to state that he was also a publican was held fatal, with *Perrins v Marine and General Travellers' Insurance Society* (1859) 2 E & E 317, ExCh, where the omission to state that an esquire was also an ironmonger had no effect, the rate of premium being the same for esquires and ironmongers; and cf *Holdsworth v Lancashire and Yorkshire Insurance Co* (1907) 23 TLR 521 (employers' liability insurance), where there was a waiver.

5 *Santer v Poland* (1924) 19 LlL Rep 29, where the date of manufacture of a motor car was held material; *Russell v Thornton* (1860) 6 H & N 140, ExCh (marine insurance), where the fact not disclosed was that the ship had been aground; *Geach v Ingall* (1845) 14 M & W 95 (life insurance); *Yorke v Yorkshire Insurance Co* [1918] 1 KB 662 (life insurance). In *Boyd v Dubois* (1811) 3 Camp 133 (marine insurance) the policy was held not to be vitiated by the non-disclosure of the fact that the goods insured had been so damaged as to be in danger of spontaneous combustion, the loss which actually took place being unconnected with their condition; but this decision was doubted in *Carr v Montefiore* (1864) 5 B & S 408 (marine insurance) per Cockburn CJ, at 425, and was disapproved in *Greenhill v Federal Insurance Co* [1927] 1 KB 65, 24 LlL Rep 383, CA (marine insurance); *Taylor v London Assurance Corpn* [1934] OR 273, where non-disclosure that the property was already in peril entitled the insurers to avoid the policy; *Anglo-African Merchants Ltd v Bayley* [1970] 1 QB 311, [1969] 1 Lloyd's Rep 268 (all risks insurance), where the assured had failed to state that some leather jerkins which he described as 'new' were war surplus goods and 20 years old, and these were held to be material facts, and, since they had not been disclosed, the policy could be avoided by the insurers. Megaw J observed (ibid, at 277): 'In relation to the fact of war surplus I am satisfied that underwriters, rightly or wrongly, but not unreasonably, regard war surplus goods, or at any rate war surplus clothing, as being goods which they classify as "hot"; that is, involving an abnormally high risk of theft. In relation to the age of the goods, underwriters would normally and reasonably be concerned with the possibility of defects, such as staining, in respect of which claims might be made and it might be a matter of great difficulty and dispute to ascertain when the damage was in fact sustained; unless, of course, a pre-insurance inspection were to be required as a condition of accepting the risk.'

6 Cf *Quin v National Assurance Co* (1839) Jo & Car 316, ExCh (fire insurance), where a building was described as a dwellinghouse occupied by a caretaker, whereas it was an unfinished house in charge of a carpenter who was engaged on work there.

7 *Bufe v Turner* (1815) 6 Taunt 338 (fire insurance). In *Versicherungs und Transport AG Daugava v Henderson* (1934) 48 LlL Rep 54, Roche J, at 58, without deciding the point, indicated that in an insurance on a building, disclosure of its contents would be material where otherwise the insurers might be under the apprehension that it was empty. Cf *A F Watkinson & Co Ltd v Hullett* (1938) 61 LlL Rep 145 (fire insurance), where there was a large stock of waste paper in the building of an insured who described himself as dealing in paper-boards.

8 Hence, the existence and the contents of a letter which would put the insurers on inquiry are material facts: *Bridges v Hunter* (1813) 1 M & S 15 (marine insurance); *Elton v Larkins* (1832) 8 Bing 198 (marine insurance).

9 *Dawsons Ltd v Bonnin* [1922] 2 AC 413, 12 LlL Rep 237 (motor insurance) per Lord Finlay, at 429. But if the risk of fire in the garage is insignificant in comparison with the other risks insured, these facts are not material: ibid. In *Johnson and Perott Ltd v Holmes* (1925) 21 LlL Rep 330, it was held not to be material to disclose to the insurer that, at the time of and prior to the insurance being effected, the garage in which the motor car was kept was being used by the Irish Republican Army.

10 *Barsalou v Royal Insurance Co* (1864) 15 ILR 3.

fire insurance policy: that a fire had broken out in an adjacent building, although it had been extinguished a few hours before the assured sent the instructions to his agent to effect the insurance;[11] that threats have been made to destroy the property;[12] or that the assured had reason to suspect that an attempt to do so will be made.[13]

2 Special motive of the assured

All facts are material which suggest that the proposed assured, in effecting the insurance, is actuated by some special motive, and not merely by ordinary prudence.[14] Thus, in an insurance upon property, it is material that the subject-matter is so greatly overvalued as to make the risk speculative.[15]

3 Greater liability of insurers

Facts which show that, in the circumstances, the liability of the insurers may be greater than would naturally be expected under an insurance of the property in question, are usually material.[16]

Thus, it is material, in a retrospective insurance, that the subject-matter is already destroyed;[17] or, under a special insurance, binding the insurers to reinstate the machinery insured, that the machinery is second-hand, seeing that the cost of reinstatement will be proportionately greater.[18]

In the case of goods entrusted to a carrier, it may be a material fact that the assured has entered into a special contract, by which the carrier is relieved from his Common Law liability.[19]

---

11 *Bufe v Turner* (1815) 6 Taunt 338.

12 *Greet v Citizens' Insurance Co* (1880) 5 AR 596, CA; cf *Kelly v Hochelaga Fire Insurance Co* (1886) 24 LCJ 298, where no importance was attached to the threats; and cf *Leen v Hall* (1923) 16 LlL Rep 100, where the fact that a house in Ireland had been occupied by forces of the Crown was held to be immaterial, having regard to the political conditions then prevailing; *Gabel v Howick Farmers' Mutual Fire Insurance Co* (1917) 40 OLR 158.

13 *Campbell v Victoria Mutual Fire Insurance Co* (1880) 45 UCR 412, where threats of personal violence by a discharged employee led the assured to suspect that his property might be burned, and hence he insured it; *Watt v Union Insurance Co* (1884) 5 NSWLR 48; *Herbert v Mercantile Fire Insurance Co* (1878) 43 UCR 384, where a question on the subject was asked. If he has any reason to suspect the conduct of the person in whose charge or under whose control the subject-matter of insurance may be, it is his duty to disclose his suspicions: *Milcher v Kingwilliamstown Fire and Marine Insurance Co* (1883) 3 Buchanan (East Dist Ct Cape) 271, where the person who had charge of the goods insured was, to the knowledge of the assured, fraudulently making away with his property.

14 *Bufe v Turner* (1815) 6 Taunt 338 (fire insurance).

15 *Hoff Trading Co v Union Insurance Society of Canton Ltd* (1929) 45 TLR 466, 34 LlL Rep 81, CA (marine insurance), where the assured failed to disclose that the value stated was speculative; *Ionides v Pender* (1874) LR 9 QB 531 (marine insurance), where Blackburn J, at 539, points out that over-valuation tends to make the assured less careful, though he does not base his judgment on that ground; *Thames and Mersey Marine Insurance Co v Gunford Ship Co* [1911] AC 529 (marine insurance), where there were several policies; cf *Canadian Bank of Commerce v Wawanesa Mutual Insurance Co* [1924] 3 WWR 822.

16 Hence, the intention of the insurers must be drawn to any unusual risk which may, in terms, fall within the policy: *T Cheshire & Co v Thompson* (1919) 35 TLR 317, CA (marine insurance).

17 *Mead v Davison* (1835) 3 Ad & El 303 (marine insurance) per Lord Denman CJ, at 308.

18 *Hewitt Bros v Wilson* [1915] 2 KB 739, CA (marine insurance). As to reinstatement, see Chapter 45.

19 *Tate v Hyslop* (1885) 15 QBD 368, CA (marine insurance), where the insurers, to the assured's knowledge, charged a higher premium in such a case; cf *Charlesworth v Faber* (1900)

Again, it has been held in the case of an 'all risks' policy in respect of pictures and objets d'art stored at the assured's office that it was a material fact that the premises would be left unoccupied except during business hours.[20]

4 'Moral hazard'

All facts are material which suggest that the proposed assured, by reason of his previous experience in matters relevant to the insurance, is not a person whose proposal can be accepted in the ordinary course of business and without special consideration.

This is sometimes known as the 'moral hazard', and has perhaps been best defined by Slesser LJ, in the following words:[1]

> 'It is elementary that one of the matters to be considered by an insurance company is entering into contractual relations with a proposed assured is the question of the moral integrity of the proposer—what has been called the moral hazard.'

Thus, it is material that the proposed assured has suffered loss in the past from the peril to be insured against,[2] or that other insurers have refused to grant[3] or to renew[4] an insurance similar to the insurance proposed.

---

5 Com Cas 408 (marine insurance) where there was an unusual clause; and cf *Marten v Nippon Sea and Land Insurance Co Ltd* (1898) 3 Com Cas 164 (marine insurance), where the contract was in the usual form.

20 *Haase v Evans* (1934) 48 LlL Rep 131 (all risks insurance).

1 *Locker and Woolf Ltd v Western Australian Insurance Co Ltd* [1936] 1 KB 408, 54 LlL Rep 211, CA (fire insurance) at 414. See further, *Roselodge Ltd (formerly Rose Diamond Products Ltd) v Castle* [1966] 2 Lloyd's Rep 113 (jewellers' block policy), where McNair J said (at 132): 'Each of these witnesses was emphatic in the view that in a jewellery insurance of this kind the moral hazard is important. Mr Archer defined the moral hazard as the risk of honesty and integrity of the assured, and in the case of a company, the honesty and integrity of any executives or key personnel (though I think he meant the risk of dishonesty and lack of integrity). The moral hazard he considered of particular importance in the case of jewellery insurance, "because of the smallness and little weight of the jewellery and because in jewellery insurance there is often a lack of documentation and jewellery is very easily disposed of". This seems to me to be a reasonable view.'

2 *Rozanes v Brown* (1928) 32 LlL Rep 98, CA (burglary insurance) per Scrutton LJ speaking of fire insurance; *Becker v Marshall* (1922) 12 LlL Rep 413, CA (burglary insurance), explained in *Ewer v National Employers' Mutual General Insurance Association Ltd* [1937] 2 All ER 193, 57 LlL Rep 172 (burglary insurance) per MacKinnon J, at 200: '[That case] is no authority for the very wide and disastrously general proposition, that one who is proposing insurance upon any subject-matter must reveal the fact that he has had during the previous course of his life claims on other policies, and other policies of every kind'; *Farra v Hetherington* (1931) 47 TLR 465, 40 LlL Rep 132 (motor insurance); *Krantz v Allan and Faber* (1921) 9 LlL Rep 410 (burglary insurance); *Morser v Eagle Star and British Dominions Insurance Co Ltd* (1931) 40 LlL Rep 254 (jewellery insurance); *Dworkin v Globe Indemnity Co of Canada* (1921) 51 OLR 159 (burglary insurance); *Simon, Haynes, Barlas and Ireland v Beer* (1946) 78 LlL Rep 337 (solicitor's indemnity insurance); *O'Keefe v London and Edinburgh Insurance Co Ltd* [1928] NI 85; *Western Assurance Co v Harrison* (1903) 33 SCR 473 where, by the condition, the question of materiality was left to the Court; cf *Anglo-American Fire Insurance Co v Hendry and Gault Bros Co* (1913) 48 SCR 577.

3 *Glicksman v Lancashire and General Assurance Co* [1925] 2 KB 593, 22 LlL Rep 179, CA; affd [1927] AC 139, 26 LlL Rep 69 (burglary insurance) per Sargant LJ, at 611 (speaking of fire insurance). But the materiality might depend upon the reason for the insurers' refusal, e g if they declined because they had a heavy insurance on adjoining property, this refusal would hardly affect the minds of other insurers who had no such insurance. In practice, questions are usually asked on these points. See also *Locker and Woolf Ltd v Western Australian Insurance Co Ltd* [1936] 1 KB 408, 54 LlL Rep 211, CA (fire insurance), where the non-disclosure was of a previous

In the case of motor insurance the previous convictions of the assured in respect of motoring offences are material.[5] So also is it material that the insured under a burglary policy[6] and a marine insurance policy[7] has a criminal record.

The fact that the insured's husband has previous convictions for receiving stolen goods and for theft has been held to be material in the case of an 'all risks' policy on jewellery.[8]

In the case of insurance on profits the fact that the assured is trading at a loss should be disclosed.[9]

In certain circumstances, the nationality[10] of the assured may be material, or even his name.[11]

---

refusal to insure the motor vehicles of the assured; *Haase v Evans* (1934), 48 LlL Rep 131 (all risks insurance), where the company had refused to insure the plaintiff's premises against burglary and theft, and this fact was not disclosed.

4 *Taylor v Yorkshire Insurance Co* [1913] 2 IR 1 (livestock insurance); *Re Yager and Guardian Assurance Co* (1912) 108 LT 38 (fire insurance); cf *Biggar v Rock Life Assurance Co* [1902] 1 KB 516 (accident insurance) per Wright J, at 523; *Holt's Motors Ltd v South-East Lancashire Insurance Co Ltd* (1930) 35 Com Cas 281, CA (motor insurance), where the insurers had intimated that they could not invite renewal. See also, *Fine v General Accident Fire and Life Assurance Corpn* [1915] App D 213, where the previous policy had been cancelled; *Claude R Ogden & Co Pty Ltd v Reliance Fire Sprinkler Co Pty Ltd* [1975] 1 Lloyd's Rep 52, Supreme Ct of Australia (public and products liability insurance).

5 *Jester-Barnes v Licenses and General Insurance Co Ltd* (1934) 49 LlL Rep 231 (motor insurance). See further, p 147, post.

6 *Schoolman v Hall* [1951] 1 Lloyd's Rep 139 (burglary insurance); *Woolcott v Sun Alliance and London Insurance Ltd* [1978] 1 All ER 1253, [1978] 1 Lloyd's Rep 629 (fire insurance), where the insured did not disclose a previous conviction for robbery; *Woolcott v Excess Insurance Co Ltd and Miles, Smith, Anderson and Game, Ltd* [1978] 1 Lloyd's Rep 633 (fire insurance), where the insured's criminal record was known to the brokers employed by the insurers. But a new trial was subsequently ordered: [1979] 1 Lloyd's Rep 231, CA. At the new trial it was proved that the brokers knew of the criminal record, and had failed to pass on this information to the insurers: *Woolcott v Excess Insurance Co Ltd and Miles, Smith, Anderson and Game Ltd (No 2)* [1979] 2 Lloyd's Rep 210. (See the judgment of Cantley J, ibid, at 216.) In *Alliance Insurance Co of Philadelphia v Laurentian Colonies and Hotels Ltd* [1953] Que QB 241 (fire insurance) the fact that a director of a company insuring a building against fire had not disclosed that in 1933 he had been convicted of living off the proceeds of prostitution and had been sentenced to five years' imprisonment was not material. The Court held that no disclosure was needed on the ground that his conviction would not seem to increase the risk of a fire loss. The decision was based on the interpretation of Article 2485 of the Civil Code, which states that: 'The insured is obliged to represent to the insurer fully and fairly every fact which shows the nature and extent of the risk, and which may prevent the undertaking of it or affect the rate of premium'; *Roselodge Ltd (formerly Rose Diamond Products Ltd) v Castle* [1966] 2 Lloyd's Rep 113 (jeweller's block policy), where it was held that the fact that the principal director of the insured company had in 1946 been convicted of bribing a police officer and fined £75 was not a material one: ibid, at 132. But the fact that the company's sales manager had been convicted in 1956 of smuggling diamonds into the United States was a material one: ibid, at 133. In *Reynolds and Anderson v Phoenix Assurance Co Ltd* [1978] 2 Lloyd's Rep 440 (fire insurance) the insurers failed to prove that a conviction of the insured 11 years earlier of receiving stolen goods was material. (See the judgment of Forbes J, ibid, at 461.)

7 *Allden v Raven, The Kylie* [1983] 2 Lloyd's Rep 444 (marine insurance).

8 *Lambert v Co-operative Insurance Society Ltd* [1975] 2 Lloyd's Rep 485, CA (all risks insurance).

9 *Stavers v Mountain* (1912) Times, 27 July, CA.

10 *The Spathari*, 1925 SC (HL) 6 (marine insurance); *Horne v Poland*, [1922] 2 KB 364, 10 LlL Rep 175, 275 (burglary insurance); *Becker v Marshall* (1922) 12 LlL Rep 413, CA (burglary insurance); *Lyons v J W Bentley Ltd* (1944) 77 LlL Rep 335 (burglary insurance) per Lewis J at 337. See further, 150, post.

11 *McCormick v National Motor and Accident Insurance Union Ltd* (1934) 49 LlL Rep 361, CA (accident insurance); *Gallé Gowns Ltd v Licenses and General Insurance Co Ltd* (1933) 47 LlL Rep 186.

Again, in the case of a trader's combined insurance policy it has been held that the insurer could avoid liability where the fact that a director of the insured company had been convicted of handling stolen property prior to the renewal of the policy was not disclosed.[12]

But the proposer need not disclose previous convictions which are 'spent'.[13]

It has been suggested that a proposer should disclose the fact of his arrest, charge and committal for trial even though in truth he was innocent but this would appear doubtful.[14]

5 Facts regarded as material by the insurers

All facts are material which are, to the knowledge of the proposed assured,[15] regarded by the insurers as material.[16]

The opinion of the insurers that a fact is material may be shown by a difference in the rate of premium charged according as the fact is present or absent.[17] In practice, however, it is usually shown by the asking of a specific question.[18]

B Facts not normally material

Facts which do not affect the risk are not material facts, and need not be disclosed.[19]

Thus, it has been held not to be a material fact that at the time of the proposal a similar insurance is in force;[20] or that the proposed insurance is a reinsurance,[1] in which case it is equally immaterial that the original premium is lower.[2]

---

12 *March Cabaret Club and Casino Ltd v London Assurance* [1975] 1 Lloyd's Rep 169, QBD. (See the judgment of May J, ibid, at 176.)

13 Rehabilitation of Offenders Act 1974, s 4. See pp 141–142, post.

14 *March Cabaret Club and Casino Ltd v London Assurance* [1975] 1 Lloyd's Rep 169 (trader's combined insurance) per May J, at 177. Cf *Reynolds and Anderson v Phoenix Assurance Co Ltd* [1978] 2 Lloyd's Rep 440 (fire insurance) per Forbes J, at 461.

15 This is essential. A mere private resolution of the insurers that the fact was to be treated as material would not be sufficient: *Tate v Hyslop* (1885) 15 QBD 368, CA (marine insurance) per Brett MR, at 376. See also *Holmes v Cornhill Insurance Co Ltd* (1949) 82 LlL Rep 575 (motor insurance), where it was proved that the proposer was aware the insurance company would not insure bookmakers, and concealed the fact that he was one.

16 *Glicksman v Lancashire and General Assurance Co* [1927] AC 139, 26 LlL Rep 69, HL (burglary insurance).

17 *Tate v Hyslop* (supra) (marine insurance) distinguished in *The Bedouin* [1894] P 1, CA (marine insurance).

18 See pp 164–166, post.

19 *Seaton v Burnand* [1900] AC 135 (solvency insurance), where it was held that the facts affecting the solvency of the principal debtor were immaterial; *Dawsons Ltd v Bonnin* [1922] 2 AC 413, 12 LlL Rep 237 (motor insurance), where on an insurance of a lorry covering third party risks and fire, the situation of the garage was held to be immaterial, having regard to the fact that the chief risks covered were, in the main, wholly unconnected with fire at the garage; *Turnbull & Co v Scottish Provident Institution* 1896 34 Sc LR 146 (life insurance) where, in an insurance by a principal on the life of his agent, it was held that the principal was not bound to disclose the fact that, before the date of the policy, the agent had given notice to terminate the agency at a date subsequent to the date of the policy.

20 *McDonnell v Beacon Fire and Life Assurance Co* (1858) 7 CP 308 (fire insurance); cf *Sibbald v Hill* (1814) 2 Dow 263, HL (marine insurance) per Lord Eldon LC, at 266.

1 *Crowley v Cohen* (1832) 3 B & Ad 478 (transit insurance) per Patteson J, at 488; *Mackenzie v Whitworth* (1875) 1 ExD 36, CA (marine insurance) per Blackburn J, at 41; *London and North Western Rly Co v Glyn* (1859) 1 E & E 652 (fire insurance) per Crompton J, at 664.

Similarly, in the case of a personal accident policy, it has been held not to be a material fact that a person described as an 'esquire' was also an ironmonger, the rates of premium of both being the same.[3]

In the case of an insurance on property, it is not a material fact that the proposed assured is not the owner of the property proposed to be insured,[4] but is only a mortgagor or mortgagee;[5] or even that his interest is merely that of a bailee.[6] Nor is it material that he has entered into a contract with a third person by which, in the event of the property proposed to be insured being lost or injured by such person, his right of action is restricted.[7] Further, in the case of motor insurance, it has been held not material that the assured had not had a driving licence for some years.[8]

Any such fact may, however, become material if made the subject of a specific question.[9]

It is further to be noted that facts are material, not in the abstract, but only as bearing upon the particular insurance proposed. The fact, therefore, which may be regarded as material in the ordinary course of insurance business, may be, in the special circumstances of the case, immaterial, e g where the fact lessens the risk, or falls within a condition or exception in the policy, or where the insurers waive its disclosure, or elect to make inquiries themselves.[10]

G FACTS WHICH NEED NOT BE DISCLOSED

Facts which would, in ordinary circumstances, be material, may become immaterial in the special circumstances of the case; and the assured is then under no obligation to disclose them.[11] Facts which may thus become immaterial may be grouped under the following classes:

1 Facts which are known to the insurers or which they may reasonably be presumed to know.
2 Facts which they could have discovered by making inquiry.
3 Facts as to which they waive information.
4 Facts tending to lessen the risk.

---

2 *Glasgow Assurance Corpn Ltd v William Symondson & Co* (1911) 16 Com Cas 109 (marine insurance) per Scrutton J, at 119.

3 *Perrins v Marine and General Travellers' Insurance Society* (1859) 2 E & E 317 (personal accident insurance).

4 *Crowley v Cohen* (supra), where there was an insurance upon canal boats; *MacKenzie v Whitworth* (1875) 1 ExD 36 at 41, Ex Ch (marine insurance); cf *James v British General Insurance Co Ltd* [1927] 2 KB 311, 27 LlL Rep 328 (motor insurance).

5 *Ogden v Montreal Insurance Co* (1853) 3 CP 497, where the mortgagor in insuring on behalf of the mortgagee omitted to state the amount of the mortgage; *Reesor v Provincial Insurance Co* (1873) 33 UCR 357, where it was held immaterial that the mortgagee was insuring on behalf of the mortgagor; *Fritzley v Germania Farmers' Mutual Fire Insurance Co* (1909) 19 OLR 49, where a mortgage was not disclosed; *Ocean Accident and Guarantee Corpn v Williams* (1915) 34 NZLR 924.

6 *London and North Western Rly Co v Glyn* (1859) 1 E & E 652 (fire insurance) per Crompton J, at 664.

7 *Tate v Hyslop* (1885) 15 QBD 368, CA (marine insurance) per Brett MR, at 375. It is otherwise where the proposed assured knows that the insurers regard the existence of such a contract as material, and vary the rate of premium accordingly: ibid.

8 *Corcos v De Rougemont* (1925) 23 LlL Rep 164 (motor insurance).

9 See pp 164–166, post.

10 See pp 137–142, post.

11 *The Bedouin* [1894] P 1, CA (marine insurance) per Lord Esher MR, at 12.

5 Facts the disclosure of which is unnecessary by reason of a condition.
6 Facts concerning 'spent' convictions.

1 Facts within actual or presumed knowledge of insurer

(a) Actual knowledge

'There are many matters as to which the insured may be innocently silent—he need not mention what the underwriter knows—*Scientia utrinque par pares contrahentes facit*. An underwriter cannot insist that the policy is void because the insured did not tell him what he actually knew; what way soever he come to the knowledge.'[12]

So where the secretary of an insurance company, which had guaranteed the solvency of a third party, knew that he was in financial difficulties, it was held that the company could not avoid liability on the ground that the insured had not disclosed this fact.[13]

As far as marine insurance is concerned, the Marine Insurance Act 1906, s 18(3), provides:

> 'In the absence of inquiry the following circumstances need not be disclosed, namely:— . . . (b) any circumstance which is known . . . to the insurer . . .'

Thus, where the underwriters knew of the age, type, condition and agreed value of a ketch, and the intended manner in which she was going to be laid up, it was not material for the assured to describe the neglected state of her topsides caulking.[14]

It is sufficient if the matter is known by the insurance company's agent.[15] Thus, in *Pimm v Lewis*[16]

> A water corn-mill was insured under a fire policy. Rice chaff which was more inflammable than pollard (i e the finer part of the husk of corn) was used in the mill, but this was not disclosed to the insurance company. The company's agent resided in the neighbourhood and knew the mill well, and looked at the premises when the proposal was made.
> *Held*, there was no duty to disclose that rice chaff was ground at the mill, for this fact was deemed to be known to the company through its agent.

(b) Presumed knowledge

'[The insured] is not bound to communicate facts or circumstances which are within the ordinary professional knowledge of an underwriter. He is not bound

---

12 *Carter v Boehm* (1766) 3 Burr 1905 at 1910 (per Lord Mansfield).

13 *Anglo-Californian Bank Ltd v London and Provincial Marine and General Insurance Co Ltd* (1904) 10 Com Cas 1.

14 *St Margaret's Trust Ltd v Navigators and General Insurance Co Ltd* (1949) 82 LlL Rep 752 (marine insurance); cf *Piper v Royal Exchange Assurance* (1932) 44 LlL Rep 103 (marine insurance), where it was not shown that the insurers knew of any facts material to the value of the yacht. See also *Bonney v Cornhill Insurance Co Ltd* (1931) 40 LlL Rep 39 (motor insurance), where the insurer knew that the motor coach was subject to a hire-purchase agreement.

15 *Pimm v Lewis* (1862) 2 F & F 778 (fire insurance); *Woolcott v Excess Insurance Co Ltd and Miles, Smith, Anderson and Game Ltd* [1978] 1 Lloyd's Rep 633 (fire insurance) where the brokers employed by the insurers knew of the insured's criminal record. (See the judgment of Caulfield J, ibid, at 638). But a new trial was subsequently ordered: [1979] 1 Lloyd's Rep 231, CA. At the new trial it was proved that the brokers knew of the criminal record, and had failed to pass on this information to the insurers: *Woolcott v Excess Insurance Co Ltd and Miles, Smith, Anderson and Game Ltd (No 2)* [1979] 2 Lloyd's Rep 210. (See the judgment of Cantley J, ibid, at 216.)

16 Supra.

to communicate facts relating to the general course of a particular trade;[17] because all these things are supposed to be within the knowledge of the person carrying on the business of insurance, and which, therefore, it is not necessary for him to be specially informed of.'[18]

In *Hales v Reliance Fire and Accident Insurance Corpn Ltd:*[19]

> A retail shopkeeper had taken out a policy against loss or damage to his shop due to fire or explosion. The business consisted of grocery, provisions, newspapers, tobacco and confectionery. For a period round Guy Fawkes Day substantial quantities of fireworks were kept on the premises in a tin box, and not in a place of safety, as required by the Explosives Act 1875. *Held,* there was no obligation in this class of insurance to disclose to the underwriters that fireworks would be, or might be on the premises during this short season, for this was a matter which the underwriters must be taken to have known.[20]

'[The underwriter] needs not to be told general topics of speculation: as for instance—the underwriter is bound to know every cause which may occasion natural perils; as, the difficulty of the voyage—the kind of seasons—the probability of lightning, hurricanes, earthquakes, etc. He is bound to know every cause which may occasion political perils; from the ruptures of States from war, and the various operations of it. He is bound to know the probability of safety, from the continuance or return of peace; from the imbecility of the enemy, through the weakness of their counsels or their want of strength, etc.'[1]

'It is also true that when a fact is one of public notoriety, as of war . . . the party proposing the insurance is not bound to communicate what he is fully warranted in assuming the underwriter already knows.'[2]

Thus, in *Leen v Hall*[3] a castle in County Kerry in Ireland was insured against damage from riot, civil commotion, war, rebellion and fire. It was destroyed in May 1921 by members of the Irish Republican Army during the troubles of that year. In an action on the policy the insurer pleaded that the insured had not disclosed that the castle had been occupied for short periods during that year by Crown Forces, and that it had been used by them for the detention of Sinn Fein prisoners. The jury found that it was not material to communicate these facts, presumably because they considered that they were common knowledge.

The insured is not bound to tell the underwriter what the law is.[4]

---

17 *Vallance v Dewar* (1808) 1 Camp 503 (marine insurance); *Charlesworth v Faber* (1900) 5 Com Cas 408. Where there are two conflicting usages, both equally well known, and the assured has, before insuring, decided which usage to follow, or contracted in accordance with one of them, it is his duty to disclose the fact, provided that it is otherwise material: *Tate v Hyslop* (1885) 15 QBD 368, CA (marine insurance), In *Tate v Hyslop* the alleged practice was held not to be general. If the insurers do not know the practice, it is their duty to inquire: *Noble v Kennoway* (1780) 2 Doug KB 510 (marine insurance) per Lord Mansfield CJ, at 512.

18 *Bates v Hewitt* (1867) LR 2 QB 595 at 611 (per Shee J).

19 [1960] 2 Lloyd's Rep 391.

20 But McNair J said that he was far from saying that he would not feel that it was a material fact to disclose that the fireworks were not kept as required by law in a secure place. It was quite clear that if it had been disclosed that fireworks were being stored in the shop under conditions not permitted by law (that would normally be a matter which would have to be disclosed), it clearly, he would have thought, would have resulted in the fireworks being properly protected, in which event it was extremely unlikely that the fire in question would ever have occurred.

1 *Carter v Boehm* (1766) 3 Burr 1905 at 1910 (per Lord Mansfield).

2 *Bates v Hewitt* (1867) LR 2 QB 595 at 605.

3 (1923) 16 LlL Rep 100, KB.

4 *The Bedouin* [1894] P 1 at 12 (per Lord Esher MR).

As far as marine insurance is concerned, the Marine Insurance Act 1906, s 18(3), states:

> 'In the absence of inquiry the following circumstances need not be disclosed, namely:—. . . (b) any circumstance which is . . . presumed to be known to the insurer. The insurer is presumed to know matters of common notoriety or knowledge, and matters which an insurer in the ordinary course of his business, as such, ought to know.'[5]

2 Facts within constructive knowledge of insurer

Actual knowledge is not essential if the insurer knew that he had the means of knowing the fact. If, for example, he knew that he could learn at Lloyd's the exact cargo which had been shipped, and chose not to ascertain it, it would be considered to be within his knowledge.[6]

If the insurer chooses to neglect the information which he receives, he cannot take advantage of his wilful blindness or negligence. If he shuts his eyes to the light, it is his own fault provided sufficient information, as far as the insured is concerned, has been placed at his disposal,[7] but the insured is still under a duty to communicate a material fact which is known to him, even though the underwriter might 'by an effort of memory and of reasoning applied to the information actually communicated' have arrived at the knowledge of the material fact concerned.[8]

3 Facts as to which information is waived

This is a principle which applies to all branches of insurance,[9] and as far as marine insurance is concerned the Marine Insurance Act 1906, s 18(3), states:

> 'In the absence of inquiry the following circumstances need not be disclosed, namely:—. . . (c) any circumstance as to which information is waived by the insurer.'[10]

But omission to make inquiry is no waiver, if the insurers are not put on inquiry.[11] Waiver is not to be easily presumed.[12]

---

5 See further, Ivamy *Marine Insurance* (4th Edn 1985), pp 46–50.

6 *Foley v Tabor* (1861) 2 F & F 663 at 672 (per Erle CJ).

7 *Bates v Hewitt* (1867) LR 2 QB 595 at 605 (per Cockburn CJ).

8 Ibid, at 609 (per Mellor J).

9 *Carter v Boehm* (1766) 3 Burr 1905 (marine insurance). The same principle applies in the case of facts as to which the assured may reasonably infer that the insurers are indifferent: *Laing v Union Marine Insurance Co Ltd* (1895) 1 Com Cas 11 (marine insurance) per Mathew J, at 15.

10 See further, Ivamy *Marine Insurance* (4th Edn 1985), pp 50–53.

11 *Greenhill v Federal Insurance Co Ltd* [1927] 1 KB 65, 24 LlL Rep 383, CA (marine insurance).

12 Ibid, per Scrutton LJ, at 85. For a case where the insurers were held to have waived disclosure of material facts regarding an old battleship being towed across the North Sea to a shipbreaker's yard, see *G Cohen, Sons & Co v Standard Marine Insurance Co Ltd* (1925) 21 LlL Rep 30 (marine insurance); *Greenhill v Federal Insurance Co* (supra), where it was held that the insurers had not waived disclosure as to the circumstances of the previous history of the cargo of celluloid before it was shipped; *Mann, Macneal and Steeves, Ltd v Capital and Counties Insurance Co Ltd* [1921] 2 KB 300, 5 LlL Rep 203, 424, CA (marine insurance), where the insurers were held to have waived disclosure by not making inquiry as to the nature of the cargo to be carried on board the insured vessel which was a wooden one, viz 100,000 gallons of petrol in 2,500 drums; *Anglo-African Merchants Ltd v Bayley* [1970] 1 QB 311, [1969] 1 Lloyd's Rep 268 (all risks insurance), where it was held that a normally prudent insurer would not have been put on inquiry as to the precise nature of some leather jerkins, viz that they were war surplus and 20 years old by reason of seeing them described as 'New Men's Clothes in Bales for Export'. Consequently the plea that the insurers, by failing to make inquiry as to the precise nature of the goods, had waived further

4 Facts tending to lessen the risk

In *Carter v Boehm*[13] Lord Mansfield illustrated this point when he said:[14]

> 'The underwriter needs not be told what lessens the risque agreed and understood to be run by the express terms of the policy . . . If he insures for three years, he need not be told any circumstance to shew it may be over in two; or if he insures a voyage, with liberty of deviation, he needs not be told what tends to shew there will be no deviation.'

As far as marine insurance is concerned, the Marine Insurance Act 1906, s 18(3), states:

> 'In the absence of inquiry, the following circumstances need not be disclosed, namely:— . . . (a) any circumstance which diminishes the risk.'

5 Facts the disclosure of which is unnecessary by reason of a condition

This principle applies whether the condition concerned is an express or implied one.[15]

As far as marine insurance is concerned, the Marine Insurance Act 1906, s 18(3), states:

> 'In the absence of inquiry, the following circumstances need not be disclosed, namely:— . . . (d) any circumstance which it is superfluous to disclose by reason of any express or implied warranty.'[16]

6 Facts relating to 'spent' convictions

After a certain length of time convictions are regarded as 'spent'.[17] But where a person is convicted and a specified type of sentence is imposed e g a sentence of imprisonment for a term exceeding 30 months or a sentence of detention during Her Majesty's pleasure, the conviction can never count as a 'spent' one.[18]

Where a question seeking information with respect to a person's previous convictions is put to him, the question must be treated as not relating to spent convictions or any circumstances ancillary to spent convictions and the answer

---

information, failed (see the judgment of Megaw J, ibid, at 279); *Arterial Caravans Ltd v Yorkshire Insurance Co Ltd* [1973] 1 Lloyd's Rep 169, QBD (fire insurance), where it was held that the insurers had not waived the insured's duty to disclose a previous loss by fire. (See the judgment of Chapman J, ibid, at 181); *Allden v Raven, The Kylie* [1983] 2 Lloyd's Rep 444 (marine insurance), where it was held that there had been no waiver of the assured's duty to disclose previous convictions (see the judgment of Parker J, ibid, at 448); *Container Transport International Inc v Oceanus Mutual Underwriting Association (Bermuda) Ltd* [1984] 1 Lloyd's Rep 476, CA (marine insurance), where the insurers were held not to have waived the non-disclosure of a claims record and a refusal by other insurers to renew a policy. (See the judgment of Kerr LJ, ibid, at 501; and that of Stephenson LJ, ibid, at 529.)

13 (1766) 3 Burr 1905.

14 Ibid, at 1910.

15 *Ross v Bradshaw* (1760) 1 Wm Bl 312 (life insurance) per Lord Mansfield CJ, at 313; *Wood v Dwarris* (1856) 11 Exch 493 (life insurance), where the policy was indisputable except in case of fraud. As to what constitutes a 'condition', see pp 277–283, post.

16 *Haywood v Rodgers* (1804) 4 East 590 (marine insurance), where it was held in view of the implied warranty of seaworthiness in a voyage policy it was unnecessary, in the absence of inquiry, to disclose the facts relating to the seaworthiness of the ship. See now the Marine Insurance Act 1906, s 39(1), as to the implied warranty of seaworthiness in the case of a voyage policy. See further, Ivamy *Marine Insurance* (4th Edn 1985), pp 299–302.

17 Rehabilitation of Offenders Act 1974, ss 1, 5.

18 Ibid, s 5(1).

thereto may be framed accordingly.[19] The person questioned must not be subjected to any liability or otherwise prejudiced in law by reason of any failure to acknowledge or disclose a spent conviction or any circumstances ancillary to a spent conviction in his answer to the question.[20]

Any obligation imposed on any person by any rule of law or by the provisions of any agreement or arrangement to disclose any matters to any other person does not extend to requiring him to disclose a spent conviction or any circumstances ancillary to a spent conviction (whether the conviction is his own or another's).[1]

The Secretary of State is empowered to make orders excluding the operation of the above provisions.[2]

H SOME EXAMPLES OF MATERIAL AND IMMATERIAL FACTS

As has been shown above, a convenient method of classification of material facts is one setting out those facts which are normally material and those which are not.[3] In the pages that follow a different method is adopted in order to show the materiality of matters relating to various types of insurance so that a broader picture may be achieved. The types of insurance which are here considered are fire, burglary, personal accident, guarantee, life, and motor.

1 Fire insurance[4]

In *Bufe v Turner*[5] the insured had a warehouse next to a boatbuilders' shop in Heligoland. The shop caught fire, but the fire was extinguished in half an hour. On the very same evening the insured instructed his agent to insure the warehouse. Two days later a fire again broke out in the shop, and spread to the warehouse. In an action on the policy the jury found that the insured should have disclosed the circumstances of the first fire. Consequently, the insurance company could avoid the policy on the ground of non-disclosure.

In *Dawsons Ltd v Bonnin*[6] Viscount Finlay pointed out that if a car were insured against fire only, the question of where it was garaged might be very material, 'for its structure and locality might affect the chances of fire or the chance of fire being extinguished'. But the case concerned a comprehensive motor policy (including fire risks), and it was proved that the risk of fire in the garage was, 'so insignificant in comparison with the other risks insured, which are those of the road, including fire on the road, which might result from self ignition, that it is ignored in fixing the premium'.

---

19 Ibid, s 4(2)(a). As to circumstances ancillary to a conviction, see ibid, s 4(5).
20 Ibid, s 4(2)(b).
1 Rehabilitation of Offenders Act 1974, s 4(3)(a).
2 Ibid, s 4(4). See Rehabilitation of Offenders Act 1974 (Exceptions) Order 1975 (SI 1975, No 1023).
3 Pp 131–142, ante.
4 See further Ivamy *Fire and Motor Insurance* (4th Edn 1984), pp 47–57.
5 (1815) 6 Taunt 338.
6 [1922] 2 AC 413, at 429, HL.

It is material for an insurance company to know that a proposer has suffered previous losses under other fire insurance policies.[7]

Disclosure should also be made of the refusal of another company to insure the proposer under a fire policy.[8]

Where valuable furs had been insured under a fire policy under the description of 'general merchandise', Scrutton LJ said that he was extremely doubtful whether a proposer would not be guilty of non-disclosure in not stating what he knew of the nature of the goods. But the case was decided on other grounds.[9]

In *Ewer v National Employers Mutual General Insurance Association Ltd*[10] it was contended that when an insured made a proposal for fire insurance, he was bound to disclose, without any question being asked about it, the fact of his ever having made a claim on any other insurance policy of any sort for the whole of his life, e g claims upon a policy on goods in transit effected by the insured in his capacity of carrier. MacKinnon J, however, held that this argument was placing the duty of disclosure too high. 'There is no trace, so far as I know, of any case in which any such duty has ever been suggested, and, as a matter of principle, I find it very difficult to believe that it can be correct.'[11]

2 Burglary insurance[12]

The fact that the property insured under a burglary policy has been overvalued has been held to be material in cases relating to the insurance of bearer shares,[13] a cinematograph film,[14] and objets d'art.[15]

In a burglary policy the non-disclosure of the nationality of the proposer was held to be material in *Horne v Poland*,[16] where he had come to this country from Romania at the age of 12, and had assumed an English name, though he had never become naturalised. This case, as was pointed out by Lush J turned on its own special facts, and he observed:[17]

> 'I cannot agree with the view which was pressed on me, and in support of which the evidence

---

7 *Condogianis v Guardian Assurance Co Ltd* [1921] 2 AC 125, 3 LlL Rep 40, PC; *Arterial Caravans Ltd v Yorkshire Insurance Co Ltd* [1973] 1 Lloyd's Rep 169, QBD (fire insurance); *Marene Knitting Mills Pty Ltd v Greater Pacific General Insurance Ltd* [1976] 2 Lloyd's Rep 631, PC (fire insurance).

8 *Arthrude Press Ltd v Eagle Star and British Dominions Insurance Co Ltd* (1924) 19 LlL Rep 373, CA; *Glicksman v Lancashire and General Assurance Co Ltd* [1927] AC 139, 26 LlL Rep 69, HL.

9 *Herman v Phoenix Assurance Co Ltd* (1924) 18 LlL Rep 371, CA Scrutton LJ observed (ibid, at 372) 'Personally, I am extremely doubtful, whether, if you insure general merchandise, and the nature of the greater part of it is valuable furs, you are not guilty of concealment in not stating what you know of the nature of the goods. I do not wish to be taken as agreeing with the view the [trial] Judge has taken that, if you go to insure general merchandise and know that two-thirds of the value insured are furs of a very valuable nature, you are not guilty of concealment if you say nothing to the underwriter except that it is general merchandise.'

10 [1937] 2 All ER 193, 57 LlL Rep 172.

11 Ibid, at 197.

12 See further Ivamy *Personal Accident, Life and Other Insurances* (2nd Edn 1980), pp 151–153.

13 *Hoff Trading Co v Union Insurance Society of Canton Ltd and De Rougemont* (1929) 34 LlL Rep 81, CA.

14 *Fournier v Valentine* (1930) 38 LlL Rep 19, where some negative films which had cost £500 had been insured for £12,000.

15 *Haase v Evans* (1934) 48 LlL Rep 131, KB.

16 [1922] 2 KB 364.

17 Ibid, at 365.

was given that the mere fact that a person is not a British subject is in all cases a material fact, so that the non-disclosure of it invalidates the policy.'[18]

The insured should disclose that he has had previous losses.[19] In this connection a previous 'loss' is sustained even if, in fact, the insurance company concerned has indemnified the insured in respect of it.[20]

In *Schoolman v Hall*[1] it was held material that the insured under a burglary policy had not disclosed that he had a criminal record some years before the insurance had been effected.

In the case of a comprehensive policy which included a loss by burglary as one of the perils insured against, it has been held that there is no duty to disclose to the insurance company the insurance history of everyone of the persons living in the house.[2] 'It may be that in certain circumstances . . . certain things may be most material and in other cases not material, and for it to be said that this is a universal rule is a view which I, for myself do not share.'[3]

The insured should disclose that another insurance company has refused to renew a policy, for this is a material fact.[4]

3 Personal accident insurance[5]

Mis-statements as to the proposer's height and weight have been held to be material.[6]

The occupation of the proposer is not necessarily material. In *Woodall v Pearl Assurance Co Ltd*,[7] where a proposer had described himself as a haulier and contractor, and the insurance company claimed that he was only a boatman, the Court of Appeal held that there had been no misdescription of his occupation. Bankes LJ said that he was glad to come to this conclusion because the effect, if he had decided otherwise, 'would be to turn policies of this class—

18 The question as to whether nationality was material was left open by the Court of Appeal in *Becker v Marshall* (1922) 12 LlL Rep 413 (Russian insured), and by Lewis J in *Lyons v J W Bentley Ltd* (1944) 77 LlL Rep 335 KB (Russian insured). See further, *Carlton v R & J Park Ltd* (1922) 10 LlL Rep 818, affd, 12 LlL Rep 246, CA, where it was contended by insurance brokers, who had been sued by the insured for negligence in not effecting a policy in accordance with his instructions, that he would not have succeeded against the insurance company in any event because he had failed to disclose that he was a Romanian and that his true name was not Ralph Carlton, but Ralph Schwartz and that this was a material fact. Sankey J however, found it unnecessary to consider this point and decided the case on other grounds.

19 *Krantz v Allan and Faber* (1921) 9 LlL Rep 410, KB; *Rozanes v Bowen* (1928) 32 LlL Rep 98, CA; *Morser v Eagle Star and British Dominions Insurance Co Ltd* (1931) 40 LlL Rep 254 (loss of jewellery in transit).

20 *Roberts v Avon Insurance Co Ltd* [1956] 2 Lloyd's Rep 240, QB (householder's comprehensive policy).

1 [1951] 1 Lloyd's Rep 139. See also *Roselodge Ltd (formerly Rose Diamond Products Ltd) v Castle* [1966] 2 Lloyd's Rep 113 (jewellers' block policy), where it was held that the insured company was guilty of non-disclosure of a material fact, viz that its sales manager had been convicted of smuggling diamonds into the United States: ibid, 133. But the Court held that the fact that the principal director of the company had in 1946 been convicted of bribing a police officer and fined £75 was not a material one: ibid 132.

2 *Lyons v J W Bentley Ltd* (1944) 77 LlL Rep 335, KB.

3 Ibid, at 338.

4 *Ascott v Cornhill Insurance Co Ltd* (1937) 58 LlL Rep 41 (burglary insurance).

5 See further Ivamy *Personal Accident, Life and Other Insurances* (2nd Edn 1980), pp 6–10.

6 *Levy v Scottish Employers' Insurance Co* (1901) 17 TLR 229, DC.

7 [1919] 1 KB 593, CA.

which ought to be, and I hope are intended to be, a simple means of persons securing protection for themselves or their families in the event of accident—into mere traps to catch the unwary'.[8]

4 Guarantee insurance[9]

In *Anglo-Californian Bank Ltd v London and Provincial Marine and General Insurance Co Ltd,*[10] which concerned a policy guaranteeing the solvency of some underwriters, the jury held that it was a material fact that the insured had not disclosed to the insurance company that the underwriters were in serious financial difficulties.[11]

In *Seaton v Burnand*[12] the insured had effected a policy which guaranteed the solvency of a person who had himself, 'guaranteed' the repayment of a loan made by the insured to a third party. The money had been lent at a very high rate of interest, and the insurance company sought to avoid liability on the ground that this fact should have been disclosed by the insured. The House of Lords held that the fact was not material.

Lord Halsbury LC observed:[13]

> 'My Lords, I entirely differ from the view that any such thing as the circumstances of the original loan could or ought to have affected the minds of those who were entering into this contract. I do not believe that any one of them would have thought any such thing . . . and the reason I say that is not that I rely upon my own judgment alone, but I look at what as a fact those businessmen did in reference to it. Did they inquire by a single question what were the circumstances of the original loan? Did they ask anything about the original loan, or how it came to be made? Not a word. What they did was what as businessmen and as sensible men would be the natural thing for them to do—they went and inquired at the bank and found out what the commercial reputation of [the guarantor] was; they were satisfied with the result of their inquiries and they entered into this contract.'

5 Life insurance[14]

'Those whose business is to insure lives calculate on the average rate of mortality, and charge a premium which on that average will prevent their being losers.'[15] Hence, facts which tend to show that the average span of life will be shortened in the case of the particular insured will be regarded as material. Usually, of course, the insurance company puts specific questions in its proposal form which the insured is required to answer.

(a) Age

The age of the insured is clearly material. Thus, in *Hemmings v Sceptre Life Association Ltd:*[16]

---

[8] Ibid, at 602.

[9] See further Ivamy *Personal Accident, Life and Other Insurances* (2nd Edn 1980), pp 315–316.

[10] (1904) 10 Com Cas 1.

[11] But the defence of non-disclosure failed because it was shown that the secretary of the insurance company knew of this fact, see p 138, ante.

[12] [1900] AC 135.

[13] [1900] AC 135 at 139.

[14] See further Ivamy *Personal Accident, Life and Other Insurances* (2nd Edn 1980), pp 75–89.

[15] *Thomson v Weems* (1884) 9 App Cas 671 at 681 (per Lord Blackburn).

[16] [1905] 1 Ch 365.

The proposer mistakenly stated that she would be 41 on her next birthday, though in fact she would have been 44.
Held, that this was a material fact. But the insurance company had continued accepting premiums in respect of the policy with knowledge of the true facts, and could, therefore, not repudiate liability on the ground of misrepresentation of the material fact.

Kekewich J observed:[17]

> '[The insurance company] might have said that the policy was granted on the basis of the assured being at the date of the proposal, 41 next birthday and that, as that fact was not admitted, and it was now proved that she was not 41 but 44 next birthday, the assured . . . could not recover on the footing of her being 41. That they had to consider in 1897, when the mistake was discovered. It seems to me that they might then, if they had thought fit, with propriety have said, 'We will return the premiums hitherto received . . . and we will receive no more unless you wish to make a new contract'. On the other hand, it was open to them to treat the policy as still subsisting and to accept the premiums on the old footing. It was a pure matter of business for the directors to say which of these two courses they would adopt. They elected to adopt the latter.'[18]

(b) Residence

This is not normally considered material, but proposal forms in practice by making the insured's answer the basis of the contract, make it so.[19] Residence means the place where he is living or residing at the time of making the proposal, and not where he has been residing before or where he is going to reside afterwards.[20]

6 Motor insurance[1]

(a) Previous accidents

The fact that a proposer has been involved in a previous accident is usually material. Thus, in *Dent v Blackmore*[2] a proposer in answer to a question in a proposal form stating 'What accidents have occurred in connection with your car during the past two years, including cost?' had replied, 'Damaged wings'. In the previous year he had had seven accidents in each of which the wings of the car had been damaged, but in one of them substantial injury was caused to a third party. The Court held that this fact was material, and should have been disclosed, and that the answer, 'damaged wings' was untrue. Consequently the underwriter could avoid liability.

Even where the insured was not actually driving at the time of the previous accident, he may be under a duty to disclose it. So, in *Trustee of G H Mundy (a Bankrupt) v Blackmore*[3] a question in a proposal form asked the proposer to state what previous accidents he had had. He replied, 'With eight cars insured at the same time a few minor accidents'. One of the insured cars which was being driven for him had been involved in a head-on crash resulting in its gearbox

---

17 *Hemmings v Sceptre Life Association Ltd* [1905] 1 Ch 365 at 369.
18 See further, *Keeling v Pearl Assurance Co Ltd* (1923) 129 LT 573, where there was an inconsistency between the date of birth and the 'age next birthday' given by the proposer, and the insurance company was held to have waived the inaccuracy.
19 *Grogan v London and Manchester Industrial Assurance Co* (1885) 53 LT 761.
20 Ibid, at 765 (per Manisty J).
1 See further Ivamy *Fire and Motor Insurance* (4th Edn 1984), pp 193–214.
2 (1927) 29 LlL Rep 9, KB.
3 (1928) 32 LlL Rep 150, Ch.

being thrown out of line and both axles being bent, the cost of repairs amounting to £130. This was held to be a material fact which ought to have been disclosed.

The accident record of a driver who to the proposer's knowledge will drive the vehicle has also been held to be a material fact. Thus, in *Dunn v Ocean, Accident and Guarantee Corpn Ltd*[4] the insurance company was entitled to repudiate liability because the proposer had not disclosed that her husband, who she knew was going to drive the car, had been involved in three accidents and had been required by one company to accept the first 20 per cent of the risk.

(b) Age of driver

Where a proposer had failed to disclose that he was only nineteen years old, an insurance company successfully claimed to avoid liability on the ground that this was a material fact.[5] Atkinson J suggested[6] that instead of proposers being asked to state, 'Age last birthday' in the proposal form, they should be required to give the date of birth. There ought to be something to make it very clear how important was the question of age. If the proposer were asked the date of birth, it would make a boy rather shrink from giving a false answer. 'It was in the interest of the public that these reckless boys should not get their protection too easily.'

(c) Previous convictions

If the insured fails to disclose his previous convictions in connection with the driving of vehicles, that will be considered a material fact, and the insurance company can avoid liability.[7]

In *Jester-Barnes v Licenses and General Insurance Co Ltd*[8] it was held that the proposer ought to have informed the company that he had been convicted of being drunk in charge of a car and driving in a manner dangerous to the public.

Even where the proposer had been convicted of drinking unconnected with any conviction for driving offences, this was still held in one case[9] to be a material fact. Evidence was given that a prudent insurer would not have issued a policy at all if he had known of such convictions.

Again, where the insured was asked the following question in a proposal form: 'Have you been convicted?' and he had not in fact been convicted of any motoring offence, and answered 'No', it was held that he should have disclosed that he had previously been convicted of garage breaking, forgery, breach of recognisances and stealing, for he had signed a declaration stating 'I have withheld no information whatever which might tend in any way to increase the risk of the insurance company or influence the acceptance of this proposal'.[10]

---

4 (1933) 47 LlL Rep 129, CA.
5 *Broad v Waland* (1942) 73 LlL Rep 263, KB.
6 Ibid, at 264.
7 *General Accident, Fire and Life Assurance Corpn Ltd v Shuttleworth* (1938) 60 LlL Rep 301, where the proposer had been convicted of a serious offence of driving a motor cycle without any certificate of insurance and had been fined and his driving licence taken away, and had been disqualified from driving for 12 months.
8 (1934) 49 LlL Rep 231, KB.
9 *Taylor v Eagle Star Insurance Co Ltd* (1940) 67 LlL Rep 136, KB.
10 *Cleland v London General Insurance Co Ltd* (1935) 51 LlL Rep 156, CA.

Not only are the proposer's own convictions but also those of persons who are likely to drive the vehicle material, e g the son,[11] husband,[12] chauffeur,[13] father,[14] of the proposer.

(d) Cancellation of other policies

In *Norman v Gresham Fire and Accident Insurance Society Ltd*[15] the view was expressed (but the case was decided on other grounds) that it was material for an insurance company to know whether or not the person, whose risk they were accepting, was a person of substance who could not only pay his premiums but also, particularly in motor insurance, was a person who did not get his policies cancelled for non-payment of premiums. That would show that they were persons who were impecunious, and therefore were not likely to spend money in order to give care and attention to their vehicles being insured.

(e) Refusals by other companies to insure or renew policies

It is a material fact that other insurance companies have refused to issue a policy[16] to the proposer, or have declined to renew an existing policy.[17]

(f) Previous losses

It has been held material for the insurance company to be informed of losses suffered by the insured on occasions prior to the issue of the policy.[18]

I PROOF OF THE MATERIALITY OF FACTS NOT DISCLOSED

There is sometimes no need to prove what facts are material, for it will be obvious to the Court that they are so. In the words of Scrutton LJ:

> '[Counsel contended] that before a Court can find that a fact is material, somebody must give evidence of the materiality. That is entirely contrary to the whole course of insurance

---

11 *Bond v Commercial Union Assurance Co Ltd* (1930) 36 LlL Rep 107, DC.

12 *Dunn v Ocean Accident and Guarantee Corpn Ltd* (1933) 47 LlL Rep 129, CA.

13 *Jester-Barnes v Licenses and General Insurance Co Ltd* (1934) 49 LlL Rep 231, KB.

14 *Zurich General Accident and Liability Insurance Co v Leven* 1940 SC 406.

15 (1935) 52 LlL Rep 292 at 301, KB.

16 *Dent v Blackmore* (1927) 29 LlL Rep 9, where the insurance company had refused to insure the plaintiff except on restricted terms; *Broad and Montague Ltd v South East Lancashire Insurance Co Ltd* (1931) 40 LlL Rep 328, where it was held that the failure to disclose the refusal to insure by two other companies avoided the obligation to return part of the premiums paid under the present policy.

17 *Cornhill Insurance Co Ltd v Assenheim* (1937) 58 LlL Rep 27, where the other insurers had written to the assured's brokers informing them that they would not invite renewal of the policy; *Holt's Motors Ltd v South East Lancashire Insurance Co Ltd* (1930) 37 LlL Rep 1, CA, where it was held that the letter from the other insurers stating that they could not invite renewal of the policy was equivalent to declining to insure.

18 *Farra v Hetherington* (1931) 40 LlL Rep 132, where the insured had not disclosed that on two previous occasions a Morris car owned by him had been 'borrowed' and subsequently recovered, and on a third occasion stolen and never recovered; *Carlton v R and J Park Ltd* (1922) 10 LlL Rep 818, where the Court held that the insured could not recover under the policy, for he had previously lost a car in a similar manner, i e it had been stolen when left in the street, and he had therefore failed to exercise due and reasonable precaution to safeguard the vehicle, as he was required to do by the policy.

litigation; it is so far contrary that it is frequently objected that a party is not entitled to call other people to say what they think is material; that is a matter for the Court on the nature of the facts. I entirely agree . . . that the nature of the facts may be such that you do not need anybody to come and say, This is material. If a shipowner desiring to insure his ship for the month of January knew that in that month she was heavily damaged in a storm, it would, with deference to Counsel who has suggested the opposite, be ridiculous to call evidence of the materiality of that fact; the fact speaks for itself.'[19]

If there is any need to prove the materiality of facts, then an expert witness can be called.[20] Such a witness in the case of marine and most branches of non-marine insurance will usually be one of those persons 'actually engaged in the occupation of insurers'.[1]

In reviewing the history of the practice of calling expert evidence, McCardie J remarked:[2]

'The view of the Courts as to expert evidence in insurance cases seems to have developed. In the days of Lord Mansfield such evidence was apparently regarded as irrelevant: see, for example, *Carter v Boehm*.[3] But the views of 150 years ago have been modified by the broader outlook of later Judges and by a clearer realisation of the utility of expert testimony as an aid to the administration of justice . . . In marine insurance cases the law to-day is not as it apparently was in 1766. Expert evidence with respect to materiality of a fact has been freely admitted in recent years by the experienced Judges who have administered, and are now administering, justice in the Commercial Court[4] . . . I can conceive that no sound distinction can be drawn between cases of marine insurance as distinguished from life, fire of other heads of insurance business . . . Expert evidence may frequently afford great assistance to the Court upon questions of novelty or doubt. If excluded, it would deprive the Court of ascertaining those considerations and views which a tribunal may well require to know, and the insurance witness would by process of law be stricken with absolute silence upon matters of vital importance to him. Judges are always free to test[5] and revise every form of expert testimony.'

Thus, as regards marine insurance, evidence of Lloyd's underwriters was held admissible to show that it was material that they should know that the valuation of a yacht was in excess of her actual value, for the reason that any

---

19 *Glicksman v Lancashire and General Assurance Co Ltd* [1925] 2 KB 593, CA at 609. In *Marene Knitting Mills Pty Ltd v Greater Pacific General Insurance Ltd* [1976] 2 Lloyd's Rep 631, PC (fire insurance) Yeldham J in the Court below preferred the evidence of one expert witness and rejected that of another as to what material facts should have been disclosed and said that in any event without any acceptable evidence he himself would have concluded that each of the previous fires were material matters which should have been disclosed. The Lordships agreed with this view. (See the judgment of Lord Fraser of Tullybelton, ibid, at 642.)

20 As to expert evidence generally, see Phipson *Law of Evidence*, 13th Edn (1982), paras 2707–2759.

1 *Yorke v Yorkshire Insurance Co* [1918] 1 KB 662 at 670.

2 Ibid, at 670. See also *L and J Hoff Trading Co v De Rougemont* (1929) 34 Com Cas 291 at 299–300. See further, *Roselodge Ltd (formerly Rose Diamond Products Ltd) v Castle* [1966] 2 Lloyd's Rep 113 (jewellers' block policy), where McNair J said (at 129): 'Until about 100 years ago it was commonly held that the fact of materiality could not be proved by expert evidence but must be determined by the jury as representing the reasonable business man—particularly apposite in the case of Lord Mansfield's jury-men; but it has long been the practice in our Courts to allow proof of this fact by the evidence of independent underwriters. (The curious may find the cases referred to and discussed in the notes to *Carter v Boehm* (1766) 3 Burr 1905 in the second volume of Smith's Leading Cases, published in 1876.)'

3 (1766) 3 Burr 1905.

4 Expert evidence was admitted in *Littledale v Dixon* (1805) 1 Bos & PNR 151; *Chaurand v Angerstein* (1791) Peake 43; *Campbell v Rickards* (1833) 5 B & Ad 840; *Berthon v Loughman* (1817) 2 Stark 258; *Rickards v Murdoch* (1830) 10 B & C 527; *Chapman v Walton* (1833) 10 Bing 57.

5 Evidence as to the materiality of an obsolete prohibition concerning the importation of arms and ammunition into Persia was disregarded in *Fracis Times & Co v Sea Insurance Co* (1898) 3 Com Cas 229.

great disparity might tempt the assured to cause her to be lost.[6] Evidence has also been admitted to show whether it was necessary to disclose that the master of a vessel had not been to sea for 20 years and had then lost his ship,[7] that a cargo was overvalued,[8] and that the charterers of a vessel insured just before the First World War broke out were of German nationality.[9]

In *Horne v Poland*,[10] which concerned a burglary policy, the evidence of the underwriters was admitted in order to show that they would not accept the risk of an alien as satisfactory. In this case one or two of the witnesses said that they did not and would not insure aliens. Lush J said that he was doubtful whether evidence of what individual witnesses would do was admissible, but it had not been objected to, and in any event he felt that in the circumstances of the case, apart from the evidence, there had been non-disclosure of a material fact.

In *Regina Fur Co Ltd v Bossom*,[11] which also related to a burglary policy, evidence was given by two underwriters to prove that it was a material fact for the purposes of the policy that the assured had had an isolated conviction for receiving stolen goods 20 years before, for this affected the 'moral hazard'.[12]

In *Becker v Marshall*,[13] another case on a burglary policy, it was proved by expert evidence that it was material in the particular circumstances to know the nationality of origin of the assured, and that the assured had changed his name.

In *Woolcott v Sun Alliance and London Insurance Ltd*[14] an underwriting manager gave evidence as to whether a proposer for a fire insurance policy should have disclosed a previous conviction for robbery.

In *Hoff Trading Co v De Rougemont*,[15] where some bearer shares were insured against loss in transit from Riga to London, underwriters and brokers were called to show that it was material to show that the assured had put an excessive and fraudulent value on them.

In the case of life insurance the evidence of a doctor will be admissible to show what facts are material. 'It must be pointed out that in questions of life insurance the matters at issue are usually physiological, medical or neuropathic. The directors of insurance companies, however, are but rarely medical men. Seldom, if at all, do they personally see the proposer. They rely to a great extent on the reports and advice of medical men. The importance or otherwise of that which should be disclosed to a life insurance company may well be appreciated only by doctors or surgeons. Medical men may, therefore, often

---

6 *Herring v Janson* (1895) 1 Com Cas 177 at 179.

7 *Thames and Mersey Marine Insurance Co v Gunford Ship Co* [1911] AC 529, HL, where it was held that this circumstance was not material.

8 *Ionides v Pender* (1874) LR 9 QB 531.

9 *Associated Oil Carriers Ltd v Union Insurance Society of Canton Ltd* [1917] 2 KB 184.

10 [1922] 2 KB 364, 10 LlL Rep 175, 275.

11 [1957] 2 Lloyd's Rep 466; affd [1958] 2 Lloyd's Rep 425, CA.

12 See pp 134–136, ante. See further, *Roselodge Ltd (formerly Rose Diamond Products Ltd) v Castle* [1966] 2 Lloyd's Rep 113 (jewellers' block policy), where evidence was given by three underwriters to prove that it was a material fact for the purposes of the policy that the principal director of the insured company had been convicted of bribing a police officer in 1946 and was fined £75 for this affected the 'moral hazard': ibid, 132 (but McNair J in fact held that the evidence was not material: ibid, 132). They also gave evidence that the conviction of the insured company's sales manager for smuggling diamonds into the United States was material: ibid, 132–133 (and his Lordship held that it was so: ibid, 133).

13 (1922) 11 LlL Rep 114; affd 12 LlL Rep 413.

14 [1978] 1 All ER 1253, [1978] 1 Lloyd's Rep 629 (fire insurance).

15 (1929) 34 Com Cas 291.

give a more useful opinion than the directors themselves as to what is or is not material or important.'[16]

Thus, in *Godfrey v Britannic Assurance Co Ltd*[17] a doctor[18] of wide experience in advising life offices as to the prudence or otherwise of accepting certain risks was called to show the materiality of the fact that the assured had been suffering from a kidney condition, and that an X-ray indicated that he had a lung infection. In this case a manager of another insurance company[19] with lifelong experience in this business also gave evidence on this point.

If no expert evidence is offered, the Court may make use of its own knowledge as to whether a fact is material, but such knowledge may not necessarily be the same as that of the ordinary man.

Thus, in *Glasgow Assurance Corpn Ltd v William Symondson & Co*,[20] where no evidence was offered on the point, Scrutton J held that in a case of *marine*[1] insurance it was not material to know that the risk had been previously refused by other underwriters saying:[2]

> 'Although in recent practice evidence has frequently been admitted of underwriters to state whether in their opinion certain facts would influence the judgment of a prudent insurer, no such evidence was tendered by either party in the case. I am, therefore, left to form my own judgment on the question from such knowledge as I have of insurance matters. The ordinary man in the street would, I am sure, think it material to know that the risk he was offered had been previously refused by six other underwriters; and many life insurance companies expressly ask the question: "Has your life been refused by any other office?" But it is elementary marine insurance law that such refusals need not be disclosed to another underwriter. The ordinary business man would, I am sure, think it material to know that the underwriter wanting to reinsure thought so badly of the risk that he was ready to pay a higher premium than he received to get rid of [it],[3] but no one has ever suggested that this need be disclosed.'

But although the Court can decide of its own motion whether something is material in a case where it is obviously material, nevertheless it should be slow to find a fact as a material one, more particularly as it would be quite possible for underwriters to protect themselves by including a suitable clause in the policy.[4]

J THE DURATION OF THE DUTY OF DISCLOSURE

The duty of disclosure continues throughout the negotiations and until at least the contract has been completed by acceptance.[5]

---

16 *Yorke v Yorkshire Insurance Co* [1918] 1 KB 662 at 671 (per McCardie J).
17 [1963] 2 Lloyd's Rep 515 QB.
18 Ibid, at 531.
19 Ibid, at 531.
20 (1911) 16 Com Cas 109.
1 As to non-marine insurance, see the quotation set out below and pp 143, 144, 148, ante.
2 (1911) 16 Com Cas 109, at 119.
3 This word would appear to have been omitted from the report. See *Glicksman v Lancashire and General Assurance Co Ltd* [1925] 2 KB 593 at 609 (per Scrutton J).
4 *Sadlers Brothers Co v Meredith* [1963] 2 Lloyd's Rep 293 at 301 per Roskill J (goods in transit policy). In this case the underwriters pleaded that the insured should have disclosed that it was their practice to leave their vehicles in the street when they were loaded with goods and merchandise. But the learned Judge found that such a practice had not been proved, and the plea of non-disclosure failed.
5 *Lishman v Northern Maritime Insurance Co* (1875) LR 10 CP 179, ExCh (marine insurance) per

In *Whitwell v Autocar Fire and Accident Insurance Co Ltd*:[6]

In a proposal form for motor insurance there was a question which asked the proposer whether any insurance company had declined his insurance. He gave the answer 'No'. This was, in fact, a true statement at the time at which he made it. But in fact, quite unknown to him, two days before the proposal was accepted another insurance company had declined to insure him. *Held,* there was no duty to disclose this fact afterwards because the contract was concluded when the proposal was accepted.

But it is usual, especially in life insurances policies, for a clause to be inserted into the contract that the risk of the insurance company is not to commence until receipt of the first premium. The effect of such a clause is that the period during which the duty to disclose exists is enlarged, so that any material fact coming to the knowledge of the insured must be disclosed right up to the moment that the first premium is paid.[7]

In *Looker v Law Union and Rock Insurance Co Ltd*:[8]

In a proposal for life insurance the proposer, in answer to a question, 'Are you now free from disease or ailment?' said, 'Yes'. Five days later the insurance company sent a conditional acceptance of the risk stating that, 'If the health of the life proposed remains meanwhile unaffected, the policy will be issued on payment of the first premium. The risk of the Company will not commence until receipt of the first premium.' Five days after the receipt of this letter he became ill, and he died within 4 days from pneumonia, but no notice of his illness was given to the company. He sent the company a cheque for the first premium, but this was dishonoured on presentation.

Held, that the insurance company was not bound to issue a policy.

Acton J based his decision on two grounds. In the course of his judgment he observed:[9]

'The rule . . . is that the acceptance is made in reliance upon the continued truth of the representations made in the proposal which it was agreed should form the basis of the contract of insurance, in the belief that there has been no material change in the risk offered, and therefore, that if anything has happened materially to increase the risk between the proposal and the acceptance, the insurance company are not bound, because that which they have made a condition of the contract going to the root of it, has not been fulfilled . . . It is also said materially to strengthen the position of the insurance company that in this case their notice . . . in terms intimated to the proposer that any subsequent acceptance by them of premium and risk would be subject to the condition that the health of the life proposed should remain meanwhile unaffected. That it had not remained unaffected cannot be disputed. It is not indeed putting it too high to say that when the insurance company accepted the premium and

---

Bramwell B, at 182; *Re Yager and Guardian Assurance Co* (1912) 108 LT 38 per Channell J, at 44: 'The time up to which it must be disclosed is the time when the contract is concluded. Any material fact that comes to his knowledge before the contract he must disclose'; *Canning v Farquhar* (1886) 16 QBD 727, CA (life insurance) per Lindley LJ, at 733; ibid, per Lord Esher MR, at 731: 'The person to be insured should not conceal any material fact, and his statement, if he makes any, should be correct . . . In this case [there] was a representation which was true at the time it was made. In insurance law that is not the material time, but the material time is the moment when the insurance is made, and the representations ought to be true then. If there had been a material change, there ought to be an alteration of the representation, and the ground for entering into the contract is altered'; *Hadenfayre Ltd v British National Insurance Society Ltd, Trident General Insurance Co Ltd and Lombard Elizabethan Insurance Co Ltd* [1984] 2 Lloyd's Rep 393 (contingency insurance), at 398 (per Lloyd J).

6 (1927) 27 LlL Rep 418.

7 *Canning v Farquhar* (1886) 16 QBD 727, CA (life insurance); *Harrington v Pearl Life Assurance Co* (1913) 30 TLR 24; affd (1914) 30 TLR 613 (life insurance); *British Equitable Insurance Co v Great Western Rly Co* (1869) 38 LJ Ch 314 (life insurance), where there was a special condition.

8 [1928] 1 KB 554.

9 Ibid, at 558.

> the risk . . ., the deceased was dying, and if the insurance company had known the facts, they would never have entertained the notion of accepting the risk for a moment. The second point . . . was that there was here a failure to discharge a duty incumbent upon all proposers of contracts of insurance such as these . . . namely, a duty to inform the insurers of any material change in the nature of the risk to be undertaken by them . . . In my opinion, the contention for the insurance company on this point also is a sound one.'

Again, where the risk under a fire policy was not to commence until the first premium had been paid, a proposer, who had insured with one company and then applied for increased insurance with another company, was held to be under a duty to disclose a refusal on the part of the original company to continue the insurance.[10] 'There still was a time at which any circumstance coming to his knowledge material to be disclosed would have to be disclosed. I quite agree that in this case it is rather hard upon the assured because I do not see anything to throw doubt upon [his] bona fides . . . or anything to show that he had the least idea that he was bound to disclose the fact which had come to his knowledge as to the refusal of the [other] company, to renew the insurance; and, if so, it was rather hard upon him, but that is the effect of this clause in the policy, which undoubtedly sometimes does work hardship to one of the parties . . . That, however, is the consequence of this law of insurance which upon the whole does justice between the parties and is rather necessary for the protection of insurers.'[11]

In *Harrington v Pearl Life Assurance Co Ltd*:[12]

> In May 1912 a proposer signed a proposal for a life insurance policy which was accepted. He was examined by the insurance company's doctor, and was passed as fit. But the proposal never came into force because the premium was not paid. He made a new proposal on October 1, 1912, stating that there had been no material change in his health since the examination. The proposal was accepted, and the policy was to come into force when the premium was paid. On November 6 he was taken ill, and on November 8 the insurance company received the premium, and he died the same day.
> *Held*, that the insurance company was under no duty to issue the policy since the circumstances had so changed, and no disclosure of them had been made.

Where a proposer had been passed as fit by the insurance company's doctor and later became alarmed about the state of his health and consulted a specialist, who told him that he was in a dangerous state of health, it was held that he should have disclosed this fact to the insurance company.[13] In answer to a question, 'Whether now and ordinarily enjoying good health', he had stated, 'Yes, and always'. 'It proved beyond all reasonable doubt that at the time when the money was paid and the policy issued, [he] knew that his.. . . answers to the . . . question . . . were no longer true, and . . . I can have no doubt that the difference between these statements and the facts as they then existed within his knowledge were of such a grave character that they certainly ought to have been communicated to the company.'[14]

But the party may agree that the insurance company is not to be at risk until the policy is actually delivered to the assured. In such a case the duty of

---

10 *Re Yager and Guardian Assurance Co Ltd* (1912) 108 LT 38 at 44 (per Channell J).
11 Ibid at 45 (per Channell J).
12 (1914) 30 TLR 613.
13 *British Equitable Insurance Co v Great Western Rly Co* (1869) 38 LJ Ch 314.
14 Ibid, at 316 (per Selwyn LJ).

disclosure will last even longer. So, in *Allis Chalmers Co v Maryland Fidelity and Deposit Co*:[15]

> A fidelity insurance policy was to come into effect from its 'issuance'. It was agreed that the company should reimburse the insured in respect of any loss sustained by larceny or embezzlement by a named employee of theirs. On March 8 a policy was executed by the insurance company, but it was not finally delivered to the insured until April 18. On April 13 the employee left the insured's office, and it was suspected by April 18 that he might have absconded. On that day the insured's manager was informed of this, and he paid the premium and obtained the policy. Shortly afterwards the insured discovered defalcations by the employee.
>
> *Held*, that they were not entitled to recover on the policy, for they should have made a disclosure of the fact that the employee had absconded, since no contract had been concluded until April 18.

Earl Loreburn observed:[16]

> 'I therefore come to the conclusion that there was no completed agreement . . . at any rate before April 18, and that prior to April 18 either party could have refused to proceed with this business of the insurance. When the policy was delivered and the premium paid on April 18, there was knowledge of a state of facts upon the part of the assured which admittedly ought to have been communicated to them; and it is agreed that in that state of facts it is impossible to recover upon the policy.'

Any material fact, therefore, which, at any stage of the negotiations comes to the knowledge of the proposed assured,[17] including any alteration of circumstances[18] which brings into existence a material fact,[19] or in consequence of which a fact previously immaterial becomes material,[20] must be at once communicated to the insurers for the purpose of enabling them to decide whether to continue or break off the negotiations: otherwise there is a failure to disclose a material fact which renders the contract voidable at the instance of the insurers.[1]

In the same way, any statement made during the negotiations which, owing to a change of circumstances become inaccurate,[2] or which is discovered by the

---

15 (1916) 114 LT 433, HL.

16 Ibid, at 434.

17 *Allis-Chalmers Co v Maryland Fidelity and Deposit Co* (1916) 114 LT 433, HL (fidelity insurance).

18 Any alteration falling within a condition against alterations (as to which, see pp 308–313, post) must be disclosed: *Quin v National Assurance Co* (1839) Jo & Car 316, ExCh (fire insurance) per Burton J, at 393.

19 *British Equitable Insurance Co v Great Western Rly Co* (1869) 38 LJ Ch 314 (life insurance); *Canning v Farquhar* (1886) 16 QBD 727, CA (life insurance), where the proposed assured had an accident by which he was seriously injured; *Canning v Hoare* (1885) 1 TLR 526 (life insurance); *Harrington v Pearl Life Assurance Co* (1913) 30 TLR 613, CA (life insurance); *Looker v Law Union and Rock Insurance Co* [1928] 1 KB 554 (life insurance). Thus, an operation between the date of the proposal and its acceptance ought to be disclosed: *Watt v Southern Cross Assurance Co* [1927] NZLR 106 (life insurance).

20 *Re Yager and Guardian Assurance Co* (1912) 108 LT 38 (fire insurance), where there was an existing policy with another company, and after the proposal in question, renewal of the policy was refused.

1 It is no excuse that the assured bona fide believed the fact to be of no importance: *Uzielli v Commercial Union Insurance Co* (1865) 12 LT 399 (marine insurance) per Mellor J, at 401.

2 *Re Marshall and Scottish Employers' Liability and General Insurance Co* (1901) 85 LT 757, where the assured, after stating that he was not proposing to insure with another company, did so before the issue of the policy; *Traill v Baring* (1864) 4 De GJ & Sm 318 (life insurance), where there was a change in the intention stated of retaining a portion of the risk; cf *Davies v London and Provincial Marine Insurance Co* (1878) 8 ChD 469 (surety) per Fry J, at 475.

proposed assured to be inaccurate,[3] must be withdrawn or corrected, as the case may be. It is immaterial that the statement was accurate, or believed to be accurate, at the time when it was made.[4] If, therefore, the proposed assured fails to withdraw or correct his original statement, there is a breach of duty which avoids the contract.

On the other hand, the duty of disclosure ceases when the contract is concluded, or the premium has been paid, or any other event specified in the policy has happened.[5] The assured need not disclose any material facts which only come to his knowledge, or any facts which only become material[6] after acceptance; nor need he withdraw or correct any statements which do not, until after acceptance, become inaccurate.

Where the policy is retrospective, the duty of disclosure applies not only to such facts as were material at the date from which the policy is to take effect, but also to all facts becoming material down to the actual date at which the contract is made.[7]

Where the assured seeks at a subsequent date to procure an alteration in the terms for his benefit,[8] his duty to make disclosure re-attaches to modified extent. He becomes bound to inform the insurers of any facts which may be material to such alteration, even though they have come to his knowledge since the completion of the original contract. He is not, however, bound to disclose any other facts which have since come to his knowledge, however material they might have been had he known them before the contract was made, inasmuch as they can have no bearing on the question of alteration.[9]

K THE EFFECT OF NON-DISCLOSURE

A failure on the part of the assured to disclose a material fact within his actual or

---

3 *Golding v Royal London Auxiliary Insurance Co Ltd* (1914) 30 TLR 350 (fire insurance), where the assured informed the agent of the insurers, who omitted to transmit the information.

4 *Canning v Farquhar* (1886) 16 QBD 727, CA (life insurance) per Lord Esher MR, at 732.

5 *Lishman v Northern Maritime Insurance Co* (1875) LR 10 CP 179, ExCh (marine insurance), following *Cory v Patton* (1872) LR 7 QB 304 (marine insurance). A misrepresentation, therefore, after the completion of contract is of no effect: *Ionides v Pacific Insurance Co* (1872) LR 7 QB 517 (marine insurance).

6 *Whitwell v Autocar Fire and Accident Insurance Co* (1927) 27 LlL Rep 418, where the insurance was declined by another company after the date of the acceptance, but before the policy was issued.

7 *Sillem v Thornton* (1854) 3 E & B 868.

8 *Sawtell v Loudon* (1814) 5 Taunt 359 (marine insurance); *Lishman v Northern Maritime Insurance Co* (1875) LR 10 CP 179, ExCh (marine insurance) per Blackburn J, at 182. The same principle applies where, after the acceptance of the original proposal, the assured agrees, on the suggestion of the insurers' agent, to take out a policy of a different class at a higher premium, in lieu of the policy originally intended and receives a cover note: *Re Marshall and Scottish Employers' Liability and General Insurance Co Ltd* (1901) 85 LT 757.

9 *Lishman v Northern Maritime Insurance Co* (supra) (marine insurance) per Blackburn J, at 182: 'Suppose the policy were actually executed, and the parties agreed to add a memorandum afterwards, altering the term: if the alteration were such as to make the contract more burdensome to the underwriters, and a fact known at that time to the assured were concealed which was material to the alteration, I should say that the policy would be vitiated. But if the fact were quite immaterial to the alteration, and only material to the underwriter as being a fact which showed that he had made a bad bargain originally, and such as might tempt him, if it were possible, to get out of it, I should say there would be no obligation to disclose it'; *Sawtell v Loudon* (supra) (marine insurance). Alteration is to be distinguished from rectification.

imputed knowledge renders the policy voidable at the option of the insurers.[10]

The assured's conduct cannot be taken into consideration as in any way affecting this result.[11] The policy is equally liable to be avoided whether his failure is attributable to fraud,[12] carelessness,[13] inadvertence,[14] indifference,[15] mistake,[16] error of judgment,[17] or even to his failure to appreciate its materiality.[18] Even his ignorance of the fact will not excuse him, if it is one which he ought to have known.[19]

As far as marine insurance is concerned, s 18(1) of the Marine Insurance Act 1906, provides:

> 'Subject to the provisions of this section, the assured must disclose to the insurer, before the contract is concluded, every material circumstance which is known to the assured, and the assured is deemed to know every circumstance which, in the ordinary course of business, ought to be known by him. If the assured fails to make such disclosure, the insurer may avoid contract.'

The insurers may, however, at any time after discovering that a material fact has not been communicated to them, waive the non-disclosure and thus affirm the policy,[20] provided that at the time of doing so, they are fully acquainted with all the circumstances of the case.[1] The mere fact that the insurers have not

---

Rectification assumes that there is already a concluded contract in existence; and, consequently, the duty of disclosure does not re-attach. As to rectification, see Chapter 24.

10 *Carter v Boehm* (1766) 3 Burr 1905 (marine insurance).

11 *Ionides v Pender* (1874) LR 9 QB 531 (marine insurance) per Blackburn J, at 537: 'It is perfectly well established that the law as to a contract of insurance differs from that as to other contracts, and that a concealment of a material fact, though made without any fraudulent intent, vitiates the policy'.

12 *Rivaz v Gerussi* (1880) 6 QBD 222, CA (marine insurance), where shipments under previous open policies had been systematically undervalued. The view expressed in *Hambrough v Mutual Life Insurance Co of New York* (1895) 72 LT 140, CA (life insurance) per Lopes LJ, at 141, that mere silence respecting a material fact, in the absence of any fraudulent intention, does not avoid the policy, unless there is an express condition to that effect, seems inconsistent with the other authorities on this subject.

13 *M'Millan v Accident Insurance Co* 1907 SC 484 per Lord Stormonth-Darling, at 493; *Cantiere Meccanico Brindisino v Janson* [1912] 3 KB 452, CA (marine insurance) per Fletcher Moulton LJ, at 469.

14 *Abbott v Howard* (1832) Hayes 381 (life insurance); cf *Lee v Jones* (1864) 17 CBNS 482 (guarantee) per Shee J, at 495.

15 *Bates v Hewitt* (1867) LR 2 QB 595 (marine insurance) per Cockburn CJ, at 607.

16 *Carter v Boehm* (1766) 3 Burr 1905 (marine insurance) per Lord Mansfield CJ, at 109.

17 *Elton v Larkins* (1832) 5 C & P 86 (marine insurance); *Morrison v Universal Marine Insurance Co* (1873) LR 8 Exch 197, ExCh (marine insurance), where the broker had made inquiries and satisfied himself that the information did not relate to the ship in question, though, as a matter of fact, it did.

18 *Dalglish v Jarvie* (1850) 2 Mac & G 231 (injunction) per Rolfe B, at 243: 'If he conceals anything he knows to be material, it is a fraud, but besides that, if he conceals anything that may influence the rate of premium which the underwriter may require, although he does not know it would have that effect, such concealment entirely vitiates the policy'. See also *Asfar & Co v Blundell* [1896] 1 QB 123, CA (marine insurance) per Lord Esher MR, at 129; *Bates v Hewitt* (supra) per Cockburn CJ, at 607; *Lindenau v Desborough* (1828) 8 B & C 586 (life insurance) per Bayley J, at 592; *Joel v Law Union and Crown Insurance Co* [1908] 2 KB 863, CA (life insurance) per Fletcher Moulton LJ, at 884.

19 See pp 123–125, ante.

20 *Armstrong v Turquand* (1858) 9 ICLR 32 (life insurance); *Morrison v Universal Marine Insurance Co* (supra); *Simon, Haynes, Barlas and Ireland v Beer* (1946) 78 LlL Rep 337 (solicitors' indemnity policy).

1 *Russell v Thornton* (1860) 6 H & N 140, ExCh (marine insurance) per Wightman J, at 143;

returned the premium to the insured has been held not to be a waiver of the non-disclosure.[2]

1 Statement by BIA and Lloyd's

In 1977 The British Insurance Association[3] and Lloyds drew up a statement of non-life insurance practice which they recommended to their members.[4] The statement applies only to non-life policy holders domiciled in the United Kingdom and insured in their private capacity only, and so far as non-disclosure and misrepresentation[5] are concerned provides:

> 'Except where fraud, deception or negligence is involved, an insurer will not unreasonably repudiate liability to indemnify a policyholder:
> *i* on the grounds of non-disclosure or misrepresentation of a material fact where knowledge of the fact would not materially have influenced the insurer's judgment in the assessment of the insurance; . . .
> [This] paragraph does not apply to marine and aviation policies.'

2 Statement by Life Offices' Association

A similar statement as to long-term insurance practice was issued by the Life Offices' Association and relates to policies effected by individuals resident in the United Kingdom in a private capacity.

The statement says that insurers will not unreasonably reject a claim. But fraud or deception will and negligence or non-disclosure or misrepresentation of a material fact may, result in adjustment or constitute grounds for rejection. In particular an insurer will not reject a claim on grounds of non-disclosure or misrepresentation of a matter that was outside the knowledge of the proposer.

Merchants' and Manufacturers' Insurance Co Ltd v Davies [1938] 1 KB 196, CA (accident insurance) per Greene MR, at 208.

2 *March Cabaret Club and Casino Ltd v London Assurance* [1975] 1 Lloyd's Rep 169 (trader's combined insurance), where May J said (ibid, at 178): 'It is true that the premium has not been returned. But waiver and estoppel require some form of representation; mere inaction, unless it is in circumstances which amount to a representation, is not enough.' See also, *Claude R Ogden & Co Pty Ltd v Reliance Fire Sprinkler Co Pty Ltd* [1975] 1 Lloyd's Rep 52, Supreme Ct of Australia (public and products liability insurance), where the acceptance of the premium and the issuing of the policy after the receipt of the proposal was not understood by any party to amount to a representation that the insurers would not avoid the policy. (See the judgment of MacFarlan J, ibid, at 65.)

3 Now The Association of British Insurers.

4 See 931 House of Commons Official Report, May 4, 1977, Written Answers, cols 218–220.

5 See Chapter 14.

CHAPTER 14

Misrepresentation

In the discharge of his duty of disclosure, the assured is required to state accurately all the facts to which the duty applies,[1] whether they are such as are material in themselves, or are shown by the asking of questions to be regarded as material by the insurer. Accuracy is equally required where the assured, with a view of inducing the insurers to enter into the contract of insurance, volunteers statements relating to facts which it is not necessary for him to disclose, and the insurers treat such statements as material[2] by acting upon them.

Statements of fact made during the negotiations are usually called 'representations'. They have fulfilled their object when the final acceptance is achieved, and form no part of the subsequent contract of insurance.[3] They must, therefore, be distinguished from statements which are contractual in their nature, and which are made part of the contract between the parties.[4]

In order to determine whether a statement is accurate, it is necessary to take into consideration the surrounding circumstances, and to construe the statement with reference to the facts of the particular case. If the statement is accurate when applied to the circumstances to which it was intended to apply, the assured has discharged his duty,[5] notwithstanding that it may be shown to be inaccurate when considered with other circumstances to which it was never intended by either party to apply.[6]

---

1 *Everett v Desborough* (1829) 5 Bing 503 (life insurance) per Park J, at 518: 'It is absolutely necessary that in every case of this description there should be the purest good faith between the parties, and the most accurate representation of all material circumstances.'

2 I e a fact which a prudent insurer would take into account when deciding whether or not to accept the risk or what premium to charge: *Highland Insurance Co v Continental Insurance Co* (1986) Times, 6 May (reinsurance).

3 A representation made after the contract is complete has no effect: *Ionides v Pacific Insurance Co* (1872) LR 7 QB 517, ExCh (marine insurance); *Pawson v Watson* (1778) 2 Cowp 785 (marine insurance) per Lord Mansfield CJ, at 778: 'If there is fraud in a representation, it will avoid the policy as a fraud, but not as part of the agreement.' See also *Roberts v Security Co* [1897] 1 QB 111, CA per Lopes LJ, at 115; *Canning v Farquhar* (1886) 16 QBD 727, CA (life insurance); *Joel v Law Union and Crown Insurance Co* [1908] 2 KB 863, CA (life insurance); and cf *British Equitable Assurance Co Ltd v Baily* [1906] AC 35 (life insurance) per Lord Lindley, at 41. They do not cease to be representations because they are recited in the policy. See p 215, post.

4 See p 161, post.

5 *Carter v Boehm* (1766) 3 Burr 1905 (marine insurance) per Lord Mansfield CJ, at 1911: 'The question therefore must always be whether there was, under all the circumstances at the time the policy was underwritten, a fair representation, or a concealment; fraudulent, if designed; or, though not designed, varying materially the object of the policy and changing the risque understood to be run.' See *Price Bros & Co Ltd v Heath* (1928) 32 LlL Rep 166, CA, where, in an insurance on timber for the protection of debenture holders, an agreed value was inserted in the policy, and it was held that this did not amount to a representation that the agreed value was the full value or that the timber was being insured for its full value.

6 *Thomson v Weems* (1884) 9 App Cas 671 (life insurance) per Lord Blackburn, at 685; *Shilling v Accidental Death Insurance Co* (1858) 1 F & F 116 (accident insurance), where the fact that the

A statement of belief or opinion as to a particular fact is not a representation that such a fact is true, but only that the belief or opinion stated is sincerely held.[7] Such a statement is not, therefore, inaccurate because the belief or opinion turns out to be erroneous.[8] It must be shown that the assured never entertained such a belief or opinion at all.[9]

The same principle is to be applied to statements of intention. The only statement of fact involved in a statement of intention is that, at the time of making it, the proposed assured honestly intended to act as stated.[10] If he never, in fact, so intended, the statement is inaccurate.[11] If he did so intend at the time of insuring, it is immaterial that he afterwards changed his mind and never carried out his intention.[12] It may be made a condition of the policy, however, that the stated intention shall be carried out.[13]

A statement may be inaccurate because it is false in the sense of being wholly untrue, and, therefore, incapable of referring to the state of facts actually

---

assured was ruptured and subject to fainting fits was held not to falsify a declaration that he had not been subject to epileptic or other fits, or that there were no other circumstances touching his occupation or habits with which the insurers ought to be acquainted; *Anderson v Pacific Fire and Marine Insurance Co* (1869) 21 LT 408, PC (marine insurance), where a representation that a ship was 'insured only for £4,000' was held in the circumstances (i e, reinsurance) to be a representation of the original amount of the insurance sought to be reinsured, and not a representation of the total amount insured upon the ship including insurances by others, and the Privy Council said, at 410: 'As between insurer and reinsurer, it being open to the owner to insure in any sum he likes, could it be taken as a misrepresentation upon which anyone could have been expected to rely in the unlimited sense contended for?'; *Golding v Royal London Auxiliary Insurance Co Ltd* (1914) 30 TLR 350 (fire insurance).

7 *Anderson v Pacific Fire and Marine Insurance Co* (1872) LR 7 CP 65 (marine insurance) per Willes J, at 69; *Irish National Insurance Co Ltd and Sedgwick Ltd v Oman Insurance Co Ltd* [1983] 2 Lloyd's Rep 453 (reinsurance), where a statement made by the brokers that the business was written on a 'first loss basis' and not on an 'excess of loss basis' was held to be one of opinion. (See the judgment of Leggatt J, ibid, at 462.)

8 *Anderson v Pacific and Marine Insurance Co* (supra), where an honest opinion as to the safety of an anchorage was given.

9 *Bowden v Vaughan* (1809) 10 East 414 (marine insurance).

10 *Benham v United Guarantee and Life Assurance Co* (1852) 7 Exch 744 (fidelity policy), where the representation related to the system to be followed including the employee's accounts, followed by *R v National Insurance Co* (1887) 13 VLR 914; *Hay v Employers' Liability Assurance Corpn* (1905) 6 OWR 459; *Grant v Aetna Insurance Co* (1862) 15 Moo PCC 516 (fire insurance), where the intention was stated in the policy; *Northern Assurance Co v Provost* (1881) 25 LCJ 211, where the statement in the policy was that the house insured was 'à être lambrissée en brique', and this was held to constitute a warranty of a promissory nature that the house would be immediately covered with brick. Cf *Provincial Insurance Co v Morgan* [1933] AC 240 (accident insurance); *de Maurier (Jewels) Ltd v Bastion Insurance Co Ltd and Coronet Insurance Co Ltd* [1967] 2 Lloyd's Rep 550 (jewellers' all risks insurance), where it was held that a warranty stating '[Warranted] road vehicles . . . fitted with locks and alarm system (approved by underwriters) and in operation' delimited and was part of the description of the risk and was not of a promissory character. (See the judgment of Donaldson J, ibid, at 558–559).

11 *Dodge v Western Canada Fire Insurance Co* (1912) 20 WLR 558, where the statement that a building was in course of construction was held to imply an intention to continue to construct it.

12 *Grant v Aetna Insurance Co* (supra); cf *Flinn v Headlam* (1829) 9 B & C 693 (marine insurance) per Lord Tenterden CJ, at 694; *Notman v Anchor Assurance Co* (1858) 4 CBNS 476 (life insurance), where the assured under a life policy obtained leave to reside abroad for a year, his intention being to go immediately, although he did not in fact go for several years. The principle is the same where the statement relates to the course of business intended to be followed; the assured is not prevented from making changes in his course of business afterwards: *Benham v United Guarantee and Life Assurance Co* (supra), distinguished in *Towle v National Guardian Assurance Society* (1861) 30 LJ Ch 900. A change of intention before the contract is complete must be communicated to the insurers: *Traill v Baring* (1864) 4 De GJ & Sm 318 (life insurance); *Re Marshall and Scottish Employers' Liability and General Insurance Co Ltd* (1901) 85 LT 757.

13 See p 307, post.

existing, e g where the proposed assured states that there are other insurances upon the same subject-matter, though there are none,[14] or that previous accidents have been minor ones, whereas they have been serious.[15]

Further, a statement though verbally accurate so far as it goes, is nevertheless false when taken in relation to other relevant facts which are not stated, e g where the proposed assured, in answer to a question as to previous proposals and their results, states that he is insured elsewhere, but omits to state that other proposals have been refused.[16] So, too, a statement that there are other insurances on the property proposed to be insured implies such other insurances are good and valid. If, therefore, they are void, the statement is inaccurate.[17]

The statement must, however, be considered as a whole, and if it is substantially accurate,[18] a trivial mis-statement[19] or an omission of immaterial details, does not render it inaccurate.[20]

Where representations have been made by the insurers during the negotiations with a view of inducing the assured to enter into the contract,[21] accuracy of statement is equally required from them in the discharge of duty of good faith towards him. This duty, though it applies to all matters relevant to

---

14 *Re Marshall and Scottish Employers' Liability and General Insurance Co* (supra); *Wainwright v Bland* (1836) 1 M & W 32 (life insurance); *MacDonald v Law Union Insurance Co* (1874) LR 9 QB 328 (life insurance); cf *Golding v Royal London Auxiliary Insurance Co Ltd* (1914) 30 TLR 350 (fire insurance), where the statement was held to be accurate, the other insurances being on different subject-matters.

15 *Mundy's Trustee v Blackmore* (1928) 32 LlL Rep 150; *Dent v Blackmore* (1927) 29 LlL Rep 9, where the statement 'damaged wings' was held to convey the impression that there had only been one accident of a trivial character, whereas there had been seven accidents involving more serious damage; cf *General Accident, Fire and Life Assurance Corpn Ltd v Campbell* (1925) 21 LlL Rep 151, where, on a reinsurance, the statement was that outstanding claims were not serious, whereas the total amount of claims was very large.

16 *London Assurance v Mansel* (1879) 11 ChD 363 (life insurance); *Cazenove v British Equitable Insurance Co* (1860) 29 LJCP 160, ExCh (life insurance) per Pollock CB, at 160; *Western Assurance Co v Harrison* (1903) 33 SCR 473, where, in answer to a question as to previous fires, the assured omitted to mention two out of three previous fires; *Re General Provincial Life Assurance Co, ex p Daintree* (1870) 18 WR 396 (life insurance); *Stibbard v Standard Fire and Marine Insurance Co of New Zealand* (1905) 5 SRNSW 473, where an answer which did not enumerate all the previous fires or claims made, but only mentioned one, was held to be a mis-statement. See further, pp 174–176, post.

17 *Hanley v Pacific Fire and Marine Insurance Co* (1883) 14 NSWLR 224.

18 *De Hahn v Hartley* (1786) 1 Term Rep 343 (marine insurance) (affirmed (1787) 2 Term Rep 186n, ExCh) per Lord Mansfield CJ, at 345; *Fowkes v Manchester and London Life Assurance and Loan Association* (1863) 3 B & S 917 (life insurance) per Blackburn J, at 924; *Quin v National Assurance Co* (1839) Jo & Car 316, Ex Ch (fire insurance), per Joy CB, at 328. With regard to marine insurance, the Marine Insurance Act 1906, s 20(4) states: 'A representation as to a matter of fact is true, if it be substantially correct, that is to say, if the difference between what is represented and what is actually correct would not be considered material by a prudent insurer.' See generally Ivamy *Marine Insurance* (4th Edn 1985), p 72. See further, pp 171–174, post.

19 *Re Universal Non-Tariff Fire Insurance Co, Forbes & Co's Claim* (1875) LR 19 Eq 485 (fire insurance); *O'Neill v Ottawa Agricultural Insurance Co* (1879) 30 CP 151, where the statement that the assured owned the property in fee simple was held not to be incorrect, though he had not yet paid for it.

20 *Morrison v Muspratt* (1827) 4 Bing 60 (life insurance) per Burrough J, at 63: 'Advantage ought not to be taken of omission of trifling circumstances'; *Perrins v Marine and General Travellers' Insurance Society* (1859) 2 E & E 317 (accident insurance), where the assured stated that he was an esquire, but omitted to state he was also an ironmonger.

21 E g *Pontifex v Bignold* (1841) 3 Man & G 63 (life insurance); *Tofts v Pearl Life Assurance Co Ltd* [1915] 1 KB 189, CA (life insurance); *Sun Life Assurance Co of Canada v Jervis* [1943] 2 All ER 425 (life insurance).

the insurance,[1] is especially applicable to statements[2] as to the nature and scope or effect of the contract into which the insurers are prepared to enter.[3]

A MODIFICATION OF THE DUTY BY CONTRACT

The policy may contain an express stipulation defining the duty of disclosure and prescribing the manner in which it is to be performed.[4] The performance of the duty then becomes contractual;[5] and if it is not performed, there is a breach of the contract of insurance as distinguished from a breach of the duty of good faith.[6]

Some stipulations merely express what, apart from contract, is required by good faith. In this case the duty of disclosure is not in any way extended or restricted. It is only made contractual.

Other stipulations, on the other hand, extend the duty of disclosure and require from the proposed assured more than is required by good faith.

Thus, a stipulation may make the accuracy of all statements made during the negotiations a condition precedent to the validity of the policy. In this case, no distinction is to be drawn between the statements that are material and statements that are immaterial,[7] unless the stipulation expressly refers only to

---

1 *Duffell v Wilson* (1808) 1 Camp 401 (insurance against militia ballot).

2 There is a misrepresentation of the effect of a written document when a statement is made, with knowledge of its real meaning, that it bears a different meaning; *Molloy v Mutual Reserve Life Insurance Co* (1906) 22 TLR 525, CA (life insurance) per Collins MR, at 527.

3 *Re Bradley and Essex and Suffolk Accident Indemnity Society* [1912] 1 KB 415, CA (employers' liability insurance) per Farwell LJ, at 430.

4 The stipulation may appear for the first time in the policy: *Cazenove v British Equitable Insurance Co* (1860) 29 LJCP 160, ExCh (life insurance); *Macdonald v Law Union Insurance Co* (1874) LR 9 QB 328 (life insurance). If the stipulation appears in the proposal form, it forms no part of the contract, unless incorporated in the policy, see pp 221–222, post. In case of variance between the form of stipulation in the policy itself and that incorporated from the proposal, the duty imposed upon the assured by the form in the proposal cannot be extended by the policy: *Fowkes v Manchester and London Life Assurance and Loan Association* (1863) 3 B & S 917 (life insurance), where the stipulation in the proposal form referred to designedly untrue statements, whereas the stipulation in the policy referred to untrue statements without any qualification; cf *Re Bradley and Essex and Suffolk Accident Indemnity Society* [1912] 1 KB 415, CA (employers' liability insurance).

5 *Anderson v Fitzgerald* (1853) 4 HL Cas 484 (life insurance) per Parke B, at 496; 'The proviso is clearly a part of the express contract between the parties, and on the non-compliance with the condition stated in the proviso, the policy is unquestionably void.' See also, *Stebbing v Liverpool and London and Globe Insurance Co* [1917] 2 KB 433 per Reading LCJ, at 437; *Yorkshire Insurance Co v Campbell* [1917] AC 218 at 224, PC (marine insurance), where, in an insurance upon a horse, an ordinary proposal form was used; *Thomson v Weems* (1884) 9 App Cas 671 (life insurance) per Lord Blackburn, at 683; *Joel v Law Union and Crown Insurance Co* [1908] 2 KB 863, CA (life insurance) per Fletcher-Moulton LJ, at 886.

6 See pp 119–121, ante.

7 *Newcastle Fire Insurance Co v Macmorran & Co* (1815) 3 Dow 255, HL (fire insurance) per Lord Eldon C, at 262: 'It is a first principle in the law of insurance, on all occasions, that where a representation is material, it must be complied with, if immaterial, that immateriality may be inquired into and shown, but that if there is a warranty, it is part of the contract, that the matter is such as it is represented to be. Therefore the materiality or immateriality signifies nothing. The only question is as to the mere facts'; *Anderson v Fitzgerald* (1853) 4 HL Cas 484 (life insurance) per Cranworth C, at 503: 'Whether certain statements are or are not material, where parties are entering on a contract of life insurance, is a matter upon which there must be a divided opinion. Nothing therefore can be more reasonable than that the parties entering into that contract

material statements.[8] Moreover, the policy is equally voidable whether the proposed assured, in making the inaccurate statement, is guilty of fraud[9] or merely of innocent misrepresentation,[10] since the statement must be true in fact, without any qualification of judgment, opinion or belief.[11]

The practice of making the accuracy of the statements in the proposal form the 'basis of the contract' was alluded to in *Provincial Insurance Co Ltd v Morgan*,[12] where Lord Wright said:[13]

> 'The policy is in a form which has in its general scheme long been in use by insurance companies, though the general scheme has exhibited many variations, some major and some minor, in detail. In that scheme there is a proposal form, signed by the assured, containing various particulars and answers to various questions, and a declaration that the answers are to be the basis of the contract and an agreement to accept the company's policy. The policy itself contains a recital incorporating the proposal and declaration, and it sets out the risk insured, certain exceptions and conditions, and a schedule embodying various particulars. Though this general scheme of policy has been, as it were, sanctified by long usage, it has often been pointed out by Judges that it must be very puzzling to assured, who may find it difficult to fit the disjointed parts together in such a way as to get a true and complete conspectus of what their rights and duties are and what acts on their part may involve the forfeiture of the insurance. An assured may easily find himself deprived of the benefits of the policy because he had done something quite innocently but in breach of a condition, ascertainable only by the dovetailing of scattered portions.'

Thus, in *Dawsons Ltd v Bonnin*:[14]

> The assured had inserted in a proposal form in respect of the insurance of a lorry, a statement that it was usually garaged at 'No 46 Cadogan Street, Glasgow'. In fact it was usually garaged at a farm on the outskirts of the city. This mis-statement had been made inadvertently and was not material. But the proposal form had included a 'basis' clause. The lorry was destroyed by fire.
> *Held*, that the insured could not recover, for the statement, though not material, was inaccurate.

Viscount Haldane said:[15]

> 'I think that the words employed in the body of the policy can only be properly construed as

---

should determine for themselves what they think to be material, and if they choose to do so, and to stipulate that unless the assured shall answer a certain question accurately, the policy or contract which they are entering into shall be void, it is perfectly open to them to do so, and his false answer will then avoid the policy.' See also, *Thomson v Weems* (1884) 9 App Cas 671 (life insurance) per Blackburn, at 683; *Condogianis v Guardian Assurance Co* [1921] 2 AC 125 at 129, PC (fire insurance).

8 *Dawsons Ltd v Bonnin* [1922] 2 AC 413, 12 LlL Rep 237 (motor insurance), where there were two conditions, one of which referred only to material mis-statements; *Re Universal Non-Tariff Insurance Fire Co, Forbes & Co's Claim* (1875) LR 19 Eq 485 (fire insurance), where there was a similar condition.

9 *London Assurance v Mansel* (1879), 11 ChD 363 (life insurance); *Hambrough v Mutual Life Insurance Co of New York* (1895) 72 LT 140, CA (life insurance).

10 *Reid & Co v Employers' Accident and Live Stock Insurance Co* 1899 1 F (Ct of Sess) 1031 (accident inurance); *Duckett v Williams* (1834) 2 Cr & M 348 (life insurance); *Macdonald v Law Union Insurance Co* (1874) LR 9 QB 328 (life insurance); *Thomson v Weems* (1884) 9 App Cas 671 (life insurance), where fraud was not alleged.

11 *Newcastle Fire Insurance Co v Macmorran & Co* (1815) 3 Dow 255, HL (fire insurance); *Fowkes v Manchester and London Life Assurance and Loan Association* (1963) 3 B & S 917 (life insurance) per Blackburn J, at 928; *Thomson v Weems* (supra) (life insurance) per Lord Fitzgerald, at 697.

12 [1933] AC 240, HL.

13 Ibid, at 98.

14 [1922] 2 AC 413, HL.

15 Ibid, at 424.

having made its accuracy a condition. The result may be technical and harsh, but if the parties have so stipulated, we have no alternative, sitting as a court of justice, but to give effect to the words agreed on. Hard cases must not be allowed to make bad law. Now the proposal, in other words the answers to the questions specifically put in it, are made basic to the contract. It may well be that a mere slip, in a Christian name, for instance, would not be held to vitiate the answer given if the answer were really in substance true and unambiguous. "*Falsa demonstratio non nocet.*" But that is because the truth has been stated in effect within the intention shown by the language used. This mis-statement as to the address at which the vehicle would usually be garaged can hardly be brought within this principle of interpretation in construing contracts. It was a specific insurance based on a statement which is made foundational if the parties have chosen, however carelessly, to stipulate that it should be so. Both on principle and in the light of authorities . . . it appears to me that when answers, including that in question, are declared to be the basis of the contract, this can only mean that their truth is made a condition, exact fulfilment of which is rendered by stipulation foundational to its enforceability.'

Similarly, in *Mackay v London General Insurance Co Ltd*:[16]

In answer to the question in a proposal form for a motor car policy, the insured had said that he had never been convicted. Some years before he had been fined 10s. for riding a motor bicycle with defective brakes. The answer which he had given was immaterial.
Held, that since the insured had warranted the truth of his statements, he could not recover under the policy, for their accuracy had been made the basis of the contract.

Swift J was most outspoken in the comments which he made, for in the course of his judgment he observed:[17]

'If he had stated the truth in its full detail, this insurance company would have jumped at receiving his premium. They would never have dreamed of rejecting his application, but after they have given him the policy and after the accident has happened and the liability is incurred, they seize upon these inaccuracies in the proposal form in order to repudiate their liability. I am extremely sorry for the plaintiff in this case. I think he has been very badly treated, shockingly badly treated. They have taken his premium. They have not been in the least bit misled by the answers which he has made. They would never have refused to take his money; they would never have refused him his policy if they had known everything which they know now. But they have seized upon this opportunity in order to turn him down and leave him without any indemnity for the liability which he has incurred. But I cannot help the position. Sorry as I am for him there is nothing that I can do to help him. The law is quite plain.'[18]

The proposed assured, may, however, expressly qualify his statements by stating that they are accurate to the best of his belief, in which case an innocent misrepresentation is not a breach of the condition precedent.[19] Stipulations of this kind are strictly construed, and it must be clearly shown that the assured agreed to be bound by them.[20]

---

16 (1935) 51 LlL Rep 201.

17 Ibid, at 202.

18 As to the inadvisability of warranting the truth of a statement made by the assured in a proposal form as to the full value of the property when the property is under-insured, see *West v National Motor and Accident Insurance Union Ltd* [1954] 2 Lloyd's Rep 461 (fire insurance).

19 *Macdonald v Law Union Insurance Co* (supra) (life insurance) per Lush J, at 331: cf *Jones v Provincial Insurance Co* (1857) 3 CBNS 65 (life insurance) per Cresswell J, at 86. The insurers, by accepting a statement with a qualification, must be presumed to waive a fuller or more complete statement.

20 *Joel v Law Union and Crown Insurance Co* [1908] 2 KB 863, CA (life insurance) per Fletcher-Moulton LJ, at 886: 'Under these circumstances, it is plainly the duty of the Court to require the insurers to establish clearly that the insured consented to the accuracy, and not the truthfulness, of his statements being made a condition of the validity of the policy. No ambiguous language suffices for this purpose. The applicant can be, and is called on to answer all questions relevant to the matter in hand. But this is merely the fulfilment of a duty—it is not

Some stipulations, however, restrict the duty of disclosure and require from the proposed assured less than is required by good faith. Thus, the stipulation may provide that the policy is to be avoided only in the event of fraud,[1] or, in the case of insurances covering several items of property, that the policy is to be avoided only as regards the item in respect of which the inaccurate statement is made.

B QUESTIONS AND ANSWERS

The insurers may, at any time during the negotiations, ask the assured questions as to any matters upon which they require information. In practice, a list of printed questions in the proposal form is usually submitted to him to answer in writing. In addition, he may be asked other questions on specific matters not covered by the questions in the proposal form. Such questions may be put and answered in writing[2] or by parol.[3]

A The effect of the questions

Where questions, whether written or verbal, are asked by the insurers, the assured's duty of disclosure is to some extent altered.

Notwithstanding the questions, the Common Law duty of disclosure remains, and the proposer must disclose material facts which are not covered by the questions.[4]

On the other hand, though the asking of questions is not conclusive, the questions show what facts are regarded by the insurers as material.

---

contractual. To make the accuracy of these answers a condition of the contract is a contractual act, and if there is the slightest doubt that the insurers have failed to make clear to the man on whom they have exercised their right of requiring full information that he is consenting thus to contract, we ought to refuse to regard the correctness of the answers given as being a condition of the validity of the policy. In other words, the insurers must prove by clear and express language the animus contrahendi on the part of the applicant; it will not be inferred from the fact that questions were answered and that the party declared that the answers were true. This is only what a witness does when he declares he has given true evidence. He is stating his belief, and not making a contract.' See also, *Anderson v Fitgerald* (1853) 4 HL Cas 484 (life insurance) per Lord St Leonards, at 507; *Thomson v Weems* (1884) 9 App Cas 671 (life insurance) per Lord Blackburn, at 682.

1 *Wood v Dwarris* (1856) 11 Exch 493 (life insurance); *Fowkes v Manchester and London Life Assurance and Loan Association* (1863) 3 B & S 917 (life insurance), followed in *Hemmings v Sceptre Life Association Ltd* [1905] 1 Ch 365 (life insurance), but distinguished in *Reid & Co v Employers' Accident and Live Stock Insurance Co* 1899 1 F (Ct of Sess) 1031 (accident insurance); *Anstey v British Natural Premium Life Association Ltd* (1908) 24 TLR 594; affd 99 LT 765 (life insurance); cf *Scottish Provident Institution v Boddam* (1893) 9 TLR 385 (life insurance). See further, *Holmes v Scottish Legal Life Assurance Society* (1932) 48 TLR 306 (life insurance), where there was an inconsistency between the policy and the rules of the Society, and the policy prevailed.

2 *Re General Provincial Life Assurance Co Ltd, ex p Daintree* (1870) 18 WR 396 (life insurance), where a letter was written asking specifically whether the insurance had been refused by other companies.

3 *Wainwright v Bland* (1836) 1 M & W 32 (life insurance); *Joel v Law Union and Crown Insurance Co* [1908] 2 KB 863, CA (life insurance), where answers to questions put by the medical examiner were written down by him, and signed by the proposed assured; *Fernand v Metropolitan Life Insurance Co* (1913) QR 44 SC 117 (life insurance), where the answers were written by the medical examiner, but were not signed by the proposed assured.

4 *Dawsons Ltd v Bonnin* [1922] 2 AC 413: 12 LlL Rep 237; *Glicksman v Lancashire and General*

> 'There is . . . no doubt that both in life and burglary insurances the insurance offices make it plain to the assured that they think it material to know whether anybody else has refused the risk. The question nearly always appears in some form or other in the proposal forms of those offices. And in my view, when it is shown to the assured that the underwriter is treating a certain fact as material, he comes under an obligation to disclose any fact of that character.'[5]

If the insurance company does not ask a question about a particular fact in the proposal form, it runs a risk for, as Scrutton LJ pointed out, it might be said: 'Well there is a material fact which you did not ask a question about, and as you did not ask a question about it, you cannot say that it was material and ought to have been disclosed.'[6]

Again, in a motor insurance case,[7] where no question in the proposal form was directed as to whether the proposer had failed to pass a driving test, Goddard LJ said:[8]

Assurance Co [1927] AC 139 (burglary insurance); *Joel v Law Union and Crown Insurance Co* [1908] 2 KB 863, CA (life insurance) per Vaughan Williams LJ, at 878, per Fletcher Moulton LJ, at 892; *Yorke v Yorkshire Insurance Co* [1918] 1 KB 662 (life insurance) per McCardie J, at 666; *Bond v Commercial Assurance Co* (1930) 35 Com Cas 171, 36 LlL Rep 107 (accident insurance); *Holt's Motors Ltd v South East Lancashire Insurance Co Ltd* (1930) 35 Com Cas 281, 37 LlL Rep 1, CA; *Wainwright v Bland* (1836) 1 M & W 32 (life insurance); *Fine v General Accident, Fire and Life Assurance Corpn* [1915] App D 213; *Steyn v Malmesbury Board of Executors and Trust and Assurance Co* [1921] CPD 96; *Schoolman v Hall,* [1951] 1 Lloyd's Rep 139, CA (jewellers' block policy) where Cohen LJ, said (at 142): 'While the insurers have stipulated that the answers to the fifteen questions 'shall be the basis of the contract', that only has the effect of preventing any argument as to the materiality of those questions should dispute arise, but it does not relieve the proposer of his general obligation at Common Law to disclose any material fact which might affect the risk which was being run, or which might affect the mind of the insurer as to whether or not he should issue a policy'; *Taylor v Eagle Insurance Co Ltd* (1940) 67 LlL Rep 136 (motor insurance), where the question in the proposal form related to the commission of *driving* offences, and it was held material that the insured had been convicted of certain drinking offences and that he had also been convicted upon charges of permitting a car to be used without a policy of insurance and of driving a car with no road fund licence in force. All these should have been disclosed.

5 *Glicksman v London and General Assurance Co Ltd* [1925] 2 KB 593, CA at 609 (per Scrutton LJ). See also the speech of Viscount Dunedin, when this case was affirmed by the House of Lords, [1927] AC 139 at 144: 'But here the whole point really comes to turn upon this— . . . that . . . the fact that a question of this sort was put showed that the insurance company thought it was material whether a proposal had been refused or not, and that that was brought to the knowledge of the claimant.' See further, *Babatsikos v Car Owners' Mutual Insurance Co Ltd* [1970] 2 Lloyd's Rep 314, Supreme Ct of Victoria, Court of Appeal (motor insurance), where Pape J said (ibid, at 323): 'Upon the issue of materiality evidence may be given by the [insurance company] as to its practice. But although such evidence is admissible as part of the circumstances existing at the time of the proposal, it does not of itself establish materiality, although it may assist the tribunal of fact to come to a conclusion on the issue. In truth it goes only part of the way—it at least establishes that the [insurance company] regarded it as material. It is conceivable that a particular insurance company may decide as a matter of policy not to insure proponents of a certain religion, or faith, and so regard it as material to be informed by the answer to a question in the proposal of the religion of the proponent. But the mere asking of the question would not make the matter material unless it were established . . . and could be so regarded by a prudent insurer, as might be the case if the intended insurance was against fire and the subject-matter of the insurance within an area where religious dissension had caused rioting and arson.'

6 *McCormick v National Motor Accident Insurance Union Ltd* (1934) 40 Com Cas 76 at 78. See also, *Newsholme Bros v Road Transport and General Insurance Co Ltd* [1929] 2 KB 356 at 363: 'The insurance companies also run the risk of the contention that matters they do not ask questions about are not material, for, if they were, they would ask questions about them' (per Scrutton LJ).

7 *Zurich General Accident and Liability Insurance Co Ltd v Morrison* [1942] 2 KB 53, 72 LlL Rep 167, CA.

8 Ibid, at 64.

'Underwriters cannot frame their questions so as to include everything that may affect any particular proposer, and the fact which ought to be disclosed may well be something peculiar to an individual case. But whether or not a person has failed in his test must, I should think, affect a very large number of proposers. The underwriter exhibits to them a long catechism in which he puts questions on matters which may affect any proposer, such as whether the car is to be used for hire, whether the person who will drive has any infirmity, or whether he had been convicted of any motoring offence, and I cannot help thinking that if it is material for the underwriter to know whether or not the proposer has failed in a test, he would ask the question.'

On the other hand, the questions serve to define the limits of what is material, and may, by requiring information of a specific sort, thus relieve the assured from the duty of disclosing facts which are not within their scope, though, if the questions have not been asked, such facts would have had to be disclosed by him in the ordinary discharge of his duty.

Thus, in a case concerning burglary insurance[9] Asquith LJ said:[10]

'It is unquestionably plain that questions in a proposal form may be so framed as necessarily to imply that the underwriter only wants information on certain subject-matters, or that within a particular subject-matter their desire for information is restricted within the narrow limits indicated by the terms of the question, and, in such a case, they may *pro tanto* dispense the proposer from what otherwise at Common Law would have been a duty to disclose everything material.'

Further, the observations of Vaughan Williams LJ in a case relating to life insurance are also pertinent:

'I think also that the insurance office may, by the requisitions for information of a specific sort, which it makes of the proposer, relieve him partially from the obligation to disclose by an election to make inquiries as to certain facts material to the risk to be insured against itself.'[11]

Thus, if the proposer for a fire policy is asked to state how many fires he has had during the last three years, the specification of a precise period will relieve him from the duty of disclosing a fire which happened five years before.

Again, an example of this effect of the questions is to be found in *Jester-Barnes v Licenses and General Insurance Co Ltd*[12], where MacKinnon J said (obiter) that if an insurance company had asked a proposer the question 'Have you or your driver during the past five years been convicted of any offence?' and he had said 'No', and that was true, he would have come without any hesitation to the conclusion that the company was not entitled, after asking that question and receiving the true answer, to take it to mean that he had failed to disclose that he had been convicted eight years ago, and that that was a material fact.

The questions may be so framed as to apply to the future as well as to the circumstances at the date of the answers, but in order to effect this, the intention must be clear.[13]

---

9 *Schoolman v Hall* [1951] 1 Lloyd's Rep 139, CA (burglary insurance).

10 Ibid, at 143. See further, *March Cabaret Club and Casino Ltd v London Assurance* [1975] 1 Lloyd's Rep 169 (trader's combined insurance), per May J, at 176.

11 *Joel v Law Union and Crown Insurance Co* [1908] 2 KB 863, CA (life insurance) at 878.

12 (1934) 49 LlL Rep 231 at 237 (motor insurance).

13 *Dawsons Ltd v Bonnin* [1922] 2 AC 413, 12 LlL Rep 237; cf *Provincial Insurance Co v Morgan* [1933] AC 240 (accident insurance); *Hearts of Oak Building Society v Law Union and Rock Insurance Co Ltd* [1936] 2 All ER 619 (liability insurance); *Woolfall and Rimmer Ltd v Moyle* [1942] 1 KB 66, [1941] 3 All ER 304, 71 LlL Rep 15, CA (employers' liability insurance); *Beauchamp v National Mutual Indemnity Insurance Co Ltd* [1937] 3 All ER 19 (liability insurance); *Hales v Reliance Fire and Accident Insurance Corpn Ltd* [1960] 2 Lloyd's Rep 391, QB (fire insurance), where the question in

B *The effect of the answers*

The effect of the answers will depend upon whether there is or is not a 'basis' clause in the proposal form.

1 Where there is a 'basis' clause

(a) The present law

The usual declaration at the foot of the proposal form that the answers are true, and that they are to be the basis of the proposed contract of insurance, makes the truth of the answers a condition precedent,[14] and the proposed assured, by signing it, signifies his agreement thereto.[15] The condition may, however, appear for the first time in the policy, in which case the assured signifies his agreement by suing on the policy.[16]

A condition will not, however, be so construed, unless its language is

---

the proposal form stated 'Are any inflammable oils or goods used or kept on the premises?' and was held to apply to the future. Consequently the insurer was entitled to avoid the policy when the insured stored fireworks on the premises shortly before October 19 with a view to their being sold on Guy Fawkes' Day; *Weber and Berger v Employers' Liability Assurance Corpn* (1926) 24 LlL Rep 321 (burglary insurance), where the question in the proposal form—'Do you keep books with a complete record of all purchases and sales, and are these books regularly entered up?' was held not to amount to a promise of conduct in the future; *Sweeney v Kennedy* (1948) 82 LlL Rep 294 (Eire Div Ct) (motor insurance), where the question in the proposal form stating: 'Are any of your drivers under 21 years of age or with less than 12 months' driving experience?' was held not to have reference to the future; *Kirkbride v Donner* [1974] 1 Lloyd's Rep 549, Mayor's and City of London Ct (motor insurance), where the question in the proposal form stated: 'Will the car to your knowledge be driven by any person under 25 years of age?' was held not to refer to the future.

14 *Dawsons Ltd v Bonnin* [1922] 2 AC 413, 12 LlL Rep 237 (accident insurance); *Glicksman v Lancashire and General Assurance Co* [1927] AC 139 (burglary insurance) per Lord Dunedin, at 143; *Anderson v Fitzgerald* (1853) 4 HL Cas 484 (life insurance) per Lord Cranworth, at 503: 'Whether certain statements are or are not material, where parties are entering into a contract of life insurance, is a matter upon which there must be a divided opinion. Nothing, therefore, can be more reasonable that the parties entering into that contract should determine for themselves what they think to be material, and if they choose to do so, and to stipulate that unless the assured shall answer a certain question accurately, the policy or contract into which they are entering shall be void, it is perfectly open to them to do so, and a false answer will then avoid the policy'; *Thomson v Weems* (1884) 9 App Cas 671 (life insurance); *Australian Widows' Fund Life Assurance Society Ltd v National Mutual Life Association of Australasia Ltd* [1914] AC 634, PC (life insurance); *Condogianis v Guardian Assurance Co* [1921] 2 AC 125, 3 LlL Rep 40, PC (fire insurance); *Stebbing v Liverpool and London and Globe Insurance Co Ltd* [1917] 2 KB 433 (burglary insurance) per Lord Reading CJ, at 437; *Levy v Scottish Employers' Insurance Co* (1901) 17 TLR 229; *Re Marshall and Scottish Employers' Liability and General Insurance Co Ltd* (1901) 85 LT 757; *Biggar v Rock Life Assurance Co* [1902] 1 KB 516; *Paxman v Union Assurance Society Ltd* (1923) 39 TLR 424, 15 LlL Rep 206 (accident insurance); *Magee v Pennine Insurance Co Ltd* [1969] 2 QB 507, [1969] 2 All ER 891, CA (motor insurance), where the insured stated that he held a driving licence, and that the car belonged to him, and both these statements were, in fact, false, though the Court found that they had not been made fraudulently. See the judgment of Lord Denning MR, ibid, at 892–893.

15 *Biggar v Rock Life Assurance Co* (supra); *Reid & Co v Employers' Accident and Live Stock Insurance Co* 1899 1 F (Ct of Sess) 1031 per Lord Traynor, at 1036; *M'Millan v Accident Insurance Co* 1907 SC 484 per Lord Stormonth-Darling at 493; *Rokkyer v Australian Alliance Assurance Co* (1908) 28 NZLR 305 (life insurance). It is immaterial that the proposal is not incorporated into the contract: *Rozanes v Bowen* (1928) 32 LlL Rep 98, CA (jewellery insurance).

16 *Cazenove v British Equitable Insurance Co* (1860) 29 LJCP 160, ExCh (life insurance); *Macdonald v Law Union Insurance Co* (1874) LR 9 QB 328 (life insurance).

sufficiently clear and amounts to a warranty that the facts stated in the answers are true.[17] Thus, Fletcher-Moulton LJ said:[18]

> 'To make the accuracy of these answers a condition of the contract is a contractual act, and if there is the slightest doubt that the insurers have failed to make clear to the man on whom they have exercised their right of requiring full information that he is consenting thus to contract, we ought to refuse to regard the correctness of the answers given as being a condition of the validity of the policy. In other words, the insurers must prove by clear and express language the *animus contrahendi* on the part of the applicant; it will not be inferred from the fact that questions were answered, and that the party interrogated declared that his answers were true.'

Where this is the case, it is open to the assured to qualify his answers by stating that they are correct to the best of his belief.[19] Sometimes the condition itself contains a similar qualification.[20]

Where the truth of the statements is made the basis of the contract, it is unnecessary to consider whether the fact inaccurately stated is material or not, or whether the assured knew or did not know the truth.[21]

(b) *Fifth Report of Law Reform Committee*

In 1957 the Law Reform Committee stated in their Fifth Report[22] that the result of the presence of a 'basis' clause in a proposal form was to render irrelevant any question either of the materiality of the information so obtained, or the honesty or care with which it was given. If the answer given was inaccurate, the insurers were at liberty to repudiate. Further, it was clear that the answering of specific questions, however detailed and searching, did not relieve the proposer from his duty to disclose material facts, although in practice, especially in life insurance, the exhaustive nature of the inquiry might be such as to make it highly improbable that any possible material fact would not be covered.[23]

The Committee recommended that 'notwithstanding anything contained in or incorporated in a contract of insurance, no defence to a claim should be

---

17 *Provincial Insurance Co Ltd v Morgan* [1933] AC 240 (accident insurance).

18 *Joel v Law Union and Crown Insurance Co* [1908] 2 KB 863, CA (life insurance) at 866.

19 *Macdonald v Law Union Insurance Co* (1874) LR 9 QB 328 (life insurance) per Lush J, at 331; cf *Jones v Provincial Insurance Co* (1857) 3 CBNS 65 (life insurance) per Cresswell J, at 86. The insurers, by accepting a statement with a qualification, must be presumed to waive a fuller or more complete statement.

20 *Pawson v Watson* (1778) 2 Cowp 785 (marine insurance) per Lord Mansfield CJ, at 788; *Jones v Provincial Insurance Co* (supra) (life insurance); *Hemmings v Sceptre Life Association Ltd* [1905] 1 Ch 365 (life insurance).

21 *Condogianis v Guardian Assurance Co* (supra); *Anderson v Fitzgerald* (supra); *Macdonald v Law Union Insurance Co* (supra); *Thomson v Weems* (1884) 9 App Cas 671 (life insurance), following *Duckett v Williams* (1834) 2 Cr & M 348 (life insurance); *Hamborough v Mutual Life Insurance Co of New York* (1895) 72 LT 140, CA (life insurance); *Paxman v Union Assurance Society* (1923) 39 TLR 424, 15 LlL Rep 206 (accident insurance); *Copp v Glasgow and London Insurance Co* (1890) 30 NBR 197; *James v Royal Insurance Co* (1908) 10 NZ Gaz LR 244; *Newcastle Fire Insurance Co v Macmorran & Co* (1815) 3 Dow 255, HL (fire insurance) per Lord Eldon LC, at 262: 'It is a first principle in the law of insurance, on all occasions, that where a representation is material, it must be complied with, if immaterial, that immateriality may be inquired into and shown, but that if there is a warranty, it is a part of the contract, that the matter is such as it is represented to be. Therefore the materiality or immateriality signifies nothing. The only question is as to the mere facts.'

22 *Conditions and Exceptions in Insurance Policies*, 1957, Cmnd 62.

23 Para 6.

maintainable by reason of any mis-statement of fact by the insured, where the insured can prove that the statement was true to the best of his knowledge and belief.'[24]

2 Where there is no 'basis' clause

Where there is no condition making the proposal the 'basis' of the contract, the inaccuracy of the answers does not entitle the insurers to repudiate liability unless it amounts to the non-disclosure or misrepresentation of a material fact.[1]

A fraudulent representation relating to a material fact avoids the contract.[2] If the fact is not material, the validity of the contract is not affected.[3]

As far as marine insurance is concerned, the insurer is entitled to avoid liability on the policy, whether the misrepresentation is fraudulent or innocent. Section 20(1) of the Marine Insurance Act 1906, states:

> 'Every material representation made by the assured or his agent to the insurer during the negotiations for the contract, and before the contract is concluded, must be true. If it be untrue the insurer may avoid the contract.'[4]

In the case of non-marine insurance, whether the insurers can avoid liability in the case of an innocent misrepresentation is not settled.

In *Graham v Western Australian Insurance Co Ltd*,[5] Roche J said that 'If there is information given, be it quite innocent, which is not a matter of contract, and never becomes a matter of contract, yet, nevertheless, if it is inaccurate, it can be used to avoid the policy or policies in question.'[6]

C The types of inaccuracy

Sometimes, the answer which is given contains a statement of fact which is directly contrary to the truth. Thus, in answer to a question as to previous

---

24 Para 14.

1 *Dawsons Ltd v Bonnin* [1922] 2 AC 413, 12 LlL Rep 237 (accident insurance); *Mutual Life Insurance Co of New York v Ontario Metal Products Co Ltd* [1925] AC 344, PC (life insurance). In *de Maurier (Jewels) Ltd v Bastion Insurance Co Ltd and Coronet Insurance Co Ltd* [1967] 2 Lloyd's Rep 550 (jewellers' all risks insurance) a representation that the locks on a car, in which the insured jewellery was being carried, were of a type giving more protection than the standard locks supplied with the vehicle, was held to be immaterial because the insurers were protected by a warranty which stated: '[Warranted] road vehicles . . . fitted with locks and alarm system (approved by underwriters) and in operation'. See the judgment of Donaldson J, ibid, at 558, where he held that the representation was false because the vehicle had no locks other than those fitted on any production model.

2 *Wheelton v Hardisty* (1857) 8 E & B 232, ExCh (life insurance) per Willes J, at 299; *Thomson v Weems* (1884) 9 App Cas 671 (life insurance) per Lord Blackburn, at 683.

3 *Anderson v Fitzgerald* (1853) 4 HL Cas 484 (life insurance) per Lord Cranworth C, at 504; '. . . if the party makes no warranty at all, but simply makes a certain statement, if that statement has been made bona fide, unless it is material it does not signify whether it is false or not false. Indeed, whether made bona fide or not, if it is not material, the untruth is quite unimportant.'

4 See further Ivamy *Marine Insurance* (4th Edn 1985), p 71.

5 (1931) 40 LlL Rep 64.

6 Ibid, at 66. See also, *Versicherungs und Transport AG Daugava v Henderson* (1934) 48 LlL Rep 54 (not appealed from on this point (1934) 49 LlL Rep 252, CA), per Roche J, at 58, where he expressed the view (though he decided on the facts that the misrepresentation in question was reckless) that all material misrepresentations, innocent or otherwise, were a ground for avoiding the policy; *Merchants and Manufacturers' Insurance Co Ltd v Hunt and Thorne and Thorne* [1941] 1 KB 295 at 318 (per Luxmoore LJ).

refusals, the assured may state that there have been none, whereas, in fact, a previous proposal has been declined.[7]

But at other times the answer may contain no statement of fact which is directly contrary to the truth. It may be true, so far as it goes; but by reason of the omission of other facts falling within the scope of the question, the answer is, in effect, inaccurate and misleading.

Thus, the assured may fail to give an alternative name by which he has been known,[8] understate the number of other insurances,[9] or of previous losses.[10] In answer to a question as to previous refusals, he may state only that negotiations with other insurers are pending, and omit to disclose the fact that there have been actual refusals.[11]

D The interpretation of the questions and answers

The scope of any particular question depends partly on the language in which it is framed,[12] and partly on the circumstances to which it is intended to relate.[13]

The statement must be considered as a whole, and a fair and reasonable construction must be adopted. The assured is under a duty to tell the whole truth. A half-truth is not enough. The answers must be construed against the background of any other information which the insurers happen to have. Where the answers are unsatisfactory, the insurers may be deemed to have waived their rights if they do not make further inquiries. Sometimes the space for the answer is left blank and here special rules apply.

---

7 *Biggar v Rock Life Assurance Co* [1902] 1 KB 516 (accident insurance); *Stott v London and Lancashire Fire Insurance Co* (1891) 21 OR 312; *Critchley v Atlas Insurance Co* (1906) 9 NZ Gaz LR 6.

8 *Gallé Gowns Ltd v Licenses and General Insurance Co Ltd* (1933) 47 LlL Rep 186 (fire insurance), where the insured had a bad financial record and a claim on a policy in other names.

9 *Wainwright v Bland* (1836) 1 M & W 32 (life insurance); *London Assurance v Mansel* (1879) 11 ChD 363 (life insurance). See also, *O'Neill v Ottawa Agricultural Insurance Co* (1879) 30 CP 151, where the number of pipe stoves was understated.

10 *Condogianis v Guardian Assurance Co* [1921] 2 AC 125, 2 LlL Rep 40, PC (fire insurance); *Reid & Co v Employers' Accident and Livestock Insurance Co* 1899 1 F (Ct of Sess) 1031 (accident insurance); *Rozanes v Bowen* (1928) 32 LlL Rep 98, CA (jewellery insurance); *Western Assurance Co v Harrison* (1903) 33 SCR 473; *Gillis v Canada Fire Assurance Co* (1904) QR 26 SC 166; *Stibbard v Standard Fire and Marine Insurance Co of New Zealand* (1905) 5 SR NSW 473.

11 *Re General Provincial Life Assurance Co, ex p Daintree* (1870) 18 WR 396 (life insurance), where the answer simply referred to pending negotiations with other insurers, whereas there had been refusals; *London Assurance v Mansel* (1879) 11 ChD 363 (life insurance), where the answer stated that the assured was insured in other offices, but omitted to state that several offices had declined the insurance; *Broad and Montague Ltd v South-East Lancashire Insurance Co* (1931) 40 LlL Rep 328 (motor insurance), where there had been refusals to renew by two companies, but only one refusal was mentioned.

12 *Connecticut Mutual Life Insurance Co of Hertford v Moore* (1881) 6 App Cas 644, PC (life insurance).

13 *Thomson v Weems* (1884) 9 App Cas 671 (life insurance) per Lord Blackburn, at 685; *Shilling v Accidental Death Insurance Co* (1858) 1 F & F 116, where the fact that the assured was ruptured and subject to fainting fits was held not to falsify a declaration that he had not been subject to epileptic or other fits, or that there were no other circumstances touching his occupation or habits with which the insurers ought to be acquainted; *Anderson v Pacific Fire and Marine Insurance Co* (1869) 21 LT 408, PC (marine insurance); *Golding v Royal London Auxiliary Insurance Co Ltd* (1914) 30 TLR 350 (fire insurance); *Ashford v Victoria Mutual Assurance Co* (1870) 20 CP 434, where an insurance on stock was not avoided by the failure to mention incumbrances on the building containing it; cf *Phillips v Grand River Farmers' Mutual Fire Insurance Co* (1881) 46 UCR 334, where it was the building that was insured, and consequently the policy was avoided by the failure to disclose incumbrances on it.

1 The statement must be considered as a whole

The statement must, however, be considered as a whole, and if it is substantially accurate,[14] a trivial mis-statement[15] or an omission of immaterial details[16] does not render it inaccurate. Thus, where an assured, having two occupations, is asked to state his occupation, his answer is not inaccurate because he states one of them only, and omits to state the other,[17] unless the fact that he has two occupations is material to the risk.[18]

2 A fair and reasonable construction must be adopted

It is a general principle that a fair and reasonable construction must be placed on the questions in the proposal form and on the answers which the proposer has given to them.

Thus, in the leading case of *Condogianis v Guardian Assurance Co*[19] Lord Shaw of Dunfermline said:[20]

---

14 *Fowkes v Manchester and London Life Assurance and Loan Association* (1863) 3 B & S 917 (life insurance) per Blackburn J, at 924; *Yorke v Yorkshire Insurance Co* [1918] 1 KB 662 (life insurance) per McCardie J, at 669; *Brewtnall v Cornhill Insurance Co Ltd* (1931) 40 LlL Rep 166 (motor insurance), where the question related to cost price, the insured giving a figure made up of the cash paid and the agreed value of another car given in part exchange. In this case Charles J said (at 168): 'If the insurance company really wish, and if their intention really is, in asking the question as to the cost price to the proposer, to have all the ingredients of the costs—not only the cash but all the ingredients—set out in their proposal form, then they should frame their question in such a way as will show to the proposer what it is that is expected of her and just what is intended.' Cf *Allen v Universal Automobile Insurance Co Ltd* (1933) 45 LlL Rep 55 (motor insurance), where the insured stated that the actual price he had paid for the car was £285, and the price was in fact £271, and the insurance company was held to be entitled to avoid the policy because he had warranted that the answers to the questions asked in the proposal form were true.

15 *Re Universal Non-Tariff Fire Insurance Co, Forbes & Co's Claim* (1875) LR 19 Eq 485 (fire insurance); *Dawsons Ltd v Bonnin* [1922] 2 AC 413, 12 LlL Rep 237 per Viscount Haldane, at 425, pointing out that a mere slip in a Christian name might be disregarded, even when there was a condition; *Laidlaw v Liverpool and London Insurance Co* (1867) 13 Gr 377, where the assured gave a round figure as the value of the property slightly in excess of the actual price; *O'Neill v Ottawa Agricultural Insurance Co* (1879) 30 CP 151 where the distance of a building was stated to be 190 feet, instead of 178 feet.

16 *Morrison v Muspratt* (1827) 4 Bing 60 (life insurance) per Burrough J, at 63: 'Advantage ought not to be taken of the omission of trifling circumstances'; *Huguenin v Rayley* (1815) 6 Taunt 186 (life insurance), where the answer as to place of residence omitted to state that the assured was in jail, and it was held to be a question for the jury whether the fact omitted was material; *Naughter v Ottawa Agricultural Insurance Co* (1878) 43 UCR 121, where the assured stated that there was no building within 100 feet, whereas there was a small outhouse 46 feet away; *Strong v Crown Fire Insurance Co* (1913) 23 OWR 701, where the assured omitted to disclose a previous trivial fire, his then insurers having continued the policy afterwards; *Burnside v Melbourne Fire Office* [1920] VLR 56 (non-disclosure of trivial loss).

17 *Perrins v Marine and General Travellers' Insurance Society* (1859) 2 E & E 317 (accident insurance), where an ironmonger described himself as an esquire, the rate of premium being the same for both; cf *Woodall v Pearl Assurance Co* [1919] 1 KB 593, CA (accident insurance).

18 *Biggar v Rock Life Assurance Co* [1902] 1 KB 516 (accident insurance). In *Holdsworth v Lancashire and Yorkshire Insurance Co* (1907) 23 TLR 521 (employers' liability insurance), where the assured was described as a joiner, whereas he was also a builder, and *Ayrey v British Legal and United Provident Assurance Co* [1918] 1 KB 136 (life insurance), where a fisherman omitted to state that he was a member of the Royal Naval Reserve, knowledge was imputed to the insurers.

19 [1921] 2 AC 125.

20 Ibid, at 130.

> 'In a contract of insurance it is a weighty fact that the questions are framed by the insurer and that if an answer is obtained to such a question which is upon a fair construction a true answer, it is not open to the insuring company to maintain that the question was put in a sense different from or more comprehensive than the proponent's answer covered. Where an ambiguity exists, the contract must stand if an answer has been made to the question on a fair and reasonable construction of that question. Otherwise the ambiguity would be a trap against which the insured would be protected by Courts of Law. Their Lordships accept that doctrine to the full, and no question is made of the soundness of it as set forth in many authorities.'

In *Connecticut Mutual Life Insurance Co of Hertford v Moore*[1]

> A question in a proposal for a policy of life assurance stated, 'Have you had any other illness, local disease, or personal injury? And if so, of what nature, how long since, and what effect upon general health?' The answer which was given was, 'No'.
> *Held,* a reasonable construction must be put on the question which must be assumed to refer to serious illnesses only.

Sir Robert P Collier said:[2]

> 'This is a question of a somewhat embarrassing character, and one which the company could hardly reasonably have expected to be answered with strict and literal truth. They could not reasonably expect a man of mature age to recollect and disclose every illness, however slight, or every personal injury, consisting of a contusion, or a cut, or a blow, which he might have suffered in the course of his life. It is manifest that this question must be read with some limitation and qualification to render it reasonable; and that personal injury must be interpreted as one of a somewhat serious or severe character.'

Where a question in a proposal form for life insurance said, 'What medical men have you consulted? when? and what for?' it was held that this did not mean that the insured had to give a list of all the doctors she had seen in her life. She had only to give a list which was sufficient for practical purposes.[3]

Similarly, some limitation must be put on a question such as 'Have any of your relations had any signs of consumption, or been insane, or had fits?' If the answer given were, 'No', and were interpreted strictly, it would mean that countless persons, many of whom could never have been known to the answerer, as, for instance, his great-grandparents, were included in the answer.[4]

The question in the proposal form for a life insurance policy stated, 'Are you now and have you always been of sober and temperate habits?' McCardie J said that these words must receive such an interpretation as would be placed upon them by ordinary men of normal intelligence and average knowledge of the world.[5] 'So interpreted, I can entertain no real doubt that they refer only to the use or abuse of alcohol. They are not applicable to the use of veronal or other soporific or narcotic drugs. They are inappropriate to what are known as "drug habits". If in the future an insurance company desires express information with respect to habits such as these, then a further question of a direct character should be added to the proposal form.'[6]

In *Austin v Zurich General Accident and Liability Insurance Co Ltd*:[7]

---

1 (1881) 6 App Cas 644, PC.
2 *Connecticut Mutual Life Insurance Co of Hertford v Moore* (1881) 6 App Cas 644, at 648, PC.
3 *Joel v Law Union and Crown Insurance Co* [1908] 2 KB 863, CA.
4 Ibid.
5 *Yorke v Yorkshire Insurance Co Ltd* [1918] 1 KB 662, at 666.
6 Ibid, at 666.
7 [1944] 2 All ER 243, 77 LlL Rep 409; affd [1945] KB 250, 78 LlL Rep 185, CA, though this point was not in issue on appeal.

A proposal form for motor insurance stated, 'Do you . . . suffer from loss, or loss of use, of limb or eye, defective vision or hearing or from any physical infirmity?' The proposer said, 'No'. The insurance company maintained that his eyes must be defective because he wore 'thick' glasses. *Held,* the answer was a true one, for his eye-sight was sufficient for the purpose of driving.

Tucker J said:[8]

'It is well known that a high proportion of people use glasses for reading but not for long distance sight, and have perfect vision for driving purposes, yet in a sense their vision is defective. I cannot suppose that such people are required to answer "Yes" to this question. Its meaning must be construed in relation to the circumstances in which it is put, and I think when occurring in a proposal form for motor insurance, it is limited to defects which in some degree affect the competence of the assured as a motor driver and have not been corrected by glasses or other means.'

Again, in *Revell v London General Insurance Co Ltd*:[9]

A question in a proposal form in respect of the insurance of a car stated: 'Have you or any of your drivers ever been convicted of any offence in connection with the driving of any motor vehicle?' The proposer answered 'No', but she and her driver had been convicted of using a motor vehicle which did not have an exterior mirror, and of not having in force a third party insurance policy. The insurance company attempted to avoid liability on the ground that the answer was untrue.
Held, by the King's Bench Division, that it could not do so, for a person reading the question might reasonably regard its purpose as being directed to the carefulness of the driver who was likely to have charge of the insured vehicle. Consequently the proposer was entitled to have answered the question in the negative.

Further, in *Corcos v De Rougemont*:[10]

In 1923 the insured was asked the following question in a proposal form relating to motor insurance:—'How long have you driven a motor car?' She answered 'Several years'. She had driven her father's car from 1907 to 1912, and a friend's car in 1915. In 1923 she bought a car and had some driving lessons.
Held, by the King's Bench Division, that the answer which had been given was a fair one. The question was ambiguous and did not obviously relate to the proposer's recent motoring experience, as the insurer had contended.

Where a question in a proposal form for a householder's insurance policy stated: 'To what extent are the premises left unattended regularly apart from holidays?', the proper way to regard the question and the answer was to treat them as being an indication of the state of affairs which existed at the time the answers were given or was going to exist within the immediate future thereafter and was going to continue so far as the assured was concerned for the period of the policy, but they did not amount to a warranty that no change would

---

8 (1944) 77 LlL Rep at 416.

9 (1935) 50 LlL Rep 114, followed in *Taylor v Eagle Star Insurance Co Ltd* (1940) 67 LlL Rep 136, where the question in the proposal form was in exactly the same words and the insured had answered 'No', but had been previously convicted of permitting a car to be used without a policy of insurance and of driving a car without there being a road fund licence in force with respect to it, and the King's Bench Division held that the answer which had been given was not an untrue one.

10 (1925) 23 LlL Rep 164. In this case the insurer failed to establish that her failure to take out a licence for some years prior to the policy constituted a material circumstance. See also, *Zurich General Accident and Liability Insurance Co Ltd v Morrison* [1942] 2 KB 53, [1942] 1 All ER 529, where the insurance company failed to show that the answer to the question in the proposal form was untrue. Here the proposer had answered 'Three years' in reply to the question 'How long have you driven motor cars?' though in fact he had failed to pass a driving test, and had held provisional licences only, but had not mentioned these circumstances.

occur.[11] To regard them as a continuing obligation to have a named individual in occupation throughout the period was putting an unreasonable interpretation on the effect of the questions and answers there appearing.[12]

Where the question is directed to a particular fact, an answer to the question as asked may be sufficient.[13]

Thus, a question as to the existence of other insurance,[14] in the absence of clear language to the contrary, is to be taken as referring only to the property proposed to be insured. The answer is not inaccurate because insurances on other property are not disclosed.[15]

Further, where the question does not in terms require the other insurers to be named, a failure to name them does not render the answer inaccurate.[16]

Similarly, where the question is whether any other insurers have declined to accept or renew the insurance, the answer is not inaccurate because the assured omits to disclose the fact that he has been refused the transfer of another person's policy,[17] or that a previous policy has been cancelled by mutual consent.[18]

3 The whole truth must be told

The fact that the answer is literally true does not protect the assured where the statement is nevertheless false when taken in relation to other relevant facts which are not stated.[19]

So in *Condogianis v Guardian Assurance Co Ltd*:[20]

> A proposal form in respect of a fire policy contained a question stating, 'Has proponent ever been a claimant on a fire insurance company in respect of the property now proposed, or any other property? If so, state when and name of company.' The answer which was given was, 'Yes'. '1917.' 'Ocean.' This answer was literally true since he had claimed against the Ocean Insurance Co in respect of the burning of a motor car. But he had omitted to state that in 1912 he had made another claim against the Liverpool and London and Globe Co in respect of the burning of another motor car.
> *Held*, the answer was not a true one.

---

11 *Hair v Prudential Assurance Co Ltd* [1983] 2 Lloyd's Rep 667 (householder's insurance), at 672 (per Woolf J).

12 Ibid, at 673 (per Woolf J).

13 *Yorke v Yorkshire Insurance Co* [1918] 1 KB 662 (life insurance); *Ogden v Montreal Insurance Co* (1853) 3 CP 497, where the mortgagor, in insuring on behalf of a mortgagee, omitted to state the amount of the mortgage; *Meyers and Paddington Motor Services Ltd v Dalgety & Co Ltd* (1926) 26 SRNSW 195.

14 As to 'other insurance', see Chapter 33.

15 *Golding v Royal London Auxiliary Insurance Co Ltd* (1914) 30 TLR 350; *Bank of Australasia v North German Insurance Co* (1898) 17 NZLR 387, where, in an insurance on a building, an inaccurate statement as to insurances on stocks was disregarded; *Metropolitan Life Insurance Co v Montreal Coal and Towing Co* (1904) 35 SCR 266 (life insurance), where, on a proposal for life insurance, two personal accident policies were not disclosed.

16 *National Protector Fire Insurance Co Ltd v Nivert* [1913] AC 507, PC (fire insurance).

17 *Golding v Royal London Auxiliary Insurance Co* (1914) 30 TLR 350 (fire insurance).

18 *Smith v Dominion of Canada Accident Insurance Co* (1902) 36 NBR 300; *Fine v General Accident Fire and Life Assurance Corpn Ltd* [1915] App D 213; *Willcocks v New Zealand Insurance Co* [1926] NZLR 805, distinguished in *Bryce v Mercantile and General Insurance Co Ltd* [1930] NZLR 231.

19 *London Assurance v Mansel* (1879) 11 ChD 363 (life insurance); *Cazenove v British Equitable Insurance Co* (1860) 29 LJCP 160, ExCh (life insurance); *Re General Provincial Life Assurance Co, ex p Daintree* (1870) 18 WR 396 (life insurance). The same principle applies to a statement disclosing one previous insurance, when there have been others: *Dent v Blackmore* (1927) 29 LlL Rep 9 (motor insurance).

20 [1921] 2 AC 125, 3 LlL Rep 40, PC.

Lord Shaw of Dunfermline said:[1]

> 'The argument of the [insured], however, was that it was sufficient to answer the question, "has the proponent ever been a claimant . . .? If so, state when and name of company?" by answering in the singular and giving one occasion and one occasion alone. Accordingly, if, say, several years ago a proponent had been a claimant under an insurance policy, it would be sufficient for him to mention that fact and to exclude from mention the further fact that every year since that occasion he had also been a claimant upon insurance companies for fire losses. It appears to their Lordships quite plain that this would be no good answer to the question, "Has proponent ever been a claimant? If so, state when?" In short, when that question is reasonably construed, it points to the insurer getting the benefit of what has been the record of the insured with regard to insurance claims. This was distinctly its intention and in their Lordships' opinion is plainly its meaning. To exclude, however, from that record what might in the easily supposed case be all its important items, however numerous these might be, and to answer the question in the singular, which again in the easily supposed case might be a colourless instance favourable to the claimant, would be to answer the question so as to misrepresent the true facts and situation and to be of the nature of a trap.'

Further, in *London Assurance v Mansel*:[2]

> In a proposal form for life insurance there was a question which stated 'Has a proposal ever been made on your life at any other office or offices? If so, where? Was it accepted at the ordinary premium, or at an increased premium, or declined?' The answer was 'Insured now in two offices for £16,000 at ordinary rates. Policies effected last year.' In fact, several insurance companies had declined to insure the life of the proposer.
> *Held,* that the answer given was not a true one.

Jessel MR observed:[3]

> 'It is to be observed that the man proposing the assurance, who knows the facts, does not answer the question. The question was, "Has the proposal been made at any office or offices; if so, where?" He does not state, "I proposed to half a dozen offices", which was the truth, but simply says, "Insured now in two offices", which, of course, must have been intended to represent an answer, and therefore would mislead the persons receiving it, who did not look at it with the greatest attention, into the belief that he was insured in two offices, and that they were the only proposals that he made. "Was it accepted at the ordinary premiums or an increased premium?" His answer is, "At ordinary rates." That is the answer to the second branch of the inquiry, but he has not answered the question, "Or declined?" The inference, therefore, which must have been intended to be produced on the mind of the person reading the answer was that it had not been declined. And in my opinion that is the fair meaning of the answer, and the assured is not to be allowed to say, "I did not answer the question".'

A further illustration is provided by *Holt's Motors Ltd v South East Lancashire Insurance Co Ltd*:[4]

> A proposal form for a motor insurance policy contained the question, "Has any company or underwriter declined to insure?' The proposer gave the answer, 'No'. In fact, another insurance company had stated that it would not renew an existing policy.
> *Held,* the answer which had been given was true in words, though untrue in substance.

Scrutton LJ said:[5]

> 'A further question arises . . . as to whether the question is answered truly: "Has any company or underwriter declined to insure?" The Lion Company said they did not invite renewal "owing to the claims experience" and [Counsel for the insured] contended: "Well, they were never asked to, and you cannot decline a thing you were never asked to do." That may be so in ordinary life; but I am quite clear, with such knowledge and experience as I have, that in the

---

1 Ibid, at 131.
2 (1879) 11 ChD 363 (life insurance).
3 Ibid, at 370.
4 (1930) 35 Com Cas 281.
5 Ibid, at 286.

> insurance world a transaction like that, though expressed in polite terms, would be treated by everybody as a declining to insure; and if so, the question has been answered wrongly.'

In the case of an insurance on partnership property, a question as to previous losses may refer only to partnership property, and a failure to disclose the previous losses of individual members of the partnership does not render the answer inaccurate[6] unless the question extends thus far.[7] Nevertheless, the previous history of the individual members may be material, and the failure to disclose it may avoid the policy.[8] Even in the case of a limited company, its insurances may be affected by the non-disclosure of events which happened before it came into existence.[9]

4 Other information in the possession of the insurers

In considering the accuracy of the answers, regard must be had not only to the statements contained in the answer itself, but also to any other information in the possession of the insurers. An answer, which when taken by itself is insufficient, may not be inaccurate when read with other answers in the proposal. Consequently, the whole of the proposal must be taken into account;[10] and where the assured submits at the same time a number of proposals relating to different properties, but referring to each other, they are all to be read together, and the accuracy of the answers determined accordingly.[11]

5 Inconsistent or unsatisfactory answers

When the answers which the proposer gives are inconsistent or unsatisfactory, and no further inquiries are made by the insurance company, and a policy is

---

6 *Davies v National Fire and Marine Insurance Co of New Zealand* [1891] AC 485, PC (fire insurance); *Ehrig and Weyer v Trans-Atlantic Fire Insurance Co* [1905] TS 557; *Burton and Watts v Batavia Sea and Fire Insurance Co* [1922] SASR 466. In *Locker and Woolf Ltd v Western Australian Insurance Co Ltd,* [1936] 1 KB 408, 54 LlL Rep 211, CA, Slesser LJ referred to this as 'a very arguable point' without deciding it.

7 The question may in terms include the previous history of individual members: *Nicholas v New Zealand Insurance Co* [1930] NZLR 699. In *Glicksman v Lancashire and General Assurance Co* [1927] AC 139 (burglary insurance) the House of Lords expressed no opinion as to whether the answer was untrue, for not disclosing the previous history of an individual partner. In *Prosser v Ocean Accident and Guarantee Corpn* (1910) 29 NZLR 1157, where the question was whether the applicants 'either collectively or individually, and if individually, either alone or in conjunction with other persons', had ever had a loss, it was held that, on an insurance by a wife, it was unnecessary to disclose a previous loss by her husband; cf *Bradbury v London Guarantee and Accident Co Ltd* (1927) 40 CLR 127, where a question as to the husband's previous losses was held not to apply to a deceased husband's fires.

8 *Glicksman v Lancashire and General Assurance Co* [1927] AC 139, HL (burglary insurance); *Becker v Marshall* (1922) 12 LlL Rep 413, CA (burglary insurance).

9 *Arthrude Press v Eagle Star and British Dominions Insurance Co* (1924) 19 LlL Rep 373, CA (fire insurance), where Bankes LJ said (at 374): 'In my opinion, reading this proposal and asking oneself what this means: "Has your insurance ever been declined by any office?" that is not referring to the individual who happens to put forward the policy (sic proposal?). It is perfectly obvious the question was and ought to have been understood as meaning: "Has this risk ever been declined by any office?"'; *Colonial Industries Ltd v Provincial Insurance Co* [1922] AppD 33; *Locker and Woolf Ltd v Western Australian Insurance Co Ltd* (1935) 153 LT 334 (fire insurance), where Swift J, in the Court below, at 335, pointed out the materiality of the previous history of a director of a company.

10 *Dear v Western Assurance Co* (1877) 41 UCR 553.

11 *McGugan v Manufacturers and Merchants Mutual Fire Insurance Co* (1879) 29 CP 494.

issued, the company cannot repudiate liability on the ground that there has not been a full disclosure, for it will be held to have waived its rights. 'If his answer is hesitating or unsatisfactory, the insurers are put upon their guard, and have the option of declining the assurance, or seeking information from other sources, or of charging a higher premium.'[12]

So in *Keeling v Pearl Assurance Co Ltd*:[13]

> There was an inconsistency between the date of birth and the age which the proposer had given in answer to a question in a proposal form for life insurance. The insurance company with knowledge of this inconsistency issued a policy.
>
> *Held*, that liability could not be repudiated on the ground of non-disclosure.

Bailhache J said:[14]

> 'The date of birth is given as November 28, 1863 . . . then the age next birthday is given as 48. Now, of course it is obvious to anybody who does the simplest subtraction sum, that a person born in 1863 would not be 48, but would be 57, in 1920. There was no reason to suppose that time had stood still for [him], and it was obvious that there was some mistake about his age, and it turns out that, in fact, 1863 is the wrong date of the birth, and that the age next birthday, instead of being 48, ought to be 49. The insurance company had that form before them, and they saw, on the face of it, that there was a mistake somewhere about the age. Obviously, it must have hit them in the eye the moment they had the proposal form. Yet, notwithstanding that, they chose to issue a policy; and if they chose to issue a policy on a proposal form which contained a mistake, obviously, on the face of it, without further inquiry, there is no ground, in my opinion, for vitiating the policy.'

6 Where the space for the answer is left blank

Where the question is not answered at all, the space for the answer being left blank, there is no inaccurate statement, since there is no statement at all, and hence there cannot be any fraud or misrepresentation or any breach of a condition warranting that the statement made was true.[15]

If the only answer open to the assured would have disclosed a fact unfavourable to the acceptance of the proposal, there is a concealment;[16] and, indeed, concealment has been defined to include the case where the assured purposely avoids answering a question, and thereby does not state a fact which it is his duty to disclose.[17]

---

12 *Thomson v Weems* (1884) 9 App Cas 671, at 694 (per Lord Watson).

13 (1923) 129 LT 573.

14 Ibid, at 574.

15 *Marcovitch v Liverpool Victoria Friendly Society* (1912) 28 TLR 188, CA (life insurance) per Lord Alverstone CJ, at 189: 'In his opinion it was difficult on the evidence to come to the conclusion that any statement had been made by the assured that there was no other policy in force. It was suggested that leaving certain columns in the proposal form blank amounted to such a statement. He could not accept the proposition that the answer of the assured to the agent that she was not aware of any other policy, and the leaving of the blank spaces by the agent amounted to a warranty by her, the untruth of which avoided the policy'; *Le Page v Canada Fire and Marine Insurance Co* (1880) 2 PEI 322; *Perrins v Marine and General Travellers' Insurance Society* (1859) 2 E & E 317 per Wightman J, at 323, suggesting that leaving a blank would be no untrue averment.

16 A failure to answer a question has been held to amount to concealment in *Taylor v Yorkshire Insurance Co* [1913] 2 IR 1 (livestock insurance), where the question related to previous insurance; see also, *Thornton-Smith v Motor Union Insurance Co Ltd* (1913) 30 TLR 139 (motor insurance), where, however, there had been a full disclosure to the agent of the insurers.

17 *London Assurance v Mansel* (1879) 11 ChD 363 (life insurance) per Jessel MR, at 369, 370, explaining *Lindenau v Desborough* (1828) 8 B & C 586 (life insurance) per Lord Tenterden CJ, at 591.

Where the space for the answer is left blank, the Court may infer that this implies that it is a negative one.

In *Roberts v Avon Insurance Co Ltd*:[18]

> The insured made a declaration in a proposal form in respect of a burglary policy that 'I have never sustained a loss in respect of any of the contingencies specified in this proposal except . . . NOTE—Give date, amount and name of insurers in respect of such loss'. The insured had recovered from another insurance company in respect of a previous burglary loss. But he did not put any words at all after the word 'except' in the declaration form.
> *Held*, that this meant that no exception existed.

Barry J said:[19]

> 'The inference to be drawn from leaving blank the two lines provided for the purpose of stating any exception can, to any reasonable applicant and to any reasonable insurer, have only one meaning, namely, that no exception exists . . . It seems to me perfectly clear that any applicant for insurance, completing this form, would appreciate without any doubt or ambiguity that the insurers required particulars of any previous loss in respect of contingencies specified to be set out on the two blank lines left for that purpose, with the date, amount and the name of the insurers who were concerned in respect of each of those losses. If that information is clearly required, it seems to me that the only inference, and the obvious inference, is that the applicant intended the blank lines to represent what I think has been described as a negative answer. As this statement is in a declaration, the obvious inference to be drawn from the applicant leaving those lines blank is there was in fact no exception to his categoric statement that he has never sustained any loss in respect of any of the contingencies specified.'

C THE ONUS OF PROOF

The issue of the policy raises the presumption that everything was rightly done.[20] Hence, the onus of proving that the assured has failed to perform the duty of disclosure or has made a misrepresentation or has broken a condition relating to disclosure lies upon the insurers.[1]

1 What must be proved

When the insurers seek to avoid the policy, the facts which they will have to prove will vary according to whether they wish to establish non-disclosure or

---

18 [1956] 2 Lloyd's Rep 240.

19 Ibid, at 249.

20 *Elkin v Janson* (1845) 13 M & W 655 (marine insurance) per Platt B, at 666.

1 *Stebbing v Liverpool and London and Globe Insurance Co* [1917] 2 KB 433 per Lord Reading CJ, at 438; *Elkin v Janson* (supra) per Parke B, at 663; *Davies v National Fire and Marine Insurance Co of New Zealand* [1891] AC 485, PC (fire insurance); *Joel v Law Union and Crown Insurance Co* [1908] 2 KB 863, CA (life insurance) per Vaughan Williams LJ, at 880; *Goldstein v Salvation Army Assurance Society* [1917] 2 KB 291 (life insurance); *Zeeman v Royal Exchange Assurance* [1919] CPD 63; *Revell v London General Insurance Co Ltd* (1934) 152 LT 258 (accident insurance); *Babatsikos v Car Owners' Mutual Insurance Co Ltd* [1970] 2 Lloyd's Rep 314, Supreme Ct of Victoria, Court of Appeal (motor insurance), per Pape J, at 318. For instances where the insurers failed to discharge the onus, see *Craig v Imperial Union Accident Assurance Co* (1894) 1 SLT 646; *Adams v London General Insurance Co* (1932) 42 LlL Rep 56 (motor insurance); *Arlet v Lancashire and General Assurance Co Ltd* (1927) 27 LlL Rep 454 (motor insurance). But the onus of proving that the fact that the insured has been guilty of a misrepresentation has been waived lies on him: *de Maurier (Jewels) Ltd v Bastion Insurance Co Ltd and Coronet Insurance Co Ltd* [1967] 2 Lloyd's Rep 550 (jewellers' all risk insurance), where it was held that the insurers by their letters to the insured had affirmed the contract. See the judgment of Donaldson J, ibid, at 559.

misrepresentation, and whether there is an express stipulation in the contract on this matter.

(a) Non-disclosure

Where non-disclosure is alleged the insurers must prove:

i That the fact not disclosed was material;
ii That it was within the knowledge of the assured; and
iii That it was not communicated to them.[2]

(b) Misrepresentation

In the case of fraudulent or innocent misrepresentation it must be shown:

i That the statement alleged to have been made was inaccurate;
ii That the statement relates to a material fact;
iii That, in the case of fraud, the assured knew the statement to be false, or did not believe it to be true, or made it recklessly, not caring whether it was true or false; or, in the case of innocent misrepresentation, ought to have known the truth; and
iv That the statement was made by the assured or by his agent.[3]

(c) Where there is an express stipulation

Where the ground of avoidance is a breach of a condition relating to non-disclosure or mis-statement the insurers are required to show:

i That by express stipulation, the duty of disclosure is made contractual;
ii That the non-disclosure or mis-statement alleged to have been made is a breach of duty as defined in the stipulation; and
iii That the assured was guilty of the alleged non-disclosure or made the alleged mis-statement.[4]

Thus, in *Stebbing v Liverpool and London and Globe Insurance Co Ltd*:[5]

> A proposal for a burglary policy stated that the proposer declared that the answers he had given were full and true ones, and that he agreed that the proposal was to the basis of the contract between him and the insurance company. The company disputed liability on the ground that his statement in the proposal form was not true.
> *Held,* that the burden of proving this lay on the insurance company.

Viscount Reading CJ said:[6]

> 'The proposal form contains a question, "Have you ever proposed for burglary insurance?" The claimant has answered, "No" and his answer is challenged by the company. He has been

---

[2] *Elkin v Janson* (supra) (marine insurance) per Alderson B, at 664; *Williams v Atlantic Assurance Co Ltd* [1933] 1 KB 81, CA (marine insurance) per Scrutton LJ, at 94: 'An underwriter pleading concealment must come [into the witness-box] and say what he was or was not told. He may not remember directly, but may be able to say that he cannot have been told this material fact: that if he had known it, he would never have dreamed of writing this policy at the ordinary rate of premium.'
[3] As to statements by agents, see pp 542–546, post.
[4] *Pearl Life Assurance Co v Johnson* [1909] 2 KB 288 (life insurance), where the only proposal produced by the insurers was not signed by the proposed assured.
[5] [1917] 2 KB 433.
[6] [1917] 2 KB 433, at 437.

asked about another policy signed by him, and he has given an explanation. The arbitrator [against whose decision this appeal is brought] is in doubt whether the answer to the question is true, and he asks the Court on whom is the burden of proof; whether on the claimant to prove that the answer is true or on the company to prove that it is false. The burden of proof, in the first instance at all events, lies on that party against whom judgment should be given if no evidence were adduced upon the issue. Assuming in this case that a loss was established and the policy put in evidence, then the claimant would be entitled to recover. If he is met by the company with the objection that his answer to a question is not true, they must establish that the answer is not true. If they fail to establish that, their objection fails. That is to say, the burden lies on the company to prove that the claimant's answer is untrue.'

2 Some examples of the evidence required

If the only question in issue is whether a fact, admittedly material, was or was not disclosed, or whether a statement, admittedly inaccurate, was or was not made, slight evidence is required to prove that the fact was not disclosed or that the statement was made.[7]

Thus, the mere issue of the policy is sufficient proof where it is clear, as in the case of a retrospective insurance upon a subject-matter which is, to the knowledge of the assured, already destroyed, that no prudent insurers would have issued the policy if they had known the true state of affairs;[8] or where the rate of premium charged by other insurers to whom full disclosure was admittedly made, leads to the conclusion that the insurers in question would not, if they had known the true state of things, have issued the policy at the rate actually charged by them.[9]

On the other hand, the fact that a higher premium than usual has been paid may be important as showing that the assured made a full disclosure.[10]

---

7 *Elkin v Janson* (supra) per Alderson B, at 665.

8 Ibid, per Parke B, at 663.

9 *Mackintosh v Marshall* (1843) 11 M & W 116 (marine insurance), where the insurers charged a premium of 30s. per cent, whereas other insurers, who were fully acquainted with the facts, charged 3 guineas per cent (see especially the judgment of Lord Abinger CB, at 123); *Tate v Hyslop* (1885) 15 QBD 368, CA (marine insurance); *Greenhill v Federal Insurance Co* [1927] 1 KB 65, CA (marine insurance) per Scrutton LJ, at 79.

10 *Bridges v Hunter* (1813) 1 M & S 15 (marine insurance) per Lord Ellenborough CJ, at 19; cf *Court v Martineau* (1782) 3 Doug KB 161 (marine insurance), where the non-disclosure of a particular fact was held not to vitiate the policy, a premium of 50 guineas per cent having been paid.

CHAPTER 15

The premium

The premium is the consideration which the insurers receive from the assured in exchange for their undertaking to pay the sum insured in the event insured against.[1]

Any consideration sufficient to support a simple contract may constitute the premium in a contract of insurance.[2] Thus, in the case of a mutual insurance association,[3] the assured is, by the terms of the contract, liable to contribute towards making good any losses which his fellow-members may sustain, either instead of or in addition to a fixed periodical payment, and is entitled in his turn to have his own losses made good by them. His liability towards his fellow-members is therefore the premium for his own insurance.[4]

In the usual course of business, however, premiums are payable in money, and it is unnecessary to consider in detail any other form of premium.

A THE AMOUNT OF THE PREMIUM

The amount of the premium is purely a matter of contract, depending on the insurers' estimate of the risk.[5] In ordinary cases no special estimate is made. Risks offered for insurance fall for the most part into well-defined classes, whatever may be the particular kind of insurance to which they belong; and the same estimate suffices for all risks of the same class. Most insurers issue tables of premiums, showing the rate charged by them for each class of risk undertaken;

1 *Sun Insurance Office v Clark* [1912] AC 443 per Lord Atkinson, at 460.

2 *British Marine Mutual Insurance Co v Jenkins* [1900] 1 QB 299 (marine insurance) per Bigham J, at 303; *Prudential Insurance Co v IRC* [1904] 2 KB 658 (life insurance) per Channell J, at 663; *Municipal Mutual Insurance Ltd v Pontefract Corpn* (1917) 116 LT 671 (fire insurance) per Sankey J, at 674; *Hampton v Toxteth Co-operative Provident Society Ltd* [1915] 1 Ch 721, CA (life insurance) per Phillimore LJ, at 735, citing *Nelson & Co v Board of Trade* (1901) 84 LT 565 (life insurance) per Lord Alverstone CJ, at 567.

3 As to mutual insurance associations, see Ivamy *Marine Insurance* (4th Edn 1985), pp 475–479.

4 *Thomas v Richard Evans & Co* [1927] 1 KB 33, CA per Lord Hanworth MR, at 52; *Lion Insurance Association v Tucker* (1883) 12 QBD 176, CA (marine insurance); *Great Britain 100 A1 SS Insurance Association v Wyllie* (1889) 22 QBD 710 (marine insurance); *British Marine Mutual Insurance Co v Jenkins* (supra) per Bigham J, at 302.

5 Hence, where a question of construction arises as to whether the words of the policy extend to cover a particular loss, the fact that the rate of premium might have been affected if the wider construction had been intended is not to be disregarded: *Re George and Goldsmiths' and General Burglary Insurance Association Ltd* [1899] 1 QB 595, CA per Collins LJ, at 611. See further, *Lower Rhine and Würtemberg Insurance Association v Sedgwick* [1899] 1 QB 179, CA (marine insurance) per Collins LJ, at 189. But see *Stone v Marine Insurance Co Ocean Ltd of Gothenburg* (1876) 1 ExD 81 (marine insurance) per Bramwell B, at 84.

in framing these tables they are guided, as far as possible by experience.[6] The premium is usually charged at the rate of so much per £100 of the sum insured.[7]

The rates ordinarily charged may be increased where the assured seeks a protection wider than that which the insurers usually agree to give in respect of property similar to that sought to be insured, and may be diminished if he is willing to accept a narrower protection or to comply with any special requirements imposed by them.[8]

The premium must be fixed by the insurers and agreed to by the proposed assured before there can be a concluded contract of insurance.[9] It does not, however, appear to be necessary that the precise amount of the premium should have been fixed and agreed to, provided that there is a definite agreement to postpone the fixing of the amount and to enter into the contract notwithstanding. Thus, the insurance may be in consideration of a premium to be arranged.[10]

In liability insurance, in particular, the policy usually prescribes the basis on

---

6 *Chapman v Pole* (1870) 22 LT 306 (fire insurance) per Cockburn CJ to the jury, at 307: 'You will do well to bear in mind that the rate of insurance is calculated upon the average of losses as compared with profits and the more the company is subjected to deception and fraud, the higher the rate of premium which they are obliged to charge.' See further, *Thomson v Weems* (1884) 9 App Cas 671 (life insurance) per Lord Blackburn, at 681: 'Those whose business it is to insure lives calculate on the average of mortality and charge a premium which on ordinary average will prevent their being losers.'

7 The premium is composed of the pure premium calculated according to the risk together with an addition for office expenses and other charges: *Re Albert Life Assurance Co, Lancaster's Case* (1871) LR 14 Eq 72n (life insurance) per Lord Cairns, at 77n. Cf *Re Argonaut Marine Insurance Co Ltd* [1932] 2 Ch 34, where the fact that the same premium was charged for a period which included transit and for storage only showed that the insurance was really one against fire and not marine losses.

8 Thus, in the case of fire insurance special discounts may be allowed where sprinklers or other fire-extinguishing appliances are available.

9 *Christie v North British Insurance Co* 1825 3 Sh (Ct of Sess) 519 (fire insurance) per Lord Boyle, at 522: 'It is impossible to assent to the doctrine that without a delivered policy there is no insurance. If the premium in this case had been agreed on, the insurance would have been effected, although no policy was delivered; but the premises here cannot be held to have been insured, the premium never having been determined on, and never having been fixed by the Phoenix Office.' See also, *Re Yager and Guardian Assurance Co* (1912) 108 LT 38 (fire insurance); *Murfitt v Royal Insurance Co Ltd* (1922) 38 TLR 334 (fire insurance) per McCardie J, at 336; *Canning v Farquhar* (1886) 16 QBD 727, CA (life insurance); *Allis-Chalmers Co v Maryland Fidelity and Deposit Co* (1916) 114 LT 433, HL per Lord Loreburn, at 434.

10 *Hyderabad (Deccan) Co v Willoughby* [1899] 2 QB 530 (marine insurance), where in the event of deviation, the goods insured were held to be covered at a premium to be arranged; *Kirby v Cosindit Societa per Azioni* [1969] 1 Lloyd's Rep 75 (builders' risks insurance) where the policy stated 'extensions held covered at a premium to be arranged', and was extended from 30 November 1967 to 31 January 1970 'at a reasonable premium', and it was held that there was no implied term that the insured would pay such part of the premium as was undisputed, and would pay it as soon as it became undisputed; *American Airlines Inc v Hope, Banque Sabbag SAL v Hope* [1973] 1 Lloyd's Rep 233, CA (aviation insurance), where some aircraft at Beirut airport were to be insured against war risks subject to an additional premium being agreed on, and it was held that the risk did not attach until it had been paid (see the judgment of Phillimore LJ, ibid, at 242, and that of Roskill LJ, ibid, at 245). As far as marine insurance is concerned, the Marine Insurance Act 1906, provides by s 31(1): 'Where an insurance is effected at a premium to be arranged, and no arrangement is made, a reasonable premium is payable.' Section 31(2) states: 'Where an insurance is effected on the terms that an additional premium is to be arranged in a given event, and that event happens but no arrangement is made, then a reasonable additional premium is payable.' See generally, Ivamy *Marine Insurance* (4th Edn 1985), pp 80–82.

which the amount of premium is to be calculated and provides for an immediate payment on account of premium and for an adjustment at the end of the year of insurance, the amount ultimately payable depending on the circumstances giving rise to liability, such as, for instance, the number of staff employed or vehicles used by the insured.[11]

Provision may be made in the policy for increasing or reducing the premium. Thus, if, during the currency of the policy, the risk is increased, an additional premium may become payable; if the risk is diminished, a proportion of the premium paid may be returned.[12] The policy may also contain a statement relating to reduction of the premium on renewal in the event of the risk having been diminished or of no claim having been made under the policy during the period of the insurance.[13]

Whether in such a case the insurers are bound to reduce the premium if a specified event has happened depends on the language used. Thus, where the question of reduction is left entirely to their judgment, the Court cannot interfere if, in the bona fide exercise of their judgment, they decline to reduce the premium.[14]

B THE PAYMENT OF THE PREMIUM

The premium may be paid by the assured, or his agent acting within the scope of his authority,[15] or, in the case of his death, by his personal representatives.[16] Sometimes the premium is payable by a third person.[17] Thus, in the case of fidelity[18] or solvency[19] insurance, the premium may be payable by the person whose fidelity or solvency is insured.

Payment by a stranger will, apparently, not be sufficient unless ratified by the assured.[20]

---

11 See generally, Ivamy *Personal Accident, Life and Other Insurances* (2nd Edn 1980), p 286.

12 *South East Lancashire Insurance Co Ltd v Croisdale* (1931) 40 LlL Rep 22 (motor insurance), where a clause providing for rebate of premium had been deleted, and a claim for premiums accordingly failed because the assured was not bound to accept a policy which had been altered.

13 As to 'no claim' bonus in motor insurance, see Ivamy *Fire and Motor Insurance* (4th Edn 1984), p 224.

14 *Manby v Gresham Life Assurance Society* (1861) 29 Beav 439 (life insurance).

15 Payment by the agent is good although the assured has not, in fact, paid him the amount of the premium: *Re Coleman's Depositories Ltd and Life and Health Assurance Association*, [1907] 2 KB 798 (employers' liability assurance); *Farquharson v Pearl Assurance Co Ltd* [1937] 3 All ER 124 (life assurance), where the policy was taken out as security for a loan, and the mortgage provided that the mortgagee might pay the premium in the case of default.

16 Payment cannot be made by the personal representatives where the policy contemplates a personal payment by the assured: *Simpson v Accidental Death Insurance Co* (1857) 2 CBNS 257.

17 See *Johnston v Ocean Accident and Guarantee Corpn Ltd* (1915) 34 NZLR 356, where a policy effected by an employer to cover accidents to an employee was held to be for the employee's benefit.

18 See *Re Economic Fire Office* (1896) 12 TLR 142, where a receipt was given for the purpose of being shown to the employer, and it was held that the insurers were estopped from denying that the premium had been paid. See further Ivamy *Personal Accident, Life and Other Insurances* (2nd Edn 1980), p 307.

19 See *Anglo-Californian Bank Ltd v London and Provincial Marine and General Insurance Co* (1904) 10 Com Cas 1, where the principal debtors paid the premiums both upon the Lloyd's policy insuring their own solvency and upon the further policy insuring the solvency of the underwriters of the first policy.

20 *Busteed v West of England Fire and Life Insurance Co* (1857) 5 I Ch R 553, at 570 (life insurance). Cf *London and Lancashire Life Assurance Co v Fleming* [1897] AC 499, PC (life insurance).

1 Mode of payment

The premium is payable in money, and payment in any other form may be refused.[21] But the insurers may, if they think fit, accept payment otherwise than in money.[22] If they have agreed, either expressly or impliedly, from the course of dealing between the parties to a particular form of payment, as, for instance, by cheque,[23] bill of exchange,[1] promissory note,[2] or settlement in account,[3] they are bound by a payment in that form.

If the form of payment adopted never results in a payment in fact, e g where the cheque or promissory note is dishonoured, the premium is to be regarded as remaining unpaid,[4] unless the insurers elected to take the cheque or promissory note in preference to cash.[5]

If, however, the cheque or note is duly honoured, the payment relates back and the premium is deemed to have been paid on the day when the cheque or note was given and not on the day when it was actually honoured.[6]

Similarly, in the case of a settlement in account, if there is a running account between the parties and the course of business is that the balance is struck periodically, whereupon the party appearing to be the debtor becomes liable to pay to the other party in cash the amount found to be due, the premium is deemed to have been paid on the day when it was debited in account to the assured, and not on the day when the actual payment of the balance is made.[7]

If the insurers authorise the assured to remit the premium by post, and it is lost or stolen in transmission, the loss falls on them,[8] provided that the remittance is sent in the usual way.[9]

---

21 The onus of proving that the premium has been paid in cash lies on the assured: *London and Lancashire Life Assurance Co v Fleming* [1897] AC 499, at 507, PC (life insurance).

22 *Manufacturers Accident Insurance Co v Pudsey* (1897) 27 SCR 374, where the premium was partly paid in cash and partly by promissory note; *New Zealand Insurance Co Ltd v Tyneside Proprietary Ltd* [1917] NZLR 569, where the premium was debited against coal supplied; *Prince of Wales Life Assurance Co v Harding* (1858) EB & E 183 (life insurance); *London and Lancashire Life Assurance Co v Fleming* (supra).

23 *Daff v Midland Colliery Owners Mutual Indemnity Co* (1913) 82 LJKB 1340, HL.

1 *Bell Brothers v Hudson Bay Insurance Co* (1911), 44 SCR 419.

2 *London and Lancashire Life Assurance Co v Fleming* (supra); *Masse v Hochelaga Mutual Insurance Co* (1878) 22 LCJ 124.

3 *Prince of Wales Life Assurance Co v Harding* (supra). Cf *Re Coleman's Depositories Ltd and Life and Health Assurance Association* [1907] 2 KB 798, CA, where the broker in the ordinary course of business credited the insurers with the premium and debited them with his commission.

4 See *Charles v Blackwell* (1877) 2 CPD 151, CA (bankers) per Cockburn CJ, at 158. Cf *Currie v Misa* (1875) LR 10 Exch 153, ExCh (affd sub nom *Misa v Currie* (1876) 1 App Cas 554) (sale of bill of exchange) per Lush J, at 163.

5 Cf *Robinson v Read* (1829) 9 B & C 449 (supplies to ship) per Parke J, at 455; *Sard v Rhodes* (1836) 1 M & W 153 (bill of exchange).

6 Cf *Marreco v Richardson* [1908] 2 KB 584, CA (statute of limitations) per Farwell LJ, at 593: 'The giving of a cheque is a payment conditional on the cheque being met, that is subject to a condition subsequent, and if the cheque is met, it is an actual payment ab initio and not a conditional one.' See also, *Hadley (Felix) & Co v Hadley* [1898] 2 Ch 680 (sale of book debts); *Nicholls v Evans* [1914] 1 KB 118 (payment of bet).

7 *Prince of Wales Life Assurance Co v Harding* (supra) (life insurance), where two companies, in the habit of reinsuring each other, by the ordinary course of business gave a receipt for each premium as it fell due, though no payment was made until the periodical settlements of account when the balance was struck and paid over by the company owing it, and it was held that a premium was paid on the day on which the receipt for it was given. Cf *Re Coleman's Depositories Ltd and Life and Health Assurance Association* (supra).

8 Cf *Norman v Ricketts* (1886) 3 TLR 182, CA (cheque), followed in *Thairlwall v Great Northern Rly Co* [1910] 2 KB 509 (dividend warrant).

The premium may, by agreement,[10] be made payable by instalments, as, for instance, where it is a lump sum payable for an insurance extending over a period of years. In this case, payment of the first instalment is a performance of a condition that the insurance is not to attach until the premium is paid.[11] The effect of the payment of the subsequent instalments is not to renew the policy but to continue a subsisting insurance.[12]

The policy continues in force throughout the period fixed for its duration, unless allowed to lapse in the meanwhile by the failure to pay a further instalment of the premium when it falls due or within any 'days of grace' that may be allowed.[13] A loss happening during the 'days of grace' is, therefore, covered even though the instalment falling due has not been paid, provided that it is paid before the 'days of grace' expire.[14]

2 Time for payment

It is not necessary, apart from an express condition in the policy, for the assured to pay the premium at any particular time.[15] As soon as there is a completed contract the insurers become liable,[16] and the assured at the same time becomes bound to pay the premium, and is, therefore, liable in an action at the suit of the insurers if he fails to do so.[17]

In practice, the policy usually contains a stipulation to the effect that the insurance is not to come into force until the premium has been paid.[18] The payment of the premium is thus made a condition precedent to the liability of the insurers, and they are not responsible for any loss happening before payment.[19] When the premium is paid and accepted after the due date, its

---

9 *Mitchell-Henry v Norwich Union Life Insurance Society* [1918] 2 KB 67, CA (treasury notes), where the remittance of a large sum by post in £1 notes was held not to be in the usual way, and the loss accordingly fell upon the sender.

10 Such an agreement may be inferred from the conduct of the insurers: *Whitehorn v Canadian Guardian Life Insurance Co* (1909) 19 OLR 535 (life insurance).

11 *Stuart v Freeman* [1903] 1 KB 47, CA (life insurance).

12 *Stuart v Freeman* [1903] 1 KB 47, CA (life assurance), distinguishing *Pritchard v Merchants' and Tradesman's Life Assurance Society* (1858) 3 CBNS 622 (life insurance).

13 As to 'days of grace', see pp 250–252, post.

14 *Phoenix Life Assurance Co v Sheridan* (1860) 8 HL Cas 745 (life insurance); *Stuart v Freeman* (supra) (life insurance). Cf *McKenna v City Life Assurance Co* [1919] 2 KB 491 (life insurance).

15 *McElroy v London Assurance Corpn* 1897 24 R (Ct of Sess) 287 per Lord Maclaren, at 291: 'If the insurance company delivers a policy, they are held to have given credit for the premium'. See also, *Kelly v London and Staffordshire Fire Insurance Co* (1883) Cab & El 47: *Thompson v Adams* (1889) 23 QBD 361, where the premium was not tendered till after loss; *Adie & Sons v Insurance Corpn Ltd* (1898) 14 TLR 544, where the loss took place after the proposal but before the policy was issued or the premium paid.

16 *Roberts v Security Co* [1897] 1 QB 111, CA.

17 *General Accident Insurance Corpn v Cronk* (1901) 17 TLR 233 (accident insurance), where it was held that the fact that the wrong form of policy was tendered did not discharge the assured from the obligation to accept the correct form of policy or to pay the premium. Cf *Star Fire and Burglary Insurance Co v Davidson & Sons* 1902 5 F (Ct of Sess) 83, where an action to recover the premium failed as the parties were not ad idem.

18 The stipulation is sometimes expressed as a condition subsequent, empowering the insurers to declare the policy void if the premium is not paid within a specified time: *Bamberger v Commercial Credit Mutual Assurance Society* (1855) 15 CB 676. Such a stipulation does not affect the duration of the policy. See p 229, post.

19 *Sharkey v Yorkshire Insurance Co* (1916) 54 SCR 92; *Sickness and Accident Assurance Association v General Accident Assurance Corpn* 1892 19 R (Ct of Sess) 977; *Tarleton v Staniforth* (1796) 1 Bos & P 471, ExCh (fire insurance), where the loss took place before a renewal premium had been paid; *Equitable Fire and Accident Office v Ching Wo Hong* [1907] AC 96, PC (fire insurance); *London and Lancashire Life Assurance Co v Fleming* [1897] AC 499, PC (life insurance). For a case in

effect is retrospective, in the absence of any agreement to the contrary.[20]

As far as marine insurance is concerned, the Marine Insurance Act 1906, s 52, provides:

> 'Unless otherwise agreed, the duty of the assured or his agent to pay the premium, and the duty of the insurer to issue the policy to the assured or his agent are concurrent conditions, and the insurer is not bound to issue the policy until payment or tender of the premium.'

There are certain cases, however, in which the insurers are, by their conduct, precluded from relying upon the non-payment of the premium and are, therefore, notwithstanding the stipulation, liable to the assured although the premium is not paid until after the loss or never paid at all. These cases are:

a Where the insurers issue a policy under seal reciting that the premium has been paid.
b Where the insurers by their conduct discharge the assured from the necessity of complying with the condition.

(a) Where the insurers issue a policy under seal reciting that the premium has been paid

If the policy is under seal, the recital may create an estoppel against the insurers and prevent them from relying upon the circumstance that the premium has not, in fact, been paid.

The language in which the stipulation is framed must be carefully scrutinised, since the effect of the recital appears to vary according to the particular stipulation used. A stipulation providing that the liability of the insurers is not to arise until the premium is 'actually paid', overrides the recital, qualifying and restricting the engagement of the insurers and converting what would otherwise be an absolute engagement into a conditional one. In this case the words of the recital are merely common form words or words of style for expressing the consideration for the insurers' engagement, which will become accurate when that engagement becomes effective;[1] and the insurers accordingly are not liable for any loss happening before the premium is paid.[2]

On the other hand, where the condition provides that no liability is to arise until the premium is 'paid', omitting the word 'actually' or any word of similar effect, the language of the condition has been held not to be strong enough to prevail against the estoppel created by the recital.[3] The insurers are, therefore, liable immediately on the execution of the policy, and it is immaterial that at

---

which the condition was held to have been performed, see *Demal v British American Live Stock Association* (1910) 14 WLR 250, where the assured insured two horses, paying the premium, one half in cash and the remainder by promissory note, and the Court having held that, as regards one of the horses, the policy never attached, held that there was a payment in full as regards the other horse.

20 *Ocean Accident and Guarantee Corpn Ltd v Cole* [1932] 2 KB 100, 43 LlL Rep 26 (accident insurance) per Avory J.

1 See *Equitable Fire and Accident Office v Ching Wo Hong* [1907] AC 96, PC, where it was held that the language of the condition prevailed; *Roberts v Security Co* [1897] 1 QB 111, CA (burglary insurance), where it was held that the recital prevailed.

2 *Equitable Fire and Accident Office v Ching Wo Hong* (supra).

3 *Roberts v Security Co* (supra), doubted and distinguished in *Equitable Fire and Accident Office v Ching Wo Hong* (supra).

the time of the loss the policy is still in their hands, provided that it has been completely executed.[4]

If the policy is not under seal, the recital that the premium has been paid does not, except in the case of a Lloyd's policy,[5] preclude the insurers from relying on the non-payment of the premium.[6]

As far as marine insurance is concerned, the Marine Insurance Act 1906, s 54, provides that:

> 'Where a marine policy effected on behalf of the assured by a broker acknowledges the receipt of the premium, such acknowledgment is, in the absence of fraud, conclusive as between the insurer and the assured, but not as between the insurer and broker.'

(b) Discharging the assured from compliance with the condition

The insurers may have wrongfully refused to accept payment of the premium when tendered to them,[7] or may have otherwise repudiated the contract contained in the policy.[8] By such refusal or repudiation, as the case may be, the assured is discharged from the obligation of performing the condition, and the insurers cannot, therefore, rely on its non-performance.

By their conduct the insurers may have waived the performance of the condition. What acts on the part of the insurers are to be regarded as a waiver will depend upon the circumstances of each particular case.[9] There is no waiver

---

4 It is to be noted, however, that in *Roberts v Security Co* (supra) there was also waiver by conduct, the loss being claimed under the cover note, and the issue of the policy being a waiver of the non-payment of the premium on the cover note: ibid, per Rigby LJ, at 116. The fact that the policy is retained by the insurers does not make it an escrow, even though the insurers are a company: ibid; *Xenos v Wickham* (1866) LR 2 HL 296 (marine insurance).

5 A Lloyd's policy contains a recital that the premium has been paid, and so far as the date of payment is concerned, the premium is, as between the underwriter and the broker, treated as having been paid on the completion of the contract. The effect of this recital is that even if the premium has not in fact been paid, the broker cannot cancel the contract without the authority of the assured: *Xenos v Wickham* (supra). The law is different in the United States: *Ruby SS Corpn Ltd v Commercial Union Assurance Co* (1933) 150 LT 38, CA (marine insurance).

6 *Newis v General Accident Fire and Life Assurance Corpn* (1910) 11 CLR 620 (fire insurance). But see *Howell v Kightley* (1856) 21 Beav 331 (affd 25 LJ Ch 341, CA) (fire insurance), where the insurers gave an ante-dated receipt, and Romilly MR, at 335, expressed the opinion that the insurers would be estopped from alleging anything contrary to the receipt. In this case, however, no question of loss before payment arose; and it is clear that there is no estoppel where such a receipt is given in ignorance of the fact that a loss has taken place; see *Pritchard v Merchants' and Tradesman's Mutual Life Assurance Society* (1858) 3 CBNS 622 (life insurance).

7 *Canning v Farquhar* (1886) 16 QBD 727, CA (life insurance) per Lord Esher MR, at 731, 732; cf *Roberts v Security Co* [1893] 1 QB 111, CA per Rigby LJ, at 117; *Daff v Midland Colliery Owners' Mutual Indemnity Co* (1913) 6 BWCC 799, HL (employers' liability insurance) per Lord Moulton, at 817, where the assured's cheque was subsequently returned. An action will lie against the insurers for damages for repudiation of the contract by refusing to accept a premium when tendered: *Honour v Equitable Life Assurance Society of United States* [1900] 1 Ch 852 (life insurance) per Buckley J, at 855.

8 *Re Albert Life Assurance Co, Cook's Policy* (1870) LR 9 Eq 703 (life insurance), where the company went into liquidation during the days of grace, and the assured was held to be absolved from the necessity of paying the premium.

9 *Masse v Hochelaga Mutual Insurance Co* (1878) 22 LCJ 124, where the acceptance of a note for the premium coupled with a recital in the policy that the premium had been paid in cash was held to amount to a waiver of condition that the insurance was not to be in force until the note had been paid; *Farquharson v Pearl Assurance Co Ltd* [1937] 3 All ER 124 (life insurance), where the premium was tendered by the mortgagee but declined by the insurers' agent who anticipated payment by the mortgagor in the ordinary way; *Peppit v North British and Mercantile Insurance Co*

unless, at the time when the act was done, the insurers knew, or had the opportunity of knowing, the true state of facts.[10] The act must further show an intention on their part to waive the condition, or must be calculated to mislead the assured into thinking that such is their intention.

Waiver is to be implied where the insurers agree to give the assured credit for the premium,[11] or to take a negotiable instrument in payment.[12] If, however, the premium is not paid at the expiration of the period of credit or the negotiable instrument is not paid at maturity, the condition precedent becomes operative.[13]

On the other hand, no waiver is to be implied from the mere delivery of the policy to the assured.[14] Nor are the insurers precluded from relying upon the non-payment of a renewal premium by reason of the fact that they have not given the assured notice that the renewal premium has become due,[15] or that on a previous occasion they had waived payment.[16]

Where the premium is payable by a third person, and the insurers have acted in such a manner as to lead the assured to believe that the premium has been paid, this may amount to a waiver on their part.[17]

3 Effect of payment

The acceptance of the premium by the insurers, in the absence of circumstances pointing to a contrary conclusion, leads to the inference that there is a

---

(1879) 13 NSR (1 R & G) 219, where the evidence showed that it was not the practice of the company to insist on performance of the condition as to renewals, and that they had in fact renewed the policy in question without insisting on prepayment of the premium; *Benson v Ottawa Agricultural Insurance Co* (1877) 42 UCR 282, where it was held that the insurers were estopped from relying on the non-payment of a note given in respect of a premium by their conduct in advising the assured not to pay the same to the agent or any one who should demand payment of the same.

10 *Sears v Agricultural Insurance Co* (1882) 32 UCCP 585, where the insurers, who had agreed to give credit for the premium but who had not been paid before the period of credit expired, were held not to have waived the benefit of a condition as to non-payment, by reason of their accepting payment in ignorance that the loss had happened, the premium being returned on discovery of the true state of facts.

11 *Prince of Wales Life Assurance Co v Harding* (1858) EB & E 183 (life insurance).

12 *London and Lancashire Life Assurance Co v Fleming* [1897] AC 499, PC (life insurance).

13 See p 184, ante. The fact that the insurers take legal proceedings to enforce payment of the negotiable instrument is not a waiver: *Manufacturers' Life Insurance Co v Gordon* (1893) 20 AR 309 (life insurance). But the position may be different if judgment is obtained and duly satisfied.

14 *Equitable Fire and Accident Office Ltd v Ching Wo Hong* [1907] AC 96, PC (fire insurance). Cf *Roberts v Security Co* [1897] 1 QB 111, CA where, however, the delivery of the policy was a waiver of the condition contained in the cover.

15 *Simpson v Accidental Death Insurance Co* (1857) 2 CBNS 257 (life insurance) per Cresswell J, at 293; *Windus v Lord Tredegar* (1866) 15 LT 108, HL (life insurance). In *Simpson v Accidental Death Insurance Co* (supra) the insurers had already sent to their agent the renewal receipt, and liability was resisted in the first instance on the ground that the assured's death was not caused by accident.

16 *Redmond v Canadian Mutual Aid Association* (1891) 18 AR 335 (life insurance), where the insurance company had given notice that in future payment must be made on the due date; *Laing v Commercial Union Assurance Co Ltd* (1922) 11 LlL Rep 54.

17 *Re Economic Fire Office Ltd* (1896) 12 TLR 142, where the agent of the insured handed over a renewal receipt to the servant whose fidelity was insured, though the renewal premium had been paid, and the master, on the faith of the receipt, continued to employ the servant.

concluded contract of insurance.[18] The assured thereupon becomes entitled to receive a policy from the insurers;[19] and even though no policy has been issued, the insurers may be precluded from denying the existence of the contract and from repudiating their consequent liability.[20]

The making of a demand for the premium leads to the same inference,[1] unless the demand is refused, in which case there is a repudiation of the contract by the assured which releases the insurers from liability.[2]

Where the insurers issue a policy to the assured or renew an existing policy, the acceptance of the premium or renewal premium, as the case may be, estops them from repudiating liability on the ground that the policy has already been avoided by reason of a breach of condition.[3] They[4] must, however, be aware of the breach at the time when they accepted payment.[5] Thus, if the insurers, knowing that the policy was procured by the fraud,[6] misrepresentation,[7] or non-disclosure[8] on the part of the assured, subsequently accept the premium, they have decided to affirm the policy, and cannot afterwards contend that the

---

18 See pp 111–112, ante.

19 *Canning v Farquhar* (1886) 16 QBD 727, CA (life insurance) per Lord Esher MR, at 731; *McElroy v London Assurance Corpn* 1897 24 R (Ct of Sess) 287 (fire insurance) per Lord Maclaren, at 291; *Christie v North British Insurance Co* 1825 3 Sh (Ct of Sess) 519 (fire insurance) per Lord Boyle, at 522. See also, *Re Norwich Equitable Fire Assurance Society, Royal Insurance Co's Claim* (1887) 57 LT 241 per Kay J, at 243; *O'Connor v Imperial Insurance Co* (1869) 14 LCJ 219.

20 *Solvency Mutual Guarantee Society v Froane* (1861) 7 H & N 5 (guarantee) per Bramwell B, speaking of the acceptance of a renewal premium.

1 *Xenos v Wickham* (1867) LR 2 HL 296 (marine insurance) per Pigot B, at p 308.

2 *Edge v Duke* (1849) 18 LJ Ch 183 (life insurance) per Shadwell V-C, at 184: 'It appears to me that although there was a demand made for the premiums, that demand was annihilated by the refusal to pay.' See also, *Salvin v James* (1805) 6 East 571 (fire insurance), where the assured refused to pay an increased premium on renewal.

3 In this case the premium must in fact be paid; a demand for the premium is not sufficient: *Lyons v Globe Mutual Fire Insurance Co* (1877) 27 CP 567; affd (1878) 28 CP 62. Cf *Pearl Life Assurance Co v Johnson* [1909] 2 KB 288 (life insurance), where the insurers were held estopped from relying upon the absence of a signed proposal, though the policy provided that the proposal was to be signed, and was to form the basis of the contract.

4 Or their agent acting on their behalf: *Wing v Harvey* (1854) 5 De GM & G 265 (life insurance), distinguished in *Newsholme Bros v Road Transport and General Insurance Co Ltd* [1929] 2 KB 356, 24 LlL Rep 247, CA (accident insurance); *Holdsworth v Lancashire and Yorkshire Insurance Co* (1907) 23 TLR 521 (accident insurance). See generally pp 292–299, post.

5 *Biggar v Rock Life Assurance Co* [1902] 1 KB 516 (accident insurance) per Wright J, at 526. *Scottish Equitable Life Assurance Society v Buist* 1877 4 R (Ct of Sess) 1076 (life insurance). Cf *Busteed v West of England Fire and Life Insurance Co* (1857) 5 IChR 553 (life insurance). In *Newcastle Fire Insurance Co v Macmorran & Co* (1815) 3 Dow 255, HL, the question was raised at 263 but not decided, as to whether, where the property insured did not answer the description at the date of the policy, a subsequent alteration bringing it within the description was sufficient, if made and communicated to the insurers before the payment of the premium.

6 *Biggar v Rock Life Assurance Co* [1902] 1 KB 516 per Wright J, at 526.

7 *Hemmings v Sceptre Life Association Ltd* [1905] 1 Ch 365 (life insurance), where the age of the assured was wrongly stated in the proposal form; *Northern Assurance Co v Provost* (1881) 25 LCJ 211. Cf *Pearl Life Assurance Co v Johnson* [1909] 2 KB 288 (life insurance); *Stone v Reliance Mutual Insurance Society Ltd* [1972] 1 Lloyd's Rep 469, CA (burglary insurance), where the Court found it unnecessary to consider whether the insurers, by continuing to collect the premiums for 3 months after they knew that the insured's answers in the proposal form were untrue, had elected to affirm the policy. (See the judgment of Lord Denning MR, ibid, at 475.)

8 *Ayrey v British Legal and United Provident Assurance Co* [1918] 1 KB 136 (life insurance); *Armstrong v Turquand* (1858) 9 ICLR 32 (life insurance); *Holdsworth v Lancashire and Yorkshire Co* (supra) (accident insurance), where the assured, who was a joiner and builder, was described in the proposal as a joiner only.

policy was voidable by reason of his breach of duty. Similarly, if they accept the premium with knowledge that the assured has broken a condition subsequent, as, for instance, by increasing the risk, they cannot insist that the policy has been avoided by the breach.[9]

4 Payment to the agent of the insurers

The payment of the premium is often made by the assured to an agent of the insurers. Whether such a payment is a payment binding on the insurers, so that they are precluded from afterwards asserting that the premium has not been paid, depends on the following considerations:

a The agent must have authority to receive payment of the premium on behalf of the insurers.
b The agent must have authority to receive payment of the premium on behalf of the insurers in the mode in which it has been made to him.

(a) The authority to receive payment

It is not necessary, in order to bind the insurers, that the assured should establish the existence of an express authority to receive payment on their behalf. An authority to do so may be implied from their conduct, and a person may, therefore, in the circumstances of the particular case, bind them by the receipt of premium from the assured, although he has already ceased to be their agent,[10] or is, in fact, for other purposes connected with the insurance, the agent of the assured.[11]

Where an existing policy is renewed, the payment of the premium to the agent through whom the insurance was originally effected, is, as a general rule,[12] and in the absence of circumstances pointing to a contrary conclusion,[13] a good payment to the insurers.[14]

---

9 *Wing v Harvey* (supra) (life insurance); *Law v Hand in Hand Mutual Insurance Co* (1878) 29 Can CP 1.

10 *Marsden v City and County Assurance Co* (1865) LR 1 CP 232 (plate glass insurance), where the agent had, unknown to the assured, left the service of the insurers and become the agent of different insurers; *Anglo-American Life Assurance Co v Le Baron* (1912) 18 RLNS 327.

11 *Kelly v London and Staffordshire Insurance Co* (1883) Cab & El 47, where a broker who habitually effected insurances for the insurers, deducting his commissions from the premiums paid, and handing over to them the balance, was held to be the agent of the insurers to receive premiums, notwithstanding a condition in the policy that any person procuring the insurance was to be deemed the agent of the assured, and not of the insurers in any circumstances whatever, or in any transactions relating to the insurance, on the ground that such condition was merely intended to prevent the insurers being bound by the broker's representations; *Bancroft v Heath* (1901) 6 Com Cas 137, CA (fire insurance).

12 In ordinary practice the renewal notice is sent to the assured through him, and the assured by the terms of the notice is instructed to pay the premium to him. The agent then completes and issues the renewal receipt, with which he has been supplied by the insurers. In such a case, he has express authority to receive the renewal premium; *Manufacturers' Accident Insurance Co v Pudsey* (1897) 27 SCR 374.

13 Such as, for instance, notice that he has ceased to be their agent: *Marsden v City and County Assurance Co* (supra). Such a notice being published on a privileged ocasion is not actionable without proof of express malice: *Nevill v Fine Art and General Insurance Co* (fire insurance) [1897] AC 68; *Citizens Life Assurance Co v Brown* [1904] AC 423, PC (libel).

14 *Wing v Harvey* (1854) 5 De G M & G 265 (life assurance); *Towle v National Guardian Assurance Society* (1861) 30 LJ Ch 900 (fidelity insurance); *Conquest's Case* (1875) 1 ChD 334, CA (life insurance). Cf *Kelly v London and Staffordshire Insurance Co* (supra); *Marsden v City and County Assurance Co* (supra).

In the case of a new insurance, though the agent may have no authority to bind the insurers, by his acceptance of the premium, to issue a policy,[15] he may have, and usually has, authority to receive payment of the whole or part of the premium on their behalf.[16] If he is supplied with official receipts to be exchanged for premiums or deposits on account of premiums, his authority to receive payment cannot be contested, though the effect of the receipt may vary according to the circumstances.[17] Further, an agent who has authority to issue a cover note,[18] or who has a duly completed policy in his possession to deliver to the assured,[19] has authority to receive payment of the premium. Even though he omits to give a receipt strictly in accordance with the official form, the payment, if duly made, may be good, as against the insurers;[20] and the same principle applies in the case of payment to a sub-agent, who is duly appointed by an agent of the insurers to receive payment on their behalf.[1]

Where the agent has authority to receive payment of premiums on behalf of the insurers, the effect of the payment is the same as if it had been made to the insurers themselves,[2] and the fact that the premiums thus received by the agent have been misappropriated by him,[3] or have not reached the insurers owing to his bankruptcy,[4] affords them no defence against a claim by the assured on the contract.

(b) The form of payment

An agent who is authorised to receive payment of premiums on behalf of the insurers, may be expressly prohibited from accepting payment otherwise than in money, and a payment in another form is, therefore, not binding upon the insurers.[5] An express prohibition is not, however, necessary, since the effect of

---

15 See pp 526–527, post. Cf *Confederation Life Association v O'Donnell* (1883) 10 SCR 92, where there was evidence that the premium had been paid, but the policy was never countersigned and delivered as required by one of the conditions, and it was held that the insurers were not liable.

16 *Kelly v London and Staffordshire Insurance Co* (supra); *Campbell v National Life Insurance Co* (1874) 24 CP 133 (life insurance). See also, *Linford v Provincial Horse and Cattle Insurance Co* (1864) 34 Beav 291 (livestock insurance), where the insurers alleged that the premium was obtained by false pretences.

17 Contrast *Wing v Harvey* (supra) with *Acey v Fernie* (1840) 7 M & W 151 (life insurance).

18 *Rossiter v Trafalgar Life Assurance Association* (1859) 27 Beav 377 (life insurance). Cf *Linford v Provincial Horse and Cattle Insurance Co* (supra) (livestock insurance), where the agent had no authority to accept the proposal. As to cover notes, see pp 103–108, ante.

19 *Kelly v London and Staffordshire Insurance Co* (supra) (fire insurance).

20 *Marshall v Western Canada Fire Insurance Co* (1911) 18 WLR 68 (renewal); *Rossiter v Trafalgar Life Assurance Association* (supra) (life insurance), where the agent's signature, which should have been written, was printed. But acceptance of the wrong premium does not bind the insurers in the absence of proof of special authority to the agent: *Kiva Hai v Northern Assurance Co Ltd* (1924) ILR 2 Ran 158. A notice in the policy that the receipt of the agent will not be admitted merely puts the assured to proof of payment: *Conquest's Case* (supra) per James LJ, at 339. A variation from the official form of receipt, if known to the person paying the money, may amount to notice of limitation of authority, and show that such person trusted the agent and not the principal: *Towle v National Guardian Insurance Society* (1861) 30 LJ Ch 900, CA per Turner LJ, at 916.

1 *Rossiter v Trafalgar Life Assurance Association* (supra) (life insurance).

2 *Acey v Fernie* (supra) per Parke B, at 155.

3 *Linford v Provincial Horse and Cattle Insurance Co* (supra) (livestock insurance) where, however, the assured failed to prove that the agent had authority to receive the premium.

4 *Rossiter v Trafalgar Life Assurance Association* (supra) (life insurance).

5 *Montreal Assurance Co v McGillivray* (1859) 13 Moo PCC 87, where it was held that the manager of an insurance company had no authority to take a promissory note. Cf *London and Lancashire Life Assurance Co v Fleming* [1897] AC 499, PC (life insurance) where payment of the premium by promissory note was authorised.

the form in which the payment is made to the agent will be governed by the ordinary rule that an agent, who is authorised to receive payment on a principal's behalf, has prima facie authority to receive payment in money only.[6] Unless, therefore, the agent is, in fact, authorised to accept payment in some other form, a payment of premium to bind the insurers must be made to him in money. Authority to receive payment in any other form must be proved by the person alleging payment.[7]

Where payment is made by cheque, the cheque is regarded as mere machinery,[8] and when the cheque is duly honoured, the payment relates back to the date when the cheque was given and is equivalent to a payment in money at that date.[9] If the cheque is dishonoured, there is no payment as against the insurers.[10]

On the other hand, an agreement by the agent to take from the assured in respect of the premium a bill of exchange or promissory note payable at a future date[11] or a post-dated cheque,[12] is not of itself a good payment, since the transaction amounts to a giving of credit, and is, therefore, in excess of the agent's ordinary authority, which does not extend to the giving of credit.[13]

Such a mode of payment may, however, be authorised by the insurers.[14] In this case, there is no payment unless the bill or note or cheque is honoured.[15] If the bill, or note, or cheque is duly paid, the insurers are bound, and it is immaterial that the agent never accounts to them for the proceeds.[16]

The agent may, however, as between himself and the assured, agree to give

---

6 *Frazer v Gore District Mutual Fire Insurance Co* (1883) 2 OR 416 where the agent allowed the premium to be set off as against his own personal debt to the assured, and gave a renewal receipt. *Pape v Westacott* [1894] 1 QB 272, CA (house agent); *Bridges v Garrett* (1870) LR 5 CP 451, ExCh (solicitor); *Pearson v Scott* (1878) 9 ChD 198 (solicitor); *Legge v Byas, Mosley & Co* (1901) 7 Com Cas 16 per Walton J, at 18, following *Sweeting v Pearce* (1861) 9 CBNS 534 (marine insurance); *The Netherholme, Hine v SS Syndicate* (1895) 72 LT 79, CA (marine insurance) per Lord Esher MR, at 81; *Tiernan v People's Life Insurance Co* (1896) 23 AR 342 (life insurance), where the agent, in payment for services rendered to the insurers by the assured, gave a receipt for the premium.

7 *Stewart v Aberdein* (1838) 4 M & W 211 (marine insurance). Such authority may be inferred from the course of business: *Manufacturers' Accident Insurance Co v Pudsey* (1897) 27 SCR 374, where the Court disregarded an express prohibition in the agent's instructions as being unknown to the assured.

8 *Pape v Westacott* [1894] 1 QB 272, CA (agency) per Lindley LJ, at 279; *Aetna Life Insurance Co v Green* (1876) 38 UCR 459 (life insurance).

9 *The Netherholme, Hine v SS Syndicate* (supra); *Marreco v Richardson* [1908] 2 KB 584, CA (statute of limitations), per Farwell LJ, at 593.

10 *Pape v Westacott* (supra) per Davey LJ, at 284, explaining *Bridges v Garrett* (supra) (agency).

11 *Montreal Assurance Co v McGillivray* (supra); *The Netherholme, Hine v SS Syndicate* (supra). Cf *London and Lancashire Life Assurance Co v Fleming* (supra).

12 A post-dated cheque is equivalent to a bill of exchange payable after date: *Forster v Mackreth* (1867) LR 2 Exch 163 (partnership). In *Newis v General Accident, Fire and Life Assurance Corpn* (1910) 11 CLR 620 (fire insurance) the assured gave an ante-dated cheque to the agent so as to make it appear that the premium had been paid before the fire, and it was held that the payment did not bind the insurers.

13 *Western Assurance Co v Provincial Insurance Co* (1880) 5 AR 190, where, on a reinsurance, the reinsurers were held not to be bound by a custom, unknown to them, among agents to give each other credit.

14 *Whitla v Royal Insurance Co* (1903) 34 SCR 191; *Bell Bros v Hudson Bay Insurance Co* (1911) 44 SCR 419.

15 *London and Lancashire Life Assurance Co v Fleming* [1897] AC 499, PC (life insurance).

16 *Commercial Union Assurance Co v Gamman* (1908) 10 NZ Gaz LR 672.

the assured credit for the amount of the premium and to pay it himself to the insurers on the assured's behalf. The agent then becomes the agent of the assured for the purpose of paying the premium, and acquires the right after paying it to sue the assured personally for the debt thus created.[17]

In this case a bill of exchange or note given by the assured to the agent is merely given either to be held by the agent as security for the debt or to be discounted for the purpose of raising money to pay the premium. It cannot, therefore, be regarded in any way as a valid payment as against the insurers, since an agreement of this kind does not itself affect the position as between the insurers and the assured, and the insurers are not bound until the premium has been paid to them by their agent.[18]

If the agent, acting in pursuance of the agreement, pays over the amount of the premium to the insurers, that is a good payment as regards the assured.[19]

An agreement by the agent to give credit to the assured and to pay the premiums on his behalf must be strictly proved, the onus of proving it resting upon the assured.[20]

Thus, where the agent has authority to receive payment by bill or note, the fact that the bill or note given to the agent by the assured was made payable to the agent personally, and not to the insurers, as is required by his authority, does not prove that such an agreement has been made.[1] Nor is it any proof of an agreement to the effect that the agent is to discount the bill or note and apply the proceeds in payment of the premium, especially in a case where the amount payable under the bill or note is the exact amount of the premium, without any allowance for discount.[2] The agent must, therefore, be regarded as receiving the bill or note on behalf of the insurers, and in the event of its dishonour they are not precluded from relying upon the non-payment of the premium.[3]

It is equally a good payment where, although no money actually passes, there is a settlement of accounts between the insurers and their agent in which the agent is debited with the premium in question.[4] A settlement of accounts is not, however, necessary; the mere fact that the agent, in accordance with his agreement with the assured, debits himself with the premium in his accounts with the insurers is a sufficient payment.[5]

---

17 *Newcastle Fire Insurance Co v Macmorran & Co* (1815) 3 Dow 255, HL (fire insurance) per Lord Eldon, at 264.

18 *London and Lancashire Life Assurance Co v Fleming* (supra), distinguished on the facts in *Steinbrecker v Mutual Life Assurance Co* (1919) 46 OLR 36 (life insurance).

19 *Kirkpatrick v South Australian Insurance Co Ltd* (1886) 11 App Cas 177, PC, where the payment was held to revive certain lapsed policies, though it was not specifically remitted by the agent or appropriated by the insurers for that purpose; *Dubuc v New York Life Insurance Co* [1925] 3 WWR 386.

20 *London and Lancashire Life Assurance Co v Fleming* [1897] AC 499, PC (life insurance).

1 *Busteed v West of England Fire and Life Insurance Co* (1857) 5 IChR 553 (life insurance).

2 *London and Lancashire Life Assurance Co v Fleming* (supra). Cf *Parrott v Anderson* (1851) 7 Exch 93 (landlord and tenant), where the agent of the landlord took from the tenant a bill for the amount of the rent. The bill was dishonoured and the agent then paid an equivalent sum to the landlord. It was held that the landlord's right to distrain depended upon whether the agent advanced the money to the tenant or to the landlord.

3 *London and Lancashire Life Assurance Co v Fleming* (supra).

4 *Newcastle Fire Insurance Co v Macmorran & Co* (1815) 3 Dow 255, HL (fire insurance) per Lord Eldon, at 264.

5 *Re Coleman's Depositories Ltd and Life and Health Assurance Association* [1907] 2 KB 798, CA (employers' liability insurance), where the broker credited the insurers with the premium and

On the other hand, if there is no agreement between the agent and the assured by which the agent is to become responsible for the premiums, the fact that the agent debits himself with the premium,[6] or is debited with it in the insurers' books,[7] cannot be regarded as a payment. In such a case, a settlement of accounts with the agent is equally insufficient to bind the insurers;[8] and even an actual payment by the agent cannot be treated by the assured as a valid payment on his behalf, unless it is, in fact, so made,[9] since the dealings between the insurers and their agent cannot affect the position as between the insurers and himself.[10]

Difficult questions may arise when the assured is also the agent of the insurers. If the course of business is that the agent is debited with the premium in the books of the insurers, but there is an agreement for credit and periodical settlement of accounts, the policy takes effect or is renewed on the due date, even if the premium, less commission, has not actually been transmitted to the insurers.[11]

Apart from any such special arrangements, the agent must do some act to show that he holds the amount of the premium as trustee for the insurers, and the mere signing of the renewal receipt is not sufficient evidence of this.[12]

C RIGHT TO CLAIM A RETURN OF PREMIUM

The right to a return of premium depends on the fact that the risk contemplated is never run,[13] and there is, in consequence, a failure of consideration in that the

---

debited them with the commission: *LaChapelle v Dominion of Canada Guarantee and Accident Insurance Co* (1907) QR 33 SC 228; *Re Law Car and General Insurance Corpn Ltd* [1911] WN 101, CA. Cf *Prince of Wales Life Assurance Co v Harding* (1858) EB & E 183 (life insurance), where reinsurers, in the ordinary course of business, gave the reassured a formal receipt for the reinsurance premium during the days of grace, but no actual payment took place until after the death of the assured, when there was the usual periodical settlement and payment of the balance, and it was held that the premium was to be deemed to have been paid when the formal receipt was given. In *Re Coleman's Depositories Ltd and Life and Health Assurance Association* (supra), where a similar practice was followed, the point that the premium had not been paid was not taken.

6 *Busteed v West of England Fire and Life Insurance Co* (1857) 5 IChR 553 (life insurance).

7 *Acey v Fernie* (1840) 7 M & W 151 (life insurance), where the agent received payment from the assured after the days of grace had expired.

8 *London and Lancashire Life Assurance Co v Fleming* (supra).

9 *Busteed v West of England Fire and Life Assurance Co* (supra), following *Acey v Fernie* (supra).

10 *Acey v Fernie* (1840) 7 M & W 151 (life insurance) per Parke B, at 155: 'It is impossible to consider the debiting of the agent with the amount of the premium as a payment on the original day . . . The only question is, "Did the company mean to make themselves liable on a new contract?" It seems to me that they did not, and that the meaning of the transaction was merely to keep their agents right, and in a case of neglect to be able to come upon them for the amount of the premium by way of penalty; but they did not mean thereby to make themselves liable for the amount of the policy.'

11 *Holliday v Western Australian Insurance Co Ltd* (1936) 54 LlL Rep 372 (fire insurance).

12 *Ingram v Caledonian Insurance Co* (1932) 42 LlL Rep 129 (fire insurance).

13 *Tyrie v Fletcher* (1777) 2 Cowp 666 (marine insurance) per Lord Mansfield CJ, at 668: 'Where the risk has not been run, whether its not having been run was owing to the fault, pleasure, or will of the insured or to any other cause, the premium shall be returned; because a policy of insurance is a contract of indemnity. The underwriter receives a premium for running the risk, of indemnifying the insured, and whatever cause it be owing to, if he does not run the risk, the consideration for which the premium or money was put into his hands fails, and therefore he

assured obtains no benefit from the protection for which he has paid.[14] If, therefore, no part of the risk is ever run, the whole of the premium must be returned. The assured may be entitled to a return of part of the premium where there has been a partial failure of consideration. The policy, however, may specify that the premium will not be returned in any event.

The right to claim a return of premium is enforceable by an action for money had and received,[15] and not by an action on the policy.[16] The Court may also, in an action for the cancellation of the policy,[17] order the premium to be returned.[18]

As far as marine insurance is concerned,[19] the Marine Insurance Act 1906, provides by s 82:

> 'Where the premium, or a proportionate part thereof, is, by this Act, declared to be returnable—
> (a) If already paid, it may be recovered by the assured from the insurer; and
> (b) If unpaid, it may be retained by the assured or his agent.'

Section 83 further states:

> 'Where the policy contains a stipulation for the return of the premium, or a proportionate part thereof,[20] on the happening of a certain event, and that event happens, the premium, or, as the case may be, the proportionate part thereof is thereupon returnable to the assured.'

Section 84(1) enacts:

> 'Where the consideration for the payment of the premium totally fails, and there has been no fraud or illegality on the part of the assured or his agents, the premium is thereupon returnable to the assured.'

In addition, s 84(2) states:

> 'Where the consideration for the payment of the premium is apportionable and there is a total failure of any apportionable part of the consideration, a proportionate part of the premium is, under the like conditions, thereupon returnable to the assured.'

---

ought to return it.' See also, *Henkle v Royal Exchange Assurance Co* (1749) 1 Ves Sen 317 (marine insurance) per Lord Hardwicke C, at 319; *Stevenson v Snow* (1761) 3 Burr 1237 (marine insurance); *Loraine v Thomlinson* (1781) 2 Doug KB 585 (marine insurance) per Lord Mansfield CJ, at 587; *Goldsmith v Martin* (1842) 4 Man & G 5 (entrance fee for race) per Tindal CJ, at 6, speaking of insurance; *Thomson v Weems* (1884) 9 App Cas 671 (life insurance) per Lord Blackburn, at 682.

14 On the other hand, a return of premium in the mistaken belief that the risk was never run does not preclude the assured from enforcing the policy: *Reyner v Hall* (1813) 4 Taunt 725 (marine insurance).

15 *Stevenson v Snow* (supra) (marine insurance) per Lord Mansfield CJ, at 1240; *Anderson v Thornton* (1853) 8 Exch 425 (marine insurance) per Parke B, at 427; *Duffell v Wilson* (1808) 1 Camp 401 (insurance against militia ballot).

16 *Castelli v Boddington* (1852) 1 E & B 66 (affd (1853) 1 E & B 879, ExCh) (marine insurance) per Lord Campbell CJ, at 79. If an action on the policy fails on the ground that the risk never commenced, the assured is, nevertheless, entitled to a return of premium: *Penson v Lee* (1800) 2 Bos & P 330 (marine insurance).

17 See pp 234–235, post.

18 *De Costa v Scandret* (1723) 2 P Wms 170 (marine insurance); *Desborough v Curlewis* (1838) 3 Y & C Ex 175 (life insurance) per Lord Abinger CB, at 177; *Barker v Walters* (1844) 8 Beav 92, at 96 (life insurance); *Joel v Law Union and Crown Insurance Co* [1908] 2 KB 431 (reversed without reference to this point, [1908] 2 KB 863, CA) (life insurance) per Lord Alverstone CJ, at 440.

19 See generally Ivamy *Marine Insurance* (4th Edn 1985), pp 82–86.

20 E g as in the Institute Time Clauses (Hulls), cl 22.

Finally, s 84(3)(b) provides:

> 'Where the subject-matter insured, or part thereof, has never been imperilled, the premium, or, as the case may be, a proportionate part thereof, is returnable: Provided that where the subject-matter has been insured "lost or not lost" and has arrived in safety at the time when the contract is concluded the premium is not returnable unless, at such time, the insurer knew of the safe arrival.'

A Right to a return of the whole of the premium

The right to a return of the whole of the premium arises in the following cases where:

1 The parties were never ad idem[1]

This is a general rule applicable to all branches of insurance.

As far as marine insurance is concerned, the Marine Insurance Act 1906, s 84(3)(a), provides:

> 'Where the policy is void . . . the premium is returnable, provided that there has been no fraud or illegality on the part of the assured; but if the risk is not apportionable, and has once attached, the premium is not returnable.'

2 The policy, which has been issued by the company, was ultra vires the company[2]

3 The policy is illegal

Where the policy is illegal, the illegality of the policy cannot be relied on by the insurers, if the facts of the case show that the assured was not in pari delicto with them, as, for instance, where the assured is induced to enter into an illegal contract by a fraudulent representation as to the legality of the contract made by their agent.[3]

---

1 *Fowler v Scottish Equitable Life Insurance Society and Ritchie* (1858) 28 LJ Ch 225 (life insurance); *Hyams v Paragon Insurance Co* (1927) 27 LlL Rep 448, where the assured was illiterate and the agent of the insurer had innocently misrepresented the extent of the contract. Cf *Biggar v Rock Life Assurance Co* [1902] 1 KB 516 per Wright J, at 525.

2 *Re Argonaut Marine Insurance Co Ltd* [1932] 2 Ch 34, where insurers of marine risks issued a fire policy; *Re Phoenix Life Assurance Co, Burgess and Stock's Case* (1862) 2 John & H 441 (marine insurance), where marine policies were issued by a life insurance company. This case was followed in *Flood v Irish Provident Assurance Co Ltd and Hibernian Bank Ltd* [1912] 2 Ch 597n, CA (life insurance), where life policies were issued by an insurance company prohibited by its memorandum of association from carrying on life insurance business, but criticised and distinguished in *Sinclair v Brougham* [1914] AC 398 (building society) per Lord Haldane C, at 417 and per Lord Sumner, at 453. But see *Re Arthur Average Association for British, Foreign and Colonial Ships, ex p Hargrove & Co* (1875) 10 Ch App 542 (marine insurance), where the assured was held not entitled to a return of premium, as having had notice that the agent granting the policy was acting ultra vires the insurers. It has been held in Canada that where the policy is void on the ground that it has not been signed in the manner prescribed by statute, the assured is not entitled to a return of premium if at the time of payment he was aware of the fact avoiding the policy: *Perry v Newcastle Mutual Fire Insurance Co* (1852) 8 UCR 363. But it is otherwise if he paid the premium in forgetfulness of the fact: ibid.

3 *Brewster v National Life Insurance Society* (1892) 8 TLR 648, CA (life insurance), where, by mistake of the agent of the insurers, the form of the policy was not in accordance with the law; *Beer v Prudential Assurance Co* (1902) 66 JP 729 (life insurance); *British Workman's and General Assurance Co Ltd v Cunliffe* (1902) 18 TLR 502, CA (life insurance), as explained in *Harse v Pearl Life Assurance Co* [1904] 1 KB 558, CA (life insurance); *Tofts v Pearl Life Assurance Co Ltd* [1915]

An agent employed to conduct negotiations for policies on behalf of insurers is not, however, an expert in insurance law,[4] and is under no greater obligation to know the law than the person with whom he is dealing.[5] An innocent misrepresentation by him as to the legality of the contract will not, therefore, entitle the assured to a return of premium.[6]

As far as marine insurance is concerned, s 84(1) of the Marine Insurance Act 1906, provides that:

> 'Where the consideration for the payment of the premium totally fails, and there has been no . . . illegality on the part of the assured or his agents, the premium is thereupon returnable to the assured.'

4 The policy has been avoided on the ground of innocent misrepresentation or non-disclosure by the assured

The assured may have been guilty of innocent misrepresentation or non-disclosure[7] in consequence of which the policy is avoided as from its inception by the insurers. In this case the policy is voidable at the election of the insurers, and if they elect to avoid it,[8] they must return the premium on the ground that the consideration for which it was paid has failed.[9]

As far as marine insurance is concerned, s 84(3)(a) of the Marine Insurance Act 1906, provides:

> 'Where the policy is . . . avoided by the insurer as from the commencement of the risk, the premium is returnable, provided that there has been no fraud or illegality on the part of the assured; but if the risk is not apportionable, and has once attached, the premium is not returnable.'

---

1 KB 189, CA (life insurance); *Hughes v Liverpool Victoria Legal Friendly Society* [1916] 2 KB 482, CA (life insurance); *Dowker and Armour v Canada Life Assurance Co* (1865) 24 UCR 591 (life insurance), where it was held that the policy was illegal under the Life Assurance Act 1774, s 2, but that the premiums might be recovered on the ground that the plaintiffs were not in pari delicto with the insurers. Cf *Re London County Commercial Reinsurance Office Ltd* [1922] 2 Ch 67 (peace insurance).

4 *Harse v Pearl Life Assurance Co* (supra) per Romer LJ, at 564.

5 *Evanson v Crooks* (1911) 106 LT 264 (life insurance) per Hamilton J, at 268.

6 *Harse v Pearl Life Assurance Co* (supra); *Phillips v Royal London Mutual Insurance Co Ltd* (1911) 105 LT 136 (life insurance); *Elson v Crookes* (1911) 106 LT 462 (life insurance). Cf *Re Hooley Hill Rubber and Chemical Co Ltd and Royal Insurance Co Ltd* [1920] 1 KB 257, CA.

7 *Anderson v Thornton* (1853) 8 Exch 425 (marine insurance) per Parke B, at 427, 428: 'In cases of insurance, material mis-statement or concealment vitiates the contract, and whether it be fraudulently made or not is a matter which is wholly immaterial, except with reference to the return of the premium . . . The representations were material, and were admitted to be so. With respect to the return of the premium, there is no doubt in my mind that the plaintiff would be entitled to recover it, as there was no fraud in the representation . . . The insurance never bound the defendant, and, consequently, the plaintiffs were entitled to the return of the premium.' See also, *Fowkes v Manchester and London Life Assurance and Loan Association* (1863) 3 B & S 917 (life insurance), followed in *Hemmings v Sceptre Life Association Ltd* [1905] 1 Ch 365 (life insurance); *Mulvey v Gore District Mutual Fire Assurance Co* (1866) 25 UCR 424 where, in his application, the assured inaccurately represented the building to have a brick chimney.

8 If the insurers treat the risk as having attached, and do not avoid the policy, the premium is not returnable: *North-Eastern 100 A SS Assurance Association v Red S SS Co* (1906) 12 Com Cas 26, CA (marine insurance) per Farwell LJ, at 37. As to what constitutes an election, see *Morrison v Universal Marine Insurance Co* (1873) LR 8 Exch 197, ExCh (marine insurance).

9 *Imperial Bank of Canada v Royal Insurance Co* (1906) 12 OLR 519, where the insurers were ordered to return the last premium, which had been received in ignorance that the policy was no longer in force.

5 There has been fraud or breach of good faith on the part of the insurers

There may have been fraud or breach of good faith on the part of the insurers, in consequence of which the assured has been induced to enter into a contract different from that which he intended to make,[10] or the policy is otherwise rendered worthless to the assured.[11]

6 The subject-matter has already been destroyed

But where the policy is intended to be retrospective,[12] it is immaterial that the risk had already ceased at the time when the policy was made, and there is no right to a return of premium.

7 The subject-matter is incapable of identification

This may occur where the assured has no property answering the description of the subject-matter contained in the policy,[13] or where the contract is otherwise void for uncertainty.[14]

8 The assured has no insurable interest in the subject-matter[15]

This is a principle which applies to all branches of insurance, but as far as marine insurance is concerned, the Marine Insurance Act 1906, s 84(3)(c), states:

> 'Where the assured has no insurable interest throughout the currency of the risk, the premium is returnable, provided that this rule does not apply to a policy effected by way of gaming or wagering.'

B Right to a return of part of the premium

In certain cases the assured may be entitled to a return of part of the premium. This may occur:

1 Where there has been over-insurance;
2 Where there is an express term to that effect in the policy; and
3 Where the company goes into liquidation.

---

10 *Carter v Boehm* (1766) 3 Burr 1905 (marine insurance) per Lord Mansfield CJ, at 1909: 'The policy would be equally void against the underwriter if he concealed . . . and an action would lie to recover the premium.' See also, *Refuge Assurance Co Ltd v Kettlewell* [1909] AC 243 (life insurance); *Mutual Reserve Life Insurance Co v Foster* (1904) 20 TLR 715, HL (life insurance); *Cross v Mutual Reserve Life Insurance Co* (1904) 21 TLR 15 (life insurance); *Merino v Mutual Reserve Life Insurance Co* (1904) 21 TLR 167 (life insurance).

11 *Duffell v Wilson* (1808) 1 Camp 401 (insurance against militia ballot), where the insurer was guilty of misrepresentation as to the date of the ballot. Cf *Barrett v Elliott* (1904) 10 BCR 461, where the policy was effected with a company not licensed to do business in Canada.

12 *Bradford v Symondson* (1881) 7 QBD 456, CA (marine insurance); *Bufe v Turner* (1815) 6 Taunt 338 (fire insurance); cf *Natusch v Hendewerk* (1881) 7 QBD 460n (marine insurance).

13 *Horneyer v Lushington* (1812) 15 East 46 (marine insurance).

14 See p 13, ante.

15 *Routh v Thompson* (1809) 11 East 428 (marine insurance).

1 Where there has been over-insurance

Where the assured is insured for an amount in excess of the sum which he can by any possibility recover in the event of the total destruction of the subject-matter of insurance, and has paid a premium in proportion, it is clear that some portion of the premium is paid without consideration, since the insurers can never become liable to pay the full amount of the insurance. So long, therefore, as the assured has acted honestly in fixing the amount for which he has insured, it seems that he is entitled to a return of the portion of the premium in excess of the actual consideration.

As far as marine insurance is concerned, the Marine Insurance Act 1906, s 84(3)(e), states:

> 'Where the assured has over-insured under an unvalued policy, a proportionate part of the premium is returnable.'

The same principle applies to liability insurance where the amount of premium depends on the amount of wages paid or number of vehicles used by the assured during the period of insurance. If the premium is paid on a larger amount of wages or a greater number of vehicles than are actually paid or used, there is an over-insurance, and there must be a return of part of the premium accordingly.

Where the over-insurance is occasioned by double insurance,[16] the assured appears equally to be entitled to a return of premium subject to the following rules:

(a) Where the different policies are all effected on the same day

In this case they are to be treated for this purpose as one insurance, and any return of premium is to be made rateably by the insurers upon all the policies in proportion to the amounts which they have respectively undertaken to pay.[17]

(b) Where the policies have been effected on different dates

In this case, although any loss falling within their scope will have to be borne rateably by all the insurers, irrespective of the date of their respective policies,[18] a return of premium is only to be made by those insurers by whose policies an over-insurance is constituted. The insurers upon the prior policy or policies would have been liable, in the event of a loss happening before the over-insurance arose, to pay the full amount covered by them, and as, therefore, in their case there is no failure of consideration, no return of premium can be claimed against them.[19]

As far as marine insurance is concerned, the Marine Insurance Act 1906, s 84(3)(f), states:

---

[16] See p 487, post.

[17] *Fisk v Masterman* (1841) 8 M & W 165 (marine insurance), where six policies were effected on the same day, the combined effect of which was to create an over-insurance, and it was held that a return of premium must be made rateably by all.

[18] See pp 488–492, post.

[19] *Fisk v Masterman* (supra), where it was held that there should be no return of premium in respect of the first set of policies, the over-insurance having been occasioned by those effected on a later date.

'. . . where the assured has over-insured by double insurance, a proportionate part of the several premiums is returnable:
Provided that, if the policies are effected at different times, and any earlier policy has at any time borne the entire risk, or if a claim has been paid on the policy in respect of the full sum insured thereby, no premium is returnable in respect of that policy, and when the double insurance is effected knowingly by the assured, no premium is returnable.'

The question is not likely to arise in connection with fire insurance except in the case of an insurance upon a particular subject-matter. Where the insurance is upon a class of objects,[20] the fact that at the time of the loss the value of the objects at risk was less than the sum or sums insured, apparently gives no right to a return of premium, since the assured is entitled at any time to secure the full benefit of the insurance by bringing objects of sufficient value within its scope, and the insurers have, therefore, run the risk of him so doing.

2 Where there is an express term in the policy

The policy frequently contains a stipulation providing for a return of part of the premium on the happening of a specified event. The events usually specified are:

(a) The determination of the policy

The insurers may reserve to themselves the right of putting an end to the policy, or the assured may be given the right to surrender it at any time upon notice. In these cases the stipulation provides for the return of a part of the premium proportionate to the unexpired part of the period of insurance.[1] It is immaterial whether the risk has or has not attached.

(b) The performance of a condition

The insurers may bind themselves to return part of the premium on the performance of a condition subsequent, the amount of premium to be returned being fixed by the stipulation.

Thus, the policy may provide that 10 per cent of the premium is to be returned on the expiration of the policy, if the assured has made no claim under it during its currency or that, if during the currency of the policy the risk is diminished, a portion of the premium, to be fixed by the insurers, is to be returned. The right of the assured to the stipulated return is not affected by the happening of a loss under the policy, so long as the condition is, in fact, performed.[2]

---

20 See pp 14–15, ante.

1 *Sun Fire Office v Hart* (1889) 14 App Cas 98, PC (fire insurance); *J H Moore & Co v Crowe* [1972] 2 Lloyd's Rep 563, Mayor's and City of London Court (motor insurance), where the policy stated: 'This policy may be cancelled by the underwriters at any time by seven days' notice by registered letter to the insured's last known address, and in such event the underwriters will return a pro rata portion of the premium upon the surrender of the policy and certificate of insurance which must be returned to underwriters within the seven days mentioned above,' and it was held that although 6 copies of the certificate had been issued to the insured, he was entitled to a refund on returning one certificate only (see the judgment of Judge Graham Rogers, ibid, at 565).

2 *Simond v Boydell* (1779) 1 Doug KB 268 (marine insurance), followed in *Aguilar v Rodgers* (1797) 7 Term Rep 421 (marine insurance); *Leevin v Cormac* (1811) 4 Taunt 483n (marine insurance).

3 Where the company goes into liquidation

Where the policy is prematurely determined by the insurers, being a company, going into liquidation during the period of insurance, the assured is entitled to prove for the value of the policy at the date of the liquidation, and thus, in effect, may become entitled to a partial return of premium.

In the case of an insurance company to which the Insurance Companies Act 1982 applies,[3] the amount of any liability of the company must be determined by the valuation regulations made under the Act.[4]

In all other cases the rules applicable to the valuation of contingent claims in a liquidation apply, and a just estimate must be made, so far as is possible of the value of the policy. There appears to be no reason in principle why the value of a current policy, if no loss happens during the liquidation, should not be estimated on the basis of a partial return of premium proportionate to the unexpired portion of the risk,[5] and it is submitted that a valuation on this basis is correct.[6] Where, however, a loss happens during the liquidation, the basis of valuation is modified, and the assured is entitled to prove for the amount of the loss.

D WHERE THERE IS NO RIGHT TO A RETURN OF PREMIUM

The fact that the assured is unable to enforce his policy against the insurers and thus loses the benefit of the protection for which he has paid does not, except in the cases specified above, entitle him to a return of premium. In particular, there is no return of premium in the following cases:

1 Where there has been no failure of consideration.

---

[3] See pp 40–41, ante.

[4] See p 85, ante.

[5] In *Re Albert Life Assurance Co, Bell's Case* (1870) LR 9 Eq 706 (life insurance), disapproved by Lord Cairns in *Lancaster's Case* (1871) LR 14 Eq 72n (life insurance), but followed by Lord Romilly MR, in *Re English Assurance Co, Holdich's Case* (1872) LR 14 Eq 72 (life insurance), the rule was laid down that in estimating the value of a current life policy the value was to be taken as the sum for which a policy of the same amount at the same premium could be purchased from a solvent office. But see now the valuation regulations made under the Insurance Companies Act 1982 with regard to the insurance companies to which Part II of the Act applies (see p 000, ante).

[6] In *Re Northern Counties of England Fire Insurance Co* (1885) 1 TLR 629 (fire insurance), Chitty J held that no part of the premium could be returned, on the ground that the assured was entitled to prove for any loss happening during the winding-up, and that consequently the company was entitled, in return for the risk which it ran of such proof, to have the benefit of the fact that no loss happened. This view, however, seems to assume a continuing liability under the policy, whereas, in truth, the policy has come to an end, and the assured has become entitled to prove for its value at the date of the liquidation. For the purpose of ascertaining this value, the fact of a subsequent loss may be taken into account, but the assured receives in the event of a loss, not the amount payable under his policy, but a sum representing the value of the policy, in the events that have happened, at the date of the liquidation; see *Re Law Car and General Insurance Corpn* (supra), per Buckley LJ, at 121. It therefore follows that, if no loss has happened, the assured is still entitled to prove for the value of the policy at the date of the liquidation, and it is submitted that the decision in *Re Northern Counties of England Fire Insurance Co* (supra) is incorrect.

2 Where though there is a failure of consideration, the failure is attributable to the conduct of the assured.
3 Where there is an express condition in the policy that the premium is to be forfeited on the happening of a specified event or events.

1 Where there is no failure of consideration

The assured is precluded from claiming a return of premium where there has been no failure of consideration. If on the face of the policy the risk has once attached, and the insurers have become liable to the assured to pay in the event of loss, the consideration for which the premium is paid is performed. The assured cannot, therefore, claim a return of premium as on a failure of consideration, although the policy for some reason or another becomes void or exhausted after the risk has attached.[7]

Thus, if the property insured is destroyed on the very day after the commencement of the policy by a cause for which the insurers have not undertaken to be answerable, such as, for instance, by an excepted peril, the assured cannot recover any portion of the premium, although the insurers are by the destruction of the property discharged from any further liability in respect of it.[8]

The same principle applies where the assured does any act which determines the policy prematurely,[9] as, for instance, by breaking a condition subsequent.[10] Nor is he entitled to a return of premium when the insurers after they have indemnified him, have, in the exercise of their right of subrogation,[11] succeeded in recovering the amount paid by them from the person responsible for the loss.[12]

If, however, the contract is not entire and the premium is capable of being

---

7 *Tyrie v Fletcher* (1777) 2 Cowp 666 (marine insurance) per Lord Mansfield CJ, at 668: 'Another rule is that if the risk of the contract of indemnity has once commenced there shall be no apportionment or return of premium after. For though the premium is estimated and the risk depends upon the nature and length of the voyage, yet, if it has commenced, though it be for only twenty-four hours or less, the risk is run; the contract is for the whole entire risk, and no part of the consideration shall be returned.'; *Moses v Pratt* (1815) 4 Camp 297 (marine insurance); *Canadian Pacific Rly Co v Ottawa Fire Insurance Co* (1907) 39 SCR 405. See also, *Wolenberg v Royal Co-operative Collecting Society* (1915) 112 LT 1036 (life insurance), where the assured who had effected insurance in respect of his mother's funeral expenses with several companies, and had received the full amount from one of them, was held not entitled to claim a return of premium from the other companies, as they had been at risk; *Provident Savings Life Society v Bellew* (1904) 35 SCR 35 (life insurance), where the assured who had paid an extra premium to cover him whilst taking part in the South African War, was not entitled to recover the premium when, in the event, he did not reach South Africa until the war was over. In accordance with the same principle an agent insuring without authority cannot recover back the premium if his principal fails to ratify the insurance, since the insurers have run the risk of the principal ratifying: *Routh v Thompson* (1811) 13 East 274 (marine insurance) per Bayley J, at 290; *Hagedorn v Oliverson* (1814) 2 M & S 485 (marine insurance).

8 *Loraine v Thomlinson* (1781) 2 Doug KB 585 (marine insurance) per Lord Mansfield CJ, at 587: 'There are two principles in these cases: 1. If the risk has never begun, the whole premium is to be returned because there was no consideration; 2. Where the risk has begun, there shall never be a return though the ship should be taken in twenty-four hours.'

9 *Langhorn v Cologan* (1812) 4 Taunt 330 (marine insurance) per Mansfield CJ, at 333.

10 *Annen v Woodman* (1810) 3 Taunt 299 (marine insurance); *Hawke v Niagara District Mutual Fire Insurance Co* (1876) 23 Gr 139.

11 See pp 465–480, post.

12 *Darrell v Tibbitts* (1880) 5 QBD 560, CA per Brett LJ, at 562.

apportioned between different risks, some of which are never run, the assured may claim a return of that portion of the premium which is referable to the risks never run.[13]

2 Failure of consideration attributable to the conduct of the assured

Where there has been a total failure of consideration, the assured may be precluded by his conduct or by the terms of his policy from claiming a return of premium. This takes place in the following cases:

(a) Where the assured has been guilty of fraud[14]

This principle applies to all branches of insurance.

As far as marine insurance is concerned, the Marine Insurance Act 1906, s 84(1), (2), states that neither the whole nor any part of the premium is returnable where the assured or his agent has been guilty of fraud.

(b) Where the contract is illegal[15]

A contract is illegal where, for instance, it is by way of gaming and wagering.[16]

As far as marine insurance is concerned, s 84(1), (2) of the Marine Insurance Act 1906, states that neither the whole or any part of the premium is returnable where there has been illegality on the part of the assured or his agents.

Until the risk has attached, the assured has a locus poenitentiae; as long as he rescinds the illegal contract before any steps have been taken to carry it out, he may claim a return of premium.[17]

If, however, the risk has once attached,[18] the assured has no longer a locus

---

[13] *Stevenson v Snow* (1761) 3 Burr 1237 (marine insurance); cf *Bermon v Woodbridge* (1781) 2 Doug KB 781 (marine insurance), where it was held that the contract was entire and consequently there could be no return of premium; *Canadian Pacific Rly Co v Ottawa Fire Insurance Co* (1907) 39 SCR 405.

[14] *Feise v Parkinson* (1812) 4 Taunt 640 (marine insurance) per Gibbs CJ, at 641: 'Where there is fraud there is no return of premium, but upon a mere misrepresentation without fraud where the risk never attached, there must be a return of premium.' See also, *Anderson v Thornton* (1853) 8 Exch 425 (marine insurance) per Parke B, at 427; *Rivaz v Gerussi* (1880) 6 QBD 222, CA (marine insurance) per Brett LJ, at 229; *Fowkes v Manchester and London Life Assurance and Loan Association* (1863) 3 B & S 917 (life insurance) per Crompton J, at 927, and per Mellor J, at 931, though Blackburn J, at 929, takes the view that there is a return of premium in the case of a fraudulent misrepresentation or concealment; *British Equitable Insurance Co v Musgrave* (1887) 3 TLR 630 (life insurance); *Prince of Wales etc Association Co v Palmer* (1858) 25 Beav 605 (life insurance), where the policy was declared void on the ground of fraud, and the premium already paid was applied in payment of costs. See also, *Wilson v Ducket* (1762) 3 Burr 1361 (marine insurance).

[15] *Lubbock v Potts* (1806) 7 East 449 (marine insurance); *Wilson v Royal Exchange Assurance Co* (1811) 2 Camp 623 (marine insurance).

[16] *Lowry v Bourdieu* (1780) 2 Doug KB 468 (marine insurance); *Andrée v Fletcher* (1789) 3 Term Rep 266 (marine reinsurance); *M'Culloch v Royal Exchange Assurance Co* (1813) 3 Camp 406 (marine insurance); *Paterson v Powell* (1832) 9 Bing 320 (bet on shares); *Howard v Refuge Friendly Society* (1886) 54 LT 644 (life insurance); *Goldstein v Salvation Army Assurance Society* [1917] 2 KB 291 (life insurance); *Re National Benefit Assurance Co Ltd* [1931] 1 Ch 46, 37 LlL Rep 153 (marine reinsurance).

[17] *Aubert v Walsh* (1810) 3 Taunt 277 (peace insurance); *Busk v Walsh* (1812) 4 Taunt 290 (peace insurance).

[18] It makes no difference that the contract was legal in its inception and did not become illegal until after the risk had attached; *Furtado v Rodgers* (1802) 3 Bos & P 191 (marine insurance).

poenitentiae. He cannot rescind the contract and claim a return of premium on the ground that no steps have been taken to carry it out, since the illegal contract comes into operation on the attaching of the risk.

Notwithstanding the attaching of the risk, however, he does not forfeit his right to a return of premium unless it is clear that he is in pari delicto with the insurers.[19] If he was fraudulently induced by them into believing that the contract was legal, the fact that the contract is illegal will not prevent him from obtaining a return of premium.[20] Similarly, where the only contract between the parties is not on the face of it illegal, and the assured never intended to enter into a contract in violation of the law, the contract actually entered into may turn out to be illegal;[1] but the assured will be entitled by reason of his bona fides to a return of premium. Thus, he may have insured in the bona fide belief that he had an interest,[2] or in the honest expectation that he would acquire an interest before loss;[3] and, although, in the absence of an interest, he cannot recover on the policy, he is not prevented from recovering the premium.

3 Express condition in the policy

The policy may contain a stipulation defining the cases in which there is to be no return of premium. The effect of the stipulation may be to deprive the assured in certain cases of the right, which, but for the stipulation, he would have had, to claim a return of premium.

Thus, a stipulation avoiding the policy in the event of any statement in the proposal being untrue[4] or in the event of a subsequent alteration of the risk[5] may further provide for forfeiture of any premium paid. Under such a stipulation, it is immaterial that the assured made the mis-statement innocently[6] or that the risk was altered in ignorance or forgetfulness of the stipulation.[7] It is equally immaterial that the premium was paid after the act

---

19 *Jaques v Withy and Reid* (1788) 1 Hy Bl 65 (lottery insurance); *Drummond v Deey* (1794) 1 Esp 151 (lottery insurance); *Allkins v Jupe* (1877) 2 CPD 375 (marine insurance). The onus of proving that he is not in pari delicto rests on the assured: *Howarth v Pioneer Life Assurance Co Ltd* (1912) 107 LT 155 (life insurance).

20 See p 198, ante.

1 *Oom v Bruce* (1810) 12 East 225 (marine insurance), where Lord Ellenborough CJ, at 226, said that the party making the insurance cannot recover the premium if he 'know it to be illegal at the time: but here the plaintiffs had no knowledge . . . and therefore no fault is imputable to them for entering into the contract.' See also, *Hentig v Staniforth* (1816) 5 M & S 122 (marine insurance); *Evanson v Crooks* (1911) 106 LT 264 (life insurance).

2 *Cousins v Nantes* (1811) 3 Taunt 513, ExCh (marine insurance) per Mansfield CJ, at 515.

3 Cf Marine Insurance Act 1906, s 84(3)(e).

4 *Duckett v Williams* (1834) 2 Cr & M 348 (life insurance), approved in *Thomson v Weems* (1884) 9 App Cas 671 (life insurance) per Lord Blackburn, at 682; *Howarth v Pioneer Life Assurance Co* (supra); *Broad and Montague Ltd v South East Lancashire Insurance Co Ltd* (1931) 40 LlL Rep 328 (motor insurance), where the proposer had falsely stated that no other insurance company had declined to insure him; *Kumar v Life Insurance Corpn of India* [1974] 1 Lloyd's Rep 147, QBD (life insurance), where the proposer had had a caesarean operation, and had answered 'No' to the question, 'Did you ever have any operation, accident or injury, if so give details.' In this case the insurer agreed to repay the premium in any event ex gratia, whatever the result of the case. (See the judgment of Kerr J, ibid, at 154.)

5 *Sparenborg v Edinburgh Life Assurance Co* [1912] 1 KB 195 (life insurance).

6 *Duckett v Williams* (supra); *Howarth v Pioneer Life Assurance Co* (supra).

7 *Sparenborg v Edinburgh Life Assurance Co* (supra).

causing the forfeiture had been committed and whilst the assured was unaware of its effect.[8]

Further a motor insurance policy may provide that in the event of a total loss of the vehicle no part of the premium will be returned.[9]

A stipulation under which the premium is forfeited is strictly construed; in particular, it must be clear that the assured as well as the insurers agreed to be bound by it.[10]

8 Ibid.

9 *Patel v London Transport Executive* [1981] RTR 29, CA (motor insurance), where the defendants, who admitted liability for an accident in which the plaintiff's car was a total loss, were held liable to reimburse him in respect of the loss of the premium for the term was a common one in motor insurance policies, and the loss of the premium was not too remote.

10 *Anderson v Fitzgerald* (1853) 4 HL Cas 484 (life insurance) per Lord St Leonards, at 507, approved in *Thomson v Weems* (supra).

PART III

The policy

CHAPTER 16

Introduction

Policies may be classified according to the description of the subject-matter or according to the amount recoverable in the case of a loss.[1] There are no restrictions on the form in which the policy is to be expressed, and the insurers are free to insert such terms in the policy as they think fit. Standard forms of policy, however, are normally used. The form and the contents of the policy will vary according as to whether the policy is issued by an insurance company or whether it is a Lloyd's form of policy.[2]

Generally the rights of the parties are governed by the terms of the policy alone. But sometimes another document, e g the proposal form is incorporated by reference into the policy, and then both the proposal form and the policy must be read together.[3]

Normally parol evidence in relation to the policy is inadmissible, but there are exceptions to this rule, e g such evidence is admissible to show that the policy is void or that it does not contain the correct terms.[4]

The date of commencement of the policy depends on the intention of the parties, and normally there will be an express term in the policy stating when it is to start. Normally the policy remains in force for the period specified in it, but may be brought to an end beforehand, e g if the parties consent or the insurance company goes into liquidation.[5]

If there has been fraud or misrepresentation on the part of the assured inducing the insurers to issue a policy, they are entitled to apply to the Court for an order that it should be delivered up to them so that it can be cancelled.[6]

If there is any material alteration in the terms of the policy made by the assured without the consent of the insurers, they are at liberty to avoid liability under it.[7]

Where the parties are agreed as to the terms of the contract, but a mistake has been made in reducing their agreement into writing, i e the policy does not properly set out the terms agreed upon, an application may be made to the Court for the rectification of the policy.[8]

On the expiration of the period of insurance the policy can usually be renewed, though often there are express terms in the policy as to whether renewal is possible and on what terms.[9] If the policy is not renewed before the current period of insurance or the 'days of grace' allowed under it, it will lapse, though in certain cases the policy may be revived.[10]

The policy sets out the details of the event which is insured against,[11] and also

1 See Chapter 17.
2 See Chapter 18.
3 See Chapter 19.
4 See Chapter 20.
5 See Chapter 21.
6 See Chapter 22.
7 See Chapter 23.
8 See Chapter 24.
9 See Chapter 25.
10 See Chapter 26.
11 See Chapter 27.

a list of exceptions specifying the circumstances in which the insurers will not be liable.[12] In certain cases where the event insured against has been brought about by the conduct of the assured, he will not be entitled to recover under the policy.[13]

Some terms of the policy amount to 'conditions' on the fulfilment of which the validity of the policy or the liability of the insurers depends.[14]

These 'conditions' deal with a variety of matters, amongst them being those relating to the alteration of the risk under the policy,[15] the assignment of the subject-matter insured under the policy,[16] and the taking out of 'other insurances' by the assured.[17]

The assured during the currency of the policy is generally entitled to assign it, though in some cases the consent of the insurers will be required.[18]

The Court is guided by certain rules of construction when the meaning of the words of the policy falls to be considered.[19]

---

12 See Chapter 28.
13 See Chapter 29.
14 See Chapter 30.
15 See Chapter 31.
16 See Chapter 32.
17 See Chapter 33.
18 See Chapter 34.
19 See Chapter 35.

CHAPTER 17

Classification of policies

All policies of insurance, whatever the kind of insurance to which they relate, may be classified in two ways:

1 According to the manner in which the subject-matter is described.
2 According to the amount recoverable in the event of loss.

1 According to the description of the subject-matter

Two types of policy fall within this class:

(a) *Policies in which the definition of the subject-matter is so precise as to confine the insurance to a specific object*

E g policies of insurance against personal accident, and policies of insurance against the loss of particular property, or loss by the defalcations of a particular employee, or by the insolvency of a particular debtor.

(b) *Policies in which the definition of the subject-matter is expressed in general terms so that the insurance is capable of applying to any object falling within the definition*

E g policies of insurance on property generally, and policies of insurance against public liability.

2 According to the amount recoverable

Two types of policy fall within this class:

a 'Unvalued' policies.
b 'Valued' policies.

(a) *'Unvalued' policies*

In the case of an 'unvalued' policy the sum to be paid to the assured is not fixed by the policy, but left to be ascertained after the loss has happened, e g in the case of policies of insurance against liability and most policies of insurance on property.

The sum specified in the policy as the amount of insurance, if any, merely indicates the amount beyond which the liability of the insurers does not extend.[1]

---

1 *Chapman v Pole* (1870) 22 LT 306 (fire insurance) per Cockburn CJ, directing the jury at 307: 'You must not run away with the notion that a policy of insurance entitles a man to recover according to the amount represented as insured by the premiums paid . . . He can only recover the real and actual value of his goods.'; *Vance v Foster* (1841) Ir Cir Rep 47 (fire insurance) per

As far as marine insurance is concerned, the Marine Insurance Act 1906, s 28, provides:

> 'An unvalued policy is a policy which does not specify the value of the subject-matter insured, but subject to the limit of the sum insured, leaves the insurable value to be subsequently ascertained, in the manner hereinbefore specified.'

(b) 'Valued' policies

In the case of a 'valued' policy the amount recoverable is fixed by the policy, e g personal accident policies and certain policies of insurance on property.

All[2] personal accident policies belong to this class, and, as the value of life or limb cannot be accurately measured,[3] the sum fixed in the policy is not open to objection on the ground of over-valuation.

In the case of an insurance on property, the value of the subject-matter may be fixed by agreement and inserted in the policy as the amount recoverable in the event of loss.

This valuation is binding,[4] except in the case of fraud[5] or mistake,[6] and dispenses the assured from the necessity of proving the value of his interest,[7] though he must still prove that he has an interest[8] in the subject-matter of insurance.

Pennefather B at 50: 'It has been truly stated that a policy of insurance is a contract of indemnity, and that while the insured may name any sum he likes as the sum for which he will pay a premium, he does not by so proposing that sum, nor does the company by accepting the risk, conclude themselves as to the amount which the plaintiff is to recover in consequence of the loss, because although the plaintiff cannot recover beyond the sum insured upon each particular item . . . he cannot recover even that sum unless he proves that he has sustained damage, and then he will recover a sum commensurate with the loss he has sustained.' Hence, a policy in express terms indemnifying the assured against loss to an amount not exceeding the sum insured on each item is not a valued policy: *Brodigan v Imperial Live Stock and General Insurance Co* [1928] WC & Ins Rep 160.

2 In *Theobald v Railway Passengers Assurance Co* (1854) 10 Exch 45 (personal accident insurance) the policy provided for a payment of £1,000 in case of death and of a proportionate part of that sum in case of personal injury, and it was held that in case of personal injury the assured was entitled to be indemnified against the expense and pain and loss immediately connected with the accident to an amount not exceeding the sum payable in case of death, and that no proportion existed between the amount of injury and the amount of loss in case of death. At the present day, personal accident policies invariably contain tables of compensation applicable to all kinds of personal injury.

3 *Theobald v Railway Passengers Assurance Co* (supra) per Alderson B, at 53.

4 *Burnand v Rodocanachi, Sons & Co* (1882) 7 App Cas 333 (marine insurance) per Lord Selborne C, at 335: 'For the purpose of the contract of insurance and for the purpose of all rights arising from that contract, it may well be that the valuation in a valued policy is conclusive, and the effect of it may be that for those purposes the assured is not entitled to say, "my loss has been greater than that which has been covered by the policy".' The valuation is not affected by an increase or diminution in the actual value of the subject-matter: *Woodside v Globe Marine Insurance Co* [1896] 1 QB 105 (marine insurance) per Mathew J, at 107.

5 An excessive valuation, out of all proportion to the real value, may be evidence of fraud: *Lewis v Rucker* (1761) 2 Burr 1167 (marine insurance) per Lord Mansfield CJ, at 1171; *Barker v Janson* (1868) LR 3 CP 303 (marine insurance) per Willes J, at 306.

6 *Barker v Janson* (supra) per Willes J, at 306.

7 *Williams v North China Insurance Co* (1876) 1 CPD 757, CA (marine insurance); *Feise v Aguilar* (1811) 3 Taunt 506 (marine insurance) per Mansfield CJ, at 507: 'It has been held again and again that it is unnecessary to prove the amount of interest under a valued policy. Therefore we must take it that the value insured is the plaintiff's interest.'

8 *Hodgson v Glover* (1805) 6 East 316 (marine insurance); *Feise v Aguilar* (supra) (marine insurance); *Lewis v Rucker* (supra) (marine insurance).

In the event of a partial loss, however, the valuation has no effect, and the assured must prove and is entitled to recover the actual amount of his loss.[9]

As far as marine insurance is concerned, the Marine Insurance Act 1906, s 27(2), states:

> 'A valued policy is a policy which specifies the agreed value of the subject-matter insured.'

Section 27(3) goes on to provide:

> 'Subject to the provisions of this Act, and in the absence of fraud, the value fixed by the policy is, as between the insurer and assured, conclusive of the insurable value of the subject intended to be insured whether the loss be total or partial.'

---

[9] See *City Tailors Ltd v Evans* (1922) 126 LT 439, CA (fire insurance) per Atkin LJ, at 444.

CHAPTER 18

The form and contents of the policy

The form and contents of an insurance policy will vary according as to whether it is issued by an insurance company or whether it is a Lloyd's form of policy.

A INSURANCE COMPANIES' POLICIES

1 The form of the policy

There are no restrictions as to the form which a policy issued by an insurance company may take. In practice, standard forms of policy are used, and these will vary from company to company.[1]

2 The contents of the policy

The contents of the policy will vary according to the type of insurance. So, too, will the contents vary from company to company.

In general, however, a policy of whatever kind may be regarded for convenience as divided into four parts:

1 The heading.
2 The body of the policy.
3 The back of the policy.
4 The docket.

1 The heading

The heading usually sets out the name of the insurers,[2] the reference number of the policy, the period for which the policy is in force,[3] the sum insured and the amount of the premium.

---

1 All policies except life policies are exempt from stamp duty: Finance Act 1970, Sch 7, para 1(2)(*b*). In the case of life policies, the stamp duty is as follows: Where the amount insured exceeds £50, but does not exceed £1,000, the duty is 5p for every £100 or part of £100 of the amount insured; where the amount insured exceeds £1,000, the duty is 50p for every £1,000 or part of £1,000 of the amount insured: ibid, Sch 7, para 17. See generally Sergeant *Stamp Duties* (8th Edn, 1982), pp 176–180 and the current Supplement.

2 In the case of a limited company the word 'limited', or an abbreviation (*Stacey & Co v Wallis* (1912) 106 LT 544 (company)) must not be omitted: Companies Act 1985, s 25.

3 A statement as to duration in the heading does not control the operative words in the policy: *Isaacs v Royal Insurance Co* (1870) LR 5 Exch 296 (fire insurance) per Cleasby B, at 301; cf *Sharkey v Yorkshire Insurance Co* (1916) 54 SCR 92, where the statement was in the margin of the proposal.

2 The body of the policy

In the body of the policy the actual contract between the parties is to be found. The following matters are usually dealt with:

a Recitals,[4] in which the fact that a proposal has been made[5] or that the premium has been paid may be stated.
b The details of the particular insurance, e g the name and address of the assured, the description of the subject-matter,[6] the amount of insurance, and the period of insurance.[7]
c The event insured against.[8]
d The premium.[9]
e The undertaking of the insurers, and exceptions from liability.[10]
f Stipulations and conditions.[11]
g Incorporation of other stipulations, including those indorsed on the policy, or contained in the proposal or other document.[12]

The policy may be expressed in general terms, and the details applicable to a particular insurance may be brought together in a schedule which is incorporated into the policy. In this case, the risk of omission or mistake in the parts which have to be filled in in writing is minimised.

3 The back of the policy

The back of the policy is a different document from the front of the policy, and nothing printed or written on the back of the policy forms part of the contract contained in the policy, unless incorporated by express reference or otherwise made part of the contract of insurance by the intention of the parties.

The matters dealt with on the back of the policy comprise:

a The conditions of the policy.
b Special terms agreed between the parties.
c The consent of the insurers.

(a) The conditions of the policy

The contract between the parties is usually expressed in broad general terms in the body of the policy. The stipulations and conditions regulating in detail the

---

4 Where the operative words are ambiguous, the recitals may be referred to for the purpose of ascertaining the meaning: *Notman v Anchor Assurance Co* (1858) 4 CBNS 476 (life insurance) per Cockburn CJ, at 480. If, however, the operative words are clear and unambiguous, they prevail: *Blascheck v Bussell* (1916) 33 TLR 74, CA per Swinfen Eady LJ, at 75; *Lazard Bros & Co Ltd v Brooks* (1932) 43 LlL Rep 372, HL (policy insuring bank against loss of securities); *Anglo-International Bank Ltd v General Accident Fire and Life Assurance Corpn Ltd* (1934) 48 LlL Rep 151, at 155 (per Lord Russell of Killowen).

5 A recital, if under seal, precludes the insurers from denying that there was a formal proposal: *Pearl Life Assurance Co v Johnson* [1909] 2 KB 288 (life insurance); cf. *Anglo-Californian Bank Ltd v London and Provincial Marine and General Insurance Co Ltd* (1904) 10 Com Cas 1, where a policy insuring the solvency of the underwriters of a particular policy recited that there were five underwriters, whereas there were, in fact, only four who were in law liable, and it was held that the insurers were bound by the recital.

6 See Chapter 4.

7 See Chapter 21.

8 See Chapter 27.

9 See Chapter 15.

10 See Chapter 28.

11 See Chapter 30.

12 See Chapter 19.

rights and duties of the parties are in practice indorsed on the back of the policy and made part of the contract by express incorporation.[13]

(b) Special terms agreed between the parties

Where such special terms are available in the ordinary course of business to any person who will pay for them, they are usually printed on a slip of paper and gummed or otherwise affixed to the policy.

If they are affixed to the face of the policy, they form part of the contract.[14] But if they are affixed to the back of the policy, they do not form part of the contract, unless clearly so intended.

(c) The consent of the insurers

Where, by a condition of the policy the consent of the insurers is required, e g in the case of the policy being assigned,[15] or the risk being increased,[16] or another insurance being effected,[17] such consent is usually required to be signified by a signed memorandum indorsed on the policy.

4 The docket

When a policy is folded, the outside portion occupies the place of a cover. Upon this there is frequently printed a docket, or summary of the policy, and there may be in addition various notices or warnings addressed to the assured.[18] These may be made part of the policy by the clause of incorporation.[19]

---

[13] *Everett v Desborough* (1829) 5 Bing 503 (life insurance) per Best CJ, at 517: 'That contract [i e the contract between the parties] is not confined to what is contained in the body of the policy, but embraces the conditions indorsed on it, and embraces the representations required by those conditions.' See also, *Solvency Mutual Guarantee Co v York* (1858) 3 H & N 588 per Pollock CB, at 593; *Gamble v Accident Assurance Co* (1869) IR 4 CL 204, where the condition in question was contained in a 'special notice' indorsed on the policy and incorporated under a reference to 'conditions, instructions, stipulations and notices'; *Muirhead v Forth and North Sea Steamboat Mutual Insurance Association* [1894] AC 72 (marine insurance), where an invalid article of association was held to be made part of the policy by incorporation; *Roper v Lendon* (1859) 1 E & E 825 (fire insurance) per Hill J, at 831; *Caledonian Insurance Co v Gilmour* [1893] AC 85 (fire insurance) per Lord Herschell LC, at 90; *Tootal, Broadhurst, Lee Co v London and Lancashire Fire Insurance Co* (1908) reported in Ivamy *Fire and Motor Insurance,* (4th Edn 1984) Appendix IV, p 403 (fire insurance) per Bigham J, at 395; *Freeze v Dominion Safety Fund Life Association* (1895) 33 NBR 238 (life insurance), where the words 'constituted as indorsed hereon' were held to incorporate an indorsement as to the time and manner of paying the premiums; and cf *Strong v Rule* (1825) 3 Bing 315 (marine insurance), where it was held that the plaintiff ought to have pleaded the indorsed regulations as well as the policy.

[14] *Bensaude v Thames and Mersey Marine Insurance Co* [1897] AC 609 (marine insurance) per Lord Halsbury C, at 612. For examples, see *Letts v Excess Insurance Co* (1916) 32 TLR 361; *Century Bank of City of New York v Mountain* (1914) 112 LT 484. CA.

[15] As to the assignment of the policy, see Chapter 34.

[16] As to the alteration of the risk, see Chapter 34.

[17] As to 'other insurance', see Chapter 33.

[18] In 1977 the Life Offices Association issued a statement relating to long-term insurance practice. It applies to such insurance effected by individuals resident in the United Kingdom in a private capacity, and says:
'Life assurance policies or accompanying documents should indicate:
a the circumstances in which interest would accrue after the assurance has matured; and
b whether or not there are rights to surrender values in the contract and, if so, what those rights are.'

[19] *Scott v Scottish Accident Insurance Co* 1889 16 R (Ct of Sess) 630.

Otherwise, they do not form part of the contract, so as to extend the obligations or diminish the rights of the assured,[20] though they may be taken into account as expressing the meaning and intention of the insurers.

B LLOYD'S POLICIES

1 The form of the policy

All Lloyd's policies are in a standard form.[1] A new form of Lloyd's marine policy was introduced in 1982, the first major change since 1778.[2]

2 The contents of the policy

A Lloyd's policy must necessarily cover the same ground and deal with the same matters as any other policy. The only points calling for attention are:

a The premium.[3]
b The liability of the underwriters.
c Conditions.[4]

(a) The premium

The policy usually contains an acknowledgment that the premium has been paid. The effect of this acknowledgment is that the assured is entitled to enforce the policy against the underwriter, although the premium has not been paid.[5]

By usage, the underwriter looks for the premium to the broker and not to the assured.[6] As between underwriter and broker the premium is treated as paid when the 'slip'[7] is initialled, irrespective of the actual date of payment. Hence, the underwriter, in addition to being liable for any loss, cannot, as against the assured, deduct the unpaid premium from the amount for which he is liable under the policy; nor, if the assured becomes entitled to a return of premium, can the underwriter refuse to refund it on the ground that he has never received it from the broker.[8] The assured, in his turn, is liable for the premium only to the broker, who may claim it although he has not actually paid the underwriter.[9]

(b) The liability of the underwriters

Though each underwriter insures the whole amount of the loss, his

---

20 *Hawke v Niagara District Mutual Fire Insurance Co* (1876) 23 Gr 139 (fire insurance); *Stoness v Anglo-American Insurance Co* (1912) 21 OWR 405 (fire insurance); cf *Rowe v London and Lancashire Fire Insurance Co* (1866) 12 Gr 311 (fire insurance), where a note at the foot of the proposal form was held not to form part of the contract.

1 As to stamp duty, see p 214, ante.

2 See Ivamy *Marine Insurance* (4th Edn, 1985), pp 104–105.

3 As to the premium, see generally Chapter 15.

4 As to conditions, see generally Chapter 30.

5 *Sweeting v Pearce* (1861) 9 CBNS 534 (marine insurance). See further, Chapter 15.

6 *Grover and Grover Ltd v Mathews* (1910) 15 Com Cas 249 (fire insurance) per Hamilton J, at 260.

7 As to the 'slip', see pp 116–118, ante.

8 *Dalzell v Mair* (1808) 1 Camp 532 (marine insurance); *Xenos v Wickham* (1863) 14 CBNS 435 (marine insurance): (reversed) (1866) LR 2 HL 296) per Blackburn J, at 457.

9 *Airy v Bland* (1774) 2 Park's Marine Insces, 8th Edn, p 811 (marine insurance).

undertaking, as expressed in the policy, limits his liability to the amount of his subscription. This liability is a several liability, not a joint liability or a joint and several liability; and the policy is, in effect, not one contract, but a number of separate contracts, one with each underwriter, expressed on the same piece of paper.[10] His liability, therefore, under his own contract is not affected by a judgment obtained against any other underwriters who may have signed the same policy, or increased by their insolvency.[11]

It is, therefore, necessary, strictly speaking, to sue each underwriter individually,[12] though, in practice, the action is usually brought against the first underwriter who signed the policy for the amount of his subscription, the remaining underwriters undertaking to abide by the result. A formal undertaking is usually given by the solicitors acting on their behalf.

(c) Conditions

Lloyd's policies generally contain exceptions; but a Lloyd's policy may contain no express conditions. It is not an uncommon practice, however, especially in connection with the more modern classes of insurance business, to insert conditions to the same effect as those used in other policies, e g conditions relating to notice and proof of loss.

3 The incorporation of other policies

Where there is another policy in existence effected by the same assured with an insurance company, it is not unusual to insert in the Lloyd's policy a clause referring to the company's policy and giving the underwriters the benefit of its terms.[13]

Where the clause provides that the Lloyd's policy is to be subject to the same conditions as the company's policy,[14] such conditions are incorporated into the Lloyd's policy, and a failure on the part of the assured to comply with them has

---

10 *Anglo-Californian Bank Ltd v London and Provincial Marine and General Insurance Co Ltd* (1904) 10 Com Cas 1 (solvency insurance) per Walton J, at 8. The existence of a partnership between underwriters is expressly prohibited by Lloyd's Act 1871, Sch V, 4(1). It is usual, however, for one underwriter to be expressly authorised to underwrite policies on behalf of several others (see *Thompson v Adams* (1889) 23 QBD 361, per Mathew J, at 362) who are called his 'names', and they are consequently liable upon the policies which he underwrites on their behalf, even though he does so fraudulently: *Hambro v Burnand* [1904] 2 KB 10 CA (solvency insurance); until notice of termination of authority is given: *Willis, Faber & Co Ltd v Joyce* (1911) 16 Com Cas 190 (marine insurance).

11 *Tyser v Shipowners' Syndicate (Reassured)* [1896] 1 QB 135 (marine insurance).

12 But a representative action may be brought by one underwriter in respect of the premium due under a reinsurance policy: *Janson v Property Insurance Co* (1913) 30 TLR 49 (motor insurance).

13 *Walker & Sons v Uzielli* (1896) 1 Com Cas 452 (fire insurance) per Mathew J, at 455; 'It is clear that the object of Lloyd's underwriters when making these fire policies is to adopt the convenient course of following the terms and conditions of insurances effected with fire insurance companies. They therefore introduce into their policies a clause giving themselves the benefit of the terms upon which those companies insure. In this case, the policy of the defendant was "warranted same premium and conditions as the Union Assurance Society", and the conditions of the policy of that company are therefore incorporated with the policy in question.' See also *Sulphite Pulp Co v Faber* (1895) 1 Com Cas 146 (fire insurance) per Lord Russell CJ, at 151.

14 The precise meaning of the word 'terms' in the usual phrase of incorporation is doubtful; it probably means terms as to risk, and cannot mean terms which are immaterial for the purpose of the contract: *Barnard v Faber* [1893] 1 QB 340, CA (fire insurance) per Lindley LJ, at 343; cf SC per Bowen LJ, at 344.

the same consequences as in the case of the company's policy. Thus, where the company's policy contains conditions providing for notice to be given of the cesser of any insurance previously effected, and for the avoidance for cancellation of the policy in the event of such notice not being duly given, a failure to give notice to the underwriters of the cesser of the company's policy relieves them from liability.[15]

In addition to incorporating its conditions, the clause may contain a statement that the rate of premium,[16] or the interest insured,[17] is to be the same as in the company's policy. This statement is to be construed as a condition precedent to the validity of the Lloyd's policy, since it is intended for the protection of the underwriters.[18] It is usually introduced by the word 'warranted', though this is immaterial since it is equally a condition precedent if the word is omitted.[19] Where, therefore, it appears that the rate of premium,[20] or the interest insured,[1] is different in the two policies, the condition is broken, and the Lloyd's policy is avoided. Similarly, where the Lloyd's policy contains a reference to the sum insured by the company's policy,[2] the accuracy of the

---

15 *Sulphite Pulp Co v Faber* (supra).

16 *Walker & Sons v Uzielli* (supra), where the premium payable under the Lloyd's policy was warranted to be the highest rate; *Sulphite Pulp Co v Faber* (supra); *Bancroft v Heath* (1901) 6 Com Cas 137, CA (fire insurance).

17 *Barnard v Faber* (supra) (fire insurance); *Sulphite Pulp Co v Faber* (supra) (fire insrance); *Walker & Sons v Uzielli* (supra) (fire insurance).

18 *Barnard v Faber* (supra) (fire insurance), where the clause was 'warranted to be on same rate, terms, and identical interest as Union Insurance Co. £800 and Glasgow Insurance Co. £700, and to follow their settlements'. In this case Bowen LJ, said (at 343): 'The object of this clause is to have other companies or underwriters in the same boat as regards the particular interest and the risk to be covered; and the clause is one which is intended unquestionably for the protection of the underwriters. When you have arrived at that, it seems to me you have arrived at half the journey's end, because there can be no adequate protection to underwriters if you relegate them to a cross-action. The clause is intended to protect them against having to pay, not to give them a right to bring an action against the man insuring with them. There are to be the same rate, the same terms, the identical interest, as in the case of the two other companies. It is, therefore, a term of this policy that there should be this promise; and if this promise is one which goes to the root of the whole engagement and transaction, then it becomes, according to the ordinary principles of ordinary law, a condition—either a condition precedent, or, if the condition is one which cannot be construed as a condition precedent and must be a condition subsequent, then it becomes a condition subsequent. That arises from the materiality of the promise which is assumed to be made, and the making of which is to be a term of the engagement or transaction into which the underwriter has entered. The same rate and identical interest are obviously so material to the transaction that we can only construe them as creating a condition precedent.'

19 *Barnard v Faber* [1893] 1 QB 340, CA, per Lindley LJ, at 342: 'What, I apprehend, the underwriters mean is this, "satisfy us that these two offices have insured the same risk, the same interest at the same rate, and we will effect this insurance." I cannot myself think that the term "warranted" is important; for I should construe this policy in precisely the same way whether the word was in or not. I do not think the policy is made plainer by the introduction of that word. I look upon part of the clause as a condition precedent. The insurance is "to be on the same rate, terms, and interest" as the two companies which are named. I regard that part as a condition precedent to the incurring of any liability at all. The remainder of the clause is a condition subsequent. Now, unless the clause is so read, in what position would the underwriters find themselves? They would then find that they had come under an obligation, and that they were thrown back upon a cross-action against the insured.'

20 *Walker & Sons v Uzielli* (1896) 1 Com Cas 452 (fire insurance); *Barnard v Faber* [1893] 1 QB 340, CA (fire insurance).

1 *Barnard v Faber* (supra).

2 Ibid.

reference is also a condition precedent, and a mis-statement of the sum so insured, therefore, discharges the underwriters from liability.[3]

The Lloyd's policy may also contain a clause to the effect that the underwriters are to follow the settlements of the company or to pay the same percentage as may be settled upon the company's policy. Under this clause, which is, strictly speaking, a condition subsequent,[4] of the policy, the assured cannot recover on the Lloyd's policy unless the liability of the company upon its policy has been established, and the amount of such liability ascertained.[5] If, therefore, the assured is precluded by any condition of the company's policy from enforcing his claim under it, the condition comes into operation and he cannot recover under the Lloyd's policy either.[6]

A further condition may provide that no payment is to be made until all other policies are exhausted, which has the effect of making the Lloyd's policy an excess insurance only.[7]

---

3 *Bancroft v Heath* (1901) 6 Com Cas 137, CA (fire insurance), where the Lloyd's policy was on stock-in-trade, contained in the building insured by the other policy.

4 *Barnard v Faber* (fire insurance) (supra) per Lindley LJ, at 342.

5 *Beauchamp v Faber* (1898) 3 Com Cas 308 (fire insurance) per Bigham J, at 311; *Sulphite Pulp Co v Faber* (1895) 1 Com Cas 146 (fire insurance) per Lord Russell CJ, at 153. But the assured would not be prevented from recovering by a wrongful repudiation of liability under the other policy. See *American Footwear Co v Lancashire and General Assurance Co* (1925) 57 OLR 305.

6 *Beauchamp v Faber* (fire insurance) (supra) per Bigham J, at 311, where the assured was unable to recover upon his other policy in consequence of his having made a fraudulent claim.

7 As to excess clauses generally, see p 433, post.

CHAPTER 19

The effect of other documents on the policy

The rights of the parties are normally governed by the terms of the policy alone. Any other document which is not incorporated into the policy has, in general, no effect. But if the terms of another document have been incorporated, then they form part of the policy and must be read as one with it.

The Court is entitled to look at other documents where there is any ambiguity as to the meaning of the words used in the policy.

A EFFECT WHERE THE OTHER DOCUMENT IS NOT INCORPORATED

Preliminary statements and documents, which are made and put forward during the negotiations, are not in themselves contractual.[1] Unless, therefore, they are incorporated into the policy, they form no part of the contract of insurance,[2] and cannot be referred to for the purpose of construing the policy or of extending or modifying the rights or duties either of the insurers or the assured in a manner inconsistent with its terms. It is immaterial whether the statement is made verbally[3] or whether it is contained in a document, e g a prospectus issued by the insurers,[4] or a proposal form filled up

---

1 *Canning v Farquhar* (1886) 16 QBD 727, CA (life insurance) per Lord Esher MR, at 731.

2 But they may amount to an independent collateral contract: *Thiselton v Commercial Union Assurance Co* [1926] Ch 888 (life insurance) per Eve J, at 894: see also, *Salvin v James* (1805) 6 East 571 (fire insurance), where the prospectus stated that losses within the days of grace were covered, notwithstanding the non-payment of the premium; *Anstey v British Natural Premium Life Association* (1908) 24 TLR 871, CA (life insurance), where the prospectus stated that after a specified period the policy would be indisputable in the absence of fraud and that no bona fide mistakes, that might have crept into the application or into any other document or statement made before the issue of the policy and accepted as the basis of the contract, would prejudice the validity of the policy. As to the indisputability of policies, see further Ivamy *Personal Accident, Life and Other Insurances* (2nd Edn, 1980), pp 101–103.

3 *Horncastle v Equitable Life Assurance Society of United States* (1906) 22 TLR 735, CA (life insurance).

4 *British Equitable Assurance Co Ltd v Baily* [1906] AC 35 (life insurance) per Lord Lindley, at 41: 'This appeal turns entirely on the contracts entered into between the insurance company and its participating policy-holders, represented by Mr. Bailey. The contracts are contained in the policies issued to them. It is contended that the applications for these policies were based on the faith of prospectuses containing statements and holding out inducements which preclude the company from making alterations in the mode of applying their profits without the consent of the policy-holders. My Lords, if these gentlemen were seeking to rescind or rectify their contracts on the ground of fraud or mistake, or were suing for damages occasioned by fraudulent misrepresentation, it would be legitimate to refer to the statements in the prospectuses on the

by the assured,[5] or the correspondence that passed between the parties.[6]

The policy may contain an express stipulation showing that the parties intend the policy to be the complete and final statement of the contract, and that nothing done during the negotiations should be considered as binding between them.[7]

B EFFECT WHERE THE OTHER DOCUMENT IS INCORPORATED

Although the policy contains the contract, it is not necessary that all the terms of the contract should actually form part of the engagement printed on the face of the policy itself. It is sufficient if they are incorporated into the policy by reference.

Where a term is thus incorporated into the policy, it is immaterial whether it is indorsed on the back of the policy, as is the usual practice in the case of conditions,[8] or whether it is contained in a separate and distinct document,[9]

---

faith of which they became policy-holders. But the complaining policy-holders are not doing anything of the sort, and the prospectuses, not being referred to in the policies, cannot, in my opinion, be legitimately referred to in order to construe the contracts into which the policy-holders have been induced to enter. These contracts are to be found in the policies themselves.' See also, *Griffiths v Fleming* [1909] 1 KB 805, CA (life insurance) per Farwell LJ, at 817.

5 *Winicofsky v Army and Navy General Assurance Association Ltd* (1919) 35 TLR 283 (burglary insurance), where a statement in the proposal that the assured would prove a loss by the production of receipts was held not to disentitle him from recovering, though he produced no receipts, on satisfying the arbitrator that he had sustained a loss; *Hare v Barstow* (1844) 8 Jur 928 (fire insurance); *Fritzley v Germania Farmers' Mutual Fire Insurance Co* (1909) 19 OLR 49, where an immaterial mis-statement in the proposal was held not to avoid the policy, although the proposal contained a warranty that the assured's statements were true, the proposal not being incorporated into the policy.

6 *Halhead v Young* (1856) 6 E & B 312 (marine insurance) per Lord Campbell CJ, at 325; see also, *Weston v Emes* (1808) 1 Taunt 115 (marine insurance). See further, *Phoenix Insurance Co of Hartford v De Monchy* (1929) 141 LT 439, 34 LlL Rep 201, HL (marine insurance), where a certificate of insurance was the contract between the parties and express incorporation of certain terms in a preceding policy was held to exclude the incorporation of the remainder; *Stolos Compania SA v Ajax Insurance Co Ltd, The Admiral C* [1981] 1 Lloyd's Rep 9, CA (marine insurance), where it was doubtful whether a term in a printed sheet annexed to a policy was incorporated into it. (See the judgment of Sir David Cairns, ibid, at 10.)

7 *Horncastle v Equitable Life Assurance Society of United States* (1906) 22 TLR 735, CA (life insurance) per Fletcher Moulton LJ, at 737.

8 *Everett v Desborough* (1829) 5 Bing 503 (life insurance) (per Best CJ, at 517: 'That contract [i e the contract between the parties] is not confined to what is contained in the body of the policy, but embraces the conditions indorsed on it, and embraces the representations required by those conditions.' See also, *Solvency Mutual Guarantee Society v York* (1858) 3 H & N 588 per Pollock CB, at 593; *Gamble v Accident Assurance Co Ltd* (1870) IR 4 CL 204, where the condition in question was contained in a 'special notice' indorsed on the policy and incorporated under a reference to 'conditions, instructions, stipulations and notices'; *Muirhead v Forth and North Sea Steamboat Mutual Insurance Association* [1894] AC 72 (marine insurance), where an invalid article of association was held to be made part of the policy by incorporation; *Roper v Lendon* (1859) 1 E & E 825 (fire insurance) per Hill J, at 831; *Caledonian Insurance Co v Gilmour* [1893] AC 85 (fire insurance) per Lord Herschell LC, at 90; *Tootal, Broadhurst, Lee Co v London and Lancashire Fire Insurance Co* (1908) Times 21 May (fire insurance); *Freeze v Dominion Safety Fund Life Association* (1895) 33 NBR 238 (life insurance), where the words 'constituted as indorsed hereon' were held to incorporate an indorsement as to the time and manner of paying the premium; cf *Strong v Rule* (1825) 3 Bing 315 (marine insurance), where it was held that the plaintiff ought to have pleaded the indorsed regulations as well as the policy.

9 A 'slip' which is pasted or otherwise affixed to the face of the policy is to be regarded as part of the policy: *Home Insurance Co of New York v Victoria-Montreal Fire Insurance Co* [1907] AC 59, PC; *Cheshire & Co v Vaughan Bros & Co* [1920] 3 KB 240, CA (marine insurance) per Scutton LJ, at

such as a schedule[10] or another policy, e g in the case of reinsurance.[11] Further, where there is another policy in existence effected by the same assured with an insurance company, it is not unusual to insert in a Lloyd's policy a clause referring to the company's policy and giving the underwriters the benefit of its terms.[12]

The contents of the proposal[13] or of any other documents employed during the preliminary negotiations may be made part of the contract by express incorporation.[14]

C LOOKING AT OTHER DOCUMENTS TO RESOLVE AMBIGUITIES

Where there is an ambiguity on the face of the policy, and a question, therefore, arises as to its meaning or effect, the Court may take into consideration any documents, such as the prospectus,[15] the proposal form,[16] a letter which the insurers have written,[17] or even the back of the policy,[18] if not incorporated into

---

254; cf *Mountain v Whittle* [1921] 1 AC 615 (marine insurance) per Lord Birkenhead LC, at 621.

10 *Sillem v Thornton* (1854) 3 E & B 868 (fire insurance), where the description of the subject-matter was contained on a separate paper referred to in the policy. This is frequently done in practice where the subject-matter comprises a large number of items.

11 *Home Insurance Co of New York v Victoria-Montreal Fire Insurance Co* [1907] AC 59 at 64, PC; *South British Fire and Marine Insurance Co of New Zealand v Da Costa* [1906] 1 KB 456 (marine insurance) per Bigham J, at 460; *Foster v Mentor Life Assurance Co* (1854) 3 E & B 48 (life insurance) per Lord Campbell CJ, at 82.

12 *Walker & Sons v Uzielli* (1896) 1 Com Cas 452 per Mathew J, at 455: 'It is clear that the object of Lloyd's underwriters when making these fire policies is to adopt the convenient course of following the terms and conditions of insurances effected with fire insurance companies. They therefore introduce into their policies a clause giving themselves the benefit of the terms upon which those companies insure. In this case the policy of the defendant was "warranted same premium and conditions as the Union Assurance Society," and the conditions of the policy of that company are therefore incorporated with the policy in question.' See also, *Sulphite Pulp Co v Faber* (1895) 1 Com Cas 146. As to the incorporation of other policies in the Lloyd's policy, see further, pp 218–220, ante.

13 In case of inconsistency between the proposal and the policy, the policy, as being the later document, prevails: *Kaufmann v British Surety Insurance Co Ltd* (1929) 45 TLR 399, 33 LlL Rep 315.

14 *Elgin Loan and Savings Co v London Guarantee and Accident Co* (1906) 11 OLR 330, following *Hay v Employers' Liability Assurance Corpn* (1905) 6 OWR 459; *Worsley v Wood* (1796) 6 Term Rep 710 (fire insurance), following *Rutledge v Burrell* (1789) 1 Hy Bl 254 (fire insurance); *Tarleton v Staniforth* (1796) 1 Bos & P 471 (fire insurance); *Sun Life Assurance Co of Canada v Jervis* [1943] 2 All ER 425, CA (life insurance). In *Youlden v London Guarantee and Accident Co* (1912) 26 OLR 75 the policy, which was for a year, did not contemplate renewal, but the assured in fact renewed his insurance, receiving a renewal receipt for an insurance 'according to the tenour' of the original policy, referring to it by number, and it was held that this incorporated the conditions of the policy.

15 *Salvin v James* (1805) 6 East 571, where the insurers had stated in a prospectus their view as to the effect of a loss during the days of grace; *Thiselton v Commercial Union Assurance Co* [1926] Ch 888 (life insurance).

16 *Hare v Barstow* (1844) 8 Jur 928 (fire insurance); *Hordern v Commercial Union Assurance Co* (1887) 56 LJPC 78 (fire insurance).

17 *R Smith & Son v Eagle Star and British Dominions Insurance Co Ltd* (1934) 50 TLR 208, CA (employers' liability insurance), where the insurers had stated in a letter after the policy had been issued that a particular disease was covered. See also, *Sun Life Assurance Co of Canada v Jervis* [1943] 2 All ER 425, CA (life insurance), where an 'illustration' was held to be part of the contract.

18 *Mardorf v Accident Insurance Co* [1903] 1 KB 584, where a policy containing insurances against accident and against disease was indorsed with a notice in general terms defining the meaning of

the policy, in which the insurers profess to set forth or explain the purport and effect of their policies, and any verbal explanations given by themselves or their agents.[19]

In this case the assured does not seek to set up a contract different from and inconsistent with the contract contained in the policy. The documents and explanations show the interpretation which the insurers themselves place on the policy, and they are, therefore, precluded by their own words from relying on any other interpretation.[20]

The onus of proving that he knew and acted upon such interpretation rests upon the assured,[1] though especially in a case where prospectuses are issued, the onus is not difficult to discharge.

'disease', and it was held that the definition applied to the accident insurance as well as the disease insurance. Cf *A-G v Cleobury* (1849) 4 Exch 65, where the docket was referred to, on a stamp question, for the purpose of showing the amount of insurance. See further, *Scott v Scottish Accident Insurance Co* 1889 16 R (Ct of Sess) 630, where the notice was referred to in the body of the policy.

19 *Bawden v London, Edinburgh and Glasgow Assurance Co* [1892] 2 QB 534, CA.

20 *Wood v Dwarris* (1856) 11 Exch 493 (life insurance) per Alderson B, at 503; *Anstey v British Natural Premium Life Association Ltd* (1908) 24 TLR 871, CA (life insurance); cf *Kaufmann v British Surety Insurance Co* (1929) 45 TLR 399 (accident insurance), where, though the proposal was incorporated, it was inconsistent with the policy.

1 *Wood v Dwarris* (supra) per Martin B, at 504.

CHAPTER 20

Parol evidence in relation to the policy

A THE GENERAL RULE

Parol evidence is not admissible to contradict[1] or vary[2] the meaning of the policy, since, after the contract is reduced into writing, the parties are not at liberty to show, by giving evidence of what passed between them at the time of effecting the policy, that they contracted otherwise than in accordance with the words in which they have chosen to express the terms of their agreement.[3]

B EXCEPTIONS TO THE GENERAL RULE

There are certain cases, however, in which parol evidence is admissible:

1 To prove that the policy is void.
2 To prove that the policy does not accurately set out the actual terms of the agreement between the parties.
3 To prove a parol condition on the faith of which the policy was made, and until the fulfilment of which the policy was not to become operative.
4 To supplement the contract by adding collateral terms.
5 To identify the subject-matter of insurance.
6 To show that a word is used in a peculiar sense.

---

1 *Levy v Scottish Employers' Insurance Co* (1901) 17 TLR 229, where the cover note provided for an insurance for 14 days unless the proposal was previously declined, and the assured sought to rely on a statement of the insurers' agent that, if he did not hear within the 14 days, he might treat himself as insured; *Anglo-Californian Bank Ltd v London and Provincial Marine and General Insurance Co Ltd* (1904) 10 Com Cas 1, where a policy insuring the solvency of the underwriters of another policy recited that 5 underwriters had subscribed the other policy, though only 4 had subscribed it in fact, and it was held that parol evidence could not be given to show that liability under the solvency policy was conditional on the fifth underwriter subscribing the other policy.

2 *Weston v Emes* (1808) 1 Taunt 115 (marine insurance), where, on an insurance of goods in ship or ships it was sought to show that, at the time of insuring, a particular ship had been excepted; cf *Halhead v Young* (1856) 6 E & B 312 (marine insurance) per Lord Campbell CJ, at 325.

3 *Johnston v Ocean Accident and Guarantee Corpn Ltd* (1915) 34 NZLR 356, where a personal accident policy was effected in the name of an employee, though the premium was paid by the employer, and it was held that parol evidence was not admissible to show that the policy was intended to cover the employer's statutory liability; *Horncastle v Equitable Life Assurance Society of United States* (1906) 22 TLR 735, CA (life insurance), where the agent, with the authority of the insurers, had represented that the value of the policy at a certain date would be a certain amount, but the policy contained no reference to this.

1 To prove that the policy is void

Where the question arises whether the policy is binding or not by reason of an alleged breach of duty, the statements of the parties, including the explanations of their agents[4] and the documents which pass between them, may be referred to for the purpose of showing whether the duty was or was not performed.[5]

In this case, there is no attempt to set up any other contract than the contract contained in the policy; and the evidence is used for the purpose of proving or disproving its binding effect. Thus, if the proposal contains a declaration that the statements in it are to be the basis of the contract, the policy is avoided by their untruth, even though the proposal is not incorporated into the policy.[6]

The onus of proving that such documents exist, or that such statements were made, and that the policy was made on the faith of them, lies on the party seeking to establish the case which they support. Thus, where the insurers seek to avoid the policy on the ground that the proposal signed by the assured contained inaccurate statements, they must prove in the first instance that there is, in fact, a proposal signed by the assured, and, if they are unable to do so, their objection to the validity of the policy fails.[7]

2 To prove that the policy does not contain the correct terms

Where the question arises whether the policy as issued contains the real contract agreed between the parties, the Court must necessarily refer to what passed between them during the negotiations, including any preliminary documents, such as a prospectus,[8] a proposal,[9] or a 'slip',[10] in order to discover whether there was ever, in fact, a concluded agreement, and if so, what were its precise terms.

In this case, an attempt is made to set up a different and inconsistent contract, the ground being that the policy does not truly exhibit the terms agreed.[11]

Evidence of conversations with the insurers or their agents, and of verbal representations made by them for the purpose of inducing the insured to enter into the contract, is also admissible for the same purpose.[12]

---

4 *Joel v Law Union and Crown Insurance Co* [1908] 2 KB 863, CA (life insurance) per Fletcher Moulton LJ, at 892.

5 *British Equitable Assurance Co Ltd v Baily* [1906] AC 35 (life insurance) per Lord Lindley, at 41; cf *Globe Savings and London Co v Employers' Liability Assurance Corpn* (1901) 13 Man R 531.

6 *Rozanes v Bowen* (1928) 32 LlL Rep 98, CA (burglary insurance).

7 *Pearl Life Assurance Co v Johnson* [1909] 2 KB 288 (life insurance).

8 *British Equitable Assurance Co Ltd v Baily* [1906] AC 35 (life insurance) per Lord Lindley, at 41; *Sun Life Assurance Co of Canada v Jervis* [1943] 2 All ER 425 (life insurance), where an 'illustration' was relied on.

9 *Griffiths v Fleming* [1909] 1 KB 805, CA (life insurance) per Farwell LJ, at 817: 'The proposals have been put in and used by both sides, and although they could not be used in an action on the policy in order to construe the policy, they could, of course, be used in an action to rectify.' As to the rectification of the policy, see pp 239–243, post.

10 *Collett v Morrison* (1851) 9 Hare 162 (life insurance), following *Motteux v London Assurance (Governor & Co)* (1739) 1 Atk 545 (marine insurance), where a policy was rectified in accordance with the 'slip'; *Rogers v Whittaker* [1917] 1 KB 942 (fire insurance); *Letts v Excess Insurance Co* (1916) 32 TLR 361 (accident insurance); *Canadian Casualty and Boiler Insurance Co v Hawthorne & Co* (1907) 39 SCR 558, where the cover note and a verbal arrangement with the agent of the insurers were referred to.

11 *Mackenzie v Coulson* (1869) LR 8 Eq 368 (marine insurance) per James V-C, at 375.

12 *Allom v Property Insurance Co* (1911) Times, 10 February.

The onus of proof lies on the party asserting that the policy is incorrect.[13]

3 To prove a parol condition

The Court will admit parol evidence to show that the policy was not to come into force until a parol condition had been fulfilled.[14]

4 To add collateral terms

Parol evidence is admissible to supplement the contract contained in the policy by adding collateral terms.[15] But such terms must not be inconsistent with the express terms of the policy.[16]

5 To identify the subject-matter of insurance

Thus, in the case of an accident insurance policy where the question was whether the person whose safety was insured had himself effected the policy or whether his son had effected it for his own benefit, evidence that the father had talked of insuring his life was admitted.[17] Similarly, in a case relating to employers' liability insurance, the Court admitted in evidence a letter from the insurers identifying a particular disease as within the risk.[18]

The description in the policy must, however, be appropriate to the subject-matter sought to be identified.[19]

6 To show that a word is used in a peculiar sense

Parol evidence is admissible to show that a word is used in a peculiar sense, differing from its ordinary meaning where the word is used with reference to a particular district, occupation, or trade, and by the usage of that district, occupation, or trade the word is understood in a peculiar sense.[20] But a usage

---

13 *Parsons v Bignold* (1846) 15 LJCR 379 (life insurance).

14 *Anglo-Californian Bank Ltd v London and Provincial Marine and General Insurance Co Ltd* (1904) 10 Com Cas 1 (solvency insurance) per Walton J, at 12: *Xenos v Wickham* (1867) LR 2 HL 296 (marine insurance); *Roberts v Security Co* [1897] 1 QB 111, CA (burglary insurance).

15 *Newman v Belsten* (1884) 28 Sol Jo 301, CA (life insurance), where the policy, which was not issued before the insured's death, was intended to be for the benefit of his wife, though no statement to this effect was contained either in the proposal or in the receipt for the premium, and Lindley LJ, at 302, pointed out that the contract was partly in writing and partly parol; *Moss v Norwich and London Insurance Association* (1922) 10 LlL Rep 395, CA, where evidence was admitted to show that an employers' liability policy was intended to cover the employer's son although the statutory liability to pay compensation did not extend to him.

16 *Horncastle v Equitable Life Assurance Society of United States* (1906) 22 TLR 735, CA (life insurance); *Boyd v Colonial Mutual Life Assurance Society* (1910) 29 NZLR 41 (life insurance).

17 *Shilling v Accidental Death Insurance Co* (1858) 1 F & F 116 (accident insurance).

18 *Smith & Son v Eagle Star and British Dominions Insurance Co Ltd* (1934) 50 TLR 208, 47 LlL Rep 88 (employers' liability insurance).

19 *Watchorn v Langford* (1813) 3 Camp 422 (fire insurance); *Hare v Barstow* (1844) 8 Jur 928 (fire insurance).

20 *Woodall v Pearl Assurance Co* [1919] 1 KB 593, CA (accident insurance), where the description of the assured was held to be accurately described as understood in the district; *Robertson v French* (1803) 4 East 130 (marine insurance) per Lord Ellenborough CJ, at 135; *Otago Farmers Cooperative Association of New Zealand v Thompson* [1910] 2 KB 145 (marine insurance); *Clift v Schwabe* (1846) 3 CB 437 (life insurance) per Parke B, at 470; *Scragg v United Kingdom Temperance and General Provident Institution* [1976] 2 Lloyd's Rep 227, QBD (Commercial Court), where evidence was admitted to show the meaning of the term 'motor racing'. (See the judgment of Mocatta J, ibid, at 231.) A mercantile usage which refers to written documents may be

will not be admitted in evidence where it is inconsistent with the express language of the policy.[1]

Further, where the word is, on the face of it, ambiguous,[2] reference may be made to the surrounding circumstances,[3] including the object with which the words were presumably introduced.[4]

C THE EFFECT OF THE ADMISSION OF PAROL EVIDENCE

Where parol evidence is admitted, the matter in issue is no longer a mere question of construction to be decided by the Court, but becomes a question of fact for the jury.[5]

---

established by parol evidence: *Foster v Mentor Life Assurance Co* (1854) 3 E & B 48 (life insurance) per Lord Campbell LJ, at 79. See further, *Imperial Marine Insurance Co v Fire Insurance Corpn* (1879) 4 CPD 166.

1 *Blackett v Royal Exchange Assurance Co* (1832) 2 Cr & J 244 (marine insurance), followed in *Hall v Janson* (1855) 4 E & B 500 (marine insurance); *Foley v Norwich Union Fire Insurance Society* (1888) 40 NSR 624. Cf *Pearson v Commercial Union Assurance Co* (1876) 1 App Cas 498 (fire insurance).

2 A latent ambiguity is not sufficient: *Hare v Barstow* (1844) 8 Jur 928 (fire insurance).

3 *Hooper v Accidental Death Insurance Co* (1860) 5 H & N 546 ExCh (accident insurance), where it was pointed out that where the assured was insured against total disablement 'from following his usual business', the nature of his business must be taken into consideration for the purpose of determining whether a particular injury entitled him to compensation; *Re Calf and Sun Insurance Office* [1920] 2 KB 366, 2 LlL Rep 304, CA where the Court, in considering the word 'premises', took into consideration the character and use of the building in question, and held that the word applied only to a part of it; *Watchorn v Langford* (1813) 3 Camp 422 (fire insurance), where 'stock-in-trade' was held not to cover a stock of linen drapery, the assured not being a linen draper; *Beacon Life and Fire Assurance Co v Gibb* (1862) 1 MooPCCNS 73 (fire insurance), where a policy on a ship was in the form of a policy on a house, and it was held that the word 'premises' in a condition against the storing of gunpowder applied to the ship; *Alliance Aeroplane Co Ltd v Union Insurance Society of Canton Ltd* (1920) 5 LlL Rep 406 (aviation insurance), where the word 'race' in connection with an insurance upon an aeroplane was held to include a competition flight to Australia, and was not restricted to a flight at racing speed. But, though regard must be had to the surrounding circumstances, in order that the policy may be read as the parties to it intended it to be read (*Union Insurance Society of Canton Ltd v George Wills & Co* [1916] AC 281 at 286, 288, PC (marine insurance)), this means having regard to the nature of the transaction and the known course of business and the forms in which such matters are carried out, and not to particular facts proved to have occurred at the inception of the transaction, or during the negotiations: *Yorkshire Insurance Co Ltd v Campbell* [1917] AC 218, PC (marine insurance) per Lord Sumner, at 225; *Kaufmann v British Surety Insurance Co Ltd* (1929) 45 TLR 399, 33 LlL Rep 315 (motor insurance), where the evidence of conversations and correspondence between the assured's brokers and the insurers to show that the expression 'private hire' included the use of the car for private pleasure was admitted.

4 *Borradaile v Hunter* (1843) 5 Man & G 639 (life insurance) per Maule J, at 563; *London and Manchester Plate Glass Co Ltd v Heath* [1913] 3 KB 411, CA (plate glass insurance) per Vaughan Williams LJ, at 417: 'If words are ambiguous, sometimes the construction put upon them by the contracting parties may be given in evidence.' But the fact that the insurers have previously paid under similar policies for losses happening in similar circumstances, does not preclude them from contending that the policy does not in fact cover the loss: ibid.

5 *Hordern v Commercial Union Assurance Co* (1887) 56 LJPC 78 (fire insurance).

CHAPTER 21

The commencement and duration of the policy

A THE COMMENCEMENT OF THE POLICY

The date at which the policy comes into force depends on the intention of the parties as shown by the language of the policy or by the circumstances of the case.[1]

Where the policy expressly provides that the period of insurance is to run from a specified day to a specified day, the first day is excluded, while the second is included.[2] Where, however, the period is stated to run from one day to the other both inclusive, both days are included in the period.[3]

The policy prima facie comes into force as soon as it is issued. The period of insurance thereupon begins and the insurers become liable, irrespective of whether the premium is paid or not.[4]

The policy, however, may provide that it is not to come into force until a specified condition, such as, e g the payment of the premium, has been fulfilled. In this case, though the period of insurance runs from the date of issue,[5] the liability of the insurers does not attach until the condition has been fulfilled.

Where the policy is ante-dated, the period of insurance runs from the

---

1 *Allis-Chalmers Co Ltd v Maryland Fidelity and Deposit Co* (1916) 114 LT 433, HL, where, though the period of insurance stated in the policy ran from March 8, 1912, to March 17, 1913, it was held that the insurance was not complete until the issue of the policy on April 18; *Scottish Metropolitan Assurance Co Ltd v Stewart* (1923) 39 TLR 407 (marine insurance); *Balfour v Beaumont* [1984] 1 Lloyd's Rep 272, CA (reinsurance), where it was held that the reinsurance policy was to take effect on a single date i e December 1, 1972, and continue in force for a period of 12 months; *Silver Dolphin Products Ltd v Parcels and General Assurance Association Ltd* [1984] 2 Lloyd's Rep 404 (marine insurance), where a certificate under an open cover stated the date on which the risk attached.

2 *South Staffordshire Tramways Co v Sickness and Accident Assurance Association* [1891] 1 QB 402, CA (driving accident insurance), where an insurance for twelve months from November 24, 1887, was held to exclude that day and to include November 24, 1888; *Sickness and Accident Assurance Association v General Accident Assurance Corpn* 1892 19 R (Ct of Sess) 977, where the effect of the same insurance was under discussion; *Isaacs v Royal Insurance Co* (1870) LR 5 Exch 296 (fire insurance) per Kelly CB, at 300. In *Dunn and Tarrant v Campbell* (1920) 4 LlL Rep 36, CA (aviation insurance) the insurance covered twelve hours' flying 'not exceeding a period of three months from the date and time of the first flight', and it was held that the policy attached during the first flight from the time of its commencement, and that, consequently, an accident happening whilst the pilot was endeavouring to rise, but before the aeroplane had left the ground, fell within its terms.

3 See *Sickness and Accident Assurance Association v General Accident Assurance Corpn* (supra).

4 *Kelly v London and Staffordshire Fire Insurance Co* (1883) Cab & El 47 (fire insurance).

5 *Salvin v James* (1805) 6 East 571 (fire insurance) per Lord Ellenborough CJ, at 582; *Armstrong v Provident Savings Life Assurance Society* (1901) 2 OLR 771 (life insurance); cf *Newcastle Fire Insurance Co v Macmorran & Co* (1815) 3 Dow 255, HL (fire insurance).

specified date and the insurers are liable although the loss may have taken place before the date of issue.

An ante-dated policy is issued where the policy is intended to replace a pre-existing contract such as the cover note.[6] In case of variance between the cover note and the policy, the assured may be able to enforce the cover note, though unable to recover on the policy.[7] An ante-dated policy is also issued where it is intended to be retrospective.[8]

B THE DURATION OF THE POLICY

The policy remains in force, in the ordinary course of events, until the expiration of the period of insurance.[9] Usually, the policy fixes the precise hour at which it is to expire; otherwise it expires at midnight of the last day specified.[10]

The policy may, however, cease to be in force at an earlier date by reason of one or other of the following causes:

1 By payment of the full sum insured under the policy.
2 By consent of the parties.
3 Under statute.
4 By breach of condition.

---

6 *Roberts v Security Co* [1897] 1 QB 111, CA; *Sickness and Accident Assurance Association v General Accident Assurance Corpn* 1892 19 R (Ct of Sess) 977. In *South Staffordshire Tramways Co v Sickness and Accident Assurance Association* [1891] 1 QB 402, CA (driving accident insurance) the cover note was to be in force till the policy was issued and there was no overlapping.

7 *Re Coleman's Depositories, Ltd and Life and Health Assurance Association* [1907] 2 KB 798, CA, where the cover note ran from December 28, and the policy, which was issued on January 9, was ante-dated to January 1; the accident happened on January 2.

8 *Bradford v Symondson* (1881) 7 QBD 456, CA (marine insurance); *Bufe v Turner* (1815) 6 Taunt 338 (fire insurance); cf *Natusch v Hendewerk* (1881) 7 QBD 460n (marine insurance).

9 The expiration of a policy may be fixed with reference to the happening of a particular event, e g the registration of a coupon or delivery to a purchaser; in this case, if the event never happens, the insurance continues indefinitely: *General Accident, Fire and Life Assurance Co v Robertson* [1909] AC 404, where a coupon provided that the holder was to be covered for twelve months from registration, and Lord Loreburn C said, at 411: 'If, however, there is no registration, then the term during which the liability continues is protracted, and protracted, as it seems to me, without limit; or if registration is delayed, then the cesser of liability is deferred accordingly.' See also, *Allagar Rubber Estates Ltd v National Benefit Assurance Co Ltd* (1922) 12 LlL Rep 110, CA (fire insurance), where goods were insured until delivery to a purchaser, and it was held that where no time limit was fixed, the insurance would end after a reasonable time for delivery. As to coupon insurance, see Ivamy *Personal Accident, Life and Other Insurances* (2nd Edn, 1980), pp 65–70.

10 *Isaacs v Royal Insurance Co* (1870) LR 5 Exch 296 (fire insurance). If the policy is made in Great Britain, Greenwich mean time applies: Interpretation Act 1978, ss 9, 23(3), except for any period during which the Summer Time Act 1972 is in operation. The time for general purposes in Great Britain is, during the period of summer time, one hour in advance of Greenwich mean time: Summer Time Act 1972, s 1(2). The period of summer time is the period beginning at 2 o'clock, Greenwich mean time, in the morning of the day after the third Saturday in March or, if that day is Easter Day, the day after the second Saturday in March, and ending at 2 o'clock, Greenwich mean time, in the morning of the day after the fourth Saturday in October: ibid, s 1(2). But Her Majesty may by Order in Council direct that the period of summer time shall be such period as specified in the Order instead of the period mentioned above, and that the time for general purposes in Great Britain shall during any part of the period of summer time, be two hours instead of one hour in advance of Greenwich mean time: ibid, s 2(1).

1 Determination by payment

Since the liability of the insurers under the policy is to pay the sum insured and no more, payment of the full sum insured discharges them from any further liability, and the policy thereupon ceases to have effect.[11] It is normally immaterial whether the policy is exhausted by a single loss or by successive losses. The policy may, however, be intended to cover all losses, however many and however large the amounts payable in respect of them, during the period of insurance.[12]

2 Determination by consent

The parties may, at any time during the period of insurance, agree to cancel[13] the policy, either for the purpose of putting an end to the contract between them or for the purpose of substituting another policy in different terms.[14]

The agreement for cancellation must, however, be clearly shown.[15] There is no effective cancellation where the parties acted under the mistaken belief that the policy was void,[16] or where the cancellation was agreed to on behalf of the assured by an agent who, in doing so, exceeded his authority.[17] On the other hand, a misunderstanding as to the precise terms of cancellation does not prevent the cancellation, if otherwise clear, from being effective.[18]

The policy may contain an express condition enabling the insurers or the assured to determine the policy before the expiration of the period of insurance.[19]

Thus, the insurers may reserve the right to determine the policy at any time, on giving notice to the assured and refunding a rateable proportion of any

---

11 *Crowley v Cohen* (1832) 3 B & Ad 478; *Gorsedd SS Co Ltd v Forbes* (1900) 5 Com Cas 413 (marine insurance); *Brewster v Sewell* (1820) 3 B & Ald 296 (fire insurance) per Abbott CJ, at 299. But a payment in the mistaken belief that a loss has happened does not put an end to the policy. It merely entitles the insurers to claim repayment of the sum paid, and the policy continues in force: *North British and Mercantile Insurance Co v Stewart* 1871 9 Macph (Ct of Sess) 534 (life insurance).

12 See pp 428–429, post.

13 This must be distinguished from cancellation by the Court on the ground of fraud, as to which see pp 234–235, post. and cf *Smith v Dominion of Canada Accident Insurance Co* (1902) 36 NBR 300, where cancellation by consent was held to be surrender, and a failure to disclose it was not a breach of a warranty that no previous policy had been cancelled.

14 *Sickness and Accident Assurance Association v General Accident Assurance Corpn* 1892 19 R (Ct of Sess) 977; *Rowe v Kenway and United Friendly Insurance Co Ltd* (1921) 8 LlL Rep 225, where such an agreement was held lawful, although its effect was to defeat the claim of the third party against the assured.

15 Cf *Russell v Thornton* (1860) 6 H & N 140, ExCh (marine insurance), where the question was whether a new contract had been substituted; *Lowlands Steam Shipping Co Ltd v North of England Protecting and Indemnity Association* (1921) 6 LlL Rep 230 (marine insurance), where it was alleged that the agreement to cancel had been entered into under a mutual mistake.

16 *Reyne v Hall* (1813) 4 Taunt 725 (marine insurance); *Adie & Sons v Insurance Corpn Ltd* (1898) 14 TLR 544 (fire insurance), where the assured had assumed that there was no contract as no policy had been issued or premium paid before the loss, but was nevertheless held entitled to recover, the Court being satisfied that there was, in fact, a contract.

17 *Xenos v Wickham* (1866) LR 2 HL 296 (marine insurance).

18 *Baines v Woodfall* (1859) 6 CBNS 657 (marine insurance).

19 Conditions of this kind must be distinguished from conditions under which the insurers are expressly empowered to declare the policy void in the event of the non-fulfilment of a condition precedent, as to which see pp 274–275, post. For an example of a policy containing conditions of both kinds, see *Bamberger v Commercial Credit Mutual Assurance Co* (1855) 15 CB 676.

premium paid.[20] The right may be limited to the circumstances specified in the condition, e g where a condition requiring notice to be given to the insurers of any increase of risk or of the cesser of other insurances, empowers the insurers, on receiving the notice, to determine the policy. The language in which the condition is framed may, however, be wide enough to cover any and every cause which could reasonably induce the insurers to desire the termination of the policy, and the effect of the condition, when so framed, is to give them the option of determining the policy at will.[1]

In either case, the policy does not cease to be in force until the insurers have complied with the requirements of the condition by giving notice to the assured and, if the policy so provides, by refunding the balance of the premium paid.[2]

Another type of condition provides that the assured may be entitled, on giving notice to the insurers, to surrender the policy before the expiration of the period of insurance and to receive back a rateable proportion of the premium and the surrender value, if any, of the policy.

In this case, the policy ceases to be in force as soon as the insurers have received the notice of surrender from the assured.[3] In the event, therefore, of a subsequent loss, the assured is not entitled to recover the amount payable under the policy, but only the balance of premium and any surrender value that may be payable under the condition. It is immaterial that at the time of the loss the policy has not been formally cancelled or the premium refunded or the surrender value paid.[4]

3 Determination by assured

An insured under an ordinary long-term insurance policy has the right to cancel it if he does so within a specified time.[5]

---

20 *London Guarantee and Accident Co v Cornish* (1905) 17 Man LR 148; *Sun Fire Office v Hart* (1889) 14 App Cas 98, PC (fire insurance); *J H Moore & Co v Crowe* [1972] 2 Lloyd's Rep 563, Mayor's and City of London Court (motor insurance), where the policy stated: 'This policy may be cancelled by the underwriters at any time by seven days' notice by registered letter to the insured's last known address, and in such event the underwriters will return a pro rata portion of the premium upon the surrender of the policy and certificate of insurance which must be returned to underwriters within seven days mentioned above', and it was held that although 6 copies of the certificate had been issued to the insured, he was entitled to a refund on returning one certificate only (see the judgment of Judge Graham Rogers, ibid, at 565).

1 *Sun Fire Office v Hart* (supra) at 104, 105. For a case where the insurers purported to cancel a policy, which had been extended from November 30, 1967 to January 31, 1970 'at a reasonable premium', on the ground that the insured had not paid such part of the premium as remained undisputed, see *Kirby v Cosindit Societa per Azioni* [1969] 1 Lloyd's Rep 75 (builders' risks insurance), where Megaw J held that there was no implied term in the policy to that effect: ibid, at 79. His Lordship also held (obiter) that even if there was such a term, the notice which the insurers gave to the insured as to the time within which the part of the premium was to be paid was unreasonable: ibid, at 80.

2 *Bamberger v Commercial Credit Mutual Assurance Co* (supra) per Jervis CJ at 694.

3 This is subject to any special conditions of the policy. See *Manitoba Farmers' Mutual Hail Insurance Co v Fisher* (1902) 14 Man LR 157, where in the case of a mutual insurance association it was held that a member could not withdraw from membership without surrendering his policy, as required by the conditions, and it was immaterial that the loss of the policy rendered it impossible for him to perform that condition; *Trudel v Cie Mutuelle de Commerce* (1920) QR 59 SC 24 (fire insurance), where the condition required seven days' notice, and it was held that the notice did not take effect until seven days after its receipt.

4 *Ingram-Johnson v Century Insurance Co* 1909 SC 1032.

5 Insurance Companies Act 1982, s 76. See pp 80–82, ante.

4 Determination under statute

If the insurers, being a company, go into liquidation, the contract of insurance contained in the policy issued by them comes to an end. The assured thereupon ceases to be protected by the policy, and acquires a right to prove against the insurers for the value of the policy on the footing of a contingent claim at the date of the liquidation.

In the case of an insurance company to which Part II of the Insurance Companies Act 1982 applies[6] the amount of any liability of the company must be determined by the valuation regulations made under the Act.[7]

In the case of a policy to which the Act does not apply, a just estimate must be made, so far as is possible of the value of the policy.

5 Determination by breach of condition

It is not the breach of every condition that affects the duration of the policy.

Where the condition broken is a condition precedent of the policy, the effect of the breach, if the insurers elect to take advantage of it, is to avoid the policy ab initio. The period of insurance never begins to run, and no claim can be made under the policy, even though the loss may have taken place before the insurers have elected to avoid the policy. Hence, it is immaterial that the actual avoidance takes place under an express condition of the policy.[8]

Where the condition broken is a condition precedent to the liability of the insurers, the only effect of the breach is to preclude the assured from enforcing any claim in respect to which there has been a breach of condition. The period of insurance continues to run and the policy remains in force. If, therefore, a subsequent loss takes place, the assured is not precluded from enforcing his claim in respect of such loss by reason of his previous breach of condition, provided that, in this case, the condition is duly performed.[9] Where, however, the condition broken is a condition subsequent of the policy, the effect of the breach, if the insurers elect to take advantage of it,[10] is to determine the period of insurance and to avoid the policy.[11] The avoidance in this case dates only from the breach. Until the breach the policy is a valid and subsisting contract of insurance, and, although the assured cannot enforce a claim arising after the breach, seeing that the policy has ceased to be in force, he is not precluded from enforcing a claim which has already arisen.[12]

The principal conditions subsequent in use relate to the following matters:

1 The alteration of the risk under the policy.[13]
2 The assignment of the subject-matter insured under the policy.[14]
3 'Other insurance.'[15]

---

[6] See pp 40–41, ante.
[7] See p 85, ante.
[8] *Bamberger v Commercial Credit Mutual Assurance Co* (1855) 15 CB 676, where the insurers were empowered to avoid the policy if the premium was not paid within a specified time.
[9] See p 291, post.
[10] *Doe d Pitt v Laming* (1814) 4 Camp 73 (fire insurance) per Lord Ellenborough CJ, at 75.
[11] See p 291, post.
[12] *Bamberger v Commercial Credit Mutual Assurance Co* (1855) 15 CB 676, per Cresswell J, at 695; *Daff v Midland Colliery Owners Indemnity Co* (1913) 6 BWCC 799, HL; see also *Baines v Holland* (1855) 10 Exch 802 (marine insurance); and cf *Sun Fire Office v Hart* (1889) 14 App Cas 98 at 103, PC (fire insurance), where the assured recovered in respect of losses happening before the cancellation.
[13] See Chapter 31.
[14] See Chapter 32.
[15] See Chapter 33.

CHAPTER 22

The cancellation of the policy

Where the insurers allege that they were induced to issue the policy by reason of the fraud, misrepresentation, or non-disclosure on the part of the assured, they are entitled to apply to the Court, on discovering the facts, for an order that the policy be delivered up to them to be cancelled. Their right to cancellation, whether on the ground of fraud,[1] misrepresentation,[2] or non-disclosure,[3] depends on the fact that the policy is thereby voidable ab initio.[4] Consequently, it never attaches, and is wholly inoperative as a contract of insurance, being mere waste paper in the hands of the assured.

The power of the Court to declare the contract void and to order cancellation of the policy, only exists where the contract is voidable ab initio by reason of a defect existing when the contract was made.[5] If the policy is in its inception valid, but events subsequently happen which will preclude the assured from enforcing any claim under it, the Court cannot, on the application of the insurers, order the policy to be cancelled or declare that the insurers are not liable on it. In this case the insurers have a good legal defence to an action on the policy, and must wait until they are sued.[6] If, however, no action on the policy is pending at the time when the events happen or are discovered to have happened, and there is a danger that the evidence of the events may be lost, the insurers may bring an action to perpetuate testimony.[7]

Similarly, where the assured alleges that he was induced to enter into the contract contained in the policy by similar conduct on the part of the insurers or

1 *Wilson v Ducket* (1762) 3 Burr 1361 (marine insurance), where the first underwriter signing the policy was by arrangement with the assured a mere decoy; *London and Provincial Insurance Co v Seymour* (1873) LR 17 Eq 85 (marine insurance); *Fenn v Craig* (1838) 3 Y & C Ex 216 (life insurance); *Traill v Baring* (1864) 4 De GJ & Sm 318 (life insurance); *Mutual Reserve Life Insurance Co v Foster* (1904) 20 TLR 715, HL (life insurance). Evidence of other frauds may be given when a systematic course of fraudulent dealing is charged: *Blake v Albion Life Assurance Co* (1878) 4 CPD 94 (life insurance); *Edinburgh Life Assurance Co v Y* [1911] 1 IR 306 (life insurance).

2 *Hoare v Bremridge* (1872) 8 Ch App 22 (life insurance), affirming and approving (1872) LR 14 Eq 522.

3 *London Assurance v Mansel* (1879) 11 ChD 363 (life insurance); *British Equitable Insurance Co v Great Western Railway Co* (1869) 38 LJCh 314 (life insurance); *British Equitable Insurance Co v Musgrave* (1887) 3 TLR 630 (life insurance).

4 The Court will not make an order for cancellation where the assured has never asserted the validity of the policy: *Sparenborg v Edinburgh Life Assurance Co* [1912] 1 KB 195 (life insurance) per Bray J at 204, following an unreported decision of Sterling J in a marine insurance case.

5 *Brooking v Maudslay, Son and Field* (1888) 38 ChD 636 (marine insurance).

6 *Thornton v Knight* (1849) 16 Sim 509 (marine insurance), where the insurers alleged that the policy was void on the ground of unseaworthiness and deviation and succeeded in proving deviation only; *Brooking v Maudslay, Son and Field* (supra).

7 *Brooking v Maudslay, Son and Field* (supra) (marine insurance); see RSC Ord 39, r 15.

their agents, he is entitled to apply to the Court for an order rescinding the contract.[8]

If the assured anticipates that the insurers will seek to avoid the policy, he may apply to the Court for a declaration that the policy is valid, but only if a claim[9] or at least a dispute has arisen.[10]

---

8 *Blake v Albion Life Assurance Co* (1878) 4 CPD 94 (life insurance); *Mutual Reserve Life Insurance Co v Foster* (1904) 20 TLR 715, HL (life insurance); *Refuge Assurance Co v Kettlewell* [1909] AC 243 (life insurance).

9 *Honour v Equitable Life Assurance Society of United States* [1900] 1 Ch 852 (life insurance).

10 *Sparenborg v Edinburgh Life Assurance Co* (supra) per Bray J, at 204. For an instance where such a declaration was made, see *Law Guarantee Trust and Accident Society Ltd v Munich Reinsurance Co* [1912] 1 Ch 138.

CHAPTER 23

The alteration of the policy

After the completion of the contract, no material alteration can be made in its terms except by mutual consent.[1] Any such alteration must also, since the policy is a written instrument, be made in writing.[2] It is usually made by an indorsement upon the policy,[3] but may be contained in a separate memorandum.[4] The consent to the alteration need not be in writing. A verbal consent is sufficient.[5] The policy may, however, contain an express stipulation prescribing the manner in which and the person by whom any alteration in the terms of the policy may be made.[6]

Where the alteration is comprised in a separate document, a failure by the assured to prove the consent of the insurers to the alteration does not preclude him from recovering on the original contract as expressed in the policy.[7] Where, however, the policy itself is altered, his failure to prove their consent to the alteration may preclude him from enforcing even the original contract.[8]

1 Methods of alteration

A policy may be altered in one or other of the following ways:

---

1 *Langhorn v Cologan* (1812) 4 Taunt 330 (marine insurance). As to the extended duty of disclosure in the case of alteration, see *Lishman v Northern Maritime Insurance Co* (1875) LR 10 CP 179 (marine insurance) per Blackburn J, at 182: 'Suppose the policy were actually executed, and the parties agreed to add a memorandum afterwards, altering the terms; if the alteration were such as to make the contract more burdensome to the underwriters, and a fact known at that time to the assured were concealed which was material to the alteration, I should say that the policy would be vitiated. But if the fact were quite immaterial to the alteration, and only material to the underwriter as being a fact which showed that he had made a bad bargain originally, and such as might tempt him, if it were possible, to get out of it, I should say there would be no obligation to disclose it.'

2 *Kaines v Knightly* (1682) Skin 54 (marine insurance); *Robinson v Tobin* (1816) 1 Stark 336 (marine insurance). Alteration of terms must be distinguished from waiver, as to which see pp 292–299, post.

3 For an example, see *Royal Exchange Assurance v Hope* [1928] Ch 179, CA (life insurance), where the period of insurance was extended.

4 For an example, see *Sickness and Accident Assurance Association v General Accident Assurance Corpn* 1892 19 R (Ct of Sess) 977, where the parties by the correspondence agreed to depart from the contract contained in the policy and to substitute for it another contract to run from a later date.

5 *A W and E Palmer v Cornhill Insurance Co* (1935) 52 LlL Rep 78 (motor insurance), where the assured had orally agreed to a variation in the policy whereby the use of the lorry was restricted to a particular area.

6 *Pigott v Employers' Liability Assurance Corpn* (1900) 31 OR 666; *Horncastle v Equitable Life Assurance Society of United States* (1906) 22 TLR 735, CA (life insurance).

7 Cf *French v Patton* (1808) 9 East 351 (marine insurance) per Le Blanc J, at 357.

8 *Fairlie v Christie* (1817) 7 Taunt 416 (marine insurance); *Laird v Robertson* (1791) 4 Bro Parl Cas 488 (marine insurance); *Langhorn v Cologan* (supra) (marine insurance); *Sanderson v Symonds* (1819) 1 Brod & Bing 426 (marine insurance).

a By the insertion of words into any part of the policy, whether by filling in blanks[9] or by interlineation;[10]
b By striking out words, with or without the substitution of different words;[11]
c By defacing the policy, or, if it is under seal, by tearing off the seal.[12]

2 The right of the insurer to avoid the contract

In order for the insurer to be able to avoid the contract two conditions must be fulfilled:

a The alteration must be in a material particular.
b The alteration must be made by the assured, or by a stranger whilst the policy is in the possession or control of the assured.

(a) The alteration must be in a material particular

The alteration must be in a material particular, i e the effect of the policy, either from a legal[13] or from a business[14] point of view, must be altered so as to make it a different instrument from what it was when executed by the insurers.[15] A correction of an obvious mistake,[16] or the insertion of a term already implied from the words actually used,[17] is not a material alteration.

In considering whether an alteration is material, its effect must be considered as at the time when it was made. If it was material then, the fact that it afterwards became immaterial is to be disregarded.[18]

(b) The policy must at the time of the alteration be in the possession or under the control of the assured

The alteration must be made by the assured, or by a stranger whilst the policy is in the possession or control of the assured.[19]

The fact that the alteration is made or assented to by an agent of the insurers

---

9 *Langhorn v Cologan* (supra) (marine insurance).

10 *Fairlie v Christie* (supra) (marine insurance); *Campbell v Christie* (1817) 2 Stark 64 (marine insurance); *Forshaw v Chabert* (1821) 3 Brod & Bing 158 (marine insurance). In *Laird v Robertson* (supra) (marine insurance) the alteration was indorsed.

11 *Fairlie v Christie* (supra), where the time of sailing stated in the policy was struck out and a different time inserted in the margin.

12 *Langhorn v Cologan* (supra) per Mansfield CJ, at 332.

13 *Davidson v Cooper* (1844) 13 M & W 343, ExCh (guarantee), where a seal was added, whereby a written guarantee was altered to a deed.

14 *Suffell v Bank of England* (1882) 9 QBD 555, CA (bank note) per Brett LJ, at 567, 568.

15 *Forshaw v Chabert* (supra) (marine insurance) per Dallas CJ, at 163.

16 Cf *Robinson v Touray* (1813) 1 M & S 217 (marine insurance); *Stephens v Australasian Insurance Co* (1872) LR 8 CP 18 (marine insurance). *Trew v Burton* (1833) 1 Cr & M 533 (arbitration award); *Waugh v Bussell* (1814) 5 Taunt 707 (bond).

17 *Clapham v Cologan* (1813) 3 Camp 382 (marine insurance); *Sanderson v Symonds* (1819) 1 Brod & Bing 426 (marine insurance); *Sanderson v McCullom* (1819) 4 Moore CP 5 (marine insurance).

18 *Forshaw v Chabert* (supra) (marine insurance), distinguishing *Sanderson v Symonds* (supra); *Langhorn v Cologan* (supra) (marine insurance).

19 *Davidson v Cooper* (1844) 13 M & W 343, ExCh (guarantee). Quaere, Whether this applies if the alteration is against the interest and in fraud of the assured; see *Lowe v Fox* (1887) 12 App Cas 206 (contract) per Lord Herschell, at 217.

does not prevent it from invalidating the policy in the hands of the assured, if made without their express sanction, except in the following cases:

i Where the agent has authority, express or implied, to make such an alteration or to assent to it;[20] or

ii Where the insurers are precluded from relying on the alteration as avoiding the policy, by reason of their having received premiums from the assured after they are, or must be taken to be, aware of the alteration;[1] or

iii Where the alteration has been made before delivery of the policy to the assured, and he was not aware that the alteration was not, in fact, the alteration of the insurers themselves, or that it was not authorised by them.[2]

If the alteration, though material, is made by the insurers themselves without the consent of the assured,[3] or by a stranger,[4] whilst the policy is not in the possession or control of the assured, its validity is not affected by such alteration, and the assured can enforce it according to its original tenor.

---

20 *Brocklebank v Sugrue* (1831) 5 C & P 21 (marine insurance), where it was suggested that the insurers might perhaps have repudiated the alteration on being informed of it.

1 *Holdsworth v Lancashire and Yorkshire Insurance Co* (1907) 23 TLR 521 (employers' liability insurance), where the knowledge of the agent was imputed to the insurers.

2 Ibid, where the assured refused to accept the policy until the alteration was made; cf *Pattinson v Luckley* (1875) LR 10 Exch 330 (building contract).

3 *Pattinson v Luckley* (supra).

4 *Henfree v Bromley* (1805) 6 East 309 (award of arbitrator).

CHAPTER 24

The rectification of the policy

Rectification means the correction of the policy. It assumes that both the insurers and the assured intended to contract on the same terms, but that by some mistake of expression, these items are not correctly stated in the policy.

Thus, Bankes LJ observed:[1]

> 'It is said . . . that it is not a correct view to suggest that it is a mutual mistake which has to be established (to entitle a party to rectification of a document). I view that contention with considerable sympathy. It seems to me much more accurate to say that if you prove that the parties have come to a definite parol agreement, and you then find in the document which was intended to carry out that definite agreement that something other than the definite agreement has been inserted, then it is right to rectify the document in order that it may carry out the real agreement between the parties. But in order to bring that doctrine into play it is necessary to establish beyond doubt that the real agreement between the parties was that which it is sought to insert in the document instead of that which appears there.'

Again, in another case[2] Slade LJ said:[3]

> 'As the law stands, the conditions which must be satisfied if rectification is to be granted on the grounds of common mistake may, in my opinion, be summarised as follows: First, there must be a common intention in regard to the particular provisions of the agreement in question, together with some outward expression of accord. Secondly, this common intention must continue up to the time of execution of the instrument. Thirdly, there must be clear evidence that the instrument as executed does not accurately represent the true agreement of the parties at the time of its execution. Fourthly, it must be shown that the instrument, if rectified as claimed, would accurately represent the true agreement of the parties at that time.'

But where the insurers and the assured each intended to contract on different terms, no case of rectification arises. The parties never having agreed on the terms of the contract, any policy issued is a nullity.

A EFFECT OF DELIVERY OF POLICY CONTAINING WRONG TERMS

The delivery of a policy containing the wrong terms does not affect the obligations of the parties. The assured is not relieved from the obligation of accepting the correct policy,[4] or from the obligation to pay the premium.[5] Nor

---

1 *Gagnière & Co v Eastern Co of Warehouses etc* (1921) 8 LlL Rep 365 at 366, CA (marine insurance). See further, *American Airlines Inc v Hope, Banque Sabbag SAL v Hope* [1974] 2 Lloyd's Rep 301, HL (aviation insurance) per Lord Diplock, at 307.

2 *Agip SpA v Navigazione Alta Italia SpA, The Nai Genova and Nai Superba* [1984] 1 Lloyd's Rep 353, CA (charter-party).

3 Ibid, at 359.

4 *General Accident Insurance Corpn v Cronk* (1901) 17 TLR 233.

5 *Solvency Mutual Guarantee Co v Freeman* (1861) 7 H & N 17; *General Accident Insurance Corpn v Cronk* (supra). The facts must show that there is already a concluded contract. If the parties have never

are the insurers discharged from the liability which they have, in fact, undertaken; for it is their duty to issue a policy in conformity with their agreement.[6]

If a loss has happened, the assured may sue the insurers on the original agreement between them;[7] or he may take steps to get the policy rectified.[8] If, however, he sues on the policy as it stands, he affirms the contract as contained in the policy, and cannot afterwards assert the existence of any other.[9] Nor can the insurers set up any contract different from that contained in the policy they have issued without rectification.[10]

B THE ADVISABILITY OF RECTIFICATION

Since the terms of the contract are to be found only in the policy, and the documents incorporated into it, the parties cannot, so long as the policy stands, refuse to be bound thereby, or rely upon any terms not contained in it.[11]

If, therefore, on the policy being tendered, the assured discovers that it does not truly set forth the real terms agreed on between the insurers and himself, he should either refuse to accept it and insist on receiving the correct policy, or, if he does not discover the incorrectness until after he has accepted it, he should take steps to get it rectified by the insertion of the correct terms.[12]

It is advisable for him to do so promptly; for by delay, he may possibly

---

reached agreement, there is no obligation on the insurers to issue a policy: *Fowler v Scottish Equitable Life Insurance Society and Ritchie* (1858) 28 LJCh 225 (life insurance): *Canning v Farquhar* (1886) 16 QBD 727, CA (life insurance). Nor is the assured bound to accept the policy tendered or to pay a premium: *Star Fire and Burglary Insurance Co v Davidson & Sons* 1903 5 F (Ct of Sess) 83 (fire insurance).

6 *Collett v Morrison* (1851) 9 Hare 162 at 176 (per Turner V-C) (life insurance): *Griffiths v Fleming* [1909] 1 KB 805 at 817, CA (per Farwell LJ) (life insurance).

7 *Pattison v Mills* (1828) 1 Dow & Cl 342, where the action was brought upon the agreement made in Scotland which was valid, and not upon the policy which was made in England and which would therefore have been void by a statute then in force if it had contained the terms of the agreement; *Wyld v Liverpool and London and Globe Insurance Co* (1876) 23 Gr 442, where the policy, as issued, did not cover certain goods which were intended to be insured and in respect of which an increased premium had been paid and a fresh cover note given, and the assured was held entitled to enforce the contract contained in the cover note; *Canadian Casualty and Boiler Insurance Co v Boulter, Davies & Co and Hawthorne & Co* (1907) 39 SCR 558, where it was held that the contract was not contained in the policy, but in the prior agreement between the assured and the insurers; *Irving v Sun Insurance Office* [1906] ORC 24, where it was held that the cover note and not the policy was the contract between the parties.

8 See pp 241–243, post.

9 *Baker v Yorkshire Fire Assurance Co* [1892] 1 QB 144 at 145: 'The plaintiff sues upon the policy and by so suing affirms it to be his contract; he cannot disaffirm a part of the very contract on which he is suing.' See also, *Newcastle Fire Insurance Co v Macmorran & Co* (1815) 3 Dow 255 at 264, HL (per Lord Eldon): *Acme Wood Flooring Co Ltd v Marten* (1904) 9 Com Cas 157 at 162 (per Bruce J); *Dawsons Ltd v Bonnin* [1922] 2 AC 413 at 432 (per Lord Cave); *Roberts v Anglo-Saxon Insurance Association* (1927) 137 LT 243 at 246, CA (per Scrutton LJ).

10 *Xenos v Wickham* (1867) LR 2 HL 296 at 324 (per Lord Cranworth).

11 *Newcastle Fire Insurance Co v Macmorran & Co* (1815) 3 Dow 255, HL at 264 (per Lord Eldon).

12 *Xenos v Wickham* (1867) LR 2 HL 296 at 324 (per Lord Cranworth) (marine insurance); *Rust v Abbey Life Assurance Co Ltd* [1978] 2 Lloyd's Rep 386 (property bond insurance), where the proposer had applied for a single premium bond policy and should have rejected the policy if it or any part of it was not what she required or had been led to expect. (See the judgment of C M Clothier QC, ibid, at 393).

preclude himself from afterwards alleging that the policy was incorrect,[13] and thus, especially where, as is usually the case, the policy is indorsed with a warning to the assured that he should read it and notify the insurers in case of any inaccuracy, enable them to rely on his acquiescence in the terms put forward by them. In the absence of circumstances creating an estoppel, however, he will not be prejudiced by delay, however lengthy. Thus, where the policy has never come into his hands, but has remained in the custody of the insurers or their agent, he is not by reason of his delay precluded from setting up what he alleges to be the real contract,[14] since in such a case he has had no opportunity of detecting the inaccuracy in the existing policy.

The insurers are equally entitled to rectification, where it appears that the policy, as issued by them, does not contain the correct terms.[15]

C THE METHODS OF RECTIFICATION

Rectification of a policy may be effected in two ways:

1 By the act of the parties.
2 By an order of the Court.

1 By the act of the parties

To rectify a policy by the act of the parties, all that is required is for the assured to notify the insurers of the inaccuracy, and for them to make or assent to its correction.[16]

2 By an order of the Court

To enable the Court to intervene, it is necessary for the party seeking its assistance to prove:

---

13 *Foster v Mentor Life Assurance Co* (1854) 3 E & B 48 at 75 (life insurance): 'The permitting the misrecital to pass without objection is an argument fairly to be used for the defendants against the plaintiffs' construction, but it is no more' (per Coleridge J). See also, *Allom v Property Insurance Co* (1911) Times 10 February, where the policy had been in the plaintiff's possession for 5 months, and no objection was taken until after the loss had occurred; *Provident Savings Life Assurance Society of New York v Mowat* (1901) 32 SCR 147 (life assurance), where the premium was raised in accordance with a condition in the policy several years after its issue; *Rust v Abbey Life Assurance Co Ltd* (supra) (property bond insurance), where the proposer delayed unreasonably in rejecting the policy. (See the judgment of C M Clothier QC, ibid, at 394.) Cf *Braund v Mutual Life and Citizens Assurance Co Ltd* [1926] NZLR 529, where the Court held the assured justified in assuming that the policy (which he had not read) accorded with the proposal, and granted rectification.

14 *Pattison v Mills* (1828) 1 Dow & Cl 342, HL (marine insurance), where the policy had been renewed without the assured having any opportunity of discovering that it varied from the contract in fact entered into. See further, *Canadian Casualty and Boiler Insurance Co v Boulter, Davies & Co and Hawthorne & Co* (1907) 39 SCR 558 (accident insurance).

15 *Rogers v Whittaker* [1917] 1 KB 942, where the claim failed; *Letts v Excess Insurance Co* (1916) 32 TLR 361 (accident insurance), where the claim succeeded. As to rectification in the case of reinsurance, see *Spalding v Crocker* (1897) 13 TLR 396 (marine insurance).

16 *Sawtell v Loudon* (1814) 5 Taunt 359 (marine insurance), where, however, the mistake was due to the broker, and the insurers were under no obligation to make the correction; cf *Robinson v Touray* (1813) 1 M & S 217 (marine insurance); *Holdsworth v Lancashire and Yorkshire Insurance Co* (1907) 23 TLR 521.

a The fact of a concluded agreement;[17]
b The terms of such agreement;[18]
c The incorrectness of the policy actually issued.[19]

There is a presumption that the policy contains the real terms between the parties;[20] and unless it is clearly proved that the policy is incorrect, rectification will be refused, and the parties remain bound by the policy as issued.[1]

---

17 *Brodigan v Imperial Live Stock and General Insurance Co* [1928] WC & Ins Rep 160; *Emanuel & Co v Weir (Andrew) & Co* (1914) 30 TLR 518 (marine insurance); *Fowler v Scottish Equitable Life Insurance Society and Ritchie* (1858) 28 LJCh 225 (life insurance); cf *Pritchard v Merchants' Life Assurance Society* (1858) 3 CBNS 622 (life insurance) per Williams J, at 640.

18 *Pasquali & Co v Traders' and General Insurance Association* (1921) 9 LlL Rep 514, where the Court refused to insert a term which had never been discussed between the parties; *Motteux v London Assurance* (1739) 1 Atk 545 (marine insurance), followed in *Collett v Morrison* (1851) 9 Hare 162 (life insurance); *Crane v Hegeman-Harris Co Inc* [1939] 1 All ER 662, [1971] 1 WLR 1390n (service contract) per Simonds J, at 664, following *Shipley UDC v Bradford Corpn* [1936] Ch 375.

19 *Letts v Excess Insurance Co* (1916) 32 TLR 361 (accident insurance) per Bailhache J, at 361: 'With regard to rectification, the law stood in this way. When two parties made a contract in clear terms which was afterwards written out in formal document, if that formal document did not express the terms of the contract, it might be rectified so as to make it conform to the original contract.'; *Maignen & Co v National Benefit Assurance Co Ltd* (1922) 38 TLR 257, 10 LlL Rep 30; *MacKenzie v Coulson* (1869) LR 8 Eq 368 (marine insurance) per James V-C, at 375; *Rogers v Whittaker* [1917] 1 KB 942, where the policy correctly represented the contract; cf *Hough v Guardian Fire and Life Assurance Co Ltd* (1902) 18 TLR 273, where the plaintiff was held entitled to a declaration that he was insured by a policy upon his property in the name of a wharfinger; *Gutheil v Delaney* (1882) 8 VLR 13, where a lessee was described as lessor, the lessors being specifically referred to later. There must be the clearest evidence of mutual mistake, *Spalding v Crocker* (1897) 13 TLR 396 (marine insurance); *Rogers v Whittaker* (supra) (fire insurance); *Allom v Property Insurance Co* (1911) Times 10 February (fire insurance). This is a question of fact: *The Aikshaw* (1893) 9 TLR 605 (marine insurance) per Gorell Barnes J, at 606; *Stanton and Stanton Ltd v Starr* (1920) 3 LlL Rep 259 (burglary insurance), where an exception on the 'slip' was not included in the policy, and the Court refused to rectify the policy as there had been no mutual mistake; *American Airlines Inc v Hope, Banque Sabbag SAL v Hope* [1974] 2 Lloyd's Rep 301, HL (aviation insurance); *American Employers Insurance Co v St Paul Fire and Marine Insurance Co Ltd* [1978] 1 Lloyd's Rep 417, District Ct of West Virginia, Northern District (marine insurance), where some barges were insured under a policy giving coverage on a 'per vessel' basis and the insurers unsuccessfully claimed rectification of the policy on the ground that the parties intended coverage to be on a 'per occurrence' basis; *Mint Security Ltd v Blair* [1982] 1 Lloyd's Rep 188 (cash in transit insurance), where the Court refused to rectify a policy by deleting a reference in it to a proposal form; *Excess Life Assurance Co Ltd v Firemen's Insurance Co of Newark New Jersey* [1982] 2 Lloyd's Rep 599 (fidelity insurance), where the claim for rectification of the extent of the cover provided by the policy failed; *Pindos Shipping Corpn v Raven, The Mata Hari* [1983] 2 Lloyd's Rep 449 (marine insurance), where the assured sought rectification of a policy by the deletion of a warranty relating to the maintenance of the class of a yacht, and the application failed; *Black King Shipping Corpn and Wayang (Panama) SA v Massie, The Litsion Pride* [1985] 1 Lloyd's Rep 437 (marine insurance), where the claim for rectification failed because the insurers failed to prove that the assured intended the inclusion of a term different from the warranty. (See the judgment of Hirst J, ibid, at 477.)

20 *Wheelton v Hardisty* (1857) 8 E & B 232 (life insurance) (revsd, without affecting this point (1858) 8 E & B 285, ExCh) per Erle J, at 263.

1 *General Accident Insurance Corpn v Cronk* (1901) 17 TLR 233, where it was held that an assured who applied for the ordinary form of policy in use by the insurers, was bound by the terms of the policy issued, if it was in the ordinary form, and it was not necessary to show that he approved of all the terms before the agreement was concluded; *Parsons v Bignold* (1846) 15 LJCh 379 (life insurance), where it was not clear whether the mistake was due to the agent of the insurers or to the incorrect information given by the assured; *Bushby v Guardian Assurance Co Ltd* [1916] App D 488, where the assured failed to prove that a condition as to the keeping of books in a fire-proof safe was not part of the original contract. Cf *Allis-Chalmers Co v Maryland Fidelity and Deposit Co* (1916) 114 LT 433, HL, per Lord Loreburn, at 434.

If, however, it appears to the Court that whilst the assured intended to contract only on the terms alleged by him, the insurers did not intend to contract except on the terms contained in the policy, and that, therefore, the parties being never ad idem, there is, in fact, no concluded contract between them, the policy will be ordered to be set aside.[2]

In order to ascertain the terms of the actual contract, reference may be made not only to such documents as are incorporated in the policy, but also to any document, such as a proposal,[3] 'slip',[4] or prospectus,[5] which is not incorporated in the policy, but which may be of assistance in showing what the contract between the parties really was. Evidence of conversations with the insurers or their agents, and of verbal representations made by them for the purpose of inducing the assured to enter into the contract, is also admissible for the same purpose.[6]

Rectification may be ordered after loss,[7] or after the policy has been renewed.[8] The Court may order that the policy be rectified where the assured,[9] or the subject-matter of insurance,[10] is wrongly described; where the amount of insurance[11] or the amount of the premium[12] is wrongly stated; or where the terms agreed on are wrongly set out in the policy issued to the assured.[13]

---

2 *Fowler v Scottish Equitable Life Insurance Society* (supra) (life insurance), where the real terms had been arranged with the agents of the insurers, but had been wrongly transmitted to the insurers owing to the fault of the assured; *Henkle v Royal Exchange Assurance Co* (1749) 1 Ves Sen 317 (marine insurance); *Billington v Provincial Insurance Co* (1879) 3 SCR 182, where an omission to indorse another insurance was attributable to the agent of the insurers whilst acting on behalf of the assured.

3 *Griffiths v Fleming* [1909] 1 KB 805, CA (life insurance) per Farwell LJ, at 817.

4 *Collett v Morrison* (supra) (life insurance), following *Motteux v London Assurance* (supra) (marine insurance), where a policy was rectified in accordance with the 'slip', *Rogers v Whittaker* (supra); *Letts v Excess Insurance Co* (supra); *Alliance Aeroplane Co v Union Insurance Society of Canton Ltd* (1920) 5 LlL Rep 341, 406 (aviation insurance), where the policy would have been rectified by inserting a clause appearing in the 'slip' which stated 'Inform usual trial flights of the machine, but not experimental as this is not the first flight at this time. Aerodrome at Acton; hangars brick built'. But no rectification was necessary in fact because the loss fell within an exception in the policy; *Eagle Star and British Dominions Insurance Co Ltd v Reiner* (1927) 27 LlL Rep 173 (marine insurance), where the policy was rectified to coincide with the terms of the 'slip'; rectification was also ordered in *Wilson Holgate & Co Ltd v Lancashire and Cheshire Insurance Corpn Ltd* (1922) 13 LlL Rep 486 (marine insurance).

5 *British Equitable Assurance Co Ltd v Baily* [1906] AC 35 (life insurance) per Lord Lindley, at 41; *Sun Life Assurance Co of Canada v Jervis* [1943] 2 All ER 425 (life insurance), where an 'illustration' was relied upon.

6 *Allom v Property Insurance Co* (supra).

7 *Henkle v Royal Exchange Assurance Co* (supra) (marine insurance); *Harley v Canada Life Assurance Co* (1911) 20 OWR 54 (life insurance), where rectification was ordered in an action on the policy.

8 *Pattison v Mills* (1828) 1 Dow & Cl 342, HL (marine insurance).

9 *Hough v Guardian Fire and Life Assurance Co* (supra) (fire insurance); *Hemmings v Sceptre Life Association* [1905] 1 Ch 365 (life insurance).

10 *Motteux v London Assurance* (supra) (marine insurance); *Henkle v Royal Exchange Assurance Co* (supra) (marine insurance).

11 *Aetna Life Insurance Co v Brodie* (1880) 5 SCR 1 (life insurance), where the Court was guided by the gross inadequacy of the premium as compared with the amount of insurance inserted in the policy; *Harley v Canada Life Assurance Co* (supra), where a clerical error was rectified, on the application of the insurers, in an action brought to recover the amount specified in the policy.

12 *Belcher v International Life Assurance Society of London* (1859) 4 Coch 35 (life insurance).

13 *Solvency Mutual Guarantee Co v Freeman* (1861) 7 H & N 17, where the conditions of the policy differed from those referred to in the proposal; *Allom v Property Insurance Co* (supra) (fire insurance), where the policy contained a warranty which the assured had never agreed to give.

CHAPTER 25

The renewal of the policy

On the expiration of the period of insurance, the policy comes to an end and the liability of the insurers ceases except in respect of claims which have already arisen.[1] The parties may, however, renew the policy by mutual consent. As a general rule, renewal is contemplated by the language of the policy and is provided for by special stipulation. The renewal is usually effected by means of a renewal receipt, given in exchange for the renewal premium;[2] but a fresh policy may be issued.

A STIPULATIONS AS TO RENEWAL

A stipulation as to renewal may be framed in three different ways:

1 A stipulation may make the policy renewable if both parties so desire.
2 The stipulation may make it renewable at the option of the assured.
3 The stipulation may bind both parties to renew it unless either party notifies the other that he does not intend to renew it.

1 Where the policy is renewable by mutual consent

The assured, by tendering the renewal premium, in the first instance makes an offer to renew the policy, which the insurers may accept or decline at pleasure; they cannot, therefore, be compelled to accept the renewal premium when tendered.[3]

If, on the other hand, the insurers invite the assured to renew the policy by sending him a renewal notice,[4] the offer to renew the policy proceeds from

---

1 *Simpson v Accidental Death Insurance Co* (1857) 2 CBNS 257; *Tarleton v Staniforth* (1796) 1 Bos & P 471, ExCh.

2 For a case where there was a dispute as to whether the premium was paid in respect of the renewal of a policy insuring premises against fire, burglary and other risks or whether it was paid in respect of a new policy insuring stock-in-trade against burglary and house-breaking, see *Protopapa v Dominion Insurance Co Ltd* [1954] 1 Lloyd's Rep 402, Ormerod J holding that the money was paid in respect of the renewal premium.

3 *Simpson v Accidental Death Insurance Co* (supra); *Tarleton v Staniforth* (supra); *Anglo-American Life Assurance Co v Le Baron* (1912) 18 RLNS 327, where the insurers promised to send the policy as soon as possible. See further, *Webb and Hughes v Bracey* [1964] 1 Lloyd's Rep 465, QB (solicitors' indemnity insurance), where the clause in the policy stated that 'in the event of non-renewal by underwriters' an extension of the cover granted was to apply, and Sachs J held that the non-renewal had to be due to some action by the underwriters, and that non-renewal in fact was due to the assured not requesting a renewal, and that accordingly the extension clause did not come into operation.

4 See p 246, post.

them, and his acceptance is signified by payment of the renewal premium. In this case they are bound to accept the renewal premium when tendered. But if the insurers offer to renew the policy at an increased premium, which the assured refuses to pay, a subsequent tender of the increased premium is inoperative,[5] even though made during the days of grace.[6]

Unless the terms of the stipulation so provide,[7] it is unnecessary for the insurers to give notice to the assured that they do not intend to renew it.[8] Their failure to do so does not preclude them from denying that they have renewed the policy.[9]

2 Where the policy is renewable at the option of the assured

The stipulation may make the policy renewable at the option of the assured. His right to claim a renewal may be absolute, in which case the policy must be renewed, if he so desires,[10] or it may, by the terms of the stipulation, be liable to be defeated if, before it is exercised, the insurers have given notice of their intention to determine the policy at the expiration of the current period.[11] In the latter case the stipulation amounts to a standing offer by the insurers to renew the policy, and the assured may accept it at any time before he has received notice of its withdrawal. On complying with the terms of the policy as to renewal, therefore, he is entitled to insist on his policy being renewed, and the insurers cannot decline to renew it unless they have first given notice of their intention not to do so.[12]

3 Where both parties must renew the policy in the absence of notice

The stipulation may provide that the policy is to continue in force for a further period unless prior to the expiration of the first period notice has been given by either party to determine it.[13] If, therefore, no such notice is given,[14] the policy

---

5 *Salvin v James* (1805) 6 East 571 (fire insurance). See further, *Doherty v Millers and Manufacturers Insurance Co* (1902) 6 OLR 78, where the fire took place whilst the question of an increased premium was under discussion.

6 As to the 'days of grace', see pp 250–252, post.

7 *Salvin v James* (supra) per Lord Ellenborough CJ, at 582.

8 *Towle v National Guardian Assurance Society* (1861) 30 LJCh 900 (guarantee policy); *Simpson v Accidental Death Insurance Co* (supra).

9 Ibid.

10 As in the case of an ordinary life policy: *Pritchard v Merchants' and Tradesman's Mutual Life Assurance Society* (1858) 3 CBNS 622 (life insurance), explained and distinguished in *Stuart v Freeman* [1903] 1 KB 47, CA (life insurance).

11 *Salvin v James* (supra) per Lord Ellenborough CJ, at 582.

12 Ibid, where, on the construction of the stipulation, the insurers could only determine the contract by giving notice within a reasonable time before the end of the current period.

13 *Solvency Mutual Guarantee Co v Froane* (1861) 7 H & N 5 (solvency insurance); *Lishman v Northern Maritime Insurance Co* (1875) LR 10 CP 179, ExCh (marine insurance); cf *Shanks v Sun Life Assurance Co* 1896 4 SLT 65 (accident insurance). See also, *Phoenix Assurance Co Ltd v Four Courts Hotel Co Ltd* [1935] IR 628, where it was intended to bind the assured to renew. But since the policy contained a clause that there was no liability upon the insurers until the premium was accepted and nothing to bind them to accept it, the policy could be determined by the assured equally with the insurers.

14 As to what is a sufficient notice, see *Re Solvency Mutual Guarantee Society, Hawthorne's Case* (1862) 31 LJCh 625 (solvency insurance), where no particular form of notice was required and it was held that a verbal notice of withdrawal given to the agent through whom the insurance had been effected was sufficient.

continues in force as a matter of course.[15] Without any act of assent on the part of either, the assured becomes liable to pay a further premium or premiums, whilst the insurers become liable in their turn to make good any loss happening during the second or any renewed period.[16]

A stipulation as to renewal contained in the original policy is not necessarily incorporated into the renewed policy, so as to make that policy in its turn renewable upon its expiration.[17] Whether the renewed policy is itself renewable or not depends on the language of the stipulation.[18]

B THE PRACTICE AS TO RENEWAL

In practice, the insurers, shortly before the expiration of the policy in force, send to the assured a 'renewal notice', intimating that the renewal premium is about to fall due.[19] The sending of this notice to the assured amounts to an offer by the insurers to renew the policy, on the footing of the original proposal or any variation of the terms indicated in the renewal notice, such as an increased premium.[20] The assured is usually required to intimate his acceptance of this offer by paying the premium for the renewed period, and unless and until he does so, the renewal does not take effect.[21] If, however, he expressly declines the offer to renew his policy, a subsequent tender of the premium will not, of itself, renew it.[1]

Where the insurers have taken no steps in the matter, the assured may tender the premium or otherwise intimate his willingness to renew the policy. In this case the offer to renew the policy comes from him, and the insurers may accept or decline it, as they think fit.[2]

On paying the premium the assured usually receives a renewal receipt on which he is entitled to rely as showing that the policy has been duly renewed. When the payment is made to an agent on the insurers' behalf, the binding effect of the payment depends on the authority of the agent to receive it.[3] If, however, the payment is otherwise good, the insurers cannot repudiate liability on the ground of a mere informality in the form of receipt actually given by the agent.[4]

---

15 *Michael v Gillespy* (1857) 2 CBNS 627 (marine insurance).

16 *Solvency Mutual Guarantee Co v York* (1858) 3 H & N 588 (solvency insurance).

17 *Solvency Mutual Guarantee Co v Froane* (supra) per Bramwell B, at 15: 'If the parties meant that the contract should be renewable in perpetuity, why not have said that it shall be a renewed contract every two years until notice be given to determine it?'

18 *Salvin v James* (1805) 6 East 571, where the policy was held to be renewable for so long as the parties pleased.

19 There is no obligation on the insurers to send such a notice; see p 245, ante. There may be an understanding between the parties that the insurers are to ask for the premium: *Isaacs v Royal Insurance Co* (1870) LR 5 Exch 296 per Kelly CB, at 301.

20 *Salvin v James* (1805) 6 East 571.

21 *Doherty v Millers and Manufacturers Insurance Co* (1902) 6 OLR 78, where no final renewal had been agreed, the premium being under discussion.

1 *Salvin v James* (supra).

2 *Tarleton v Staniforth* (1794) 5 Term Rep 695.

3 *Anglo-American Life Assurance Co v Le Baron* (1912) 18 RLNS 327, where the agent had ceased to be employed by the insurers; see further, p 190, ante. As to the agent's right to commission on renewal, see *McNiel v Law Union and Rock Insurance Co Ltd* (1925) 23 LlL Rep 314.

4 *Moore v Halfey* (1883) 9 VLR 400, where the agent gave a renewal receipt upon a form of cover

Statement by BIA and Lloyd's

In 1977 The British Insurance Association[5] and Lloyd's drew up a statement of non-life insurance practice which they recommended to their members.[6] The statement applies only to non-life policyholders domiciled in the United Kingdom and insured in their private capacity only, and, as far as the renewal of a policy is concerned, provides:

> 'Renewal notices should contain a warning about the duty of disclosure including the necessity to advise changes affecting the policy which have occurred since inception or last renewal date, whichever was the later.'

C THE EFFECT OF RENEWAL

Whether the renewal of a policy is a continuation of the original contract or the making of a new contract is a question of importance in view of its effect on the duty of disclosure[7] and the operation of conditions subsequent.[8]

1 The situations to be considered

The effect of a renewal appears to depend on the manner in which renewal is dealt with by the policy. Three situations may arise:

- a Where the policy provides for its continuation by renewal unless a particular event takes place.
- b Where the policy stipulates that it is not to continue unless renewed by mutual consent.
- c Where the policy is silent on the question of renewal.

(a) Provision for renewal unless particular event takes place

Where the policy (e g the ordinary form of life policy) expressly provides for its continuation by renewal beyond the specified period of insurance, unless a particular event, such as the giving of notice or the non-payment of the premium takes place, the renewal is a continuation of the original contract.[9] The contract comes to an end on the happening of the specified event.[10] But,

---

note for an original insurance, and it was held that a limitation of liability for fourteen days did not apply, the agent having authority to renew the policy. As to the effect of an informal receipt, see generally, p 191, ante.

5 Now the Association of British Insurers.

6 See 931 House of Commons Official Report, 4 May, 1977, Written Answers, cols 218–220.

7 As to non-disclosure and misrepresentation generally, see Chapters 12 and 13, ante.

8 As to conditions subsequent, see generally, p 275, post.

9 *Re Anchor Assurance Co, ex p Heron* (1870) 5 Ch App 632 (life insurance) per Lord Hatherley LC, at 638: 'A policy of insurance is not exactly a new contract every year, but is a contract made once for all with a condition to be performed de anno in annum and if the condition is not performed in any year, the contract is at an end.' See also, *Re Manchester and London Life Assurance and Loan Association* (1870) 5 Ch App 640 (life insurance), per Lord Hatherley LC, at 642; and cf *Pritchard v Merchants' and Tradesman's Life Assurance Society* (1858) 3 CBNS 622 (life insurance) per Willes J, at 644. On the other hand, Lord Ellenborough CJ in *Want v Blunt* (1810) 12 East 183, 190 (life insurance) was of the opinion that the payment of a renewal premium was, in the case of a life policy, making a new insurance, though under the former policy.

10 *Re Anchor Assurance Co* (supra) (life insurance) per Lord Hatherley LC, at 638.

until it happens, the contract continues in full operation, the insurers being bound to accept the renewal premium, if tendered, at the original rate.[11]

The first issue of the policy is the completion of the contract and the duty of disclosure is exhausted once and for all.[12] Facts which were not then material need not be disclosed afterwards, if they should become material,[13] and the insurers cannot refuse to renew the policy on the ground that, owing to a change of circumstances, the risk has been greatly increased.[14]

On the other hand, any breach of duty during the original negotiations renders the policy liable to be avoided, however often it may have been renewed.[15] Similarly, the breach of a condition subsequent avoids the policy once and for all, and not merely during the current period of insurance.[16] The period of insurance does not, in fact, affect the duration of the policy; it merely fixes the basis on which the premium is calculated and the time when it is to be paid. The insurers may, however, by accepting a renewal premium with knowledge of a breach of duty[17] or breach of condition,[18] preclude themselves from denying that the policy continues in force.

(b) Where the policy is not to continue unless renewed by mutual consent

Where the policy expressly stipulates that it is not to continue in force beyond the period of insurance, unless renewed by mutual consent, the renewal appears to be equivalent to the making of a new contract.[19]

The insurers, being at liberty to renew the policy or not at pleasure, are not bound to accept the premium, when tendered;[20] they may refuse it altogether,[21] or they may make their consent to the renewal conditional on an increased premium being paid,[1] or on the terms of the contract being otherwise varied.

---

11 *Pritchard v Merchants' and Tradesman's Mutual Life-Assurance Society* (supra) per Willes J, at 643. See *Jones Construction Co v Alliance Assurance Co Ltd* [1961] 1 Lloyd's Rep 121, CA (contractors' all risks insurance), where the clause in the policy stated that 'the insurers will indemnify the insured for loss arising during the period stated in the schedule or any subsequent period in respect of which the insured shall have paid and the insurers accepted the premium required for this extension of the terms of this policy', and it was held that the self-extending provision had not come into operation as the premium had not been paid and had not been accepted.

12 *Canning v Farquhar* (1886) 16 QBD 727, CA (life insurance).

13 *Lishman v Northern Maritime Insurance Co* (1875) LR 10 CP 179, ExCh (marine insurance).

14 *Pritchard v Merchants' and Tradesman's Life Assurance Society* (supra) per Willes J, at 643.

15 *Joel v Law Union and Crown Insurance Co* [1908] 2 KB 863, CA (life insurance).

16 *Wing v Harvey* (1854) 5 De GM & G 265 (life insurance), where, however, there was, in the circumstances, a waiver; *Sparenborg v Edinburgh Life Assurance Co* [1912] 1 KB 195 (life insurance).

17 *Hemmings v Sceptre Life Association* [1905] 1 Ch 365 (life insurance); *Ayrey v British Legal and United Provident Assurance Co* [1918] 1 KB 136 (life insurance); cf *Armstrong v Turquand* (1858) 9 ICLR 32 (life insurance).

18 *Wing v Harvey* (supra).

19 *Stokell v Heywood* [1897] 1 Ch 459; *Carpenter v Canadian Railway Accident Insurance Co* (1909) 18 OLR 388; *Youlden v London Guarantee and Accident Co* (1913) 28 OLR 161; *McDonnell v Carr* (1833) Hay & Jo 256 (fire insurance); cf *Last v London Assurance Corpn* (1884) 12 QBD 389 (fire insurance) per Day J, at 400.

20 *Tarleton v Staniforth* (1794) 5 Term Rep 695 (affd (1796) 1 Bos & P 471, ExCh) (fire insurance); cf *Towle v National Guardian Assurance Society* (1861) 30 LJCh 900, CA, per Turner LJ, at 915.

21 *Simpson v Accidental Death Insurance Co* (1857) 2 CBNS 257 per Cresswell J, at 296.

1 *Salvin v James* (1805) 6 East 571 (fire insurance).

Moreover, the duty of disclosure reattaches[2] so far as the facts to be disclosed are material.[3] All representations, therefore, made at the inception are deemed to be repeated on the renewal unless corrected.[4] Hence, any material facts which were not disclosed or were misrepresented during the original negotiations, must, if they are still material, be fully disclosed or accurately stated, as the case may be, before renewal; any facts which have become material during the current period of insurance must also be disclosed.[5] On the other hand, the fact that the original policy was or became void because of a breach of duty or a breach of condition does not, it is submitted, affect the validity of the renewed policy, if the cause of avoidance has ceased to operate before the renewal.[6] Thus, an inaccurate answer to a question relating to 'other insurance' may affect the validity of the original policy; but if, before renewal, the other insurance has been allowed to lapse, there is no misrepresentation or breach of condition so far as the renewal is concerned, and the renewed policy is, therefore, it is submitted, valid.[7]

(c) Where the policy is silent on the question of renewal

Where the policy is silent on the question of renewal, any renewal is probably a

---

2 *Martin v National Union Society* 1906 13 SLT 914; *Pim v Reid* (1843) 6 Man & G 1 (fire insurance) per Cresswell J, at 15.

3 Where the policy contains special conditions as to disclosure, these conditions do not necessarily apply on renewal: *Simpson SS Co Ltd v Premier Underwriting Association Ltd* (1905) 10 Com Cas 198 (marine insurance), where a condition in a policy, which contained a renewal clause, provided that information as to other insurance should be delivered to the insurers when the proposal was transmitted, and Bigham J, at 202, doubted whether the condition applied on the renewal, seeing that no proposal was transmitted on the renewal.

4 *Re Wilson and Scottish Insurance Corpn* [1920] 2 Ch 28; *Roy v Sun Insurance Office* [1927] SCR 8 (fire insurance); *Martin v Home Insurance Co* (1870) 20 CP 447.

5 *Carpenter v Canadian Railway Accident Insurance Co* (supra), where the renewal premium was paid after an accident, which was not notified to the insurers before payment; *Pim v Reid* (supra) per Cresswell J, at 15, followed in *Re Wilson and Scottish Insurance Corpn* (supra); cf *Hanley v Pacific Fire and Marine Insurance Co* (1883) 14 NSWLR 224 (fire insurance), where it was doubted whether the assured on renewing a policy was bound to disclose the fact that during the year the risk had been declined by other insurers.

6 As to 'other insurance', see Chapter 33.

7 The contrary has been held in Canada: *Liverpool and London and Globe Insurance Co v Agricultural Savings and Loan Co* (1902) 33 Can SCR 94 (fire insurance). It is submitted that the view expressed in the text is correct; otherwise assuming the policy to have been continuously renewed, the insurers would be entitled to repudiate liability for a loss happening twenty years or more after the lapse of the undisclosed policy, notwithstanding the fact that the policy, long after the lapse, had been assigned and that the assignee had paid premium after premium in the belief that he was protected by a valid policy. In the case of a life policy or other continuing contract the position is different, since the assured is given, on the faith of the original representations, rights which the insurers cannot take away or alter during the continuation of the policy. But in the case of other classes of insurance, where the assent of the insurers is required before a renewal beyond the original period can become operative, if the original representations, though untrue when first made, are in fact true when the policy is renewed, it is difficult to see in what way the insurers are prejudiced. Assuming that in deciding to assent to the renewal they are guided by the original representations, they have before them the truth, and are not induced to renew the policy by any misrepresentation or concealment. See further, *Howard v Lancashire Insurance Co* (1885) 11 SCR 92, where, however, there was a condition providing that renewals were to be based on the original application, except so far as varied in writing.

new contract.[8] The duty of disclosure is the same when the insured is applying for a renewal as it is when he is applying for the original policy.[9]

2 Some express terms as to whether renewal is a new contract

There has been considerable difference of opinion whether the renewal of a policy by mutual consent is a continuation of the original contract or the making of a new contract. Many policies have been drafted on the assumption that renewal is a mere continuation, and consequently, express stipulations have been inserted to assimilate the rights of the insurers on renewal to what their rights would be on the making of a new contract.

Thus, the policy may expressly provide that the insurers are not bound to renew the policy, that the period of the renewed insurance is to be the subject of agreement, that the premium may be increased, that the assured is to apply for renewal upon a fresh proposal form[10] or give notice of any fresh material facts, or that the policy is to be void if its continuation is procured by fraud or misrepresentation.

If the view that renewal in this case is a new contract is correct, these stipulations are unnecessary.[11]

D DAYS OF GRACE

A policy which requires renewal ought, strictly speaking, to be renewed at or before the expiration of the current period of insurance, since, at the expiration of the period, the policy lapses and the assured ceases to be covered.[12] The policy or renewal notice frequently contains a stipulation enabling the assured to renew the policy, after its expiration, on payment of the premium during a further period, known as 'days of grace'.[13] In the absence of such a stipulation, the assured is not entitled to days of grace; and the policy may contain an

---

8 Renewal is to be distinguished from extension of the period of insurance before its expiration; this is a mere variation in one of the terms of the original contract: *Royal Exchange Assurance v Hope* [1928] Ch 179 CA (life insurance), distinguished in *Prudential Assurance Co Ltd v IRC* [1935] 1 KB 101 (life insurance), where the alteration indorsed on the policy increased the amount payable.

9 *Lambert v Co-operative Insurance Society* [1975] 2 Lloyd's Rep 485, CA (all risks insurance) at 487 (per MacKenna J). In that case the insurers were held entitled to repudiate liability on the ground that the insured, when the original policy was effected, had failed to disclose her husband's previous conviction for receiving stolen goods, and also, at the time for the renewal of the policy, had not disclosed another conviction of his for conspiracy to steal and theft of goods between the date when the original policy was effected and the date of renewal. See also *March Cabaret Club and Casino Ltd v London Assurance Ltd* [1975] 1 Lloyd's Rep 169 (trader's combined insurance), where a director's previous conviction for handling stolen property prior to the renewal of the policy was not disclosed.

10 Or that the statements in the proposal are to be deemed to be repeated in each renewal.

11 Thus, apart from any stipulation, the premium may be increased on renewal: *Salvin v James* (1805) 6 East 571 (fire insurance); and the assured is bound to disclose facts becoming material during the continuance of the original policy: *Pim v Reid* (1843) 6 Man & G 1 (fire insurance) per Cresswell J, at 15.

12 See pp 253–254, post.

13 See, e g *Webb and Hughes v Bracey* [1964] 1 Lloyd's Rep 465 QB (solicitors' indemnity insurance), where 15 days' grace was allowed for the renewal of the policy, and the assured failed to make a request for renewal within the required period.

express stipulation requiring the renewal premium to be paid before the expiration of the policy.[14]

1 The classes of stipulation

Days of grace only become important in the event of a loss happening during the days of grace and before the premium has been paid. The rights of the parties in this case vary according to the form of stipulation used. The following classes of stipulation may be distinguished:

a Stipulations under which the insurers are liable for any loss happening during the days of grace, notwithstanding the non-payment of the premium before the loss.
b Stipulations under which the insurers are not liable for any loss happening before the renewal premium is paid.

(a) Where the insurers are liable even though the premium has not been paid before the loss

The insurers will be liable where the stipulation, in effect, extends the original period of insurance by the days of grace.[15] In this case there is, strictly speaking, no question of renewal, since the loss is covered by the original policy, and it is, therefore, immaterial whether the renewal premium has been paid or not.[16]

A stipulation in the policy may provide that the insurers are to be liable if the premium is paid before the days of grace expire.[17] A stipulation in this form does not extend the original period of insurance,[18] or preclude the insurers from giving notice that they do not intend to renew unless an increased premium is paid.[19] If, therefore, the assured has declined to pay the increased premium or has otherwise indicated his intention not to renew the policy, the stipulation has no effect and the insurers are not liable, there being no policy in existence at the time of the loss.[20]

Where, however, the parties have done nothing to determine the policy, payment of the premium at any time during the days of grace is equivalent to payment on the day when it fell due;[1] there is, therefore, a subsisting policy at

---

14 *Stokell v Heywood* [1897] 1 Ch 459.

15 *Doe d Pitt v Shewin* (1811) 3 Camp 134 (fire insurance), explained in *Simpson v Accidental Death Insurance Co* (1857) 2 CBNS 257 per Cresswell J, at 283; *McDonnell v Carr* (1833) Hayes & Jo 256 (fire insurance), where the condition provided that the policy, which was expressed to be for a year, should not be valid for more than fifteen days after the time limited unless the premium and stamp duty for renewal should be paid within that time. Cf *Tarleton v Staniforth* (1794) 5 Term Rep 695 per Lord Kenyon CJ, at 699. See further, *Fitton v Accidental Death Insurance Co* (1864) 17 CBNS 122 at 127, where the policy was to remain in force during the days of grace, whether renewed or not.

16 *McDonnell v Carr* (supra). Cf *Bamberger v Commercial Credit Mutual Assurance Society* (1855) 15 CB 676, where the insurers, under a condition in the policy empowering them either to declare the policy void for non-payment of premium during the days of grace or to enforce payment, had declared the policy void.

17 *Salvin v James* (1805) 6 East 571 (fire insurance), distinguishing *Tarleton v Staniforth* (1796) 1 Bos & P 471 ExCh (fire insurance).

18 *Simpson v Accidental Death Insurance Co* (supra) per Cresswell J, at 295.

19 *Salvin v James* (supra) per Lord Ellenborough CJ, at 581.

20 Ibid.

1 *Stuart v Freeman* [1903] 1 KB 47, CA (life insurance) per Mathew LJ, at 55, dissenting from *Pritchard v Merchants' and Tradesman's Life-Assurance Society* (1858) 3 CBNS 622 (life insurance);

the date of the loss. Moreover, the insurers cannot, after the loss, decline to accept the premium if tendered,[2] since to allow them to refuse it would render the stipulation of little effect.[3]

If the stipulation contemplates a payment by the assured personally, a tender by his personal representatives during the days of grace does not renew the policy.[4] Thus, under a personal accident policy containing a stipulation to this effect, the insurers are not liable where the assured, during the days of grace, sustains an accident within the meaning of the policy, from which he dies, although his executors afterwards, before the days of grace expire, tender the renewal premium.[5]

(b) *Where the insurers are not liable for any loss happening before the renewal premium is paid*

The insurers may repudiate liability on this ground where the stipulation gives the insurers an option, exercisable at any time, to accept or decline the renewal.[6] Hence, if they refuse to accept the premium, there is no policy in existence under which they can be held liable,[7] and there is nothing in the language of the stipulation to preclude them from refusing to accept the premium after loss.

Sometimes the stipulation expressly provides that they are not to be liable for any loss happening before the renewal premium is paid.[8]

McKenna v City Life Assurance Co [1919] 2 KB 491 (life insurance) per Scrutton LJ, at 497. Cf *Farquharson v Pearl Assurance Co Ltd* [1937] 3 All ER 124 (life insurance), where tender on behalf of the assured was held sufficient.

2 It is, therefore, immaterial that they accepted in ignorance of the loss: *Stuart v Freeman* (supra), where, however, the failure was to pay a quarterly instalment, the current year not having expired.

3 *Salvin v James* (supra) per Lord Ellenborough CJ, at 582: 'The effect of the third article and the advertisement are to give the parties an option for fifteen days to continue the contract or not; with this advantage on the part of the assured, that if a loss should happen during the fifteen days though he has not paid his premium, the office shall not after such loss determine the contract; but that it shall be considered as having been renewed.' See also, *Simpson v Accidental Death Insurance Co* (supra) per Cresswell J, at 298.

4 *Want v Blunt* (1810) 12 East 183 (life insurance); *Pritchard v Merchants' and Tradesman's Life-Assurance Society* (supra) (life insurance), distinguished in *Stuart v Freeman* (supra) (life insurance).

5 *Simpson v Accidental Death Insurance Co* (supra).

6 *Tarleton v Staniforth* (supra) (fire insurance).

7 *Simpson v Accidental Death Insurance Co* (supra), where there was another stipulation dealing with liability during the days of grace and before payment.

8 *Tarleton v Staniforth* (supra). Cf. *Phoenix Life Assurance Co v Sheridan* (1860) 8 HL Cas 745 (life insurance).

CHAPTER 26

Lapse and revival of the policy

A policy which is not renewed at or before the expiration of the current period of insurance or of the days of grace, if any, is said to 'lapse', and the assured cannot enforce it in respect of any claim arising afterwards.[1] It may, however, be 'revived' at any time by mutual consent, and the insurers may be precluded by their contract from relying on its lapse.[2]

A request for the premium made by the insurers after lapse is an offer on their part to revive the policy, and the payment of the premium by the assured is his acceptance of the offer; hence, a refusal to pay the premium prevents any revival taking place.[3] Similarly, a tender of the premium by the assured is an offer on his part to revive the contract, and the receipt and retention of the premium by the insurers[4] constitute their acceptance of the offer.[5] Before agreeing to revive the policy, the insurers may impose fresh terms and

---

1 *Employers' Insurance Co of Great Britain v Benton* 1897 24 R (Ct of Sess) 908, where repayment of a debenture in 1897 was insured conditionally on payment of an annual premium, and it was held that the failure of the assured to pay the annual premium in 1895 caused a lapse, though it was then apparent that the debenture would not be repaid; *Duffel v Wilson* (1808) 1 Camp 401; *Webb and Hughes v Bracey* [1964] 1 Lloyd's Rep 465, QB (solicitors' indemnity insurance), where the assured had made no application for the renewal of the policy within the 15 days' grace, and consequently an extension clause in the policy did not apply; *Doe d Pitt v Shewin* (1811) 3 Camp 134 (fire insurance) per Lord Ellenborough CJ, at 137; *Acey v Fernie* (1840) 7 M & W 151 (life insurance) per Parke B, at 156; *Phoenix Life Assurance Co v Sheridan* (1860) 8 HLCas 745 (life insurance), where the premium was payable in instalments; *Handler v Mutual Reserve Fund Association* (1904) 90 LT 192, CA (life insurance) per Collins MR, at 195; *McKenna v City Life Assurance Co* [1919] 2 KB 491 (life insurance). Hence, the insurers may recover back the amount of a loss which they have paid by mistake, forgetting that the policy had lapsed: *Kelly v Solari* (1841) 9 M & W 54 (life insurance). See further as to lapse generally, *R v Powell* (1884) 15 Cox CC 568, CCR, where the guilt of the prisoners depended upon whether the policy had lapsed.

2 *Handler v Mutual Reserve Fund Association* (supra) per Mathew LJ, at 194: 'It was open to the plaintiff to show a new contract of insurance, (1) by showing an actual agreement on the lapse of the policy; (2) by showing that he had been misled by the conduct of the defendants in inducing him to think the policy was still a subsisting policy'; *Kirkpatrick v South Australian Insurance Co* (1886) 11 App Cas 177, PC; *Howell v Kightley* (1856) 21 Beav 331. An agent, however, cannot revive a lapsed policy by receiving the premium unless he has authority to do so: *Acey v Fernie* (supra); *British Industry Life Assurance Co v Ward* (1856) 17 CB 644 (life insurance); *Busteed v West of England Life Assurance Co* (1857) 5 IChR 553 (life insurance) *Towle v National Guardian Assurance Society* (1861) 30 LJCh 900, CA (fidelity insurance).

3 *Edge v Duke* (1849) 18 LJCh 183 (life insurance).

4 Receipt by an agent who has no authority to contract does not constitute a revival: *Acey v Fernie* (supra), followed in *Busteed v West of England Fire and Life Insurance Co* (supra).

5 *Kirkpatrick v South Australian Insurance Co* (supra).

conditions[6] and, if they do so, there is no revival unless and until the terms and conditions imposed are accepted and performed by the assured.[7]

Any conduct on the part of the insurers which reasonably leads the assured to believe that the policy is still a subsisting policy precludes them from relying on its lapse.[8] Thus, the giving of a receipt containing ambiguous phraseology which may reasonably be construed to mean that the policy is still alive, is, perhaps, sufficient.[9]

A revival is not a continuation of the old contract, but the making of a new contract.[10] Thus, although, in practice, a revived policy is usually ante-dated to the expiration of the last period of insurance under the lapsed policy, a claim arising before the actual date of revival is not covered,[11] unless the parties clearly so intended.[12] Acceptance of the premium by the insurers in ignorance of the loss is not sufficient proof of intention.[13]

---

6 *Handler v Mutual Reserve Fund Association* (supra). The policy may contain an express condition providing for its revival on payment of a fine and proof that the circumstances have not materially altered: *Pritchard v Merchants' and Tradesman's Life-Assurance Society* (1858) 3 CBNS 622 (life insurance).

7 *Handler v Mutual Reserve Fund Association* (supra) (life insurance), where the revival was conditional on the assured being in good health; *Canada Life Assurance Co v Taafe* (1911) QR 21 KB 204 (life insurance), where the revival was conditional on a cash payment. Cf *Rainbow v Juggins* (1880) 5 QBD 422, CA (life insurance) per Bramwell LJ, at 423. Mere retention of the premium in ignorance of a breach of condition does not show an agreement to revive: *Handler v Mutual Reserve Fund Association* (supra), where the premium was accepted and retained in ignorance of the fact that the assured was in bad health. But it is otherwise if the insurers are acquainted with the facts: *Supple v Cann* (1858) 9 ICLR 1 (life insurance), where subsequent premiums had been accepted without objection: *Campbell v National Life Insurance Co* (1874) 24 CP 133 (life insurance), where the insurers knew that the assured had met with an accident.

8 *Handler v Mutual Reserve Fund Association* (supra) per Mathew LJ, at 194.

9 Ibid, per Collins MR, at 193.

10 *Doe d Pitt v Shewin* (supra) (fire insurance); *Kirkpatrick v South Australian Insurance Co* (supra) (fire insurance); *Handler v Mutual Reserve Fund Association* (supra) per Mathew LJ, at 194. See also, *Stokell v Heywood* [1897] 1 Ch 459 (accident insurance), which is really a case of lapse and revival. Cf *Western Australian Bank v Royal Insurance Co* (1908) 5 CLR 533, where the plaintiffs, who were mortgagees of the property insured, paid a premium on the mortgagor's policy after the days of grace had expired, and it was held that there was a new contract upon which the plaintiffs could sue in their own name. The language of the stipulation in the policy dealing with renewal does not effect the position: *Handler v Mutual Reserve Fund Association* (supra).

11 *Pritchard v Merchants' and Tradesman's Mutual Life Assurance Society* (1858) 3 CBNS 622 (life insurance), where the premium was paid and accepted after the death of the life insured. Cf *Doe d Pitt v Shewin* (supra); *Carpenter v Canadian Railway Accident Insurance Co* (1908) 18 OLR 388, where, however, the receipt of the renewal premium did not bind the insurers.

12 *Pritchard v Merchants' and Tradesman's Life Assurance Society* (supra) per Byles J, at 645; ' "Dead or alive"—which would be equivalent to "lost or not lost" in a marine policy—seems to be excluded by the terms of the policy and the third condition.' As to ante-dated policies, see pp 229–230, ante.

13 *Carpenter v Canadian Railway Accident Insurance Co* (supra); *Pritchard v Merchants' and Tradesman's Life Assurance Society* (supra).

CHAPTER 27

The perils insured against in the policy

The peril insured against may be any peril in respect of which the assured seeks and the insurers are willing to give protection.[1] Certain perils are of every-day occurrence and are insured against in the ordinary course of business. Other perils can only be insured against with difficulty, if at all.

The perils insured against will, of course, vary in accordance with the class of insurance.[2]

For the purpose of ascertaining what is the peril insured against, reference must be made to its description in the policy.[3] It must, therefore, be described with accuracy and precision;[4] for, although the words used to describe it are to be construed liberally,[5] they are still restricted to their plain and ordinary meaning[6] and do not extend to other perils which, though analogous in their operation, do not fairly fall within the scope of the words actually used.[7] The

---

1 Cf *Seaton v Burnand* [1900] AC 135 per Lord Halsbury LC, at 140: 'Of course, the transaction itself of guaranteeing the solvency of somebody who is to be a security for somebody else's debt is, I admit, a somewhat extraordinary transaction . . . I was not aware, until this case, that such a transaction as this, any more than the determinations of judicial tribunals, is now made the subject of policies at Lloyd's.'

2 The perils insured against in the various types of insurance are considered in detail in other volumes of this work.

3 See pp 17–18, ante.

4 *Morrison and Mason v Scottish Employers' Liability and Accident Assurance Co* 1888 16 R (Ct of Sess) 212, where an insurance expressed to be against liability under or by virtue of the Employers' Liability Act 1880, was held not to cover the employer's liability at Common Law, notwithstanding that the workman might, if he had chosen, have sued the employer under the Act; *Soole v Royal Insurance Co Ltd* [1971] 2 Lloyd's Rep 332, QBD, where a developer intending to develop property which was subject to a restrictive covenant effected a policy whereby he was to be indemnified by the insurers in the event of any person within 30 years 'claiming' to be entitled to enforce the covenant, and it was held that the claim initiated by a third party before the commencement of the policy was within its ambit (see the judgment of Shaw J, at 338).

5 See pp 356–360, post.

6 *Stanley v Western Insurance Co* (1868) LR 3 Exch 71 (fire insurance), where the word 'gas' in the phrase 'explosion by gas' was held to mean 'coal gas'. See further, pp 339–350, post.

7 *Re George and Goldsmiths' and General Burglary Insurance Association* [1899] 1 QB 595, CA per Collins LJ, at 609, 610; *Debenhams Ltd v Excess Insurance Co Ltd* (1912) 28 TLR 505; *Century Bank of City of New York v Mountain* (1914) 112 LT 484, CA; *Stott (Baltic) Steamers Ltd v Marten* [1916] 1 AC 304 (marine insurance); *Borradaile v Hunter* (1843) 5 Man & G 639 (life insurance) per Maule J, at 653, followed in *Clift v Schwabe* (1846) 3 CB 437 (life insurance); cf *Wootton v Lichfield Brewery Co* [1916] 1 Ch 44, CA, distinguishing *Williams v Lassell and Sharman Ltd* (1906) 22 TLR 443. On the other hand, an accident which falls within the terms of the policy is covered, even though the particular kind of accident is of rare occurrence and was probably not thought of when the policy was framed: *Pugh v London, Brighton and South Coast Rly Co* [1896] 2 QB 248, CA, per Smith LJ, at 254.

peril which causes the loss must be the peril described in the policy, and no other.[8] If, however, the peril causing the loss is the peril described in the policy, it is immaterial that it is also a peril which might have been insured against under a different species of policy.[9]

---

8 *Re George and Goldsmiths' and General Burglary Insurance Association* [1899] 1 QB 595, CA, where it was held that acts which constituted burglary or housebreaking within the meaning of Common Law did not entitle the assured to recover if they did not fall within the definition in the policy; *Waterkyn v Eagle Star and British Dominions Insurance Co Ltd* (1920) 5 LlL Rep 42, where a policy insuring against the insolvency of a Russian Bank directly due to damage or destruction of premises through riot or civil commotion was held not to cover insolvency due to confiscation by the Bolsheviks; *Morrison and Mason v Scottish Employers' Liability and Accident Assurance Co* 1888 16 R (Ct of Sess) 212, where the workman might have enforced his employer's statutory liability instead of proceeding, as he did, at Common Law.

9 *Reischer v Borwick* [1894] 2 QB 548, CA (marine insurance) per Lindley LJ, at 551. But the policy may contain a stipulation providing that it is not to apply to particular kinds of loss capable of being covered by another kind of insurance.

CHAPTER 28

The exceptions in the policy

The peril insured against is usually described in the policy in general terms, and it is the practice of insurers with the view of qualifying their undertaking, to introduce exceptions which expressly exclude their liability where the loss is caused or the peril brought into operation by certain specified causes.

A THE VARIETY OF THE EXCEPTIONS USED

The exceptions introduced by the insurers will vary in accordance with the type of insurance concerned, e g in the case of motor insurance there is often an exception stating that the insurers will not be liable where the vehicle is being driven in an unroadworthy condition;[1] whereas in the case of personal accident insurance an exception is usually inserted excluding liability for death or disablement from disease.[2]

B THE EXCEPTIONS TO BE FOUND IN MOST TYPES OF POLICY

Certain exceptions, however, are to be found in almost every type of policy. They may be classified as follows:

1 Exceptions relating to particular causes which, though falling within the description of the peril in the policy, fall equally within the scope of a different species of policy.
2 Exceptions relating to causes for which the insurers are not prepared to accept liability.
3 Exceptions relating to causes which are not intended to fall within the scope of the description in the policy, but which may possibly do so on account of the general words in which the peril insured against is described.
4 Exceptions relating to the conduct of the assured.

---

1 As in *Clarke v National Insurance and Guarantee Corpn Ltd* [1964] 1 QB 199, [1963] 3 All ER 375, CA (motor insurance) where 9 people were being carried in a car designed to carry 4, and it was held that the exception applied and that the insurers were not liable; *A P Salmon Contractors Ltd v Monksfield* [1970] 1 Lloyd's Rep 387, Mayor's and City of London Court (motor insurance), where the policy stated that the insurers were not to be liable 'if the vehicle is driven or used in an unsafe condition', and it was held that the faulty loading of a lorry had no effect on the safety of the vehicle, and that accordingly the vehicle was not 'used in an unsafe condition' (see the judgment of Judge Graham Rogers, ibid, at 390).

2 The various exceptions used in insurance policies are considered in detail in the other volumes of this work.

1 Exceptions relating to causes falling within another policy

Exceptions of this sort exclude the liability of the insurers where the cause of the loss or of the peril coming into operation is itself a peril which is, in common practice, insured against by a different species of policy. Thus, in insurances against theft or damage to property generally, it is usual to except loss which is capable of being covered by a fire policy, in which case theft of the property insured or damaged during a fire is not covered.[3]

Another type of exception excludes the liability of the insurers where there is actually in existence a policy belonging to a different species of insurance, which covers the loss. In this case a question of great difficulty arises if both policies contain the exception.

2 Exceptions relating to causes for which the insurers are not to be liable

There are certain causes which, though they may rarely occur, are calculated if they do occur, to bring the peril insured against into general operation and to cause losses of such magnitude that the liability of the insurers is, in consequence, likely to be increased far beyond what it would be in the ordinary course of business. The usual exceptions of this class relate to the following causes:

- a Foreign enemy.
- b Riot.
- c Civil commotion.
- d Military or usurped power.
- e Insurrection.
- f Hostilities.
- g Civil war.

(a) Foreign enemy

This phrase implies the existence of a war between the State of which the assured is a member and a foreign State.[4] Whether a particular state of hostilities amounts to 'war' is a question of fact in each case.[5]

(b) Riot

This word is to be construed in its ordinary legal meaning.[6] It involves a tumultuous[7] disturbance of the peace by three persons[8] or more.[9] Mere

---

[3] Such theft or damage being, unless expressly excepted, covered by a policy. But the fire must be the proximate cause of the loss, otherwise, the exception does not apply: *Marsden v City and County Assurance Co* (1866) LR 1 CP 232.

[4] *Drinkwater v London Assurance Co* (1767) 2 Wils 363; cf *Butler v Wildman* (1820) 3 B & Ald 398 (marine insurance) per Abbott CJ, at 402.

[5] *Kawasaki Kisen Kabushiki Kaisha of Kobe v Bantham SS Co Ltd* [1939] 2 KB 544 (charter-party) per Greene MR, at 558.

[6] *London and Lancashire Fire Insurance Co Ltd v Bolands Ltd* [1924] AC 836 (burglary insurance) per Lord Finlay, at 843.

[7] It is not necessary that the tumult should be accompanied by noise: *Motor Union Insurance Co Ltd v Boggan* (1923) 130 LT 588, HL (accident insurance) per Lord Birkenhead, at 591.

[8] It is immaterial that the persons are soldiers, and that the acts amount to mutiny and take place

malicious injury to property done by three or more persons does not constitute a riot.[10]

(c) Civil commotion[11]

This phrase is used to indicate a stage between a riot and a civil war.[12] It has been defined to mean an insurrection of the people for general purposes though not amounting to a rebellion.[13] But it is probably not capable of any very

---

in a military camp: *Pitchers v Surrey County Council* [1923] 2 KB 57, CA (riot). But in *Pan American World Airways Inc v Aetna Casualty and Surety Co* [1974] 1 Lloyd's Rep 207 (District Ct. for Southern District of New York) (aviation insurance), Frankel DJ, said (ibid, at 234): 'The Court concludes that if assemblages numbering as few as three could ever make 'riots', for insurance purposes, they do not to-day'. The decision was subsequently affirmed by the US Ct of Appeals: [1975] 1 Lloyd's Rep 77.

9 1 Hawkins, PC, c 65; *Drinkwater v London Assurance Co* (supra). To constitute a riot, five elements must be present: (i) a number of persons, not less than three; (ii) a common purpose; (iii) execution or inception of the common purpose; (iv) an intent on the part of the number of persons to help one another by force, if necessary, against any persons who may oppose them in the execution of the common purpose; (v) force or violence, not merely used in and about the common purpose, but displayed in such a manner as to alarm at least one person of reasonable firmness and courage: *Field v Metropolitan Police Receiver* [1907] 2 KB 853 (riot) per Phillimore J, at 860, approved in *Motor Union Insurance Co v Boggan* (supra), and in *Athens Maritime Enterprises Corpn v Hellenic Mutual War Risks Association (Bermuda) Ltd, The Andreos Lemos* [1983] QB 647, [1983] 1 All ER 590, [1982] 2 Lloyd's Rep 483 (marine insurance), at 492 (per Staughton J). See also, *Johnson and Perrott Ltd v Holmes* (1925) 21 LlL Rep 330 (motor insurance), where the policy covered loss by riot and civil commotion except where the loss was caused under military or police authority, and the car concerned was removed by armed men and never seen again, and it was held that the loss was *prima facie* a loss by riot and civil commotion; *Pan American World Airways Inc v Aetna Casualty and Surety Co* (supra) where the hijacking of a plane by two persons, even though they were later joined by a third person to help with its demolition was held not to be a 'riot' because there was no tumultuous conduct. (See the judgment of Frankel DJ, ibid, at 234.) The decision was subsequently affirmed by the US Ct of Appeals: [1975] 1 Lloyd's Rep 77; *Athens Maritime Enterprises Corpn v Hellenic Mutual War Risks Association (Bermuda) Ltd, The Andreos Lemos,* supra (marine insurance), where a gang of men armed with knives attacking a vessel and taking equipment and materials from her was held to be a riot, but the insurers were not liable because the loss was not caused by the riot. (See the judgment of Staughton J, ibid, at 492.)

10 *Field v Receiver of Metropolitan Police* (supra) per Phillimore J, at 859.

11 Cf *Langdale v Mason* (1780) 2 Park's Marine Insurances 8th Edn 965, where the Gordon Riots were held to be a civil commotion, with *London and Manchester Plate Glass Co Ltd v Heath* [1913] 3 KB 411, CA (plate glass insurance), where the organised breaking of windows by suffragettes was held not to be a civil commotion. The exception does not apply where the case is one of malicious burning: *Craig v Eagle Star and British Dominions Insurance Co* [1922] WC & Ins Rep 324; cf *American Tobacco Co v Guardian Assurance Co* (1925) 69 Sol Jo 621, CA.

12 *Bolivia Republic v Indemnity Mutual Marine Assurance Co Ltd* [1909] 1 KB 785, CA (marine insurance) per Farwell LJ, at 801: *Lindsay and Pirie v General Accident Fire and Life Assurance Corpn Ltd* [1914] App D 574; cf *Rogers v Whittaker* [1917] 1 KB 942 per Sankey J, at 944; *Levy v Assicurazioni Generali* [1940] AC 791, [1940] 3 All ER 427, 67 LlL Rep 174, PC (fire insurance).

13 *Langdale v Mason* (supra) per Lord Mansfield CJ, at 967, 968, approved in *London and Manchester Plate Glass Co v Heath* (supra). This has been explained to mean a rising of a considerable number of the population for purposes of general mischief: *Lindsay and Pirie v General Accident Fire and Life Assurance Corpn* (supra), followed in *Orenstein Arthur Coppel Ltd v Salamandra Fire Insurance Co* [1915] SAR (TPD) 497. See also *Spinney's (1948) Ltd v Royal Insurance Co Ltd* [1980] 1 Lloyd's Rep 406 (fire insurance), where Mustill J said (ibid, at 438): 'I find nothing in the authorities to hold that a civil commotion must involve a revolt against the government, although the disturbances must have sufficient cohesion to prevent them from being the work of a mindless mob.'

precise definition.[14] The element of turbulence or tumult is essential.[15] An organised conspiracy to commit criminal acts, where there is no tumult or disturbance until after the acts, does not amount to civil commotion.[16] It is not, however, necessary to show the existence of any outside organisation at whose instigation the acts were done.[17]

The words 'popular rising' in the phrase 'civil commotion assuming the proportions or amounting to a popular rising' have no recognised technical meaning and often mean the same as 'insurrection'.[18] Where there is a distinction, it probably lies in the greater spontaneity and looser organisation of a popular rising. There must be some unanimity of purpose among those participating, and the purpose must involve the displacement of the government. It is doubtful whether a violent attack by one section of the population on the other on grounds e g of religion or race, would be described as a rising. The word 'proportions' is sometimes used to mean shape or configuration, but in the context of the phrase concerned signifies 'dimensions'. One cannot identify precisely the dimensions of a popular rising. All that one can say is that it must involve a really substantial proportion of the populace, although obviously not all the population need participate, and there should be tumult and violence on a large scale.[19]

(d) Military or usurped power[20]

This phrase includes not only the acts of foreign enemies engaged in warfare within the realm[1] or of subjects of the Crown engaged in external rebellion,[2] but also the acts done by the forces of the Crown in repelling the enemy or suppressing the rebellion.[3] So far as foreign enemies and the forces of the Crown

---

14 The different terms used to some extent overlap, and the distinction between them is one of degree, as to which no hard and fast rule can be laid down: *Lindsay and Pirie v General Accident Fire and Life Assurance Corpn* (supra). Hence, a particular case may be a case both of riot and civil commotion: *Motor Union Insurance Co v Boggan* (supra) (accident insurance) per Lord Birkenhead, at 591.

15 *London and Manchester Plate Glass Co v Heath* [1913] 3 KB 411, CA (plate glass insurance) per Buckley LJ, at 417: 'Commotion connotes turbulence or tumult and, I think, violence or intention to commit violence', approved in *Cooper v General Accident, Fire and Life Assurance Corpn Ltd* (1923) 128 LT 481, 13 LlL Rep 219, HL (accident insurance); *Pan American World Airways Inc v Aetna Casualty and Surety Co* (supra), where Frankel DJ said (ibid), at 234): 'Civil commotion occurs in a locale—a city, a county, perhaps a country, or an area. It is essentially a kind of domestic disturbance.' If a state of civil commotion exists, it is immaterial that there was no commotion at the actual time and place where the loss happened: ibid; or that the loss happened during a temporary suspension of conflict or tumult: *Lindsay and Pirie v General Accident Fire and Life Assurance Corpn* (supra).

16 *London and Manchester Plate Glass Co v Heath* (supra) per Buckley LJ, at 418.

17 *Lindsay and Pirie v General Accident, Fire and Life Assurance Corpn* (supra).

18 See p 262, post.

19 *Spinney's (1948) Ltd v Royal Insurance Co Ltd* [1980] 1 Lloyd's Rep 406 (fire insurance) at 438 (per Mustill J).

20 The phrase does not mean 'usurped military power': *Rogers v Whittaker* [1917] 1 KB 942, per Sankey J, at 945.

1 *Drinkwater v London Assurance Co* (1767) 2 Wils 363; *Rogers v Whittaker* (supra), where the fire was caused by a bomb dropped from a Zeppelin.

2 *Drinkwater v London Assurance Co* (supra) per Wilmot CJ, at 364; *Langdale v Mason* (1780) 2 Park's Marine Insurances 8th Edn 965 per Lord Mansfield CJ, at 966, referring to the Rebellion of 1745.

3 *Curtis & Sons v Mathews* [1919] 1 KB 425, CA, where the claim rose out of a fire caused by the bombardment of the General Post Office in Dublin by the forces of the Crown during the Irish Rebellion in 1916.

are concerned, the application of the phrase calls for no detailed consideration. As regards civilian subjects of the Crown its application, however, presents difficulties. The phrase is ambiguous, and its meaning may vary according to the subject-matter to which it is applied.[4] It clearly applies to an armed and organised rebellion, which has got to such a head as to be under authority[5] and to assume the power of government by making laws and punishing disobedience to them.[6] The phrase, however, is probably not capable of being precisely defined.[7] It may, therefore, be of wider application. At the same time there must be facts which justify the application of the phrase.[8] There must be something in the nature of warfare,[9] something which is more in the nature of war or civil war than of riot or civil commotion;[10] and the persons taking part must be guilty of high treason.[11] Further, there must probably be some kind of organisation.[12]

---

4 *Drinkwater v London Assurance Co* (supra) per Wilmot CJ, at 364; *Langdale v Mason* (supra) per Lord Mansfield CJ, at 966.

5 *Langdale v Mason* (supra) per Lord Mansfield CJ, at 966.

6 *Drinkwater v London Assurance Co* (supra) per Bathurst J, at 363; *Pan American World Airways Inc v Aetna Casualty and Surety Co* [1974] 1 Lloyd's Rep 207 (District Ct for Southern District of New York) (aviation insurance), where an aircraft was blown up at Cairo airport by the Popular Front for the Liberation of Palestine, and it was held that the loss was not due to 'military or usurped power', Frankel DJ observing (ibid, at 229): 'They had not at any pertinent time seized or controlled any territory over the opposition of the Jordanian government. They "occupied" a training camp at Salt while the fedayeen were being tolerated generally—a barren and exiguous facility containing some caves, tents and rudimentary structures. Then they "seized" Dawson's Field . . . But that strip was an unoccupied area on a desert plateau. Neither the uncontested occupation of the Salt camp nor the brief episode at Dawson's Field constituted such "control of territory" as the phrase ['military or usurped power'] connotes'. The decision was subsequently affirmed by the US Ct of Appeals: [1975] 1 Lloyd's Rep 77.

7 *Curtis & Sons v Mathews* [1919] 1 KB 425, CA, per Bankes LJ, at 429.

8 *Curtis & Sons v Mathews,* as reported [1918] 2 KB 825, per Roche J, at 828: 'A riot does not, it is true, become a war or a caucus a usurped power merely because grandiloquent words are used to describe them.'

9 *Drinkwater v London Assurance Co* (supra) per Wilmot CJ, at 365.

10 *Curtis & Sons v Mathews* [1918] 2 KB 825 per Roche J, at 828, 829: 'I am satisfied that what occurred was more than a riot and more than a civil commotion . . . I am satisfied that Easter week in Dublin was a week not of mere riot, but of civil strife amounting to warfare waged between military and usurped powers and involving bombardment.' See also, SC [1919] 1 KB 425, CA per Bankes LJ, at 429; *Rogers v Whittaker* [1917] 1 KB 942 per Sankey J, at 945. Hence, in *Drinkwater v London Assurance Co* (1767) 2 Wils 363 the exception was held not to apply to a bread riot.

11 *Drinkwater v London Assurance Co* (supra) per Wilmot CJ, at 365; *Curtis & Sons v Mathews* [1918] 2 KB 825 per Roche J, at 829; *Spinney's (1948) Ltd v Royal Insurance Co Ltd,* supra (fire insurance) at 435: 'There remains the much more difficult question whether constructive treason is the only test for usurped power. Is it enough to show a mob in posture of war, acting with a common intent and some degree of leadership, in pursuance of aims which properly lie within the prerogative of the Sovereign? Or are there other requirements: in particular that the events should amount to a rebellion or insurrection? It seems to me that in the present context the answer must be "No" ' (per Mustill J).

12 *Curtis & Sons v Mathews* [1919] 1 KB 425, CA, per Bankes LJ, at 429: 'I do not propose to attempt to give a definition of what constitutes "usurped power". In this policy which we have to construe the words are "war, bombardment, military or usurped power". It does not seem to me to be very material to consider what in this clause usurped power means in view of the finding of fact by the learned Judge that the damage was directly caused by the bombardment. But assuming that it is material to consider the meaning of "usurped power" I will merely say this: Usurped power seems to me to mean something more than the action of an unorganised rabble. How much more I am not prepared to define. There must probably be action by some more or less organised body with more or less authoritative leaders.'

The usurpation consists of the arrogation to itself by the mob of a law-making and law-enforcing power which properly belongs to the sovereign.[13]

(e) Insurrection

This word means a rising of the people in open resistance against established authority with the object of supplanting it.[14]

(f) Hostilities

This word does not refer to the mere existence of a state of war. There must be acts or operations of hostility,[15] committed by persons acting as agents of an enemy government or of an organised rebellion, and not by private individuals acting entirely on their own initiative.[16]

(g) Civil war

A civil war is a war which has the special characteristic of being civil, i e internal rather than external. The words do not simply denote a violent internal conflict on a large scale. A decision on whether such a war exists will generally involve a consideration of (i) whether it can be said that the conflict was between opposing 'sides'; (ii) what were the objects of the 'sides' and how did they set about pursuing them; and (iii) what was the scale of the conflict, and of its effect on public order and the life of the inhabitants. It must be possible to say of each

---

13 *Spinney's (1948) Ltd v Royal Insurance Co Ltd,* supra (fire insurance) at 433 (per Mustill J).

14 *Lindsay and Pirie v General Accident, Fire and Life Assurance Corpn Ltd* [1914] AppD 574; 'As regards "rebellion" I adopt the definition in the Oxford English Dictionary (Murray) ". . . organised resistance to the ruler or government of one's country; insurrection, revolt." To this I would add that the purpose of the resistance must be to supplant the existing rulers or at least to deprive them of authority over part of their territory. The dictionary defines "insurrections" in a similar manner, but also suggests the notion of an incipient or limited rebellion. I believe that this reflects the distinction between two exceptions as they are used in the present clause, subject to the rider that a lesser degree of organisation may also mark off an insurrection from a rebellion. But with each exception there must be action against the government with a view to supplanting it.'; *Spinney's (1948) Ltd v Royal Insurance Co Ltd,* supra (fire insurance), at 436 (per Mustill J).

15 *Britain SS Co v R* [1921] 1 AC 99 (marine insurance) per Lord Wrenbury, at 133; *Spinney's (1948) Ltd v Royal Insurance Co Ltd,* supra (fire insurance) per Mustill J, at 437: 'The term "hostilities" refers to acts or operations of war committed by belligerents; it presupposes an existing state of war . . . There seems no reason to doubt that the exception applies to acts committed in the course of a civil war; and perhaps also to an organised armed rebellion.'

16 *Atlantic Mutual Insurance Co v King* [1919] 1 KB 307 (marine insurance) per Bailhache J, at 310; cf *Nobel's Explosives Co v British Dominions General Insurance Co* [1918] WC & Ins Rep 106; *Pan American World Airways Inc v Aetna Casualty and Surety Co* [1974] 1 Lloyd's Rep 207 (District Ct for Southern District of New York) (aviation insurance), where an aircraft was blown up at Cairo airport by the Popular Front for the Liberation of Palestine, and it was held that the loss was not due to 'war' or 'warlike operations', Frankel DJ observing (ibid, at 230): 'There is no warrant . . . for reading the phrase "warlike operations" to encompass the infliction of international violence by political groups neither employed by nor representing governments upon civilian citizens of non-belligerent powers and their property at places far removed from the locale or the subject of any warfare'. The decision was subsequently affirmed by the US Ct of Appeals: [1975] 1 Lloyd's Rep 77; ' "warlike operations" includes such operations as belligerents have recourse to in war even though no state of war exists. Nevertheless, the acts must be done in the context of a war.'; *Spinney's (1948) Ltd v Royal Insurance Co Ltd,* supra, (fire insurance), at 437 (per Mustill J).

fighting man that he owes allegiance to one side or another, and to identify each side by reference to a community of objective, leadership and administration. It does not necessarily follow that the objectives of all those on any one side must be identical but there must be some substantial community of aim which the allies have banded together to promote by the use of force. There need not always be only two sides, but if the factions are too numerous, the struggle is no more than a melée without the clear delineation of combatants which is one of the distinguishing features of war. A desire to seize or retain the reins of state is not the only motive which can ever put the contestants into a state of civil war. There would be such a war if the objective was not to seize complete political power but to force changes in the way in which power was exercised without fundamentally changing the existing political structure. There would also be a civil war if the participants were activated by tribal, racial or ethnic animosities. It is possible to build up a list of matters which should be considered when deciding on whether internal strife has reached the level of civil war, e g the number of combatants, the number of military and civilian casualties, the amount and nature of the armaments employed, the relative sizes of the territory occupied by the opposing sides, the degree to which the populace as a whole is involved in the conflict, the extent to which each faction purports to exercise legislative, administrative and judicial powers over the territories which it controls.[17]

3 Exceptions inserted ex abundanti cautela

Such exceptions are in many cases unnecessary, but are inserted for the purpose of placing the intention beyond doubt.[18]

4 Exceptions relating to the conduct of the assured

These also may include the conduct of persons for whom the assured is, or is deemed to be, responsible.[19]

C THE CONSTRUCTION OF EXCEPTIONS

Since exceptions are inserted in the policy mainly for the purpose of exempting the insurers from liability for a loss which, but for the exception, would be covered by the policy, they are construed against the insurers with the utmost

---

[17] *Spinney's (1948) Ltd v Royal Insurance Co Ltd,* supra, (fire insurance) at 430 (per Mustill J).

[18] *Borradaile v Hunter* (1843) 5 Man & G 639 (life insurance) per Erskine J, at 658: 'The very object of a proviso like the present, is to take out of the operation of the general terms of the policy, death resulting from causes which would otherwise fall within the general scope of the contract, although, ex abundanti cautela, it also includes cases which the law itself would except, as those of criminal suicides, and death by sentence of the law or duelling.' See also, *Cole v Accident Assurance Co Ltd* (1889) 5 TLR 736, CA per Bowen LJ at 737; *Curtis & Sons v Mathews* [1918] 2 KB 825 per Roche J, at 830; *Burger v Indemnity Mutual Marine Assurance Co* [1900] 2 QB 348 (marine insurance), where the Court was of the opinion that an exception excluding liability for loss of life or personal injury from the scope of the policy was unnecessary, being inserted ex abundanti cautela.

[19] See pp 269–270, post.

strictness.[20] It is the duty of the insurers to except their liability in clear and unambiguous terms.[1]

[20] *Cornish v Accident Insurance Co* (1889) 23 QBD 453, CA per Lindley LJ, at 456: 'In a case on the line, in a case of real doubt, the policy ought to be construed most strongly against the insurers; they frame the policy and insert the exceptions. But this principle ought only to be applied for the purpose of removing a doubt, not for the purpose of creating a doubt, or magnifying an ambiguity, when the circumstances of the case raise no real difficulty.' See also, *Lake v Simmons* [1927] AC 487 per Lord Sumner, at 509; *Cole v Accident Assurance Co Ltd* (1889) 5 TLR 736, CA, where the Court held with reluctance that the exception applied; *Re United London and Scottish Insurance Co Ltd, Brown's Claim* [1915] 2 Ch 167, CA; *A P Salmon Contractors Ltd v Monksfield* [1970] 1 Lloyd's Rep 387, Mayor's and City of London Ct, (motor insurance) per Judge Graham Rogers, at 389, where it was held that an exception stating that the insurers would not be liable in respect of death or bodily injury to any person 'caused by the spreading of material or substance from the insured vehicle or load carried by such vehicle' did not exclude the accidental fall of part of the load from a lorry. (See the judgment of Judge Graham Rogers, ibid, at 390.)

[1] *Re Etherington and Lancashire and Yorkshire Accident Insurance Co* [1909] 1 KB 591, CA per Farwell LJ, at 601: 'Where there are clear words which prima facie import liability on the part of the company, and it is said that their effect is cut down by a subsequent proviso, I think we are bound to see that the terms of the proviso are clear and not repugnant.' See also, *Smith v Accident Insurance Co* (1870) LR 5 Exch 302, per Kelly CB, who dissented from the rest of the Court on the main point of the case, at 309; *Sangster's Trustees v General Accident Assurance Corpn Ltd* 1896 24 R (Ct of Sess) 56.

CHAPTER 29

The conduct of the assured

The fact that the peril insured against was brought into operation by an act on the part of the assured or of a person for whom he is or may be responsible does not necessarily take away the liability of the insurers for any loss that may be sustained in consequence.[1] The effect of the act depends partly on its nature and partly on the special stipulations, if any, of the policy.

A NEGLIGENT ACTS

Negligence, whether on the part of the assured himself[2] or of his employees,[3] does not exempt the insurers from liability though the loss is caused thereby, for one of the objects of insurance is to protect the assured against the consequences of negligence.

In the words of Lord Denman CJ:[4]

> 'There is no doubt that one of the objects of insurance against fire is to guard against the negligence of servants and others; and, therefore, the simple fact of negligence has never been held to constitute a defence. But it is argued that there is a distinction between the negligence of servants or strangers, and that of the assured himself. We do not see any ground for such a distinction; and are of opinion that, in the absence of all fraud, the proximate cause of the loss only is to be looked to.'

In a case concerning marine insurance[5] Parke B remarked:[6]

> 'But the assured makes no warranty to the underwriters . . . that the master or crew shall do their duty during the voyage; and their negligence or misconduct is no defence to an action on the policy, where the loss has been immediately occasioned by the perils insured against . . .

---

1 *Gordon v Rimmington* (1807) 1 Camp 123 (marine insurance), where a ship was set on fire by her master to avoid imminent capture, and the insurers were held liable for her loss on the grounds expressed, per Lord Ellenborough CJ, at 123, 124: 'Fire is expressly mentioned in the policy as one of the perils against which the underwriters undertake to indemnify the assured; and if the ship is destroyed by fire, it is of no consequence whether this is occasioned by a common accident or by lightning, or by an act done in duty to the State. Nor can it make any difference whether the ship is destroyed by third persons, subjects of the King, or by the captain and crew acting with loyalty and good faith.'

2 *Cornish v Accident Insurance Co* (1889) 23 QBD 453, CA, per Lindley LJ, at 457.

3 *A-G v Adelaide SS Co* [1923] AC 292 (charter-party) per Lord Wrenbury, at 308, speaking (inter alia) of motor insurance; *Re Etherington and Lancashire and Yorkshire Accident Insurance Co* [1908] 1 KB 591, CA per Kennedy LJ, at 601; *Global Tankers Inc v Amercoat Europa NV and Rust, The 'Diane'* [1977] 1 Lloyd's Rep 61 (guarantee insurance), where the failure of the anti-corrosive painting of a vessel's tanks was due to a fault on the part of the insured paint manufacturers' inspector.

4 *Shaw v Robberds* (1837) 6 Ad & El 75 at 84, (fire insurance).

5 *Dixon v Sadler* (1839) 5 M & W 405.

6 Ibid, at 414.

> nor can any distinction be made between the omission by the master and crew to do an act which ought to be done, or the doing an act which ought not, in the course of the navigation. It matters not whether a fire which causes a loss be lighted improperly or, after being properly lighted, be negligently attended; whether the loss of an anchor, which renders the vessel unseaworthy, be attributable to the omission to take proper care of it, or to the improper act of shipping it or cutting it away; nor could it make any difference whether any other part of the equipment were lost by mere neglect or thrown away or destroyed in the exercise of an improper discretion, by those on board. If there be any fault in the crew, whether of omission or commission, the assured is not to be responsible for its consequences.'

The effect of this decision is reproduced as far as marine insurance is concerned by the Marine Insurance Act 1906, s 55(2)(a) which states:

> 'The insurer . . . unless the policy otherwise provides . . . is liable for any loss proximately caused by a peril insured against, even though the loss would not have happened but for the misconduct or negligence of the master or crew . . .'

It is unnecessary to consider the nature of the act constituting negligence, whether it is the doing of an act which ought not to have been done or the doing of a proper act in an improper manner.[7] The degree of negligence does not appear to be material.[8]

B WILFUL ACTS

A wilful act, whether of misfeasance[9] or omission,[10] which brings the peril

---

7 *Dixon v Sadler* (supra) (marine insurance).

8 *Tinline v White Cross Insurance Association Ltd* [1921] 3 KB 327 (motor insurance), where the assured was driving at an excessive speed and successfully claimed an indemnity in respect of an act of criminal negligence, which resulted in his conviction for manslaughter; *James v British General Insurance Co Ltd* [1927] 2 KB 311, 27 LlL Rep 328 (motor insurance), where the assured was drunk; see contra, *O'Hearn v Yorkshire Insurance Co* (1921) 50 OLR 377 (affd 51 OLR 130) in which case (which was decided a few days before *Tinline v White Cross Insurance Association Ltd* (supra)) the assured, who was drunk at the time, drove a car at 40 mph along a main street and killed a workman who was doing repairs on a railway track on the roadway at a place protected by red lights, and the Court, whilst recognising the legality of insurances against negligence, held that there was no indemnity in the case of criminal conduct. Further, an indemnity against the costs of defending criminal proceedings is valid, though the extent of the indemnity depends upon the language of the policy; see *James v British General Insurance Co Ltd* (supra), where the assured was held entitled to the cost of police court proceedings, but not to the cost of his defence at Assizes.

9 *Tinline v White Cross Insurance Association* (supra) per Bailhache J, at 332; *Trinder, Anderson & Co v Thames and Mersey Marine Insurance Co* [1898] 2 QB 114, CA (marine insurance) per Smith LJ, at 123; *Midland Insurance Co v Smith* (1881) 6 QBD 561 (fire insurance); *Haseldine v Hosken* [1933] 1 KB 822, 44 LlL Rep 127, CA (solicitors' indemnity policy), where the assured was unaware of the illegality of a champertous agreement entered into between himself and his client, though it was manifestly unlawful and constituted an indictable offence, and he was accordingly held unable to recover on the policy, for it did not cover claims for damages for champerty and maintenance brought against him by a third party. In *Global Tankers Inc v Amercoat Europa NV and Rust, The Diane* [1977] 1 Lloyd's Rep 61 (guarantee insurance), where the failure of the anti-corrosive painting of a vessel's tanks was due to a fault on the part of the insured paint manufacturers' inspector, it was not suggested that the default was a wilful one. (See the judgment of Kerr J, ibid, at 67.)

10 *Bell v Carstairs* (1811) 14 East 374 (marine insurance); *Jameson v Royal Insurance Co* (1873) IR 7 CL 126 (fire insurance); *Pan American World Airways Inc v Aetna Casualty and Surety Co* [1974] 1 Lloyd's Rep 207 (District Ct for Southern District of New York) (aviation insurance), where an aircraft was destroyed at Cairo airport by the Popular Front for the Liberation of Palestine, and it was held that the loss was not caused by the wilful misconduct of the owners. (See the judgment of Frankel DJ, ibid, at 237.) The decision was subsequently affirmed by the US Ct of Appeals: [1975] 1 Lloyd's Rep 77.

insured against into operation, if amounting to misconduct,[11] exempts the insurers from liability.[12]

The ground of the exemption, however, is not so much the misconduct[13] as the breach of good faith involved in making a claim in such circumstances.[14] On the other hand, the policy is not avoided by a mere intention to commit a wrongful act which is never carried out, and the assured is not precluded from enforcing the policy if the peril subsequently comes into operation without any misconduct on his part.[15]

It has also been held that it would be against public policy for the insured to succeed in any claim he might make on the insurers.

Thus, in *Gray v Barr (Prudential Assurance Co Ltd Third Party)*:[16]

> The insured was covered under a 'hearth and home' policy in respect of all sums which he might become legally liable to pay as damages for bodily injury to any person caused by accident. His wife developed a liaison with another man, and the insured went to his house with a loaded shotgun and fired a shot into the ceiling to frighten him. A struggle ensued and the gun went off killing the other man. The insured admitted liability and claimed an indemnity from the insurers.

---

11 *Thompson v Hopper* (1858) EB & E 1038, ExCh (marine insurance); *Dudgeon v Pembroke* (1877) 2 App Cas 284 (marine insurance); *Trinder Anderson & Co v North Queensland Insurance Co* (1897) 2 Com Cas 216 (marine insurance) per Kennedy J, at 223, citing *Midland Insurance Co v Smith* (supra); cf *Gordon v Rimmington* (1803) 1 Camp 123 (marine insurance), where the wilful act was justifiable.

12 But the Motor Insurers' Bureau will be liable to a third party injured by an uninsured driver even though that driver intentionally causes the injury, and would for that reason have been unable to recover on his own policy of insurance if he had been insured: *Hardy v Motor Insurers' Bureau* [1964] 2 QB 745, [1964] 2 All ER 742, CA (motor insurance). Lord Denning MR said (at 746): 'If the motorist is guilty of a crime involving a wicked and deliberate intent, and he is made to pay damages to an injured person, he is not entitled to recover on the policy. But if he does not pay the damages, then the injured third party can recover against the insurers under s 207 of the Road Traffic Act 1960 [now s 149 of the Road Traffic Act 1972]; for it is a liability which the motorist under the statute was required to cover. The injured third party is not affected by the disability which attached to the motorist himself. So here the liability of [the driver] to the [third party] was a liability which [he] was required to cover by a policy of insurance, even though it arose out of his wilful and culpable criminal act. If [he] had been insured, he himself would be disabled from recovering from the insurers. But the injured third party would not be disabled from recovering from them. Seeing that he was not insured, the [Bureau] must treat the case as if he were. [It] must pay the injured third party, even though [the driver] was guilty of felony.' (See also the judgments of Pearson LJ, at 749–750, and Diplock LJ, at 752); *Gardner v Moore* [1984] AC 548, [1984] 1 All ER 1100, [1984] 2 Lloyd's Rep 135, HL (see the judgment of Lord Hailsham of St Marylebone LC, ibid, at 140–141). As to the Motor Insurers' Bureau, see Ivamy *Fire and Motor Insurance* (4th edn, 1984), pp 347–365.

13 But see *Moore v Woolsey* (1854) 4 E & B 243 (life insurance) per Lord Campbell CJ at 254: 'If a man insured his life for a year, and commits suicide within the year, his executors cannot recover on the policy, or the owner of a ship who insures her for a year cannot recover upon the policy if within the year he causes her to be sunk; a stipulation that, in either case, upon such an event, the policy should give a right of action would be void.'

14 *Thompson v Hopper* (supra) (marine insurance) per Bramwell B, at 1045; cf *R v Robinson* [1915] 2 KB 342, CCA, where it was held that a jeweller who arranged a sham burglary and falsely represented to the police that a burglary had been committed on his premises, hoping that, on the face of the police report, his insurers might be induced to make a payment under his burglary policy, could not be convicted of attempting to obtain money from the insurers by false pretences, the truth having been discovered before he communicated with the insurers.

15 Cf *Barrett v Jermy* (1849) 3 Exch 535 (fire insurance) per Parke B, at 543.

16 [1971] 2 QB 554, [1971] 2 All ER 949, CA. See the judgment of Lord Denning MR, ibid, at 957, that of Salmon LJ, ibid, at 964, and that of Phillimore LJ, ibid, at 970. The Court of Appeal also held that the death of the other man had not been caused by 'accident.' See further, Ivamy *Personal Accident, Life and Other Insurances* (2nd Edn, 1980), pp 223–224.

Held, the claim failed for the insured was guilty of deliberate violence and it would be against public policy to allow him to recover the sum insured.

The exemption from liability extends to the similar acts of third persons done with the privity or consent of the assured.[17] In the absence of privity or consent, the assured, if not guilty himself of misconduct, is not precluded from recovering.[18]

If the act amounts to a crime, the insurers must, if they resist claim on this ground,[19] satisfy the jury that the alleged crime was committed. The evidence brought forward must be sufficient to justify a conviction on the criminal charge.[20] In the absence of clear proof that the act was criminal, the presumption against crime must prevail, and the assured will be entitled to recover. To preclude the assured from recovering, it must be shown that the crime was committed by him or with his privity or consent. If the assured is not in any way responsible for the crime, he may recover, though the loss was caused by the criminal act of a third person.[21]

A wilful act is excused where it is committed for the purpose of averting a greater danger,[1] or, perhaps, for the purpose of saving human life.[2]

Where the policy covers two assured, who are not joint owners, in respect of their respective interest, the wilful act by one of the assured does not prevent the other assured from bringing an action on the policy.[3]

Thus, in *Lombard Australia Ltd v NRMA Insurance Ltd*:[4]

---

17 *Midland Insurance Co v Smith* (supra) (fire insurance) per Watkin Williams J, at 568; cf *Logan v Hall* (1847) 4 CB 598 (fire insurance) per Maule J, at 622; and see *Visscherij Maatschappij Nieuw Onderneming v Scottish Metropolitan Assurance Co* (1922) 38 TLR 458, CA (marine insurance), where the assured's privity was inferred.

18 *Midland Insurance Co v Smith* (supra) (fire insurance); *Samuel (P) & Co v Dumas* [1924] AC 431 (marine insurance) per Lord Sumner, at 462; cf *Thomas v Tyne and Wear SS Freight Insurance Association* [1917] 1 KB 938 (marine insurance), where the ship was unseaworthy in two respects, the assured being privy to the one and not to the other, which caused the loss.

19 It is not advisable to raise this defence, if there is adequate reason for resisting the claim on other grounds; see *Britton v Royal Insurance Co* (1866) 4 F & F 905 (fire insurance) per Willes J, at 908: 'The real question was whether there had been fraud, and he should advise his jury that, if satisfied that there was, they need not enter into the question of arson, and that it would be better to avoid entering unnecessarily into what would be virtually an inquiry into a criminal charge. If there was arson, it could only have been with a view to effectuate a fraud, and it was so extremely inconvenient to embarrass a civil suit with a collateral inquiry into a charge of felony that he deemed it better to put it out of the case.'

20 *Thurtell v Beaumont* (1823) 1 Bing 339 (fire insurance); *Goulstone v Royal Insurance Co* (1858) 1 F & F 276 (fire insurance); *Britton v Royal Insurance Co* (supra); *Prosser v Ocean Accident and Guarantee Corpn* (1910) 29 NZLR 1157 (fire insurance).

21 *Midland Insurance Co v Smith* (supra). Thus, insurances may be effected to cover loss by theft, riot, or malicious damage generally. See, as far as marine insurance is concerned, e g the Institute Strike Clauses (Cargo). See generally Ivamy *Marine Insurance* (4th Edn, 1985), p 214.

1 *Re Etherington and Lancashire and Yorkshire Accident Insurance Co* [1909] 1 KB 591, CA per Vaughan Williams LJ, at 599; *Gordon v Rimmington* (1807) 1 Camp 123 (marine insurance); *Stanley v Western Insurance Co* (1868) LR 3 Exch 71 (fire insurance) per Kelly CB, at 74.

2 In practice, where an express exception is inserted covering the conduct of the insured, this is usually excluded from the scope of the exception. In *Trew v Railway Passengers' Assurance Co* (1861) 6 H & N 839, Cockburn CJ, at 842, asked during the argument, whether if a person rushed into a burning house to save his child and was burnt to death, that would be death from 'accident' within the meaning of the policy. Counsel for the insurers said that it would not be, since the assured voluntarily entered the house, but no opinion was expressed by the Court.

3 *Lombard Australia Ltd v NRMA Insurance Ltd* [1969] 1 Lloyd's Rep 575, Supreme Court of New South Wales, Court of Appeal.

4 [1969] 1 Lloyd's Rep 575, Supreme Court of New South Wales, Court of Appeal.

A proposal was made by the hire-purchaser of a car which he was obtaining on hire-purchase terms from a finance company. The policy which was issued covered the car against 'accidental loss'. The hire-purchaser committed suicide by deliberately driving the car into a tree. The finance company claimed under the policy.
Held that the claim succeeded. It was clear that the policy constituted a several promise to each of the assured. The deliberate action of the hire-purchaser in causing damage to the car did not prejudice the finance company's claim that the loss was derived from accidental causes.

As far as marine insurance is concerned, the Marine Insurance Act 1906, s 55(2)(a) provides:

'The insurer is not liable for any loss attributable to the wilful misconduct of the assured . . .'[5]

C EXPRESS STIPULATIONS IN THE POLICY

The conduct of the assured and of the persons for whom he is responsible may be dealt with by express stipulations in the policy. The stipulations in use may be classified as follows:

1 Stipulations which merely put into words what is already implied by law.
2 Stipulations which extend the exceptions implied by law.
3 Stipulations which diminish the exceptions implied by law.

1 Stipulations expressing what is already implied

This class includes stipulations which refer generally to wilful misconduct,[6] and stipulations specifying the acts which, having reference to the circumstances of the particular insurance, would probably be regarded, even in the absence of the stipulation, as wilful misconduct, e g in the case of personal accident insurance, engaging in a duel. An express stipulation may also exclude the insurers' liability if his death or disablement is caused by the insured's own criminal act.[7]

2 Stipulations extending the exceptions implied by law

Such stipulations may be sub-divided into:

a Stipulations excepting acts which are ambiguous in their nature, e g in the case of personal accident insurance, wilful exposure to obvious risk.[8]

---

5 See further, Ivamy *Marine Insurance* (4th Edn, 1985), pp 232–247.

6 See, as far as marine insurance is concerned, the Institute Cargo Clauses (A), cl 4(1), which expressly states that the policy does not cover loss, damage or expense attributable to the wilful misconduct of the assured. See generally Ivamy *Marine Insurance* (4th Edn, 1985), p 256.

7 *Marcel Beller Ltd v Hayden* [1978] 1 Lloyd's Rep 472 (personal accident insurance), where the offences of dangerous driving and driving under the influence of drink were held to be sufficiently serious to qualify as 'the insured person's own criminal act'. (See the judgment of Judge Edgar Fay, ibid, at 479.)

8 *Cornish v Accident Insurance Co* (1889) 23 QBD 453 (personal accident insurance), where the insurers were not to be liable for an accident caused 'by exposure of the insured to obvious risk of injury'; *Marcel Beller Ltd v Hayden* (supra) (personal accident insurance), where the clause exempted the insurers from liability for death or disablement resulting from 'deliberate exposure to exceptional danger (except in an attempt to save human life)', and it was held that, on the evidence, the insured by driving under the influence of drink had not deliberately exposed himself to exceptional danger. (See the judgment of Judge Edgar Fay, ibid, at 478.)

b Stipulations excepting acts which, though not wrongful in themselves, are from their nature calculated to bring the peril into operation, e g in personal accident insurance, engaging in mountaineering or steeple-chasing.

c Stipulations excepting acts of negligence;[9] such stipulations may be framed in general terms or may specify the particular acts of negligence excepted.

d Stipulations excepting acts of persons for whom the assured is responsible, e g members of his household or business staff; such stipulations are usually confined to acts of criminal misconduct.

3 Stipulations diminishing the exceptions implied by law

Such stipulations may be sub-divided into:

a Stipulations which apply only in favour of an assignee for value, though the assured or persons claiming through him otherwise than for value cannot take advantage of them.[10]

b Stipulations of general application.

---

9 *Re George and Goldsmiths' and General Burglary Insurance Association Ltd* [1899] 1 QB 595, CA per Lord Russell CJ, at 602.

10 *Moore v Woolsey* (1854) 4 E & B 243 (life insurance) per Lord Campbell CJ, at 254.

CHAPTER 30

The conditions of the policy

A policy of insurance usually contains or incorporates a variety of terms.

Some terms are known as 'conditions' on the fulfilment of which the validity of the policy or the liability of the insurers depends.

Other terms, however, do not amount to 'conditions'.[1] Non-fulfilment of these does not affect the validity of the policy nor the liability of the insurers, but entitles them to recover in a cross-action such damages as they may have sustained by reason of the non-fulfilment.

A THE CLASSIFICATION OF CONDITIONS

Conditions may be classified:

1 As implied and express conditions.
2 According to the time when they come into operation.

1 Implied and express conditions

(a) Implied conditions

There are certain conditions which govern the validity or effect of every policy of insurance unless it clearly appears to have been the intention of the parties to exclude them[2] or to modify their operation;[3] and it is therefore unnecessary for them to be expressed in the policy. The implied conditions are the following:

i That the parties shall observe good faith towards each other at all material times and in all material particulars;
ii That there is a subject-matter of insurance in existence at the time when the policy is effective;

---

[1] *London Guarantee Co v Fearnley* (1880) 5 App Cas 911 (fidelity insurance) per Lord Blackburn, at 915; *Re Bradley and Essex and Suffolk Accident Indemnity Society* [1912] 1 KB 415, CA (employers' liability insurance) per Fletcher Moulton LJ, at 427; *Barnard v Faber* [1893] 1 QB 340, CA (fire insurance) per Bowen LJ, at 343, 344; *W and J Lane v Spratt* [1969] 2 Lloyd's Rep 229 (goods in transit insurance) at 236: 'By a "condition" I mean a contractual term of the policy, any breach of which by the assured will in the event of a loss arising otherwise payable under the policy afford underwriters a defence to any claim irrespective of whether there is any causal connection between the breach of the contractual term and the loss. By a "warranty" I mean a contractual term of the policy, a breach of which will not of itself afford a defence to underwriters unless there is the necessary causal link between the breach and the loss which is the subject of the claim under the policy' (per Roskill J).

[2] *Fowkes v Manchester and London Life Assurance and Loan Association* (1863) 3 B & S 917 (life insurance) per Blackburn J, at 930; *Joel v Law Union and Crown Insurance Co* [1908] 2 KB 863, CA (life insurance) per Vaughan Williams LJ, at 878.

[3] *Jones v Provincial Insurance Co* (1857) 3 CBNS 65 (life insurance).

iii That the subject-matter of insurance is so described in the policy as clearly to identify it and to define the risk undertaken by the insurers;
iv That the assured has an insurable interest in the subject-matter of insurance.

These are the only conditions which may be implied in any policy of insurance.[4] If it is wished to impose any further obligations on the assured and to make their fulfilment a condition, it is necessary to insert in the policy express stipulations to that effect.[5]

Thus, it is not an implied condition of the policy:

i That all representations made by the assured during the negotiations shall be true;
ii That the policy shall not attach until the premium is paid;
iii That the risk shall not, during the currency of the policy, be altered;
iv That the assured shall not, during the currency of the policy, effect a similar policy with other insurers;
v That the assured shall give particulars of his claim to the insurers before instituting proceedings on the policy;
vi That, if, at the time of the loss, there are other subsisting insurances covering the same subject-matter, the insurers shall not be liable to the assured for more than a rateable proportion of the loss.

(b) Express conditions

It is the practice of insurers to insert in their policies express conditions to the effect of those conditions which would otherwise be implied by law. Such conditions may have the effect of extending or restricting the scope of the implied conditions, or of excluding any condition not clearly expressed. It is, therefore, necessary in any particular case to consider the language of the condition employed.

Thus, by virtue of an express condition, a misrepresentation or non-disclosure of a material fact may not avoid the whole policy, as it would do in the absence of the condition; it may avoid it as regards the particular portion of the subject-matter in respect of which the misrepresentation or non-disclosure is committed, without affecting the validity of the policy in respect of the remaining portions of the subject-matter.[6]

It is further open to the parties to make any stipulation in the policy a condition[7] provided that their intention to do so is clearly shown.[8] It is immaterial for what purpose it is introduced.[9]

---

4 For examples of such conditions being modified or excluded, see *Pennsylvania Co for Insurances on Lives and Granting Annuities v Mumford* [1920] 2 KB 537, 2 LlL Rep 351, CA, where the policy was expressed to include security believed to be in the assured's possession; *March (Earl) v Pigot* (1771) 5 Burr 2802 (wager), where the subject-matter had already ceased to exist, followed in *Mead v Davison* (1835) 3 Ad & El 303 (marine insurance); *Jones v Provincial Insurance Co* (supra), where the proposed assured was required only to state what he knew.

5 *London and North Western Rly Co v Glyn* (1859) 1 E & E 652 (fire insurance) per Erle J, at 633; *Baxendale v Harvey* (1859) 4 H & N 445 (fire insurance); *Joel v Law Union and Crown Insurance Co* (supra).

6 *Daniel v Robinson* (1826) Batt 650 (fire insurance).

7 *Thomson v Weems* (1884) 9 App Cas 671 (life insurance) per Lord Blackburn, at 683; 'It is competent to the contracting parties, if both agree to it and sufficiently express their intention so

A stipulation, which would not otherwise be a condition, may be made a condition by express language for the purpose of protecting the insurers.[10] The breach of a stipulation which is not a condition has no effect on the validity of the policy or on the liability of the insurers; however greatly the breach of the stipulation may have prejudiced them, they remain liable on the policy,[11] and their only remedy is an action for damages, a remedy which, in practice, affords them little or no protection.[12] In order to secure the fulfilment of the stipulation, therefore, it is the practice of insurers to make the various stipulations to which they attach importance conditions, on the fulfilment of which the validity of the policy or the liability of the insurers depends.

There is no obligation on the insurers to relate a condition to a particular aspect of the policy.[13]

---

to agree, to make the actual existence of anything a condition precedent to the inception of the contract; and if they do so, the non-existence of that thing is a good defence. And it is not of any importance whether the existence of that thing was or was not material; the parties would not have made it part of the contract if they had not thought it material, and they have a right to determine for themselves what they shall deem material.' See also, *Dawsons Ltd v Bonnin* [1922] 2 AC 413 per Lord Haldane, at 423; *Anderson v Fitzgerald* (1853) 4 HLCas 484 (life insurance) per Lord Cranworth, at 503; *Gamble v Accident Assurance Co Ltd* (1869) IR 4 CL 204. Thus, an alteration in the articles of association of a mutual insurance company, though invalid as an alteration owing to non-compliance with the statutory requirements, may, if printed on the policy, be valid as a condition, and therefore binding on the members: *Muirhead v Forth and North Sea Steamboat Mutual Insurance Association* [1894] AC 72 (marine insurance). As to mutual insurance, see Ivamy *Marine Insurance* (4th Edn, 1985), pp 475–479.

8 *Braunstein v Accidental Death Insurance Co* (1861) 1 B & S 782 (accident insurance) per Blackburn J, at 799; 'I quite admit that parties may make what they please a condition precedent, but it must be shown that they so intended'; *Thomson v Weems* (1884) 9 App Cas 671 (life insurance) per Lord Blackburn, at 682, following *Anderson v Fitzgerald* (1853) 4 HL Cas 484 (life insurance) per Lord St Leonards, at 507. See also, *Joel v Law Union and Crown Insurance Co* [1908] 2 KB 863, CA (life insurance) per Fletcher Moulton LJ, at 886.

9 *De Hahn v Hartley* (1786) 1 Term Rep 343 (marine insurance) (affirmed (1787) 2 Term-Rep 186n, ExCh) per Lord Mansfield CJ, at 345; *Newcastle Fire Insurance Co v Macmorran & Co* (1815) 3 Dow 255, HL per Lord Eldon C, at 258; *Thomson v Weems* (supra) per Lord Watson, at 689.

10 *London Guarantee Co v Fearnley* (1880) 5 App Cas 911 per Lord Blackburn, at 915: 'It has long been the practice of companies insuring against fire for the purpose of their own security, to incorporate in the policies, by reference to their proposals, various stipulations for matters to be done by the assured making a claim before the company is to pay them and (as the remedy by action for not complying with the stipulation would not afford them any protection) to make the fulfilment of those conditions a condition precedent to their obligation to pay. There was much controversy on the subject about a century ago; but since the case of *Worsley v Wood* (1796) 6 Term Rep 710 (fire insurance) it has been settled law that this mode of protecting themselves is effectual.' See also *Lancashire Insurance Co v IRC* [1899] 1 QB 353 (accident insurance) per Bruce J, at 359; *Barnard v Faber* [1893] 1 QB 340, CA (fire insurance) per Bowen LJ, at 343; *Newcastle Fire Insurance Co v Macmorran & Co* (1815) 3 Dow 255, HL per Lord Eldon LC, at 262.

11 *Ballantine v Employers' Insurance Co of Great Britain* 1893 21 R (Ct of Sess) 305, where a post-mortem was refused, though not unreasonably demanded.

12 *Gamble v Accident Assurance Co Ltd* (1869) IR 4 CL 204; *London Guarantee Co v Fearnley* (1880) 5 App Cas 911 per Lord Blackburn, at 915; *Re Coleman's Depositories Ltd and Life and Health Assurance Association* [1907] 2 KB 798, CA per Fletcher Moulton LJ, at 809; *HTV Ltd v Lintner* [1984] 2 Lloyd's Rep 125 (entertainment risk insurance), at 128 (per Neill J).

13 *New India Assurance Co Ltd v Chow alias Chong* [1972] 1 Lloyd's Rep 479, PC (motor insurance) per Viscount Dilhorne, at 482, the question being whether a condition stating that the insured must maintain the vehicle in an efficient condition still stood in view of the fact that a comprehensive policy form had been adapted to cover third-party risks only.

The principal express conditions in use relate to the following matters:[14]

- i Misrepresentation, misdescription, or non-disclosure in any material particular;
- ii Increase of risk;
- iii Alienation of interest;
- iv Payment of the premium;
- v Notice and particulars and proofs of loss;
- vi Fraudulent claims;
- vii Rights of the insurers upon loss;
- viii The existence of other insurances;
- ix Arbitration.[15]

2 Classification of conditions with reference to time of operation

Conditions may also be classified with reference to the time when they come into operation. These may be divided into:

- a Conditions precedent to the validity of the policy;
- b Conditions subsequent of the policy; and
- c Conditions precedent to the liability of the insurers.

(a) Conditions precedent to validity of the policy

Such conditions relate to matters which precede the formation of the contract contained in the policy, and which are, or are agreed by the parties[16] to be, essential to its validity.[17] They must be fulfilled; otherwise the policy never attaches, but is void ab initio.[18]

---

14 See *Andrews v Patriotic Assurance Co (No. 2)* (1886) 18 LRIr 355 (fire insurance) per Palles CB, at 361: 'You would expect to find provisions relating to the conduct of the assured and those over whom he had control, provisions affecting or possibly making void the policy in case of fraud in its making or procurement, or in the event of circumstances which increase the actual risk above that which was contemplated and paid for and perhaps clauses . . . providing against anything more than a complete indemnity being recovered by the assured.'

15 In 1956 the British Insurance Association and Lloyd's stated that the members of the Association and Lloyd's Underwriters had agreed to refrain in general from insisting upon the enforcement of arbitration clauses if the insured preferred to have the question of liability, as distinct from amount, determined by a Court in the United Kingdom. This arrangement does not apply where the terms of the insurance are contained in a policy which has been specially negotiated and in which an arbitration clause has been inserted by express agreement between the parties. Nor does it apply to marine insurance; to contracts of reinsurance; or to certain aspects of aircraft insurance, e g insurance against the loss of or damage to an aircraft, the insured's liability to third parties or to passengers in the aircraft, or to loss of or damage to, or liability in respect of, cargo consigned by air. See Law Reform Committee Fifth Report *Conditions and Exceptions in Insurance Policies,* 1957, Cmnd 62, para 13.

16 *Thomson v Weems* (supra) per Lord Blackburn, at 682; *Joel v Law Union and Crown Insurance Co* [1908] 2 KB 863, CA (life insurance) per Fletcher Moulton LJ, at 886.

17 *Barnard v Faber* [1893] 1 QB 340, CA (fire insurance) per Bowen LJ, at 344: 'These are to be the same rate, the same terms, the identical interest, as in the case of the other two companies. It is, therefore, a term of the policy that there should be this promise; and if this promise is one which goes to the root of the whole engagement and transaction, then it becomes, according to the ordinary principles of ordinary law, a condition—either a condition precedent, or, if the condition is one which cannot be construed as a condition precedent, and must be a condition subsequent, then it becomes a condition subsequent. That arises from the materiality of the promise which is assumed to be made, and the making of which is to be a term of the engagement or transaction into which the underwriter has entered. When you have got as far as that, it is

Thus, it is or may be made a condition precedent of the policy;

i That the assured shall discharge his duty of disclosure;[19]
ii That all statements made during the negotiations by the assured shall be true;[20]
iii That the subject-matter of insurance is in existence;
iv That the subject-matter of insurance is adequately described;[21]
v That the assured has an insurable interest in the subject-matter of insurance.[22]

(b) Conditions subsequent of the policy

Such conditions relate to matters which arise after the formation of the contract contained in the policy, and which are, or are agreed by the parties to be essential to its continued validity.[1] They must be fulfilled; otherwise the policy ceases to attach, and, though not void ab initio, may be avoided as from the date of the breach.[2]

Thus, it is or may be made a condition subsequent of the policy:

i That the assured shall not voluntarily alienate his interest in the subject-matter of insurance;[3]
ii That the assured shall not alter the risk as defined in the policy;[4]
iii That the assured shall not effect a similar policy with other insurers;[5]
iv That either or both of the parties shall be entitled to determine the contract on notice;[6]
v That the assured shall not be guilty of fraud in connection with any claim put forward under the policy.[7]

---

clear that it is the term as regards the risk which is material. A term as regards the risk must be a condition. Then let us look back at what the particular words are—the "same rate and identical interest." The "same rate and identical interest" are obviously words so material to the transaction that we can only construe them as creating a condition precedent.'

18 *Thomson v Weems* (1884) 9 App Cas 671 (life insurance) per Lord Blackburn, at 683. The word 'void' in this connection appears to mean no more than 'voidable': *Armstrong v Turquand* (1858) 91 ICLR 32 (life insurance) per Christian J, at 42, where there is a long discussion on the use of the word 'void' in insurance policies and the previous authorities are considered. See further, *Equitable Life Assurance Society of United States v Reed* [1914] AC 587, PC (life insurance) per Lord Dunedin, at 596; *Holland v Russell* (1863) 4 B & S 14, ExCh (marine insurance) per Erle CJ, at 16; *Doe d Pitt v Laming* (1814) 4 Camp 73 (fire insurance) per Lord Ellenborough CJ, at 75. The insurers may therefore waive the breach of condition, see pp 292–298, post.

19 As to the duty of disclosure, see Chapter 13.

20 See pp 167–168, ante.

21 As to the description of the subject-matter, see pp 13–18, ante.

22 As to insurable interest, see Chapter 5.

1 *Barnard v Faber* [1893] 1 QB 340, CA (fire insurance) per Bowen LJ, at 343.

2 *Glen v Lewis* (1853) 8 Exch 607 (fire insurance); *Sun Fire Office v Hart* (1889) 14 App Cas 98, PC (fire insurance); *Sulphite Pulp Co v Faber* (1895) 1 Com Cas 146 (fire insurance); *Equitable Fire and Accident Office v Ching Wo Hong* [1907] AC 96, PC (fire insurance) where, on the facts, there was no breach; *Wing v Harvey* (1854) 5 De GM & G 265 (life insurance), where, however, there was a waiver of the breach; *Marcovitch v Liverpool Victoria Friendly Society* (1912) 28 TLR 188 (life insurance), where the insurers failed to prove a breach.

3 As to assignment of the subject-matter, see Chapter 32.

4 As to alteration of the risk, see Chapter 31.

5 As to 'other insurance', see Chapter 33.

6 See pp 231–232, ante.

7 As to fraudulent claims, see pp 407–411, post.

(c) Conditions precedent to the liability of the insurers

Such conditions relate to matters arising after a loss under the policy and define the circumstances in which the liability of the insurers is to arise.[8] They must be fulfilled; otherwise the liability of the insurers never arises.[9]

It is, or may be made, a condition precedent to the liability of the insurers:

- i That the premium shall be paid;[10]
- ii That notice, particulars and proof of loss shall be given within a prescribed time:[11]
- iii That the assured shall assist the insurers to investigate and ascertain the cause and extent of the loss;
- iv That the liability of the insurers shall be determined by arbitration;
- v That the liability of other insurers under similar policies covering the same loss shall be taken into account.[12]
- vi That no admission of liability or offer or promise of payment shall be made without the written consent of the insurers.[13]
- vii That if the insurers disclaim liability to the insured, he must institute legal proceedings against them within a specified period of the date of the disclaimer.[14]

In January 1957 the Law Reform Committee in their Fifth Report[15] stated that the presence of such clauses was a very valuable protection to the insurers since their function was usually to facilitate prompt investigation after a loss, to ensure control by the insurers of any litigation or negotiations with third parties, or to protect their interest in matters of salvage or subrogation.[16] They were not normally calculated to be prejudicial to an insured who took the trouble to read his policy, except perhaps the condition, common in certain types of policy, which required notice of loss to be given within so many days.[17] Circumstances might arise which rendered compliance with such a condition impossible, e g where the discovery of one irregularity on the part of an employee led to the discovery of a series of embezzlements in the past, the

---

8 *London Guarantee Co v Fearnley* (1880) 5 App Cas 911 per Lord Blackburn, at 915.

9 *Gamble v Accident Assurance Co Ltd* (1869) IR 4 CL 204, followed in *Patton v Employers' Liability Assurance Corpn* (1887) 20 LRIr 93; *Cawley v National Employers' Accident and General Assurance Association Ltd* (1885) 1 TLR 255; *Cassel v Lancashire and Yorkshire Accident Insurance Co Ltd* (1885) 1 TLR 495; *Stoneham v Ocean Railway and General Accident Insurance Co* (1887) 19 QBD 237 per Cave J, at 241; *British General Insurance Co v Mountain* [1920] WC & Ins Rep 245, HL; *Re Williams and Lancashire and Yorkshire Accident Insurance Co's Arbitration* (1902) 19 TLR 82; *Worsley v Wood* (1796) 6 Term Rep 710 (fire insurance), followed in *Mason v Harvey* (1853) 8 Exch 819 (fire insurance); *Oldman v Bewicke* (1786) 2 HyBl 577n (fire insurance); *Roper v Lendon* (1859) 1 E & E 825 (fire insurance), followed in *Elliott v Royal Exchange Assurance Co* (1867) LR 2 Exch 237 (fire insurance); *Re Carr and Sun Fire Insurance Co* (1897) 13 TLR 186, CA (fire insurance).

10 See Chapter 15.

11 See Chapter 39.

12 See pp 430–431, post.

13 See e g *Terry v Trafalgar Union Insurance Co Ltd* [1970] 1 Lloyd's Rep 524, Mayor's and City of London Court (motor insurance), where this type of condition was held not to be contrary to public policy. (See the judgment of Judge Graham Rogers, ibid, at 526.)

14 *Walker v Pennine Insurance Co Ltd* [1980] 2 Lloyd's Rep 156, CA (motor insurance).

15 *Conditions and Exceptions in Insurance Policies*, 1957, Cmnd 62.

16 Para. 9.

17 Para. 9.

presence of such a clause in a fidelity policy taken out to insure against such losses would entitle the insurers to refuse compensation for any of the losses except the last.[18]

B WHAT CONSTITUTES A CONDITION

The question whether a particular stipulation is a condition or not depends on the intention of the parties,[19] as shown in the language which they have selected to express their meaning.[20] It is not a question of fact, but a question of pure construction, to be determined by the Court in accordance with the ordinary rules of construction after looking at all the terms of the policy.[1] A condition need not be expressed in precise technical language;[2] nor need it occupy any particular place in the policy.[3]

A stipulation which, in addition to imposing an obligation on the assured, further requires that his failure to perform it shall render the policy null and

---

18 Para 9.

19 *Braunstein v Accidental Death Insurance Co* (1861) 1 B & S 782 (accident insurance) per Blackburn J, at 799; *Provincial Insurance Co Ltd v Morgan* [1933] AC 240 (accident insurance) per Lord Buckmaster, at 246; *Fawcett v Liverpool, London and Globe Insurance Co* (1868) 27 UCR 225, where it was held that the question whether a certificate demanded by the insurers was within the condition was for the Court; *Welch v Royal Exchange Assurance* [1939] 1 KB 294, [1938] 4 All ER 289, 62 LlL Rep 83, CA (fire insurance), where it was held that a clause in the policy providing that 'the insured shall also give to the (company) all such proofs and information with respect to the claim as may reasonably be required . . . No claim under this policy shall be payable unless the terms of this condition have been complied with' was a condition precedent to the assured's right to recover; *Jones v Provincial Insurance Co Ltd* (1929) 35 LlL Rep 135 (motor insurance), where it was held that the obligation of the insured to maintain the vehicle in an efficient condition was a condition precedent to the liability of the insurers.

20 *Weir v Northern Counties of England Insurance Co* (1879) 4 LRIr 689 (fire insurance) per Lawson J, at 692: 'No precise form of words is necessary to make a condition precedent, but the question must depend on the intention of the parties to be collected from the instrument.' See also, *Wheelton v Hardisty* (1857) 8 E & B 232, ExCh (life insurance) per Martin B, at 297, applying *Stokes v Cox* (1856) 1 H & N 533, ExCh (life insurance); *Thomson v Weems* (1884) 9 App Cas 671 (life insurance) per Lord Blackburn, at 682, citing *Anderson v Fitzgerald* (1853) 4 HL Cas 484 (life insurance) per Lord St Leonards, at 507; *Joel v Law Union and Crown Insurance Co* [1908] 2 KB 863, CA (life insurance) per Fletcher Moulton LJ at 886.

1 *Stoneham v Ocean, Railway and General Accident Insurance Co* (1887) 19 QBD 237 per Mathew J, at 239. See further, *Allan Peters (Jewellers) Ltd v Brocks Alarms Ltd* [1968] 1 Lloyd's Rep 387, at 391 (burglary insurance), where it was held (obiter) that a condition in a fire and burglary insurance policy relating to the setting of a burglar alarm only applied to the burglary section and not to the whole of the policy. As to the construction of the policy, see pp 331–369, post.

2 *Weir v Northern Counties of England Insurance Co* (1879) LRIr 689 (fire insurance) per Lawson J, at 692.

3 But it has been suggested in the case of the conditions of a stringent nature that they should be placed in a conspicuous part of the policy; *Doe d Pitt v Laming* (1814) 4 Camp 73 (fire insurance) per Lord Ellenborough CJ, at 76; or that special attention should be called to them in the proposal: *Re Bradley and Essex and Suffolk Accident Indemnity Society* [1912] 1 KB 415, CA (employers' liability insurance) per Farwell LJ, at 431, stating that it was the duty of the insurers to draw attention in the proposal form to the condition which would be imposed by the policy. This view is difficult to reconcile with the cases in which it has been held that the contract is a contract to take the ordinary form of policy issued by the insurers: *Acme Wood Flooring Co Ltd v Marten* (1904) 9 Com Cas 157 per Bruce J, at 162; and that the delivery of the policy to the insured is notice of the clauses in it and makes them part of the contract: *Equitable Fire and Accident Office Ltd v Ching Wo Hong* [1907] AC 96 at 100, PC. See also, *Macdonald v Law Union Insurance Co* (1874) LR 9 QB 328 (life insurance) per Blackburn J, at 332.

void,[4] or preclude him from recovering under the policy,[5] is clearly intended to be a condition.[6]

In the same way, if the performance of the obligation is declared to be the basis of the contract,[7] the stipulation is to be construed as a condition. On the other hand, a declaration that its performance is to be of the essence of the contract, is not, perhaps, sufficient proof of intention to make the stipulation a condition.[8]

A stipulation which on the face of it is called a condition precedent,[9] warranty[10] or proviso[11] will usually be construed as a condition precedent. The use of the word 'condition' alone is not in itself decisive.[12]

---

4 *Mason v Harvey* (1853) 8 Exch 819; *Life and Health Assurance Associated Ltd v Yule* 1904 6 F (Ct of Sess) 437; *Sulphite Pulp Co v Faber* (1895) 1 Com Cas 146 (fire insurance); *Stoneham v Ocean Railway and General Accident Insurance Co* (1887) 19 QBD 237 (accident insurance) per Mathew J, at 240.

5 *Re Coleman's Depositories Ltd and Life and Health Assurance Association* [1907] 2 KB 798, CA. A stipulation that in default no action shall be brought or payment made has the same effect: *Weir v Northern Counties of England Insurance Co* (supra) per Lawson J, at 693.

6 *London Guarantee Co v Fearnley* (1880) 5 App Cas 911 (fidelity insurance) per Lord Selborne C, at 920. The practice of inserting general declarations that all the stipulations of the policy shall be conditions precedent has been criticised in *Re Bradley and Essex and Suffolk Accident Indemnity Society* [1912] 1 KB 415, CA (employers' liability insurance) per Farwell LJ, at 432, and in *Pictorial Machinery Ltd v Nicolls* (1940) 164 LT 248 per Humphreys J, at 250.

7 *Dawsons Ltd v Bonnin* [1922] 2 AC 413, 12 LlL Rep 237; *Anderson v Fitzgerald* (1853) 4 HL Cas 484 (life insurance); *Wheelton v Hardisty* (1857) 8 E & B 232 (life insurance); *Thomson v Weems* (1884) 9 App Cas 671 (life insurance); *Australian Widows' Fund Life Assurance Society v National Mutual Life Association of Australasia Ltd* [1914] AC 634, PC (life insurance); *Stebbing v Liverpool and London and Globe Insurance Co Ltd* [1917] 2 KB 433 (burglary insurance); *Yorkshire Insurance Co Ltd v Campbell* [1917] AC 218, PC (marine insurance); *Bell v Lever Bros Ltd* [1932] AC 161 (mistake) per Lord Atkinson, at 225, speaking of insurance.

8 A stipulation requiring immediate notice of an accident and providing that 'time shall be of the essence of this condition' has been held to be a condition in *Gamble v Accident Assurance Co Ltd* (1889) IR 4 CL 204, where the notice was not given owing to the instantaneous death of the assured and there being no one capable of giving it, and, in *Re Williams and Lancashire and Yorkshire Accident Insurance Co's Arbitration* (1902) 19 TLR 82, where the assured did not give notice for three months, and where Bigham J said (at 12): 'The arbitrator had found that immediate notice was not given . . . That, in his opinion, decided the case, but he had no hesitation in saying that the giving of immediate notice was a condition precedent to the employers' right to indemnity under the policy. Clause 3 said "time shall be the essence of this condition", and when he read the whole of the clause and remembered how essential it was that the circumstances under which a claim might be made should be speedily brought to the knowledge of the insurance company, he was satisfied that it was intended by the parties that time should be of the essence of the contract.' In *Elliott v Royal Exchange Assurance Co* (1867) LR 2 Exch 237 (fire insurance) Bramwell B (at 246) said that he preferred the phrase 'essential term' to the phrase 'condition precedent'. For other cases in which the word 'essential' has been used to express the nature of a condition precedent, see *Anderson v Fitzgerald* (supra) (life insurance) per Parke B, at 498; *Roper v Lendon* (1859) 1 E & E 825 (fire insurance) per Lord Campbell CJ, at 829, 830; *Dawsons Ltd v Bonnin* (supra) per Lord Haldane, at 424. On the other hand, in *Re Coleman's Depositories Ltd and Life and Health Assurance Association* [1907] 2 KB 798, CA, Bray J in the Court below appears to have decided the case mainly on the ground that he could not construe the word 'essence' as being equivalent to condition precedent, and, though in the Court of Appeal the decision was based on other grounds, Vaughan Williams LJ, at 804, who, however, doubted, and Buckley LJ, at 813, were not disposed to differ from Bray J on this point.

9 *Caledonian Insurance Co v Gilmour* [1893] AC 85 (fire insurance).

10 *Newcastle Fire Insurance Co v Macmorran & Co* (1815) 3 Dow 255, HL (fire insurance), followed in *Hambrough v Mutual Life Insurance Co of New York* (1895) 72 LT 140, CA (life insurance); *Barnard v Faber* [1893] 1 QB 340, CA (fire insurance); *Sulphite Pulp Co v Faber* (1895) 1 Com Cas 146 (fire

A stipulation relating to matters which clearly go to the root of the whole contract,[13] such as a term directly affecting the risk,[14] or which are essential to the existence of liability on the part of the insurers,[15] will be construed as a condition.[16] The nature of the contract, even without any express stipulation to that effect, makes it clear that the parties intended to give the stipulation the effect of a condition.[17] No particular form of words is, therefore, necessary;[18] the matters to which the stipulation relate are so material[19] that the intention of the parties to make the stipulation a condition is beyond doubt, and necessarily involved in the mere fact that the stipulation is made,[20] seeing that it is inconceivable that the insurers would have contracted on the footing that the stipulation was to be enforced only by a cross-action by the insurers against the assured after loss.[1]

Thus, a stipulation to the effect that the assured will not, during the continuance of the policy, commit suicide[2] or that the rate of premium is the same as that payable under another policy,[3] or that the death of an insured animal is to be duly certified by a qualified veterinary surgeon[4] or that

---

insurance); *Walker & Sons v Uzielli* (1896) 1 Com Cas 452 (fire insurance); *Bancroft v Heath* (1901) 6 Com Cas 137, CA (fire insurance), where, however, Vaughan Williams LJ, at 140 doubted on account of the subject-matter to which the stipulation related; *Palatine Insurance Co v Gregory* [1926] AC 90, 93, PC (fire insurance); *Anderson v Fitzgerald* (supra) per Lord Cranworth, at 504; *Dawsons Ltd v Bonnin* [1922] 2 AC 413 per Lord Finlay, at 428.

11 *Cassel v Lancashire and Yorkshire Accident Insurance Co Ltd* (1885) 1 TLR 495; *London Guarantee Co v Fearnley* (1880) 5 App Cas 911.

12 *Stoneham v Ocean Railway and General Accident Insurance Co* (1887) 19 QBD 237 per Mathew J, at 239.

13 *Barnard v Faber* [1893] 1 QB 340, CA (fire insurance) per Bowen LJ, at 343, 344; 'It is, therefore, a term of the policy that there should be this promise; and if this promise is one which goes to the root of the whole engagement and transaction, then it becomes, according to the ordinary principles of ordinary law, a condition—either a condition precedent, or, if the condition is one which cannot be construed as a condition precedent and must be a condition subsequent, then it becomes a condition subsequent'; cf *Bancroft v Heath* (1901) 6 Com Cas 137, CA (fire insurance) per Vaughan Williams LJ, at 140. See also, *Stavers v Curling* (1836) 3 Bing NC 355 (contract) per Tindal CJ, at 368; *Homes v Scottish Legal Life Assurance Society* (1932) 48 TLR 306 (life insurance).

14 *Barnard v Faber* (supra) per Bowen LJ, at 344; *Bancroft v Heath,* as reported (1900), 5 Com Cas 110 per Mathew J, at 114; cf SC, supra, where the doubts expressed by Vaughan Williams LJ, at 140, were based on the fact that it was not quite clear how the risk was affected.

15 *Roper v Lendon* (1859) 1 E & E 825 (fire insurance), where a stipulation providing for the delivery of particulars within a specified time was construed to be a condition.

16 *Barnard v Faber* (supra) per Bowen LJ, at 343; cf *London Guarantee Co v Fearnley* (supra) per Lord Watson, at 918.

17 *Wheelton v Hardisty* (supra) per Bramwell B, at 300.

18 *Barnard v Faber* (supra) per Lindley LJ, at 342; *Weir v Northern Counties of England Insurance Co* (supra) per Lawson J, at 692.

19 *Barnard v Faber* (supra) per Bowen LJ, at 343.

20 *Worsley v Wood* (1796) 6 Term Rep 710 (fire insurance).

1 *Barnard v Faber* (supra) (fire insurance) per Bowen LJ, at 343: 'The clause is one which is intended unquestionably for the protection of the underwriters. When you have arrived at that, it seems to me, you have arrived at half your journey's end, because there can be no adequate protection to underwriters if you relegate them to a cross-action. The clause is intended to protect them against having to pay, not to give them a right to bring an action against the man insuring with them'; *Bancroft v Heath* (supra) per Vaughan Williams LJ, at 140; *Ellinger & Co v Mutual Life Insurance Co of New York* [1905] 1 KB 31, CA (life insurance) per Stirling LJ, at 38.

2 *Ellinger & Co v Mutual Life Assurance Co of New York* (supra).

3 *Barnard v Faber* (supra).

4 *Burridge & Son v F H Haines & Sons Ltd* (1918) 118 LT 681.

particular kinds of goods are not to be kept on the premises,[5] is to be construed as a condition, the breach of which avoids the policy.

A stipulation relating to matters which do not go to the root of contract, or which are not essential to the liability of the insurers, but are merely collateral to the main contract,[6] is not to be construed as a condition[7] unless the stipulation on the face of the policy clearly and precisely shows that it was the intention of the parties to make its fulfilment a condition precedent.[8] It is the duty of the insurers, since the stipulation is framed by them for their protection,[9] to make it clear that the stipulation is intended to be a condition.[10] Where, therefore, the words used are ambiguous, the stipulation will not be construed as a condition.[11]

A stipulation which is grouped with a number of other stipulations under the general heading of 'conditions' or 'conditions precedent' is not, merely on that account, necessarily to be construed as a condition precedent;[12] and it makes no difference that the policy contains an express declaration that the stipulations comprised under the heading are to be conditions precedent.[13] Though the effect of the heading or declaration is the same as if a similar heading or declaration was repeated at the beginning of each separate stipulation,[14] it

---

5 *Dobson v Sotheby* (1827) Mood & M 90 (fire insurance).

6 *Lancashire Insurance Co v IRC* [1899] 1 QB 353 per Bruce J, at 359.

7 See, for instance, *Ballantine v Employers' Insurance Co of Great Britain* 1893 21 R (Ct of Sess) 305, where the refusal of a post-mortem, which was not unreasonably demanded in accordance with a stipulation in the policy, was held not to release the insurers from liability.

8 *Wheelton v Hardisty* (1857) 8 E & B 232 (life insurance) per Martin B, at 297; *W and J Lane v Spratt* [1969] 2 Lloyd's Rep 229 (goods in transit insurance), where it was held that a clause stating that 'The insured shall take all reasonable precautions for the protection and safeguarding of the goods and/or merchandise and use such protective appliances as may be specified in the Policy and all vehicles and protective devices shall be maintained in good order . . .' was held not to be a condition. There was nothing in the clause itself to describe it as a condition. See the judgment of Roskill J, at 236. His Lordship also held that on its true construction the clause did not impose on the insured an obligation to vet their staff with due diligence before they employed them: ibid, at 237; *HTV Ltd v Lintner* [1984] 2 Lloyd's Rep 125 (entertainment risk insurance), where a clause in the policy which stated 'The insured shall use due diligence and do and concur in doing all things reasonably practicable to avoid or diminish any loss of or damage to the property herein insured' was held not to be a condition. (See the judgment of Neill J, ibid, at 128.)

9 *London Guarantee Co v Fearnley* (1880) 5 App Cas 911 per Lord Blackburn, at 915.

10 *Re Bradley and Essex and Suffolk Accident Indemnity Society* [1912] 1 KB 415, CA per Farwell LJ, at 430, 431; *Baxendale v Harvey* (1859) 4 H & N 445 (fire insurance) per Pollock CB, at 451; *Black King Shipping Corpn and Wayang (Panama) SA v Massie, The Litsion Pride* [1985] 1 Lloyd's Rep 437 (marine insurance) at 469 (per Hirst J).

11 *Gamble v Accident Assurance Co Ltd* (1870) IR 4 CL 204; *Re Etherington and Lancashire and Yorkshire Accident Insurance Co* [1909] 1 KB 591, CA; *Re Bradley and Essex and Suffolk Accident Indemnity Society* (supra); *Thomson v Weems* (1884) 9 App Cas 671 (life insurance) per Lord Blackburn, at 682; *Cowell v Yorkshire Provident Live Assurance Co* (1901) 17 TLR 452 (life insurance); *Black King Shipping Corpn and Wayang (Panama) SA v Massie, The Litsion Pride*, supra (marine insurance), where a 'held covered' clause made no mention of a condition or condition precedent, and gave no hint whatsoever that failure to give the information as soon as practicable would result in loss of cover, and it was held that the clause should not be construed as a condition. (See the judgment of Hirst J, ibid, at 469–470.)

12 *Stoneham v Ocean Railway and General Accident Insurance Co* (1887) 19 QBD 237.

13 In *Re Bradley and Essex and Suffolk Accident Indemnity Society* [1912] 1 KB 415, CA, Farwell LJ, at 432 thought that such a provision was objectionable.

14 *London Guarantee Co v Fearnley* (supra) per Lord Watson, at 918; *Ellinger & Co v Mutual Life Insurance Co of New York* [1905] 1 KB 31, CA (life insurance) per Collins LJ, at 35.

raises, at most, a general inference of intention, which is liable to be rebutted.[15]

The stipulations which, in practice, are grouped together under such a heading, relate to all sorts of matters, some going to the root of the contract, others involving mere matters of detail;[16] they also vary in their language, some containing a provision that in case of non-fulfilment the policy is to be void,[17] others containing no such provision,[18] and some of them may, from their nature, be incapable of being construed as conditions precedent.[19] In this case, the inference is that the heading is nothing more than a general indication of the character of the stipulations which follow it, and that the several stipulations are to be judged independently as meaning what they individually say; those which are intended to be conditions precedent show themselves to be so intended either by the subject-matter to which they relate or by express words,[20] and the remaining stipulations, therefore, are not to be construed as conditions precedent.[1]

A stipulation must be construed as a whole; if part of it is[2] or is not[3] a condition precedent, the rest of it equally is or is not a condition precedent. Where several independent stipulations imposing different obligations are combined in one clause or 'condition' or the policy, the clause or condition may be treated by the Court as being severable. One or more of its stipulations may be construed as conditions precedent, whilst the others may be construed otherwise.[4]

---

15 *Re Bradley and Essex and Suffolk Accident Indemnity Society* (supra), where the majority of the Court held that a stipulation requiring a proper wages book to be kept by the assured was not a condition precedent, notwithstanding the express declaration that the due observance and fulfilment of the conditions of the policy was to be a condition precedent to any liability of the insurers.

16 *Re Coleman's Depositories Ltd and Life and Health Assurance Association* [1907] 2 KB 798, CA, per Buckley LJ, at 813.

17 As in *Re Marshall and Scottish Employers' Liability and General Insurance Co Ltd* (1901) 85 LT 757.

18 *Stoneham v Ocean Railway and General Accident Insurance Co* (1887) 19 QBD 237 per Cave J, at 241.

19 *London Guarantee Co v Fearnley* (1880) 5 App Cas 911 per Lord Blackburn, at 916; *Re Bradley and Essex and Suffolk Accident Indemnity Association* (supra) per Cozens-Hardy MR, at 241.

20 *London Guarantee Co v Fearnley* (supra) per Lord Watson, at 918; *Re Coleman's Depositories Ltd and Life and Health Assurance Association* (supra) per Buckley LJ, at 813.

1 *Stoneham v Ocean Railway and General Accident Insurance Co Ltd* (supra) per Cave J, at 241; *Re Coleman's Depositories Ltd and Life and Health Assurance Association* (supra) per Buckley LJ, at 813.

2 *Roper v Lendon* (1859) 1 E & E 825 (fire insurance), where the stipulation required particulars of loss to be delivered within fifteen days, and, it being admitted that the stipulation was a condition precedent, so far as it related to delivery of particulars, it was held that it was equally a condition precedent as regards the time within which the delivery of particulars was to be made.

3 *Re Bradley and Essex and Suffolk Accident Indemnity Society* (supra), where a stipulation providing for the adjustment of premium and for the delivery after the expiration of the policy of an account of wages paid during the period of insurance contained a provision that the assured was to keep a proper wages book, and it was held that the stipulation was one and entire and that, therefore, the provision as to keeping the wages book was not a condition precedent.

4 Thus, in *Roper v Lendon* (supra), where condition 15 of the policy contained a stipulation relating to the delivery of particulars, and also an arbitration clause, it was held that the delivery of particulars in accordance with the terms of the stipulation was a condition precedent, but that arbitration was not. In *London Guarantee Co v Fearnley* (supra), where the same condition of the policy provided that the assured was, if required, to prosecute the defaulting employee and also to assist the insurers to obtain reimbursement from the employee of any moneys which they should become liable to pay, it was held that, although the provision as to assisting the insurers to obtain reimbursement could not be a condition precedent, as it could not apply until they had become liable, the provision requiring the assured to prosecute was a condition precedent.

The mere fact that the stipulation appears on the face of the policy does not necessarily render it a condition precedent.[5] In this respect fire insurance appears to resemble life insurance and to differ from marine insurance where it has long been the rule that statements bearing on the risk introduced into the policy are to be construed as warranties.[6]

On the other hand, the stipulation is not prevented from being a condition precedent by the fact that it does not appear on the face of the policy. It may be endorsed on the policy, or may be contained in another and separate document, such as the proposal, provided that it is incorporated into the policy by express words or otherwise. The question whether such a stipulation is a condition precedent is determined in the same way as if it were contained in the policy itself.

Where a stipulation thus incorporated is inconsistent with a stipulation contained in the policy itself, the question as to which of the two is to be taken as the true condition precedent intended by the parties is a matter of construction. Prima facie, the policy, being the later document, prevails;[7] but if the stipulation contained in the policy is more disadvantageous to the assured, the maxim *verba chartarum fortius contra proferentem accipiuntur* applies, and the incorporated stipulation is taken to express the real intention of the parties.[8]

Although generally a stipulation which is expressed to be a condition precedent will be construed as one, this rule will not apply where the stipulation appears to be so capricious and unreasonable that the Court ought not to enforce it.[9] Thus, a stipulation empowering the insurers to terminate the

---

5 *Gilbert v National Insurance Co* (1848) 12 ILR 143; contra *Quin v National Insurance Co* (1839) Jo & Car 316 per Joy CB, at 340, following the marine rule.

6 *Thomson v Weems* (1884) 9 App Cas 671 (life insurance) per Lord Blackburn, at 684: 'In policies of marine insurance I think it is settled by authority that any statement of a fact bearing upon the risk introduced into the written policy is, by whatever words and in whatever place, to be construed as a warranty, and prima facie at least that the compliance with that warranty is a condition precedent to the attachment of the risk. I think that on the balance of authority the general principles of insurance law apply to all insurances, whether marine, life, or fire . . . but I do not think that this rule as to the construction of marine policies is also applicable to the construction of life policies.'

7 *Kaufmann v British Surety Insurance Co Ltd* (1929) 45 TLR 399, 33 LlL Rep 315 (accident insurance); *Izzard v Universal Insurance Co Ltd* [1937] AC 773 (accident insurance) per Lord Wright, at 780.

8 *Fowkes v Manchester and London Life Assurance Association* (1863) 8 LT 309 (life insurance); cf *Wood v Dwarris* (1856) 11 Exch 493 (life insurance), *Re Bradley and Essex and Suffolk Accident Indemnity Society* [1912] 1 KB 415, CA (employers' liability insurance). As to the contra proferentem rule, see pp 362–368, post.

9 *London Guarantee Co v Fearnley* (1880) 5 App Cas 911 (fidelity insurance) per Lord Watson, at 919; 'When the parties to a contract of insurance choose in express terms to declare that a certain condition of the policy shall be a condition precedent, that stipulation ought, in my opinion, to receive effect, unless it shall appear either to be so capricious and unreasonable that a Court of Law ought not to enforce it, or to be *sua natura* incapable of being made a condition precedent'; *Daff v Midland Colliery Owners Mutual Indemnity Co* (1913) 6 BWCC 799, HL (employers' liability insurance) per Lord Moulton, at 823; *Home Insurance Co of New York v Victoria-Montreal Fire Insurance Co* [1907] AC 59, at 64, PC; *Pictorial Machinery Ltd v Nicolls* (1940) 164 LT 248 per Humphreys J, at 250; cf *Re Bradley and Essex and Suffolk Accident Indemnity Society* [1912] 1 KB 415, CA (employers' liability insurance); but see *Gamble v Accident Assurance Co Ltd* (1869) IR 4 CL 204, per Pigot CB, at 214: 'A most unreasonable condition . . . would still be binding, if its meaning was clear. If the words were capable of two constructions, we might adopt one which was reasonable and reject one which was not. But the language . . . is clear and unambiguous, and we cannot free either of the parties from a contract which they have both

insurance at any future time on account of a past delay of the assured in payment of the premium, or a payment elsewhere than at the place specified, by reason of such payment not being made a payment in strict accordance with the policy, might well be held to be unreasonable.[10] Further, it has been doubted whether a stipulation in a fire policy for a definite period that, in case of the death of the assured during the period, the policy may be continued by the personal representatives, provided that an indorsement to that effect is made within three months after his death, can be construed as a condition.[11]

Where the stipulation is in its nature incapable of being made a condition precedent, the Court will not construe it as one. Thus, a stipulation which does not relate to time at all is not a condition precedent;[12] and a stipulation which relates to things to be done after the payment under the policy is due, such as, e g assisting the insurers to obtain reimbursement of the amount which they have paid,[13] is not a condition precedent, but a condition subsequent.[14]

The time for performance must, however, by the terms of the stipulation be necessarily postponed until after the date for payment under the policy; and the fact that no time for performance is specified does not show that the obligation must be treated as if its performance was referable to a period subsequent to such date, and could not be insisted on at an earlier period.

Even where the stipulation is, on its face, capable of being fulfilled either before or after the date of payment, the fact that the parties have expressly declared it to be a condition precedent is sufficient to limit the time for performance to the antecedent period.[15]

C WHETHER PERSONAL FULFILMENT OF THE CONDITION BY THE ASSURED IS NECESSARY

The responsibility for the fulfilment of a condition lies in the first instance on the

---

made for themselves, because we may think it was very unwise in one of the parties to engage in it.'; *Farr v Motor Traders' Mutual Insurance Society* [1920] 3 KB 669, CA per Bankes LJ, at 673: 'If the question and answer amount to a warranty, then, however absurd it may appear, the parties have made a bargain to that effect, and if the warranty is broken, the policy comes to an end.'; *Wilkinson v Car and General Insurance Corpn* (1913) 110 LT 468, CA per Lord Reading CJ, at 472.

10 *Daff v Midland Colliery Owners Mutual Indemnity Co* (1913) 6 BWCC 799, HL (employers' liability insurance) per Lord Moulton, at 823.

11 *Doe d Pitt v Laming* (1814) 4 Camp 73 (fire insurance) per Lord Ellenborough CJ, at 75. A condition requiring the assured to pay half the costs of an arbitration upon the policy is not so unreasonable and oppressive as to prevent the arbitration clause from being enforced; *Clough v County Live Stock Insurance Association Ltd* (1916) 85 LJKB 1185. A condition enabling the insurers to determine the policy at will on refunding a rateable proportion of the premium is not unreasonable, though it might be otherwise if the condition involved the avoidance of the policy ab initio or forfeiture of the premium paid: *Sun Fire Office v Hart* (1889) 14 App Cas 98, PC (fire insurance). Similarly, a condition which differentiates between military service at home and abroad and avoids the policy in the event of the assured voluntarily enlisting and serving abroad, without the consent of the insurers, is not void on the ground of public policy: *Duckworth v Scottish Widows' Fund Life Assurance Society* (1917) 33 TLR 430 (life insurance).

12 *Re Bradley and Essex and Suffolk Accident Indemnity Society* [1912] 1 KB 415, CA (employers' liability insurance), where several conditions of this kind are referred to.

13 *London Guarantee Co v Fearnley* (1880) 5 App Cas 911 (fidelity insurance) per Lord Blackburn, at 916.

14 *Barnard v Faber* [1893] 1 QB 340, CA, per Bowen LJ at 343, 344.

15 *London Guarantee Co v Fearnley* (1880) 5 App Cas 911 (fidelity insurance) per Lord Watson, at 919, 920.

assured;[16] and the condition may by reason of its subject-matter or by its express terms require him to fulfil it personally. Thus, where the policy provides for payment of a renewal premium by the assured personally, payment after his death, but during the days of grace, by his personal representatives is not sufficient.[17]

Except, however, where the condition involves or prescribes acts to be done by the assured personally, they may be done by his agent,[18] or personal representatives,[19] or trustee in bankruptcy,[20] or even, it seems, by a stranger on his behalf.[1]

Sometimes a condition requires acts to be done or left undone by third persons, in which case there is no fulfilment of the condition unless such persons do or leave undone the acts contemplated; nevertheless the assured is responsible.

D BREACH OF CONDITION

1 What constitutes a breach

In order to ascertain what constitutes a breach of a condition, it is necessary to consider not only the precise language in which the condition is framed,[2] and the circumstances to which it is intended to apply,[3] but also the act which the assured has, in fact, done or left undone.[4]

---

16 Cf *Andrews v Patriotic Assurance Co (No. 2)* (1886) 18 LRIr 355 (fire insurance) per Palles CB, at 361.

17 *Simpson v Accidental Death Insurance Co* (1857) 2 CBNS 257; *Want v Blunt* (1810) 12 East 183 (life insurance); *Pritchard v Merchants' and Tradesman's Mutual Life-Assurance Society* (1858) 3 CBNS 622 (life insurance).

18 *Patton v Employers' Liability Assurance Corpn* (1887) 20 LRIr 93; *Davies v National Fire and Marine Insurance Co of New Zealand* [1891] AC 485, PC (fire insurance), where the condition was performed by a partner on behalf of his firm.

19 *Cawley v National Employers' Accident and General Assurance Association Ltd* (1885) 1 TLR 255, where the fact that the conditions were expressed to be conditions precedent 'to the right of the assured' without mention of the personal representatives was held to be immaterial, the contract being with the assured and his personal representatives; *Verelst's Administratrix v Motor Union Insurance Co Ltd* [1925] 2 KB 137, where the condition was assumed to apply to a personal representative.

20 *Re Carr and Sun Fire Insurance Co* (1897) 13 TLR 186, CA (fire insurance), where the trustee's claim was sent in too late.

1 *Patton v Employers' Liability Assurance Corpn* (1887) 20 LRIr 93 per Murphy J, at 100; cf *Shiells v Scottish Assurance Corpn Ltd* 1889 16 R (Ct of Sess) 1014.

2 *Provincial Insurance Co Ltd v Morgan* [1933] AC 240 per Lord Wright, at 254: 'In insurance a warranty or condition . . . must be strictly though reasonably construed.'

3 *Dobson v Sotheby* (1827) Mood & M 90 (fire insurance) per Lord Tenterden CJ at 92; *Baxendale v Harvey* (1859) 4 H & N 445 per Pollock CB, at 451; *North British and Mercantile Insurance Co v London, Liverpool, and Globe Insurance Co* (1877) 5 ChD 569, CA, where a condition against double insurance was held not to apply except where the same property was the subject-matter of insurance, and the interests were the same; *Re Birkbeck Permanent Benefit Building Society, Official Receiver v Licenses Insurance Corpn* [1913] 2 Ch 34 (mortgage insurance), where a condition requiring notice of assignment was held not to require the assent of the insurers; *Norwich Union Fire Insurance Society, Ltd v South African Toilet Requisite Co Ltd* [1924] App D 212, where a condition as to the keeping of books was held to apply only to transactions with third persons, so that a failure to make entries of goods removed to a branch store was not a breach of the condition.

4 *Equitable Fire and Accident Office Ltd v Ching Wo Hong* [1907] AC 96, PC, where a condition requiring notice to be given of any additional insurance was held not to be broken by an omission to give notice of an insurance which, on its terms, never became operative; *National*

Where the condition is general in its terms, and does not enter into a precise and detailed specification of what is required, a reasonably substantial compliance with it is sufficient. The insurers cannot, therefore, rely on the fact that the performance is incomplete in the sense that the terms of the condition might have been more closely complied with, provided that the matters, as to which there has been a failure in performance, are not so material as to prevent what has been done from being reasonably considered as a performance.[5]

As regards matters with which the condition specifically deals, a literal performance is required,[6] a substantial performance only being insufficient. If, therefore, the condition goes into details, the details must be literally fulfilled,[7]

Protector Fire Insurance Co Ltd v Nivert [1913] AC 507 (fire insurance), where a similar condition was held not to be broken by the omission to communicate the substitution of other polices with different insurers for those already declared.

5 *Mason v Harvey* (1853) 8 Exch 819 (fire insurance) per Pollock CB, at 891.

6 *Roper v Lendon* (1859) 1 E & E 825 (fire insurance) per Lord Campbell CJ, at 829; *Benham v United Guarantee and Life Assurance Co* (1852) 7 Exch 744 (fidelity insurance) per Pollock CB, at 752.

7 *Worsley v Wood* (1796) 6 Term Rep 710 where a condition requiring a certificate from the Minister, church wardens and reputable inhabitants was not fulfilled by a certificate from reputable inhabitants only, even though the refusal of the Minister and church wardens to certify was unreasonable; *Haworth & Co v Sickness and Accident Assurance Association* 1891 18 R (Ct of Sess) 563, where the accounts, instead of being sent to customers direct, were sent to the traveller for collection; *Scott's Executor v Southern Life Association* (1909) 7 TH 223, where a written demand for arbitration had to be made within six months, otherwise the assured was to be deemed to have abandoned the claim, and it was held that a written demand for payment without mention of arbitration was not sufficient; *Larouche v Merchants' and Employers' Guarantee and Accident Co* (1920) QR 59 SC 376, where it was a condition that the assured should be attended by a legally qualified doctor, and it was held that the assured, who had fractured his foot, could not recover, as he had been attended by a bone-setter; *Jacobson v Yorkshire Insurance Co Ltd* (1933) 49 TLR 389 (burglary insurance), where a condition requiring the insured to keep proper books of account with a complete record of all purchases or sales was held not to be fulfilled by keeping records of purchases only; *Newcastle Fire Insurance Co v Macmorran & Co* (1815) 3 Dow 255, HL (fire insurance), followed in *Re Universal Non-Tariff Fire Insurance Co Forbes & Co's Claim* (1875) LR 19 Eq 485; *Want v Blunt* (1810) 12 East 183 (life insurance); *Jones v Provincial Insurance Co Ltd* (1929) 35 LlL Rep 135 (motor insurance), where the absence of the footbrake on the car constituted a breach of the condition to keep the vehicle in an efficient state; *National Farmers' Union Mutual Insurance Society Ltd v Dawson* [1941] 2 KB 424, 70 LlL Rep 424 (motor insurance), where the insured by driving when under the influence of alcohol was guilty of a breach of a condition providing that 'the insured shall keep every motor car insured by this policy in an efficient state of repair, and shall use all care and diligence to avoid accidents and to prevent loss and to employ only steady and sober drivers'; *Brown v Zurich General Accident and Liability Insurance Co Ltd* [1954] 2 Lloyd's Rep 243 (motor insurance), where the use of very smooth tyres on the front wheels of a van showed a lack of reasonable care to maintain the vehicle in an efficient state, and was consequently a breach of a condition in the policy imposing such a duty on the insured; *McInnes v National Motor and Accident Insurance Union Ltd* [1963] 2 Lloyd's Rep 415 (Sheriff Court of Lanark) (motor insurance), where Sheriff-Substitute Middleton held that the condition stating that the insured was to maintain the vehicle in 'efficient condition' meant that the vehicle had to be capable of doing what was normally and reasonably required of it, and directed that the outcome of the case was to await further proof of the facts alleged to constitute a breach of the condition. He did not follow the decision of Sellers J, in *Brown v Zurich General Accident and Liability Insurance Co Ltd,* (supra) that the words 'efficient condition' meant 'efficient condition for the purpose for which it was going to be used, namely to run upon the roads', for he considered that no such limitation of the meaning of the words was justified; *Bennett v Yorkshire Insurance Co Ltd* [1962] 2 Lloyd's Rep 270, QB (burglary insurance), where the insurers proved that the assured was in breach of a condition which provided that he was to keep 'a complete record of all purchases and sales'; *Vaughan Motors and Sheldon Motor Services Ltd v Scottish General Insurance Co Ltd* [1960] 1 Lloyd's Rep 479 (money in

transit policy), where the assured was found to have broken a condition requiring that a complete record of the money in transit and on the premises should be kept in some place other than the safe; *Richardson v Roylance* (1933) 47 LlL Rep 173 (cash in transit policy), where the assured, who had kept the money in a padlocked wooden box, was held to have broken a condition that the money was to be placed 'in a locked safe or strong room'; *London Crystal Window Cleaning Co Ltd v National Mutual Indemnity Insurance Co Ltd* [1952] 2 Lloyd's Rep 360 (employers' liability insurance), where the assured was held not to have broken a condition that he should 'take all reasonable precautions to prevent accidents' because, on the facts, safety belts had been supplied for the general use of the window cleaner, and he was well aware that such safety belts were available for use, though he was not wearing one at the time of the accident. Lord Goddard CJ held that the assured carried on their business in an ordinary way and in not such a manner as to invite accidents; *Garthwaite v Rowland* (1948) 81 LlL Rep 417 (Mayor's and City of London Court) (employers' liability insurance), where the assured had failed to comply with a condition of the policy requiring him to supply to the underwriters a correct account of all wages, salaries and other earnings paid to the employees during the period of insurance; *Woolfall and Rimmer Ltd v Moyle* [1942] 1 KB 66, [1941] 3 All ER 304, 71 LlL Rep 15, CA (employers' liability insurance), where it was held that the assured had complied with a condition requiring him 'to take reasonable precautions to prevent accidents, and to comply with all statutory regulations', for he had entrusted to a competent foreman the task of providing suitable and safe materials for scaffolding; *Hassett v Legal and General Assurance Society Ltd* (1939) 63 LlL Rep 278 (public liability insurance), where the assured had failed to comply with a condition stating that the insurers should be informed of any proceeding, brought against him; *Pictorial Machinery Ltd v Nicholls* (1940) 67 LlL Rep 461 (public liability insurance), where the assured was found not to have broken a condition that he should take 'all reasonable safeguards and precautions against accident' in that, although they had permitted a boy of 16 to carry 2 quart bottles of a dangerously inflammable liquid from their premises without providing any receptacle for their carriage, this was in accordance with the practice of the trade. In *Liverpool Corpn v T & H R Roberts (a firm) (Garthwaite, Third Party)* [1964] 3 All ER 56, [1965] 1 WLR 938 (motor insurance), where a condition in the policy stated that: 'The insured shall take all due and reasonable precautions to safeguard the property insured and to keep it in a good state of repair. The underwriters shall not be liable for damage or injury caused through driving the motor vehicle in an unsafe condition either before or after the accident', the Court held that the first sentence of the condition imposed on the insured a personal obligation to take due and reasonable precautions, but that if the insurers had proved only a casual negligence or failure on the part of an employee to carry out his duty, there would not by reason of that alone be any breach of the obligation on the part of the insured under the first sentence of the condition. But, on the facts, the insured had failed to take due and reasonable precautions to keep the vehicle in a good state of repair, and therefore were in breach of the obligation imposed by the first sentence. It was also held in this case that the second sentence did not impose a separate and absolute obligation independent of the obligation in the first sentence of the condition. The words of the second sentence were preceded by the first sentence, and the second sentence expressed the consequences in terms of contractual liability of a failure on the part of the insured to exercise the duty imposed by the first sentence; *Dickinson v Del Solar* [1930] 1 KB 376, 34 LlL Rep 445 (motor insurance), where it was held that a member of the Peruvian Legation who was involved in an accident, and acting on the instructions of the Peruvian Minister had not pleaded diplomatic privilege, had not broken a condition of the policy requiring him not in any way to act to the detriment or prejudice of the insurance company's interests; *Rendlesham v Dunne (Pennine Insurance Co Ltd Third Party)* [1954] 1 Lloyd's Rep 192 (motor insurance) (Westminster County Court), where it was held that the driving of a car by a learner driver unaccompanied by a holder of a full driving licence did not constitute a breach of a condition requiring the assured to safeguard the insured vehicle from loss and damage. Judge Herbert considered that the clause in the policy was concerned with the physical condition of the car and did not apply to damage to the car caused, e g by the negligent driving of the assured or driving by someone in contravention of the terms of the driving licence issued to a learner driver; *Conn v Westminster Motor Insurance Association Ltd* [1966] 1 Lloyd's Rep 407, CA (motor insurance), where it was held that the insured had broken a condition relating to a taxi-cab requiring him to take all reasonable steps to maintain it in efficient condition, for its two front tyres were in a deplorable state. (For the evidence on this point, see ibid, 411–415.) But it was also held that he had not broken the above condition in so far as it related to the brakes, for the insurers had not shown that he had failed to take all reasonable steps to maintain them in an efficient condition. For the evidence on this point, see ibid, 409–411, 414; *Allan Peters (Jewellers) Ltd v Brocks Alarms Ltd* [1968] 1 Lloyd's Rep 387 at 394 (burglary insurance), where it was held (obiter) that the insured were not in breach by their own actions of a condition concerning the setting of a burglar

and it is no defence for the assured to assert that such details are immaterial.[8]

Thus, in *Roberts v Eagle Star Insurance Co Ltd*:[9]

A burglary policy made it a condition precedent to the insurance company's liability that a

---

alarm; *Farrell v Federated Employers' Insurance Association Ltd* [1970] 3 All ER 632, 2 Lloyd's-Rep 170, CA, where it was held that there had been a breach of a condition which stated: 'Every writ served on the employer shall be notified or forwarded to the [insurers] immediately on receipt'; *Terry v Trafalgar Insurance Co Ltd* [1970] 1 Lloyd's Rep 524, Mayor's and City of London Court (motor insurance), where it was held that the insured had broken a condition which stated: 'No liability shall be admitted or legal expenses be incurred, nor any offer promise or payment made to third parties without the company's written consent.' (See the judgment of Judge Graham Rogers, ibid, at 526–527); *Monksfield v Vehicle and General Insurance Co Ltd* [1971] 1 Lloyd's Rep 139, Mayor's and City of London Court (motor insurance), where the insured had broken a condition that written notice should be given to the insurers as soon as possible after the occurrence of any accident; *Marzouca v Atlantic and British Commercial Insurance Co Ltd* [1971] 1 Lloyd's Rep 449, PC (fire insurance), where there was a condition that the insurance would cease to attach if the building insured became 'unoccupied and so remain for a period of more than 30 days', and it was held that the condition was broken for there was no one in the building for a period of 51 days; *New India Assurance Co Ltd v Chow alias Chong* [1972] 1 Lloyd's Rep 479, PC (motor insurance), where the insured was held to have broken a condition stating that he was to mantain a lorry 'in an efficient condition'; *Farnham v Royal Insurance Co Ltd* [1976] 2 Lloyd's Rep 437 (fire insurance), where the insured was held to have broken a condition concerning the alteration of the risk; *Global Tankers Inc v Amercoat Europa NV and Rust, The Diane* [1977] 1 Lloyd's Rep 61 (guarantee insurance), where a condition as to the application of anti-corrosive painting to a vessel's tanks had not been broken; *Victor Melik & Co Ltd v Norwich Union Fire Insurance Society Ltd and Kemp* [1980] 1 Lloyd's Rep 523 (burglary insurance), where the insured were held not to have broken a condition that the burglar alarm was to be 'kept in efficient working order' and 'kept in full operation at all times when the premises are unattended'; *Cox v Orion Insurance Co Ltd* [1982] RTR 1 (motor insurance), where the insured was held to have breached a condition requiring him to give the insurers notice of an accident; *Mint Security Ltd v Blair* [1982] 1 Lloyd's Rep 188 (cash in transit insurance), where the insured were held to have broken a condition that equipment and personnel and procedures as described in the proposal form should not be varied by the insured to the insurers' detriment without their knowledge and approval; *Berliner Motor Corpn and Steiers Lawn and Sports Inc v Sun Alliance and London Insurance Ltd* [1983] 1 Lloyd's Rep 320 (products and public liability insurance), where the insured was held to be in breach of giving notice of a claim by a third party; *Exchange Theatre Ltd v Iron Trades Mutual Insurance Co Ltd* [1984] 1 Lloyd's Rep 149, CA (fire insurance), where it was held that the insured had not broken a condition as to the alteration of a building whereby the risk of destructional damage is increased merely by bringing into it a petrol generator and a quantity of petrol (see the judgment of Eveleigh LJ, ibid, at 153); *Linden Alimak Ltd v British Engine Insurance Ltd* [1984] 1 Lloyd's Rep 416 (extraneous damage insurance), where the insured were held to have broken a condition concerning the increase of the risk to a gantry crane (see the judgment of Webster J, ibid, at 423); *Pioneer Concrete (UK) Ltd v National Employers Mutual General Insurance Association Ltd* [1985] 2 All ER 395, [1985] 1 Lloyd's Rep 274 (public liability insurance), where the insured were in breach of a condition regarding the giving of notice of a claim (see the judgment of Bingham J, ibid, at 279); *Insurance Co of Africa v Scor (UK) Reinsurance Co Ltd* [1985] 1 Lloyd's Rep 312, CA (reinsurance), where the reassured's failure to co-operate with the reinsurers was held not to be a breach of a condition; *Aluminium Wire and Cable Co Ltd v Allstate Insurance Co Ltd* [1985] 2 Lloyd's Rep 280 (public liability insurance), where the insured was held not to have broken a condition requiring him to exercise reasonable care to prevent accidents; *Port-Rose v Phoenix Assurance Co plc* [1986] NLJ Rep 333 (all risk insurance), where leaving a bag containing jewellery valued at £29,000 momentarily unattended was held not to be a breach of a condition of the policy.

8 *Benham v United Guarantee and Life Assurance Co* (1852) 7 Exch 744, per Pollock CB at 752; *Blackhurst v Cockell* (1789) 3 Term Rep 360 (marine insurance) per Buller J, at 361; *Yorkshire Insurance Co Ltd v Campbell* [1917] AC 218 at 224, PC (marine insurance); *Re Universal Non-Tariff Fire Insurance Co Forbes & Co's Claim* (supra) per Malins V-C, at 494; *Bancroft v Heath* (1901) 6 Com Cas 137, CA (fire insurance); *Thomson v Weems* (1884) 9 App Cas 671 (life insurance) per Lord Blackburn, at 583; *Pearson v Commercial Union Assurance Co* (1876) 1 App Cas 498; *Condogianis v Guardian Assurance Co* [1921] 2 AC 125 at 129, PC (fire insurance); *Dawsons Ltd v Bonnin* [1922] 2 AC 413, 12 LlL Rep 237 (motor insurance).

9 [1960] 1 Lloyd's Rep 615.

burglar alarm 'shall be put into full and proper operation whenever the premises are closed for business or left unattended'. The premises were broken into, and some furs were stolen. In an action on the policy,

Held, the assured could not recover because he had not put the alarm into operation before he left the premises.

Again, in *Princette Models Ltd v Reliance, Fire and Accident Corpn Ltd*:[10]

Some ladies' dresses were insured under a 'goods in transit' policy, which provided that the insurance company would not be liable should they be stolen from an unattended motor vehicle 'unless all doors and windows were left closed, securely locked and properly fastened'. The dresses were stolen from an unlocked vehicle.

Held, the insurance company was not liable.

Nor can he claim that part only of the condition is essential, and that the rest of it may be rejected, since the condition must be taken as a whole.[11] The condition is, however, performed when all that the condition actually requires has, in fact, been done.[12] The assured cannot be called upon to do more, and it is not open to the insurers to allege that a literal performance is not sufficient for their purpose, since they could have made the condition more stringent in its terms.[13]

On the other hand, the assured cannot substitute other terms and conditions in lieu of those which the parties to the contract have originally made.[14]

---

10 [1960] 1 Lloyd's Rep 49.

11 *Worsley v Wood* (1796) 6 Term Rep 710 (fire insurance), where the condition required a certificate of the loss from the Minister and church wardens and some reputable householders of the parish, and the assured put forward a certificate signed by four reputable householders, but not by the Minister or the church wardens; *Roper v Lendon* (1859) 1 E & E 825 (fire insurance), where it was held that time was of the essence of the condition.

12 *Fidelity and Casualty Co of New York v Mitchell* [1917] AC 592, PC, where it was held that a warranty as to soundness of health was sufficiently complied with if the assured would have been passed as sound by a doctor, though there might be a disease latent in his system; *Shiells v Scottish Assurance Corpn* 1889 16 R (Ct of Sess) 1014 (accident insurance), where a condition providing for a notice to be sent to the company's office was held to be performed by the giving of notice to an agent, who immediately transmitted it to the office, although the condition further provided that notice to an agent should not be a sufficient compliance with the condition; *Whitehead v Price* (1835) 2 Cr M & R 447 (fire insurance).

13 *Smith v Dominion of Canada Accident Insurance Co* (1902) 36 NBR 300, where the assured warranted that no previous policy had been cancelled, and it was held that the determination of a previous policy by consent was a surrender, and not a cancellation within the meaning of the warranty; *Ward v Law Property Assurance and Trust Society* (1856) 4 WR 605, where a condition requiring notice of any liability being incurred under the policy was held to refer to criminal misconduct whereby it was clear that liability was incurred, and did not require the assured to give notice before he had ascertained that the facts discovered gave rise to a claim under the policy; *Byrne v Muzio* (1881) 8 LRIr 396, where the condition was held not to require notice of acts of dishonesty prior to the policy; *Re Birkbeck Permanent Benefit Building Society, Official Receiver v Licenses Insurance Corporation,* [1913] 2 Ch 34, where a condition requiring a notification of assignment of the policy was held not to require the insurers' consent; *Hide v Bruce* (1783) 3 Doug KB 213 (marine insurance), where a warranty that a ship had 20 guns was held not to require her to carry sufficient men to work them; *Blackhurst v Cockell* (1789) 3 Term Rep 360 (marine insurance), where a warranty that a ship was safe on a particular day was held to be fulfilled if the ship was safe at any time of that day, and the assured recovered, notwithstanding that the ship was lost at 8 am on that day (see now on this point, Marine Insurance Act 1906, s 38, and Ivamy, *Marine Insurance* (4th Edn 1985), p 285); *National Protector Fire Insurance Co Ltd v Nivert* [1913] AC 507, PC (fire insurance), where it was held, under a condition relating to double insurance, to be sufficient for the assured to disclose the amount of the other insurance, without naming the other insurers.

14 *Worsley v Wood* (1796) 6 Term Rep 710 (fire insurance) per Lord Kenyon CJ, at 719; cf *Want v Blunt* (1810) 12 East 183 (life insurance) per Lord Ellenborough CJ, at 187.

The cause of the breach of condition is immaterial. The breach may be deliberately committed by the assured,[15] or it may be due to his negligence,[16] inadvertence,[17] or error of judgment,[18] or even to his ignorance of the facts bringing the condition into operation.[19] It makes no difference whether he was honest or guilty of fraud.[20]

There is equally a breach where the failure to fulfil the condition is due to circumstances beyond the assured's control, as, for instance, where a third person declines to do an act required by the condition;[1] for the fact that in the events that happen fulfilment of the condition is rendered impossible does not excuse its non-fulfilment.[2] Where, however, the condition is impossible of fulfilment ab initio, it is a nullity, and the failure to fulfil it has no effect upon the validity of the policy.[3] Thus, where a condition in a personal accident policy required a report to be furnished by the assured's medical attendant, the failure to furnish a report might not be fatal if he had no medical attendant.[4]

There is no breach of the condition where he does not know and has had no opportunity of knowing of the existence of the condition at the time when it ought to have been fulfilled.[5] Thus, a condition in an employer's liability insurance policy prescribing the time within which notice of the accident is to be given to the insurers is not broken by the assured's failure to give the notice within the prescribed time, if at the time of the accident the policy was still in the possession of the insurers, since the condition does not bind him.[6]

The onus of proving his knowledge or opportunity of knowledge, as the case may be, lies on the insurers.

A mere intention to commit a breach of condition does not of itself constitute a breach.[7]

---

15 *Borradaile v Hunter* (1843) 5 Man & G 639 (life insurance), followed in *Clift v Schwabe* (1846) 3 CB 437 (life insurance).

16 *Gamble v Accident Assurance Co* (1869) IR 4 CL 204 (accident insurance).

17 *Re Williams and Lancashire etc Accident Insurance Co's Arbitration* (1902) 19 TLR 82.

18 *Lindenau v Desborough* (1828) 8 B & C 586 (life insurance) per Bayley J, at 592; *Joel v Law Union and Crown Insurance Co* [1908] 2 KB 863, CA (life insurance) per Moulton LJ, at 883.

19 *Cassel v Lancashire and Yorkshire Accident Insurance Co Ltd* (1885) 1 TLR 495 (accident insurance), where the assured was not aware that he had sustained an injury until long after the time fixed in the policy for giving notice; *Rhodes v Union Insurance Co* (1883) 2 NZLR 106, where the assured failed to give notice of the loss of the licence of the insured hotel through ignorance of the fact.

20 *Thomson v Weems* (1884) 9 App Cas 671 (life insurance) per Lord Blackburn, at 683.

1 *Worsley v Wood* (1796) 6 Term Rep 710 (fire insurance); *Oldman v Bewicke* (1786) 2 HyBl 577n (fire insurance).

2 *Gamble v Accident Assurance Co* (supra), distinguishing *Taylor v Caldwell* (1863) 3 B & S 826 (contract).

3 *Worsley v Wood* (supra) per Lord Kenyon CJ, at 718.

4 *Patton v Employers' Liability Assurance Corpn* (1887) 20 LRIr 93 (accident insurance) per Harrison J, at 99.

5 *Re Coleman's Depositories Ltd and Life and Health Assurance Association* [1907] 2 KB 798, CA (employers' liability insurance), where the policy was still in the hands of the insurers; *Canadian Casualty and Boiler Insurance Co v Hawthorne & Co* (1907) 39 Can SCR 558; *Pattison v Mills* (1828) 1 Dow & Cl 342, HL (fire insurance).

6 *Re Coleman's Depositories Ltd and Life and Health Assurance Association* (supra), where the cover note issued had no conditions.

7 *Simpson SS Co Ltd v Premier Underwriting Association Ltd* (1905) 10 Com Cas 198 (marine insurance) per Bigham J, at 201.

2 Burden of proving a breach

The burden of proving that a condition has been broken rests on the insurers.[8]

The words of the policy, however, may change the burden of proof and make it the duty of the insured to prove that he has not broken a condition. But in order for them to have this effect the words must be clear.

In *Bond Air Services Ltd v Hill*:[9]

> A Lloyd's aircraft policy contained a condition stating, 'The insured and all persons in his employment . . . shall duly observe the statutory orders, regulations and directions relating to air navigation for the time being in force'. Another clause stated that the observance and performance by the insured of the conditions of the policy were of the essence of the contract and were conditions precedent to his right to recover. The insurance company denied liability for the loss of the aircraft, claiming that the burden of proving that the condition had been complied with lay on the insured.
> *Held,* that the burden of proving that there was a breach of condition still lay on the insurance company.

Lord Goddard CJ said:[10]

> 'But I cannot find that [some earlier][11] cases have ever been regarded, either in any judgment or in the opinion of eminent text writers as throwing doubt on what I think is axiomatic in insurance law, that, as it is always for an insurer to prove an exception, so it is for him to prove the breach of a condition which would relieve him from liability in respect of a particular loss. The [insurance company's] contention no doubt is that, by providing that the observance of conditions is to be a condition precedent to his liability to pay, the policy has shifted the onus on to the [insured]. I do not doubt that the parties to a policy can use words which would relieve insurers of the onus and cast it on the assured, as they might with regard to any other matter affecting an insurer's liability . . . but, in my opinion much clearer words than are used here would be necessary to change what I think, certainly for a century and probably for much longer, has always been regarded as a fundamental principle of insurance law, that it is for the insurers who wish to rely on a breach of condition to prove it.'

3 The effect of a breach

A breach of condition affects the rights not only of the assured, but also, in the absence of an express condition to the contrary,[12] of his personal representative,[13] trustee in bankruptcy,[14] or assignee[15] or any other person claiming through the assured.[16]

---

8 *Barrett v Jermy* (1849) 3 Exch 535 per Parke B, at 542; *Farnham v Royal Insurance Co Ltd* [1976] 2 Lloyd's Rep 437 (fire insurance) at 441 (per Ackner J).

9 [1955] 2 QB 417.

10 Ibid, at 427.

11 *Geach v Ingall* (1845) 14 M & W 95: *Ashby v Bates* (1846) 15 M & W 589.

12 *Jackson v Forster* (1859) 1 E & E 470 (life insurance). Such a condition, as a rule, operates in favour of assignees for value only; see pp 451–452, post. It applies only to subsequent acts, except in the case of an assignment amounting to a new contract between the insurers and the assignee; see p 452, post. It does not prevent the policy being vitiated by the prior act of the assured: *Small v United Kingdom Marine Mutual Insurance Association* [1897] 2 QB 311, CA (marine insurance) per Smith LJ, at 315; *Scottish Amicable Life Assurance Society v Fuller* (1867) Ir 2 Eq 53 (life insurance); *Omnium Securities Co v Canada Fire Mutual Insurance Co* (1882) 1 OR 494, followed in *Liverpool and London and Globe Insurance Co v Agricultural Savings and Loan Co* (1902) 33 SCR 94.

13 *Cawley v National Employers' Accident and General Assurance Association Ltd* (1885) 1 TLR 255.

14 *Jackson v Foster* (supra) (life insurance); *M'Entire v Sun Fire Office* (1895) 29 ILT 103 (fire insurance); *Re Carr and Sun Fire Insurance Co* (1897) 13 TLR 186, CA (fire insurance).

15 *Scottish Amicable Life Assurance Society v Fuller* (supra) (life insurance); *Scottish Equitable Life Assurance Society v Buist* 1877 4 R (Ct of Sess) 1076 (life insurance).

16 A person, such as a mortgagee of the subject-matter, who does not claim through him, is not

The insurers can rely on a breach of condition even though the breach has not prejudiced them.[17]

(a) The usual effect

The precise effect of the breach depends, however, on the nature of the condition broken, for it will vary according as to whether the condition is one precedent to the validity of the policy or whether it is a condition subsequent or whether it is a condition precedent only to the liability of the insurers.

i Condition precedent to the validity of the policy

A condition precedent to the validity of the policy must be performed before the policy can become operative.[18] If, therefore, a loss happens before it is performed, it is immaterial whether the loss is occasioned by the failure to perform it or not. The assured cannot recover on the policy, even in respect of property covered thereby to which the condition does not relate, or as to which it is not broken.[19] In the absence of fraud, however, he is entitled to the return of any premiums which he may have paid as on a failure of consideration.[20]

ii Condition subsequent of the policy

The breach of a condition subsequent avoids the policy from the date of the breach.[1] The assured cannot, therefore, recover in respect of any loss happening afterwards,[2] even though the loss is in no way caused or affected by the breach.[3] If, however, the loss takes place before the breach, he is not precluded from recovering in respect of it, since the policy, at the time of the loss, was still operative.[4]

iii Condition precedent to the liability of the insurers

The breach of a stipulation which is a condition precedent only to the

---

affected: *Samuel (P) & Co Ltd v Dumas* [1924] AC 431 (marine insurance); cf *Graham Joint Stock Shipping Co Ltd v Merchants' Marine Insurance* [1924] AC 294, 17 LlL Rep 44, 241 (marine insurance), where the mortgagee had no independent title.

17 *Pioneer Concrete (UK) Ltd v National Employers Mutual General Insurance Association Ltd* [1985] 2 All ER 395, [1985] 1 Lloyd's Rep 274 (public liability insurance), where there was a breach concerning the giving of notice of a claim. (See the judgment of Bingham J, ibid, at 279.) As to giving notice of a claim, see pp 395–401.

18 *Newcastle Fire Insurance Co v Macmorran & Co* (1815) 3 Dow 255, HL, per Lord Eldon LC, at 259.

19 *Hibbert v Pym* (1783) 2 Park 696 (marine insurance); *Sacks v Western Assurance Co* [1907] 5 TH 257, where the condition provided that the assured should keep his books in a fire-proof safe at night, and it was held that, though the condition related only to stock, nothing could be recovered in respect of fixtures: *Silverstone v North British and Mercantile Insurance Co* [1903] ORC 73, where there was a similar condition.

20 *Britton v Royal Insurance Co* (1866) 4 F & F 905, per Willes J, at 909.

1 Sometimes on the true construction of the condition the policy is only suspended on breach and re-attaches if and when the breach is remedied. See pp 304–305, post. Cf *Provincial Insurance Co Ltd v Morgan* [1933] AC 240 (accident insurance).

2 *Glen v Lewis* (1853) 8 Exch 607.

3 *Garrett v Provincial Insurance Co* (1860) 20 UCR 200, where there was a condition that 12 pailfuls of water should be kept in each flat of the building.

4 *Sun Fire Office v Hart* (1889) 14 App Cas 98, PC (fire insurance); *Daff v Midland Colliery Owners' Mutual Indemnity Co* (1913) 6 BWCC 799, HL (employers' liability insurance); *Hare v Travis* (1827) 7 B & C 14 (marine insurance); *Kewley v Ryan* (1794) 2 HyBl 343 (marine insurance); *Baines v Holland* (1855) 10 Exch 802 (marine insurance); cf *Pim v Reid* (1843) 6 Man & G 1 (fire insurance) per Maule J, at 13.

liability of the insurers, does not affect the validity of the policy, but prevents the assured, in case of loss, from recovering anything under the policy, unless and until, where it is still possible, the condition is performed.[5] In such a case, therefore, he is not entitled to any return of premium.[6]

A breach does not, however, affect the validity of the policy, but only precludes the assured from recovering for the loss in respect of which the breach is committed; he is not precluded from recovering for a subsequent loss during the currency of the policy, provided that on the second occasion the condition is fulfilled.[7]

(b) Where a particular penalty is provided

Where the insurers have stipulated for a particular penalty for breach of a stipulation, e g an increased premium, they are limited to that penalty and cannot avoid the policy.[8]

4 Waiver of breach of condition

(1) Waiver by the insurers: What constitutes a waiver

The insurers may, if they think fit, elect[9] to waive the breach of any condition, and thus affirm the policy. If they so elect, the policy is treated as in force in the same way as if the condition had been performed.[10] There is, however, no waiver, unless the insurers are fully acquainted with the facts relating to the breach.[11]

---

5 *Gamble v Accident Assurance Co Ltd* (1869) IR 4 CL 204, followed in *Patton v Employers' Liability Assurance Corpn* (1887) 20 LRIr 93; *Cawley v National Employers' Accident and General Assurance Association Ltd* (1885) 1 TLR 255; *Cassel v Lancashire and Yorkshire Accident Insurance Co* (1885) 1 TLR 495; *Stoneham v Ocean Railway and General Accident Insurance Co* (1887) 19 QBD 237 per Cave J, at 241; *British General Insurance Co v Mountain* [1920] WC & Ins Rep 254, HL; *Re Williams and Lancashire and Yorkshire Accident Insurance Co's Arbitration* (1902) 19 TLR 82; *Worsley v Wood* (1796) 6 Term Rep 710 (fire insurance), followed in *Mason v Harvey* (1853) 8 Exch 819 (fire insurance); *Oldman v Bewicke* (1796) 2 HyBl 577n (fire insurance); *Roper v Lendon* (1859) 1 E & E 825 (fire insurance), followed in *Elliott v Royal Exchange Assurance Co* (1867) LR 2 Exch 237 (fire insurance); *Re Carr and Sun Fire Insurance Co* (1897) 13 TLR 186, CA (fire insurance).

6 See pp 202–203, ante.

7 *Hood's Trustees v Southern Union General Insurance Co of Australasia* [1928] Ch 793, CA per Tomlin J, at 806; *Reid & Co v Employers' Accident and Live Stock Insurance Co* 1899 1 F (Ct of Sess) 1031, where Lord Trayner was of the opinion that, in the absence of an express condition, a fraudulent claim did not avoid the policy, but only avoided the claim, leaving the policy as a current obligation untouched.

8 *London Loan and Savings Co of Canada v Union Insurance Co of Canton Ltd* (1925) 56 OLR 590.

9 The election may take place after loss: *Canada Landed Credit Co v Canada Agricultural Insurance Co* (1870) 17 GR 418.

10 *Holland v Russell* (1863) 4 B & S 14, ExCh (marine insurance); *Towle v National Guardian Insurance Society* (1861) 30 LJCh 900 per Knight Bruce LJ, at 911; *Morrison v Universal Marine Insurance Co* (1873) LR 8 Exch 197, ExCh (marine insurance), where, on the facts, there was no election; cf *Hemmings v Sceptre Life Association Ltd* [1905] 1 Ch 365 (life insurance); *Barrett v Jermy* (1849) 3 Exch 535 (fire insurance).

11 *M'Entire v Sun Fire Office* (1895) 29 ILT 103; *McCormick v National Motor and Accident Insurance Union Ltd* (1934) 49 LlL Rep 361, CA (accident insurance) per Scrutton LJ, at 365: 'The duty to take action (avoid the contract) does not arise (1) unless you know all the facts—being put on inquiry is not sufficient: you must know the facts—and (2) unless you have a reasonable time to make up your mind. You are not bound the moment the statement is made to you to make up your mind at once; you are entitled to a reasonable time to consider—to a reasonable time to

The insurers may also dispense the assured from the necessity of performing a condition, or may be estopped by their conduct from insisting upon its performance, and in these cases a failure to perform the condition may be disregarded.

(a) Waiver of breach already committed

It is not necessary that a waiver of a breach of condition should be in writing, unless there is an express condition to that effect. A parol waiver by the insurers, or by their agent, acting within the scope of his authority,[12] is sufficient.

There may also be a waiver by conduct;[13] if the insurers do an act which can be justified only on the footing that the policy is in force, they are precluded from contending that the policy is avoided by the breach of condition.[14] There must be some positive act done by them which is inconsistent with the avoidance of the policy.[15]

They are equally precluded from relying on the breach where their conduct misleads the assured and induces him to alter his position in the belief that the

---

make inquiries'; *Locker and Woolf Ltd v Western Australian Insurance Co Ltd* [1936] 1 KB 408, 54 LlL Rep 211, CA, where taking possession of salvage in ignorance of a breach was not an election to waive; *Victor Melik & Co Ltd v Norwich Union Fire Insurance Society Ltd and Kemp* [1980] 1 Lloyd's Rep 523 (burglary insurance) per Woolf J, at 534: 'That really means that what happened here was at best the giving of information to the insurers of a limited nature. There was not full knowledge, and what is more, there was no positive act by the insurers but mere inactivity and mere inactivity in these circumstances is insufficient to amount to a waiver.'; *Phillips v Grand River Farmers' Mutual Fire Insurance Co* (1881) 46 UCR 334, where a resolution of the directors of the company to pay the loss, followed by an assessment to meet it, in ignorance of a breach of condition, was held not to constitute a waiver. Nor is there a waiver when the premium is received in ignorance of the true facts: *Busteed v West of England Fire and Life Insurance Co* (1857) 5 IChR 553 (life insurance).

12 See pp 298–299, post.

13 But a condition may expressly provide that the conduct of the insurers, e g in taking steps to appraise the loss, is not to be taken as a waiver.

14 *Yorkshire Insurance Co Ltd v Craine* [1922] 2 AC 541, 11 LlL Rep 1, PC, where the insurers after receiving an imperfect claim took possession of the assured's premises under a condition of the policies; *Globe Savings and Loan Co v Employers' Liability Assurance Corpn* (1900) 13 Man R 531, where the employers notified the insurers of the loss, but failed to give the formal notice prescribed by the condition, and the insurers took steps themselves to investigate the fact; *Jones v Bangor Mutual Shipping Insurance Society Ltd* (1889) 61 LT 727 (marine insurance), where a policy was issued with knowledge that a condition against double insurance had been broken; *Allan Peters (Jewellers) Ltd v Brocks Alarms Ltd* [1968] 1 Lloyd's Rep 387 at 394 (burglary insurance), where it was held (obiter) that the failure of the insurers' surveyor to notice that the window grille at the insured premises had not been electrically connected did not constitute a waiver by the insurers of the breach of the condition concerned; *Farrell v Federated Employers Insurance Association Ltd* [1970] 2 Lloyd's Rep 170, CA (employers' liability insurance), where the insurers were held not to have waived a breach of a condition stating: 'Every writ served on the [insured] shall be notified or forwarded to the [insurers] immediately' (see the judgment of Lord Denning MR, ibid, at 171); *Hadenfayre Ltd v British National Insurance Society Ltd* [1984] 2 Lloyd's Rep 393 (contingency insurance), where the insurers were held to have waived an implied condition concerning an alteration of the risk. (See the judgment of Lloyd J, ibid, at 401.)

15 *Armstrong v Turquand* (1858) 9 ICLR 32 (life insurance); *Hemmings v Sceptre Life Association Ltd* [1905] 1 Ch 365 (life insurance). The mere sending of a claim form to be filled in is not sufficient: *James v Royal Insurance Co* (1907) 10 NZ Gaz LR 244 (fire insurance). But a demand for a post-mortem, which is assented to by the assured's widow, necessarily implies that the policy is in force, since, if there was no policy, the insurers would have no right to demand it: *Donnison v Employers' Accident and Live Stock Insurance Co* 1897 24 R (Ct of Sess) 681.

policy is valid.[16] Thus, the acceptance of the premium[17] or the proceeding to arbitration on the footing that the policy is valid,[18] with actual knowledge of the breach, is a waiver.

On the other hand, conduct which does not mislead the assured does not constitute a waiver.[19] An intention to waive cannot be inferred from mere silence,[20] or even from equivocal acts on the part of the insurers which are unknown to the assured.[1] Thus, a failure to give notice that a renewal premium has not been paid does not preclude the insurers from relying on its non-payment.[2] Similarly, the failure to raise a particular ground of objection is not in itself a waiver,[3] though the taking of objection on other grounds may be a waiver of the ground of objection which is not specifically raised.[4]

When the insurers discover that there has been a breach of a condition entitling them to avoid liability under the policy, they can elect to refuse to pay the sum insured or to accept liability or to delay their decision. Mere lapse of time does not lose them their right ultimately to decide to refuse to indemnify. The lapse of time only operates against them if thereby there is prejudice to the insured or if in some way rights of third parties intervene or if the delay is so long that the Court feels that the delay in itself is of such a length as to be evidence that they have in truth decided to accept liability.[5]

Thus, in *Allen v Robles (Compagnie Parisienne de Garantie, Third Party)*:[6]

---

16 *Whyte v Western Assurance Co* (1876) 22 LCJ 215, PC; *Morrison v Universal Marine Insurance Co* (1873) LR 8 Exch 197, ExCh (marine insurance) per Honyman J, at 205.

17 *Wing v Harvey* (1854) 5 De GM & G 265 (life insurance), where the assured had gone abroad in breach of a condition; *Armstrong v Turquand* (supra); *Hemmings v Sceptre Life Association* (supra), where the assured's age was mis-stated; *Ayrey v British Legal and United Provident Assurance Co* [1918] 1 KB 136 (life insurance); *Beasant v Northern Life Assurance Co* [1923] 1 WWR 362 (life insurance), where a condition requiring notice and extra premium if the assured joined the militia was waived by receipt of three years' ordinary premium with knowledge of his enlistment; cf *Handler v Mutual Reserve Fund Association* (1904) 90 LT 192, CA (life insurance), where the premium was accepted on certain conditions.

18 *Lampkin v Ontario Marine and Fire Insurance Co* (1855) 12 UCR 578 (fire insurance); *Canadian Mutual Fire Insurance Co v Donovan* (1878) 2 Stephen's Quebec Digest 406 (fire insurance).

19 *Morrison v Universal Marine Insurance Co* (supra), where the issue of the policy was a mere formality, the contract being complete on the initialling of the 'slip', and the assured did not contend that he was misled; *Equitable Fire and Accident Office Ltd v Ching Wo Hong* [1907] AC 96, PC (fire insurance); *Handler v Mutual Reserve Fund Association* (supra); cf *Sun Fire Office v Hart* (1889) 14 App Cas 98 at 102, PC (fire insurance).

20 *Whyte v Western Assurance Co* (supra).

1 *Acey v Fernie* (1840) 7 M & W 151 (life insurance), where debit of the premium to the agent in the books of the company, an act unknown to the assured, did not waive a breach of the condition for payment of premium on the due date, followed in *Busteed v West of England Insurance Co* (1857) 5 IChR 553 (life insurance); *Manufacturers' Life Insurance Co v Gordon* (1893) 20 OAR 309 (life insurance), where the policy continued to be carried on the books of the insurers as an existing policy, and was included in the official returns.

2 *Simpson v Accidental Death Insurance Co* (1857) 2 CBNS 257 per Cresswell J, at 293; *Windus v Lord Tredegar* (1866) 15 LT 108, HL (life insurance). Even a demand for the premium is not sufficient: *Edge v Duke* (1849) 18 LJCh 183 (life insurance).

3 *Whyte v Western Assurance Co* (supra).

4 *Fowlie v Ocean Accident and Guarantee Corpn* (1902) 33 SCR 253, where reliance upon an exception, coupled with lapse of time, amounted to a waiver of full proof of loss; cf *Accident Insurance Co of North America v Young* (1891) 20 SCR 280, where a refusal to pay on the ground that death was due to disease did not amount to a waiver of notice within the specified time.

5 *Allen v Robles (Compagnie Parisienne de Garantie, Third Party)* [1969] 2 Lloyd's Rep 61, CA (motor insurance) per Fenton Atkinson LJ, at 64.

6 [1969] 2 Lloyd's Rep 61, CA.

By a condition in a motor insurance policy the insured was required to advise the insurers 'immediately he has knowledge of a claim and at the latest within 5 days . . .' On April 9, 1967 he drove his car in such a dangerous manner that he collided with a house belonging to a third party, and caused him personal injuries. In July 1967 he informed the insurers that a claim had been made against him by the third party. On November 29, 1967 the insurers informed the third party that they would only pay for his personal injuries and loss of earnings. The third party obtained a judgment for £1,131 against the insured in respect of the damage to the house. The insured now claimed that the delay until November 29, 1967 was unreasonable and that the insurers had lost their right to repudiate liability on the policy.
Held, that the insurers had not lost the right to repudiate, for the insured had not been prejudiced nor was the delay of such a length as to be evidence that they had accepted liability.

(b) Waiver of future performance of condition

Where the insurers seek to avoid the policy or to resist liability on the ground that the assured has failed to comply with a condition of the policy, the assured will, nevertheless, be entitled to recover, if he is able to show that he has previously been dispensed by the insurers from the obligation of performing the condition in question, and that, in the circumstances, no breach of it has, therefore, been committed.[7]

For this purpose he must prove that he was, in fact, dispensed by the insurers from performance,[8] or that the insurers are estopped from asserting that the condition continues to be in force. The waiver or estoppel must relate to the particular policy or claim.[9]

Where the policy contains a condition relating to waiver, an express waiver of fulfilment should be in accordance with the terms.[10] Any such condition may, however, be waived by conduct.[11]

Even where there is no express waiver, there may be a waiver by conduct where the insurers have rendered the fulfilment of the condition impossible, e g where, in an insurance upon a horse, a condition required the death of the horse to be duly certified by a qualified veterinary surgeon acting on behalf of the assured, and the insurers by their own veterinary surgeon destroyed the horse

---

7 *Barrett v Jermy* (1849) 3 Exch 535; *Victor Melik & Co Ltd v Norwich Union Fire Insurance Society Ltd and Kemp* [1980] 1 Lloyd's Rep 523 (burglary insurance), where the insurers were held not to have waived a condition that a burglar alarm was to be 'kept in efficient working order' and 'kept in full operation at all times when the premises are unattended'; *Mint Security Ltd v Blair* [1982] 1 Lloyd's Rep 188 (cash in transit insurance), where the insurers were held not to have waived a condition that equipment and personnel and procedures as described in the proposal form should not be varied by the insured to the insurers' detriment without their knowledge and approval.

8 *Everett v Desborough* (1829) 5 Bing 503 (life insurance); *Ashford v Victoria Mutual Assurance Co* (1870) 20 CP 434, where the assured was about to answer certain questions in the proposal, when the agent of the insurers told him that it was unnecessary. Such a dispensation may be inferred by the jury from the correspondence: *Pim v Reid* (1843) 6 Man & G 1.

9 *Sun Fire Office v Hart* (1889) 14 App Cas 98, PC, where there was a request for delay in the commencement of proceedings; *London and Manchester Plate Glass Co Ltd v Heath* [1913] 3 KB 411, CA (plate glass insurance), where there had been payment under a similar policy under similar circumstances.

10 An express waiver is not necessarily absolute; it must be construed with reference to the circumstances: *Re Carr and Sun Fire Insurance Co* (1897) 13 TLR 186, CA (fire insurance), where an extension of time for sending in the claim was granted for the purpose of enabling certain named persons to work out the figures, and it was held that the extension did not last longer than the time which those persons actually took to work out their arithmetic.

11 *Marcovitch v Liverpool Victoria Friendly Society* (1912) 28 TLR 188 (life insurance).

so that it could not be subsequently examined on behalf of the assured.[12]

The conduct of the insurers may render the fulfilment of the condition unnecessary,[13] eg by wrongfully repudiating the policy or their liability thereunder before it becomes necessary for the assured to perform it,[14] or by refusing to fulfil their part of the condition[15] or by otherwise preventing him from performing it.[16]

Further, the conduct of the insurers[17] may lead the assured reasonably to believe that they do not insist on the condition being fulfilled.[18]

---

12 *Burridge & Son v F H Haines & Sons Ltd* (1918) 118 LR 681; *Re Albert Life Assurance Co, Cook's Policy* (1870) LR 9 Eq 703 (life insurance), where the assured could not pay the premium on the due date because the insurers had gone into liquidation; *Smith v Commercial Union Insurance Co* (1872) 33 UCR 69, where it was held that the fact that after the fire the defendants took possession of the goods that remained and prevented the plaintiffs from giving the account required by a condition of the policy, was a perfect excuse for their non-compliance with such condition.

13 *E Hulton & Co v Mountain* (1921) 37 TLR 869, 8 LlL Rep 249, CA (litigation insurance); *Irving v Sun Insurance Office* [1906] ORC 24, where, though the assured failed to give immediate notice of the fire, the insurers had received timely notice from their agent; *Barratt Bros (Taxis) Ltd v Davies (Lickiss, First Third Party), Milestone Motor Policies at Lloyd's (Second, Third Party)* [1966] 2 Lloyd's Rep 1, CA (motor insurance), where the insured had broken a condition requiring him to forward to the insurers a notice of an intended prosecution in connection with an accident in which he was involved, and it was held that a letter to him from the insurers stating that they had heard from the police about the intended prosecution amounted to a waiver of the breach of condition. Salmon LJ, observed (at 6): 'In my judgment, any reasonable person receiving that letter would have concluded that the [insurers], having learnt all about the intended prosecution, no longer required him to notify them of it . . .' *Farrell v Federated Employers Insurance Association Ltd* [1970] 3 All ER 632 [1970] 2 Lloyd's Rep 170, CA.

14 *Parker & Co (Sandbank) v Western Assurance Co* [1925] WC & Ins Rep 82, applying *Re Coleman's Depositories Ltd and Life and Health Association* [1907] 2 KB 798, CA (employers' liability insurance); *Shiells v Scottish Assurance Corpn Ltd* 1889 16 R (Ct of Sess) 1014 (accident insurance), where the assured was held to be discharged from the duty of sending in a report of the loss. But the assured is bound by a clause making arbitration a condition precedent to action unless the repudiation of the insurers goes to the length of denying the existence of the contract: *Heyman v Darwins Ltd* [1942] AC 356 (contract) per Viscount Simon C, at 366, where the decision in *Jureidini v National British and Irish Millers' Insurance Co Ltd* [1915] AC 499 is strongly criticised.

15 *Strong v Harvey* (1825) 3 Bing 304 (marine insurance), where, on the refusal of the insurers to adjust the loss, the assured was allowed to sue at once on the policy, though a condition provided that losses were to be paid within three months after adjustment.

16 There is no waiver where the insurers merely state that they do not consider themselves liable, without giving their reasons, since they may be relying upon the non-performance of the particular condition: *Whyte v Western Assurance Co* (1876) 22 LCJ 215, PC (fire insurance).

17 It is immaterial that they did not intend their conduct to operate as a waiver: *Toronto Rly Co v National British and Irish Millers' Insurance Co Ltd* (1914) 111 LT 555, CA (fire insurance) per Scrutton J, at 563: 'Conditions precedent may be waived by a course of conduct inconsistent with their continuing validity, even though the contracting party does not intend his conduct to have that result. This is especially so if the course of conduct leads the other party to spend time and incur expense in a proceeding which he would not have undertaken had he not been led, by the conduct of the other party, to think that he was relieved, by concurring in those proceedings, from the other course of conduct and conditions prescribed by the policy.' This case was followed in *Burridge & Son v Haines & Sons* (supra).

18 *Burridge & Son v Haines & Sons* (supra), where the insurers, after erroneously stating that the policy required the death of the horse insured to be proved by a certificate from their own veterinary surgeon, went on to inform the assured that they would pay if he could satisfy them by other evidence that the death was covered by the policy, and this was held to be a waiver of a condition requiring the death to be duly certified by a qualified veterinary surgeon; *Harrison v Douglas* (1835) 3 Ad & El 396 (marine insurance), where the insurers by making a payment into Court were held to have waived the objection that the time of action had not arrived; *Kaffarian Colonial Bank v Grahamstown Fire Insurance Co* (1885) 5 Buchanan (East Dist Ct Cape) 61, where

Thus, the issue of a policy under seal containing a recital that the premium has been paid is a waiver of a condition in the cover note that no liability is to arise until the premium is paid.[19] Similarly, the renewal of a policy is a waiver of any condition which, to the knowledge of the insurers, cannot be[20] or has not been fulfilled.[1] In the absence of knowledge, the renewal is not a waiver.[2]

On the other hand, the fact that the insurers have admitted liability under previous policies without relying on a particular exception, does not preclude them from relying on the exception in the case of a subsequent policy; and it is immaterial that the application of the exception could equally have been raised on the facts of the previous cases.[3]

(c) Waiver must be pleaded

To put forward a plea of waiver, whether before or after breach, of a condition precedent to the right of action contained in a policy is a very serious step. It is quite obvious that it is essential in the interests of justice that the insurance company in such circumstances should have its attention called beforehand to

---

the acceptance of a verbal notice was held to be a waiver of a written notice; *Newcastle Fire Insurance Co v Macmorran Co* (1815) 3 Dow 255, HL (fire insurance) per Lord Eldon LC, at 263; *Pim v Reid* (1843) 6 Man & G 1 (fire insurance), where the correspondence showed that the insurers did not insist on the delivery of particulars; *Scottish Amicable Heritable Securities Association v Northern Assurance Co* 1883 11 R (Ct of Sess) 287 (fire insurance), where the conduct of the insurers in dealing with the assured on the footing of a payment in money to be fixed by arbitration precluded them from afterwards claiming the right to reinstate; *Toronto Rly Co v National British and Irish Millers' Insurance Co* (1914) 111 LT 555, CA (fire insurance), where, after the loss had been adjusted with the assent of the insurers, in a manner inconsistent with the conditions of the policy, the insurers demanded proof of loss in accordance with the conditions, and it was held that by their conduct they had waived their right not only to demand such proof, but also to insist upon a condition fixing the time before which the action could not be brought; *Provident Savings Life Society v Bellew* (1904) 35 SCR 35 (life insurance), where the giving of permission to members of the Canadian Contingent to take part in the South African War was a waiver of a restriction against travelling in the torrid zone; *Whitehorn v Canadian Guardian Life Assurance Co* (1909) 19 OLR 535 (life insurance), where the premium had always been paid in driblets; *Victor Melik & Co Ltd v Norwich Union Fire Insurance Society Ltd and Kemp* [1980] 1 Lloyd's Rep 523 (burglary insurance), where there was no conduct on the part of the insurers which could amount to a representation that a condition in the policy would not be relied on. A letter written 'without prejudice' is not a waiver: *Sun Fire Office v Hart* (1889) 14 App Cas 98 at 102, PC (fire insurance).

19 *Roberts v Security Co* [1897] 1 QB 111 CA per Rigby LJ, at 116; cf *Equitable Fire and Accident Office Ltd v Ching Wo Hong* [1907] AC 96, PC (fire insurance).

20 *Sulphite Pulp Co v Faber* (1895) 1 Com Cas 146 (fire insurance) per Lord Russell of Killowen CJ, at 153; cf *Pritchard v Merchants' and Tradesman's Life-Assurance Society* (1858) 3 CBNS 622 (life insurance), where the revival of the policy in ignorance of the assured's death was held not to be a waiver of a condition requiring him to be in good health at the time when the policy was revived.

1 *Supple v Cann* (1858) 9 ICLR 1 (life insurance); *Handler v Mutual Reserve Fund Association* (1904) 90 LT 192, CA (life insurance); *Northern Assurance Co v Provost* (1881) 25 LCJ 211, where the policy contained a clause to the effect that the house insured was *à être lambrissée en brique*, and after the expiration of a year, the insurers accepted a renewal premium while the house was still, to their knowledge, in the same state and had not been covered with brick, and it was held that they could not take advantage of the clause.

2 *Pritchard v Merchants' and Tradesman's Life Assurance Society* (supra); *Handler v Mutual Reserve Fund Association* (supra).

3 *London and Manchester Plate Glass Co Ltd v Heath* [1913] 3 KB 411, CA; cf *Sun Fire Office v Hart* (1889) 14 App Cas 98, PC (fire insurance).

the fact that it is intended to rely on an issue of the kind upon which evidence can be called.[4]

Where the assured failed to plead waiver, and no application was made at the trial for leave to introduce such a plea, it was held that the Judge was wrong in considering the issue at all.[5]

(2) Waiver by agent of insurers

Where the insurers, as is usually the case, are represented in their dealings with the assured by an agent, a waiver on the part of their agent, whether of performance or of breach, may be binding on them so as to preclude them from relying on the assured's failure to perform a condition.

To constitute a waiver binding on the insurers, it must be shown that:

a The act done by the agent must be an act which would amount to a waiver if done by the insurers themselves.[6]

b The act must fall within the authority which the agent, in fact, possesses,[7] or which he is held out by the insurers as possessing.[8]

Thus, where an agent has authority to receive and give receipts for the premium on behalf of the insurers, his acceptance of a premium with knowledge of a breach of condition is a waiver of the breach binding upon the insurers.[9]

There is, however, no waiver where the act done falls outside the agent's authority.[10] Thus, an agent whose authority is limited to receiving premiums

---

4 *Brook v Trafalgar Insurance Co Ltd* (1947) 79 LlL Rep 365, CA (motor insurance) per Scott LJ, at 367.

5 Ibid.

6 *Wing v Harvey* (1854) 5 De GM & G 265 (life insurance) per Knight-Bruce LJ, at 269; cf *Davies v National Fire and Marine Insurance Co of New Zealand* [1891] AC 485, PC, where it was held that on the facts there was no waiver. Hence, the mere failure of the agent to take objection is not a waiver: *O'Connor v Commercial Union Insurance Co* (1878) NSR (3 R & C) 119; cf *Hayden v Stadacona Insurance Co* (1877) 2 PEI 242, where, on the assured objecting to the condition against double insurance, the agent told him that he could insure elsewhere.

7 *Houghton & Co v Nothard Lowe and Wills* [1928] AC 1 (contract) per Lord Dunedin, at 14. A particular agent, such as the manager of the head office, may, by the terms of the policy, be given express authority to waive a condition: *Atlas Assurance Co v Brownell* (1899) 29 SCR 537. In *Provincial Assurance Co v Roy* (1879) 2 Stephen's Quebec Digest, 400, an agent of the insurers took part, on their behalf, in a settlement of the assured's claim, and it was held that his act amounted to a waiver of a breach of the condition against double insurance, although the telegram under which he had acted had been incorrectly transmitted, the words 'decide to take part' being transmitted instead of 'decline to take part'.

8 *Davies v National Fire and Marine Insurance Co of New Zealand* [1891] AC 485, PC, where the Court declined to decide the question of authority; *National Benefit Life and Property Co v McCoy* (1918) 57 SCR 29, where it was held that the general agent of a foreign insurance company waived the breach of a condition against subsequent insurance by appointing an adjuster to settle the claim, and thus bound the company; *Brocklebank v Sugrue* (1831) 5 C & P 21 (marine insurance).

9 *Wing v Harvey* (1854) 5 De GM & G 265 (life insurance), where the assured had gone to reside outside the limits of the policy; *Ayrey v British Legal and United Provident Assurance Co* [1918] 1 KB 136 (life insurance), where there was a concealment; *Scott v Accident Association of New Zealand* (1888) 6 NZLR 263; cf *Re Economic Fire Office* (1896) 12 TLR 142 (fidelity insurance); *Newsholme Bros v Road Transport and General Insurance Co Ltd* [1929] 2 KB 356, 24 LlL Rep 247, CA (accident insurance).

10 *Torrop v Imperial Fire Insurance Co* (1896) 26 SCR 585, where the agent had no authority to waive a forfeiture by transfer of interest; *Kline Bros & Co v Dominion Fire Insurance Co* (1912) 47 SCR 252, where the agent had no authority to assent to the removal of property; cf. *British Industry Life Assurance Co v Ward* (1856) 17 CB 644 (life insurance).

during the days of grace, cannot waive the non-payment by receiving the premium afterwards and thus revive a lapsed policy.[11]

Similarly, a loss adjuster who is employed by the insurers to adjust the loss, cannot bind the insurers by waiving a condition as to proofs of loss.[12] Again, a local agent has no usual authority to waive a condition concerning the giving of notice of loss to the head office of the insurance company within a specified time.[13]

In some cases the policy may contain a condition expressly prohibiting or limiting waiver by an agent or prescribing the mode in which a waiver is to be made.[14]

5 Statement by BIA and Lloyd's

In 1977 The British Insurance Association[15] and Lloyd's drew up a statement of non-life insurance practice which they recommended to their members.[16] The statement applies only to non-life policyholders domiciled in the United Kingdom and insured in their private capacity only, and so far as a breach of a condition is concerned provides:

> 'Except where fraud, deception or negligence is involved, an insurer will not unreasonably repudiate liability to indemnify a policyholder . . . (ii) on the grounds of a breach of warranty or condition where the circumstances of the loss are unconnected with the breach.
>
> [This] paragraph does not apply to marine and aviation policies.'

---

[11] *Acey v Fernie* (1840) 7 M & W 151 (life insurance), distinguished in *Wing v Harvey* (supra) and in *Re Economic Fire Office* (supra).

[12] *Atlas Assurance Co v Brownell* (1899) 29 SCR 537, followed in *Commercial Union Assurance Co v Margeson* (1899) 29 SCR 601; *Hyde v Lefaivre* (1902) 32 SCR 474.

[13] *Brook v Trafalgar Insurance Co Ltd* (1947) 79 LlL Rep 365, CA (motor insurance). See further as to the facts of the case, p 527, post. For the 'usual authority' of agents, see pp 525–529, post.

[14] *M'Millan v Accident Insurance Co* 1907 SC 484 (accident insurance); *Atlas Assurance Co v Brownell* (supra).

[15] Now The Association of British Insurers.

[16] See 931 House of Commons Official Report, 4 May, 1977, Written Answers, cols 218–220.

CHAPTER 31

The alteration of the risk under the policy

The risk that the event insured against will or will not happen necessarily depends on the subject-matter of insurance and its attendant circumstances, and the insurers, in accepting the insurance, are guided by the state of the subject-matter and the circumstances existing at the date of the policy.[1]

The description inserted in the policy of the subject-matter and its circumstances, therefore, serves to define the risk undertaken by the insurers,[2] and any alteration made during the currency of the policy which affects the subject-matter or its circumstances as so described is an alteration of the risk since the state of facts contemplated by the insurers no longer exists in its entirety.

There is, however, no alteration of the risk where an alteration, though apparently on the face of it an alteration of the risk, is not a real alteration of the risk at all, but such an alteration as, on the true construction of the policy, might be taken to have been within the contemplation of the parties at the time when they entered into the contract.[3]

Nor is there any alteration of the risk where the alteration does not affect the description in the policy, even though it increases the danger of loss, since the risk as defined in the policy remains the same.[4]

---

1 *Sillem v Thornton* (1854) 3 E & B 868 (fire insurance) per Lord Campbell CJ, at 884.

2 *Shaw v Royce Ltd* [1911] 1 Ch 138 per Warrington J, at 148; *Law Guarantee Trust and Accident Society Ltd v Munich Reinsurance Co* [1912] 1 Ch 138 per Warrington J, at 154; *Shaw v Robberds* (1837) 6 Ad & El 75 (fire insurance) per Lord Denman CJ, at 82.

3 *Law Guarantee Trust and Accident Society Ltd v Munich Reinsurance Co* (supra) per Warrington J, at 153, 154: 'The defendant company rests its case upon the general principle applicable in all cases of insurance that the obligation of the insurer is confined to the particular risk insured, and that if the risk in respect of which the claim is made against the insurers differs from the risk he has insured, he is not liable to make good that claim . . . It is hardly necessary to enlarge upon that principle, but I take it that it involves this. The alteration, if there has been an alteration, must be a real alteration of the risk; if what appears on the face of it to be an alteration of the conditions is only such an alteration as, on the true construction of the contract of insurance might be taken to have been within the contemplation of the parties at the time they entered into the contract; then, of course, though apparently an alteration, it is no real alteration at all, because the fact that such an alteration might take place was an element in the contract itself.' See also, *Gorman v Hand-in-Hand Insurance Co* (1877) IR 11 CL 224 (fire insurance) per Palles CB, at 236; *Re Albert Life Assurance Co, Bell's Case* (1870) LR 9 Eq 706 (life insurance) per James V-C, at 719.

4 *Baxendale v Harvey* (1859) 4 H & N 445 (fire insurance) per Pollock CB, at 449: 'This is a mere increase of danger. It is like the case of a person who has an oven on his premises and instead of using it for baking bread he uses it for some other purpose. If a person who insures his life goes up in a balloon, that does not vitiate his policy.' SC at 452: 'The Society, having had notice of the nature of the risk, were not entitled to any notice by reason of the increase of danger. A person who insures may light as many candles as he pleases in his house, though each additional candle

Alterations of the risk fall into three classes:

1 Alterations in the subject-matter of insurance;
2 Changes of locality;
3 Changes of circumstances, such as, for instance, in the user of the subject-matter or in the trade or business carried on by the assured.

A THE EFFECT OF AN ALTERATION

Sometimes the effect of an alteration is that the policy ceases to apply. This occurs where the identity of the subject-matter is destroyed.

In other cases the effect is that the operation of the policy is merely suspended.

1 Where the policy ceases to apply

Where the alteration destroys the identity of the subject-matter as described in the policy, there is not so much an alteration of the risk as the substitution of a different risk; the policy, therefore, ceases to apply in as much as the insurers have never undertaken the new risk.[5]

Thus, in a burglary policy, a description of the locality, in which the property insured is situated, may form a necessary part of the description of the subject-matter, as, for instance, where property insured under a general description is described as being in a particular house or shop. In this case the property, on its removal from the specified locality, ceases to answer the description and the policy no longer applies.[6]

---

increases the danger of setting the house on fire.' See also, *Toulmin v Inglis* (1808) 1 Camp 421 (marine insurance) per Lord Ellenborough CJ, at 422: 'It is impossible to say that everything which increases the risk vacates the insurance, or this effect would be produced by taking on board a cask of gun-powder or any other inflammable matter'; *Thompson v Hopper* (1858) EB & E 1038, ExCh (marine insurance) per Willes J, at 1049, approved in *Trinder Anderson & Co v Thames and Mersey Marine Insurance Co* [1898] 2 QB 114, CA (marine insurance) per Collins LJ, at 128.

5 *Wembley Urban District Council v Poor Law and Local Government Officers Mutual Guarantee Association Ltd* (1901) 17 TLR 516 per Wills J, at 516; *Shaw v Royce Ltd* (supra) per Warrington J, at 148; *Thompson v Hopper* (supra) (marine insurance) per Willes J, at 1049, explaining *Sillem v Thornton* (supra) (fire insurance); *Pearson v Commercial Union Assurance Co* (1876) 1 App Cas 498 (fire insurance) per Lord Chelmsford, at 506, and per Lord O'Hagen, at 510; cf *Stuart v Horse Insurance Co* 1893 1 SLT 91, 108, where the horse insured was used for work materially differing from that specified in the proposal; *Newcastle Fire Insurance Co v Macmorran & Co* (1815) 3 Dow 255, HL (fire insurance), where the policy was held void because the building insured was wrongly described, and it was immaterial that the policy contained a clause that it was not to attach until the premium was paid, and an alteration was made before the premium was paid bringing the building within the description; *Hadenfayre Ltd v British National Insurance Society Ltd* [1984] 2 Lloyd's Rep 393 (contingency insurance), where the sum which a demolition company was to pay for the purchase of a site was to be paid by instalments of £6,000 per week and the instalments were reduced to £3,000 per week, and it was held that this constituted a material variation of the risk. (See the judgment of Lloyd J, ibid, at 400.)

6 *Gorman v Hand-in-Hand Insurance Co* (supra) (fire insurance), where a policy on horses and agricultural machines described as being in a particular place was held not to cover them when removed, though it re-attached on their return; *McClure v Lancashire Insurance Co* (1860) 6 IrJur 63 (fire insurance), where a new locality had been substituted by agreement and the property insured was burnt before it had been removed. Cf *Pearson v Commercial Union Assurance Co* (supra), where under a fire policy upon a ship 'lying in the Victoria Docks, with liberty to go

Similarly, in fidelity insurance, a description of the employee's office or duties may form a necessary part of the description of the subject-matter, and apart from any condition in the policy, a change in the office[7] or duties[8] described may involve the substitution of a different risk which the policy was not intended to cover.

A motor policy is usually identified with a particular vehicle, although the insured may be protected when he is driving another vehicle. But when the vehicle is sold, the insured is no longer covered whilst driving another vehicle.[9]

In accordance with the same principle, a change in the constitution of a firm,[10] or a change of business,[11] may deprive the assured of his protection.

Where, on the other hand, the identity of the subject-matter is not affected, an alteration of the risk, whether in the subject-matter,[12] its locality or circumstances,[13] has, in general, no effect on the policy,[14] and it is immaterial

---

into dry-dock', it was held that the ship was not covered whilst in the River for a collateral purpose after leaving the dry-dock, and Lord Cairns C, said at 503: 'It is unnecessary to speculate whether the risk would or would not be greater while the ship was in the River than when it was in the dock . . . it is difficult to say that the respondents have defined the risk which they are willing to undertake, and that risk cannot be enlarged beyond the ordinary meaning of the words upon any theory that the difference of risk is immaterial.'

7 *Cosford Union v Poor Law and Local Government Officers' Mutual Guarantee Association Ltd* (1910) 103 LT 463, where a policy covering the act of an assistant overseer was held not to apply to defalcations committed by the servant in his capacity as clerk to the parish council.

8 *Wembley Urban District Council v Poor Law and Local Government Officers' Mutual Guarantee Association* (supra), where a clerk was, during the currency of the policy, charged with the duty of paying the workmen employed by the council; *Hay v Employers' Liability Assurance Corporation* (1905) 6 OWR 459.

9 *Rogerson v Scottish Automobile and General Insurance Co Ltd* (1931) 146 LT 26, 41 LlL Rep 1, HL.

10 *McLachlan v Accident Insurance Co of North America* (1888) MLR 4 SC 365, where the insurance was on partners in a firm as such; *Solvency Mutual Guarantee Co v Freeman* (1861) 7 H & N 17, where the policy became void on the retirement of a partner.

11 See *Smellie v British General Insurance Co* [1918] WC & Ins Rep 233, where the policy applied only to accidents happening in connection with work done on particular premises; and cf *Watchorn v Langford* (1813) 3 Camp 422 (fire insurance), where a person who was not a linen draper purchased on speculation a stock of linen goods, which were held not be covered notwithstanding the word 'stock-in-trade' in the policy. The position is different where an alteration in trade does not affect the identity of the subject-matter; see *Pim v Reid* (1843) 6 Man & G 1 (fire insurance) per Tindal CJ, at 19.

12 *Thompson v Hopper* (1858) EB & E 1038, ExCh (marine insurance) per Willes J, at 1049: 'In effect, there being no violation of the law and no fraud on the part of the assured, an increase of risk to the subject-matter of insurance, its identity remaining, though such increased risk be caused by the assured, if it is not prohibited by the policy, does not avoid the insurance.' See also, *Shaw v Robberds* (1837) 6 Ad & El 75 per Lord Denman CJ, at 82; *Baxendale v Harvey* (1859) 4 H & N 445 per Martin B, at 450; *Trinder Anderson & Co v Thames and Mersey Marine Insurance Co* [1898] 2 QB 114 (marine insurance) per Collins LJ, at 128.

13 *Pim v Reid* (supra) per Maule J, at 22: 'It has been argued that, independently of the express provisions of the policy, if hazardous articles, or a hazardous trade were introduced upon the premises with the knowledge or assent of the assured, after the policy was effected, it would be thereby avoided. But I conceive the law to be otherwise; and that, in the absence of fraud, such an alteration would not vitiate the policy.' But sometimes the introduction of hazardous articles will change the identity of the risk: *Beauchamp v National Mutual Indemnity Insurance Co Ltd* [1937] 3 All ER 19 (liability insurance). See also, *R v National Insurance Co* (1887) 13 VLR 914, where it was held that the assured could recover although the loss was due to the fact that the intended course of business was not followed; *Tyson v Gurney* (1789) 3 Term Rep 477 (marine insurance), where, on a policy on goods in a neutral ship, it was held to be sufficient that the ship was neutral when she sailed; *Dent v Smith* (1869) LR 4 QB 414 (marine insurance), where the nationality of the ship was changed during the voyage and the amount payable under the policy thereby

whether the assured is responsible or not for the alteration,[15] or whether the alteration increases the danger of loss[16] and, in fact, conduces to the loss.[17] Any such alteration made during the currency of the policy must, however, if material, be communicated to the insurers before the policy is renewed; otherwise the renewal is void.[18]

But although the alteration of the risk does not affect the identity of the subject-matter, the policy may still be avoided where:

---

increased. See now on this point, Marine Insurance Act 1906, s 37, and Ivamy *Marine Insurance* (4th Edn, 1985), pp 286–287. See further, *Shaw v Robberds* (supra) (fire insurance); and cf *Jenkins v Heycock* (1853) 8 Moo PCC 351 (marine insurance), where it was held that in a time policy the implied warranty of seaworthiness was not a continuing warranty. See now on this point, Marine Insurance Act 1906, s 39(5), and Ivamy *Marine Insurance* (4th Edn, 1985), pp 302–306; *Mitchell Conveyor and Transport Co v Pulbrook* (1933) 45 LlL Rep 239 (policy concerning loss caused by defective workmanship in construction of building), where the variation of the proportions of granite chippings and the cement used in the flooring was held not to have varied the risk. Roche J observed (at 245): 'I am unable to assent to the proposition that the mere fact that the risk increased after the policy was effected covering that risk, avoids the policy or frees the underwriter from liability. If authority were needed for quite such a universal proposition, the case of *Pim v Reid* (1843) 6 Man & G 1, is sufficient authority. Of course, it depends what is the subject-matter of the insurance and what are the conditions of the insurance; and, of course, where a voyage is the subject-matter, the change of voyage would avoid the policy and free the underwriter from liability, and if there was an insurance here that the underwriter would insure the work to be done by the plaintiff company under the contract, whether by express words or necessary implication, in terms that the works were to be done in a certain way and no other, then the variations in the works might either avoid the policy or render the loss from the increased risk irrecoverable. But so far from that being the case, there is, as might be expected in a construction contract of this magnitude, express provision for all sorts of variations; and accordingly I do not find, either by express words or by implication, any provision that the variation of the works, although it may increase the risk attaching to the work, will avoid the policy.'

14 In *Sillem v Thornton* (1854) 3 E & B 868 (fire insurance) a contrary view was taken, the Court holding that the description in the policy amounted to a warranty against subsequent alteration, and consequently that an alteration increasing the risk avoided the policy, although there was no condition against it. Though the decision was correct on the actual facts, the reasoning and opinion of the Court as to the effect of a subsequent alteration must be regarded as unsound; see *Stokes v Cox* (1856) 26 LJEx 113, ExCh (fire insurance) per Willes J, at 113: 'In *Sillem v Thornton* the description in the policy was untrue. At the time of the execution of the policy the premises described as of two storeys were, in fact, of three; therefore, whatever is said in *Sillem v Thornton* as to a subsequent alteration making a policy void must have been extra-judicial..' See also, *Thompson v Hopper* (supra) per Willes J, at 1049: 'I may add that there is a case, *Sillem v Thornton,* which turned mainly upon a question of identity of the subject-matter intended to be insured at the time of the insurance, and may be sustained on that ground, notwithstanding our present decision. That part of the judgment in that case which discusses the above point (i e the effect of a subsequent alteration) was not called for by the facts; and if it was intended to negative the proposition just stated, we ought to overrule it.' In *Stokes v Cox* as reported (1856) 1 H & N 533, Cockburn CJ, at 540, decided the question of the effect of the alteration made upon the condition in the policy, and said that it was unnecessary to express an opinion as to the effect of the alteration in the absence of condition against it.

15 *Thompson v Hopper* (supra) per Willes J, at 1049; *Shaw v Robberds* (supra); *Pim v Reid* (supra).

16 *Pim v Reid* (supra) per Coltman J, at 21. It was suggested during the argument in *Barrett v Jermy* (1849) 3 Exch 535, that, independently of the condition in question, if a fire was occasioned by the circumstances increasing the risk, the insurers might not be liable, though the policy would not be affected if the fire happened through some independent cause; and this suggestion was assented to by Parke and Rolfe BB: *Stokes v Cox* (1856) 1 H & N 533, ExCh per Willes J, at 539.

17 *Shaw v Robberds* (supra); but see *Stokes v Cox* (supra) per Willes J, at 536.

18 *Pim v Reid* (supra) per Cresswell J, at 25.

a The alteration is in breach of good faith,[19] as, for instance, where it is made fraudulently with intent to defraud the insurers.[20]
b The alteration is a breach of a condition subsequent of the policy.

2 Where the alteration merely suspends the operation of the policy

There are certain cases in which the alteration does not affect the validity of the policy, but merely suspends its operation whilst the alteration continues. These cases are:

a Where there is an express condition of the policy to that effect.
b Where it is the intention of the parties that the policy should be suspended only, and not avoided.

(a) Express condition in the policy

Thus, a motor vehicle policy may contain a condition suspending its operation whilst the vehicle is under repair; or an employers' liability insurance may be suspended whilst the insured's employees are on strike.[1]

(b) Intention that the policy should be suspended only

A policy which is intended to cover accidents happening only in a particular locality or in particular circumstances, necessarily ceases to attach upon a change of locality[2] or circumstances,[3] as the case may be.

---

19 See *Denison v Modigliani* (1974) 5 Term Rep 580 (marine insurance), distinguished in *Moss v Byrom* (1795) 6 Term Rep 379 (marine insurance); *Garrels v Kensington* (1799) 8 Term Rep 230 (marine insurance), where a warranty of neutrality was deliberately broken by the misconduct of those on board the ship. The cases of *Horneyer v Lushington* (1812) 15 East 46 (marine insurance), and *Oswell v Vigne* (1812) 15 East 70 (marine insurance), are probably to be explained on the same ground.

20 *Pim v Reid* (supra) (fire insurance) per Maule J, at 22; *Thompson v Hopper* (supra) (marine insurance) per Willes J, at 1049; *Jenssen v Commercial Insurance Co* (1885) 4 Juta's R (Cape) 20, where the assured, having insured his store as such, subsequently used it also as a canteen, this having been his intention from the first. Cf *Reid v Gore District Mutual Fire Insurance Co* (1854) 11 UCR 345, where the assured, after effecting the policy, which contained a condition against alteration increasing the risk, put up a steam-engine in one of the buildings insured. It was proved that he had been previously told by the agent of the insurers that, if he put up the engine, he would have to apply for leave and pay an additional premium, that he endeavoured to obtain an insurance elsewhere, but was refused, the risk being considered too hazardous, and that he acknowledged that he knew that the policy was void because he had made no arrangement with the insurers in consequence of the additional risk.

1 In such cases, provision may be made for a proportionate return of premium.

2 *Smellie v British General Insurance Co* [1918] WC & Ins Rep 233; *Pigott v Employers' Liability Assurance Corpn* (1900) 31 OR 666; *Pearson v Commercial Union Assurance Co* (1876) 1 App Cas 498 (fire insurance); *Gorman v Hand-in-Hand Insurance Co* (1877) IR 11 CL 224 (fire insurance); cf *McClure v Lancashire Insurance Co* (1860) 6 IrJur 63 (fire insurance), where it was held that after removal had been sanctioned, the property insured was no longer covered in the original locality.

3 *Farr v Motor Traders' Mutual Insurance Society* [1920] 3 KB 669, CA, where accidents happening whilst a taxi-cab was being worked in two shifts were held not to be covered, followed in *Roberts v Anglo-Saxon Insurance Association* (1927) 137 LT 243, 27 LlL Rep 313, CA, where the insured car was being used for a different purpose; *Provincial Insurance Co Ltd v Morgan* [1933] AC 240, HL, where the original purpose had been resumed; *Murray v Scottish Automobile and General Insurance Co Ltd* 1929 SC 49, where a car habitually used for a different purpose was held not to be covered in the garage, as this was merely incidental to its ordinary employment for such purpose; *Stuart v Horse Insurance Co* 1893 1 SLT 91, 108, where the horse insured was doing different work.

If, subsequently, the original position is restored, a question may arise, in the event of an accident happening in the original locality or in the original circumstances, whether the alteration has put an end to the policy or merely suspended it during the continuance of the alteration. The answer to the question depends on the construction to be placed upon the language of the particular policy.[4]

If the language used amounts to a condition against alteration, the policy is avoided and does not reattach when the original position is restored.[5]

In some cases, however, it is clear from the nature of the subject-matter that the alteration must have been within the contemplation of the parties, and the policy accordingly reattaches.[6] Thus, if horses are insured whilst in a stable, their removal from the stable suspends the operation of the policy, but it reattaches on their return.[7]

Similarly, an insurance against liability for accidents, whether to workmen[8] or third persons[9] arising out of work carried on at particular premises, does not cover accidents happening in consequence of work carried on elsewhere; but the fact that work may be carried on elsewhere does not affect the validity of the policy as regards accidents happening upon the premises specified.

B IMPLIED CONDITIONS AS TO MAKING ALTERATIONS

The description in the policy of the subject-matter usually includes statements as to locality, user, or other circumstances,[10] which are not required for its identification, and an alteration in the circumstances described does not, therefore, prevent the subject-matter from being identified.

It is necessary to consider with what object such statements are inserted in the policy, and how far they prohibit an alteration in the circumstances described. The following cases may be distinguished:

1 Where the policy contains an express condition against alterations.
2 Where there is no express condition against alterations.

1 Where the policy contains an express condition against alterations

Where the policy contains an express condition against alterations, the statements in the description define the risk undertaken by the insurers and

---

4 Contrast *Whitehead v Price* (1835) 2 CrM & R 447 (fire insurance), where a statement in the proposal that a mill was worked by day only was treated as a condition, with *Farr v Motor Traders' Mutual Insurance Society* (supra), where a statement in the proposal that a taxi-cab was driven in one shift per twenty-four hours was held not to be a condition, but merely a description of the risk covered.

5 *Whitehead v Price* (supra), followed in *Mayall v Mitford* (1837) 6 Ad & El 670 (fire insurance), where the mill was expressly warranted to be worked by day only; cf *Way v Modigliani* (1787) 2 Term Rep 30 (marine insurance).

6 *Farr v Motor Traders' Mutual Insurance Society* (supra); *Pearson v Commercial Union Assurance Co* (1873) LR 8 CP 548, ExCh (fire insurance) per Blackburn J, at 549.

7 *Gorman v Hand-in-Hand Insurance Co* (supra) (fire insurance).

8 *Pigott v Employers' Liability Assurance Corpn* (supra).

9 *Smellie v British General Insurance Co* (supra).

10 Such statements may be framed in the negative.

furnish the standard by which any subsequent alterations are to be measured.[11]

They are not in themselves contractual; if they are accurate at the time of insuring, the assured has discharged his obligation and is not precluded by their presence in the policy from making alterations.[12] Any alteration, therefore, to be prohibited, must fall within the scope of the express condition; any other alteration may be made with impunity.[13]

2 Where there is no express condition against alterations

Where there is no express condition against alterations, the effect of a statement in the description depends upon whether it is to be construed as a mere representation or as amounting to a contract that the circumstances shall remain as described throughout the duration of the policy.

A statement in terms referring to the future, if construed as a mere representation, is a representation of an intention honestly entertained at the date of the policy and nothing more; it does not prohibit the assured from changing his intention and thereby bringing about an alteration in the circumstances described.[14]

---

11 *Stokes v Cox* (1856) 1 H & N 320 (reversed (1856) 1 H & N 533, Ex Ch) (fire insurance) per Bramwell B, the dissenting Judge whose views were accepted in the Exchequer Chamber at 335: 'What would have been the meaning (of the words in question) had they stood alone it is not necessary to decide. They are found in a description of the premises as they then were, which is required by the conditions, and found in connection with some things clearly not warranted and other expressly warranted. And they may well mean, and I believe in fact do mean, nothing more than "this is the now description" on which the insurers act (which, if false, would vitiate the policy), but for the continuance of which or any part they provide, if at all, by other stipulations.'

12 *Shaw v Robberds* (1837) 6 Ad & El 75 (fire insurance) per Lord Denman CJ, at 82: 'The third condition points to the description of the premises at the time of insuring; and that description was, in this instance, quite correct. Nothing which occurred afterwards, not even a change of business, could bring the case within the condition which was fully performed when the risk attached.'

13 See pp 309–310, post.

14 *Benham v United Guarantee and Life Assurance Co* (1852) 7 Exch per Pollock CB, at 752: 'The manner in which the question is put, the other question with which it is associated, and the decisions upon policies of insurance lead me to the conclusion that the answer was not expected to be upon the part of the office, or meant to be on the part of the plaintiff, anything more than a declaration of the course intended to be pursued; and if that answer was made bona fide and honestly, it does not prevent the plaintiff from maintaining this action.' See also, *Grant v Aetna Insurance Co* (1862) 15 Moo PCC 516, where a steamship, having been insured against fire by a fire policy for twelve months, was described in the policy as 'now lying in the T. Dock, Montreal, and intended to navigate the St. Lawrence'; and the insured was held entitled to recover although the ship never left the dock, the fire having taken place one month before the expiration of the policy, the reason being stated at 527: 'If they (the words "intended to navigate the St. Lawrence") import an agreement that the ship shall navigate in the manner described in the policy, there being an engagement contained in the policy, they must be considered a warranty, and the engagement not being performed, whether the engagement is material or not material, the insurers are discharged.' The judgment proceeds to state that it was a matter of construction, but that in the opinion of the Court the words were not a warranty, but a mere representation 'that an intention to employ the ship in the manner described was bona fide entertained by the insured at the time the policy was effected.' Cf *Grant v Equitable Fire Insurance Co* (1864) 14 LCR 469, where the same steamer was described as '(now in T Dock) navigating the St. Lawrence'. See also, *McGibbon v Imperial Insurance Co* (1881) 14 NSR (2 G & R) 6, where it was held that a policy on a building described as occupied as a water-power sawmill was not avoided, although it had not been so used up to the time of the fire owing to a shortage of water. See further, *Weber and Berger v Employers' Liability Assurance Corpn* (1926) 24 LlL Rep 321, where

If, on the other hand, the statement is construed as contractual, it is an undertaking by the assured that the circumstances shall continue as described,[15] and any alteration therein is prohibited.[16]

A statement not in terms referring to the future, if construed as a representation, is fulfilled at the date of the policy and is not affected by any subsequent alteration;[17] if, on the other hand, it is contractual, it must be construed as co-extensive with the risk, unless there is something to limit its duration,[18] and any alteration in the circumstances described must, therefore, be regarded as prohibited during the currency of the policy.[19]

Whether in a particular case the statement is a representation or contractual is a matter of construction, to be determined with reference to all the circumstances of the case;[20] the fact that it is inserted in the policy does not prevent it from being construed as a representation.[1]

A statement expressing a future intention,[2] or a statement which merely assists in the identification of the subject-matter,[3] or which adds a detail to its description or is otherwise a natural adjunct of the description,[4] is, in the

---

a statement in the proposal that books were kept with a complete record of purchases and sales and were regularly entered up was held not to amount to a promise; and cf *R v National Insurance Co* (1887) 13 VLR 914, where a statement as to the direction as to the checking of a clerk's accounts was held to be a mere statement of intention; *Hay v Employers' Liability Assurance Corpn* (1905) 6 OWR 459, where it was held that in the case of a new employee statements as to checks were merely statements of intention; *Grain Claims Bureau Ltd v Canadian Surety Co* [1927] 3 WWR 1, where a statement naming the accountants by whom the accounts would be examined was held not to be a continuing warranty, and was not broken by the employment of a different firm; *Hearts of Oak Building Society v Law Union and Rock Insurance Co Ltd* [1936] 2 All ER 619 (liability insurance); *Dawsons Ltd v Bonnin* [1922] 2 AC 413; *Woolfall and Rimmer Ltd v Moyle* [1942] 1 KB 66, CA (employers' liability insurance); *Beauchamp v National Mutual Indemnity Insurance Co Ltd* [1937] 3 All ER 19 (liability insurance); *Hales v Reliance Fire and Accident Insurance Corpn Ltd* [1960] 2 Lloyd's Rep 391, QB (fire insurance); *Sweeney v Kennedy* (1948) 82 LlL Rep 294 (motor insurance).

15 *Towle v National Guardian Assurance Society* (1861) 30 LJCh 900, distinguishing *Benham v United Guarantee and Life Assurance Co* (supra).

16 *Benham v United Guarantee and Life Assurance Co* (supra) per Pollock CB, at 752: 'Suppose that, instead of examining the accounts every fortnight, the institution had adopted, as a more convenient mode of securing the fidelity of their secretary, the practice of sending the money every day to a banker, and that on one occasion when some was left, the secretary absconded with it, would the policy be avoided? If this is a warranty, it must be construed strictly; and therefore, although the institution had found out a better mode of checking the accounts, they would, nevertheless, be obliged to go through the idle ceremony of having them examined by a finance committee.'

17 *Shaw v Robberds* (1837) 6 Ad & El 75 (fire insurance), where the description of a kiln as 'for drying corn' was held not to refer to the future.

18 *Pearson v Commercial Union Assurance Co* (1876) 1 App Cas 498 (fire insurance). See also, *Hoffman v Marshall* (1835) 2 Bing NC 383 (marine insurance) per Tindal CJ, at 390.

19 *Farr v Motor Traders' Mutual Insurance Society* [1920] 3 KB 669, CA: *Stuart v Horse Insurance Co* 1893 1 SLT 91, 108, where the horse insured was stated in the proposal to be used for cart or lorry, and the accident took place while it was drawing a wagon at a railway siding.

20 *Benham v United Guarantee and Life Assurance Co* (supra) per Pollock CB, at 752; *Grant v Aetna Insurance Co* (supra).

1 *Grant v Aetna Insurance Co* (supra).

2 Ibid.

3 *McGibbon v Imperial Insurance Co* (1881) 14 NSR (2 G & R 6) (fire insurance), where a building was described as occupied as a water-power sawmill, though it had not been so used up to the time of the loss on account of a shortage of water.

4 *Shaw v Robberds* (supra).

absence of anything pointing to a contrary conclusion, to be regarded as a representation.[5]

If, however, the statement does more than amplify the description of the subject-matter and adds a description of circumstances which it is unnecessary to mention unless the statement is intended to be contractual, it is difficult to avoid the conclusion that it was so intended, since there is otherwise no apparent reason why it should have been inserted in the policy, and it must therefore be construed as prohibiting any alteration in the circumstances described during the currency of the policy.[6]

C EXPRESS CONDITIONS AS TO MAKING ALTERATIONS

The policy usually contains a condition by which the making of subsequent alterations affecting the subject-matter is either prohibited altogether or more or less restricted.

The effect of the condition depends on its terms. Usually, the policy is avoided by a breach of the condition; but in some cases it is so framed as merely to suspend the policy whilst the alteration continues. Where the policy is avoided by the breach, it is immaterial to consider, in case of loss, whether the loss is attributable to the prohibited alteration or not, since the policy has ceased to be operative.[7]

By the terms of the condition the effect of the breach is usually limited to the property affected by the alteration;[8] otherwise, the policy may be avoided as a whole.

The policy is not, however, avoided ab initio, the avoidance takes effect only from the time of the breach.[9] The assured therefore remains entitled to enforce the policy in respect of any claim which has already arisen.

There is no breach of condition if the alteration which is made is not of such a character as to be covered by its terms, since such conditions are strictly construed.[10] Where, however, the alteration is, in fact, a breach of the

---

5 Thus, it can hardly be contended that a statement in a personal accident policy that the assured's health is good, is contractual in the sense that his health is to continue good during the currency of his policy; it is a mere representation of the state of his health at the date of the contract.

6 *Dobson v Sotheby* (1827) Mood & M 90 (fire insurance); *Pearson v Commercial Union Assurance Co* (1876) 1 App Cas 498 (fire insurance).

7 *Glen v Lewis* (1853) 8 Exch 607 per Parke B, at 617; *Beacon Life and Fire Assurance Co v Gibb* (1862) 1 Moo PCC NS 73 at 99; *Roberts v Anglo-Saxon Insurance Association* (1927) 137 LT 243, CA, per Bankes LJ, at 245.

8 *Sun Fire Office v Hart* (1899) 14 App Cas 98, PC (fire insurance); *Farnham v Royal Insurance Co Ltd* [1976] 2 Lloyd's Rep 437 (fire insurance).

9 *Pim v Reid* (1843) 6 Man & G 1 per Maule J, at 13.

10 *Re George and Goldsmiths' and General Burglary Insurance Association Ltd* [1899] 1 QB 595, CA, per Smith LJ, at 609: 'Again, by the second condition of the policy the assured is to take all precautions as regards securing all doors and windows and other means of entrance or otherwise, and by the third condition the policy is to become void if the assured suffers any change altering the state of the premises in which the property insured is situate. Does this mean, if the assured omits to secure the inside door of the showcase or suffers an alteration of his showcase, the policy is to be void? Clearly not.' See also, *Catholic School Commission v Provident etc Co* (1913) QR 44 SC 97, where a condition requiring notice to be given by the assured of any default on the part of the contractors insured was held not to require notice to be given of a dissolution of partnership; *Shaw v Robberds* (1837) 6 Ad & El 75 (fire insurance) per Lord

condition, the purpose for which it was made, or the fact that it was made without the assent or even the knowledge of the assured, cannot be taken into consideration.[11]

The types of prohibition or restriction

The prohibition or restriction may be confined to a particular class or classes of alterations specified in the policy, or may be so wide as to cover alterations of any nature whatsoever.

The different forms which the condition may take may be classified under the following heads:

a Conditions prohibiting alterations absolutely.
b Conditions prohibiting increase of risk.
c Conditions prohibiting alterations without notice.
d Conditions prohibiting increase of risk without sanction.

(a) Conditions prohibiting alterations absolutely

By such a condition the making of alterations is prohibited absolutely. The prohibition may be:

i General, extending to any alteration whatsoever; or
ii Qualified, prohibiting alterations of the kind or kinds specified.

In either case the making of a prohibited alteration avoids the policy,[12] and it is immaterial that the alteration is of a trivial character, or that it does not increase the risk,[13] provided that it falls within the scope of the condition.[14]

Denman CJ, at 83; *Mayall v Mitford* (1837) 6 Ad & El 670 (fire insurance) per Lord Denman CJ, at 673, following *Whitehead v Price* (1935) 2 Cr M & R 447 (fire insurance); *Stokes v Cox* (1856) 1 H & N 533, ExCh (fire insurance) per Cockburn CJ, at 540; *Barrett v Jermy* (1849) 3 ExCh 535 (fire insurance) per Parke B, at 543, 544; *Baxendale v Harvey* (1859) 4 H & N 445 (fire insurance) per Pollock CB, at 452; *Thompson v Equity Fire Insurance Co* [1910] AC 592, PC (fire insurance), where the condition exempted the insurers from liability 'for loss or damage occurring while gasoline is stored or kept in the building insured', and it was held that the condition was not broken by the fact that the assured kept a small quantity of gasoline for use in a cooking stove, although the fire was, in fact, caused thereby.

11 *Kuntz v Niagara District Fire Insurance Co* (1866) 16 CP 573; *Rhodes v Union Insurance Co* (1883) 2 NZLR 106, in both of which cases the policy was held to have been avoided by breach of condition against alteration, although the plaintiff, who was mortgagee of the premises insured and assignee of the policy, had no knowledge of the alteration. But the condition may apply only to alterations within the control of the assured: *Merrick v Provincial Insurance Co* (1857) 14 UCR 439; *Heneker v British-America Assurance Co* (1864) 14 CP 57; *Peck v Phoenix Mutual Insurance Co* (1881) 45 UCR 620; *Copp v Glasgow and London Insurance Co* (1890) 30 NBR 197.

12 *Thompson v Equity Fire Insurance Co* (supra); *Hales v Reliance Fire and Accident Insurance Corporation Ltd* [1960] 2 Lloyd's Rep 391, QB (fire insurance), where the insured in answer to the question in the proposal form asking whether any inflammable oils or goods were kept on the premises had stated 'lighter fuel', and had stored fireworks on the premises during the currency of the risk. McNair J held that the warranty was a continuing one. The insurer was therefore entitled to avoid liability because the policy contained a condition stating, 'Every Warranty to which the Policy is, or may be, made subject, shall from the time the warranty attaches apply and continue to be in force during the whole currency of the Policy, and non-compliance with any such Warranty, whether it increases the risk or not, shall be a bar to any claim here-under . . .'

13 *Sovereign Fire Insurance Co v Moir* (1887) 14 SCR 612, where the assured added to the business described in the policy another and less hazardous business, and was held to have broken the condition.

14 *Thompson v Equity Fire Insurance Co* (supra).

(b) Conditions prohibiting increase of risk

By such a condition the making of such alterations as increase the risk is prohibited. Provided that the identity of the subject-matter remains, the assured is not precluded from making any alteration, however extensive, so long as the risk is not thereby increased; for until there is an increase of risk, the condition cannot be broken.[15]

Whether any particular alteration increases the risk is a question of fact,[16] and must be proved by the insurers.[17]

To establish a breach of condition it is not, however, sufficient to show that the risk has been increased. The question remains whether the alteration falls within the terms of the particular condition employed.

Two classes of such conditions are to be distinguished:

- i Conditions which are so widely framed as to embrace *any alteration whatsoever,* and to avoid the policy, whether the alteration increasing the risk is permanent or temporary.[18]
- ii Conditions which contemplate alterations of a *permanent character only.* Under such a condition a mere temporary alteration does not avoid the policy,[19] even though it increases the risk and, in fact, causes the loss.[20]

(c) Conditions prohibiting alterations without notice

By such a condition the making of alterations is prohibited unless notice is given to the insurers.

Two classes of such conditions are to be distinguished:

---

[15] *Stokes v Cox* (1856) 1 H & N 533, ExCh; *Barrett v Jermy* (1849) 3 Exch 535 per Parke B, at 543.

[16] *Baxendale v Harvey* (1859) 4 H & N 445, where it appears (see 28 LJ Ex 236, 237) that the defendant unsuccessfully objected to the question being left to the jury; *Ottawa and Rideau Forwarding Co v Liverpool and London and Globe Insurance Co* (1869) 28 UCR 518; *Guardian Insurance Co v Willshire and Feeley* (1911) 13 WALR 210, where the finding of the jury that the risk had not been increased was set aside as against the undisputed evidence. In *Date v Gore District Mutual Insurance Co* (1865) 15 CP 175 it was held that an increase of risk in one part of the building was counter-balanced by a diminution of risk in another part, and that there was therefore on the whole no increase of risk; but the correctness of this finding is open to question.

[17] *Barrett v Jermy* (1849) 3 Exch 353 per Parke B, at 542; *Anglo-American Fire Insurance Co v Morton* (1912) 46 SCR 653, where a billiard room was changed into a restaurant; *Guerin v Manchester Fire Assurance Co* (1898) 29 SCR 139, where a private dwelling-house was used as a hotel; *Kourzswki v Metropolitan Fire Association of Canada* (1922) 55 NSR 81, where the removal of property into a building changed its character; *Linden Alimak Ltd v British Engine Insurance Ltd* [1984] 1 Lloyd's Rep 416 (extraneous damage insurance), where the insurers proved that there had been a material change in the risk to a gantry crane (see the judgment of Webster J, ibid, at 423).

[18] *Shaw v Robberds* (1837) 6 Ad & El 75 per Lord Denman CJ, at 82; *Dobson v Sotheby* (1827) Mood & M 90.

[19] *Barrett v Jermy* (supra) per Parke B, at 545; *Shaw v Robberds* (supra) per Lord Denman CJ, at 82, 83; *Quin v National Assurance Co* (1839) Jo & Car 316 per Joy CB, at 330, distinguishing the use of premises as a carpenter's shop from the casual presence of a carpenter called in to do an occasional job; *Baxendale v Harvey* (1859) 4 H & N 445; *Ottawa and Rideau Forwarding Co v Liverpool and London and Globe Insurance Co* (1869) 28 UCR 518; *Stanford v Imperial Guarantee and Accident Insurance Co of Canada* (1908) 18 OLR 562, where a condition against engaging temporarily in a more hazardous employment was held, in the case of a commercial traveller, to be broken by his acting gratuitously on a trial trip as a brakesman.

[20] *Shaw v Robberds* (supra).

i Conditions in which the prohibition is general in its terms, amounting to an absolute prohibition of alterations without notice

In this case any alteration, however immaterial, is, in the absence of notice, a breach of the condition, and avoids the policy.[1]

The fact that it is of a temporary character[2] or that the risk is not increased thereby[3] cannot be taken into consideration.

ii Conditions which define the classes of alteration which are not to be made without notice

No notice need be given when the alteration made does not fall within its terms;[4] for in this case neither the alteration nor the failure notice avoids the policy.

(A) TIME FOR GIVING NOTICE

The time when the notice should be given, whether before or after the alteration is made, depends on the particular condition. The terms of the condition may be such as to permit of the notice being given after the alteration has been effected;[5] in this case, unless the condition specifies a time within which the notice is to be given, it will be sufficient if given within a reasonable time.[6] If notice is given within the requisite time, there is no breach of the condition, and the assured may recover, notwithstanding that the loss may have taken place after the alteration and before the notice. It is for the insurers to prove the absence of notice.[7]

(B) SANCTION OF THE INSURERS

The condition may provide not only for the giving of notice, but also for

---

1 *Glen v Lewis* (1853) 8 Exch 607, where the introduction of a steam-engine for experimental purposes, which was only used on one occasion, avoided the policy; *Rhodes v Union Insurance Co* (1883) 2 NZLR 106, where the assured was ignorant of the alteration.

2 *Glen v Lewis* (supra).

3 *Lindsay v Niagara District Mutual Fire Insurance Co* (1869) 28 UCR 326, where it was held, on a condition prohibiting any condition to the insured building without notice, that it was unnecessary for the insurers to prove that the risk had been increased, and that they were entitled to succeed on proving the addition without notice; *Merrick v Provincial Insurance Co* (1857) 14 UCR 439, where, on a condition avoiding the policy if the building containing the goods insured should be used for any trade or business denominated hazardous unless agreed to by the insurers, it was held that the policy was avoided by the fact that a hazardous trade had been carried on without notice to the insurers, and that no question as to increase of risk thereby was left for the jury.

4 *Baxendale v Harvey* (supra) per Pollock CB, at 451; *Stokes v Cox* (1856) 1 H & N 533, ExCh per Cockburn CJ, at 540; *Barrett v Jermy* (supra).

5 *Canada Landed Credit Co v Canada Agricultural Insurance Co* (1870) 17 Gr 418, where the condition related to the premises insured becoming unoccupied.

6 *Pim v Reid* (1843) 6 Man & G 1 per Coltman J, at 21; *Canada Landed Credit Co v Canada Agricultural Insurance Co* (supra); *Rhodes v Union Insurance Co* (1883) 2 NZLR 106, where sixty days was held to be more than a reasonable time; *Linden Alimak Ltd v British Engine Insurance Ltd* [1984] 1 Lloyd's Rep 416 (extraneous damage insurance), where the insurers were to be notified 'forthwith'.

7 *Barrett v Jermy* (1849) 3 Exch 535 per Parke B, at 542. Notice to an agent is sufficient: *Ansley v Watertown Insurance Co* (1888) 15 QLR 256; unless the condition provides otherwise: *Peck v Agricultural Insurance Co* (1890) 19 OR 494.

obtaining the sanction of the insurers to the alteration.[8] There may also be an express provision that such sanction must be obtained before the alteration is to be made;[9] or the terms of the condition may contemplate the giving of the sanction afterwards.[10] The assured cannot safely make any of the prohibited alterations without first obtaining the sanction of the insurers,[11] unless the condition clearly contemplates that such sanction may follow the alteration. Even in this case it is more prudent for him to obtain it first.

The sanction of the insurers may be refused altogether, or may only be granted in consideration of an increased premium. If, notwithstanding the refusal of the insurers, the alteration is persisted in, the condition applies and the policy is avoided by the making of a prohibited alteration.

The policy will similarly be avoided where the sanction is given in consideration of an increased premium, if such premium is not paid, since the terms upon which the sanction has been given have never been performed, and the sanction has therefore never taken effect.[12]

Where, however, the condition provides that a breach is to avoid the policy only as regards that part of the subject-matter insured which is affected by the alteration, the policy will remain in force as to the remainder; but the insurers may, to meet such a case, by the terms of the condition, reserve the right to terminate the whole insurance effected by the policy.[13]

The assured is not bound, on obtaining the consent of the insurers and paying the increased premium, if any, to make the alteration at once; unless a time is prescribed by the insurers, he may make it at any time during the currency of the policy.[14] The condition may provide that the sanction of the insurers is to be signified by a memorandum indorsed on the policy.[15] The insurers may, however, waive the necessity for this memorandum, or may be estopped by their acts or conduct from relying upon its absence.[16]

---

8 Where the condition merely requires a notice, the sanction of the insurers is not necessary; *Re Birkbeck Permanent Building Society, Official Receiver v Licenses Insurance Corpn* [1913] 2 Ch 34 (mortgage insurance).

9 *McClure v Lancashire Insurance Co* (1860) 6 IrJur NS 63, where removal of the insured property was prohibited without consent.

10 *Barrett v Jermy* (supra), where the condition was that the alteration must be immediately notified; *Peck v Phoenix Mutual Insurance Co* (1881) 45 UCR 620, where the condition provided for the avoidance of the policy 'unless the change be promptly notified'; but see *Re Birkbeck Permanent Building Society, Official Receiver v Licenses Insurance Corpn* (supra) per Neville J, at 37.

11 See *Glen v Lewis* (1853) 8 Exch 607 per Parke B, at 618. In this case the condition required notice of alteration to be given and an increased premium to be paid.

12 Cf *Harvey v Mutual Fire Insurance Co of Prescot* (1862) 11 UCR 294.

13 *Sun Fire Office v Hart* (1889) 14 App Cas 98, PC.

14 *Notman v Anchor Assurance Co* (1858) 4 CBNS 476 (life insurance), where the assured paid an additional premium for permission to go abroad for a year, but did not go abroad for some years afterwards.

15 The agent through whom the insurance was originally effected may be authorised to indorse the requisite memorandum in ordinary case of alteration. But an unauthorised indorsement by the agent is not binding upon the insurers: *Kline Bros & Co v Dominion Fire Insurance Co* (1912) 47 SCR 252.

16 *Wing v Harvey* (1854) 5 De GM & G 265 (life insurance), where a condition against going abroad without licence was waived by the receipt of premiums; *Armstrong v Turquand* (1858) 9 ICLR 32 (life insurance); *Smith v Commercial Union Insurance Co* (1872) 33 UCR 69, where the assured had sent his policy to the company for endorsement, and it was returned to him without endorsement accompanied by a statement that all had been done under the policy and conditions that was necessary; cf *Peck v Phoenix Mutual Insurance Co* (supra); *Canada Landed Credit Co v Canada Agricultural Insurance Co* (supra).

(d) Conditions prohibiting increase of risk without sanction

By such a condition, which is the one most usually employed in practice, the prohibition is confined to the making of such alterations as increase the risk,[17] and at the same time the obligation is imposed upon the assured of obtaining the sanction of the insurers.

To avoid the policy, therefore, it is necessary to show not only that the alteration in queston increases the risk, but also that the sanction of the insurers has not been obtained. The condition usually provides that the sanction is to be signified by indorsement on the policy. This provision is an important factor in determining whether the particular condition avoids the policy in the case of alterations other than those of a permanent character.[18]

Where, after an alteration increasing the risk has been sanctioned by the insurers, and duly indorsed on the policy, a second alteration is made which, though increasing the original risk, does not amount to an increase of risk compared with the alteration sanctioned, the policy is probably avoided.[19]

---

[17] *Shanly v Allied Traders' Insurance Co Ltd* (1925) 21 LlL Rep 195, where the interposition of variety turns at a cinema was held not to increase the risk, the building having formerly been a theatre; *Farnham v Royal Insurance Co Ltd* [1976] 2 Lloyd's Rep 437, (fire insurance), where the insured allowed welding repair work on metal cargo containers to be carried out in a barn, and it was held that the condition as to the alteration of the risk had been broken. (See the judgment of Ackner J, ibid, at 443); *Exchange Theatre Ltd v Iron Trades Mutual Insurance Co Ltd* [1984] 1 Lloyd's Rep 149, CA (fire insurance), where the policy stated that there should be no alteration in a building whereby the risk of destructional damage was increased, and it was held that there had been no alteration by a petrol generator and a quantity of petrol being brought into the building. (See the judgment of Eveleigh LJ, ibid, at 153.)

[18] *Barrett v Jermy* (1849) 3 Exch 535 per Parke B, at 545: 'It does not mean that the mere casual use for any of the hazardous purposes is to avoid the policy, but something of a permanent character of which notice had been given to the insurance company, so that an indorsement might have been made on the policy, but the use on one or more occasions would not avoid the policy.' See also, *Pim v Reid* (1843) 6 Man & G 1 at 18 (reporter's note).

[19] In *Campbell v Liverpool and London Fire and Life Insurance Co* (1869) 13 LCJ 309 it was held that the policy was not avoided, although the second alteration had been neither sanctioned nor indorsed on the policy; but see *Sovereign Fire Insurance Co v Moir* (1887) 14 SCR 612, where the condition prohibited the carrying on of hazardous trades without the sanction of the insurers, and it was held to be broken by the establishment of a trade which was classed as hazardous, although such trade was in fact less dangerous than the trade originally allowed by the policy, and although there was therefore no increase of risk. The condition in use has the effect of restricting the sanction to the actual alteration sanctioned.

CHAPTER 32

The assignment of the subject-matter insured under the policy

The assured does not necessarily retain his interest in the subject-matter of insurance throughout the currency of the policy.

Usually the policy contains an express clause setting out the result of any assignment by the assured. Further, the subject-matter may have been assigned by operation of law in the case of his death or bankruptcy. It may have been sold or given away. A trust may have been created in respect of it, or it may have been mortgaged. If it were originally owned by a partnership, a change in the constitution of the firm may have come about, or the firm may have been turned into a limited company. It, therefore, becomes necessary to consider the effect of such types of assignment on the validity of the policy.

The subject-matter of insurance in the case of personal accident insurance and life insurance is from its nature unassignable. In all other classes of insurance the subject-matter is capable of being assigned.

An assignment of the subject-matter of insurance by virtue of an agreement between the assured and the assignee may affect the validity of the policy by reason of the rule that the assured must at the date of the loss possess an insurable interest.

If the insurance relates to specific property, whether directly, as in the case of an insurance on the property itself, or indirectly, as in the case of an insurance against the liability arising out of its ownership, it is clear that the property insured may be assigned, and that the liability insured against necessarily passes with the property. If the insurance does not relate to specific property, but to a class of property, the assignment of a particular object falling within the class affects neither the ownership of the class nor the liability arising therefrom.[1] But the class may be assigned as a whole, as, for instance, on the sale of a business, and any subsequent liability arising from its ownership necessarily devolves on its new owner.

A EXPRESS CONDITIONS AGAINST ASSIGNMENT

The policy usually contains an express condition to the effect that the policy is to cease to be in force if the subject-matter passes from the assured otherwise

1 Consequently, the sale, e g of articles forming part of the assured's stock-in-trade, is not an assignment of his stock-in-trade for the purposes of an insurance upon his stock-in-trade.

than by will or by operation of law.[2] The position under a condition to this effect does not materially[3] differ from what would be the position in its absence.[4] Such a condition usually applies only to an absolute transfer.[5]

Sometimes the condition is framed more strictly and the policy may be avoided though the assignment is by way of mortgage or charge or by way of leasing or sub-letting,[6] unless the consent of the insurers thereto is obtained.[7] On the other hand, the condition may permit absolute assignment in certain cases, as, for instance, on the retirement of a partner,[8] or on the sale of a business.

There is no breach of a condition against the assignment of the subject-matter until the assignment is complete.[9]

B ASSIGNMENT BY OPERATION OF LAW

Where the assignment takes place by operation of law, as on the death[10] or bankruptcy[11] of the assured, the insurable interest of the assured in the

---

2 *Reilly Bros v Mercantile Mutual Insurance Co* (1928) 30 WALR 72, where in the case of a policy expressly covering the respective interests of the parties under a hire-purchase agreement, the condition was held to be broken by the making of a sub-hire-purchase agreement. A compulsory sale, e g by a mortgagee is probably not to be regarded as an assignment by operation of law since it is ultimately the result of an act done by the assured; see *Pyman v Marten* (1907) 13 Com Cas 64, CA (marine insurance) per Lord Alverstone CJ, at 67.

3 The only possible difference is in the case where the subject-matter passes by will, as to which see infra, note 10.

4 Enemy capture is not within a condition expressly referring to sale or transfer to new management: *Pyman v Marten* (supra).

5 But a particular policy may be intended to cover the property, irrespective of its transfer: *Brady v Irish Land Commission* [1921] 1 IR 56.

6 *National Protector Fire Insurance Co Ltd v Nivert* [1913] AC 507, PC.

7 See *Wilkinson v Coverdale* (1793) 1 Esp 74 (fire insurance).

8 Or it may contain a condition the effect of which is to avoid the policy in such an event: *McLachlan v Accident Insurance Co of North America* (1888) 4 MLRSC 365; *Solvency Mutual Guarantee Co v Freeman* (1861) 7 H & N 17.

9 *Forbes & Co v Border Counties Fire Office* 1873 11 Macph (Ct of Sess) 278 (fire insurance); cf *Collingridge v Royal Exchange Assurance Corpn* (1877) 3 QBD 173, CA (fire insurance); *Rayner v Preston* (1881) 18 ChD 1, CA (fire insurance); *Castellain v Preston* (1883) 11 QBD 380, CA (fire insurance).

10 Devolution on intestacy is clearly an assignment by operation of law. Devolution under a will is probably to be regarded in the same way, but in that case the transfer to the person ultimately entitled takes place by the act of the assured, and is capable of being regarded as a breach of the condition express or implied against assignment of the subject-matter: see *Rayner v Preston* (1881) 18 ChD 1, CA per Cotton LJ, at 8, criticising *Durrant v Friend* (1852) 5 De G & Sm 343 (marine insurance). The point is, however, of little practical importance, as the usual condition against assignment of the subject-matter contains an express exception in favour of transfer by will as well as by operation of law.

11 *Jackson v Forster* (1860) 1 E & E 470, ExCh (life insurance) per Cockburn CJ, at 471. In *Re Birkbeck Permanent Benefit Building Society, Official Receiver v Licenses Insurance Corpn* [1913] 2 Ch 34 (mortgage insurance) it was held that a sale by the trustee in bankruptcy or liquidator was an assignment by operation of law. But this was a case of an unregistered company where an order had been made vesting the property of the company in the liquidator. In the case of a limited company, its property does not vest in the liquidator on a winding-up, and, therefore, the decision does not apply to an assignment by the liquidator of such a company, the assignment being a voluntary assignment: *Re Farrow's Bank* [1921] 2 Ch 164, CA (company).

subject-matter of insurance is transferred to the personal representatives[12] or trustee in bankruptcy,[13] and the validity of the policy is not affected.

C SALE OR GIFT OF SUBJECT-MATTER

Where the assignment is by the voluntary act of the assured, e g in the case of a sale or a gift, the validity of the policy depends on whether the assured, after the assignment, retains his insurable interest in the subject-matter.

An absolute conveyance[14] of the subject-matter from the assured to a purchaser,[15] accompanied by the receipt of the agreed price, divests the assured of his interest in the subject-matter.[16] He cannot, therefore, in the event of its subsequent destruction, e g by fire, recover on any policy by which it may have been insured, since he has suffered no loss, and there is consequently nothing to which the right of indemnity can attach.[17]

The validity of a policy is not affected by the mere fact that the assured has entered into a contract to convey the subject-matter on insurance,[18] even though, as between the assured and the purchaser, the risk has passed to the purchaser.[19]

---

12 *Durrant v Friend* (supra) (marine insurance); *Doe d Pitt v Laming* (1814) 4 Camp 73 (fire insurance).

13 Bankruptcy Act 1914, ss 38(1), 167.

14 By a conveyance is meant the actual transfer of the property in the subject-matter from the assured to the purchaser. In the case of a building this is effected by the execution of a deed. In the case of chattels it may be effected by the mere terms of the contract.

15 The transfer may be shown by the fact of the transferee going into immediate possession, and also taking over the benefit of an existing policy: *Doe d Pearson v Ries* (1832) 8 Bing 178 per Bosanquet J, at 185.

16 *Collingridge v Royal Exchange Assurance Corpn* (1877) 3 QBD 173 (fire insurance) per Lush J, at 177, where the first took place before the conveyance; *Ecclesiastical Comrs for England v Royal Exchange Assurance Corpn* (1895) 11 TLR 476 (fire insurance), where the fire took place after the conveyance; *Robson v Liverpool, London and Globe Insurance Co* (1900) Times, 23 June, CA, per Romer LJ; *Bacon v Providence Washington Insurance Co* (1914) QR 47 SC 71; *Powles v Innes* (1843) 11 M & W 10 (marine insurance), explaining *Sparkes v Marshall* (1836) 2 Bing NC 761 (marine insurance).

17 *Rayner v Preston* (1881) 18 ChD 1, CA, per Cotton LJ, at 7: 'The fact that the insured had parted with all interest in the property insured would be an answer to the claim on the principle that the contract is one of indemnity only.' See also, *Garden v Ingram* (1852) 23 LJCh 478, per Lord St Leonards, at 481; *North British and Mercantile Insurance Co v Moffatt* (1871) LR 7 CP 25, where teas which had been sold by the assured, and for which they had been paid, were held not to be covered by a policy on 'merchandise the assured's own, in trust or on commission, for which they are responsible', there being no obligation on the assured to insure, the fact that the assured had voluntarily paid to the purchasers the value of the teas destroyed making no difference; *Ecclesiastical Comrs v Royal Exchange Assurance Corpn* (supra) (fire insurance); *Rogerson v Scottish Automobile and General Insurance Co Ltd* (1931) 146 LT 26, HL (accident insurance); *Ocean Accident and Guarantee Corpn v Williams* (1915) 34 NZLR 924.

18 *Collingridge v Royal Exchange Assurance Corpn* (supra) (fire insurance), where a notice to treat in respect of the insured's building had been given to the assured by the Metropolitan Board of Works, the amount of compensation payable had been assessed by arbitration, and the assured's title to the building accepted, but the premises had been burned before execution of the conveyance, and the assured was held entitled to recover the full amount of his insurance, without regard to the dealings between the Board and himself; *Ardill v Citizen's Insurance Co* (1893) 20 OR 605, where there was a contract to pull down the building and sell the material.

19 As was the case in *Collingridge v Royal Exchange Assurance Corpn* (supra) (fire insurance), for 'the risk of fire was the Corporation's risk from the time of the notice to treat' (*Phoenix Assurance Co v Spooner* [1905] 2 KB 753, per Bigham J, at 756).

The existence of the contract does not, in itself, divest the assured of his insurable interest, which continues by reason of his legal ownership of the subject-matter; and he acquires a further interest arising out of the possibility of the purchaser refusing to carry out the contract, and thereby throwing the loss on him.[20]

In the case of a fire policy, where the fire takes place before the sale is completed by the execution of the conveyance and the receipt of the price, the assured is entitled to recover to the full extent of his loss within the limits of the policy. The existence of the contract and even the certainty that the assured will finally suffer no loss at all because of the purchaser's intention to complete, and his undoubted solvency, cannot be taken into account as diminishing the amount recoverable.[1]

Where, however, the sale is afterwards completed, and the price paid, the assured has, in the events that have happened, suffered no loss. He cannot, therefore, either enforce the policy, or, if he has received the proceeds of the policy, retain both the proceeds and the price for his own benefit.[2]

A conveyance of the subject-matter, unaccompanied by the receipt of the price, does not apparently affect the validity of the policy, if the fire takes place before the assured has parted with his lien as unpaid vendor.[3] Although the conveyance divests him of his legal ownership, he nevertheless retains, by virtue of his lien, an insurable interest sufficient to keep the policy alive, and it is immaterial that it is reduced from a legal interest to a mere equitable one. He, therefore, is entitled, as in the previous case, to enforce his policy, so long as such interest remains. If, however, he parts with his lien before he has received his price, his insurable interest under the policy is extinguished, in as much as his relationship to the subject-matter of insurance has ceased to exist. He has no longer a right to look to the subject-matter as securing payment of the price; his sole right is a personal right as an ordinary creditor against the purchaser himself.[4]

If the price has been paid, but the conveyance of the subject-matter has not been completed, the assured retains an insurable interest by virtue of his legal ownership. The policy therefore remains in force, notwithstanding such payment.[5] But in the event of a loss before completion, the assured, not being damnified by the loss, will not be entitled to enforce it against the insurers for his own benefit, although, if the conditions of the Law of Property Act 1925, s 47 are fulfilled,[6] he may enforce it for the benefit of the purchaser. Where, however, the assured has contracted with the purchaser to be responsible for the safety of the subject-matter, the position will be different; and, unless the

---

20 *Castellain v Preston* (1883) 11 QBD 380, CA (fire insurance), per Brett LJ, at 385.

1 *Collingridge v Royal Exchange Assurance Corpn* (supra) (fire insurance).

2 *Castellain v Preston* (supra) (fire insurance).

3 Cf Sale of Goods Act 1979, s 41.

4 Sale of Goods Act 1979, s 43.

5 *Castellain v Preston* (supra) (fire insurance). In *Bank of New South Wales v North British and Mercantile Insurance Co* (1881) 2 NSWLR 239 the Court, which might have been influenced by the subsequent execution of a formal conveyance by the assured, held that the assured in such a case had no insurable interest. This, however, seems on principle to be incorrect. The assured's right is to be ascertained as at the date of the loss, and at that he clearly had some interest, although the fact that he had been paid and was therefore not damnified by the loss, disentitled him to recover.

6 See p 445, post.

language of the policy is prohibitive, the value of the subject-matter will be recoverable by the assured.[7]

The contract under which the assignment of the subject-matter takes place may contain a provision that the assured is to keep alive an existing policy for the benefit of the purchaser.[8] Where, as is usually the case, the consent of the insurers is obtained to what is to all intents and purposes an assignment of the policy,[9] no difficulty can arise.

The effect of the provision, in the absence of such consent, does not appear to have been discussed, but it would seem that there must be no condition in the policy precluding the assured from contracting with a purchaser in the terms of the provision.[10] So long as the assured retains some interest in the subject-matter,[11] such a provision may be valid, not only as between the assured and the purchaser, but also against the insurers. Although the contract may effect a change in the nature of his interest, it does not put an end to it. Nor is its value necessarily diminished, since the contract may amount to an undertaking by the assured to be responsible in the event of any loss. In this case, at any rate, there seems to be no reason[12] why he should not be entitled to enforce the policy in respect of such interest,[13] provided that he is not prohibited from so doing by the terms of the policy.

Where there is no such undertaking, he may perhaps be entitled to enforce his policy for the benefit of the purchaser on the ground that, at the time of effecting it, he intended to cover the whole interest in the subject-matter.[14] It is more probable, however, that he cannot effectively do so, since the handing over of the sum received under the policy would be a mere voluntary payment on his part, and would not deprive the insurers of their right to have the purchase money taken into account.[15]

If before loss the assured parts with his interest in the subject-matter, the policy comes to an end, by reason of the cesser of the interest on which it was

---

7 *Martineau v Kitching* (1872) LR 7 QB 436, per Blackburn J, at 458.

8 *Doe d Pearson v Ries* (1832) 8 Bing 178; *Poole v Adams* (1864) 33 LJCh 639; *North British and Mercantile Insurance Co v Moffatt* (1871) LR 7 CP 25; *Martineau v Kitching* (supra); *Rayner v Preston* (1881) 18 ChD 1, CA, per James LJ, at 6; *Caledonian Insurance Co v Montreal Trust Co* [1932] SCR 581, where the liquidator was in possession as trustee of the purchasers; cf *Paine v Meller* (1801) 6 Ves 349; *Powles v Innes* (1843) 11 M & W 10 (marine insurance), per Parke B, at 13.

9 As in *Garden v Ingram* (1852) 23 LJCh 478, where the insurers were willing to pay the purchaser; *Darrell v Tibbitts* (1880) 5 QBD 560, CA, where it was the purchaser who had received payment under the policy.

10 *Rayner v Preston* (1881) 18 ChD 1, CA (fire insurance) per Cotton LJ, at 6.

11 As where a seller, having been paid, remains in possession of the goods: *North British and Mercantile Insurance Co v Moffatt* (supra) (fire insurance) per Keating J, at 31; *Martineau v Kitching* (supra).

12 Cf *Reed v Cole* (1764) 3 Burr 1512 (marine insurance), where an assured, who had sold the ship insured under an agreement with the purchaser to pay £500 if a loss happened within three months, was held entitled to recover on the ground that he still had an interest in the ship. He had not parted with all his interest in it, but remained interested quoad this loss.

13 Since any money received under the policy is in effect to be applied towards the purchase money, no question of indemnification aliunde appears to arise, and the insurers could not therefore raise it as against the assured.

14 It may, however, be urged that the only interest which he intended to cover was his own, and that he did not, at the time of insuring intend to cover any other.

15 Cf *North British and Mercantile Insurance Co v Moffatt* (1871) LR 7 CP 25 (fire insurance), where the assured had voluntarily paid over the amount of the loss to the purchaser, who had already paid for the goods destroyed.

based.[16] Where, by his agreement with the purchaser, the assured does not undertake to be liable in the event of a loss, his right, if any, to enforce the policy does not depend on the interest which he had at the date of effecting the policy, and the rules relating to continuity of interest in the assured apply.[17] The policy, therefore, would not be revived, and the assured would not be able to enforce the policy in respect of any loss happening after the cesser of interest.

D CREATION OF A TRUST OR MORTGAGE

Where the assignment of the subject-matter, though in its terms purporting to be absolute,[18] is only a nominal assignment without consideration, and is not intended to divest the assured of his interest, the validity of the policy is not affected. The assured remains fully interested in the subject-matter, although his interest is now an equitable one only.[19] It is thus to be distinguished from an assignment which, although made without consideration, is intended to operate by way of gift, and which, therefore wholly divests the assured of his interest in the subject-matter.

Similarly, the creation of a mortgage or charge on the subject-matter by the assured does not in the absence of an express condition to that effect[20] affect the validity of his policy, because he is not entirely divested of his interest, since he retains an equity of redemption,[1] and generally also the possession of the subject-matter.[2]

---

16 *Robson v Liverpool, London and Globe Insurance Co* (1900) Times, 23 June, CA; *Tattersall v Drysdale* [1935] 2 KB 174, 52 LlL Rep 21 (accident insurance), following *Rogerson v Scottish Automobile and General Insurance Co Ltd* (1931) 146 LT 26, HL (accident insurance), in each of which the assured had parted with the motor car insured for which he had substituted another of similar make.

17 See pp 26–29, ante.

18 *Ward v Beck* (1863) 13 CBNS 668 (marine insurance), per Willes J, at 673; *Caledonian Insurance Co v Montreal Trust Co* [1932] SCR 581.

19 *Montreal Assurance Co v McGillivray* (1859) 13 Moo PCC 87, per Smith J (in the Court below), at 98.

20 The usual condition against parting with interest otherwise than by will or operation of law is not sufficient: *Bull v North British Canadian Investment Co and Imperial Fire Insurance Co* (1888) 15 AR 421, approving *Sands v Standard Insurance Co* (1879) 26 Gr 113; *Wade v Rochester German Fire Insurance Co* (1911) 19 OR 99 (assignment for the benefit of creditors); *Minucoe v London, Liverpool and Globe Insurance Co* (1925) 26 SRNSW 325 (bill of sale). The condition must refer specifically to a mortgage: *Russ v Mutual Fire Insurance Co of Clinton* (1869) 29 UCR 73; or at least refer to a change of title or interest: *Citizens' Insurance Co v Salterio* (1894) 23 SCR 155; *Torrop v Imperial Fire Insurance Co* (1896) 26 SCR 585; *O'Neill v Ottawa Agricultural Insurance Co* (1879) 30 CP 151.

1 If he parts with his equity of redemption to the mortgagee, his interest ceases and the policy comes to an end: *Pinhey v Mercantile Fire Insurance Co* (1901) 2 OLR 296.

2 *Garden v Ingram* (1852) 23 LJCh 478 (fire insurance), per Lord St Leonards, at 479: 'When a man insures property under an absolute covenant to insure, and then assigns and charges the lease to secure a sum of money, he still retains his interest in the property subject to the charge.' See also, *Alston v Campbell* (1779) 4 Bro Parl Cas 476 (marine insurance); *Hibbert v Carter* (1787) 1 Term Rep 745 (marine insurance); *Hutchinson v Wright* (1858) 25 Beav 444 (marine insurance); *Ottawa Agricultural Insurance Co v Sheridan* (1880) 5 SCR 157, where the assured sold the property, but reserved the right to redeem it; *Parsons v Queen Insurance Co* (1878) 29 CP 188, where warehouse receipts for goods were transferred to a bank as collateral security. Where a mortgagee specifically insures his interest as mortgagee, it has been held that his policy ceases to be operative after foreclosure, the nature of the interest insured having been completely changed: *Gaskin v Phoenix Insurance Co* (1866) 11 NBR (6 All) 429.

E CHANGE IN A PARTNERSHIP

The effect of a change in the constitution of an assured firm is open to some doubt. In the case of the retirement of a partner it may be said that, as the contract contained in the policy is a joint contract, the assignment of his interest by the retiring partner to the remaining partners is a breach of the condition against assignment of the subject-matter.

On the other hand, the interest of the remaining partners continues, and the retiring partner remains liable for the debts of the partnership contracted prior to his retirement.[3]

This second view is considered to be more probably correct, particularly as there is no question of the introduction of any element which the insurers might have been unwilling to accept on risk.[4]

The admission of a new partner will, however, have a different effect, and it is considered that the policy will be avoided. The new partner may be a person whom the insurers will not wish to insure or whom they are only prepared to insure on different terms.[5] Similarly, the taking of a partner by a person, who at the date of the policy was carrying on business alone, is a breach of the condition.

If, however, the subject-matter of the insurance is the property of one partner, although used by the firm, any policy effected by that partner will not be avoided by a subsequent change in the firm. It is, therefore, advisable in either case to notify the change in the firm to the insurers, and to obtain from them their consent to the continuance of the insurance. It is not, however, the change in the firm, but the assignment of the property insured to the new firm, that affects the policy. If, therefore, a loss takes place before the assignment is completed, the old firm may enforce it.[6]

When a partnership is changed into a limited company to which the subject-matter of insurance is assigned, any existing policy of insurance is avoided by reason of the transfer.[7]

---

3 Partnership Act 1890, s 17(2).

4 In *Jenkins v Deane* (1933) 150 LT 314 (accident insurance) Goddard J, at 318, expressed this view, though he did not find it necessary, on the facts of the case, to decide the question. Prior to this, the only English authority appears to be *Solvency Mutual Guarantee Co v Freeman* (1861) 7 H & N 17 (solvency insurance), where there was a special condition. Decisions in other countries similarly turn on special facts; see *Forbes & Co v Border Counties Fire Office* 1873 11 Macph (Ct of Sess) 278, where the transfer from the old firm to the continuing partners had not been effectively carried out; *Klein v Union Fire Insurance Co* (1883) 3 OR 234, where the retiring partner had himself a continuing interest under a covenant to insure; *Robert v Equitable Fire Insurance Co* (1912) QR 44 SC 205, where the policy was issued after the death of one of the partners; *Ferguson v National Fire and Marine Insurance Co of New Zealand* (1886) 7 NSWLR 392.

5 *Jenkins v Deane* (supra) (accident insurance), per Goddard J, at 317, where, however, he points out that there may be a different result in accident insurance.

6 *Forbes & Co v Border Counties Fire Office* 1873 11 Macph (Ct of Sess) 278; *Mann and Hobson v Western Assurance Co* (1860) 19 UCR 314.

7 *Levinger v Licenses and General Insurance Co Ltd* (1936) 54 LlL Rep 68 (accident insurance); *A G Peuchen Co v City Mutual Fire Insurance Co* (1891) 18 AR 446, where the members of the former partnership held nearly all the shares in the company.

CHAPTER 33

Other insurance

The assured is not prohibited by law from effecting as many policies as he pleases on the same subject-matter and against the same risk, and the existence of several policies at the same time does not affect the validity of the individual insurances, though his rights under any particular policy may, in the event of a claim arising, be modified.[1]

The usual question in the proposal form as to 'other insurance', though it requires the proposed assured to disclose not only such insurances as exist at the time of answering the question, but also any further insurances which he may effect between the date of answering and the issue of the policy,[2] extends no further and does not impose on him the duty of informing the insurers of any insurances effected after the issue of the policy.

1 Express conditions relating to 'other insurance'

The policy may, however, contain a condition requiring any such insurances to be notified. Such a condition is either a condition subsequent of the policy,[3] providing that a failure to notify is to avoid the policy, or a condition precedent to the liability of the insurers,[4] providing that no claim is to be valid in the absence of notification.[5]

The notification of other insurances is usually required by the condition to be indorsed by or on behalf of the insurers. The necessity for indorsement may, however, be waived.[6]

The duty imposed by the condition of notifying other insurances does not involve the duty of notifying the insurers that an existing policy has been allowed to lapse.[7] This duty may, however, be imposed by an express condition.[8]

---

1 *Scottish Amicable Heritage Securities Association v Northern Assurance Co* 1883 11 R (Ct of Sess) 287 (fire insurance) per the Lord Justice Clerk (Moncrieff), at 303. As to contribution between the different policies, see Chapter 48.

2 *Re Marshall and Scottish Employers' Liability and General Insurance Co* (1901) 85 LT 757.

3 *Chapman v Lancashire Insurance Co* (1875) 2 Stephens' Digest 407, PC (fire insurance); *Equitable Fire and Accident Office Ltd v Ching Wo Hong* [1907] AC 96, PC (fire insurance).

4 *Citizens' Insurance Co of Canada v Parsons* (1881) 7 App Cas 96, PC (fire insurance); cf *Sulphite Pulp Co of Canada v Faber* (1895) 1 Com Cas 146 (fire insurance), where, on the construction of the particular policy, the stipulation was held not to be a condition.

5 The impossibility of notifying before loss would, apparently, be no defence: *Australian Agricultural Co v Saunders* (1875) LR 10 CP 668 (fire insurance) per Blackburn J, at 675.

6 *Marcovitch v Liverpool Victoria Friendly Society* (1912) 28 TLR 188 (life insurance).

7 *Hordern v Commercial Union Assurance Co* (1884) 5 NSWLR 309 (fire insurance), affirmed without reference to this point: (1887) 56 LJPC 78.

8 *Sulphite Pulp Co v Faber* (supra), where the policy was to cease to attach till notification, and the insurer was given the option to cancel.

2 What constitutes 'other insurance'

To constitute 'other insurance' within the meaning of the condition:

a The other policies must be intended to cover the same risk as that covered by the policy containing the condition.
b The other policies must be valid and subsisting contracts of insurance.
c The other policies must be additional insurances.

(a) Same risk

The policies must be intended to insure the same interest in the same subject-matter and the same peril.[9] A subsequent insurance which, in certain contingencies only, may cover a portion of the same risk and which involves the mere possibility of an accidental overlapping,[10] is not 'other insurance' within the meaning of the condition.[11]

(b) Valid and subsisting policies[12]

It is not necessary that formal policies should have been issued. The issue of a cover note or the entry into a binding contract of insurance[13] is sufficient. On the other hand, there is no 'other insurance' within the meaning of the condition if the other insurance was never completed,[14] and it is immaterial that a formal policy was issued if it is, in fact, void[15] or is treated by the parties to it as void.[16]

---

9 *Australian Agricultural Co v Saunders* (supra) per Bramwell B, at 674.

10 As in *Australian Agricultural Co v Saunders* (supra) (fire insurance), where a fire policy covered goods in transit on land, and the failure of the assured to notify the insurers of a marine policy subsequently effected, which happened to cover them whilst temporarily in a warehouse awaiting shipment, was held not to be a breach of a condition providing that no claim should be recoverable if the property insured should be previously or subsequently insured elsewhere, unless the insurers were notified; cf *American Surety Co of New York v Wrightson* (1910) 16 Com Cas 37, where one policy was a fidelity insurance, a separate sum being insured in the case of each of the assured's servants, whilst the other policy covered in one lump sum dishonesty and negligence of servants, dishonesty of strangers, fire, burglary and other risks, and Hamilton J doubted whether there was really a case of double insurance at all.

11 *Australian Agricultural Co v Saunders* (supra) per Blackburn J, at 675: 'I cannot think it would be a reasonable construction of the words to hold that the particulars of the marine insurance ought to have been notified to the company merely because it might happen that during the transit some loss by fire might occur which the marine policy might cover. The mere possibility of an accidental overlapping of the two policies was not, as it seems to me, what was aimed at.'

12 *Equitable Fire and Accident Office Ltd v Ching Wo Hong* [1907] AC 96, PC (fire insurance).

13 Probably the effecting of a policy binding in honour though not in law is sufficient to constitute a breach of the condition: *Roddick v Indemnity Mutual Insurance Co* [1895] 1 QB 836 (marine insurance) per Kennedy J, at 839 et seq, doubted in SC [1895] 2 QB 380, CA, but approved in *Thames and Mersey Marine Insurance Co v Gunford Ship Co* [1911] AC 529 (marine insurance) per Lord Alverstone CJ, at 538.

14 Cf *Lishman v Northern Maritime Insurance Co* (1875) LR 10 CP 179, ExCh (marine insurance).

15 *Equitable Fire and Accident Office Ltd v Ching Wo Hong* (supra), where the second policy never took effect owing to the non-payment of the premium.

16 Ibid, at 99.

(c) Additional insurances

The condition has no application where an existing policy which is allowed by the condition is renewed or replaced by another policy issued by different insurers.[17] The duty of notifying the change of insurance may, however, be imposed by an express condition.

[17] *National Protector Fire Insurance Co Ltd v Nivert* [1913] AC 507 (fire insurance), where the fact that the substituted policies were for slightly larger amounts was considered, in the circumstances, immaterial; cf *General Insurance Co of Trieste (Assicurazioni Generali) v Cory* [1897] 1 QB 335 (marine insurance), where the effecting of a further insurance to cover an estimated deficiency on an existing policy was held not to be a breach of a warranty that the ship should not be insured beyond a specified amount.

CHAPTER 34

The assignment of the policy

The contract contained in the policy, being a purely personal one, does not run with the subject-matter of insurance in the same way as certain contracts are said to run with the land.[1]

An assignment of the subject-matter, therefore, does not of itself operate as an assignment of the policy so as to substitute the assignee for the original assured and to enable him to enforce it in his own name.[2] Nor does it give the assignee any rights in connection with the policy. In the event, therefore, of a subsequent loss the assignee of the subject-matter cannot, in the absence of some special agreement,[3] call on the assured to enforce the policy for his benefit, or to pay over any moneys which the assured may have already received under it.[4]

A WHAT CONSTITUTES A VALID ASSIGNMENT

Before the assignee of the subject-matter can in his own name enforce the contract contained in the policy, it is necessary that the policy should be validly assigned to him.[5] To constitute a valid assignment the following conditions must be fulfilled:

a Where necessary, the consent of the insurers must be obtained; and
b The assignment of the policy must be contemporaneous with the assignment of the subject-matter.

(a) Consent of the insurers

The policy may contain an express prohibition against its being assigned

---

[1] *Rayner v Preston* (1881) 18 ChD 1, CA (fire insurance), per Brett LJ, at 11, applying *North of England Pure Oil-Cake Co v Archangel Insurance Co* (1875) LR 10 QB 249 (marine insurance) and *Powles v Innes* (1843) 11 M & W 10 (marine insurance): 'The contract of insurance is a mere personal contract. It is not a contract which runs with the land . . . ; it is a mere personal contract and unless it is assigned no suit or action can be maintained upon it except between the original parties to it.' See also, *Phoenix Assurances Co v Spooner* [1905] 2 KB 753, per Bigham J, at 756; *Gill v Yorkshire Insurance Co* (1913) 24 WLR 389.

[2] *Paine v Meller* (1801) 6 Ves 349 per Lord Eldon C, at 351: 'The house is bought, not the benefit of any existing policy . . . The question, whether insured or not, is with the vendor solely, not with the vendee, unless he . . . makes it matter of contract with the vendor that the vendee shall buy according to that fact, that the house is insured'; *North of England Pure Oil-Cake Co v Archangel Insurance Co* (supra) per Quain J, at 255, citing *Powles v Innes* (supra): 'On the sale of a thing insured, no interest in the policy passes to the vendee, unless, at the time of the sale, the policy be assigned expressly or impliedly,' See also, *Poole v Adams* (1864) 33 LJCh 639; *Rayner v Preston* (supra) per Brett LJ, at 10.

[3] *Paine v Meller* (supra). [4] *Rayner v Preston* (supra).

[5] *Rayner v Preston* (supra) per Brett LJ, at 11.

without notice to the insurers and without obtaining their consent. Unless the condition provides otherwise, the insurers may give or withhold their consent at pleasure.[6] There is, therefore, no reason why they should not, as a condition of the consent, vary the terms of the policy, as, for instance, by requiring the assignee to pay a higher premium. Where, however, the condition merely requires notice, the insurers are bound to indorse the assignment on the policy.[7] An express condition, however, is not necessary, in the case of a fire policy or a liability insurance policy[8] which is not and never was, either at Common Law or in Equity,[9] assignable without such consent on account of its personal nature.[10] It is, therefore, necessary to obtain the consent of the insurers to the assignment, and, if any particular form of indicating their consent is prescribed, it should be obtained in that form.[11]

But, unless there is an express prohibition, a policy of marine insurance may be assigned,[12] and the assignee is entitled to sue in his own name.[13]

Similarly, the consent of the insurers is not necessary in the case of an assignment of a life policy, and the assignee is entitled to sue in his own name.[14]

Where the consent of the insurers is required, an assignment of the policy without their consent renders the policy voidable only,[15] and the policy, therefore, remains in force until they elect to avoid it.

The assignee, on obtaining their consent at any time after the assignment, is apparently entitled to enforce the policy. By giving their consent, the insurers

---

6 *Re Birkbeck Permanent Benefit Building Society, Official Receiver v Licenses Insurance Corpn* [1913] 2 Ch 34 (mortgage insurance) per Neville J, at 37; cf *Sun Fire Office v Hart* (1889) 14 App Cas 98, PC (fire insurance).

7 *Re Birkbeck Permanent Benefit Building Society, Official Receiver v Licenses Insurance Corpn* (supra) (mortgage insurance).

8 *Peters v General Accident Fire and Life Assurance Corpn Ltd* [1938] 2 All ER 267, 60 LlL Rep 311, CA.

9 *Lynch v Dalzell* (1729) 4 Bro Parl Cas 431; *Sadlers' Co v Badcock* (1743) 2 Atk 554.

10 *Sadlers' Co v Badcock* (supra) per Lord Hardwicke, at 556: 'To whom and for what loss are [the insurers] to make satisfaction? Why to the person insured, and for the loss he may have sustained: for it cannot properly be called insuring the thing, for there is no possibility of doing it, and therefore must mean insuring the person from damage'; *Lynch v Dalzell* (supra) in which case counsel for the Sun Fire Office used the following words which have always been regarded as correctly stating the law: 'These policies are not insurances of the specific things mentioned to be insured, for nobody could warrant against accidents: nor do such insurances attach on the reality or in any manner go with the same as incident thereto by any conveyance or assignment, but they are only special agreements with the persons insuring against such loss or damage as they should sustain.'

11 *Wilkinson v Coverdale* (1793) 1 Esp 74.

12 Marine Insurance Act 1906, s 50(1): 'A marine policy is assignable unless it contains terms expressly prohibiting assignment. It may be assigned either before or after loss.' See further, Ivamy *Marine Insurance* (4th Edn, 1985), p 315.

13 Marine Insurance Act 1906, s 50(2): 'Where a marine policy has been assigned so as to pass the beneficial interest in such policy, the assignee of the policy is entitled to sue thereon in his own name; and the defendant is entitled to make any defence arising out of the contract which he would have been entitled to make if the action had been brought in the name of the person by or on behalf of whom the policy was effected.' See further, Ivamy *Marine Insurance* (4th Edn, 1985), pp 315–316.

14 Policies of Assurance Act 1867, s 1: 'Any person or corporation now being or hereafter becoming entitled, by assignment or other derivative title, to a policy of life assurance, and possessing at the time of action brought the right in equity to receive and the right to give an effectual discharge to the assurance company liable under such policy for monies thereby assured or secured, shall be at liberty to sue at law in the name of such person or corporation to recover such monies.' See further, Ivamy *Personal Accident, Life and Other Insurances* (2nd Edn, 1980), pp 105–106.

15 *Doe d Pitt v Laming* (1814) 4 Camp 73 (fire insurance) per Lord Ellenborough CJ, at 75.

are estopped from denying the validity of the policy.[16] They may further be precluded by their subsequent conduct, or by their dealings with the assignee, from relying on the fact that their consent was not given in the proper form, or even on the fact that it was not given at all.

In practice, insurance policies except in the case of marine insurance usually contain an express condition regulating their assignment. The condition may provide that, on an assignment of the subject-matter otherwise than by will or operation of law, the policy is to cease to be in force unless, by the consent of the insurers, to be signified by indorsement on the policy, it is continued to the assignee.

Sometimes the condition dispenses with the consent of the insurers. Thus, under a condition to the effect that the policy is to cease to be in force unless notice of the assignment is given and unless the assignment is indorsed on the policy, the insurers have no power to withhold their consent, but must indorse the policy, if so required, on receiving notice.[17]

Similarly, the condition may provide that, on a change in a firm, the policy is to continue in force and to enure for the benefit of the new firm.

(b) Contemporaneity of assignment of the policy and the subject-matter

To constitute a valid assignment of the policy, the assignment must accompany a transfer of interest in the subject-matter.[18] The assignment of the policy can only be made, therefore, to the assignee of the subject-matter and at the same time as the assignment of the subject-matter[19] or in pursuance of a contemporaneous agreement.[20]

Since it is a transfer of the insurance as a whole, a transfer to any other person than such assignee would be a transfer to a person without an insurable interest and the policy would, therefore, become void.[21]

Moreover, as the original assured retains and the assignee does not acquire the insurable interest until the actual transfer of the subject-matter, the policy, if not assigned until after the assignment of the subject-matter, has already ceased to be in force,[1] whilst if assigned before the assignment of the subject-matter, it ceases to be in force on coming to the hands of a person who, as yet, has no insurable interest in the subject-matter.[2]

---

16 *Doe d Pitt v Laming* (supra) (fire insurance) per Lord Ellenborough CJ, at 75, where the indorsement was not obtained until after the expiration of the time limited by the condition, and the Court held that there had been no breach of a covenant to insure.

17 *Re Birkbeck Permanent Benefit Building Society, Official Receiver v Licenses Insurance Corpn* [1913] 2 Ch 34 (mortgage insurance).

18 *Lloyd v Fleming* (1872) LR 7 QB 299 (marine insurance) per Blackburn J, at 302: 'An attempted transfer to the beneficial interest in the policy, before loss, to a person having no beneficial interest in the subject-matter is inoperative.'

19 *Gill v Yorkshire Insurance Co* (1913) 24 WLR 389, where an assignment made after the sale of the insured animal was held to give the buyer no rights without the insurers' consent; *Powles v Innes* (1843) 11 M & W 10 (marine insurance). The transfer of the policy may be evidence of a transfer of interest: *Doe d Pearson v Ries* (1832) 8 Bing 178, at 185.

20 *North of England Pure Oil-Cake Co v Archangel Insurance Co* (1875) LR 10 QB 249 (marine insurance) per Cockburn CJ, at 253.

21 *Lloyd v Fleming* (supra) (marine insurance) per Blackburn J, at 302.

1 *North of England Pure Oil-Cake Co v Archangel Insurance Co* (supra) (marine insurance) per Cockburn CJ, at 253.

2 *Lloyd v Fleming* (supra) (marine insurance) per Blackburn J, at 302.

As far as marine insurance is concerned, the Marine Insurance Act 1906, s 51 provides that:

> 'Where the assured has parted with or lost his interest in the subject-matter insured, and has not, before or at the time of so doing, expressly or impliedly agreed to assign the policy, any subsequent assignment of the policy is inoperative.'[3]

B THE FORM OF THE ASSIGNMENT

No particular form of assignment appears to be necessary to complete the rights of the assignee as against the insurers, since the validity of the assignment depends, not on the form in which it is made, but on the consent of the insurers.

As far as marine insurance is concerned, the Marine Insurance Act 1906, s 50(3), states:

> 'A marine policy may be assigned by indorsement thereon or in other customary manner.'[4]

The assignment of the policy cannot be regarded as an assignment of an ordinary chose in action since it depends for its validity both on the assignee's possession of an interest in the subject-matter, and on the giving of their consent by the insurers, and therefore, the rules governing the validity of an assignment of a chose in action, whether legal, or equitable are inapplicable.

The assignment of the policy does not of itself confer any rights on the assignee as against the insurers, even though he possesses or acquires an interest in the subject-matter of insurance. By giving their consent, they render themselves liable to the assignee whether the policy has been duly assigned by a formal assignment, or whether it has merely been transferred to him by manual delivery in pursuance of an understanding between the original assured and himself.

Since, therefore, before giving their consent they may require such evidence of the assignee's title as they think desirable, they cannot, it is apprehended, resist liability on the ground of any informality in the assignment.[5]

C ASSIGNMENT BY OPERATION OF LAW

On the death,[6] or bankruptcy,[7] of the assured, the policy devolves on his personal representatives or trustee in bankruptcy, as being part of his estate and

---

3 See Ivamy *Marine Insurance* (4th Edn, 1985), p 321.

4 See e g *J Aron & Co v Miall* (1928) 98 LJKB 204, 31 LlL Rep 242, CA (marine insurance), where it was held that a policy indorsed in blank and assigned in accordance with the custom of marine insurance in England passed to the assignee all rights held by the assignor in the policy. See further, Ivamy *Marine Insurance* (4th Edn, 1985), pp 319–320.

5 They are not precluded by their consent from resisting liability upon other grounds; see pp 329–330, post. They may also resist liability on the ground that their consent to the assignment had been obtained by a mis-statement: *Johnstone v Niagara District Mutual Insurance Co* (1863) 13 CP 331.

6 *Doe d Pitt v Laming* (1814) 4 Camp 73 (fire insurance) per Lord Ellenborough CJ, at 75; cf *Jackson v Forster* (1860) 1 E & E 463, 470, ExCh (life insurance) per Williams J, at 471.

7 *Re Carr and Sun Fire Insurance Co* (1897) 13 TLR 186, CA (fire insurance); cf *Jackson v Forster* (supra); *Manchester Fire Assurance Co v Wykes* (1875) 33 LT 142 (fire insurance); *Re Bennett, ex p Official Receiver* [1907] 1 KB 149 (life insurance).

not merely because of its connection with the subject-matter.[8] In the case of a subsequent loss, the trustee in bankruptcy is entitled to sue on the policy in his official name.[9] No specific assignment of the policy appears to be necessary though a condition may require the policy to be indorsed.[10]

Whilst the policy is in the hands of the personal representatives or trustee in bankruptcy, it may be enforced for the benefit of the estate[11] not only in respect of claims which have arisen before the death or bankruptcy, and which have devolved upon them as claims,[12] but also in respect of claims arising afterwards.[13]

Where, in the administration of the estate, they transfer the subject-matter of insurance to a beneficiary or purchaser, they may assign the policy also, this being equally with the original devolution an assignment by operation of law as being consequent on and rendered necessary by the death or bankruptcy of the assured,[14] and the beneficiary[15] or purchaser[16] thereupon becomes entitled to the benefit of the policy.[17]

---

8 *Mildmay v Folgham* (1797) 3 Ves 471 (fire insurance), where, as the law then stood, the subject-matter devolved on his heir-at-law, whilst the policy devolved on the assured's personal representative. This position was changed by the Land Transfer Act 1897, s 1(1), so that now both the policy and the subject-matter pass to the personal representative. Policies of insurance are not within the doctrine of reputed ownership: Bankruptcy Act 1914, s 38(c); *Re Moore, ex p Ibbetson* (1878) 8 ChD 519, CA (life insurance); *Colonial Bank v Whinney* (1886) 11 App Cas 426 (shares) per Lord Blackburn, at 440.

9 Bankruptcy Act 1914, s 76. That is to say, he sues as 'the trustee of the property of —— a bankrupt', inserting the name of the bankrupt. He may, however, apparently sue in his own name: *Leeming v Lady Murray* (1879) 13 ChD 123 (life insurance), at 127.

10 See *Doe d Pitt v Laming* (1814) 4 Camp 73 (fire insurance), where Lord Ellenborough CJ thought the condition unreasonable. In practice the policy is usually indorsed.

11 This is subject to the Third Parties (Rights against Insurers) Act 1930, which provides by s 1(1) that 'Where a person . . . is insured against liabilities to third parties which he may incur, then—(a) in the event of the insured becoming bankrupt . . . if, either before or after that event, any such liability . . . is incurred by the insured, his rights against the insurer under the contract in respect of the liability shall notwithstanding anything in any act or rule of law to the contrary, be transferred to and vest in the third party to whom the liability was so incurred.' See e g *Murray v Legal and General Assurance Society Ltd* [1970] 2 QB 495, [1969] 3 All ER 794 (employers' liability insurance); *Farrell v Federated Employers Insurance Association Ltd* [1970] 3 All ER 632, [1970] 1 WLR 1400, CA (employers' liability insurance).

12 *Hood's Trustees v Southern Union General Insurance Co of Australasia* [1928] Ch 793, CA, where it was held that the trustee was not bound by a subsequent release of the insurers executed by the assured and accompanied by a surrender of the policy; *McEntire v Potter & Co* (1889) 22 QBD 438 (marine insurance); *Marriage v Royal Exchange Assurance Co* (1849) 18 LJCh 216 (fire insurance); *Logan v Hall* (1847) 4 CB 598 (covenant to insure) per Maule J, at 613. As they succeed only to the rights of the assured in respect of the claim, they must not only perform any conditions precedent which fall to be performed by them (*Re Carr and Sun Fire Insurance Co* (supra) per Lord Esher MR, at 186); but are also liable to be defeated by breach of condition on the part of the assured: ibid; *M'Entire v Sun Fire Office* (1895) 29 ILT 103 (fire insurance).

13 They are equally liable in this case to be defeated by a breach of condition on the part of the assured: *Jackson v Forster* (1860) 1 E & E 470, ExCh (life insurance), where the assured committed suicide after bankruptcy.

14 *Re Birkbeck Permanent Benefit Building Society, Official Receiver v Licenses Insurance Corpn* [1913] 2 Ch 34.

15 *Durrant v Friend* (1851) 5 De G & Sm 343 (marine insurance), where, though the legatee of specific chattels, which perished at the same time as the testator, failed to recover, it was assumed that he would have been entitled to the benefit of the policy, if he had shown that the chattels were in existence after the testator's death; *Mildmay v Folgham* (1797) 3 Ves 471 (fire insurance), where it was held that the heir-at-law of the assured to whom the subject-matter of insurance had descended, could not have had the benefit of the policy, which had devolved upon the

D THE EFFECT OF THE ASSIGNMENT OF THE POLICY

On the completion of the assignment, the rights and duties of the original assured devolve on the assignee, who becomes, to all intents and purposes, the assured under the policy which he may accordingly enforce in his own name.[18] He is, therefore, entitled, in the event of a loss subsequently taking place, to retain for his own benefit the whole amount received from the insurers under the policy, and cannot be compelled, where the amount received happens to exceed his own loss, to hand over the surplus to the original assured, unless there is an agreement to that effect.[19]

Nor will any act done by the original assured after the assignment affect the validity of the policy.[20]

The assignee becomes liable to fulfil the conditions of the policy, and his failure to do so avoids the policy or prevents him from recovering according to the nature of the condition.[1]

Further, however, he takes the policy subject to equities, since the assignment

---

executors, unless it was assigned to him. In *Rayner v Preston* (1881) 18 ChD 1, CA (fire insurance) Cotton LJ, at 8, appears to doubt the correctness of the view taken in *Durrant v Friend* (supra). It is submitted, however, that this doubt is not justified. Seeing that the policy is not determined by the death of the assured, it is difficult to understand why it should be prematurely determined afterwards in consequence of an act done reasonably and even necessarily in due course of administration. The personal representatives cannot themselves enforce the policy after they have transferred the subject-matter of insurance, and unless they can lawfully assign it to the beneficiary, it must cease to exist. If a sale were to become necessary during the administration, presumably the principle of *Re Birkbeck Permanent Benefit Building Society, Official Receiver v Licenses Insurance Corpn* (supra) would apply, and the policy could be assigned to the purchaser. An assignment to a beneficiary is, it is submitted, equally with the original devolution upon the personal representatives an assignment by operation of law.

16 *Re Birkbeck Permanent Benefit Building Society, Official Receiver v Licenses Insurance Corpn* (supra).

17 The devolution of the policy on death or bankruptcy is not, in practice, dealt with by an express condition. The usual condition defining the circumstances in which the policy may be continued after an assignment of the subject-matter expressly excepts assignments by will or operation of law; and from the existence of the exceptions it may be inferred that, in the case of these assignments, the parties intended that the policy should continue as a matter of course; see *Re Birkbeck Permanent Benefit Building Society, Official Receiver v Licenses Insurance Corpn* (supra) per Neville J, at 38: '*Doe d Goodbehere v Bevan* ((1815) 3 M & S 353 (covenant in lease)) clearly shows that prima facie a contractual restriction of assignment does not apply to the assignment by a person on whom the property has devolved by operation of law, and who is under an obligation to assign. Of course, you may have so contracted as to include such a case, but the mere condition against assignment does not prima facie include it. And that this condition was not intended to include it is, I think, to be found not only from the general construction which ought to be placed upon such a condition, but also from the fact that we have in the conditions a direct elimination of the case of the passing of a policy by operation of law. I do not think, therefore, it was even intended to apply to an assignment by a person in whom the policy became vested, not by a voluntary act of the insured, but by the operation of law and who was then under an obligation to assign to someone else.'

18 *Western Australian Bank v Royal Insurance Co* (1908) 5 CLR 533.

19 *Landauer v Asser* [1905] 2 KB 184 (marine insurance), following *Ralli v Universal Marine Insurance Co* (1862) 4 De GF & J 1, CA (marine insurance), discussed in *Strass v Spillers and Bakers Ltd* [1911] 2 KB 759 (marine insurance), where there was an agreement as to the value of the policies to be handed over. Cf *Harland and Woolff v J Burstall & Co* (1901) 84 LT 324 (marine insurance).

20 *Burton v Gore District Mutual Fire Insurance Co* (1865) 12 Gr 156; *Black v National Insurance Co* (1879) 24 LCJ 65.

1 *Re Carr and Sun Fire Insurance Co* (1897) 13 TLR 186, CA (fire insurance), where the trustee in bankruptcy of the assured failed to put in a claim within the prescribed time.

is the assignment of an existing contract, and must therefore bear the consequences of any act or omission of the original assured before the assignment.[2] Thus, if during the negotiations, the original assured was guilty of fraud or non-disclosure, the policy, being voidable ab initio, may be avoided by the insurers notwithstanding assignment subsequently to an innocent assignee;[3] and the fact that the insurers consented to the assignment does not in itself preclude them from electing afterwards to avoid the policy.[4]

The form of their consent and the circumstances in which it was given, however, amount to a new contract, and, therefore, place the assignee in a better position than the original assured.[5]

Similarly, where the insured property has been seized and condemned as enemy property and lawful prize, an assignee of a policy effected by an enemy alien[6] in respect of it has no rights under it, for it could not have been enforced by the assured.[7]

---

2 *Re Car and Sun Fire Insurance Co* (supra) (fire insurance), where the trustee in bankruptcy failed also to recover on the claim previously made by the assured on the ground that it was fraudulent; *M'Entire v Sun Fire Office* (1895) 29 ILT 103 where after a compromise with the trustee in bankruptcy it was discovered that the assured had committed a breach of condition avoiding the policy, and it was held that the insurers were not bound by the compromise; *Scottish Amicable Life Assurance Society v Fuller* (1867) IR 2 Eq 53 (life insurance); *Williams v Atlantic Assurance Co Ltd* [1933] 1 KB 81, CA; cf *Manchester Fire Assurance Co v Wykes* (1875) 33 LT 142, CA (fire insurance).

3 See *William Pickersgill & Sons Ltd v London and Provincial Marine and General Insurance Co Ltd* [1912] 3 KB 614 (marine insurance). Aliter, if the interest of an innocent mortgagee is not by way of assignment: *P Samuel & Co v Dumas* [1924] AC 431 (marine insurance).

4 *Omnium Securities Co v Canada Fire and Mutual Insurance Co* (1882) 1 OR 494, approved in *Liverpool and London Globe Insurance Co v Agricultural Savings and Loan Co* (1902) 33 SCR 94; *North British and Mercantile Insurance Co v Tourville* (1895) 25 SCR 177.

5 *Chapman v Gore District Mutual Insurance Co* (1876) 26 CP 89, where the assignee applied for a new insurance, making full disclosure, but, at the suggestion of the insurance agent, accepted an assignment of the old policy.

6 As to 'enemy aliens', see Chapter 56.

7 *Bank of New South Wales v South British Insurance Co Ltd* (1920) 4 LlL Rep 266, 384, CA (marine insurance).

CHAPTER 35

The construction of the policy

The construction of a policy of insurance[1] is a question for the Court.[2] When words in a policy have once been judicially interpreted, they will be construed in the same way should their meaning be in issue in a subsequent case. But when the words have not been previously interpreted, the Court is guided by certain principles of general application. The size of print in insurance policies is immaterial.

A CONSTRUCTION AND THE DOCTRINE OF PRECEDENT

Where the Court has already decided the meaning of words used in a policy of insurance, the doctrine of precedent will be applied, and the same interpretation will be given should the meaning of the same words be in issue in a later case.

This principle has been described in a number of ways in the decided cases. 'We are asked to construe an expression in a mercantile document of ancient origin, interpreted by decisions that have stood for more than a century. In such a case the only safe rule for a Court is stare decisis.'[3] 'Nor have we a decision of any Court on the meaning of these precise words, by which we should consider ourselves bound.'[4] 'If a construction had already been put on a clause precisely similar in any decided case, we should defer to that authority.'[5] 'It seems to me that it would be a bold thing to argue against a judgment of the full Court of King's Bench presided over by Lord Mansfield, and 150 years after it has been accepted as the law during that period by every English tribunal.'[6]

Thus, the interpretation given to the words 'social, domestic and pleasure purposes' in a motor insurance policy by Du Parcq J in *Passmore v Vulcan Boiler and General Insurance Co Ltd*[7] in 1936 was followed by Pilcher J in *Browning v*

---

1 The principles of construction are the same as in the case of other contracts: *Robertson v French* (1803) 4 East 130 (marine insurance) per Lord Ellenborough, at 135; *Carr v Montefiore* (1864) 5 B & S 408, ExCh (marine insurance); *Smith v Accident Insurance Co* (1870) LR 5 Exch 302 (accident insurance) per Martin B, at 307; *West India Telegraph Co v Home and Colonial Insurance Co* (1880) 6 QBD 51, CA (marine insurance) per Brett LJ at 58; contra, *Stewart v Merchants Marine Insurance Co* (1885) 16 QBD 619 CA (marine insurance) per Lord Esher MR, at 626, 627, disapproving *Blackett v Royal Exchange Assurance Co* (1832) 2 Cr & J 244 (marine insurance).

2 *Clift v Schwabe* (1846) 3 CB 437 (life insurance) per Parke B, at 469; *Simond v Boydell* (1779) 1 Doug KB 268 (marine insurance) per Buller J, at 277.

3 *Becker Gray & Co v London Assurance Corpn* [1918] AC 101 at 108 (per Lord Dunedin).

4 *Clift v Schwabe* (1846) 3 CB 437 at 470 (per Parke B).

5 *Glen v Lewis* (1853) 8 Exch 607 at 618 (per Parke B).

6 *Andersen v Marten* [1908] AC 334 at 340 (per Lord Halsbury).

7 (1936) 54 LlL Rep 92.

Phoenix Assurance Co Ltd[8] in 1960, and again by Lawton J in *McGoona v Motor Insurers' Bureau and March*[9] in 1969.

Further, where words are merely put in as a variation of those previously used, and which are exactly the same as those which have received a judicial construction, the same meaning will be given to them.[10]

But the general principle will not apply where the words are not the same. Thus, in one case Atkin LJ said 'On a question of construction I protest against one case being treated as an authority in another unless the language and the circumstances are substantially identical.'[11] Further, Buckley LJ observed in another case: 'Authorities may determine principles of construction, but a decision upon one form of words is no authority upon the construction of another form of words.'[12]

Another example of the application of the doctrine of precedent is provided by *Louden v British Merchants' Insurance Co Ltd*:[13]

> An insured under a motor insurance policy was killed in an accident. There was no doubt that he was drunk at the time. The insurance company sought to avoid liability on the ground that he had died from bodily injury 'sustained whilst under the influence of drugs or intoxicating liquor', liability for which was excepted under the policy.
> *Held,* these words were not uncertain as to their meaning and effect should be given to them. They had been interpreted in a case in 1877, and the meaning given to them there should be applied on the present case.

Lawton J said:[14]

> 'The words used in the exemption clause of the policy before me have probably been used for many years in policies giving assurance against injury. Counsel for the [insurance company] referred to *Mair v Railway Passengers Assurance Co Ltd.*[15] The policy in that case provided that the assurance should not extend to any death or injury happening while the assured was under the influence of intoxicating liquor. The case came before Lord Coleridge CJ and Denman J. . . . Both learned Judges construed the words "while the assured is under the influence of intoxicating liquor", although it may not have been necessary for the purposes of their judgment to do so. Neither seems to have thought that the words were so uncertain as to be incapable of construction. Both were of the opinion that these words connoted a disturbance of the faculties. Lord Coleridge CJ using the words, "As disturbs the balance of a man's mind",[16] and Denman J the words, "Disturbing the quiet, calm, intelligent exercise of the faculties"[17]. . . . In those circumstances I find that the words were not so uncertain as to be incapable of construction, and I adopt the construction in *Mair v Railway Passengers Assurance Co Ltd*[18] albeit they have been expressed in mid-19th century idiom. I add no gloss as to do so might add confusion when none have existed among insurers and policy holders during the past 84 years.'

---

8 [1960] 2 Lloyd's Rep 360. See the judgment of Pilcher J, ibid, at 367.

9 [1969] 2 Lloyd's Rep 34, where Lawton J said (ibid, at 44): '[*Passmore v Vulcan Boiler and General Insurance Co Ltd*] having been decided a long time ago, a number of cases have been looked at and, as far as I can see, as Counsel has pointed out, there is nothing in the reports to show that any judge has ever disapproved of the principle.'

10 *Lawrence v Accidental Insurance Co Ltd* (1881) 7 QBD 216 at 220 (per Denman J). See also, *Re Etherington and Lancashire and Yorkshire Accident Insurance Co* [1909] 1 KB 591, CA.

11 *Re Calf and Sun Insurance Office* [1920] 2 KB 366 at 382.

12 *Re Coleman's Depositories Ltd and Life and Health Assurance Association* [1907] 2 KB 798.

13 [1961] 1 Lloyd's Rep 154.

14 Ibid, at 157.

15 (1877) 37 LT 356.

16 Ibid, at 358.

17 Ibid, at 359.

18 Supra.

B THE PRINCIPAL RULES OF CONSTRUCTION

The principal rules of construction may be stated in the following terms:

1 The intention of the parties must prevail.
2 The whole of the policy must be looked at.
3 The written words will be given more effect than the printed words.
4 The policy must be construed in accordance with the ordinary laws of grammar.
5 The ordinary meaning of the words will be adopted.
6 The meaning of a particular word may be limited by the context.
7 The words of the policy must be taken to mean what they say.
8 The words of the policy must, if possible, be construed liberally.
9 In case of ambiguity the reasonable construction is to be preferred.
10 In case of ambiguity the 'contra proferentem' rule will be applied.
11 Where the words are repugnant to each other, the Court will exhaust every means to reconcile the inconsistencies.
12 An express term overrides any implied term which is inconsistent with it.
13 Where a matter left uncertain in the policy afterwards becomes ascertained, the ascertained part will be treated as if it had been inserted in the original policy.

1 The intention of the parties must prevail

The cardinal rule of construction is that the intention of the parties must prevail.[19] But the intention is to be looked for on the face of the policy,[20] including any documents incorporated therewith,[21] in the words in which the parties have themselves chosen to express their meaning.[22] The Court must not

---

19 *Drinkwater v London Assurance Corpn* (1767) 2 Wils 363 (fire insurance) per Wilmot CJ, at 364; *Tarleton v Staniforth* (1794) 5 Term Rep 695 (fire insurance) per Lord Kenyon CJ, at 699; *Braunstein v Accidental Death Insurance Co* (1861) 1 B & S 782 (accident insurance) per Blackburn J, at 799. See e g *Lombard Australia Ltd v NRMA Insurance Ltd* [1969] 1 Lloyd's Rep 575, Supreme Court of New South Wales, Court of Appeal (motor insurance), where it was held that where a car owned by a finance company was let out to a hire-purchaser under a hire-purchase agreement, and was insured by the hire-purchaser in his own name and in that of the finance company, it was the intention of the parties that the policy should constitute a several promise to the finance company and to the hire-purchaser in respect of the respective interests. See the judgment of Wallace A-CJ (ibid, at 576) and that of Holmes JA (ibid, at 578–580).

20 *M'Swiney v Royal Exchange Assurance* (1849) 14 QB 634, ExCh (marine insurance) per Parke B at 661; *Want v Blunt* (1810) 12 East 183 (life insurance) per Lord Ellenborough CJ, at 187; *Borradaile v Hunter* (1843) 5 Man & G 639 (life insurance) per Maule J, at 653; *Beacon Life and Fire Assurance Co v Gibb* (1862) 1 Moo PCCNS 73 at 97, PC (fire insurance).

21 E g the proposal: *South Staffordshire Tramways Co v Sickness and Accident Assurance Association* [1891] 1 QB 402, CA, where the proposal was referred to for the purpose of ascertaining the meaning of the word 'accident' in the policy; *Re George and Goldsmiths' and General Burglary Insurance Association Ltd* [1899] 1 QB 595, CA (burglary insurance) per Lord Russell CJ, at 605; *Yorkshire Insurance Co v Campbell* [1917] AC 218, PC (marine insurance), where the difficulties involved are pointed out.

22 *Re George and Goldsmiths' and General Burglary Insurance Association* (supra) (burglary insurance) per Collins LJ, at 610; *Weir v Northern Counties of England Insurance Co* (1879) 4 LRIr 689 (fire insurance); *Victor Melik & Co Ltd v Norwich Union Fire Insurance Society Ltd and Kemp* [1980] 1 Lloyd's Rep 523 (burglary insurance) at 530: 'In order to interpret this clause it is necessary to gather the intent from the words used by the parties to the policy and I am satisfied that the

speculate as to their intention, apart from their words,[23] but may, if necessary, interpret the words by reference to the surrounding circumstances.[1] At the same time, it must be borne in mind that a special policy is not, as a rule, prepared to meet the particular case. The policy is in a stock form, and the Court must consider the effect of a particular construction upon other cases.[2] Further, if the precise form of words has already been before the Court, the previous construction is binding.[3]

2 The whole of the policy must be looked at

The whole of the policy must be looked at,[4] and not merely a particular clause.[5] In *Hamlyn v Crown Accidental Insurance Co Ltd*:[6]

> The insured had effected a policy against 'any bodily injury caused by violent, accidental, external and visible means'. A clause exempted the insurance company from being liable in respect of injuries arising from 'natural disease or weakness, or exhaustion consequent upon

---

Norwich Union could not have intended that the policy should have been interpreted in that way, and equally that the insured would not have intended it to be interpreted in this way.' (per Woolf J).

23 *Pearson v Commercial Union Assurance Co* (1863) 15 CBNS 305 per Erle CJ, at 313; *Re George and Goldsmiths' and General Burglary Insurance Association* [1899] 1 QB 595, CA (burglary insurance) per Collins LJ, at 611.

1 *Watchorn v Langford* (1813) 3 Camp 422; *Union Insurance Society of Canton Ltd v George Wills & Co* [1916] AC 281 at 286, 288, PC (marine insurance), distinguished in *Yorkshire Insurance Co Ltd v Campbell* [1917] AC 218 at 225, PC (marine insurance).

2 *Re Etherington and Lancashire and Yorkshire Insurance Co* [1909] 1 KB 591, CA (accident insurance) per Vaughan Williams LJ, at 597.

3 *Clift v Schwabe* (1846) 3 CB 437 (life insurance); *Lawrence v Accidental Insurance Co Ltd* (1881) 7 QBD 216 (accident insurance) per Denman J, at 220. See generally, pp 331–332, ante.

4 *Braunstein v Accidental Death Insurance Co* (1861) 1 B & S 782 (accident insurance) per Blackburn J, at 799; *Cornish v Accident Insurance Co* (1889) 23 QBD 453, CA (accident insurance) per Lindley LJ, at 456: 'To ascertain the true meaning of the [clause] the whole document must be studied'; *Re George and Goldsmiths' and General Burglary Insurance Association Ltd* [1899] 1 QB 595, CA (burglary insurance) per Lord Russell CJ, at 605; *Pennsylvania Co for Insurances on Lives and Granting Annuities v Mumford* [1920] 2 KB 537, CA (theft insurance) per Lord Sterndale MR, at 543; *Notman v Anchor Assurance Co* (1858) 4 CBNS 476 (life insurance) per Cockburn CJ, at 480, where the recital was referred to for the purpose of ascertaining the period of insurance; cf *Stoneham v Ocean Railway and General Accident Insurance Co* (1887) 19 QBD 237 per Cave J, at 241; *Equitable Fire and Accident Office Ltd v Ching Wo Hong* [1907] AC 96 at 100, PC (fire insurance); *Pocock v Century Insurance Co Ltd* [1960] 2 Lloyd's Rep 150 (Leeds Assizes) (personal accident insurance); *W and J Lane v Spratt* [1970] QB 480, [1970] 1 All ER 162, [1969] 2 Lloyd's Rep 229 (goods in transit insurance), where a clause stated that 'The insured shall take all reasonable precautions for the protection and safeguarding of the goods and/or merchandise and use such protective appliances as may be specified in the policy and all vehicles and protective devices shall be maintained in good order.' and it was held that the clause did not impose on the insured an obligation to vet their staff with due diligence before they took them on. Roskill J said (ibid, at 237): 'I think there is force in [Counsel's] arguments . . . secondly, that if one looks at this clause as a whole, the impression that it leaves on someone reading it is that it is not intended to cover the whole field but is limited to what, on a reasonable reading of the clause, is that which is mentioned in the clause, namely, the need to protect and safeguard the goods and merchandise.'

5 *Hamlyn v Crown Accidental Insurance Co Ltd* [1893] 1 QB 750, CA (accident insurance) per Lopes LJ, at 754: 'The policy must be read in the way in which a person of ordinary intelligence would read it, and in construing this particular clause we must not confine our attention to that clause, but must look to the whole of the policy'; *City Tailors Ltd v Evans* (1921) 126 LT 439, CA (fire insurance) per Atkin LJ, at 444: 'One has to construe the policy as a whole, giving effect to every word except in so far as it appears plain that any of the provisions were not intended to apply to the particular contract.'

6 [1893] 1 QB 750, CA.

disease'. He stooped to pick up a marble which had been dropped by a child, and dislocated the cartilage of his knee. The insurance company contended that there were no external or visible means which caused the accident, and that it was therefore not liable.
Held, the word 'external' was to be contrasted with 'internal' causes of injury, such as disease, mentioned in the clause above, and so the injury was caused by external means and the insured could recover.

Lord Esher MR said:[7]

'The word "external" is that which has caused the most doubt; but I feel that in this policy, looking, as we are bound to, at the rest of the policy, and the things that are excepted from it, the expression must be taken to mean the antithesis of "internal". If the injury had happened by reason of something internal, it would not be within the policy; but that is not the case, and I think we must say that because the cause of the injury was not internal it must have been "external".'

Lopes LJ observed:[8]

'Then comes the word "external", and in construing that word it is important to bear in mind the other part of the policy which deals with matters internal. Looking at the contrast between matters external and matters internal, it is suggested that the resistance of the floor supplies the external cause. I think a more obvious cause is the act of reaching after the marble and the wrench which accompanied that act. That stooping and reaching after the marble was certainly not an internal cause, but was, in my opinion, an external cause within the policy.'[9]

Hence, the same words, as a rule, bear the same meaning throughout the policy.

Thus, in *South Staffordshire Tramways Co v Sickness and Accident Assurance Association Ltd*[10] a tramway company effected a policy of insurance in respect of 'claims for personal injury in respect of accidents caused by vehicles'. The policy limited the amount of the liability of the insurance company to '£250 in respect of any one accident'. A tramcar overturned, and 40 people were injured. The tramway company had to pay them £833, and then claimed to be reimbursed from the insurance company. The Court of Appeal held that the term 'accident' in the policy meant injury in respect of which a person claimed compensation from the tramway company, and that the liability of the insurance company was not limited to £250, but that the whole amount could be recovered. In the course of his judgment Bowen LJ observed:[11]

'What is the meaning of the term "one accident" further on in the policy? It seems to me that, if

---

7 Ibid, at 753.

8 Ibid, at 754.

9 For other examples, see *Gale v Motor Union Insurance Ltd* [1928] 1 KB 359, where a condition excluding liability if the risk was covered elsewhere was held to be qualified by the contribution clause; *Canadian Casualty and Boiler Insurance Co v Hawthorne & Co* (1907) 39 SCR 558, where the Court construed an exception against loss by freezing to mean loss immediately caused by freezing, the policy being expressed to be against 'immediate' loss by leakage, etc, and held that damage caused by the escape of water from a pipe which had burst through the water in it freezing did not fall within the exception, but was covered by the policy; *Simon Brooks Ltd v Hepburn* [1961] 2 Lloyd's Rep 43, QB (Commercial Court) (all risks insurance), where the policy stated that it gave cover in respect of 'all risks of loss and damage from whatsoever cause arising . . . whilst anywhere in the United Kingdom including the Assured's own addresses . . . Excluding larceny and theft in respect of shop portion of Louisette Ltd', and the Court held that in the circumstances, the reference was to the premises of Louisette Ltd at the time that the policy was effected, and that a loss which had occurred at other premises at which Louisette Ltd subsequently carried on business was not excluded.

10 [1891] 1 QB 402.

11 [1891] 1 QB 402, at 407.

> in the previous part of the policy the word "accident" is used as meaning accident to the person, it must receive the same construction in the phrase limiting the liability of the [insurance company].'

Fry LJ said:[12]

> 'Then the policy proceeds to say that "the Association shall pay to the assured the sum of £250 in respect of any one accident". I think the word "accident" is there used in the same sense as in the earlier part of the policy, and that the meaning is "in respect of any single injury to person or property accidentally caused".'

Again, the word 'theft' in a policy concerning injury was held to have the same meaning in the recitals as in the main body of the policy.[13]

But it does not necessarily follow that the converse is true, for sometimes it has been held that where the words are expressed in a different form, their meaning is really the same. Thus in *Burridge & Son v F H Haines & Sons*[14] it was held that in the case of a policy concerning a horse, the phrase 'damage by external and visible means' was the same as 'death attributable to external and visible injury', which appeared in another clause. Shearman J said that it was unfortunate and gave rise to argument that one found two phrases meaning the same thing, but using different language, and in different sections of the policy and observed:

> 'But this is not a conveyance, but a document dealing with different contingencies by insurance as between businessmen, and I do not entertain any doubt that the words . . . "accidental external and visible injury" do not in the least refer to signs of any injury of the body of the animal killed, but that the whole meaning of it is injury caused by violence and that "accidental external and visible" means violence external and visible, and "death solely attributable to accident" means violence, and these words "accidental external and visible" are in effect the same as the words "caused by external and visible means".'[15]

At the same time, the object of a particular clause must be considered,[16] and the same words may bear different meanings in different clauses.[17]

3 The written words will be given more effect than the printed words

An insurance policy sets out the terms and conditions of the contract in a

---

12 Ibid, at 408. See also *Forney v Dominion Insurance Co Ltd* [1969] 1 Lloyd's Rep 502 (solicitors' indemnity insurance), where the policy limited the insurers' liability in respect of any one claim or number of claims arising out of the same occurrence to £3,000, and Donaldson J held that the policy contemplated that a number of claims might arise out of the same occurrence, and observed (ibid, at 508): 'This seems to me to indicate that a number of persons may be injured by a single act of negligence by the insured—in other words that "occurrence" in this context is looked at from the point of view of the insured.'

13 *Lake v Simmons* [1927] AC 487; see particularly the speech of Viscount Sumner, at 507. See also, per Lord Blanesburgh, at 514.

14 (1918) 118 LT 681.

15 Ibid, at 686.

16 *Borradaile v Hunter* (1843) 5 Man & G 639 (life insurance) per Maule J, at 653. Hence, the operative part of the policy prevails over the recital: *Blascheck v Bussell* (1916) 33 TLR 74, CA (accident insurance) per Swinfen Eady LJ, at 75.

17 *Shera v Ocean Accident and Guarantee Corpn* (1900) 32 OR 411, where the word 'immediately' was held in one part of the policy to refer to causation, and in another part, to time; *Andrews v Patriotic Assurance Co (No 2)* (1886) 18 LRIr 355 (fire insurance) per Palles CB, at 362, pointing out that the word 'property' may mean in the same instrument both 'building' and 'interest', according to the context.

standard printed form. But to this form the parties may have added further words and clauses either in handwriting or in typescript. The question then arises as to what is the relation between the written and the printed words in the policy. The Courts have evolved the rule that both the printed and the written words must be taken into consideration. 'Prima facie all the words which the policy contains . . . are words of contract to which effect must be given.'[18] 'In construing a policy of insurance the Court certainly cannot consider whether it be in writing or in print or partly in writing and partly in print.'[19]

But when there is a conflict between the printed and the written clauses, greater consideration will be paid to the written clauses. The written words are the immediate language and terms selected by the parties themselves for the expression of their meaning; the printed words, on the other hand, are a general formula adapted equally to their case and that of all other contracting parties upon similar occasions and subjects.

> 'The only difference between policies of assurance and other instruments in this respect is that the greater part of the printed language of them being invariable and uniform has acquired from use and practice a known and definite meaning and that the words superadded in writing . . . are entitled, nevertheless, if there should be any reasonable doubt upon the sense and meaning of the whole, to have a greater effect attributed to them than to the printed words, in as much as the written words are the immediate language and terms selected by the parties themselves for the expression of their meaning, and the printed words are a general formula adapted equally to their case and that of all other contracting parties upon similar occasions and subjects.'[20]

Again,

> 'The ordinary and general rule in the case of a policy of insurance, of course, is that we must construe the policy as we find it; it is in a printed form with written parts introduced into it and we are to take the whole together, both the written and the printed parts. Although it has sometimes been endeavoured to be argued that we ought to bestow no more attention on the written part than on the printed part which are uniform in most policies of insurance, there is no doubt that we do and ought to make a difference between them. The part that is especially put into a particular instrument is naturally more in harmony with what the parties are intending than the other, although it must not be used to reject the other or to make it have no effect.'[1]

The printed words are not necessarily intended to stand as part of the contract in any particular case[2] since, through carelessness or in the hurry of business, the parties may have omitted to delete the superfluous or inapplicable

---

18 *Yorkshire Insurance Co Ltd v Campbell* [1917] AC 218 at 224, PC (per Lord Sumner).

19 *Foster v Mentor Life Assurance Co* (1854) 3 E & B 48 at 82 (per Lord Campbell CJ).

20 *Robertson v French* (1803) 4 East 130 at 136 (per Lord Ellenborough CJ); *Western Assurance Co of Toronto v Poole* [1903] 1 KB 376 (marine insurance) per Bigham J, at 389; cf *Brunton v Marshall* (1922) 10 LlL Rep 689 (fire insurance). See further the same principle applied in cases concerning the carriage of goods by sea, e g *G H Renton & Co Ltd v Palmyra Trading Corpn of Panama* [1957] AC 149 at 168, HL (per Lord Morton); and *Glynn v Margetson & Co* [1893] AC 351, HL.

1 *Joyce v Realm Marine Insurance Co* (1872) LR 7 QB 580 at 583 (per Blackburn J). See further, *Kaufmann v British Surety Insurance Co Ltd* (1929) 33 LlL Rep 315 at 318 (per Roche J); *General Accident Fire and Life Assurance Corpn Ltd v Midland Bank Ltd* [1940] 2 KB 388, CA, per Greene MR, at 402.

2 *South British Fire and Marine Insurance Co of New Zealand v Da Costa* [1906] 1 KB 456 (marine insurance) per Bigham J, at 460.

words from the form or to alter the printed words so as to make them conform exactly to the contract which they intended to make.[3]

At the same time, the print must be construed with the writing as far as possible;[4] it is not to be rejected if not repugnant to or inconsistent with what is written.[5] If, however, the writing shows it to be inapplicable, the print must be disregarded.[6]

Thus, in a case concerning marine insurance[7] Atkin LJ said:[8]

> 'We are asked by the plaintiffs to confine our attention to the typewritten clause. That does not seem to me to be the proper mode of construing the policy which is partly in print and partly in writing. You must look at the documents as a whole, and if, of course, you find that there are printed clauses which are inconsistent with that which has been obviously the particular matter of agreement as expressed in writing, why then you may fairly and properly eliminate the printed clauses so far as they are inconsistent with the clauses, written or typewritten, which the parties clearly had in contemplation as part of their contract; but if the clauses are not inconsistent, then there is no reason why you should not give full effect to the whole document.'

Where part of the print is struck out, it is not settled whether the words struck out can be looked at for the purpose of discovering the intention of the parties;[9]

---

3 *Western Assurance Co of Toronto v Poole* (supra) per Bigham J, at 389, 390, citing *Cunard SS Co Ltd v Marten* [1902] 2 KB 624 (marine insurance) per Walton J, at 627. In *Western Assurance Co of Toronto v Poole* (supra) two policies had been issued by different underwriters upon the same ship, in one of which certain printed words were struck out, though in the other they were left untouched, and Bigham J, at 389, pointed out that both policies had the same effect.

4 *Hydarnes SS Co v Indemnity Mutual Marine Assurance Co* [1895] 1 QB 500, CA (marine insurance), per Rigby LJ, at 508: 'I agree that, where there are general words in a contract which may have an application to a state of things existing under the contract, the Court ought to be very cautious in rejecting them, even though they are common form, in the absence of very strong reasons for doing so.'

5 *Nigel Gold Mining Co Ltd v Hoade* [1901] 2 KB 849 per Mathew J, at 853.

6 *Hydarnes SS Co v Indemnity Mutual Marine Assurance Co* (supra), where all parties knew that the printed words could not apply to the particular port the name of which was inserted in the policy; *Home Insurance Co of New York v Victoria-Montreal Fire Insurance Co* [1907] AC 59, PC (fire insurance), where a reinsurance was expressed in a typewritten slip attached to an ordinary form of fire policy, and the terms in the policy form applicable only to an original insurance were rejected; *City Tailors Ltd v Evans* (1921) 126 LT 439, CA (profit insurance), where a printed condition prescribing the method of ascertaining the profits was disregarded as being inapplicable to a case where the profits were valued; *Australian Widows' Fund Life Assurance Society Ltd v National Mutual Life Association of Australasia Ltd* [1914] AC 634, at 642, PC (life insurance), where a statement in a reinsurance policy that the risk was accepted upon the same terms and conditions as those upon which the original policy was granted was held not to incorporate clauses of the original policy which contradicted express provisions of the reinsurance policy; *Dudgeon v Pembroke* (1877) 2 App Cas 284 (marine insurance); cf *Mountain v Whittle* [1921] 1 AC 615 (marine insurance) per Lord Sumner, at 630.

7 *Farmers' Co-operative Ltd v National Benefit Assurance Co* (1922) 13 LlL Rep 417, 530, CA (marine insurance).

8 Ibid, at 533.

9 *Wyllie v Povah* (1907) 12 Com Cas 317 (marine insurance) per Pickford J, at 323; *M A Sassoon & Sons Ltd v International Banking Corpn* [1927] AC 711, PC (letter of credit) per Lord Sumner, at 721; *Ambatielos v Anton Jurgens Margarine Works* [1923] AC 175 at 185, where Lord Finlay held that the deleted words should not be looked at. Cf *Louis Dreyfus v Parnaso Cia Naviera SA* [1959] 1 QB 498 at 515; *Thomasson Shipping Co v Henry W Peabody & Co of London* [1959] 2 Lloyd's Rep 296 at 301. See generally, Scrutton *Charter-parties and Bills of Lading*, 19th Edn (1984) p 21, where the view is taken that 'it has been a matter of controversy whether the Court may look at deletions from a printed form as showing the intention of the parties, but the weight of authority is now in favour of the view that the Court may not look at deletions'.

but the fact that they have been struck out is not to be entirely disregarded.[10]

4 The grammatical construction will be adopted

The general rule is that the grammatical meaning of the words used in the policy will be adopted.[11]

But this may not always be possible for, as Lord Esher MR pointed out in connection with a policy of marine insurance:[12]

> 'Now, to say that the language of these Lloyd's policies can be construed according to strict grammar is, as has often been observed, next to impossible. The phraseology used in them is in many respects regardless of grammar, but the meaning of it has been understood for many years among shipowners and mercantile men in a certain sense. Still, one must examine the language of this memorandum or warranty, and construe it, having regard, as far as possible, to ordinary rules of grammar.'

Where, however, the intention is clear, the grammatical construction must give way. Thus, in another case on marine insurance Lawrence J said:[13]

> 'It is wonderful, considering how much property is at stake upon instruments of this description, that they should be drawn up with so much laxity as they are, and that those who are interested should not apply to some man whose habits of life and professional skill will enable him to adapt the words of the policy to the intention professed by the parties. In construing these instruments we must always look for what was the intention of the parties without confining ourselves to a strict grammatical construction; for it is impossible in many instances so to construe them, without departing widely from the object intended. Thus, we find a policy meant to cover a risk of goods only, will have words relating for the most part to an insurance on ship, to which it would extend but for some loose memorandum.'

Obvious grammatical errors may be corrected,[14] and immaterial blanks and surplusage may be rejected.[15]

5 The words are to be construed in their ordinary meaning

This rule has been constantly stated in a variety of ways.

'The same rule of construction which applies to all other instruments applies

---

[10] See *Fracis, Times & Co v Sea Insurance Co* (1898) 3 Com Cas 229 (marine insurance), where Bigham J, at 234, referred to the fact that certain words were struck out on the suggestion of the insurers as supporting the good faith of the assured.

[11] *Weir v Northern Counties of England Insurance Co* (1879) 4 LRIr 689 at 693 (per Lawson J); *Lewis Emanuel & Son Ltd v Hepburn* [1960] 1 Lloyd's Rep 304 (strikes contingency insurance). See p 343, post for the facts of this case; *Balfour v Beaumont* [1984] 1 Lloyd's Rep 272, CA (reinsurance), where the reinsurance slip policy stated: 'To reimburse the Reinsured for all sums payable in respect of liability occurring under the London Market Products Line Slip which includes products policies placed on a vertical basis with American Domestic Insurers (mainly USAIG and AAU) and similar products policies', and it was held that these words were an apt description in broad terms of the nature of the various policies provided for in the Line Slip, Sir John Donaldson MR observing (ibid, at 275): 'As a simple matter of language, if "similar products policies" had been intended to extend the scope of the cover to facultative insurances, as contrasted with parenthetically explaining the scope of the Line Slip, we would have expected the description of the interest to read "and *under* similar products policies".'

[12] *Price & Co v A1 Ships' Small Damage Insurance Association* (1889) 22 QBD 580 at 584.

[13] *Marsden v Reid* (1803) 3 East 572 (marine insurance) at 579; *Re Athenaeum Life Assurance Co, ex p Eagle Insurance Co* (1858) 4 K & J 549 (life insurance) per Wood V-C, at 555; *Phoenix Insurance Co of Hartford v De Monchy* (1929) 141 LT 439 (marine insurance) per Lord Sumner, at 445.

[14] *Glen's Trustees v Lancashire and Yorkshire Accident Insurance* 1906 8 F (Ct of Sess) 915 (accident insurance), where the word 'not' was struck out from the printed clause.

[15] *Sears v Agricultural Insurance Co* (1882) 32 CP 585.

equally to . . . a policy of insurance, viz that it is to be construed according to its sense and meaning as collected, in the first place, from the terms used in it, which terms are themselves to be understood in their plain, ordinary and popular sense . . .'[16] 'The words of the policy are to be construed not according to their strictly philosophical or scientific meaning, but in their ordinary and popular sense.'[17] 'All I have to do is to look at the words which (the parties) have used, and try to give them their plain and common sense meaning.'[18] 'The (matter) must in my opinion be interpreted according to the ordinary and natural meaning of the words used, if that meaning be plain and unequivocal and there be nothing in the context to qualify it.'[19] 'A policy of insurance is subject to the same rules of construction as any other written contract. The words used in it must be given their plain, ordinary meaning in the context of the policy looked at as a whole, subject to any special definitions contained in the policy.'[20] 'The words . . . must receive such an interpretation as would be placed upon them by ordinary men of normal intelligence and average knowledge of the world.'[21] 'The general rule of construction is that words used in documents must receive their primary signification unless the context of the instrument or surrounding circumstances show that the secondary meaning expresses the real intention of the parties or unless the words are used in connection with some place, trade or the like in which they have acquired the secondary meaning as their customary meaning quoad hoc.'[22] 'I am satisfied that . . . I should construe the words according to the understanding of business people so as to make their meaning realistic and such as to give business efficacy to the agreement between the parties.'[1]

Thus, in *Leo Rapp Ltd v McClure*:[2]

Stocks of metal were insured against theft 'whilst in warehouse anywhere in the United Kingdom'. Some metal was loaded on to a lorry parked in an open space in a locked compound enclosed by a thick brick wall topped by barbed wire, and was stolen.

Held, the loss was not covered by the policy because the compound did not constitute a warehouse.

Devlin J observed:[3]

'It seems to me abundantly clear that at the material time these goods were in a yard and not a

---

16 *Robertson v French* (1803) 4 East 130 at 135 (per Lord Ellenborough CJ).

17 *Stanley v Western Insurance Co* (1868) LR 3 Exch 71 at 73 (per Kelly CB).

18 *Re George and Goldsmiths' and General Burglary Insurance Association Ltd* [1899] 1 QB 595 at 610 (per Collins LJ).

19 *Thomson v Weems* (1884) 9 App Cas 671 at 687 (per Lord Watson).

20 *Jason v British Traders' Insurance Co Ltd* [1969] 1 Lloyd's Rep 281 (personal accident insurance) per Fisher J, at 290.

21 *Yorke v Yorkshire Insurance Co Ltd* [1918] 1 KB 662 at 666 (per McCardie J).

22 *Yangtze Insurance Association v Indemnity Mutual Marine Assurance Co* [1908] 2 KB 504 at 509, CA (per Farwell LJ).

1 *J Lowenstein & Co Ltd v Poplar Motor Transport (Lymn) (Gooda, Third Party)* [1968] 2 Lloyd's Rep 233 (goods in transit insurance) at 238 (per Nield J).

2 [1955] 1 Lloyd's Rep 292, QB (Lloyd's Burglary, Theft and Fire Policy (Commercial Form)). See also *Firmin and Collins Ltd v Allied Shippers Ltd (Alder, Third Party)* [1967] 1 Lloyd's Rep 633 ('all risks' insurance), where Lyell J held that the words 'whilst in a public warehouse' in their ordinary meaning did not apply to premises consisting of an archway under a railway, and that consequently goods stored there did not fall within a policy in respect of goods for which they were responsible 'whilst in the insured's and/or any public warehouse'. The evidence as to the nature of the premises is set out ibid, at 637–638.

3 [1955] 1 Lloyd's Rep at 293. His Lordship also said (ibid, at 293): 'If one has regard, as, of

warehouse . . . When the Court is construing words in an insurance policy, it must give them their ordinary natural meaning. The question is, therefore, what is the ordinary natural meaning of a warehouse. It suggests to me some sort of building . . . and these goods were not in a building, but were in a yard, and upon that short ground I shall give my judgment.'

Again, in *Rogers v Whittaker*:[4]

A bomb from an enemy Zeppelin during an air raid damaged a building, which was insured under a policy excluding the insurer's liability for damage resulting from 'insurrection, riots, civil commotion or military or usurped power'.
Held, 'military power' included *foreign* military power, and so the insurer was not liable.

Further, in *Thompson v Equity Fire Insurance Co*:[5]

A building, which was destroyed by fire, had been insured under a policy excluding liability for loss while gasoline was 'stored or kept' in it. The fire was caused by a small quantity of gasoline in a stove used for cooking purposes. No other gasoline was used in the building.
Held, the insurance company was liable, because 'kept or stored' implied a considerable amount of gasoline or at least keeping it in stock for trading purposes.

Lord Macnaghten said:[6]

'What is the meaning of the words "stored or kept" in collocation and in the connection in which they are found? They are common English words with no very precise or exact signification. They have a somewhat kindred meaning and cover very much the same ground. The expression . . . seems to point to the presence of a quantity not inconsiderable, or at any rate not trifling in amount, and to import a notion of warehousing or depositing for safe custody or keeping in stock for trading purposes. It is difficult if not impossible to give an accurate definition of the meaning, but if one takes concrete cases, it is not very difficult to say whether a particular thing is "stored or kept" . . . No one probably would say that a person who had a reasonable quantity of tea in his house for domestic use was "storing or keeping" tea there, or (to take the instance of benzine . . .) no one would say that a person who had a small bottle of benzine for removing grease spots or cleansing purposes of that sort was "storing or keeping" benzine.'

In *Princette Models Ltd v Reliance Fire and Accident Insurance Corpn Ltd*:[7]

A goods in transit policy stated that the insurance company would not be liable for ladies' dresses stolen from a vehicle 'unless any door, window, windscreen . . . lock or fastener has been smashed by violent forceable means wherever entry, access or theft has been effected.'
Held, that the word 'wherever' meant any place on the van from which the dresses had been stolen.

Pearson J (as he then was) said:[8]

'What is the meaning of the word "wherever"? Does it mean: "In any case in which" which is sometimes, I think, the meaning of the word "where" in Acts of Parliament and other places; "where" sometimes means "in any case in which". Or does it mean "wherever" in the sense of the situation of the ground? That is to say, in this case, in Dean Street, or in some particular square foot of Dean Street? Or does it mean in any place on the van? In my view, the right construction is that it means on the van. It refers to some place on the van. As between "wherever" referring to place and "wherever" referring to any case in which, one should

---

course, one is entitled to have regard, to what is the object of the policy, it is plain that the object of the policy is concerned with the question of security, not with the purpose of the store. It does not matter at all to the underwriters why the goods are to be stored there. What does matter to them is the nature of the place where the goods are being stored.'

4 [1917] 1 KB 942.
5 [1910] AC 592, PC.
6 Ibid, at 596.
7 [1960] 1 Lloyd's Rep 49.
8 Ibid, at 56.

> prefer the reference to place, because that is the primary meaning. The word "wherever" refers primarily to place and one ought to give it that meaning unless there is some reason for giving it some other meaning.'

There are many other examples of the application of this rule.

Goods were considered to be 'in store' (within the meaning of a policy insuring them in the course of transit) whilst they were in the possession of a depository company on its premises for the purpose of storage, and were being stored by it in some vans in the open air.[9] Jersey, in popular language has been held to be 'within the United Kingdom' for the purpose of a life insurance policy.[10] 'Gas' in a fire policy meant ordinary illuminating coal gas,[11] and not vapour given off in the course of extracting oil from shoddy.[12] Where an accident policy stated that no claim could be made if the insured were in charge of a 'vehicle', this term included a bicycle.[13] A hotel yard was not a 'garage' for the purpose of a burglary policy, for the word connoted some sort of building with a roof providing shelter from above.[14] 'Collapse' of a building, in its primary sense, denotes falling, or breaking down or giving way through external pressure or loss of rigidity or support, and it does not cover intentional destruction or demolition of a building by housebreakers.[15] The term 'subsidence', i e movement in a vertical direction, includes, in its popular sense 'settlement' which strictly speaking means movement in a lateral direction.[16] The words 'sober and temperate' in a proposal form in respect of life insurance were held to refer only to the use or abuse of alcohol. They were not applicable to the use of veronal or other soporific or narcotic drugs.[17]

An assured under a jewellery policy insuring her against 'loss' was held entitled to recover from the insurance company in respect of a pearl necklace which she had 'lost', although three months later it was found in the collar of her evening cloak.[18] 'It is, of course, true that a thing may be mislaid yet not lost, but in my opinion, if a thing has been mislaid and is missing or has disappeared and a reasonable time has elapsed to allow of diligent search and of recovery, and such diligent search has been made and has been fruitless, then the thing may properly be said to be lost.'[19]

Fireworks are 'inflammable', for the word 'inflammable' means something

---

9 *Wulfson v Switzerland General Insurance Co Ltd* [1940] 3 All ER 221.

10 *Stoneham v Ocean, Railway and General Accident Insurance Co Ltd* (1887) 19 QBD 237. But in *Navigators and General Insurance Co Ltd v Ringrose* [1962] 1 All ER 97, CA (marine insurance), where a catamaran was insured 'whilst within the United Kingdom ashore or afloat' and she was dismasted 28 miles off Portland Bill, it was held that the loss did not fall within the policy, and that in any case the Channel Islands were not part of the United Kingdom. Davies LJ (ibid, at 100) said that he thought that it was unnecessary for the Court to express any view as to the correctness of the decision in *Stoneham v Ocean, Railway and General Accident Insurance Co* (supra).

11 *Stanley v Western Insurance Co* (1868) LR 3 Exch 71.

12 Woollen yarn obtained by tearing to shreds refuse woollen rags which, with the addition of new wool, is made into a kind of cloth.

13 *Hansford v London Express Newspaper Ltd* (1928) 43 TLR 349; *Harper v Associated Newspapers Ltd* (1927) 43 TLR 331.

14 *Barnett and Block v National Parcels Insurance Co Ltd* [1942] 1 All ER 221; affd [1942] 2 All ER 55n, 73 LlL Rep 17.

15 *D Allen & Sons Billposting Ltd v Drysdale* [1939] 4 All ER 113, 65 LlL Rep 41.

16 Ibid.

17 *Yorke v Yorkshire Insurance Co Ltd* [1918] 1 KB 662.

18 *Holmes v Payne* (1930) 37 LlL Rep 41.

19 Ibid, at 45 (per Roche J).

which increases the fire risk by reason of the fact that the goods have an inherent quality of being easily set on fire. If a person were asked the simple question, 'Are fireworks inflammable?', he would not have the slightest doubt in answering the question, 'Yes', although he might have the recollection that sometimes on a wet November evening when having a firework party it was difficult to set them alight.[20]

An assured under an 'all risks' policy in respect of some skins was held to have suffered a 'loss' within the meaning of the policy when he had sent them to a firm for processing, and the firm wrongfully retained them under an alleged general lien, and refused to release them.[1]

In a case where a policy was effected by some fruit importers, and contained a term that it covered 'physical loss or damage or deterioration' caused by strikes, a loss of market caused by delay arising out of a strike was held not to be recoverable.[2] 'All these three possible misfortunes are of the same kind; they are all of a physical kind occurring to the goods themselves. It is physical loss, physical damage and physical deterioration.'[3] 'Even if I am not right on the grammatical construction, I should still hold that in view of the subject-matter being dealt with and the way in which those words are placed in this phrase, one could understand each of the three words "loss", "damage" and "deterioration" as applying to physical happenings and not merely to financial happenings such as loss of market, and in my view those are the decisive considerations to be taken into account here.'[4]

Again, a schoolgirl was held to be 'ordinarily residing with her father (the insured)' although she was away at a boarding school for 70 per cent of the year, for this circumstance was entirely outweighed by the fact that the connection with the parents' home and household had never been severed, and that they intended to maintain the connection while her mode of living remained under their control.[5]

Smith J remarked:[6]

> 'The words "ordinarily residing with" are common English words and here there is no context requiring that they should be given other than their natural meaning in accordance with the accepted usage of English. Even in such circumstances, however, there can be difficulty and doubt as to their applicability to particular sets of facts, because the conception to which the words have reference does not have a clearly definable content or fixed boundaries. It is a conception as to the extent of the association and the strength of the connection between two persons as members of one household or domestic establishment; and whether the extent and strength of the connection are such, in any given case, as to make the words fairly applicable, is a question of degree. Moreover, that question depends upon an assessment of a combination of factors; and combinations may be found to be adequate though they differ widely, both in the weighting of factors and in the identity of the factors present.'

Where a jeweller's stock-in-trade policy contained an exception stating that the insurance company was not to be liable where the jewellery was 'entrusted'

---

20 *Hales v Reliance Fire and Accident Insurance Corpn Ltd* [1960] 2 Lloyd's Rep 391.

1 *London and Provincial Leather Processes Ltd v Hudson* [1939] 2 KB 724, [1939] 3 All ER 857, 64 LlL Rep 352.

2 *Lewis Emanuel & Sons Ltd v Hepburn* [1960] 1 Lloyd's Rep 304 (strikes contingency insurance).

3 Ibid, at 308 (Pearson J).

4 Ibid, at 309.

5 *Clarke v Insurance Office of Australia Ltd* [1965] 1 Lloyd's Rep 308 (Supreme Court of Victoria).

6 Ibid, at 310.

to a customer, it was held that no 'entrusting' had taken place where possession of them had been obtained by larceny by a trick.[7]

'Gold' in an insurance upon 'gold, tin, diamonds, jewellery etc' has been held to include gold coin.[8] A 'dwelling house' is not an apt term to cover a building in the course of construction,[9] nor does the word 'goods' include wearing apparel[10] or personal effects.[11] 'Iron' does not include 'steel'.[12] A 'bill of exchange' does not include a document in the form of a bill of exchange, but which is a conditional order for the payment of money.[13]

Where an aviation policy excluded the liability of the insurers if the aeroplane was 'racing', it was held that 'racing' in its ordinary and natural meaning signified engaging in a race, and was not necessarily confined to travelling at the highest speed. Hence the aeroplane, which crashed whilst competing for a prize to be offered to the first machine to fly from Hounslow to Australia, was not covered by the policy.[14]

In a marine insurance policy the word 'war' has been held to include a 'civil war'.[15]

For the purpose of a marine insurance policy a flying boat has been held not to be a 'ship or vessel', for such words connoted a hollow structure intended to be used in navigation and capable of free and ordered movement. The ability of a flying boat to navigate was merely incidental to its real work which was to fly.[16] Nor was a pontoon with a crane fixed on it a 'ship or vessel', for the primary purpose for which the pontoon was designed and adapted was to float and to lift, and not to navigate. Adaptability for navigation was an essential element of a 'ship or vessel'.[17]

In the case of a householder's comprehensive insurance policy covering liability to the public 'for all sums which the assured may be held legally liable to pay in respect of claims made by any person for damage to property caused by accident', the assured was held entitled to recover in respect of damages which he had to pay his neighbour for injury to the neighbour's house by the roots of a tree growing in the assured's garden, for this amounted to damage 'caused by accident'.[18] But if the brickwork of a house catches a disease from a tree, this would not be damage 'caused by accident'.[19]

A house is not 'in the custody or control of' a person when he occupies it

---

7 *Lake v Simmons* [1927] AC 487, 27 LlL Rep 153, HL.

8 *National Bank of South Africa v Standard Marine Insurance Co* (1915) 139 LTJo 27.

9 *Quin v National Assurance Co* (1839) Jo & Car 316 (fire insurance) per Joy CB, at 330.

10 *Ross v Thwaites* (1776) 1 Park's Marine Insurances, 8th Edn 23 (marine insurance).

11 *Brown v Stapyleton* (1827) 4 Bing 119 (marine insurance).

12 *Hart v Standard Insurance Co* (1889) 22 QBD 499, CA (marine insurance) per Bowen LJ, at 502, pointing out, however, that 'steel goods' would fall within an exception excluding 'iron goods'.

13 *Palmer v Pratt* (1824) 2 Bing 185 (marine insurance).

14 *Alliance Aeroplane Co v Union Society of Canton* (1920) 5 LlL Rep 341, 406 (aviation insurance).

15 *Pesquerias y Secaderos de Bacalao de Espana SA v Beer* [1949] 1 All ER 845n, 82 LlL Rep 501, HL (marine insurance).

16 *Polpen Shipping Co Ltd v Commercial Union Assurance Co Ltd* [1943] KB 161, [1943] 1 All ER 162, 74 LlL Rep 157 (marine insurance).

17 *Merchants Marine Insurance Co Ltd v North of England Protecting Indemnity Association* (1926) 26 LlL Rep 201, CA (marine insurance).

18 *Mills v Smith (Sinclair, Third Party)* [1963] 1 Lloyd's Rep 168 QB (householder's comprehensive insurance).

19 Ibid, at 175 (per Paull J).

merely for the purpose of looking after the owner's children who are staying there.[20]

In a 'goods in transit' policy 'transit' was held to mean the passage or carriage of goods from one place to another, and the goods were still being carried and, therefore, were still in transit even though the lorry in which they were being carried was temporarily parked.[1] It was the movement of the goods which mattered, and not the movement of the vehicle or other means of conveyance in which they were being carried.[2]

Where a policy insured a bank against loss if securities in its possession were stolen by one of its employees 'between any houses or places situate within 100 miles of Philadelphia', and the securities in question were misappropriated by an employee whilst being conveyed from the vault room to the reception room, it was held that the loss was not covered by the policy, for moving securities from one part to another in the same building put them in transit, if at all, from one part to another part of the same place and not from one place to another.[3]

Where an assured under a motor policy handed over the car to a motor agent for the purposes of sale, and the agent then disposed of it for his own purposes, and it was shown that recovery of it was uncertain, this constituted a conversion and a 'loss' within the meaning of the policy.[4] But where the assured under a motor policy was induced by false pretences to part with the possession of and property in the car in exchange for a worthless cheque, that did not amount to a 'loss'. What was lost was the proceeds of sale and not the car[5].

Where a local authority organised a venture course in North Wales, and had agreed with the plaintiff, who was subsequently injured whilst rock climbing during the course, 'to take out a special policy to cover any injury that might possibly be sustained during the course', it was held that the words meant that the policy must be one which was unrestricted in amount.[6]

---

20 *Oei v Foster (formerly Crawford) and Eagle Star Insurance Co Ltd* [1982] 2 Lloyd's Rep 170 (householder's insurance) at 177 (per Glidewell J).

1 *Sadler Bros Co v Meredith* [1963] 2 Lloyd's Rep 293, QB (goods in transit insurance).

2 Ibid, at 308 (per Roskill J). The learned Judge said (at 307) that obviously an exhaustive definition of 'transit' was impossible, and undesirable, and that certainly he did not propose to attempt one. See further, *Crows Transport Ltd v Phoenix Assurance Co Ltd* [1965] 1 All ER 596, CA (goods in transit policy), where Lord Denning MR held that the goods were 'temporarily housed during the course of transit' if they were housed as an incident of the transit, and Danckwerts LJ held that they were in transit from the moment that they left the customer's premises and remained in transit until they reached their destination, and that the housing of them temporarily on the assured's premises was part of the transit; *SCA (Freight) Ltd v Gibson* [1974] 2 Lloyd's Rep 533, QBD (Commercial Ct) (goods in transit insurance), where the transit began at least when the insured books were loaded on the lorry.

3 *Pennsylvania Co for Insurances on Lives and Granting Annuities v Mumford* [1920] 2 KB 537, 2 LlL Rep 351, CA (theft insurance).

4 *Webster v General Accident Fire and Life Assurance Corpn Ltd* [1953] 1 QB 520, [1953] 1 All ER 663, [1953] 1 Lloyd's Rep 123.

5 *Eisinger v General Accident Fire and Life Assurance Corpn Ltd* [1955] 2 All ER 897, [1955] 2 Lloyd's Rep 95. See also, *Lim Trading Co v Haydon* [1968] 1 Lloyd's Rep 159, Singapore High Court, at 161 (Lloyd's In and Out stockbroker's policy), where Counsel argued that even if it were held that the transaction concerned amounted to a loss by 'theft' within the meaning of the policy, it was not in respect of a loss of a security covered by the policy since the insured were merely deprived of the proceeds of the cheques. Buttrose J, however, found it unnecessary to deal with this argument, and decided the case on other grounds.

6 *Woolford v Liverpool County Council* [1968] 2 Lloyd's Rep 256, where Roskill J said (ibid, at 258):

Where a 'slip' in respect of a jewellers' all risk insurance policy stated 'locks and alarms fitted to cars owned by assured by Hartwood Alarms, Ltd or other approved alarm systems,' the word 'approved' was held not to mean 'approved by the underwriters' but of a type which had the approval of underwriters generally.[7]

Further, the words 'cars owned by assured' meant cars which a reasonable insured would describe as 'the company's cars'. This description included cars of which the company was a hirer under a hire-purchase agreement, but excluded cars of which the company was a hirer without an option to purchase.[8]

The word 'locks' meant locks having a greater security value than that provided by those supplied by car manufacturers on ordinary production models.[9]

The words 'and in operation' in a warranty stating '[Warranted] road vehicles . . . fitted with locks and alarm system (approved by underwriters) and in operation' mean 'switched on' and so far as the person using the alarm system knows, fully operative, even though unknown to him two of the contact switches are subject to a fault of an intermittent character. They do not mean 'fully operative' in fact, subject only to a possible qualification if it is rendered inoperative by some act of a third party in contemplation of, or in preparation for the commission of the act which eventually led to the loss.[10]

Where an 'all risks' policy in respect of some manuscripts stated that the insurers were to be liable up to £1,000 in the event of 'the destruction or loss of any manuscripts or documents resulting in the necessity for the assured to rewrite, including all costs of research, preparation and the like,' it was held that on the loss of the manuscripts the insurers were liable even though the books had not been rewritten. The costs of rewriting merely quantified the loss.[11]

Where a contractors' all risks insurance policy had been effected in connection with the building of a railway bridge, and contained a clause stating that the insurers were not to be liable for 'loss or damage arising from faulty design', and the bridge collapsed due to the piers supporting it being swept away by flood water and being subjected to greater transverse forces than had been realized, it was held that the insurers were not liable, for the loss had been caused by 'faulty design'. According to the ordinary meaning of the word, 'faulty design' meant defective design. It was erroneous to confine the words to

---

'As a matter of ordinary English language in relation to insurance a "policy to cover any injury" seems to me to mean a policy which will insure the beneficiary of that policy against the consequences of any injury which may be sustained by him or her, and when one sees that those words "to cover any injury" are followed by the words "that might possibly be sustained during the course", the use of the adverb "possibly" in that context suggests that the intention is not only to provide reassurance to parents but also, which is more important, to provide a cover of considerable width, for there is no restriction in relation to the terms, as I have already said, nor is there any restriction in relation to the quantum of the cover.'

7 *de Maurier (Jewels) Ltd v Bastion Insurance Co Ltd and Coronet Insurance Co Ltd* [1967] 2 Lloyd's Rep 550. See the judgment of Donaldson J, ibid, at 557.

8 Ibid, at 557 (per Donaldson J).

9 Ibid, at 560 (per Donaldson J).

10 Ibid. See the judgment of Donaldson J, ibid, at 559.

11 *Frewin v Poland* [1968] 1 Lloyd's Rep 100, QBD (Commercial Court). See the judgment of Donaldson J, ibid, at 102.

the personal failure or non-compliance with standards which would be expected of designing engineers.[12]

A caesarean is an 'operation', both as a matter of ordinary English and as a matter of medical terminology.[13]

Where a family are living in a house in the sense that they are sleeping there, having most of their meals there, watching television there, there with their own children and incidentally looking after the children of the owners, they are, while they are there, 'occupying' the house.[14]

But it is a mistake for a lawyer to attempt a definition of ordinary words and to substitute other words for them. The best way is to take the words in their ordinary sense and apply them to the facts.[15] 'I deprecate any attempt to expound the meaning or further to define words . . . which are common words in everyday use, having a perfectly ordinary and clear meaning.'[16]

Thus, in *Starfire Diamond Rings Ltd v Angel*:[17]

> A Jewellers Block Policy covered jewellery against theft and contained a clause excluding theft from a vehicle 'which not being garaged (is) left unattended'. Its driver went 37 yards away from it in order to relieve himself.
> *Held*, the car was 'unattended' and a claim under the policy failed.

Lord Denning MR said:[18]

> 'The meaning of "left unattended" is, I think, best found by considering the converse. If a car is "attended", what does it mean? I think it means that there must be someone able to keep it under observation, that is, in a position to observe any attempt by anyone to interfere with it, and who is so placed as to have a reasonable prospect of preventing any unauthorized interference with it.'

'Collect' in a clause stating that claims under a marine insurance policy are to be 'collected' by a named broker means 'collected in cash', and is incapable of

---

12 *Queensland Government Railways and Electric Power Transmission Pty Ltd v Manufacturers' Mutual Insurance Ltd* [1969] 1 Lloyd's Rep 214, High Court of Australia, where Barwick CJ said (ibid, at 217): 'We have not found sufficient ground for reading the exclusion in this policy as not covering loss from faulty design, when, as here, the piers fell because their design was defective although . . . not negligently so. The exclusion is not against loss from "negligent designing", and the latter is more comprehensive than the former'. See also the judgment of Windeyer J where he said (ibid, at 219): 'It seems to me that into, the question whether [the piers] were of faulty design there has been intruded unnecessarily a consideration of whether the faults of the design was the result of fault in the designer. In other words fault in the sense of shortcoming in the static quality and character of a thing has become involved with fault in the sense of shortcomings in conduct and action.'

13 *Kumar v Life Insurance Corpn of India* [1974] 1 Lloyd's Rep 147 at 154 (per Kerr J) (life insurance).

14 *Oei v Foster (formerly Crawford) and Eagle Star Insurance Co Ltd* [1982] 2 Lloyd's Rep 170 (householder's insurance) at 174 (per Glidewell J).

15 *Starfire Diamond Rings Ltd v Angel* [1962] 2 Lloyd's Rep 217 at 219 (per Lord Denning MR).

16 Ibid, at 219 (per Upjohn LJ).

17 [1962] 2 Lloyd's Rep 217, CA.

18 Ibid, at 219. The words of Lord Denning MR set out in the text above were cited with approval by Phillimore J in *Ingleton of Ilford Ltd v General Accident Fire and Life Assurance Corpn Ltd* [1967] 2 Lloyd's Rep 179 (goods in transit insurance), where the policy contained an exception clause in terms identical with those in *Starfire Diamond Rings Ltd v Angel* (supra), and it was held that the lorry from which the goods were stolen had been 'left unattended', for its driver had gone into a shop at which he was delivering goods and had stayed there for 15 minutes, and was unaware that the vehicle had been stolen. For the evidence on this point, see [1967] 2 Lloyd's Rep at 181–182.

meaning 'brought into account between brokers and insurers in the manner customary in the market'.[19]

The word 'explosion' in its ordinary meaning includes an eruption without a chemical reaction.[20] But it has also been held to mean an event that was violent, noisy and one which was caused by a very rapid chemical or nuclear reaction, or the bursting out of gas or vapour under pressure.[1]

(a) Technical words

When technical words are used in an insurance policy, they will be given their technical meaning.

'[The] terms [of the policy] are themselves to be understood in their plain ordinary and popular sense, unless they have generally in respect of the subject-matter, as by the known usage of trade . . . acquired a peculiar sense distinct from the popular sense of the same words.'[2]

'The Court must adopt the usual rules, and construe the provisos or conditions, as well as the other parts of the instrument, according to the ordinary meaning of the language used; except that terms of art, or technical words, must be understood in their proper sense, unless the context controls or alters their meaning . . .'[3]

In considering the meaning of the word 'average' in a marine insurance policy, Lord Esher MR said that '"average" as used in this connection, is clearly a technical expression, and it has a well-established mercantile signification. It means a partial as distinguished from a total loss'.[4]

Further, in the clothing trade goods are never described as 'new' (e g in invoices or other trade documents) unless they are Government surplus goods. If they are Government surplus goods, and are unused, they may be described as 'new', despite the fact that they are not of recent manufacture.[5]

A 'sprint event' in which the competitors are timed against the clock and are started individually at intervals of 10 to 30 seconds and are given instructions not to overtake has been held not to fall within the words 'motor racing' as used in that sport.[6]

---

19 *Stolos Cia SA v Ajax Insurance Co Ltd, The Admiral C* [1981] 1 Lloyd's Rep 9, CA (marine insurance). (See the judgment of Lord Denning, ibid, at 10.)

20 *Canadian General Electric Co Ltd v Liverpool and London and Globe Insurance Co Ltd* (1980) 106 DLR (3d) 750 (Ont. CA) (fire insurance), where a manufacturing plant was insured against damage caused by fire or explosion, and an overheated pressure tank ruptured as a result of water being poured on to it in order to cool it down, and it was held that an 'explosion' had occurred.

1 *Commonwealth Smelting Ltd v Guardian Royal Exchange Assurance Ltd* [1984] 2 Lloyd's Rep 608 (property insurance) at 608 (per Staughton J). In that case the claim for damage to the blower house when a blower disintegrated failed because the predominant cause of the damage was centrifugal disintegration of the impeller and not explosion. (See the judgment of Staughton J, ibid, at 612). The decision was subsequently affirmed: [1986] 1 Lloyd's Rep 121, CA. (See the judgment of Parker LJ, ibid, at 126.)

2 *Robertson v French* (1803) 4 East 130 at 135 (per Lord Ellenborough CJ).

3 *Clift v Schwabe* (1846) 3 CB 437 at 469 (per Parke B).

4 *Price & Co v A1 Ships' Small Damage Insurance Association* (1889) 22 QBD 580 at 584. See further, Ivamy *Marine Insurance* (4th Edn, 1985), p 411.

5 *Anglo-African Merchants Ltd and Exmouth Clothing Co Ltd v Bayley* [1969] 1 Lloyd's Rep 268 (all risks insurance) at 278 (per Megaw J).

6 *Scragg v United Kingdom Temperance and General Provident Institution* [1976] 2 Lloyd's Rep 227, QBD (Commercial Ct), where the insurers knew of the restricted meaning of 'motor racing' as spoken to by the plaintiff's witnesses. (See the judgment of Mocatta J, ibid, at 233).

There is no usage that the words 'pavement limit' and the phrase 'any one loss between vehicles and premises and vice versa' in a cash in transit insurance policy mean the limit at risk from the point of acceptance by a security company until stowed in a vehicle and from a vehicle to the security company's customer.[7]

(b) Technical Legal Words

Technical legal words must be given their strict technical meaning.[8]

Thus, in *London and Lancashire Fire Insurance Co Ltd v Bolands Ltd*:[9]

> A burglary policy relating to premises used as a bakery excluded the liability of the insurance company if loss or damage resulted from a 'riot'. Four armed men held up the employees with revolvers and seized money in a cashier's office. There was no other disturbance at all in the neighbourhood.
> *Held*, this constituted a 'riot' and the insured could not recover under the policy.

Lord Sumner said:[10]

> 'It is true that the uninstructed layman probably does not think in connection with the word "riot" of such a scene as is described in the case stated. How he would describe it I know not, but he probably thinks of something if not more picturesque at any rate more noisy. There is, however, no warrant for saying that when the (clause) uses a word which is emphatically a term of legal art, it is to be confined in the interpretation of the policy to circumstances which are only within the popular notions on the subject, but are not within the technical meaning of the word.'

Similarly the word 'embezzlement' in a fidelity policy was construed in the same way as it would have been if it had appeared in an indictment charging a person with the crime of embezzlement.[11] The word 'enter' in a burglary policy included entering the premises through an open door, and also a situation in which a person lawfully on the premises broke and entered one room on the premises.[12]

Again, in the case of a householder's comprehensive policy where the policy provided cover 'in respect of all sums for which the assured (as occupier) . . . may be held legally liable',[13] it was held that these words were words of 'legal art' and covered those liabilities which the law imposed upon the occupier because he was the occupier, and admitted of no ambiguity.[14]

Conversely, where a householder's comprehensive policy stated that the

---

7 *Mint Security Ltd v Blair* [1982] 1 Lloyd's Rep 188 at 194 (per Staughton J).

8 *Lake v Simmons* [1927] AC 487, HL, per Lord Sumner, at 509; *Saqui and Lawrence v Stearns* [1911] 1 KB 426, CA, per Farwell LJ, at 436.

9 [1924] AC 836, HL.

10 Ibid, at 847. See also the speech of Viscount Finlay (at 844): 'That there was a riot here in the circumstances in which this money was taken I think it is perfectly impossible to doubt. Force was used; and it is clear that those who were conducting the operations felt that they had force behind them and that they could control the situation. That amounted to a riot . . .'.

11 *Debenhams Ltd v Excess Insurance Co Ltd* (1912) 28 TLR 505. See further, *Lim Trading Co v Haydon* [1968] 1 Lloyd's Rep 159, Singapore High Court (Lloyd's In and Out stockbroker's policy), where the transaction concerned was held to be the obtaining of shares by false pretences and not 'theft', and accordingly was not a loss covered by the policy.

12 *Re Calf and the Sun Insurance Office* [1920] 2 KB 366.

13 Within the principle stated by Lord Sumner in *London and Lancashire Fire Insurance Co Ltd v Bolands Ltd* [1924] AC 836 at 846.

14 *Sturge v Hackett* [1962] 3 All ER 166, [1962] 1 Lloyd's Rep 626, CA (householder's comprehensive policy): affirming the interpretation of these words given by McNair J in the Court below: [1962] 1 Lloyd's Rep 117, QB.

insurers were liable for the amount of damages arising out of the insured's 'liability at law attaching only as owner (not occupier) of the house', the words 'as owner' were apt to describe not the capacity of the insured or history of the liability, but the character of the liability itself.[15]

The word 'theft' must be given the same meaning as it has in the criminal law.[16]

It has, however, been pointed out that the word 'suicide' is not a technical term,[17] and the word 'forged' was held in one case to have been used merely to describe an existing state of fact and not as a term of art.[18]

But sometimes the context may indicate that the words, though normally of technical significance, are not to be given their technical meaning.

Thus, in *Algemeene Bankvereeniging v Langton*:[19]

> A Lloyd's banker's policy was issued in London for the protection of a Belgian bank, and covered property 'lost or destroyed or otherwise made away with by fire, burglary, theft, robbery, or hold-up'. One of its bank managers issued bonds to customers without the bank's consent, and appropriated the money resulting from their sale.
> *Held,* the loss fell within the policy, for the words were not to be construed, in the circumstances of the case, in a technical sense.

Maugham LJ observed:[20]

> 'I do not doubt that the law of the contract is English, but I think that the loss which is intended to be covered by the policy is a loss which must be incurred in Belgium; that it is quite wrong in principle to construe the words . . . "fire, burglary, theft, robbery, or hold-up" as if those words could only be construed in a technical sense according to English law . . . I object to the notion that ordinary commercial men in this country . . . would contend that the (words) should be read as if (they) were drawn in the form that was applicable only to crimes which would be treated as burglary, theft, robbery . . . or hold-up if the crimes were being investigated in this country . . . The policy is obviously to be construed as if it related to a loss by crimes or misdemeanours perpetrated in that foreign country, and to be punished . . . according to the laws of the foreign country. I would add this, that there is nothing in the [words] which leads me to suppose that [they are] intended to have a very technical significance because it contains some phrases which are not known to English law as technical phrases . . . I do not think you will find the words 'made away with' in a statute or even in an ordinary book on criminal practice.'

---

15 *Rigby v Sun Alliance and London Insurance Ltd* [1980] 1 Lloyd's Rep 359, where Mustill J said (ibid, at 364): 'To my mind [the words "as owner"] denote the status of the insured as owner is an integral part of the cause of action against him, and not merely that in practice he would never have found himself in the position of receiving a claim and being held liable if he had not been the owner of the premises . . . In my view, the added words "solely" and ("not occupier") made the extent of the cover quite clear. If "attaching as owner" means "attaching to the insured in his capacity as owner", then the phrase as a whole must mean "attaching to the owner in his capacity as owner and in no other capacity, and particularly not in his capacity as occupier." '

16 *Grundy (Teddington) Ltd v Fulton* [1981] 2 Lloyd's Rep 666 (property insurance) at 670 (per Stuart-Smith J). The decision was subsequently affd by the Court of Appeal [1983] 1 Lloyd's Rep 16.

17 *Clift v Schwabe* (1846) 3 CB 437 (life insurance), where Rolfe B said (at 462, 463): 'The word "suicide" is not, as it appears to me, a word of art, to which any legal meaning is to be affixed different from that which it is popularly understood to bear . . . But, after all, our decision must rest entirely on what is the ordinary meaning of the term.'

18 *Equitable Trust Co of New York v Henderson* (1930) 47 TLR 90 (policy covering loss by means of forged documents).

19 (1935) 40 Com Cas 247, CA.

20 Ibid, at 259. See also, *Re George and Goldsmiths' and General Burglary Insurance Association Ltd* [1899] 1 QB 595, CA (burglary insurance), where the policy covered burglary and theft 'as hereinafter defined'.

6 The meaning may be limited by the context

The meaning of a word is to be ascertained with reference to its context,[1] and may be restricted[2] or modified thereby.[3]

---

1 *Hooper v Accidental Death Insurance Co* (1860) 5 H & N 546 per Wightman J, at 559; *Fitton v Accidental Death Insurance Co* (1864) 17 CBNS 122 per Byles J, at 135; *Drinkwater v London Assurance Corpn* (1767) 2 Wils 363 (fire insurance); *Watchorn v Langford* (1813) 3 Camp 422 (fire insurance); *Rogers v Whittaker* [1917] 1 KB 942 (fire insurance) per Sankey J, at 943; *Clift v Schwabe* (1846) 3 CB 437 (life insurance) per Parke B, at 469; *Elliott v Royal Exchange Assurance Co* (1867) LR 2 Exch 237 per Martin B, at 245.

2 *Curtis & Sons v Mathews* [1919] 1 KB 425, CA, where there was an exception against confiscation or destruction by the government of the country in which the insured property was situated, and it was held that the collocation of the words showed that the exception referred to destruction that was deliberate in the same sense as confiscation would be deliberate, and hence, accidental destruction by the forces of the Crown in the course of military operations did not fall within it; *Joel v Harvey* (1857) 5 WR 488 (fire insurance), where the meaning of 'stock-in-trade' was in question; *Fowkes v Manchester and London Life Assurance and Loan Association* (1863) 3 B & S 917 (life insurance), where the word 'untrue' meant according to the context, 'designedly untrue'; *Menzies v North British Insurance Co* 1847 9 Dunl (Ct of Sess) 694, where the reinstatement clause showed that the policy was intended to apply to buildings, and not to profits; *Borradaile v Hunter* (1843) 5 Man & G 639 (life insurance), where the Court refused to limit the exception to felonious suicide, there being nothing in the context, when taken as a whole, to show that the parties had any such intention.

3 *Stoneham v Ocean Railway and General Accident Insurance Co* (1887) 19 QBD 237 per Mathew J, at 240; *Re Coleman's Depositories Ltd and Life and Health Assurance Association* [1907] 2 KB 798, CA, per Buckley LJ, at 813; *Williams v Lloyd's Underwriters* [1957] 1 Lloyd's Rep 118 (personal accident insurance), where it was held that the assured was unable 'to resume his normal calling or occupation of any kind', and therefore entitled to the benefit payable under the policy in respect of 'permanent total disablement', for although gainfully employed as a watchman, he was unable to resume his pre-accident work as a steel worker; *Cathay Pacific Airways Ltd v Nation Life and General Assurance Co Ltd* [1966] 2 Lloyd's Rep 179 (aircrew disablement insurance), where McNair J held that a pilot suffered a 'permanent total disablement' within the meaning of the policy where a medical board set up under the current licensing regulations found on reasonable grounds (a) that he suffered from a physical incapacity which rendered him inelegible to hold a pilot's licence; and (b) that that incapacity was of a permanent character, and the licensing authority acting on those findings reasonably held that he was permanently inelegible to hold a licence. For the evidence leading to the conclusion that he was inelegible, see ibid, pp 183–187; *Queensland Government Railways and Electric Power Transmission Pty Ltd v Manufacturers' Mutual Insurance Ltd* [1969] 1 Lloyd's Rep 214, High Court of Australia, (contractors' all risk insurance), where it was held that the words 'faulty design' in the context of the policy which related to the construction of a bridge swept away by flood water, were not to be confined to personal failure or non-compliance with standards which would be expected of designing engineers, and Windeyer J observed (ibid, at 218): 'Doubtless a faulty design can be the product of fault on the part of the designer. But a man may use skill and care, he may do all that in the circumstances could reasonably be expected of him, and yet produce something which is faulty because it will not answer the purpose for which it was designed.' In *Kearney v General Accident Fire and Life Assurance Corpn Ltd* [1968] 2 Lloyd's Rep 240 (employers' liability insurance) a building which had originally been built as an aircraft hangar but which was in the course of being converted into a factory, was held still to be a hangar for the purpose of a clause in a policy which exempted the insurers from liability in the case of employees engaged in 'work' in connection with gasometers, towers, steeples, bridges, viaducts, blast furnaces, colliery overhead winding gear, hangars . . . Nield J observed (ibid, at 244): 'But construing the whole of this [exception] . . . I reach the conclusion . . . that what the insurance company had in mind was the physical characteristics of the building. It seems to me that this [exception] is setting out a number of descriptions of work which involve special hazard or danger. They are not all concerned with height, but most of them are—gasometers, towers, steeples, and so on—and hangars, I think, must have been regarded by the insurers as involving danger of people falling from a height.'; *Laurence v Davies (Norwich Union Fire Insurance Society Ltd, Third Party)* [1972] 2 Lloyd's Rep 231, Exeter Crown Court (motor insurance), where, in the context, the words 'motor car' were sufficient to apply to a van. (See the judgment of Dunn J, ibid, at 233); *Young v*

Thus, in *Pocock v Century Insurance Co Ltd*:[4]

> A personal accident insurance policy stated that the insurance company would pay the insured a weekly sum in respect of 'temporary total disablement from attending to business of any and every kind.'
> *Held,* that a person could not be said to attend to business simply because he was capable of doing some minor part of the work involved in that business.

Mr Commissioner Molony QC said:[5]

> 'The phrase must be looked at as a whole and in its context; and . . . what attention is directed to is attending to business of any sort, which might be that of a wholesale grocer doing the business nominated in this case or might be some substituted business to which a person might turn; and in order to bring the clause into operation, the question is whether a man is fit to go to business, to use a vernacular expression. Is he able to attend to a business of the nominated or substituted type? My view is that a person cannot be said to attend the business in that sense because he is capable of doing—perhaps rather badly—some minor part of the work involved in that or any other sort of business.'

Again, in *Jaglom v Excess Insurance Co Ltd*:[6]

> Jewellery was insured under a 'slip'[7] which stated that it was covered whilst in the assured's bank, and that it was agreed 'to extend this policy in respect of items taken out of the bank' in accordance with rates specified in the schedule. The insured was robbed of one of the items of jewellery whilst she was taking it to be repaired. It had never been in the custody of the bank.
> *Held,* the loss was covered. The word 'extend' in the context of the 'slip' meant no more than that the insurers were accepting a second risk in addition to the first. The use of the words 'taken out of the bank' did no more than reflect the fact that the bank custody risk came first on the 'slip' and that it was no doubt contemplated that the jewellery would be more in the bank than out of it.

Where from the context[8] it appears that the parties intended to use the word in a special and peculiar sense, and not in a meaning which it might otherwise

---

Sun Alliance and London Insurance Ltd [1976] 2 Lloyd's Rep 189, CA (master block policy), where the word 'flood' in a policy providing cover for loss or destruction or damage caused by 'storm, tempest or flood' was held to mean something which had some element of violence, suddenness or largeness about it, and not to apply to a natural seepage of water which damaged a lavatory. (See the judgment of Shaw LJ, ibid, at 191); *Rowlinson Construction Ltd v Insurance Co of North America (UK) Ltd* [1981] 1 Lloyd's Rep 332 (contractors' public liability policy), where a question arose as to whether a contract to build a retaining wall beside a river involved 'bridges or other work in or over water or tidal or coastal areas', and, in the context of the policy, which also related to 'any other bridges, tunnels or dams or weirs', it was held that it did not. (See the judgment of Lloyd J, ibid, at 335); *Mint Security Ltd v Blair* [1982] 1 Lloyd's Rep 188 (cash in transit insurance), where, in the context, the word 'premises' in the phrase 'any one loss between vehicles and premises and vice versa' was held to mean 'buildings'. (See the judgment of Staughton J, ibid, at 194); *Petrofina (UK) Ltd v Magnaload Ltd* [1984] QB 127, [1983] 3 All ER 33, [1983] 2 Lloyd's Rep 91 (contractors' all risks insurance), where in the context of the policy the word 'sub-contractors' included 'sub-sub-contractors'. (See the judgment of Lloyd J, ibid, at 94); *Commonwealth Smelting Ltd v Guardian Royal Exchange Assurance Ltd* [1984] 2 Lloyd's-Rep 608 (property insurance), where a blower house was insured against 'fire, lightning and explosion', and it was held that the word 'explosion' should be construed in the light of its association with the other two perils, though that approach did not give more than minimal assistance. (See the judgment of Staughton J, ibid, at 612). The decision was subsequently affirmed: [1986] 1 Lloyd's Rep 121, CA. (See the judgment of Parker LJ, ibid, at 126).

4 [1960] 2 Lloyd's Rep 140 (Leeds Assizes).

5 Ibid, at 154.

6 [1971] 2 Lloyd's Rep 171, QBD (Commercial Court). See the judgment of Donaldson J, ibid, at 176.

7 No policy was ever issued. As to the 'slip', see pp 116–118, ante.

8 *Robertson v French* (1803) 4 East 130 (marine insurance) per Lord Ellenborough CJ, at 136; *Borradaile v Hunter* (1843) 5 Man & G 639 (life insurance) per Maule J, at 653.

bear, the word must be construed in accordance with their intention.[9] Further, the language of one condition may narrow the effect of another.[10] Where a question is raised whether a particular stipulation is a condition precedent or not, it will not be construed as a condition precedent, if the parties clearly show on the face of the policy itself when they mean a stipulation to operate as a condition precedent, and the stipulation in question is not thus shown to be a condition precedent.[11]

(a) The ejusdem generis rule

Where specifications of particular things belonging to the same genus precede a word of general signification, the latter word is confined in its meaning to things belonging to the same genus,[12] and does not include things belonging to a different genus.[13]

This rule is known as the 'ejusdem generis' rule, and its application must in every case depend on the precise terms, subject-matter and context of the clause in the policy under construction.[14]

---

9 *Watchorn v Langford* (1813) 3 Camp 422 (fire insurance), where, from the collocation of the words 'household furniture, linen and wearing apparel', it was held that 'linen' meant household linen, and hence a stock of linen drapery was not covered; cf *Cole v Accident Insurance Co Ltd* (1889) 5 TLR 736, CA, where it was argued that from the context the word 'poison' in an exception was restricted to cases where the poison was intentionally taken by the assured, but the Court pointed out that the exception included disease, war, and riot, for which the assured would not be responsible, and held that the word was not restricted by the context but extended to cover a case where poison was taken by mistake; *Re United London and Scottish Insurance Co Ltd, Brown's Claim* [1915] 2 Ch 167, CA (accident insurance), where an exception against 'anything inhaled' was held not to be restricted to cases of voluntary inhalation.

10 *Fowkes v Manchester and London Assurance Association* (1863) 3 B & S 917 (life insurance); *Williamson v Commercial Union Insurance Co* (1876) 26 CP 591; *Doull v Western Insurance Co* (1886) 6 R & G 478. As to when a stipulation will be construed as a 'condition', see pp 277–283, ante.

11 *Home Insurance Co of New York v Victoria-Montreal Fire Insurance Co* [1907] AC 59 at 64, PC; *Re Bradley and Essex and Suffolk Accident Indemnity Society* [1912] 1 KB 415, CA (employers' liability insurance).

12 *Lake v Simmons,* [1927] AC 487 per Lord Sumner, at 507; *Palmer v Naylor* (1854) 10 Exch 382, ExCh (marine insurance) per Coleridge J, at 389; *Stoomvaart Maatschappij Sophie H v Merchants Marine Insurance Co Ltd* (1919) 122 LT 295, HL (marine insurance) per Lord Birkenhead LC, at 296; *King v Travellers' Insurance Association Ltd* (1931) 48 TLR 53 (baggage insurance).

13 An exception against wilful exposure to obvious risk must be read with the other acts enumerated in it so that it does not include the case of an assured who, being a good swimmer, goes out to bathe from a boat at night: *Sangster's Trustees v General Accident Assurance Corpn Ltd* 1896 24 R (Ct of Sess) 56. In the question 'Have you had chronic dyspepsia or any other disease?' the word 'disease' refers to maladies as serious as chronic dyspepsia or which might, in the way it might, increase the risk, and does not include attacks of acute dyspepsia or ordinary indigestion: *IOF v Turmelle* (1910) QR 19 KB 261 (life insurance), where the further question 'For what disease or diseases have you consulted a physician?' was construed in accordance with the same principle.

14 *Sun Fire Office v Hart* (1889) 14 App Cas 98, PC (fire insurance) per Lord Watson, at 103: 'It is a well-known canon of construction that where a particular enumeration is followed by such words as "or other" the latter expression ought, if not enlarged by the context, to be limited to matters ejusdem generis with those specially enumerated. The canon is attended with no difficulty except in its application. Whether it applies at all, and if so, what effect should be given to it, must in every case depend upon the precise terms, subject-matter and context of the clause under construction.' See further, *Chandris v Isbrandtsen-Moller Co Inc* [1951] 1 KB 240 (carriage of goods by sea) where Devlin J said (at 244): 'A rule of construction cannot be more than a guide to enable the Court to arrive at the true meaning of the parties. The ejusdem generis rule means that there is implied into the language which the parties have used, words of restriction that are

In *King v Travellers' Insurance Associations Ltd*:[15]

> A policy of insurance against accidental loss of baggage contained a clause stating: 'Jewellery, watches, field-glasses, cameras, and other fragile or specially valuable articles must be separately declared and valued.' The insured claimed for the loss of a Persian lamb fur coat. *Held,* that a fur coat was not a 'specially valuable article' within the meaning of the above condition.

Rowlatt J said:[16]

> 'The question I have to ask myself is whether furs are specially valuable articles in the same sort of sense that jewellery, watches, field-glasses and cameras are fragile or specially valuable articles. That I think is the modern plain English translation of the application here of the ejusdem generis rule. Are furs specially valuable articles in the sense exemplified by the particular instance named? I do not think that they are. Furs are a commonplace article of dress in the case of every woman of any sort of comfortable means. The fact that the purchase of some furs affords scope for extravagance and vanity so that a woman can purchase furs at fantastic prices does not, to my mind, show that furs as a class, being a commonplace article of dress, are fragile or specially valuable articles in the same sort of way as jewellery, watches, field-glasses and cameras are fragile or specially valuable articles.'

Further, in *Mair v Railway Passengers Assurance Co Ltd*:[17]

> A clause in a life assurance policy excluded the insurance company from being liable if the assured met his death as a result of one of a wide variety of causes, '. . . by his travelling by railway in a different carriage from those provided for the conveyance of passengers, or entering or leaving a carriage whilst a train is in motion . . . or riding races or steeple-chases or generally by his wilfully exposing himself to any unnecessary danger or peril'. The insured accosted a woman in the street, and was knocked down by the man in whose company she was, and died as a result of injuries which had been inflicted upon him.
> *Held,* that the insurance company could not rely on the exclusion clause, since what had happened could not be considered to be ejusdem generis with the perils enumerated in the clause.

Lord Coleridge CJ said:[18]

> 'I think [the clause] must be construed by the expressions that go before; the danger or peril which is pointed at must be a peril ejusdem generis with those which are specified in the more particular language of the policy . . . I cannot bring my mind to think that any such thing was pointed at as a man . . . morally or immorally going up and speaking to a woman and in the

---

not there. It cannot be right to approach a document with the presumption that there should be such implication. We must ascertain the meaning of the parties from the words they have used. Of course, the first approach will often show quite plainly that the words are used far more widely than the parties could have intended . . . The so-called rule is, in short, really only a recognition of the fact that parties with their minds concerned with the particular objects about which they are contracting are apt to use words, phrases or clauses which taken literally are wider than they intend.' He then went on to say (at 246): 'If the ejusdem generis principle is a rule of automatic application, it becomes of the first importance to determine exactly what the rule is. If it is merely, as I think, an aid to ascertaining the intention of the parties, no point of controversy need arise. If there is something to show that the literal meaning of the words is too wide, then they will be given such other meaning as seems best to consort with the intention of the parties. In some cases it may be that they would seem to indicate a genus; in others that they perform the simpler office of expanding the meaning of each enumerated item. If a genus cannot be found, doubtless, that is one factor indicating that the parties did not intend to restrict the meaning of the words used. But I do not take it to be universally true that whenever a genus cannot be found, the words must have been intended to have their literal meaning, whatever other indications there may be to the contrary.'

15 (1931) 48 TLR 53.

16 Ibid, at 55.

17 (1877) 37 LT 356.

18 Ibid, at 358. But see the judgment of Denman J, ibid, at 359.

> course of speaking to a woman getting knocked down by somebody who thought that he had a right to protect her. I cannot think that is wilful exposure to unnecessary danger or peril, coming after this proviso "or entering or leaving a carriage whilst the train is in motion . . . or riding races or steeple-chases and so on".'

In the case of a marine insurance policy where a yacht was strained whilst being docked for the purpose of having her bottom cleaned, this circumstance was held to be ejusdem generis with a peril of the sea and other perils set out in the Institute Yacht Clauses, and therefore the assured was entitled to recover in respect of the damage which had been sustained.[19]

The rule applies not merely where there is a common characteristic running through or underlying the previous words,[20] but also where several distinct cases are enumerated leading to a common result or intended to be met by a common remedy.[1]

Where, on the other hand, the preceding words do not contain a mere specification of particulars, but the description of a complete genus, if not of two different genera, the word is to be given its full signification, and the ejusdem generis rule has no application.[2]

Thus, in an exception against insurrection, riots, civil commotion, or military or usurped power, there are really two exceptions, one against riot and the other against war. The words 'military or usurped power' are not qualified by the preceding words, but refer to events of a different character, and, therefore, include the acts of foreign enemies.[3]

(b) General words followed by words of limitation

Where a word of general signification is followed by words of limitation or definition, which introduce words of narrower signification, the first word is not to be taken in its full sense, but must be construed as limited by and applying only to the particulars specified.

Thus, an insurance on a corn dealer's 'stock-in-trade consisting of corn, seed, hay, straw, fixtures and utensils in business' does not cover hops or malting.[4]

---

19 *The Lapwing* [1940] P 112 (marine insurance).

20 *Sangster's Trustees v General Accident Assurance Corpn Ltd* 1896 24 R (Ct of Sess) 56 per Lord Robertson, at 58.

1 *Thames and Mersey Marine Insurance Co v Hamilton, Fraser & Co* (1887) 12 App Cas 484 (marine insurance) per Lord McNaghten, at 502. In accordance with the same principle, where a clause defining the risk as limited to land risks is followed by another clause defining the scope of the insurance in general terms which, apart from the first clause, would be construed as extending to marine risks, the second clause is to be regarded as controlled by the first: *Ewing & Co v Sicklemore* (1918) 35 TLR 55, CA.

2 *Sun Fire Office v Hart* (1889) 14 App Cas 98, PC (fire insurance), where a condition empowering the insurers to terminate the policy if they should wish to do so from various specified reasons 'or from any other cause whatsoever' was held to give them the option of terminating the policy at will; cf *Cole v Accident Insurance Co Ltd* (1889) 61 LT 227 (affirmed 5 TLR 736, CA) per Mathew J, at 228; *Re United London and Scottish Insurance Co Ltd, Brown's Claim* [1915] 2 Ch 167, CA (accident insurance).

3 *Rogers v Whittaker* [1917] 1 KB 942 (fire insurance) per Sankey J, at 944; cf *Curtis & Sons v Mathews* [1919] 1 KB 425, CA, where, in an insurance against loss caused 'by war, bombardment, military or usurped power or by aerial craft (hostile or otherwise)', it was held that the earlier words were to be considered as including the acts of the forces of the Crown and were not cut down by the qualification 'hostile or otherwise' which had been inserted ex abundanti cautela after the words 'aerial craft'.

4 *Joel v Harvey* (1858) 5 WR 488 (fire insurance).

Similarly, where a clause framed in general terms and capable of a wider significance (e g a declaration that the answers to questions are correct and true, which declaration, together with the proposal, is to be the basis of the contract), is followed by another clause of narrower significance (e g a provision avoiding the policy in the event of any fraudulent concealment or designedly untrue statement in the proposal, which is superfluous and unnecessary if the first clause is to bear the wider significance), the second clause is to be regarded as explanatory of the first and limiting its application accordingly.[5]

7 The words mean what they say

The words of the policy must be construed to mean what they say,[6] unless there is some strong ground for putting a different construction on the words from what they naturally import.[7] If, therefore, the policy is framed in language so precise, express and strong as to admit of one construction only, this construction must be adopted, however unreasonable it may be,[8] since it is not the province of the Court to make for the parties a reasonable contract.[9]

The Court is at liberty to correct a misnomer e g a mere clerical error.[10]

8 The words must be construed liberally

The words of the policy must, if possible, be construed liberally, so as to give effect to the intention of the parties.[11]

---

5 *Fowkes v Manchester and London Life Assurance Association* (1863) 3 B & S 917 (life insurance) per Cockburn CJ, at 925. Cf *Reid & Co v Employers' Accident Insurance Co* 1899 1 F (Ct of Sess) 1031, where *Fowkes v Manchester and London Life Assurance Association* (supra) was distinguished on the ground that the proposal was not incorporated in the policy, and it was held that the warranty contained in the declaration was not limited by the condition in the policy to cases of fraudulent misrepresentation.

6 *Winspear v Accident Insurance Co* (1880) 6 QBD 42, CA, per Coleridge CJ, at 45; *Cassel v Lancashire and Yorkshire Accident Insurance Co Ltd* (1885) 1 TLR 495 per Pollock B, at 496.

7 *Borradaile v Hunter* (1843) 5 Man & G 639 (life insurance) per Coltman J, at 663.

8 *Gamble v Accident Assurance Co* (1869) IR 4 CL 204 per Pigot CB, at 214; *Cole v Accident Assurance Co Ltd* (1889) 5 TLR 736, CA per Lord Esher MR, at 737; *Re United London and Scottish Insurance Co Ltd, Brown's Claim* [1915] 2 Ch 167, CA per Lord Cozens-Hardy MR, at 170; *Farr v Motor Traders Mutual Insurance Society* [1920] 3 KB 669, CA per Bankes LJ, at 673; *Joel v Law Union and Crown Insurance Co* [1908] 2 KB 863, CA (life insurance) per Fletcher Moulton LJ, at 886.

9 *Re George and Goldsmiths' and General Burglary Insurance Association Ltd* [1889] 1 QB 595, CA (burglary insurance) per Collins LJ, at 609.

10 *Nittan (UK) Ltd v Solent Steel Fabrication Ltd trading as Sargrove Automation and Cornhill Insurance Co Ltd* [1981] 1 Lloyd's Rep 633, CA (product liability insurance), where the Court construed the words 'Sargrove Electronic Controls Ltd' as a concern called 'Sargrove Automation'. See the judgment of Brightman LJ (ibid, at 639), where he said: 'In my opinion, in construing a document, the Court is at liberty, as a matter of construction, to correct a misnomer. A misnomer is not, in my view, a mistake which requires the equitable remedy of rectification. The misnomer may be a mere clerical error. A simple example would be the use in a conveyance of the expression "the vendor" where clearly "the purchaser" was intended. It is not necessary to rectify the conveyance to enable it to be read and take effect as the parties intended.' (See also the judgment of Lord Denning MR, ibid, at 637, and that of Griffiths LJ, ibid, at 641). As to the rectification of the policy, see pp 239–243, ante.

11 *Sheridan v Phoenix Life Assurance Co* (1858) EB & E 156 (life insurance) per Pollock CB, at 165: 'If there be a doubt, we think of all instruments that come before us, none requires a more liberal construction than a life policy.'; *Pelly v Royal Exchange Assurance Co* (1757) 1 Burr 341 (marine insurance) per Lee CJ, at 349: 'It is certain that in construction of policies, the *strictum jus* or *apex juris* is not to be laid hold on; but they are to be construed largely, for the benefit of trade, and for the assured'; *Barnard v Faber* [1893] 1 QB 340, CA (fire insurance) per Lindley LJ, at 342:

The object of the parties being to make a contract of insurance, any construction which defeats that object or renders the contract practically illusory is to be rejected.[12]

A literal construction leading to a result which is absurd or otherwise manifestly contrary to the real intention of the parties is not to be adopted,[13] and the words used must be construed with qualifications.[14]

On the other hand, the words of the policy are not to be extended beyond their ordinary meaning in order to comprehend a case which is within their object[15] and which the parties would probably have desired to include, if it had occurred to them[16] for that would be to give effect to an intention which is not expressed.[17]

'When you have a clause which is consistent with the ordinary habits of men if you interpret it one way, and which is utterly inconsistent with their ordinary habits if you interpret it another, I prefer the former interpretation, that is, supposing the language admits of a double interpretation.' See also, *Pim v Reid* (1843) 6 Man & G 1 (fire insurance) per Tindal CJ, at 20; *Borradaile v Hunter* (1843) 5 Man & G 639 (life insurance) per Erskine J, at 657.

12 See also, *Braunstein v Accidental Death Insurance Co* (1861) 1 B & S 782, where 'proof satisfactory to the directors' was held to mean 'reasonably satisfactory'; *Smellie v British General Insurance Co* [1918] WC & Ins Rep 233, where a condition requiring notice of any accident to be given within three days was held to mean that notice was only to be given when it was made clear that the insurers might be involved; *Pearson v Commercial Union Assurance Co* (1876) 1 App Cas 498 (fire insurance) per Lord Penzance, at 507; *SCA (Freight) Ltd v Gibson* [1974] 2 Lloyd's Rep 533, QBD (Comercial Ct) (goods in transit insurance) per Ackner J, at 535.

13 *Sangster's Trustees v General Accident Assurance Corpn Ltd* 1896 24 R (Ct of Sess) 56 per Lord Stormonth-Darling, at 57n, pointing out that the exception against wilful exposure to unnecessary danger, if literally construed, would exclude the majority of accidents, seeing that everyone who travels by land or sea wilfully exposes himself to danger, and, if he travels for pleasure, does so unnecessarily; *Accident Insurance Co of North America v McFee* (1891) MLR 7 QB 255, where it was held that the insurers could not rely on an exception against getting on or off a train in motion in the case of an assured who was described in the proposal as superintendent of a railway and whose duties required him to get on and off trains in motion; *Burridge & Son v F H Haines & Sons Ltd* (1918) 118 LT 681, where a policy upon a horse provided for an indemnity against 'death attributable to accidental, external and visible injury', and it was held that the assured was entitled to recover although the accident which caused the horse's death left no mark of injury visible on its skin; *Daff v Midland Colliery Owners Mutual Indemnity Co* (1913) 6 BWCC 799, HL, per Lord Moulton, at 823; *Australian Agricultural Co v Saunders* (1875) LR 10 CP 668, ExCh (fire insurance) per Bramwell B, at 674; *Beauchamp v Faber* (1898) 3 Com Cas 308 (fire insurance) per Mathew J, at 342; *Borradaile v Hunter* (1843) 5 Man & G 639 (life insurance) per Erskine J, at 657, pointing out that the phrase 'die by his own hands' could not be taken literally; *Clift v Schwabe* (1846) 3 CB 437 (life insurance) per Patteson J, at 465.

14 *Cornish v Accident Insurance Co* (1889) 23 QBD 453, CA; *Connecticut Mutual Life Insurance Co of Hertford v Moore* (1881) 6 App Cas 644, at 648, PC (life insurance), pointing out that the questions in the proposal form cannot always be answered with strict and literal truth, but must be read with limitations and qualifications so as to make them reasonable.

15 *Borradaile v Hunter* (1843) 5 Man & G 639 (life insurance) per Maule J, at 653; cf *Century Bank of New York v Mountain* (1914) 112 LT 484, CA, where a policy protecting a banker against loss by the fraudulent taking of coin, etc., was held not to cover a loss by the fraudulent obtaining of credit. On the other hand, the policy applies to an accident falling within its terms, although such accident may be of rare occurrence and was never thought of when the policy was framed: *Pugh v London, Brighton and South Coast Rly Co* [1896] 2 QB 248, CA, per Smith LJ, at 253.

16 *Re George and Goldsmiths' and General Burglary Insurance Association* [1889] 1 QB 595, CA, per Collins LJ, at 609, 610: 'We have not to deal with any general principle of law, but merely to construe the agreement made by the parties. They have chosen to frame for themselves a definition of burglary and housebreaking for the purposes of their contract, and by that definition their rights in this case must be determined. It is no part of our province to make for the parties a reasonable contract, and if, as I think, they have not altogether succeeded in doing

---

[*Footnote 17 on p 358*]

Thus, a death may be 'accidental' in the sense that it is unforeseen and unexpected. But unless it is further caused by accidental means, it does not fall within the scope of a personal accident policy in the ordinary form,[18] nor of a public liability policy covering the insured in respect of any sum he may be liable to pay as damages for bodily injury to any person 'caused by accident'.[19]

Where the interests of two insured in a subject-matter which is insured 'against accidental loss or damage' are different, and one of the insured deliberately causes damage to it, this does not prevent the other insured from claiming under the policy, for, as far as he is concerned, the damage has been caused by 'accident'.[20]

In *Cornish v Accident Insurance Co*[1] a policy had been effected against accidental death or injury, and contained a statement exempting the insurance company from liability for any accident which happened 'by exposure of the insured to obvious risk of injury'. One of the questions which arose concerned the meaning of the word 'obvious'. In the course of his judgment Lindley LJ said:[2]

---

so for themselves, we cannot do so for them. I think the vice of the decision of the Divisional Court, if I may say so, is that they sought to make for the parties a contract which should be reasonable from all points of view, and such as the parties, if they had had in their minds all the matters which have been brought before us in agreement, might very probably have made for themselves. But I am not called upon to find for the parties that which they have not found for themselves. All I have to do is to look at the words which they have used, and try to give them their plain and commonsense meaning.' Cf *Gorman v Hand-in-Hand Insurance Co* (1877) IR 11 CL 224 (fire insurance), where two ricks of hay were insured in terms so specific that it was held that the insurance applied only to the two ricks existing at the date of the policy.

17 *Ward v Law Property Assurance and Trust Society* (1856) 4 WR 605, where a condition in a fidelity policy requiring notice to be given of any liability being incurred was held not to require the employer to give notice of facts which aroused his suspicions.

18 *Clidero v Scottish Accident Insurance Co* 1892 19 R (Ct of Sess) 355; *Re Scarr and General Accident Assurance Corpn* [1905] 1 KB 387; *Marcel Beller Ltd v Hayden* [1978] 1 Lloyd's Rep 472 (personal accident insurance), where the insured was killed when driving a car negligently after consuming too much alcohol, and it was held that the death was an accident for the predisposing cause, although it led to the taking of a risk, was neither deliberately run nor actually appreciated. (See the judgment of Judge Edgar Fay, ibid, at 478).

19 *Gray v Barr (Prudential Assurance Co Ltd, Third Party)* [1971] 2 QB 554, [1971] 2 All ER 949, CA, where the insured threatened another man with a loaded shotgun and fired into the ceiling to frighten him, and the gun went off a second time in a struggle which ensued, and it was held that the death of the other man was not 'caused by accident'. (See the judgments of Lord Denning MR, ibid, at 957, and that of Phillimore LJ, ibid, at 949. Salmon LJ however said (ibid, at 963) that he considered that death was 'caused by accident', but was not the type of accident covered by the policy.)

20 *Lombard Australia Ltd v NRMA Insurance Ltd* [1969] 1 Lloyd's Rep 575, Supreme Court of New South Wales, Court of Appeal (motor insurance), where the interests of a finance company and the hire-purchaser of a car which was let out to him by the company under a hire-purchase agreement were held to be separately insured under one policy, and the finance company was held to be entitled to sue under the policy in respect of damage to the vehicle caused by the hire-purchaser deliberately running it into a tree in order to commit suicide. The Court held that the damage was caused by 'accident', Wallace A-CJ, observing (ibid, at 577): 'The word "accidental" like so many other words has different meanings according to its particular context but here the question whether the loss was accidental can only be decided from an examination of the conduct and activities of the claimant for indemnity because the indemnity was a several one. On this basis the claim of the owner in the present case is unanswerable.' See also, the judgment of Holmes JA (ibid, at 580): 'I am satisfied that so far as the claimant in this case was concerned the damage to the motor car was accidental, even though it was deliberate so far as the actor was concerned.'

1 (1889) 23 QBD 453.

2 Ibid, at 456.

'The words are "exposure of the insured to obvious risk of injury". These words suggest the following questions: Exposure by whom? Obvious when? Obvious to whom? It is to be observed that the words are very general. There is no such word as "wilful", or "reckless" or "careless', and to ascertain the true meaning of the exception the whole document must be studied and the object of the parties to it must be steadily borne in mind. The object of the contract is to insure against accidental death and injuries, and the contract must not be construed so as to defeat that object, nor so as to render it practically illusory. A man who crosses an ordinary crowded street is exposed to obvious risk of injury; and if the words in question are construed literally, the [insurance company] would not be liable in the event of an insured being killed or injured in so crossing, even if he was taking reasonable care of himself. Such a result is so manifestly contrary to the real intention of the parties that a construction which leads to it ought to be rejected.'

Further, in *Re Etherington and Lancashire and Yorkshire Accident Insurance Co.*[3] a policy stated that it only insured against death where the accident was the direct or proximate cause thereof, but not where the direct or proximate cause was disease or another intervening cause, even although the disease or other intervening cause might itself have been aggravated by such accident. Vaughan Williams LJ remarked:[4]

'We have to construe this policy not merely in reference to this particular case; we must recollect that it is a document in the form which is used for the regular issue of policies by the company to persons who are desirous of insuring with them, and one must consider whither the construction contended for by the company would lead, if we were to adopt it. As far as I can see, if we adopted it, the result would be that it would be very difficult to establish the liability of the insurance company in any case except where the accident resulted in what may be called death on the spot. There is always in every other case a possibility of some supervening cause, and it would be very difficult for anyone to look forward with any certainty to a sum being receivable on the policy if we were to put such a construction as was suggested upon a policy in this form. I think that some limitation of the terms of the proviso contained in the policy ought to be welcomed by the insurance companies themselves, for otherwise, in my opinion the number of cases in which the policy could be enforced against the company would be so very much reduced that the practical result would soon be that very few persons would care to insure.'

In *Trew v Railway Passengers' Assurance Co*[5] one of the issues was the interpretation of a clause in a policy which provided that, 'If at any time during his life . . . the assured shall sustain any injury caused by accident or violence . . . and if the assured shall die from the effects of such injury within three calendar months', the insurance company would be liable. It was contended that the insured had died by drowning, and that drowning was not one of the cases covered by the policy.

Cockburn CJ said:[6]

'[Counsel] ingeniously argued that the policy only applies to cases where from accident or violence some injury occurs from which death may or may not ensue; and if it ensues within three months, the sum assured is payable. But he contended, in effect, that where the cause of death produces immediate death without the intervention of any external injury, the policy does not apply; and whereas from the action of the water there is no external injury, death by

---

3 [1909] 1 KB 591.

4 Ibid, at 597.

5 (1861) 6 H & N 839.

6 Ibid, at 844. See also *Jason v British Traders' Insurance Co Ltd* [1969] 1 Lloyd's Rep 281, where it was assumed for the purpose of the action that a coronary thrombosis causing a clot to form occurring as a result of stress suffered by the insured in a motor accident was 'a bodily injury sustained in an accident.' But Fisher J said (ibid, at 290): 'It seems to me a strained and unnatural use of words to call either the anxiety or the change in the blood or the clot itself "a bodily injury sustained in the accident".'

the action of the water is not within the meaning of this policy. That argument, if carried to its extreme length, would apply to every case where death was immediate. If a man fell from the top of a house, or overboard from a ship, and was killed; or if a man was suffocated by the smoke of a house on fire, such cases would be excluded from the policy, and the effect would be that policies of this kind, in many cases of death resulting from accident, would afford no protection whatever to the assured. We ought not to give those policies a construction which will defeat the protection of the assured in a large class of cases. We are therefore of opinion that, if there was evidence for the jury that the deceased died from drowning, that was a death by accident within the terms of this policy.'

9 A reasonable construction will be preferred

In any case of ambiguity where the words of the policy are capable of two constructions, the reasonable construction is to be preferred as representing the presumed intention of the parties.[7]

Thus, a stipulation in a contract of mutual insurance[8] which provides that when a member's protection has been determined by reason of his failure to pay a call[9] he shall not be entitled to any indemnity, is to be construed as referring to the future only, and not as depriving him of any indemnity to which he has become entitled before the determination of his contract.[10]

In *Hooper v Accidental Death Insurance Co*:[11]

A solicitor had taken out an accident policy, which contained a clause that the insurance company would pay him £5 per week if he sustained any bodily injury of so serious a nature 'as wholly to disable him from following his usual business, occupation or pursuits'. He sprained his ankle severely and was confined to his bedroom for some weeks, being unable to get downstairs. He was prevented from attending at various places at which he was required to complete purchases for his clients.

Held, that he was so disabled as to be incapable of following his usual occupation within the meaning of the policy, and that the company was liable to pay the sum named.

In giving judgment Wightman J said:[12]

'We are all of opinion that the plaintiff, having received such an injury that he was obliged to

---

7 *Hooper v Accidental Death Insurance Co* (1860) 5 H & N 546, ExCh, per Wightman J, at 559; *Gamble v Accident Assurance Co Ltd* (1869) IR 4 CL 204 (accident insurance) per Pigot CB, at 214; *Century Bank of City of New York v Mountain* (1914) 112 LT 484, CA (insurance of securities) per Kennedy LJ, at 486; *London Guarantee Co v Fearnley* (1880) 5 App Cas 911 per Lord Blackburn, at 916; *E Hulton & Co Ltd v Mountain* (1921) 37 TLR 869, CA per Bankes LJ, at 870; *North British and Mercantile Insurance Co v London, Liverpool and Globe Insurance Co* (1877) 5 ChD 569 (fire insurance) per Jessel MR, at 576; *Barnard v Faber* [1893] 1 QB 340, CA (fire insurance) per Lindley LJ, at 342; *Gorman v Hand-in-Hand Insurance Co* (1877) IR 11 CL 224 (fire insurance), where, in the case of an insurance upon horses and agricultural implements which were described as being in a particular place, but the contemplated use of which necessarily rendered frequent removal from the specified place essential, it was held on the construction of a condition as to removal, that removal did not absolutely put an end to the insurance, but that the insurance only ceased pro tempore, until their return. Cf *Farr v Motor Traders Mutual Insurance Society* [1920] 3 KB 669, CA. See also, *John Martin of London Ltd v Russell* [1960] 1 Lloyd's Rep 554 (Commercial Court) (all risks insurance), where the insurer's contention that the cover ceased if the consignee did not intend to send the goods to a 'final warehouse', did not give a reasonable business like meaning to a clause stating that 'this insurance continues until the goods are delivered to the consignees' or other final warehouse at the destination named in the policy.'

8 As to 'mutual insurance', see Ivamy *Marine Insurance* (4th Edn, 1985), pp 475–479.

9 As to 'calls', see ibid, at pp 476–477.

10 *Daff v Midland Colliery Owners Mutual Indemnity Co* (1913) 6 BWCC 799, HL.

11 (1860) 5 H & N 546.

12 Ibid, at 559.

lie on a sofa in his room, and being unable to put his foot to the ground or come downstairs, had received an injury which "wholly disabled him from following his usual business or employment". Great stress has been laid on the word "wholly" as applicable to the word "disabled". In order to ascertain its meaning we must look at the other words in the sentence. From what is he to be wholly disabled? From following his usual occupation. When, as shown in this case, he was confined to his room and unable to see his clients, surely it is a reasonable construction to say that he was "wholly disabled" from following his usual occupation.'

In *London Guarantee Co v Fearnley*:[13]

A fidelity policy contained a clause stating that 'the employer shall if and when required by the company . . . use all diligence in prosecuting the employed to conviction for any fraud or dishonesty . . . in consequence of which a claim shall have been made under this policy, and shall . . . give all information and assistance to enable the company to sue for and obtain reimbursement, by the employed, or by his estate, of any moneys which the company shall have become liable to pay'. A sum of money was embezzled by the insured's servant, but the insured, although requested to do so by the company, did not prosecute him.
Held, the clause amounted to a condition precedent and since the insured had not complied with it, he was unable to recover under the policy.

Lord Blackburn pointed out that:[14]

'The provision in question as to the employer, when required, using all diligence in prosecuting the employed to conviction is coupled with a stipulation that he shall give all assistance to enable the company to obtain reimbursement from the employed or his estate is different; that latter stipulation is not and cannot be a condition precedent to the obligation of the company to pay: the company cannot be entitled to reimbursement till it has, at least, become liable to pay. It seems to me likely that those who framed the policy stipulated for the prosecution by the employer, with a view to facilitate reimbursement, and I do not think the words such as to require us to put this construction on the instrument, a construction which seems to me unreasonable. I think that the two matters are separate and independent, and the meaning of the first part of the stipulation is that the employer, who is not entitled to recover except for loss by embezzlement, shall, if required, subject his proof to the test of bringing it before a magistrate, and so subjecting it to the defence of the person accused of embezzlement, before the directors are called on to say whether the proof is satisfactory. The stipulation thus understood is one not at all unreasonable, and it is one the nature of which makes it necessary, for the protection of the company, that it should be made a condition precedent to an action for damages, for not doing this would give the company no redress.'

In *E Hulton & Co Ltd v Mountain*:[15]

An insurance policy had been effected by a newspaper against actions for libel in respect of articles which appeared in it. The policy contained a clause stating, 'In the event of a claim occurring likely to exceed the amount retained by the assured at their own risk, no costs shall be incurred without the consent of the underwriters.'
Held, this clause only meant that the consent of the underwriters should be obtained at every important stage of the proceedings.

In giving judgment Bankes LJ observed:[16]

'In my view the words of the policy, "no costs shall be incurred without the consent of the underwriters" literally construed, mean that at every stage of the proceedings involving costs the consent of the underwriters must be applied for. A clause, however, must be construed reasonably. Application for consent was a necessary condition precedent, and it must be shown either that an express application was made and express consent given, or that the necessity for making it was waived, or that the consent was implied. The application for the consent of the underwriters should be made at every important stage of the proceedings. When the consent was applied for and given for defending an action, if the action resulted in favour of the assured

[13] (1880) 5 App Cas 911.
[14] Ibid, at 916.
[15] (1921) 8 LlL Rep 249.
[16] Ibid, at 250.

and there was an appeal, it would be necessary to apply and obtain consent to oppose the appeal, and if the appeal resulted in a new trial being ordered, application and consent would be necessary before proceeding to defend the new trial.'

Again, where a burglary policy contains a condition that a burglar alarm is to be 'kept in efficient working order', the word 'kept' implies within it a requirement that before there can be a breach of the condition by the insured he must be aware of the facts which give rise to the alarm not being in efficient working order, or if he is not aware of those facts, he should at least be in a position where, exercising common care, he should have known of those facts.[17] Further, he must be given a sufficient opportunity to have the alarm installed once more in proper working order.[18]

10 The 'contra proferentem' rule

A well known rule of construction is the '*contra proferentem*' rule—or to state it in full—*verba chartarum fortius accipiuntur contra proferentem.*

The principle is found stated in a number of passages in the reports. 'There is one perfectly good rule of construction which has bound underwriters for very many years, and that is that if they choose the language, if it is their language, then the document must be construed *contra proferentem,* which means to say against the person who put the language into the document upon which he is relying or upon which anybody relies.'[19] 'It is extremely important with reference to insurance, that there should be a tendency rather to hold for the assured than for the company, where any ambiguity arises upon the face of the policy.'[20] 'I start with the consideration that it has been established by the authorities that in dealing with the construction of policies, whether they be life, or fire, or marine policies, an ambiguous clause must be construed against rather than in favour of the company.'[1] 'It is a well known principle of insurance law that if the language of a warranty in a policy is ambiguous, it must be construed against the underwriter who has drawn the policy and has inserted the warranty for his own protection.'[2] There is no doubt that if the phrase used in the policy is . . . ambiguous, that meaning must be chosen, which is the less favourable to the underwriters who have put forward the policy.'[3] 'In

17 *Victor Melik & Co Ltd v Norwich Union Fire Insurance Society Ltd and Kemp* [1980] 1 Lloyd's Rep 523 (burglary insurance), at 530 (per Woolf J).

18 Ibid, at 530 (per Woolf J).

19 *Metal Scrap and By-products Ltd v Federated Conveyors Ltd* [1953] 1 Lloyd's Rep 221 at 227 (per Croom Johnson J).

20 *Fitton v Accidental Death Insurance Co* (1864) 17 CBNS 122 at 135 (per Willes J).

1 *Re Etherington and Lancashire and Yorkshire Accident Insurance Co* [1909] 1 KB 591 at 596 (per Vaughan Williams LJ).

2 *Simmonds v Cockell* [1920] 1 KB 843 at 845 (per Roche J).

3 *English v Western* [1940] 2 KB 156 at 165 (per Clauson LJ). See further, *Tarleton v Staniforth* (1794) 5 Term Rep 695 at 699: 'I admit that . . . the words of the covenantor according to Lord Bacon, *fortius accipiuntur contra proferentem*' (per Lord Kenyon CJ); *Anderson v Fitzgerald* (1853) 4 HL Cas 484 at 507: '[The policy] is, of course, prepared by the company, and if therefore there should be any ambiguity in it, must be taken according to law more strongly against the person who prepared it.' (per Lord St Leonards); *Braunstein v Accidental Death Insurance Co* (1861) 1 B & S 782 at 799: 'I quite admit that the parties may make what they please a condition precedent, but it must be shown that they so intended. Here the stipulation is the language of one party, and *verba fortius accipiuntur contra proferentem*' per Blackburn J); *Joel v Law Union and Crown Insurance Co* [1908] 2 KB 863 at 890: 'It is a case in which the principle of taking such a

case of ambiguity the contra proferentem rule will apply, but apart from this there is no rule of law which requires me to strain the language of the policy in favour of or against the insured person. It is a bargain by which, in consideration of a relatively small premium, the insurance company agrees to make substantial payments in certain events, and it would be no less of an injustice to compel payment in events not falling within the meaning of the words used in the policy than to deny payment in events falling within such meaning.'[4]

---

document as this *contra proferentes* ought to be applied in the strongest way' (per Fletcher Moulton LJ); *Lake v Simmons* [1927] AC 487 at 508: 'The language is the insurers' own, and in an exception it must be read *contra proferentes*' (per Lord Sumner); *Weir v Northern Counties of England Insurance Co* (1897) 4 LRIr 689 at 693 (per Lawson J); *Hooper v Accidental Death Insurance Co* (1860) 5 H & N 546 at 557, ExCh (per Pollock CB); *Harris v Scaramanga* (1872) LR 7 CP 481 (marine insurance) at 497 (per Brett J); *National Protector Fire Insurance Co Ltd v Nivert* [1913] AC 507 at 513, PC; *Cowell v Yorkshire Provident Life Assurance Co* (1901) 17 TLR 452 (life insurance); *Fowkes v Manchester and London Life Assurance Association* (1863) 3 B & S 917; *Winter v Employers Fire Insurance Co* [1962] 2 Lloyd's Rep 320 (State of Florida, Civil Court, Duval County) (marine insurance), where damage sustained by a motor boat 14 miles off the US coast was held to have taken place 'within the limits of the continental United States of America.'; *Gerhardt v Continental Insurance Companies and Firemen's Insurance Co of Newark* [1967] 1 Lloyd's-Rep 380 (Supreme Court of New Jersey) (houseowner's comprehensive policy), where it was held that the insurance company could rely on an exemption clause. Mr Justice Jacobs said (at 384): 'Nowhere was there any straightforward and unconditional statement that the policy was not intended to protect the insured against a workmen's compensation claim by a resident employee injured at the insured's home.'; *Woolford v Liverpool County Council* [1968] 2 Lloyd's Rep 256, which concerned not a policy itself but a failure by a local authority to effect a policy in respect of a venture course in North Wales on which the plaintiff was injured whilst rock climbing. The local authority was under a contractual duty to 'take out a special insurance policy to cover any injury that might possibly be sustained during the course'. Counsel for the local authority argued that the words 'to cover any injury' meant no more than a cover which would result in a benefit 'consistent with what is usually done in these cases'. Roskill J refused to accept this contention, and said (ibid, at 259): 'It is for [the local authority] as the party putting forward those words, if they wish to impose any limitation on their apparent width, to see that suitable clear words restricting the ordinary prima facie meaning of the language which they have seen fit to use appear in the sentence in question'; *W and J Lane v Spratt* [1969] 2 Lloyd's Rep 229 (goods in transit insurance), where it was held that a clause stating that 'the insured shall take all reasonable precautions for the protection and safeguarding of the goods and/or merchandise and use such protective appliances as may be specified in the policy and all vehicles and protective devices shall be maintained in good order', did not impose on the insured an obligation to vet their staff with due diligence before they employed them. Roskill J observed (ibid, at 237): 'I think there is force in Counsel's arguments, first, that this is a clause for the benefit of the underwriters, and therefore if underwriters wish to say that it is to extend not merely to what I have called physical precautions but is to cover selection of staff, the clause ought so to state in express terms'; *Kirkbride v Donner* [1974] 1 Lloyd's Rep 549, Mayor's and City of London Ct (motor insurance), where the question in a proposal form stated: 'Will the car to your knowledge be driven by any person under 25 years of age?' was construed *contra proferentem*, and held not to relate to the future, Deputy Judge Tibber saying (ibid, at 553): 'It seems to me that this document has got to be construed against the insurance company and I just cannot accept that there was no clear way which the insurance company could put this intention. It is perfectly simple to find a form of words to express the construction for which the defendants contend.'; *Consolidated-Bathurst Export Ltd v Mutual Boiler and Machinery Insurance Co* (1980) 112 DLR (3d) 49 (Can SC) (property insurance), where the word 'accident' was defined as meaning a sudden and accidental occurrence to the object but stated that 'accident' should not mean, inter alia, corrosion, and it was held that the definition was ambiguous and should be construed *contra proferentem*.

4 *Jason v British Traders Insurance Co Ltd* [1969] 1 Lloyd's Rep 281 (personal accident insurance) per Fisher J, at 290.

Thus, the *contra proferentem* rule was applied in *Houghton v Trafalgar Insurance Co Ltd*:[5]

> A motor insurance cover note excluded 'loss, damage and/or liability caused or arising whilst [the] car is . . . conveying any load in excess of that for which it was constructed.' The vehicle was carrying a driver and five passengers. The insurance company contended that it was not liable because the car was conveying a 'load in excess of that for which it was constructed'.
> *Held*, that the company was liable.

Somervell LJ said:[6]

> 'If there is any ambiguity, it is the [company's] clause and the ambiguity will be resolved in favour of the assured. In my opinion, the words relied on, "any load in excess of that for which it was constructed," only clearly cover cases where there is a weight load specified in respect of the motor vehicle, be it lorry or van. I agree that the earlier words in the clause obviously are applicable to an ordinary private car in respect of which there is no such specified weight load. But there was, of course, no evidence as to whether this was a form which was used for lorries as well as ordinary private motor cars. I do not think that matters. We have to construe the words in their ordinary meaning, and I think those words only clearly cover the case which I have put. If that is right, they cannot avail the insurance company in the present case.'

Denning LJ said that it would surprise most car owners to be told that if they squeezed in an extra passenger, one more than the ordinary seating capacity, they thereby lost the benefit of the insurance policy. If the clause had such an interpretation, he would regard it almost as a trap. He was glad to find the clause did not bear that extended interpretation. It was only applicable to cases where there was a specified weight which must not be exceeded, as in the case of lorries.

Romer LJ said that it would be a serious thing for a motorist involved in a collision, if he were told that the particular circumstances of the accident excluded him from the benefit of the policy. He thought that any clause or provision that purported to have that effect ought to be clear and unambiguous so that the motorist knew exactly where he stood. The provision was neither clear nor unambiguous. If applied to a private motor car, he had not the slightest idea what it meant.

Again, in *English v Western*:[7]

> A 17 year old boy had taken out a motor car insurance policy. He and his sister both lived with their father. His sister was injured in a motor accident, whilst the assured was driving. The insurers claimed that they were not liable because the policy contained an exception stating that it excluded death of or injury to 'any member of the assured's household', and that it meant any member of the same household of which the assured was a member.
> *Held*, that the policy might mean 'any member of a household of which the assured was the head'. Since there was a doubt, it should be construed against the insurers. Consequently they were liable on the policy.

Clauson LJ said:[8]

> 'It may well be that one would have expected the underwriters—possibly for very good reasons—to have intended the phrase to carry the wider connotation. But that seems to me to be quite immaterial if one once reaches the conclusion that the phrase is ambiguous. If the underwriters desired the wider meaning to be placed on it, it was their duty to make that desire clear by using unambiguous language . . . I find myself bound to hold that the phrase of exception covers only the narrower class, the member of a household of which the [assured] is head; and accordingly, the case is not a case within the exception and the underwriters are liable.'

---

5 [1953] 2 Lloyd's Rep 503, CA.
6 Ibid, at 504.
7 [1940] 2 KB 156.
8 Ibid, at 165.

Again, in the case of a burglary policy containing a warranty that 'the said premises are always occupied', it was held not to be broken when on the day on which the burglary took place the premises were left unoccupied between 2.30 pm and 11.30 pm except that the insured returned there to change his clothes at 7 pm. The Court applied the *contra proferentem* rule, and said that the warranty did not mean that the premises were never to be left unattended, but that they were to be used continuously and without interruption for occupation as a residence, which they had been in the present case.[9]

In a motor insurance policy where there was an ambiguity as to the meaning of the expression 'private hire', the Court applied the *contra proferentem* rule, and held that the words included the use of the vehicle for private pleasure.[10]

Further, where a householder's comprehensive insurance policy contained a condition stating that 'the insured shall at all times maintain the building in a proper state of repair', and a new floor was being erected and was inadequately supported, and the whole of the front of the building collapsed, it was held (obiter) that the insurers could not rely on the condition, for it was ambiguous and was not in point while the building was being reconstructed.[11]

Again, in a motor insurance policy the words 'motor car' were deemed to have the same meaning as they had under the Road Traffic Act 1960, s 253(2)[12] (i e, a mechanically propelled vehicle constructed to carry a load or passengers and the weight of which unladen does not exceed 3 tons), and accordingly applied to a van, the unladen weight of which was 1 ton 6 cwt 43 lbs, the Court rejecting the condition that the vehicle could not be properly described as a 'car'.[13]

If the party who proffers an instrument uses ambiguous words in the hope that the other side will understand them in a particular sense, and that the Court which has to construe the instrument will give them a different sense, they ought to be construed in that sense in which a prudent and reasonable man on the other side would understand them.[14]

'It is the duty of underwriters or insurance companies if they seek to rely upon a question in a proposal form, to state their question in clear and unambiguous terms, and I think that extends to this, they must state in such terms as can be understood by the persons who are likely to be required to answer them, which includes persons of humble rank and perhaps not the highest intelligence.'[15]

But sometimes the rule will be applied against the insured.

---

9 *Simmonds v Cockell* [1920] 1 KB 843, 2 LlL Rep 230 (buglary insurance).

10 *Kaufmann v British Surety Insurance Co Ltd* (1929) 45 TLR 399, 33 LlL Rep 315.

11 *S and M Hotels Ltd v Legal and General Assurance Society Ltd* [1972] 1 Lloyd's Rep 157, QB. (See the judgment of Thesiger J, ibid, at 165.)

12 Now Road Traffic Act 1972, s 190(2).

13 *Laurence v Davies (Norwich Union Fire Insurance Society Ltd, Third Party)* [1972] 2 Lloyd's Rep 231, Exeter Crown Court (motor insurance), where Dunn J said (ibid, at 233): 'I accept [Counsel's] submission that if insurers desire to place some meaning on words like "motor car" or "motor cycle" or "private motor car" or "motor vehicle" other than those contained in the Road Traffic Act, they should make it abundantly clear in the policy, and, if they fail to do so, then the words will be deemed to have those meanings.'

14 *Fowkes v Manchester and London Life Assurance Association* (1863) 3 B & S 917 at 930 (per Blackburn J).

15 *Hales v Reliance Fire and Accident Insurance Corpn Ltd* [1960] 2 Lloyd's Rep 391 at 396 (per McNair J).

Thus, in *Condogianis v Guardian Assurance Co*:[16]

A question in a proposal form said: 'Has proponent ever been a claimant on a fire insurance company in respect of the property now proposed, or any other property, if so, state when and name of company?' The proposer's answer was: 'Yes. 1917. Ocean.' That answer was literally true, because in 1917 he had claimed against that company in respect of a burning of a motor car. But in 1912 he had made a claim against another company in respect of a similar loss. By the terms of the policy the particulars given by the proposer were to be express warranties. *Held*, that the answer was untrue, for the question could not be read as being intended to have the limited scope which would make the answer true.

Lord Shaw of Dunfermline observed:[17]

'But upon the other hand, the principle of a fair and reasonable construction of the question must also be applied in the other direction, that is to say, there must also be a fair and reasonable construction of the answer given; and if on such a construction the answer is not true, although upon extreme literalism it may be correct, then the contract is equally avoided.'

Again, in *Bartlett & Partners Ltd v Meller*[18] the *contra proferentem* rule was applied against an assured who had submitted through a broker a 'slip' for acceptance.

Where the insurer amends a 'slip' which has been submitted to him for acceptance, the amendment may be construed against him.[19]

But there is one important qualification to the doctrine. 'In a case on the line, in a case of real doubt, the policy ought to be construed most strongly against the insurers; they frame the policy and insert the exceptions. But this principle ought only to be applied for the purpose of removing a doubt, not for the purpose of creating a doubt, or magnifying an ambiguity, when the circumstances of the case raise no real difficulty.'[20] 'But one must not use the rule to create the ambiguity—one must find the ambiguity first.'[1]

---

16 [1921] 2 AC 125.

17 Ibid, at 130. See further, *Birrell v Dryer* (1884) 9 App Cas 345 (marine insurance) per Lord Blackburn at 352.

18 [1961] 1 Lloyd's Rep 487. See also, *A/S Ocean v Black Sea and Baltic General Insurance Co Ltd* (1935) 51 LlL Rep 305, CA, at 307: 'If it were necessary, I think it is clear that the party within the *proferentes* doctrine is the assured who by his agent brings a slip to Lloyd's underwriters or the underwriters for the company and says: "This is what I want; how much are you going to charge me?" and then the underwriter fixes the price of what he is going to pay upon the conditions on which he is asked to underwrite the risk . . .' (per Greer LJ); *American Airlines Inc v Hope, Banque Sabbag SAL v Hope* [1973] 1 Lloyd's Rep 233, CA (aviation insurance) per Roskill LJ, at 250. In *de Maurier (Jewels) Ltd v Bastion Insurance Co Ltd and Coronet Insurance* [1967] 2 Lloyd's Rep 550 (jewellers' all risks insurance) Donaldson J held (obiter) that the *contra proferentem* principle would apply to a 'slip', but as a matter of construction it did not do so because the words in the 'slip' were not ambiguous. His Lordship observed (ibid, at 559): 'Whatever may be the origin of this principle of construction in relation to contracts of insurance, I do not think that it is now confined to policies. If it were so confined, one would have the curious situation that the same words in a slip meant one thing and in a policy another, notwithstanding that the contract contained in or evidenced by the slip entitled the assured to receive and the underwriter to issue a policy in the terms set out in the slip.'

19 *Jaglom v Excess Insurance Co Ltd and Gilbert Smith* [1971] 2 Lloyd's Rep 171, QBD (Commercial Court), at 177 (per Donaldson J).

20 *Cornish v Accident Insurance Co Ltd* (1889) 23 QBD 453 at 456, CA (per Lindley LJ); *Nittan (UK) Ltd v Solent Steel Fabrication Ltd trading as Sargrove Automation and Cornhill Insurance Co Ltd* [1981] 1 Lloyd's Rep 633, CA (product liability insurance) at 641 (per Griffiths LJ).

1 *Cole v Accident Assurance Co Ltd* (1889) 5 TLR 736 at 737 (per Lindley LJ); *Yorkshire Insurance Co Ltd v Campbell* [1917] AC 218, PC (marine insurance) per Lord Sumner, at 223; *Drinkwater v London Assurance Corpn* (1767) 2 Wils 363; *London and Lancashire Fire Insurance Co Ltd v Bolands Ltd* [1924] AC 836 (burglary insurance) per Lord Sumner, at 848; *Kruger v Mutual Benefit Health and*

Thus, in *Cole v Accident Assurance Co Ltd*:[2]

A personal accident policy contained a clause which excepted the insurance company from being liable if death occurred through poison. The insured by mistake took a poisonous mixture instead of medicine and died immediately. It was contended that the exception in the policy did not apply when the poison was taken by pure accident, and that the exception must be construed strongly against the insurance company.
Held, that there was no ambiguity. The death was caused by poison, and, therefore, the company was not liable.

Again, in *Alder v Moore*:[3]

A professional football player, who was insured under a Personal Accident Insurance Scheme,[4] suffered 'permanent total disablement', and was paid £500 by the underwriter, after signing an undertaking as required by the policy that he would take no part 'as a playing member in any form of professional football' in the future. One of the clauses in the policy stated that 'member' 'shall mean a person of the male sex who is registered with the [Football Players and Trainers] Union'. The insured ceased to be a member of the Union, but later made a remarkable recovery from his injuries and played professional football again, whereupon the underwriter claimed the return of the £500. The insured however, maintained that the sum was not due because it only had to be returned if he played football whilst he was a member of the Union.
Held, by the Court of Appeal[5] that the sum must be returned. The words of the policy were clear, and the *contra proferentem* rule did not apply.

Accident Association [1944] OR 157; *Condogianis v Guardian Assurance Co* [1921] 2 AC 125, PC (fire insurance). *de Maurier (Jewels) Ltd v Bastion Insurance Co Ltd and Coronet Insurance Co Ltd* [1967] 2 Lloyd's Rep 550 (jewellers' all risks insurance), where it was held that the *contra proferentem* rule did not apply to a clause in a 'slip' stating '[Warranted] road vehicles . . . fitted with locks and alarm system (approved by underwriters) and in operation', for the clause was not ambiguous, Donaldson J said (ibid, at 560): '"Locks" in my judgment in the context of this contract . . . must at least mean locks having a greater security than that provided by those supplied by the manufacturers of cars on ordinary production models'; *Stolberg v Pearl Assurance Co Ltd* [1970] 2 Lloyd's Rep 421, Supreme Ct of British Columbia (public liability insurance), where the *contra proferentem* rule was not applied, for the meaning of the words 'the insured' was clear (see the judgment of Wilson CJ, ibid, at 424); *Marzouca v Atlantic and British Commercial Insurance Co Ltd* [1971] 1 Lloyd's Rep 449, PC (fire insurance), where the meaning of a condition stating that the insurance was to cease to attach if the building insured became 'unoccupied and so remain for a period of more than 30 days' was clear and unambiguous and consequently the *contra proferentem* rule was not applied (see the judgment of Lord Hodson, ibid, at 452); *Pickford & Black Ltd v Canadian General Insurance Co* [1976] 2 Lloyd's Rep 108, (contractor's public liability insurance), Supreme Court of Canada, where the language employed in the preamble to an endorsement making it subject to the exclusions in the policy was held not to lead to an ambiguity which would justify invoking the *contra proferentem* rule. (See the judgment of Ritchie J, ibid, at 111); *Jaglom v Excess Insurance Co Ltd and Gilbert Smith* (supra), where the meaning of the amendment to the 'slip' made by the insurer was clear and the *contra proferentem* rule was not applied (see the judgment of Donaldson J, ibid, at 177). As to amendments to the 'slip' made by insurers, see p 117, ante; *Nittan (UK) Ltd v Solent Steel Fabrication Ltd trading as Sargrove Automation and Cornhill Insurance Co Ltd,* supra (product liability insurance), where the *contra proferentem* rule was not applied, for there was no ambiguity in an exception excluding liability for 'injury, loss or damage caused by or arising out of the failure of any such goods to perform their intended function'. (See the judgment of Griffiths LJ, ibid, at 641).

2 (1889) 5 TLR 736.

3 [1960] 2 Lloyd's Rep 325, CA.

4 Which had been arranged between Lloyd's underwriters and the Association Football Players and Trainers Union.

5 Sellers and Devlin LJJ, and Slade J. Slade J, did not refer in his judgment to the *contra proferentem* rule. Devlin LJ, however, (at 332) said that if he were to go into the point, he would want to invoke a rule of construction rather wider than the *contra proferentem* rule, for the undertaking and the clause from which it sprang were most unusual impositions to put upon an assured. He said that it could be strongly argued that if underwriters wished to get the money back again on the

Sellers LJ said in the course of his judgment:[6]

> 'The [insured] had, however, declared and agreed in consideration of the payment to him of the £500 as follows: "I will take no part as a playing member of any form of professional football in the future", which I read as meaning, "I will take no part in any form of professional football in the future as a playing member" (or more briefly, "as a player"). So read I do not find it doubtful or ambiguous. The stipulation with regard to partaking in any form of professional football is as a playing member (or player), not as a spectator, or trainer or referee, manager, or in any other capacity. I cannot read it as referring in any way to the [insured's] membership of the Union . . . I can see no ground for invoking the *contra proferentem* rule which cannot defeat the clear meaning of the words.'

11 The court will try to reconcile the inconsistencies

If words or phrases are found in the same policy which are repugnant to each other, the Court will exhaust every means in its power to reconcile the inconsistencies.[7] If the intention of the parties can be ascertained, that part of the policy which is repugnant thereto will be disregarded.[8] Otherwise, the ordinary rule of construction applies and the earlier of two repugnant clauses will be received in preference to the later, where there is no special reason to the contrary.[9] Where, however, there is an inconsistency between the wording of the policy and that in the proposal or other earlier document, the policy is to be regarded as the true intention of the parties in the absence of valid evidence to the contrary.[10]

12 Express terms override implied terms

An express term in the policy overrides any implied term which is inconsistent with it.

Thus, in a case concerning a life insurance policy,[11] Blackburn J, said:[12]

> 'The express mention of fraudulent concealment and designedly untrue statement fairly leads to the construction that the declaration parts with the implied tacit agreement that any untrue particulars should vitiate the policy, and that it means that, if there were a designedly untrue statement, the policy should be void and not otherwise.'

13 Subsequent ascertainment of matters originally uncertain

Where that which is left indeterminate in the policy, whether it be time, or place, or quantum, becomes fixed and ascertained in the manner stipulated by

---

happening of a certain event, they must define the event in clear and unambiguous language so that the assured could know exactly what he could not do. He preferred, however, to base his judgment on another ground.

6 [1960] 2 Lloyd's Rep 325 at 329.

7 *Squire v Ford* (1851) 9 Hare 47 per Turner V-C at 57: 'If a deed can operate in two ways, one consistent with the intent, and the other repugnant to it, the Court will be ever astute so to construe it, as to give effect to the intent.'

8 *Western Assurance Co of Toronto v Poole* [1903] 1 KB 376 (marine insurance) per Bigham J, at 389.

9 *Forbes v Git* [1922] 1 AC 256, PC (building contract) per Lord Wrenbury, at 259.

10 *Izzard v Universal Insurance Co Ltd* [1937] AC 773 (accident insurance) per Lord Wright, at 780; *Kaufmann v British Surety Insurance Co* (1929) 45 TLR 399, 33 LlL Rep 315 (accident insurance).

11 *Fowkes v Manchester and London Life Assurance Association* (1863) 3 B & S 917.

12 Ibid, at 930.

the contracting parties, it must be treated just as if it had been an original term of the policy.[13]

Thus, an insurance on 'goods to be declared' will be construed as if the goods subsequently declared had been expressly named in the policy.

C THE SIZE OF PRINT IN INSURANCE POLICIES

In the course of his judgment in *Koskas v Standard Marine Insurance Co Ltd.*[14] Sankey J said that the policy which he had to construe was extremely difficult to read. The main provisions were printed partly in type, partly in large type and partly in print which was quite legible and of a large character, but when one came to the particular clause which was in issue between the parties, it was the smallest print it was possible to imagine. He did not mean to say it was like the Lord's Prayer on a threepenny piece or anything like that, but if one looked at it, the clause was in the smallest print of the whole of the page. He, therefore, felt that it should be ignored. But this view was not upheld in the Court of Appeal[15], for Bankes LJ said:[16]

> 'I desire to say that I should not have been able to agree with Sankey J's view that because the clause which is relied upon appears in such small print it must not be taken to be part of the contract and binding upon both parties. It is quite true that it is in small print, but I think it is in sufficiently distinct print and comparing it with many bills of lading and other documents which one sees, one realises that it is much plainer than a great many documents about which a similar criticism has never been suggested.'

Scrutton LJ said:[17]

> 'I can only say with a long experience, that both underwriters and shipowners have given me much more illegible clauses and much more difficult clauses to read, and I can read this with comparative ease; and I am rather afraid of the doctrine that you can get out of clauses by saying that they are difficult to read. There may be extreme cases. I have in mind the bill [of lading] of a well known shipping line printed on red paper which was calculated to produce blindness in anyone reading it. I am not saying that in no case can you get out of it on the point of illegibility, but this case does not appear to me to be a case in which that doctrine should be applied.'

---

13 *London Guarantee Co v Fearnley* (1880) 5 App Cas 911 per Lord Watson, at 920.
14 (1926) 25 LlL Rep 363.
15 (1927) 27 LlL Rep 59.
16 Ibid, at 61.
17 Ibid, at 62.

PART IV

The claim

CHAPTER 36

Introduction

Should a loss take place under the policy, the assured may decide to make a claim under it, but he is only entitled to do so if the policy is a valid and subsisting one.

Thus, the parties may not be ad idem or the offer of the proposer[1] may not have been accepted[2] by the insurer. There may have been non-disclosure or misrepresentation of a material fact entitling the insurer to avoid liability under the policy.[3] The premium may not have been paid in a case where the policy states that it is not to come into force until this has been done.[4] The policy must not have been avoided through an alteration by the assured in a material particular,[5] nor must it have expired before the loss takes place.[6] There must have been no breach of a condition entitling the insurers to avoid liability.[7]

To entitle the assured to enforce the policy, the event insured against must have happened. There can be no claim unless there is a loss caused by the peril insured against.[8]

The peril and the loss must, therefore, stand to each other in the relation of cause and effect.[9] A loss which is not caused by the peril does not fall within the policy[10] Thus, if the peril never comes into existence, a loss sustained by the

---

1 See Chapter 8.

2 See Chapter 9.

3 See Chapters 13 and 14. See further, Chapter 22 as to the right of the insurers to cancel the policy in such circumstances.

4 See Chapter 15.

5 See Chapter 23.

6 See Chapter 21.

7 See Chapters 30, 31, 32 and 33.

8 *Martin v Travellers' Insurance Co* (1859) 1 F & F 505; *Hamlyn v Crown Accidental Insurance Co* [1893] 1 QB 750, CA; *Pugh v London, Brighton and South Coast Rly Co* [1896] 2 QB 248, CA; *Debenhams, Ltd v Excess Insurance Co Ltd* (1912) 28 TLR 505; *Young v Trustee, Assets and Investments Insurance Co* 1893 21 R (Ct of Sess) 222; *Laird v Securities Insurance Co Ltd* 1895 22 R (Ct of Sess) 452; *MacVicar v Poland* (1894) 10 TLR 566; *Murdock v Heath* (1899) 80 LT 50; *Dane v Mortgage Insurance Corpn* [1894] 1 QB 54, CA; *Finlay v Mexican Investment Corpn* [1897] 1 QB 517; *Molinos de Arroz v Mumford* (1900) 16 TLR 469; *Curtis & Co v Head* (1902) 18 TLR 771, CA; *Captain Boyton's World's Water Show Syndicate Ltd v Employers' Liability Assurance Corpn* (1895) 11 TLR 384. As to the perils insured against under the policy, see Chapter 27.

9 *Isitt v Railway Passengers' Assurance Co* (1889) 22 QBD 504 per Wills J, at 511.

10 *Re Scarr and General Accident Assurance Corpn* [1905] 1 KB 387 per Bray J, at 395: 'In my opinion there never was any accident here at all, and consequently the plaintiff fails in bringing the case within the terms of the policy.' See also, *Sinclair v Maritime Passengers' Assurance Co* (1861) 3 E & E 478, where death by sunstroke was held not to have arisen from accident within the meaning of the policy; *McKechnie's Trustees v Scottish Accident Insurance Co* 1889 17 R (Ct of Sess) 6, where it did not appear whether death was due to accident or to disease; *Clidero v Scottish Accident Insurance Co* 1892 19 R (Ct of Sess) 355, where there was no evidence of accident; *Re George and Goldsmiths' and General Burglary Insurance Association Ltd* [1899] 1 QB 595, CA, where entrance was obtained by stealth, and not by force as required by the policy; *Century Bank of the City of New York*

assured for the purpose of averting an accident in the anticipation that, if the peril comes into existence, it will result in loss, is not caused by the peril and is, therefore, not covered by the policy.[11] If, on the other hand, the peril has come into existence, a loss sustained by the assured in the anticipation that, if the peril continues to exist, it will cause a greater loss, may be caused by the peril, even though the peril never operates directly on the subject-matter of insurance.[12]

Further, the loss must not fall within an exception,[13] nor must it have come about as a result of the conduct of the assured, e g where he has intentionally caused it to happen.[14] Difficult questions may arise as to the actual moment

---

v Mountain (1914) 112 LT 484, CA, where money obtained from a bank by a customer whose account, owing to a fraud, was in credit, was held not to be taken out of the bank's possession by fraudulent means within the meaning of the policy; *Waterkyn v Eagle, Star and British Dominions Insurance Co* (1920) 5 LlL Rep 42, where a deposit at a Russian Bank was insured against loss arising from the insolvency of the bank directly due to damage or destruction of the premises through riot or civil commotion, etc., and it was held that the policy did not apply where the deposit was confiscated and the bank rendered unable to carry on business by the acts of the Bolsheviks; *Walker v British Guarantee Association* (1852) 18 QBD 277, where the failure to pay over moneys received was due to the servant having been robbed; *London and Manchester Plate Glass Co Ltd v Heath* [1913] 3 KB 411, CA, where the insurance was against damage by riot or civil commotion, and there was no riot or civil commotion; *Pasquali & Co v Traders' and General Insurance Association* (1921) 9 LlL Rep 514, where the loss was due to defects of manufacture; *Morrison and Mason v Scottish Employers' Liability and Accident Assurance Co* 1888 16 R (Ct of Sess) 212, where the insurance did not extend to cover liability at Common Law, which liability in fact arose, and it was held to be immaterial that the injured workmen might have enforced the employer's statutory liability; *Scott v McIntosh* (1814) 2 Dow 322, HL, where a militia ballot was illegally conducted and it was held that the insurers were not liable to protect the assured against its consequences, seeing that it imposed no real obligation on the assured to serve or provide a substitute; *Tatham v Hodgson* (1796) 6 Term Rep 656 (marine insurance), where slaves insured against perils of the seas died from starvation, owing to a failure of provisions occasioned by an extraordinary delay in the voyage from bad weather; *Oddy v Phoenix Assurance Co Ltd* [1966] 1 Lloyd's Rep 134, Cornwall Assizes (householder's comprehensive insurance), where the bungalow was damaged by the collapse of a wall due to persistent rain, and it was held that this did not constitute a loss by 'storm' or 'tempest'; *S and M Hotels Ltd v Legal and General Assurance Society Ltd* [1972] 1 Lloyd's Rep 157, QB (householder's comprehensive insurance), where the collapse of a hotel was held to be due to the over-stressing of supports used in the addition of a new floor, and not to a 'storm' which was one of the perils insured against (see the judgment of Thesiger J, ibid, at 181).

11 *Kacianoff v China Traders' Insurance Co Ltd* [1914] 3 KB 1121, CA (marine insurance), where cargo insured against loss arising from capture was re-landed after shipment and sold by the assured as it was anticipated that if the cargo went forward, it would be lost by capture, and the Court held, distinguishing *Butler v Wildman* (1820) 3 B & Ald 398 (marine insurance) and *The Knight of St Michael* [1898] P 30 (marine insurance), that the assured could not recover the loss on the sale as the peril had never begun to operate; *Hadkinson v Robinson* (1803) 3 Bos & P 388 (marine insurance), where the original port of destination was closed to British ships; *Becker, Gray & Co v London Assurance Corpn* [1918] AC 101 (marine insurance], where a German ship with British goods on board, took refuge in a neutral port for the duration of the war; *Joseph Watson & Son Ltd v Firemen's Fund Insurance Co of San Francisco* [1922] 2 KB 355; 12 LlL Rep 133 (marine insurance), where the damage was done in the mistaken belief that the cargo was on fire.

12 *Butler v Wildman* (1820) 3 B & Ald 398 (marine insurance), where insured bullion was thrown overboard by the master to avoid capture by an enemy ship, which was already preparing to attack; *The Knight of St Michael* [1898] P 30 (marine insurance), where a cargo of coals had begun to heat and there was imminent danger of spontaneous combustion if it was not immediately discharged; cf *Pugh v London, Brighton and South Coast Rly Co* [1896] 2 QB 248, CA; *Re Etherington and Lancashire and Yorkshire Accident Insurance Co* [1909] 1 KB 591, CA per Vaughan Williams LJ, at 599; *Stanley v Western Assurance Co* (1868) LR 3 Exch 71 (fire insurance) per Kelly CB, at 74.

13 See Chapter 28.

14 See Chapter 29.

when the loss took place and as to the date on which it was discovered to enable the assured to claim under the policy.[15] The insurers will only be liable if the loss is proximately caused by one of the perils insured against.[16]

There are various requirements usually found in policies as to the method of making a claim and the time within which it must be made.[17]

Further, the claim will not succeed unless the insurers admit it or the assured succeeds in discharging the burden of proving that the loss has taken place and that his claim is justified.[18]

15 See Chapter 37.
16 See Chapter 38.
17 See Chapter 39.
18 See Chapter 40.

CHAPTER 37

The time of the loss

The legal position as to the time of the loss will vary according as to whether there are or are not express terms in the policy relating to this matter.

1 No express terms

The event insured against must take place during the period of insurance.[1] The event has taken place when the peril insured against has operated upon the subject-matter of insurance to the detriment of the assured. The loss is, therefore, caused when the peril operates on the subject-matter,[2] and it is

[1] *Hough & Co v Head* (1885) 55 LJQB 43, CA (marine insurance) per Lord Esher MR, at 44: 'The insurance is not that no accident shall happen, but is always against a loss which the assured may suffer by reason of an accident to his property. In the case of a time policy the loss against which he is insured must take place within the time fixed, otherwise it is not a true policy'. See also *Carpenter v Canadian Railway Accident Insurance Co* (1909) 18 OLR 388 where the accident happened after an invalid renewal; *London Guarantee and Accident Co v Cornish* (1905) 17 Man LR 148, where the insurers had given notice to cancel, but had subsequently agreed to continue the insurance; *Constructive Finance Co Ltd v English Insurance Co Ltd* (1924) 19 LlL Rep 144, HL, where a policy against losses under hire-purchase agreements only covered losses happening whilst the agreements were in existence and not losses happening after the agreements had determined; *Moore v Evans* [1918] AC 185 (jewellery insurance), where there was no evidence that any loss had taken place during the period of insurance; *Mitsui v Mumford* [1915] 2 KB 27 (war insurance), where goods lying in Antwerp were not seized by the Germans during the period of insurance; *Campbell & Phillipps Ltd v Denman* (1915) 21 Com Cas 357 (war insurance), where the goods were not seized until after the expiration of the policy; *Duffel v Wilson* (1808) 1 Camp 401 (insurance against militia ballot), where the ballot did not take place until after the policy had expired, and it was held that the assured could not recover; *South Staffordshire Tramways Co v Sickness and Accident Assurance Association* [1891] 1 QB 402, CA, where the policy was held not to have expired at the time of the accident; *Sickness and Accident Assurance Association v General Accident Assurance Corpn* 1892 19 R (Ct of Sess) 977, where the accident took place before the policy came into force; *Parkin v Tunno* (1809) 11 East 22 (marine insurance), where the ship was lost after the voyage insured had come to an end; *Ellerbeck Collieries Ltd v Cornhill Insurance Co Ltd* [1932] 1 KB 401, CA (employers' liability insurance) where, in a case of individual disease, the date of the certificate was held to be the date of the accident; *Electro Motion Ltd v Maritime Insurance Co Ltd and Bonner* [1956] 1 Lloyd's Rep 420 (all risks insurance), where the question was whether the diesel engine found damaged on arrival at the destination had been damaged before or during the transit.

[2] *University of New Zealand v Standard Fire and Marine Insurance Co* [1916] NZLR 509, where it was held that the material time was the date of the embezzlement which fell outside the period of insurance, and that, consequently, the assured could not recover, notwithstanding that fraudulent acts for the purpose of concealment had been committed subsequently during the period of insurance; cf *Employers' Insurance Co of Great Britain v Benton* 1897 24 R (Ct of Sess) 908, where, on a policy insuring the repayment of a debenture in 1897, it was held that there could be no failure to pay until 1897, and consequently the fact that it became clear long before that a loss would be incurred did not relieve the assured from the duty of paying the annual premiums reserved by the policy.

immaterial that the fact or extent of the loss is not discovered, or the full effect of the peril made manifest until after the expiration of the policy.[3]

Difficult questions may, however, arise when the peril is in existence at the time when the period of insurance begins or expires. Where the peril has already operated on the subject-matter of insurance when the period of insurance begins, and no fresh peril intervenes, the loss sustained, though it may take place during the period of insurance, is not covered, seeing that it is attributable solely to a cause which operated before the policy came into force.[4]

If, however, the peril continues to operate after the period of insurance has begun and the loss is attributable solely to its operation during the period of insurance, the assured is entitled to recover unless he was aware that the peril had already begun to operate and concealed the fact from his insurers.[5]

In the case of a loss attributable to the operation of the peril, partly before the commencement of the policy, and partly afterwards, it is probable that, if the loss is capable of being apportioned, the assured will be entitled to recover such part of his loss as can be shown to be due to the operation of the peril during the period of insurance.[6] But the assured may, in some cases, be precluded from recovering even this part of the loss if the subject-matter has been so far affected by the peril as no longer to correspond with the description in the policy.

Where the peril is in existence at the time when the policy expires,[7] and the

---

3 *Knight v Faith* (1850) 15 QB 649 (marine insurance) per Lord Campbell CJ, at 667; *Daff v Midland Colliery Owners' Indemnity Co* (1913) 6 BWCC 799 (employers' liability insurance) per Lord Moulton, at 820.

4 *Demal v British America Live Stock Association* (1910) 14 WLR 250, where the evidence showed that the horse insured was before noon on 18 July, the date fixed for the commencement of the insurance, inoculated with the disease from which it died, although the symptoms were not noticed until the following day, and it was held that the assured could not recover; *Buchanan v Faber* (1899) 4 Com Cas 223 (marine insurance), where the ship insured became a total loss after the date of the policy in consequence of the damage previously sustained; *Hutchins Bros v Royal Exchange Assurance* [1911] 2 KB 398, CA (marine insurance), where a hidden defect became manifest during the currency of the policy. This may be made clear by the terms of the policy: *Sharkey v Yorkshire Insurance Co* (1916) 54 SCR 92, where the insurance was expressly limited to death from accident or disease occurring or contracted after the commencement of liability.

5 *Bufe v Turner* (1815) 6 Taunt 338 (fire insurance), where the policy was avoided by reason of the failure to disclose the existence of the fire.

6 There appears to be no direct authority on the point. But in the case of burglary insurance, e g if a burglary happens to be in progress at the time when the policy begins, there seems no reason why the assured should not recover for the goods taken after it has begun.

7 It is submitted that the law is as stated in the text is correct. The point is, however, not free from difficulty. Some difficulty is created by the following passage from *Lockyer v Offley* (1786) 1 Term Rep 252 (marine insurance) per Willes J, at 260: 'It would be a dangerous doctrine to lay down that the insurer should in all cases be liable to remote consequential damages. This has been compared to a death's wound received during the voyage, which subjected the ship to a subsequent loss. To this point the case of *Meretony v Dunlope* (1783), seems very material. That was an insurance on a ship for 6 months, and 3 days before the expiration of the time she received her death's wound, but by pumping was kept afloat till 3 days after the time; there the verdict was given for the insurer' (this is the correct reading: see 15 QB 664n), 'which was confirmed by the Court. I will put another case. Suppose an insurance on a man's life for a year, and some short time before the expiration of the term he receives a mortal wound, of which he dies after the year, the insurer would not be liable.' This passage was criticised in *Coit v Smith* (1802) (3 Johnson's New York, Supreme Court, etc Cases 16), and is thus dealt with in *Knight v Faith* (1850) 15 QB 649 (marine insurance) per Lord Campbell CJ, at 667: 'We very much doubt whether any such doctrine ever was laid down by Lord Mansfield in *Meretony v Dunlope*; and the decision of the Court may have proceeded on a totally different ground. The doctrine

loss is complete before the expiration of the policy, the insurers will be liable.[8] But where the loss is wholly attributable to the operation of the peril after the expiration of the policy, it is not recoverable.[9]

Where, on the other hand, the loss may be wholly attributable to the operation of the peril before the expiration of the policy, though its existence, nature, or extent is not ascertained until afterwards, it is recoverable.[10]

Where the loss is attributable partly to the operation of the peril before the expiration of the policy and partly to its continued operation afterwards, the

---

being contrary to the principle of insurance law, that the insurer is liable for a loss actually sustained from a peril insured against during the continuance of the risk.' In *Knight v Faith* (supra) (marine insurance) it was expressly held that if a ship was injured by perils of the sea during the period of insurance, the assured was not precluded by the fact that she was kept afloat until the policy expired, from recovering either a total or a partial loss according to the fact. Lord Campbell CJ, at 668, also pointed out that *Lockyer v Offley* (supra) the proximate cause of the loss was the seizure, which did not take place until the policy had expired. It is submitted that the view taken in *Knight v Faith* (supra) is correct. The test must be what is the event insured against and whether it happens during the period of insurance. The mere happening of the peril is not sufficient; there must be a loss within the period of insurance, the facts which happen subsequently not constituting a new loss, but merely showing the character of the loss which has already taken place. If, on the other hand, there is no loss during the period of insurance, the event insured against has not happened, and it is immaterial that the loss was due to a cause arising during the period of insurance. Thus, in *Lockyer v Offley* (supra) there was no loss till the seizure; in *Mitsui v Mumford* [1915] 2 KB 27 (war insurance) the goods, though lying in a warehouse in Antwerp, had not been seized by the Germans during the currency of the policy; in *Campbell & Phillipps Ltd v Denman* (1915) 21 Com Cas 357 (war insurance) the goods were not seized by the Germans until after the policy had expired; see also, *Moore v Evans* [1918] AC 185 (jewellery insurance). Similarly, in *Hough & Co v Head* (1885) 55 LJQB 43, CA (marine insurance), where there was an insurance on loss of hire arising under a charter-party for accidents occurring between certain dates, it was held that the assured could not recover for loss of hire arising after the policy had expired, although the loss of hire was due to an accident occurring between the specified dates, seeing that he had suffered no loss during the time for which he was insured; cf *Michael v Gillespy* (1857) 2 CBNS 627 (marine insurance), where the loss of hire took place during the currency of the policy. It is, therefore, submitted that the analogy of a life policy taken in *Lockyer v Offley* (supra) (marine insurance) is not a true one, since, in the case of a life policy, the event insured against is death within the period of insurance. The point is also referred to, but not decided in *Montoya v London Assurance Co* (1851) 6 Exch 451 (marine insurance).

8 *Isaacs v Royal Insurance Co Ltd* (1870) LR 5 Exch 296 (fire insurance), where the fire took place just before midnight of the last day of the policy; cf *South Staffordshire Tramways Co v Sickness and Accident Assurance Association* [1891] 1 QB 402, CA.

9 Thus, the seizure of a ship after the completion of her voyage for a cause of forfeiture accruing during the voyage is not covered by a voyage policy; *Lockyer v Offley* (supra); if the assured under a life policy for a year shortly before the policy expires receives a mortal wound from which he dies after the policy has expired, the insurers are not liable: ibid per Willes J, at 260; see also, *Hough & Co v Head* (supra) (marine insurance); *Mitsui v Mumford* (supra) (war insurance); *Campbell & Phillipps Ltd v Denman* (supra) (war insurance); *Moore v Evans* (supra) (jewellery insurance).

10 Thus, if a ship is injured by perils of the sea during the period of insurance, the assured is not precluded from recovering by the fact that she is kept afloat until the policy expires, and he may, according to the facts, recover for either the total or partial loss: *Knight v Faith* (1850) 15 QB 649 (marine insurance); if a neutral ship, insured against seizure, is seized and, after the expiration of the policy, condemned, for carrying contraband, the loss is within the policy: *Andersen v Marten* [1908] AC 334 (marine insurance) per Lord Loreburn C, at 338, HL; [1908] 1 KB 601, CA, per Fletcher Moulton LJ, at 609. It therefore follows that, in the case of a personal accident policy, as opposed to a life policy, if the assured receives by accident, during the currency of the policy, a mortal wound from which he dies after the policy has expired, the insurers will be liable; the policy, however, may contain a condition fixing the period within which death must take place.

insurer will be liable if the operation of the peril during the period of insurance can be regarded as the proximate cause of the loss.

2 Express terms

In order to obviate difficulties the policy may contain express stipulations relating to the time of loss or of its discovery. Thus, the policy may cover all losses discovered during its currency, irrespective of the time when they were actually sustained;[11] or it may limit the right of recovery to losses notified within a specified period.[12]

11 *Pennsylvania Co for Insurances on Lives and Granting Annuities v Mumford* [1920] 2 KB 537; 2 LlL Rep 351, CA (theft insurance), where the policy, which was effected in 1916, covered all losses which the assured might, during its currency, discover that they had sustained at any time since 1909; *Maxwell v Price* [1960] 2 Lloyd's Rep 155 (High Court of Australia) (solicitors' indemnity policy), where the assured was indemnified against any claims during the policy period for breach of professional duty as solicitor by reason of any negligent act, error or omission whenever and wherever it was committed, even though the breach in question had taken place before he had joined the partnership.

12 *New Zealand University v Standard Fire and Marine Insurance Co* [1916] NZLR 509, where the policy covered losses incurred within 12 months prior to notice of claim, and it was held that time ran from the date of the embezzlement by which the assets of the assured were diminished, and not from the date of later fraudulent acts committed for the purpose of concealment; *T H Adamson & Sons v Liverpool and London and Globe Insurance Co Ltd* [1953] 2 Lloyd's Rep 355 (cash in transit policy), where the policy provided that 'The insured shall, immediately upon the discovery of any loss, give notice thereof in writing to the company . . . The company shall be under no liability hereunder in respect of any loss which has not been notified to the company within fourteen days of its occurrence', and it was held that the insured, who had notified the insurance company immediately that it was discovered that an employee had been systematically embezzling money given to him each week for the purpose of purchasing National Insurance stamps over a period of 2 years, was not entitled to claim an indemnity in respect of the full sum (£2,366) which had been embezzled, but only in respect of those losses which had been notified within the period of 14 days. These amounted to only £50.

CHAPTER 38

The doctrine of proximate cause

One of the underlying principles of insurance law is the doctrine of 'Proximate Cause'. In this chapter the meaning of the term is shown. The application of the doctrine will vary according as to whether the issue to be decided is 'Was the loss caused by a peril insured against?' or whether it is 'Was the loss caused by an excepted cause?' In some cases the policy may modify or exclude the doctrine.

A THE MEANING OF 'PROXIMATE CAUSE'

Every event is the effect of some cause. It cannot, however, be treated as isolated; it is not an effect attributable solely to the operation of the cause working independently of everything else. It is necessarily preceded and led up to by a succession of events, but for which it would not, or might not, have happened. Hence, it is nothing more than the last link in a chain of causes and effects which might be prolonged indefinitely into the past. The law, however, refuses to enter into a subtle analysis,[1] or to carry back the investigation further than is necessary.[2] It looks exclusively to the immediate and proximate cause,[3]

---

1 *Hamilton, Fraser & Co v Pandorf & Co* (1887) 12 App Cas 518 (charter-party), where damage to a cargo of rice caused by seawater escaping through a hole in a pipe gnawed by rats was held to be damage by 'dangers and accidents of the sea', and it was said per Lord Halsbury LC, at 524: 'A subtle analysis of all the events which led up to, and in that sense *caused* a thing, may doubtless remove the first link in the chain so far that neither the law nor the ordinary business of mankind can permit it to be treated as a cause affecting the legal rights of the parties to a suit. In this case the existence of the rats on board, their thirst, the hardness of their teeth, the law of gravitation which caused the water to descend upon the rice, the ship being afloat, the pipe being lead, and its capacity of being gnawed, each of these may be represented as the cause of the water entering, but I do not assent to the view that this contract can have a different meaning attached to it according as you regard each step in the chain of events as the origin out of which the damage ultimately arises.'

2 *Lawrence v Accidental Insurance Co Ltd* (1881) 7 QBD 216 per Watkin Williams J, at 221: 'It seems to me that the well-known maxim of Lord Bacon, which is applicable to all departments of the law, is directly applicable to this case. Lord Bacon's language in the *Maxims of the Law*, reg 1, runs thus:— "It were infinite for the law to consider the causes of causes, and their impulsions one of another; therefore it contenteth itself with the immediate cause". Therefore, I say according to the true principle of law, we must look at only the immediate and proximate cause of death, and it seems to me impracticable to go back ultimately to the birth of the person, for if he had never been born the accident would not have happened.'

3 *Everett v London Assurance* (1865) 19 CBNS 126 per Willes J, at 133: 'We are bound to look to the immediate cause of the loss or damage, and not to some remote or speculative cause. Speaking of the injury no person would say that it was caused by fire. It was occasioned by a concussion or disturbance of the air caused by fire elsewhere. It would be going into the causes of causes to say that this was an injury caused by fire to the property insured. The rule "*In jure non remota causa sed proxima spectatur*" determines this case.' See also, *Walker v London and Provincial Insurance Co* (1888) 22 LRIr 572 per Palles CB, at 577; *Ionides v Universal Marine Insurance Co* (1863) 14 CBNS 259

all causes preceding the proximate cause being rejected as too remote.[4]

The doctrine of proximate cause, which is common to all branches of insurance,[5] is based on the presumed intention of the parties as expressed in the contract into which they have entered.[6] But it must be applied with good sense, so as to give effect to, and not to defeat that intention.[7] Its application, therefore, depends on the broad principle that the policy was intended to cover any loss which can fairly be attributed to the operation of the peril,[8] rather than

---

(marine insurance) per Willes J, at 289: 'In ascertaining the relative rights of the parties you are not to trouble yourself with distant causes, or to go into a metaphysical distinction between causes efficient and material and causes final; but you are to look exclusively to the immediate and proximate cause of the loss.'

4 *Marsden v City and County Assurance Co* (1865) LR 1 CP 232 (plate glass insurance) per Erle CJ, at 239: 'No doubt the remote cause of the damage was fire; but the proximate cause was the lawless violence of the mob. I think that the general rule of insurance law that the proximate and not the remote cause of the loss is to be regarded, is the rule which must govern our decision.'; *Becker, Gray & Co v London Assurance Corpn* [1918] AC 101 (marine insurance) per Lord Sumner, at 113: 'In a contract of indemnity . . . the insurer promises to pay in a certain event and in no other, namely, in case of loss caused in a certain way, and the question is whether the loss was caused in that way, and whether the event occurred, and the remote causes of this state of things do not become material.' See also, *Winspear v Accident Insurance Co* (1880) 6 QBD 42, CA; *Mardorf v Accident Insurance Co* [1903] 1 KB 584; *Shaw v Robberds* (1837) 6 Ad & El 75 (fire insurance) per Lord Denman CJ, at 84.

5 *Ionides v Universal Marine Insurance Co* (1863) 14 CBNS 259 (marine insurance) per Erle J, at 285; *Marsden v City and County Assurance Co* (1865) LR 1 CP 232 (plate glass insurance) per Willes J, at 240; *Winspear v Accident Insurance Co* (1880) 6 QBD 42, CA (accident insurance); *Tootal, Broadhurst, Lee Co v London and Lancashire Fire Insurance Co* (1908) Times 21 May (fire insurance) per Bigham J; *Re Etherington and Lancashire and Yorkshire Insurance Co* [1909] 1 KB 591, CA (accident insurance) per Kennedy LJ, at 601.

6 *Becker, Gray & Co v London Assurance Corpn* [1918] AC 101 (marine insurance) per Lord Sumner, at 112: 'There is no mystery about it. Cause and effect are the same for underwriters as for other people. Proximate cause is not a desire to avoid the trouble of discovering the real cause or the "commonsense cause", and, though it has been and always should be rigorously applied in insurance cases, it helps one side no oftener than the other. I believe it to be nothing more nor less than the real meaning of the parties to a contract of insurance. I venture to say so because eminent Judges have sometimes differed on the point [referring to *Leyland Shipping Co Ltd v Norwich Union Fire Insurance Society* [1917] 1 KB 873, CA (marine insurance) per Scrutton LJ, at 892, calling the rule a Judge-made rule] . . . I dare say few assured have any distinct view of their own on this point, and might not even see it if it were explained to them; but what they intend individually does not depend upon what they understand individually. If it is implied in the nature of the bargain, then they intend it in law, just as much as if they said it in words. I think that it is so implied. Indemnity involves it apart from decisions. In effect it is the act of the parties.' See also, *De Vaux v Salvador* (1836) 4 Ad & El 420 (marine insurance) per Lord Denman CJ, at 431; *Leyland Shipping Co v Norwich Union Fire Insurance Society* [1918] AC 350 (marine insurance) per Lord Shaw, at 369.

7 *Reischer v Borwick* [1894] 2 QB 548, CA (marine insurance) per Lindley LJ, at 550, approved in *Leyland Shipping Co v Norwich Union Fire Insurance Society* (supra), cf *Coxe v Employers' Liability Assurance Corpn Ltd* [1916] 2 KB 629 per Scrutton J, at 634.

8 *Fitton v Accidental Death Insurance Co* (1864) 17 CBNS 122; *Re Etherington and Lancashire and Yorkshire Accident Insurance Co* [1909] 1 KB 591, CA. But the loss must be such as is within the contemplation of the parties. Thus, a 'collision liability' clause in a marine insurance policy does not protect the shipowner against liability for loss of life; *Taylor v Dewar* (1864) 5 B & S 58 (marine insurance), disapproving *Coey v Smith* 1860 22 Dunl (Ct of Sess) 955 (marine insurance); *Burger v Indemnity Mutual Marine Assurance Co* [1900] 2 QB 348 (marine insurance), where an express exception to this effect was, in the opinion of the Court, inserted ex abundanti cautela. As to the 'collision liability' clause, see Ivamy *Marine Insurance* (4th Edn 1985), pp 170–176.

on drawing nice distinctions between the varieties of phrases used in particular policies[9] to express the causation of the loss.[10]

As far as marine insurance is concerned, the Marine Insurance Act 1906, s 55(1) provides:

> 'Subject to the provisions of this Act, and unless the policy otherwise provides, the insurer is liable for any loss proximately caused by a peril insured against, but, subject as aforesaid, he is not liable for any loss which is not proximately caused by a peril insured against.'[11]

Wherever there is a succession of causes which must have existed in order to produce the loss,[12] or which has in fact contributed,[13] or may have contributed[14] to produce it, the doctrine of proximate cause has to be applied for the purpose of ascertaining which of the successive causes is the cause to which the loss is to be attributed within the intention of the policy.[15]

---

9 See *Becker, Gray & Co v London Assurance Corpn* [1918] AC 101 (marine insurance) per Lord Sumner, at 114: 'It must be admitted that the terminology of causation in English Law is by no means ideal. it would be better for a little plain English. I think "direct cause" would be a better expression that "causa proxima". Logically, the antithesis of proximate cause is not real cause but remote cause. Lord Ellenborough uses causa causans as its equivalent in *Gordon v Rimmington* (1807) 1 Camp 123; Abbott CJ, speaks of "immediate cause" in *Walker v Maitland* (1821) 5 B & Ald 171; Lord Fitzgerald of 'direct and immediate cause' in *Cory v Burr* (1883), 8 App Cas 393; and my noble and learned friend Lord Loreburn of "direct cause" in *British and Foreign Insurance Co Ltd v Samuel Sanday & Co* [1916] 1 AC 650. Many similar expressions might be quoted.' The following are phrases which have been used: 'caused by' (*Trew v Railway Passengers' Assurance Co* (1861) 6 H & N 839; *Hamlyn v Crown Accidental Insurance Co Ltd* [1893] 1 QB 750, CA); 'caused by, arising from or traceable to' (*Coxe v Employers' Liability Assurance Corpn Ltd* [1916] 2 KB 629 where, however, the addition of the words 'directly or indirectly' excluded the doctrine of proximate cause); 'occasioned by or through', 'occasioned by or happening through' (*Tootal, Broadhurst, Lee Co v London and Lancashire Fire Insurance Co* (1908) Times 21 May (fire insurance); cf *Reynolds v Accidental Insurance Co* (1870) 22 LT 820); 'originating from' (*Marsden v City and County Assurance Co* (1866) LR 1 CP 232 (plate glass insurance); 'consequences of' (*Ionides v Universal Marine Insurance Co* (1863) 14 CBNS 259 (marine insurance)); 'direct and sole cause of' (*Fitton v Accidental Death Insurance Co* (1864) 17 CBNS 12; *Lawrence v Accidental Insurance Co Ltd* (1881) 7 QBD 216; *Mardorf v Accidental Insurance Co* [1903] 1 KB 584); 'direct or proximate cause of' (*Re Etherington and Lancashire and Yorkshire Accident Insurance Co* [1909] 1 KB 591, CA; 'direct effect of' (*Winspear v Accident Insurance Co* (1880) 6 QBD 42, CA); 'from effects of injury caused by' (*Isitt v Railway Passengers' Assurance Co* (1889) 22 QBD 504); 'directly, independently and exclusive of all other causes' (*Fidelity and Casualty Co of New York v Mitchell* [1917] AC 592, PC); 'occasioned through riot or civil commotion' (*Cooper v General Accident, Fire and Life Assurance Corpn Ltd* (1923) 128 LT 481, HL per Lord Dunedin, at 485); 'in consequence of warlike operations' (*Ocean SS Co Ltd v Liverpool and London War Risks Insurance Association Ltd* [1946] KB 561, [1946] 2 All ER 355, CA); 'injury or damage arising directly or indirectly from ownership or occupation of any land or buildings' (*Oei v Foster (formerly Crawford) and Eagle Star Insurance Co Ltd* [1982] 2 Lloyd's Rep 170 (householder's insurance).

10 *Lawrence v Accidental Insurance Co* (supra) per Denman J, at 220. Hence, the particular words used to express causation may be disregarded: *Marsden v City and County Assurance Co* (supra) per Willes J, at 240.

11 See further, Ivamy *Marine Insurance* (4th Edn 1985), pp 225–232.

12 *Pink v Fleming* (1890) 25 QBD 396, CA (marine insurance) per Lord Esher MR, at 397; *Reynolds v Accidental Insurance Co* (supra), where the assured, whilst bathing, became insensible and was drowned in water a foot deep.

13 *Winspear v Accident Insurance Co* (supra), where the assured was seized with a fit whilst fording a stream and drowned, followed in *Lawrence v Accidental Insurance Co* (supra), where the assured fell in a fit in front of a train and was killed; *Cawley v National Employers' Accident and General Assurance Association Ltd* (1885) 1 TLR 255, where the accident would not have caused death but for the assured's state of health; *Wadsworth v Canadian Railway Accident Insurance Co* (1913) 28 OLR 537, where the policy provided for payment of benefit on a different scale according as the injury was

The application of the doctrine varies according as the question is whether the loss was caused by the peril insured against or whether the peril was brought into operation by an excepted cause.

B WAS THE LOSS CAUSED BY A PERIL INSURED AGAINST?

The doctrine of proximate cause must be applied for the purpose of ascertaining whether the loss was caused by the peril insured against. Its application will vary according as to whether:

1 The last of the successive causes happens to be the peril insured against.
2 The peril insured against is not the last cause but a preceding cause.
3 The causes are not successive but concurrent in their operation.

1 Where the last cause is the peril insured against

Where the last of the successive causes happens to be the peril insured against, the loss is caused by the peril insured against.[16] There is no necessity to inquire into the preceding causes and to ascertain which of them brought the peril into

---

caused by a burning building or by fits, and the assured in a fit dropped a lantern which set fire to the building in which he was; *Gray v Barr (Prudential Assurance Co Ltd, Third Party)* [1971] 2 QB 554, [1971] 2 All ER 949, CA (public liability insurance), where the insured threatened another man with a loaded gun and fired into the ceiling to frighten him, and subsequently the other man was killed in a struggle in which the gun was accidentally fired a second time.

14 *Isitt v Railway Passengers Assurance Co* (supra), where the assured, whilst confined to bed in consequence of an accident, was seized with pneumonia caused by cold; *Re Etherington and Lancashire and Yorkshire Accident Insurance Co* (supra), where pneumonia followed upon the accident.

15 *Leyland Shipping Co Ltd v Norwich Union Fire Insurance Society Ltd* [1918] AC 350 (marine insurance) per Lord Shaw, at 369: 'To treat proxima causa as the cause which is nearest in time is out of the question. Causes are spoken of as if they were distinct from one another as beads in a row or links in a chain, but if this metaphysical logic has to be referred to—it is not wholly so, the chain of causation is a handy expression, but the figure is inadequate. Causation is not a chain, but a net. At each point influences, forces, events, precedent and simultaneous, meet; and the radiation from each point extends indefinitely. At the point where these various influences meet it is for the judgment as upon a matter of fact to declare which of the causes thus joined at the point of effect was the proximate and which was the remote cause . . . The cause which is truly proximate is that which is proximate in efficiency. That efficiency may have been preserved although other causes may meantime have sprung up which have not yet destroyed, or truly conquered it, and it may culminate in a result of which it still remains the real efficient cause to which the event can be ascribed'; *Gray v Barr (Prudential Assurance Co Ltd, Third Party)* [1971] 2 Lloyd's Rep 1, CA (public liability insurance) per Lord Denning MR, at 5: 'Ever since [*Leyland Shipping Co Ltd v Norwich Union Fire Insurance Society Ltd* (supra)] in 1918 it has been settled in insurance law that the "cause" is that which is the effective or dominant cause of the occurrence, or, as it is sometimes put, what is in substance the cause, even though it is more remote in point of time, such cause to be determined by common sense'.

16 *Trew v Railway Passengers' Assurance Co* (1861) 6 H & N 839, ExCh; *Reynolds v Accidental Insurance Co* (1870) 22 LT 820; *Marsden v City and County Insurance Co* (1866) LR 1 CP 232; *Green v Elmslie* (1794) Peake 278 (marine insurance), where a ship insured against capture only was driven ashore by a storm, and remaining uninjured, was seized by the enemy and it was held to be a loss by capture; cf Anon (1618) Poph 136 (deodand), where a man riding through a stream was drowned owing to his horse stumbling, and it was held that, as his death was found by the coroner's jury to be caused *per cursum aquae,* the horse was not a deodand, for the water and not the horse was the cause of his death.

operation,[17] unless the further question arises whether the peril was brought into operation by an excepted cause.[18]

2 Where the peril insured against is not the last cause

Where the peril insured against is not the last cause, but a preceding cause, it is necessary to consider whether the last cause is so intimately connected, either immediately or by transmission through a chain of circumstances, with the preceding cause that the loss which is the effect of the last cause is nonetheless the effect of the preceding cause, and is, therefore, within the policy as being caused by the peril insured against.[19]

It is necessary to distinguish between two cases:

a Where there is no break in the sequence of causes.
b Where the sequence of causes is interrupted.

(a) Where there is no break in the sequence of causes

Where there is no break in the sequence of causes from the peril insured against to the last cause, each cause in the sequence being the reasonable[20] and probable[21] consequence, directly and naturally resulting[1] in the ordinary

---

17 *Winspear v Accident Insurance Co* (1880) 6 QBD 42, CA; *Lawrence v Accident Insurance Co Ltd* (1881) 7 QBD 216 per Watkin Williams J, at 221; *Pink v Fleming* (1890) 25 QBD 396, CA (marine insurance) per Lord Esher MR, at 397; cf *Redman v Wilson* (1845) 14 M & W 476 (marine insurance), where a ship having been damaged by negligent loading and becoming leaky in consequence, was run ashore to prevent her sinking and to save her cargo, and the Court held that there was a loss by perils of the sea, notwithstanding the prior negligence and subsequent voluntary stranding.

18 See pp 389–393, post.

19 It is immaterial that the loss may also be covered by a policy insuring against the last cause: *Reischer v Borwick* [1894] 2 QB 548, CA (marine insurance) per Lindley LJ, at 551: unless there is a condition to that effect.

20 *Stanley v Western Insurance Co* (1868) LR 3 Exch 71 (fire insurance) per Kelly CB, at 74: 'Any loss resulting from an apparently necessary and bona fide effort to put out a fire, whether it be by spoiling the goods by water, or throwing articles of furniture out of the window, or even the destroying of a neighbour's house by an explosion for the purpose of checking the progress of the flames, in a word, every loss that clearly and proximately results, whether directly or indirectly from the fire, is within the policy', approved in *Canada Rice Mills Ltd v Union Marine and General Insurance Co Ltd* [1941] AC 55, PC (marine insurance) per Lord Wright, at 71, where rice became overheated because ventilators had to be closed to prevent the incursion of sea water. See also, *Shiells v Scottish Assurance Corpn Ltd* 1889 16 R (Ct of Sess) 1014, where the killing of a horse by an unqualified veterinary surgeon after it had received a fatal injury was held to be a case of death and not of injury within the meaning of a condition requiring the horse, in the event of injury, to be attended by a qualified veterinary surgeon; *Dyson v Rowcroft* (1803) 3 Bos & P 474 (marine insurance), where a cargo was so much damaged that it had to be thrown overboard; *Butler v Wildman* (1820) 3 B & Ald 398 (marine insurance), where the master of a ship on the point of being captured threw bullion overboard to prevent it falling into the hands of the enemy, and it was held to be a loss by enemies; *Montoya v London Assurance Co* (1851) 6 Exch 451, where tobacco, which was stowed in proximity to hides, was damaged in flavour owing to the putrefaction of the hides caused by perils of the sea, and it was held that the damage to the tobacco was caused by perils of the sea; *The Knight of St Michael* [1898] P 30 (marine insurance), where the loss of freight upon a cargo landed to avert imminent danger of fire was held to be a loss by fire.

21 *Isitt v Railway Passengers' Assurance Co* (1889) 22 QBD 504, where the assured while confined to bed through an accident, caught a cold, which developed into pneumonia, and it was held that, as the accident rendered him unusually susceptible to cold, and as the catching cold and the pneumonia were attributable to the state of health consequent on the accident, his death

course of events[2] from the cause which precedes it, the peril insured against is the cause of the loss within the meaning of the policy.[3]

Thus, where an accidental fall, whether from a horse or otherwise, is followed by disease which is either caused by the fall itself[4] or directly attributable to the enfeebled condition of the assured in consequence of the fall,[5] the death, though caused by disease, is proximately caused by the accidental fall.

Similarly, death due to a surgical operation rendered necessary by the accident is death by accident.[6]

Again, where a passenger in getting out of a train slips on the step of a carriage and is injured, the proximate cause of the injury is the fact that he has been travelling by train, and the accident is therefore a 'railway accident' within the meaning of a policy against railway accidents.[7]

The operation of the doctrine of proximate cause is not affected by the number of causes that may intervene between the peril and the loss. Thus, a

---

resulted from the effects of injury caused by accident within the meaning of the policy; *Bondrett v Hentigg* (1816) Holt NP 149 (marine insurance), where goods landed from a wreck were stolen by the inhabitants of the coast, and it was held that they were lost by perils of the sea; *Montoya v London Assurance Co* (supra) (marine insurance); cf *Re Scarr and General Accident Corpn* [1905] 1 KB 387, where there was no accident, the death being the probable consequence of the act done by the assured in his then bodily condition.

1 *Isitt v Railway Passengers' Assurance Co* (supra); *Re Etherington and Lancashire and Yorkshire Accident Insurance Co* [1909] 1 KB 591, CA; *Gabay v Lloyd* (1825) 3 B & C 793 (marine insurance), where horses on board a ship, being frightened in a storm, broke down their stalls and kicked one another, and it was held that death so caused was a loss by perils of the sea.

2 *Pugh v London, Brighton and South Coast Rly Co* [1896] 2 QB 248, CA, where a railway-signalman, in endeavouring to prevent an accident, sustained a nervous shock caused by the excitement and fright which arose in consequence of the immediate and serious responsibility thrown upon him; *Liberty National Bank of New York v Bolton* (1925) 21 LlL Rep 3, CA, where the proceeds of bonds fraudulently abstracted by a bank clerk and sold on his instructions, were paid into the bank by the brokers and fraudulently withdrawn by the clerk, and it was held that, though the proceeds had come to the hands of the bank, the loss was directly attributable to the abstraction of the bonds.

3 *Reischer v Borwick* [1894] 2 QB 548, CA (marine insurance), where a ship insured against collision ran upon a snag which made a hole in her, and sunk some days afterwards whilst being towed to a port of repair owing to a plug which had been placed in the hole being forced out, approved in *Leyland Shipping Co v Norwich Union Fire Insurance Society Ltd* [1918] AC 350 (marine insurance); *William France, Fenwick & Co Ltd v Merchants' Marine Insurance Co Ltd* [1915] 3 KB 290, CA (marine insurance), where an insured ship came into collision with a second ship, the impact being slight, but the second ship, in consequence, collided with a third ship, doing considerable damage, for which the insured ship was held liable, and it was held that the damages payable in respect of the third ship were damages in consequence of a collision.

4 *Fitton v Accidental Death Insurance Co* (1864) 17 CBNS 122, where the accident was followed by hernia; *Fidelity and Casualty Co of New York v Mitchell* [1917] AC 592, PC, where the tuberculosis latent in the assured's system would have remained harmless but for the accident.

5 *Isitt v Railway Passengers' Assurance Co* (supra), where the accident was followed by pneumonia; *Re Etherington and Lancashire and Yorkshire Accident Insurance Co* (supra), where the accident was followed by pneumonia.

6 *Fitton v Accidental Death Insurance Co* (supra); *Isitt v Railway Passengers' Assurance Co* (supra), where it was admitted by the defendants' Counsel during the argument that if the assured had suffered an accident rendering amputation of a limb necessary and had died under the operation, the defendants would clearly be liable; cf *Shiells v Scottish Assurance Corpn Ltd* 1889 16 R (Ct of Sess) 1014.

7 *Theobald v Railway Passengers' Assurance Co* (1854) 10 Exch 45; cf *Powis v Ontario Accident Insurance Co* (1901) 1 OLR 54, where the assured, who was insured against injuries whilst riding as a passenger on a public conveyance, was injured whilst entering a public conveyance after he had put his foot on the step, and was held entitled to recover.

scratch may produce septicaemia, which develops into septic-pneumonia resulting in death. Nevertheless, the death is proximately caused by the scratch.[8]

In these cases, though the loss is not the immediate result of the operation of the peril upon the subject-matter of insurance, there is, nevertheless, no break in the chain of causation, which leads, through a succession of causes, directly from the peril to the loss.[9] They are so intimately connected, the one with the other, that but for the operation of the peril, the loss would not have happened.[10] The relation of cause and effect is, therefore, established between them;[11] the intermediate causes are themselves brought into existence by the peril, and constitute the instruments by which it produces its ultimate result.

(b) Where the sequence of causes is interrupted.

If, on the other hand, the sequence of causes is interrupted by the intervention of a fresh cause which is not the reasonable or probable consequence[12] directly and naturally resulting[13] in the ordinary course of events[14] from the peril insured against[15] but is an independent cause,[16] the cause of the loss within the

---

8 *Mardorf v Accident Insurance Co* [1903] 1 KB 584 (accident insurance); cf *Isitt v Railway Passengers' Assurance Co* (1889) 22 QBD 504.

9 *Re Etherington and Lancashire and Yorkshire Accident Insurance Co* [1909] 1 KB 591, CA, per Vaughan Williams LJ, at 598, 599: 'When the disease or other cause is dependent on the accident, I think it is right to say that the term (direct or proximate cause) covers in such a case not only the immediate result of the accident, but also all those things which may fairly be considered as results usually attendant upon the particular accident in question . . . In my opinion, it is impossible to limit that which may be regarded as the proximate cause to one part of the accident. The truth is that the accident itself is ordinarily followed by certain results according to its nature, and, if the final step in the consequences so produced is death, it seems to me that the whole previous train of events must be regarded as the proximate cause of the death which results'; *Pesquerias y Secaderos de Bacalao de Espana SA v Beer* (1947) 80 LlL Rep 318, CA (marine insurance), where the seizure of ships in the course of civil commotion preceding the outbreak of the Spanish Civil War was held to be the proximate cause of their loss or damage in subsequent warlike operations; *Smith v Cornhill Insurance Co Ltd* [1938] 3 All ER 145 (motor insurance), where a car was found lying on its side, and in a river not far off, the driver was found with her feet stuck in the mud, and water a few inches over her head. Atkinson J held that death resulted solely from bodily injury caused by the accident, and was therefore covered by the policy. Death was due to shock on entering the water, but such entry did not amount to a novus actus interveniens breaking the chain of causation starting with the accident.

10 *Isitt v Railway Passengers' Assurance Co* (supra) per Wills J, at 512; cf *Butler v Wildman* (1820) 3 B & Ald 398 (marine insurance); *William France, Fenwick & Co v Merchants' Marine Insurance Co* [1915] 3 KB 290, CA (marine insurance).

11 *Isitt v Railway Passengers' Assurance Co* (supra) per Wills J, at 511.

12 *Gregson v Gilbert* (1783) 3 Doug KB 232 (marine insurance), where the master, getting out of his reckoning and running short of water, threw some slaves overboard, and it was held that the loss of the slaves was not a loss by perils of the sea.

13 *De Vaux v Salvador* (1836) 4 Ad & El 420 (marine insurance), where, on an apportionment of the damages arising out of a collision in which both ships were to blame, it was held that the insurers of one of the ships were not liable for their proportion of the damage, as the loss was not the necessary or proximate effect of the perils of the sea, but arose out of an arbitrary provision of the law of nations; *Pink v Fleming* (1890) 25 QBD 396, CA (marine insurance), where goods were landed whilst the ship was under repair in consequence of a collision, and afterwards re-shipped, and damage to the goods caused by handling during the landing and re-shipment was held not to be damage consequent on collision within the meaning of the policy.

14 *Isitt v Railway Passengers' Assurance Co* (supra) per Wills J, at 511.

15 Thus, where, under a charter-party, the charterer is given the option, if the ship becomes inefficient, of ceasing to pay hire, the loss of hire arising from the exercise of this option, if the ship becomes inefficient through perils of the sea, is not a loss by perils of the sea: *Inman SS Co v Bischoff* (1822) 7 App Cas 670 (marine insurance); but it is otherwise if the charter-party provides for

meaning of the policy is not the peril insured against, but the intervening cause.[17]

It is immaterial that, in the particular circumstances, the effect of the peril on the subject-matter of insurance is to render it more susceptible to the operation of the intervening cause. The peril is exhausted when it has produced its natural result, which is not the loss under discussion.[18]

To produce the loss a fresh cause must intervene and operate on the result produced by the peril; the relation of cause and effect, therefore, does not exist between the peril insured against and the loss. Thus, where a person weakened by a railway accident is run over in the street by a bus which, owing to his weakness, he is unable to avoid, his death is due, not to the railway accident, but to a foreign and independent cause, i e the street accident.[19]

Similarly, loss of profits[20] and other consequential loss[1] cannot be recovered

---

the automatic cesser of hire in such a case: *The Bedouin* [1894] P 1, CA (marine insurance).

16 *Fitton v Accidental Death Insurance Co* (1864) 17 CBNS 122 per Williams J, at 133; *Re Etherington and Lancashire and Yorkshire Accident Insurance Co* (supra) (accident insurance) per Vaughan Williams LJ, at 600; *Leyland Shipping Co Ltd v Norwich Union Fire Insurance Society Ltd* [1918] AC 350 (marine insurance) per Lord Shaw, at 370.

17 *Clan Line Steamers Ltd v Board of Trade* [1928] 2 KB 557, CA (charter-party) per Scrutton LJ, at 371; 'Suppose an insurance is effected against consequences of railway operations, and a misguided person commits suicide by jumping in front of a train. Would that be a consequence of a railway operation within the meaning of the policy? To me it appears that the proximate cause of the death is the man's own act.'

18 *Jones v Schmoll* (1785) 1 Term Rep 130n (marine insurance), where, in an insurance on slaves against mutiny, it was held that the policy covered slaves who were killed in the mutiny, or who subsequently died of their wounds or bruises received in the mutiny, even though accompanied by other causes, but not slaves who received no injury in the mutiny, but who committed suicide or died of disappointment in consequence of the mutiny failing; *Tatham v Hodgson* (1796) 6 Term Rep 656 (marine insurance), where a number of slaves died from starvation owing to a shortage of provisions due to an extraordinary delay in the voyage from bad weather, and it was held that their deaths were due to natural causes, and not to perils of the sea; *Taylor v Dunbar* (1869) LR 4 CP 206 (marine insurance), where a ship carrying meat was delayed by a storm, in consequence of which the meat became putrid and had to be thrown overboard, and it was held that the loss of the meat was not a loss by perils of the sea; *Quellec Le et Fils v Thomson* (1916) 115 LT 224 (marine insurance), where a ship insured against war risks including extinction of lights was wrecked on Cape de la Hogue, the light on which had been extinguished owing to the war, and it was held that, as the master was not steering by the light and probably could not have seen it on account of the weather, even if it had been lit, the extinction of the light was too remote a cause of the loss; *William France, Fenwick & Co v North of England Protecting and Indemnity Association* [1917] 2 KB 522 (marine insurance), where a policy against the consequences of hostilities was held not to cover damage caused by the ship striking against the submerged wreck of another ship which had been sunk a few hours before by a German submarine.

19 *Isitt v Railway Passengers' Assurance Co* (1889) 22 QBD 504 per Wiles J, at 512; cf *Wallace v Employers' Liability Assurance Co* (1912) 21 OWR 249, where the assured after alighting from a tramcar, stepped back on to it to avoid a motor car and was injured, and the Court held that he was not entitled to recover the special compensation payable under the policy in respect of injury while a passenger on a public conveyance.

20 *Theobald v Railway Passengers' Assurance Co* (1854) 10 Exch 45 per Pollock CB, at 58: 'We think that, in considering the damage done to the traveller, the consequential mischief of losing some profit is not to be taken into consideration; otherwise a passenger whose time or business is more valuable than that of another would for precisely the same personal injury receive a greater remuneration than that other. What the insurance company calculate on indemnifying the party against is the expense and pain and loss immediately connected with the accident, and not remote consequences that may follow according to the business or profession of the passenger.' See also, *Re Wright and Pole* (1834) 1 Ad & El 621 (fire insurance), where it was held that, under an insurance on the assured's interest in an inn, loss sustained by the refusal of persons to go to the inn while under repair was not recoverable.

1 *Molinos De Arroz v Mumford* (1900) 16 TLR 469, where the assured unsuccessfully claimed for

under an ordinary policy, since they are not proximately caused by the peril insured against.[2] In these cases the chain of causation is broken, and the connection between the peril and the loss is not causal but accidental.

3 Where the causes are concurrent

Where the causes are not successive but concurrent in their operation, and continue to operate on the subject-matter of insurance until they cause the loss, the loss is attributable to one cause as much as to the other.[3]

If, therefore, one of the causes is the peril insured against, the cause of the loss within the meaning of the policy is the peril, the existence of the concurrent cause and the fact that it, too, may be the cause of the loss within the meaning of another policy being disregarded.[4]

---

deterioration in respect of goods which, but for the warlike operation insured against would have been sold in the ordinary course of business before seizure; *Taylor v Dewar* (1864) 5 B & S 58 (marine insurance), where it was held that the policy did not cover the assured's liability for loss of life in a collision; *Rogers & Co v British Shipowners' Mutual Protection Association Ltd* (1896) 1 Com Cas 414 (marine insurance), where an insurance protecting a shipowner against 'any claim or demand' which he should become liable to pay and 'costs and charges (inter alia) in respect of any illness' was held not to cover expenses properly incurred by the assured in obtaining substitutes for a crew disabled by sickness or in cleaning and disinfecting the ship; *Shelbourne & Co v Law Investment and Insurance Corpn* [1898] 2 QB 626 (marine insurance), where an insurance on barges against loss or damage by collision was held not to cover loss in consequence of the detention of the barges during repairs after a collision; *Re Wright and Pole* (1834) 1 Ad & El 621 (fire insurance), where the rent of the inn and the expense of hiring other premises whilst the inn was being repaired were also held not to be recoverable.

2 Such losses may, however, be specifically insured against: *Re Wright and Pole* (supra), per Lord Denman CJ, at 623. See generally Ivamy *Personal Accident, Life and Other Insurances* (2nd Edn, 1980), p 141, and Ivamy *Fire and Motor Insurance* (4th Edn, 1984), pp 75–79.

3 *Crown Bank v London Guarantee and Accident Co* (1908) 17 OLR 95, where the policy covered both dishonesty and negligence of servants, and the loss was occasioned by the dishonesty of one servant and the negligence of another; *Hagedorn v Whitmore* (1816) 1 Stark 157 (marine insurance), where cargo on board a ship seized and taken in tow by a man-of-war was injured in consequence by reason of bad weather, and the loss was held to be a loss by perils of the sea, and apparently, also, a loss by capture. It is important to distinguish a case in which, though both the peril and the other cause appear at first sight to conduce to the loss concurrently, only one of them is, in fact, in operation; see *Trew v Railway Passengers' Assurance Co* (1861) 6 H & N 839, ExCh, where it was pointed out that death from natural causes such as apoplexy, whilst the assured was swimming, would not be within the policy; *Hahn v Corbett* (1824) 2 Bing 205 (marine insurance), where a ship having been wrecked off an enemy coast, the cargo was taken from the wreck by the authorities, and it was held that there was a loss by perils of the sea, not a loss by capture; *Andersen v Marten* [1908] AC 334 (marine insurance), where a ship after capture was lost by perils of the sea.

4 *Dudgeon v Pembroke* (1877), 2 App Cas 284 (marine insurance) per Lord Penzance, at 297: '"Causa proxima et non remota spectatur" is the maxim by which these contracts of insurance are to be construed, and any loss caused immediately by the perils of the sea is within the policy, though it would not have occurred but for the concurrent action of some cause which is not within it'; *Grill v General Iron Screw Collier Co* (1866) LR 1 CP 600 (bill of lading) per Willes J, at 611: 'I may say that a policy of insurance is an absolute contract to indemnify for loss by perils of the sea, and it is only necessary to see whether the loss comes within the terms of the contract and is caused by perils of the sea; the fact that the loss is partly caused by things not distinctly perils of the sea does not prevent it coming within the contract'; *Reischer v Borwick* [1894] 2 QB 548, CA (marine insurance) per Lindley LJ, at 551: 'The fact that some fresh cause arises, without which the injury would not have led to further loss, is, I think, in such a case far from conclusive. Policies may be so worded as to overlap and cover some risks common to them all. The sinking of the ship was proximately caused by the internal injuries produced by the collision and by water reaching and getting through the injured parts whilst she was being towed to a place of repair.

It is, therefore, immaterial whether the onset of the other cause preceded[5] or followed[6] the peril in point of time, or whether the other cause was the cause[7] or effect[8] of the peril, or a cause which intervened independently.[9]

Thus, where the assured is drowned while bathing, his death is caused by accident, and it is immaterial that he fell into the water in a fainting fit, and that the water into which he fell was so shallow that he could not have been drowned if he had not remained unconscious.[10]

Similarly, where the assured is injured in an accident, and, whilst confined to his room, catches a cold which, in consequence of his weak state of health, develops into pneumonia and ends fatally, his death is caused by the accident.[11]

C WAS THE LOSS CAUSED BY AN EXCEPTED CAUSE?

The question frequently arises whether the peril insured against or an excepted cause is the cause of the loss within the meaning of the policy.

If the peril and the excepted cause operate independently on the subject-matter of insurance and the consequences of each are separate and can be distinguished with precision, there is no real difficulty. Once the facts are ascertained, it is clear that the consequence of the peril, being unconnected with the excepted cause, is a loss covered by the policy.[12]

Thus, under a personal accident policy, if the assured is killed by accident, it

---

The sinking was due as much to one of these causes as the other, each was as much the proximate cause of the sinking as the other, and it would, in my opinion, be contrary to good sense to hold that the damage by the sinking was not covered by this policy. I feel the difficulty of expressing in precise language the distinction between causes which co-operate in producing a given result. When they succeed at intervals which can be observed, it is comparatively easy to distinguish them and to trace their respective effects; but under other circumstances, it may be impossible to do so. It appears to me, however, that an injury to a ship may fairly be said to cause its loss if, before that injury is or can be repaired, the ship is lost by reason of the existence of that injury, i e under circumstances which, but for that injury would not have affected her safety.' See also, *Arcangelo v Thompson* (1811) 2 Camp 620 (marine insurance), where the assured was held entitled to recover for a loss by capture, though the evidence showed that the ship was captured by the collusion of the master, and the assured might have recovered for a loss by barratry.

5 *Hagedorne v Whitmore* (1816) 1 Stark 157 (marine insurance).

6 *Bondrett v Hentigg* (1816) Holt NP 149 (marine insurance), where goods landed from a wreck were destroyed and plundered by the inhabitants of the coast, and it was held that they were lost by perils of the sea; *Reischer v Borwick* [1894] 2 QB 548, CA (marine insurance).

7 *Reynolds v Accidental Insurance Co* (1870) 22 LT 820.

8 *Isitt v Railway Passengers' Assurance Co* (1889) 22 QBD 504; *Re Etherington and Lancashire and Yorkshire Accident Insurance Co* [1909] 1 KB 591, CA.

9 *Hagedorne v Whitmore* (supra) (marine insurance), where loss of cargo by perils of the sea whilst the ship was in the hands of captors by mistake was held a loss by capture. The intervention of an independent cause is frequently dealt with by an exception.

10 *Reynolds v Accidental Insurance Co* (supra); cf *Winspear v Accident Insurance Co Ltd* (1880) 6 QBD 42, CA; *Lawrence v Accident Insurance Co* (1881) 7 QBD 216.

11 *Isitt v Railway Passengers' Assurance Co* (supra); *Re Etherington and Lancashire and Yorkshire Accident Insurance Co* (supra), where the assured died of pneumonia caused by the lowering of vitality consequent on the shock of a fall whilst hunting, the ride home and a subsequent journey to London next day to attend to business.

12 *Stanley v Western Insurance Co* (1868) LR 3 Exch 71 (fire insurance) per Kelly CB, at 74. The onus of proving what part of the loss is due to the peril insured against lies upon the assured: ibid per Martin B, at 75; and there may be an express condition to that effect: *Re Hooley Hill Rubber and Chemical Co Ltd and Royal Insurance Co Ltd* [1920] 1 KB 257 at 264, CA (fire insurance).

is immaterial that, at the time of the accident, he was suffering from an excepted disease which might have proved fatal if he had lived long enough, but which in no way contributed to the accident from which he, in fact, died.[13]

It is equally clear that the consequence of the excepted cause, being unconnected with the peril, is not a loss covered by the policy.

Thus, under a personal accident policy, the fact that the assured has sustained an accident does not entitle him to maintain a claim for injuries due not to the accident but to an excepted disease,[14] and it is immaterial that the existence of the disease was unsuspected by him, and would not have been detected but for the investigations rendered necessary by the accident.[15]

The question becomes more difficult when the consequence cannot be assigned with precision either to the peril or to the excepted cause, but appears to be the result of their combined operation, but for which it would or might not have happened. In this case recourse must be had to the doctrine of proximate cause for the purpose of ascertaining whether there is a loss within the meaning of the policy.

Though the doctrine is applied in the same way as in dealing generally with the cause of the loss, it is convenient to consider its application to excepted causes in detail. The application will depend on:

1 Whether the peril insured against is preceded by an excepted cause.
2 Whether the peril insured against precedes an excepted cause.
3 Whether the loss is caused by the action of two concurrent and independent causes.

1 Where the peril insured against is preceded by an excepted cause

Where the peril insured against, though undoubtedly causing the loss, is preceded in point of time by an excepted cause, there is no loss within the meaning of the policy if the excepted cause can be regarded as its proximate cause.

If the peril insured against is the reasonable and probable consequence, directly and naturally resulting in the ordinary course of events from the excepted cause, the excepted cause is the cause of the loss within the meaning of the policy,[16] since there is no break in the sequence of causes, and the relation of cause and effect between the excepted cause and the loss is, therefore, established.[17]

Thus, a farmer who is neither short-sighted nor deaf, attempting in broad

---

13 *Hope's Trustees v Scottish Accident Insurance Co* 1896 3 SLT 252.

14 *Fitton v Accidental Death Insurance Co* (1864) 17 CBNS 122, where leave was given to the defendants to amend their plea by alleging that the death of the assured arose from hernia occasioned by internal causes; cf *McKechnie's Trustees v Scottish Accident Insurance Co* 1889 17 R (Ct of Sess) 6, where the assured was thrown out of a cart, but it was not clear whether he died from the accident or from disease of the kidneys.

15 *Burnett v British Columbia Accident and Employers' Liability Co* (1914) 28 WLR 425.

16 *Letts v Excess Insurance Co* (1916) 32 TLR 361; *Walker v London and Provincial Insurance Co* (1888) 22 LRIr 572 (fire insurance); *Tootal, Broadhurst, Lee Co v London and Lancashire Fire Insurance Co* (1908) Times 21 May.

17 Cf *Tait v Levi* (1811) 14 East 481 (marine insurance), where the master through ignorance mistook an enemy port for his port of destination, and the assured was held not to be entitled to recover for the loss of the ship owing to the breach of the implied warranty to employ a competent master.

daylight to cross a railway main line in front of an approaching train which he ought to have noticed, exposes himself to obvious risk of injury; and, if he is killed by the train, his death, though caused by accident, is attributable to his want of care and falls within the scope of an exception relating to exposure to obvious risk of injury.[18]

It is not necessary for the excepted cause to remain in operation down to the loss; it is sufficient that it has started the chain of circumstances leading to the loss.[19] The whole circumstances beginning from the excepted cause constitute one accident; the intervention of the peril insured against is merely the natural and probable consequence of the excepted cause.[20]

Where, on the other hand, the sequence of causes is broken, the peril insured against being a fresh and independent cause, whose connection with the excepted cause is accidental only and not causal, the cause of the loss within the meaning of the policy is the peril, and not the excepted cause.[1] The intervention of the peril insured against is an accidental consequence of the excepted cause; and there is, therefore, a new accident, which the exception does not exclude.

Thus, the death of a person falling from a railway platform in a fit and being killed by a passing train is not proximately caused by the fit.[2]

Similarly, where a shop window is broken by a disorderly mob brought together by a fire on adjacent premises, the cause of the breakage is the act of the mob, and not the fire.[3]

Again, where a person who has been injured by a shell is killed by a passing car because, owing to his crippled condition, he is unable to get out of the way, the war is not the cause of his death within the meaning of an exception against the consequences of hostilities;[4] nor is an isolated act of burglary committed during an air raid a loss caused by hostilities within the meaning of a similar exception.[5]

---

18 *Cornish v Accident Insurance Co* (1889) 23 QBD 453, CA, following *Lovell v Accident Insurance Co* (1874) unreported, where Cockburn CJ held that a person taking a short cut along a railway line was exposing himself to obvious risk; *Walker v Railway Passengers' Assurance Co* (1910) 129 LTJo 64, where the assured was found dead at the foot of a cliff, and the inference from the facts was that while walking along the top he had gone carelessly too near the edge and had fallen over.

19 *Mair v Railway Passengers' Assurance Co Ltd* (1877) 37 LT 356, where, in the case of an exception against death or injury whilst under the influence of intoxicating liquor, it was held to be sufficient that he was under the influence of intoxicating liquor at the time when the injury which resulted in death was sustained; *MacRobbie v Accident Insurance Co* 1886 23 ScLR 391.

20 See generally, *Leyland Shipping Co Ltd v Norwich Union Fire Insurance Society Ltd* [1918] AC 350 (marine insurance).

1 *Lawrence v Accident Insurance Co* (1881) 7 QBD 216 per Watkin Williams J, at 222; *Walker v London and Provincial Insurance Co* (1888) 22 LRIr 572 (fire insurance) per Palles CB, at 577.

2 *Lawrence v Accident Insurance Co* (supra), following *Winspear v Accident Insurance Co Ltd* (1880) 6 QBD 42, CA, where, in consequence of the fit, the assured fell into water and was drowned; cf *Wadsworth v Canadian Railway Accident Insurance Co* (1913) 28 OLR 537, where the assured sustained fatal injuries by a fire caused by him dropping a lantern in a fit, and it was held that the scale of compensation for injuries by fits, which differed from the scale applicable to injuries caused by fire, applied.

3 *Marsden v City and County Assurance Co* (1866) LR 1 CP 232, where there was an exception against loss originating from fire.

4 *Leyland Shipping Co Ltd v Norwich Union Fire Insurance Society Ltd* as reported in [1917] 1 KB 873, CA (marine insurance) per Scrutton LJ, at 897; cf *Ionides v Universal Marine Insurance Co* (1863) 14 CBNS 259 (marine insurance), where, during the American Civil War a ship was wrecked on Cape Hatteras, the Confederates having extinguished the light.

5 *Winicofsky v Army and Navy General Assurance Association Ltd* (1919) 88 LJKB 1111.

2 Where the peril insured against precedes an excepted cause

Where the peril insured against precedes an excepted cause which actually produces the loss, there is a loss within the meaning of the policy if, notwithstanding the operation of the excepted cause, the peril insured against is to be regarded as the proximate cause of the loss.

If there is a causal connection between the peril and the loss, the excepted cause being merely a link in the chain of causation in as much as it is a reasonable and probable consequence of the peril, the peril is the cause of the loss within the meaning of the policy.

Thus, where an accident is followed, in the ordinary course of events, without the intervention of any extraneous cause, by a disease causing death, the death is caused by the accident, not by the disease; it is, therefore, immaterial that the particular disease is excepted by the policy.[6]

Where, on the other hand, the excepted cause is a fresh and independent cause intervening between the peril and the loss, the excepted cause is the cause of the loss within the meaning of the policy, since the connection between the peril and the loss is merely accidental.[7]

Thus, where a man weakened by an accident is attacked by a disease wholly unconnected with the accident, an exception against disease applies.[8]

3 Where the loss is caused by the action of two concurrent and independent causes

Where the loss is caused by the action of two concurrent and independent causes, one of which is the peril insured against and the other an excepted cause,

---

6 *Fitton v Accidental Death Insurance Co* (1864) 17 CBNS 122, where hernia caused by an accidental fall was held not to be within an exception against hernia; *Mardorf v Accident Insurance Co* [1903] 1 KB 584, where septicaemia and septic-pneumonia resulting from the scratch were held not to be within an exception against any intervening cause; *Re Etherington and Lancashire and Yorkshire Accident Insurance Co* [1909] 1 KB 591, CA, where an exception against 'disease or other intervening cause' was held to refer to the disease or cause intervening, which is independent of the accident and the ordinary results of the accident and, therefore, not to be applicable where the disease which intervened was a natural sequela of the accident; *Accident Insurance Co of North America v Young* (1891) 20 SCR 280, where erysipelas followed a wound. It is not easy to reconcile these cases with the cases dealing with exceptions in a fire policy against explosion, namely, *Stanley v Western Insurance Co* (1868) LR 3 Exch 71 (fire insurance), followed in *Re Hooley Hill Rubber & Chemical Co Ltd and Royal Insurance Co Ltd* [1920] 1 KB 257 at 264, CA (fire insurance), and *Curtis and Harvey (Canada) Ltd v North British and Mercantile Insurance Co* [1921] 1 AC 303, PC (fire insurance).

7 *Livie v Janson* (1810) 12 East 648 (marine insurance) per Lord Ellenborough CJ, at 653: 'If, for instance, a ship meet with sea-damage which checks her rate of sailing, so that she is taken by an enemy from whom she could otherwise have escaped; though she would have arrived safe but for the sea-damage, the loss is to be ascribed to the capture, not to the sea-damage; and thereupon the principle that causa proxima non remota spectatur.' See also, *Cory v Burr* (1883) 8 App Cas 393 (marine insurance), where a ship insured against barratry of the master, but warranted free of capture and seizure, was seized and confiscated by the Spanish Revenue Authorities in consequence of the master engaging in smuggling, and it was held that the loss was caused by capture and seizure and not by the master's barratry.

8 *Cawley v National Employers' Accident and General Assurance Association Ltd* (1885) 1 TLR 255, where the death of the assured caused by the dislodgement, in consequence of a fall, of a gall stone, was held to be covered by an exception against death arising from or accelerated or promoted by any disease or any natural cause arising within the system of the assured, whether accelerated by accident or not; *Re Etherington and Lancashire and Yorkshire Accident Insurance Co* (supra) per Kennedy LJ, at 603.

the loss is not within the policy, since it may be accurately described as caused by the excepted cause, and it is immaterial that it may be described in another way which would not bring it within the exception.[9]

Thus, where an employee of the assured is an accessory before the fact to the theft of the assured's goods by strangers, the loss is within an exception against theft by the assured's employees.[10]

Again, in *Jason v British Traders' Insurance Co Ltd*[11]

> The insured had effected a personal accident insurance policy which stated that the insurers would pay the sum insured if he should 'sustain in any accident bodily injury resulting in and being—independently of all other causes—the exclusive, direct and immediate cause of the injury or disablement'. The policy also stated that no benefit was to be payable in respect of 'death, injury or disablement directly or indirectly caused by or arising or resulting from or traceable to . . . any physical defect or infirmity which existed prior to an accident'. The insured suffered a coronary thrombosis caused by stress when he was involved in a motor accident, a clot forming in such a way as to occlude the coronary artery, which was narrowed by a pre-existing arterial disease.[12] The insured claimed under the policy in respect of the injury which he had suffered.
> *Held,* the claim failed. The bodily injury was not 'independently of all other causes the exclusive . . . cause of the disablement'. There were two concurrent causes, the pre-existing arterial disease and the formation of the clot. These two causes were independent of each other, and the thrombosis would not have occurred unless both had operated. If there were any doubt about the matter, it was removed by the words of the exception clause set out above.[13]

D MODIFICATION OR EXCLUSION OF THE DOCTRINE OF PROXIMATE CAUSE

The policy may, however, by the terms in which the exception is framed, modify the application of the doctrine of proximate cause or exclude it altogether,[14] and the assured may be disentitled from recovering although the loss is only remotely caused by the excepted cause.

Thus, where the assured, an officer in command of soldiers guarding a

---

9 *Saqui and Lawrence v Stearns* [1911] 1 KB 426, CA, per Fletcher Moulton LJ, at 435; cf *Lawrence v Accident Insurance Co* (1881) 7 QBD 216 per Watkin Williams J, at 221; *John Cory & Sons v Burr* (1883) 8 App Cas 393, HL (marine insurance) at 400 per Lord Blackburn; *Samuel (P) & Co Ltd v Dumas* [1924] AC 431, HL (marine insurance) at 467 per Lord Sumner; *Wayne Tank and Pump Co Ltd v Employers' Liability Assurance Corpn Ltd* [1973] 2 Lloyd's Rep 237, CA (public liability), where the insured company, which carried on business as engineers and installers of storage devices, constructed a storage tank at a plasticine mill and the mill was destroyed when a pipe caught fire partly due to electric current being left switched on by the insured's employee and partly due to the pipe's unsuitability to carry stearine in a heated condition, and it was held that the insurers could rely on exception of liability for loss 'caused by the nature of goods supplied by the insured' (see the judgment of Cairns LJ, ibid, at 241, and that of Roskill LJ, ibid, at 245).

10 *Saqui and Lawrence v Stearns* (supra).

11 [1969] 1 Lloyd's Rep 281.

12 For the evidence, see ibid, at 287–288.

13 See the judgment of Fisher J, ibid, at 290.

14 *Tootal, Broadhurst, Lee Co v London and Lancashire Fire Insurance Co* (1908) Times 21 May where the policy excepted fire occasioned by earthquake, and Bigham J said: 'The rule of insurance law as to proximate cause may not apply where there is a special contract. Earthquake cannot, as I understand, proximately cause fire. If the jerking caused by the earthquake occasioned burning coals to be thrown out of a grate on to some material, I doubt whether in that case, according to the rule, the proximate cause is the earthquake at all. The proximate cause is the burning coal falling on the material. The remote cause is earthquake which causes the burning coal to jump out of the grate on to the material.'

railway, is killed by a train whilst inspecting his men, at a time when it is exceptionally dark owing to the lights being obscured under military regulations, his death is to be regarded as caused by war within the meaning of an exception which includes war as a remote cause.[15]

[15] *Coxe v Employers' Liability Assurance Corpn Ltd* [1916] 2 KB 629, where it was suggested that if the assured had not been in a place of special danger in the course of his military duties, and had not been killed by a special danger prevailing at that place, but had been merely caused by the war to be in a particular place, and had been killed by something, e g lightning, which had nothing to do with war, the excepted cause of death might have been too remote; *Oei v Foster (formerly Crawford) and Eagle Star Insurance Co Ltd* [1982] 2 Lloyd's Rep 170 (householder's insurance), where the doctrine of proximate cause was excluded by the addition of the words 'directly or indirectly' to a clause in the policy providing for an indemnity in respect of a 'claim for injury arising from ownership or occupation of any land or buildings'. In *Mardorf v Accident Insurance Co* [1903] 1 KB 584 the decision turned on the meaning of 'intervening cause', and the effect of the phrase 'directly or otherwise' in the exception was not discussed.

CHAPTER 39

The making of a claim

When the loss has taken place, the assured becomes entitled to enforce the policy and the insurers become liable to pay the amount of the loss in accordance with its terms. The respective rights and duties of the parties are usually defined by the stipulations of the policy.

No claim is maintainable on a policy of insurance unless all the conditions precedent and subsequent of the policy have been duly performed, since it is essential that at the time of the loss the policy should be valid. Moreover, there are certain duties as regards the making of the claim imposed on the assured by law or by the stipulations of the policy.[1] The due performance of these duties may be made a condition precedent to the liability of the insurers.[2]

The duties of the assured as regards the making of a claim are:

a To give notice of the loss;
b To furnish particulars of the loss;
c To furnish proofs of loss;
d To make no fraudulent claim.

If the assured makes a claim and it is rejected by the insurers, he may, in certain circumstances, be entitled to complain to the Insurance Ombudsman Bureau.

A NOTICE OF LOSS

The duty of giving notice of loss seems to exist apart from any stipulation in the policy, seeing that the fact of the loss is one which the assured, as having control of the subject-matter, must be assumed to know, whilst the insurers cannot reasonably be expected to have any private knowledge whatsoever of the state or condition of the subject-matter at any particular time.

Further, the duty of good faith seems to impose the obligation of giving notice so that the insurers may be in a position to take the necessary steps for ascertaining the cause and extent of the loss.

---

1 The insurers cannot, by inserting a new term in the claim form sent to the assured to be filled in, impose upon him further or additional duties: *Beeck v Yorkshire Insurance Co* (1909) 11 WALR 88 (livestock insurance).

2 *Worsley v Wood* (1796) 6 Term Rep 710 (fire insurance). The assured's personal representatives (*Cawley v National Employers' Accident and General Assurance Association Ltd* (1885) 1 TLR 255; *Harvey v Ocean Accident and Guarantee Corpn* [1905] 2 IR 1, CA) and trustee in bankruptcy (*Re Carr and Sun Fire Insurance Co* (1897) 13 TLR 186, CA (fire insurance)) are equally bound. Such conditions, however, so far as policies of motor vehicle insurance are concerned, are of no effect in connection with third-party claims in respect of death or bodily injury; Road Traffic Act 1972, s 148(2). See generally Ivamy *Fire and Motor Insurance* (4th Edn 1984), p 333.

In practice, the policy almost invariably contains a condition requiring the assured to give notice, and specifying the manner in which it is to be given.[3] Whether a failure to give the required notice merely suspends the assured's rights under the policy until it is actually given, or whether, by his failure, he loses his rights under the policy altogether, depends on the language in which the particular condition is framed.

Unless the stipulation expressly provides to the contrary,[4] the giving of notice is regulated by the following rules:

1 The notice need not be in writing.
2 The notice need not be given by the assured himself.
3 The notice need not be given to the insurers personally.
4 The notice should be given within the prescribed time.

1 The notice need not be in writing

In the absence of an express condition to the contrary,[5] the notice of loss need not be in writing, a verbal notice being sufficient.[6] Where there is an express condition that the notice must be in writing, the assured must fulfil the condition, and he is not absolved by reason of the fact that the insurers may have received notice of the loss either verbally or from another source,[7] unless the performance of the condition is waived by acceptance of notice in another form.[8]

2 The notice need not be given by the assured himself

In the absence of an express condition to the contrary, the notice of loss need not be given by the assured himself.[9] It is sufficient if it is given by his agent,[10] or by

---

3 See eg *Forney v Dominion Insurance Co Ltd* [1969] 1 Lloyd's Rep 502 (solicitors' indemnity insurance), where the policy stated: 'The insured shall as a condition precedent to their right to be indemnified under this Policy give to the Insurers immediate notice in writing of any claim made upon them or of any occurrence of which they may become aware which may subsequently give rise to a claim.' See also *Farrell v Federal Employers' Insurance Association Ltd* [1970] 3 All ER 632, CA (employers' liability insurance); *Monksfield v Vehicle and General Insurance Co Ltd* [1971] 1 Lloyd's Rep 139, Mayor's and City of London Court (motor insurance).

4 Any express stipulation may be waived.

5 E g as in *Brook v Trafalgar Insurance Co Ltd* (1947) 79 LlL Rep 365, CA (motor insurance), where the policy stated that 'notice of any accident or loss must be given in writing to the company at its head office'.

6 *Re Solvency Mutual Guarantee Society Hawthorne's Case* (1862) 31 LJCh 625 (solvency insurance), where verbal notice of withdrawal was held sufficient.

7 *Prairie City Oil Co v Standard Mutual Fire Insurance Co* (1910) 19 Man R 720, where the insurers received notice from their own agent, but there was an express condition requiring the assured to give notice in writing forthwith.

8 *Globe Savings and Loan Co v Employers' Liability Assurance Corpn* (1901) 13 Man LR 531 where, though no formal notice, as required by the condition, was given, information was promptly communicated to the insurers and acted upon by them; *Kaffarian Colonial Bank v Grahamstown Fire Insurance Co* (1885) 5 Buchanan (East Dist Ct Cape) 61; *Devlin v Westminster Fire Insurance Co* (1925) 1 WWR 482; *Sproul v National Fire Insurance Co* (1925) 58 NSR 32.

9 Thus, notice may be given by one partner on behalf of the firm: *Davies v National Fire and Marine Insurance Co of New Zealand* [1891] AC 485, 489, PC (fire insurance); *Mason v Western Assurance Co* (1859) 17 UCQB 190, where it was held unnecessary that notice should be given by all the owners of the property insured.

10 *Davies v National Fire and Marine Insurance Co of New Zealand* (supra) at 490.

any person purporting to act on his behalf.[11] In the case of his death it may be given by his personal representatives.[12] In fact, it is immaterial from what source the insurers receive notice provided that they receive it before the expiration of the time within which the notice must be given.[13] Hence, the notice is good, although received from their own agent.[14]

3 The notice need not be given to the insurers personally

The notice need not, as a general rule, be given to the insurers personally. It is sufficient if it is given to an agent who is authorised to receive notice on their behalf. The assured is entitled to assume, in the absence of information to the contrary, that the agent through whom he negotiated the policy has authority to receive notice of loss, and a notice given to such agent will, therefore, be binding upon the insurers,[15] even where he has ceased, without the knowledge of the assured, to be their agent before the happening of the loss.[16]

The policy may, however, by its conditions require the notice to be given to the insurers themselves at their head office and not to an agent.[17]

Thus, in a case concerning motor insurance[18] the policy provided:

> 'Notice of any accident or loss must be given in writing to the company at its head office immediately upon the occurrence of such accident or loss . . . In the event of failure to comply with the terms of this condition, and in particular, if within 7 days after such accident or loss has occurred, the company has not been notified as above set forth, then all benefit under this policy shall be forfeited.'

A local agent of the insurance company has no 'usual authority' to waive compliance by the assured with this condition.[19] But a notice given by the assured to their agent will be effectual as against them if the agent duly

---

11 *Patton v Employers' Liability Assurance Corpn* (1887) 20 LRIr 93 (accident insurance).

12 Ibid.

13 *Abel v Potts* (1800) 3 Esp 242 (marine insurance).

14 *Shiells v Scottish Assurance Corpn Ltd* 1889 16 R (Ct of Sess) 1014 (accident insurance); *Irving v Sun Insurance Office* [1906] ORC 24.

15 *Gale v Lewis* (1846) 9 QB 730 (life insurance), where notice of assignment given to the agent was held sufficient, distinguishing *Re Hennessy* (1842) IR 5 Eq 259 (life insurance), where it was held that notice of an assignment given to the agent, who was himself the assignor, was insufficient; *McQueen v Phoenix Mutual Fire Insurance Co* (1879) 4 SCR 660; *Williams v Canada Farmers' Mutual Fire Insurance Co* (1876) 27 CP 119, where it was held that the insurers had held out their agent as having authority to receive notice. But notice to the broker, who negotiated the policy on behalf of the assured, is not sufficient: *Roche v Roberts* (1921) 9 LlL Rep 59 (livestock insurance).

16 *Marsden v City and County Assurance Co* (1865) LR 1 CP 232 (plate glass insurance); *Re Solvency Mutual Guarantee Society, Hawthorne's Case* (supra); cf *Imperial Bank of Canada v Royal Insurance Co* (1960) 12 OLR 519, where it was held that the fact that a subsequent insurance was effected by a sub-agent of the insurer's general agent who had also acted in procuring the earlier insurance, was not of itself to be regarded as affecting the insurers with constructive notice of the subsequent insurance.

17 *Re Williams and Lancashire and Yorkshire Accident Insurance Co's Arbitration* (1903) 19 TLR 82 (employers' liability insurance); *Hendrickson v Queen Insurance Co* (1870) 31 UCR 547, where it was held that a verbal notice of other insurances to the agent was insufficient, since the policy provided that notice should be given to the company and indorsed on the policy. See further, *Employers' Liability Assurance Corpn v Taylor* (1898) 29 SCR 104, where the notice was to be given either to the head office at Boston or to the agent whose name was indorsed on the policy.

18 *Brook v Trafalgar Insurance Co Ltd* (1947) 79 LlL Rep 365, CA (motor insurance).

19 (1947) 79 LlL Rep 365, CA. See further, p 527, post, as to the 'usual authority' of insurance agents, especially pp 525–529, post.

transmits to them within the proper time the notice which he has received.[20] The assured, however, takes the risk of the agent failing to transmit the notice, and if he fails to do so, there is no valid notice to the insurers within the meaning of the condition.[1]

4 The notice should be given within the prescribed time

The notice should be given within the prescribed time, i e within the time fixed by the stipulation, or within a reasonable time, as the case may be.[2] What is a reasonable time depends on the circumstances.[3] The reason for this rule is that if notice is not given within the required period, the insurers may well be prejudiced by the greater difficulty of ascertaining the true facts relating to the loss.[4] The condition usually provides for the notice to be given 'forthwith' or 'as soon as possible' after its occurrence.[5] Whether in a particular case the condition has been fulfilled is a matter of fact.[6]

---

20 *Shiells v Scottish Assurance Corpn Ltd* (supra); *Gill v Yorkshire Insurance Co* (1913) 24 WLR 389, where the agent telegraphed to the head office.

1 *Re Williams and Lancashire and Yorkshire Accident Insurance Co's Arbitration* (supra); *Shiells v Scottish Assurance Corpn Ltd* (supra) (accident insurance) per Lord MacDonald at 1020; *Accident Insurance Co of North America v Young* (1892) 20 SCR 280, where the agent failed to transmit the notice until after the expiration of the time prescribed; *Evans v Railway Passengers' Assurance Co* (1912) 21 OWR 442; *Roche v Roberts* (supra).

2 *Hadenfayre Ltd v British National Insurance Society Ltd, Trident General Insurance Co Ltd and Lombard Elizabethan Insurance Co Ltd* [1984] 2 Lloyd's Rep 393 (contingency insurance), at 402 (per Lloyd J), where the statement in the text above was expressly approved.

3 *O'Flynn v Equitable Fire Insurance Co* (1866) 1 Roscoe's R (Cape) Sup Ct 372, where the notice of other insurances given two months after the fire was held not to have been given within a reasonable time; *Verelst's Administratrix v Motor Union Insurance Co Ltd* [1925] 2 KB 137, where notice was given by the administratrix of the assured as soon as possible after the discovery of the policy; *Baltic Insurance Association of London Ltd v Cambrian Coaching and Goods Transport Ltd* (1926) 25 LlL Rep 195, where a delay of three weeks was held not to amount to a breach of the condition since the driver concerned in the accident had duly notified the accident, but the notice was not passed on for several days; *Warne v London Guarantee Accident Co* (1900) 20 CLT 227, where notice two months after the accident was held to be 'immediate' notice, if given as soon as serious consequences were apprehended; *London Guarantee and Accident Co v Hochelaga Bank* (1893) QR 3 QB 25, where notice was given the day after the employee disappeared; *Parent v Merchants' Insurance Co* (1918) QR 54 SC 106, where notice given on the day when the assured was informed that an accident apparently harmless had resulted in serious consequences, was held to be 'immediate' notice. Cf *Montreal Harbour Comrs v Guarantee Co of North America* (1894) 22 SCR 542, where notice a week after the defalcations were discovered was held not to be in time; *Vezey v United General Commercial Insurance Corpn Ltd* (1923) 15 LlL Rep 63 (jewellery insurance), where the loss was not reported until 7 weeks after it had occurred; *Hadenfayre Ltd v British National Insurance Society Ltd,* supra (contingency insurance), where the notice of the claim was held to have been given within a reasonable time. (See the judgment of Lloyd J, ibid, at 402).

4 *Re Williams and Lancashire and Yorkshire Accident Insurance Co's Arbitration* (1902) 19 TLR 82 (employers' liability insurance) per Bigham J, at 82; *Gamble v Accident Assurance Co* (1869) IR 4 CL 204 (accident insurance) per Pigot CB, at 214.

5 *Webster v General Accident Fire and Life Assurance Corpn Ltd* [1953] 1 QB 520 (motor insurance); *Verelst's Administratrix v Motor Union Insurance Co Ltd* [1925] 2 KB 137 (motor insurance); *Farrell v Federated Employers' Insurance Association Ltd* [1970] 3 All ER 632, CA; *Monksfield v Vehicle and General Insurance Co Ltd* [1971] 1 Lloyd's Rep 139, Mayor's and City of London Court (motor insurance); *Pioneer Concrete (UK) Ltd v National Employers Mutual General Insurance Association Ltd* [1985] 2 All ER 395, [1985] 1 Lloyd's Rep 274 (public liability insurance).

6 *Re Williams and Lancashire and Yorkshire Accident Insurance Co's Arbitration* (supra), where it was held that a notice given nearly three months after the accident was clearly no compliance with the condition; *Monksfield v Vehicle and General Insurance Co Ltd* (supra), where the insured broke a

Whether a stipulation as to the giving of notice within the required time is a condition precedent or not depends on the intention of the parties, as shown in the language of the condition,[7] and the consequences of a breach of the stipulation vary accordingly.

The insurers are entitled to rely on a breach of a condition concerning the giving of notice whether or not the breach has caused prejudice to them.[8]

(a) Where the stipulation as to time is made a condition precedent

Where the stipulation as to time is made a condition precedent, the assured must give notice within the prescribed time.[9] If he fails to do so, he will be precluded from enforcing the policy,[10] even though circumstances beyond his control have rendered it impossible for him to give the notice within the prescribed time, and it has, in fact, been given at the earliest opportunity.[11]

---

condition that written notice should be given to the insurers as soon as possible after the occurrence of any accident. If the condition provides for immediate notice within fourteen days, a notice given at any time within fourteen days is sufficient: *Mason v Western Assurance Co* (1859) 17 UCR 190. See further *Brook v Trafalgar Insurance Co Ltd* (1947) 79 LlL Rep 365, CA (motor insurance), where the assured notified the insurance agent of the loss of the car, but failed to send the notice to the head office of the company within the prescribed time, as he was required to do under the terms of the policy; *Webster v General Accident Fire etc* (supra), where the condition was waived.

7 *Stoneham v Ocean, Railway and General Accident Insurance Co* (1887) 19 QBD 237 (accident insurance) per Mathew J, at 239.

8 *Pioneer Concrete (UK) Ltd v National Employers Mutual General Insurance Association Ltd* [1985] 1 Lloyd's Rep 274, at 281 (per Bingham J).

9 *Re Williams and Lancashire and Yorkshire Accident Insurance Co's Arbitration* (supra) per Bigham J, at 82; cf *Re Coleman's Depositories Ltd and Life and Health Assurance Association* [1907] 2 KB 798. CA (employers' liability insurance) per Vaughan Williams LJ, at 804.

10 *Ralston v Bignold* (1853) 22 LTOS 106; *Roper v Lendon* (1859) 1 E & E 825; *Cawley v National Employers' Liability Accident and General Assurance Association Ltd* (1885) 1 TLR 255 (accident insurance); *Hollister v Accident Association of New Zealand* (1887) 5 NZLR 49; *Accident Insurance Co of North America v Young* (1891) 20 SCR 280; *Employers' Liability Assurance Corpn v Taylor* (1898) 29 SCR 104; *Evans v Railway Passengers' Assurance Co* (1912) 21 OWR 442; *Montreal Harbour Comrs v Guarantee Co of North America* (supra); *Elliott v Royal Exchange Assurance Co* (1867) LR 2 Exch 237 (fire insurance).

11 Thus, it is immaterial that the failure to give notice is due to the character of the accident: *Gamble v Accident Assurance Co* (1869) IR 4 CL 204, where owing to the sudden character of the accident and its resulting in instantaneous death, there was nobody capable of giving the required notice, followed in *Patton v Employers' Liability Assurance Corpn* (1887) 20 LRIr 93 (accident insurance); or to the omission of the assured to inform his relatives of the existence of the policy: *Gamble v Accident Assurance Co* (supra), where there was a time limit; or to the fact that it was not discovered until after the expiration of the prescribed time that an accident had happened within the meaning of the policy: *Cassel v Lancashire and Yorkshire Accident Insurance Co* (1885) 1 TLR 495, where the assured met with an accident in July, but did not discover until the following March that he had sustained injury; cf *Gill v Yorkshire Insurance Co* (1913) 24 WLR 389, where a condition requiring notice of illness to be given within twenty-four hours was held to be sufficiently performed if notice was given within twenty-four hours of knowledge of the illness, though the illness had commenced three days before. See further, *Re Williams and Lancashire and Yorkshire Accident Insurance Co's Arbitration* (supra), where the assured did not send in the notice until the workers who had been injured made a claim upon them. In the case of liability insurance, it has been held that time does not begin to run until it is clear that the insurers may be involved; *Smellie v British General Insurance Co* [1918] WC & Ins Rep 233; cf *General Motors Ltd v Crowder* (1931) 40 LlL Rep 87. Where the stipulation as to time does not apply, a failure to give notice within the time required thereby has no effect: *Re Coleman's Depositories Ltd and Life and Health Assurance Association* (supra), where the policy containing the condition was not issued until after the accident, at the time of which the assured was protected by a cover note which did not contain any such condition.

Sometimes, however, the policy may provide for an extension of time in certain events or contingencies, such as, for instance, in the case of a personal accident policy, where the accident takes place outside the United Kingdom or outside Europe. Further, the particular cause of delay may be excluded by the condition.[12]

(b) Where the stipulation as to time is not made a condition precedent

Where the stipulation as to time is not made a condition precedent, a failure to give notice within the prescribed time will not preclude the assured from recovering, provided that he does, in fact, give notice at some time or other to the insurers.[13] He will, however, be liable to the insurers for any damages which they may have sustained by reason of his failure.[14]

(c) Waiver of requirements as to notice

It is competent for the insurers to waive any of the requirements of the policy as to notice. What amounts to a waiver will depend on the circumstances.[15]

(d) Statement by BIA and Lloyd's

In 1977 The British Insurance Association[16] and Lloyd's drew up a statement of non-life insurance practice which they recommended to their members.[17] The statement applies only to non-life policyholders domiciled in the United Kingdom and insured in their private capacity only, and so far as the time for giving notice of a claim is concerned provides:

> 'Under the conditions regarding notification of a claim, the policyholder shall not be asked to do more than report a claim and subsequent developments as soon as reasonably possible except in the case of legal processes and claims which a third party requires the policyholder to notify within a fixed time, where immediate advice may be required.'

---

[12] *Ward v Law Property Assurance and Trust Society* (1856) 2 WR 605, where a condition requiring notice within six days of any liability being incurred was held to refer to criminal misconduct, and consequently the assured, on receiving evidence that his servant had been guilty of embezzlement, was not bound to give notice until he had ascertained that the servant had been guilty of criminal misconduct.

[13] *Stoneham v Ocean Railway and General Accident Co* (1887) 19 QBD 237. Presumably the making of a claim would be sufficient.

[14] *Re Coleman's Depositories Ltd and Life and Health Assurance Association* [1907] 2 KB 798, CA (employers' liability insurance).

[15] *Hadwin v Lovelace* (1809) 1 Act 126, PC; *Donnison v Employers' Accident and Live Stock Insurance Co Ltd* 1897 24 R (Ct of Sess) 681 (accident insurance), where the insurers, after receiving a notice which was out of time, required a post-mortem examination; *Labbé v Equitable Mutual Fire Assurance Co* (1906) QR 29 SC 143, where the insurers after receiving an informal notice, offered a sum in settlement; *Walker v Western Assurance Co* (1859) 18 UCR 19 (accident insurance), where the insurers had agreed that the question to be tried related only to the cause and manner of the loss; *Kaffarian Colonial Bank v Grahamstown Fire Insurance Co* (1885) 5 Buchanan (East Dist Ct Cape) 61, where a verbal notice had been accepted; *Carbray v Strathcona Fire Insurance Co* (1915) QR 47 SC 212, where an informal notice was acted on; *Canadian Railway Accident Insurance Co v Haines* (1911) 44 SCR 386, where the condition was held to be waived by a tender before action of a sum which the insurers contended to be the amount payable, and by a plea of tender in the defence; *Webster v General Accident Fire and Life Assurance Corpn Ltd* [1953] 1 QB 520, [1953] 1 All ER 663, [1953] 1 Lloyd's Rep 123 (motor insurance), where a requirement that notice of the loss should be given in writing 'as soon as possible after the occurrence of . . . loss' was waived.

[16] Now The Association of British Insurers.

[17] See 931 House of Commons Official Report, 4 May 1977, Written Answers, cols 218–220.

(e) *Statement by Life Offices' Association*

A statement of long-term insurance practice has been issued by the Life Offices' Association. It applies to such insurance effected by individuals resident in the United Kingdom in a private capacity, and says:

> 'Under any conditions regarding a time limit for notification of a claim, the claimant will not be asked to do more than report a claim and subsequent developments as soon as reasonably possible.'

B PARTICULARS OF LOSS

Apart from any stipulation to the contrary, the assured is not bound in the event of loss to make his claim against the insurers at any particular time before his claim is barred by the Limitation Act 1980, or to support it by any proofs before action is brought.

But it is the almost invariable practice of insurers, for the purpose of enabling them to form a judgment as to the reality and extent of the loss alleged to have been sustained by the assured.[18] to insert in the policy an express condition that the assured must deliver to the insurers within a specified time after the loss a claim in writing containing full particulars of the loss or damage in respect of which the claim is made, and that, unless he complies with this condition, no claim under the policy is to be payable.[19]

Whether the assured has complied with the condition or not depends in each case on the language of the particular condition employed.[20]

---

18 *Worsley v Wood* (1796) 6 Term Rep 710 per Lord Kenyon, at 718: 'These insurance companies who enter into very extensive contracts of this kind are liable . . . to great frauds and impositions; common prudence therefore suggests to them the propriety of taking all possible care to protect them from frauds when they make these contracts'; *Gamble v Accident Assurance Co* (1869) IR 4 CL 204 (accident insurance) per Pigot CB, at 214; 'In order to protect themselves against unfounded or aggravated claims it was very urgent that [the company] should, in every instance in which a casualty should occur likely to originate a claim against them, have the earliest opportunity when the facts should be recent, and when evidence could be more easily and satisfactorily procured than it could be after the lapse of any considerable time, of inquiring into the circumstances of the casualty, the nature of the injury, and the position of the insured.' See also, *Mason v Harvey* (1853) 8 Exch 819 per Pollock CB, at 821; *Hiddle v National Fire and Marine Insurance Co of New Zealand* [1896] AC 372, at 376, PC.

19 *London Guarantee Co v Fearnley* (1880) 5 App Cas 911, approving *Worsley v Wood* (supra) (fire insurance); *Lancashire Insurance Co v IRC* [1899] 1 QB 353, per Bruce J, at 359; *Oldman v Bewicke* (1796) 2 HyBl 577n (fire insurance); *Routledge v Burrell* (1789) 1 HyBl 254 (fire insurance); *Mason v Harvey* (supra); *Penney v Goode* (1853) 2 WR 49 (fire insurance); *Roper v Lendon* (1859) 1 E & E 825 (fire insurance) per Lord Campbell CJ, at 830. A mere statement in the proposal that the assured proposes to prove any loss by the production of receipts from the sellers does not amount to a condition precluding him from proving his loss in another way: *Winicofsky v Army and Navy General Assurance Co* (1919) 35 TLR 283 (burglary insurance). There may be an express condition requiring particular books to be kept: *Jacobson v Yorkshire Insurance Co Ltd* (1933) 49 TLR 389; *Le Riche v Atlas Insurance Co* [1913] CPD 697; *Papas v General Accident, Fire and Life Assurance Corpn Ltd* [1916] CPD 619; *Shame's Trustee v Yorkshire Insurance Co Ltd* [1922] TPD 259.

20 For examples of cases where it was held that such a condition had not been complied with, see *Cook v Scottish Imperial Insurance Co* (1884) 5 NSWLR 35, where the assured omitted to state what articles were destroyed and their value, as required by the condition, although he gave an account with the names of the persons from whom he had purchased goods since he began business, stating the value of such goods, and the value of the goods sold by him and of the salvage, and evidence was given that the account was as particular and detailed an account as

The various stipulations in use necessarily vary in the details required according to the nature of the insurance. They are, however, framed on the same general lines and usually provide as follows:

1 The assured is required to deliver particulars of the loss.
2 The particulars to be delivered must be given with such details as are reasonably practicable.
3 The particulars should be delivered within the prescribed time.

1 Delivery of the particulars of the loss

The assured is required to deliver particulars of the loss. For this purpose, a 'claim form' is usually provided by the insurers in which the assured is required to state the cause, nature, and extent of the loss.

2 Sufficient details must be given

The particulars to be delivered must be given with such details as are reasonably practicable.[21] Whether the details given are sufficient to satisfy the condition is a question of degree, depending partly on the means of information at the claimant's disposal,[1] and partly on the time within which the particulars have to be delivered.[2]

Unless the stipulation otherwise provides,[3] the delivery of particulars does not preclude the assured from delivering further particulars which were omitted from the first statement by mistake, ignorance, carelessness, or inadvertence.[4] The insurers may also reserve the right to require the delivery of further particulars.

---

the assured could have delivered within the time; *Cameron v Monarch Assurance Co* (1858) 7 CP 212; *L'Union Fire, Accident and General Insurance Co Ltd v Klinker Knitting Mills Pty Ltd* (1938) 59 CLR 807, where the assured only gave particulars of some of the items claimed, and was held not entitled to recover any part of his loss.

21 *Mason v Harvey* (supra) per Pollock CB, at 820. The performance of the condition in this respect may be waived: *Fowlie v Ocean Accident and Guarantee Corpn* (1902) 33 Can SCR 253, where no objection was raised to the particulars until two years after the insured's death.

1 *National Trust Co v Sterling Accident and Guarantee Insurance Co of Canada* (1916) QR 51 SC 481, where the insurers were informed that the assured had been lost in The Titanic; *National Bank of Australasia v Brock* (1864) 1 WW & AB 208; *Hiddle v National Fire and Marine Insurance Co of New Zealand* (supra), where the assured had in their possession at the time of forwarding the particulars, the material for furnishing fuller, more detailed, and better particulars.

2 *National Trust Co v Sterling Accident and Guarantee Insurance Co of Canada* (supra); *Hiddle v National Fire and Marine Insurance Co of New Zealand* (supra).

3 *Vance v Forster* (1841) IR Cir Rep 47 (fire insurance) per Pennefather B, at 52: 'I do not think that the plaintiff is concluded by the account which he furnished to the company. It may be evidence to go to the jury that any addition is fraudulent, but I think it is going too far to say that no addition is to be made. There is no stipulation in the policy that the plaintiff shall be precluded from going any further than the account which it is required to furnish.'

4 *Mason v Harvey* (1853) 8 Exch 819 (fire insurance) per Pollock CB, at 820; *Cammell v Beaver and Toronto Mutual Fire Insurance Co* (1876) 39 UCR 1. The fact that the assured has made a claim which has been paid does not prevent him from subsequently making a claim in respect of further loss arising out of the same accident: *Prosser v Lancashire and Yorkshire Accident Insurance Co* (1890) 6 TLR 285, CA, where the assured, after claiming in respect of an accident, received a sum 'in full discharge', of the claim, and it was held that this did not preclude him from claiming in respect of a subsequent total disablement from the same accident. Cf *Elliott v Royal Exchange Assurance Co* (1867) LR 2 Exch 237 (fire insurance) per Pigott B, at 247; *Kent v Ocean Accident and Guarantee Corpn* (1909) 20 OLR 226.

3 The particulars should be delivered within the prescribed time

The particulars should be delivered within the prescribed time, i e within the time fixed by the stipulation or a reasonable time, as the case may be.

The stipulation as to time may be of the essence of the condition, so as to render it obligatory on the assured to furnish the particulars within the prescribed time, and may thus be a condition precedent to the liability of the insurer.[5]

On the other hand, the stipulation may not be a condition precedent and the assured may be entitled, notwithstanding the stipulation as to time, to furnish particulars at any time, even after the expiration of the prescribed period, although, until he has done so, he is unable to enforce his claim.[6]

Whether the stipulation is a condition precedent or not is purely a question of construction, depending on the language of the particular policy. The stipulation when standing alone in the policy,[7] or when coupled with a statement to the effect that in default of compliance therewith no claim shall be payable under the policy, is clearly a condition precedent.[8]

On the other hand, where the stipulation is coupled with a declaration that no claim is to be payable until the requisite particulars are furnished, the question as to the effect of the stipulation is one on which different opinions have been expressed. It has been held that the furnishing of particulars within the prescribed time is a material part of the contract, and that the stipulation is, therefore, a condition precedent notwithstanding the declaration.[9] This construction, however, fails to give any effect to the declaration, the addition of which is, upon this construction, unnecessary.

Effect can only be given to the declaration by treating it as enlarging the time, and thus precluding the insurers from relying on the stipulation as to time being a condition precedent; and, in accordance with this view, it has been held that the stipulation is not a condition precedent.[10] The latter construction

---

5 *Elliott v Royal Exchange Assurance Co* (1867) LR 2 Exch 237. Cf *Lancashire Insurance Co v IRC* [1899] 1 QB 353 (accident insurance) per Bruce J, at 359.

6 *Weir v Northern Counties of England Insurance Co* (1879) 4 LRIr 689 per Lawson J, at 692. Cf *Welch v Royal Exchange Assurance* [1939] 1 KB 294, [1938] 4 All ER 289, 62 LlL Rep 83, CA, where the wording of the condition was that no claim should be paid 'unless' the condition had been fulfilled, and it was held too late to tender the proofs after proceedings had been begun.

7 *Roper v Lendon* (1859) 1 E & E 825, where the condition provided that: 'All persons insured by this company sustaining any loss or damage by fire shall forthwith give notice thereof to the directors or secretary of this company . . . , and within fifteen days after such fire deliver as particular an account of their loss or damage as the nature of the case will admit of', and Lord Campbell CJ, at 830 said: 'The whole of the condition, relating to the delivery of particulars of loss, must be taken *tale quale*. When, therefore, it is conceded that a delivery of such particulars before action is essential, it follows from the wording of the condition, that the delivery must be within fifteen days after loss. And the condition so construed is a very reasonable one; it being obviously of great importance to the defendants' company to know, as soon as possible after a loss, the amount claimed by the assured.' This statement was approved in *Elliott v Royal Exchange Assurance Co* (supra) per Martin B, at 244. See also, *Mason v Harvey* (1853) 8 Exch 819, following *Worsley v Wood* (1796) 6 Term Rep 710; *Atlas Assurance Co v Brownell* (1899) 29 SCR 537; *Anderson v Norwich Fire Insurance Society* (1918) QR 53 SC 409; *Gran v Colonial Insurance Co of New Zealand* (1884) 2 QLJ 53.

8 *Stoneham v Ocean, Railway and General Accident Insurance Co* (1887) 19 QBD 237 (accident insurance) per Cave J, at 241.

9 *Whyte v Western Assurance Co* (1875) 22 LCJ 215, PC; *Commercial Union Assurance Co v Margeson* (1899) 29 SCR 601; *Hollander v Royal Insurance Co* (1885) 4 SC 66.

10 *Weir v Northern Counties of England Insurance Co* (1879) 4 LRIr 689; *Lafarge v London, Liverpool and*

appears to be the more correct one, especially in view of the fact that it is the duty of the insurers, if they intend to make a stipulation a condition precedent, to make their intention clear.

Where the stipulation as to time is a condition precedent, the failure of the assured, from whatever cause, to furnish particulars within the time prescribed puts an end to the insurers' liability,[11] and the assured cannot by a subsequent delivery of particulars revive his rights against them.[12]

Nor are they estopped from relying on the objection by reason of the fact that, after the particulars are sent in, they merely decline to admit liability, since they may have declined to admit liability on the very ground that the particulars have been delivered too late.[13]

If, however, there is an express repudiation of liability on other grounds after receipt of the particulars, the condition must be regarded as waived.[14]

A repudiation of liability before the particulars are due discharges the assured from his obligation to furnish them within the prescribed time.[15]

The insurers may, however, extend the time if they think fit, and sometimes the condition expressly empowers them to do so, though this is unnecessary. An extension of time is exhausted when the purpose for which it was granted, as, for instance, the working out of figures, has been fulfilled and a delivery afterwards is too late.[16]

The insurers may also waive the requirement as to time,[17] or by their subsequent conduct preclude themselves from objecting to the particulars as having been delivered out of time;[18] but a mere failure to take objection on this

---

Globe Insurance Co (1873) 17 LCJ 237; *Bowes v National Insurance Co* (1880) 20 NBR 437; *Western Australian Bank v Royal Insurance Co* (1908) 5 CLR 533.

11 The fact that the assured has been adjudicated bankrupt does not entitle the trustee in bankruptcy to any further time: *Re Carr and Sun Fire Insurance Co* (1897) 13 TLR 186, CA.

12 *Whyte v Western Assurance Co* (1875) 22 LCJ 215, PC. But he is entitled to revise his claim though the time limit has expired: *Northern Suburban Property and Real Estates Co Ltd v British Law Fire Insurance Co* (1919) 1 LlL Rep 403, where the revision was due to the fact that the builders employed by the assured had withdrawn their estimate of the cost of repairs, and the assured after the time limit had expired substituted the estimates of different builders.

13 Ibid.

14 *Kelly v Hochelaga Fire Insurance Co* (1886) 24 LCJ 298; *Accident Insurance Co of North America v Young* (1891) 20 SCR 280.

15 *Shiells v Scottish Assurance Corpn Ltd* 1889 16 R (Ct of Sess) 1014 (accident insurance); *Morrow v Lancashire Insurance Co* (1898) 29 OR 377; *Adams v Glen Falls Insurance Co* (1916) 37 OLR 1; *Irving v Sun Insurance Office* [1906] ORC 24; *Passaportis v Guardian Assurance Co Ltd* [1916] SR 14.

16 *Re Carr and Sun Fire Insurance Co* (supra).

17 *Toronto Rly Co v National British and Irish Millers' Insurance Co Ltd* (1914) 111 LT 555, CA (fire insurance), where the method of dealing with the loss adopted differed from that prescribed by the policy; *Cann v Imperial Fire Insurance Co* (1875) 10 NSR (1 R & C) 240, where the assured, who was absent at the time of the fire, was told to get the information as soon as possible after his return home; *Robins v Victoria Mutual Fire Insurance Co* (1881) 6 AR 427, where the assured gave verbal particulars, and was told that nothing more need be done; *Western Assurance Co v Pharand* (1902) QR 11 KB 144, where the delay was due to the investigations of the insurers; *Mount Royal Insurance Co v Benoit* (1906) QR 15 KB 90, where the insurers stated that they were investigating the circumstances of the loss.

18 *Yorkshire Insurance Co v Craine* [1922] 2 AC 541, 11 LlL Rep 1, PC, where the insurers, by taking and keeping possession of the assured's premises, were estopped from disputing the validity of the claim; *Bowes v National Insurance Co* (1880) 20 NBR 437, where the insurers afterwards adjusted the loss, without raising any objection as to the delay, although the assured did not accept the adjustment; *Donnison v Employers' Accident and Live Stock Insurance Co* 1897 24 R (Ct of Sess) 681, where the insurers insisted on a post-mortem; *Lamkpin v Ontario Marine and Fire Insurance Co* (1855) 12 UCR 578, where the insurers entered into a correspondence as to

ground does not amount to a waiver of the condition,[19] even though the insurers whilst repudiating liability, are demanding that particulars be furnished.[20]

Where the insurers waive a stipulation as to time, this does not amount to an indefinite extension of time, and the particulars must be delivered, if no time is mentioned, within a reasonable time.[1]

C THE METHODS OF PROVING THE LOSS

The insurers are usually empowered, by a stipulation in the policy, to call on the assured to prove that the loss is covered by the policy,[2] and to verify the particulars given by such documentary or other proofs as they may require. Delivery of proofs, if required, is usually[3] a condition precedent to the liability of the insurers.[4]

In requiring proofs, however, or in deciding whether the proofs given are sufficient, the insurers cannot act capriciously, unreasonably, or unjustly, by requiring evidence which is not necessary to satisfy them on any reasonable view of the case. It is sufficient if the assured lays before them evidence with which reasonable men would be satisfied,[5] and it is unnecessary to show that the insurers have been, in fact, satisfied.[6]

---

furnishing better particulars, and subsequently refused to pay on account of some suspicious circumstances; *Caldwell v Stadacona Fire and Life Insurance Co* (1883) 11 SCR 212; *Hammond v Citizens' Insurance Co of Canada* (1886) 26 NBR 371, where the assured gave prompt notice of the fire and applied for a claim form which was not sent to him by the insurers until after the time for the claim had expired; but see *Niagara District Mutual Fire Insurance Co v Lewis* (1862) 12 CP 123, where it was held that a mere proposal to arbitrate did not amount to a waiver; *Quon v British and European Insurance Co* [1928] 3 WWR 545, where the assured was arrested on a charge of arson immediately after the fire, and though he had instructed an assessor to prepare proofs of loss, they were not prepared until after acquittal.

19 *Whyte v Western Assurance Co* (1875) 22 LCJ 215, PC.

20 *Re Coleman's Depositories Ltd and Life and Health Assurance Association* [1907] 2 KB 798, CA (employers' liability insurance) per Vaughan Williams LJ, at 805; *Goodwin v Lancashire Fire and Life Insurance Co* (1873) 18 LCJ 1; *Hollander v Royal Insurance Co* (1885) 4 SC 66.

1 *Re Carr and Sun Fire Insurance Co* (1897) 13 TLR 186, CA, per Lord Esher MR, at 186; *Kanneneyer N O v Sun Insurance Co* (1896) 13 Cape SCR 451.

2 *Harvey v Ocean Accident and Guarantee Corpn* [1905] 2 IR 1, 26. A mere notice of loss is not sufficient to satisfy the stipulation, even though it specifies the time, place and cause of the loss: *Johnston v Dominion of Canada Guarantee and Accident Insurance Co* (1908) 17 OLR 462.

3 *Hollister v Accident Association of New Zealand* (1887) 5 NZLR 49; *Johnston v Dominion of Canada Guarantee and Accident Insurance Co* (supra); *London Guarantee Co v Fearnley* (1880) 5 App Cas 911 per Lord Blackburn, at 916; *Oldman v Bewicke* (1786) 2 HyBl 577n (fire insurance); *Routledge v Burrell* (1789) 1 HyBl 254 (fire insurance); *Worsley v Wood* (1796) 6 Term Rep 710 (fire insurance). In another case, *Cowell v Yorkshire Provident Life Assurance Co* (1901) 17 TLR 452 (life insurance), a stipulation providing for proof of interest was held not to be a condition precedent, the policy containing a provision for the settlement of disputes by a County Court Judge.

4 *Globe Savings and Loan Co v Employers' Liability Assurance Corpn* (1901) 13 Man R 531, where the assured, though precluded from recovering owing to a breach of the condition, was held to be recouped the expenses incurred, under another condition, in prosecuting the defaulting servant.

5 *Braunstein v Accidental Death Insurance Co* (1861) 1 B & S 782 per Wightman J, at 794; *Trew v Railway Passengers' Assurance Co* (1860) 6 Jur NS 759; *Macdonald v Refuge Assurance Co* 1890 17 R (Ct of Sess) 955, where the presumption against suicide was applied; *Ballantine v Employers' Insurance Co of Great Britain* 1893 21 R (Ct of Sess) 305, where a request for a post-mortem was apparently considered unreasonable; *National Trust Co v Sterling Accident and Guarantee Co of Canada* (1916) QR 51 SC 481, where proof by affidavit that the assured had perished in the wreck of a steamer on which he was a passenger was held to be sufficient; *Moore v Woolsey* (1854)

[*Footnote 6 on p 406*]

The nature of the proofs that may be required must necessarily vary according to the nature of the insurance. For instance, in fire insurance the proofs may consist of books of account,[7] vouchers, and invoices,[8] whether original or copies,[9] or of plans, specifications, and estimates,[10] and the assured may be required to supplement the information therein contained by a written or verbal explanation.

Similarly in a case of an 'all risks' insurance policy in respect of some metal stored in a warehouse, the insurers put the assured to strict proof of the loss, and he adduced in evidence the stock cards which had been kept, though, in the result, he failed to show the exact quantity which had been lost.[11]

The stipulation usually provides that the assured may further be required to make a statutory declaration[12] verifying the proof of his claim and particulars.[13] If by the terms of the stipulation the statutory declaration is

---

4 E & B 243 (life insurance); *London Guarantee Co v Fearnley* (1880) 5 App Cas 911 (fidelity insurance) per Lord Blackburn, at 916; *J R Mooney and Co v Pearl Assurance Co* [1942] 4 DLR 13 (fidelity insurance); cf *Harvey v Ocean Accident and Guarantee Corpn* (supra), where the facts pointed equally to accident or suicide and the presumption against suicide was held not to be sufficient to satisfy the condition; *Doyle v City of Glasgow Life Assurance Co* (1884) 53 LJCh 527 (life insurance), where the directors were held entitled to require further evidence of death notwithstanding that an order presuming death had been made under the Cestui que Vie Act 1707.

6 *Moore v Woolsey* (supra) per Lord Campbell, at 256. it is immaterial that the particular proofs required, e g banking accounts, when inspected, do not contain any matter tending to justify refusal to pay the claim: *Welch v Royal Exchange Assurance* [1939] 1 KB 294, [1938] All ER 289, 62 LlL Rep 83, CA (fire insurance).

7 This may include banking accounts controlled by the assured, though in the name of another: *Welch v Royal Exchange Assurance* (supra) (fire insurance), where a fire had occurred on the assured's premises, and the insurance company requested information as to the bank accounts used and controlled by him for the purposees of his business, and he failed to give information of bank accounts in his mother's name which were used and controlled by him for the purpose of his business.

8 *Carter v Niagara District Mutual Insurance Co* (1868) 19 CP 143, where the assured did not verify his claim by reference to books or other vouchers as required by the condition, following *Greaves v Niagara District Mutual Fire Insurance Co* (1865) 25 UCR 127; *Cinqmars v Equitable Insurance Co* (1857) 15 UCR 143, where the assured refused to produce certain vouchers; *Mulvey v Gore District Mutual Fire Assurance Co* (1866) 25 UCR 424, where the particulars stated the total value of goods, and were accompanied by some accounts of goods sold to the assured which showed only charges of 'goods per invoice', which were held insufficient; *Gordon v Transatlantic Fire Insurance Co* [1905] TH 146, where the condition provided, inter alia, that the assured must furnish all documents which might reasonably be required, and it was held that the production of certain vouchers which were asked for was a condition precedent.

9 If the books and vouchers are burned, the condition as to their production does not apply: *Perry v Niagara District Mutual Fire Insurance Co* (1877) 21 LCJ 257, where it was held that an affidavit by the assured of the amount of the loss was sufficient. In *Kibzcy v Home Insurance Co* [1918] 2 WWR 541 it was held that the assured was not bound to procure copies of invoices.

10 *Fawcett v Liverpool and London and Globe Insurance Co* (1868) 27 UCR 225, where a builder's certificate was required.

11 *Atlantic Metal Co Ltd v Hepburn* [1960] 2 Lloyd's Rep 42 (Commercial Court] (all risks insurance).

12 The form of the statutory declaration cannot be dictated by the insurers in the absence of a term in the stipulation to that effect; the assured is entitled to frame the declaration as he chooses: *Beeck v Yorkshire Insurance Co* (1909) 11 WALR 88 (livestock insurance), where the form of declaration put forward by the insurers contained a series of questions, concluding with a condition forfeiting the claim and avoiding the policy if any answer were untrue. The declaration must be bona fide demanded: *Cameron v Times and Beacon Fire Insurance Co* (1857) 7 CP 234; and may be waived: *Blow v Guardian Assurance Co* (1922) 22 SRNSW 154.

13 The making of a false statutory declaration is a misdemeanour: Statutory Declarations Act 1835, s 21; see *R v Boynes* (1843) 1 Car & Kir 65.

sufficient prima facie evidence that the loss falls within the policy, the fact that a statutory declaration has been required does not dispense the assured from the onus of proving his loss at the trial.[14]

The insurers may, by their conduct, waive their right to demand proofs in accordance with the condition.[15] They may also, where the proofs are insufficient, waive any objection to them on that ground;[16] but a mere failure to take objection does not amount to a waiver.[17] Where, however, the insurers take objection to the particulars on other grounds, their silence as to the insufficiency of the particulars may be evidence of a waiver.[18]

On the other hand, a demand for particulars and proofs of loss is not a waiver on any other ground of forfeiture which may exist.[19]

Where no time is fixed for the delivery of proofs, they may be delivered at any time before the claim is statute-barred.[20]

D FRAUDULENT CLAIMS

Since it is the duty of the assured to observe the utmost good faith in his dealings with the insurers throughout, the claim which he puts forward must be honestly

---

14 *Watts v Simmons* (1924) 18 LlL Rep 87 at 177 (jewellery insurance), where the policy provided that 'A statutory declaration by the assured with regard to any claim hereunder that he believes it to be a loss within the meaning of the insurance, and further that he has no reason to suspect or believe that such loss has been caused by an excepted risk or is in any respect a loss from which the underwriters are by the terms of this policy declared free from liability, shall be sufficient prima facie evidence that the loss is not of the character excluded by this policy'.

15 *Fowlie v Ocean Accident and Guarantee Corpn* (1902) 33 SCR 253; *Pim v Reid* (1843) 6 Man & G 1 (fire insurance); *Toronto Rly Co v National British and Irish Millers' Insurance Co* (1914) 111 LT 555, CA (fire insurance).

16 *Pim v Reid* (supra), where it was held that the jury might infer from the correspondence that there was a waiver; *Canadian Mutual Fire Insurance Co v Donovan* (1879) 2 Stephen's Quebec Digest 406 where the insurers proceeded to arbitration on the claim with knowledge of all the facts; *Canada Landed Credit Co v Canada Agricultural Insurance Co* (1870) 17 Gr 418, where the insurers made no objection until after the action had been brought; *Bowes v National Insurance Co* (1880) 20 NBR 437; *Bull v North British Canadian Investment Co* (1888) 15 AR 421. But there may be an express condition that the insurers are not to be held to have waived any requirement by any steps which they may take to appraise the loss: *Prevost v Scottish Union and National Insurance Co* (1897) QR 14 SC 203. A waiver by an agent is not binding unless it is within his authority: *Mason v Hartford Fire Insurance Co* (1875) 37 UCR 437; *Commercial Union Assurance Co v Margeson* (1899) 29 SCR 601, following *Atlas Assurance Co v Brownell* (1899) 29 SCR 537.

17 *Mason v Andes Insurance Co* (1873) 23 CP 37; *O'Connor v Commercial Union Insurance Co* (1878) 12 NSR (3 R & C) 119, where the insurers' agent made no objection to the excuse for non-compliance with the condition put forward by the assured, distinguished in *Herkins v Provincial Insurance Co* (1878) 12 NSR (3 R & C) 176.

18 *McManus v Aetna Insurance Co* (1865) 11 NBR (6 All) 314; *Glagovsky v National Fire Insurance Co of Hartford* [1913] 1 WWR 573.

19 *Abrahams v Agricultural Mutual Assurance Association* (1876) 40 UCR 175; *McDermott v Western Canada Fire Insurance Co* (1913) 24 WLR 375, where the proofs were not demanded until the time had expired.

20 *Harvey v Ocean Accident and Guarantee Corpn* [1905] 2 IR 1 CA (accident insurance). But if the assured has failed to produce the required proofs at the time when he commences proceedings, and a reasonable time for compliance has already elapsed, he cannot fulfil the conditions by producing the proofs thereafter; *Welch v Royal Exchange Assurance* [1939] 1 KB 294, [1938] 4 All ER 289, 62 LlL Rep 83, CA (fire insurance), where the assured had failed to give full information to the insurance company when requested to do so, but had supplied the information when the claim went to arbitration.

made; and, if it is fraudulent, he will forfeit all benefit under the policy whether there is a condition to that effect or not.[1] The assured must make a full disclosure of the circumstances of the case.[2]

It is equally the duty of the insurers to the public and to their shareholders, if they are a company, to insist on a full and searching investigation into the case, where there are circumstances of grave suspicion.[3]

There is usually an express condition in the policy to the effect that if the claim is in any respect fraudulent,[4] or if any fraudulent means or devices are used by the assured, or anyone acting on his behalf, to obtain any benefit under the policy, all benefit under it is to be forfeited.[5]

Thus, the Lloyd's 'All Risks' policy provides:

---

1 *Britton v Royal Insurance Co* (1866) 4 F & F 905 per Wills J, at 909: 'The contract of insurance is one of perfect good faith on both sides, and it is most important that such good faith should be maintained. It is the common practice to insert in fire policies conditions that they shall be void in the event of a fraudulent claim, and there was such a condition in the present case. But a condition is only in accordance with legal principle and sound policy . . . if there is a wilful falsehood or fraud in the claim, the insured forfeits all claim whatever upon the policy'; *Black King Shipping Corpn and Wayang (Panama) SA v Massie, The Litsion Pride* [1985] 1 Lloyd's Rep 437 (marine insurance) per Hirst J, at 518: 'I am prepared to hold that the duty not to make fraudulent claims and not to make claims in breach of duty of utmost good faith is an implied term of the policy.' See also, *Thurtell v Beaumont* (1823) 1 Bing 339 (fire insurance); *Goulstone v Royal Insurance Co* (1858) 1 F & F 276 (fire insurance) per Pollock CB, at 279: 'If the claim was fraudulent, the plaintiff cannot recover.'; *McKirby v North British Insurance Co* 1858 20 Dunl (Ct of Sess) 463; and cf *Goldstone v Osborn* (1826) 2 C & P 550. If, after a fraudulent claim is sent in, the assured is adjudicated bankrupt, his trustee in bankruptcy is equally precluded from recovering: *Re Carr and Sun Fire Insurance Co* (1897) 13 TLR 186, CA (fire insurance), followed in *Cassim's Estate v London Assurance Corpn* [1914] SAR (NPD) 6. In *Reid & Co v Employers' Accident and Live Stock Insurance Co* 1899 1 F (Ct of Sess) 1031 Lord Trayner was of opinion that in the absence of an express condition the claim would be avoided, but the policy would remain in force. But this, it is submitted, is not in accordance with the English authorities.

2 *Shepherd v Chewter* (1808) 1 Camp 274 (marine insurance) per Lord Ellenborough CJ, at 275.

3 *Chapman v Pole* (1870) 22 LT 306 (fire insurance) per Cockburn CJ addressing the jury, at 307: 'In consequence of the observations which have been made upon the conduct of the insurance company, I feel it to be my duty to say that I consider that in insisting on a full and searching examination into the case in a Court of Justice, the defendants, the Sun Fire Insurance Society, have only discharged their duty to their shareholders and the public. If you think . . . that . . . with reference either to the quantity or the value of the goods the plaintiff knowingly preferred a claim he knew to be false and unjust, then he is entitled to recover nothing.'

4 The word 'false', when used in a condition of this kind in connection with the word 'fraudulent', means 'false to the knowledge of the assured': *Steeves v Sovereign Fire Insurance Co* (1840) 20 4 NBR 394, where it was held that a plea alleging that the plaintiff falsely swore the cash value of the property insured to be $500 was bad, because it did not state that he did so 'knowingly and wilfully'; *Harrison v Western Assurance Co* (1902) 35 NSR 488; revsd on other grounds (1903) 33 CanSCR 473.

5 *Lek v Mathews* (1927) 29 LlL Rep 141, HL (theft insurance) per Lord Sumner at 145: 'As to the construction of the false claim clause, I think that it refers to anything falsely claimed, that is, anything not so unsubstantial as to make the maxim de minimis applicable, and is not limited to a claim which as to the whole is false. It means claims as to particular subject-matters in respect to which a right to indemnity is asserted, not the mere amount of money claimed without regard to the particulars or the contents of the claim, and a claim is false not only if it is deliberately invented, but also if it is made recklessly, not caring whether it is true or false but only seeking to succeed in the claim.' In *Central Bank of India Ltd v Guardian Assurance Co and Rustomji* (1936) 54 LlL Rep 247, PC (fire insurance) the policy provided that: 'If any claim be in any respect fraudulent or if any false declaration be made or used in support thereof or if any fraudulent means or devices are used by the insured or anyone acting on his behalf to obtain any benefit under this policy . . . all benefit under this policy shall be forfeited.' For a similar clause, see *Harris v Evans* (1924) 19 LlL Rep 303, 346 (fire insurance).

> 'If the assured shall make any claim knowing the same to be false or fraudulent, as regards amount or otherwise, this Policy shall become void and all claim hereunder shall be forfeited.'

It is immaterial, therefore, whether the fraud affects the whole or only part of the claim,[6] though at the same time it must have some relation to the claim itself.[7]

The question whether the claim is fraudulent or not is a question for the jury.[8] The particular kind of fraud practised is immaterial. The claim may be fraudulent in that the assured has suffered no loss within the meaning of the policy,[9] or in that although he has suffered a loss, it was not caused by the peril insured against.[10] It may contain false statements of fact[11] or it may be supported by fraudulent evidence.[12]

---

6 *Britton v Royal Insurance Co* (1866) 4 F & F 905. Thus, where the insurance is on buildings and contents, a fraudulent declaration as to the value of the contents prevents the assured from recovering even in respect of the buildings: *Cashman v London and Liverpool Fire Insurance Co* (1862) 10 NBR (5 All) 246; *Lek v Mathews* (supra), where the assured had put forward fraudulent claims in relation to part of the stamp collection which was insured under the policy; *Harris v Waterloo Mutual Fire Insurance Co* (1886) 10 OR 718; *Maple Leaf Milling Co Ltd v Colonial Assurance Co* [1917] 2 WWR 1091. But in the case of a composite policy insuring several parties for their different interests, e g a company, the landlords of its premises, and mortgagees, a fraudulent claim by one does not prevent the other parties from recovering: *General Accident, Fire and Life Assurance Corpn Ltd v Midland Bank Ltd* [1940] 2 KB 388, CA per Greene MR, at 417. Aliter if the policy is a joint one.

7 *Crowley v Agricultural Mutual Assurance Association of Canada* (1871) 21 CP 567, where a false statement that all premiums had been paid was held not to fall within the condition, following *Ross v Commercial Union Assurance Co* (1867) 26 UCR 559, where the assured falsely stated his title to the property insured; *Steeves v Sovereign Fire Insurance Co* (1880) 20 NBR 394.

8 *Goulstone v Royal Insurance Co* (1858) 1 F & F 276.

9 *Britton v Royal Insurance Co* (1866) 4 F & F 905; *Phillips v Chapman* (1921) 7 LlL Rep 139, where the burglary was a pretence; *Cuppitman v Marshall* (1924) 18 LlL Rep 277, where a claim upon a burglary policy was held fraudulent on the grounds that the books showed the goods claimed for were not on the premises, and that the alleged burglary did not in fact take place; *Dome Mining Corpn Ltd v Drysdale* (1931) 41 LlL Rep 109 (dredger insurance), where the assured put forward a claim to a total loss when he had good reason to believe that it was only partial; *Herbert v Poland* (1932) 44 LlL Rep 139 (fire insurance), where the assured claimed that a bungalow had been accidentally destroyed by fire, and the Court found that the building had been set alight intentionally; *Shoot v Hill* (1936) 55 LlL Rep 29, where a claim under a jewellery policy was held to be fraudulent as the alleged burglary never took place, but had been an 'inside job' on the part of the insured, 'the appearance of an entry into the shop and a theft of articles from it has been staged and . . . in truth and in fact there was nothing at all in the shape of a robbery from the shop'. (Branson J, at 37.) A claim in respect of alleged damage by fire to the premises caused by the supposed thief, i e in that the contents of every case and drawer was also found to be fraudulent (see pp 38–9); *Herman v Phoenix Assurance Co Ltd* (1928) 18 LlL Rep 371, CA (fire insurance), where furs alleged by the insured to be on the premises at the time of the fire were not there at all, and the Court of Appeal held that the claim was a fraudulent one. Evidence was called by the insurance company to show that, in the case of furs alleged to be burnt, traces of the burnt skin, heads and other indestructible parts of the furs are usually found. But in the present case no ash consistent with burnt furs was found. See further, *R v Boynes* (1843) 1 Car & Kir 65, where the prisoner was indicted for making a false statement of loss; *Watkins & Davis Ltd v Legal and General Assurance Co Ltd* [1981] 1 Lloyd's Rep 674 (fire insurance), where the insurers proved that a fire in a warehouse had been deliberately started by the assured; *S & M Carpets (London) Ltd v Cornhill Insurance Co Ltd* [1982] 1 Lloyd's Rep 423, CA (fire insurance), where a fire in a carpet shop had been deliberately started by the assured's managing director.

10 *Thompson v Hopper* (1858) EB & E 1038 (marine insurance) per Bramwell B, at 1046.

11 *Smith v Queen Insurance Co* (1868) 12 NBR (1 Han) 311, where the assured falsely stated that he was absent at the time of the fire.

12 *R v Boynes* (supra), where the statutory declaration furnished by the assured was accompanied by a forged certificate; *Newis v General Accident Fire and Life Assurance Corpn* (1910) 11 CLR 620,

More usually, the fraudulent claim consists of an exaggeration of the extent of the loss. In dealing with exaggerated claims it is necessary to bear in mind that the assured may honestly over-estimate his loss,[13] and sometimes it may have been due to a mistake.[14] In any case the extent and value of the loss are largely matters of opinion.[15]

An exaggerated claim is to be considered fraudulent in the following cases:

1 Where the assured clearly intended to defraud the insurers:[16]
2 Where the over-estimate of his loss is so excessive as to lead to the inference that the assured cannot have made the claim honestly, but must have intended to defraud the insurers;[17]

---

where an ante-dated cheque for the premium was given after the fire; *Singh v Yorkshire Insurance Co Ltd* (1917) 17 NSWLR 312, where false evidence was given before the arbitrator; *Harris v Evans* (1924) 19 LlL Rep 303, 346 (fire insurance), where the assured hoped to support a fraudulent claim by their stock sheet; *Albion Mills Co v H Babington Hill* (1922) 12 LlL Rep 96 (fire insurance), where there were alterations in the stock books: *Wisenthal v World Auxiliary Insurance Corpn Ltd* (1930) 38 LlL Rep 54 (burglary insurance), where the jury found that fraudulent means or devices were used by the insured in concealing a stock book and facts and documents relating to a banking account; *Grunther Industrial Developments Ltd and GID Ltd v Federated Employers Insurance Association Ltd* [1976] 2 Lloyd's Rep 259, CA (consequential loss insurance), where the jury found that the claim was not fraudulent and that the documents supporting it has not been forged; *Black King Shipping Corpn and Wayang (Panama) SA v Massie, The Litsion Pride* [1985] 1 Lloyd's Rep 437 (marine insurance), where a letter had been concocted and false information invented in order to deceive the insurers. (See the judgment of Hirst J, ibid, at 507).

13 *Newcastle Fire Insurance Co v MacMorran & Co* (1815) 3 Dow 255, HL (fire insurance) per Lord Eldon, at 262; *Wood v Masterman* (1822) cited in Ellis *Law of Fire and Life Assurance and Annuities,* 2nd Edn p 14 (fire insurance), where Lord Tenterden CJ, told the jury that if they thought that the plaintiff had overrated the amount or value of his loss from mere mistake or misapprehension, they would find only for such loss or damage as he had actually incurred; but if, on the other hand, they thought that he had done so with a fraudulent intent, then they should find a verdict for the defendant; *Chapman v Pole* (1870) 22 LT 306 (fire insurance) per Cockburn CJ, at 307; *South African Assurance Co v Dunstan* (1894) 1 Off Rep (Transvaal) 272; *Prosser v Ocean Accident and Guarantee Corpn* (1910) 29 NZLR 1157; *London Assurance v Clare* (1937) 57 LlL Rep 254 (fire insurance), where Goddard J in directing the jury (at 268), said that mere exaggeration was not conclusive evidence of fraud, for a man might honestly have an exaggerated idea of the value of his stock.

14 *Park v Phoenix Insurance Co* (1859) 19 UCR 110, where it was held that the insurers must prove that the over-valuation by the assured was not due to a mistake; *Devlin v Westchester Fire Insurance Co* [1925] 3 DLR 1109.

15 *Harrison v Western Assurance Co* (1903) 33 SCR 473; *McGibbon v Imperial Fire Insurance Co* (1881) 14 NSR (2 G & R) 6; *Northern Assurance Co v Provost* (1881) 25 LCJ 211, where an apparent over-valuation of buildings was held not to be fraudulent.

16 *Chapman v Pole* (supra); *Grenier v Monarch Fire and Life Assurance Co* (1859) 3 LCJ 100; *Seghetti v Queen Insurance Co* (1866) 10 LCJ 243; *Haase v Evans* (1934) 48 LlL Rep 131 (all risks insurance).

17 *Northern Assurance Co v Provost* (supra), where an excess of 20 per cent was held not to be evidence of fraud; *Critchley v Atlas Insurance Co* (1906) 9 NZGazLR 6, where it was held that, if the loss exceeded the sum insured, an excessive claim was no proof of fraud, unless the exaggeration was very gross; *Worsley v Wood* (1796) 6 Term Rep 710, where the claim was for £7,000 and the jury awarded £3,000; *Levy v Baillie* (1831) 7 Bing 349, where the plaintiff claimed £1,085 and the jury awarded £500; *Goulstone v Royal Insurance Co* (1858) 1 F & F 276, where the assured claimed £200 in respect of property worth £50; *Chapman v Pole* (1870) 22 LT 306, where the assured claimed (inter alia) £30 for the contents of a room, the real value of which was £3, and £33 for crockery worth a few shillings; *Beauchamp v Faber* (1898) 3 ComCas 308, where the assured claimed £11,600, and the umpire found the value of the stock to be only £4,656; *Hodgkins v Wrightson* (1910) Times 24 March (burglary insurance), where the claim was for £507 and the jury awarded £150; *Central Bank of India Ltd v Guardian Assurance Co Ltd* (1936) 54 LlL Rep 247, PC, where the actual loss was found to be 43,000 rupees on a claim for over 4,000,000 rupees;

3 Where the over-estimate, though not deliberately put forward with the directly fraudulent intent of inducing the insurers to pay the full amount claimed, is designedly made for the purpose of fixing a basis upon which to negotiate with the insurers.[18]

This condition, like any other condition, may be waived;[19] but no waiver is to be inferred from the fact that the insurers refrain from requiring further proofs[20] or refer the question of the amount of the loss to loss adjusters.[1]

A claim which is honestly made in the mistaken belief that a loss has happened, has no effect on the validity of the policy.[2]

The insurers are not entitled to recover as damages for breach of contract the expenses incurred in investigating a fraudulent claim.[3]

Larocque v Royal Insurance Co (1878) 23 LCJ 217, where the assured claimed more than double the amount subsequently proved to be the amount of the loss; *McLeod v Citizens' Insurance Co* (1897), 13 NSR 21, where the assured stated that the building insured was worth $2,000, though its real value was not more than $500; *Gervais v Liverpool, London and Globe Insurance Co* (1920) QR 57 SC 407, where a carriage bought for $7 was insured for $300, being valued by the assured at $600; cf *McMillan v Gore District Mutual Fire Insurance Co* (1870) 21 UP 123, where the assured, who was charged with fraud and arson, had claimed a sum twelve times greater than the amount awarded by the jury, and the Court granted a new trial although the defence of arson failed; and see *Meagher v London and Lancashire Fire Insurance Co* (1881) 7 VLR 390; *London Assurance v Clare* (1937) 57 LlL Rep 254 (fire insurance), where a claim was made for £81,000 in respect of stock which had earlier been offered for sale at £20,000, and was held to be fraudulent; *Harris v Evans* (1924) 19 LlL Rep 303, 346 (fire insurance), where the insured claimed that a loss of £4,701 had been incurred, and the insurer contended that the claim was exaggerated to such an extent that the insured must have known that it was false.

18 *Norton v Royal Fire and Life Assurance Co* (1885) Times 12 August, CA, where the decision of the Court below ((1885) 1 TLR 460) was revsd on the ground that the view that the plaintiff had made a statement which he knew to be false in order that the company might act upon it seemed hardly to have been presented to the jury, and the Court was, therefore, of opinion that the verdict obtained on that point was unsatisfactory; cf *Chapman v Pole* (supra). But in *Ewer v National Employers' Mutual General Insurance Association Ltd* [1937] 2 All ER 193 there was held to be no fraud where the assured claimed the cost price of new articles in replacement, though he knew that this was probably only a bargaining figure; see further, *London Assurance v Clare* (1937) 57 LlL Rep 254 (fire insurance), where Goddard J, in directing the jury (at 268) said that 'mere exaggeration was not conclusive evidence of fraud for a man might honestly have an exaggerated idea of the value of the stock, or suggest a high figure as a bargaining price.'

19 *British American Assurance Co v Wilkinson* (1876) 23 Gr 151, where the claim was compromised.

20 *Cashman v London and Liverpool Fire Insurance Co* (1862) 10 NBR (5 All) 246, where it was held that the fact that an officer of the isurers had given evidence at a magisterial enquiry into the cause of the fire, held under a statute, was no evidence of waiver.

1 *Larocque v Royal Insurance Co* (supra).

2 *North British and Mercantile Insurance Co v Stewart* 1871 9 Macph (Ct of Sess) 534 (life insurance), where it appeared that the life insured was not dead.

3 *London Assurance v Clare* (1937) 57 LlL Rep 254 (fire insurance), where Goddard J said (at 270): '(The insurers) repudiated the contract and they did not pay thereby getting, of course, a great advantage because they did not have to pay what they would have had to pay if the claim had not been fraudulent. They pay nothing, and any part of the expenses that they have been put to which is properly regarded as costs, no doubt the Taxing Master will take into account when he is dealing with the question of costs; but to treat this sum as damages for a breach of contract seems to me to be going beyond anything that has ever been done before, and no authority has been suggested or cited to me which would suggest that the Courts have ever applied the principle of damages for breach of contract to such a matter . . . I find some difficulty in envisaging how they are in a worse position than they would have been in if it had been an honest claim, in which case they would still have to investigate. But apart from that, I think the damages are far too remote to be said to be damages for breach of contract.'

E THE INSURANCE OMBUDSMAN BUREAU

In 1981 the Insurance Ombudsman Bureau[4] was set up to deal with claims of dissatisfied policyholders. A considerable number of insurance companies are members of the scheme which the Bureau operates.[5]

A claimant, whose insurance company is a member, is entitled to submit a claim to the Insurance Ombudsman for decision if:

- (i) it has been considered by senior management of the insurance company;
- (ii) the claimant has not instituted proceedings in a court of law or made reference to arbitration unless proceedings have been discontinued or the reference has been withdrawn prior to final judgment;
- (iii) the claim has not been considered previously (unless new evidence is now available); and
- (iv) the claim has been received by the Bureau within 6 months of the insurance company making its decision known to the claimant.

The Ombudsman has power to make an award binding on the insurance company up to £100,000.

The scheme relates only to policies issued in the United Kingdom, and to policies effected by or for the benefit of natural persons. It does not apply to industrial assurance policies.

---

4 The address of the Bureau is 31 Southampton Row, London WC1B 5HJ.

5 A list of the members of the scheme is contained in the Bureau's Annual Report for 1984, pp 43–47.

CHAPTER 40

Burden of proof

It is necessary to consider the question of the burden of proof of the loss and also the burden of proof that the loss falls within an exception. Further, it is important to realize that in some cases the undertaking of the insurer is a qualified one and this may affect the burden.

A PROOF OF LOSS

1 On whom the burden lies

The onus of proving that the loss was caused by a peril insured against lies on the assured.[1] Unless he discharges the onus, the claim must fail.[2]

Thus, in *AB v Northern Accident Insurance Co*[3] a claim was made under a policy against accidental blood poisoning by a medical man who alleged that he had been accidentally infected with syphilis through cutting his finger whilst operating on a patient, who, at the time, he did not suspect to be suffering from syphilis. But, as he refused to name the patient, for reasons of medical etiquette, and did not call another doctor who had previously attended her, and knew

1 *British and Foreign Marine Insurance Co v Gaunt* [1921] 2 AC 41 (marine insurance) per Lord Sumner, at 58.

2 *Re Scarr and General Accident Assurance Corpn* [1905] 1 KB 387 (personal accident insurance), where the assured died from dilatation of the heart due to extra exertion, and it was held on the facts that there was no accident; *Tootal, Broadhurst, Lee Co v London and Lancashire Fire Insurance Co* (1908) Times 21 May (fire insurance); *Austin v Drewe* (1816) 6 Taunt 436 (fire insurance); *London and Manchester Plate Glass Co v Heath* [1913] 3 KB 411, CA (plate glass insurance); *Century Bank of New York v Mountain* (1914) 112 LT 484, CA (insurance of securities); *Whitehead v Hullett* (1946) 79 LlL Rep 410 (all risks insurance), where the assured failed to establish that the necklace was stolen from him on a particular day when he attended the Law Courts; *Weyerhaeuser v Evans* (1932) 43 LlL Rep 62 (personal accident insurance), where the personal representatives of the assured failed to prove that there was any accident or accidental injury causing the pimple, and consequently had not discharged the onus of showing that the death of the assured was due to bodily injury by accident; *Prudential Staff Union v Hall* [1947] KB 685, 80 LlL Rep 410 (burglary insurance) where the assured failed to prove that any loss by burglary or housebreaking had taken place, and the claim failed; *Richard Aubrey Film Productions Ltd v Graham* [1960] 2 Lloyd's Rep 101 (all risks insurance), where the assured was put to strict proof that a film negative had been stolen and succeeded in proving it: *NE Neter & Co Ltd v Licenses and General Insurance Co Ltd* [1944] 1 All ER 341, 77 LlL Rep 202 (marine insurance), where there was insufficient proof that the proximate cause of the damage to the cargo was the rough weather experienced on the voyage; *Anderson v Norwich Union Fire Insurance Society Ltd* [1977] 1 Lloyd's Rep 253, CA, where the policy covered damage due to 'storm, tempest or flood', and the insured failed to show that the damage to the house was caused by the peril insured against; *Rhesa Shipping Co SA v Edmunds, The Popi M* [1985] 2 All ER 712, [1985] 1 WLR 948, HL (marine insurance), where the assured was held not to have discharged the burden of proving that the vessel was lost by perils of the sea; *Courtaulds plc and Courtaulds (Belgium) SA v Lissenden* [1986] 1 Lloyd's Rep 368 (contingency insurance), where the assured failed to prove that a loss had been 'sustained on account of forgery or fabrication of securities'.

3 1896 24 R (Ct of Sess) 258.

that she was suffering from syphilis, it was held that he had failed to discharge the onus of proof.

In all cases the insurer is entitled to require the assured to give strict proof that a loss has been incurred. Where this course is adopted, the insurer is not entitled to put forward some affirmative case which has not been pleaded or alleged.

In *Regina Fur Co Ltd v Bossom*:[4]

> Furs were insured under an 'all risks' insurance policy. The insurance company denied liability and put the insured to strict proof of the claim that they had, in fact, been stolen.
> *Held,* the burden of proving the loss by theft was on the assured, and on the facts of the case, this burden had not been discharged.

Lord Evershed MR observed:[5]

> 'I think that a defendant—whether he is an underwriter or any other kind of defendant—is entitled to say, by way of defence, "I require this case to be strictly proved, and admit nothing". Where such is the defence, the onus remains throughout upon the plaintiffs to establish the case they are alleging. Where such is the form of pleading, it is not only obligatory upon the defendants but it is not even permissible for them to proceed to put forward some affirmative case which they have not pleaded or alleged; and it is not, therefore, right that they should, by cross-examination of the plaintiffs or otherwise, suggest such an affirmative case. The defendants are acting correctly if they follow the course adopted in this case—that is, so to challenge, at each point, and by proper evidence, where it is advisable, and by cross-examination, the case which the plaintiffs seek to make good.'

Sellers LJ, said that in order to succeed the insured had to prove a loss of goods covered by the policy due to a risk insured against, and that obligation remained nonetheless where the evidence called by the underwriter might establish or tend seriously to show that a crime had been committed by the claimant. If the evidence of all the witnesses and the effect of all the documents left the Court in doubt on the question whether or not there had been a fortuitous loss—i e by breaking and entering and stealing—the insured would not be entitled to judgment as he would not have established the fact that the loss of the goods was due to a risk insured by the policy.[6]

The burden of proving that he did not cause the loss himself does not lie on the insured.

Thus, in *Slattery v Mance*:[7]

> A yacht was insured under a marine insurance policy. It was totally destroyed by fire, which was one of the perils insured against. Arson was alleged by the underwriter.
> *Held,* once it was shown that the loss was caused by fire, the plaintiff had made out a prima facie case, and the onus was on the underwriter to show that on a balance of probabilities the fire was caused or connived at by the plaintiff.

Salmon J said:[8]

> 'In my judgment once it is shown that the loss has been caused by fire, the plaintiff has made out a prima facie case and the onus is upon the defendant to show on a balance of probabilities

---

4 [1958] 2 Lloyd's Rep 425, CA.

5 Ibid, at 428. This direction as to the form of pleading was followed by McNair J in *Roselodge Ltd (formerly Rose Diamond Products Ltd) v Castle* [1966] 2 Lloyd's Rep 113 (jewellers' block policy) at 119, 120. His Lordship, however, observed (ibid, at 120): 'The difference between putting up an affirmative case of fraud and seeking to establish by cross-examination that the plaintiffs' chief witness is putting forward a false story with perjured evidence is I feel rather fine.'

6 [1958] 2 Lloyd's Rep at 434.

7 [1962] 1 Lloyd's Rep 60.

8 Ibid, at 62; *S & M Carpets (London) Ltd v Cornhill Insurance Co Ltd* [1981] 1 Lloyd's Rep 667 (fire insurance) at 668 (per Watkins J); affd [1982] 1 Lloyd's Rep 423, CA. *Watkins & Davis Ltd v Legal and General Assurance Co Ltd* [1981] 1 Lloyd's Rep 674 (fire insurance) at 677 (per Neill J).

that the fire was caused or connived at by the plaintiff. Accordingly, if at the end of the day, the jury come to the conclusion that the loss is equally consistent with arson as it is with an accidental fire, the onus being on the defendant, the plaintiff will win on that issue.'

In that case the learned Judge also observed that the principle of the Common Law was that he who asserted must prove, and that there was no principle and no authority that he knew of for the proposition that when the facts were peculiarly within the knowledge of the person against whom the assertion, e g of arson was made, the onus shifted to that person.[9]

2 Degree of proof required

The assured is not, however, required to prove the cause of the loss conclusively. All that he need do is to establish a prima facie case.[10]

Thus, in one case[11] Lord Guthrie said:[12]

> 'Outside the region of mathematics, proof is never anything more than probability. It is for the Court in each case to say whether the probability is so slight, or so equally balanced by counter-probabilities, that nothing more results than a surmise; or whether the probabilities are so strong and so one-sided as to amount to legal proof. The abstract possibility of mistake can never be excluded.'

When he has done this, the onus shifts to the insurers to show that the loss was not caused by a peril insured against, and unless they prove this conclusively, they have not discharged the onus cast on them.[13]

Thus, in the case of personal accident insurance, if the assured dies after an accident, the onus of proving that the death is due to the accident and not to natural causes lies on the person claiming under the policy; and if he is unable to establish a prima facie case of accident, his claim must fail.[14]

Where, however, the more natural and reasonable inference to be drawn from the circumstances in which the death takes place, is that the death was accidental, the claimant has discharged the onus.[15]

---

9 [1962] 1 Lloyd's Rep 60, at 62.

10 *Gorman v Hand-in-Hand Insurance Co* (1877) IR 11 CL 224 (fire insurance); *Ross v Hunter* (1790) 4 Term Rep 33 (marine insurance); *MacDonald v Refuge Assurance Co* 1890 17 R (Ct of Sess) 955 (personal accident insurance); *Macbeth & Co v King* (1916) 115 LT 221 (marine insurance).

11 *Nobel's Explosive Co v Britih Dominions General Insurance Co* [1918] WC & Ins Rep 106.

12 Ibid, at 108.

13 *Samuels v Tompson* (1910) Times 12 November (burglary insurance), where the insurers denied that there had been a burglary, and there being evidence that the theft, if any, had not been committed from the outside, failed to account for one only of the persons who might have committed it. Where there is evidence on both sides proper to be left to the jury, the appellate tribunal will not interfere with the verdict of the jury. It must be shown that the verdict was one which could not reasonably have been found upon the evidence before the jury: *Atkinson v Dominion of Canada Guarantee and Accident Co* (1908) 16 OLR 619; *Pawsey & Co v Scottish Union and National Insurance Co* (1908) Times 17 October, PC (fire insurance).

14 *McKechnie's Trustees v Scottish Accident Insurance Co* 1889 17 R (Ct of Sess) 6, where the assured was thrown out of a cart and died, and the evidence left it doubtful whether the death was due to the accident or to kidney disease.

15 *Trew v Railway Passengers' Assurance Co* (1861) 6 H & N 839, where the assured went to bathe and disappeared, a naked body being afterwards washed up 200 miles away, which there was evidence to identify as his; *Ballantine v Employers' Insurance Co of Great Britain* 1893 21 R (Ct of Sess) 305, where the assured fell into the water whilst fishing and was drowned, and the insurers contended that the death was due to disease; *Young v Maryland Casualty Co* (1909) 14 BCR 146, where the assured who had gone to fish was found lying in 27 inches of water; *Youlden v London Guarantee and Accident Co* (1912) 26 OLR 75, where the assured died after lifting a weight, and it was held that, as lifting the weight was a possible cause of death, and the only one of several possible causes which in fact did exist, the inference was to be drawn that it was the cause of death.

In particular, where it is proved that the assured was found drowned, in circumstances equally consistent with accident or suicide, the inference to be drawn from the proved facts is that the death was accidental since there is a presumption of law against suicide.[16]

Thus, Lord MacDonald said:[17]

> 'There might be many cases in which, where the insurance is against death by accident, nothing at all could be recovered if it was essential that the pursuer must prove conclusively that the cause of death was accident, not suicide. In my opinion, if the pursuer brings forward evidence of the death having happened in such a manner as naturally points to accident, she fulfils all that is incumbent on her. To call upon the pursuer to disprove negatively other causes of death, would be to put upon her a burden which is not according to a fair reading of the contract.'

In the case of fire insurance, direct evidence as to the cause of the fire is not always available, and accordingly the success or failure of the claim depends upon whether the onus of proof, upon the materials before the Court, has been discharged. Where the property is actually burned, the loss is, in fact, caused by fire and the policy, therefore, covers it, unless the insurers succeed in establishing that the fire was originated by an excepted cause. Where the result of the evidence is to leave the cause of the fire in doubt, the insurers have not discharged the onus of proof and the assured, therefore, will succeed.[18]

Further, if the insurers rely on the defence of arson by or with the privity of the assured, the charge, being in effect a criminal charge, must be strictly proved.[19] Hence, where the evidence leaves it open whether the loss was caused by accidental fire or by arson, the assured must recover since the presumption against crime operates in his favour.[20]

---

16 *Harvey v Ocean Accident and Guarantee Corpn* [1905] 2 IR 1, CA; *Moretti v Dominion of Canada Guarantee and Accident Assurance Co* [1923] 3 WWR 1; *London Life Insurance Co v Lang Shirt Co's Trustee* [1929] SCR 117, where it was held that, to rebut the presumption, the facts must not be merely consistent with suicide, but must be inconsistent with any other rational conclusion.

17 *MacDonald v Refuge Assurance Co* 1890 17 R (Ct of Sess) 955 at 957.

18 *Gorman v Hand-in-Hand Insurance Co* (1877) IR 11 CL 224 (fire insurance); *Tootal, Broadhurst, Lee Co v London and Lancashire Fire Insurance Co* (1908) Times 21 May (fire insurance); *Pawsey & Co v Scottish Union and National Insurance Co* (1908) Times 17 October, PC (fire insurance).

19 *Herbert v Poland* (1932) 44 LlL Rep 139 (fire insurance) per Swift J, at 142, where a defence of arson succeeded. A plea of arson is rarely used in practice, and should be as far as possible avoided since a plea of fraud will be sufficient, if proved, to defeat the assured's claim. See *Britton v Royal Insurance Co* (1866) 4 F & F 905 per Willes J, at 908: 'The real question was whether there had been fraud, and he should advise the jury that, if satisfied that there was, they need not enter into the question of arson, and that it would be better to avoid entering unnecessarily into what would be virtually an inquiry into a criminal charge. If there was arson, it could only have been with a view to effectuate a fraud; and it was so extremely inconvenient to embarrass a civil suit with a collateral inquiry into a charge of felony that he deemed it better to put it out of the case.' See also, *Newcastle Fire Insurance Co v MacMorran & Co* (1815) 3 Dow 255, HL (fire insurance) per Lord Eldon, at 261; *Goulstone v Royal Insurance Co* (1858) 1 F & F 276 (fire insurance) per Pollock CB, at 279; *Prosser v Ocean, Accident and Guarantee Corpn* (1910) 29 NZLR 1157 (fire insurance); *Watkins and Davis Ltd v Legal and General Assurance Co Ltd* [1981] 1 Lloyd's Rep 674 (fire insurance), where the insurers proved that a fire in a warehouse had been deliberately started by the assured (see the judgment of Neill J, ibid, at 680–681); *S and M Carpets (London) Ltd v Cornhill Insurance Co Ltd* [1982] 1 Lloyd's Rep 423, CA (fire insurance), where the insurers established that a fire in a carpet shop had been started by the assured's managing director; and cf *Maguire v Liverpool and London Fire and Life Insurance* (1857) 7 LCR 343, where the Court refused to stay the proceedings until the assured had been tried upon a pending charge of arson.

20 *Thurtell v Beaumont* (1823) 1 Bing 339 (fire insurance); *Britton v Royal Insurance Co* (1866)

If the property is not actually burned, but the facts proved are sufficient upon a balance of probabilities to enable an inference to be drawn as to the cause of loss, the onus of proof is discharged and the assured will succeed or fail according as the inference is drawn that the cause of loss falls within the policy or not.

If, on the other hand, the facts proved are insufficient to enable any inference to be drawn at all, the assured must fail, since he has not proved that the loss was caused by fire.

In the case of an 'all risks' policy, it is sufficient to show that the loss was caused by a casualty or something accidental without proving the exact nature of the casualty or accident which caused the loss.[1]

B PROOF THAT THE LOSS FALLS WITHIN AN EXCEPTION

1 On whom the burden lies

(a) The general rule

When the assured has proved a prima facie case of loss within the policy, the insurers are entitled to show that the loss falls within an exception.[2]

The burden of proving that the loss was caused by an excepted peril lies upon them. Thus, in a case relating to fire insurance[3] Bigham J, in summing up to the jury, said:

> 'The excuses for refusing to pay are to be found indorsed upon the policies, and they are as much part of the contract as that which is expressed on the front of the policy, by which they undertake to pay in the event of fire. The only difference is this, and it is an important difference, and one that you must bear in mind, that, whereas it is for the [insured] to show that their goods have been burned, it is for the [insurers] to show to your satisfaction that the circumstances which constitute an excuse for non-payment of the claim has in fact arisen. To use common legal language, the onus of proof, so far as the excuse goes, is an onus which rests upon the [insurance] company . . . And, finally, you must remember that this is what is called an exception in the policy, and it is for the [insurers] to satisfy you that the exception has arisen which excuses them. They must not leave your minds in any reasonable doubt about it, because if they do, they may have not discharged the burden which is upon them.'

(b) Modification by the terms of the policy

The general rule that the onus of proving that the loss falls within an exception

---

4 F & F 905 (fire insurance); *MacDonald v Refuge Assurance Co* 1890 17 R (Ct of Sess) 955 (personal accident insurance); *Harvey v Ocean, Accident and Guarantee Corpn* [1905] 2 IR 1, CA (personal accident insurance); cf *Dominion Trust Co v New York Life Insurance Co* [1919] AC 254, PC (life insurance).

1 *British and Foreign Marine Insurance Co v Gaunt* [1921] 2 AC 41, 7 LlL Rep 62. Cf *Theodorou v Chester* [1951] 1 Lloyd's Rep 204, where Croom-Johnson J held that the assured under an 'all risks' policy was required to prove that the loss was due to an abnormal peril, and that he was also required to disprove any counter-theory put forward by the insurers which was designed to show that the loss had been caused by abnormal transit risks.

2 *Gorman v Hand-in-Hand Insurance Co* (1877) IR 11 CL 224 (fire insurance) per Palles CB, at 230; *Hurst v Evans* [1917] 1 KB 352 (jewellery insurance); cf *Walker v Railway Passengers' Assurance Co* (1910) 129 LT Jo 64, CA (personal accident insurance).

3 *Tootal, Broadhurst, Lee Co v London and Lancashire Fire Insurance Co* (1908) Times 21 May (fire insurance).

lies on the insurers, may be modified by the terms of the policy, and the onus of proof may accordingly be shifted so as to require the assured to prove, as part of his case, that the loss does not fall within an exception.[4] The question whether the onus of proof has been shifted, and, if so, to what extent, depends upon the language of the particular policy.

Sometimes the policy contains a condition by the terms of which the assured is required to prove to the satisfaction of the insurers that the loss was not caused by an excepted peril. In such a case the condition does not directly affect the onus of proof in the event of proceedings being taken to enforce the claim. If the insurers rely on an exception, the onus of proof is not shifted. The effect of the condition is merely to require the assured, as part of the preliminary proof, to satisfy the insurers as to the cause of the loss, and it is performed when the assured has furnished proofs which ought to have satisfied the insurers as reasonable men.

The insurers may contest the claim on the ground that the condition has not been performed; but the issue thus raised is only a subsidiary one.

The policy, on the other hand, may expressly shift the onus of proof in any proceedings that may be taken to enforce the claim, by imposing upon the assured the obligation of proving that the loss was not caused by an excepted peril. The onus of proof may be shifted by an express condition to that effect.[5]

In the case of fire insurance, the policy sometimes contains a condition that if a fire takes place at a time when an excepted peril, such as an earthquake or a civil commotion, is in operation, the insurers are not to be liable for any loss occasioned by the fire, unless the assured proves that the fire arose independently.

Such a condition leaves the insurers subject to the onus of proving that the excepted peril was in operation at the time of the fire. But once they have discharged this onus, it shifts to the assured.[6] The assured must then prove that the fire was not, in fact, caused by earthquake,[7] or civil commotion,[8] as the case may be, and, if he fails to discharge the onus, he cannot recover.[9]

---

4 *Levy v Assicurazioni Generali* [1940] AC 791, PC (fire insurance) per Luxmoore LJ, at 798: 'As a matter of agreement between parties, the onus of proof of any particular fact, or of its non-existence, may be placed on either party in accordance with the agreement made between them.' In this case the policy provided that 'any loss or damage happening during the existence of abnormal conditions . . . arising out of or in connection with any of the said occurrences shall be deemed to be loss or damage which is not covered by this insurance, except to the extent that the insured shall prove that such loss or damage happened independently of the existence of such abnormal conditions. In any action, suit or other proceeding, where the company alleges that by reason of the provisions of this condition any loss or damage is not covered by this insurance, the burden of proving that such loss or damage is covered shall be upon the insured.'

5 *Re Hooley Hill Rubber and Chemical Co Ltd and Royal Insurance Co Ltd* [1920] 1 KB 257, CA (fire insurance) per Scrutton LJ, at 273.

6 *Motor Union Insurance Co Ltd v Boggan* (1923) 130 LT 588, HL (motor insurance) per Lord Birkenhead, at 590; *Lindsay and Pirie v General Accident Fire and Life Assurance Corpn Ltd* [1914] App D 574.

7 *Pawsey & Co v Scottish Union and National Insurance Co* (1908) Times, 17 October, PC.

8 *Lindsay and Pirie v General Accident Fire and Life Assurance Corpn Ltd* (supra); *Levy v Assicurazioni Generali* (supra) (fire insurance).

9 The onus is not discharged merely by adducing evidence which is not contradicted by other evidence called by the insurers. It is for the jury to decide whether on the evidence the onus has been discharged: *Winnipeg Electric Co v Geel* [1932] AC 690, PC.

2 Degree of proof required

The insurers must produce affirmative evidence of facts supporting their contention, and such evidence must be sufficient to be submitted to the jury.[10] If they fail to produce such evidence, they have not discharged the onus of proof, and the assured accordingly succeeds in his claim.[11]

Thus, in the case of a personal accident insurance policy, if the claimant establishes a prima facie case of death by accident, it will be for the insurers to prove that the death was not due to accident, but to suicide.

The onus of proof is sufficiently discharged if on the balance of probabilities the proper inference to be drawn from the facts is that the loss falls within the exception.[12]

If, however, the insurers discharge the onus of proof laid upon them, the onus shifts back to the assured and he must prove either that his claim falls within an exception to that exception[13] or that, in the circumstances, the exception has no application, e g by reason of waiver,[14] or that, if it does apply, it does not apply to the whole of the loss.[15] In the latter case, the assured must prove what part of the loss is not caused by the excepted peril; and if he fails to discharge the onus of proof in this respect, the whole of the loss will be regarded as falling within the exception.

---

10 *Stormont v Waterloo Life and Casualty Assurance Co* (1858) 1 F & F 22 (life insurance).

11 *Motor Union Insurance Co v Boggan* (1924) 130 LT 588, HL (motor insurance) per Lord Birkenhead, at 590; *Smith v Accident Insurance Co* (1870) LR 5 Exch 302 (personal accident insurance); *Cornish v Accident Insurance Co* (1889) 23 QBD 453, CA (personal accident insurance) per Lindley LJ, at 456; *Canadian Railway Accident Co v Haines* (1911) 44 SCR 386, where the assured when last seen was drunk, and, on his body being found in a river some months later, it was held that the onus of proving that he was drunk at the time of his death lay on the insurers; *Gorman v Hand-in-Hand Insurance Co* (1877) IR 11 CL 224 (fire insurance); *Stormont v Waterloo Life Assurance Co* (supra) (life insurance); *Luciani v British American Assurance Co* (931) 65 OLR 687; *Law Union and Rock Insurance Co v De Wet* [1918] SAR 663, where liability vas denied on the ground that the fire was caused by an explosion.

12 *Cooper v General Accident, Fire and Life Assurance Corpn Ltd* (1923) 128 LT 481, HL (motor insurance), where the insured car was stolen from a garage near Cork and it was held that, having regard to the circumstances, the proper inference to be drawn was that the car was seized by rebels for use in their operations, and not that it was stolen by ordinary thieves, and consequently the loss fell within the exception against 'civil commotion'. In this case Viscount Cave observed (at 483): 'If the loss is occasioned through—that is, if it took place in consequence of—a civil commotion, then it appears to me that the case falls within the exception and there is no need to prove a commotion at the actual time and place where the loss happened'; cf *Dominion Trust Co v New York Life Insurance Co* [1919] AC 254, PC (life insurance); distinguished in *London Life Insurance Co v Lang Shirt Co's Trustee* [1929] SCR 117. See further, *Boggan v Motor Union Insurance Co* (1923) 16 LlL Rep 64, HL (motor insurance), where the insured's chauffeur was stopped by armed men and blindfolded and taken to a farm, and it was held that the loss of the car fell within an exception of 'civil commotion and riot'. In this case Lord Birkenhead said (at 65): 'The circumstances are not those of normal theft. They differ in almost every important incident from what you would expect would happen in the case of an ordinary theft. In the case of an ordinary theft of a motor car the thieves might be expected to remove themselves as quickly as possible from the scene . . . There is an assumption of organisation which differs profoundly from the circumstances of an ordinary theft.'

13 *Rowett, Leaky & Co Ltd v Scottish Provident Institution* [1927] 1 Ch 55, CA (life insurance) per Warrington LJ, at 69.

14 *Re Hooley Hill Rubber and Chemical Co Ltd and Royal Insurance Co Ltd* [1920] 1 KB 257, 1 LlL Rep 3, 25, CA (fire insurance), where the point was not persisted in.

15 *Stanley v Western Insurance Co* (1868) LR 3 Exch 71 (fire insurance) per Martin B, at 75.

C WHERE THE UNDERTAKING OF THE INSURER IS QUALIFIED

In an ordinary case, the undertaking of the insurers is expressed in general terms. If the insurers wish to qualify it, they do so by means of exceptions excluding certain forms of the peril. Hence, it is sufficient for the assured to bring himself prima facie within the terms of the policy, leaving it to the insurers to prove that the case in fact falls within an exception.

A different method of qualification may, however, be adopted. The undertaking itself may be qualified, and the insurers may contract to insure the assured against certain forms only of the peril. If the undertaking is qualified in terms referring to the excluded forms of the peril, the qualification, so far as the scope of the policy is concerned, is equivalent to an exception.

Thus, to take a convenient illustration from fire insurance, an insurance against fire, with an exception against incendiary fires, has the same effect as an insurance against non-incendiary fire. The difference is in a sense a mere difference of phraseology; but it has a material bearing on the onus of proof.

To entitle the insured to recover, he must bring himself within the terms of the qualified undertaking. He must, therefore, prove that the loss was caused not merely by the peril, but by the particular form of it defined in the policy, and this involves, in the case of an insurance against non-incendiary fire, proof that the fire is not an incendiary fire.

1 The principles to be applied

A general statement of the principles to be applied in considering the relation of the burden of proof to the perils excepted in an insurance policy were well stated by Bailhache J in *Munro, Brice & Co v War Risks Association Ltd.*[16] This was a case relating to marine insurance, but the rules there enunciated apply to all cases of insurance. In the course of his judgment he said:[17]

> 'This review of the authorities confirms me in my view that, as the law now stands, when in an action upon a policy of marine insurance the assured has proved that his ship was sunk at sea, he has made out a prima facie case against his underwriters on that policy, and that it is for them to set up the "free of capture and seizure" exception and to bring themselves within it if they can. The rules now applicable for determining the burden of proof in such a case as the present may, I think be stated thus:
>
> 1 The plaintiff must prove such facts as bring him prima facie within the terms of the promise.
> 2 When the promise is qualified by exceptions, the question whether the plaintiff need prove facts which negative their application does not depend upon whether the exceptions are to be found in a separate clause or not. The question depends upon an entirely different consideration, namely, whether the exception is as wide as the promise, and thus qualifies the whole of the promise, or whether it merely excludes from the operation of the promise particular classes of cases which, but for the exception, would fall within it, leaving some part of the general scope of the promise unqualified. If so, it is sufficient for the plaintiff to bring himself prima facie within the terms of the promise, leaving it to the defendant to prove that, although prima facie within its terms, the plaintiff's case is, in fact, within the excluded exceptional class.

---

16 [1918] 2 KB 78 (marine insurance). The judgment was later reversed on the facts: [1920] 3 KB 94, CA. But the rules which the learned Judge expounded in the Court below may still be regarded as the basic principles.

17 [1918] 2 KB 78, at 88.

Illustrations of this rule are actions against common carriers and the analogous cases in which a promisor undertakes to perform a given act unless excused by certain events, as, for example a vendor to deliver, strikes excepted; a charterer to load a ship in a given number of lay-days, subject to the usual exceptions now found in charter-parties.

3 When a promise is qualified by an exception which covers the whole scope of the promise, a plaintiff cannot make out a prima facie case unless he brings himself within the promise as qualified. There is ex hypothesi no unqualified part of the promise for the sole of his foot to stand upon. As an instance I take a marine policy with the particular average franchise. There, reading the promise and the exception together, the promise is not a promise to pay particular average or to pay particular average except in certain events. It is a promise to pay particular average exceeding 3%. To bring himself within that promise a plaintiff must show more than a particular average loss; he must show a particular average loss exceeding 3% . . .

4 Whether a promise is a promise with exceptions or whether it is a qualified promise is in every case a question of construction of the instrument as a whole: see per Palles CB in *Gorman v Hand-in-Hand Insurance Co.*[18]

5 In construing a contract with exceptions it must be borne in mind that a promise with exceptions can generally be turned by an alteration of phraseology into a qualified promise. The form in which the contract is expressed is, therefore, material.'

It must be emphasised that in each case it is a matter of construction whether the words in the policy are to be regarded as a promise with an exception or as a qualified promise.

2 Promise with an exception

In *Macbeth & Co v King*[19] and *British and Burmese Steam Navigation Co Ltd v Liverpool and London War Risks Insurance Association Ltd*,[20] which concerned vessels that had disappeared without trace during the enemy submarine campaign in the First World War, Bailhache J held that in an action on a marine insurance policy insuring against loss by perils of the sea with a clause excepting 'loss by capture, seizure, and consequences of hostilities', it was not necessary for the assured to prove that the ship was not lost by the excepted causes.[1]

The policies of motor insurance concerned in two cases arising out of the troubles in Ireland after the First World War were construed as promises with exceptions, and the insurers had to show that the loss fell within an exception clause relating to various causes including riot and civil commotion.[2]

Further, in *Re National Benefit Assurance Co Ltd*,[3] which concerned a policy on goods which had been lost in transit from Novorossisk to Rostoff-on-Don during the war between the Bolsheviks and the White Russians, Maugham J held that it was for the underwriters to bring themselves, if they could, within an exception clause relating to 'all claims arising from delay'.

---

[18] (1877) IR 11 CL 224.

[19] (1916) 86 LJKB 1004.

[20] (1917) 34 TLR 140.

[1] Bailhache J gave a similar decision in *Munro, Brice & Co v War Risks Association Ltd* [1918] 2 KB 78 though his judgment was reversed by the Court of Appeal on the facts: [1920] 3 KB 94. But the correctness of his decision in *Macbeth & Co v King* (supra) and *British and Burmese Steam Navigation Co Ltd v Liverpool and London War Risks Insurance Association Ltd* (supra) had been doubted by Roche J in *Compania Maritima of Barcelona v Wishart* (1918) 87 LJKB 1027.

[2] *Cooper v General Accident, Fire and Life Assurance Corpn Ltd* (1923) 128 LT 481, 13 LlL Rep 219, HL; *Motor Union Insurance Co v Boggan* (1923) 130 LT 588.

[3] (1933) 45 LlL Rep 147.

Again, in *Greaves v Drysdale*,[4] which concerned an action on a burglary policy, Branson J held that once the assured had proved a loss within the terms of the policy, he was entitled to succeed unless the underwriter could prove that the loss was occasioned by 'members of the assured's staff or household or inmates of the above-mentioned premises.'

3 Qualified promise

A difficult question arises in the case of policies covering not specific perils, such as fire or theft, but loss or damage generally. If a general insurance of this kind is qualified by an exception, e g where the policy is against loss due to any cause except theft by servants, it is possible to regard the qualification as forming part of the definition of the peril.

Thus, in *Hurst v Evans*[5] there was a policy on jewellery which contained a clause exempting the underwriter from liability in case of 'theft or dishonesty by any servant . . . of the assured'. Lush J said that it was impossible to hold that the onus was on the underwriter. To do so would produce absurd results. This was not a case of an insurance against loss caused by some specified reason such as fire or theft. If the contention of the assured were right, he need only aver a loss of jewellery, and it would be for the underwriter to prove that amongst the multitude of causes which might have occasioned the loss, the actual cause was dishonesty of a servant. The assured, however, in his opinion, had to prove that the loss was one against which the defendant had agreed to indemnify him, but in fact he had felt the gravest suspicion whether his own servant was not the cause of the loss.[6]

Since, however, the qualification is expressed by means of an exception, there does not seem to be any reason for making a distinction between general insurance and insurances against specific perils;[7] and it is probable that the ordinary rule applies, and that the onus of proof lies on the insurers, wherever the qualification is so expressed.[8]

---

4 (1935) 53 LlL Rep 16. But the actual decision of the trial Judge was reversed on the facts by the Court of Appeal (1936) 55 LlL Rep 95.

5 [1917] 1 KB 352.

6 *Hurst v Evans* (supra) was not cited in *Greaves v Drysdale* (supra), where Branson J seems to have regarded a similar policy as a promise with exceptions and held that the burden of proof was on the underwriter.

7 Contrast *Samuels v Tompson* (1910) Times 12 November (burglary insurance) where the insurers failed to prove that the theft was committed by a servant, with *Hurst v Evans* (supra).

8 See *Munro, Brice & Co v War Risks Association* [1918] 2 KB 78 (marine insurance), disapproving *Hurst v Evans* (supra).

PART V

The settlement of the claim

CHAPTER 41

Introduction

When the insurers have accepted liability for the claim put forward by the assured,[1] or have been forced to do so as a result of a legal action brought against them or as a result of an arbitration award[2] in favour of the assured, they are under a duty to pay.[3]

Normally the assured is quite free to employ the sum of money which he has received from the insurers in any way he pleases. But in some cases either as a result of a statute or a right conferred by contract other persons may have a right to the proceeds.[4]

Sometimes either before or after the loss the assured assigns to a third party the proceeds of the policy.[5]

In the case of certain types of insurance, instead of paying a sum of money in respect of the loss, the insurers either by virtue of the terms of the contract or of the provisions of the Fires Prevention (Metropolis) Act 1774, have the power of 'reinstatement', i e to replace the insured goods which have been lost or to restore property which has been destroyed or damaged by fire. Sometimes the assured is under a duty to reinstate.[6]

After the insurers have paid for the loss, they are entitled to be subrogated to the rights of the assured.[7]

In some cases the assured may have received indemnification from a person other than the insurers either before or after the loss, and then the question arises as to whether the insurers still have to pay, or, if they have already paid, whether the money can be recovered.[8]

In certain cases where the assured is covered by more than one insurance policy, and one of the insurers concerned has paid for the loss, that insurer has the right to claim 'contribution' from the other insurers concerned.[9]

---

1 For a case where the insured argued that the insurers by taking over the conduct of legal proceedings brought against him by a third party had admitted that the loss fell within the policy, see *Soole v Royal Insurance Co Ltd* [1971] 2 Lloyd's Rep 332, QBD (insurance against claim being brought by third party for breach of restrictive covenant).

2 The law of arbitration is outside the scope of this work, and the reader is referred to Russell *Law of Arbitration* 20th Edn (1982).

3 See Chapter 42.

4 See Chapter 43.

5 See Chapter 44.

6 See Chapter 45.

7 See Chapter 46.

8 See Chapter 47.

9 See Chapter 48.

CHAPTER 42

Payment of the loss

The assured is not entitled to payment until such time as the amount recoverable has, or ought to have, been ascertained.[1]

The Court will not assist an insured to recover the sum insured if to do so would conflict with public policy, e g it will not enforce a contract of insurance in respect of goods which are knowingly imported by him into this country in breach of the customs regulations.[2]

The policy usually contains an express condition that no claim shall be payable until all the requisite particulars have been furnished. It may, in addition, fix a definite number of days before which no claim is to be payable,[3] and may further limit the time within which the claim is to be made on it.[4]

The first matter to be considered is the calculation of the amount recoverable. The loss may not be payable in full due to the presence of clauses in the policy limiting the amount which is recoverable. Sometimes the assured, due to a 'franchise' clause having been inserted in the policy, cannot recover unless the loss exceeds a specified percentage. Payment must usually be made to the assured, and normally it must be made in cash, sometimes with interest being payable in addition. The insurers cannot recover money paid under a mistake of law, but it is otherwise if the mistake is one of fact. In certain cases they may be willing to make an 'ex gratia' payment.

A THE CALCULATION OF THE AMOUNT RECOVERABLE

The object of calculating the amount recoverable is to ascertain the pecuniary

1 *Randall v Lithgow* (1884) 12 QBD 525. See further, *Chandler v Poland* (1933) 44 LlL Rep 349 (burglary insurance), where the sum payable had been agreed by assessors acting on behalf of the insurers, and it was held that a binding agreement had been made and not one subject to the approval of the underwriters; *Frewin v Poland* [1968] 1 Lloyd's Rep 100 (all risks insurance), where the policy contained a Mutual Assessors Clause which stated: 'In the event of loss arising under this Policy the Underwriters and the Assured shall appoint an Assessor to be mutually agreed upon whose findings shall be binding upon both parties.' In commenting on the use of this clause Donaldson J said (ibid, at 102): 'This may be a most useful clause, but the insurance market may like to consider whether its general adoption would not give rise to very considerable problems.' His Lordship then proceeded to give examples of the difficulties which might arise: ibid, at 103.

2 *Geismar v Sun Alliance and London Insurance Ltd and Alliance Assurance Co Ltd* [1977] 2 Lloyd's Rep 62 (theft insurance). Different considerations would apply in cases of unintentional importation or of innocent possession of uncustomed goods: ibid, at 69 (per Talbot J).

3 The period in this case runs from the time when the particulars are delivered: *Rice v Provincial Insurance Co* (1858) 7 CP 548: *Hatton v Provincial Insurance Co* (1858) 7 CP 555.

4 For an example of a policy containing a stipulation to this effect, see *Fitton v Accidental Death Insurance Co* (1864) 17 CBNS 122.

value of the loss, since the obligation of the insurers is to make good the loss by a payment of money.[5]

1 Valued policies

Where the policy under which the claim of the assured arises is a valued policy, the valuation placed on the subject-matter in the policy except in the case of fraud or mistake, conclusively establishes the sum required for the purpose of a full indemnity.[6] The assured is, therefore, dispensed from the necessity of dealing with questions of amount, and is entitled, on proving the fact of his loss, to recover the full amount insured on the subject-matter of insurance.[7]

Thus, a personal accident policy usually specifies the various sums payable according to the nature and effect of the injury sustained. A liability policy of whatever kind binds the insurers to pay any sum for which, in the event insured against, the assured becomes legally liable, the amount of his liability being a matter of calculation in proceedings to which they are not parties, and their obligation being to pay him the amount when calculated, subject to the limits of the policy.[8] Similarly, solvency policies of all kinds and fidelity policies relate to pecuniary losses in the first instance.[9]

As far as marine insurance is concerned, the Marine Insurance Act 1906, s 27(3), provides:

> 'Subject to the provisions of this Act, and in the absence of fraud, the value fixed by the policy is, as beween the insurer and assured, conclusive of the insurable value of the subject intended to be insured, whether the loss be total or partial.'[10]

2 Unvalued policies

Where the policy is an unvalued one, the amount of insurance specified in the

---

[5] *Rayner v Preston* (1881) 18 ChD 1, CA (fire insurance) per Brett LJ, at 9: 'The only result of the policy, if an accident which is within the insurance happens, is a payment of money'; *Prudential Insurance Co v IRC* [1904] 2 KB 658 (life insurance) per Channell J, at 603: 'Where you insure a ship or a house you cannot insure that the ship shall not be lost or the house burned, but what you do insure is that a sum of money shall be paid on the happening of a certain event.' In certain classes of insurance, the insurers may reserve the right of reinstatement. See pp 455–460, post.

[6] But the valuation is only conclusive between the assured and the insurers issuing the policy, and not as regards other policies: *Bousfield v Barnes* (1815) 4 Camp 228.

[7] *Re Law Car and General Insurance Corpn Ltd* [1913] 2 Ch 103, CA, per Cozens-Hardy MR, at 118; *Feise v Aguilar* (1811) 3 Taunt 506 (marine insurance); *Irving v Manning* (1847) 6 CB 391, HL (marine insurance); *Burnand v Rodocanachi, Sons & Co* (1882) 7 App Cas 333 (marine insurance) per Lord Selborne C, at 335. In some cases the practical result may be to give the assured more than a true indemnity: *Maurice v Goldsbrough Mort & Co Ltd* [1939] AC 452, [1939] 3 All ER 63, 64 LlL Rep 1, PC. Where the loss is partial, the agreed value must be taken into account just as in the case of a total loss: *Elcock v Thompson* [1949] 2 KB 755, 82 LlL Rep 892 (fire insurance), where the assured was held entitled to recover upon the basis of the percentage of the depreciation of the real value due to the fire as applied to the agreed value.

[8] Thus, in *Forney v Dominion Insurance Co Ltd* [1969] 1 Lloyd's Rep 502, a solicitors' indemnity insurance policy stated that the insurers liability was limited '(a) in respect of any one claim or number of claims arising out of the same occurrence the sum of £3,000; (b) in respect of all claims . . . the sum of $15,000.'

[9] See e g *Excess Life Assurance Co Ltd v Firemen's Insurance Co of Newark New Jersey* [1982] 2 Lloyd's Rep 599 (fidelity insurance), where the policy limited the liability of losses caused by sales representatives and general agents to US$1,000,000.

[10] As to valued policies in marine insurance, see Ivamy *Marine Insurance* (4th Edn 1985), pp 93–97.

policy does not necessarily reprsent the measure of indemnity.[11] It may, thefore, be disregarded in this connection, except as fixing the maximum sum for which the insurers may be held liable.[12] The assured must prove the extent and value of his loss,[13] and the amount recoverable will be calculated accordingly. The amount thus calculated may correspond with the amount of insurance, but it is recoverable not as being the sum specified in the policy, but as being the sum which has been proved to be required for a full indemnity.[14]

As far as marine insurance is concerned, the Marine Insurance Act 1906, s 28, states:

> 'An unvalued policy is a policy which does not specify the value of the subject-matter insured, but, subject to the limit of the sum insured, leaves the insurable value to be subsequently ascertained, in the manner hereinbefore specified.'[15]

In the case of certain classes of property insurance, e g insurance against burglary or damage, it may, and usually does, become necessary to measure the value of the loss and to consider on what basis the value is to be calculated.[16]

3 Successive losses

The fact that the assured has already recovered in respect of a loss under the policy does not prevent him from recovering for a second loss and any number of subsequent losses during the period of insurance.[17]

---

11 *Vance v Forster* (1841) Ir Cir Rep 47 (fire insurance) per Pennefather B, at 50: 'It has been truly stated that a policy of insurance is a contract of indemnity, and that while the insured may name any sum he likes as the sum for which he will pay a premium, he does not, by so proposing that sum, nor does the company by accepting the risk, conclude themselves as to the amount which the plaintiff is to recover in consequence of the loss—because, although the plaintiff cannot recover beyond the sum insured upon each particular item . . . he cannot recover even that sum unless he proves that he has sustained damage, and then he will recover a sum commensurate to the loss which he has sustained; and therefore what the jury have to inquire is, what is the actual damage sustained by the plaintiff on the subjects of insurance in consequence of the fire?' See also *Chapman v Pole* (1870) 22 LT 306 (fire insurance) per Cockburn CJ, at 307.

12 *Westminster Fire Office v Glasgow Provident Investment Society* (1888) 13 App Cas 699 (fire insurance) per Lord Selborne, at 711; *Hercules Insurance Co v Hunter* 1836 14 Sh (Ct of Sess) 1137; *Vance v Forster* (supra). Hence, if the amount of the loss exceeds the sum insured, the assured can only recover the sum insured: *Curtis & Sons v Matthews* (1918) 119 LT 78, at 81.

13 *Williams v Atlantic Assurance Co Ltd* [1933] 1 KB 81, CA (marine insurance), where the claim failed because the assured could not prove the value of the lost goods.

14 *Vance v Forster* (supra). Therefore until the amount has been fixed, there is no attachable debt in the hands of the insurers: *Randall v Lithgow* (1884) 12 QBD 525. For a case of an unvalued policy relating to a motor car, see *Edney v De Rougemont* (1927) 28 LlL Rep 215 (motor insurance), where the Official Referee took the life of the car at 5 years, and allowed a depreciation of 25 per cent for the first year, and 20 per cent for each of the next two years, and said that £15 should be allowed for the value of the vehicle at the end of its life.

15 As to unvalued policies in marine insurance, see Ivamy *Marine Insurance* (4th Edn, 1985), pp 97–100.

16 See e g *Reynolds and Anderson v Phoenix Assurance Co Ltd* [1978] 2 Lloyd's Rep 440 (fire insurance), where it was held that the true view as to the value was whether the owner for any reason which would appeal to an ordinary man in his position would rebuild the property if he obtained replacement damages or whether his claim for damages was a mere pretence, and that on the facts the insured was entitled to the means to reinstate the property (see the judgment of Forbes J, ibid, at 453); *Pleasurama Ltd v Sun Alliance and London Insurance Ltd* [1979] 1 Lloyd's Rep 389 (fire insurance), where a bingo hall was burnt down, and it was held that the measure of indemnity was the cost of reinstatement and not the difference between the market value of the insured property immediately before the fire and its value immediately after the fire (see the judgment of Parker J, ibid, at 393).

17 *Re Law Car and General Insurance Corpn* (supra) (employers' liability insurance) per Cozens-

As far as marine insurance is concerned, the Marine Insurance Act 1906, s 77(1), states:

> 'Unless the policy otherwise provides, and subject to the provisions of this Act, the insurer is liable for successive losses, even though the total amount of such losses may exceed the sum insured.'

Section 77(2) provides:

> 'Where, under the same policy, a partial loss, which has not been repaired or otherwise made good, is followed by a total loss, the assured can only recover in respect of the total loss . . .'[18]

The policy may, however, fix a maximum sum beyond which the liability of the insurers is not to extend, in which case the policy is exhausted as soon as the maximum sum has been paid; or it may limit the number of claims allowable in respect of a particular kind of loss.

Sometimes the policy contains what is called a 'self-renewing' or 'automatic reinstatement' clause, providing that, on the happening of a loss, subject to a further premium becoming payable, the policy is to remain in force for the full amount of insurance.[19]

4 Simultaneous losses

The same principle applies where the same occurrence gives rise to a number of losses, each of which is sufficient to support a claim against the insurers.[20]

Thus, where a motor accident involves the assured in liability to a number of persons, he is entitled to be indemnified by the insurers against the whole of his liability, unless precluded by the terms of the policy.

Even a limitation on the amount payable may apply only to the liability to a particular individual; and payment in respect of a particular claim of the full amount specified in the policy does not necessarily discharge the insurers from

---

Hardy MR, at 118: 'For it must not be forgotten that a workman is not taken out of the policy by the receipt of a weekly payment. The policy covers any future accidents during the currency of the policy to the same workman, or, in most cases, to any other workman who may take his place.' See also, *Prosser v Lancashire and Yorkshire Accident Insurance Co Ltd* (1890) 6 TLR 285, CA (accident insurance) per Lord Esher MR, at 286; *Pennsylvania Co for Insurances on Lives and Granting Annuities v Mumford* [1920] 2 KB 537, 2 LlL Rep 351, CA (theft insurance); *Crowley v Cohen* (1832) 3 B & Ad 478 (insurance on canal boats); *Joyce v Kennard* (1871) LR 7 QB 78 (insurance by carriers) per Lush J, at 83; *Blackett v Royal Exchange Assurance Co* (1832) 2 Cr & J 244 (marine insurance); *Stewart v Merchants' Marine Insurance Co* (1885) 16 QBD 619, CA (marine insurance); and cf *Sun Fire Office v Hart* (1889) 14 App Cas 98, PC (fire insurance), where there were ten successive fires. See further, *Lidgett v Secretan* (1871) LR 6 CP 616 (marine insurance), where a partial loss occurred under one policy and before the repairs were completed there was a total loss, and it was held that the insured were entitled to recover on the second policy without reference to their claim on the first.

18 See e g *British and Foreign Insurance Co Ltd v Wilson Shipping Co Ltd* [1921] 1 AC 188, 4 LlL Rep 197, 371, HL (marine insurance), where the vessel sustained partial damage from marine risks which was temporarily but not permanently repaired, and was later a total loss from war risks. See generally, Ivamy *Marine Insurance* (4th Edn, 1985), pp 440–441.

19 For an example, see *American Surety Co of New York v Wrightson* (1910) 103 LT 663; *Pennsylvania Co for Insurances on Lives and Granting Annuities v Mumford* (supra) (theft insurance); *Pauls v National Union Fire Insurance Co* [1932] 2 WWR 558 (motor insurance).

20 See *Prosser v Lancashire and Yorkshire Accident Insurance Co* (1890) 6 TLR 285, CA (accident insurance), where the assured, after being paid the claim which he put forward, was allowed to maintain an action upon a further claim based upon subsequent disablement arising out of the accident and not contemplated in the first claim; and cf *Kent v Ocean Accident and Guarantee Corpn* (1909) 20 OLR 226, where the settlement of the first claim was held binding.

liability to indemnify the assured up to the limit fixed by the policy in respect of each succeeding claim which may be put forward.[1] To discharge the insurers from further liability, the policy must make it clear that once the maximum sum has been paid their liability is to cease.

B LIMITATION ON THE AMOUNT RECOVERABLE

When a loss has occurred, the assured will not necessarily be paid the full amount of it by reason of:

1 a contribution clause;
2 an average clause;
3 an excess clause;
4 a clause specifying that a smaller sum will be payable in certain circumstances; or
5 a limitation imposed by a statute.

1 Contribution clause

The policy may, and usually does, contain a condition, usually known as the 'contribution clause', to the effect that, if at the time of any destruction or damage happening to the property insured by it, there is any other insurance effected by or on behalf of the assured covering any of the property destroyed or damaged, the liability of the insurers upon the policy in question is to be limited to their rateable proportion of such destruction or damage.

In this case the right of contribution is so far modified as to limit the amount which the assured is himself entitled to recover under the policy.[2]

---

1 *South Staffordshire Tramways Co v Sickness and Accident Assurance Association* [1891] 1 QB 402, CA, where the assured recovered £833, the amount of their liability to forty persons injured in a tramway accident, notwithstanding the limitation in the policy of £250 'in respect of any one accident'; cf *Pennsylvania Co v Mumford* (supra) (theft insurance).

2 *North British and Mercantile Insurance Co v London, Liverpool and Globe Insurance Co* (1877) 5 ChD 569, CA (fire insurance) per James LJ, at 582. In *Farmers Fire and Hail Insurance Co v Philip* [1924] 2 WWR 205, where there was a special clause permitting 'total concurrent insurance including this policy up to 75 per cent of the value', it was held that the clause merely limited liability in case of concurrent insurance, and if there were no concurrent insurance, the insurers were liable for the full sum insured. Cf *Gale v Motor Union Insurance Co Ltd* [1928] 1 KB 359, 26 LlL Rep 65 (accident insurance), where each policy excluded liability if there were cover under another policy and each contained a rateable proportion clause, and it was held that each should bear half the loss. In *Weddell v Road Transport and General Insurance Co Ltd* [1932] 2 KB 563 (accident insurance) the position was the same except that only one policy had a rateable proportion clause, and it was held that the insured could enforce his whole claim against the insurer he chose. Rowlatt J said (at 567): 'It is to be borne in mind that the risk covered by the clause as to a relative or friend is an extension of the scope of the policy. It gives protection to a person other than the assured. So, as to the clause in the Cornhill Company's policy covering the assured when driving a car not belonging to him, is it an extension of the primary purpose of the policy, which is to cover risks to and in connection with a particular car or cars of the assured mentioned in the schedule? The general purpose of the proviso seems to be to make such extension operate only as a secondary cover, available only in the absence of other insurance regarded as primary, not including (one would suppose) other insurance also of a secondary character. In my judgment it is unreasonable to suppose in each case the proviso in the other policy) with the result that, on the ground in each case that the loss is covered elsewhere, it is covered nowhere. On the contrary, the reasonable construction is to exclude from the category of co-existing cover

He cannot, therefore, demand payment in full from the insurers under such a policy, but only the proportion for which they are liable after all policies subsisting at the time of the loss have been taken into consideration.[3]

The right of contribution may be excluded or limited by the terms of the policy. The policy may contain an express condition excluding contribution altogether; or it may, as in the case of the form known as an 'excess policy', apply only to the balance of the loss remaining after payment in full has been made under other policies. In this case, if there are other policies covering the same property, no question of contribution arises and the assured must exhaust the other policies first.[4]

A contribution clause may, however, contain a provision that if any other insurance effected by or on behalf of the assured is expressed to cover any of the property insured, but is subject to any provisions whereby it is excluded from ranking concurrently with the policy containing the clause either in whole or in part or from contributing rateably to the loss, the liability of the insurers under such policy is to be limited to such proportion of the loss as the sum insured bears to the value of the property.

The presence of this provision in the other policy does not affect the liability of the excess or non-contributory policy, which by reason of its own terms cannot be called into contribution.[5]

---

any cover which is expressed to be itself cancelled by such co-existence, and to hold in such cases that both companies are liable, subject, of course, in both or either case to any rateable proportion clause which there may be.' See also *National Employers Mutual General Insurance Association Ltd v Haydon* [1980] 2 Lloyd's Rep 149, CA (professional indemnity insurance).

3 *North British and Mercantile Insurance Co v London, Liverpool and Globe Insurance Co* (supra) (fire insurance) per Baggallay JA, at 588: 'I am bound to say that in my opinion it [i e the contribution clause] in effect, although it may not be very clearly expressed, really amounts to this, that where there are several policies and where there, in point of fact, is a double insurance, then in order to do away with the old practice of the insured recovering the whole from one of the several insurance offices, and then the one from whom it was recovered being put to obtain contribution from the others, this clause was put in to say that the insured should, in the first instance, proceed against the several insurance companies for the aliquot parts for which they are liable in consequence of that condition'; *Scottish Amicable Heritable Securities Association v Northern Assurance Co* 1883 11 R (Ct of Sess) 287 (fire insurance) per Lord Moncrieff, at 303: 'In the case of double insurances of the same interest with different insurance companies, the assured will not be entitled to recover more than the full amount of the loss he has suffered. It might, on strict legal principle, have been thought that in such cases the assured might select the debtor from whom that amount should be demanded, with the result to him of extinguishing all further claim. But for obvious reasons, both of private right and public policy, in cases of double insurance, this rule of practice has been carried somewhat further, and common insurers of the same interest over the same property may make their right to rateable contribution available in a question with the common creditor.'; SC (in the Court below) ibid, per Lord McLaren, at 290n, 291n: 'The clause of contribution could have had no other object or purpose than to reduce the liability of the subscribing companies to that of underwriters, that is, a liability which the assured should be entitled to recover the full amount of his claim in payments from the several contributories, but should not be entitled, in case of a partial loss, to throw the loss on one or more contributories to the exclusion of the others.' See also, *Nichols & Co v Scottish Union and National Insurance Co* 1885 14 R (Ct of Sess) 1094 (fire insurance) per Cave J, at 1095.

4 There may be contribution between two or more excess policies.

5 Cf *Re Lloyd's Fire Policies and Beaver Speciality Co* [1941] 4 DLR 192, where a fire policy contained a clause requiring the insured to maintain a concurrent policy for a proportion of the risk or be his own insurer for that amount, but he did not do so, taking out merely an excess policy. On a partial loss it was held that the co-insurance clause did not enure to the benefit of the excess insurers who were liable to pay the difference between the proportionate liability of the first insurers and the amount of the loss.

2 Average clause

Policies insuring goods, and occasionally other policies, contain a stipulation called an 'average clause' which provides that if, at the time of the loss, the sum insured is less than the value of the subject-matter of insurance, the assured is to be considered as his own insurer for the difference, and is to bear a rateable proportion of the loss accordingly.

Thus, in the case of fire insurance, a clause usually states:

> 'Whenever a sum insured is declared to be subject to Average, if the Property covered thereby shall at the breaking out of any fire or at the commencement of any destruction or damage to the property by any other peril insured against be collectively of greater value than such sum insured, then the Assured shall be considered as being his own Insurer for the difference and shall bear a rateable share of the loss accordingly.'

This condition is commonly called the 'first'[6] or 'pro rata' condition of average. The effect of this condition is that, though in the case of a total loss the assured receives the whole sum insured, he is, in the event of the loss being partial, entitled to receive only a fractional part of it, the fraction having the sum as numerator and the value of the subject-matter as denominator.

Thus, if a policy containing the condition is for £4,000 upon a subject-matter of the value of £5,000, and the loss is £1,000, the insurer will pay $\frac{4000}{5000}$ths of £1,000, i e £800, and the assured will have to bear the balance of the loss, i e £200 himself. In one case Bailhache J expressed the view, though it was necessary for the decision, that an average clause is now so universally inserted in fire policies on goods that he would read into it a contract with warehousemen to be insurers of goods deposited with them.[7]

Where a Lloyd's policy is declared to be 'subject to average', a condition in similar terms is to be implied, and the effect of the condition is the same although specific portions of the property covered by the Lloyd's policy are also covered by other policies.[8]

The words 'property covered thereby' contained in the average clause set out above mean the property covered by the policy which contains the declaration, and mean that the average clause has no relation to any other policy.[9]

In the case of marine insurance, there is no need for an average clause to be inserted in the policy, for s 81 of the Marine Insurance Act 1906, has the same effect. The section provides that:

> 'Where the assured is insured for an amount less than the insurable value or in the case of a valued policy, for an amount less than the policy valuation, he is deemed to be his own insurer in respect of the uninsured balance.'[10]

In the absence of an average clause, a policy of insurance, other than a policy of marine insurance, is not subject to average, and the assured is entitled to recover the whole amount of his loss up to the sum insured, whether the loss is total or only partial.[11]

---

6 For the 'second' condition of average, see p 503, post.

7 *Carreras v Cunard SS Co* [1918] 1 KB 118, at 123.

8 *Acme Wood Flooring Co v Marten* (1904) 9 Com Cas 157 (fire insurance).

9 Ibid, per Bruce J, at 162.

10 See further, Ivamy *Marine Insurance* (4th Edn, 1985), p 405.

11 *Fifth Liverpool Starr-Bowkett Building Society v Travellers' Accident Insurance Co* (1893) 9 TLR 221; *Anglo-Californian Bank v London and Provincial Marine and General Insurance Co Ltd* (1904) 10 Com Cas 1, per Walton J, at 9; *Vance v Forster* (supra) per Pennefather B, at 50; *Sillem v Thornton* (1854) 3 E & B 868 (fire insurance) per Lord Campbell CJ, at 888.

Thus, in the case of a fidelity guarantee policy in respect of £100, the assured was entitled to the sum even though the loss caused by an employee's embezzlement amounted to £150.[12]

3 Excess clause

Where there is an excess clause, e g in the case of motor insurance policies and public liability insurance policies,[13] the policy specifies a certain sum up to which the assured must bear liability, e g 'the first £100'.

Thus, in the case of motor insurance the effect of such a clause is to relieve the insurers from responsibility for minor accidents altogether, and, in the case of other accidents, to give the assured the right of indemnity only in so far as the loss incurred exceeds the specified limit.[14]

Where there is an excess clause in the policy, and the company makes a bona fide settlement of a claim for damages brought against the insured by a third party, the company will be entitled to recover, e g the first £100 (or such other sum stated in the excess clause), from him.[15]

Another stipulation in use is framed for the purpose of throwing a definite proportion of the loss on the assured, irrespective of the sum insured or the relation which it bears to the value of the subject-matter.[16] The stipulation may provide that the assured is to be his own insurer for a specified portion of any loss,[17] in which case an insurance of the balance elsewhere avoids the policy.[18]

Another form of the stipulation more particularly used in agricultural insurances provides that the insurers are not to be liable for more than a specified portion of any loss. The stipulation in this form contains no express prohibition against insuring the balance elsewhere, and it is submitted that the assured is at liberty to do so, if he can find insurers willing to take the risk.[19]

---

12 *Fifth Liverpool Starr-Bowkett Building Society v Travellers Accident Insurance Co* (supra).

13 See e g *Trollope and Colls Ltd v Haydon* [1977] 1 Lloyd's Rep 244, CA (contractors' liability insurance), where a clause stated: 'Underwriters will be liable for all claims up to £100,000 in the aggregate but warranted the contractors shall bear the first £25 of each and every claim.'

14 In the case of successive losses the excess clause applies to each loss as being a separate transaction: *Equitable Trust Co of New York v Whittaker* (1923) 17 LlL Rep 153 (policy insuring bank against loss by taking forged documents); *Philadelphia National Bank v Price* [1938] 2 All ER 199, 60 LlL Rep 257, CA (policy insuring bank against loss by taking forged documents); *Government Insurance Office of New South Wales v Atkinson-Leighton Joint Venture* (1980) 31 ALR 193 (Aust HC) (policy insuring against damage in connection with construction of coastal embankment).

15 *Beacon Insurance Co Ltd v Langdale* [1939] 4 All ER 204, 65 LlL Rep 57 (motor insurance), where a pedal cyclist had to pay the first £5 to the insurance company which had made a bona fide settlement in the common interest of themselves and the insured.

16 See *Re Law Guarantee Trust and Accident Society Ltd, Liverpool Mortgage Insurance Co's Case* [1914] 2 Ch 617, CA, per Scrutton LJ, at 645.

17 This phrase is, strictly speaking, incorrect; all that it means is that the assured must bear the risk himself: *Grey v Ellison* (1856) 1 Giff 438 (life insurance) per Stuart V-C, at 442, 443.

18 *Muirhead v Forth and North Sea Steamboat Mutual Insurance Association* [1894] AC 72 (marine insurance); *Traill v Baring* (1864) 4 De GJ & Sm 318 (life insurance). The policy is not, however, avoided by a second insurance effected in contemplation of the insolvency of the insurers upon the original policy, and intended only to cover the estimated amount of their deficiency: *General Insurance Co of Trieste (Assicurazioni Generali) v Cory* [1897] 1 QB 335 (marine insurance). In this case there is a double insurance, and the assured cannot recover, under both policies, more than the amount which he was originally at liberty to insure: ibid, per Mathew J, at 341.

19 There is no condition that the balance is not to be insured; the assured does not warrant that the balance is uninsured. All that the policy does is to limit his right against the insurers, not to impose a further duty upon him. He is clearly at liberty to effect further insurance where the

4 Clause specifying smaller sum payable in certain circumstances

A clause in a life insurance policy may specify that a smaller sum is payable if the insured dies whilst engaged in certain activities.[20]

Further, a clause in a cash in transit insurance policy may limit the liability of the insurers to a smaller sum where the loss occurs 'between vehicles and premises and vice versa.'[1]

Again, liability for a loss under a goods in transit insurance policy was held to be limited where the goods lost consisted of non-ferrous metals.[2]

5 Limitation by statute

The amount recoverable may also be limited by the provisions of a statute.[3]

C FRANCHISE CLAUSES

Where there is a 'franchise clause', any loss which occurs will have to be borne by the assured provided that it does not exceed a specified percentage.

The effect of the clause is that the assured has no claim upon the insurers unless the loss exceeds the specified amount. When the loss exceeds this limit, he will be entitled to recover the whole of the loss and not merely the excess.

D TO WHOM PAYMENT IS TO BE MADE

Payment must be made to the assured himself,[4] unless the insurers have duly assented to the assignment of the policy,[5] or unless the proceeds of the policy, as distinguished from the policy itself, have been validly assigned,[6] in which cases payment must be made to the assignee, and his receipt is a sufficient discharge to the insurers.[7]

---

insurers have limited their liability to a specific sum, if such sum represents only a portion of the value of the subject-matter. It is submitted that it cannot make any difference that the limit of liability is measured, not by a specific sum, but by a reference to the amount of loss in the particular case.

20 See e g *Scragg v United Kingdom Temperance and General Provident Institution* [1976] 2 Lloyd's Rep 227, QBD (Commercial Ct) (life insurance), where the sum payable was limited if the insured died as a result of engaging in motor racing, motor speed hill climbs, motor trials or rallies.

1 *Mint Security Ltd v Blair* [1982] 1 Lloyd's Rep 188, where the loss in those circumstances was limited to £20,000.

2 *Avandero (UK) Ltd v National Transit Insurance Co Ltd* [1984] 2 Lloyd's Rep 613.

3 See e g *Harker v Caledonian Insurance Co* [1980] 1 Lloyd's Rep 556, HL (motor insurance), where the British Honduras Motor Vehicles Insurance (Third Party Risks) Ordinance 1958 enabled the insurers to limit their liability to $4,000 in respect of third party risks.

4 Payment to the wrong person does not discharge the insurers: *Swan and Cleland's Graving Dock and Slipway Co v Maritime Insurance Co and Croshaw* [1907] 1 KB 116 (marine insurance); *Robarts v Tucker* (1851) 16 QB 560, ExCh (life insurance), where a bill of exchange was given by the insurers and paid by their bankers under a forged indorsement.

5 See Chapter 34.

6 See Chapter 44.

7 Law of Property Act 1925, s 136(1)(c); *Ottley v Gray* (1847) 16 LJCh 512 (life insurance); *Desborough v Harris* (1855) 5 De GM & G 439 (life insurance); *Curtin v Jellicoe* (1863) 13 IChR 180 (life insurance).

In the event of the death or bankruptcy[8] of the assured, or, in the case of an assignment, of the assignee,[9] his personal representative,[10] or trustee in bankruptcy,[11] as the case may be, is entitled to be paid as representing his estate.

Payment may also be made to the judgment creditor if garnishee proceedings are taken after the amount payable has been ascertained.[12]

Except where the policy otherwise provides[13] or where a case of estoppel arises against the insurers,[14] the rights of any person claiming through the assured are no greater than those of the assured himself.[15]

Payment may also be made to an agent of the assured, who is duly authorised to receive payment on his behalf.[16] The agent must thereupon account to his

---

8 In cases to which the Third Parties (Rights against Insurers) Act 1930, applies, the rights of the assured in his policy, so far as it covers liability to third parties, vest, on his bankruptcy in the third party. In the case of a company, the vesting takes place if the company is wound up or if its property is taken possession of by debenture holders: ibid, s 1(1). See generally, Ivamy *Fire and Motor Insurance* (4th Edn, 1984), pp 326–332.

9 *Glynn v Locke* (1842) 3 Dr & War 11 (life insurance).

10 *Mildmay v Folgham* (1797) 3 Ves 471 (fire insurance); *John v Bradbury* (1866) LR 1 P & D 245; *Re Pollock* 1889 26 ScLR 515; *Re Lambert, Public Trustee v Lambert* (1916) 84 LJCh 279; *Durrant v Friend* (1851) 5 De G & Sm 343 (marine insurance); *Johnston v Ocean Accident and Guarantee Corpn Ltd* (1915) 34 NZLR 356, where the question was whether a policy effected by the employers in the name of an employee enured for the benefit of the employers, and it was held that the employee's personal representative was entitled to recover. If the assured was a trustee, his personal representative must account to the *cestui que trust* for any money received under the insurance: *Payne v Payne* (1908) Times, 6 November.

11 *Logan v Hall* (1847) 4 CB 598 (fire insurance) per Maule J, at 613; *Berndtson v Strang* (1868) 3 Ch App 588 (marine insurance); *McEntire v Potter & Co* (1889) 22 QBD 438 (marine insurance); *Hood's Trustees v Southern Union General Insurance Co of Australasia* [1928] Ch 793, CA (accident insurance); cf *Re Bennett, ex p Official Receiver* [1907] 1 KB 149 (life insurance); see also, *Marriage v Royal Exchange Assurance Co* (1849) 18 LJCh 216, where a mortgagee applied for an injunction to restrain the insurers from paying the policy money to the assured, the mortgagor, and the Court refused to order payment of the money into Court, on the ground that, as the assured had become bankrupt, his assignees in bankruptcy had not yet been made parties. But where property, belonging to a partner and insured by him in his own name, is in the order and disposition of his firm, which becomes bankrupt after its destruction by fire, the proceeds of the policy do not pass to the trustee in bankruptcy of the firm: *Re Bakewell, ex p Smith* (1819) Buck 149.

12 *Randall v Lithgow* (1884) 12 QBD 525 (fire insurance), where garnishee proceedings were taken before the amount due under the policy had been ascertained, and the insurers submitted to the order without objecting that there was no debt then due; *Israelson v Dawson* [1933] 1 KB 310, CA (accident insurance); *Electric Printing Works v Cooper* (1923) 14 LlL Rep 125, where a garnishee order was refused as, although the amount of the loss had been agreed, the insurers contended that the insurance was subject to average.

13 Such a provision may be made in favour of assignees for valuable consideration.

14 *Randall v Lithgow* (1884) 12 QBD 525 (fire insurance).

15 *Borradaile v Hunter* (1843) 5 Man & G 639 (life insurance), where the assured committed suicide; *Re Carr and Sun Fire Insurance Co* (1897) 13 TLR 186, CA (fire insurance), where the trustee failed on account of the assured having made a fraudulent claim; *M'Entire v Sun Fire Office* (1895) 29 ILT 103 (fire insurance), where the assured had broken a condition; *Dickson v Provincial Insurance Co* (1874) 24 CP 157, where the trustee in bankruptcy was defeated by reason of a double insurance effected by him in ignorance of the fact that there was a policy already in existence; *Jackson v Forster* (1860) 1 E & E 470, ExCh (life insurance), where the trustee in bankruptcy was held not to be entitled to claim the benefit of a condition exempting the policy from forfeiture if third persons had acquired interests.

16 Trustees may apoint a banker or solicitor as agent to receive and give a discharge for money payable under a policy, by permitting the agent to have the custody of and produce the policy with a receipt signed by the trustee: Trustee Act 1925, s 23(c). As to the authority of an agent,

principal for the whole of the money received, and cannot withhold all or part on the ground that other persons are interested in the policy.[17]

In the case of a joint policy, payment may be made to any one of the joint assured, and his receipt is a sufficient discharge.[18] Where several persons have joined in effecting a composite policy for their respective rights and interests, the policy monies should be paid to each according to the amount of the loss, and, if any of the assured receives more than this, he holds the balance for the benefit of the other parties to the insurance who have not been indemnified.[19]

Where conflicting claims are made to the policy money, there is no statutory provision, as there is in the case of life insurance, enabling the insurers to obtain relief by paying the money into Court,[20] except where the proceeds of the policy have been legally assigned.[1]

They are entitled, however, to interplead,[2] provided that they have themselves no interest in the policy money, and that the claims really do conflict.[3] In the course of the interpleader proceedings, they may be directed to pay the money into Court,[4] and they may thus obtain a valid discharge against all claimants.[5]

To entitle the insurers to interplead, the amount due to the assured must have been ascertained,[6] and there must be, in fact, adverse claims for payment of

---

see pp 524–532, post. For a case where it was alleged to be a term in the policy that a claim could be collected only by a broker named in it, and it was held that it was doubtful whether such a term had been incorporated into the policy, see *Stolos Cia SA v Ajax Insurance Co Ltd, The Admiral C* [1981] 1 Lloyd's Rep 9, CA (marine insurance).

17 *Roberts v Ogilby* (1821) 9 Price 269 (marine insurance); *Dixon v Hamond* (1819) 2 B & Ald 310 (marine insurance), both cited in *Blaustein v Maltz, Mitchell & Co* [1937] 2 KB 142, CA (agency) per Slesser LJ, at 152.

18 *Penniall v Harborne* (1848) 11 QB 368 per Lord Denman J, at 376; *Powell v Brodhurst* [1901] 2 Ch 160 (mortgage).

19 *General Accident, Fire and Life Assurance Corpn Ltd v Midland Bank Ltd* [1940] 2 KB 388, CA, per Greene MR, at 414.

20 Life Insurance Companies (Payment into Court) Act 1896, is, as its name shows, confined to life assurance companies: ibid, s 2. Nor does the Trustee Act 1925, s 63(1), which enables trustees to make a payment into Court, apply, since the insurers are not trustees: *Matthew v Northern Assurance Co* (1878) 9 ChD 80 (life insurance); although a petitioner asking for payment out of Court of any money so paid in, cannot avail himself of the objection: *Re Haycock's Policy* (1876) 1 ChD 611 (life insurance), followed in *Re Sutton's Trusts* (1879) 12 ChD 175 (deposit at bank). As to the right of a life insurance company to pay money into Court, see further, Ivamy *Personal Accident, Life and Other Insurances* (2nd Edn, 1980), pp 116–117.

1 Law of Property Act 1925, s 136.

2 *Paris v Gilham* (1813) Coop G 56 (fire insurance), distinguished in *Sun Insurance Office v Galinsky* [1914] 2 KB 545, CA, where the dispute was not as to who was entitled to the benefit of the policy monies, but as to the nature of the obligation of the insurers; *Prudential Assurance Co v Thomas* (1867) 3 ChApp 74 (life insurance); *English and Scottish Mercantile Investment Co v Brunton* [1892] 2 QB 700, CA (fire insurance); but the money may be paid over by the insurers under an agreement reserving the rights of the parties: *Re Barker, ex p Gorely* (1864) 4 De GJ & Sm 477. In *Randall v Lithgow* (1884) 12 QBD 525 (fire insurance) the insurers, by their conduct, lost the right to interplead.

3 There must be a case of real doubt: *Desborough v Harris* (1855) 5 De G M & G 439 (life insurance): cf *Myers v United Guarantee and Life Assurance Co* (1855) 7 De G M & G 112, CA (life insurance).

4 For an instance, see *English and Scottish Mercantile Investment Co v Bruton* [1892] 2 QB 700, CA (fire insurance).

5 RSC Ord 17, r 5.

6 *Randall v Lithgow* (1884) 12 QBD 525, where the insurers had submitted to a garnishee before the amount due had been ascertained, and it was held that the insurers could not interplead as

such amount.[7] If some of the claimants ask for payment, whilst others are insisting on reinstatement by the insurers under their statutory obligation in the case of a fire policy,[8] the claims are not adverse, but inconsistent, since they presume different obligations, and the insurers cannot interplead.[9]

E THE FORM OF PAYMENT

Payment must be made in cash, unless the assured agrees to accept some other form of payment.[10]

Where the assured has agreed to take payment by means of a bill of exchange, he may, on its dishonour, sue either upon the bill,[11] or on the original consideration. If, however, he has taken the bill in full discharge of the insurers' obligation, he can sue only on the bill.[12]

Where the value of the subject-matter is estimated in foreign currency, but payment of the amount of the loss has to be made in English money, the amount recoverable is calculated at the rate of exchange current at the time when the payment falls due.[13]

An agent, who is authorised to collect payment from the insurers on behalf of the assured, has no implied authority to take a bill of exchange in payment,[14] and the insurers will not be discharged by a payment in that form, even though the bill is discounted by the agent, and honoured by them at maturity, unless the proceeds have come into the hands of the assured.[15] Where, however, the

---

between the garnishees and the trustees to whom the assured had assigned the debt due from the insurers after it had been ascertained.

7 *Sun Insurance Office v Galinsky* [1914] 2 KB 545, CA, where it was doubtful whether there was any claim for payment.

8 Fires Prevention (Metropolis) Act 1774. See pp 460–462, post.

9 *Sun Insurance Office v Galinsky* (supra), where the lessor claimed reinstatement and the lessee claimed payment.

10 *Times Fire Assurance Co v Hawke* (1859) 28 LJEx 317 (fire insurance) per Bramwell B, at 318: 'As between the company and [the assured] the contract was one of indemnity, and they might have agreed to take a wall, or a load of barley in satisfaction.'

11 As to the effect of suing on the bill, see *Re State Fire Insurance Co, ex p Meredith* (1863) 32 LJCh 300 (fire insurance), where it was held that the assured in proving in the liquidation of an insurance company was not bound, as regards a bill given in payment of the loss, by a clause contained in the policy limiting the liability of the shareholders; *Herald v Connah* (1876) 34 LT 885, where the manager of an insurance company who had accepted a bill drawn upon him for the amount of the loss, was held personally liable.

12 *Sayer v Wagstaff, re Sanders, ex p Wagstaff* (1844) 14 LJCh 116 (promissory note); *Strong v Hart* (1827) 6 B & C 160 (payment of freight).

13 *Thellusson v Bewick* (1793) 1 Esp 77 (marine insurance); *Anderson v Equitable Life Assurance Society of United States* (1926) 134 LT 557, CA (life insurance); *Buerger v New York Life Assurance Co* (1927) 137 LT 43, CA (life insurance). There may be a special clause fixing the rate of exchange: *Howard, Houlder & Partners Ltd v Union Marine Insurance Co Ltd* (1922) 38 TLR 515, HL (marine insurance). Cf *Assicurazioni Generali v Selim Cotran* [1932] AC 268, PC (life insurance), where an alteration in the currency payable had been made by the Treaty of Lausanne, 1923; *Sturge & Co v Excess Insurance Co Ltd* [1938] 4 All ER 424, 62 LlL Rep 128 (bond insurance), where it became illegal to enforce a clause in the bonds requiring payment in the equivalent value of gold.

14 *Sweeting v Pearce* (1861) 9 CBNS 534 (marine insurance) per Bramwell B, at 540. As to payments to agents, see generally pp 524–532, post.

15 *Hine Bros v SS Insurance Syndicate Ltd* (1895) 72 LT 79, CA (marine insurance).

payment is made by cheque, it may be regarded as a payment in cash, if the cheque is duly honoured.[16]

F THE PAYMENT OF INTEREST

A policy does not bear interest as a matter of course[17] from the time when the policy money becomes payable. It is only awarded, if the Court thinks fit, as damages for the wrongful detention of money which ought to have been paid.[18]

Interest may, however, be awarded[19] from the date of the loss,[20] or a later date,[1] as damages for the wrongful detention of money which ought to have been paid.[2]

---

16 Ibid, per Lord Esher MR, at 82.

17 *Webster v British Empire Mutual Life Assurance Co* (1880) 15 ChD 169, CA (life insurance) per James LJ at 174, overruling *Crossley v City of Glasgow Life Assurance Co* (1876) 4 ChD 421 (life insurance), which was followed in *Re Rosier's Trusts* (1877) 37 LT 426 (life insurance); *Kingston v McIntosh* (1808) 1 Camp 518 (marine insurance); *Higgins v Sargent* (1823) 2 B & C 348 (life insurance).

18 *Webster v British Empire Mutual Life Assurance Co* (supra) per James LJ, at 174. If the insurers go into liquidation, the assured may be allowed to prove for interest: *Re State Fire Insurance Co* (1864) 34 LJCh 436 (fire insurance), including interest given by foreign law: *Re State Fire Insurance Co, ex p Meredith* (1863) 32 LJCh 300 (fire insurance).

19 Under the Supreme Court Act 1981, s 35A(1). In *Burts and Harvey Ltd and Alchemy Ltd v Vulcan Boiler and General Insurance Co Ltd* [1966] 1 Lloyd's Rep 354 (consequential loss insurance) Lawton J said (ibid, at 354) that there was no reason why the insurance company should not pay interest at a rate which bore some relation to commercial rates of interest, and ordered the company to pay interest at 6 per cent per annum on the amount due. He also said that he accepted that for some months after the happening of the contingency which gave rise to the claim, it was reasonable that the parties should negotiate to find out exactly how much was due. Negotiations had been made exceedingly difficult by the fact that the indemnity provisions of the policy were particularly inappropriate to this particular case. That was not the fault of the assured. 'If insurance companies will issue policies which contain conditions which are inappropriate in a particular case, they can hardly say that it is the fault of the assured that it has been difficult to find out how much is due': ibid, at 354.

20 *Sillem v Thornton* (1854) 3 E & B 868 (fire insurance); *Montreal Assurance Co v M'Gillivray* (1857) 2 LCJ 221 (revsd without affecting this point (1859) 13 MooPCC 87).

1 *Macbeth & Co Ltd v Maritime Insurance Co Ltd* (1908) 24 TLR 559 (marine insurance) per Walton J, at 560: 'It was an ordinary practice in cases of this kind to allow interest from a date which would have given a reasonable time for adjustment and payment of the claim if there had been no dispute as to legal liability.' If no question of liability arises and an adjustment is a mere matter of form, interest may be allowed from the date of the claim: ibid. Interest was awarded in *Meyer-See v Mountain* (1916) Times, 3 March, from the date of the writ. In *Macbeth & Co Ltd v Maritime Insurance Co* (supra), where the House of Lords reversed the decisions of the courts below and decided in favour of the plaintiffs, interest was awarded from the date of the judgment at the trial, the date selected by the plaintiff. See further, *Mackie v European Assurance Co* (1869) 21 LT 102, where interest was awarded from, apparently, the date of repudiation; *J Gliksten & Son v State Assurance Co* (1922) 10 LlL Rep 604, where it was awarded from the date of the writ. The logical date is that at which payment becomes due under the conditions of the policy. In *Burts and Harvey Ltd and Alchemy Ltd v Vulcan Boiler and General Insurance Co Ltd (No 2)* [1966] 1 Lloyd's Rep 354 (consequential loss insurance) a chemical plant, which was the subject of a consequential loss insurance policy, broke down on 4 June 1961, and the insurers were held liable to indemnify the insured in respect of what would have been the production of the plant from 4 June 1961 to 6 August 1961, when production recommenced. Interest on the sum due, however, was awarded only from 30 November 1962, when the insured first called on the insurers to pay. For previous proceedings in the case, see [1966] 1 Lloyd's Rep 161. As to the rate of interest awarded, see supra; *Forney v Dominion Insurance Co Ltd* [1969] 1 Lloyd's Rep 502 (solicitor's indemnity insurance), where the Court awarded interest at the rate of 7 per cent from the moment when the insured had paid damages to the clients, who had brought actions for negligence against him. See the order made by Donaldson J, ibid, at 510.

Normally where strict proof is insisted on by the insurance company and the assured proves his case, interest on the amount claimed up to the date of judgment will be awarded. But in one case concerning a claim under a householder's comprehensive policy relating to jewellery, interest on the amount was disallowed in view of the circumstances and, in particular, the conflicting claims by the husband and wife as to the ownership of the goods.[3]

Payment of interest is sometimes, however, regulated by a special condition in the policy.[4]

G PAYMENT BY MISTAKE

Where the insurers have paid under a mistake, whether they are entitled to recover the money so paid will depend on whether the mistake was one of law or of fact.

1 Mistake of law

Where the insurers have paid the assured in the mistaken belief that they were liable, they will not be entitled to recover the money back where the payment was made under a mistake of law.[5]

2 Mistake of fact

The right to recover money paid by mistake arises only where the mistake is one of fact.[6] It is immaterial how the mistake came to be made. It may be due to fraud on the part of the assured,[7] or merely to ignorance,[8] inadvertence, or forgetfulness[9] on the part of the insurers.

The only question is what was the state of the insurers' mind at the time of making the payment.[10] If at that time they believed, on the facts as present to

---

2 *Webster v British Empire Life Assurance Co* (supra) (life insurance); *Re Waterhouse's Policy* [1937] Ch 415, [1937] 2 All ER 91 (life insurance). Such interest is subject to income tax: *Riches v Westminster Bank Ltd* [1947] AC 390, [1947] 1 All ER 469, HL (interest). *Forney v Dominion Insurance Co Ltd* (supra) (solicitor's indemnity insurance), where the insurers had wrongfully repudiated liability under the policy with the result that the insured had incurred costs in defending actions brought against him.

3 *Knoller v Evans* (1936) 55 LlL Rep 40 (householder's comprehensive policy).

4 For an example, see *Fitton v Accidental Death Insurance Co* (1864) 17 CBNS 122.

5 *Bilbie v Lumley* (1802) 2 East 469 (marine insurance); *Kelly v Solari* (1841) 9 M & W 54 (life insurance) per Lord Abinger CB, at 58; *Re Home and Colonial Insurance Co Ltd* [1930] 1 Ch 102 (marine insurance), at 106, where the liquidator stated that he would have paid the assured even if he had known that no stamped policies had been issued.

6 *Bilbie v Lumley* (supra). But they cannot recover as damages for breach of contract expenses to which they have been put in investigating a fraudulent claim which ultimately leads to an order for repayment of the policy monies: *London Assurance v Clare* (1937) 57 LlL Rep 254.

7 *Assicurazioni Generali de Trieste v Empress Assurance Corpn Ltd* [1907] 2 KB 814 (marine insurance), where the reinsurers were held entitled to recover from the original insurers the sum paid by way of reinsurance.

8 *De Hahn v Hartley* (1786) 1 Term Rep 343, affd (1787) 2 Term Rep 186n, ExCh (marine insurance), where a loss had been paid in ignorance of a breach of warranty; *Irving v Richardson* (1831) 2 B & Ad 193 (marine insurance), where there was a double insurance; *Lefevre v Boyle* (1832) 3 B & Ad 877 (life insurance), where the policy was voidable on account of fraud.

9 *Kelly v Solari* (supra) (life insurance).

10 Ibid, per Lord Abinger CB, at 58: 'I think the knowledge of the facts which disentitles the party from recovering, must mean a knowledge existing in the mind at the time of payment.'

their minds, that they were liable to pay, it is immaterial whether they did not know and could not have known the true facts till after the payment,[11] or whether they had known them previously and, but for their carelessness, would have known them at the time,[12] or whether they could, if they had made inquiries, have discovered them before payment.[13]

If the payment has been made in the first instance to an agent on behalf of the assured, the insurers are entitled to recover it back from the agent,[14] provided that the agent has not paid the money over to his principal before notice of their claim.[15]

The action is an action for money had and received.[16]

3 Some examples of mistakes of fact

The insurers will be entitled to the return of money paid under the policy where at the time of payment they believed that there was a valid policy in existence, whereas, in fact, the policy was voidable ab initio,[17] or had, in the events that had happened, become voidable,[18] or had already been allowed to lapse.[19]

A claim for repayment exists where, at the time of payment they believed that a loss had happened within the meaning of the policy, whereas, in fact, the assured had suffered no loss,[20] or, if he had suffered a loss, the loss was not caused by a peril insured against,[1] or was caused by an excepted cause.[2]

Where the insurers at the time of payment believed that the loss sustained by the assured was greater than in fact it is, they will be entitled to recover the sum which they had paid. The mistake in this case may be due to the fact that the

---

11 *De Hahn v Hartley* (supra); *Irving v Richardson* (supra); *Lefevre v Boyle* (supra).

12 *Kelly v Solari* (supra), where the policy, which was in the possession of the insurers, had been marked 'lapsed' for non-payment of premium, but the insurers afterwards paid the sum insured, having forgotten that the policy had lapsed.

13 *Kelly v Solari* (supra) (life insurance) per Lord Abinger, at 58, and per Parke B, at 59. Cf *Darrell v Tibbitts* (1880) 5 QBD 560, CA (fire insurance) per Cotton LJ, at 565.

14 *Buller v Harrison* (1777) 2 Cowp 565 (marine insurance), followed in *Scottish Metropolitan Assurance Co v P Samuel & Co Ltd* [1923] 1 KB 348 (marine insurance).

15 *Holland v Russell* (1863) 4 B & S 14, ExCh (marine insurance); *General Accident, Fire and Life Assurance Corpn Ltd v Midland Bank Ltd* [1940] 2 KB 388, [1940] 3 All ER 252, CA, where cheques had been made payable to all the assured jointly under a policy for their respective interests and the cheques had been endorsed and passed to one of the assured who alone had suffered loss, and it was held that the other assured were mere conduit pipes and not liable.

16 *Kelly v Solari* (supra) (life insurance).

17 *Lefevre v Boyle* (1832) 3 B & Ad 877 (life insurance); *Holland v Russell* (1863) 4 B & S 14, ExCh (marine insurance); cf *Home and Colonial Insurance Co v London Guarantee and Accident Co* (1928) 45 TLR 134 (marine insurance).

18 *De Hahn v Hartley* (supra) (marine insurance), where a condition precedent was broken; cf *M'Entire v Sun Fire Office* (1895) 29 ILT 103 (fire insurance).

19 *Kelly v Solari* (supra) (life insurance); cf *Lower Rhine and Würtenberg Insurance Association v Sedgwick* [1899] 1 QB 179, CA (marine insurance).

20 *North British and Mercantile Insurance Co v Stewart* 1871 9 Macph (Ct of Sess) 534 (life insurance), where the life insured was not dead, and it was held that, the assured having acted bona fide, the policy remained in force; cf *Holmes v Payne* [1930] 2 KB 301, 37 LlL Rep 41 (jewellery insurance).

1 *Norwich Union Fire Insurance Society Ltd v Price Ltd* [1934] AC 455, 49 LlL Rep 55, PC (marine insurance), where subsequent investigation showed that the fruit, the subject of the insurance, was sold because it was ripening and not as a result of a peril of the sea; cf *Mills v Alderbury Union* (1849) 3 Exch 590 (guarantee).

2 *Buller v Harrison* (1777) 2 Cowp 565 (marine insurance); *London Assurance Co v Clare* (1937) 57 LlL Rep 254; *Queen Insurance Co v Devinney* (1878) 25 Gr 394.

assured has omitted to credit the insurers with sums received or receivable from other sources in diminution of the loss,[3] or to an over-estimate of its amount.[4]

The money which has been paid by the insurers will also be recoverable where it is discovered that the assured had no insurable interest.[5]

If the assured has put forward a claim which he knew to be excessive, he forfeits all benefit under the policy and must return the whole sum received.[6] In any other case, he is only liable to return the excess beyond the sum which, on the true facts, is recoverable under the policy.[7]

4 Exceptions to the general rule

The insurers cannot, however, rely on the fact that they were unacquainted with the true state of facts at the time of payment where the payment was made under a compromise,[8] unless the assured acted fraudulently in connection with the compromise.[9] If, however, they discover the mistake before payment, they are not bound by the compromise.[10]

Thus, in *Magee v Pennine Insurance Co Ltd*:[11]

> In a proposal for a motor insurance policy the insured stated that he was the owner of the car and had a driving licence. The insurers issued the policy which extended to any person driving with the insured's consent. The insured's son drove the car and it was accidentally damaged. The insured made a claim under the policy, and the insurers offered £385 in settlement of the claim and this was accepted by the insured. Later it was discovered that the statements of the

---

3 *Irving v Richardson* (1831) 2 B & Ad 193 (marine insurance); *Darrell v Tibbitts* (1880) 5 QBD 560, CA (fire insurance); *Law Fire Assurance Co v Oakley* (1888) 4 TLR 309 (fire insurance).

4 *North British and Mercantile Insurance Co v Moffatt* (1871) LR 7 CP 25 (fire insurance).

5 *Piper v Royal Exchange Assurance* (1932) 44 LlL Rep 103 (marine insurance).

6 *London Assurance v Clare* (supra); *Assicurazione Generali de Trieste v Empress Assurance Corpn Ltd* [1907] 2 KB 814 (marine insurance); cf *Queen Insurance Co v Devinney* (supra).

7 *Irving v Richardson* (supra) (marine insurance); *North British and Mercantile Insurance Co v Moffatt* (supra) (fire insurance). This, of course, will be the whole sum, if the assured had been fully indemnified aliunde: *Darrell v Tibbitts* (supra) (fire insurance).

8 *Pennsylvania Co for Insurances on Lives and Granting Annuities v Mumford* [1920] 2 KB 537, 2 LlL Rep 351, CA; *Holmes v Payne* [1930] 2 KB 301, 37 LlL Rep 41; *Brooks v MacDonnell* (1835) 1 Y & C Ex 500 (marine insurance); cf *Re Norske Lloyd Insurance Co Ltd* [1928] WN 99 (marine insurance).

9 *Herbert v Champion Ltd* (1809) 1 Camp 134 (marine insurance) per Lord Ellenborough CJ, at 136: 'If money has been paid, it cannot be recovered back without proof of fraud; but a promise to pay will not in general be binding, unless founded on a previous liability'; *Queen Insurance Co v Devinney* (supra); but see *British American Assurance Co v Wilkinson* (1876) 23 Gr 151.

10 *Shepherd v Chewter* (1808) 1 Camp 274 (marine insurance); *M'Entire v Sun Fire Office* (1895) 29 ILT 103 (fire insurance), where, after the compromise, the insurers discovered that the policy had been avoided by a breach of condition.

11 [1969] 2 All ER 891, CA (motor insurance), where Lord Denning MR said (ibid, at 894): 'It is clear that when the insurance company and the plaintiff made this agreement to pay £385, they were both under a common mistake which was fundamental to the whole agreement. Both thought that the plaintiff was entitled to claim under the policy of insurance, whereas he was not so entitled. The common mistake does not make the agreement to pay £385 a nullity, but it makes it liable to be set aside in equity. This brings me to a question which has caused me much difficulty. Is this a case in which we ought to set the agreement aside in equity? I have hesitated on this point, but I cannot shut my eyes to the fact that the plaintiff had no valid claim on the insurance policy; and if he had no claim on the policy, it is not equitable that he should have a good claim on the agreement to pay £385; seeing that it was made under a fundamental mistake, it is not fair to hold the insurance company to an agreement which it would not have dreamt of making if it had not been under a mistake.' See also the judgment of Fenton Atkinson LJ, ibid, at 896.

insured as to the ownership of the car and the driving licence were false, so the insurers could have repudiated liability. They now claimed that they were under no liability to pay the £385, for they had entered in the compromise on the assumption that the policy was a valid one. *Held,* that the insurers were not liable.

The money is also irrecoverable where the payment was made under compulsion of legal process,[12] unless the assured has acted unfairly or unconscionably.[13]

Further, no recovery is possible where the payment was made without reference to the real state of affairs, the insurers having deliberately waived enquiry,[14] or where the payment was made ex gratia.[15]

H EX GRATIA PAYMENTS

Insurers may, and frequently do, make payments to the assured[16] in respect of losses for which they are not legally liable under the terms of their policies.[17] Such payments, which are known as 'ex gratia payments', are usually made in cases of hardship, for the purpose of not only relieving the particular assured, but also of enhancing the reputation of the insurers for fair dealing.[18]

Sometimes the insurers make a payment only in the form of a loan to be returned if the assured fails to establish the insurers' liability under the policy.

The fact that the insurers have made an ex gratia payment under a particular policy does not preclude them from disputing their liability under a subsequent policy, although the words of both policies and the circumstances of both losses are the same.[19]

Ex gratia payments are made in the ordinary course of insurance business, and, if made by an insurance company, are not ultra vires the company.[20]

---

12 *Marriot v Hampton* (1797) 7 Term Rep 269 (money paid by mistake).

13 *Ward & Co v Wallis* [1900] 1 QB 675 (work and labour) per Kennedy J, at 678, 679, distinguishing *Marriot v Hampton* (supra). The fact that the insurers have been compelled to pay the amount of the loss by legal process does not prevent them from recovering the amount so paid if the assured is afterwards indemnified aliunde: *Law Fire Assurance Co v Oakley* (1888) 4 TLR 309 (fire insurance). As to indemnification aliunde, see Chapter 47.

14 *Kelly v Solari* (1841) 9 M & W 54 (life insurance) per Parke B, at 59: 'If, indeed the money is intentionally paid, without reference to the truth or falsehood of the fact, the plaintiff meaning to waive all enquiry into it, and that the person receiving shall have the money at all events, whether the fact is true or false, the latter is certainly entitled to retain it'; cf *Home and Colonial Insurance Co v London Guarantee and Accident Co Ltd* (1928) 45 TLR 134 (marine insurance).

15 *Kelly v Solari* (supra) (life insurance) per Rolfe B, at 59. As to ex gratia payments, see infra.

16 An ex gratia payment cannot be claimed by a trustee in bankruptcy as against an assignee of the proceeds to whom it has been paid over by the assured: *Wills v Wells* (1818) 8 Taunt 264 (life insurance), where the trustee in bankruptcy recovered 2d for conversion of the parchment on which the policy was written. On the other hand, a trustee receiving an ex gratia payment must account for it to his cestui que trust: *Rayner v Preston* (1881) 18 ChD 1, CA (fire insurance) per James LJ, at 15.

17 *Taunton v Royal Insurance Co* (1864) 2 Hem & M 135, where the losses were caused by an explosion of gunpowder, and were within an exception in the various policies concerned.

18 *Tomkinson v South-Eastern Rly Co* (1887) 35 ChD 675 (company) per Kay J, at 678, 679, discussing *Taunton v Royal Insurance Co* (supra).

19 *London and Manchester Plate Glass Co Ltd v Heath* [1913] 3 KB 411, CA (plate glass insurance), where the question was whether the loss was caused by the peril insured against.

20 *Taunton v Royal Insurance Co* (supra) (fire insurance), where the Court refused, on the application of a shareholder, to restrain the company from making such payments, approved in *Breay v Royal British Nurses' Association* [1897] 2 Ch 272, CA (company).

Payment under an ultra vires policy cannot, however, be defended as an ex gratia payment, and the directors must refund to the shareholders any payments so made.[1]

An ex gratia payment cannot be recovered under a reinsurance.[2]

1 *Evanson v Crooks* (1911) 28 TLR 123 (life insurance) per Hamilton J, at 124.

2 *Chippendale v Holt* (1895) 73 LT 472 (marine insurance) per Mathew LJ, at 473. But a reinsurance treaty usually makes special provisions for ex gratia payments. See generally, Ivamy *Personal Accident, Life and Other Insurances* (2nd Edn, 1980), pp 334–335.

CHAPTER 43

The application of the proceeds of the policy

A THE GENERAL RULE

The assured, on being paid his insurance money by the insurers, may, as a general rule, deal with it as he thinks fit.[1]

The mere fact that some other person has an interest of some kind in the property destroyed does not give him any right, as against the assured, to the proceeds of the policy.[2]

Thus, a tenant for life or a tenant in tail, who is under no obligation to insure the settled property, but who does insure out of his own pocket,[3] is entitled, as against the remainderman under the settlement, to retain for his own benefit any money received from the insurers in consequence of the destruction of the settled property,[4] unless his intention in insuring was to protect the interest of the remainderman as well as his own.[5]

---

1 *Rayner v Preston* (1881) 18 ChD 1, CA, per Cotton LJ, at 6; *Re Law Guarantee Trust and Accident Society Ltd, Liverpool Mortgage Insurance Co's Case* [1914] 2 Ch 617, CA (debenture insurance) per Kennedy LJ, at 639. As to his duty to reinstate the property see pp 462–464, post.

2 *Gillespie v Miller, Son & Co* 1874 1 R (Ct of Sess) 423 per Moncrieff, at 433: 'He alone reaps the benefit who creates the insurance. When the insured has been indemnified, the contract of the insurer has been fully executed, and the person who effects the insurance is not bound to communicate the benefit of his insurance to any third party, whatever his interest in the subject insured.' See also, *Collingridge v Royal Exchange Assurance Corpn* (1877) 3 QBD 173; *Maurice v Goldsbrough Mort & Co Ltd* [1939] AC 452, [1939] 3 All ER 63, PC; *Rayner v Preston* (1881) 18 ChD 1, CA; and cf *Durrant v Friend* (1851) 5 De G & Sm 343 (marine insurance), where a legatee of chattels was held not to be entitled to the proceeds of an insurance upon them effected by the testator, as against the executor, the chattels and the testator have been lost in the same ship, and the legatee being unable to prove that the testator perished first. As to the presumption of the survivorship see now Law of Property Act 1925, s 184, and *Re Grosvenor, Peacey & Grosvenor* [1944] Ch 138, [1944] 1 All ER 81, CA (will); *Re Dellow's Will Trusts, Lloyds Bank Ltd v Institute of Cancer Research* [1964] 1 All ER 771, [1964] 1 WLR 451 (will).

3 *Warwicker v Bretnall* (1882) 23 ChD 188, explaining on this ground *Rook v Worth* (1750) 1 Ves Sen 460 per Lord Hardwicke, at 461; *Cruickshank v Robarts* (1821) 6 Madd 104.

4 *Warwicker v Bretnall* (supra) following *Seymour v Vernon* (1852) 21 LJCh 433;*Gaussen v Whatman* (1905) 93 LT 101; *Re Bladon, Dando v Porter* [1911] 2 Ch 350 (licence compensation) per Neville J, at 354, speaking of fire insurance; cf *Watson v Brutton* (1830), cited Ellis, pp 177, 178. This is subject to the right of the remainderman, in the case of realty to claim reinstatement, in which case the tenant for life is not entitled to a charge in respect of the premiums paid; *Re Quicke's Trusts, Poltimore v Quicke* [1908] 1 Ch 887, where the tenant for life was held entitled to the insurance money in respect of the settled chattels. It is immaterial that, as between the assured and the insurers, the assured was not entitled to recover the full amount: *Dalgleish v Buchanan* (1854) 16 Dunl (Ct of Sess) 332 per Lord Ivory, at 338.

5 Cf *Parry v Ashley* (1829) 3 Sim 97, where a person, who was both devisee of property subject to a charge and executrix, renewed a policy on the property, and it was held that the proceeds of the policy were subject to the charge, the renewal having ben made in her capacity as executrix,

He may, nevertheless, if he thinks fit, abandon all claim to the money, and make a gift of it to the remainderman, in which case it will not pass to his personal representatives after his death.[6]

Similarly, as a general rule, neither the lessor nor the lessee[7] has any right as such to share in the proceeds of any policy effected by the other in respect of the demised property.

B EXCEPTIONS TO THE GENERAL RULE

But in some cases a right to the proceeds is conferred by statute or by contract.

1 Right conferred by statute

A right to the proceeds of a policy is conferred by statute in the case of:

a A contract for the sale or exchange of property.
b A mortgage by deed.
c Property subject to a trust or settlement.

(a) Contract for the sale or exchange of property

In the case of a contract for the sale or exchange of property, which is insured by the vendor, if a fire takes place between the date of the contract and completion, the purchaser is entitled to the benefit of the proceeds of the policy,[8] subject to the following conditions:

i there must be no stipulation to the contrary contained in the contract;
ii the consent of the insurers, if required, must be obtained;[9] and
iii the premium must be apportioned and paid by the purchaser as from the date of the contract.[10]

Apart from the statute or special contract, the purchaser has no claim against the proceeds of the vendor's policy.[11]

(b) Mortgage by deed

In the case of a mortgage by deed, where the mortgaged property is insured by the mortgagor in accordance with the mortgage deed or with the consent of the mortgagee, or where the mortgagor is liable under the mortgage deed for the

---

commented on in *Warwicker v Bretnall* (1882) 23 ChD 188; *Castellain v Preston* (1883) 11 QBD 380, CA, per Bowen LJ, at 398.

6 *Norris v Harrison* (1817) 2 Madd 268, as explained in *Warwicker v Bretnall* (supra), and in *Rayner v Preston* (1881) 18 ChD 1, CA. But the tenant for life is entitled to a reasonable time for considering whether the money is to be applied in rebuilding: *Gaussen v Whatman* (1905) 93 LT 101, where the money was invested for 14 years in the names of the trustees of the settlement, and it was held that the tenant for life had not abandoned his right.

7 *Leeds v Cheetham* (1827) 1 Sim 146, followed in *Lofft v Dennis* (1859) 1 E & E 474.

8 Law of Property Act 1925, s 47(1). The same rule applies, with the necessary modifications, to a sale or exchange by an order of the Court: ibid, s 47(3).

9 In some cases the policy may contain a special condition rendering their consent necessary.

10 Law of Property Act 1925, s 47(2).

11 *Paine v Meller* (1801) 6 Ves 349; *Poole v Adams* (1864) 33 LJCh 639; *Edwards v West* (1878) 7 ChD 858; *Rayner v Preston* (1881) 18 ChD 1, CA. For the converse case, where the insurance was effected by the purchaser, see *Bartlett v Looney* (1876–7) 3 VLR 14.

maintenance of the insurance, the mortgagee is entitled to require that the proceeds of the policy shall be applied in or towards the discharge of the mortgage money. But this right is without prejudice to any obligation to the contrary imposed by law or by special contract.[12]

Apart from the statute or special contract, neither the mortgagor nor the mortgagee[13] has any claim against the proceeds of a policy effected by the other.

(c) Property subject to a trust or settlement

In the case of property subject to a trust or settlement, if such property is insured under any trust, power or obligation,[14] the money receivable[15] under the policy in the event of a loss by fire, is capital money for the purposes of the trust or settlement,[16] and is to be dealt with in accordance with the provisions of the statute.[17]

2 Right conferred by contract

If the policy is effected by the assured in pursuance of a contract, express[18] or implied,[19] under which other persons interested are to share in the benefit of the insurance, he must, on receiving payment from the insurers, account to such persons for their shares.

The same principle applies where, though there is no contract between the parties, the assured, at the time of effecting the policy, intended[20] to cover not only his own interest in the subject-matter of insurance, but also the interest of the person claiming to share in the proceeds of the insurance. In this case the assured is in the position of a trustee in respect of the amount attributable to

---

12 Law of Property Act 1925, s 108(4).

13 *Lees v Whiteley* (1866) LR 2 Eq 143; *Sinnott v Bowden* [1912] 2 Ch 414 per Parker J, at 419; *Halifax Building Society v Keighley* [1931] 2 KB 248; *Re McMillan Estate and Calgary Brewing and Malting Co Ltd* [1929] 3 WWR 202.

14 This includes property insured by a tenant for life impeachable for waste: Trustee Act 1925, s 20(1).

15 If receivable by any person other than the trustees of the trust or settlement, such person must use his best endeavours to obtain payment and, after deducting the costs and obtaining payment, pay over the residue to the trustees or, if there are no trustees, into Court: Trustee Act 1925, s 20(2).

16 Ibid, s 20(1).

17 Ibid, s 20(3).

18 *Cochran & Son v Leckie's Trustee* 1906 8 F (Ct of Sess) 975; *Maurice v Goldsbrough Mort & Co Ltd* [1939] AC 452, [1939] 3 All ER 63, 64 LlL Rep 1 PC.

19 *Martineau v Kitching* (1872) LR 7 QB 436, per Blackburn J, at 458; *Reynard v Arnold* (1875) 10 Ch App 386. Such a contract may be implied from the existence of a covenant to insure, coupled with an undertaking to lay out the proceeds in reinstatement; *Garden v Ingram* (1852) 23 LJCh 478 per Lord Cranworth LC, at 479, explained in *Lees v Whiteley* (1866) LR 2 Eq 143, per Kindersley V-C, at 149, and *Rayner v Preston* (1881) 18 ChD 1, CA, per Cotton LJ, at 7; but not from the existence of a covenant to insure alone; *Lees v Whiteley* (supra).

20 *Hepburn v A Tomlinson (Hauliers) Ltd* [1966] AC 451, [1966] 1 All ER 418, HL (goods in transit policy), where the policy showed that there was an intention on the part of the carriers to insure the proprietary interest of the owners of the goods as well as their own interest. See especially the judgment of Lord Reid at 422–423. For other cases showing intention, see *Waters v Monarch Fire and Life Assurance Co* (1856) 5 E & B 870 (fire insurance) and *London and North Western Rly Co v Glyn* (1859) 1 E & E 652 (fire insurance); *Petrofina (UK) Ltd v Magnaload Ltd* [1984] QB 127, [1983] 3 All ER 33, [1983] 2 Lloyd's Rep 91 (contractors' all risks insurance), where a head contractor was held to be able to insure the entire contract works in his own name and that of all his sub-contractors. (See the judgment of Lloyd J, ibid, at 96.)

such person's interest,[1] but only to the extent of the balance after recouping his own loss.[2]

A person having a right to the proceeds of a policy may enforce it against the assured in an action for money had and received.[3]

If the assured is responsible to some other person for the safety of the subject-matter, he must, in the event of fire, make good its loss.[4] For this purpose he may avail himself of the proceeds of any insurance effected by him, but the existence of the insurance does not confer on the person entitled to be indemnified any right as such to the proceeds,[5] unless it was the assured's intention at the time of insuring to confer it.

Where the assured has received from the insurers an amount in excess of the value of the interest or interests which he intended to insure, the fact that such excess expressly represents the value of some other person's interest, gives that person no right to claim it.[6]

The insurers, indeed, may be entitled to recover it back as being more than a full indemnity to the assured.[7] But if they do not choose to do so, a person whose interest the assured never intended to protect cannot avail himself of it against the wishes of the assured.[8]

---

1 *London and North Western Rly Co v Glyn* (1859) 1 E & E 652 per Wightman J, at 660: 'They must . . . be considered as having insured the goods, which they held in trust as carriers, for the benefit of the owners, for whom they will hold the amount recovered, as trustees, after deducting what is due in respect of their own charges upon the goods'; and at 661: 'It is true that this insurance is in the nature of a voluntary trust undertaken by the plaintiffs without the knowledge of the cestuis que trustent, the owners of the goods; but it is a trust clearly binding on the plaintiffs in equity, who will hold the amount which they will now recover, in the first place for the satisfaction of their own claims and in the next, as to the residue, in trust for the owners.' See also, *Waters v Monarch Life Assurance Co* (1856) 5 E & B 870, per Campbell CJ, at 881; *Re Bladon, Dando v Porter* [1911] 2 Ch 350 (licence compensation) per Neville J, at 354, speaking of fire insurance; *Payne v Payne* (1908) Times, 6 November (motor insurance); *Gillespie v Miller, Son & Co* 1874 1 R (Ct of Sess) 423; *Mutual Fire Insurance Co v Paquet Co* (1912) QR 21 KB 419; *Hepburn v A Tomlinson (Hauliers) Ltd* [1966] 1 All ER 418, HL (goods in transit policy); *Petrofina (UK) Ltd v Magnaload Ltd*, supra (contractors' all risks insurance).

2 *Martineau v Kitching* (1872) LR 7 QB 436; *Gillett v Mawman* (1808) 1 Taunt 137. But his own loss is limited to accrued loss, and no account may be taken of profit or other benefit he would have received if the property had not been destroyed: *Maurice v Goldsbrough Mort & Co Ltd* [1939] 3 All ER 63, 64 LlL Rep 1, PC.

3 *Sidaways v Todd* (1818) 2 Stark 400.

4 If there is an obligation to insure and the contract is frustrated, the Court, in assessing what monies ought to be recovered or retained by either party, may take into account insurance monies; otherwise insurance is not within the application of this Act: Law Reform (Frustrated Contracts) Act 1943, ss 1(5), 2(5)(b).

5 *Dalgleish v Buchanan* (1854) 16 Dunl (Ct of Sess) 332.

6 *Dalgleish v Buchanan* (supra) per Lord Ivory, at 338: 'If I insure a third party's property in which I have no insurable interest, whatever objection the insurance office may on that account take to my own title to recover, yet if I do recover—by assent of the insurance office or otherwise—that most assuredly could never raise up a title in the third party—an absolute stranger to the whole transaction—to come against me with a demand to deliver up to him what I had thus—it may be without a good legal title—recovered from another party with whom or with whose rights he does not connect himself directly or indirectly.' See also, *Armitage v Winterbottom* (1840) 1 Man & G 130; and cf *Grant v Hill* (1812) 4 Taunt 380 (marine insurance), where the assured had recovered monies under a policy although he had no insurable interest, and it was held that the person in whom he had averred the interest to be in his action against the insurers had no claim against him, on the ground that the mere fact of insuring in another person's name gives that person no claim to the proceeds of the insurance.

7 *Castellain v Preston* (1883) 11 QBD 380, CA.

8 *Armitage v Winterbottom* (supra); *Dalgleish v Buchanan* (supra).

CHAPTER 44

The assignment of the proceeds of the policy

Where the right to receive the sum payable under the policy in the event of loss is alone assigned, it is not necessary that the assignee should possess or acquire any beneficial interest in the subject-matter itself, since it is not the assured's interest in the subject-matter, but his interest in the sum payable that is assigned.[1] No question, therefore, arises as to the avoidance of the policy by reason of the assignee's want of interest in the subject-matter.[2] The assignment of the proceeds does not substitute a new assured, but merely a new creditor who succeeds to the assured's rights in respect of the sum payable under the policy.

A WHERE THE LOSS HAS ALREADY TAKEN PLACE

Where a loss has already taken place, the right of the assured to recover the sum payable under the policy is an ordinary chose in action,[3] and it may, therefore, like any other chose in action, be assigned by the assured before payment.[4]

For such an assignment, the consent of the insurers is not necessary.[5] The assignment is, therefore, not a breach of the condition in the policy prohibiting an assignment without consent.[6] Though the policy itself may apparently be assigned,[7] it is safer to assign the right only and not the policy, especially in the

---

1 *Lloyd v Fleming* (1872) LR 7 QB 299 (marine insurance); *North American Accident Insurance Co v Newton* (1918) 57 SCR 577.

2 See pp 19–24, ante. Moreover, a mortgagee can assign his right to recover the whole proceeds and not merely the amount of his pecuniary interest, though there is an obligation to account for the balance: *Williams v Atlantic Assurance Co Ltd* [1933] 1 KB 81, CA (marine insurance) per Scrutton LJ, at 97.

3 *Lloyd v Fleming* (1872) LR 7 QB 299 (marine insurance) per Blackburn J, at 302, 303: 'After a loss the policy of insurance and the right of action under it might, like any other chose in action, be transferred in equity.' See also, *Re Foster* (1873) IR 7 Eq 294.

4 *Hamilton v Snowden* [1880] WN 58, 175, CA; *Randall v Lithgow* (1884) 12 QBD 525; *Green v Brand* (1884) Cab & El 410, where an assignment of the policies after the fire to trustees upon trust to pay and divide the moneys received among creditors was held valid; *Blanchard v Sun Fire Office* (1890) 6 TLR 365, where an assignment to one of the arbitrators appointed in an arbitration upon the policy was held to invalidate the award; *English and Scottish Mercantile Investment Co v Brunton* [1892] 2 QB 700, CA; *Bank of Toronto v St Lawrence Fire Insurance Co* [1903] AC 59, PC, where the assignment was in pursuance of a previous undertaking to assign in the event of a fire; *Re Foster* (supra), where the letter which was alleged to transfer the right was held not to amount to an equitable assignment.

5 See *Brice v Bannister* (1878) 3 QBD 569, CA (assignment of debt).

6 *Waydell v Provincial Insurance Co* (1862) 21 UCR 612.

7 *Kerr v Hastings Mutual Fire Insurance Co* (1887) 41 UCR 217.

case where the loss is partial only, since the policy, if specifically assigned, is by the assignment rendered void as to the balance.

Though the assignment is valid against the insurers, it does not give the assignee an absolute right to payment. Its effect is only to transfer to the assignee the existing rights of the assured, and the insurers may therefore, as against the assignee, make use of any defences which would, at the time when the assignment was completed, have been available against the assured,[8] unless the policy otherwise provides.[9]

Thus, as far as marine insurance is concerned, the Marine Insurance Act 1906, s 50(2), provides:

> '. . . and the defendant [i e the insurer] is entitled to make any defence arising out of the contract which he would have been entitled to make if the action had been brought in the name of the person by or on behalf of whom the policy was effected.'[10]

Further, all conditions precedent to the insurers' liability must be duly performed by the assured.[11]

B WHERE THE LOSS HAS NOT YET TAKEN PLACE

During the currency of the policy, and before loss, the assured may assign the right which he may subsequently acquire, in the event of a loss taking place, to receive the sum payable under his policy. Such an assignment, whether it is absolute, or whether it is by way of mortgage or charge only, is not an assignment of the contract contained in the policy but only of the assured's beneficial interest therein.[12]

In the case of life policies, what is commonly called an assignment of the policy is really an assignment of the right to receive the proceeds of the policy, and not an assignment of the policy itself; for this would amount to an insurance

---

8 Law of Property Act 1925, s 136.

9 Cf *Jackson v Forster* (1860) 1 E & E 470, ExCh (life insurance), where an exception against suicide did not apply to bona fide assignees for value.

10 See further, Ivamy *Marine Insurance* (4th Edn, 1985), pp 316–319. In *First National Bank of Chicago v West of England Shipowners Mutual Protection and Indemnity Association (Luxembourg), The Evelpidis Era* [1981] 1 Lloyd's Rep 54 (marine insurance) the assignment could not be brought within the Marine Insurance Act 1906, s 50(2) by reason of the provisions of a letter of undertaking that the Association was allowed to pay claims directly to the shipowners or the shipowners' creditors until it had received notice to the contrary. (See the judgment of Mocatta J, ibid, at 64).

11 *Re Carr and Sun Fire Insurance Co* (1897) 13 TLR 186, CA (fire insurance), where the assured had failed to furnish proofs of loss within the time required, and it was held that this precluded the trustee in bankruptcy from recovering; *Miller-Morse Hardware Co v Dominion Fire Insurance Co* [1922] 1 WWR 1097, where it was held that the assignee was affected by the fraud of the assured in furnishing proofs of loss, whether the fraud was committed before or after the assignment.

12 *Richards v Liverpool and London Fire and Life Insurance Co* (1866) 25 UCR 400, where it was held that the assignment of a policy to a mortgagee of the insured premises was valid, as being a transfer of the assured's beneficial interest in the policy only, and not, therefore, in violation of the principle that fire policies are not assignable; cf *Bank of Toronto v St Lawrence Fire Insurance Co* [1903] AC 59, PC (fire insurance), where the assignment, though not made till after the loss, was made in pursuance of the previous undertaking to assign the policy in the event of a loss; *Kruse v Seeley* [1924] 1 Ch 136, where a money-lender was ordered to assign for the benefit of the debtor any policy of insurance or furniture of the debtor in his possession.

on a different life. Assignments of life policies in this sense have always been treated as valid in equity.[13]

Similarly, accident policies have also been treated as assignable.[14] There does not seem to be any reason why an assignment of the beneficial interest in a contract of fire insurance should not be valid.[15] There is no doubt that the proceeds of marine insurance policies can be assigned.[16]

It is no objection that the contract involves both rights and responsibilities, and cannot therefore be assigned in its entirety without the consent of the other party,[17] or even that an assignment of the contract in its entirety is prohibited.[18] Nor is the assignment invalid on the ground that the contract is still executory, and there is no existing right of action,[19] or that there is at the time of the assignment no chose-in-action in existence.[20]

---

13 *Chowne v Baylis* (1862) 31 Beav 351 (life insurance); cf *Re Griffin, Griffin v Griffin* [1902] 1 Ch 135, CA (life policy issued under Friendly Societies Act 1875, s 15(3)), even when the terms of the policy prohibit a legal assignment: *Re Turcan* (1888) 40 ChD 5, CA (life insurance).

14 *Stokell v Heywood* [1897] 1 Ch 459 (accident insurance), where it was held that the right to the proceeds of an existing policy in the event of a loss which had not yet happened passed under the words 'all and singular the lands, tenements and hereditaments, goods, chattels and moneys, credits, estates and effects whatsoever and wheresoever' in a deed of assignment, although the right to the proceeds of a policy renewed subsequently did not. Cf *Re Turcan* (supra), where two personal accident policies, which, however, the Court treated as life policies, were held to fall within a covenant in a marriage settlement to settle after-acquired property.

15 This seems to follow from the fact that the beneficial interest in a contract is, as a general rule, assignable in equity: *Tolhurst v Associated Portland Cement Manufacturers* [1903] AC 414 (assignment of contract to supply goods) per Lord MacNaughten, at 420. There is only one English reported case on the subject, i e *London Investment Co v Montefiore* (1864) 9 LT 688, where a fire policy was assigned to secure a loan along with the lease of the insured premises, and it was held that the assignee was not entitled, after loss, to maintain an action at law in his own name to recover the sum payable under the policy, in the absence of an express contract on the part of the insurers to pay it over. The Court did not, however, deal with the question whether or not the assignment was valid in equity, and after the Judicature Act 1873, a different decision might have been given. The existence of mortgages of fire policies is also recognised in *Garden v Ingram* (1852) 23 LJCh 478; *Browne v Price* (1858) 4 CBNS 598 (life insurance).

16 Marine Insurance Act 1906, s 50(2), which states: 'Where a marine policy has been assigned so as to pass the beneficial interest in such policy, the assignee of the policy is entitled to sue thereon in his own name . . .'. See, further, Ivamy *Marine Insurance* (4th Edn, 1985), pp 315–316.

17 *Torkington v Magee* [1902] 2 KB 427 (assignment of executor's contract to sell reversionary interest) (revsd on the facts [1903] 1 KB 644, CA) per Channell J, at 431–432.

18 *Re Turcan* (1888) 40 ChD 5, CA (life insurance) per Cotton LJ, at 9.

19 *Torkington v Magee* (supra).

20 *Tailby v Official Receiver* (1888) 13 App Cas 523 (future book debts) per Lord Watson at 533: 'The rule of equity which applies to the assignment of future choses-in-action is, as I understand it, a very simple one. Choses-in-action do not come within the scope of the Bills of Sale Acts, and though not yet existing, may nevertheless be the subject of present assignment. As soon as they come into existence, assignees who have given valuable consideration will, if the new chose-in-action is in the disposal of their assignor, take precisely the same right and interest as if it had actually belonged to him, or had been within his disposition and control at the time when the assignment was made.' SC per Lord MacNaughten at 543: 'It has long been settled that future property, possibilities and expectancies are assignable in equity for value. The mode or form of assignment is absolutely immaterial, provided the intention of the parties is clear. To effectuate the intention an assignment for value, in terms present and immediate, has always been regarded in equity as a contract binding on the conscience of the assignor and so binding the subject-matter of the contract when it comes into existence, if it is of such a nature and so described as to be capable of being ascertained and identified.' See also, *Brown v Tanner* (1868) 3 ChApp 597 (assignment of future freight); *Re Irving, ex p Brett* (1877) 7 ChD 419 (assignment of future dividends in bankruptcy); *Re Pyle Works* (1890) 44 ChD 534, CA (assignment of uncalled capital).

It is not necessary for the assignee of the beneficial interest in the contract to possess or to acquire any interest in the subject-matter of insurance,[21] though he may do so as a collateral part of the transaction.[1]

Nor is the consent of the insurers to the assignment required, even if the policy contains a condition against assignment without their consent,[2] or even an express condition that the policy shall not be assignable in any case whatever,[3] since the assignment does not alter the relations of the original parties to the contract, and consequently, does not prevent the personal factor in the contract of insurance from having its full operation.[4]

The policy continues to subsist, depending for its existence on the continuance of the assured's interest and on his performance of the duties imposed upon him personally by the nature of the contract, whilst the assignment relates merely to the application of the proceeds of the insurance, and takes effect only in the event of a loss.[5]

The assignment of the right to receive sums which may become payable under the policy is equally subject to equities, and the assignee is liable to be defeated not only by the acts and omissions of the assured before the assignment,[6] but also his acts and omissions afterwards.[7]

Even the fact that the insurers have expressly consented to the assignment

---

21 *McPhillips v London and Mutual Fire Insurance Co* (1896) 23 AR 524, (fire insurance).

1 This will be the case where the property insured is mortgaged and the proceeds of the policy are assigned as collateral security; see e g *London Investment Co v Montefiore* (1864) 9 LT 688 (fire insurance).

2 *McPhillips v London Mutual Fire Insurance Co* (supra) (fire insurance).

3 *Re Turcan* (1888) 40 ChD 5, CA (life insurance) per Cotton LJ, at 10: 'I think the condition was inserted in order to prevent the insured from availing himself of his power to assign the policy and to give the assignee a right to receive the money from the office. But though he could not assign the policy, I think it would have been a sufficient compliance with the covenant (ie to settle after-acquired property) if he had executed a declaration of trust for the trustees of the settlement, just as he might have done before the passing of the Act of 1867. Then he could not have assigned the policy or given his trustees the power to receive the money, but he might have given them all the benefit of the money when it was received. And I think he could have given them the same benefit in the present case by executing a declaration of trust.'

4 Consequently, a breach of condition by the assignor even after the date of the assignment will, as a general rule, avoid the policy and thus defeat the assignee: *Mechanics Building and Savings Society v Gore District Mutual Fire Insurance Co* (1878) 3 AR 151.

5 Hence, the validity of the assignment cannot be questioned on the ground of the personal nature of the contract, as was the case in *Kemp v Baerselman* [1906] 2 KB 604, CA (contract to supply goods), where it was held that an assignment even of the beneficial interest was prohibited where the contract involved a personal element.

6 *William Pickersgill & Sons Ltd v London and Provincial Marine and General Insurance Co Ltd* [1912] 3 KB 614 (marine insurance); *Scottish Amicable Life Assurance Society v Fuller* (1867) IR 2 Eq 53 (life insurance); *Scottish Equitable Life Assurance Society v Buist* 1877 4 R (Ct of Sess) 1076 (life insurance); *Thomson v Weems* (1884) 9 App Cas 671 (life insurance).

7 *Whyte v Western Assurance Co* (1875) 22 LCJ 215, PC (fire insurance), where the assignee was precluded from recovering by the assured's failure to furnish the necessary proofs of loss; *Amicable Society v Bolland* (1830) 2 Dow & Cl 1 (life insurance); *Central Bank of India v Guardian Assurance Co Ltd* (1936) 54 LlL Rep 247, PC, where a fraudulent claim was made by the mortgagor; *Kanady v Gore District Mutual Fire Insurance Co* (1879) 44 UCR 261, where it was held that the assignee of a policy was prevented from recovering by reason of the assignor's breaches of condition against alienation and double insurance; cf *King v Phoenix Assurance Co* [1910] 2 KB 666, CA (employers' liability insurance). The assured may expressly covenant with the assignee not to do any act which avoids the policy: *Hawkins v Coulthurst* (1864) 5 B & S 343 (life insurance); but the doing of such an act is not a breach of a covenant to do all acts requisite for keeping the policy on foot: *Dormay v Borrodaile* (1847) 10 Beav 335 (life insurance).

does not improve the assignee's position, or preclude them from resisting liability on the ground that the policy is invalid,[8] unless their conduct amounts to a representation that at the date of the assignment there is a valid contract in existence, e g where the proposed assignee made inquiries of the insurers and was informed that the policy was valid, or unless a new contract, which is not to be affected by the subsequent conduct of the assured, is created between the assignee and the insurers by the terms of their consent.[9]

The material date for ascertaining the rights of the parties is the date at which such rights become effective, and unless at that date the policy is in force and the liability of the insurers has arisen, no claim can be successful.[10]

The policy, may, however, provide that if it is afterwards bona fide assigned[11] to an assignee[12] for valuable consideration,[13] it may be enforced for the benefit of the assignee, notwithstanding a breach of condition by the assured.[14]

C THE FORM OF THE ASSIGNMENT

In general, there are no statutory provisions relating to the form in which an assignment of the proceeds of the policy must be made.

But as far as marine insurance is concerned, the Marine Insurance Act 1906, s 50(3), provides;

> 'A marine policy may be assigned by indorsement thereon or in other customary manner.'[15]

---

8 *Kuntz v Niagara District Fire Insurance Co* (1866) 16 CP 573; *Stanstead and Sherbrooke Mutual Fire Insurance Co v Gooley* (1899) QR 9 KB 324; cf *Cormier v Ottawa Agricultural Insurance Co* (1881) 20 NBR 526, where an indorsement making the loss payable to the mortgagee to the extent of his interest was held to be neither a contract by the insurers to pay the mortgagee, nor an assignment, and consequently the mortgagee was precluded from recovering by reason of a breach of condition by the mortgagor.

9 *Burton v Gore District Mutual Fire Insurance Co* (1865) 12 Gr 156, approved but distinguished in *Mechanics Building Socieyty v Gore District Mutual Fire Insurance Co* (1878) 3 AR 151; *Western Australian Bank v Royal Insurance Co* (1908) 5 CLR 533.

10 *Stokell v Heywood* [1897] 1 Ch 459 (accident insurance), where the assignees were held not entitled to the proceeds of a renewed policy, the policy assigned to them having expired without any claim.

11 An equitable assignment is sufficient: *Cook v Black* (1842) 1 Hare 390 (life insurance); *Dufaur v Professional Life Insurance Co* (1858) 25 Beav 599 (life insurance), where the words of the condition 'legally assigned' were held to mean 'validly and effectually assigned'. The provision does not protect the original assured, even though the insurance is in respect of a third person: *Rowett, Leakey & Co Ltd v Scottish Provident Institution* [1927] 1 Ch 55, CA (life insurance).

12 Including the insurers themselves: *White v British Empire Mutual Life Assurance Co* (1868) LR 7 Eq 394 (life insurance), distinguished in *Royal London Mutual Insurance Society Ltd v Barrett* [1928] Ch 411 (life insurance).

13 A past consideration is not sufficient: *Wigan v English and Scottish Law Life Assurance Association* [1909] 1 Ch 291 (life insurance). A trustee in bankruptcy is not an assignee for valuable consideration within the meaning of the condition: *Jackson v Forster* (1860) 1 E & E 470, ExCh (life insurance).

14 *Ballantyne's Trustees v Scottish Amicable Life Assurance Society* [1921] WC & Ins Rep 263 (life insurance). Where the assignment is to secure a debt, the insurers are not entitled, on payment of the sum due under the policy, to an assignment of any other securities held by the assignee or to an apportionment of the debt between such securities and the policy: *Solicitors' and General Life Assurance Society v Lamb* (1864) 2 De G J & Sm 251, CA (life insurance), followed in *City Bank v Sovereign Life Assurance Co* (1884) 50 LT 565 (life insurance).

15 See further, Ivamy *Marine Insurance* (4th Edn, 1985), pp 319–320.

Further, in relation to life insurance policies,[16] the Policies of Assurance Act 1867, s 5, states:

> 'Any such assignment may be made either by indorsement on the policy or by a separate instrument in the words or to the effect set forth in the schedule hereto,[17] such indorsement or separate instrument being duly stamped.'

Except, therefore, where the policy expressly provides to the contrary,[18] the beneficial interest in it may be assigned in equity, whether the assignment is before or after loss, and whether it is absolute or by way of mortgage or charge, by any form of assignment so long as the intention is clear,[19] and provided that it is recognised in equity as sufficient.[20]

To complete the assignee's title it is necessary for notice of the assignment to be given to the insurers.[21] In the event of a claim arising under the policy, any action must, if the assignment is equitable only, be brought in the name of the assured.[1]

The right to receive the money under the policy may, however, be assigned by way of a legal assignment. The assignment must comply with the requirements of the Law of Property Act 1925, s 136, i e must be an absolute assignment in writing signed by the assured, of which express notice in writing has been given to the insurers.

---

16 In *Re Turcan* (1888) 40 ChD 5, CA, where the effect of the statute was discussed, the Court does not seem to have attached any importance to the fact that the principal policy in question was not a life policy, but a personal accident policy. It is submitted that the Policies of Assurance Act 1867, does not apply to personal accident policies. The Act applies only to companies carrying on life assurances business (ibid, s 7) so that companies carrying on personal accident insurance business apart from life insurance business are not within its scope. Moreover, a personal accident policy is not an instrument by which payment 'on the happening of any contingency depending on the duration of human life, is assured' (ibid).

17 This schedule states the form of words which may be used viz 'I, AB . . . of, &c, in consideration of, &c, do hereby assign unto CD, of, &c, his executors, administrators, and assigns, the [within] policy of assurance granted, &c, [here describe the policy]. In witness, &c.' See further, Ivamy *Personal Accident, Life and Other Insurances* (2nd Edn, 1980), pp 106–107.

18 *Re Turcan* (1888) 40 ChD 5, CA.

19 *Tailby v Official Receiver* (1888) 13 AppCas 523 (future book debts) per Lord MacNaughten, at 543; cf *Crossley v City of Glasgow Life Assurance Co* (1876) 4 ChD 421 (life insurance), where a letter from the assured accompanying the deposit of the policy, asking the proposed assignee to instruct his solicitor to prepare an assignment, was held not to be sufficient. See further, *Re Foster* (1873) IR 7 Eq 294 (fire insurance), where the document was held not to be sufficient.

20 In practice the assignment is usually indorsed on the policy, or on the cover note, as the case may be: *O'Connor v Imperial Insurance Co* (1869) 14 LCJ 219. See further *Chowne v Baylis* (1862) 31 Beav 351 (life insurance); *Spencer v Clarke* (1878) 9 ChD 137 (life insurance); *Re King, Sewell v King* (1869) 14 ChD 179 (life insurance), folowing *Fortescue v Barnett* (1834) 3 My & K 36 (life insurance). In *Howes v Prudential Assurance Co* (1883) 48 LT 133 (life insurance) it was held that an equitable assignment of a policy must be in writing, and that a verbal assignment, coupled with delivery of the policy, was not sufficient to entitle the assignee to the proceeds of the policy. It is difficult to see why writing should be necessary. A verbal assignment of a marine policy, coupled with delivery, was sufficient before the Policies of Marine Assurance Act 1868: *Powles v Innes* (1843) 11 M & W 10; and, even if this arose out of a usage peculiar to marine insurance, it shows that writing cannot be universally essential to the validity of an equitable assignment; cf *Maugham v Ridley* (1863) 8 LT 309 (life insurance), where on the deposit of a policy to secure a debt, there was a verbal understanding that the deposit would properly secure not only the existing, but also any further advances.

21 *Re Foster* (1873) IR 7 Eq 294 (fire insurance); *Re Hennessy* (1842) IR 5 Eq 259 (life insurance).

1 But see *William Brandt's Sons & Co v Dunlop Rubber Co* [1905] AC 454 (assignment of debt) per Lord MacNaughten, at 462.

Where the assignment takes place after loss, at a time when the loss has been admitted, and the amount payable has been ascertained, there is no doubt that such an assignment can be made since there is actually a debt in existence capable of being legally assigned.[2]

Where, however, though the assignment is made after loss, the loss has not been admitted, or the sum payable ascertained, or where the assignment is made before loss, different considerations apply, for in these cases there is no existing debt. If, therefore, the assignment purports to be an assignment of a specific sum, it is not a good legal assignment.[3]

There is, however, an existing contract, and although the contract cannot be assigned in its entirety, the benefit of the contract appears, therefore, to be a legal chose in action within the meaning of the statute;[4] and if the assignment purports to assign it, and does not deal with a specific sum, the assignee is probably entitled to sue the insurers in his own name.[5]

Where, on notice of the assignment being given to the insurers they expressly contract with the assignee to pay him the sum assigned when it falls due, the question as to whether the assignment is legal or equitable only becomes immaterial. In this case, the assignee's rights as against the insurers depend not so much on his assignment from the assured as on their express contract with himself, and he is, therefore, entitled under this contract to sue them in his own name.[6]

---

2 A legal assignment of part of the proceeds cannot be made: *Re Steel Wing Co* [1921] 1 Ch 349, following *Forster v Baker* [1910] 2 KB 636, CA (assignment of debt) and not following *Skipper and Tucker v Holloway and Howard* [1910] 2 KB 630 (assignment of debt); *Williams v Atlantic Assurance Co Ltd* [1933] 1 KB 81, CA (marine insurance).

3 *Re Steel Wing Co* (supra).

4 Which distinguishes between an assignment of a debt and an assignment of a chose in action: *Re Moore, ex p Ibbetson* (1878) 8 ChD 519, CA (life insurance), per Jessel MR, at 520.

5 In *English and Scottish Mercantile Investment Co v Brunton* [1892] 2 QB 700, CA, the point does not appear to have been taken. The validity of a legal assignment before loss seems to be established; see *Torkington v Magee* [1902] 2 KB 427 (assignment of a contract to sell a reversionary interest) per Channell J, at 431–432; see also, *Manchester Brewery Co v Coombs* [1901] 2 Ch 608 per Farwell J, at 619, adopting the language of the Colonial Court (not of the Judicial Committee of the Privy Council as stated per Farwell J) in *King v Victoria Insurance Co* [1896] AC 250: 'Since the Judicature Act 1873, the right to sue on those covenants is a chose in action within s 25(6)' [now Law of Property Act 1925, s 136] 'the term "chose in action" in that section has been said in the Privy Council . . . to include all "rights the assignment of which a Court of Law or equity would before the Act have considered normal".' As to the validity of an assignment after loss, cf *Dawson v Great Northern and City Rly Co* [1905] 1 KB 260 (compensation under Lands Clauses Consolidation Act 1845, s 68).

6 *London Investment Co v Montefiore* (1864) 9 LT 688 per Erle CJ, at 688.

CHAPTER 45

Reinstatement

The liability of the insurers to make good the loss under the policy is a liability to do so by a payment in money.[1] Though any other mode of discharging their liability may be substituted with the consent of the assured,[2] they cannot without his consent insist on making good the loss by what is usually known as 'reinstatement', i e by replacing what is lost or repairing what is damaged.[3] Nor can they, after payment of the loss, insist, in the absence of any contract or statute to that effect, that the assured shall himself expend money paid in reinstatement.[4]

In some cases a third person has the right to compel the assured to reinstate the property.

A REINSTATEMENT BY THE INSURERS

The insurers are entitled to reinstate the property either as a result of a contract to that effect, or, where the property insured is a house or a building, and it is damaged by fire, as a result of the powers given to them under the Fires Prevention (Metropolis) Act 1774.

1 Reinstatement under contract

(a) The reinstatement clause

The policy, however, usually contains in the appropriate branches of insurance, e g fire, burglary, plate glass, steam boiler and motor vehicle insurance, a 'reinstatement clause', which confers on the insurers the option of making good the loss by reinstatement. The contract contained in the policy, nevertheless, remains a contract to pay a sum of money, subject to the right of the insurers, if they think fit, to substitute a different mode of discharging their liability.[5]

The clause is intended to benefit the insurers and to protect them from liability to pay the full pecuniary value of the loss, if the loss can be more

---

1 *Rayner v Preston* (1881) 18 ChD 1, CA (fire insurance) per Brett LJ, at 9.

2 *Times Fire Assurance Co v Hawke* (1859) 28 LJEx 317 (fire insurance) per Bramwell B, at 318: 'As between the company and the assured, the contract was one of indemnity and they might have agreed to take a wall, or a load of barley in satisfaction.'

3 *Anderson v Commercial Union Assurance Co* (1885) 55 LJQB 146, CA (fire insurance) per Lord Esher MR, at 148; and per Bowen LJ, at 149.

4 *Re Law Guarantee Trust and Accident Society Ltd, Liverpool Mortgage Insurance Co Ltd's Case* [1914] 2 Ch 617, CA (debenture insurance) per Kennedy LJ, at 639; *Queen Insurance Co v Vey* (1867) 16 LT 239 (fire insurance).

5 *Rayner v Preston* (supra) (fire insurance) per Brett LJ, at 9.

cheaply made good otherwise.[6] Hence, the assured cannot take advantage of the clause and insist on reinstatement if the insurers do not elect to reinstate;[7] nor on the other hand, can he prevent them from reinstating if they have elected to do so.[8]

Further, an assignee of the proceeds of the policy, even where the insurers have assented to the assignment, cannot prevent them from exercising their option to reinstate, since by virtue of his assignment he acquires no larger right than the assignor.

(b) Time within which election is to be made

The policy may specify a period before or after the expiration of which the option is to be exercised.[9] Usually it contains no reference to time at all, in which case the option must be exercised within a reasonable time. Sometimes the insurers are expressly empowered to exercise their option at any time, even after the amount of the loss or damage has been adjusted or ascertained or an arbitration award or a judgment has been made or obtained.

The insurers may, however, before the expiration of the time allowed for the purpose, deprive themselves of their right to elect by their conduct, e g where they have dealt with the assured on the footing that he is to be indemnified by means of a money payment.[10]

They may also waive their right. But a waiver is not to be presumed from the mere fact that they have taken steps in conjunction with the assured to ascertain the amount of the loss, since, until this has been done, they are not in a position to decide whether to make good the loss by payment or reinstatement.[11]

The assured may also waive the requirement as to time.

(c) The mode of election

The insurers may expressly notify the assured that they intend to exercise their option and reinstate the property insured, in which case no difficulty arises. At the same time, an express election is not necessary. There may be a binding

---

6 *Anderson v Commercial Union Assurance Co* (supra) (fire insurance) per Bowen LJ, at 149.

7 Ibid, per Bowen LJ, at 149.

8 *Bissett v Royal Exchange Assurance Co* (1821) 1 Sh (Ct of Sess) 174 (fire insurance).

9 Ibid, where the condition provided for reinstatement at the end of 60 days after notice of loss.

10 *Scottish Amicable Heritable Securities Association Ltd v Northern Assurance Co* 1833 11 R (Ct of Sess) 287; *Lalande v Phoenix Insurance Co of Hartford* (1918) QR 54 SC 461, where the insurers had consented to arbitration as to amount; cf *Sutherland v Sun Fire Office* 1852 14 Dunl (Ct of Sess) 775, where there was a mere reference to valuators to ascertain the amount of the loss.

11 *Sutherland v Sun Fire Office* (supra) per Lord Anderson, at 777; 'I am not prepared to say that such a condition may not be waived or barred. But a strong case must be made out . . . Now one observation is that the power to reinstate could not be exercised immediately on the loss. Until a claim was made by the pursuer accompanied by evidence of the loss it would be unreasonable to expect a settlement. It is only after this is done that the company can determine how they are to exercise their option. But it is said that there was an arbitration. If there had been an arbitration . . . there would have been an end to the case. But it is not alleged on the record that there was an arbitration. On the contrary, it is the statement of the pursuer himself that there was not an out-and-out reference, but a remit to these parties to ascertain as far as possible the amount of loss by damage to the stock . . . Therefore I cannot hold that the reference to valuators could supersede the right of the company to reinstate.'

election by conduct, where the insurers have so conducted themselves as to mislead the assured into thinking that they intend to reinstate.[12]

Since, however, it would be unreasonable to expect that the insurers would elect to reinstate unless and until they had all the materials before them requisite for their guidance in deciding which of the two courses open to them would be more advantageous, no act by them for the purpose of ascertaining the extent of the loss or damage, or the cost of reinstatement, can fairly be considered an election under which they are bound to reinstate.[13]

It may, indeed, be made an express term of the policy that the insurers are not called upon to elect, unless and until they have obtained all such information, and all such plans and estimates as may be deemed necessary or expedient for the purpose.

(d) The effect of the election

The insurers, by exercising their option, substitute a different mode of discharging their obligation under the policy.[14] Their contract is no longer a contract to pay a sum of money, but a contract to reinstate the property insured.[15] They cannot withdraw from it,[16] and, although they are not compellable to perform it specifically,[17] they are liable for the consequences of a failure to perform it adequately.[18]

If the whole or any part of the property insured is destroyed, it is their duty, in the case of a building, to rebuild it, or, in the case of goods, to replace them by goods of a corresponding description and quality, so far as may be necessary, in either case, to make good the loss. If the property is damaged, and capable of being restored to its condition by reinstatement or repair, it is their duty to reinstate or repair it.[19]

---

12 Where the consent of the third person is necessary before reinstatement can be made, there is no binding election until such consent has been obtained: *Bank of New South Wales v Royal Insurance Co* (1880) 2 NZLR 337.

13 *Sutherland v Sun Fire Office* (supra) per the Lord President at 778.

14 There is no fresh contract, and it is therefore unnecessary for the assured to show an insurable interest beyond the time of the loss: *Bank of New South Wales v Royal Insurance Co* (supra).

15 *Brown v Royal Insurance Co* (1859) 1 E & E 853 (fire insurance) per Lord Campbell CJ, at 858: 'The case stands as if the policy had been simply to reinstate the premises in case of fire; because, where a contract provides for an election, the party making the election is in the same position as if he had originally contracted to do the act which he has elected to do.'

16 *Sutherland v Sun Fire Office* (supra) per Lord Ivory, at 779.

17 *Home District Mutual Insurance Co v Thompson* (1847) 1 E & A 247.

18 *Times Fire Assurance Co v Hawke* (1859) 28 LJ Ex 317 (fire insurance); *Brown v Royal Insurance Co* (1859) 1 E & E 853 (fire insurance); *Robson v New Zealand Insurance Co* [1931] NZLR 35; *Alchorne v Favill* (1825) 4 LJ OSCh 47 (fire insurance); *Davidson v Guardian Royal Exchange Assurance* [1979] 1 Lloyd's Rep 406, Inner House, Second Division of the Court of Session (motor insurance), where the insurers elected to get a damaged car repaired and the repairs took 40 weeks whereas a reasonable time for their completion was about 8 weeks, and it was held that they were in breach of an implied term of the contract to see that the repairs were executed in a reasonable time, and were liable to the insured for the loss of use of the vehicle. Lord Kissen said (ibid, at 409) that the policy was the occasion for the breach of contract in that the breach was caused by the manner in which the insurers tried to carry out their contractual obligation to repair, but the policy was otherwise irrelevant to the claim; *Leppard v Excess Insurance Co Ltd* [1979] 2 All ER 668, [1979] 1 WLR 512, [1979] 2 Lloyd's Rep 91, CA (fire insurance), where a cottage was destroyed by fire, and the question was whether the insured was entitled to the cost of reinstatement or the amount of the loss actually suffered.

19 *Anderson v Commercial Union Assurance Co* (1885) 55 LJQB 146, CA (fire insurance) per Lord

In the case of goods, there is, as a rule, no reason why this duty should not be literally fulfilled, even where there is a total loss of the subject-matter, since there is usually an available market in which the requisite equivalent can, if necessary, be bought.[20]

In the case of a building, however, it would be unreasonable to demand from the insurers a literal performance of their duty, for it is impracticable to restore every minute detail of a building. They will, therefore, have fulfilled their duty when the restored building is substantially the same as before.[1]

If, however, it falls short of the original building in any material respect, they have not rebuilt or reinstated it within the meaning of the policy, and are accordingly liable to the assured for damages for their failure to do so.[2]

If, on the other hand, the effect of the reinstatement is to give the assured a better building than before, they cannot in the absence of an agreement to that effect, compel him to bear a portion of the cost, even though they have, in fact, exceeded the sum which it was necessary for them to expend in the due performance of their duty.[3]

Unless, therefore, the policy so provides,[4] the insurers cannot limit their expenditure to the sum insured and excuse themselves from not completing their contract by showing that the reinstatement will be more expensive than they had anticipated, or even that it has become impossible owing to circumstances beyond their control.[5] They are bound by their election and must perform their contract or pay damages for not performing it.[6]

Esher MR, at 148: 'We have come to the conclusion that the words "reinstate" and "replace" should be thus applied; if the property is wholly destroyed, the company may, if they choose, instead of paying the money to replace the things by others which are equivalent; or, if the goods insured are damaged but not destroyed, may exercise the option to reinstate them—i e to repair them and put them in the condition in which they were before the fire.'

20 *Sutherland v Sun Fire Office* (supra) per Lord Anderson, at 778: 'Reinstatement is replacement of the stock in forma specifica.'

1 *Times Fire Assurance Co v Hawke* as reported in (1858) 1 F & F 406 per Channell B, at 407: 'As to the main question the defendant was only bound to put the house substantially in the same state as before the fire and was not bound to púll down the old walls and rebuild them entirely on account of any defects in their foundation.' For a special condition, see *Alleyn v La Cie d'Assurance de Quebec* (1861) 11 LCR 394, where the reinstated premises had to be passed by experts before the assured could be compelled to take them.

2 *Alchorne v Favill* (1825) 4 LJ OS Ch 47 (fire insurance), where the insurers were prevented by a Building Act from making the building project into the street beyond the line of the adjacent houses, as it did before, and consequently the premises erected by them were of inferior value; *Kaffarian Colonial Bank v Grahamstown Fire Insurance Co* (1885) 5 Buchanan (East Dist Ct Cape) 61, where the building as reinstated by the insurers was not of equal value to the one destroyed, and the Court gave judgment against the insurers for the difference.

3 *Brown v Royal Insurance Co* (1859) 1 E & E 853 (fire insurance) per Crompton J, at 860; cf *Vance v Forster* (1841) Ir Cir Rep 47. The policy may provide for an allowance to be made to the insurers if the reinstated building is of greater value than the building destroyed.

4 *Young v New Zealand Insurance Co* (1910) 12 NZ Gaz LR 315. The limitation of liability would not apply where the insurers were in default, e g where the work of reinstatement was badly done. Cf *Swift v New Zealand Insurance Co Ltd* [1927] VLR 249.

5 *Alchorne v Favill* (1825) 4 LJ OS Ch 47 (fire insurance); *Brown v Royal Insurance Co* (1859) 1 E & E 853 (fire insurance), where the Commissioners of Sewers, after the insurers had begun to reinstate, condemned the premises as being dangerous; *Anderson v Commercial Union Assurance Co* (1885) 55 LJQB 146, CA (fire insurance) per Bowen LJ, at 150.

6 *Brown v Royal Insurance Co* (supra) per Crompton J, at 860: 'The defendants are bound by their election, and if the performance has become impossible, or (which is all they have shown) more expensive than they had anticipated, still they must either perform their contract or pay damages for not performing it.'

In the case of a fire policy, where a fire breaks out during the reinstatement and again destroys the property, the insurers are not in any way excused, but must complete the work. During the progress of reinstatement they are their own insurers; and the happening of the subsequent fire does not concern the assured, who remains entitled to insist on the due performance by the insurers of their obligation without crediting them with what they have already expended.[7]

Where it becomes impossible to reinstate goods in their original locality because the building in which they were situated has been destroyed, or because the assured has no longer a right of access thereto, the insurers are not discharged from their duty to reinstate the goods insured, but the assured may require them to do so within a reasonable distance of the original locality.

Further, if the insurers have not already elected to reinstate, they are not deprived of their right to do so. The assured cannot insist on a money payment merely because it is impossible to reinstate the goods in the locality where they were before the fire.[8]

The insurers are also responsible for the manner in which the rebuilding or reinstatement is carried out. Thus, if, owing to bad workmanship, the work has to be done over again by the assured, they are liable to him for the expense to which he may have been put, although they will in their turn have a right to be reimbursed by the person to whom they delegated the work, and who was directly responsible for its defects.[9]

(e) The duties of the assured

The policy usually provides that the assured is at his own expense to furnish the insurers with such plans, documents, books and information, as may be reasonably required for the purpose of reinstatement.[10]

Apart from any such provision, it is his duty to facilitate the work of reinstatement by all means in his power; and he must not, therefore, interfere with the insurers or prevent them from performing the work. Thus, if he refuses to permit them to go on to the land on which the insured building stood, or, if it

---

7 *Smith v Colonial Mutual Fire Insurance Co* (1880) 6 VLR 200, where a second fire occurred during reinstatement, and the insurers claimed that they were entitled to credit for the amount already spent; cf *Brown v Royal Insurance Co* (supra).

8 *Anderson v Commercial Union Assurance Co* (supra) per Lord Esher MR, at 148: 'The condition says nothing as to locality and therefore it is idle on the part of the company to say that if locally in which the things were is destroyed, they may elect to reinstate or replace, and then do neither. But the plaintiff was equally wrong. His proposition that, if the goods could not be reinstated or replaced in the place where they were before, either because that place was destroyed, or because he could not legally get there, he therefore had a right to be paid in money, and the option of the company was taken away. I cannot think that is right . . . If the plaintiff could not get the things put back where they were before the fire, he has a right to say that the company should do what is reasonable—that is, if he could not go back to the same place, he might take the things to a place within a reasonable distance, and ask them to repair the things there, or might say, "Take them to your own place and repair them".'

9 *Times Fire Assurance Co v Hawke* (1859) 28 LJEx 317 (fire insurance); *Braithwaite v Employers' Liability Assurance Corpn* [1964] 1 Lloyd's Rep 94 (burglary insurance), where the insurers were held to be entitled to reject a replica of a brooch made by a firm of jewellers since it was inferior to the brooch insured, and the assured had rightly refused to accept it as a replacement.

10 If, upon the construction of the particular provision, the plans etc., have to be furnished before election, they must be furnished, if the insurers so require, although reinstatement has been rendered impossible: *Young v New Zealand Insurance Co* (1910) 12 NZ Gaz LR 315.

appears that he has no title to it and cannot, therefore, provide them with a site upon which to rebuild, he is guilty of a breach of duty, which discharges them from their obligation to reinstate,[11] and, apparently, from all obligation under the policy, since the original contract to pay a sum of money no longer exists, but has already been replaced by the contract to reinstate.

2 Reinstatement under the Fires Prevention (Metropolis) Act 1774

The Fires Prevention (Metropolis) Act 1774,[12] contains certain provisions relating to the reinstatement of houses and other buildings. It does not apply to trade fixtures[13] or personal property of any kind.[14] The object of these provisions is to deter evilly-disposed persons from wilfully setting fire to their property for the purpose of obtaining the insurance money, and thereby endangering the lives and fortunes of the public.[15]

Although the statute is a local Act, the provisions relating to reinstatement have been held not to be confined in their application to the district to which the statute specially applies (i e 'the cities of London and Westminster and the liberties thereof and the parishes, precincts and places within the weekly bills of mortality, the parishes of St Mary-le-bow, Paddington, St Pancras, and St Luke at Chelsea, in the County of Middlesex'), but to be applicable to the whole of England.[16]

The statute authorises and requires the governors or directors of the insurance company with which any house or building which may be burned down, demolished, or damaged by fire, is insured, to apply the insurance money in rebuilding, reinstating or repairing such house or building where:

- a there is reason to suspect that the assured, whether he is the owner or occupier of the property insured or otherwise, has been guilty of fraud, or of wilfully setting such property on fire;[17] or
- b the insurers are requested to reinstate the property upon the request of any person interested in or entitled to it.

---

11 Cf *Roberts v Bury Improvement Comrs* (1870) LR 5 CP 310 (building contract).

12 See Appendix A, pp 627–628.

13 *Re Barker, ex p Gorely* (1864) 4 De GJ & Sm 477.

14 *Re Quicke's Trusts, Poltimore v Quicke* [1908] 1 Ch 887.

15 *Simpson v Scottish Union Insurance Co* (1863) 1 Hem & M 618 per Wood V-C, at 628: 'The object of the provision is in the interest of the public to prevent persons from fraudulently setting fire to their houses, and this is a fraud, which, of course, might be committed by the owner or the tenant. The company themselves are to rebuild in order that they may see that the money is really laid out in reinstating the property.'

16 *Sinnott v Bowden* [1912] 2 Ch 414, following *Re Barker, ex p Gorely* (1864) 4 De GJ & Sm 477; *Re Quicke's Trusts, Poltimore v Quicke* [1908] 1 Ch 887. In *Rayner v Preston* (1881) 18 ChD 1, CA, the statute was assumed to apply to Liverpool. The provisions do not apply to Scotland: *Westminster Fire Office v Glasgow Provident Investment Society* (1888) 13 App Cas 699 per Lord Watson, at 716; nor to Ireland: *Andrews v Patriotic Assurance Co (No 2)* (1886) 18 LRIr 355 per Palles CB, at 368. But doubts have been expressed as to whether the statute should not be confined to the Metropolitan area: *Westminster Fire Office v Glasgow Provident Investment Society* (supra) per Lord Selborne at 713, and Lord Watson, at 716, doubting *Re Barker, ex p Gorely* (supra). The point was raised, but no opinion expressed, in *Simpson v Scottish Union Insurance Co* (supra) per Wood V-C, at 629, and in *Vernon v Smith* (1821) 5 B & Ald 1 per Abbott CJ, at 5.

17 If, however, fraud or arson on the part of the assured can be proved as distinct from suspected, the insurers will repudiate liability and no question of the application of the Act arises: *Logan v Hall* (1847) 4 CB 598 per Maule J, at 623.

The Act does not apply to policies subscribed by Lloyd's underwriters.[18]

The persons entitled to claim reinstatement under the statute[19] include owners;[20] lessors[1] and lessees,[2] or tenants from year to year;[3] tenants for life and remaindermen;[4] and mortgagors or mortgagees.[5]

An insured, who is also the owner of the property, has no right under the statute to claim reinstatement.[6]

The right does not arise until a distinct request to reinstate the property insured has been made to the insurers by the person entitled to claim reinstatement.[7] He cannot himself do the work of reinstatement and then call on them to pay over to himself the amount payable under the assured's policy.[8] In the absence of any such request, therefore, the insurers are justified in paying over the insurance money to the assured.[9]

If the insurers fail to reinstate the property insured on request, the person claiming reinstatement may obtain an injunction to restrain them from paying over the insurance money to the assured.[10] He may, perhaps, also be entitled to

---

18 *Portavon Cinema Co Ltd v Price and Century Insurance Co Ltd* [1939] 4 All ER 601 per Branson J, at 607.

19 The right to claim reinstatement is not displaced by a garnishee order *nisi* attaching the policy money: *Sinnott v Bowden* [1912] 2 Ch 414; but it does not invest the person interested with an insurance on the property: *Portavon Cinema Co Ltd v Price and Century Insurance Co Ltd* (supra).

20 A purchaser pending completion, being the equitable owner, is probably entitled to claim the right: *Rayner v Preston* (1881) 18 ChD 1, CA, per James LJ, at 15. Cotton LJ, at 7, declined to express an opinion.

1 *Vernon v Smith* (1821) 5 B & Ald 1; *Penniall v Harborne* (1848) 11 QB 368.

2 *Wimbledon Park Golf Club v Imperial Insurance Co* (1902) 18 TLR 815. The lessee may claim reinstatement under a policy in the joint names of himself and the lessor: *Paris v Gilham* (1813) Coop G 56, where the insurers were held entitled to interplead, distinguished in *Sun Insurance Office v Galinsky* [1914] 2 KB 545, CA.

3 *Simpson v Scottish Union Insurance Co* (1863) 1 Hem & M 618.

4 *Re Quicke's Trusts, Poltimore v Quicke* [1908] 1 Ch 887.

5 *Sinnott v Bowden* [1912] 2 Ch 414, not following *Westminster Fire Office v Glasgow Provident Investment Society* (1888) 13 App Cas 699 per Lord Selborne, at 714; *Re Barker, ex p Gorely* (1864) 4 De GJ & Sm 477; *Stinson v Pennock* (1868) 14 Gr 604; *Carr v Fire Assurance Association* (1887) 14 OR 487.

6 *Reynolds and Anderson v Phoenix Assurance Co Ltd* [1978] 2 Lloyd's Rep 440 (fire insurance) per Forbes J, at 462: 'That the assured person and the person serving the notice should ever be one and the same person I am quite sure never entered the heads of the draftsmen of the Act or of the Parliament who passed it. This is shown by the final provisions. These allow for the assured to give a sufficient security to the insurance company that he will himself spend the insurance money on reinstatement, or to arrange for the insurance money to be divided appropriately between himself and the other person interested in the building. Neither of these provisions would be at all appropriate to a case where it was the assured who made the request. The whole scheme of the section is to prevent the insurance money being paid to an assured who might make away with it.'

7 The request need not be in writing, but should refer to the statute; a mere claim to have the insurance paid to the claimant or for his benefit is not sufficient: *Simpson v Scottish Union Insurance Co* (supra) per Wood V-C, at 627. The request must, it is submitted, be made before payment to the assured.

8 Ibid, per Wood V-C, at 628: 'The Act of Parliament points to a request of this kind in order that the company may cause the money to be paid out in rebuilding, and I think it is clear that they could not pay the money to the owner . . . The policy of the Act . . . does not in any case give the owner the right to rebuild and claim the money, but requires the work to be done by the company; if this were otherwise, the purpose of the Act might be defeated by the landlord taking the policy money when there was a covenant by the tenant to rebuild.' See also *Sun Insurance Office v Galinsky* [1914] 2 KB 545, CA.

9 *Simpson v Scottish Union Insurance Co* (supra).

10 *Wimbledon Park Golf Club v Imperial Insurance Co* (1902) 18 TLR 815 per Wright J, at 816.

a mandamus to compel them to reinstate,[11] but he cannot recover damages for loss suffered by reason of the insurers' default.[12]

The reinstatement is to be effected by the insurers, unless, within 60 days after the adjustment of the claim, the assured gives a sufficient security to them that he will himself expend the insurance money in reinstatement,[13] or unless the insurance money is within that time settled and disposed of amongst the contending parties[14] to the satisfaction and approbation of the insurers.

The insurers cannot be compelled to expend more on reinstatement than the amount of the insurance.[15] But they are under no duty to reinstate the property unless the assured is entitled to maintain a claim under the policy.[16]

B REINSTATEMENT BY THE ASSURED

When the assured has received from the insurers the sum payable under his policy, he may, as a rule, deal with it as he pleases. He cannot, therefore, be compelled to expend it in reinstatement,[17] unless he has entered into a contract to do so,[18] or unless the duty of reinstating the property out of the proceeds of his insurance is imposed on him by statute.

Thus, if premises demised under a lease, which contains no covenant relating to reinstatement,[19] are destroyed by fire, the lessee is not entitled to call on the lessor to reinstate them out of the proceeds of a policy effected by the lessor for the protection of his own interest alone.[20] Nor can the lessor obtain the benefit of a policy which the lessee has taken out to cover his interest as lessee only, by requiring the lessee to apply the proceeds of his policy in reinstatement.[1]

But in some cases, although there is no express term in the contract that the

---

11 In *Simpson v Scottish Union Insurance Co* (supra) Wood V-C held that mandamus would lie. The contrary opinion was expressed in *Wimbledon Park Golf Club v Imperial Insurance Co* (supra), where the view was taken that the insurers were not empowered by the statute to enter upon the land, and the Court accordingly would not order them to commit a trespass; but see *Sun Insurance Office v Galinsky* (supra), where the Court refused to decide the point, and Kennedy LJ, at 560, whilst doubting the correctness of the report of *Wimbledon Park Golf Club v Imperial Insurance Co* (supra), expressed the opinion that the decision, if correctly reported, was irreconcilable with *Simpson v Scottish Union Insurance Co* (supra).

12 *Mylius v Royal Insurance Co Ltd* [1928] VLR 126, where the person claiming failed to recover loss of rent and profits suffered owing to the unreasonable delay of the insurers in reinstatement.

13 The person claiming reinstatement may object to the sufficiency of the bond, and the Court may allow the insufficiency to be rectified: *Wimbledon Park Golf Club v Imperial Insurance Co* (supra).

14 This includes persons who, though not interested in the policy money, are interested in the property insured and are insisting upon the policy money being laid out in reinstatement: *Sinnott v Bowden* [1912] 2 Ch 414 per Parker J, at 420.

15 Fires Prevention (Metropolis) Act 1774, s 83.

16 *Matthey v Curling* [1922] 2 AC 180 per Younger LJ, at 219. Thus, where the lessee's policy is avoided through misdescription, the lessee cannot claim reinstatement: *Auckland City Corpn v Mercantile General Insurance Co* [1930] NZLR 809; nor where the assured is guilty of fraud or arson: *Logan v Hall* (1847) 4 CB 598.

17 *Leeds v Cheetham* (1827) 1 Sim 146.

18 Such contracts are frequently made between mortgagors and mortgagees and between lessors and lessees: *Swan and Cleland's Graving Dock and Slipway Co v Maritime Insurance Co and Croshaw* [1907] 1 KB 116 (marine insurance) per Channell J, at 122, speaking of fire insurance.

19 A covenant to insure is not of itself sufficient: *Lees v Whiteley* (1866) LR 2 Eq 143.

20 *Leeds v Cheetham* (supra), where the lessee was under covenant with his lessor to repair followed in *Lofft v Dennis* (1859) 1 E & E 474, where there was no covenant to repair.

1 *Lees v Whiteley* (supra).

assured will apply the money received in reinstating the property, the Court may imply a term to this effect.[2]

1 Duty imposed by contract

Where a duty to employ the proceeds of a policy of insurance in reinstating the property destroyed is alleged to have been created by a contract, the existence of the contract must be clearly established.

Thus, there is no implied contract between the assured and the insurers that he will so apply his insurance money. But it may be shown that payment was made by the insurers on the faith of an express promise by him to do so, in which case an action lies for his failure to reinstate.[3]

Even the fact that the assured is under contract, either to the person claiming reinstatement or to a third person, to repair[4] or to insure[5] the premises in respect of which the insurance money has been paid, will not establish the duty. It must be shown that there is, in fact, a further contract to expend the money, when received, in reinstatement,[6] and that such contract is enforceable at the time when reinstatement is claimed.[7]

2 Duty imposed by statute

A duty to expend the money received under a policy in reinstating the insured property is expressly created by statute in the case of:

a Property subject to a trust or settlement.
b Mortgaged property.
c Ecclesiastical property.

(a) Property subject to a trust or settlement

In the case of property subject to a trust or settlement, the money receivable under a policy kept under any trust, power or obligation may be applied by the trustees, or, if in Court, under the direction of the Court, in reinstatement of the property destroyed or damaged, subject to the conditions imposed by the statute.[8]

(b) Mortgaged property

In the case of mortgaged property, all moneys received on an insurance effected under statute, or an insurance for the maintenance of which the mortgagor is

---

2 *Mumford Hotels Ltd v Wheler* [1964] Ch 117, [1963] 3 All ER 250, CA.

3 *Queen Insurance Co v Vey* (1867) 16 LT 239.

4 *Leeds v Cheetham* (supra); cf *Andrews v Patriotic Assurance Co (No 2)* (1886) 18 LRIr 355.

5 *Lees v Whiteley* (supra). A covenant to insure in the name of the lessor is broken by the lessee adding his own name notwithstanding the fact that the Fires Prevention (Metropolis) Act 1774, s 83, entitles the lessor to insist on the insurance money being employed in reinstating the premises: *Penniall v Harborne* (1848) 11 QB 368.

6 *Garden v Ingram* (1852) 23 LJCh 478, as explained in *Rayner v Preston* (1881) 18 ChD 1, CA, per Cotton LJ, at 8; see also, *Matthey v Curling* [1922] 2 AC 180.

7 *Reynard v Arnold* (1875) 10 Ch App 386.

8 Trustee Act 1925, s 20(4). Nothing in the section is to prejudice or affect the right of any person to require reinstatement, whether under any statute or otherwise: ibid, s 20(5).

liable under the mortgage deed, must, if the mortgagee so requires, be applied by the mortgagor in reinstatement.[9]

(c) Ecclesiastical property

If a liability in respect of damage to a parsonage house arises under a policy, and the insurance office[10] elects to pay the insurance money instead of making good the damage at the expense of the office, the Parsonages Board must make good the damage, provided that

- a the damage may be made good with such alterations as the Board may with the consent of the incumbent and the patron determine;
- b the whole or part of the damage may, if the Board so determine with such consent, be not made good.[11]

---

9 Law of Property Act 1925, s 108(3); *Sinnott v Bowden* [1912] 2 Ch 414, holding that the statute applied to a policy existing at the date of the mortgage and renewed afterwards.

10 I e the Ecclesiastical Insurance Office Ltd or such office as may be selected by the Parsonages Board and approved by the Church Commissioners: Repair of Benefice Buildings Measure 1972, s 12.

11 Ibid, s 12(3), as amended by Endowments and Glebe Measure 1976, s 47(4), Sch 8. Any moneys received by the Board under any insurance policy effected under the 1972 Measure must, so far as they are not applied for the purposes of s 12(3) or to meet any liability covered by the policy be paid to the Church Commissioners and any net proceeds of the demolition under this Measure of any outbuildings of any parsonage house must be paid to them. The Commissioners must hold all moneys so paid as if they were moneys arising from a sale of the parsonage house under the Acts and Measures relating to such sales and may apply them accordingly: Repair of Benefice Buildings Measure 1972, s 19(4) as amended by Endowments and Glebe Measure 1976, s 47(4). Sch 8.

CHAPTER 46

Subrogation

A THE NATURE OF SUBROGATION

1 The types of policies to which subrogation applies

In the case of all policies of insurance which are contracts of indemnity the insurers, on payment of the loss, by virtue of the doctrine of 'subrogation', are entitled to be placed in the position of the assured, and succeed to all his rights and remedies against third parties in respect of the subject-matter of insurance.

Thus, subrogation applies to marine insurance policies[1] and to many non-marine policies, e g a fire,[2] motor,[3] jewellery,[4] contingency insurance providing cover against non-receipt of money within a given time,[5] fidelity,[6] burglary,[7] solvency,[8] insurance of securities,[9] and export credits guarantee policy.[10]

But it does not apply to life insurance[11] nor to personal accident insurance,[12] for these are not contracts of indemnity.

2 The history of the doctrine

In *John Edwards & Co v Motor Union Insurance Co Ltd*[13] the history of the doctrine of subrogation was outlined by McCardie J who observed:[14]

> 'The doctrine of subrogation must be briefly considered. It was derived by our English Courts from the system of Roman Law. It varies in some important respects from the doctrine as applied in that system and indeed the actual term "subrogation" does not, I think, appear in Roman Law in relation to the subjects to which it has been applied by English Law; see Dixon on *The Law of Subrogation*, 1862, Philadelphia, Chapter 1. The doctrine has been widely applied in our English body of law, e g to sureties and to matters of ultra vires as well as to insurance. In connection with insurance it was recognised ere the beginning of the eighteenth century . . . It is curious to observe how this doctrine of subrogated equity gradually entered in

1 Marine Insurance Act 1906, s 79. See further, Ivamy *Marine Insurance* (4th Edn, 1985), pp 455–460.

2 *Castellain v Preston* (1883) 11 QBD 380, CA.

3 *Page v Scottish Insurance Corpn Ltd* (1929) 140 LT 571, CA; *Horse, Carriage and General Insurance Co v Petch* (1916) 33 TLR 131.

4 *Allgemeine Versicherungs Gesellschaft Helvetia v German Property Administrator* [1931] 1 KB 672, CA.

5 *Meacock v Bryant & Co* [1942] 2 All ER 661, 74 LlL Rep 53.

6 *Employers Liability Assurance Corpn v Skipper and East* (1887) 4 TLR 55; *London Guarantee Co v Fearnley* (1880) 5 App Cas 911.

7 *Symons v Mulkern* (1882) 46 LT 763.

8 *Parr's Bank v Albert Mines Syndicate* (1900) 5 Com Cas 116.

9 *Finlay v Mexican Investment Corpn* [1897] 1 QB 517: *Dane v Mortgage Insurance Corpn* [1894] 1 QB 54, CA.

10 *Re Miller Gibb & Co Ltd* [1957] 2 All ER 266, [1957] 1 Lloyd's Rep 258.

11 *Dalby v India and London Life Assurance Co* (1854) 15 CB 365.

12 See *Theobald v Railway Passengers Assurance Co* (1854) 10 Exch 45 at 53: 'This is not a contract of indemnity, because a person cannot be indemnified for the loss of life, as he can in the case of a house or ship.' (per Alderson B); *Bradburn v Great Western Rly Co* (1874) LR 10 Exch 1.

13 [1922] 2 KB 249.

14 Ibid, at 252.

to the substance of insurance law and at length became a recognised part of several branches of the general Common Law. In *Mason v Sainsbury*[15] Lord Mansfield said, "Every day the insurer is put in the place of the insured", and Buller J in the same case in approving judgment for the plaintiff insurer said: "Whether this case be considered on strict legal principles or upon the more liberal principles of insurance law the plaintiff is entitled to recover".[16] These more liberal principles were based upon equitable considerations . . . This equity springs, I conceive, solely from the fact that the ordinary and valid contract of marine insurance is a contract of indemnity only.'

3 The principle of indemnity

Although the assured is prima facie entitled, on performing the requisite conditions, to receive the full amount of his loss within the limits of the policy, he must nevertheless be content with an indemnity. Any means of diminishing or extinguishing the loss which may exist must be brought into account in some way or other, since he cannot be allowed to make a profit out of his insurance.

The doctrine of subrogation has been adopted solely for the purpose of preventing the assured from recovering more than a full indemnity,[17] by placing the insurers in the position of the assured.[18]

The insurers are, therefore, entitled as between the assured and themselves, 'to the advantage of every right of the assured, whether such right consists in contract, fulfilled or unfulfilled, or in remedy for tort capable of being insisted on or already insisted on, or in any other right, whether by way of condition or otherwise, legal or equitable, which can be, or has been exercised or has accrued, and whether such right could or could not be enforced by [them] in the name of the assured, by the exercise or acquiring of which right or condition the loss against which the assured is insured can be or has been diminished.'[19]

As far as marine insurance is concerned, the Marine Insurance Act 1906, s 79(1) provides:

> 'Where the insurer pays for a total loss, either of the whole, or in the case of goods any apportionable part, of the subject-matter insured, he thereupon becomes entitled to take over the interest of the assured in whatever may remain of the subject-matter so paid for, and he is thereby subrogated to all the rights and remedies of the assured in and in respect of that subject-matter as from the time of the casualty causing the loss.'

---

15 (1782) 3 Doug KB 61 at 64.

16 Ibid, at 64.

17 *Castellain v Preston* (1883) 11 QBD 380, CA (fire insurance) per Brett LJ, at 387: 'That doctrine does not arise upon any terms of the contract of insurance; it is only another proposition which has been adopted for the purpose of carrying out the fundamental rule [i e indemnity] which I have mentioned, and it is a doctrine in favour of the underwriters or insurers in order to prevent the assured from recovering more than a full indemnity; it has been adopted solely for that reason.'; *Simpson v Thomson* (1877) 3 App Cas 279 (marine insurance) per Lord Cairns LC, at 284: 'I know of no foundation for the right of underwriters [i e to subrogation] except the well-known principle of law, that where one person has agreed to indemnify another, he will, on making good the indemnity, be entitled to succeed to all the ways and means by which the person indemnified might have protected himself against or re-imbursed himself for the loss. It is on this principle that the underwriters of a ship that has been lost are entitled to the ship in specie if they can find and recover it, and it is on the same principle that they can assert any right which the owner of the ship might have asserted against a wrong-doer for damage for the act which has caused the loss.'

18 *Castellain v Preston* (supra) per Brett LJ, at 388: *Randal v Cockran* (1748) 1 Ves Sen 98 (marine insurance); *Blaauwpot v Da Costa* (1758) 1 Eden 130 (marine insurance).

19 This definition was given in *Castellain v Preston* (supra) per Brett LJ, at 388, and was intended to express the doctrine of subrogation in the largest possible form; also ibid per Bowen LJ at 404: 'It is said that the law only gives the underwriters the right to stand in the assured's shoes as to rights which arise out of, or in consequence of, the loss. I venture to think that there is absolutely no authority for that proposition. The true test is, can the right to be insisted on be deemed to be one the enforcement of which will diminish the loss? In this case the right, whatever it be, has

Section 79(2) goes on to state:

> 'Subject to the foregoing provisions, where the insurer pays for a partial loss, he acquires no title to the subject-matter insured, or such part of it as may remain, but he is thereupon subrogated to all the rights and remedies of the assured in and in respect of the subject-matter insured as from the time of the casualty causing the loss, in so far as the assured has been indemnified, according to this Act, by such payment for the loss.'

If the third person is also insured, the result is that the loss ultimately falls on his insurers.[20]

The right of subrogation may be modified by agreement between the insurers concerned so far as it affects their respective rights and liabilities. Thus, in the case of two insured motor vehicles colliding, the respective insurers may have a 'knock-for-knock' agreement,[1] under which there is no subrogation, the damage to each vehicle being borne by its owner's insurers. If, however, the policy covering one of the vehicles is void, the 'knock-for-knock' agreement does not apply, and a case of subrogation arises.[2]

The right of subrogation exists whether the loss is total or partial,[3] but there is

---

been actually enforced, and all we have to consider is whether the fruit of that right after it is enforced does not belong to the insurers. It is insisted that only those payments are to be taken into consideration which have been made in respect of the loss. I ask why, and where is the authority? If the payment diminishes the loss, to my mind, it falls within the application of the law of indemnity. On this point I should like to pause one instant to consider the definition which Brett LJ has given. It does seem to me that, taking his language in the widest sense, it substantially expresses what I should wish to express with only one small appendage that I desire to make. I wish to prevent the danger of his definition being supposed to be exhaustive by saying that if anything else occurs outside it, the general law of indemnity must be looked at.'; *Darrell v Tibbitts* (1880) 5 QBD 560, CA, per Brett LJ, at 563; 'The doctrine is well-established that where something is insured against loss either in a marine or a fire policy, after the assured has been paid by the insurers for the loss, the insurers are put into the place of the assured with regard to every right given to him by the law respecting the subject-matter insured, and with regard to every contract which touches the subject-matter insured, and which contract is affected by the loss or the safety of the subject-matter insured by reason of the peril insured against.': *Burnand v Rodocanachi, Sons & Co* (1882) 7 App Cas 333 (marine insurance) per Lord Blackburn, at 339: 'The general rule of law (and it is obvious justice) is that where there is a contract of indemnity (it matters not whether it is a marine policy or a policy against fire on land or any other contract of indemnity) and a loss happens, anything which reduces or diminishes that loss reduces or diminishes the amount which the indemnifier is bound to pay; and if the indemnifier has already paid it, then, if anything which diminishes the loss comes into the hands of the person to whom he has paid it, it becomes an equity that the person who has already paid the full indemnity is entitled to be recouped by having that amount back.'; See also, *Phoenix Assurance Co v Spooner* [1905] 2 KB 753; on appeal (1906) 22 TLR 695.

20 *North British and Mercantile Insurance Co v London, Liverpool and Globe Insurance Co* (1877) 5 ChD 569, CA (fire insurance).

1 The meaning of the term 'knock for knock' agreement was referred to by Sir Boyd Merriman P in *Morley v Moore* [1936] 2 KB 359 at 361: 'We have not before us . . . the terms of this agreement, but again we are informed that the purpose of this agreement is that each insurance company pays its own assured without question that which the assured is entitled to receive under the particular policy and that both of them do their utmost to discourage either of their own assureds from making claims against the other, or, putting it in another way, the insurance companies amongst themselves do not insist upon their assured bringing such action as they may be entitled to bring against the party insured by the other insurance company.' See further, *Bourne v Stanbridge* [1965] 1 All ER 241, CA (motor insurance), *Hobbs v Marlowe* [1978] AC 16, [1977] 2 All ER 241, HL (motor insurance) and Ivamy *Fire and Motor Insurance* (4th Edn, 1984), pp 293–296.

2 *Bell Assurance v Licenses and General Insurance Corpn and Guarantee Fund Ltd* (1923) 17 LlL Rep 100, CA.

3 *Simpson v Thomson* (1877) 3 App Cas 279 (marine insurance) per Lord Blackburn, at 292.

no subrogation under a void policy.[4] Thus, in *John Edwards & Co v Motor Union Insurance Co Ltd*:[5]

> A vessel was insured under a ppi policy. It was run into and sunk by another ship whose owners admitted liability. The insurance company paid the assured the sum stated in the policy, and then claimed that it was entitled by reason of the doctrine of subrogation to the sum which the owners of the wrongdoing vessel had paid by way of damages.
> *Held,* that they were not so entitled since the doctrine of subrogation did not apply to a ppi policy.

McCardie J observed:[6]

> 'It will be observed that the whole basis of the subrogative doctrine is founded on a binding and operative contract of indemnity, and that it is from such a contract only that the equitable results and rights . . . derive their origin . . . If then the right of subrogation rests upon payment under a contract of indemnity, how does the matter stand when the policy of insurance is an honour policy only? In my judgment such a policy is not a contract of indemnity at all. It is the negation of such a contract . . . If then the policy before me is to be deemed a mere wager and not a contract of indemnity, it follows that there is no juristic scope for the operation of the principle of subrogation. The essential basis of subrogation is wholly absent.'

The insurers may, however, by the terms upon which they settle the assured's claim,[7] or by their conduct towards the assured,[8] debar themselves from afterwards asserting their rights. Subrogation may also be excluded by the terms of the policy or by usage of the trade in which the policy is effected.[9]

The insurer may waive the right of subrogation,[10] and the policy may contain an implied term that he will not exercise the right.[11]

Further, the right of subrogation cannot be exercised against a co-insured,[12] nor against a person for whose joint benefit the subject-matter has been insured e g against a tenant where premises have been insured against fire and it is the mutual intention of him and of the landlord that the insurance should be for the benefit of both of them.[13]

B WHEN SUBROGATION ARISES

The right of subrogation does not arise unless and until the insurers have

---

4 *John Edwards & Co v Motor Union Insurance Co Ltd* [1922] 2 KB 249 (marine insurance).

5 [1922] 2 KB 249.

6 Ibid, at 254.

7 *Blaauwpot v Da Costa* (1758) 1 Eden 130 (marine insurance), where it was held that the Royal Exchange Assurance, having settled the loss with the assured and renounced all benefit of salvage, were not entitled to claim the benefit of any subsequent satisfaction received by the assured in respect of his loss, followed in *Brooks v MacDonnell* (1835) 1 Y & C Ex 500 (marine insurance), where the insurers having declined an offer of abandonment compromised by paying 35 per cent of the claim, and it was held that they were not entitled to any portion of a sum subsequently awarded to the assured in respect of the loss.

8 But they must have so acted as to estop themselves and make it inequitable for them to insist on the position which they must, by their conduct as between them and the assured be deemed to have abandoned: *West of England Fire Assurance Co v Isaacs* [1896] 2 QB 377 (affd [1897] 1 QB 226, CA) per Collins J, at 385.

9 *Tate v Hyslop* (1885) 15 QBD 368, CA (marine insurance).

10 *The Marine Sulphur Queen* [1970] 2 Lloyd's Rep 285, District Court, Southern District of New York (marine insurance).

11 *The Yasin* [1979] 2 Lloyd's Rep 45 (marine insurance).

12 *Petrofina (UK) Ltd v Magnaload Ltd* [1984] QB 127, [1983) 3 All ER 35 (contractors' all risk insurance).

13 *Mark Rowlands Ltd v Berni Inns Ltd* [1986] QB 211, [1985] 3 All ER 473, CA (fire insurance).

admitted the assured's claim,[14] and have paid[15] the sum payable under the policy.[16]

They are not entitled to call on him to exercise his rights against third persons before payment, so as to diminish their own liability towards him,[17] or to have such rights taken into account in estimating the amount of such liability;[18] and, therefore, the fact that they are fully aware of his rights and do not call upon him to exercise them does not preclude them from afterwards claiming the benefit of subrogation.[19]

If, however, the assured has already exercised his right and his loss has been thereby diminished, the position is different, and any benefit so received must be taken into consideration in estimating the insurer's liability.

The effect of payment is to subrogate the insurers to the rights of the assured in respect of the subject-matter. They thereupon become identified with him,[20]

---

14 *Midland Insurance Co v Smith* (1881) 6 QBD 561 per Watkin Williams J, at 564.

15 *Page v Scottish Insurance Corpn* (1929) 140 LT 571, CA (accident insurance) per Scrutton LJ, at 575. If the payment is by way of loan only, presumably there is no subrogation. See further, *City Tailors Ltd v Evans* (1921) 91 LJKB 379 at 385: 'When [the underwriter] has paid, and not till then, he is subrogated to any legal rights which the assured had which might reduce the loss . . .' (per Scutton LJ); *John Edwards & Co v Motor Union Insurance Co Ltd* [1922] 2 KB 249 at 255: 'In my view the essence of the matter is that subrogation springs not from payment only but from actual payment conjointly with the fact that it is made pursuant to the basic and original contract of indemnity'. (per McCardie J); Marine Insurance Act 1906, s 79(1): 'Where the insurer pays for a total loss . . . of the subject-matter insured, . . . he is thereby subrogated to all the rights and remedies of the assured in and in respect of that subject-matter as from the time of the casualty causing the loss.' There is a similar provision in s 79(2) as regards subrogation when the insurer pays for a partial loss; *Yorkshire Insurance Co Ltd v Nisbet Shipping Co Ltd* [1962] 2 QB 330, [1961] 2 All ER 487, [1961] 1 Lloyd's Rep 479 QB (marine insurance). The words 'subject-matter insured' in s 79(1) in relation to cargo insurance mean the goods, and if their owner is awarded damages for their loss and also interest against a third party, and the insurer pays for the loss, the insurer is entitled to claim both the sum awarded by way of damages and also that part of the interest arising after the settlement of the insured's claim, for the resulting judgment is a single judgment based on a single cause of action: *H Cousins and Co Ltd v D & C Carriers Ltd* [1970] 2 Lloyd's Rep 397, CA (marine insurance). (See the judgment of Lord Widgery LCJ, ibid, at 400–401.) For subrogation in marine insurance, see generally Ivamy *Marine Insurance* (4th Edn, 1985) pp 455–460.

16 *Mason v Sainsbury* (1782) 3 Doug KB 61, approved in *Simpson v Thomson* (1877) 3 App Cas 279 (marine insurance) per Lord Blackburn, at 293; *Quebec Fire Insurance Co v St Louis* (1851) 7 Moo PCC 286 per Parke B, at 316 (according to Willes J in *Lidgett v Secretan* (1871) LR 6 CP 616, 621, n, (marine insurance) this case is inaccurately reported); *Castellain v Preston* (supra) per Brett LJ, at 389; *Page v Scottish Insurance Corpn* (supra) (accident insurance), where it was held that the insurers were not subrogated to the assured's right of action in respect of damages to the insured car in as much as they were disputing liability in respect of third party risks; *Scottish Union National Insurance Co v Davis* [1970] 1 Lloyd's Rep 1, CA (motor insurance), where the insurers were held not to be entitled to a sum recovered by the insured from third parties in respect of the damage to his car, because the insurers had not indemnified the insured, and consequently the right of subrogation did not arise. (See the judgment of Russell LJ, ibid, at 4).

17 *Dickenson v Jardine* (1868) LR 3 CP 639 (marine insurance).

18 *Darrell v Tibbitts* (1880) 5 QBD 560, CA, per Brett LJ, at 561, 562; *Collingridge v Royal Exchange Assurance Corpn* (1877) 3 QBD 173. In *Castellain v Preston* (supra) Cotton LJ, at 394, used language which is capable of being construed to mean that the insurers before payment may insist on having such rights taken into consideration, but he is there dealing with the rights of the insurers to recover from the assured sums paid by third persons and pointing out that the payment of the loss by the insurers without taking into account such sums does not preclude them from recovering; cf *Darrell v Tibbitts* (supra) per Cotton LJ, at 565.

19 *West of England Fire Insurance Co v Isaacs* [1897] 1 QB 226, CA; affg and approving [1896] 2 QB 377, where Collins J, at 383–385, criticises the dicta of Cotton LJ referred to in the preceding note.

20 *Mason v Sainsbury* (1782) 3 Doug KB 61 per Buller J, at 65: 'The principle is that the insurer and the insured are one.' This was followed in *North British and Mercantile Insurance Co v London, Liverpool and Globe Insurance Co* (1877) 5 ChD 569, CA, per James LJ, at 581.

and are entitled to stand in his shoes not merely as to rights which arise out of or in consequence of the loss,[21] but as to all rights by the exercise of which the loss will be diminished.[22]

C THE RIGHTS IN RESPECT OF WHICH SUBROGATION ARISES

The principal rights in respect of which the insurers may be entitled to subrogation are the following:

1 Rights arising out of tort.
2 Rights arising out of contract.
3 Rights under statute.
4 Rights over the subject-matter.

1 Rights arising out of tort

The tort must be connected with the loss, so as to make the tortfeasor[23] responsible in damages to the assured.[24] In this case the insurers succeed, on payment of the loss, to the assured's rights of action against the tortfeasor.[1]

Thus, in the case of a fidelity policy, the insurers, after payment, are entitled to claim against the defaulter reimbursement of the amount which they have paid.[2] In the case of a burglary policy, they are entitled to claim the proceeds of the burglary if they can be traced.[3] In the case of a policy against damage to

21 *North British and Mercantile Insurance Co v London, Liverpool and Globe Insurance Co* (supra) per Jessel MR, at 576.

22 *Castellain v Preston* (1883) 11 QBD 380, CA, per Brett LJ, at 387, 388: 'But it being admitted that the doctrine of subrogation is to be applied merely for the purpose of preventing the assured from obtaining more than a full indemnity, the question is whether that doctrine as applied in insurance law can be in any way limited. Is it to be limited to this, that the underwriter is subrogated into the place of the assured so far as to enable the underwriter to enforce a contract or to enforce a right of action? Why is it to be limited to that, if, when it is limited to that, it will, in certain cases, enable the assured to recover more than the full indemnity? The moment it can be shown that such a limitation of doctrine would have that effect, then, as I said before, in my opinion, it is contrary to the foundation of the law as to insurance, and must be wrong.'; *Rankin v Potter* (1873) LR 6 HL 83 (marine insurance) per Blackburn J, at 118: 'On general principles of equity, not at all peculiar to marine insurance, he who recovers on a contract of indemnity must, and does, by taking the satisfaction from the person indemnifying him, cede all his right, in respect of that for which he obtains indemnity.'

23 If the assured is the person who has caused the damage, the right of subrogation cannot be asserted at all: *Simpson v Thomson* (1877) 3 App Cas 279 (marine insurance) per Lord Cairns LC, at 284: 'But this right of action for damages they must assert not in their own name, but in the name of the person insured, and if the person insured be the person who has caused the damage, I am unable to see how the right can be asserted at all'. This was followed in *Midland Insurance Co v Smith* (1881) 6 QBD 561 per Watkin Williams J, at 564, 565.

24 *North British and Mercantile Insurance Co v London, Liverpool and Globe Insurance Co* (fire insurance) per Mellish LJ, at 584; *Assicurazioni Generali de Trieste v Empress Assurance Corpn Ltd* [1907] 2 KB 814 (marine insurance); *The Charlotte* [1908] P 206, CA (marine insurance); *Groom v Great Western Rly Co* (1892) 8 TLR 253 (fire insurance); *King v Victoria Insurance Co* [1896] AC 250 at 256, PC (fire insurance); *Law Fire Assurance Co v Oakley* (1888) 4 TLR 309 (fire insurance).

1 *King v Victoria Insurance Co* (supra); *Northern Assurance Co v Manitoba Pool Elevators* [1928] 3 WWR 154; *Gough v Toronto and York Radical Rly Co* (1918) 42 OLR 415.

2 *London Guarantee Co v Fearnley* (1880) 5 App Cas 911 per Lord Blackburn, at 916.

3 *Symons v Mulkern* (1882) 46 LT 763: cf *Employers' Liability Assurance Corpn v Skipper and East* (1887) 4 TLR 55, where the action was brought to recover the proceeds of cheques indorsed without authority and cashed by the defendant.

goods such as, e g a car, they are entitled to claim damages from the person responsible.[4]

Further, in the case of fire insurance, the insurers have been held to be entitled to recover damages against a railway company in respect of a fire caused by negligence,[5] or against an incendiary;[6] and they are entitled to enforce any rights of compensation which the assured may possess against a public authority.

Again, where a third party has been injured by the negligent driving of a car by an employee of the assured, the insurers, on payment of an indemnity to the assured in respect of the damages which he has had to pay to the third party, are entitled to sue the employee in order to recoup themselves.[7]

2 Rights arising out of contract

If the contract in question imposes on a third person the obligation of making compensation to the assured in respect of the loss, the benefit of the obligation clearly passes to the insurers.[8]

Thus, where the goods insured are lost or destroyed in the hands of a bailee, such as a carrier, the insurers may sue the bailee on the contract of bailment.[9]

Similarly, where an employee whose fidelity is insured is guilty of defalcations, they may enforce the rights of the employer under a guarantee given to secure the employee's fidelity;[10] or his rights against the banker whose negligence has enabled the defalcations to be committed.[11]

The same principle applies in the case of solvency insurance, where the insurers succeed to the rights of the assured against the debtor and, if the debt is guaranteed, his guarantors are, therefore, entitled to enforce payment of the debt insured or of the guarantee.[12]

So also, in the case of a fire policy, where a house which is demised to a tenant

---

4 *Horse, Carriage and General Insurance Co v Petch* (1916) 33 TLR 131. But at the present time motor insurers usually have a 'knock-for-knock' agreement under which there is no subrogation, the damage to each vehicle being borne by its owner's insurers. See, e g *Morley v Moore* [1936] 2 KB 359, CA (motor insurance); *Bourne v Stanbridge* [1965] 1 All ER 241, CA (motor insurance); *Hobbs v Marlowe* [1978] AC 16, [1977] 2 All ER 241, HL. See further, Ivamy *Fire and Motor Insurance* (4th Edn, 1984), pp 293–296.

5 *Groom v Great Western Rly Co* (1892) 8 TLR 253; *Guardian Fire and Life Assurance Co v Quebec Railway Light and Power Co* (1906) 36 SCR 676.

6 *Otter Mutual Fire Insurance Co v Rand* (1913) 25 OWR 568, where the action was brought against a lunatic and failed.

7 *Lister v Romford Ice and Cold Storage Co Ltd* [1957] AC 555, [1957] 1 All ER 125, [1956] 2 Lloyd's Rep 505, HL.

8 *North British and Mercantile Insurance Co v London, Liverpool and Globe Insurance Co* (1877) 5 ChD 569 per Jessel MR, at 576; *Parr's Bank v Albert Mines Syndicate* (1900) 5 Com Cas 116 (solvency insurance).

9 *Dufourcet v Bishop* (1886) 18 QBD 373 (marine insurance). There is, of course, no subrogation where, by the terms of the contract with the assured, the carrier is not liable for the loss: *Thomas & Co v Brown* (1899) 4 Com Cas 186 (marine insurance). The existence of a special contract with the carrier affecting his liability may therefore be a material fact which ought to be disclosed; *Tate v Hyslop* (1885) 15 QBD 368, CA (fire insurance). In *Thomas & Co v Brown* (supra) the contract was implied. See further, *North British and Mercantile Insurance Co v London, Liverpool and Globe Insurance Co* (supra) and *Maurice v Goldsbrough Mort and Co Ltd* [1939] AC 452, 64 LlL Rep 1, PC.

10 *London Guarantee and Accident Co v Cornish* (1905) 17 Man LR 148, where the action failed on the ground that the guarantee did not relate to the transaction in question.

11 *Bank of Montreal v Dominion Gresham Guarantee and Casualty Co* [1930] AC 659, PC.

12 *Parr's Bank v Albert Mines Syndicate* (1900) 5 Com Cas 116.

under a covenant to repair or rebuild it and which is insured by the landlord on his own behalf, is burned,[13] the benefit of the covenant to rebuild or repair[14] passes to the insurers upon payment.

The doctrine of subrogation is not, however, confined to contracts imposing the obligation of making good the loss; it extends to any contract relating to the subject-matter of insurance,[15] which entitles the assured to be put by the other contracting party into as good a position as if the loss insured against had not happened.[16]

It is immaterial that the contract which is sought to be enforced is not a contract, either directly or indirectly, for the preservation of the property insured, and that the contract of insurance is a collateral contract wholly distinct from it, since the loss is, in fact, lessened by its fulfilment and affected by its non-fulfilment.[17]

Thus, where the subject-matter of insurance is a house which the assured, as owner, has contracted to sell to a purchaser, and which is burned before completion of the purchase, the insurers are entitled, on payment of the loss, to the benefit of the assured's lien as unpaid vendor,[18] though they are perhaps not entitled to insist upon specific performance of the contract of purchase.[19]

Similarly, where a mortgagee effects an insurance upon the mortgaged property to the amount of the mortgage debt for his own benefit solely, and not for the benefit of the mortgagor as well as himself,[20] the payment of a full indemnity by the insurers in the event of a loss entitles them to succeed to his rights against the mortgagor.[1]

Further, if a person is, by contract with the assured, under an obligation to

---

13 *Darrell v Tibbitts* (1880) 5 QBD 560, CA, per Brett LJ, at 562, following *North British and Mercantile Insurance Co v London, Liverpool and Globe Insurance Co* (supra); *Castellain v Preston* (1883) 11 QBD 380, CA, per Brett LJ, at 391; *Enlayde Ltd v Roberts* [1917] 1 Ch 109 at 116; cf *West of England Fire Insurance Co v Isaacs* [1897] 1 QB 226, CA, where the sub-lessor was under a covenant to his sub-lessee.

14 Apparently they can compel the tenant to repair: *Darrell v Tibbitts* (supra) per Thesiger LJ, at 568.

15 *Castellain v Preston* (supra) per Cotton LJ, at 395. The doctrine does not extend to contracts which are independent of the subject-matter, though they can only be fulfilled by its means: *Sea Insurance Co v Hadden* (1884) 13 QBD 706, CA (marine insurance) per Brett MR, at 713. Thus, in the case of fire insurance, the landlord's insurers would not be subrogated to his right to recover rent from the tenant.

16 *Castellain v Preston* (supra) per Brett LJ, at 390, 392. It has been suggested that there may possibly be some contracts so entirely independent of the subject-matter of the insurance as to put the assured in the position of being more than fully indemnified in the event of a loss: *Darrell v Tibbitts* (supra) per Thesiger LJ, at 567. But it is difficult to see what such contract can be. Cf *Meacock v Bryant & Co* [1942] 2 All ER 661, 74 LlL Rep 53 (debt insurance).

17 *Castellain v Preston* (supra) per Bowen LJ, at 404.

18 Ibid, per Bowen LJ, at 405.

19 Ibid, per Brett LJ, at 390, and per Bowen LJ, at 405, declining to decide whether the insurers could insist on specific performance in deference to the doubts expressed by Cotton LJ on the point, which doubts do not appear either in the report or in the shorthand note.

20 In which case there is no subrogation: *Nichols & Co v Scottish Union and National Insurance Co* 1885 14 R (Ct of Sess) 1094.

1 *North British and Mercantile Insurance Co v London Liverpool and Globe Insurance Co* (1877) 5 ChD 569 per Mellish LJ, at 583; *Burton v Gore District Mutual Fire Insurance Co* (1865) 12 Gr 156, where, on paying the amount of the mortgage debt, the insurers were held entitled to an assignment of the mortgage; *North British and Mercantile Insurance Co v McLellan* (1892) 21 SCR 288; cf *Goldie v Bank of Hamilton* (1899) 31 OR 142.

insure the subject-matter, the benefit of the contract to insure passes to the insurers.[2]

Similarly, in the case of a sale of goods if, by the terms of the contract of sale, the buyer remains liable to pay for them, notwithstanding that they have been destroyed before delivery, the insurers, on a policy effected by the seller are entitled, after payment, to sue the buyer for the price.[3]

3 Rights under statute

If the assured would be able to recover, under the terms of a statute, the whole or part of his loss, the insurers are subrogated to his right.[4] In fire insurance, this particularly arises in the case of destruction of or damage to property as a result of riot.[5]

4 Rights over the subject-matter

Where, notwithstanding the happening of a total loss, there is a sufficient amount of salvage which possesses some value, the assured cannot claim both to receive from the insurers a full indemnity for his loss and to retain the salvage, since he would thus be more than fully indemnified.

It is his duty, therefore, on receiving payment in full, to hand over to the insurers the salvage.[6] The title of the insurers thereupon relates back to the date when the loss took place, e g the date of the fire in the case of fire insurance, and they become to all intents and purposes owners of the salvage as from that date,[7] and are, therefore, entitled to take to themselves any advantage to be derived from such ownership.[8]

Since, however, the ownership of the salvage may carry with it onerous and expensive responsibilities, a difficult question arises, as to whether the property

---

2 *Enlayde Ltd v Roberts* [1917] 1 Ch 109.

3 *Gill v Yorkshire Insurance Co* (1913) 24 WLR 389 (livestock insurance).

4 *Ellerbeck Collieries Ltd v Cornhill Insurance Co Ltd* [1932] 1 KB 401, CA (employers' liability insurance) per Scrutton LJ, at 411.

5 Riot (Damages) Act 1886, s 2(2).

6 *Rankin v Potter* (1873) LR 6 HL 83 (marine insurance) per Blackburn J, at 118: 'There is no notice of abandonment in cases of fire insurance, but the salvage is transferred on the principle of equity expressed by Lord Hardwicke in *Randal v Cockran* (1748) 1 Ves Sen 98) (marine insurance) "that the person who originally sustains the loss was the owner, but after satisfaction made to him the insurer".' See also, *Kaltenbach v Mackenzie* (1878) 3 CPD 467, CA (marine insurance) per Brett LJ, at 470, 471; *Dane v Mortgage Insurance Corpn* [1894] 1 QB 54, CA (insurance of securities) per Lord Esher MR, at 61; *Holmes v Payne* [1930] 2 KB 301 (jewellery insurance).

7 *London Assurance Co v Sainsbury* (1783) 3 Doug KB 245 (affd ExCh) per Lord Mansfield CJ, at 253; *Simpson v Thomson* (1877) 3 App Cas 279 (marine insurance) per Lord Blackburn, at 292; *Randal v Cockran* (supra) (marine insurance).

8 *Rankin v Potter* (supra) per Blackburn J, at 119: 'When, therefore, the party indemnified has a right to indemnity and has elected to enforce his claim, the chance of any benefit from an improvement in the value of what is in existence and the risk of any loss from its deterioration are transferred from the party indemnified to those who indemnify; and therefore if the state of things is such that steps may be taken to improve the value of what remains, or to preserve it from further deterioration, such steps, from the moment of election, concern the party indemnifying, who, therefore ought to be informed promptly of the election to come upon him, in order that he may, if he pleases, take steps for his own protection.' See also, *Case v Davidson* (1816) 5 M & S 79 (marine insurance), where it was held that an abandonment of the ship transferred freight subsequently earned to the underwriters on ship, and Abbott J was of opinion, at 87, that 'an abandonment is equivalent to a sale of the ship.'; *Stewart v Greenock Marine Insurance Co* (1848) 2 HL Cas 159 (marine insurance); and cf *Skipper v Grant* (1861) 10 CBNS 237 per Byles J, at 250.

in the salvage passes to them as from the date of the loss by the fact of payment, or whether they are entitled to exercise an option in the matter so that the property does not pass to them unless they think fit to take over the salvage. It is probable that the latter alternative is correct, and that they may therefore refuse to take over the salvage, if, by so doing, they would be incurring liabilities to third persons.[9]

D THE EXERCISE OF THE RIGHT OF SUBROGATION

The rights to which the insurers are subrogated, must, as a general rule, be enforced in the name of the assured.[10] The mere fact of subrogation does not entitle them to enforce such rights in their own names.[11]

To enable them to do so, it is necessary either that a statute should confer upon them a right of action,[12] or that the assured should make a formal

[9] This appears to be the view taken in the Marine Insurance Act 1906, s 79(1): *Allgemeine Versicherungs-Gesellschaft Helvetia v German Property Administrator* [1931] 1 KB 672, CA (jewellery insurance) per Scrutton LJ, at 688); see also, *Arrow Shipping Co v Tyne Improvement Comrs, The Crystal* [1894] AC 508 (marine insurance) per Lord Herschell, at 519, declining to decide whether the underwriters were liable as 'owners' for the expense of removing a wreck; *Elgood v Harris* [1896] 2 QB 491 (marine insurance) per Collins J, at 494, suggesting that the passing of the property is perhaps subject to disclaimer; *Boston Corpn v Fenwick & Co Ltd* (1923) 129 LT 766 (removal of wrecks) per Bailhache J, at 769. See generally, Ivamy *Marine Insurance* (4th Edn, 1985), pp 392–394.

[10] *Symons v Mulkern* (1882) 46 LT 763; *Dickenson v Jardine* (1868) LR 3 CP 639 (marine insurance) per Willes J, at 644; *Mason v Sainsbury* (1782) 3 Doug KB 61 (fire insurance), followed in *Clark v Blything (Inhabitants)* (1823) 2 B & C 254 (fire insurance). The position is different where the case is really one of double insurance and the insurers are seeking contribution: *Austin v Zurich General Accident and Liability Insurance Co Ltd* [1945] KB 250, [1945] 1 All ER 316, CA (accident insurance) per MacKinnon LJ, at 288. For a case where the insurers were entitled under a term of the policy to sue in the name of the assured, and did so without first consulting the assured, see *Lister v Romford Ice and Cold Storage Co Ltd* [1957] AC 555, [1957] 1 All ER 125, [1956] 2 Lloyd's Rep 505, HL. But the insurers cannot sue in the name of an assured which is a limited company that has been wound up for the assured had no cause of action: *M H Smith (Plant Hire) Ltd v Mainwaring (trading as Inshore)* (1986) Times, 10 June (marine insurance).

[11] *London Assurance Co v Sainsbury* (1783) 3 Doug KB 245 (affd ExCh) per Lord Mansfield CJ, at 253: 'The relation of the plaintiffs is by the insurance which is a contract of indemnity. It follows that in respect of salvage the insurer stands in the place of the insured and vice versa as to damage. I take it to be a maxim, that as against the person sued, the action cannot be transferred. As between the parties themselves the law has long supported it for the benefit of commerce, but the assignee must sue in the name of the assignor, by which the defence is not varied.' See also, *Midland Insurance Co v Smith* (1881) 6 QBD 561 per Watkin Williams J, at 565; *Simpson v Thomson* (1877) 3 App Cas 279 (marine insurance) per Lord Blackburn, at 293; *Wealleans v Canada Southern Rly Co* (1894) 21 AR 297; revsd on another point 24 SCR 309. See further, *Oriental Fire and General Insurance Co Ltd v American President Lines Ltd and Cotton Trading Corpn of San Francisco* [1968] 2 Lloyd's Rep 372, High Court of Bombay (marine insurance), where it was held that an insurer subrogated to the rights of the assured under the Indian Transfer of Property Act (since repealed and re-enacted by the (Indian) Marine Insurance Act 1963) was not entitled to bring an action in his own name against a wrongdoer. Even though the policy expressly gives the insurers the right to control litigation, they have themselves no locus standi: *Murfin v Ashbridge and Martin* [1941] 1 All ER 231, CA (accident insurance). The insurers are not entitled in the event of the person liable becoming a bankrupt to prove against his estate in their own names: *Re Blackburne, ex p Strouts* (1892) 9 Morr 249.

[12] Such a right appears to be conferred by s 4(1) of the Riot (Damages) Act 1886, where the insurers are subrogated to the assured's rights of compensation against the police authority in cases of damage done by riot. It therefore follows that *London Assurance Co v Sainsbury* (supra) is no longer law as applied to its own peculiar facts, though the general principles laid down remain unaffected.

assignment[13] to them of his right of action in respect of the subject-matter.[14]

Thus, in *Compania Colombiana de Seguros v Pacific Steam Navigation Co*:[15]

> The consignees of a cargo of electric cables which were damaged during a voyage from England to Colombia, recovered the sum insured from the insurers, and assigned to them their right of action against the shipowners. The insurers gave notice of the assignment to the shipowners, and then brought an action in their own names.
> *Held*, that they were entitled to do so.

Roskill J observed:[16]

> 'Where before 1873 Equity would have compelled the assignor to exercise his rights against the contract-breaker or tortfeasor for the benefit of the assignee, those rights can, since 1873, be made the subject of a valid legal assignment and subject to due compliance with the requirements of the statute [i e the Law of Property Act 1925] as to notice, can be enforced at law. Equity always, before 1873, compelled an assured to lend his name to enforce his underwriter's rights of subrogation against a contract-breaker or tortfeasor. It follows, therefore, that the only possible objection to such rights being now enforceable at law is that such enforcement would involve the enforcement of a bare cause of action in contract or in tort. But, . . . if that is so, why did Equity act as Equity did act before 1873 in relation to the enforcement of subrogation rights? I think that the answer is because the enforcement of such rights was never regarded as the enforcement of a mere cause of action, but as the enforcement of a cause of action legitimately supported by the underwriter's interest in recouping himself in respect of the amount of the loss which he has paid under the policy as a result of the acts, neglects or defaults of the actual contract-breaker or tortfeasor . . . I think that an assignment by an assured to his underwriter of the assured's rights against the contract-breaker or tortfeasor is enforceable by the underwriter in the underwriter's own name, provided, of course, that the other requirements of s 136 of the Law of Property Act 1925, are satisfied.'

Where, however, the right of action is not directly connected with the loss, but only arises after the loss out of the ownership of the subject-matter, the insurers, if they have taken over the salvage, may enforce it in their own names, since it is their own right as owners of the salvage, and not a merely derivative right depending on the assured's right of property.[17]

E THE DUTIES OF THE ASSURED

In as much as the rights which pass to the insurers by virtue of subrogation are merely the rights of the assured,[18] the insurers being unable to maintain any

---

[13] Under the Law of Property Act 1925, s 136(1). Such a formal assignment is not infrequently made. Probably there cannot be an assignment of part of the rights of the assured: *James Nelson & Sons v Nelson Line (Liverpool) Ltd* [1906] 2 KB 217, CA (marine insurance) per Cozens-Hardy LJ, at 225. In *Quebec Fire Insurance Co v St Louis* (1851) 7 Moo PCC 286, where the insurers, who had paid the amount due under the policy, about three-fourths of the loss, brought the action, under a formal assignment which was apparently invalid, for the sum they had paid, it was suggested, at 319, that the defendants would have the right to have the assured joined as co-plaintiff.

[14] *King v Victoria Insurance Co* [1896] AC 250, PC, where it was an express term of the assignment that the assured's name was not to be used; *Employers' Liability Assurance Corporation v Skipper and East* (1887) 4 TLR 55 (fidelity insurance); *Westminster Fire Office v Reliance Marine Insurance Co* (1903) 19 TLR 668 (marine insurance); *Royal Exchange Assurance Corpn of London v Kingsley Navigation Co* [1923] AC 235, PC.

[15] [1964] 1 All ER 216.

[16] Ibid, at 230.

[17] *Page v Scottish Insurance Corpn* (1929) 140 LT 571, CA (accident insurance) per Scrutton LJ, at 575; cf *Simpson v Thomson* (1877) 3 App Cas 279 (marine insurance) per Lord Blackburn at 292.

[18] *James Nelson & Sons v Nelson Line (Liverpool) Ltd* [1906] 2 KB 217, CA (marine insurance) per Collins LJ, at 223; *Finlay v Mexican Investment Corpn* [1897] 1 QB 517 (insurance of securities), where the rights of the assured as a debenture-holder had been modified after the issue of the

claim against third persons in their own right, certain obligations are imposed on the assured with the view of securing to the insurers the full benefit of the subrogation. These obligations are the following:

1 The assured must assist the insurers in enforcing any claims which he may have against third persons in respect of the loss; and
2 the assured must do no act by which the insurers may be prejudiced.

1 Duty to give assistance to the insurers

The assured must assist the insurers in enforcing any claims which he may have against third persons in respect of the loss.[19] This is sometimes expressly provided for by a condition in the policy,[20] though such a condition is unnecessary.

Thus, it is his duty to permit them to use his name in any action which they may desire to bring for this purpose.[1] If he refuses, the Court may compel him to do so on receiving an indemnity in respect of the costs to be incurred.[2]

2 Duty not to prejudice the insurers' position

The assured must do no act by which the insurers may be prejudiced.[3] He is, therefore, not entitled, without their sanction, to enforce any claim arising out of the loss himself, and he may, on their application, be restrained from so

---

policy; *Austin v Zurich General Accident and Liability Insurance Co Ltd* [1945] KB 250, CA (accident insurance). Hence, a neutral underwriter has no claim in the case of enemy goods: *The Gothland* [1916] P 239n (marine insurance).

19 *Dane v Mortgage Insurance Corpn* [1894] 1 QB 54, CA (insurance of securities) per Lord Esher MR, at 61: 'If the assured does obtain anything by way of salvage out of the subject-matter insured, he must account for that to the underwriter; and, further than that, if anything is obtainable by way of salvage, he has no right to say to the underwriter that he will not take any step in order to obtain such salvage; he is bound to assist underwriters in obtaining it. For instance, in the present case, if the bank had not failed, but had remained in perfect credit, and it had on some untenable ground refused to pay the plaintiff at the time when, according to the deposit note, payment was due, the plaintiff would not be bound first to sue the bank . . . She would be entitled to receive payment from the defendants, the insurers; but then, if, after they had paid her, the bank, discovering their mistake, were to pay her the amount of the deposit, she would be bound to account for it to the defendants; or, on the other hand, if the bank still refused to pay, she would be bound to allow the defendants to sue in her name. All that is well understood law with regard to insurance.'

20 For the effect of such a condition, see *London Guarantee Co v Fearnley* (1880) 5 App Cas 911 (fidelity insurance).

1 *Dane v Mortgage Insurance Corpn* (supra). As to the relations between solicitors nominated by the insurers and the assured, see *Groom v Crocker* [1939] 1 KB 194, CA, per Greene MR, at 202.

2 *Duus, Brown & Co v Binning* (1906) 11 Com Cas 190 (marine insurance); *King v Victoria Insurance Co* [1896] AC 250, PC; *Northern Assurance Co v Manitoba Pool Elevators* [1928] 3 WWR 154, where the Court held that as the claim to which the insurers were subrogated lay in tort, they ought to be allowed to use the assured's name, notwithstanding a formal assignment.

3 *West of England Fire Insurance Co v Isaacs* [1897] 1 QB 226, CA (fire insurance) per Lord Esher MR, at 229: 'Any remedy which the defendant has against anybody in respect of the damage is subrogated to them (i e the plaintiffs), and the defendant has no right to deal with such a claim to the prejudice of the plaintiffs.'; *Boag v Standard Marine Insurance Co Ltd* [1937] 2 KB 113, at 129: 'Had the assured in any way prejudiced their right of recovery so as to deprive the [insurer] of the benefits of subrogation, the assured would have incurred a personal liability to the [insurer] to the extent of the prejudice so caused.' (per Scott LJ).

doing.[4] If he is allowed to prosecute his claim without interference and succeeds, he must account to his insurers for the amount originally paid under his policy.[5]

Similarly, if he releases third persons from their liability to himself arising out of the loss, or enters into a compromise with them by which the amount payable by them in respect of their liability is diminished, as, for instance, where the amount so payable is arrived at by taking into account the sum already paid by the insurers,[6] he must account to them not merely for what he has received, but for what he has lost by reason of his act, and must pay over to them the full value of the rights and remedies which he has just released or compromised.[7] By his act the insurers are debarred from asserting in his name any claim against the persons formerly liable,[8] seeing that any defence available against the assured, including a release or compromise of his claim,[9] is still available notwithstanding that the action is brought for the benefit of the insurers.[10]

Similarly, any attempt by the assured to contract out of the rights of subrogation is either ineffective or renders him liable to the insurers for the value of the right of which he has disposed.[11]

F THE DEFENCES AVAILABLE TO THE PARTY SUED

Where an action is brought on behalf of the insurers to enforce the rights to which they are subrogated, the person responsible to the assured for the loss

---

4 *Law Fire Assurance Co v Oakley* (1888) 4 TLR 309 (fire insurance) per Mathew J, at 309. As to where the assured has not been fully indemnified, see pp 468–470, ante.

5 *Horse, Carriage and General Insurance Co Ltd v Petch* (1916) 33 TLR 131 (accident insurance); *Law Fire Assurance Co v Oakley* (supra).

6 *Phoenix Assurance Co v Spooner* [1905] 2 KB 753 (fire insurance).

7 *West of England Fire Insurance Co v Isaacs* [1896] 2 QB 377; affd [1897] 1 QB 226, CA) per Collins J, at 383: 'I do not know that the precise point has ever been decided; that is to say, that the insurance company can come against the assured, and recover from him, not the amount of a benefit he has received, but the amount of benefit he has lost—a benefit to which they had the right to be subrogated, but which in the events that have happened has been lost to them. But I think it follows as a matter of principle from the decision, cited in argument, if indeed it is not covered by the dicta or some of the reasoning by which those principles are arrived at and enunciated in the cases referred to.' In this case it was a term of the compromise that no action should be brought for breach of any covenent. See further, *Horse, Carriage and General Insurance Co v Petch* (supra) (accident insurance), where an action by an executor claiming damages in respect of the death of the assured and also in respect of the insured motor car was settled for a lump sum, no specific amount being appropriated to the motor car, and it was held that the executor must be deemed to have received the full value of the motor car.

8 *The Millwall* [1905] P 155, CA (marine insurance) where the insurers were not allowed to prosecute an appeal which the assured had abandoned.

9 The opinion expressed in *Smidmore v Australian Gas Light Co* (1881) 2 NSWLR 219 (where, however, the Court held on the facts that the release applied only to the uninsured part of the loss), that a release by the assured given to a tortfeasor, together with an undertaking not to allow his name to be used in any proceedings, does not preclude the insurers after payment from maintaining an action in the assured's name, if sound, can only be justified on the ground that the tortfeasor was aware of the insurers' claim at the time when he received his release. If he had been ignorant of the insurers' rights, the release would have extinguished his liability as regards the insurers as well as the assured.

10 *London Assurance Co v Sainsbury* (1783) 3 Doug KB 245 (affd ExCh) per Lord Mansfield CJ, at 254: 'As against the person sued the right of action cannot be transferred nor the defence varied.'

11 *Boag v Standard Marine Insurance Co Ltd* [1937] 2 KB 113 (marine insurance) per Lord Wright MR, at 124; *Canadian Transport Co Ltd v Court Line Ltd* [1940] AC 934, [1940] 3 All ER 112 (charter-party).

cannot resist liability on the ground that the assured has already received a full indemnity from the insurers,[12] since the effect of a successful defence on this ground would be that the defendant would be receiving the benefit of the policy without paying the premium.[13]

Nor can he resist liability on the ground that the insurers have paid the assured for a loss in respect of which they were not liable, provided that they have acted in good faith.[14]

On the other hand, he is entitled to treat the insurers as being, in fact, the real plaintiffs, and to raise a defence which is available only against them and not against the nominal plaintiff. Thus, he may rely on a term in the policy by which the insurers have relinquished their rights against himself,[15] or he may object that the insurers are enemy aliens and, therefore, disentitled to maintain their claim.[16]

G THE EFFECT OF SUBROGATION

After the payment of a full indemnity, whether in respect of a total or a partial loss, the insurers are entitled to take the place of the assured and are subrogated to all his rights and remedies.

But they are under an obligation to account to him for any profit which they may have made from the exercise against third persons of any rights of action which may have existed.

Thus, in *Yorkshire Insurance Co Ltd v Nisbet Shipping Co Ltd*:[17]

> A ship was insured for £72,000. She became a total loss in 1945 as a result of a collision with a Canadian Government vessel. The insurers paid the £72,000 to the assured, and then claimed damages from the Canadian Government. This action was successful, but meanwhile the

---

[12] The person responsible cannot therefore insist on the insurers being made a party to the action: *Symons v Mulkern* (1882) 46 LT 763 (transit insurance).

[13] *Mason v Sainsbury* (1782) 3 Doug KB 61 (fire insurance), where the insurers, having paid the amount of a loss occasioned by the demolition of a house by rioters, were held entitled to recover against the Hundred in the name of their assured, and Lord Mansfield CJ, at 64, said: 'The question then, comes to this, can the owner, having insured, sue the Hundred? Who is first liable? If the Hundred, it makes no difference; if the insurers, then it is a satisfaction, and the Hundred is not liable. But the contrary is evident from the nature of the contract of insurance. It is an indemnity. Every day the insurer is put in place of the insured. In every abandonment it is so. The insurer uses the name of the insured . . . upon the principles of policy . . . I am satisfied that it is to be considered as if the insurers had not paid a farthing.' This was approved in *Yates v Whyte* (1838) 4 Bing NC 272 (marine insurance). See also, *London Assurance Co v Sainsbury* (1783) 3 Doug KB 245 (affd ExCh) per Buller J, at 249, stating that he had acted in a former action in allowing the insurance to be taken into account in estimating the third person's liability; *Darrell v Tibbitts* (1880) 5 QBD 560, CA (fire insurance) per Brett LJ, at 562, following *North British and Mercantile Insurance Co v London, Liverpool and Globe Insurance Co* (1877) 5 ChD 569, CA (fire insurance); *Ballymagauran Co-operative Agricultural and Dairy Society Ltd v Cavan and Leitrim County Councils* [1915] 2 IR 85, CA.

[14] *Mason v Sainsbury* (supra) (fire insurance); *King v Victoria Insurance Co* [1896] AC 250 at 254, 255, PC (fire insurance). But he may raise the defence that the policy was not a valid insurance and that, consequently, there is no right of subrogation available under it: *John Edwards & Co v Motor Union Insurance Co* [1922] 2 KB 249, 11 LlL Rep 122 (marine insurance).

[15] *Thomas & Co v Brown* (1899) 4 Com Cas 186 (lighterman's insurance) per Mathew J, at 192.

[16] *The Palm Branch* [1916] P 230 (war insurance), where goods seized as prize were claimed on behalf of enemy underwriters who had paid the loss to the neutral owners.

[17] [1961] 2 All ER 487, QB (marine insurance).

Pound Sterling had been devalued in 1949 and the loss, when quantified and converted into English currency, came to nearly £127,000. The assured then repaid the £72,000 to the insurers and claimed that they were entitled to keep the balance, i e about £55,000. *Held,* by the Queen's Bench Division, that this contention succeeded.

In the course of his judgment Diplock J stated the principle applicable in the following way:[18]

> 'It follows that in my view the insurer's rights in this case were limited to recovering from the assured the amount overpaid, that is to say, the £72,000. He is entitled to no more. The principle, I think is a simple one. It renders irrelevant any consideration of the particular concatenation of circumstances which enable the assured to recover from the Canadian Government a sum in sterling in excess of the value of the ship at the time of the casualty . . . The simple principle which I apply is that the insurer cannot recover under the doctrine of subrogation now embodied in s 79 of the Marine Insurance Act 1906,[19] anything more than he has paid.'

If, however, the assured is not fully indemnified, by reason of the fact that he was under-insured at the time of the loss,[20] and the amount of his loss exceeds the sum recovered from the insurers, different considerations apply.[1]

The assured is not to be deprived of his right to obtain a full indemnity. The insurers, therefore are not subrogated to the whole of his rights in respect of the loss; and he may enforce it himself by action against the person responsible.[2]

---

18 Ibid, at 494, QB (marine insurance).

19 The words of this section are set out at 467, ante. For other cases illustrative of the principle, see *Stewart v Greenock Marine Insurance Co* (1848) 2 HL Cas 159 (marine insurance); *Thames and Mersey Marine Insurance Co v British and Chilian SS Co* [1916] 1 KB 30, CA (marine insurance), where the loss was total; *Goole and Hull Steamtowing Co Ltd v Ocean Marine Insurance Co Ltd* [1928] 1 KB 589, 29 LlL Rep 242 where the loss was partial; *Boag v Standard Marine Insurance Co Ltd* [1937] 1 All ER 714 at 720; *Glen Line Ltd v A-G* (1930) 36 Com Cas 1, where Lord Atkin, drawing the distinction between the rights of abandonment and the rights of subrogation said (at 13, 14): 'And it is to be noted that in respect of abandonment the rights exist on a valid abandonment, whereas in respect of subrogation they only arise on payment; and that subrogation will only give the insurer rights up to twenty shillings in the pound on what he has paid.'

20 As to the position of the insurers after payment under a valued policy, where the loss exceeds the valuation, see *North of England Iron SS Insurance Association v Armstrong* (1870) LR 5 QB 244 (marine insurance) doubted in *Burnand v Rodocanachi* (1882) 7 App Cas 333 (marine insurance) (per Lord Blackburn, at 342); and cf *Tunno v Edwards* (1810) 12 East 488 (marine insurance), where the loss was treated as partial, the insurers paying 50 per cent. of the valuation, and it was held that they were not entitled to share a sum received subsequently from the captors of the goods insured which represented half the proceeds of the goods, although it amounted to more than the valuation in the policy. An analysis of the effect of the decision in *North of England Iron Steamship Insurance Association v Armstrong* (supra) is to be found in the judgment of Diplock J in *Yorkshire Insurance Co Ltd v Nisbet Shipping Co Ltd* [1961] 2 All ER 487, QB at 492–3.

1 *Globe and Rutgers Fire Insurance Co v Truedell* (1927) 60 OLR 227.

2 *Morley v Moore* [1936] 2 KB 359, CA (accident insurance) where the assured had to bear the first £5 of loss under his policy, and the insurers settled the balance with the insurers for the other party on a 'knock-for-knock' basis, but the insured was held entitled to sue for the full amount of his claim. Sir Boyd Merriman P said (obiter) (at 367): 'I hope that the result of this judgment will be that plaintiffs will realise that they still have whatever may be their full rights accompanied by whatever duties result from the exercise of those rights, notwithstanding arrangements made behind the scenes between insurance companies. If, contrary to the opinion that I have been expressing, the combined effect of arrangements where by the assured is regarded as his own insurer for a certain proportion of the loss and this agreement colloquially known as a 'knock-for-knock' agreement is used seriously to prejudice insured persons when insisting upon the whole of their legal rights, I should wish to consider whether the agreement were contrary to public policy.' *Morley v Moore* was applied by the Court of Appeal (Sellers and Davies LJJ: Salmon LJ, dissenting) in *Bourne v Stanbridge* [1965] 1 All ER 241, where it was held

They are not entitled to prevent him from so doing; nor will the Court interfere with his conduct of the action, if he undertakes that he will claim for the full amount of his loss, without deducting the sum recovered from the insurers under his policy, and that he will not compromise the action except in good faith.[3] In the absence of express agreements as to costs, the costs will be apportioned in accordance with the respective interests of the assured and the insurers in the litigation.[4] If he recovers anything in the action over and above that portion of the loss which falls upon himself, he will hold it as trustee on behalf of the insurers.[5]

Where a bailee is insured against liability to his bailor and the bailor is insured under the same policy, the insurer cannot exercise a right of subrogation against the bailee.[6]

Similarly there is no right of subrogation in the case of contractors and sub-contractors engaged on a common enterprise under a building contract.[7]

---

there was no ground of misconduct on which the County Court Judge could properly exercise his discretion to deprive the insured of Scale 3 costs, since the insured's right to sue for the full amount of damage to his car was not affected by any 'knock for knock' agreement made between his own insurance company and that of the other motorist involved in the collision.

3 *Commercial Union Assurance Co v Lister* (1874) 9 Ch App 483, where a building insured against fire but not for its full value, was destroyed by a fire alleged to have been caused by the negligence of a municipal corporation, and it was held that the owner, who had brought an action for damages against the corporation, could not be deprived of the conduct of the action at the suit of the insurers, upon his undertaking to sue for the whole amount of the damage, although he would be liable for anything done by him in violation of any equitable duty towards them. This case arose upon an interlocutory application and did not finally determine the question: *Page v Scottish Insurance Corpn* (1929) 140 LT 571, CA (accident insurance) per Scrutton LJ, at 576. In *Globe and Rutgers Fire Insurance Co v Truedell* (1927) 60 OLR 227, where the position is fully discussed, it was held that the Court could not interfere with or control the assured in the prosecution or the settlement of the claim against third parties except to require him in prosecuting or settling it to act with diligence and good faith having regard to the fact that the insurers were interested. Cf *Re Driscoll* [1918] 1 IR 152 (fire insurance).

4 *Duus, Brown and Co v Binning* (1906) 11 Com Cas 190 (marine insurance).

5 *Commercial Union Assurance Co v Lister* (supra) (fire insurance) per Jessel MR, at 484; *The Commonwealth* [1907] P 216, CA (marine insurance) per Gorell Barnes P, at 222, 223, where the assured was held entitled to retain a proportion of the monies recovered from third parties in the ratio of the amount by which he was his own insurer to that of the insurance monies which he had been paid; *National Fire Insurance Co v McLaren* (1886) 12 OR 682; cf *Re Blackburne, ex p Strouts* (1892) 9 Morr 249, where a landlord, who had recovered £273 from his insurers, was admitted to prove in the bankruptcy of the tenant for £440, the full amount of loss in respect of his tenant's covenant to reinstate, and it was suggested that the landlord would not be bound to hand over anything to the insurers until he had received 20s in the pound in respect of his own loss.

6 *Petrofina (UK) Ltd v Magnaload Ltd* [1984] QB 127, [1983] 3 All ER 33, [1983] 2 Lloyd's Rep 91 (contractors' all risks insurance) at 98 (per Lloyd J).

7 Ibid, at 99 (per Lloyd J).

CHAPTER 47

Indemnification aliunde

In those contracts of insurance which are contracts of indemnity it follows that, since the assured is only entitled to an indemnity, in estimating the amount for which the insurers are liable under the policy, any payment or benefit received by the assured, which has the effect of diminishing or extinguishing the loss, must be taken into account.[1]

Such a payment or benefit may be received either before or after the insurer settles the claim of the insured.

A INDEMNIFICATION BEFORE PAYMENT

The loss sustained by the assured may be partially or in some cases wholly made good from other sources, before payment by the insurers, whose liability is correspondingly diminished or extinguished. The action of the assured is founded on the nature of the damnification as it really is at the time of action brought.[2] The contract of the insurers is to make good the loss; and, if the loss is made good aliunde, the insurers are not liable, since there is no loss.[3]

The assured may receive a sum of money or other benefit from a third person which has the effect of diminishing or extinguishing the loss. Whether such person is under some liability to the assured in consequence of the destruction of the subject-matter, and makes the payment in discharge of his liability,[4] or

---

1 *Burnand v Rodocanachi* (1882) 7 App Cas 333 (marine insurance) per Lord Blackburn, at 339: 'The general rule of law is that where there is a contract of indemnity . . . and a loss happens, anything which reduces or diminishes that loss reduces or diminishes the amount which the indemnifier is bound to pay.' See also, *Brotherston v Barber* (1816) 5 M & S 418 (marine insurance) per Lord Ellenborough CJ, at 411, following *Hamilton v Mendes* (1761) 2 Burr 1198 (marine insurance) per Lord Mansfield CJ, at 1210; *Castellain v Preston* (1883) 11 QBD 380, CA (fire insurance) per Cotton LJ, at 393; *Godsall v Boldero* (1807) 9 East 72 (life insurance), the principle of which still applies to contracts of indemnity; *Law v London Indisputable Life Policy Co* (1855) 1 K & J 223 (life insurance) per Wood V-C, at 228.

2 *Hamilton v Mendes* (supra) (marine insurance) per Lord Mansfield CJ, at 1210.

3 *Law v London Indisputable Life Policy Co* (supra) (life insurance) per Wood V-C, at 228.

4 *Fifth Liverpool Star-Bowkett Building Society v Travellers' Accident Insurance Co* (1893) 9 TLR 221; *Bruce v Jones* (1863) 1 H & C 769 (marine insurance), where a portion of the loss had already been received under other policies; *Darrell v Tibbitts* (1880) 5 QBD 560, CA (fire insurance) per Brett LJ, at 562, applying *North British and Mercantile Insurance Co v London, Liverpool and Globe Insurance Co* (1877) 5 ChD 569 (fire insurance); *Castellain v Preson* (supra) per Cotton LJ, at 393; *Law Fire Assurance Co v Oakley* (1888) 4 TLR 309 (fire insurance). See also, *Mathewson v Western Assurance Co* (1859) 10 LCR 8, where a mortgagee was held not entitled to recover upon a policy covering his own interest, on the ground that the mortgagor had reinstated the mortgaged property before action brought, and the mortgagee's security was therefore undiminished.

whether he makes it voluntarily with the intention of assisting the assured to bear his loss,[5] is immaterial.

In either case the assured must give the insurers credit for the sum which he has been paid, or for the value of the benefit which he has received, as the case may be. He cannot, therefore, recover as against them more than the balance, if any, of his loss, since, if he were allowed to claim a full indemnity from them, and to retain the payments or benefits already received from third persons, he would be more than fully indemnified.

The assured cannot, however, be compelled in the absence of an express stipulation to that effect,[6] to have recourse to third persons first and to exercise any rights which he may have against them, for the purpose of relieving the insurers.[7] He has the right, if he thinks fit, to insist on being paid by the insurers in full.[8]

B INDEMNIFICATION AFTER PAYMENT

After the insurers have paid to the assured the amount recoverable under the policy, the assured remains liable to account to them for any benefit which he subsequently received from a third person in respect of the loss,[9] and which results in diminishing or extinguishing the loss against which the insurers have indemnified him.[10]

This liability is based on the principle of indemnity, and is intended to prevent the assured from retaining what is in effect a double indemnity.[11]

---

5 *Godsall v Boldero* (1807) 9 East 72 (life assurance) which, though overruled in *Dalby v India and London Life Assurance Co* (1854) 15 CB 365 (life insurance), correctly states the principle applicable to contracts of indemnity, cf *Curtis & Sons v Mathews* [1918] 2 KB 825 per Roche J, at 832. See further, *R v Shaw* (1901) 27 VLR 70.

6 For an example, see *Constructive Finance Co Ltd v English Insurance Co Ltd* (1924) 19 LlL Rep 144, HL.

7 *Fifth Liverpool Star-Bowkett Building Society v Travellers' Accident Insurance Co* (1893) 9 TLR 221, where a condition requiring the deduction of moneys payable by the employer was held to have no application where the employer was a company in liquidation, and the amount due to the employee had not been ascertained; *Dickenson v Jardine* (1868) LR 3 CP 639 (marine insurance).

8 *Darrell v Tibbitts* (1880) 5 QBD 560, CA (fire insurance) per Brett LJ, at 561; *West of England Fire Insurance Co v Isaacs* [1897] 1 QB 226, CA (fire insurance). The insurers, therefore, do not, by failing to insist that the assured's rights against third persons shall be taken into account before payment of the loss, lose the right to have them taken into account afterwards: *West of England Fire Insurance Co v Isaacs* [1897] 2 QB 377 per Collins J, at 383, in the Court below.

9 The mere fact that the property insured is recovered after payment of the loss does not entitle the insurers to repayment: *Holmes v Payne* [1930] 2 KB 301, 37 LlL Rep 41; cf *Goldberg v Employers' Liability Assurance Corpn* [1922] 1 WWR 529, where, by the terms of the policy, the loss was payable within a specified period, and it was held that the recovery of the stolen car from the thief after the expiration of the period did not relieve the insurers from liability to pay its value.

10 *Castellain v Preston* (1883) 11 QBD 380, CA, per Brett LJ, at 390–391; *King v Victoria Insurance Co* [1896] AC 250 at 256, PC (fire insurance). The assured, in consequential loss insurance, is not bound to account for profits subsequently earned: *City Tailors Ltd v Evans* (1921) 126 LT 439, CA, except possibly where he uses the same staff: ibid, per Atkin LJ, at 445. Similarly, if one of two unique china vases is insured and destroyed, it is immaterial that the remaining one, by the destruction, has become more unique and more valuable: ibid, per Scrutton LJ, at 443.

11 *Darrell v Tibbitts* (1880) 5 QBD 560, CA (fire insurance), where it was held that if, after payment by the insurers, the assured receives compensation for his loss from other sources, the insurers are entitled to recover from him any sum received by him in excess of the loss actually sustained by

So, where the Export Credits Guarantee Department of the Board of Trade issued to a firm of exporters a policy in respect of a buyer's inability to pay for the goods, which had been sold to him, on account of his inability to transfer currency owing to foreign exchange control difficulties, it was held that the Department, which had paid the sum due under the policy, was entitled to claim the sum which the buyer finally paid when the controls were relaxed.[12]

If, therefore, the assured in spite of receiving the benefit, is no more than fully indemnified, as, for instance, where the actual loss which he has sustained is far in excess of the amount paid by the insurers under the policy, and the sum or benefit received from the third person does not, when added to such amounts, exceed the actual loss, the liability to account does not arise.[13]

1 The insurers' right to benefit

Though the exercise of the liability of the assured to account for any benefit received is clear, and the fact that it is based on the principle of indemnity is beyond question, there is some difficulty in defining the nature of the right of the insurers, or in saying on what grounds the liability of the assured may be enforced. The right of the insurers may be a right to recover back what they have paid, or it may be merely a right to the benefit of what the assured has received; and the distinction may depend on the grounds on which it is justified. The difficulty has been said to be rather one of form than of substance.[14] There are cases, however, in which the nature of the right becomes material. If the benefit received by the assured is the payment of a sum which purports to be a full indemnity, but which is less than the amount already paid by the insurers,[15] the amount for which the assured must account necessarily differs according to the view adopted as to the nature of the insurers' right.

The following views have been formulated:

a The right of the insurers depends on the doctrine of subrogation,[16] which is not confined to the enforcing of remedies, but confers on the insurers the right to receive the advantage of any remedy which has been applied by the assured to himself.[17]

b The right of the insurers depends on an implied contract that the assured is to hold for the benefit of the insurers or pay over to them

---

him, and Brett LJ, at 562, said: 'If the company cannot recover the money back, it follows that the landlord will have the whole extent of his loss as to the building made good by the tenants and will also have the whole amount of the loss paid by the insurance company. If that it so, the whole doctrine of indemnity would be done away with; the landlord would be not merely indemnified, he would be paid twice over.'

12 *Re Miller Gibb & Co Ltd* [1957] 2 All ER 266, [1957] 1 Lloyd's Rep 258.

13 *Tunno v Edwards* (1810) 12 East 488 (marine insurance).

14 *Darrell v Tibbitts* (1880) 5 QBD 560, CJ (fire insurance) per Brett LJ, at 562.

15 See *Law Fire Assurance Co v Oakley* (1888) 4 TLR 309 (fire insurance), where the insurers had paid £25, and the assured recovered in an action against a tortfeasor £23.

16 *Darrell v Tibbitts* (supra) per Brett LJ, at 563, and per Thesiger LJ, at 568. As to subrogation, see Chapter 46.

17 *Castellain v Preston* (1883) 11 QBD 380, CA (fire insurance), per Brett LJ, at 389, and per Bowen LJ, at 403, followed in *Assicurazioni Generali de Trieste v Empress Assurance Corpn Ltd* [1907] 2 KB 814 (marine insurance), where Pickford J referring to the above passages, said at 820: 'I am by no means sure the passages are only dicta. I think the learned Judges were stating the principle on which their decision proceeded, but in any case they are dicta of such authority that I think I am bound to follow them and that they cover this case'.

whatever he may afterwards receive from other sources in respect of the loss.[18]

c The right of the insurers depends on a promise on the part of the assured, which is to be implied from the payment by the insurers of the amount of the loss, that if the loss is afterwards made good from other sources, he will repay them what he has received from those sources.[19]

d The right of the insurers depends on the fact that the insurers made their payment on the condition that the assured had, in fact, sustained the loss for which he made his claim, and they are, therefore, entitled, on it turning out that he has sustained no loss at all, to maintain an action for money had and received to recover what they paid.[20]

2 The cases in which the right arises

The cases in which the insurers may become entitled to have a payment made to the assured brought into account are:

a Where the payment is made by a tortfeasor.
b Where the payment is made under a contract.
c Where the payment is made as a gift.

(a) Where the payment is made by a tortfeasor

Where the payment is made by the person to whose negligence or default the loss is to be attributed,[1] the payment is clearly made by way of compensation for

---

18 *Darrell v Tibbitts* (supra) per Cotton LJ, at 565; *King v Victoria Insurance Co* [1896] AC 250, at 252, PC. The opinion has been expressed, on the one hand, that he is a trustee for the insurers to the extent of the money received: *Symons v Mulkern* (1882) 46 LT 763 (transit insurance); and, on the other hand, that he is a mere debtor: *Stearns v Village Main Reef Gold Mining Co Ltd* (1905) 10 Com Cas 89, CA (insurance on bullion) per Stirling LJ, at 98.

19 *Darrell v Tibbitts* (supra) per Brett LJ at 562, 563. The right has, however, been said to be not a right to recover back what has been paid, but merely a right to the benefit of what is received by the assured: ibid, per Cotton LJ, at 564; *Castellain v Preston* (1883) 11 QBD 380, CA (fire insurance) per Cotton LJ, at 393, 396.

20 *Darrell v Tibbitts* (supra) per Thesiger LJ, at 568; *Law Fire Assurance Co v Oakley* (1888) 4 TLR 309 (fire insurance); and cf *Horse, Carriage and General Insurance Co Ltd v Petch* (1916) 33 TLR 131 (accident insurance). This view appears to be the most satisfactory one, though it is contrary to the view expressed in *Darrell v Tibbitts* (supra) per Brett LJ, at 562, 563: 'I do not think that the money can be recovered back upon the ground that the consideration for the payment of the money has wholly failed: because the premium upon the policy is part of the consideration, and no one supposes that the premium is to be returned.' It may, however, be pointed out that the reason given is not very satisfactory, since the recovery of the money does not avoid the policy, and the contract of insurance remains in force for whatever period is fixed for its duration; why, therefore, any question should arise as to return of premium it is difficult to understand.

1 Where the payment is made in respect of a loss not covered by the policy, the insurers cannot claim the benefit of it: *Sea Insurance Co v Hadden* (1884) 13 QBD 706, CA (marine insurance), where insurers on ship, who paid for a constructive total loss by collision, were held not to be entitled to claim from the owners the compensation which they had received from a tortfeasor for loss of freight; cf *Assicurazioni Generali de Trieste v Empress Assurance Corpn Ltd* [1907] 2 KB 814 (marine insurance), where Pickford J, at 820, pointed out that damages for libel published incidentally in, and arising out of, the insurance transaction would not be taken into account.

the loss,[2] whether it is recovered in an action of tort for damages,[3] or whether it is made voluntarily by the tortfeasor.

The assured cannot, therefore, be allowed to retain it, in addition to the sum paid by the insurers under the policy covering the loss, since he would thus receive a double indemnity.[4] The assured is, however, entitled to an allowance in respect of the costs incurred in maintaining any necessary action to recover the compensation.[5]

(b) Where the payment is made under a contract

If the contract imposes on the person making the payment a liability towards the assured to make good the loss which he has sustained, as, e g where such person is a carrier, or a tenant under a covenant to repair,[6] such payment, being a discharge of the liability, operates as an indemnification of the assured in respect of the loss against which he had insured, and for which he has already received an indemnity from the insurers.

The effect, therefore, of the payment is that he is doubly indemnified, and he cannot retain the payment as against the insurers.[7]

It is not, however, necessary that the payment should have been made in respect of the loss, or that the person making good the payment should by the terms of the contract be required to make good the loss. The contract need not in any way relate to the loss, provided that it relates to the subject-matter of insurance, the principle of indemnity being equally applicable so long as the effect of the payment is to diminish or extinguish the loss.[8]

(c) Where the payment is made as a gift

The fact that the payment is made voluntarily by a third person as a gift,[9] or even as a matter of grace by a person who is in fact, though not in law, responsible for the loss,[10] does not necessarily preclude the insurers from

---

2 It is immaterial, in the case of a valued policy, that the compensation is based upon a different valuation: *Thames and Mersey Marine Insurance Co v British and Chilian SS Co* [1916] 1 KB 30, CA (marine insurance).

3 *Law Fire Assurance Co v Oakley* (supra) (fire insurance), where part of the money received by the assured from the tortfeasor was in respect of personal injuries, and no claim was made by the insurers to that part.

4 *Darrell v Tibbitts* (supra) per Brett LJ, at 562.

5 *Hatch, Mansfield & Co v Weingott* (1906) 22 TLR 366 (guarantee), followed in *Crown Bank v London Guarantee and Accident Co* (1908) 17 OLR 95; *Assicurazioni Generali de Trieste v Empress Assurance Corpn Ltd* (supra) (marine insurance); *Baloise Fire Insurance Co v Martin* [1937] 2 DLR 24. Where an action involves claims, some of which are for the benefit of the insurers, and others in which the insurers are not interested, the Court has no power, on taxation, to apportion the costs between the assured and the insurers: *Re Taxation of Costs, Re TAM* [1937] 2 KB 491 [1937] 3 All ER 113, CA.

6 *Darrell v Tibbitts* (1880) 5 QBD 560, CA.

7 Ibid, per Brett LJ, at 562, and per Cotton LJ, at 564.

8 *Castellain v Preston* (1883) 11 QBD 380, CA (fire insurance), where the assured, after payment, received the full price from the purchaser of the house insured.

9 *Randal v Cockran* (1748) 1 Ves Sen 98 (marine insurance); *Blaauwpot v Da Costa* (1758) 1 Eden 130 (marine insurance).

10 *Brooks v MacDonnell* (1835) 1 Y & C (Ex) 500 (marine insurance), where a British ship was condemned as a blockade-runner by the Brazilian Government, which, some years later, made a payment as compensation under a convention with the British Government; *Stearns v Village Main Reef Gold Mining Co Ltd* (1905) 10 Com Cas 89, CA (insurance on bullion), where the

claiming the benefit of it, if it results in diminishing or extinguishing the loss which the assured has sustained.

The right of the insurers depends solely on the intention with which the payment was made, and its effect on the position of the assured.[11]

To enable the insurers to claim the right, the following conditions must be fulfilled:

i The payment must have been made with the intention on the part of the donor of diminishing or extinguishing the loss in respect of which the insurers have already indemnified the assured.[12]

ii The insurers must not have been excluded by the donor from the benefit of the payment.[13]

To enable them to benefit it is not necessary that they should be expressly referred to by the terms of the gift; it is sufficient if the gift, on a fair and legitimate construction of its terms, operates in favour of the insurers.[14]

iii The effect of the payment must be to extinguish the loss or reduce it to an amount less than the sum already paid by the insurers.

If the assured's loss exceeds the sum so paid, and the payment relates only to the excess, having been made with the intention of making good, not his whole loss, but only such portion of it as should not have been covered by insurance,[15] no question of double indemnity can arise, since the assured, by receiving and retaining both sums, is not more than fully indemnified.

Transvaal Government made a return to the assured of gold which it had commandeered. It may be noted that in no reported case has any claim been made in respect of private gifts; all the cases relate to grants of public money made by the Government of a State.

11 Cf *Castellain v Preston* (supra) per Bowen LJ, at 404: 'Suppose that a man who has insured his house has it damaged by fire, and suppose that his brother offers to give him a sum of money to assist. The effect on the position of the underwriters will depend on the real character of the transaction. Did the brother mean to give the money for the benefit of the insurers as well as for the benefit of the assured? If he did, it seems to me the insurers are entitled to the benefit, but if he did not, but only gave it for the benefit of the assured . . . then the gift was not given to reduce the loss, and it falls within *Burnand v Rodocanachi* ((1882) 7 App Cas 333 (marine insurance)) . . . If it was given to reduce the loss and for the benefit of the insurers as well as the assured, the case would fall on the other side of the line, and be within *Randal v Cochran* (1748) 1 Ves Sen 97 (marine insurance)'.

12 *Burnand v Rodocanachi* (supra) per Lord Blackburn, at 341; *Stearns v Village Main Reef Gold Mining Co Ltd* (supra) per Vaughan Williams LJ, at 94.

13 *Burnand v Rodocanachi* (supra) (marine insurance) per Lord Selborne C, at 338, distinguishing *Randal v Cockran* (supra) (marine insurance), and *Blaauwpot v Da Costa* (supra) (marine insurance). For an explanation of the distinction, see *Castellain v Preston* (supra) (fire insurance) per Brett LJ, at 389: 'In *Burnand v Rodocanachi* the foundation of the judgment, to my mind, was that what was paid by the United States Government could not be considered as salvage, but must be deemed to have been only a gift. It was only a gift to which the assured had no right at any time until it was placed in their hands. I am aware that with regard to the case of reprisals, or that which a person whose vessel has been captured got from the English Government by way of reprisal, the sum received has been stated to be, and perhaps in one sense was, a gift of his own Government to himself, but it was always deemed to be capable of being brought within the range of the law as to insurance, because the English Government invariably made the "gift", so invariably, that as a matter of business it had come to be considered as a matter of right'.

14 *Burnand v Rodocanachi* (supra (marine insurance) per Lord Selborne, at 338, following *Randal v Cockran* (supra) (marine insurance), and *Blaauwpot v Da Costa* (supra) (marine insurance).

15 As was the case in *Burnand v Rodocanachi* (supra), which concerned a valued policy.

CHAPTER 48

Contribution

In insurances on property or against liability, which are contracts of indemnity, the assured cannot, however many policies he may have effected, recover more than a full indemnity.[1]

Where there is no condition to the contrary, the assured may select the policy under which to claim his indemnity—if that alone is sufficient for the purpose—and the insurers on that policy cannot resist liability on the ground that there are other policies in existence which the assured might have equally enforced.

As far as marine insurance is concerned, s 32(2) of the Marine Insurance Act 1906 states:

> 'Where the assured is over-insured by double insurance—(a) the assured, unless the policy otherwise provides, may claim payment from the insurers in such order as he may think fit, provided that he is not entitled to receive any sum in excess of the indemnity allowed by this Act.'

Section 32(1) defines 'double insurance' in the following way:

> 'Where two or more policies are effected by or on behalf of the assured on the same adventure and interest or any part thereof, and the sums insured exceed the indemnity allowed by this Act, the assured is said to be over-insured by double insurance.'

A THE MEANING OF 'CONTRIBUTION'

When the insurers have discharged their liability,[2] however, they are entitled, as between themselves and the other insurers, to call on the latter to bear their

1 *Morgan v Price* (1849) 4 Exch 615 (marine insurance) per Parke B, at 620; 'The second policy was effected on the same vessel, and in exactly the same sum, and upon the same terms; and in such case the payment by one insurer acts by way of satisfaction to the other'; *Godin v London Assurance Co* (1758) 1 Burr 489 (marine insurance) per Lord Mansfield CJ, at 492; *Newby v Reed* (1763) 1 WmBl 416 (marine insurance); *Rogers v Davis* (1777) 2 Park's Marine Inscc 8th Edn, p 601 (marine insurance); *North British and Mercantile Insurance Co v London, Liverpool and Globe Insurance Co* (1877) 5 ChD 569, CA (fire insurance) per James LJ, at 581; *Scottish Amicable Heritable Securities Association v Northern Assurance Co* 1883 11 R (Ct of Sess) 287 (fire insurance) per Lord Moncrieff), at 303: 'That principle (i e contribution) or rather that rule of practice depends on the doctrine—one not of law only but of common reason—that a man who insures his interest in property against loss by fire, whether that interest is that of a proprietor or that of a creditor, cannot recover from the insurer a greater amount than he has lost by the contingency insured against. So, in the case of double insurances of the same interest with different insurance companies, the assured will not be entitled to recover more than the full amount of the loss which he has suffered'; *Wolenberg v Royal Co-operative Collecting Society* (1915) 84 LJKB 1316 (life insurance); cf *Bruce v Jones* (1863) 1 H & C 769 (marine insurance).

2 But not before: *Williams v North China Insurance Co* (1876) 1 CPD 757, CA (marine insurance) per Jessel MR, at 768.

share of the loss and pay their proportion of the amount already paid under the first policy.[3] This right is called the 'right of contribution'.

Thus, as far as marine insurance is concerned, s 80 of the Marine Insurance Act 1906 provides that:

> '(1) Where the assured is over-insured by double insurance, each insurer is bound, as between himself and the other insurers, to contribute rateably to the loss in proportion to the amount for which he is liable under his contract.
>
> (2) If any insurer pays more than his proportion of the loss, he is entitled to maintain an action for contribution against the other insurers, and is entitled to the like remedies as a surety who has paid more than his proportion of the debt.'[4]

The right of contribution does not depend on contract, but on principles of equity.[5]

B WHEN THE RIGHT OF CONTRIBUTION ARISES

To give rise to a right to contribution the following conditions must be fulfilled:

1 All the policies concerned must comprise the same subject-matter.
2 All the policies must be effected against the same peril.
3 All the policies must be effected by or on behalf of the same assured.
4 All the policies must be in force at the time of the loss.
5 All the policies must be legal contracts of insurance.
6 No policy must contain any stipulation by which it is excluded from contribution.

1 Same subject-matter

The policies need not be restricted to the same subject-matter. Each may cover a wider whole, but the subject-matter in respect of which the claim to contribution arises must be common to all.[6]

On the other hand, it is not necessary that the amount of insurance should be

---

3 *Newby v Reed* (supra); *Davis v Gildart* (1777) 2 Park's Marine Inscc 8th Edn, p 424 (marine insurance); *Godin v London Assurance Co* (supra) (marine insurance), applied to fire insurance in *North British and Mercantile Insurance Co v London, Liverpool and Globe Insurance Co* (supra) per Baggallay LJ, at 587. The insurers should bring the action in their own name and not in the form of subrogation: *Austin v Zurich General Accident and Liability Insurance Co Ltd* [1945] KB 250, CA (accident insurance) per MacKinnon LJ, at 258.

4 See further, Ivamy *Marine Insurance* (4th Edn, 1985), p 461.

5 *Godin v London Assurance Co* (1758) 1 Burr 489 (marine insurance) per Lord Mansfield CJ, at 492: 'If the insured is to receive but one satisfaction, natural justice says that the several insurers shall all of them contribute *pro rata* to satisfy that loss against which they have all insured.' See also, *American Surety Co of New York v Wrightson* (1910) 16 Com Cas 37 (fidelity insurance) per Hamilton J, at 49.

6 *American Surety Co of New York v Wrightson* (1910) 16 Com Cas 37 (fidelity insurance) per Hamilton J, at 56; *Godin v London Assurance Co* (1758) 1 Burr 489 (marine insurance) per Lord Mansfield CJ, at 492; *North British and Mercantile Insurance Co v London, Liverpool and Globe Insurance Co* (1877) 5 ChD 569, CA (fire insurance); *Boag v Economic Insurance Co Ltd* [1954] 2 Lloyd's Rep 581, where it was held that a lorry load of tobacco insured under an all risks transit policy never formed part of the stock-in trade at the assured's premises, and was not covered by a fire policy, and consequently there was no right to demand contribution from the insurers under the fire policy.

the same in all.[7] It is sufficient if, at the time of the loss, some portion at least of the property destroyed happens to fall within the scope of all.

2 Same peril

The policies may include other perils, differing in the different policies, but the peril which causes the loss must be common to all.[8]

3 Same assured

The policies must cover a common interest, i e they must all be in favour of a common assured. It is not sufficient that the policies all relate to the same physical object.[9] They must also relate to the same interest in such object.

They must, therefore, be effected by the same assured, or by some person on his behalf.[10]

Where the assured under one policy is a distinct person from the assured under the other, each having a separate interest in himself, and neither policy being intended for the benefit of the assured under the other, no right of contribution arises, notwithstanding that the policies all relate to the same object, and to the same risk.[11] In such a case, the insurers under each policy are to be identified with their respective assured.[12]

---

7 *American Surety Co of New York v Wrightson* (supra), where one of the policies limited the liability of the insurers to $2,500 in any one case of dishonesty, and the other policy covering the assured against loss up to £40,000, without any limitation in any particular case, and the actual amount misappropriated was $2,680.

8 *North British and Mercantile Insurance Co v London, Liverpool and Globe Insurance Co* (supra) (fire insurance) per James LJ, at 581; *American Surety Co of New York v Wrightson* (supra) (fidelity insurance), where the policies in question were so widely different in their scope that Hamilton J, at 56, came to the conclusion that the ordinary rule of contribution was inapplicable.

9 *North British and Mercantile Insurance Co v London, Liverpool and Globe Insurance Co* (1877) 5 ChD 569, CA (fire insurance) per Jessel MR, at 577: 'What is the meaning of the words "covering the same property". They cannot mean the actual chattel; the most absurd consequences would follow if you read those words in the sense. I am satisfied that this condition was put in to apply to cases where it is the same property that is the subject-matter of the insurance, and the interests are the same'; *Nichols & Co v Scottish Union and National Insurance Co* 1885 14 R (Ct of Sess) 1094 (fire insurance) per Cave J, at 1095: 'The question in this case is whether . . . the insurance with the Lancashire Company does cover the same interest as that effected with the Scottish Union and National Co. If the interests are the same, . . . then the clause . . . applies and the plaintiff is only entitled to recover a proportion of the loss or damage from the defendants. If, on the other hand, the interests are different, . . . then there is nothing in common between the two and the paragraph does not apply'; *Scottish Amicable Heritable Securities Association Ltd v Northern Assurance Co* (1883) 11 R (Ct of Sess) 287 (fire insurance) per Lord Craighill, at 293; *Andrews v Patriotic Assurance Co (No 2)* (1886) 18 LRIr 355 (fire insurance) per Palles CB, at 261 et seq.

10 *Godin v London Assurance Co* (1758) 1 Burr 489 (marine insurance) per Lord Mansfield CJ, at 492: 'Where a man makes a double insurance on the same thing, in such a manner that he can clearly recover, against several insurers in distinct policies, a double satisfaction, the law certainly says that he ought not to recover doubly for the same loss, but be content with one single satisfaction for it. And if the same man really, and for his own proper account, insures the same goods doubly, though both insurances be not made in his own name, but one or both of them in the name of another person, yet that is just the same thing, for the same person is to have the benefit of both policies. And if the whole should be recovered from one, he ought to stand in the place of the insured, to receive contribution from the other who was equally liable to pay the whole'.

11 *North British and Mercantile Insurance Co v London, Liverpool and Globe Insurance Co* (supra) (fire insurance); *Scottish Amicable Heritable Securities Association Ltd v Northern Assurance Co* (supra) (fire insurance); *Andrews v Patriotic Assurance Co (No 2)* (fire insurance).

12 *North British and Mercantile Insurance Co v London, Liverpool and Globe Insurance Co* (supra) (fire insurance) per James LJ, at 581, following *Mason v Sainsbury* (1782) 3 Doug KB 61.

Their rights and liabilities as between themselves, therefore, depend on the right of subrogation, and not on the right of contribution. If the assured under one policy has any rights against the assured under the other policy, by the exercise of which his loss may be extinguished or diminished, his insurers are, on payment under their policy, subrogated to such rights against the second assured, who in his turn may call upon his own insurers to relieve him of his responsibility.[13] The ultimate result is, therefore, that the insurers under the second policy, so far from being able to call on the first insurers to contribute towards the loss, may be compelled to bear it all themselves, and to refund to the first insurers the sums which they have paid to the first assured.[14]

Thus, where separate insurances are effected by different persons on the same subject-matter solely for the protection of their respective interests, e g by a bailor and a bailee,[15] or by a landlord and a tenant,[16] or by a first and a second mortgagee,[17] or by a mortgagor and a mortgagee,[18] respectively—liability under each policy must be separately assessed, and the existence of the other policies must, so far as any question of contribution is concerned, be disregarded.

If, on the other hand, the policy effected by the bailee or mortgagee is by arrangement between the parties intended to cover the full value of the subject-matter, and to protect the interest of the bailor or mortgagor as well as the interest of the bailee or mortgagee, then a second policy effected by the bailor or mortgagor independently for his own benefit covers the same interest as the first

---

13 *North British and Mercantile Insurance Co v London, Liverpool and Globe Insurance Co* (supra) (fire insurance) per Mellish LJ, at 583–584: 'It was not a contract of indemnity to indemnify Barnett (i e the wharfinger) against the claim of Rodocanachi (i e the merchant) but it was a further contract which Rodocanachi got for his own security. If Rodocanachi had upon the invitation of Barnett gone against the office in the first instance, if it is true that Barnett was under an absolute liability to Rodocanachi to make good the entire loss, what was there to prevent the office from availing themselves of the right to sue Barnett in Rodocanachi's name? To such an action as that I am at a loss to see how, between Rodocanachi and Barnett, the language of Rodocanachi's policy of insurance or the language of Barnett's policy of insurance could have the slightest effect. Rodocanachi's case would be that Barnett ought to return him the goods he had, or ought to pay him the value of them, and if Barnett said "You ought to have sued somebody else", the reply would have been, "What is that to you? You owe me the goods; you are primarily liable".' As to subrogation, see Chapter 46.

14 *North British and Mercantile Insurance Co v London, Liverpool and Globe Insurance Co* (supra) (fire insurance) per Mellish LJ, at 585.

15 Ibid, per Mellish LJ, at 584.

16 *Portavon Cinema Co Ltd v Price and Century Insurance Co Ltd* [1939] 4 All ER 601; *Andrews v Patriotic Assurance Co (No 2)* (1886) 18 LRIr 355 (fire insurance). In *Reynard v Arnold* (1875) 10 Ch App 386 an apportionment of the loss had in fact been made between the two policies effected by the landlord and the tenant without objection, and, therefore, the legality of the apportionment was not called in question.

17 *North British and Mercantile Insurance Co v London, Liverpool and Globe Insurance Co* (supra) (fire insurance) per Jessel MR, at 577; *Scottish Amicable Heritable Securities Association Ltd v Northern Assurance Co* 1883 11 R (Ct of Sess) 287. It is immaterial that the mortgagor is made a party to both policies in respect of his right of reversion only, and undertakes to pay the premium, since the policies are intended to protect the several interests of the different mortgagees: *Westminster Fire Office v Glasgow Provident Investment Society* (1888) 13 App Cas 699 (fire insurance) per Lord Watson, at 715.

18 *Nichols & Co v Scottish Union and National Insurance Co* 1885 14 R (Ct of Sess) 1094 (fire insurance) per Cave J, at 1096.

policy. There is then a double insurance, and a case of contribution arises.[19]

It should, however, be pointed out that in the case of fire insurance, by a rule of the Fire Offices' Committee it has been provided that contribution is to take place between the insurers on different policies in certain cases where the policies all relate to the same subject-matter, notwithstanding that the interests covered by them are not the same.[20] This rule only applies as between the insurers themselves, and cannot affect the rights of the assured under each policy.[21] Nor does it have any binding force against insurers other than those who are members of the Fire Offices' Committee.

4 Policies in force

All the policies must be in force at the time of the loss. If, at the time of the loss, one of the policies has already lapsed, or has not yet attached, there is no double insurance and consequently no case of contribution arises.[22]

---

19 *Nichols & Co v Scottish Union and National Insurance Co* (supra) (fire insurance), where the first policy was effected in the name of certain trustees for the mortgagees, a building society, under an agreement incorporating certain rules which provided that the mortgagees were to insure the mortgaged property at the cost of the mortgagors, and that any insurance monies received were to be applied in discharging the mortgage debt, or, at the option of the mortgagees, in reinstatement; and the second policy was effected by the mortgagors for their own benefit, and it was held that it was a case for contribution, the first policy covering the interest of the mortgagor, as well as that of the mortgagee.

20 This rule was made in consequence of the decision of the Court of Appeal in *North British and Mercantile Insurance Co v London, Liverpool and Globe Insurance Co* (1877) 5 ChD 569, CA (fire insurance). It states 'Where there are two or more subsisting insurances in the names of persons having different rights and liabilities inter se covering the same Building of any kind, and/or the rent thereof (but not including Insurances covering different undivided shares in Buildings—whether the fact that the Insurance applies to an undivided share only appears on the face of the Policy or not), or the same Contents of Private Houses, Offices, Churches, Chapels, Schools, Hotels, Theatres, or Retail Shops, or the same Farming Stock, any loss shall, as between the Offices, be apportioned rateably amongst all such insurances without regard to the rights or liabilities of the Insured inter se. For the purposes of this Rule a "subsisting Insurance shall be deemed an Insurance effected by, or on behalf of, anyone having at the time of the breaking out of the fire an insurable interest in the subject-matter of the Insurance, and in respect of which Insurance the Insuring Company, if there were no other than current Insurance covering such subject-matter, would be legally liable to the Insured".' It is noteworthy that insurances on merchandise are not included in the rule.

21 An exception to this rule appears to have arisen in *Halifax Building Society v Keighley* [1931] 2 KB 248, where mortgagees, in accordance with the mortgage deed, insured in the joint names, and, the mortgagor having effected a separate insurance in his own name, the respective insurers paid their proportions of the loss to mortgagee and mortgagor, but the mortgagee was unable to recover from the mortgagor the policy monies he had received under his policy. Had there been no second policy, the insurers under the first would have paid the whole loss which would have been paid to the mortgagee who would have been entitled to apply it in reduction of the mortgage debt.

22 *Sickness and Accident Assurance Association v General Accident Assurance Corpn* 1892 19 R (Ct of Sess) 977 (accident insurance), where the second policy had not attached as the premium had not been paid. But there is contribution where the policy is avoided only after loss: *Weddell v Road Transport and General Insurance Co Ltd* [1932] 2 KB 563, 41 LlL Rep 69 (accident insurance). See further, *Jenkins v Deane* (1933) 103 LJKB 250, 47 LlL Rep 342 (motor insurance), where there was no proof that the second policy was a subsisting policy covering the loss for which the second insurers were liable; *National Employers Mutual General Insurance Association Ltd v Haydon* [1980] 2 Lloyd's Rep 149, CA (professional indemnity insurance).

Again, no right of contribution exists if the insurance company from whom contribution is claimed can repudiate liability under its policy on the ground that the insured has broken a condition.[1]

5 Valid and effective contracts

All the policies must be legal contracts of insurance. There is no contribution where the insurance, even though expressed in the form of a policy, is not legally binding.[2]

6 Contribution not excluded by terms of policies

No policy must contain any stipulation by which it is excluded from contribution.[3]

Sometimes a loss caused by a particular peril is capable of being covered by two or more different kinds of policies, the one kind of policy specifically insuring against the peril in question, whilst the other policy defines the peril insured against in terms wide enough to cover it. Thus, a loss by fire or burglary may fall within the terms of a policy of plate glass insurance or insurance against accidental loss. In this case, the policy giving the wide protection may contain a condition excluding it from contribution where the loss is covered by a more specific insurance.

Notwithstanding that all the above conditions may be fulfilled, the difference in the scope and character of the policies may be so great that it may be open to question whether the principle of contribution applies as between them at all.[4]

---

1 *Monksfield v Vehicle and General Insurance Co Ltd* [1971] 1 Lloyd's Rep 139, Mayor's and City of London Court (motor insurance), where no right of contribution arose because the insurer from whom contribution was claimed was entitled to repudiate liability on the ground that the insured had broken a condition stating that written notice should be given as soon as possible after the occurrence of any accident. (See the judgment of Judge Graham Rogers, ibid, at 141, where he said: 'It cannot be an equitable result that an insurance company which had no notice of an accident, had no say in the handling of the claim, and for whom . . . there was no opportunity "to investigate the rights or wrongs of it", should be called upon to make a contribution in a case in which it would quite clearly have had the right to repudiate if the claim had been brought under the terms of its own policy. The defendants are entitled to take advantage of the conditions in their policy and in my view are not liable for contribution.')

2 *Woods v Co-operative Insurance Society* 1924 SC 692 (fire insurance), where it was held that the benefit payable to the assured under a newspaper scheme which expressly excluded contractual liability could not be taken into account. But the contribution clause is occasionally so framed as to bring invalid and ineffective policies into account.

3 *Niger Co Ltd v Guardian Assurance Co* (1922) 13 LlL Rep 75. But in *Gale v Motor Union Insurance Co Ltd* [1928] 1 KB 359, 26 LlL Rep 65 (accident insurance), where two policies contained the usual contribution clause and each contained also a condition excluding liability if the risk were covered by another policy, it was held that the policies were not mutually exclusive and that a case of contribution arose; *Monksfield v Vehicle and General Insurance Co Ltd* [1971] 1 Lloyd's Rep 139, Mayor's and City of London Court (motor insurance), where the car driver was insured under his own policy, and both policies contained a clause stating that the insurance company concerned was not liable if the driver was entitled to an indemnity under any other policy. See also, *Weddell v Road Transport and General Insurance Co* (supra), where there was no contribution clause in one of the policies. But in this class of case there appears to be not so much a double insurance as a merely accidental over-lapping: *Australian Agricultural Co v Saunders* (1875) LR 10 CP 668, ExCh (fire insurance). See further, *National Employers Mutual General Insurance Association Ltd v Haydon* [1980] 2 Lloyd's Rep 149, CA (professional indemnity insurance).

4 In *American Surety Co of New York v Wrightson* (1910) 103 LT 663, where one of the policies was an ordinary fidelity policy, the other policy being a Lloyd's policy covering not only loss arising

C THE ENFORCEMENT OF THE RIGHT OF CONTRIBUTION

Since the right of contribution between different insurers depends, where it exists at all, on an equitable right arising out of the fact that the first insurers have paid more than ought fairly to be paid by them, it follows that they are entitled to enforce it in their own names.[5]

D THE APPORTIONMENT OF THE LOSS

The liability of the insurers under the different policies is to be estimated by applying the same rules whether the assured recovers payment in full from the insurers on one policy only, and leaves them to claim contribution from the insurers under the other policies, or whether, by the operation of the contribution clause, he is restricted from claiming in the first instance more than their due proportion from the insurers on each policy, since, in both cases, the ultimate liability must be the same.

The apportionment of a loss between the different policies by which it is covered, is governed, in the main, by various rules of practice which have been adopted more or less uniformly by the different insurers. Such rules are not entirely satisfactory, and it is difficult to see precisely on what principles they are based.

In practice, a distinction is drawn between policies which are 'specific', i e those which are not subject to average, and those which are subject to average.

1 Specific policies

The assured is entitled to be indemnified against loss in accordance with the terms of his insurance. No method of apportionment must, therefore, be adopted by which any portion of the loss is to fall on him except where the policies so provide, unless and until the aggregate amounts insured under the two policies have been exhausted.

The rules by which a loss is apportioned in the case of specific policies will vary according to whether the policies are 'concurrent' or 'non-concurrent'.

The policies are said to be 'concurrent' when they both apply to the same property or group of property, every group being insured separately in each policy for equal, or different, amounts.

---

from the dishonesty of clerks but also loss by fire or burglary, Hamilton J, whilst deciding the case in accordance with the defendant's admission that something was due, left the question open whether the case was in fact one for contribution at all.

5 *Sickness and Accident Assurance Association v General Accident Assurance Corpn* 1892 19 R (Ct of Sess) 977 (accident assurance) per Lord Low, at 980: 'The claim of an underwriter, who has indemnified the insured, to claim contribution from the other underwriters cannot be founded on the doctrine of subrogation, because an assignee can have no higher right than his cedent, and a shipowner who has received a full indemnity from one underwriter can never make any claim against another underwriter. The answer, therefore, to the claim of an underwriter who had paid, if made only in the right and as an assignee of the insured, would be that the contract was one of indemnity and that the insured had already been indemnified.' In *American Surety Co of New York v Wrightson* (1910) 103 LT 663 the plaintiffs were insurers who had paid the full amount for which they were liable under their policy.

They are said to be 'non-concurrent' when, although they both cover the property which is destroyed, such property is not insured separately either alone or in the same group in both policies, but is in one or both policies, as the case may be, grouped with other property in one insurance, so that the two policies do not refer solely to the same subject-matter.

(a) Where the policies are concurrent

Where the policies are concurrent, the liability under both policies arises in the same circumstances, since they are identical in risk, subject-matter and interest.

Both sets of insurers may be regarded as underwriters of one common policy underwritten by them for the sum specified in their respective policies.[6] The apportionment is, therefore, made in accordance with the rule applied in the case of marine insurance policies[7] which is equally applicable to fire policies.[8] Where both policies are effected for the same amounts of insurance, the loss is, therefore, in practice apportioned equally between them. If their respective amounts of insurance differ, such amounts will be aggregated together, and each policy will be liable for the proportion of the loss which its amount of insurance bears to the aggregate amount insured by both policies.[9]

This method of apportionment has been justified by comparing the insurers on the different policies to co-sureties,[10] who have guaranteed a common debt and whose individual liability is, therefore, regulated by the sum for which they have each undertaken to be responsible.[11]

It may be pointed out, however, that it is not an entirely true analogy to compare the insurers on different policies to co-sureties. In the case of each

---

6 *Scottish Amicable Heritable Securities Association Ltd v Northern Assurance Co* (1883) 11 R (Ct of Sess) 287 (fire insurance) per Lord McLaren, at 290n; *Newby v Reed* (1763) 1 Wm Bl 416 (marine insurance).

7 Marine Insurance Act 1906, s 80(1), which provides: 'Where the assured is over-insured by double insurance, each insurer is bound, as between himself and the other insurers, to contribute rateably to the loss in proportion to the amount for which he is liable under his contract.' The ambiguity of the words in this section 'contribute rateably to the loss in proportion to the amount for which he is liable under his contract' has been pointed out in *American Surety Co of New York v Wrightson* (1910) 16 Com Cas 37 (fidelity insurance) per Hamilton J, at 54. The words are capable of being construed as referring either to the insurers' possible liability under the contract, which is measured only by the amount of insurance, or to their actual liability in the particular case, assuming that their policy stood alone.

8 *North British and Mercantile Insurance Co v London, Liverpool and Globe Insurance Co* (1877) 5 ChD 569, CA (fire insurance) per Mellish LJ, at 583.

9 Thus, if insurer A insures for £500, and insurer B for £150 property which is damaged to the extent of £100, A would pay $\frac{500}{650}$ths of £100, i e £76.925 and B would pay $\frac{150}{650}$ths of £100, i e £23.075. The English practice appears to have been followed in *Eacrett v Gore District Mutual Fire Insurance Co* (1903) 6 OLR 592, where certain property, the value of which at the time of the trial was $9,274.62, was insured under policy A for $3,000 and under policy B for $7,000, and it was held upon a partial loss taking place amounting to $6,250, that policy A was liable for three-tenths of the loss.

10 This comparison is criticised in *American Surety Co of New York v Wrightson* (1910) 16 Com Cas 37 (fidelity insurance) per Hamilton J, at 55.

11 *Deering v Earl Winchelsea* (1787) 2 Bos & P 270 (guarantee) per Eyre CB, at 273, speaking of the sureties bound under different instruments: 'They are bound as effectually quoad contribution as if bound in one instrument, with this difference only, that the sums in each instrument ascertain the proportion, whereas if they were all joined in the same engagement, all contribute equally.' See also, *Pendlebury v Walker* (1841) 4 Y & C Ex 424 (guarantee) per Alderson B, at 441; *Ellesmere Brewery Co v Cooper* [1896] 1 QB 75 (guarantee) per Lord Russell CJ, at 81.

surety there is always a possibility that the principal debtor may incur a debt equal to the full amount of the guarantee. In the case of each set of insurers, on the other hand, it does not necessarily follow that they will ever become liable for the full amount of their insurance. Their liability cannot, even in the event of the total destruction of the subject-matter, extend beyond its value, however greatly such value may be exceeded by the amount of the insurance.

It appears to be, therefore, a more just and equitable method of apportioning the loss to take the liability under each policy as the basis of apportionment, and to make the amount to be contributed by each depend on its independent liability rather than upon the accident that a particular sum was specified in the policy, although it might well be that in no conceivable circumstances could the insurers ever be called upon to pay it.[12]

(b) Where the policies are non-concurrent

Where the policies are non-concurrent, the apportionment of the loss between them gives rise to questions of great difficulty. Although, in the facts of a particular case, there is a common liability occasioned by a common peril, yet the liability under each policy depends on different circumstances. The scope and character of the two policies may be widely different.

One of them may be a policy of insurance against fire only, whilst the other may insure against a number of perils of which fire is only one.[13] Moreover, since one or both of the policies must include in one insurance property other than that in respect of which the claim for apportionment is made, the amount of insurance cannot be regarded as exclusively appropriated to cover the common subject-matter.

A further complication arises where the loss extends beyond the common subject-matter, and includes other property which is covered by one policy alone.

It is accordingly difficult to ascertain how far the two policies are to be

---

12 Cf *Scottish Amicable Heritable Securities Association v Northern Assurance Co* 1883 11 R (Ct of Sess) 287 (fire insurance) per Lord McLaren, at 290n, 291n: 'The clause of contribution could have had no other object or purpose than to reduce the liability of the subscribing companies to that of underwriters, that is, a liability under which the assured should be entitled to recover the full amount of his claim in payments from the several contributories, but should not be entitled, in case of partial loss, to throw the loss on one or more contributories to the exclusion of the others . . . The divisor to be applied to the sum assured by the Northern Company (if the contract is a fair one) must be the ratio of the aggregate liabilities of the contributories to the actual loss'. It may be pointed out that some forms of the contribution clause expressly provide that the insurers are not to be liable for more than their rateable proportion of the aggregate liability under all the insurances covering the property. The 'independent liability' basis was applied in *Commercial Union Assurance Co Ltd v Hayden* [1977] 1 Lloyd's Rep 1, CA (public liability insurance). (See the judgment of Cairns LJ, ibid, at 12, and that of Stephenson LJ, ibid, at 13.)

13 Cf *American Surety Co of New York v Wrightson* (1910) 16 Com Cas 37 (fidelity insurance), where the plaintiff company's policy covered any loss or damage caused by the bad faith or dishonesty of any employee of an American bank, a separate sum being insured in the case of each individual employee, whereas a Lloyd's policy, underwritten by the defendant and others, and containing a self-renewing clause, covered in one lump sum not only loss by the bad faith or dishonesty of the bank's employees, but also loss by their negligence and, in addition, loss by the dishonesty of persons who were not employees of the bank, and losses by fire and burglary, etc; and the question was in what proportion the plaintiff company and the underwriters of the Lloyd's policy should contribute to a loss caused by the misappropriation of an employee of the bank.

treated as together insuring the common subject-matter, and to formulate the rules by which, in such a case, the apportionment of the common loss is to be made. Even as to the principles which are to be applied, there is no clear guidance. Certain working rules are to some extent followed by those responsible for calculating the details of the apportionment. These rules are to be regarded as merely laying down a rough and ready method of apportioning the loss, without reference to any satisfactory principle, and for this reason have been adversely criticised.

Moreover, they are not by any means universally recognised, and it cannot be said that there is any settled or uniform practice.[14] It may, therefore, be useful to consider the different principles on which it may be suggested that the apportionment should be made, and to indicate the manner in which they are to be applied. For this purpose it will be convenient to differentiate the case in which the loss affects the common subject-matter only from the case in which the loss extends to other property not covered by both policies.

i Where the loss affects the common subject-matter only

Where the whole of the property destroyed falls within the scope of both policies, the usual method is to apportion the loss in proportion to their respective amounts of insurance, as if the policies were concurrent.[15]

The objection to this method of apportionment is that it treats both policies as if the obligations of both were identical, and makes no allowance for the fact that, though the policies contain a common element, they are not limited to one and the same subject-matter, and may further differ widely in their scope and character. The difference between the two policies, however, should not, it is submitted, be wholly disregarded, especially in view of the fact that it has been suggested that such difference may be so great as to preclude any question of contribution between them from ever arising.[16]

No method of apportionment, therefore, can be considered satisfactory unless it takes into account the difference between the policies. It has been suggested that this may be done by ascertaining the respective values of the different subject-matters insured by each policy, and distributing the sum insured by each policy amongst them in proportion to such values. The sum thus allocated under each policy to the common subject-matter is then to be treated as the basis upon which the loss is to be apportioned, as if the two policies were concurrent.

The objection to this method is that the common subject-matter is treated as if it were separately insured by each policy, although it is not so in fact,[17] and

14 *American Surety Co of New York v Wrightson* (supra) (fidelity insurance) per Hamilton J, at 54.

15 Thus, where insurer A's policy is for £1,000 on subject matters I and II, and insurer B's policy is for £100 on subject-matter II only, and the sole loss is £100 on subject-matter II, insurer A would pay $\frac{1000}{1100}$ths of £1,000, i e £91, and insurer B $\frac{100}{1100}$ths of £100, i e £9.

16 *American Surety Co of New York v Wrightson* (supra) (fidelity insurance) per Hamilton J, at 56: 'It appears to me that the problem of discovering some terms which can be rateably compared with one another between two policies so widely different as these is one that differentiates so much from the simple rule of double insurance—namely, same interest, same assured, same adventure, same risk, and different amounts— as to make a consideration drawn from those hardly applicable, and make it desirable to leave open the question whether anything that can be called contribution in the nature of double insurance arises in such a case as this.'

17 *American Surety Co of New York v Wrightson* (supra) (fidelity insurance) per Hamilton J, at 55.

the apportionment proceeds on the hypothesis that the liability of the insurers under each policy is limited by the sum on which the apportionment is based, whereas the liability is, in reality, limited only by the amount of the insurance; for, if either policy had stood alone, the insurers under it would have been liable to pay the full value of the subject-matter, provided that the amount of the insurance was for the purpose sufficient.

Another method which has been suggested is that the word 'rateable' in the contribution clause should be construed as applying to liabilities, and that each policy should, in the first instance, be treated as though it stood alone, the liability of the insurers on it in respect of the common subject-matter being calculated independently of the other policy. The loss is then to be apportioned between the two policies in proportion to the two sums measuring their respective liability.[18]

The principle on which this method is based is the same as that which is known as the 'independent liability' principle,[19] and which is, in fact, applied under the existing working rules for the purpose of apportioning losses between average policies.[20] It has also been applied by the Court to the analogous case of two insurances covering the same loss occasioned to the assured by the dishonesty of the same employee.[1]

The adoption of the 'independent liability' principle seems, therefore, to be justified by authority. Nor does there appear to be any objection to it on the grounds of fairness. The only factor common to both policies is the existence of their common liability, and this liability can only be measured by taking into consideration the independent liability of each in respect of the same loss.

The principle, moreover, is equally capable of being applied where in one of the policies the amount of the insurance, and consequently the liability of the insurers, fall short of the full amount of the loss. In this case the whole loss is to be apportioned on the basis of the respective liabilities; for to make the more extensive policy liable for the excess over the common obligation, and to divide the balance between the two policies in proportion to their then respective liabilities, i e in equal shares, would be to disregard the specific limitation of liability in the other policy.[2]

ii Where the loss extends to other property not covered by both policies.

Where part only of the property destroyed falls within the scope of both policies, and the remainder is covered by one policy only, the method of apportionment in use is merely a practical working rule. It is not based on any principle, other than that of taking the mean between figures which results from the application

---

18 Thus, if insurer A's policy is for £1,000 on subject-matters I and II, and insurer B's policy is for £100 on subject-matter II, and the loss is £100 on II, A's policy, if standing alone, would be liable for £100 and B's policy if standing alone, would be liable for £100 in respect of the loss on II, and therefore by this method each policy would pay £50.

19 See p 495, ante.

20 This appears to be the case even though the average clause is, in the particular circumstances, inoperative. It is difficult to understand why one principle should be applied in the case of purely specific insurances and a different principle applied in the case of insurances which are, in the events that happen, specific, merely because in the latter case an average condition which, in the circumstances, has no effect appears in the policies.

1 *American Surety Co of New York v Wrightson* (supra) (fidelity insurance).

2 Ibid.

of two different methods of apportionment. These two methods, in their turn, appear to be based on the principle of apportioning the loss in proportion to the amounts of insurance under the respective policies,[3] but, as will be seen, the principle is not applied in a very satisfactory manner.

By the first method, the loss which is greater in amount is dealt with first. If it is covered by one policy only, its amount is deducted from the amount of insurance specified in such policy. The loss which is common to both policies is then apportioned between them in the proportion which the amount of insurance under the second policy bears to the balance left over on the first policy.

If, on the other hand, the loss which is common to both policies is the greater loss, it is apportioned between them in a similar manner, and the balance of the amount of insurance under the policy which alone covers the other loss is carried over to meet it.

By the second method, the lesser loss is taken first and dealt with in the same way. There is a considerable difference in the apportionment of the loss common to both policies as worked out by the two methods, and the working rule by which the mean between them is taken is a compromise.[4]

---

3 In *McCausland v Quebec Fire Insurance Co* (1894) 25 OR 330, where there were three policies, one on the front portion of a building, another on the rear portion, and a third covering the whole building, the apportionment was based solely on the amounts of the respective insurances as if the policies were concurrent policies on the building, without reference to the division in the first two policies. See also, *First Unitarian Congregation of Toronto Trustees v Western Assurance Co* (1886) 26 UCR 175, where a similar method was adopted. This method is not consistent with the English practice, nor does it appear to be correct on principle.

4 The following are examples of the way in which the 'mean' rule is worked:—

Example 1

Where the greater loss is covered by one policy only:

Insurer A's policy is for £200 on subject-matters I and II; insurer B's policy is for £100 on subject-matter II only; the loss is £100 on subject-matter I and £50 on subject-matter II.

The greater loss (*viz.* that of £100) is covered only by A's policy. By the first method, taking the greater loss first, therefore, the amount of this loss, £100, is deducted from the amount of A's policy, leaving the balance of £100 to contribute pro rata with B's policy for £100 towards the loss of £50 on subject-matter II. On II therefore, both A and B are liable for $\frac{100}{200}$ths of £50, i e £25 each.

Thus, by the first method A on I is liable for £100, and on II for £25, i e £125 in all, while B is liable for £25 on II.

By the second method (taking the lesser loss first) the loss of £50 on subject-matter II is apportioned pro rata between the amounts of A's and B's policies, i e £200 and £100. Thus, A is liable for $\frac{200}{300}$ths of £50, i e £33 on II and B is liable for $\frac{100}{300}$ths of £50, i e £17 on II, and the balance of A's policy, i e £167, is carried to meet the loss of £100 on subject-matter I.

By this method, therefore, A on I is liable for £100, and on II for £33, i e £133 in all, while B is liable for £17 on II.

The total of A's liability by both methods is £258, and of B's liability £42. Thus taking the mean, A will pay £129 and B will pay £21.

Example 2

Where the loss which is common to both policies is the greater loss:

Insurer A's policy is for £200 on subject-matters I and II. Insurer B's policy is for £100 on subject-matter II only; the loss is £50 on subject-matter I and £100 on subject-matter II.

By taking the greater loss (viz the loss on II) first and apportioning it pro rata between the amounts of A's and B's policies, A is liable for $\frac{200}{300}$ths of £100, i e £66, and B is liable for $\frac{100}{300}$ths of £100, i e £34. There is thus £134 remaining of A's policy to meet the loss of £50 on I. A's total liability, therefore, by this method is £116, and B's liability £34.

By taking the lesser loss (viz the loss on I) first and deducting it from the amount of A's policy,

Where the subject-matters separately insured by one or other of the policies are numerous, or where there is a large number of policies to be taken into account, it may become impossible, from the practical point of view, to work out in detail all the various combinations of which the subject-matters and policies are capable, and to take the mean of all the results, which must necessarily vary according to the order in which each subject-matter and policy is taken.

It is, therefore, the working rule in these cases to make two apportionments only, the first beginning with the greatest loss and working through the losses in order of magnitude down to the least, and the second beginning with the least loss and working upwards. In this way, the two extreme apportionments are obtained, and the mean is taken between them.

This method breaks down, and is wholly abandoned, where the result of taking the mean would be to throw a portion of the loss on the assured, since the effect of it would be to deprive him of his indemnity. It is, therefore, usual in this case to apportion the loss by the first method alone, and the apportionment is made upon the basis of taking the greatest loss first, without taking into consideration the different result which the second method would give. If, however, by the first method a portion of the loss is still thrown on the assured, the apportionment is made by the second method alone, and the least loss is taken first.[5]

The continuance of the present method of apportionment can only be defended on the ground that an apportionment of the loss must be made in some way or other, that it is entirely favourable to the assured, and that the insurers have, in fact, for many years usually apportioned their losses in accordance with it. In so far as it is based upon any principle at all, the principle is that of apportionment in proportion to the amounts of insurance, a principle which, as has already been seen, works unsatisfactorily, where the loss sustained by the assured is common to both policies.

The objections to that principle apply equally here, and it, therefore, remains to be considered whether an apportionment on the basis of the liabilities under the two policies is not more satisfactory, both as leading to a more equitable distribution of the loss between the contributing policies, and as being more in accordance with the legal principles. It must not be forgotten in this connection that the assured has certain legal rights under each of the policies, and he cannot be prevented by any arrangement between different insurers from exercising them, as and when he thinks fit.

What, therefore, is required is a basis of apportionment which will, in case of need, be binding not merely on the insurers among themselves,[6] but also on the assured, and which will prevent him from defeating any arrangement to which

---

and carrying forward the balance of A's policy, i e £150, to contribute with B's policy to the loss on II, and apportioning the loss on II, i e £100 pro rata between the balance of A's policy and the amount of B's policy, the result will be that A's liability is £50 on I and £60 on II, i e £110 in all and B's liability is £40.

The total of A's liability by both methods is £226, and of B's liability £74. Thus, taking the mean, A will pay £113 and B £37.

5 The following is an actual example of such an apportionment: Insurer A's policy was for £300 on subject-matters I and II, and insurer B's policy was for £300 on subject-matter I only, and the loss was £500 on I and £80 on II. In this case the method of taking the lesser loss had to be adopted.

6 The present practice cannot bind those insurers who do not agree to abide by it.

the insurers may come. For this purpose the basis of apportionment should be established on a principle which is capable of universal application, and which will work equitably and satisfactorily wherever it is applied. Such a principle must, in some way or other, afford a standard by which the policies may be compared, and, at the same time, give due weight to their respective differences.

The only principle which fulfils this requirement is the principle of basing the apportionment of loss on the liabilities of the respective policies, and not on their amounts of insurance, a principle which has been already advocated in the case where the only loss is that which is common to both policies.

There is a certain difficulty in determining the precise method in which this principle is to be applied, but the following method has been advocated.[7]

The policy which has the wider scope is taken first. The loss which is covered by this policy only[8] is separated from the loss which is common to both policies, and a calculation is made of the amount of each. The aggregate liability of the first policy for both losses is then ascertained, and the sum representing it is distributed between the two losses in the proportion which the separate loss bears to the common loss. The amount thus allocated to the common loss is, for the purpose of apportionment, treated as the amount of liability upon the first policy in respect of that loss. The amount of liability on the second policy in respect of the same loss is ascertained by the application of the 'independent liability' principle, and the common loss is ultimately apportioned between the two policies in proportion to their respective amounts of liability.[9]

This method, however, appears to be open to several objections. In the first place by separating the two losses under the first policy, and distributing the liability of the first insurers between the two losses, it treats the first policy as though it were in reality two separate policies. To do this is to overlook the fact that on the first policy there is only one loss, and not two, and to make a contract different from that which the parties have themselves made.[10]

Moreover, where the amount of the separate loss is at least equal to the total sum insured by the first policy, the effect of distributing the loss in accordance with this method is to reduce the amount payable in respect of the separate loss below a full indemnity, and to carry over part of the sum insured to meet the loss common to both policies. Since, however, by reason of the existence of the second policy, the whole of the sum carried over may not be required for this purpose, the balance remains, apparently, in the hands of the first insurers, and the assured is therefore a loser to the extent by which the amount payable in

---

7 This method appears to have been adopted in *Bloomfield v London Mutual Fire Insurance Co* (1906) QR 29 SC 143, where it was held upon a question of contribution arising between insurers of merchandise under a general policy, and insurers upon special policies covering a portion of the same merchandise, that the sum insured by the general policy must be divided into as many parts as there were special policies, and proportionately to the losses on each, and that the loss on each portion should be apportioned between the general policy and the special policy covering it in the proportion that the sum insured by the policy referable to that portion bore to the general sum insured by the special policy.

8 For convenience, the part of the loss which is covered by one policy will be referred to as the separate loss, and the part of the loss which is covered by both policies as the common loss.

9 Thus, if insurer A's policy was for £200 on subject-matters I and II, and insurer B's policy was for £100 on subject-matter II only, and the loss was £200 on I and £50 on II, the liability of A would be £160 on I and £40 on II, while the liability of B would be £50 on II. A would, therefore, pay £160 on I and £22 on II, and B would pay £28 on II.

10 The first policy is by its terms liable to make good the whole loss within its limits.

respect of the separate loss was reduced, although the aggregate sums for which he insured under both policies may exceed the amount of the total loss sustained.

It, therefore, follows that, although in respect of the common loss the assured receives a full indemnity, yet he is not fully indemnified in respect of the separate loss, in as much as there is still a balance on the first policy, which he has not received.

It has been suggested that the assured must be content to stand a loser in this case, since he has not placed his insurances correctly. The answer to this is that, however unbusinesslike he may have been in placing his insurances, each policy is a separate contract which he is entitled to enforce in accordance with its terms,[11] and that it is a term in his contract with the first insurers that they shall make good the loss covered by their policy up to the limits of his insurance with them.

A more satisfactory method of applying the principle of 'independent liability' will be, it is submitted, to estimate the liability of the insurers on the first policy upon the basis that their liability for each portion of the loss covered by their policy is, within the limits of the insurance, co-extensive with the loss. It is impossible to hold that by their policy they have undertaken any greater liability in respect of one portion of the loss than in respect of the other; and, although it becomes necessary to separate the amount of the loss under this policy into two portions for the purpose of ascertaining how far there is a double insurance, the contract under it cannot be affected by such separation, and the policy still remains an insurance upon the whole property covered thereby. The existence of the second policy only affects the sum ultimately payable under the first policy in respect of the common loss. The liability, therefore, of the first policy for the common loss must be ascertained in the same manner as if such loss were the only loss, and the ultimate apportionment will be made between the two policies in the proportion which the liability of the first policy bears to that of the second policy.[12]

Assuming that the separate loss is equal to the sum insured by the first policy, the insurers under this policy can have no defence if the assured chooses to restrict his claim against them to it, and to demand payment in full. It cannot be said that the insurers are entitled to insist on his making a more extensive claim, there being no condition in the contract compelling him to do so, or that their liability in respect of the separate loss, which would be co-extensive with such loss if it stood alone, is to be reduced by reason of the happening of the common loss.

Nor does the contribution clause appear to affect the position, since there has been no double insurance over the property in respect of which the claim is made.

Further, if the assured subsequently claims the balance of the loss from the insurers on the second policy, they will be liable, in the absence of a contribution

---

11 *Bruce v Jones* (1863) 1 H & C 769 (marine insurance) per Martin B, at 777.

12 Thus, in the example given in footnote 4, p 498, ante, the amount of the loss to which insurer A's policy applies is £250, and A's liability calculated independently is, therefore, £200, being the amount of his insurance. Insurer B's policy applies only to the loss on II, and his liability calculated independently is £50. Insurer A's liability for this loss, if his was the only policy, and this was the only loss, would be £50 also. Therefore, B contributes £25, and A, after bearing £25 of the loss on II, remains liable for £175, the assured not being fully insured.

clause, to indemnify him up to the full amount of their insurance, without reference to the co-existing insurance, since the assured has received nothing under the first policy in respect of this loss. The effect of the contribution clause, however, is to limit the liability of the second insurers to their rateable proportion of the loss.

The fact that the first policy has already been exhausted should, it is submitted, be disregarded, since, at the date of the loss, there was another policy in existence, and accordingly, by the terms of the condition, the second insurers are not liable to pay a full indemnity themselves, but only their rateable proportion of the loss. For the purpose, therefore, of ascertaining the amount which the second insurers are to pay, the liability of the first insurers in respect of the common loss must be taken into account. The fact that the assured is not entitled to receive anything from the first insurers, inasmuch as the sum payable under their policy is already exhausted, cannot, it is submitted, affect the legal right of the second insurers to have their own liability estimated on the basis of the common insurance, or increase the amount to be paid by them.

Some effect must be given to the words of the condition, which clearly show that the liability of the second insurers is not to be measured by the amount of the assured's loss, nor by the difference between such amount and the amount actually received as an indemnity under the first policy. By reason of the existence of the first policy at the time of the loss, the liability of the second insurers is limited as from the time of the loss; and the assured's failure, from whatever cause, to obtain from the first insurers their proportion, whether because the first policy is exhausted, or because he omits to make the claim under it within the time prescribed, or otherwise, cannot deprive the second insurers of the benefit of the limitation.

The effect of this is that the assured will lose in respect of the common loss that proportion which would have been paid by the first policy if it had not been already exhausted by payment in respect of the separate loss, and he is therefore to that extent under-insured. That this is the case is clearly shown if the order in which the claims are made is reversed. If the assured first claims payment in respect of the common loss, the amount payable between the two policies will be apportioned in accordance with their respective liabilities, and the balance will be carried over to meet the separate loss.

It will thus be seen that the assured must necessarily be a loser by this method, though to a lesser degree than by the first suggested method. But the result is arrived at by the application of legal principles, and relieves the insurers, who have, in fact, limited their liability, and not those who are in any event liable for the separate loss which they alone have undertaken to bear.[13]

As regards the manner in which the common loss is to be apportioned between the two policies, the only satisfactory basis is to estimate the respective liabilities on the 'independent liability' principle. In this way it becomes unnecessary to treat the first policy, which has the wider scope, as if it were two insurances, and to distribute its liability between the two losses in proportion to their respective amounts.

---

[13] Though this conclusion appears to be in accordance with legal principles, it should be pointed out that the contribution clause was apparently drafted merely for the purpose of adjusting the rights of the respective insurers inter se, and was not intended to restrict their liability or to throw any portion of his loss upon the assured, where he had in the aggregate insured for amounts sufficient to cover the whole.

Such a method has the defect of making the extent of the liability of the first policy not only for the common loss, but also for the separate loss, vary according to circumstances, since the greater the amount of the common loss in proportion to the separate loss, the greater becomes the liability of the first policy for such loss, and the smaller its liability for the separate loss.

Yet the fact that the first policy is, in any event, liable to pay the whole amount of the separate loss, and might in certain circumstances be liable to pay the whole of the common loss, cannot be disregarded. Nor does it seem consistent that the proportionate liabilities of the two policies between themselves should depend upon the accidental circumstance that a portion of the assured's loss happens to fall outside the common insurance. Whatever the position of the first policy, the liability of the second policy must surely be constant.

By adopting the 'independent liability' principle, the apportionment is put upon a clear and satisfactory basis. Moreover, a consistent and uniform method, and a method which accords with legal principles, is applied to all non-concurrent policies.

2 Average policies

The policy may, however, contain a condition providing that in certain circumstances some portion of the loss is to be borne by the assured himself. The policy is then said to be 'subject to average'.

(a) The two conditions of average

There are two conditions relating to average:

i The first condition of average:

This condition is sometimes known as the pro rata condition of average and does not apply unless the assured is under-insured. Its effect is that, in the event of a partial loss of the subject-matter of insurance, the assured cannot recover the whole amount of his loss within the limits of the policy, but only such proportion of the loss as the amount of insurance bears to the full value of the subject-matter at the time. Where, however, the subject-matter is totally destroyed, he is entitled to be paid the full sum insured.[14]

ii The second condition of average:

This condition usually states that:

> 'But if any of the Property included in such Average shall at the breaking out of any Fire be also covered by any other more Specific Insurance, i e by an Insurance which at the time of such Fire applies to part only of the Property actually at risk and protected by this Insurance and to no other Property whatsoever, then this Policy shall not insure the same except only as regards any excess of value beyond the amount of such more Specific Insurance or Insurances, which said excess is declared to be under the protection of this Policy and subject to Average as aforesaid.'

---

[14] As the first condition of average, see generally, p 432, ante.

(b) The application of the two average conditions

The second condition of average is in practice treated as being nothing more than a contribution clause apportioning the loss in a particular manner between the two policies concerned, and not as an average condition.

In comparing policies for the purpose of ascertaining whether the condition applies, their respective ranges are taken as the basis of comparison. If they are both identical in range and insure the same items of property and no more, neither is more specific than the other, and the condition does not apply. Similarly, it does not apply if the two ranges cannot be compared owing to the fact that each policy covers, in addition to the items common to both, a variety of items not covered by the other,[15] since in this case also neither policy can be said to be more specific than the other.

If, however, the ranges of the two policies are capable of being compared as, e g where all the items covered by one policy fall within the scope of the other policy, which covers other items in addition, the second policy is of greater range than the first policy. The first policy is, therefore, more specific than the second, and the condition is brought into operation.

(c) The apportionment of the loss

For the purpose of apportioning the loss between the two policies, the second average condition is applied independently of the existence of the first, and the second or less specific policy, equally when it is a full insurance as when it is an under-insurance, is not required to contribute anything until the first and more specific policy is exhausted.

The effect of the second condition is, in practice, to make the second policy an insurance of the excess of value beyond the amount insured by the more specific policy. It does not merely limit the sum payable by the second policy in the case where there is a common loss, but excludes the items common to both policies from the operation of the second policy, either wholly or partially according as the more specific policy is a full or under-insurance.

Thus, where the actual loss is covered by the second policy only, the basis on which the amount of the loss is to be borne by the assured himself under the first condition of average is to be calculated, is not the value of the whole property stated to be insured by the second policy, but only its value after deducting the amount covered by the more specific policy.[16]

---

15 As, e g where different kinds of property are insured by the two policies, or where, though the kind of property insured is the same, the policies apply to different places.

16 Thus, if the more specific policy is for £1,000 and covers goods in warehouse X, the value of which is £1,000, and the second policy is for £1,000 upon goods in warehouse X and in warehouse Y, the value of which latter goods is £3,000, the amount payable under the second policy upon a loss happening in warehouse Y is not calculated upon the total value of the property purported to be insured, i e £4,000, but upon £3,000 only, the value of the contents of warehouse Y, since the goods in warehouse X are fully covered by the more specific policy. The second policy therefore pays $\frac{1000}{3000}$ths of the loss and not $\frac{1000}{4000}$ths. On the other hand, in comparing the range of the second policy with a third policy, also containing the condition, different considerations appear to apply. Thus, if the third policy covered goods in warehouse Y and in warehouse Z, and there happened to be no goods in warehouse Z at the time of the loss in warehouse Y, the third policy is apparently more specific than the second, since the latter in fact cover the goods in warehouse X, though with a limitation in consequence of the existence of the first policy.

The present practice, although it probably carries out the intention of the framers of the second average condition, and works fairly both to the assured and to the different insurers, can hardly be regarded as based on a strict interpretation of the condition. The condition is badly worded, and is in consequence somewhat difficult to understand or to apply.

It is to be observed that it is a term in a contract between the assured and a particular set of insurers. It confers no contractual rights on any other persons, even though they may also be insurers of the same property. Its legal effect is merely to regulate the amount recoverable by the assured under the policy containing it. It must, therefore, be compared with other conditions of a similar nature in the policy.

Thus, as has already been seen,[17] the contribution clause, as against the assured, reduces the amount which he would otherwise be entitled to recover, provided that a certain state of facts exists. It is not the presence of the contribution clause in the policy that limits the liability of the insurers, but the existence of other policies.

Similarly, the first average condition reduces the amount recoverable by the assured, but only in the event of his being under-insured. Without an under-insurance, the first average condition is inoperative. As regards the second average condition, the practice is to treat it as being merely a narrower contribution clause, under which the insurers under the second policy, instead of bearing the loss equally with the insurers under the more specific policy, are enabled to throw the burden wholly upon the latter until the more specific policy is exhausted.

The practice, as between the two sets of insurers, appears to be justified, since to apply the principle of contribution in any other way would be to disregard the terms under which the second policy is alone to be liable for the common loss. At the same time, the practice apparently goes too far. It assumes that the second average condition is commensurate in its terms with the contribution clause, and that the existence of a more specific policy is sufficient to bring it into operation. This is, however, not the case, since the condition does not purport to apply to any property covered by the more specific policy; it adds the qualification 'if included in such average'. These words, coupled with the position of the second average condition, seem to point to some connection with the first average condition, and to indicate that the property to which the second condition applies is to be ascertained in some way or other by reference to the first.

If this is so, it is clear that the policy must necessarily contain a first average condition, and thus make the property insured subject to average, since otherwise no part of the property covered by the policy would be included in any average at all. Moreover, unless there is an under-insurance, the first average condition has no effect. It may, therefore, be argued that, if the insurance by the policy containing it is full, the second average condition is equally precluded from coming into operation, since property to which the first average condition cannot be applied cannot reasonably be regarded as 'included in such average', and therefore as falling within the description in the policy.

It is difficult to see why the second condition should have been made to

---

[17] See pp 430–431, ante.

depend on the first. The practice, however, of applying the condition in every case treats the condition as though it was framed in general terms, and disregards the fact that it begins with a qualification. The qualification imposed may be absurd, but it might become important where the first insurers became insolvent after the loss or where they challenged the correctness of an apportionment on the usual lines.

The first condition sometimes appears in a modified form by which it is provided that the policy is to be subject to average if the sum insured upon the property specified in the condition, either separately or in one amount with other property, shall, at the breaking out of any fire, be less than three-fourths of the value of such property.[18] This form of condition is often employed in insurances on agricultural produce, and its effect is that the policy is, for the purpose of contribution, treated as a specific policy, unless the assured is under-insured to the extent required by the condition.

Where a question of contribution arises between policies which are subject to the first condition of average, the basis of apportionment is, in every case, the sum by which the liability of the insurers under each policy is measured, after making the requisite allowance for the portion of the loss which, in the event of the value of the subject-matter exceeding the sum insured, must be borne by the assured himself.

Where the policies are concurrent, the apportionment is worked out in the same way as where policies are specific and concurrent, except that it is calculated on the proportion which the respective liabilities, and not the respective amounts of insurance, bear to each other.[19]

Where the policies are non-concurrent, the liability of each policy is ascertained in accordance with the 'independent liability' principle, whether there is only a loss common to both policies, or whether there is also a portion of the loss which is covered only by one of them. Accordingly, the liability of each policy in respect of the loss which it covers is ascertained without reference to the existence of the other, and the common loss is apportioned between them in proportion to their respective liabilities.[20]

Where the second condition of average is contained in one or both of the policies, the liability of the policy with the greater range only arises in respect of the excess of the common loss not covered by the more specific policy,[1] and, in

---

18 *Eckhardt v Lancashire Insurance Co* (1900) 31 SCR 72.

19 It may be pointed out that in the case of concurrent policies containing the first condition of average, an apportionment on the basis of the amounts of insurance will give the same result. It seems, however, more consistent to base the apportionment upon the liabilities as in the case where the policies are non-concurrent.

20 *Acme Wood Flooring Co v Marten* (1904) 9 Com Cas 157 (fire insurance) per Bruce J, at 163. E g insurer A's policy is for £500 on subject-matter I, and insurer B's policy is for £700 on subject-matters I and II. The value of subject-matter I is £600 and of subject-matter II £500. The loss on I is £400, and there is no loss on II. Both policies contain the first condition of average. A's liability is $\frac{500}{600}$ths of £400, i e £333. B's liability is $\frac{700}{1100}$ths of £400, i e £254. As the liabilities of A and B in the aggregate amount to more than the loss, A and B will pay pro rata on £333 and £254 respectively, i e A will pay £227 and B £173.

1 Thus, if both policies contain the second condition, insurer A's policy being for £1,000 on subject-matters I and II, and insurer B's policy for £1,500 on subject-matters I, II and III, and the values of the subject-matters are respectively I £1,000, II £600, and III £950, B's policy having the greater range will be liable for only so much of the loss on I and II as represents the excess after A's policy has been exhausted, and for the loss on III. Thus, A's liability is $\frac{1000}{1600}$ths of the loss on I and II, and B's liability is £1,500 over the total values of the three subject-matters,

practice, it is only called upon to contribute towards the common loss after the more specific policy has been exhausted.

In the same way, if there is a third policy of still greater range, the second policy, though less specific than the first policy, is more specific than the third, which cannot, therefore, be called upon to contribute till the second is in its turn exhausted. Where the condition is inapplicable by reason of the range of the two policies being so different that it cannot be used as a basis of comparison, the basis of apportionment is the 'independent liability' principle, and the common loss is apportioned accordingly.

Where the loss which takes place falls outside the range of the more specific policy, and is covered by the second policy only, it is nevertheless necessary to take into account the existence of the more specific policy. The proportion of the loss to be borne by the assured under the first condition of average is to be determined not by the total value of the property to which the second policy applies, but by its value after making allowance for the amount covered by the more specific policy.

Where one policy is an average policy, and the other is a specific policy containing the condition making it subject to average on account of the existence of the second policy,[2] both policies become subject to average in respect of the common loss, and the loss will be apportioned as though both policies had been from their commencement subject to average.

Similarly, where, in addition to average and specific policies, there is also a third policy containing the second condition, the loss will be apportioned in the same way. The average and the specific policies will clearly, as between themselves, bear their share of the loss in proportion to their respective liabilities. As regards the third policy, if it is of a different range and cannot be treated as being of a greater range than the others, the 'independent liability' principle must be applied, and the loss will ultimately be apportioned in proportion to the liabilities of the three policies. If, however, it is of a greater range, the loss in the first instance will be apportioned as between the two other policies, and the third policy will only be resorted to for the excess after the others are exhausted.

---

i e £2,550 less £1,000 the amount of A's policy, or $\frac{1500}{1550}$ths of the excess of the loss on I and II over A's liability and of the loss on III.

2 If the specific policy does not contain such a condition, the only satisfactory manner of apportioning the loss is upon the independent liability principle. Cf the following minute of the Fire Offices' Committee dated 27 June 1883: 'Whenever property damaged by fire is insured by non-average policies and also by average policies which are subject to the pro rata clause only, the loss to be apportioned among the several insurances in the proportion of their several liabilities, the liability of each to be independently ascertained as if no other insurance existed on the property in question.'

PART VI

Agency in insurance transactions

CHAPTER 49

Introduction

Every stage in the contract of insurance, from the inception of the negotiations to the receipt of the payment of the loss, involves to a greater or lesser degree the employment of agents.

On the part of the insurers, agents are universally employed; insurance companies must necessarily act through agents,[1] whilst underwriters are usually associated in syndicates, one member of the syndicate acting as agent for the others.[2]

The assured may be compelled by usage to employ an insurance broker,[3] or he may find it convenient to do so; apart from this, any duty imposed upon the assured under the contract may be performed by an agent on his behalf,[4] unless, on the construction of the policy, personal performance is required.[5]

It may, therefore, be useful to show how the general principles of the law of agency are to be applied to insurance business.

There are three relationships to be considered:

1 The relationship between the principal and the agent.[6]
2 The relationship between the principal and third parties.[7]
3 The relationship between the agent and third parties.[8]

Further, the course of business at Lloyd's[9] and the fact that insurance brokers must be registered under the Insurance Brokers (Registration) Act 1977,[10] should also be noted.

---

1 *Re Norwich Equitable Assurance Society, Royal Insurance Co's Claim* (1887) 57 LT 241 (fire insurance) per Kay J, at 246: 'An insurance company act by agents. Its directors are agents, it effects all its policies by agents. Everyone knows that these companies have agents all over this country and, if they have foreign business, all over the world'; *Newsholme Bros v Road Transport and General Insurance Co Ltd* [1929] 2 KB 356, CA (accident insurance) per Scrutton LJ, at 362.

2 See *Hambro v Burnand* [1904] 2 KB 10, CA.

3 An agreement between different insurers not to pay commission to persons effecting their own insurance in order to encourage the employment of insurance brokers is lawful: *Workman and Army and Navy Auxiliary Co-operative Supply Ltd v London and Lancashire Fire Insurance Co* (1903) 19 TLR 360.

4 *Patton v Employers' Liability Assurance Corpn* (1887) 20 LRIr 93 per Murphy J, at 100; *Davies v National Fire and Marine Insurance Co of New Zealand* [1891] AC 485, PC (fire insurance), where notice of loss was given by an agent.

5 Thus, where a stipulation contemplates a personal payment of the premium by the assured, a tender by his personal representative during the days of grace does not renew the policy: *Want v Blunt* (1810) 12 East 183 (life insurance); *Pritchard v Merchants' and Tradesman's Mutual Life-Assurance Society* (1858) 3 CBNS 622 (life insurance), distinguished in *Stuart v Freeman* [1903] 1 KB 47, CA (life insurance); *Simpson v Accidental Death Insurance Co* (1857) 2 CBNS 257.

6 See Chapter 50.

7 See Chapter 51.

8 See Chapter 52.

9 See Chapter 53.

10 See Chapter 54.

CHAPTER 50

The relationship between the principal and the agent[1]

When an agent is appointed, he has certain rights against his principal and also has duties to perform. Where the agent is guilty of a breach of duty, certain consequences will follow.

A THE RIGHTS OF THE AGENT[2]

The rights of an agent against the principal are:

1 The right to claim commission.
2 The right to an indemnity.
3 The right to claim a lien.

1 Commission

The agent has the right to receive from the principal the agreed remuneration;[3] in insurance business, agents, whether employed by the insurers or by the assured,[4] are usually remunerated by commission.[5]

Sometimes commission will be payable to the agent even though the agency

[1] In this chapter only those portions of the law of Agency which are of particular importance in insurance transactions are referred to. For the relationship between the principal and the agent in general, the reader is referred to the standard textbooks on the subject, e g *Bowstead on Agency* 15th Edn (1985); R Powell *The Law of Agency* 2nd Edn (1961).

[2] See generally, Bowstead op cit, pp 208–278; Powell op cit, pp 329–377.

[3] *Times Life Assurance and Guarantee Co v Swann* (1854) 23 LTOS 114 (life insurance), where an agent, after his dismissal, claimed commission on premiums on insurance obtained by him and by his sub-agents, and it was held that he was entitled to commission when he accounted, and that the right to commission ceased when the duty to account ceased. For a case where there was no agreement as to the amount of remuneration to be paid to assessors employed by the insured to deal with a claim against the insurers of a building damaged by fire, and the Court held that a reasonable amount would be $7\frac{1}{2}$ per cent. of the sum recovered, see *Hugh v Allen & Co Ltd v Holmes* [1969] 1 Lloyd's Rep 348, CA.

[4] The fact that commission is not paid directly by the assured to the agent employed to effect an insurance, but is, in the ordinary course of business, deducted by the agent from the premium before payment over to the insurers, does not constitute the agent the agent of the insurers: *Bancroft v Heath* (1900) 5 Com Cas 110 (affd (1901) 6 Com Cas 137, CA) (fire insurance) per Mathew J, at 115; cf *Power v Butcher* (1829) 10 B & C 329 (marine insurance).

[5] The agent is entitled to commission on renewal if he is the efficient cause of bringing about the renewal: *McNiel v Law Union and Rock Insurance Co Ltd* (1925) 23 LlL Rep 314. For a case where it was alleged that the brokers were only entitled to one half of the commission, and had to share the remaining half with the shipowners who had effected the insurance, see *McNiel, Ripley & Coulson v SS Mutual Underwriting Association Ltd* (1940) 67 LlL Rep 142.

has been terminated. Whether he is so entitled is, of course, a matter of the construction of the terms of the contract in each case.[6]

2 Indemnity

The agent has a right to be reimbursed any sums expended on the principal's behalf. Thus, if he has paid the premium out of his own pocket, he is entitled to be repaid the amount of the premium with interest.[7]

Further, if the agent of the assured has, in ordinary course of business, rendered himself personally liable to the insurers for payment of the premium, he is entitled to be indemnified by the assured to the extent of his liability.[8]

3 Lien

The agent of the assured, who, on payment of the premium receives the policy from the insurers, may retain it and refuse to hand it over to the assured until the amount of the premium has been paid to him by the assured.[9]

Necessity for proper performance of duties

These rights depend on the due performance by the agent of his duties on the

---

6 Thus, in *Gold v Life Assurance Co of Pennsylvania* [1971] 2 Lloyd's Rep 164, QBD, an agent was held to be entitled to commission on the first premiums on life insurance business introduced by him, even though the premiums had been paid to the insurers by the insured after the agency had been terminated (see the judgment of Donaldson J ibid, at 170).

7 *Airy v Bland* (1774) 2 Park's Marine Insurances, 8th Edn 811 (marine insurance); *Natusch v Hendewerk* (1871) 7 QBD 460, n. (marine insurance); *Universo Insurance Co of Milan v Merchants' Marine Insurance Co* [1897] 2 QB 93, CA (marine insurance); *Dixon v Hovill* (1828) 4 Bing 665 (marine insurance).

8 *Airy v Bland* (supra); *Power v Butcher* (1829) 10 B & C 329 (marine insurance). But in *Wilson v Avec Audio-Visual Equipment Ltd* [1974] 1 Lloyd's Rep 81, CA (burglary insurance) the broker did not prove that he had rendered himself personally liable, and the case was merely one of an agent who had chosen, apparently because he was under a mistaken belief as to his legal position vis-à-vis the liquidator of the insurance company to assume a personal liability to him, and having done so, in his turn sought to make his principal liable (see the judgment of Edmund Davies LJ ibid, at 83). The Court also held that even if the broker initially had authority to pay the premium for the principal, the authority had been revoked before he did so (see the judgment of Buckley LJ ibid, at 84).

9 *Fisher v Smith* (1878) 4 App Cas 1 (marine insurance); *Busteed v West of England Insurance Co* (1878) 5 Ir ChR 553 (life insurance). If the policy, after being handed over to the assured, comes again into the agent's hands, the lien revives: *Levy v Barnard* (1818) 8 Taunt 149 (marine insurance). In marine insurance the broker has a lien for the general balance of his account: *Mann v Forrester* (1814) 4 Camp 60 (marine insurance); Marine Insurance Act 1906, s 53(2), unless excluded in the circumstances of the particular case: *Fairfield Shipbuilding and Engineering Co Ltd v Gardner, Mountain & Co Ltd* (1911) 104 LT 288 (marine insurance), where the question whether the lien extended to the proceeds of the policy was not decided: *Scottish Metropolitan Assurance Co Ltd v P Samuel & Co Ltd* [1923] 1 KB 348 (marine insurance), where there was a payment by mistake. It does not appear to have been decided whether a general lien exists in other branches of insurance; presumably, such a lien may be implied from the course of business or from usage. As to the question of the revival of a general lien, which has been lost on parting with possession, see *Near East Relief v King, Chasseur & Co Ltd* [1930] 2 KB 40 (marine insurance) where Wright J said (at 44):—'Generally, a lien which is lost on parting with possession is resumed; but there is authority for the proposition that the rule does not apply to a general lien if after possession is parted with and before possession is resumed, the person claiming the general lien becomes aware that his immediate employer is only an agent and not a principal.' As to particular and general liens of a marine insurance broker, see further, Ivamy *Marine Insurance* (4th Edn 1985), pp 333–337.

principal's behalf. They do not exist in the case of unauthorised transactions, as, for instance, an insurance differing materially from that which the agent was employed to effect,[10] or an insurance effected without any authority at all,[11] unless it is ratified by the principal.[12]

Nor do they exist where the transaction, though authorised, proves abortive to the principal by reason of the agent's breach of duty, e g where a policy is avoided by the agent's fraud or concealment,[13] or where the transaction is unlawful, e g in the case of an insurance prohibited by statute.[14]

On the other hand, the agent, if wrongfully prevented by the principal from earning commission, may recover damages.[15]

B THE DUTIES OF THE AGENT[16]

The chief duties which an agent owes to the principal are the following:

1. To carry out the transaction which he is employed to carry out.
2. To obey his instructions and to act strictly in accordance with the terms of his authority.
3. To act with reasonable and proper skill.
4. To account to the principal for money received.
5. To deal honestly with the principal.

1 Duty to carry out the transaction

It is the duty of the agent to carry out the transaction which he is employed to carry out,[17] or, if it is impossible for him to do so, to inform the principal promptly in order to prevent him from suffering loss through relying on the successful completion of the transaction by the agent.

Thus, an agent employed to effect[18] or renew[19] an insurance must effect it or

---

10 *Barron v Fitzgerald* (1840) 6 Bing NC 201 (life insurance), where an agent employed to effect a policy in the names of A and B insured in the name of A, B and C, and was held not to be entitled to recover the premium which he had paid.

11 *Warwick v Slade* (1811) 3 Camp 127 (marine insurance), where the authority had been revoked, and it was held that the agent could recover neither commission nor the premium paid by him to the underwriter.

12 *Barron v Fitzgerald* (supra) per Bosanquet J, at 205.

13 See *Hill v Featherstonhaugh* (1831) 7 Bing 569 per Tindal CJ, at 571.

14 *Ex p Mather* (1797) 3 Ves 373 (marine insurance).

15 See generally, *Simpson v Lamb* (1856) 17 CB 603 per Jervis CJ, at 615. But in the case of an agent appointed by the insurers, the insurers do not necessarily bind themselves to carry on the business for the purpose of enabling him to earn commission: *Re English and Scottish Marine Insurance Co, ex p Maclure* (1870) 5 Ch App 737 (marine insurance), where, on the voluntary winding-up of the company, the agent was not allowed to prove for loss of commission for the unexpired portion of the period for which he was employed; cf *Stirling v Maitland* (1864) 5 B & S 840 (life insurance), where the terms of appointment provided for payment of compensation if the agent were displaced, and it was held that the insurers by transferring their business to another company and winding-up had displaced the agent: *Watson v Royal Insurance Co* [1896] 1 QB 41, CA (fire insurance).

16 See generally, Bowstead op. cit, pp 138–156, Powell op. cit, pp 302–322.

17 In the absence of express instructions to insure, a duty to insure may be implied from usage or from the circumstances of the case: *Hurrell v Bullard* (1863) 3 F & F 445 (marine insurance).

18 *McNeill v Millen & Co* [1907] 2 IR 328, CA, where the owner of a motor car, which was being repaired by the defendants, was prevented from insuring it by the representation of the

renew it effectively, or, if he is unable to do so, must notify his principal of his inability as soon as possible so as to enable the principal to take steps to insure elsewhere.

If, however, it is impossible to effect the insurance at all, on account of its illegality,[20] or if it is impossible to give notice in time to enable the principal to insure elsewhere,[21] a failure to notify promptly is not a breach of duty.

2 Duty to obey his instructions

It is the duty of the agent to obey his instructions and to act strictly in accordance with the terms of his authority or, as regards matters on which they are silent, the usual course of business.[1]

If the instructions are clear and precise, the agent departs from them at his peril;[2] he is not, as a general rule, at liberty to exercise his discretion,[3] unless expressly authorised to do so. If he has a discretion, it is not to be inferred that he is guilty of a breach of duty because it appears that, in the circumstances, he has exercised his discretion wrongly, and that, if he had exercised it differently, the transaction could or might have proved more advantageous to the principal.[4] Thus, an agent employed to effect an insurance, with a discretion as to the choice of insurers, is not bound to go to the insurers offering to insure at the lowest premium.[5]

The same rule applies where the agent's instructions are ambiguously expressed and capable of different interpretations. If the interpretation placed

---

defendants that they had insured the car for him; *Smith v Lascelles* (1788) 2 Term Rep 187 (marine insurance) per Ashhurst J, at 188; *Callander v Oelrichs* (1838) 5 Bing NC 58 (marine insurance); *Turpin v Bilton* (1843) 5 Man & G 455 (marine insurance); *Hurrell v Bullard* (1863) 3 F & F 445 (marine insurance); *Dickson & Co v Devitt* (1916) 21 Com Cas 291 (marine insurance), where the mistake was due to the broker's clerk and might have been corrected if the assured had examined the documents; *Cock, Russell & Co v Bray Gibb & Co Ltd* (1920) 3 LlL Rep 71, where it was alleged that the insurance brokers were guilty of unreasonable delay in effecting the insurance.

19 *Wilkinson v Coverdale* (1793) 1 Esp 74 (fire insurance).

20 *Webster v De Tastet* (1797) 7 Term Rep 157 (insurance on slaves). If, however, the illegality applies to part only of the transaction so that the insurance, though void pro tanto would not be wholly void, the agent is guilty of a breach of duty; *Glaser v Cowie* (1813) 1 M & S 52 (marine insurance), where it was further suggested that an honour policy might have been obtained.

21 *Hurrell v Bullard* (supra); *Great Western Insurance Co of New York v Cumliffe* (1874) 9 Ch App 525 (marine insurance).

1 *Smith v Cologan* (1788) 2 Term Rep 188 n. (marine insurance) per Buller J, at 189 n.; *Glaser v Cowie* (supra).

2 *Barron v Fitzgerald* (1840) 6 Bing NC 201 (life insurance), where the instructions were to effect the policy in the names of two particular persons, and a third name was added. But where the agent is employed to effect an insurance with such names as should be to his principal's satisfaction, it is sufficient if he insures with unexceptionable names, and the names need not be submitted to the principal for his previous approbation: *Dixon v Hovill* (1828) 4 Bing 665 (marine insurance).

3 *Wallace v Tellfair* (1786) 2 Term Rep 188 n. (marine insurance), where the agent employed to insure, instructed a broker to effect a policy, but at too low a premium.

4 *Comber v Anderson* (1808) 1 Camp 523 (marine insurance), where the loss fell within an exception in the policy actually effected, though other insurers issued policies without the exception; *Tasker v Scott* (1815) 6 Taunt 234 (marine insurance), where the holder of a bill of exchange drawn by the master of a ship for necessaries insured it under a power conferred by the bill, and it was held that he had a discretion whether to insure it under a time policy or under a voyage policy; *Letts v Excess Insurance Co* (1916) 32 TLR 361, where, however, the instructions were, apparently, precise and were exactly followed.

5 *Moore v Mourgue* (1776) 2 Cowp 479 (marine insurance).

by the agent on the instructions is one which they may reasonably bear, there is no breach of duty in that the principal intended a different construction to be placed upon them, and if such construction had been adopted, the transaction would not have resulted in loss to the principal.[6]

3 Duty to use proper skill

It is the duty of the agent, in the exercise of the authority entrusted to him, to act with reasonable and proper care, skill and diligence.[7]

If he is a professional agent, such as a broker, the standard by which the duty is to be measured is that of persons of experience and skill in his profession[8] and in the place where he was employed to perform it;[9] if he is not a professional agent, he is to be judged by what an ordinary person might reasonably have been expected to do in the circumstances.[10]

---

6 *Fomin v Oswell* (1813) 3 Camp 357 (marine insurance); *James Vale & Co v Van Oppen & Co Ltd* (1921) 37 TLR 367 (marine insurance), where the agent was held entitled to construe a direction to insure against 'all risks' as meaning all the risks covered by an ordinary marine policy; *Provincial Assurance Co v Roy* (1879) 10 RLOS 643 (fire insurance), where the agent assented to an arrangement with other insurers on the face of a telegram informing him that his principals had 'decided' to take part, whereas the telegram should have stated that they 'declined'; see generally, *Ireland v Livingston* (1872) LR 5 HL 395 (agency).

7 *Mallough v Barber* (1815) 4 Camp 150 (marine insurance); *Park v Hammond* (1816) 6 Taunt 495 (marine insurance); *Hurrell v Bullard* (1863) 3 F & F 445 (marine insurance). Hence his duty is sufficiently discharged if he effects the policy in the usual form: *James Vale & Co v Van Oppen & Co Ltd* (supra), with which contrast *Enlayde Ltd v Roberts* [1917] 1 Ch 109 (fire insurance) per Sargent J, at 121; *Yuill v Scott Robson* [1907] 1 KB 685, CA (marine insurance), where a policy put forward by the seller of cattle as an 'all risks' policy, excepted capture, seizure and detention, and it was held that the policy was not in accordance with the contract, though as between broker and underwriter it might have been sufficient.

8 *Chapman v Walton* (1833) 10 Bing 57 (marine insurance) per Tindal CJ, at 63: 'The action is brought for the want of reasonable and proper care, skill and judgment shown by the defendant under certain circumstances in the exercise of his employment as a policy-broker. The point, therefore, to be determined, is not whether the defendant arrived at a correct conclusion upon reading the letter, but whether, upon the occasion in question, he did nor did not exercise a reasonable and proper care, skill and judgment. This is a question of fact, the decision of which appears to us to rest upon this further inquiry, viz whether other persons exercising the same profession or calling, and being men of experience and skill therein, would or would not have come to the same conclusion as the defendant. For the defendant did not contract that he would bring to the performance of his duty on this occasion an extraordinary degree of skill, but only a reasonable and ordinary proportion of it'; *Hood v West End Motor Car Packing Co* [1917] 2 KB 38, CA (marine insurance) per Scrutton LJ, at 47. In *Roselodge Ltd v Bray Gibb (Holdings) Ltd* [1967] 2 Lloyd's Rep 99 (jewellery block policy) Roskill J, pointed out the harm which is done to the reputation of a firm of brokers even when an allegation of negligence which has been made against them is withdrawn. He observed (at 100): '[Counsel] has withdrawn those charges and has agreed that they are without foundation, but I think that it is right that I should say . . . that I have not yet heard one single word which would justify any allegation of negligence against [the brokers]. Sometimes when these cases are brought alleging negligence against people of high professional repute the damage is done, however much the charges may subsequently be withdrawn, but if anything I can say and have said in the last five minutes can undo any damage which may already have been done, that at least should be said and publicized in fairness to the [brokers] in this case.' The broker employed by the proposer owes no duty of care or skill to the insurers: *Empress Assurance Corpn v CT Bowring & Co Ltd* (1905) 11 Com Cas 107 (marine insurance); *Glasgow Assurance Corpn Ltd v Symondson & Co* (1911) 16 Com Cas 109 (marine insurance) per Scrutton J, at 110.

9 *Connecticut Fire Insurance Co v Kavanagh* [1892] AC 473, at 480, PC (fire insurance).

10 It is immaterial that he acts voluntarily, and not for reward: *Wallace v Tellfair* (1786), as cited in *Wilkinson v Coverdale* (1793) 1 Esp 74, 75, 76, (fire insurance) per Buller J: 'Although there was

Whether he has actually acted with the required degree of skill depends in each case on the circumstances.[11]

---

no consideration for one party's undertaking to procure an insurance for another, yet where a party voluntarily undertook to do it, and proceeded to carry his undertaking into effect by getting a policy underwritten, but did it so negligently or unskilfully that the party could derive no benefit from it, in that case he should be liable to an action'. See also, *Wilkinson v Coverdale* (supra), where the vendor of premises undertook to get a policy renewed on the purchaser's account, but the policy was void owing to the vendor's failure to procure the endorsement of the policy to the purchaser as required by the conditions; *Baxter & Co v Jones* (1903) 6 OLR 360, where a broker who undertook gratuitously to effect further insurances and to notify the previous insurers, effected the insurances, but failed to notify the previous insurers.

11 *Avondale Blouse Co Ltd v Williamson and Geo Town* (1948) 81 LlL Rep 492 (burglary insurance); *Lyons v J W Bentley Ltd* (1944) 77 LlL Rep 335 (burglary insurance); *United Mills Agencies Ltd v Harvey Bray & Co* [1951] 2 Lloyd's Rep 631 (insurance of goods for export); *General Accident, Fire and Life Assurance Corpn Ltd v J H Minet & Co Ltd* (1943) 74 LlL Rep 1, CA (aircraft reinsurance); *Michaels v Valentine* (1923) 16 LlL Rep 244 (burglary insurance); *Transport and Trading Co Ltd v Olivier & Co Ltd* (1925) 21 LlL Rep 379 (marine insurance); *Strong and Pearl v S Allison & Co Ltd* (1926) 25 LlL Rep 504 (yacht insurance); *King (or Fiehl) v Chambers and Newman (Insurance Brokers) Ltd* [1963[2 Lloyd's Rep 130 (jewellery insurance); *United Marketing Co v Hasham Kara* [1963] 1 Lloyd's Rep 331, PC (fire insurance), where an insurance agent was held liable to an insured whose goods had been destroyed by fire because he had not taken steps to renew the policy in spite of instructions to do so, so that at the time of the fire no policy was in existence and the insurance company had rightly repudiated liability; *Coles v Sir Frederic Young (Insurances) Ltd* (1929) 33 LlL Rep 83 (motor insurance); *British Citizens Assurance Co v L Woolland & Co* (1921) 8 LlL Rep 89 (marine insurance), where the broker had failed to disclose to the insurer the fact that the vessel which was to be insured was a sailing ship; *Waterkeyn v Eagle Star and British Dominions Insurance Co Ltd and Price Forbes & Co Ltd* (1920) 5 LlL Rep 42 (risk of insolvency of bank); *Osman v J Ralph Moss Ltd* [1970] 1 Lloyd's Rep 313, CA (motor insurance), where an insurance broker was held liable for recommending the insured to insure with a company known to be in financial difficulties (see the judgment of Sachs LJ, ibid, at 315; that of Edmund Davies LJ, ibid, at 317; and that of Phillimore LJ, ibid, at 319); *O'Connor v B D B Kirby & Co* [1971] 1 Lloyd's Rep 454, CA (motor insurance), where an insurance broker, who filled in a proposal form wrongly and gave it to the proposer to check, was held not to have been negligent for it was the proposer's duty to see that the details inserted in the form were correct (see the judgment of Davies LJ, ibid, at 459, and that of Karminski LJ, ibid, at 459. Cf the judgment of Megaw LJ, ibid, at 461, where he said that the broker's duty was to use such care as was reasonable in ensuring that the answers recorded to the questions in the form accurately represented the answers given to him by the proposer, and that the duty was not a duty to ensure that every answer was correctly recorded); *Everett v Hogg, Robinson and Gardner Mountain (Insurance) Ltd* [1973] 2 Lloyd's Rep 217, QBD (Commercial Court) (reinsurance), where the brokers misrepresented a material fact and the reinsurers repudiated liability under the reinsurance policy; *Claude R Ogden & Co Pty Ltd v Reliance Fire Sprinkler Co Pty Ltd* [1975] 1 Lloyd's Rep 52, Supreme Ct of Australia (public and products liability insurance), where the brokers had misrepresented and failed to disclose material facts to the insurers who repudiated liability; *Ackbar v C F Green & Co Ltd* [1975] QB 582, [1975] 2 All ER 65 (motor insurance), where the brokers omitted to obtain passenger insurance cover; *Warren v Henry Sutton & Co* [1976] 2 Lloyd's Rep 276, CA, (motor insurance), where the brokers falsely represented to the insurers that a second driver who was to be added to the insured's policy had no previous convictions, and the insurers repudiated liability; *Cherry Ltd v Allied Insurance Brokers Ltd* [1978] 1 Lloyd's Rep 274 (consequential loss insurance), where the brokers negligently advised the insured that a double insurance was in force; *Woolcott v Excess Insurance Co Ltd and Miles, Smith, Anderson and Game Ltd* [1978] 1 Lloyd's Rep 633 (fire insurance), where brokers employed by the insurers failed to inform them that the insured had a criminal record. But a new trial was subsequently ordered [1979] 1 Lloyd's Rep 231, CA. At the new trial it was proved that the brokers knew of the criminal record and had failed to pass on this information to the insurers: *Woolcott v Excess Insurance Co Ltd and Miles, Smith, Anderson and Game Ltd (No 2)* [1979] 2 Lloyd's Rep 210. (See the judgment of Cantley J, ibid, at 216); *McNealy v Pennine Insurance Co Ltd West Lancashire Insurance Brokers Ltd and Carnell* [1978] 2 Lloyd's Rep 18, CA (motor insurance), where the brokers ought to have asked the principal whether he fell within a list of

A broker will be held guilty of negligence if he expresses an unqualified opinion on a point of law, unless he has taken reasonable care to furnish himself with such information as would entitle him to give that opinion.

Thus, in *Sarginson Bros v Keith Moulton & Co Ltd*[12]

> Insurance brokers informed their clients that their timber was uninsurable under the War Risks Insurance Act 1939. The timber was destroyed by enemy action, but the information was incorrect and it was insurable.
> *Held,* the brokers, although they were not lawyers, were liable as they had not taken sufficient care to see that their advice was correct.

Hallett J observed:[13]

> 'In my view, if people occupying a professional position take it upon themselves to give advice upon a matter directly connected with their own profession, then they are responsible for seeing that they are equipped with a reasonable degree of skill and a reasonable stock of information so as to render it reasonably safe for them to give that particular piece of advice . . . No one is under obligation to give advice on [these] difficult matters. If they are going to give advice, they can always qualify their advice and make it plain that is a matter which is doubtful or upon which further investigation is desirable, but if they do take it upon themselves to express a definite and final opinion, knowing, as they must have known in this case, that their clients would act upon that, then I do think they are responsible without having taken reasonable care to furnish themselves with such information, of whatever kind it be, as will render it reasonably safe, in the view of a reasonably prudent man to express that opinion.'

But a broker is under no legal duty to inform the assured of the terms of a cover note as soon as it is ready.

Thus, in *United Mills Agencies Ltd v Harvey Bray & Co*[14]

> Insurance brokers were instructed to insure goods for export. There was a slight delay in sending to the assured a cover note stating details of the insurance effected.
> *Held,* there was no duty to forward a cover note to the assured as soon as it was completed.

McNair J observed:[15]

> 'Evidence was called . . . that it is the practice of . . . insurance brokers . . . that when cover has been placed, the clients are notified as soon as possible. That seems to me to be good business

---

risks including whole time and part time musicians which were not acceptable to the insurers; *Victor Melik & Co Ltd v Norwich Union Fire Insurance Society Ltd and Kemp* [1980] 1 Lloyd's Rep 523 (burglary insurance), where the brokers would have been held liable for failing to raise with the insurers a matter as requested by the insured, but were held not to be liable, because the insurers had not proved a breach of a condition and so themselves were liable in respect of the loss. (See the judgment of Woolf J, ibid, at 534); *Reardon v Kings Mutual Insurance Co (Gollon Third Parties)* (1981) 120 DLR (3d) 196, Supreme Court of Nova Scotia, Trial Division (property insurance), where an insurance agent failed to advise the proposer that the risk in respect of a hay barn had not been accepted by the insurers; *Mint Security Ltd v Blair* [1982] 1 Lloyd's Rep 188 (cash in transit insurance), where the brokers failed to inform the insured that an earlier proposal had been incorporated into the policy; *Commonwealth Insurance Co of Vancouver v Groupe Sprinks SA, Compagnie Française d'Assurances Européenes, J H Minet & Co Ltd and C E Heath & Co (Marine) Ltd* [1983] 1 Lloyd's Rep 67 (reinsurance), where the reinsurance brokers were held not to be in breach of their duty to procure valid and effective reinsurance; *Dunbar v A and B Painters Ltd and Economic Insurance Co Ltd and Whitehouse & Co* [1985] 2 Lloyd's Rep 616 (employers' liability insurance), where the proposal form completed by the brokers did not disclose that the previous insurers had required an increased premium.

12 (1943) 73 LlL Rep 104 (Birmingham Assizes); *Fraser v B N Furman (Productions) Ltd (Miller Smith & Partners, Third Party)* [1967] 3 All ER 57, CA (employers' liability insurance) where the brokers had failed to effect an employers' liability insurance policy; *Roselodge Ltd v Bray, Gibb (Holdings) Ltd* [1967] 2 Lloyd's Rep 99 (jewellers' block insurance) where the insured unreservedly withdrew allegations of negligence in regard to advice about insurance matters given by the brokers.

13 (1943) 73 LlL Rep at 107.

14 [1951] 2 Lloyd's Rep 631.

15 Ibid, at 643.

and prudent office management, but, on the evidence, I am completely unable to hold that it is part of the duty owed by the broker to the client so to notify him, in the sense that failure so to notify him would involve him in legal liability. No case was spoken to in which any broker had ever been held liable or had ever paid any client money in respect of such failure. It seems to me to put quite an unreasonable burden on a broker to say that as a matter of law, apart from prudent practice, he is bound to forward the cover note as soon as possible. It is no doubt prudent to do so, both to allay the client's anxiety and possibly to enable the client to check the terms of the insurance. That is a very different thing from saying it is part of his duty.'

Again, an agent employed to effect an insurance must procure a policy which the principal can enforce; he must, therefore, do no act in the course of the negotiations by which the policy may be rendered useless to the assured. Hence, a failure to make full disclosure as a result of which the policy[16] or its renewal[17] is avoided by the insurers is a breach of duty towards the assured.

Similarly, an agent of the insurers employed to deal with the loss, must not, either by fraud or by negligence, induce the insurers to pay a loss for which to his knowledge they are not liable.[18]

In accordance with the same principle, the agent must act personally and not delegate the performance of his duties to another,[19] unless delegation is permissible by the terms of the employment[20] or in the ordinary course of business.[21]

4 Duty to account

It is the duty of the agent, when employed to receive payment on his principal's behalf, to act with due diligence in collecting the amounts payable to his principal, and to pay over to the principal such sums as he may have received in the course of his employment.[22]

Thus, if the assured employs an agent to collect the amount due on the policy, the agent must collect it promptly,[1] and payment must be received in a form

---

16 *Maydew v Forrester* (1814) 5 Taunt 615 (marine insurance); *Claude R Ogden & Co Pty Ltd v Reliance Fire Sprinkler Co Pty Ltd* [1975] 1 Lloyd's Rep 52, (Can SC) (public and products liability insurance). Even innocent non-disclosure through an honest mistake of judgment is sufficient: *Holland v Russell* (1863) 4 B & S 14 (marine insurance). But no action lies where, although there was non-disclosure, the policy was in any case void: *T Cheshire & Co v Vaughan Bros & Co* [1920] 3 KB 240, 3 LlL Rep 213, CA (marine insurance), where the agent was guilty of nondisclosure in carrying out his instructions to effect a ppi policy.

17 *Coolee Ltd v Wing, Heath & Co* (1930) 47 TLR 78 (employers' liability insurance).

18 *Connecticut Fire Insurance Co v Kavanagh* (supra), where, however, the claim for negligence was raised too late.

19 This does not apply to merely ministerial acts; thus, a policy issued in pursuance of a 'slip' initialled by the agent, acting under a power of attorney from his principal, may be signed by a clerk: *Mason v Joseph* (1804) 1 Smith KB 406 (marine insurance).

20 *Cahill v Dawson* (1857) 3 CBNS 106 (marine insurance), where there was a difference of opinion in the Court as to whether the delegation was a breach of duty.

21 *Coolee Ltd v Wing, Heath & Co* (supra), where the country broker employed a Lloyd's broker: *Rossiter v Trafalgar Life Assurance Association* (1859) 27 Beav 377 (life insurance) where it was held that the principal agent for the company in Australia was empowered to appoint sub-agents; cf *W H and F J Horniman & Co Ltd v Hill, Brewer and Jenkins Ltd* (1925) 22 LlL Rep 333, where it was held that a broker, who had ceased to be a member of Lloyd's though this was not known to the assured, could not delegate the duty of collecting a loss to a Lloyd's broker, and accordingly the Lloyd's broker was accountable to the assured for the amount collected as money had and received, and could not rely upon a set-off against the assured's broker.

22 He is equally liable to account for money received by a sub-agent: *National Employers' Mutual General Insurance Association Ltd v Elphinstone* [1929] W N 135.

1 *Bousfield v Creswell* (1810) 2 Camp 545 (marine insurance).

authorised by the principal;[2] otherwise any loss occasioned by the breach of duty falls on the agent.[3]

Moreover, the agent cannot after receiving the amount from the insurers, refuse to pay it over to the principal;[4] and it is immaterial that the insurance by virtue of which it was received was illegal.[5]

Where an agency agreement made between an insurance company and a broker states that any premiums held by him are the property of the company, he is not entitled to use those premiums to obtain alternative cover for an insured with other insurers, if the insurance company concerned goes into liquidation.[6] All that he can do is to prove in the liquidation for a pro rata return of the insured's premium.[7]

5 Duty to act honestly

It is the duty of the agent to deal honestly with his principal, and not to act in any way detrimental to his interest in collusion with the third person.[8]

Thus, the agent employed to effect an insurance on behalf of the assured must not take a secret commission[9] from the insurers, and must account to the assured for any secret commission received.[10] Further, an agent employed by

---

2 *J McCarthy v F F Dixon & Co (London) Ltd* (1924) 19 LlL Rep 29, 58 (motor insurance), where the assured's agent was authorised to receive payment from the broker who had been paid by the underwriters in respect of a loss relating to a motor car, and the broker paid the agent partly in cash and partly in account, and it was held that the full sum must be paid in cash to the assured by the broker.

3 *Andrew v Robinson* (1812) 3 Camp 199 (marine insurance); *Wilkinson v Clay* (1815) 6 Taunt 110 (marine insurance).

4 *Dixon v Hammond* (1819) 2 B & Ald 310 (marine insurance) per Abbott CJ, at 313; *Roberts v Ogilby* (1821) 9 Price 269 (marine insurance); or to the trustee in bankruptcy: *McEntire v Potter & Co* (1889) 22 QBD 438 (marine insurance), where the broker paid over the proceeds to the assured in ignorance of his bankruptcy. In *Wolf and Korkhaus v Tyser & Co* (1921) 8 LlL Rep 340 the brokers would have been liable to account to the principals for the money which they themselves had wrongfully paid to a third party, but were not held liable in fact because the principals had elected to pursue their rights against the third party, thus releasing the brokers from liability.

5 *Tenant v Elliott* (1797) 1 Bos & P 3 (marine insurance), where the policy was in contravention of a statute, but the insurers paid the loss without objection.

6 *Vehicle and General Insurance Co Ltd v Elmbridge Insurances* [1973] 1 Lloyd's Rep 325, Mayor's and City of London Court, where the agreement stated: 'All monies received on behalf of the Company in your capacity as an Agent of the Company are at all times the property of, and received for, and in trust, to pay the same to the Company and can in no way form part of your personal estate or have any connection with any business you may transact apart from that done on behalf of the Company'.

7 Ibid. As to a pro rata return of premium, see p 201, ante.

8 *Connecticut Fire Insurance Co v Kavanagh* [1892] AC 473, PC (fire insurances), where the agent was charged with fraudulently transferring an insurance to the insurers after loss, but the transfer was held to be bona fide having been made without communication with the assured.

9 This includes discounts for punctual payment: *Queen of Spain v Parr* (1869) 39 LJCh 73 (marine insurance); cf *Leete v Wallace* (1888) 58 LT 577 (life insurance), where the same person acted as agent for both parties; *Taylor v Walker* [1958] 1 Lloyd's Rep 490, where the assessors' fee was paid by the insurance company without the knowledge of the assessors' principal.

10 *Workman and Army and Navy Auxiliary Co-operative Supply Ltd v London and Lancashire Fire Insurance Co* (1903) 19 TLR 360 (fire insurance) per Kekewich J, at 362: 'It was perfectly plain that, if one instructed an agent to effect an insurance for him and that agent received a commission, without any agreement expressed or implied, that the commission should be for his own benefit, the commission belonged to the person whose property was being insured, and not to the agent. Of course, if one employed an insurance broker, it might fairly be inferred that he was to have the

the insurers to conduct the negotiations must not, in concert with the proposed assured, conceal from them or misrepresent to them any material facts within his knowledge.[11]

C THE CONSEQUENCES OF A BREACH OF DUTY[12]

The consequences of a breach of duty by an agent towards the principal are:

1 He forfeits all his rights against the principal.
2 He is liable to the principal for all loss resulting from the breach of duty.
3 He can be dismissed instantly.
4 He can be punished criminally.

1 Forfeiture of all his rights

The agent forfeits all rights against his principal under the transaction in respect of which the breach of duty is committed.

Thus, an agent, who takes a secret commission from the insurers, can claim no commission from the assured, and if he has already received it, must repay it.[13] If the insurance which he is employed to effect proves abortive by reason of his breach of duty, he can claim neither his commission[14] nor the reimbursement of money expended[15] nor indemnification against liability incurred[16] in connection with the abortive insurance.

2 Liability for all loss sustained

The agent is liable to the principal for all loss sustained by the principal in consequence of the agent's breach of duty. Thus, the assured may, on the happening of a loss, find himself unable to recover its amount from the insurers because the agent wilfully omitted to effect the insurance,[17] or failed to effect it

---

commission. On the other hand, if one employed a solicitor, it was not his business, and the solicitor was accountable to his client.' See also, *Re Lord Berwick, Lord Berwick v Lane* (1900) 81 LT 797, CA (life insurance). There is, however, no duty to account where the principal is aware that the agent is receiving commission from the other party: *Great Western Insurance Co of New York v Cunliffe* (1874) 9 Ch App 525 (marine insurance); *Baring v Stanton* (1876) 3 ChD 502, CA (marine insurance); *Jordy v Vanderpump* [1920] WN 64 (life insurance); or where the receipt of commission is justified by usage: *Rucker v Lunt* (1863) 3 F & F 959 (marine insurance).

11 See p 548, post.

12 See generally, Bowstead op cit, pp 240–244, 252; Powell op cit, pp 322–327.

13 *Andrews v Ramsay & Co* [1903] 2 KB 635 (agency).

14 *Denew v Daverell* (1813) 3 Camp 451 (agency).

15 *Barron v Fitzgerald* (1840) 6 Bing NC 201 (life insurance), where the insurance, instead of being effected in two names, was effected in three names, and it was held that the premiums paid could not be recovered, the Court pointing out that the addition of the third name might render it difficult for the principal to receive the benefit of the policy; cf *Lewis v Samuel* (1846) 8 QB 685 (agency); and cf *Tasker v Scott* (1815) 6 Taunt 234 (marine insurance), where there was a proper exercise of discretion.

16 *Dixon v Hovill* (1828) 4 Bing 665 (marine insurance), where, however, the breach of duty, if any, had been waived.

17 *McNiell v Millen & Co* [1907] 2 IR 328, CA; *Tickel v Short* (1750–51) 2 Ves Sen 239 (marine insurance), where the agent, who represented contrary to the fact that he had insured, was chargeable as if he had insured; *Smith v Price* (1862) 2 F & F 748 (marine insurance); *Rudd Paper Box Co v Rice* (1912) 20 OWR 979.

and neglected to notify the assured of his failure promptly,[18] or because the agent failed to effect the proper insurance[19] or was guilty of conduct entitling the insurers to avoid the policy[20] or to refuse payment.[1]

In these cases the agent does not, by reason of his conduct, become an insurer so as to be liable in any event for the exact amount which was or which ought to have been insured; he is liable only in damages for his breach of duty.[2]

Again, in *Osman v Ralph J Moss Ltd*[3]

> An insurance broker negligently advised the insured to insure with a motor insurance company known to be in financial difficulties. Later a winding up order was made against the company and the policy was valueless. The broker failed to advise the insured that he was not effectively insured, but merely advised him to insure with another company. The insured was involved in an accident and had to pay damages to a third party. He had also been fined for driving whilst uninsured, and had paid the premium to the insurance company.
> *Held*, that the insured was entitled to recover the damages he had paid to the third party,[4] the amount of the fine,[5] and the premium.

The damages[6] may, in a proper case, be measured by the amount which the

---

18 *Cock, Russell & Co v Bray Gibb & Co Ltd* (1920) 3 LlL Rep 71; *Smith v Lascelles* (1788) 2 Term Rep 187 (marine insurance); *Callander v Oelrichs* (1838) 5 Bing NC 58 (marine insurance); *Great Western Insurance Co of New York v Cunliffe* (1874) 9 Ch App 525 (marine insurance).

19 *Harding v Carter* (1781) 1 Park's Marine Inscc, 8th ed 4 (marine insurance), where the policy effected did not cover the plaintiff's interest; *Turpin v Bilton* (1843) 5 Man & G 455 (marine insurance), where a proper policy was not obtained; *Hurrell v Bullard* (1863) 3 F & F 445 (marine insurance), where the policy was not effected with responsible insurers; *Dickson & Co v Devitt* (1916) 21 Com Cas 291 (marine insurance), where the fact that the assured could have discovered that his instructions had not been followed was held to be immaterial; cf *Wallace v Tellfair* (1786) 2 Term Rep 188n. (marine insurance), where no policy could be effected as the agent was not willing to pay a sufficient premium.

20 *Coolee Ltd v Wing, Heath & Co* (1930) 47 TLR 78 (employers' liability insurance), where the insurers were not informed on renewal that the risk had been increased; *Connors v London and Provincial Insurance Co* [1913] WC & Ins Rep 408 (life insurance) where the agent filled up the proposal inaccurately.

1 *Wilkinson v Coverdale* (1793) 1 Esp 74 (fire insurance), where a condition requiring indorsement of the policy was not complied with; *March Cabaret Club and Casino Ltd v Thompson & Bryan Ltd* [1975] 1 Lloyd's Rep 169, QBD (traders' combined insurance), where the insured contended that the fire assessors had not submitted a claim within 30 days as required by a condition in the policy.

2 *Charles v Altin* (1854) 15 CB 46 (marine insurance) per Jervis CJ, at 63; *Everett v Hogg, Robinson & Gardner Mountain (Insurance) Ltd* [1973] 2 Lloyd's Rep 217, QBD (Commercial Court) (reinsurance), where the brokers were held to be liable to pay the reassured two-thirds of the loss which the reassured claimed that he had suffered by reason of the reinsurers repudiating liability under a reinsurance policy on the ground that the brokers had misrepresented a material fact, for, on the evidence, the reinsurers would have compromised the claim in view of the friendly relations existing between them and the reassured (see the judgment of Kerr J, ibid, at 224).

3 [1970] 1 Lloyd's Rep 313, CA.

4 But only part of the costs, for the insured ought to have taken immediate steps to say that he would submit to judgment for the amount claimed by the third party: ibid, at 316 (per Sachs LJ).

5 But the insured was entitled to recover only part of the costs in relation to the fine, for it had been imposed partly in respect of driving without being insured, and partly for careless driving: ibid, at 316 (per Sachs LJ).

6 The damages may be nominal only: *Cahill v Dawson* (1857) 3 CBNS 106 (marine insurance), where the proceeds were wrongfully withheld by a sub-agent employed by the agent to effect the insurance: cf *Smith v Cologan* (1788) 2 Term Rep 188n. (marine insurance); or may be less than the sum insured; *Charles v Altin* (supra) per Jervis CJ, at 63; See *Turpin v Bilton* (supra).

assured would have received if the agent had duly performed his duty,[7] and, in addition, if the agent had effected a policy which proved abortive, may include the costs of an action reasonably brought on the abortive policy.[8] No action lies, however, where the breach of duty arises in connection with a policy which is illegal[9] or void.[10]

The same principles apply in the case of an agent of the insurers. Thus, where an agent, by a fraudulent transfer in his books after loss, induces the insurers to accept liability for the loss, although they were never at risk, he is liable to them for the amount paid by them in respect of the loss[11].

3 Dismissal

Where the agent is guilty of committing a breach of duty, e g by disclosing confidential information to a third party, the principal can dismiss him instantly.[12]

Even though the agent has been employed under contract for a period, the principal is entitled to dismiss him summarily where he is guilty of a breach of duty.[13]

4 Criminal liability

The agent, if the breach of duty consists in taking a secret commission or in acting in concert with a third person to defraud his principal, may be punished under the Prevention of Corruption Act 1906.

---

7 *Coolee Ltd v Wing, Heath & Co* (supra), where both the country brokers and the Lloyd's brokers were guilty of negligence, and were both held liable for the amount of the loss; *Wilkinson v Coverdale* (supra); *Great Western Insurance Co of New York v Cunliffe* (supra). A deduction must be made for premium that would have been paid: *Charles v Altin* (supra) per Jervis CJ, at p 64; *Ackbar v C F Green & Co Ltd* [1975] QB 582, [1975] 2 All ER 65, (motor insurance) where the broker's client was a passenger in a lorry and was injured, and could not claim compensation from the insurer because the broker had not effected a policy covering injury to passengers, and it was held that an action against the broker was one which lay in contract and not one in respect of personal injuries, and so was not barred after 3 years under the Limitation Act 1939, s 2(1), as amended by the Law Reform (Limitation of Actions, etc) Act 1954, s 2(1).

8 See Arnould *The Law of Marine Insurance and Average* (16th edn, 1981); cf *Maydew v Forrester* (1814) 5 Taunt 615, (marine insurance), where the assured was held entitled to recover from the agent the amounts paid by the insurers under their policy and repaid to them by the assured on discovery of the agent's non-disclosure of a material fact.

9 *Webster v De Tastet* (1797) 7 Term Rep 157 (insurance on slaves).

10 It is immaterial whether the policy is void ab initio: *T Cheshire & Co v Vaughan Bros & Co* [1920] 3 KB 240, 3 LlL Rep 213, CA (marine insurance); or is avoided by reason of a breach of condition: *Delany v Stoddart* (1785) 1 Term Rep 22 (marine insurance), where deviation was alleged.

11 *Connecticut Fire Insurance Co v Kavanagh* [1892] AC 473, PC (fire insurance), where, in the circumstances, the charge of fraud was unsuccessful: see further, *Stoness v Anglo-American Insurance Co* (1912) 21 OWR 405; *Independent Cash Mutual Fire Insurance Co v Winterborn* (1913) 24 OWR 6, where the agent, contrary to his instructions, insured grain elevators.

12 See, e g *L S Harris Trustees Ltd (trading as L S Harris & Co) v Power Packing Services (Hermit Road) Ltd* [1970] 2 Lloyd's Rep 65, QB, where fire insurance assessors employed by the insured to prepare a claim in respect of a fire disclosed to a third party confidential information relating to the insured's policy, and the insured were held to be entitled to dismiss them summarily. (See the judgment of Paull J, at 68).

13 *Swale v Ipswich Tannery Co* (1906) 11 Com Cas 88 (fire insurance), where the manager of a tannery company, whose duty it was to advise the company as to its insurances, received secret commissions from the insurers with whom the insurances were effected, and it was held that the company, on discovering the facts, was entitled to dismiss him summarily, notwithstanding a provision in his contract of service providing for six months' notice.

CHAPTER 51

The relationship between the principal and third parties[1]

The general rule is that the principal is liable to the third party for any act done by the agent which falls within the agent's authority. In certain circumstances the principal is entitled to ratify the agent's unauthorised acts, and thus is enabled to take advantage of them vis-à-vis the third party, though, if he does so, he himself becomes contractually bound to the third party.

In some cases the knowledge of the principal is deemed to be the knowledge of the agent, and vice versa.

A THE AUTHORITY OF THE AGENT

1 The types of authority

Where the principal seeks, as against third parties, to take the benefit of an act done by another person on his behalf, the question whether the act was done with or without authority is of little importance, since an unauthorised act may, as a rule be ratified.[2]

Where, however, it is a question of the principal's liability to third parties, the existence, nature and extent of the alleged agent's authority are material factors to be taken into consideration. The principal will be liable to the third party if the act of the agent falls within:

a His express or implied authority.
b His usual authority.
c His apparent authority.

(a) Express and implied authority

All acts falling within the express authority of the agent bind the principal. There is express authority wherever the agent's authority in terms applies to the act in question.[3] Thus, where a broker is instructed to effect an insurance on behalf of a proposed assured, or an underwriter is authorised to sign policies on behalf of a syndicate, the principals are, in both cases, bound by any policy which is in accordance with the agent's instructions. The assured is, therefore,

[1] In this chapter only those portions of the law of Agency which are of particular importance in insurance transactions are referred to. For the relationship between principal and third parties in general, the reader is referred to the standard textbooks on the subject, e g Bowstead op cit, pp 279–424; Powell op cit, pp 148–247.

[2] See generally, Bowstead op cit, pp 51–84; Powell op cit, pp 120–147.

[3] *Acey v Fernie* (1840) 7 M & W 151 (life insurance) per Parke B, at 155.

liable to pay the premium,[4] and the syndicate is responsible for any loss.[5]

The principal is also bound by any act necessarily involved in the execution of the agent's express authority. Thus, an agent employed to effect an insurance on behalf of the proposed assured has authority to disclose all material facts to the insurers, and to describe the risk proposed to be insured;[6] the proposed assured is, therefore, responsible for his agent's non-disclosure or misdescription.[7] So also an agent employed to effect the insurance has authority to sign the proposal form and declaration on behalf of the proposed assured.[8]

Thus, in *Zurich General Accident and Liability Insurance Co Ltd v Rowberry*[9]

> Brokers were instructed to effect a policy of insurance in respect of continental travel. By mistake they stated in the proposal form that the destination of the assured was Paris whereas it was, in fact, Nice. The assured refused to pay the premium on the ground that the policy which was issued covered travel between London and Paris only.
> *Held*, by the Court of Appeal that the insurance company was entitled to the premium because the assured had given the brokers authority to negotiate a form of policy within the broad limits of the proposal form, which related to France, and that they were, therefore, entitled to nominate Paris as the destination.

An agent may be expressly authorised by the insurers to issue a cover note[10] or bind them to issue a policy to the proposer.[11]

Again, where the agent of the insurers had authority to handle the accounts under a reinsurance treaty,[12] it was held that he had authority to initial the accounts and thereby bind the reinsurers.[13]

(b) Usual authority

Although an agent may have been given no express instructions by his principal, by the very position which he holds he may have a 'usual authority' to do certain acts.

Thus, in the case of the insurers, an agent may be employed to negotiate the terms of a proposal and to induce the proposed assured to make a proposal which the insurers are willing to accept.[14] By virtue of this employment, the agent has authority to explain the meaning of the questions in the proposal

---

4 *Wolff v Horncastle* (1798) 1 Bos & P 316 (marine insurance) per Buller J, at 323. Hence, if the protection given by the policy varies according to the rate of premium, the assured is only entitled to the protection corresponding to the premium paid: *Letts v Excess Insurance Co* (1916) 32 TLR 361, where a higher premium was charged to cover war risks.

5 *Hambro v Burnand* [1904] 2 KB 10 (guarantee policy).

6 *Bancroft v Heath* (1901) 6 Com Cas 137, CA (fire insurance).

7 *Allen v Universal Automobile Insurance Co Ltd* (1933) 45 LlL Rep 55 (motor insurance), where the agent of the insured described the car as a new one, whereas in fact it had been severely burnt in a fire and had then been bought by the insured and reconditioned.

8 *Foster v Mentor Life Assurance Co* (1854) 3 E & B 48 (life insurance).

9 [1954] 2 Lloyd's Rep 55, CA.

10 See pp 103–108, ante.

11 *Woolcott v Excess Insurance Co Ltd and Miles, Smith, Anderson and Game Ltd* [1978] 1 Lloyd's Rep 633 (fire insurance). But a new trial was subsequently ordered: [1979] 1 Lloyd's Rep 231, CA.

12 As to reinsurance treaties, see Ivamy *Personal Accident, Life and Other Insurances* (2nd Edn, 1980), pp 326–329.

13 *River Thames Insurance Co Ltd v Al Ahleia Insurance Co SAK* [1973] 1 Lloyd's Rep 2, CA.

14 *Bawden v London, Edinburgh and Glasgow Assurance Co* [1892] 2 QB 534, CA, per Lord Esher MR, at 539.

form;[15] he may settle the terms of the proposal,[16] or decide the limits within which disclosure is to be made,[17] and he may even have authority to issue a cover note[18] or to receive the premium. If he has authority to receive the premium, he may also have authority, on receiving it, to waive the breach of a condition.[19] He may further, unless the policy provides otherwise, receive notice to determine the policy[20] or notice of loss.[21]

But an agent employed by the insurers to carry out the negotiations on their behalf, has, as a general rule, no usual authority to bind them to issue a policy,[22] though he may have authority to issue a cover note.[23] He has no authority to fill in the answers to the questions in the proposal form or to vary the terms of the contract,[24] whether expressed in the cover note[25] or in the policy.[1] Similarly, an

---

15 *Joel v Law Union and Crown Insurance Co* [1908] 2 KB 863, CA (life insurance) per Fletcher Moulton LJ, at 891.

16 *Bawden v London, Edinburgh and Glasgow Assurance Co* (supra) (per Lindley LJ, at 540, as explained in *Levy v Scottish Employers' Insurance Co* (1901) 17 TLR 229, per Wills J, at 230.

17 *Hough v Guardian Fire and Life Assurance Co* (1902) 18 TLR 273 (fire insurance), where the agent filled up the proposal in the name of a wharfinger and not in the name of the owner; *Naughter v Ottawa Agricultural Insurance Co* (1878) 43 UCR 121 (fire insurance), where the agent said that certain facts were not worth mentioning; cf *Holdsworth v Lancashire and Yorkshire Insurance Co* (1907) 23 TLR 521; *Montreal Assurance Co v McGillivray* (1859) 13 Moo PCC 87, 124, PC (fire insurance).

18 *Stockton v Mason, Vehicle and General Insurance Co Ltd and Arthur Edward (Insurance) Ltd* [1978] 2 Lloyd's Rep 430, CA (motor insurance), where the broker had a usual authority to issue a cover note and did not advise the insured that the cover in respect of a substituted car had been altered until after an accident had occurred, and it was held that the insurers were liable for he was acting as their agent. (See the judgment of Lord Diplock, ibid, at 432).

19 *Scott v Accident Association of New Zealand* (1888) 6 NZLR 263; *Wing v Harvey* (1854) 5 De GM & G 265 (life insurance); *Ayrey v British Legal and United Provident Assurance Co* [1918] 1 KB 136 (life insurance).

20 *Re Solvency Mutual Guarantee Society, Hawthorne's Case* (1862) 31 LJCh 625.

21 *Marsden v City and County Assurance Co* (1866) LR 1 CP 232.

22 *Linford v Provincial Horse and Cattle Insurance Co* (1864) 34 Beav 291; *M'Elroy v London Assurance Corpn* 1897 24 R (Ct of Sess) 287 (fire insurance); *Stockton v Mason, Vehicle and General Insurance Co Ltd and Arthur Edward (Insurance) Ltd* (supra), where Lord Diplock said (ibid, at 431) that the implied authority of a broker did not extend to entering into the complete policy of insurance which was substituted for the cover note and was for a fixed period. Similarly, a local agent of an insurance company has no usual authority to grant or contract to grant policies on behalf of his company: *Claxton and Pilling v Licenses and General Insurance Co* (1925) Manchester Assizes, 5 July, Frazer J.

23 *Mackie v European Assurance Society* (1869) 21 LT 102 (fire insurance); *Rossiter v Trafalgar Life Assurance Association* (1859) 27 Beav 377 (life insurance); *Wilkinson v General Accident Fire and Life Assurance Corpn Ltd* [1967] 2 Lloyd's Rep 182 (motor insurance), where a car dealer was also an agent of the insurance company and was only authorised to grant temporary cover notes; *London Borough of Bromley v Ellis (A Luff & Son, Third Parties)* [1971] 1 Lloyd's Rep 97, CA (motor insurance), where the brokers had full authority from the insurers to issue cover notes. (See the judgment of Lord Denning MR, ibid, at 98).

24 Misrepresentation by the agent of the legal effect of the contract is not binding on the insurers, and if acted on by the assured creates no estoppel against them: *Re Hooley Hill Rubber and Chemical Co Ltd and Royal Insurance Co* [1920] 1 KB 257, 1 LlL Rep 2, 25 (fire insurance). Nor has an agent, whose authority is limited to the granting of temporary cover notes, any authority to grant a contract entirely different from that already granted by the insurance company: *Wilkinson v General Accident Fire and Life Assurance Corpn Ltd* [1967] 2 Lloyd's Rep 182 (motor insurance), where it was held that the agent had no authority to grant to the insured cover in respect of third party risks only when driving cars not belonging to him provided that he had the consent of the owners, for the policy granted by the insurance company covered the insured only so long as he remained the owner of the insured vehicle, and in fact he had sold it to a third party.

25 *Levy v Scottish Employers' Insurance Co* (1901) 17 TLR 229.

1 *Pigott v Employers' Liability Assurance Corpn* (1900) 31 OR 666, where the policy was indorsed to

agent employed to receive premiums has no authority to give credit;[2] even if he receives the premium, he does not necessarily bind the insurance company either to issue,[3] or renew,[4] or, after lapse, to revive[5] the policy.

Again, a local agent has no usual authority to waive a condition concerning the giving of notice of loss to the head office of the company within a specified time.

Thus, in *Brook v Trafalgar Insurance Co Ltd*[6]

> A motor insurance policy provided that:—'Notice of any accident or loss must be given in writing to the company at its head office immediately upon the occurrence of such accident or loss . . . In the event of failure to comply with the terms of this condition and in particular, if within 7 days after such accident or loss has occurred, the company has not been notified as above set forth, then all benefit under this policy shall be forfeited.' The assured's car was lost by fire on 17 December, 1943. He reported the matter to Nelson, the company's provincial agent, on 18 December, and was then supplied with a claim form. He completed it on 3 January, 1944, and returned it to Nelson, who sent it to the company.
> *Held* by the Court of Appeal, that the claim was out of time, and that there was no evidence to show that Nelson had authority to waive the express condition of written notice having to be sent to the company's head office.

In the course of his judgment Scott LJ said:[7]

> 'The learned Judge[8] [in the Court below] relied upon the fact that Nelson's name is mentioned against the printed word "Agent" in the schedule to the policy. He treats that as amounting to conclusive evidence that Nelson had authority on behalf of the company to waive the express condition of written notice having to be sent to the company's head office. In my view . . . that would have been an erroneous inference. It is common knowledge to everybody that policies are issued at the instance of agents who procure the business and who get a small commission on the premium for doing so. That is the sense which prima facie the printed word "Agent" at the bottom of the policy bears; it appears there for the simple reason that it so serves as a record for the office files of the company as to who was the person entitled to commission. To suggest that the word "Agent" in front of the name there gives the commission agent authority to take the place of the company and waive an express condition requiring that written notice should be sent to the head office of the company when they have dozens of agents all over the country of that type, is, I venture to think, ridiculous.'

An underwriter who is authorised to act on behalf of his syndicate may use his discretion as to what insurances he will accept on its behalf, and, therefore,

---

cover another place; *McKinlay v Life and Health Insurance Association* 1905 13 SLT 102, where a limit in respect of any one accident was held binding notwithstanding a different agreement with the agent of the insurers; *Fowler v Scottish Equitable Life Insurance Society* (1858) 28 LJCh 225 (life insurance); *Comerford v Britannic Assurance Co* (1908) 24 TLR 593 (life insurance); *Boid v Colonial Mutual Life Assurance Society Ltd* (1910) 29 NZLR 41 (life insurance); cf *Horncastle v Equitable Life Assurance Society of the United States* (1906) 22 TLR 735, CA (life insurance), where it was assumed that the agent had authority, but the variation, being by parol, was excluded as inconsistent with the policy; *Ayrey v British Legal and United Provident Assurance Co* [1918] 1 KB 136 (life insurance) per Atkin J, at 141.

2 See pp 191–193, ante.

3 *Linford v Provincial Horse and Cattle Insurance Co* (supra).

4 *Towle v National Guardian Assurance Society* (1861) 30 LJCh 900, CA.

5 *Carpenter v Canadian Railway Accident Insurance Co* (1909) 18 OLR 388, where the agent gave a renewal receipt in exchange for a promissory note after the accident; cf *Scott v Accident Association of New Zealand* (1888) 6 NZLR 263, where the agent had authority to accept new insurances, and was accordingly held authorised to bind the insurers by receiving the renewal premium after the due date; *Acey v Fernie* (1840) 7 M & W 151 (life insurance); *British Industry Life Assurance Co v Ward* (1856) 17 CB 644 (life insurance).

6 (1947) 79 LlL Rep 365, CA (motor insurance).

7 (1947) 79 LlL Rep 365 at 367, CA.

8 Stable J.

policies signed by him in its name binds the syndicate as though he had signed them in the names of all members of the syndicate.[9] He has a usual authority to settle the amount of a loss,[10] or agree to refer a dispute arising under the policy to arbitration.[11]

Directors[12] or authorised officers of an insurance company[13] or persons represented as such[14] bind the company by their agreements to issue policies,[15] and by the policies which they, in fact, issue in its name.[16] They may waive a breach of condition[17] or accept as satisfactory answers to questions which ought to have been deemed unsatisfactory.[18] The usual authority even of these agents is, however, limited.[19] Thus, they cannot bind the insurers by entering into a contract which exceeds the known limits of their authority,[20] such as, for instance in the case of an insurance company, an ultra vires policy[1] or, apparently, a parol contract of insurance.[2]

But no usual authority is possessed by clerks and salaried employees of the

---

9 *Hambro v Burnand* [1940] 2 KB 10, CA; *Willis, Faber & Co Ltd v Joyce* (1911) 104 LT 576 (marine insurance), where the agent acted after his authority had expired.

10 *Richardson v Anderson* (1805) 1 Camp 43n. (marine insurance).

11 *Goodson v Brooke* (1815) 4 Camp 163 (marine insurance).

12 *Newsholme Bros v Road Transport and General Insurance Co* [1929] 2 KB 356, CA, per Scrutton LJ, at 370, 374; *Re Norwich Equitable Fire Assurance Society, Royal Insurance Co's Claim* (1887) 57 LT 241 (fire insurance).

13 *Re Arthur Average Association, ex p Cory and Hawksley* (1875) 32 LT 525 (marine insurance); *Prince of Wales Assurance Co v Harding* (1858) EB & E 183 (life insurance) followed in *Agar v Athenaeum Life Assurance Society* (1858) 3 CBNS 725 (issue of debenture). The same principle applies in the case of colonial managers: *Rossiter v Trafalgar Life Assurance Association* (1859) 27 Beav 377 (life insurance).

14 *Re County Life Assurance Co* (1870) 5 Ch App 288 (life insurance).

15 *Re Athenaeum Life Assurance Society, ex p Eagle Insurance Co* (1858) 4 K & J 549 (life insurance).

16 *Prince of Wales Assurance Co v Harding* (supra); *Re Athenaeum Life Assurance Society* (supra). The same principle applies where a negotiable instrument, signed by such officers, is given in payment of a loss: *Allen v Sea Fire and Life Assurance Co* (1850) 9 CB 574 (marine insurance); *Gordon v Sea Fire Life Assurance Society* (1857) 1 H & N 599 (marine insurance).

17 *Wing v Harvey* (supra) per Knight Bruce LJ, at 269.

18 *Montreal Assurance Co v McGillivray* (1859) 13 MooPCC 87 at 124 (fire insurance); cf *Newsholme Bros v Road Transport and General Insurance Co* (supra), explaining *Ayrey v British Legal and United Provident Assurance Co* [1918] 1 KB 136 (life insurance).

19 Contrast *Pontifex v Bignold* (1841) 3 Man & G 63 (life insurance), where an insurance company was held responsible for the fraudulent misrepresentations of its secretary made for the purpose of inducing the plaintiff to insure with the company, with *Newlands v National Employers' Accident Association Ltd* (1885) 54 LJQB 428, CA (agency), where the representations were made for the purpose of inducing the plaintiff to apply for shares.

20 *Baines v Ewing* (1866) LR 1 Exch 320 (marine insurance), where there was a known limit of amount; *Wilkinson v General Accident Fire and Life Assurance Corpn Ltd* [1967] 2 Lloyd's Rep 182 (motor insurance), where the insured knew that the authority of the agent was limited to the granting of temporary cover notes.

1 *Hambro v Hull and London Fire Assurance Co* (1858) 3 H & N 789 (marine insurance) where the directors of a company authorised to carry on fire insurance business only, issued marine policies; *Re Arthur Average Association, ex p Cory and Hawksley* (1875) 32 LT 525 (marine insurance); *Montreal Assurance Co v McGillivray* (1859) 13 MooPCC 87 at 124 (fire insurance). But if the assured has acted in good faith, he can enforce an *ultra vires* policy against the company in a case where the issue of the policy was decided on by the directors: Companies Act 1985, s 35. See p 6, ante.

2 *Davies v National Fire and Marine Insurance Co of New Zealand* [1891] AC 485 at 495, PC (marine insurance); cf *Murfitt v Royal Insurance Co* (1922) 38 TLR 334 (fire insurance), where it was held that, in the circumstances, there was authority to make a parol contract; *Parker & Co (Sandbank) v Western Assurance Co* [1925] WC & Ins Rep 82 (fire insurance).

insurers whose duty it is to perform merely ministerial acts, nor by persons who introduce business for a commission,[3] and whose authority is limited to the transmission of proposals to the insurers.[4] Thus, a person, who is merely employed to introduce business, has no power to bind the insurers by the issue of a cover note, or by the receipt of the premium, in the absence of an express authority to do so.[5] Nor has he any authority to accept a proposal.[6] The authority of such an agent may, however, be extended by the conduct of the insurers;[7] thus, if they allow him to collect premiums and to deduct his commission therefrom before handing them over, he is their agent to receive premiums.[8]

(c) Apparent authority

The principal will be bound when he has held out a person as his agent, and he will be liable to third parties for all acts which fall within the agent's apparent authority.

In this case it is immaterial whether the agent exceeded his express authority,[9] or whether he was never, in fact, an agent and had no authority to represent the principal at any time.[10] Thus, an agent, who has been in the habit of receiving premiums on behalf of the insurers, may bind them by the receipt of a particular premium,[11] and they may be affected with notice of the circumstances attending its payment.[12] An agent entrusted with blank signed policies and renewal receipts may bind the insurers by any policy or renewal receipt which he fills in and issues.[13] In accordance with the same principle, the

---

3 *Bawden v London, Edinburgh and Glasgow Insurance Co* [1892] 2 QB 534, CA, per Lord Esher MR, at 539.

4 *Bancroft v Heath* (1900) 5 Com Cas 110 (fire insurance) (affd (1901) 6 Com Cas 137, CA), per Mathew J, at 115; *Zurich General and Liability Insurance Co Ltd v Buck* (1939) 64 LlL Rep 115 (motor insurance), where it was held that the agent's authority was merely to receive and forward the proposal to the insurance company, and that the insurance company was not bound by any agreement between the agent and the proposer as to the form of the policy to be issued.

5 *Linford v Provincial Horse and Cattle Insurance Co* (1864) 34 Beav 291; *Summers v Commercial Union Insurance Co* (1881) 6 SCR 19.

6 *Canadian Fire Insurance Co v Robinson* (1901) 31 SCR 488.

7 *Murfitt v Royal Insurance Co Ltd* (1922) 38 TLR 334 (fire insurance), where, on the special facts of the case, it was held that the agent had authority to give verbal cover.

8 *Kelly v London and Staffordshire Fire Insurance Co* (1883) Cab & El 47 (fire insurance).

9 *Holdsworth v Lancashire and Yorkshire Insurance Co* (1907) 23 TLR 521, following *Wing v Harvey* (1854) 5 De GM & G 265 (life insurance).

10 *Re County Life Assurance Co* (1870) 5 Ch App 288 (life insurance), where the persons signing the policy as directors and secretary had never been validly so appointed; cf *Barrett v Deere* (1828) Mood & M 200 (agency), where payment to a thief masquerading as a cashier was held to be good.

11 *Kelly v London and Staffordshire Fire Insurance Co* (1883) Cab & El 47 (fire insurance), where the authority of the agent was in other respects limited by the terms of the policy; cf *Re Economic Fire Office Ltd* (1896) 12 TLR 142, where the premium was payable by the employee, and the agent of the insurers gave him a receipt, though the premium was not paid in order that it might be shown to the employers; and cf *Towle v National Guardian Assurance Society* (1861) 30 LJCh 900, CA, where there was held to be no renewal, the receipt being unauthorised.

12 *Scott v Accident Association of New Zealand* (1888) 6 NZLR 263, where an agent accepted a renewal premium after the due date; *Wing v Harvey* (supra), where a renewal premium was received by the agent with knowledge that a condition had been broken.

13 *Kelly v London and Staffordshire Insurance Co* (supra); cf *Neal v Erving* (1793) 1 Esp 61 (marine insurance); *Haughton v Ewbank* (1814) 4 Camp 88 (marine insurance).

insurers cannot repudiate an alteration indorsed on a policy by an agent who has been held out by them as authorised to indorse on policies alterations in their terms.[14]

Again, where a person was appointed as chairman of a negotiating committee of reinsurers to settle disputes under a reinsurance treaty, it was held that, on the evidence, he had apparent authority to make a settlement which was binding on them.[15]

Further, Lloyd's Policy Signing Office has been held to have apparent authority to sign policies binding on underwriters as if they had signed them themselves.[16]

An unauthorised act may, however, be repudiated by the principal provided that he acts promptly and before the position of the third party has been altered to his prejudice. Hence, the insurers cannot, after loss, rely on the fact that the agent, in issuing the policy, had exceeded his express authority.[17]

But the principal cannot, by a secret limitation of the agent's authority, prevent the agent from binding him by acts falling within his apparent authority.[18]

2 The termination of the agent's authority

As far as the relationship between the principal and the agent is concerned, the authority of an agent may be withdrawn at any time.[19]

But as far as third parties who have already dealt with him as an agent are concerned, his authority may, according to the circumstances, continue until they have received notice to the contrary. It is then immaterial whether the act done falls within the express[20] or apparent authority,[21] which the agent possessed before the withdrawal.

Thus, a policy signed on behalf of the insurers by an agent, who formerly had authority to sign policies on their behalf, binds them, though the authority had been withdrawn before it was signed, unless the assured had been notified of the withdrawal;[22] and a notice of loss given to the agent through whom the policy was effected is, in the absence of a condition to the contrary, a valid notice, although the agent had, before the loss, ceased to represent the insurers, provided that the assured was not aware of it.[1]

3 Where the act of the agent does not bind the principal

Any acts which fall outside the scope of the agent's authority, either because the

---

14 *Brocklebank v Sugrue* (1831) 5 C & P 21 (marine insurance).

15 *Eagle Star Insurance Co Ltd v Spratt* [1971] 2 Lloyd's Rep 116, CA (see the judgment of Lord Denning MR, ibid, at 127).

16 Ibid. (See the judgment of Lord Denning MR, ibid, at 128.)

17 *Mackie v European Assurance Society* (1869) 21 LT 102 (fire insurance) per Malins V-C, at 105.

18 *Manufacturers' Accident Insurance Co v Pudsey* (1879) 27 SCR 374, where an agent and district manager, who was entrusted with renewal receipts, gave credit for the premium contrary to his private instructions, the Court being of the opinion that the giving of credit was within his apparent authority. See generally, *Edmunds v Bushell and Jones* (1865) LR 1 QB 97 (agency).

19 *Warwick v Slade* (1811) 3 Camp 127 (marine insurance).

20 *Willis, Faber & Co v Joyce* (1911) 104 LT 576 (marine insurance).

21 *Marsden v City and County Assurance Co* (1866) LR 1 CP 232; *Conquest's Case* (1875) 1 ChD 334, CA (life insurance).

22 *Willis, Faber & Co v Joyce* (supra).

1 *Marsden v City and County Assurance Co* (supra).

alleged agent has no authority to represent the principal,[2] or because his express or usual or implied or apparent authority does not extend that far,[3] do not bind the principal.

Thus, a disclosure of a material fact to the solicitor acting for the insurers is not a disclosure to the insurers.[4] Similarly, payment of the premium to their agent, if not made in the proper form,[5] or at the proper time,[6] is not necessarily a payment to the insurers.

Again, an admission of liability made by the driver of a vehicle after an accident is not an admission of liability by an agent of his employer within the meaning of a condition in a motor insurance policy providing that the assured should not by his agent make any admission of liability, since the driver is not, in the absence of express authority, the agent of his employer to make admissions.[7] Further, where the principal had instructed his agent to insure some goods against war risks for 3 months, and the agent asked a firm of brokers to insure them for 'one or three months as obtainable', and the insurance policy was arranged for a period of one month only, it was held that the principal was not liable for the payment of the premium because the agent had acted without authority.[8]

4 The effect of the agent's fraud

An act which otherwise falls within the agent's authority does not cease to bind the principal because it was done fraudulently.[9] It is immaterial whether the agent was acting in his own interest and in fraud of the principal[10] or for the supposed benefit of the principal.[11]

If the principal successfully repudiates responsibility for the act on the ground that it was unauthorised, he must account to the third party for any benefit which he may have received, since he cannot benefit by his agent's fraud and at the same time repudiate what the agent has done.[12]

A breach of duty on the part of the assured's agent in concert with the insurers confers rights on the assured as against them. Thus, insurers who have

---

2 *Anglo-Californian Bank Ltd v London and Provincial Marine and General Insurance Co Ltd* (1904) 10 Com Cas 1; *Bancroft v Heath* (1900) 5 Com Cas 110 (fire insurance) (affirmed (1901) 6 Com Cas 137, CA) per Mathew J, at 115.

3 *Levy v Scottish Employers' Insurance Co* (1901) 17 TLR 229; *Linford v Provincial Horse and Cattle Insurance Co* (1864) 34 Beav 291; *Xenos v Wickham* (1867) LR 2 HL 296 (marine insurance); *McElroy v London Assurance Corpn* 1897 24 R (Ct of Sess) 287 (fire insurance); *Comerford v Britannic Assurance Co* (1908) 24 TLR 593 (life insurance).

4 *Tate v Hyslop* (1885) 15 QBD 368, CA (marine insurance).

5 See pp 184–185, ante.

6 *Carpenter v Canadian Railway Accident Insurance Co* (1909) 18 OLR 388; *Acey v Fernie* (1840) 7 M & W 151 (life insurance); *British Industry Life Assurance Co v Ward* (1856) 17 CB 644 (life insurance).

7 *Tustin v Arnold & Sons* (1915) 84 LJKB 2214, where the view was expressed that even if the admission were admissible in evidence as part of the res gestae, it would not constitute a breach of the condition.

8 *Sedgwick, Collins & Co Ltd v Highton* (1929) 34 LlL Rep 448 (war risk insurance).

9 *Hambro v Burnand* [1904] 2 KB 10, CA; *Lloyd v Grace, Smith & Co* [1912] AC 716.

10 *Hambro v Burnand* (supra); *Lloyd v Grace, Smith & Co* (supra).

11 *Blackburn, Low & Co v Vigors* (1887) 12 App Cas 531 (marine insurance); *Hambrough v Mutual Life Insurance Co of New York* (1895) 72 LT 140, CA (life insurance); cf *Pontifex v Bignold* (1841) 3 Man & G 63 (life insurance).

12 *Refuge Assurance Co Ltd v Kettlewell* [1909] AC 243 (life insurance).

paid a secret commission to the agent of the assured, are liable to the insured in damages; the insured is entitled to claim the amount of the secret commission from the agent but cannot claim both damages and the secret commission and must elect between the two remedies.[13]

Further, if the agent in concert with the insurers fraudulently makes a compromise of the assured's claim, the compromise agreement can be set aside at the instance of the assured.[14]

B RATIFICATION[15]

An act which does not fall within the agent's authority, whether express, implied, usual or apparent, becomes binding on the principal if it is ratified. Ratification takes place where the principal adopts the unauthorised act and makes it his own. It may be either express or implied from conduct, e g where he takes the benefit of the act with knowledge of the circumstances in which it was done.[16]

It is immaterial whether the unauthorised act was done without authority by a person who was in no sense the agent of the principal at the time,[17] or whether it was done in excess of authority by a person who was, at the time, his agent for other purposes.[18]

1 Conditions necessary for a valid ratification

To constitute a valid ratification the following conditions must be fulfilled:

(a) The person doing the unauthorised act must purport to do it as agent and not on his own behalf[19]

Thus, if a person effects an insurance in his own name, there being nothing to show the insurers that any other person is interested in the insurance, the insurance is personal to the person actually effecting it; such person cannot

---

[13] *Mahesan v Malaysia Government Officers' Co-operative Housing Society Ltd* [1979] AC 374, [1978] 2 All ER 405, PC, disapproving *Salford Corpn v Lever* [1891] 1 QB 168, CA. The insurers may also be liable criminally under the Prevention of Corruption Act 1906, s 1(1).

[14] *Taylor v Walker* [1958] 1 Lloyd's Rep 490. 'I find that there was a payment . . . of 40 guineas to Mr. Blackwell and that it was a bribe or payment of a secret commission, in that [the third party] made the payment to Mr. Blackwell, the agent of the [assured], with whom they were dealing: they made it to Mr. Blackwell knowing Mr. Blackwell was acting as agent for the [assured] . . . and they failed to disclose to the [assured] that they had made that payment . . . The fact that Mr. Blackwell assured them that he had disclosed the payment to his principal is of no avail to them. If they themselves did not communicate the payment to the [assured], they have to accept the risk of the agent not doing so either. The course which they took, in my view, can only be validated by actual disclosure to the [assured] and there was none. Therefore I hold that the settlement was voidable at the option of the [assured].' (Per Havers J, at 513.)

[15] See generally, Bowstead op cit, pp 51–84, Powell op cit, pp 120–147.

[16] See *Hunter v Parker* (1840) 7 M & W 322 (sale of ship) per Parke B, at 342.

[17] See *Ancona v Marks* (1862) 7 H & N 686 (agency).

[18] *Hunter v Parker* (supra).

[19] *Wolff v Horncastle* (1798) 1 Bos & P 316 (marine insurance); *Walters v Monarch Fire and Life Assurance Co* (1856) 5 E & B 850 (fire insurance), followed in *London and North Western Rly Co v Glyn* (1859) 1 E & E 652 (fire insurance).

afterwards allege that he intended to insure on behalf of a principal, and the alleged principal cannot ratify the insurance.[20]

(b) The principal purporting to ratify the unauthorised act must be the principal whom the agent had in contemplation and on whose behalf he intended to act[1]

The principal need not be named.[2] It is sufficient if he belongs to a contemplated class, e g where an insurance purports to be on behalf of all persons interested or of those it may concern.[3] A person falling within the description of the principal in the policy cannot, however, ratify it, if it appears that he was not such a person as the agent had in contemplation.[4]

(c) The principal must, at the time of the act alleged to constitute ratification,[5] *have full knowledge of all the circumstances relevant to the unauthorised act*[6] *or, at least, must have waived further inquiry*[7]

(d) The principal must be in existence at the time when the unauthorised act was done[8]

This is important only in the case of limited companies and other corporate bodies. Thus, a policy issued by an agent on behalf of an insurance company before its actual incorporation cannot be ratified by the company afterwards.[9] A new policy must be issued after the incorporation of the company.[10]

---

20 *Watson v Swann* (1862) 11 CBNS 756 (marine insurance), where the agent, having failed to effect a policy in accordance with the instructions, sought to declare his principal's goods under an open policy which he had previously effected on his own behalf.

1 *Boston Fruit Co v British and Foreign Marine Insurance Co* [1906] AC 336 (marine insurance).

2 *Hagedorn v Oliverson* (1814) 2 M & S 485 (marine insurance); *Watson v Swann* (1862) 11 CBNS 756 (marine insurance) per Erle CJ, at 769.

3 An insurance in this form, though usual in marine insurance, is rarely used in other branches of insurance.

4 *Watson v Swann* (supra) per Willes J, at 771; *Byas v Miller* (1897) 3 Com Cas 39 (marine insurance), where the principal on behalf of whom the agent effected the insurance repudiated it as being in excess of his instructions, and the agent sought to give the benefit of insurance to the plaintiff; *Boston Fruit Co v British and Foreign Marine Insurance Co* (supra), where the charterers of a ship unsuccessfully sought to ratify a policy effected by the owners, which, though in terms sufficiently wide, was not, according to the evidence, intended to cover them.

5 *Bell v Janson* (1813) 1 M & S 201 at 204 (marine insurance), where at the time that the insurance was effected instructions to insure were on the way, and it was held that such instructions could not be relied on as constituting a ratification.

6 *Busteed v West of England Insurance Co* (1857) 5 IChR 553 (life insurance), where the insurers received renewal premiums from their agent in ignorance of the fact that the policy had lapsed, following *Acey v Fernie* (1840) 7 M & W 151 (life insurance); cf *London and Lancashire Life Assurance Co v Fleming* [1897] AC 499 at 508 (life insurance).

7 See *Fitzmaurice v Bayley* (1856) 6 E & B 868 (agency); and cf *Wing v Harvey* (1854) 5 De GM & G 265 (life insurance).

8 See *Kelner v Baxter* (1866) LR 2 Cp 174 (agency).

9 See *Gunn v London and Lancashire Assurance Co* (1862) 12 CBNS 694 (fire insurance), where the agreement was with the promoter; *Kelner v Baxter* (supra). The person who issued the policy is personally liable to the assured: Companies Act 1985, s 36(4). See Pennington *Company Law* (5th Edn, 1985), p 105.

10 See *Howard v Patent Ivory Manufacturing Co* (1888) 38 ChD 156 (company).

(e) The principal must, by law, be capable of doing the unauthorised act[11]

This also is important only in the case of limited companies and other corporate bodies, whose powers are limited by their memorandum of association or other instruments constituting them. An insurance company which is formed for the purpose, as defined in its memorandum of association, of carrying on a specified kind of insurance business[12] cannot carry on any other kind of insurance business, unless its memorandum of association is first altered according to law.[13] It cannot, therefore, ratify policies of insurance issued by its directors, which do not fall within the scope of the memorandum of association so as to enforce them against the assured.[14]

(f) The principal must not be precluded by his conduct from ratifying the unauthorised act[15]

Thus, an unequivocal expression of determination not to adopt or to ratify or to be bound by the act binds the principal.[16]

2 The effect of ratification

The effect of ratification is that the act ratified is, in contemplation of law, the act of a duly appointed agent, acting on behalf of the principal and in pursuance of the principal's prior instructions.[17] The act, therefore, becomes the act of the principal, by which he is entitled to benefit and for which he is responsible. Thus, an unauthorised insurance, when ratified by the assured or by the insurers, as the case may be, becomes a valid insurance. The assured is, therefore, liable for the premium,[18] and the insurers are liable for any loss which may subsequently happen.[19]

---

11 See *Ashbury Railway Carriage and Iron Co v Riche* (1875) LR 7 HL 653 (company).

12 The memorandum of association may be framed in terms sufficiently wide to cover other kinds of insurance business: *Re Norwich Provident Insurance Society Bath's Case* (1878) 8 ChD 334 (fire insurance), where a life insurance company authorised 'generally to make and effect insurances against all and every kind of risk, special or general . . . upon such terms and conditions as may seem reasonable and expedient, having due regard to the business of an insurance company' was held entitled to issue policies of fire insurance.

13 Under the Companies Act 1985, s 4. See p 5, ante.

14 But the assured if he has acted in good faith is entitled to enforce the policy against the company if the issue of the policy has been decided on by the directors: Companies Act 1985, s 35(1). See p 6, ante.

15 A repudiation of the act, addressed by the principal to the professing agent, but not communicated to the third person, is not sufficient: *Simpson v Eggington* (1855) 10 Exch 845 (agency).

16 *Boston Fruit Co v British and Foreign Marine Insurance Co* [1906] AC 336 (marine insurance) per Lord Atkinson, at 342, 343.

17 *Wolff v Horncastle* (1798) 1 Bos & P 316 (marine insurance) per Heath J, at 324: 'While the ship is in safety where is the difference whether the agent insure without order, and the principal afterwards approve of the insurance, or first receive the order and then insure?' See also, *Routh v Thompson* (1811) 13 East 274 (marine insurance).

18 *New Zealand Insurance Co Ltd v Tyneside Proprietary Ltd* [1917] NZLR 569; cf *Wolff v Horncastle* (supra) per Buller J, at 323; *Robinson v Gleadow* (1835) 2 Bing NC 156 (marine insurance) per Park J, at 161.

19 *Routh v Thompson* (supra); *Wolff v Horncastle* (supra).

3 Ratification after loss

(a) Marine insurance

In marine insurance, it is clear that an unauthorised insurance may be ratified even after the principal has heard of the loss. Ratification after loss is an anomaly.[20] It is to be regarded as an exception to the general principle that there can only be a ratification where the principal could at the time of ratification make the same contract as that ratified.[1] At the same time the validity of a ratification after loss is established both by the authority of decided cases[2] and by statute.[3] Moreover, it has been recognised as a legitimate exception to the general principle, in as much as the loss insured against is very likely to happen before ratification, and it must be taken that an insurance effected subject to ratification involves that possibility as the basis of the contract.[4]

(b) Non-marine insurance

The question of ratification after loss has also been considered in connection with fire insurance;[5] and it may be assumed that, in the case of any other kind of insurance, the principles applicable to fire insurance will be followed rather than those which may be peculiar to marine insurance.

In the case of fire insurance, it will depend on the circumstances whether the loss can be ratified. Two types of situation are to be distinguished:

i The person effecting the unauthorised insurance may himself be interested in the subject-matter.

ii The person effecting the unauthorised insurance may have no interest in the subject-matter.

i Insurances by persons interested

In many cases a person who has an interest in the subject-matter of insurance is

---

20 *Williams v North China Insurance Co* (1876) 1 CPD 757, CA (marine insurance) per Cockburn CJ, at 764; and per Jessel MR, at 766; *Grover & Grover Ltd v Mathews* [1910] 2 KB 401 (fire insurance) per Hamilton J, at 404.

1 *Williams v North China Insurance Co* (supra) per Jessel MR, at 766. For an example, see *Dibbens v Dibbens* [1896] 2 Ch 348 (partnership), where it was held that an option to purchase exercised by an agent without authority within the period fixed for its exercise could not be ratified after the expiration of that period.

2 See, e g *Routh v Thompson* (supra); *Hagedorn v Oliverson* (1814) 2 M & S 485 (marine insurance); *Williams v North China Insurance Co* (supra).

3 Marine Insurance Act 1906, s 86: 'Where a contract of marine insurance is in good faith effected by one person on behalf of another, the person on whose behalf it is effected may ratify the contract even after he is aware of a loss'. See, e g *Hansen v Norske Lloyd Insurance Co* (1919) 1 LlL Rep 66, 185.

4 *Williams v North China Insurance Co* (supra) per Cockburn CJ, at 764.

5 See *Waters v Monarch Fire and Life Assurance Co* (1856) 5 E & B 870 (fire insurance), followed in *London and North Western Rly Co v Glyn* (1859) 1 E & E 652 (fire insurance); *Grover & Grover Ltd v Mathews* [1910] 2 KB 401 (fire insurance); *Ferguson v Aberdeen Parish Council* 1916 SC 715 (fire insurance). A similar question was raised in *London Guarantee and Accident Co v Cornish* (1905) 17 Man LR 148, where the Colonial Manager of an insurance company had endorsed a cancelled fidelity policy with a continuation clause, and it was held in an action upon a counter-security given to the company that, in the absence of evidence that he had authority to do so, the company had failed to prove that the policy was continued.

desirous of effecting an insurance which will cover the interests of other persons interested in the subject-matter, and will insure for their benefit as well as his own.

Thus, it is the practice of bailees to whom goods are entrusted for carriage, safe custody and the like purposes,[6] to effect insurances by the terms of which they are, in the event of the goods entrusted to them being destroyed by fire whilst in their possession, to recover not merely the value of their own interest in such goods, but their full value.

In the same way, a mortgagee, whether legal or equitable,[7] or a tenant for life,[8] or for years,[9] or the holder of any similar interest,[10] may find it convenient to cover the interest of the mortgagor or remainderman, or as the case may be.

An insurance of this kind is a valid insurance.[11] It is not a joint insurance since the interests of each assured are different;[12] the other persons interested

---

[6] *Martineau v Kitching* (1872) LR 7 QB 436 per Blackburn J, at 458: 'It is very common for a warehouseman to keep up very large and extensive floating policies to cover the goods in his hands, and let it be known generally that he was doing so, so that people would come to him in hopes that they would have the benefit of that insurance in case of loss. In that case, I think the Court might very properly draw the inference that it was part of the understood bargain that persons dealing with him would have the benefit of that insurance.' For examples of such insurances, see *Waters v Monarch Fire and Life Assurance Co* (1856) 5 E & B 870 (fire insurance); *London and North Western Rly Co v Glyn* (1859) 1 E & E 652 (fire insurance); *Re Pastoral Finance Association Ltd* (1922) 23 SR NSW 43; *Hepburn v A Tomlinson (Hauliers) Ltd* [1966] AC 451, [1966] 1 All ER 418, HL (goods in transit insurance).

[7] *Ebsworth v Alliance Marine Insurance Co* (1873) LR 8 CP 596 (marine insurance) per Bovill CJ, at 609: 'Prima facie, an insurance by a mortgagee whether legal or equitable, would cover only his own particular interest in the goods, but if the insurance was, as between him and the underwriters, intended to cover the interest of all parties and the whole value of the goods, there would be no objection to a legal mortgagee insuring in his own name to cover all the interests and the entire value of the goods: and we think there is equally no objection to an equitable mortgagee or a person who stands in a similar position insuring in a like manner'; *Woolcott v Sun Alliance and London Insurance Ltd* [1978] 2 All ER 1253, [1978] 1 WLR 493 (fire insurance), where a building society had a block policy of insurance and the names of the insured were expressed to be the society as mortgagees and the mortgagors mentioned in the record sheets. See also, *Castellain v Preston* (1883) 11 QBD 380, CA, per Bowen LJ, at 398, 399; *Nichols & Co v Scottish Union and National Insurance Co* (1885) 2 TLR 190, more fully reported 14 R (Ct of Sess) 1094; *Seaman v West* (1884) 5 Russ & GNS 207, where a mortgagee, who had insured on behalf of the mortgagor and himself, was held entitled to enforce the policy, although he had already recovered the amount of his own loss under another policy; *Chartered Trust and Executor Co v London, Scottish Assurance Corpn Ltd* (1923) 39 TLR 608 (marine insurance), where the innocent mortgagees of a scuttled ship were entitled to recover from the underwriters the value of their interest at the time of the loss; *Hordern v Federal Mutual Insurance Co of Australia* (1924) 25 SFNSW 267.

[8] *Castellain v Preston* (supra) per Bowen LJ, at 399, 400, 401.

[9] *Enlayde Ltd v Roberts* [1917] 1 Ch 109 per Sargant J, at 117; *Mutual Fire Insurance Co v Paquet Co* (1912) QR 21 KB 419.

[10] Such as an unpaid vendor: *Keefer v Phoenix Insurance Co* (1903) 1 Com LR (Can) 1.

[11] *Waters v Monarch Fire and Life Assurance Co* (1856) 5 E & B 870 (fire insurance) per Lord Campbell CJ, at 881.

[12] *General Accident, Fire and Life Assurance Corpn Ltd and Drysdale v Midland Bank, Ltd* [1940] 2 KB 388, CA, per Greene MR, at 405: 'How then can there be a joint insurance in any true sense of that phrase of the interest of a freeholder in freehold premises and the interest of a debenture holder holding a floating charge on that mass of property, including, among other things, these premises? There is no joint risk; there is no joint interest; the measure of loss suffered by these two parties will be different, calling for a different measure of indemnity, and, accordingly, it seems to me that there is no joint element about the thing at all. Such a policy, in my judgment, may be more accurately described as a composite policy, because it comprises, for reasons of obvious convenience, in one piece of paper, the interests of a number of persons who connection with the

are entitled accordingly to participate in the benefit of it.[13] The person effecting the insurance is to be regarded as an agent insuring on their behalf.[14] It is no objection to the validity of the insurance that the insurance was not, in fact, authorised or that its existence was only made known to the other persons interested after the loss.[15] The insurance is subject to the marine insurance rule[16] that an insurance by an agent may be ratified even after loss;[17] and they are entitled, therefore, notwithstanding the loss, to ratify the act done on their behalf.[18]

Further, it is no objection that the person insuring owed no duty to the other persons interested to effect the insurance[19] and was in no way responsible to them for the safety of the subject-matter.[20]

On the other hand, it is essential that, at the time of insuring, he should intend to cover their interests as well as his own.[21] So long as his intention is clear,[1] it was at one time thought that it was unnecessary for him to disclose it to

---

subject-matter of the insurance makes it natural and reasonable that the whole matter should be dealt with in one policy'; *Woolcott v Sun Alliance and London Insurance Ltd* [1978] 1 Lloyd's Rep 629 (fire insurance), where the interests of a building society as mortgagee and those of a mortgagor under a block policy of insurance were held to be different. (See the judgment of Caulfield J, ibid, at 631). See also, *Lombard Australia Ltd v NRMA Insurance Ltd* [1969] 1 Lloyd's Rep 575, Supreme Court of New South Wales, Court of Appeal (motor insurance), where it was held that where a proposal was made by a hire-purchaser of a car in his own name and in that of the finance company which was letting it to him under a hire-purchase agreement, the policy issued by the insurers could not be considered a 'joint policy', but constituted a separate promise to each of them with regard to their respective interests. Wallace A-CJ, said (ibid, at 576): 'The intention of the parties emerging from the provisions themselves in the policy is beyond debate—for example, a clause of the policy described as "s. 17" provides that the company shall pay "to the assured or the husband or wife of the assured as the case may be" and this promise can only be given if it be accepted as was so obviously the intention of the parties that the promise of the insurance company to the two entities who together constituted the "assured" was a several promise to each of them and not a promise to them jointly.' See also, the judgment of Walsh JA, ibid, at 577, and that of Holmes J A, ibid, at 579–580.

13 *Brady v Irish Land Commission* [1921] 1 IR 56.

14 This is clearly the case, where the insurance is effected by a bailee, e g a warehouseman: *Waters v Monarch Fire and Life Assurance Co* (supra); or a carrier: *London and North-Western Rly Co v Glyn* (1859) 1 E & E 652. The other insurances referred to probably depend on the same principle; see *Seaman v West* (supra).

15 *Waters v Monarch Fire and Life Assurance Co* (supra) per Lord Campbell CJ, at 881; *London and North Western Rly Co v Glyn* (supra) per Wightman J, at 662.

16 Marine Insurance Act 1906, s 86; *Routh v Thompson* (1811) 13 East 274 (marine insurance); *Hagedorn v Oliverson* (1814) 2 M & S 485 (marine insurance); *Williams v North China Insurance Co* (1876) 1 CPD 757, CA.

17 *Waters v Monarch Fire and Life Assurance Co* (supra) per Lord Campbell CJ, at 881.

18 *The Cairnsmore, The Gunda* [1921] 1 AC 439 at 441, PC (prize).

19 *London and North-Western Rly Co v Glyn* (supra) per Erle J, at 262.

20 *Waters v Monarch Fire and Life Assurance Co* (supra), where the bailees were warehousemen; *London and North-Western Rly Co v Glyn* (supra), where the bailees were carriers, but were protected by the Carriers Act 1830, s 1.

21 *Waters v Monarch Fire and Life Assurance Co* (supra; *London and North-Western Rly Co v Glyn* (supra); *Castellain v Preston* (1883) 11 QBD 380, CA, per Bowen LJ, at 398; *Yangtze Insurance Association v Lukmanjee* [1918] AC 585, PC (marine insurance). But the intention must appear from the terms of the policy: *Hepburn v A Tomlinson (Hauliers) Ltd* [1966] 1 All ER 418 at 422–423 (per Lord Reid).

1 *Chambers v Phoenix Assurance Co* (1915) 34 NZLR 435, where the insurers charged premiums on the full value. In the case of an insurance by a mortgagee, the intention to cover the interests of the mortgagor is shown by an agreement to apply the policy moneys in discharge of his mortgage debt; *Nichols & Co v Scottish Union and National Insurance Co* (1885) 2 TLR 190, more fully reported 14 R (Ct of Sess) 1094.

the insurers,[2] unless there is a condition in the policy to that effect, but this view has now been held to be incorrect.[3]

ii Insurances by persons having no interest

A person, who has no interest in the subject-matter of insurance and who is not even in possession of it, may nevertheless insure it on behalf of its owner or some other person interested in it. In this case it has been held that ratification cannot take place after the principal has heard of the loss, and that he cannot therefore enforce the policy.[4]

4 Where the policy covers persons other than the assured

A policy of insurance may contain a stipulation extending its protection to a

---

2 See *Rayner v Preston* (1881) 18 ChD 1, CA, per Brett LJ, at 10. In the case of bailees, the present form of the policy requires disclosure; in the case of limited owners and the like, it is not usual to make disclosure.

3 *Hepburn v A Tomlinson (Hauliers) Ltd* [1966] 1 All ER 418, HL (goods in transit insurance) per Lord Reid, at 422–423.

4 *Grover & Grover Ltd v Mathews* [1910] 2 KB 401 (fire insurance) per Hamilton J, at 404: 'It appears to me that the judgments in *Williams v North China Insurance Co* (1876) 1 CPD 757 (marine insurance), which is a decision of the Court of Appeal, compel me to say that it was too late for ratification; because, as it appears to me, the Court of Appeal recognised that a rule which permits a principal to ratify an insurance even after the loss was known to him was an anomalous rule which it was not, for business reasons, desirable to extend, and which, according to the authorities, had existed only in connection with marine insurance. No case has been cited to me which suggests that this anomalous rule ought to be extended to fire insurance'. It is thought, however, that this ruling may have been given per incuriam. In the first place, the decision in *Williams v North China Insurance Co* appears to have turned on another point. All the Judges of the Court agreed that ratification of the loss in question was valid and no criticism was passed on the rule. Indeed, Pollock B, at 770 said: 'As a question of mercantile convenience, I think it very desirable that ratification of an insurance under such circumstances should be permissible'. Secondly, the attention of Hamilton J was not drawn to *Waters v Monarch Fire and Life Assurance Co* (1856) 5 E & B 870, in which case the Court accepted without hesitation the marine rule of ratification as applying in fire insurance. It is true that that case dealt with an insurance by a bailee, and not by a mere agent, but in so far as he insured on behalf of the owners of the goods, he insured as agent, and, as he insured without authority, his act required ratification. In referring to the question of ratification, Lord Campbell CJ, at 881, said: 'The authorities are clear that an insurance made without orders may be ratified.' This cannot be regarded as a mere dictum, since the assured's right to recover the full sum insured depended upon the principle here laid down. Nor can it be said that Lord Campbell was dealing only with the case of bailees who had themselves an interest in the subject-matter: on the contrary, it is evident that he was here laying down a general principle and applying the marine rule to fire insurance. The authorities to which he was referring were presumably those cited in argument, namely, *Routh v Thompson* (1811) 13 East 274 (marine insurance), and *Hagedorn v Oliverson* (1814) 2 M & F 485 (marine insurance), in neither of which does it appear that the agent himself had any interest, and both of which were cases of ratification after loss. It is therefore possible that, if *Waters v Monarch Fire and Life Assurance Co* (supra) had been cited in *Grover & Grover Ltd v Mathews,* the decision might have been different. Support for this argument may be found in *Graham v Western Australian Insurance Co Ltd* (1931) 40 LlL Rep 64 (reinsurance) per Roche J, at 67: 'I can only say that, of course, I accept Mr Justice Hamilton's decision, but it is on an entirely different point, it throws no light on this question, in my judgment, whatsoever, and there is no such principle that parties cannot agree that an insurance shall cover risks to be declared, and that in proper cases these risks should include risks as to which the fire has already happened before the declaration is made'. See further, *Mackie v European Assurance Society* (1869) 21 LT 102, and *Giffard v Queens Insurance Co* (1869) 12 NBR 432, in both of which cases the assured intended to insure with a particular company through its agent, and did not discover, until after the loss, that the agent had insured with a different company.

class of persons who are not named, but designated in the policy in general terms.

Thus, a burglary policy issued in respect of a private house may cover the property of all persons residing in the house in question including the members of the assured's family, domestic servants and visitors, whilst a motor vehicle policy may insure relatives or friends[5] of the assured or members of his household,[6] against personal injuries sustained or liability to third parties incurred by such persons while driving the insured's car. So far as motor vehicle insurance is concerned, the existence of such a stipulation has been recognised by statute,[7] and no question of its legality can arise within the limits of the statutory recognition.

In the case of a burglary policy, however, or of a policy covering liability for damage to property, in respect of which no statutory provision has been made, it is necessary to consider how far such a stipulation is valid. The assured has no insurable interest in the private and exclusive property of the individual members of his family[8] or of his guests; nor is he concerned with the liability arising out of an accident for which a relative or friend is alone legally responsible.

In neither case is there any loss personal to the assured against which he requires an indemnity and the policy is enforceable, if at all, for the benefit of the person who has actually sustained the loss or incurred the liability and who alone requires indemnity. The validity of this kind of insurance appears to depend on ratification. It is analogous to an insurance on behalf of those whom it may concern; the assured in whose name the policy stands is to be regarded as an agent effecting insurance on behalf of the persons falling within the description in the policy.[9]

If, therefore, as will probably be the case, the insurance is unauthorised, it will have to be ratified by the person concerned; and if the ratification takes place before loss, there is no reason why the policy should not be enforced for his

---

5 A person may be a 'friend' within the meaning of such a provision, though not on terms of social equality: *Pailor v Cooperative Insurance Society Ltd* (1930) 38 LlL Rep 237, CA.

6 *English v Western* [1940] 2 KB 156, [1940] 2 All ER 515, 67 LlL Rep 45, CA.

7 Road Traffic Act 1972, s 145(3), (4).

8 But in *Goulstone v Royal Insurance Co* (1858) 1 F & F 276 a husband was held to have an insurable interest in furniture belonging to his wife. See also, *Griffiths v Fleming* [1909] 1 KB 805 at 815 (per Vaughan Williams LJ) as to the wife's insurable interest in her husband's property; *Patterson v Central Canada Insurance Co* (1910) 15 WLR 123, where the husband claimed in respect of his wife's furs, and wearing apparel; *Muldover v Norwich Union Fire Insurance Co* (1917) 40 OLR 532, where the insurance was held to cover the property of the assured's parents and brothers and sisters all living in the same house.

9 *Ferguson v Aberdeen Parish Council* 1916 SC 715; cf *Williams v Baltic Insurance Association of London Ltd* [1924] 2 KB 282, 19 LlL Rep 126 (motor insurance), where there was ratification before loss. It may be contended, however, that an insurance of this kind contemplates the possibility of a loss before ratification; see *Williams v North China Insurance Co* (1876) 1 CPD 757, CA (marine insurance) per Cockburn CJ, at 764. In *Re Lambert, Public Trustee v Lambert* (1916) 114 LT 453 (accident insurance) Eve J assumed that under a newspaper coupon insurance purporting to include the wife of a subscriber in the benefit of the insurance, the insurance money would be payable to the wife, if an accident happened to her. See also *Vandepitte v Preferred Accident Insurance Corpn of New York* [1933] AC 70, PC (accident insurance). The difficulty was removed as regard war damage insurance by s 66 of the War Damage Act 1941, which expressly legalised the insurances of private chattels of a member of the assured's household or a domestic servant, even if the assured had no insurable interest.

benefit.[10] If, however, the insurance is not ratified till after the loss, the ratification will be too late, and he will, therefore, be unable to recover.[11]

The policy may be enforced either by the assured as trustee for the person entitled to benefit[12] or by such person himself.[13]

C KNOWLEDGE OF THE PRINCIPAL OR OF THE AGENT[14]

Though a transaction carried out through an agent is, in contemplation of law, the transaction of the principal, it is nevertheless, in point of fact, carried out by a person other than the principal. It may, therefore, happen that facts material to the transaction are known to the one and not known to the other, in which case the question arises how far the knowledge of the one is to be imputed to the other.

This question is of special importance in connection with the discharge of the duty of disclosure, though it arises at any stage of the contract, whenever notice or knowledge of a fact becomes material.[15] Thus, the insurers may be bound by notice of a breach of condition,[16] by notice of assignment,[17] by notice of loss,[18] or by the knowledge of any material communication[19] if received or acquired by their agent within the scope of his authority,[20] although the notice or

---

10 *Williams v Baltic Insurance Association of London Ltd* (supra).

11 *Ferguson v Aberdeen Parish Council* (supra) (fire insurance), where the policy purported to cover the property of servants, and it was held that an employee whose property had been burned could not recover from the assured any part of the amount paid by the insurers, such amount not, in fact, covering their own loss. It may be pointed out, however, that *Grover & Grover Ltd v Mathews* [1910] 2 KB 401 (fire insurance), whether it be correctly decided or not (see p 538, ante), was a case of an insurance on behalf of a particular insured, and it is therefore, strictly speaking, not precisely in point. The insurances in question relate to a class and it may be contended that they contemplate the possibility of ratification after loss, and thus fall within the reasoning of *Williams v North China Insurance Co* (1876) 1 CPD 757, CA (marine insurance) per Cockburn CJ, at 764.

12 *Williams v Baltic Insurance Association of London Ltd* (supra); *Gale v Motor Union Insurance Co* [1928] 1 KB 359.

13 In *Re Lambert, Public Trustee v Lambert* (1916) 114 LT 453, where a newspaper coupon insurance provided that the wife of a subscriber should be entitled to certain benefits, and the widow of the subscriber claimed the insurance money paid in respect of her husband's death, the Court held that her claim must fail as the provision in the coupon as to benefit did not entitle her to receive the insurance money as against her husband's personal representative, but was intended to give her the benefit of the same insurance as her husband; the right of the wife to enforce the coupon, though referred to in argument, was not dealt with in the judgment.

14 See generally, Bowstead op cit, pp 412–420; Powell op cit, pp 239–244.

15 *Marsden v City and County Assurance Co* (1866) LR 1 CP 232.

16 *Wing v Harvey* (1854) 5 De GM & G 265 (life insurance) distinguished in *Busteed v West of England Fire and Life Insurance Co* (1857) 5 IChR 553 life insurance). See generally, pp 284–299, ante.

17 *Gale v Lewis* (1846) 9 QB 730 (life insurance). See generally on assignment pp 324–330, ante.

18 *Marsden v City and County Assurance Co* (1866) LR 1 CP 232.

19 *Re Solvency Mutual Guarantee Society, Hawthorne's Case* (1862) 31 LJCh 625, where the assured gave notice to the agent of his refusal to renew the policy, (see pp 298–299, ante); *Kirkpatrick v South Australian Insurance Co* (1886) 11 App Cas 177, PC (fire insurance), where knowledge of a telegram undoubtedly received at the head office was imputed to the insurers, though the telegram was not forthcoming. Cf *General Accident, Fire and Life Assurance Co v Robertson* [1909] AC 404 per Lord Loreburn LC, at 411.

20 *Wilson v Salamandra Assurance Co of St Petersburg* (1903) 8 Com Cas 129 (marine insurance), where it was held that the knowledge of Lloyd's agents was not to be imputed to individual members of Lloyd's; *Re Hennessy* (1842) IR 5 Eq 259 (life insurance); *Smith v Excelsior Life*

communication never actually reached them. The policy may, however, contain a condition requiring notice to be given to the insurers themselves and not to an agent, in which case, notice to an agent is not sufficient,[1] unless actually transmitted to the insurers by the agent.[2]

1 Imputed knowledge in general

(a) Principal's knowledge imputed to agent

Third parties dealing with an agent are entitled to assume that the principal has communicated to his agent all facts within his knowledge which are material to the transaction which the agent is employed to carry out.[3] For the purposes of the transaction the knowledge of the principal is imputed to the agent, and the principal cannot rely on his agent's actual ignorance of the truth.[4]

(b) Agent's knowledge imputed to principal

Third parties are further entitled to assume that every agent employed by the principal has communicated or will communicate all material facts which have come to his knowledge in the course of his employment,[5] and which it is his duty to communicate to his principal.[6]

The knowledge of the agent in question is imputed to the principal, as from the time when it would have reached him if the agent had done his duty,[7] and the principal cannot rely upon his own ignorance.

This rule is, however, subject to the following limitations:

- i *The person whose knowledge is sought to be imputed to the principal must be acting as agent for the principal in the transaction in which the knowledge is material.*[8]
- ii *The agent must have actual knowledge of the fact in question at the time when such knowledge is relevant to the transaction.*

It is not sufficient that he possessed the knowledge at an earlier stage of the transaction, unless it was his duty to have retained the fact within his knowledge until it became material.[9]

Assurance Co (1912) 22 OWR 863 (life insurance), where the assured, to the knowledge of the local agent of the insurers, engaged in a prohibited employment, and it was held that the agent's knowledge was not to be imputed to the insurers. If the agent of the insurers in charge of the negotiations exceeds his authority by agreeing to issue a policy containing particular terms, and the insurers issue a policy containing different terms, there is no contract, and knowledge of the terms on which the assured intended to contract is not imputed to the insurers: *Fowler v Scottish Equitable Life Insurance Society and Ritchie* (1858) 28 LJCh 225 (life insurance).

1 *Re Williams and Lancashire and Yorkshire Accident Insurance Co's Arbitration* (1902) 19 TLR 82.

2 *Shiells v Scottish Assurance Corpn Ltd* 1889 16 R (Ct of Sess) 1014.

3 *Mackintosh v Marshall* (1843) 11 M & W 116 (marine insurance), where the instructions to the agent contained false information; *Bufe v Turner* (1815) 6 Taunt 338 (fire insurance), where the principal wrote to his agent instructing him to insure, but did not mention that a fire in an adjoining building had just been extinguished.

4 *Webster v Foster* (1795) 1 Esp 407 (marine insurance).

5 *Blackburn v Haslam* (1888) 21 QBD 144 (marine insurance) per Pollock B, at 153.

6 *Blackburn, Low & Co v Vigors* (1887) 12 App Cas 531 (marine insurance) per Lord Watson, at 541.

7 *Proudfoot v Montefiore* (1867) LR 2 QB 511 (marine insurance), where the information was sent by letter instead of by cable.

8 See pp 548–552, post.

9 See *Molyneux v Hawtrey* [1903] 2 KB 487, CA (lease).

iii *The agent must have acquired the knowledge in the course of his employment as agent and in pursuance of his duty to his principal.*

It is not sufficient that he acquired the knowledge before the employment began,[10] or in some other capacity,[11] unless it was his duty to place his knowledge, however acquired, at his principal's disposal.[12]

iv *The third person must not be aware at any material time that the agent has not, in fact, communicated or does not intend to communicate his knowledge to his principal.*[13]

2 Imputed knowledge in insurance transactions

The general principles set out above are of particular importance in insurance transactions. They may be conveniently considered under the following heads:

a In relation to the assured and his agent; and
b In relation to the insurers and their agent.

(a) In relation to the assured and his agent

The rules relating to imputed knowledge apply, in the case of the assured, for the most part during the negotiations leading up to the policy, and it is, therefore, necessary to consider how far they affect the duty of disclosure. They also apply at other stages of the insurance.

i Duty of disclosure

It is the duty of the agent,[14] as representing the proposed assured in the

---

[10] *Ballantine v Employers' Insurance Co of Great Britain* 1893 21 R (Ct of Sess) 305, where a demand for a post-mortem was addressed to the solicitors who afterwards acted in the action.

[11] *Tate v Hyslop* (1885) 15 QBD 368, CA (marine insurance), where notice of a material fact was given to the solicitor acting for the insurers; cf *Re Hennessy* (1842) IR 5 Eq 259 (life insurance), where the agent, whose knowledge of an assignment of the policy was sought to be imputed to the insurers, was himself the assignor.

[12] *Blackburn, Low & Co v Vigors* (supra) per Lord Halsbury C, at 539; *Gale v Lewis* (1846) 9 QB 730 (life insurance), distinguishing *Re Hennessy* (supra).

[13] Cf *Bawden v London, Edinburgh and Glasgow Assurance Co* [1892] 2 QB 534, CA, where the insured was illiterate and did not know that the proposal form had not been properly filled in, with *Biggar v Rock Life Assurance Co* [1902] 1 KB 516; and see 548, post.

[14] Including any person acting on the proposed assured's behalf and taking any part in the negotiations; *Fitzherbert v Mather* (1785) 1 Term Rep 12 (marine insurance). It will depend on the facts whether the statement is made by the agent in his capacity of agent of the assured or as the agent of the insurers. See *St Margaret's Trust Ltd v Navigators and General Insurance Co Ltd* (1949) 82 LlL Rep 752, (marine insurance), where the agent stated that the ketch was 'quite sound', and it was held that he had made this statement as the agent of the insurers. Morris J observed (at 765): 'In what capacity was Mr Walmisley giving his expression of opinion? It seems to me that he was doing so, as I have said, in his capacity as someone who was to get business for the defendant company; and he was giving them his view, based upon his knowledge as the owner for some weeks, and as the vendor; he was giving his view to the insurance company for whom he acted in regard to this craft. He had not been asked by [the assured] to express any opinion, and the insurance company by their proposal form had indicated the matters in regard to which they wanted the answers of [the assured]. [The assured] did not himself think that there was further information that it was material to disclose. In these circumstances, in my judgment, the defence that this policy is null and void because of a misstatement made by the agent of the assured, or someone acting for the assured, is not well-founded. It is quite obvious that many situations may arise, and each will have to be determined according to its own facts. If someone who is the general agent for an insurance company received a proposal form in regard to a motor car, and if

negotiations, to disclose to the insurers all material facts which are within his knowledge, however acquired,[15] or which ought to have come to his knowledge in the ordinary course of business.[16]

Any failure to discharge this duty, whether by non-disclosure or by misrepresentation, entitles the insurers to avoid the policy[17] as against the proposed assured, since he has delegated the duty of disclosure to his agent and is responsible for the manner in which it is performed.[18]

It is, therefore, immaterial whether the agent was guilty of an intentional concealment[19] or of fraud[20] or whether he did not disclose a particular fact because he honestly thought that it was not material,[1] or misrepresented it in the honest belief that what he stated was true.[2]

It is equally immaterial whether the proposed assured expressly instructed the agent to disclose the fact in question,[3] or whether he gave the agent general instructions to disclose all material facts and keep nothing back,[4] or whether he simply left everything to the agent, and did not know that he had not performed his duty.[5]

---

he wrote a covering letter, unknown to the proposer, setting out his view as to the motor car, it would have to be very carefully considered in each particular case whether what was said was said in the capacity of agent for the insurance company, or whether it was said in the capacity of agent for the proposer.'

15 *Blackburn, Low & Co v Vigors* (supra) per Lord Macnaghten at 542; *Bancroft v Heath* (1901) 6 Com Cas 137, CA. It is immaterial that the information was acquired in confidence: *Blackburn v Haslam* (supra).

16 *London General Insurance Co v General Marine Underwriter's Association* [1921] 1 KB 104, 4 LlL Rep 382 CA (marine insurance). See also, Marine Insurance Act 1906, s 19 '. . . Where an insurance is effected for the assured by an agent, the agent must disclose to the insurer—(a) every material circumstance which is known to himself, and an agent to insure is deemed to know every circumstance which in the ordinary course of business ought to be known, or to have been communicated to, him. . . .'. See further, Ivamy *Marine Insurance* (4th Edn, 1985) pp 41–44.

17 *Rozanes v Bowen* (1928) 32 LlL Rep 98, CA (jewellery insurance). Where there is no breach of duty, e g where the non-disclosure (*Court v Martineau* (1782) 3 Doug KB 161 (marine insurance)) or misrepresentation (*Flinn v Headlam* (1829) 9 B & C 693 (marine insurance)) is not, in the circumstances, material, the validity of the policy is not affected.

18 In *Blackburn, Low & Co v Vigors* (supra) (marine insurance) per Lord Macnaghten, at 543, takes the view that concealment by an agent is not a case of knowledge imputed to the principal, but a direct breach of duty on the part of the agent who is, equally with the principal, bound to disclose all material facts within his knowledge; cf SC (1886) 17 QBD 553, CA, per Lord Esher MR, at 559.

19 *Blackburn v Haslam* (1888) 21 QBD 144 (marine insurance).

20 *Hambrough v Mutual Life Insurance Co of New York* (1895) 72 LT 140, CA (life insurance).

1 *Krantz v Allan* (1921) 9 LlL Rep 410 (burglary insurance), where the agent made a bona fide mistake; *Rickards v Murdock* (1830) 10 B & C 527 (marine insurance); *Russell v Thornton* (1860) 6 H & N 140, ExCh (marine insurance); *Holland v Russell* (1863) 4 B & S 14, ExCh (marine insurance).

2 *Ionides v Pacific Insurance Co* (1872) LR 7 QB 517, ExCh (marine insurance); *Anderson v Pacific Fire and Marine Insurance Co* (1872) LR 7 CP 65 (marine insurance); *Bancroft v Heath* (1901) 6 Com Cas 137, CA (fire insurance).

3 *Gedge v Royal Exchange Assurance* [1900] 2 QB 214 (marine insurance).

4 *Seaton v Burnand* [1900] AC 135, where, however, in the circumstances, the policy was not avoided.

5 *Biggar v Rock Life Assurance Co* [1902] 1 KB 516, per Wright J, at 524, approved in *McMillan v Accident Insurance Co* 1907 SC 484 (accident insurance); *Life and Health Assurance Association Ltd v Yule* 1904 6 F (Ct of Sess) 437; cf *Russell v Thornton* (supra), where the assured sent a copy of a letter which he received during the negotiations, and which contained material facts to the agent, who did not communicate it to the insurers; *Evans v Ward* (1930) 37 LlL Rep 177 (motor insurance).

It is the duty of the proposed assured, since he appoints the agent to represent him in the negotiations and to perform the duty of disclousre on his behalf, to place the agent in possession of all the material facts which the proposed assured would have been bound to disclose to the insurers, if he himself had been conducting the negotiations.[6] An omission or mis-statement on the part of the agent which, if judged solely from the agent's state of knowledge, would have no effect on the validity of the policy may, when the proposed assured's knowledge is imputed to the agent, amount to non-disclosure[7] or misrepresentation[8] entitling the insurer to avoid the policy. It is immaterial whether the proposed assured neglected to communicate his knowledge to the agent because he did not think the knowledge material,[9] or whether he designedly employed an agent who was ignorant of the truth.[10]

It is equally immaterial that the proposed assured himself did not know the truth if, as between himself and the insurers, he should have known of it; and the doctrine of imputed knowledge may become applicable although neither the proposed assured nor the agent employed to effect the policy had any knowledge of the truth.

Where it is the duty of any agent in the employment of the proposed assured to obtain and communicate to the principal information relating to the subject-matter of insurance, the knowledge of the agent relative to the subject-matter is imputed to the principal.[11] Thus, an agent who is entrusted with the care and management of the subject-matter, is bound to keep the principal acquainted with its state and condition, and the insurers are entitled to assume that the agent has performed this duty.[12] If this duty is not performed, the insurer may avoid the policy, although the proposed assured himself did not know the truth, and, therefore, could not communicate it to the agent who actually negotiated the policy.[13]

---

6 *Vallance v Dewar* (1808) 1 Camp 503 (marine insurance) per Lord Ellenborough CJ, at 507: 'The rule is that the broker must communicate what is in the special knowledge of the assured.'

7 *Webster v Foster* (1795) 1 Esp 407 (marine insurance), where the insurers asked questions which the agent was unable to answer; *Gandy v Adelaide Insurance Co* (1871) LR 6 QB 746 (marine insurance), where, however, the jury found the fact, which had not been disclosed, to be immaterial; *Bufe v Turner* (1815) 6 Taunt 338 (fire insurance), where the assured, immediately after a fire on adjacent premises had been apparently extinguished, sent instructions by an extraordinary conveyance to his agent to effect an insurance, but omitted to mention the fire, which broke again and destroyed the assured's premises.

8 *Stribley v Imperial Marine Insurance Co* (1876) 1 QBD 507 (marine insurance).

9 *Bufe v Turner* (1815) 6 Taunt 338 (fire insurance) where the jury acquitted the assured of any fraud or dishonest design.

10 *Webster v Foster* (1795) 1 Esp 407 (marine insurance).

11 *Blackburn, Low & Co v Vigors* (1887) 12 App Cas 531 (marine insurance) per Lord Macnaghten, at 542: 'There is nothing unreasonable in imputing to a shipowner who effects an insurance on his vessel all the information with regard to his own property which the agent to whom the management of that property is committed possessed at the time and might in the ordinary course of things have communicated to his employer. In such a case it may be said without impropriety that the knowledge of the agent is the knowledge of the principal.'

12 *Proudfoot v Montefiore* (1867) LR 2 QB 511 (marine insurance) per Cockburn CJ, at 521, approved in *Blackburn, Low & Co v Vigors* (supra per Lord Halsbury C, at 537. See also ibid, per Lord Watson, at 541.

13 *Fitzherbert v Mather* (1785) 1 Term Rep 12 (marine insurance) where the agent sent information which was correct at the time, but could have sent another letter containing news that the ship was lost; *Gladstone v King* (1813) 1 M & S 35 (marine insurance), where the master, in writing to his owners, omitted to state that the ship had struck a rock; *Proudfoot v Montefiore* (supra) where

The knowledge of any particular agent is only imputed to the proposed assured so far as it affects the transaction in which the agent is employed. Thus, the knowledge of an agent entrusted with the care or management of the subject-matter of insurance is imputed to the proposed assured in any negotiations for its insurance, since his employment is to take care of the subject-matter, and his knowledge of its state or condition equally concerns every proposed insurance.[14]

If, on the other hand, the agent whose knowledge is in question is employed to effect a particular insurance, his knowledge of the state or condition of the subject-matter is imputed to the proposed assured, not generally, but only in connection with such insurance.[15]

So far as the particular insurance is concerned, the employment of the agent need not continue until the policy is actually effected; if, during the negotiations, the principal takes the business out of the agent's hands, it is sufficient for him to continue the negotiations begun by the agent and avail himself of them by using and adopting what the agent had done, since there is one entire transaction and the contract is founded on negotiations which are tainted.[16]

The agent's knowledge, however, is not imputed to the proposed assured in transactions with which the agent had no concern.[17] Thus, a different insurance on the same subject-matter, effected through another agent who is ignorant of its state or condition, is valid if the first agent made no communication in fact to the proposed assured, who was, therefore, unacquainted with the truth at the time of the second insurance.[18]

Persons to whom the proposed assured refers the insurers for information are not necessarily his agents,[19] and their knowledge of the truth is not necessarily imputed to him so as to make him responsible for any inaccuracy in their statements.[20] The policy may, however, contain a condition by which the proposed assured warrants that their statements are true.[1]

---

the agent sent the information by letter instead of by telegram; *Blackburn, Low & Co v Vigors* (supra) per Lord Halsbury C, at 537; cf *Stewart v Dunlop* (1785) 4 Bro Parl Cas 483 (marine insurance) where the clerk to whom material information had to be given failed to inform his principal. The view taken in *Gladstone v King* (supra), followed in *Stribley v Imperial Marine Insurance Co* (1876) 1 QBD 507 (marine insurance), that the innocent non-communication of a material fact by the agent merely creates an exception from policy, cannot be regarded as correct; see *Blackburn, Low & Co v Vigors* (supra) per Lord Halsbury LC, at 536, and per Lord Watson, at 540.

14 *Blackburn, Low & Co v Vigors* (supra) per Lord Watson, at 541.

15 *Blackburn v Haslam* (1888) 21 QBD 144 (marine insurance) distinguishing *Blackburn, Low & Co v Vigors* (supra) (marine insurance).

16 *Blackburn v Haslam* (supra) per Pollock B, at 153.

17 *Blackburn, Low & Co v Vigors* (supra) per Lord Halsbury C, at 537, and per Lord Watson, at 540, explained in *Blackburn v Haslam* (supra) per Pollock B, at 153.

18 *Blackburn v Haslam* (supra).

19 In so far as they may be agents, they are merely agents for the purpose of giving the information required; for a failure to disclose material facts within their knowledge as to which no specific enquiry is made, the assured is not responsible: *Huckman v Fernie* (1838) 3 M & W 505 (life insurance).

20 *Wheelton v Hardisty* (1857) 8 E & B 232, ExCh (life insurance).

1 The earlier cases (*Maynard v Rhode* (1824) 1 C & P 360 (life insurance); *Morrison v Muspratt* (1827) 4 Bing 60 (life insurance); *Everett v Desborough* (1829) 5 Bing 503 (life insurance); *Rawlins v Desborough* (1840) 2 Mood & R 328 (life insurance)), in so far as they lay down the rule that persons referred to for information are, in giving such information, impliedly agents of the

ii Knowledge at other stages of the insurance

The doctrine of imputed knowledge applies equally at any other stage of the insurance at which knowledge of the particular facts may become material.

Thus, where a policy is applied for through an agent, the agent's knowledge of the terms of the policy is imputed to the assured, who cannot, therefore, object that the policy includes terms not contained in the proposal form.[2]

Similarly, where after loss, particulars of loss are furnished, such particulars are to be regarded as insufficient if it appears that, although his books have been destroyed, the assured could, nevertheless with the assistance of persons in his employment, have furnished a more detailed account;[3] and, if they are false to the knowledge of the person employed to prepare them, the assured, by adopting them and putting them forward, makes them his own, and the claim based upon them is, therefore, to be regarded as fraudulent.

(b) In relation to the insurers and their agent

In the case of the insurers, the doctrine of imputed knowledge may apply at any stage of the insurance.[4] The correct application of the doctrine, however, gives rise to questions of difficulty, particularly with reference to the discharge of the duty of disclosure, and to cases where the proposal form is filled in by their agent.

i Duty of disclosure

For the knowledge of the agent to be imputed to the insurance company it must be shown that:

a The agent was in fact the agent of the insurers

The onus of showing that he was their agent lies on the assured. Thus, the mere fact that the person in question has received a commission from the

---

assured, must be regarded as no longer authoritative; they may, however, be supported on the ground that the policies in question contained a stipulation that the truth of the statements made by the persons referred to should be the basis of the contract: *Wheelton v Hardisty* (supra) per Lord Campbell CJ, at 271 et seq, and per Pollock CB and Willes J, at 292.

2 *Sanderson v Cunningham* [1919] 2 IR 234, CA (fire insurance).

3 *Nixon v Queen Insurance Co* (1893) 23 SCR 26 (fire insurance).

4 E g as in *Evans v Employers' Mutual Insurance Association Ltd* (1935) 52 LlL Rep 51, CA (motor insurance), where the knowledge of a clerk entrusted with the job of comparing the proposal form with the claim form was imputed to the company. Greer LJ, observed (at 54):—'I think the knowledge of Mitchell [i e the clerk], to whom in the ordinary course of their business the Association entrusted the duty of comparing the claim forms with the proposal forms so as to ascertain whether there was any discrepancy between them, fixes the Association with the knowledge of that which came to the knowledge of Mr. Mitchell. . . . The Association are not entitled in law to say that they were not aware of the contents of documents such as the proposal form and the claim form, which at their request the claimant addressed to them. They must be treated as having received the information contained in these two documents, and they cannot be heard to say that they did not know their contents . . . If there be no evidence that the company has delegated the ascertainment of the relevant facts to some officer of the company, it may well be that nothing short of knowledge by the board of directors will bind the company . . . If it be established by evidence that the duty of investigating and ascertaining the facts has been delegated in the ordinary course of the company's business to a subordinate official, the company will in law be bound by his knowledge for the same reasons that they are affected by the knowledge of the board of directors.'

insurers in respect of the policy was held not to be sufficient to show that he was their agent.[5]

b The agent must have authority to acquire the knowledge

Thus, a disclosure to their solicitor, who is not concerned in the insurance, is not sufficient for the knowledge to be imputed to the insurers.[6]

Knowledge which he does not acquire in the course of his employment, but which he already possesses when his employment begins, such as, e g knowledge of a previous refusal acquired when he was acting for different insurers, is not imputed to them.[7]

If the proposed assured, or the agent conducting the negotiations on his behalf, makes a full and accurate disclosure of every material fact to the agent conducting the negotiations on behalf of the insurers, the duty of disclosure is performed.[8] The proposed assured has a right to expect that the agent will transmit to the insurers all that he has been told, and that the agent will do so accurately. He is, therefore, not responsible if the agent, by inadvertence, mistake or fraud, transmits an imperfect statement, whether by omitting to state some of the facts which he was told, or by mis-stating them.[9]

It is for the assured, however, to prove that he has made a sufficient disclosure, and that he is not in any way responsible for the imperfect or inaccurate statement.[10]

Though the insurers act on an imperfect statement which would avoid the policy if made by the proposed assured directly to them, it is the statement of their own agent, and its imperfection is due to an act for which they, and not the assured, must accept responsibility. The validity of the policy is therefore not affected.[11]

Knowledge of the facts which the agent has or ought to have ascertained in the course of his own investigations into the circumstances of the risk is imputed

---

5 *Bancroft v Heath* (1901) 6 Com Cas 137, CA; *Rozanes v Bowen* (1928) 32 LlL Rep 98, CA; *Equitable Life Assurance Society v General Accident Assurance Corpn* 1904 12 SLT 348; cf *Letts v Excess Insurance Co* (1916) 32 TLR 361, per Bailhache J, at 362.

6 *Tate v Hyslop* (1885) 15 QBD 368, CA (marine insurance). See also, *Wilkinson v General Accident Fire and Life Assurance Corpn Ltd* [1967] 2 Lloyd's Rep 182 (motor insurance), where the agent had aquired the knowledge of the sale of the insured car as a car dealer, and not as the agent of the insurance company.

7 *Taylor v Yorkshire Insurance Co* [1913] 2 IR 1; *O'Keefe v London and Edinburgh Insurance Co Ltd* [1928] NI 85, CA (fire insurance).

8 *Joel v Law Union and Crown Insurance Co* [1908] 2 KB 863, CA (life insurance).

9 *Parsons v Bignold* (1846) 15 LJCh 379 (life insurance), as explained in *Re Universal Non-Tariff Fire Insurance Co, Forbes & Co's Claim* (1875) LR 19 Eq 485 (fire insurance) per Malins V-C, at p 495; *Ayrey v British Legal and United Provident Assurance Co* [1918] 1 KB 136 (life insurance); *City of London Fire Insurance Co v Smith* (1887) 15 SCR 69 (fire insurance), where the word 'boards' in the agent's handwriting was read by the insurers as 'bricks', *Woolcott v Excess Insurance Co Ltd and Miles, Smith, Anderson & Game Ltd* [1978] 1 Lloyd's Rep 633 (fire insurance), where the brokers employed by the insurers failed to inform them of the insured's criminal record. But a new trial was subsequently ordered: [1979] 1 Lloyd's Rep 231, CA. At the new trial it was proved that the brokers knew of the criminal record and had failed to pass on this information to the insurers: *Woolcott v Excess Insurance Co Ltd and Miles, Smith, Anderson and Game Ltd (No 2)* [1979] 2 Lloyd's Rep 210. (See the judgment of Cantley J, ibid, at 216).

10 *Parsons v Bignold* (supra) (life insurance), where the assured failed to discharge the onus of proof.

11 The same principle applies where the proposed assured makes a mis-statement which he subsequently points out to the agent and corrects: *Golding v Royal London Auxiliary Insurance Co* (1914) 30 TLR 350 (fire insurance); cf *Ayrey v British Legal and United Provident Assurance Co* (supra) (life insurance).

to the insurers; and the proposed assured is not responsible for the agent's failure to bring such facts to their actual knowledge.[12]

c The agent was not guilty of a fraud on the insurers

Where the agent, acting in concert with the proposed assured, conceals or misrepresents any material facts within his knowledge or assists the proposed assured in concealing or misrepresenting them, his conduct is a fraud on the insurers and his knowledge of the truth is not imputed to them.[13]

ii Where the proposal form is filled in by the agent

a The present law

The application of the doctrine of imputed knowledge is considerably affected by the existence of a written proposal, signed by the proposed assured. It is then a condition precedent to the validity of the policy that all material facts stated in the proposal should be accurately stated.[14] If there is a mis-statement in the proposal but the agent is unaware of the true facts, the agent has no knowledge which can possibly be imputed to the insurers,[15] and the mere fact that he transmits the proposal to the insurers does not prevent the policy from being avoided.[16]

The agent may, however, know the truth, and he may even be responsible for the mis-statement. It not unfrequently happens in practice that the answers to the questions are filled in by the agent of the insurers and that the answers are inaccurate, and it then becomes necessary to inquire how far the fact that the answers, as they reach the insurers, are in the handwriting of their agent, affects the doctrine of imputed knowledge.

On this question two conflicting views have been held. According to the first view, which has been severely criticised,[17] the knowledge of the agent, acquired during the negotiations,[18] is imputed to the insurers, and the policy is

---

[12] *Bawden v London, Edinburgh and Glasgow Insurance Co* [1892] 2 QB 534, CA, as explained in *Newsholme Bros v Road Transport and General Insurance Co Ltd* [1929] 2 KB 356, 24 LlL Rep 247, CA (motor insurance); *Re Universal Non-Tariff Fire Insurance Co, Forbes & Co's* (supra) (fire insurance); *Pimm v Lewis* (1862) 2 F & F 778 (fire insurance).

[13] *Biggar v Rock Life Assurance Co* [1902] 1 KB 516 (accident insurance); *Newsholme Bros v Road Transport and General Insurance Co* [1929] 2 KB 356, CA (motor insurance) per Scrutton LJ, at 375; *Dunn v Ocean Accident and Guarantee Corpn Ltd* (1933) 50 TLR 32, 47 LlL Rep 129, CA (accident insurance); *Burnett v British Columbia Accident and Employers' Liability Co* (1914) 28 WLR 425.

[14] If the proposal is made the basis of the contract, the question of materiality does not arise, and all statements in the proposal must be true. See pp 161–164, ante.

[15] *Newsholme Bros v Road Transport and General Insurance Co* [1929] 2 KB 356, CA (motor insurance) per Scrutton LJ, at 376.

[16] *Parsons v Bignold* (1846) 15 LJCh 379 (life insurance). The same principle applies where the agent fills up the proposal, if he merely takes down what he is told: *Perrins v Marine etc Insurance Society* (1859) 2 E & E 317; *Davies v National Fire and Marine Insurance Co of New Zealand* [1891] AC 485, PC (fire insurance).

[17] See *M'Millan v Accident Insurance Co* 1907 SC 484 (accident insurance), following *Life and Health Assurance Association Ltd v Yule* 1904 6 F (Ct of Sess) 437 (liability insurance); *Taylor v Yorkshire Insurance Co* [1913] 2 IR 1 (livestock insurance).

[18] Knowledge which the agent acquired previously from other sources is not to be imputed: *O'Keefe v London and Edinburgh Insurance Co Ltd* [1928] NI 85, CA; *Taylor v Yorkshire Insurance Co* (supra).

accordingly valid, whether there was an omission[19] or mis-statement.[20] According to the second view, the agent's knowledge is not imputed to the insurers, and they are entitled to avoid the policy on the ground that the duty of disclosure has not been discharged.[21]

The second view, which has been accepted by the Court of Appeal,[1] is based on the principle that the proposal is the document on which the insurers act in deciding whether to accept or decline the insurance; it is the basis of the contract, and the validity of the policy depends on its accuracy. The insurers, therefore, are entitled to assume that it is accurate and the knowledge of any fact inconsistent with the proposal is not to be imputed to them merely because the person responsible for the inaccuracy knew the truth and happened to be the agent who introduced the insurance.[2] The agent,[3] in filling in the answers, ceases to be the agent of the insurers.[4] He becomes the agent of the proposed assured, and therefore his knowledge cannot be imputed to the insurers.

On the contrary, by signing the proposal,[5] the proposed assured adopts the

---

19 *Bawden v London, Edinburgh and Glasgow Assurance Co* [1892] 2 QB 534, CA (accident insurance), where the assured was illiterate and did not know that the omitted information was required, followed in *Hough v Guardian Fire and Life Assurance Co* (1902) 18 TLR 273, where, in the case of an insurance upon goods stored at a wharf, the agent filled in a proposal in the wharfinger's name, as arranged by the parties who believed that a policy in the wharfinger's name would cover the owner's interest, and the insurers were held, by reason of the agent's knowledge of the insurances, to be estopped from denying that the owner was not covered thereby, and in *Holdsworth v Lancashire and Yorkshire Insurance Co* (1907) 23 TLR 521 (accident insurance), where the agent described the assured in the proposal form as a joiner, although he was, to the agent's knowledge, a joiner and builder; see also, *Thornton-Smith v Motor Union Insurance Co* (1913) 30 TLR 139 (accident insurance); *Kaufmann v British Surety Insurance Co Ltd* (1929) 45 TLR 399, 33 LlL Rep 315 (accident insurance). In *Stone v Reliance Mutual Insurance Society Ltd* [1972] 1 Lloyd's Rep 469, CA (burglary insurance), Lord Denning MR said (ibid, at 475) that he thought that *Bawden v London, Edinburgh and Glasgow Assurance Co* (supra) was correctly decided, and that it would have been most unjust if the insurers had been allowed to repudiate liability.

20 *Brewster v National Life Insurance Society* (1892) 8 TLR 648, CA (life insurance); *Keeling v Pearl Assurance Co Ltd* (1923) 129 LT 573 (life insurance).

21 *Biggar v Rock Life Assurance Co* [1902] 1 KB 516 (accident insurance); see also, *Levy v Scottish Employers' Insurance Co* (1901) 17 TLR 229 (accident insurance); *Paxman v Union Assurance Society Ltd* (1923) 39 TLR 424, 15 LlL Rep 206 (accident insurance); *M'Millan v Accident Insurance Co* 1907 SC 484 (accident insurance); *Life and Health Assurance Association Ltd v Yule* 1904 6 F (Ct of Sess) 437 (liability insurance); *Taylor v Yorkshire Insurance Co* [1913] 2 IR 1 (livestock insurance).

1 *Newsholme Bros v Road Transport and General Insurance Co* [1929] 2 KB 356, 24 LlL Rep 247, CA (accident insurance), where the cases are reviewed, followed in *Dunn v Ocean Accident and Guarantee Corpn Ltd* (1933) 50 TLR 32, 47 LlL Rep 129, CA (accident insurance) and in *Facer v Vehicle and General Insurance Co Ltd* [1965] 1 Lloyd's Rep 113, QB (motor insurance).

2 The position might be different if the person knowing the truth had authority to make the contract: see *Newsholme Brothers v Road Transport and General Insurance Co* (supra) per Scrutton LJ, at 374; and cf *Ayrey v British Legal and Provident Assurance Co* [1918] 1 KB 136 (life insurance).

3 The same principle applies where the proposal form is filled in by a sub-agent of the insurance company: *Facer v Vehicle and General Insurance Co Ltd* (supra) (motor insurance).

4 But see *Stone v Reliance Mutual Insurance Society Ltd* [1972] 1 Lloyd's Rep 469, CA (burglary insurance), where it was held that the agent who had mistakenly stated in the proposal form that no previous policy had lapsed and that no previous loss had been sustained, was held to be the insurers' agent in spite of a declaration made by the proposer that the agent was his agent. Megaw LJ (ibid, at 475), and Stamp LJ (ibid, at 477) both stressed the point that the case turned on its own special facts.

5 If the only proposal produced is not signed or authorised by the proposed assured, the insurers cannot rely upon its inaccuracy: *Pearl Life Assurance Co v Johnson* [1909] 2 KB 288 (life insurance).

answers as his own,[6] and makes himself responsible for any inaccuracy in them.[7] The particular circumstances in which he came to sign the proposal are to be disregarded. He may expressly approve the answers before signing the proposal;[8] or he may choose to sign it without reading them[9] or pointing out any incomplete or inaccurate answer.[10] It is, however, immaterial whether he has had the opportunity of reading them or not; if he signs the proposal before completion and leaves it to the agent to fill in the answers and forward the completed proposal to the insurers, he is none the less responsible for any inaccuracy.[11]

The circumstances in which the inaccuracy arose are equally to be disregarded. The proposed assured may have given the agent the correct information, and the agent, in filling the answers, may have forgotten or misunderstood it;[12] or the agent may have filled up the answers without asking any questions, believing that he was acquainted with the truth.[13]

Even the fact that the statements in the proposal are a mere invention of the agent does not absolve the proposed assured from responsibility or preclude the insurers from relying upon their inaccuracy.[14]

Different considerations apply where the proposal, as filled up by the agent, contains no false statements, but the insurers seek to avoid the policy on the ground that some further fact ought to have been disclosed. In this case, the basis of the contract, so far as it rests upon the proposal, is not affected. If the fact has been disclosed to the agent by the proposed assured, or has otherwise come to the agent's knowledge in the course of his employment, there does not seem to be any valid reason why the agent's knowledge should not be imputed to the insurers.

Though the agent, in filling up the proposal, may go outside the scope of his authority and become for that purpose the agent of the proposed assured, he remains for all the purposes of his employment the agent of the insurers. The

---

6 *Rokkyer v Australian Alliance Assurance Co* (1908) 28 NZLR 305 (life insurance).

7 He will, therefore, have a right of action against the agent for negligence or breach of duty in filling up the answers inaccurately: *Connors v London and Provincial Assurance Co* [1913] WC & Ins Rep 408 (life insurance). See pp 516–519, ante.

8 *Quin v National Assurance Co* (1839) Jo & Car 316 (fire insurance) per Joy CB, at 341.

9 The Court presumes that he has read them: *New York Life Insurance Co v Fletcher* (1886) 117 US 519 (life insurance), approved in *Biggar v Rock Life Assurance Co* [1902] 1 KB 516, and in *Taylor v Yorkshire Insurance Co* (supra). In *Facer v Vehicle and General Insurance Co Ltd* [1965] 1 Lloyd's Rep 113, QB (motor insurance) the Court expressly found that the insured had not read the proposal form.

10 *Newsholme Bros v Road Transport and General Insurance Co* (supra). If he points out the inaccuracy and corrects it, the insurers cannot rely upon the original inaccuracy; *Golding v Royal London Auxiliary Insurance Co Ltd* (1914) 30 TLR 350 (fire insurance); cf *Holdsworth v Lancashire and Yorkshire Insurance Co* (1907) 23 TLR 521.

11 *Parsons v Bignold* (1846) 15 LJCh 379 (life insurance); *Connors v London and Provincial Insurance Co* (supra) (life insurance); *Billington v Provincial Insurance Co* (1879) 3 SCR 182, where the assured signed a proposal form, the agent promising to fill in the amount of an existing insurance, which he failed to do; *Re Samson and Atlas Insurance Co Ltd* (1909) 28 NZLR 1035, where the proposal form was filled in by a clerk of the insurers, but there was no evidence that he was their agent for any purpose connected with the insurance.

12 *Newsholme Bros v Road Transport and General Insurance Co* (supra); *M'Millan v Accident Insurance Co* (supra).

13 *Life and Health Assurance Association Ltd v Yule* 1904 6 F (Ct of Sess) 437.

14 *Biggar v Rock Life Assurance Co* (supra), approved in *Newsholme Bros v Road Transport and General Insurance Co* (supra). See also *Phoenix Assurance Co Ltd v Berechree* (1906) 3 CLR 946.

proposed assured is entitled to assume that the agent knows what ought to be stated and what may be omitted, and it is submitted that the proposed assured is not responsible for the agent's failure to pass on the information to the insurers, notwithstanding the fact that the proposal has been filled up by the agent.

Thus, if the proposal omits to state the fact that the proposed assured has only one eye,[15] or carries on another business as well as the business described in the proposal,[16] knowledge of the fact is to be imputed to the insurers, provided that the proposed assured is not personally responsible for any breach of the duty of disclosure and the omission to state it is solely the fault of the agent.

The same considerations may apply where, though there is a mis-statement in the proposal, it is not one which ought to have been detected by the proposed assured if he had read the answers carefully, but relates to a matter upon which he is entitled to seek guidance from the agent as representing the insurers. In this case, he does not know and has no reason to suspect that the statement is inaccurate: he signs the proposal in reliance on the agent's accuracy. The mis-statement is not merely a mis-statement made by the agent in filling up the proposal; it is a mistake in a matter falling within the scope of his duty to the insurers.[17] Thus, if the assured is in doubt as to the description of the property proposed to be insured, he may reasonably ask the agent to inspect it, and it is difficult to see why he is not entitled to assume that the description, as inserted in the proposal, is accurate.[18]

For the purpose of preventing any difficulty, the policy may contain a condition that the rights of the insurers as regards non-disclosure or misrepresentation are not to be affected by any knowledge of or notice to their agent unless communicated to the insurers and acknowledged by them in writing.[19] The condition may also state that the agent in filling in the proposal form or otherwise is to be deemed to be agent of the assured[20] and not of the

---

15 *Bawden v London, Edinburgh and Glasgow Assurance Co* [1892] 2 QB 534, CA (accident insurance).

16 *Holdsworth v Lancashire and Yorkshire Insurance Co* (1907) 23 TLR 521.

17 In *Perry v British General Insurance Co* (24 January 1923, unreported) the agent who was told that the proposed assured had paid £325 for his car and had spent £125 on repairs, advised him to insert £450 in the proposal as the cash price and it was held that the agent's knowledge was to be imputed to the insurers. There appears to be no reason why the decision should have been different if, instead of dictating the answer, the agent had written it out himself: cf *Splents v Lefevre* (1864) 11 LT 114, ExCh (life insurance), where there was a misrepresentation as to the age of the life insured, and the insurers were held bound on the ground that the assured had himself no personal knowledge, but signed the proposal in the belief that the agent knew the age and had inserted it correctly. There is the difficulty that the proposed assured warrants the truth of the statements in the proposal; but he does not warrant the agent's infallibility. See further, *Drysdale v Union Fire Insurance Co* (1890) 8 SC 63, where the agent, after inspecting the property, did not correctly describe it in the proposal, and the assured signed the proposal in reliance on the agent's correctness, and without intentional non-disclosure; *Mahomed v Anchor Fire and Marine Insurance Co* (1913) 48 SCR 546, where the details were filled in by the district manager after the property had been inspected both by himself and by his agent; cf *Dawsons Ltd v Bonnin*, [1922] 2 AC 413 per Lord Finlay, at 427.

18 *Drysdale v Union Fire Insurance Co* (supra); *Mahomed v Anchor Fire and Marine Insurance Co* (supra).

19 *M'Millan v Accident Insurance Co* 1907 SC 484 (accident insurance); *Life and Health Assurance Association Ltd v Yule* 1904 6 F (Ct of Sess) 437; *Billington v Provincial Insurance Co* (1879) 3 SCR 182; *Peck v Agricultural Insurance Co* (1890) 19 OR 494; cf *Levy v Scottish Employers' Insurance Co* (1901) 17 TLR 229.

20 But the condition may expressly provide that for certain acts of the agent the company will be responsible: *Hastings Mutual Fire Insurance Co v Shannon* (1878) 2 SCR 394, where it was provided that the company was responsible for all surveys made by the agent personally, followed in *Quinlan v Union Fire Insurance Co* (1883) 8 AR 376.

insurers.[1] Under such a condition a full disclosure to the agent is not a disclosure to the insurers, and the assured cannot rely on the knowledge of the agent as making good the deficiencies in the proposal.[2] If, however, the agent transmits to the insurers the information which he has received, the insurers have actual knowledge, and there may be a sufficient compliance with the condition, according to the language in which it is framed.[3] In the case of such a condition it is necessary that it should expressly refer to the agent of the insurers, otherwise his knowledge will be imputed to his principals.[4]

b Fifth Report of Law Reform Committee

In January 1957 the Law Reform Committee stated in their Fifth Report[5]

---

1 *Kelly v London and Staffordshire Fire Insurance Co* (1883) Cab & El 47 (fire insurance), where the condition provided that any person procuring the insurance was to be deemed the agent of the assured, and not of the company, in any circumstances whatever or in any transactions relating to the insurance, and it was held that the condition was intended to prevent the insurers from being bound by the agent's representations; *Johnstone v Niagara District Mutual Insurance Co* (1863) 13 CP 331, where the policy was held invalid on the ground of the non-disclosure of the mortgage though the agent knew of its existence and the insurers subsequently assented to the assignment of the policy to the mortgagee, in the belief that the mortgage was subsequent to the policy; *Bleakley v Niagara District Mutual Insurance Co* (1869) 16 Gr 198, where it was held that the applicant was bound by a false statement contained in the application, although such a statement was inserted by the agent and was the answer to a question never put to the applicant by him; *Sowden v Standard Fire Insurance Co* (1880) 5 AR 290, where the assured signed a blank proposal form and gave it to the agent to fill in after inspecting the building; see also, *Jumna Khan v Bankers and Traders Insurance Co Ltd* (1925) 37 CLR 451. But, in deciding what information is necessary, he is the agent of the insurer. *Naughter v Ottawa Agricultural Insurance Co* (1878) 43 UCR 121, where the agent told the assured that a certain mortgage was not worth mentioning, and himself stated in answer to question as to incumbrances that there were none; *Benson v Ottawa Agricultural Insurance Co* (1877) 42 UCR 282, where the agent told the assured that it was unnecessary, in answer to a question in the proposal as to neighbouring buildings, to state that there was a blacksmith's shop within 86 feet of the building to be insured; *Facer v Vehicle and General Insurance Co Ltd* [1965] 1 Lloyd's Rep 113, QB (motor insurance), where the proposal form signed by the insured stated: 'I . . . further agree that if this Proposal in any particular is filled in by any other person, such person shall be deemed my agent and not the agent of the Company'; *Stone v Reliance Mutual Insurance Society Ltd* [1972] 1 Lloyd's Rep 469, CA (burglary insurance), where the insured had signed a declaration in the proposal form stating that 'in so far as any part of this proposal is not written by me the person who had written same has done so by my instructions and as my agent for that purpose', but it was held that the insurers could not rely on this declaration in order to repudiate liability on the ground that the insured had not disclosed material facts, for he had completed the proposal form for the insured on their instructions (see the judgment of Lord Denning MR, ibid, at 475, and that of Megaw LJ, ibid, at 476).

2 *Life and Health Assurance Association Ltd v Yule* 1904 6 F (Ct of Sess) 437; *M'Millan v Accident Insurance Co* 1907 SC 484; cf *Shiells v Scottish Assurance Corpn Ltd* 1889 16 R (Ct of Sess) 1014 per Lord MacDonald, at 1020; *Re Williams and Lancashire and Yorkshire Accident Insurance Co's Arbitration* (1902) 19 TLR 82, where notice of a claim was given to the agent.

3 *Ayrey v British Legal and United Provident Assurance Co* [1918] 1 KB 136 (life insurance), where the information was transmitted to the District Manager of the insurers, and it was held that this was sufficient, as the condition did not make it necessary to give the information direct to the head office; cf *Shiells v Scottish Assurance Corpn* (supra), where notice of loss was given to an agent, who transmitted it to the head office of the insurers.

4 *Gallagher v United Insurance Co* (1893) 19 VLR 228, where the condition provided that 'any person other than the assured who may have procured the insurance shall be deemed to be the agent of the assured, and not of the company under any circumstances whatsoever in any transaction relating to the insurance', and it was held not to apply where 'the person other than the assured' was in fact the authorised agent of the insurers.

5 *Conditions and Exceptions in Insurance Policies,* 1957, Cmnd 62.

that the result of the present position as set out above was that insurers could repudiate liability because an agent had been allowed by the proposer to fill up the proposal form, and had carelessly or deliberately falsified therein the oral information given to him by the proposer.[6]

The Committee recommended that 'any person who solicits or negotiates a contract of insurance shall be deemed, for the purpose of the formation of the contract, to be the agent of the insurers, and that the knowledge of such person shall be deemed to be the knowledge of the insurers.'[7]

---

6 Para 7.
7 Para 14.

CHAPTER 52

The relationship between the agent and third parties

Where an agent contracts for a principal he has certain rights and liabilities under the contract which he has made. If he had no authority to enter into the contract, he may be sued by the third party for breach of warranty of authority. In some cases he may be liable in tort to the third party.

A RIGHTS AND LIABILITIES UNDER THE CONTRACT

1 Where he acts for a named or unnamed principal

An agent cannot, as a general rule, enforce a contract which he has effected on behalf of a named principal or of a principal whose existence he has disclosed to the third party but whose name he has not given. Nor can he be made liable on the contract.[1] Thus, the agent of the insurers, through whom the policy is effected, cannot, therefore, as such, sue the assured for the payment of the premium.[2] Further, an agent who effects or issues a policy on behalf of a principal is not, as a general rule, personally liable for the premium or for the amount of the loss, as the case may be.[3]

Sometimes, however, the contract may be so worded that, even though the principal is disclosed, the agent may incur personal liability.[4] So also may the

[1] See generally, Bowstead op cit, pp 424–505; Powell op cit, pp 260–267.

[2] *Gray v Pearson* (1870) LR 5 CP 568 (marine insurance); *Evans v Hooper* (1875) 1 QBD 45, CA (marine insurance).

[3] See generally, *Lewis v Nicholson* (1852) 18 QB 503 (agency) per Lord Campbell CJ, at 511. As to personal liability by usage, see infra.

[4] E g as in *Bowers (Maghull) Ltd v Morton* (1940) 67 LlL Rep 1, CA (motor insurance), where the broker was held liable for the cost of the repairs because he had sent to the garage proprietors concerned a letter stating: 'With reference to the repairs you are carrying out to [the] car I shall be glad if you will release this car when the repairs are completed and obtain a satisfaction note from my insured and send same to me together with your account for the repairs when they will receive my immediate attention.' For cases in which agents of the insurers have rendered themselves liable upon bills of exchange, see *Jones v Jackson* (1870) 22 LT 828 (marine insurance); *Herald v Connah* (1876) 34 LT 885 (fire insurance); and cf *Pepper v Green* (1865) 2 Hem & M 478 (life insurance); *Pepper v Henzell* (1865) 2 Hem & M 486 (life insurance). For cases where the insurers had authorized a garage to carry out repairs to an insured car, and were held to have contracted as principals in the transaction and therefore personally liable for the cost, see *Cooter & Green Ltd v Tyrrell* [1962] 2 Lloyd's Rep 377, CA; *Godfrey Davis Ltd v Culling and Hecht* [1962] 2 Lloyd's Rep 349, CA; *Brown and Davis Ltd v Galbraith* [1972] 2 Lloyd's Rep 1, CA. In *Cooter & Green Ltd v Tyrrell* (supra) and *Godfrey Davis Ltd v Culling and Hecht* (supra) the Court of Appeal did not hold that there was no contract at all between the owner of the vehicle and the repairers: *Charnock v Liverpool Corpn* [1968] 3 All ER 473 at 476, CA (per Harman LJ). All that the Court of Appeal decided was that there was no liability on the part of the owner to

agent be personally liable by usage. Thus, by the usage of Lloyd's the broker is personally liable to the underwriter for the premium.[5] Similarly, the country broker and not his principal is liable to the Lloyd's broker.[6]

As far as marine insurance is concerned, the Marine Insurance Act 1906, s 53(1) provides:

> 'Unless otherwise agreed, where a marine policy is effected on behalf of the assured by a broker, the broker is directly responsible to the insurer for the premium . . .'

2 Where he acts for an undisclosed principal

Where he contracts on behalf of an undisclosed principal, the position is different.[7] Thus, the agent of the assured may sue upon a policy which he has effected in his own name.[8] Again, the agent of the insurers may sue as holder of a negotiable instrument given in payment of the premium.[9] Further, an agent signing a policy in his own name without qualification or indication that it is signed by him as agent only on behalf of a principal, is personally liable on the policy.[10]

B LIABILITY FOR BREACH OF WARRANTY OF AUTHORITY

An agent effecting an unauthorised insurance, which the principal refuses or fails to ratify,[11] is not liable to the insurers for the premium.[12] But, if he has already paid it, he cannot recover it back, since the insurers have run the risk of the principal ratifying the insurance.[13]

It is, however, the duty of an agent to know his authority, and if the insurers

---

pay the repairers for the repairs which they had contracted with the insurers to do: ibid, at 476, 477 (per Harman LJ). See also the judgment of Salmon LJ, ibid, at 476, where he said: 'As I read those cases, they are no authority at all for the proposition that when a car owner who is insured takes his car into a garage and arranges with the garage to repair it at the insurers' expense, the garage is under no contractual liability to him to do the work carefully and skilfully and with reasonable expedition.' Further, in *Brown & Davis Ltd v Galbraith* (supra), it was held that there were two contracts with the repairers: (i) the contract with the insurers under which they became liable to pay; and (ii) one with the car owner under which he was entitled to have the work properly done. On the evidence, however, there was nothing from which it could be implied that the owner ever contracted to pay for the repairs (see the judgment of Cairns LJ, ibid, at 7, that of Buckley LJ, ibid, at 8, and that of Sachs LJ, ibid, at 9).

5 See pp 559–562, post.

6 *Holmwoods, Back and Mawson Ltd v Peel & Co* (1923) Times, 27 January.

7 See generally, Bowstead op cit, pp 312–325; Powell op cit, p 267.

8 *Sunderland Marine Insurance Co v Kearney* (1851) 16 QB 925 (marine insurance) per Lord Campbell CJ, at 939. In this case the insurers may rely on a defence available against the agent only, such as, e g payment by a settlement in account: *Gibson v Winter* (1833) 5 B & Ad 96 (marine insurance) per Lord Denman CJ, at 102.

9 See *Newcastle Fire Insurance Co v Macmorran & Co* (1815) 3 Dow 255, HL (fire insurance) per Lord Eldon LC, at 264; *Macdonald v Smaill* (1893) 25 NSR 440 (life insurance), where the agent was so described in the instrument.

10 *Re Arthur Average Association, ex p Cory and Hawksley* (1875) 32 LT 525 (marine insurance).

11 If it is ratified, the agent is in the same position as if he had had authority throughout. As to ratification, see pp 532–540, ante.

12 See *Lewis v Nicholson* (supra) (agency) per Lord Campbell CJ, at 511.

13 *Routh v Thompson* (1811) 15 East 274 (marine insurance) per Bayley J, at 290.

sustain any loss by reason of the unauthorised insurance, they will be entitled to sue the agent for breach of warranty of authority.[14]

The same principle applies where the agent of the insurers issues a policy without authority. In this case, the assured will be entitled in the event of a loss to recover from the agent the amount which would have been payable by the insurers if the policy had been valid.[15]

C LIABILITY IN TORT

A broker employed by the assured owes no duty of care or skill to the insurers to whom he offers an insurance; for these duties arise out of contract and are owed only to the principal by whom he is employed.[16]

Hence, no action lies against him at the suit of the insurers for failing to disclose a material fact[17] or for making an erroneous statement,[18] if it is clear that he honestly believed that the fact was not material or that it was true, as the case may be.

Where, on the other hand, he wilfully misrepresents a material fact, he is guilty of fraud and, therefore, liable to the insurers for the consequences.[19] Similarly, an agent of the insurance company who wilfully misrepresents the position of the company whereby the proposed assured is induced to effect an insurance with the company, is guilty of fraud and liable accordingly.[20]

Where the purchaser of a car asked the insurance brokers acting for the insurance company to arrange for the policy in respect of it to be transferred to him, and they forwarded the proposal form to the company, which refused to accept it, and cancelled the policy, the brokers were liable to him for damages for negligence because they had failed to inform him that he was not insured.[21]

---

14 See generally as to breach of warranty of authority, Bowstead op cit, pp 457–465; Powell op cit, pp 253–260; *Starkey v Bank of England* [1903] AC 114 (agency).

15 See *Firbank's Executors v Humphreys* (1886) 18 QBD 54, CA (agency); *Harris v McRobert* (1924) 19 LlL Rep 5, 135, HL (fire insurance), where the assured brought an action for damages for breach of warranty of authority against an agent, who had purported to alter the policy, and the agreement was repudiated by the insurance company.

16 *Glasgow Assurance Corpn Ltd v W Symondson & Co* (1911) 16 Com Cas 109 (marine insurance); cf *Empress Assurance Corpn Ltd v C T Bowring & Co Ltd* (1905) 11 Com Cas 107 (marine insurance), where the brokers, in declaring reinsurances risks under open covers, were alleged to have misstated the amounts of premiums charged by their principals, the reassured, and it was held that no action would lie against them at the suit of the reinsurers. But these cases were not followed by Hobhouse J in *General Accident Fire and Life Assurance Corpn v Tanter, The Zephyr* [1984] 1 Lloyd's Rep 58 (reinsurance), where it was held that the broker owed a duty of care to the insurers where there was an express signing down indication. His Lordship said (ibid, at 84) that he considered that they were no longer authoritative following the decision of the House of Lords in *Hedley, Byrne & Co Ltd v Heller & Partners Ltd* [1964] AC 465, [1963] 2 All ER 575, [1963] 1 Lloyd's Rep 485, HL.

17 *Holland v Russell* (1863) 4 B & S 14 (marine insurance) per Erle CJ, at 16; *Glasgow Assurance Corpn Ltd v W Symondson & Co* (supra) (marine insurance).

18 *Glasgow Assurance Corpn Ltd v W Symondson & Co* (supra) (marine insurance).

19 *Holland v Russell* (supra) (marine insurance) per Erle CJ, at 16.

20 *Pontifex v Bignold* (1841) 3 Man & G 63 (life insurance).

21 *Bromley London Borough Council v Ellis (A Luff & Sons, Third Parties)* [1971] 1 Lloyd's Rep 97, CA (motor insurance). See the judgment of Lord Denning MR, ibid, at 99; 'I know that the brokers were not [the purchaser's] agents. They were agents for the insurance company; but nevertheless, they were also under a duty to use reasonable care to [the purchaser]. He had asked them to arrange the transfer of the insurance. They had undertaken the duty of arranging the transfer. They had taken the proposal form from him and got it filled in. They were clearly under a duty to arrange the transfer with reasonable care so as to see that he was protected.'

CHAPTER 53

The course of business at Lloyd's

Insurances of all kinds[1] are effected at Lloyd's, and in relation to the law of agency it is of particular importance to notice that the course of business is mainly regulated by usage.

Though a usage binds the members of Lloyd's in their dealings with each other, it does not necessarily bind the assured. A usage which adversely affects his position is unreasonable and does not bind him, unless he is shown to be cognisant of it and to have assented to it.[2] He may expressly authorise dealings to be concluded on his behalf in accordance with the usage,[3] or he may adopt them afterwards;[4] and a general knowledge and assent may be presumed from the fact that he is in the habit of dealing at Lloyd's.[5]

A THE CLASSES OF MEMBERS AT LLOYD'S

There are two classes of members at Lloyd's:

(1) Underwriters who undertake liability upon contract of insurance;[6] and

---

1 *Seaton v Burnand* [1900] AC 135 per Lord Halsbury LC, at 140; *Saqui and Lawrence v Stearns* [1911] 1 KB 426, CA; *Tannenbaum & Co v Heath* [1908] 1 KB 1032, CA (fire insurance) per Lord Alverstone, CA, at 1035; *American Surety Co of New York v Wrightson* (1910) 16 Com Cas 37, where the Lloyd's policy covered also fire and burglary; *Wimble, Sons & Co v Rosenberg & Sons* [1913] 3 KB 743, CA (sale of goods) per Hamilton LJ, at 761; *London and Manchester Plate Glass Co v Heath* [1913] 3 KB 411, CA; *Nigel Gold Mining Co Ltd v Hoade* [1901] 2 KB 849, where there was a special stipulation that the policy was not to be regarded as a policy of sea insurance. See further, *London County Cycling and Athletic Club v Beck* (1897) 3 Com Cas 49 (insurance on receipts of cycling meetings); *T Dunn and W G Tarrant v Campbell* (1920) 4 LlL Rep 36, which was one of the first cases on aviation insurance.

2 *Legge v Byas, Mosley & Co* (1901) 7 Com Cas 16 per Walton J, at 19; *Sweeting v Pearce* (1861) 9 CBNS 534 (marine insurance); *Acme Wood Flooring Co v Marten* (1904) 9 Com Cas 157 (fire insurance) per Bruce J, at 162.

3 *Sweeting v Pearce* (supra) per Bramwell B, at 541.

4 *Russell v Bangley* (1821) 4 B & Ald 395 (marine insurance), where the assured was held not to have adopted them.

5 *Bartlett v Pentland* (1830) 10 B & C 760 (marine insurance) per Lord Tenterden CJ, at 770; *Stewart v Aberdein* (1838) 4 M & W 211 (marine insurance).

6 The fact that a Lloyd's underwriter makes default in the payment of a loss under a Lloyd's policy imposes no liability upon Lloyd's itself: *Industrial Guarantee Corpn v Lloyd's Corpn* (1924) 19 LlL Rep 78 (solvency insurance); see also, *Rozanes v Bowen* (1928) 32 LlL Rep 98, CA, where Scrutton LJ discussed the position of Lloyd's. Nor do either Lloyd's or a group of underwriters fall within the description of 'governors or directors' of insurance offices for the purposes of the Fires Prevention (Metropolis) Act 1774, s 83; *Portavon Cinema Co Ltd v Price and Century Insurance Co Ltd* [1939] 4 All ER 601 per Branson J, at 607. Where a person uses advertising material stating that his business procedures are insured by Lloyd's, the falsity of the claim does not affect any business of the Corporation of Lloyd's, but it does affect the business of all underwriters who are members of Lloyd's, and they can apply for an injunction to prevent him from doing so: *Scott v Tuff-Kote (Australia) Pty Ltd* [1976] 2 Lloyd's Rep 103, New South Wales, Supreme Court (Equity Division). (See the judgment of Needham J, ibid, at 108).

(2) Brokers who act as intermediaries between underwriters and persons wishing to effect insurances with them.[7]

Though partnerships between underwriters[8] are forbidden by usage, it is usual for underwriters to associate themselves for business purposes into 'syndicates'. One of the members of the 'syndicate' takes the active part in the business and is given authority to underwrite policies in the names of the other members of the syndicate, who are known as the 'names', and who do not themselves take any active part in the business.[9]

B THE NEED TO EMPLOY A BROKER

By the usage of Lloyd's, an underwriter does not do business directly with the general public, but only with a broker who is a member of Lloyd's, the underwriter and the broker dealing with each other as principals. A proposal for insurance cannot, therefore, be submitted to the underwriter by the proposed assured himself or by a broker who is not a member of Lloyd's; a Lloyd's broker must be employed for the purpose.

So far as the making of the contract is concerned, the proposed assured is bound by the usage and must employ a Lloyd's broker to act on his behalf, since the underwriter is entitled to prescribe the terms on which alone he is prepared to do business.

As soon as the contract is made, however, privity of contract is established between the underwriter and the assured, who may, if he thinks fit, disregard the usage in any matters arising subsequently under the contract, and deal directly with the underwriter.[10]

---

[7] See *Thompson v Adams* (1889) 23 QBD 361 (fire insurance); *Bancroft v Heath* (1901) 6 Com Cas 137 (fire insurance); *Grover & Grover Ltd v Mathews* [1910] 2 KB 401 (fire insurance). Sometimes there is an underwriting agent between the broker and the underwriters: *Glanvill, Enthoven & Co v IRC* (1924) 131 LT 818, CA (revenue). Neither the Lloyd's broker nor any person introducing the business to the Lloyd's broker is in any sense an agent of the underwriter, and his knowledge of a material fact is not to be imputed to the underwriter: *Rozanes v Bowen* (1928) 32 LlL Rep 98, CA (jewellery insurance); *General Accident, Fire and Life Assurance Corpn Ltd v Midland Bank Ltd* [1940] 2 KB 388 per Greene MR, at 418; *Anglo-African Merchants Ltd and Exmouth Clothing Co Ltd v Bayley* [1969] 1 Lloyd's Rep 268 (all risks insurance), where there were three brokers between the assured and the insurers. (See the judgment of Megaw J on this point, ibid, at 276.) For a case concerning disciplinary proceedings against a Lloyd's broker, see *Moran v Lloyd's* [1981] 1 Lloyd's Rep 423, CA, where it was held that the rules of natural justice had no application to a preliminary inquiry whether a charge was to be made, and that it was sufficient that those who were holding the preliminary inquiry should be honest men doing their best to come to a right decision. (See the judgment of Lord Denning MR, ibid, at 427).

[8] Cf *Aubert v Maze* (1801) 2 Bos & P 371 (marine insurance).

[9] *Thompson v Adams* (supra) per Mathew J at 362. As to the liability of the 'names', see *Hambro v Burnand* [1904] 2 KB 10, CA. As to the respective rights of the 'names' and the trustee in bankruptcy of the underwriter as regards the books of the trustee, see *Re Burnand, ex p Baker, Sutton & Co* [1904] 2 KB 68, CA (bankruptcy), where it was held that, the agency of the debtor having come to an end, the trustee had no right to the exclusive possession of the books, and that he was entitled to reasonable facilities for inspection and making extracts.

[10] *Dalzell v Mair* (1808) 1 Camp 532 (marine insurance), where the assured claimed a return of premium; *De Gaminde v Pigou* (1812) 4 Taunt 246 (marine insurance), where the assured claimed for a loss under the policy; *MacFarlane v Giannacopulo* (1858) 3 H & N 860 (marine insurance), where the assured had already applied to the broker for payment.

C THE RELATIONSHIP BETWEEN THE ASSURED, THE BROKER AND THE UNDERWRITER

As a broker who carries on his business at Lloyd's is in the habit of submitting the various 'slips'[11] which he may have put forward to the underwriters with whom he habitually does business, and as it would be inconvenient to treat each 'slip' as a separate transaction entered into between the underwriter and the particular assured, it is the practice for the underwriter and the broker to treat each other as principals.

In all matters relating to the placing of insurance the insurance broker is the agent of the assured, and of the assured only.[12]

Although it is the practice at Lloyd's,[13] when a claim arises under a policy, for the underwriters to instruct the broker who placed the insurance to obtain a report from loss adjusters as to the claim, and thus become the underwriters' agent for this purpose without being allowed to disclose the contents of the report to the assured, or to the assured's legal advisers, without the underwriters' express consent, the practice has not been upheld by the Courts.[14]

If an insurance broker, before he accepts instructions to place an insurance, discloses to his client that he wishes to act according to the above practice, and if the client, fully informed as to the broker's intention to accept such instructions from the insurers and as to the possible implications of such collaboration between his agent and the opposite party, is prepared to agree that the broker may so act, good and well. In the absence of such express and fully informed consent, it would be a breach of duty on the part of the insurance broker so to act.[15]

---

11 As to the nature and purpose of the 'slip', see generally, pp 116–118, ante.

12 *Anglo-African Merchants Ltd and Exmouth Clothing Co Ltd v Bayley* [1969] 1 Lloyd's Rep 268 (all risks insurance) per Megaw J, at 279, where his Lordship stated that he did not think that this proposition of law had ever been in doubt among lawyers, and said that he hoped that it was not in doubt among insurance brokers or insurers. See also *Rozanes v Bowen* (1928) 32 LlL Rep 98 at 101 (per Scrutton LJ).

13 And also in the non-Lloyd's insurance market: *Anglo-African Merchants Ltd and Exmouth Clothing Co Ltd v Bayley* (supra), at 279.

14 *Anglo-African Merchants Ltd and Exmouth Clothing Co Ltd v Bayley* (supra), at 279–280, where Megaw J cited with approval the words of Scrutton LJ in *Fullwood v Hurley* [1928] 1 KB 498, at 502: 'No agent who has accepted an employment from one principal can in law accept an engagement inconsistent with his duty to the first principal . . . unless he makes the fullest disclosure to each principal of his interest, and obtains the consent of each principal to the double employment . . .'; *North and South Trust Co v Berkeley* [1970] 2 Lloyd's Rep 467, QB (marine insurance), where Donaldson J (ibid, at 479) said that he regarded the practice of an underwriter using a broker as his agent in communicating with claims assessors 'as wholly unreasonable and therefore incapable of being a legal usage.'; *Eagle Star Insurance Co Ltd v Spratt* [1971] 2 Lloyd's Rep 116, CA, where Megaw LJ (ibid, at 130) criticized the brokers for acting both for the reassured and the reinsurers without the reassured's consent.

15 *Anglo-African Merchants Ltd and Exmouth Clothing Co Ltd v Bayley* (supra) at 280 (per Megaw J), where his Lordship observed (ibid, at 280): 'The potential dangers and undesirable consequences are obvious in any case, where, as here, an agent permits himself, without the express consent of his principal, to make a compact with the opposite party whereby he is supplied with information which he is, or may be, precluded from passing on to his principal. Such a relationship with the insurer inevitably, even if wrongly, invites suspicion that the broker is hunting with the hounds while running with the hare. It readily leads to consequences such as occurred in this case where a broker refused to comply with a proper request from his principal's solicitors, but sought, or accepted advice from the adverse party's solicitors as to how he should

Where the underwriters do employ the broker, who placed the insurance, to obtain the loss adjusters' report, the broker cannot be compelled by the insured to hand over the report to him.[16]

The underwriter looks to the broker for his premium,[17] and through the broker, as a rule, on the happening of a loss, he receives notice of any claim.

In the ordinary course of business it is likely that at any given moment there will be a considerable number of premiums due from the broker to the underwriter on new insurances, and at the same time there may be claims payable by the underwriter to the broker in respect of losses covered by existing policies. To make or to receive separate payments in respect of each transaction as the payments fall due would lead to an unnecessary amount of trouble. It is not, therefore, the practice of the broker to pay the premium on each insurance to the underwriter at the time when the 'slip' is initialled or the policy signed. All premiums as they fall due, and all claims as they become payable, are debited or credited as the case may be, in the books of both. The balance is struck quarterly, and a payment made of the sum shown to be due either to the broker or to the underwriter, as the case may be.

As regards any particular policy, however, the premium is treated by the broker and the underwriter as having been paid on the completion of the contract, and the policy contains a statement that the premium has been paid.

The assured is not, as a rule, liable for the premium to the underwriter, but only to the broker.[18]

As far as marine insurance is concerned, the Marine Insurance Act 1906, s 54 states:

> 'Where a marine policy effected on behalf of the assured by a broker acknowledges the receipt of the premium, such acknowledgement is, in the absence of fraud, conclusive as between the insurer and the assured, but not as between the insurer and broker.'

The underwriter cannot, therefore, repudiate liability under the policy as against the assured on the ground that has never received it from the broker;[19]

---

act vis-à-vis his principal. If the insurer desires to obtain an assessor's report, he can obtain it through some other channel than the assured's agent, the broker who has placed the insurance. If the insurer thinks it would be helpful in arriving at a fair settlement of a claim that the assured's broker should see the whole or part of the assessor's report, he can disclose it to the broker; but not in the absence of the express consent of the assured, subject to a condition that the agent shall withhold relevant information from his principal.'

16 *North and South Trust Co v Berkeley* (supra, where Donaldson J said (ibid, at 481); '[The brokers], in acting for the defendant, were undertaking duties which inhibited the proper performance of their duties towards the plaintiffs, but, in so far as they acted for the defendant underwriter, they were not acting in the discharge of any duty towards the plaintiffs. [The brokers] wore the plaintiffs' hat and the underwriter's hat side by side and in consequence, as was only to be expected, neither hat fitted properly. The plaintiffs had a legitimate complaint on this account and can claim damages if and to the extent that the partial dislodgment of their hat has caused them loss or damage. But what the plaintiffs ask in these proceedings is to be asked to see what [the brokers] were keeping under the underwriter's hat and for that there is no warrant.'

17 *Grover & Grover Ltd v Mathews* (1910) 15 Com Cas 249 (marine insurance) per Hamilton J, at 260.

18 *Power v Butcher* (1829) 10 B & C 329 (marine insurance) per Parke J, at 347; *Universo Insurance Co of Milan v Merchants' Marine Insurance Co* [1897] 2 QB 93, CA (marine insurance). The broker can sue the assured for the premium, even though he has not paid the underwriters: *Airy v Bland* (1774) 2 Park's Marine Insurance, 8th Edn, 811 (marine insurance); and, if he has paid it, he has a lien upon the policy, unless otherwise agreed: *Fisher v Smith* (1878) 4 App Cas 1 (marine insurance).

19 *Sweeting v Pearce* (1861) 9 CBNS 534 (marine insurance); cf *Thompson v Adams* (1889) 23 QBD 361 per Mathew J, at 363.

nor can he deduct it from the amount payable to the assured in respect of a loss.

On the other hand, the assured may, if he thinks fit, on the happening of a loss, make his claim on the underwriter direct without the intervention of a broker.[20]

Even where the claim is put forward through the broker, who is entrusted with the policy for this purpose, a settlement in account between him and the underwriter does not necessarily bind the assured.[21] The possession of the policy is, indeed, evidence of the broker's authority to act in all matters relating to the claim on the assured's behalf.[22] But, so far as the receipt of payment is concerned, his authority, even when accompanied by the possession of the policy, does not justify him in receiving payment otherwise than in money.[23]

The usage of Lloyd's by which a settlement of accounts is, as between the broker and the underwriter, regarded as a payment is an unreasonable usage and does not bind the assured or discharge the underwriter from his liabilities on the policy, unless it is shown that the assured was aware of the usage.[24]

The assured, however, is bound by the settlement in account where he expressly authorises the broker to receive payment of the loss by a settlement in this way,[25] and where the broker's authority to receive payment by a settlement is to be implied from the fact that he is employed by a person who is acquainted with the usage.[1]

He is also bound where he ratifies the payment, as, for instance, by calling

---

20 *De Gaminde v Pigou* (1812) 4 Taunt 246 (marine insurance) per Mansfield CJ, at 248.

21 But the assured may, after the settlement, sue the broker for the amount of his loss, and the broker cannot resist liability on the ground that he never in fact received payment under the settlement: *Wilkinson v Clay* (1815) 6 Taunt 110 (marine insurance); *Andrew v Robinson* (1812) 3 Camp 199 (marine insurance).

22 *Xenos v Wickham* (1863) 14 CBNS 435, ExCh (marine insurance) (revsd (1867), LR 2 HL 296) per Blackburn J, at 464.

23 *Bartlett v Pentland* (1830) 10 B & C 760 (marine insurance); *Legge v Byas, Mosley & Co* (1901) 7 Com Cas 16 (livestock insurance) per Walton J, at 19.

24 *Pollard, Ashby & Co (France) Ltd v Franco-British Marine Insurance Co Ltd* (1920) 5 LlL Rep 286 (marine insurance); *Sweeting v Pearce* (1861) 9 CBNS 534 (marine insurance), followed in *Legge v Byas, Mosley & Co* (supra) (livestock insurance); *Todd v Reid* (1821) 4 B & Ald 210 (marine insurance); *Scott v Irving* (1830) 1 B & Ad 605 (marine insurance); *Matveieff & Co v Crossfield* (1903) 8 Com Cas 120 (marine insurance); *McCowin Lumber and Export Co v Pacific Marine Insurance Co* (1922) 38 TLR 901, 12 LlL Rep 496 (marine insurance); cf *Acme Wood Flooring Co v Marten* (1904) 9 Com Cas 157 per Bruce J, at 162: 'I think that where a person insures with Lloyd's, and obtains from Lloyd's a policy in the form ordinarily granted by Lloyd's, he must be taken to accept the terms expressed in the policy and to agree with the meaning which the words ordinarily bear. The decided cases with regard to the authority of brokers at Lloyd's are, I think, not inconsistent with this view. It may well be that a person dealing with Lloyd's and having no express notice of the customs of Lloyd's regulating the authority of brokers is not bound by such customs. But I think it is different with regard to the terms expressed on the face of the contract which is handed to and accepted by the assured.' The existence of the usage had been negatived in the case of motor reinsurance: *Provincial Insurance Co Ltd v Crowder* (1927) 27 LlL Rep 28. As to the position where the payment is, as to part, covered by the broker's authority, the cases are conflicting; cf. *Scott v Irving* (supra) (marine insurance), where a payment partly in a form authorized and partly by settlement in account was held to bind the principal so far as the part payment in the form authorized was concerned, with *Legge v Byas, Mosley & Co* (supra) (livestock insurance), and *MacFarlane v Giannacopulo* (1858) 3 H & N 860 (marine insurance).

25 *Scott v Irving* (supra) (marine insurance) per Parke J, at 614; *Stewart v Aberdein* (1838) 4 M & W 211 (marine insurance).

1 *Scott v Irving* (supra) (marine insurance) per Parke J, at 614; *Stewart v Aberdein* (supra) (marine insurance) per Lord Abinger CB, at 228; *Sweeting v Pearce* (supra) (marine insurance) per Bramwell B, at 541; *Matveieff & Co v Crossfield* (supra) (marine insurance); cf *Gabay v Lloyd* (1825) 3 B & C 793 (marine insurance).

upon the broker to pay over the amount of the loss in which case it is no defence that the broker has never in fact received payment under the settlement,[2] or by suing the underwriter on the settlement in the name of the broker.[3]

As between the broker and the underwriter, a settlement in account, or even an actual payment of the amount of the loss in cash, does not bind the underwriter, if made under a mistake of fact. He is, therefore, entitled to recover from the broker the money so paid or allowed in settlement, unless and until the broker in good faith has paid over the money to the assured or has otherwise altered his position to his prejudice.[4] A mere debiting of himself in the accounts with the assured is not for this purpose sufficient.[5] Where, however, the money has been paid over or accounted for to the assured by the broker, the assured alone is liable to be sued by the underwriter.[6]

Similarly, the assured, though he is not liable to the underwriter for the premium, may, if he becomes entitled to a return of premium, enforce his right directly against the underwriter, and the underwriter is liable even though he has never received the original premium from the broker employed by the assured.[7]

---

2 *Andrew v Robinson* (1812) 3 Camp 199 (marine insurance); *Wilkinson v Clay* (1815) 6 Taunt 110 (marine insurance). In accordance with the same principle the broker cannot, after paying the assured the amount due under the policy, recover any portion back on the ground that he has not received it himself from the underwriter: *Edgar v Bumstead* (1808) 1 Camp 411 (marine insurance).

3 *Gibson v Winter* (1833) 5 B & Ad 96 (marine insurance).

4 *Holland v Russell* (1863) 4 B & S 14, ExCh (marine insurance).

5 *Buller v Harrison* (1777) 2 Cowp 565 (marine insurance).

6 *Holland v Russell* (supra) (marine insurance).

7 *Dalzell v Mair* (1808) 1 Camp 532 (marine insurance); *Xenos v Wickham* (1863) 14 CBNS 435 (marine insurance) (reversed (1866) LR 2 HL 296) per Blackburn J, at 457.

CHAPTER 54

Registration of insurance brokers

The purpose of the Insurance Brokers (Registration) Act 1977[1] is (i) to set up an Insurance Brokers Registration Council;[2] (ii) to provide for the registration and training of insurance brokers;[3] and (iii) to regulate the conduct of such brokers and to establish rules for disciplinary proceedings in respect of them.[4]

A THE INSURANCE BROKERS REGISTRATION COUNCIL

The Insurance Brokers Registration Council has the general function of carrying out the powers and duties conferred on them by the Act.[5] It is constituted in accordance with the Schedule to the Act.[6]

1 Constitution

The Council consists of:[7]

i 12 persons chosen to represent registered insurance brokers[8] of whom one shall be the Chairman of the Council.

ii 5 persons nominated by the Secretary of State.[9]

---

1 The Act is set out in Appendix I, pp 653–669, post.

2 See infra.

3 See pp 566–571, post.

4 See pp 572–581, post.

5 Insurance Brokers (Registration) Act 1977, s 1(1). The Council is a body corporate with perpetual succession and a common seal: ibid, s 1(1).

6 Ibid, s 1(2).

7 Ibid, Sched, para 1. The Secretary of State may, after consulting the Council, amend the provisions of the Schedule so as to vary the number of members and the manner in which they are chosen or appointed: ibid, Sched, para 10. An order under para 10 must not be made unless a draft of the order has been approved by resolution of each House of Parliament, ibid, s 28(3).

8 I e registered under the Act.

9 Of these persons one must be a barrister, advocate or solicitor, one a member of a recognised body of accountants, and one a person appearing to the Secretary of State to represent the interests of persons who are or may become policyholders of insurance companies: Insurance Brokers (Registration) Act 1977, Sched, para 1. The persons chosen to represent registered insurance brokers in the first instance were to be nominated by the British Insurance Brokers' Association: ibid, Sched, para 2(1). On the retirement of such persons the persons chosen to represent registered insurance brokers are to be elected in accordance with a scheme made by the Council and approved by order of the Secretary of State: ibid, Sched, para 2(2). The Secretary of State may approve a scheme as submitted to him or subject to such modifications as he thinks fit: ibid, Sched, para 2(3). Where he proposes to approve a scheme subject to modifications, he must notify the modifications to the Council and consider any of the observations of the Council thereon: Insurance Brokers (Registration) Act 1977, Sched, para 2(3). In the exercise of any functions under para 2 due regard must be had to the

The term of office of

a members nominated by the British Insurance Brokers' Association is such period not exceeding 4 years as may be fixed by a scheme made by the Council and approved by the Secretary of State;
b members elected by registered insurance brokers is such period as may be fixed by the scheme;
c members nominated by the Secretary of State is such period not exceeding 3 years as may be fixed by him.[10]

A member of the Council may at any time, by notice in writing to the registrar,[11] resign his office.[12] A person nominated or elected to fill a casual vacancy among the members of the Council holds office during the remainder of the term of office of the person whose vacancy he has filled.[13] Any vacancy other than a casual vacancy must be filled before the date on which the vacancy occurs.[14] A person ceasing to be a member of the Council is eligible to be again nominated or elected a member.[15]

2 General powers

The Council has power to do anything which in their opinion is calculated to facilitate the proper discharge of their functions.[16] In particular, they have power[17]

i to appoint, in addition to a registrar, such officers and servants as the Council may determine;
ii to pay to the members of the Council or their committees such fees for attendance at meetings of the Council or their committees and such travelling and subsistence allowances while attending such meetings or while on any other business of the Council as the Council may determine;
iii to pay to their officers and servants such remuneration as the Council may determine;
iv as regards any officers or servants in whose case they may determine to do so, to pay to, or in respect of them, such pensions and gratuities, or provide and maintain for them such superannuation schemes[18] as the Council may determine;

---

desirability of securing that the Council includes representatives of all parts of the United Kingdom: ibid, Sched, para 2(5). A scheme can be varied or revoked by a subsequent scheme made and approved as above: ibid, Sched, para 2(2). An order under para 2 of the Schedule must not be made unless a draft of the order has been approved by resolution of ech House of Parliament. The scheme at present in force is set out in the Insurance Brokers Registration Council Election Scheme Approval Order 1980 (SI 1980/62). See Appendix II, post.

10 Ibid, Sched, para 4(1).
11 I e the registrar of the Council appointed under s 8(1): ibid, s 29(1).
12 Ibid, Sched, para 5.
13 Ibid, Sched, para 6(1).
14 Ibid, Sched, para 6(2).
15 Ibid, Sched, para 7.
16 Ibid, Sched, para 8(1). The powers of the Council and any of its committees may be exercised notwithstanding any vacancy, and no proceedings of the Council or of any of its committees are invalidated by any defect in the nomination or election of a member: ibid, Sched, para 8(3).
17 Ibid, Sched, para 8(2).
18 Whether contributory or not.

v to borrow[19] such sums as the Council may from time to time require for performing any of their functions under the Act.

The Council may make standing orders for regulating the proceedings including the quorum of the Council and of any committee.[20]

3 Power to appoint committees

The Council may set up a committee for any purpose and may delegate to it any functions exercisable by them except

i the power to make rules under the Act;
ii any functions expressly conferred on any committee set up under the provisions of the Act;
iii subject to any express provision for delegation in the rules, any functions expressly conferred on the Council by rules under the Act.[1]

The number of members of a committee and their term of office must be fixed by the Council.[2]

A committee may include persons who are not members of the Council, but at least two-thirds of the members of every such committee must be members of the Council.[3]

Every member of a committee who at the time of his appointment was a member of the Council, on ceasing to be a member of the Council, also ceases to be a member of the committee.[4]

4 Accounts

The Council must keep proper accounts of all sums received or paid by them and proper records in relation to the accounts.[5]

The Council must appoint auditors who must be members of a recognised body of accountants.[6]

The Council must cause their accounts to be audited annually by the auditors to the Council.[7] As soon as is practicable after the accounts for any period have been audited the Council must cause them to be published and

---

19 Subject to the provisions of the Borrowing (Control and Guarantees Act) 1946, s 1 and of any order under those provisions for the time being in force.

20 Insurance Brokers (Registration) Act 1977, Sch, para 9. Orders must not be made under this paragraph with respect to the proceedings of the Disciplinary Committee: ibid, Sched, para 9. As to the Disciplinary Committee, see 576, post.

1 Ibid, s 21(1).

2 Ibid, s 21(2).

3 Ibid, s 21(3).

4 Ibid, s 21(4). But a member of the Council is not deemed to have ceased by reason of retirement to be a member of it if he has again been nominated or elected not later than the day of his retirement: ibid, s 21(4).

5 Ibid, s 25(1).

6 Ibid, s 25(2). The expression 'recognised body of accountants' means any one of the following: the Institute of Chartered Accountants in England and Wales; the Institute of Chartered Accountants of Scotland; the Association of Certified Accountants; the Institute of Chartered Accountants in Ireland; any other body of accountants established in the United Kingdom and for the time being recognised for the purposes of the Companies Act 1985, s 389(1)(a) by the Secretary of State: ibid, s 29(1).

7 Ibid, s 25(3).

must send a copy of them to the Secretary of State together with the report of the auditors on them.[8]

5 Rules

Rules made by the Council relating to the keeping of the register and the making of entries and alterations in them[9] the requirements for carrying on business,[10] professional indemnity,[11] the constitution of the Investigating Committee,[12] the constitution of the Disciplinary Committee[13] and its procedure,[14] do not come into operation until approved by order of the Secretary of State.[15]

The Secretary of State may approve rules relating to the procedure of the Disciplinary Committee either as submitted to him or subject to such modifications as he thinks fit.[16] But where he proposes to make any such rules subject to modifications, he must notify the modifications to the Council and consider any of their observations on them.[17]

After consulting the Council he may by order vary or revoke any rules relating to the registration procedure, the practising requirements or professional indemnity.[18]

B THE REGISTRATION AND TRAINING OF INSURANCE BROKERS

1 Registration

(a) Insurance brokers' register

The Council must establish and maintain a register of insurance brokers containing the names, addresses and qualifications, and such other particulars as may be prescribed[19] of all persons who are entitled under the provisions of the Act to be registered and apply in the prescribed manner to be so registered.[20]

(b) Qualifications for registration

A person is entitled to be registered in the register if he satisfies the Council

---

8 Insurance Brokers (Registration) Act 1977, s 25(3).
9 Under s 8 of the Act. See p 569, post.
10 Under s 11 of the Act. See p 572, post.
11 Under s 12 of the Act. See p 573, post.
12 Under s 14 of the Act. See p 576, post.
13 Under s 19 of the Act. See p 578, post.
14 See p 578, post.
15 Insurance Brokers (Registration) Act 1977, s 27(1). The power to make orders exercisable by statutory instrument and any order made under the Act may be varied or revoked by a subsequent order so made: ibid, s 28(1). The statutory instrument is subject to annulment in pursuance of a resolution of either House of Parliament: ibid, s 28(2).
16 Ibid, s 27(2).
17 Ibid, s 27(2).
18 Ibid, s 27(3). An order under this subsection must not be made until a draft of the order has been approved by resolution of each House of Parliament: ibid, s 28(3).
19 'Prescribed' means prescribed by rules under the Act: Insurance Brokers (Registration) Act 1977, s 29(1).
20 Ibid, s 2.

1 that he holds a qualification approved by the Council, being a qualification granted to him from an approved institution; or
2 that he holds a qualification recognised by the Council, being a qualification granted outside the United Kingdom; or
3 that he has carried on business as an insurance broker, or as a whole-time agent acting for two or more insurance companies in relation to insurance business, for a period of not less than 5 years[1]; or
4 that he holds a qualification recognised by the Council and has carried on business as an insurance broker, or as a whole-time agent acting for two or more insurance companies in relation to insurance business, for a period of not less than 3 years; or
5 that he has been employed by a person carrying on business as an insurance broker or a whole-time agent acting for two or more insurance companies in relation to insurance business, for a period of not less than 5 years[2]; or
6 that he holds a qualification recognised by the Council and has been employed by a person carrying on business as an insurance broker or as a whole-time agent for two or more insurance companies in relation to insurance business, or by an insurance company, for a period of not less than 3 years; or
7 that he has knowledge and practical experience of insurance business which is comparable to that of a person who has carried on business as an insurance broker for a period of 5 years; or
8 that he holds a qualification recognised by the Council and has knowledge and practical experience of insurance business which is comparable to that of a person who has carried on business as an insurance broker for a period of 3 years.[3]

A person is not entitled to be registered in the register unless he also satisfies the Council

a as to his character and suitability to be a registered insurance broker; and
b in a case falling within paragraphs 1, 2, 5 and 6 above that he has had adequate practical experience in the work of an insurance broker; and
c if he is carrying on business as an insurance broker at the time when the application is made, that he is complying with the rules.[4]

The Secretary of State may, after consulting the Council, by order provide that any of the above requirements be omitted or shall have effect subject to such amendments as may be specified in it.[5]

---

1 This refers to a period during which a person has carried on business providing him with adequate practical experience in the work of an insurance broker: *Pickles v Insurance Brokers Registration Council* [1984] 1 All ER 1073, [1984] 1 WLR 748. (See the judgment of McCullough J ibid at 1078–1079.)
2 This refers to a period during which a person has been employed by a person carrying on business which has provided him with adequate practical experience in the work of an insurance broker: ibid. (See the judgment of McCollough J ibid, at 1078–1079.)
3 Insurance Brokers (Registration) Act 1977, s 3(1).
4 Ibid, s 3(2).
5 Ibid, s 3(4). An order under this subsection must not be made unless a draft of the order has been approved by resolution of each House of Parliament: ibid, s 28(3).

A person is entitled to be registered in the register if he satisfies the Council that he or a partnership of which he is a member is accepted as a Lloyd's broker by the Committee of Lloyd's.[6]

(c) List of bodies corporate

The Council must establish and maintain a list of bodies corporate carrying on business as insurance brokers containing the names, principal place of business and such other particulars as may be prescribed[7] of all bodies corporate which are entitled to be enrolled and apply in the prescribed manner to be so enrolled.[8]

A body corporate is entitled to be enrolled if it satisfies the Council

a that a majority of its directors are registered insurance brokers; or
b in the case of a body corporate having only one director, that he is a registered insurance broker; or
c in the case of a body corporate having only two directors, that one of them is a registered insurance broker, and that the business is carried on under his management.[9]

A body corporate is not entitled to be enrolled in the list unless it also satisfies the Council that it is complying with the requirements of the rules for carrying on business.[10]

A body corporate is entitled to be enrolled in the list if it satisfies the Council that it is accepted as a Lloyd's broker by the Committee of Lloyd's.[11]

(d) Appeals against refusal to register or enrol

Before refusing an application for registration or an application for enrolment the Council must give the person by whom or the body corporate by which the application was made an opportunity of appearing before and being heard by a committee of the Council.[12]

Where the Council refuses any application to register or to enrol, the Council must, if so required by the person by whom or the body corporate by which the application was made, within 7 days from notification of the decision, serve on that person or body a statement of the reasons therefor.[13]

A person or body corporate whose application is so refused may within 28 days from

a notification of the decision, or
b if a statement of reasons had been required, service of the statement,

appeal against the refusal to the Court.[14]

---

6 Ibid, s 3(4).
7 'Prescribed' means prescribed by rules under the Act: Insurance Brokers (Registration) Act 1977, s 29(1).
8 Ibid, s 4(1). The rules at present in force are the Insurance Brokers Registration Council (Registration and Enrolment) Rules Approval Order 1978 (SI 1978/1395), as amended. See Appendix II, post.
9 Ibid, s 4(2).
10 Ibid, s 4(3).
11 Ibid, s 4(4).
12 Ibid, s 5(1).
13 Ibid, s 5(2).
14 Ibid, s 5(3). 'Court' means the High Court: ibid, s 29(1).

The Council may appear as respondent on any such appeal.[15] On the hearing of the appeal the Court may make such order as it thinks fit, and its order is final.[16]

(e) Form of register and list

The register and list must be kept by the registrar of the Council.[17]

The Council may make rules with respect to the form and keeping of the register and list and making entries and alterations in it, and in particular

- a regulating the making of applications for registration or enrolment and providing for the evidence to be produced in support of any such applications;
- b providing for the notification to the registrar of any change in the particulars required to be entered in the register or list;
- c prescribing a fee to be charged on the entry of a name in, or the restoration of a name to, the register or list;
- d prescribing a fee to be charged in respect of the retention in the register or list of any name in any year subsequent to the year in which that name was first entered in the register or list;
- e providing for the entry in the register of qualifications (whether approved qualifications or not) possessed by persons whose names are registered and for the removal of such qualifications from the register, and prescribing a fee to be charged in respect of the entry;
- f authorising the registrar to refuse to enter a name in, or restore it to, the register or list until a fee prescribed for the entry or restoration has been paid and to erase from the register or list the name of a person who or body corporate which, after the prescribed notices and warnings, fails to pay the fee prescribed in respect of the retention of that name in the register or list;
- g authorising the registrar to erase from the register or list the name of a person who or body corporate which, after the prescribed notices and warnings, fails to supply information required by the registrar with a view to ensuring that the particulars entered in the register or list are correct;
- h prescribing anything required or authorised to be prescribed by the provisions of the Act relating to the register or list.[18]

Rules which provide for the erasure of a name from the register or list on failure to pay a fee must provide for its restoration on the making of the prescribed application and on payment of that fee and any additional fee prescribed in respect of the restoration.[19]

Rules prescribing fees may provide for the charging of different fees in

---

15 Ibid, s 5(4). For the purpose of enabling directions to be given as to the costs of any such appeal the Council is deemed to be a party thereto, whether they appear on the hearing of the appeal or not: ibid, s 5(4).

16 Ibid, s 5(5).

17 Insurance Brokers (Registration) Act 1977, s 8(1).

18 Ibid, s 8(2). The rules at present in force are the Insurance Brokers Registration Council (Registration and Enrolment) Rules Approval Order 1978 (SI 1978, No 1395) as amended. See Appendix II, post.

19 Insurance Brokers (Registration) Act 1977, s 8(3).

different classes of cases and for the making of arrangements for the collection of fees with such body or bodies as may be prescribed.[20]

(f) Publication of register and list

The Council must cause the register and list to be printed and published as often as they think fit.[1]

Where the register or list is not published in any year, the Council must cause any alteration in the entries in the register or list which have been made since the last publication to be printed and published within that year.[2]

A copy of the register and list purporting to be printed by the Council is evidence in all proceedings that the individuals specified in the register are registered in it or, as the case may be, that the bodies corporate specified in the list are enrolled in it.[3] The absence of the name of any individual or body corporate from any such copy of the register or list is evidence, unless the contrary is shown, that he is not registered or, as the case may be, that it is not enrolled in it.[4]

In the case of an individual whose name or a body corporate the name of which does not appear in any copy of the register or list as altered a certified copy, under the hand of the registrar, of the entry relating to that individual or body corporate in the register or list is evidence of the entry.[5]

2 Training

The Council has power to approve educational institutions and qualifications, and to supervise such institutions and qualifying examinations.

(a) Approval of educational institutions and qualifications

The Council may approve any institution where the instruction given to persons being educated as insurance brokers appears to the Council to be such as to secure to them adequate knowledge and skill for the practice of their profession.[6]

The Council may approve any qualification which appears to them to be granted to candidates who reach such a standard at a qualifying examination as to secure to them such knowledge and skill.[7]

Where the Council has refused to approve an institution or qualification as suitable for any purpose, the Secretary of State, on representations being made to him within one month of the refusal, may, if he thinks fit, after considering the representations and after consulting the Council, order the Council to approve the institution or qualification as suitable for the purpose.[8]

The Council must publish from time to time a list of approved educational institutions and approved qualifications.[9]

(b) Supervision of educational institutions and qualifying examinations

It is the duty of the Council to keep themselves informed of the nature of the

---

[20] Ibid, s 8(4).
[1] Ibid, s 9(1).
[2] Insurance Brokers (Registration) Act 1977, s 9(2).
[3] Ibid, s 9(3).
[4] Ibid, s 9(3).
[5] Ibid, s 9(4).
[6] Ibid, s 6(1).
[7] Ibid, s 6(2).
[8] Ibid, s 6(3).
[9] Ibid, s 6(4).

instruction given by any approved educational institution to persons being educated as insurance brokers and of the examinations on the result of which approved qualifications are granted.[10] For the purposes of this duty the Council may appoint persons to visit approved educational institutions and to attend at the examinations held by the bodies which grant approved qualifications.[11]

It is the duty of visitors so appointed to report to the Council as to the sufficiency of the instruction given by the institution visited by them, or of the examinations attended by them, and as to any other matters relating thereto and as to any other matters as may be specified by the Council either generally or in any particular case.[12] But no visitor must interfere with the giving of any instruction or the holding of any examination.[13]

Where it appears to the Council, as a result of a report or otherwise,

a that the instruction given by any approved educational institution to persons being educated as insurance brokers or the examinations taken by such persons are not such as to secure the possession by them of adequate knowledge and skill for the practice of their profession; and
b that for that reason the approval of the institution or qualification in question should be withdrawn.

the Council must give notice to the institution or body of their opinion, sending with it a copy of any report on which their opinion is based.[14]

On receipt of the notice the institution or body may, within such period[15] as the Council may have specified in the notice, make to the Council observations on the notice and any report sent with it or objections to the notice and report.[16]

As soon as may be after the expiration of the period specified in the notice the Council must determine whether or not to withdraw their approval of the institution or qualification, as the case may be, taking into account any observation or objections made by the institution or body.[17]

The Council must give notice in writing of any decision to withdraw approval of an institution or qualification to the institution or body concerned. The decision does not take effect until one month from the date of the giving of the notice or, if during that time the institution or body makes representations with respect to the decision to the Secretary of State, until the representations are finally dealt with.[18]

Where the Council has decided to withdraw approval of an institution or qualification, the Secretary of State, on representations being made to him within one month from the giving of the notice of the decision, may if he thinks fit, after considering the representations and after consulting the Council, order the Council to annul the withdrawal of approval.[19]

---

10 Ibid, s 7(1).
11 Insurance Brokers (Registration) Act 1977, s 7(2). The Council may pay to visitors such fees and travelling and subsistence allowances as the Council may determine: ibid, s 7(9).
12 Ibid, s 7(3).
13 Ibid, s 7(3).
14 Ibid, s 7(4).
15 Not being less than one month: ibid, s 7(5).
16 Ibid, s 7(5).
17 Ibid, s 7(6).
18 Ibid, s 7(7).
19 Ibid, s 7(8).

C THE REGULATION OF CONDUCT, DISCIPLINARY PROCEEDINGS AND PENALTIES

The Council are responsible for the regulation of the conduct of insurance brokers and for disciplinary proceedings. There are penalties for pretending to be registered.

1 Regulation of conduct

The Council must draw up a code of conduct, impose requirements for the carrying on of business and make rules concerning professional indemnity.

(a) Code of conduct

The Council must draw up and may from time to time revise a statement of the acts and omissions, which, if done or made by registered insurance brokers or enrolled bodies corporate in particular circumstances, constitute in the opinion of the Council unprofessional conduct.[20]

The statement serves as a guide to registered brokers and enrolled bodies corporate and persons concerned with the conduct of registered insurance brokers and enrolled bodies corporate.[1] But the mention or lack of mention in it of a particular act or omission is not conclusive of any question of professional conduct.[2]

(b) Requirements for carrying on business

The Council must make rules requiring practising insurance brokers and enrolled bodies corporate to ensure

- a that their businesses have working capital of not less than such amount as may be prescribed;
- b that the value of the assets of their businesses exceeds the amount of the liabilities of their businesses by not less than such amount as may be prescribed; and
- c that the number of insurance companies with which they place insurance business, and the amount of insurance business which they place with each insurance company, is such as to prevent their businesses from becoming unduly dependent on any particular insurance company.[3]

The Council must also make rules requiring practising insurance brokers[4] and enrolled bodies corporate

- a to open and keep accounts for money received by them from persons with whom they do business;

---

20 Insurance Brokers (Registration) Act 1977, s 10(1). The Code of Conduct at present in force is set out in the Insurance Brokers Registration Council (Code of Conduct) Approval Order 1978 (SI 1978/1394). See Appendix II, post.

1 Insurance Brokers (Registration) Act 1977, s 10(2).

2 Ibid, s 10(2).

3 Ibid, s 11(1).

4 Practising insurance brokers' means 'a registered insurance broker who is carrying on business as an insurance broker': ibid, s 29(1).

b to hold money so received in such manner as may be prescribed;
c to keep such accounting records showing and explaining the transactions of their businesses as may be prescribed; and
d to prepare and submit to the Council at such intervals as may be prescribed balance sheets and profit and loss accounts containing such information as may be prescribed for the purpose of giving a true and fair view of the state of their businesses.[5]

Rules may empower the Council

a to require practising insurance brokers and enrolled bodies corporate to deliver at such intervals as may be prescribed reports given by qualified accountants[6] and containing such information as may be prescribed for the purpose of ascertaining whether or not the rules have been complied with;
b to require practising brokers and enrolled bodies corporate to deliver at such intervals as may be prescribed statements made by them and containing such information as may be prescribed for the purpose of ascertaining whether or not the rules are being complied with; and
c to take such other steps as they consider necessary or expedient for the purpose of ascertaining whether or not the rules are being complied with.[7]

(c) Professional indemnity

The Council must make rules for indemnifying

a practising insurance brokers and former practising insurance brokers, and
b enrolled bodies corporate and former enrolled bodies corporate

against losses arising from claims in respect of any description of civil liability incurred by them, or by employees of theirs, in connection with their businesses.[8]

The Council must also make rules for the making of grants or other payments

---

[5] Insurance Brokers (Registration) Act 1977, s 11(2).

[6] An accountant is qualified to give reports for the purpose of the rules if he is a member of a recognised body of accountants or is for the time being authorised by the Secretary of State under the Companies Act 1985, s 389(1)(*b*): ibid, s 11(4). As to the meaning of the expression 'recognised body of accountants', see p 565, footnote 6, ante. An accountant is not qualified to give such reports

a in relation to a practising insurance broker, if he is an employee or partner of, or an employee of a partner of the practising insurance broker;
b in relation to an enrolled body corporate, if he is not qualified for appointment as auditor of the enrolled body corporate: Insurance Brokers (Registration) Act 1977, s 11(5).

A Scottish firm of accountants is qualified to give such reports if, but only if, all the partners are so qualified: ibid, s 11(6).

[7] Ibid, s 11(3). The rules may make different provision for different circumstances, and may specify circumstances in which persons are exempt from any of the requirements of the rules: ibid, s 11(7). The rules at present in force are the Insurance Brokers Registration Council (Accounts and Business Requirements) Rules Approval Order 1979 (SI 1979/489), as amended. See Appendix II, post.

[8] Ibid, s 12(1). The rules at present in force are the Insurance Brokers Registration Council (Indemnity Insurance and Grants Scheme) Rules Approval Order 1979 (SI 1979/408). See Appendix II, post.

for the purpose of relieving or mitigating losses suffered by persons in consequence of

- a negligence or fraud or other dishonesty on the party of practising insurance brokers or enrolled bodies corporate or of employees of theirs, in connection with their businesses; or
- b failure on the part of practising insurance brokers or enrolled bodies corporate to account for money received by them in connection with their businesses.[9]

For the purpose of providing such an indemnity and of enabling grants or other payments to be made, rules

- a may authorise the Council to establish and maintain a fund or funds;
- b may authorise or require the Council to take out and maintain insurance with authorised insurers;[10]
- c may require practising insurance brokers or enrolled bodies corporate or any specified description of practising insurance brokers or enrolled bodies corporate to take out and maintain insurance with authorised insurers.[11]

Rules

- a may specify the terms and conditions on which indemnity or a grant or other payment is to be available and any circumstances in which the right to it is to be excluded or modified;
- b may provide for the management, administration and protection of any fund[12] and require practising insurance brokers or enrolled bodies corporate or any description of practising brokers or enrolled bodies corporate to make payments to any such fund;
- c may require practising insurance brokers or enrolled bodies corporate or any description of practising insurance brokers or enrolled bodies corporate to make payments by way of premium on any insurance policy maintained by the Council;[13]
- d may prescribe the conditions which such a policy must satisfy;
- e may authorise the Council to determine the amount of any payments required by the rules, subject to such limits, or in accordance with such provisions, as may be prescribed;
- f may specify circumstances in which, where a registered insurance broker or an enrolled body corporate for whom indemnity is provided has failed to comply with the rules, the Council or insurers may take proceedings against him or them or it in respect of sums paid by way of indemnity in connection with a matter in relation to which there has been a failure to comply with the rules;
- g may specify circumstances in which, where a grant or other payment is

---

9 Insurance Brokers (Registration) Act 1977, s 12(2).

10 Authorised insurers' means 'a person permitted under the Insurance Companies Act 1982': to carry on insurance business of class 13 or of classes 1, 2, 14, 15, 16 and 17 in Schedule 2 to the Insurance Companies Act 1982: ibid, s 29(1).

11 Ibid, s 12(3).

12 Maintained under s 12(3)(a).

13 Under s 12(3)(b).

made in consequence of the act or omission of a practising insurance broker or enrolled body corporate, the Council or insurers may take proceedings against him or it in respect of the sum so paid;

h may make different provision for different circumstances, and may specify circumstances in which practising insurance brokers or enrolled bodies corporate are exempt from any of the rules;

i may empower the Council to take such steps as they consider necessary or expedient to ascertain whether or not the rules are being complied with; and

j may contain incidental, procedural or supplementary provisions.[14]

2 Disciplinary proceedings

Disciplinary cases are investigated by an Investigating Committee, which has power to refer them to a Disciplinary Committee. Names can be erased from the register for crime, unprofessional conduct etc, and can be restored by the Disciplinary Committee. Entries in the register or list can be erased on the ground of fraud or error. There are provisions for an appeal from the Disciplinary Committee to the Council. The procedure of the Disciplinary Committee is regulated by rules made for the purpose. Legal assessors to the Disciplinary Committee must be in attendance at its proceedings.

(a) Investigating Committee

The Council must set up a committee, to be known as the Investigating Committee, for the preliminary investigation of cases in which

a it is alleged that a registered insurance broker or enrolled body corporate is liable to have his or its name erased from the register or list on any ground specified in s 15 of the Act;[15] or

b a complaint is made to the Council by or on behalf of a member of the public about a registered insurance broker or an enrolled body corporate.[16]

A disciplinary case must be referred to the Investigating Committee who must then carry out a preliminary investigation of it.[17] Unless they are satisfied that there is insufficient evidence to support a finding that the registered insurance broker or enrolled body corporate is liable to have his or its name erased from the register or list, the Committee must refer the case, with the results of their investigation, to the Disciplinary Committee.[18]

The Council must make rules as to the constitution of the Investigating Committee.[19]

---

[14] Insurance Brokers (Registration) Act 1977, s 12(3).

[15] See p 576, post.

[16] Insurance Brokers (Registration) Act 1977, s 13(1). Any such case is referred to for the purposes of the Act as a 'disciplinary case': ibid, s 13(1).

[17] Ibid, s 13(2).

[18] Ibid, s 13(2).

[19] Ibid, s 13(3). The rules at present in force are the Insurance Brokers Registration Council (Constitution of the Investigating Committee) Rules Approval Order 1978 (SI 1978/1456). See Appendix II, post.

(b) Disciplinary Committee

The Council must set up a committee, to be known as the Disciplinary Committee, for the consideration and determination of disciplinary cases referred to them by the Investigating Committee and of any other cases of which they have cognisance under the provisions of the Act.[20]

The Council must make rules as to the constitution of the Disciplinary Committee, the time and places of the meetings of the Committee, the quorum and mode of summoning its members.[1] The rules must secure that a person, other than the chairman of the Council, who has acted in relation to any disciplinary case as a member of the Investigating Committee does not act in relation to that case as a member of the Disciplinary Committee.[2]

(c) Erasure from the register for crime, unprofessional conduct etc

If a registered insurance broker or enrolled body corporate

- a is convicted by any court in the United Kingdom of any criminal offence, not being an offence which, owing to its trivial nature or the circumstances under which it was committed, does not render him or it unfit to have his or its name on the register or list; or
- b is judged by the Disciplinary Committee to have been guilty of unprofessional conduct,

the Disciplinary Committee may, if they think fit, direct that the name of the insurance broker or body corporate shall be erased from the register or list.[3]

If it appears to the Disciplinary Committee that a registered insurance broker or an enrolled body corporate has contravened or failed to comply with any rules made under s 11[4] or s 12[5] of the Act, and that the contravention or failure is such as to render the insurance broker unfit to have his name on the register or the body corporate unfit to have its name on the list, the Disciplinary Committee may, if they think fit, direct that the name of the insurance broker or body corporate be erased from the register or list.[6]

Where

- a the name of a director of an enrolled body corporate is erased from the register under s 15(1),[7] or
- b a director of any enrolled body corporate is convicted of an offence under the Act, or
- c the name of a registered insurance broker employed by an enrolled body corporate is erased from the register under s 15(1)[8] and the act or omission constituting the ground on which it was erased was instigated

---

20 Insurance Brokers (Registration) Act 1977, s 14(1).
1 Ibid, s 14(2).
2 Ibid, s 14(3). The rules at present in force are the Insurance Brokers Registration Council (Constitution of the Disciplinary Committee) Rules Approval Order 1978 (SI 1978/1457). See Appendix II, post.
3 Insurance Brokers (Registration) Act 1977, s 15(1).
4 Which relates to the requirements for carrying on business. See p 572, ante.
5 Which relates to professional indemnity. See p 573, ante.
6 Insurance Brokers (Registration) Act 1977, s 15(2).
7 Supra.
8 Supra.

or connived at by a director of the body corporate, or, if the act or omission was a continuing act or omission, a director of the body corporate had or reasonably ought to have had knowledge of the continuance of it,

the Disciplinary Committee may, if they think fit, direct that the name of the body corporate be erased from the list.[9]

If the Disciplinary Committee are of opinion as respects an enrolled body corporate that the conditions for enrolment in s 4[10] are no longer satisfied, the Disciplinary Committee may, if they think fit, direct that the name of the body corporate be erased from the list.[11]

When the Disciplinary Committee direct that the name of an individual or body corporate be erased from the register or list, the registrar must serve on that individual or body a notification of the direction and a statement of the Committee's reasons for it.[12]

(d) *Restoration of names*

Where the name of an individual or body corporate has been erased from the register or list under such a direction, the name of that individual or body corporate must not again be entered in the register or list unless the Disciplinary Committee, on application made to them, otherwise direct.[13] An application for the restoration of a name to the register or list must not be made to the Disciplinary Committee within 10 months of the date of erasure or within 10 months of a previous application for restoration.[14]

(e) *Erasure on ground of fraud or error*

If it is proved to the satisfaction of the Disciplinary Committee that any entry in the register or list has been fraudulently or incorrectly made, the Disciplinary Committee may, if they think fit, direct that the entry be erased from the register or list.[15]

An individual may be registered or a body corporate enrolled notwithstanding that his or its name has been erased under the above provision.[16] But if it was erased on the ground of fraud, that individual or body corporate must not be registered or enrolled except on an application to the Disciplinary

---

9 Insurance Brokers (Registration) Act 1977, s 15(3). But the Disciplinary Committee must not take a case into consideration during any period within which proceedings by way of appeal may be brought which may result in this subsection being rendered inapplicable in that case or while any such proceedings are pending: ibid, s 15(3).

10 See p 568, ante.

11 Insurance Brokers (Registration) Act 1977, s 15(4). Where a registered insurance broker dies while he is a director of an enrolled body corporate he is deemed for the purposes of this subsection to have continued to be a director of that body until the expiration of a period of 6 months beginning with the date of his death or until a director is appointed in his place, whichever first occurs: ibid, s 15(5).

12 Ibid, s 15(6). Any notice may, without prejudice to any other method of service but subject to any provision to the contrary be served by post: ibid, s 26.

13 Ibid, s 16(1).

14 Ibid, s 16(2).

15 Ibid, s 17(1).

16 Ibid, s 17(2).

Committee.[17] On any such application the Disciplinary Committee may, if they think fit, direct that the individual or body corporate must not be registered or enrolled until the expiration of such period as may be specified in the direction.[18]

Where the Disciplinary Committee direct that the name of an individual or body corporate be erased from the register or list, the registrar must serve on that individual or body a notification of the direction and a statement of the Committee's reasons for it.[19]

(f) Appeals

At any time within 28 days from the service of a notification that the Disciplinary Committee have under s 15[20] or s 17[1] directed that the name of an individual or body corporate be erased from the register or list, that individual or body may appeal to the Council.[2]

The Council may appear as respondent on any such appeal.[3] For the purpose of enabling directions to be given as to the costs of any such appeal the Council is deemed to be a party thereto, whether they appear on the hearing of the appeal or not.[4]

Where no appeal is brought against a direction under s 15 or s 17, or where such an appeal is brought but withdrawn or struck out for want of prosecution, the direction takes effect on the expiration of the time for appealing or, as the case may be, on the withdrawal or striking out of the appeal.[5]

Where an appeal is brought against a direction under s 15 or s 17, the direction takes effect if and when the appeal is dismissed and not otherwise.[6]

(g) Procedure of Disciplinary Committee

The Council must make rules as to the procedure and the rules of evidence to be observed in proceedings[7] before the Disciplinary Committee, and in particular

a for securing that notice that the proceedings are to be brought is given, at such time and in such manner as may be specified in the rules, to the individual or body corporate alleged to be liable to have his or its name erased from the register or list;

---

17 Ibid, s 17(2).
18 Ibid, s 17(2).
19 Insurance Brokers (Registration) Act 1977, s 17(3).
20 See p 576, ante.
1 See p 577, ante.
2 Insurance Brokers (Registration) Act 1977, s 18(1).
3 Ibid, s 18(2).
4 Ibid, s 18(2).
5 Ibid, s 18(3).
6 Ibid, s 18(4).
7 'Proceedings' means 'proceedings under this Act, whether relating to disciplinary cases or otherwise': ibid, s 20(6). The Disciplinary Committee may administer oaths, and any party to the proceedings may sue out writs of subpoena and testificandum and duces tecum, but no person can be compelled under any such writ to produce any document which he could not be compelled to produce at the trial of an action: ibid, s 19(1). The provisions of the Supreme Court Act 1981, s 36 or of the Attendance of Witnesses Act 1854 apply in relation to any proceedings before the Disciplinary Committee as they apply to causes or matters in the High Court: ibid, s 19(2).

b for securing that any party to the proceedings, if he so requires, is entitled to be heard by the Disciplinary Committee;

c for enabling any party to the proceedings to be so represented by counsel or solicitor or (if the rules so provide and the party so elects) by a person of such other description as may be specified in the rules;

d for requiring proceedings before the Disciplinary Committee to be held in public except in so far as may be specified in the rules;

e for requiring, in cases where it is alleged that a registered insurance broker or enrolled body corporate has been guilty of unprofessional conduct, that where the Disciplinary Committee judge that the allegation has not been proved, they record a finding that the insurance broker or body corporate is not guilty of such conduct in respect of the matters to which the allegation relates;

f for requiring, in cases where it is alleged that a registered insurance broker or enrolled body corporate is liable to have his or its name erased from the register or list,[8] that where the Disciplinary Committee judge that the allegation has not been proved, they record a finding that the insurance broker or body corporate is not guilty of the matters alleged.[9]

Before making the rules the Council must consult such organisations representing the interests of insurance brokers and bodies corporate carrying on business as insurance brokers as appear to the Council requisite to be consulted.[10]

(h) Assessors to Disciplinary Committee

For the purposes of advising the Disciplinary Committee on questions of law arising in proceedings before them there must be in all such proceedings an assessor to the Committee.[11]

The power of appointing assessors is exercisable by the Council.[12] But if no assessor appointed by them is available to act at any particular proceedings, the Disciplinary Committee may appoint an assessor to act at those proceedings.[13]

The Lord Chancellor may make rules as to the functions of the assessors. In particular, rules may contain such provisions for securing

a that where an assessor advises the Disciplinary Committee on any question of law as to evidence, procedure or any other matters specified in the rules, he does so in the presence of every party, or person representing a party, to the proceedings, who appears at them, or, if the advice is tendered after the Disciplinary Committee have begun to deliberate as to their findings, that every such party or person representing a party is informed what advice the assessor has tendered;

---

8 Under s 15(2). See p 576, ante.

9 Insurance Brokers (Registration) Act 1977, s 19(4). The rules at present in force are the Insurance Brokers Registration Council (Procedure of the Disciplinary Committee) Rules Approval Order 1978 (SI 1978/1457). See Appendix II, post.

10 Insurance Brokers (Registration) Act 1977, s 19(5).

11 Ibid, s 20(1). He must be a barrister or solicitor of not less than 10 years' standing: ibid, s 20(1), 'Proceedings' means 'proceedings under this Act, whether relating to disciplinary cases or otherwise': ibid, s 19(6).

12 Ibid, s 20(2).

13 Ibid, s 20(2).

b that every such party or person representing a party is informed if in any case the Disciplinary Committee do not accept the advice of the assessor on any such question,

and such incidental and supplementary provisions as appear to the Lord Chancellor expedient.[14]

An assessor may be appointed either generally or for any particular proceedings or class of proceedings.[15] He holds and vacates office in the terms of the instrument under which he is appointed.[16]

Any remuneration paid by the Council to persons appointed to act as assessors is at such rates as the Council may determine.[17]

3 Penalties

Any individual who wilfully

a takes or uses any style, title or description which consists of or includes the expression 'insurance broker'[18] when he is not registered in the register, or
b takes or uses any name, title, addition or description falsely implying, or otherwise pretends that he is registered in the register

is liable on summary conviction to a fine not exceeding the prescribed sum[19] under the Magistrates' Courts Act 1980, s 32(2), or on conviction on indictment to a fine.[20]

Any body corporate which wilfully

a takes or uses any style, title or description which consists of or includes the expression 'insurance broker' when it is not enrolled in the list, or
b takes or uses any name, title, addition or description falsely implying, or otherwise pretends, that it is enrolled in the list

is liable on summary conviction to a fine not exceeding the prescribed sum[1] under the Magistrates' Courts Act 1980, s 32(2), or on conviction on indictment to a fine.[2]

Where a practising insurance broker dies, then, during the period of 3 months beginning with his death or such longer period as the Council may in any particular case allow, the above provisions do not prevent his personal representatives, his surviving spouse or any of his children or trustees on behalf of his surviving spouse or any of his children from taking or using in relation to

---

14 Insurance Brokers (Registration) Act 1977, s 20(3). The power to make rules is exercisable by statutory instrument: ibid, s 20(b). The rules at present in force are the Insurance Brokers Registration Council (Disciplinary Committee) Legal Assessor Rules 1978 (SI 1978/1503). See Appendix II, post.
15 Insurance Brokers (Registration) Act 1977, s 20(4).
16 Ibid, s 20(4).
17 Ibid, s 20(5).
18 The expression insurance broker includes references to 'assurance broker', 'reinsurance broker' and 'reassurance broker': ibid, s 22(3).
19 I e £1,000 or such sum as is for the time being substituted for this definition by an order in force under the Magistrates' Courts Act 1980, s 143(1): Magistrates' Courts Act 1980, s 32(9).
20 Insurance Brokers (Registration) Act 1977, s 22(1).
1 See footnote, supra.
2 Insurance Brokers (Registration) Act 1977, s 22(2).

his business, but in conjunction with the name in which he carried it on, any title which he was entitled to take or use immediately before his death.[3]

Similarly, where a practising broker becomes bankrupt, then, during the period of 3 months beginning with the bankruptcy or such longer period as the Council may in any particular case allow, the above provisions do not prevent his trustee in bankruptcy from taking or using in relation to his business, but in conjunction with the name in which he carried it on, any title which he was entitled to take or use immediately before the bankruptcy.[4]

Where an offence under the Act which has been committed by a body corporate is proved to have been committed with the consent or connivance of, or to be attributable to any neglect on the part of any director, manager, secretary or other similar officer of the body corporate, or any person purporting to act in any such capacity, he as well as the body corporate is guilty of that offence and is liable to be proceeded against and punished accordingly.[5]

---

3 Ibid, s 23(1).
4 Ibid, s 23(2).
5 Ibid, s 24.

PART VII

Miscellaneous

CHAPTER 55

Conflict of laws

The business of insurance, as carried on by English insurers, is not confined exclusively to England and Wales, but extends to countries which are outside the jurisdiction of the English courts. On the other hand, insurers who are not English are entitled to carry on insurance business in England, provided that they comply with the statutory requirements of the Insurance Companies Act 1982.[1] Moreover, there is a considerable amount of reinsurance business carried on between English and foreign insurers.

It, therefore, becomes necessary to consider how far the English Courts are empowered to decide questions arising under contracts of insurance where the subject-matter of insurance is situated outside the jurisdiction, or where one of the contracting parties is not resident within the jurisdiction.[2] Further, it is necessary to ascertain whether such questions, where they fall within the jurisdiction of the English Courts, are to be decided by reference to the law of England, or to some other system of law, and in the latter case by what method the law applicable is to be discovered.[3]

A THE JURISDICTION OF THE ENGLISH COURTS

The High Court of Justice clearly has jurisdiction where the contract of insurance is made in England, and is to be performed in England, even though the insurers are not domiciled within the jurisdiction, provided that the requisite steps are taken to bring them before the Court. Except in the case of Scottish or Irish insurers, there is no difficulty in doing so, since all foreign insurers carrying on business in the United Kingdom must have a duly registered address for service situate in each part of the United Kingdom in which they carry on business.[4]

---

1 See Chapter 6.

2 The details of the Conflict of Laws are outside the scope of this book and the reader is referred to the standard books on the subject, e g Dicey and Morris *Conflict of Laws* (10th Edn, 1980): C M Schmitthoff, *The English Conflict of Laws* (3rd Edn, 1954). The question of the jurisdiction of the English Courts is dealt with in Dicey and Morris at pp 149–257 and in Schmitthoff at pp 420–457.

3 As to the law which governs the contract, see Dicey and Morris, op cit, pp 747–828, and Schmitthoff, op cit, pp 105–149.

4 Companies Act 1985, s 691. Apart from this provision service out of the jurisdiction can be ordered under RSC Ord 11, r 1(f). This will be necessary where the contract is made abroad, but provides for payment of losses to be made in England; cf *Mutzenbecher v La Aseguradora Espanola* [1906] 1 KB 254, CA (wrongful dismissal), where the contract was made abroad between a foreign insurance company and the agent whom it proposed to employ in England, and the dismissal took place in England.

Insurers who are domiciled in Scotland or Ireland, whether they are incorporated or not, must, however, be sued in Scotland or Ireland as the case may be, and cannot be sued in England,[5] unless, as is usually the case,[6] they have expressly bound themselves to accept service of any proceedings against them through an agent in England, or unless they are similarly bound by their conduct.[7]

Where, on the other hand, the insurers are domiciled in England, an action will lie against them whether the contract of insurance was made in England or abroad,[8] and the place where the contract is to be performed is for the purpose of jurisdiction immaterial.[9] The English Courts have jurisdiction in such a case, notwithstanding that the subject-matter of insurance may be foreign immovable property, inasmuch as no question of title is involved, and the contract is one of a purely personal character.

The jurisdiction of the English Courts may, however, be ousted where it is the manifest intention of the parties that the English Courts shall not have

---

5 RSC Ord 11, r 1 (f); *Jones v Scottish Accident Insurance Co* (1886) 17 QBD 421 (accident insurance), where the policy had been issued through an agent within the jurisdiction to whom the premiums were paid; *Watkins v Scottish Imperial Insurance Co* (1889) 23 QBD 285 (life insurance), where the company had its registered office in Scotland, but had branch offices in England, and a head branch office in London.

6 Similar provisions are inserted in policies issued by English companies as to acceptance of service in Scotland or Ireland.

7 *Moloney v Tulloch* (1835) 1 JoExIr 114 (life insurance), where an English company was held by its conduct to have agreed to accept service of proceedings in Ireland, and Pennefather B said (at 115): 'The decision of the Court does not assume that the merits are the one way or the other; but says that a company which has dealt in this country; which holds an office in this country for the receipt of premiums; where the entire contract is made; and where the office is still open for future contracts, does by such contract enter into an engagement that for all purposes of suit their office here shall be considered as their dwelling-house . . . The holding open an office in this country by an insurance company, where in point of fact the contract is made, though the instrument may be formally completed in London, is an undertaking on the part of the company that their office is to be considered their residence, not only for the purpose of receiving premiums, but also of enforcing contract.' See also, *M'Cullagh v Wood* (1838) 1 Craw & D 264 (Law and Equity Ir) (life insurance). In *Oesterreichische Export A-G v British Indemnity Insurance Co Ltd* [1914] 2 KB 747, CA (marine insurance), service on a Scottish company was allowed under RSC Ord 11, r 1 (g).

8 *New York Life Insurance Co v Public Trustee* [1924] 2 Ch 101, CA (life insurance), where the contract was made in New York, but the insurers were domiciled in London as well as in New York.

9 RSC Ord 11, r 1 (c). The English Court might, however, decline to exercise its jurisdiction on the ground that the court of the foreign country was the more convenient. The judgment of a foreign court may be enforced in this country by action, or by registration under the Foreign Judgments (Reciprocal Enforcement) Act 1933, in the case of countries to which that Act has been applied by Order in Council (see RSC Ord 71, and notes thereto in the *Supreme Court Practice* 1985). In the case of proceedings by action, a stay may be granted to enable the defendants to take proceedings in the foreign court to set aside the judgment: *Myakka Lumber Co v Lancashire and General Assurance Co Ltd* (1927) 28 LlL Rep 5, CA; *Sheehy v Professional Life Assurance Co* (1857) 3 CBNS 597, ExCh (life insurance); but payment under it is a complete bar: *Equitable Life Assurance Co v Perrault* (1882) 26 LCJ 382 (life insurance). It is no defence to an action on a foreign judgment that the insurers are an English company, if the company was incorporated for the purpose of carrying on of business in the foreign country concerned, and the proceedings there were regular: *Waydell v Provincial Insurance Co* (1862) 21 UCR 612, where a judgment duly obtained in New York by an assignee of the policy was held enforceable against a Canadian insurance company. As to the enforcement of Scottish and Irish judgments in England, see Judgments Extension Act 1868.

jurisdiction,[10] or where the contract of insurance, though made in England, is wholly to be performed abroad, and both the assured and the insurers are foreigners.[11]

B THE 'PROPER LAW' OF THE CONTRACT

The proper law of the contract, i e the system of law by reference to which the contract was made or that with which the transaction has its closest and most real connection,[12] is to be determined by finding the intention of the parties.[13]

The English Court is not, however, deprived of its jurisdiction by reason of its appearing that the parties intended their contract to be governed by the law of a foreign country, any more than a foreign court would be deprived of jurisdiction in the case of the policy being governed by English law.[14] In such a case the English Court must endeavour to ascertain the foreign law applicable, and apply it to the best of its ability.[15] The application of this law may sometimes involve a combination of English law and the municipal law of the foreign country.[16]

---

10 *Austrian Lloyd SS Co v Gresham Life Assurance Society Ltd* [1903] 1 KB 249, CA (life insurance), where the policy issued in Budapest by the agent of an English company contained a condition expressly agreeing to the jurisdiction of the court of Budapest. But the intention of the parties must be clearly shown: *Buenos Ayres and Ensenada Port Rly Co v Northern Rly Co of Buenos Ayres* (1877) 2 QBD 210 (rent).

11 *St Gobian, Chauny and Cirey Co v Hoyermann's Agency* [1893] 2 QB 96, CA (sale of goods).

12 *Bonython v Commonwealth of Australia* [1951] AC 201 at 219, PC per Lord Simonds. See further, *Re United Railways of the Havana and Regla Warehouses Ltd* [1960] 2 All ER 332 at 364, HL (per Lord Morris); *Rossano v Manufacturers Life Insurance Co Ltd* [1963] 2 QB 352, [1962] 2 All ER 214, [1962] 1 Lloyd's Rep 187, QB (Commercial Court) (life insurance).

13 *Spurrier v La Cloche* [1902] AC 446, PC, following *Hamlyn & Co v Talisker Distillery* [1894] AC 202 (contract): *R v International Trustee for Protection of Bondholders Aktiengesellschaft* [1937] AC 500 (contract) per Lord Atkin, at 529; *First Russian Insurance Co v London and Lancashire Insurance Co* [1928] Ch 922, 31 LlL Rep 151; *Lloyd v Guibert* (1865) LR 1 QB 115, ExCh (charter-party) per Willes J, at 120, 122, stating that the question is not so much by what general law the parties intended that the transaction should be governed, but rather to what general law it is just to presume that they have submitted themselves in the matter; *Jacobs v Credit Lyonnais* (1884) 12 QBD 589, CA (contract) per Bowen LJ, at 600.

14 *Parken v Royal Exchange Co* 1846 8 Dunl (Ct of Sess) 365 (life insurance), where it was held that, although the policy in question was an English policy, issued by an English company, and although the pursuer was domiciled in England, the Scottish Courts were competent to try the case; *Thomson v North British Mercantile Insurance Co* 1868 6 Macph (Ct of Sess) 310 (life insurance).

15 *Re Suse and Sibeth, ex p Dever* (1887) 18 QBD 660, CA (life insurance) per Lord Esher MR, at 664. The lex fori is presumed to be the law governing the contract unless the lex loci is proved to be different: *Canadian Fire Insurance Co v Robinson* (1901) 31 SCR 488. Thus, in *Gold v Life Assurance Co of Pennsylvania* [1971] 2 Lloyd's Rep 164, QBD, a contract for the employment of an agent to sell life insurance policies issued by his principals was held to be governed by English law, for although the contract was probably governed by the law of one of the States in the USA, no evidence had been given on that point. (See the judgment of Donaldson J, who said (ibid, at 167): 'I have to apply the presumption, which is perhaps the most presumptuous of English law, that the foreign country adopts or at any rate has an exactly similar law to that of the law of England.')

16 *Shaik Sahied Bin Abdullah Bajerai v Sockalingam Chettiar* [1933] AC 342, PC (moneylending), where the law of the Straits Settlements provided that the law of England should apply in all questions with respect to insurance and mercantile law generally, per Lord Atkin, at 344: 'If a question of insurable interest arose on a claim on a fire policy, the law as to what constituted an insurable

The proper law must be determined as at the date of the making of the contract, though the Court will, of course, give effect to changes in that proper law which arise after the making of the contract.[17]

1 Where there is an express provision in the policy

If the policy expressly provides that it is to be governed either wholly or partially[18] by the law of a particular country, the intention of the parties is clear,[19] and the law of that country must be applied accordingly.[20] The intention is equally clear where the policy provides that the insurers agree to be bound in all things by the jurisdiction and decision of the courts of a particular country.[1]

2 Where there is no provision in the contract

Where there is no provision in the contract relating to the law to be applied, the intention of the parties must be ascertained by reference to the language of the policy and the surrounding circumstances.[2]

---

interest would be determined by the law of England; but the application of the principle in Singapore might depend upon the law of landlord and tenant, bills of sale, or the administration of deceased persons' estates, none of which in themselves form part of mercantile law.'

17 *Rossano v Manufacturers Life Insurance Co Ltd* [1962] 1 Lloyd's Rep 187, QB (Commercial Court) (life insurance) per McNair J, at 199; *Kahler v Midland Bank Ltd* [1950] AC 24, [1949] 2 All ER 621 (exchange control); *Zivnostenka Banka National Corpn v Frankman* [1950] AC 57, [1949] 2 All ER 671, HL (exchange control).

18 The extent to which the foreign law is incorporated is a mere question of construction of the policy: *Re Suse and Sibeth, ex p Dever* (1887) 18 QBD 660, CA, per Fry LJ, at 688.

19 For a case where the contract contained inconsistent provisions as to the law which governed the contract, see *Ocean SS Co Ltd v Queensland State Wheat Board* [1941] 1 KB 402 [1941] 1 All ER 158, CA (carriage of goods).

20 *Greer v Poole* (1880) 5 QBD 272 (marine insurance) per Lush J, at 274; *Jacobs v Credit Lyonnais* (1884) 12 QBD 589, CA (contract) per Bowen LJ, at 599; cf *Montgomery v Liebenthal* [1898] 1 QB 487, CA (sale of goods), where the contract contained a clause providing not only that the English Court or English arbitrators, as the case might be, should have exclusive jurisdiction over all disputes arising under the contract, but also that such disputes should be settled by English law whatever the domicil, residence or place of business of the contracting parties might be or become.

1 *Royal Exchange Assurance Corpn v Sjoforsakrings Aktiebolaget Vega* [1902] 2 KB 384, CA (marine insurance).

2 *British South Africa Co v De Beers Consolidated Mines Ltd* [1910] 2 Ch 502, CA (mortgage) per Kennedy LJ, at 523: 'Now in ascertaining the proper law of a contract, that which we have to seek is the intention of the contracting parties . . . To this intention, in the absence of express declaration on their part, we must be guided by applying to the language of the contract itself sound ideas of business convenience and sense, and by justly appraising the inferences to be drawn from the nature of the transaction, and the place and circumstances of its machinery and of its contemplated performance'; *Armadora Occidental SA v Horace Mann Insurance Co* [1977] 2 Lloyd's Rep 406, CA (marine insurance), where an American policy contained a 'follow London' clause, and it was held that the clause was of paramount importance and that the policy was to be interpreted according to English law. (See the judgment of Lord Denning MR, ibid, at 412); *Amin Rasheed Shipping Corpn v Kuwait Insurance Co* [1984] AC 50, [1983] 2 All ER 884, [1983] 2 Lloyd's Rep 365, HL (marine insurance), where a policy was issued by insurers in Kuwait, was in the English language only and followed meticulously the wording of the Lloyd's SG policy, and it was held that the proper law of the contract was English law. (See the judgment of Lord Diplock, ibid, at 370–371.)

(a) The 'presumptions'

In order to ascertain the intention of the parties the Courts are guided by various 'presumptions'. These relate to:

- i The place where the contract is made.
- ii The place where payment is to be made.
- iii The form in which the policy is framed.
- iv The position where the terms of the policy are valid in one country, but not in another.

i The place where the contract is made

The law applicable is, prima facie, presumed to be that of the place where the contract is made.[3] This presumption is not, however, conclusive,[4] and may be rebutted by evidence of a contrary intention.[5]

Contracts made through agents

In dealing with a policy of insurance effected with English insurers through an agent resident abroad, the place where the contract is to be regarded as having been made depends on the powers of the agent.

Where the agent has himself power to bind his principal by the contracts which he makes, the contract will be made in the place where the agent is, since the position is the same as if the principal were there himself.[6]

Where the agent's powers are limited, and it is his duty to transmit all proposals for insurance to his principals in England, who alone have power to decide as to their acceptance or rejection, no contract comes into existence until there is an acceptance by them of a particular proposal.[7] In this case the contract is made in England, although the acceptance has to be transmitted abroad.[8]

---

[3] *Jacobs v Credit Lyonnais* (supra) per Bowen LJ, at 600, citing *Robinson v Bland* (1760) 1 WmBl 234 (contract), and *Lloyd v Guibert* (1865) LR 1 QB 115 (charter-party) per Willes J, at 122; *Pattison v Mills* (1828) 1 Dow & Cl 342, HL, where an English fire insurance company, through an agent in Scotland, insured a ship against loss by fire, such an insurance being then forbidden by English law, but not by Scots law, and it was held that the assured was entitled to recover upon the agreement as made in Scotland, and that he was not bound by a limitation inserted in the policy, without his knowledge, by the Head Office in London; *Peninsular and Oriental Steam Navigation Co v Shand* (1865) 3 Moo PCCNS 272, 290 (carrier); *Citizens' Insurance Co of Canada v Parsons* (1881) 7 App Cas 96, PC; *Scottish Provident Institution v Cohen & Co* 1888 16 R (Ct of Sess) 112 (life insurance); cf *Waydell v Provincial Insurance Co* (1862) 21 UCR 612, where a policy granted by a Canadian company was held assignable in accordance with the law of New York, as having been made in New York.

[4] *Royal Exchange Assurance Corpn v Sjoforsakrings Atkiebolaget Vega* (supra) per Cozens-Hardy LJ, at 396.

[5] *Re Missouri SS Co* (1889) 42 ChD 321, CA (bill of lading) per Cotton LJ, at 338.

[6] *Pattison v Mills* (1828) 1 Dow & Cl 342, HL (fire insurance) per Lord Lyndhurst LC, at 382. See further, Dicey and Morris, op cit, pp 911–917.

[7] But where the agent has authority to issue a cover note, the contract contained in the cover note will be made at the place where the cover note is issued by the agent: *Pattison v Mills* (supra) (fire insurance).

[8] *Parken v Royal Exchange Assurance Co* 1846 8 Dunl (Ct of Sess) 365 (life insurance); cf *Redpath v Sun Mutual Insurance Co* (1869) 14 LCJ 90, where it was held that a contract of insurance made by an agent in Montreal was void, the company being incorporated by the law of New York and being restricted by its charter and byelaws to entering into contracts in New York by its presidents or vice-presidents.

Where the policy itself is issued in England, the contract as contained in the policy is made in England.[9] But the assured is not, by the issue of the policy, necessarily precluded from relying on the original agreement from which the policy resulted, and he may, therefore, contend that the original agreement is the real contract, and that it is governed by the law of the place where it is made.[10]

ii The place of payment

Where the policy expressly provides for the payment either of premiums or of losses or of both at a particular place,[11] there is a presumption that the parties intended the law of that place to govern the incidents of the payment,[12] and even the whole contract, if the whole of the performance is to take place there.

The presumption is not, however, conclusive, and may be rebutted by the express or implied intention of the parties to be deduced from other circumstances of the case.[13]

Even where the payment is to be made abroad, the parties may still intend their rights and liabilities to be governed by English law, or they may, on the other hand, intend to incorporate the foreign law so far as it is necessary to

---

9 *Sanderson v Cunningham* [1919] 2 IR 234, where a policy was issued in London and sent by post to brokers in Dublin; *Clarke v Union Fire Insurance Co* (1884) 6 OR 223, where the policy was held to be an Ontario policy, being signed and sealed in Ontario, though sent to an agent of the insurers in New York; cf *O'Leary v Law of Integrity Insurance Co* [1912] 1 IR 479 (life insurance), where the policy, though sealed in England was, in the contemplation of the parties, not to be completely binding on either party until delivery in Dublin; *Richardson v Army, Navy and General Assurance Association* [1924] 2 IR 96 (life insurance).

10 *Pattison v Mills* (supra); *Ruby SS Corpn Ltd v Commercial Union Assurance Co* (1933) 150 LT 38, CA (marine insurance), where the right of the broker to cancel the policy on the ground of the non-receipt of the premium in spite of a recital in the policy that the premium had been paid, was determined by the law of the country where the relation of principal and agent was created.

11 In the absence of any such provision, the place of payment will be the insurers' or the assured's place of business according as the payment is of premiums or losses: *Robey v Snaefell Mining Co* (1887) 20 QBD 152 (sale of goods to Isle of Man); *Hassall v Lawrence* (1887) 4 TLR 23 (sale of goods to Australia); *Rein v Stein* [1892] 1 QB 753, CA (sale of goods to Germany); *Thompson v Palmer* [1893] 2 QB 80, CA (work and labour in Spain).

12 *Lloyd v Guibert* (1865) LR 1 QB 115, ExCh (charter-party) per Willes J, at 125, 126; *Cook v Scottish Equitable Life Assurance Society* (1872) 26 LT 571 (life insurance) cf *Mildred, Goyeneche & Co v Maspons* (1883) 8 App Cas 874 (marine insurance); *Austrian Lloyd SS Co v Gresham Life Assurance Society Ltd* [1903] 1 KB 249, CA (life insurance); *Adelaide Electric Supply Co Ltd v Prudential Assurance Co Ltd* [1934] AC 122 (company) per Lord Wright, at 151.

13 *Jacobs v Credit Lyonnais* (1884) 12 QBD 589, CA (contract) per Bowen LJ, at 601: 'The place of performance is necessarily in many cases the place where the obligations of the contract will have to be enforced, and hence, as well as for other reasons, has been introduced another canon of construction, to the effect that the law of the place of fulfilment of a contract determines its obligation. But this maxim . . . must, of course, give way to any inference that can legitimately be drawn from the character of the contract, and the nature of the transaction. In most cases no doubt where a contract has to be wholly performed abroad, the reasonable presumption may be that it is intended to be a foreign contract determined by foreign law; but this prima facie view is in its turn capable of being rebutted by the expressed or implied intention of the parties as deduced from other circumstances. Again, it may be that the contract is partly to be performed in one place and partly in another. In such a case the only certain guide is to be found in applying sound ideas of business, convenience, and sense to the language of the contract itself, with a view to discovering from it the true intention of the parties.' In the case of a policy made in a foreign country, where no special provision is made, a demand for payment after a loss should be made by the assured at the head office in that country before the insurers can be sued in England; cf *Equitable Life Assurance Co v Perrault* (1882) 26 LCJ 382 (life insurance).

regulate the method and manner of payment,[14] without altering any of the incidents which attach to the contract according to English law.[15]

iii The form in which the policy is framed

The fact that the policy is framed in the usual form leads to the inference that the parties intended that their rights under the contract should be governed by the law of England.[16]

This intention is, however, made clearer where there are specific references in the policy to English law, e g to the Arbitration Act 1950. In this case, the fact that the policy was made abroad may be disregarded.[17]

iv Terms valid in one country only

Where the contract contains stipulations which are valid by the law of one country, but invalid by the law of another country, it must be presumed to have been the intention of the parties that the law which would make the contract valid in all particulars is to be the proper law of the contract.[18] But this presumption may be rebutted by the presence of other incidents in the contract.[19]

3 Immateriality of locality of subject-matter

The locality of the subject-matter of insurance, even in the case of immovable property, does not appear to have any bearing on the question of what law is to be regarded as the proper law of the contract.

The rule that where the contract affects immovables situated out of the jurisdiction, the lex loci rei sitae in general, at least, must be taken as the proper law of the contract, has no application. The subject-matter of the contract is to be distinguished from the subject-matter of insurance. The contract itself cannot fairly be regarded as in any way affecting the immovable property

---

14 *Re State Fire Insurance Co, ex p Meredith and Convers' Claim* (1863) 32 LJ Ch 300, where, payment for the loss being made by bills of exchange drawn in Canada, which were dishonoured, it was held that the assured was entitled to prove, in the winding-up of the insurance company, for the full amount payable on the bills of exchange together with the interest and damages allowed by Canadian law, notwithstanding that the policy limited the claim under it to the capital of the company. Cf *St Pierre v South American Stores (Gath & Chaves) Ltd and Chilean Stores (Gath & Chaves) Ltd* [1937] 3 All ER 349, CA (lease), where Chilean law was held to apply even though the lease provided for an option, which was exercised, for payment of rent in England.

15 *Jacobs v Credit Lyonnais* (1884) 12 QBD 589, CA (contract) per Bowen LJ, at 601.

16 *Harris v Scaramanga* (1872) LR 7 CP 481 (marine insurance); *Greer v Poole* (1880) 5 QBD 272 (marine insurance); *Royal Exchange Assurance Corpn v Sjoforsakrings Aktiebolaget Vega* [1902] 2 KB 384, CA (marine insurance) per Collins MR, at 394; ibid, per Cozens-Hardy LJ, at 396.

17 *Spurrier v La Cloche* [1902] AC 446, PC, where the contract was made in Jersey; *Wilson v National Live Stock Insurance Co* [1914] WC & Ins Rep 169, CA (livestock insurance) per Holmes LJ, at 172; cf *Norske Atlas Insurance Co v London General Insurance Co* (1927) 43 TLR 541 (marine insurance), where the fact that the arbitration was to be held in Norway led to the inference that Norwegian law was intended to apply.

18 *Re Missouri SS Co* (1889) 42 ChD 321, CA (bill of lading); cf *Norske Atlas Insurance Co v London General Insurance Co* (1927) 43 TLR 541 (marine insurance).

19 *Maritime Insurance Co Ltd v Union Von Assecuranz 1865* (1935) 52 LlL Rep 16 (marine insurance), where there were provision for payment in sterling and for London arbitration in a policy invalid by English law owing to non-compliance with the requirements of the Stamp Acts.

which happens to be the subject-matter of insurance, since it is merely a contract to pay a sum of money in a certain event.

The fact that the event must be connected with some particular property, and that the right to recover on the contract must depend upon an interest in such property, cannot bring the contract within the rule, seeing that neither the ownership nor the possession of the property is affected by the contract, either directly or indirectly.[20]

C WHEN THE LAW OF ENGLAND MUST ALWAYS BE APPLIED

There are certain cases in which the law of England must be applied, even though the law generally applicable to the policy may be that of a foreign country. These cases are:

1 Where the policy is one which, by reason of some defect in form, is not enforceable by English law.[1]

2 Where the policy is one the making of which is prohibited by English law or is otherwise inconsistent with English ideas of public policy.[2]

D ASSIGNMENT

The question whether a policy of insurance relating to property situated abroad or the proceeds of the policy, as against the insurers, can be assigned or not, depends upon the law governing the policy.[3]

But the validity of the assignment itself, assuming that it is capable of being carried out lawfully in some way or other, is governed by the law of the country where it takes place, since the subject-matter of the assignment is a chose in action which has, for this purpose, no locality.[4]

---

20 Cf *British South Africa Co v De Beers Consolidated Mines Ltd* [1910] 2 Ch 502, CA (revsd without affecting this point [1912] AC 52), where a contract to give a mortgage on foreign land was held to be a contract to give an English mortgage, subject to such rights of redemption and such equities as the law of England regards as necessarily incident to a mortgage; *Buenos Ayres and Ensenada Port Rly Co v Northern Rly Co of Buenos Ayres* (1877) 2 QBD 210 (rent), where the contract under which the plaintiff's claim arose was made at Buenos Aires and related to a railway station and the works there.

1 *Leroux v Brown* (1852) 12 CB 801 (verbal contract not to be performed within the year). The absence of the stamp required by a foreign revenue law may be disregarded, if the policy is not thereby invalidated by the foreign law, but is only inadmissible in evidence in the foreign court; *Bristow v Sequeville* (1850) 5 Exch 275 (receipt). But if the policy is rendered void, it is equally void in England: *Alves v Hodgson* (1797) 7 Term Rep 241 (promissory note).

2 Thus, if the policy is a wager policy, the English law will probably prevail; see *Moulis v Owen* [1907] 1 KB 746, CA (cheque in payment of gambling debt) per Collins MR, at 753; ibid, per Cozens-Hardy LJ, at 756.

3 *Colonial Bank v Cody and Williams* (1890) 15 App Cas 267 (transfer of shares) per Lord Herschell, at 283; *New York Life Insurance Co v Public Trustee* [1924] 2 Ch 101, CA (life insurance).

4 *Lee v Abdy* (1886) 17 QBD 309 (life insurance); *Scottish Provident Institution v Cohen & Co* 1888 16 R (Ct of Sess) 112 (life insurance); *Republica de Guatemala v Nunez* [1927] 1 KB 669, CA (assignment of debt); *Waydell v Provincial Insurance Co* (1862) 21 UCR 612. In *Kelly v Selwyn* [1905] 2 Ch 117 (assignment of reversionary interest), a subsequent assignment was held in accordance with English law to prevail over a previous assignment without notice, although the latter assignment was held valid by the law of the country where it was made.

CHAPTER 56

The effect of war upon the contract[1]

An enemy alien,[2] being by law incapable of contracting with a British subject, cannot, during the continuance of hostilities between the country with which he is to be identified and Great Britain,[3] enter into a valid contract of insurance with British insurers.[4]

On the other hand, if, after the execution of a policy, the assured becomes an enemy alien by reason of the outbreak of war between his country and Great Britain, the policy, not being unlawful in its inception, is not avoided, but is only suspended in its operation during the continuance of the war.[5]

Where a loss has taken place before the outbreak of war, the assured may, on the conclusion of peace, but not before, sue on the policy.[6]

Where the loss takes place after the conclusion of peace, it takes place under a valid contract, and the assured is entitled to recover in respect of it.[7]

Where the loss takes place during hostilities, it is clear that if the loss is

---

1 As to this subject generally, see G J Webber *The Effect of War on Contracts*, 2nd Edn (1946), especially pp 277–280 (life insurance) and pp 295–363 (property insurance).

2 Including a corporation: *Janson v Driefontein Consolidated Mines* [1902] AC 484 (marine insurance) per Lord Lindley, at 505.

3 To constitute an enemy alien, the existence of a war between belligerent states is essential: *Eastern Carrying Insurance Co v National Benefit Life and Property Assurance Co Ltd* (1919) 35 TLR 292.

4 *Janson v Driefontein Consolidated Mines* (supra) per Lord Davey, at 499. The law as stated is the Common Law and is subject to special legislation enacted for the purpose of any particular war. See Trading with the Enemy Act 1939, and the Statutory Rules and Orders made thereunder.

5 An executory contract is abrogated on the outbreak of war, since it involves trading with the enemy which is assumed to be beneficial to him: *Ertel Bieber & Co v Rio Tinto Co* [1918] AC 260 (sale of goods) per Lord Atkinson, at 277. An executed contract, however, is one which has been so far carried out that it does not require intercourse with the enemy: *Ottoman Bank v Jebara* [1928] AC 269 (sale of goods). A contract of insurance is of the latter class: *Seligman v Eagle Insurance Co* [1917] 1 Ch 519 (life insurance). An executory contract with a neutral is abrogated only if its performance will probably enure to the benefit of an enemy: *Schering Ltd v Stockholmes Enskilda Bank Aktiebolag* [1944] Ch 13, [1943] 2 All ER 486, CA (contract).

6 *Janson v Driefontein Consolidated Mines* (supra) per Lord Davey, at 499; *Harman v Kingston* (1811) 3 Camp 150 (marine insurance); *Flindt v Waters* (1812) 15 East 260 (marine insurance); *Ex p Boussmaker* (1806) 13 Ves 71 (claim in bankruptcy). But the insurers may agree not to raise the defence that the assured is, at the time of action brought, an enemy alien: *Janson v Driefontein Consolidated Mines* (supra).

7 Since the contract is not one which in its terms must necessarily be performed during the period of hostilities, the outbreak of hostilities does not of itself make performance unlawful or impossible as was the case in *Esposito v Bowden* (1857) 7 E & B 763 (charter-party), and hence the contract is not discharged. It appears, therefore to be capable of being revived when peace is made. The marine insurance cases cited below seem to assume that the policy continues to exist after the outbreak of war; see also, *Furtado v Rogers* (1802) 3 Bos & P 191 (marine insurance); *Seligman v Eagle Insurance Co* (supra). The position is different in the case of a treaty of obligatory reinsurance, since the basis of the contract is destroyed; see *Eastern Carrying Insurance Co v National Benefit Life and Property Assurance Co Ltd* (1919) 35 TLR 292; *Ertel Bieber & Co v Rio Tinto Co* [1918] AC 260 (sale of goods).

directly connected with such hostilities, e g where, in the case of fire insurance, the fire is occasioned in the course of military operations, whether on the part of the British Forces,[8] or their allies,[9] or of the assured's own countrymen,[10] the assured is, quite apart from any express condition in the policy, prohibited from recovering on the ground of public policy.

A similar prohibition applies even where the loss is wholly unconnected with the existence of the hostilities, e g in the case of an ordinary loss by fire.[11]

The prohibition applies only to claims made by enemy aliens. As British subjects are not precluded from enforcing against enemy aliens claims arising under contracts which were made before the outbreak of war, provided that the difficulties of service of the writ can be overcome, British insurers are, therefore, entitled in the case of an enemy assured to receive, and if necessary, to enforce payment of premiums.[12] Further, in the case of enemy insurers, a British assured may receive payment or enforce a claim under his policy.[13]

In determining whether a person is an enemy alien or not, it is not his nationality, i e the fact that he is a subject of a hostile state, so much as his place of business during the war that is important.[14]

Although the prima facie disability arising from nationality is not removed by mere residence in British Dominions without a licence, express or implied, from the Crown,[15] the subject of a hostile state who is carrying on business in British Dominions, or in a foreign country, is not, for the purposes of a contract of insurance, to be deemed an enemy alien.[16]

---

8 *Kellner v Le Mesurier* (1803) 4 East 396 (marine insurance); *Janson v Driefontein Consolidated Mines* [1902] AC 484 (marine insurance) per Lord Davey, at 499; cf *The Gothland* [1916] P 239n (prize), where neutral insurers were held to have no claim in the case of enemy goods, for which they paid a total loss; *The Palm Branch* [1916] P 230 (prize), where a similar claim by enemy insurers in respect of neutral goods failed.

9 *Brandon v Curling* (1803) 4 East 410 (marine insurance).

10 *Janson v Driefontein Consolidated Mines* (supra) per Lord Brampton, at 502.

11 *Brandon v Curling* (supra) per Lord Ellenborough, at 417: 'So that where the insurance is upon goods generally, a proviso to this effect shall in all cases be considered as engrafted therein, viz, "*provided that this insurance shall not extend to cover any loss happening during the existence of hostilities between the respective countries of the assured and assurer.*" Because during the existence of such hostilities the subjects of one country cannot allowably lend their assistance to protect by insurance the property and commerce of the subjects of the other.' This was approved in *Janson v Driefontein Consolidated Mines* (supra) per Lord Lindley, at 508; see *Seligman v Eagle Insurance Co* [1917] 1 Ch 519 (life insurance) per Neville J, at 526. But the treaty of peace may make special provision for preserving the validity of the policy: *Excess Insurance Co Ltd v Mathews* (1925) 23 LlL Rep 71.

12 *Seligman v Eagle Insurance Co* [1917] 1 Ch 519 (life insurance), where the premium was tendered by a surety.

13 *W L Ingle Ltd v Mannheim Continental Insurance Co* [1915] 1 KB 227 (marine insurance) where the loss took place during hostilities; *Robinson & Co v Continental Insurance Co of Mannheim* [1915] 1 KB 155 (marine insurance), where the pleadings had been closed before the outbreak of war.

14 *Janson v Driefontein Consolidated Mines* [1902] AC 484 (marine insurance) per Lord Lindley, at 505. Invasion of friendly territory, resulting in the enemy being in effective control, gives the area an enemy character and disqualifies local residents, however friendly disposed in fact, from suing in the British Courts: *Sovfracht V/O v Van Udens Scheepvaart en Agentuur Maatschappij (NV Gebr)* [1943] AC 203, [1943] 1 All ER 76 (arbitration).

15 *Boulton v Dobree* (1808) 2 Camp 163 (marine insurance) per Lord Ellenborough CJ, at 165.

16 *Wells v Williams* (1697) 1 Ld Raym 282 (licence to trade). But unless the enemy alien is in British Dominions with such an express or implied licence, his right to sue in the Courts is suspended: *Porter v Freudenberg* [1915] 1 KB 857, CA (rent); *Thurn and Taxis (Princess) v Moffitt* [1915] 1 Ch 58 (libel).

On the other hand, the subject of a neutral,[17] or even a British subject,[18] will, by carrying on business there, or even by voluntarily residing there, be treated for these purposes as enemy alien.[19]

The stringency of this rule, may, however, be relaxed by treaty, Order in Council, or licence.[20] Where an enemy alien is thus enabled to contract, he acquires the right to enter into contracts of insurance,[1] and to enforce them in his own name during the war.[2]

---

17 *Sorenson v R, The Baltica* (1858) 11 Moo PCC 141 (sale of a ship).

18 *Porter v Freudenberg* (supra) per Lord Reading CJ, at 869.

19 See also the definition of 'enemy' in the Trading with the Enemy Act 1939, s 2.

20 *Esposito v Bowden* (1857) 7 E & B 763, ExCh (charter-party) per Willes J, at 793. As to the effect of an Order in Council, see *Clemontson v Blessig* (1855) 11 Exch 135 (sale of goods).

1 *Kensington v Inglis* (1807) 8 East 273 (marine insurance); *Flindt v Scott* (1814) 5 Taunt 674 (marine insurance).

2 *Morgan v Oswald* (1812) 3 Taunt 554 (marine insurance); cf *Fayle v Bourdillon* (1811) 3 Taunt 546 (marine insurance).

CHAPTER 57

The protection of policyholders

The Policyholders Protection Act 1975[1] establishes the Policyholders Protection Board, and enables it to assist policyholders who have been or may be prejudiced in consequence of the inability of authorised insurance companies carrying on business in the United Kingdom to meet their liabilities under policies which have been issued. The Act gives the Board power to impose levies on the insurance industry for the purpose.

A THE POLICYHOLDERS PROTECTION BOARD

1 Constitution

The Board consists of 5 members to be appointed by the Secretary of State together with any persons appointed by him to be alternate members.[2] Of the persons appointed

- a at least 3 must be members who are directors, chief executives or managers of authorised insurance companies; and
- b at least one must be a person appearing to the Secretary of State to be qualified to represent the interests of policyholders of authorised insurance companies.[3]

The Secretary of State may appoint, in respect of each member of the Board, a person to perform his duties as a member in his absence. A person so appointed is to be an alternate member of the Board and may take part in its proceedings in the absence of the member in respect of whom he was appointed.[4]

A person appointed as an alternate member of the Board in respect of a person who is a director, chief executive or manager of an authorised insurance company must himself be such a director, chief executive or manager.[5] A person appointed as an alternate member in respect of a person appearing to the Secretary of State to be qualified to represent the interests of policyholders of authorised insurance companies must himself be a person appearing to the Secretary of State to be so qualified.[6]

The Secretary of State must consult persons appearing to him to be representative of the interests of authorised insurance companies before

---

1 The Act is set out at pp 628–653, post.
2 Policyholders Protection Act 1975, Sch 1, para 1(1).
3 Ibid, Sch 1, para 1(2).
4 Ibid, Sch 1, para 1(3).
5 Ibid, Sch 1, para 1(4).
6 Ibid, Sch 1, para 1(4).

appointing a person who is a director, chief executive or manager of an authorised insurance company to be a member or alternate member of the Board.[7]

2 Appointment and tenure of members

Any appointment of a member by the Secretary of State is for a term not exceeding 2 years.[8] The term of the appointment of an alternate member must not exceed the term or the remainder of the term, as the case may be, of the member in respect of whom he is appointed.[9] The Secretary of State has power to re-appoint a person as a member or alternate member on his ceasing to hold office in either capacity, or at any time thereafter.[10]

The Secretary of State must appoint one of the members to be the chairman.[11] If the chairman ceases to be a member, he ceases to be chairman.[12]

The members and alternate members (including the chairman) hold and vacate office in accordance with the terms of their respective appointments.[13]

A person may at any time resign his office as a member, as an alternate member or as chairman by giving to the Secretary of State a notice in writing signed by that person and stating that he resigns that office.[14]

If the Secretary of State is satisfied that a member or an alternate member

a is incapacitated by physical or mental illness; or
b is otherwise unable or unfit to discharge his functions,

the Secretary of State may by notice in writing given to the person in question remove him from office as member or alternate member, as the case may be.[15] His office thereupon becomes vacant.[16]

Where before the end of the term for which he was appointed a member dies or vacates office,[17]

a the alternate member in respect of that member may act as member in his place until a person is appointed to fill his office as member; and
b the Secretary of State may vary the terms of appointment of the alternate member on appointing a person to fill the office vacated by the member in question.[18]

3 Remuneration and compensation

The Board must pay to each member or alternate member such remuneration

---

7 Policyholders Protection Act 1975, Sch 1, para 1(5).
8 Ibid, Sch 1, para 2(1).
9 Ibid, Sch 1, para 2(1).
10 Ibid, Sch 1, para 2(2).
11 Ibid, Sch 1, para 3(1).
12 Ibid, Sch 1, para 3(2).
13 Ibid, Sch 1, para 4(1).
14 Ibid, Sch 1, para 4(2).
15 Ibid, Sch 1, para 4(3).
16 Ibid, Sch 1, para 4(3).
17 Under paras 4(2) or 4(3) above.
18 Policyholders Protection Act 1975, Sch 1, para 4(4).

and such travelling, subsistence or other allowances as the Board may determine.[19]

If a person ceases to be a member or alternate member and it appears to the Secretary of State that there are special circumstances which make it right that that person should receive compensation, the Secretary of State may require the Board to pay to that person a sum of such amount as the Secretary of State may with the consent of the Minister for the Civil Service determine.[20]

4 Powers and procedure

The Board may invest any funds held by them which appear to them to be surplus to their requirements for the time being

a in any investment for the time being falling within Part II or Part III of Sch 1 to the Trustee Investments Act 1961; or
b in any investment approved for the purpose by the Secretary of State.[1]

Further, the Board has power to do anything incidental or conducive to the proper performance of their functions under the Act.[2] The measures open to the Board under any provision of the Act which authorises or requires the Board to take any measures appearing to them to be appropriate for any purpose include in particular

a the making of payments to any person on such terms[3] and conditions as the Board think fit;
b the giving of guarantees or indemnities to or in favour of any person; and
c the making of any other agreement or arrangement with or for the benefit of any person.[4]

The Board has power to regulate their own procedure.[5]

A member or an alternate member who is in any way directly or indirectly interested[6] in any matter falling to be considered by the Board must disclose the nature of his interest at a meeting of the Board, and the disclosure must be recorded in the minutes of the meeting. The member or alternate member in question must not take part in any deliberation or decision of the Board with respect to that matter.[7]

---

19 Policyholders Protection Act 1975, Sch 1, para 5(1). Any determination of the Board with respect to the remuneration to be paid to any member or alternate member is subject to the approval of the Secretary of State, and the Secretary of State must not give his approval without the consent of the Minister for the Civil Service: ibid, Sch 1, para 5(2).
20 Ibid, Sch 1, para 6.
1 Ibid, Sch 1, para 7(1).
2 Ibid, Sch 1, para 7(2).
3 Including terms requiring repayment, in whole or in part.
4 Policyholders Protection Act 1975, Sch 1, para 7(3).
5 Ibid, Sch 1, para 8.
6 Whether as being a member or policyholder of an insurance company or in any other matter whatsoever.
7 Policyholders Protection Act 1975, Sch 1, para 9(2). This sub-paragraph does not apply in relation to any interest of a member or alternate member arising from any connection with an insurance company where the only connection of the company in question with the matter under consideration arises from the fact that it has agreed or may agree to take a transfer of all or any part of the insurance business of a company in liquidation or of a company which is a company in financial difficulties within the meaning of s 16: Policyholders Protection Act 1975, Sch 1, para 9(2). As to a company in financial difficulties within the meaning of s 16, see p 609, post.

A notice given by a member or alternate member at a meeting of the Board to the effect that he is a member or a policyholder of a specified insurance company and is to be regarded as interested in any matter affecting that company which falls to be considered by the Board after the date of the notice is a sufficient disclosure of his interest in any such matter.[8]

A member or alternate member need not attend in person at a meeting of the Board in order to make a disclosure which he is required to make if he takes reasonable steps to secure that the disclosure is made by a notice which is taken into consideration and read at such a meeting.[9]

The validity of any proceedings of the Board is not affected by any vacancy among the members or by any defect in the appointment of any member or of an alternate member or by any failure to comply with the requirements as to disclosure mentioned above.[10]

5 Performance of functions

The Board may authorise any member or alternate member or any other person who is either an employee or agent of theirs to perform on their behalf such of their functions[11] as are specified in the authorisation.[12]

6 Instruments and contracts

The fixing of the common seal of the Board must be authenticated by the chairman or some other person authorised by the Board to act for that purpose.[13]

A document purporting to be duly executed under the seal of the Board must be received in evidence and, unless the contrary is proved, is deemed to be so executed.[14]

7 Accounts, audit and annual report

It is the duty of the Board

a to keep proper accounts and proper records in relation to the accounts; and

b to prepare in respect of each financial year[15] a statement of accounts, in such form as the Secretary of State may direct, showing the state of affairs and income and expenditure of the Board.[16]

A statement of accounts prepared in accordance with the above provisions must be audited by auditors appointed by the Board.[17]

---

8 Policyholders Protection Act 1975, Sch 1, para 9(3).

9 Ibid, Sch 1, para 9(4).

10 Ibid, Sch 1, para 10.

11 Including the function conferred on them by para 11.

12 Policyholders Protection Act 1975, Sch 1, para 11.

13 Ibid, Sch 1, para 12.

14 Ibid, Sch 1, para 13.

15 'Financial year' means a period of 12 months ending with March 31 in any year: ibid, s 32(1).

16 Ibid, Sch 1, para 14(1).

17 Ibid, Sch 1, para 14(2). A person is not qualified to be appointed as auditor by the Board unless he is a member of one or more of the following bodies:

i the Institute of Chartered Accountants in England and Wales;

ii the Institute of Chartered Accountants of Scotland;

iii the Association of Certified Accountants;

It is the duty of the Board as soon as possible after the end of each financial year to prepare, in such manner as the Secretary of State may direct, a report on the performance of their functions during that year.[18]

The Board must publish the statement of accounts and the report in respect of each financial year at such time and in such manner as the Secretary of State may direct.[19]

8 Guidance by the Secretary of State

The Secretary of State may from time to time, after consultation with the Board, give them guidance with respect to the performance of any of their functions under the Act. It is the duty of the Board to perform the functions in question in such a manner as they consider is in accordance with the guidance for the time being given to them.[20]

No guidance must be given to the Board unless a draft of the document containing it has been approved by a resolution of each House of Parliament.[1]

B THE GENERAL SCOPE OF THE BOARD'S FUNCTIONS

The functions of the Board are exercisable in relation to policyholders and others who have been or may be prejudiced in consequence of the inability of insurance companies to meet their liabilities under policies issued or securities given by them only in cases where the insurance companies in question are authorised insurance companies.[2]

A policyholder is eligible for the assistance or protection of the Board[3] only in respect of a policy which was a United Kingdom policy at the material time.[4]

C THE BOARD'S DUTIES IN CASE OF COMPANIES IN LIQUIDATION

The Board's functions are exercisable where in the case of any authorised insurance company

---

iv the Institute of Chartered Accountants in Ireland;

v any other body of accountants established in the United Kingdom and for the time being recognised for the purpose of the Companies Act 1985, s 389(1)(a) by the Secretary of State;

but a Scottish firm may be so appointed if each of the partners in it is so qualified: ibid, Sch 1, para 14(3).

18 Ibid, Sch 1, para 14(4).

19 Ibid, Sch 1, para 14(5).

20 Ibid, s 2(1).

1 Ibid, s 2(2).

2 Ibid, s 3(1). An insurance company is an authorised insurance company if it is authorised under the Insurance Companies Act 1982, s 3 or s 4 to carry on business of any class in the United Kingdom: ibid, s 3(2).

3 In accordance with any provisions of ss 6 to 16 of the Act. See pp 601–610, post.

4 Policyholders Protection Act 1975, s 4(1). A policy of insurance is a United Kingdom policy at any time when the performance by the insurer of any of his obligations under the contract evidenced by the policy would constitute the carrying on by the insurer of insurance business of any class in the United Kingdom: ibid, s 4(2).

a a resolution has been passed, in accordance with the provisions of the Companies Act 1985 for the voluntary winding up of the company, otherwise than merely for the purpose of reconstruction or of amalgamation with another insurance company; or

b without any such resolution having been passed beforehand, an order has been made for the winding up of the company by the Court under the Act of 1985.[5]

1 Compulsory insurance

Where a policy

i satisfies the requirements of the Riding Establishments Act 1964, s 1(4A)(d)[6] or the Employers' Liability (Compulsory Insurance) Act 1969, s 1[7] or Part VI of the Road Traffic Act 1972;[8] or

ii evidences a contract of insurance effected for the purposes of the Nuclear Installations Act 1965, s 19,[9]

or a security in respect of third party risks given by an authorised insurance company satisfies the requirements of Part VI of the Road Traffic Act 1972,[10] it is the duty of the Board to secure that a sum equal to the full amount of any liability of a company in liquidation towards any policyholder or security holder under the terms of any such compulsory insurance or security is paid to the policyholder or security holder as soon as reasonably practicable after the beginning of the liquidation.[11]

It is the duty of the Board to secure that a sum equal to 90 per cent of the amount of any liability of a company in liquidation towards a private policyholder[12] under the terms of any compulsory insurance policy, being a liability arising otherwise than in respect of a liability of the policyholder which

---

5 Policyholders Protection Act 1975, s 5(1).

6 See post.

7 See Ivamy *Personal Accident, Life and Other Insurances* (2nd Edn, 1980), pp 292–296.

8 See Ivamy *Fire and Motor Insurance* (4th Edn, 1984), pp 299–318.

9 See Ivamy *Personal Accident, Life and Other Insurances* (2nd Edn, 1980), pp 264–265.

10 Policyholders Protection Act 1975, s 6(1)(2).

11 Ibid, s 6(4). This subsection does not apply by reference to any liability of a company in liquidation under the terms of a policy otherwise than in respect of a liability of the policyholder which is a liability subject to compulsory insurance: ibid, s 6(5). 'A liability subject to compulsory insurance' means any liability required under any of the enactments mentioned in s 6(1) to be covered by insurance or (as the case may be) by insurance or by some other provision for securing its discharge: ibid, s 6(3). 'The beginning of the liquidation' means the passing of a resolution for the voluntary winding up of the company or the making of a winding up order, as the case may be: ibid, s 5(5). The duty of the Board under s 6(4) does not apply:

a in the case of any policy unless it was a United Kingdom policy at the beginning of the liquidation; or

b in the case of any security in respect of third-party risks unless it would have been a United Kingdom policy at the beginning of the liquidation if it had been an insurance policy and the contract governing the security had been a contract of insurance; ibid, s 6(7).

12 'Private policyholder' means a policyholder who is either:

a an individual: or

b a partnership or other unicorporated body of persons all of whom are individuals: ibid, s 6(7).

is a liability subject to compulsory insurance, is paid to the policyholder as soon as reasonably practicable after the beginning of the liquidation.[13]

2 Third-party risks against insurance companies in road traffic cases

It is the duty of the Board to secure that a sum equal to the full amount of any liability of a company in liquidation in respect of a sum payable to a person entitled to the benefit of a judgment under the Road Traffic Act 1972, s 149[14] is paid to that person as soon as reasonably practicable after the beginning of the liquidation.[15]

3 General policies other than compulsory insurance policies

It is the duty of the Board to secure that a sum equal to 90 per cent of the amount of any liability of a company in liquidation towards a private policyholder[16] under the terms of any general policy[17] which was a United Kingdom policy at the beginning of the liquidation is paid to the policyholder as soon as reasonably practicable after the beginning of the liquidation.[18]

4 Limits on the Board's duties

The Board is not required to secure any sum for a policyholder in respect of a policy of a company in liquidation which was a United Kingdom policy at the beginning of the liquidation or (as the case may be) for a person entitled to the benefit of a judgment by reference to any liability (or any part of any liability) of a company in liquidation which is duplicated by the liability of any other authorised insurance company which is not a company in liquidation.[19]

5 Long term policies

It is the duty of the Board to secure that a sum equal to 90 per cent of the

---

13 Ibid, s 6(6). The duty of the Board under this subsection does not apply:
a in the case of any policy, unless it was a United Kingdom policy at the beginning of the liquidation; or
b in the case of any security in respect of third-party risks, unless it would have been a United Kingdom policy at the beginning of the liquidation if it had been an insurance policy and the contract governing the security had been a contract of insurance: ibid, s 6(8).

14 See Ivamy *Fire and Motor Insurance* (4th Edn, 1984), 337–345.

15 Policyholders Protection Act 1975, s 7.

16 'Private policyholder' has the same meaning as in s 6(6): ibid, s 8(3). See footnote 12, supra.

17 'General policy' means any policy evidencing a contract the effecting of which constituted the carrying on of general business of any class other than class 5, 6, 7, 11 or 12, not being a contract of reinsurance: Policyholders Protection Act 1975, s 8(4). As to these classes, see p 31, ante.

18 Policyholders Protection Act 1975, s 8(2).

19 Policyholders Protection Act 1975, s 9(1). A liability of a company towards a policyholder is duplicated by the liability of another company for the purposes of this subsection in so far as that other company is also under a liability, under the terms of any general policy which was a United Kingdom policy at the beginning of the first mentioned company's liquidation, to make any payment to or on behalf of the policyholder in respect of the matter to which the liability of the first-mentioned company relates: ibid, s 9(2). A liability of a company in respect of a sum payable under the Road Traffic Act 1972, s 149 to a person entitled to the benefit of a judgment is duplicated by the liability of another company in so far as that other company is also liable under s 149 of that Act to pay any sum to that person in respect of the same judgment: ibid, s 9(3).

amount of any liability of a company in liquidation towards any policyholder of a long term policy[20] which was a United Kingdom policy at the beginning of the liquidation is paid to the policyholder as soon as reasonably practicable after the beginning of the liquidation.[1]

6 Future benefits under long term business

It is the duty of the Board, as soon as reasonably practicable after the beginning of the liquidation, to make arrangements for securing continuity of insurance for every policyholder of a company in liquidation who is a policyholder in respect of a long term policy which was a United Kingdom policy at the beginning of the liquidation.[2]

Such a duty extends only to securing that the policyholder will receive 90 per cent. of any future benefit[3] under his policy, subject to and in accordance with terms corresponding so far as seems to the Board to be reasonable in the circumstances to the terms which would have applied under the policy.[4]

For the purpose of securing continuity of insurance for any policyholders of a company in liquidation the Board may take such measures as appear to them to be appropriate

a for securing or facilitating the transfer of the long term business of the company, or of any part of that business, to another authorised insurance company; or
b for securing the issue by another authorised insurance company to the policyholders in question of policies in substitution for their existing policies.[5]

Where a long term policy of a company in liquidation contains terms relating to matters other than future benefits under the policy, the Board's duty extends also to securing that the policy after any transfer of business in which it is included or (as the case may be) any policy issued in substitution for the policy in question contains terms relating to those matters which correspond so far as appears to the Board to be reasonable in the circumstances to the terms first mentioned.[6]

During any period while the Board are seeking to make arrangements for

---

20 'Long term policy' means any policy evidencing a contract the effecting of which constituted the carrying on of long term business, not being a contract of reinsurance: ibid, s 10(1).

1 Ibid, s 10(2).

2 Ibid, s 11(3). Any duty of the Board under this subsection is subject to compliance on the policyholder's part with any conditions imposed by the Board with respect to the payment, in any case or in any class or description of case, of sums which would have fallen due from policyholders of a company in liquidation by way of premiums under long term policies if the company had not gone into liquidation: ibid, s 11(11).

3 'Future benefit' in relation to any long term policy of a company in liquidation, means any benefit provided for under the policy which has not fallen due to be paid by the company before the beginning of the liquidation: ibid, s 11(1). Any bonus provided for under a policy is not to be treated as a future benefit unless it was declared before the beginning of the liquidation: ibid, s 11(2).

4 Ibid, s 11(4).

5 Policyholders Protection Act 1975, s 11(5). Arrangements made by the Board under this subsection are not required to cover any future benefit under a policy in so far as any sums have been paid to the policyholder in pursuance of s 11(7) by reference to that benefit: ibid, s 11(8).

6 Ibid, s 11(6).

securing continuity of insurance for any policyholders of a company in liquidation, it is the Board's duty to secure that 90 per cent of any future benefit under a long term policy which would have fallen due to be paid to any of those policyholders during that period is paid to the policyholder in question as soon as reasonably practicable after the time when the benefit in question would have fallen due under the policy (but subject to and in accordance with any other terms which would have applied under the policy).[7]

Where it appears to the Board that it is not reasonably practicable to secure continuity of insurance for any policyholder of a company in liquidation, it is the duty of the Board to pay to the policyholder a sum equal to 90 per cent of the value attributed to his policy for the purposes of any claim in respect of his policy in the winding up of the company, as soon as reasonably practicable after any such claim is admitted.[8]

7 Disproportionate benefits under long term policies

If it appears to the Board, in the case of any long term policy of a company in liquidation which was a United Kingdom policy at the beginning of the liquidation, that the benefits provided under it are or may be excessive in any respect, having regard to the premiums paid or payable and to any other term of the policy, the Board must refer the policy to an independent actuary.[9]

Where an actuary to whom the policy is referred makes to the Board a report in writing

a stating, with respect to any of the benefits provided for under the policy, that in his view the benefit or benefits in question are excessive; and
b recommending accordingly that any liability of the company under the policy or any future benefit[10] under the policy should be treated as reduced or (as the case may be) disregarded,

the Board may determine in the light of any recommendation contained in his report that the liability or benefit to which the recommendation relates should be treated as reduced or disregarded.[11]

---

7 Ibid, s 11(7). Any duty of the Board under this subjection is subject to compliance on the policyholder's part with any conditions imposed by the Board with respect to the payment, in any case or in any class or description of case, of sums which would have fallen due from policyholders of a company in liquidation by way of premiums under long term policies if the company had not gone into liquidation: ibid, s 11(11).

8 Ibid, s 11(9). The Secretary of State may by regulations made by statutory instrument
a require the Board, in a case to which s 11(9) applies, to pay to the policyholder at his option, instead of the sum there mentioned, a sum equal to 90 per cent of the value of the future benefits under his policy, or of such of those benefits as may be specified by the regulations, determined in such manner as the regulations may provide;
b make such provision as appears to him to be appropriate with respect to the time within which and the manner in which the Board are to perform any of their functions under s 11 (including any function conferred on them by virtue of paragraph (*a*)): ibid, s 11(10).

9 Policyholders Protection Act 1975, s 12(1).

10 'Future benefit' has the same meaning as in s 11: ibid, s 12(6).

11 Ibid, s 12(3). Where the Board so determines, the liability or benefit in question shall be treated as reduced or (as the case may be) disregarded for the purposes of the application of s 10, of any provision of s 11(3) to (7), or of any provision of any regulations made under s 11(10) (as the case may require) in relation to the policy in question: ibid, s 12(3).

In any case where

a a claim has been admitted in the winding up of a company in respect of any policy which is the subject of a report by an actuary; and
b that report indicates, or the actuary makes to the Board a further report in writing indicating, what value would in his view have been attributed to the policy in the winding up if any future benefit under the policy to which any recommendation in the report relates had been treated as reduced or disregarded in accordance with the recommendation in determining the claim in respect of the policy in the winding up,

the Board may determine, in the light of the value indicated in the actuary's report, that the value attributed to the policy in question for the purposes of the claim in respect of the policy in the winding up shall be treated as reduced for the purpose of calculating the sum payable to the policyholder.[12]

D GENERAL PROVISIONS WITH RESPECT TO THE BOARD'S DUTIES

1 Performance of duties

Where it appears to the Board, in the case of any policy of a company in liquidation

a that payment in respect of any sums falling due under the policy could have been made to a person other than the policyholder; or
b that any sums paid under the policy would have been subject to any trust, charge or other agreement binding on the policyholder;

the Board may secure the payment of any sum payable to the policyholder[13] or pay any sum so payable[14] (in whole or in part) to that other person or (as the case may be) to the person appearing to the Board to be entitled under the trust, charge or agreement in question, instead of to the policyholder.[15]

Any payment made to a person other than the policyholder is treated as a payment to the policyholder, and may be made on such conditions (with respect to the total or partial assignment to the Board of any rights of the recipient against the policyholder or any other person, or otherwise) as the Board think fit.[16]

The Board may secure the payment of any sum payable to a policyholder[17] or payable[18] to a person entitled to the benefit of a judgment, and of any sum they are authorised to secure for a person other than the policyholder,[19] by either or both of the following methods:

---

12 Ibid, s 12(5). Where the Board so determine, the value so attributed to the policy is treated as reduced for that purpose: ibid, s 12(5).
13 In accordance with any of the provisions of ss 6 to 10 or in accordance with s 11(7).
14 In accordance with s 11(9) or (10).
15 Policyholders Protection Act 1975, s 13(1).
16 Ibid, s 13(1).
17 In accordance with any of the provisions of ss 6 to 10 or in accordance with s 11(7).
18 Under s 7.
19 By virtue of s 13(1).

a by themselves making payments in respect of the sum in question; or
b by securing by any measures appearing to them to be appropriate that such payments are made by any other person.[20]

The Board is not required[1] to make any payment or to incur any other expenditure at a time when it appears to the Board that the funds available to them for such expenditure, together with any funds they may raise by means of a levy[2] which might be applied on such expenditure, fall short of what they may require.[3] Accordingly, the Board may:

a postpone making any payment, or any part of any payment, they propose to make; and
b postpone taking any measures involving expenditure on their part;

from time to time, until it appears to them that their funds are adequate to meet the expenditure they propose to incur.[4]

Any duty of the Board to assist a policyholder of a company in liquidation[5] is subject to compliance on his part with any conditions imposed by the Board with respect to the total or partial assignment to the Board of

a his rights under or in respect of the policy;
b any rights he may have in respect of any payments made by him to the liquidator by way of premiums under the policy since the beginning of the liquidation; and
c any rights he may have against any other persons in respect of any event giving rise to any liability of the company under the policy.[6]

Any duty of the Board to secure the payment of any sum payable to[7] a person entitled to the benefit of a judgment is subject to compliance on his part with any conditions imposed by the Board with respect to the total or partial assignment to the Board of any rights he may have against any other persons in respect of any event giving rise to the liability of the company in liquidation by reference to which that sum is so payable.[8]

In connection with imposing any conditions with respect to the assignment to them of any rights the Board may make any arrangement which appears to them to be appropriate with any person on whom the conditions are imposed with respect to the manner in which they are to apply any sums they may receive by virtue of the rights in question.[9]

The Secretary of State may by regulations made by statutory instrument provide for a transfer to and the vesting in the Board by virtue of the regulations, in such circumstances as may be specified in them,

---

20 Policyholders Protection Act 1975, s 13(2).
1 By any provision of ss 6 to 11.
2 Under s 19 or s 21. See pp 611–612, 616–617, post.
3 Policyholders Protection Act 1975, s 13(3).
4 Ibid, s 13(3).
5 By any of the measures provided for by ss 6 to 11.
6 Policyholders Protection Act 1975, s 13(4).
7 Under s 7.
8 Policyholders Protection Act 1975, s 13(5).
9 Ibid, s 13(6).

a of any such rights of a policyholder to whom the Board have given assistance by any of the measures provided for [10] above;
b of any rights of a person for whom the Board have secured any payment[11]; and
c of any rights which a person to whom any payment has been made[12] may have against the policyholder in respect of the policy or any sums falling due under it or against any other persons in respect of any event giving rise to any liability of the policyholder by virtue of which the payment in question was made.[13]

The regulations may also provide for the manner in which the Board are to apply any sums received by them by virtue of any rights vested in them by the regulations.[14]

2 Exclusion and modification of Board's duties

Any payment made by any person other than the Board to the policyholder, to a person entitled to the benefit of a judgment, or to any other person, being a payment which is referable to any liability[15] of a company in liquidation[16] must be treated as reducing any sum payable to the policyholder or to a person entitled to the benefit of the judgment by reference to that liability.[17]

Where it appears to the Board in respect of a long term policy of a company in liquidation,

a that any other person has made a payment to the policyholder or to any other person which is referable to any liability of the company which was outstanding at the beginning of the liquidation or which is otherwise required[18] to be taken into account in relation to the policy; or
b that any other person has taken any other measures for assisting or protecting the policyholder[19] which ought to be taken into account for the purpose of excluding or modifying any of their duties[20] towards the policyholder,

any payment made

a by reference to any valuation of a long term policy of a company in liquidation or of any of the benefits provided for under any such policy; or
b by reference to any future benefits[1] under a long term policy of a company in liquidation,

---

10 By ss 6 to 11 as are mentioned in s 13(4).
11 In accordance with s 7 as are mentioned in s 13(5).
12 By virtue of s 13(1).
13 Policyholders Protection Act 1975, s 13(7).
14 Ibid, s 13(7).
15 As is mentioned in s 6, 7 or 8.
16 A payment is referable to a liability of a company in liquidation if it has the effect of reducing or discharging, or is otherwise made by reference to, that liability or any liability of the policyholder or any other person from which that liability arises.
17 Policyholders Protection Act 1975, s 14(1).
18 In accordance with s 14(3).
19 Whether measures of a like description to those open to the Board under s 11(5) or otherwise.
20 Under ss 10 and 11.
1 'Future benefit' has the same meaning as in s 11: Policyholders Protection Act 1975, s 14(9). See p 603, ante.

must be taken into account,[2] whether it was made to the policyholder or to any other person.[3]

Any sums secured[4] by the Board for a policyholder of a company in liquidation or for any other person by reference to any future benefits under a long term policy must be treated as reducing any sum payable[5] to the policyholder in respect of that policy.[6]

The Board may postpone taking any measures[7] in any case where it appears to the Board that, independently of any measures they may take, any other person (not being the liquidator) may make any payment or take any measures which would[8] affect any of their duties in relation to the case in question.[9]

E THE BOARD'S POWERS TO ASSIST POLICYHOLDERS OF COMPANIES IN LIQUIDATION

In any case where it appears to the Board to be desirable to do so, the Board may,

- a make payments to or on behalf of policyholders who are eligible for assistance,[10] on such terms and on such conditions as the Board think fit; or
- b secure that payments are made to or on behalf of any such policyholders by the liquidator or the provisional liquidator by giving him an indemnity covering any such payments or any class or description of such payments.[11]

---

2 For the purpose of s 14(2)(*a*).

3 Policyholders Protection Act 1975, s 14(2)(3). In a case to which s 14(2) applies nothing in ss 10 and 11 requires the Board to take any measures for assisting the policyholder in respect of the long term policy in question where it appears to the Board to be inappropriate to do so in view of any such payment or other measures of assistance or protection as are mentioned in s 14(2): Policyholders Protection Act 1975, s 14(4). In any case to which s 14(2) applies, other than one falling within s 14(4), the Board may treat any sum payable to the policyholder in accordance with s 10 or s 11(7), (9) or (10) and any sum to be secured for the policyholder by virtue of s 11(4) as reduced to any extent appearing to them to be appropriate in the circumstances of the case: ibid, s 14(5).

4 Under s 11(7).

5 In accordance with s 11(9) or (10).

6 Policyholders Protection Act 1975, s 14(6).

7 Provided for by ss 6 to 11.

8 By virtue of s 14(1), (4) or (5).

9 Policyholders Protection Act 1975, s 14(7).

10 A policyholder is eligible for assistance:
- a if he is a policyholder in respect of a general policy or a long term policy of a company in liquidation which was a United Kingdom policy at the beginning of the liquidation; or
- b if he is a policyholder in respect of a general policy or a long term policy of a company in provisional liquidation which was a United Kingdom policy at the time when the provisional liquidator was appointed: ibid, s 15(2).

An authorised insurance company, not being a company in liquidation, is a company in provisional liquidation for the purposes of s 15 if a provisional liquidator has been appointed in respect of the company under the Companies Act 1985, s 532: ibid, s 15(1).

11 Ibid, s 15(3). The indemnity which the Board may give the liquidator or provisional liquidator under s 15(3)(b) includes an indemnity given to him for the benefit of the company with the object of protecting the company against loss, and not merely protecting the liquidator personally: *Policyholders Protection Board v Official Receiver* [1976] 2 All ER 58, [1976] 1 WLR 447. (See the judgment of Brightman J, ibid, at 63).

F THE BOARD'S POWERS TO PROTECT POLICYHOLDERS OF COMPANIES IN FINANCIAL DIFFICULTIES

1 Transfers of business, etc

The Board may exercise powers[12] conferred on them for the purpose of safeguarding policyholders of a company in financial difficulties[13] who are eligible[14] for protection or any class or description of such policyholders to any extent appearing to the Board to be appropriate in any case or in any class or description of case, against loss arising from the financial difficulties of the company.[15]

The Board may take any measures appearing to them to be appropriate for securing or facilitating the transfer of all or any part of the insurance business carried on by a company in financial difficulties to another authorised insurance company on terms[16] appearing to the Board to be appropriate in any case or in any class or description of case.[17]

In any case where it appears to the Board that it would be practicable to secure the purpose of safeguarding policyholders by giving assistance to the company in financial difficulties to enable it to continue to carry on insurance business, the Board may take such measures as appear to them to be appropriate for giving such assistance.[18]

The Board may make the giving of assistance[19] to a company in financial difficulties conditional on the reduction of any liabilities or benefits provided for under any policies of the company to any extent appearing to them to be appropriate in any case or in any class or description of case.[20]

The Board must not exercise any power conferred on them[1] in any case where it appears to the Board that

---

12 By s 16(3) or (4).

13 An authorised insurance company, not being a company in liquidation, is a company in financial difficulties for the purpose of s 16 if:
- a it is a company in provisional liquidation within the meaning of s 15;
- b it has been proved, in any proceedings on a petition for the winding up of the company under the Companies Act 1985, to be unable to pay its debts; or
- c an application has been made to the Court under the Companies Act 1985, s 425 for the sanctioning of a compromise or arrangement proposed between the company and its creditors or any class of them (whether or not any of its members are also parties thereto) and the terms of the compromise or arrangement provide for reducing the liabilities or the benefits provided for under any of the company's policies: ibid, s 16(1).

14 A policyholder is eligible if he is a policyholder in respect of a general policy or a long term policy of the company which was a United Kingdom policy at the relevant time: ibid, s 16(9). 'The relevant time' means
- a in a case falling within s 16(1)(a), the time when the provisional liquidator was appointed;
- b in a case falling within s 16(1)(b), the time when the winding up petition was presented; and
- c in a case falling within s 16(1)(c), the time when the application was made under the Companies Act 1985, s 425: Policyholders Protection Act 1975, s 16(6).

15 Policyholders Protection Act 1975, s 16(2).

16 Including terms reducing the liabilities or the benefits provided for under any policies.

17 Policyholders Protection Act 1975, s 16(3).

18 Ibid, s 16(4).

19 Under s 16(4).

20 Policyholders Protection Act 1975, s 16(5).

1 By s 16(3) or (4).

a persons who were members of the company at the relevant time;[2] or
b persons who had any responsibility for or who may have profited from the circumstances giving rise to the company's financial difficulties;

would benefit to any material extent as a result of any measures the Board may take.[3]

The Board must not take any measures[4] for the purpose of safeguarding any policyholders in any case where it appears to the Board that to take whatever measures may be required for the assistance of the policyholders in question under sections 6 to 11[5] in the event of the company's going into liquidation would cost them less than to take the measures in question under s 16(3) or (4).[6]

2 Long term business

The Board must not take any measures in pursuance of s 16(3) or (4) for the purpose of safeguarding any policyholders of a company in financial difficulties in respect of long term policies of the company, other than the measures allowed by s 17(2), in any case where it appears to the Board that to take those other measures would cost them more than to take measures allowed by s 17(2).[7]

The measures allowed by s 17(2) are any measures open to the Board under s 16(3) or (4) which involve the imposition by the Board, as a prerequisite of their incurring any expenditure or liabilities for that purpose, of conditions requiring

a the reduction of all liabilities of the company under relevant long term policies[8] and of all benefits provided for under any such policies which have not fallen due to be paid by the company before the date when the reduction is to take effect, to 90 per cent of the amount which would otherwise have been payable in accordance with the terms of the policies; and
b the reduction of all premiums under any such policies which have not fallen due before that time to 90 per cent of the amount which would otherwise have been so payable.[9]

If it appears to the Board, in the case of any long term policy of a company in financial difficulties which was a United Kingdom policy at the relevant time,[10] that the benefits provided for under it are or may be excessive in any respect,

---

2 For the meaning of 'the relevant time', see p 609, footnote 14, ante.
3 Policyholders Protection Act 1975, s 16(6). The Board must disregard for the purposes of s 16(6) any benefit which may accrue to any such persons as are there mentioned who are policyholders of the company in financial difficulties in their capacity as such: ibid, s 16(7).
4 In pursuance of s 16(3) or (4).
5 See pp 601–604, ante.
6 Policyholders Protection Act 1975, s 16(8).
7 Policyholders Protection Act 1975, s 17(1).
8 A long term policy is a 'relevant long term policy' for the purposes of s 17(2) if it is included in any transfer secured or facilitated by the Board under s 16(3) or by virtue of any assistance given by the Board under s 16(4): ibid, s 17(2).
9 Ibid, s 17(2). The benefits mentioned in s 17(2)(a) do not include any bonus provided for under a policy unless it was declared before the time when any such reduction of liabilities and benefits under that policy as is mentioned in that paragraph is to take effect: ibid, s 17(3).
10 As defined in s 16(6). See p 609, footnote 14, ante.

having regard to the premiums paid or payable and to any other terms of the policy, the Board must refer the policy to an independent actuary.[11]

Where an actuary to whom a policy is referred makes to the Board a report in writing

a stating, with respect to any of the benefits provided for under the policy, that in his view the benefit or benefits in question are excessive; and
b recommending[12] that any such benefit should be treated as reduced or (as the case may be) disregarded,

the Board may determine in the light of any recommendation contained in the actuary's report that any benefit to which that recommendation relates be treated as reduced or disregarded.[13]

Where the Board determine that the benefit in question be disregarded, the conditions[14] must include conditions requiring the cancellation of that benefit or (as the case may be) of any liability representing that benefit.[15]

Where the Board determine that the benefit in question shall be treated as reduced, s 17(2)(*a*)[16] applies in relation to the policy as if the amount of that benefit or (as the case may be) of any liability representing that benefit, as reduced in accordance with the Board's determination, were the amount which would otherwise have been payable in accordance with the terms of the policy.[17]

G LEVIES ON INTERMEDIARIES

Where

a the Board have incurred or propose to incur any long term business expenditure[18] in relation to a company in liquidation or a company which is a company in financial difficulties;[19] and
b it appears to the Board that the company in question has accountable intermediaries,

it is the duty of the Board to impose a levy on those intermediaries.[20]

---

11 Policyholders Protection Act 1975, s 17(4).
12 For the purposes of any measures to be taken by the Board in pursuance of s 16(3) or (4).
13 Policyholders Protection Act 1975, s 17(5).
14 Mentioned in s 17(2).
15 Ibid, s 17(6).
16 See p 610, ante.
17 Policyholders Protection Act 1975, s 17(7).
18 'Long term business expenditure' means:
a any expenditure of the Board under s 10 or s 11;
b any expenditure attributed by the Board under s 18(3) to long term business expenditure: ibid, s 18(2).
By s 18(3) the Board may in the case of
a any expenditure under s 15 or 16;
b any expenditure in repaying or servicing loans; and
c any expenditure on their administrative expenses in performing their functions under the Act;
attribute that expenditure to general business expenditure or to long term business expenditure, or partly to the one and partly to the other, in such manner as may appear to them to be reasonable in the circumstances of the case: ibid, s 18(3).
19 Within the meaning of s 16.
20 Policyholders Protection Act 1975, s 19(1).

1 Accountable intermediary

A person is an accountable intermediary of a company if,

a he has acted as an intermediary for the company[1] in relation to any relevant long term contract[2] of the company; and
b his income from the company in respect of his services (whether as an intermediary or otherwise) in relation to such contracts for either or each of the 2 years comprised in the 2 years immediately before the beginning of the liquidation in a case of a company in liquidation exceeded his exempt income level for the year in question.[3]

An individual is not an accountable intermediary of a company if the services in question were performed in pursuance of a contract of exclusive agency with the company.[4]

2 Income liable to levy

The income of an accountable intermediary of a company which is liable to a levy is:

a one-half of any amount by which his income from the company in respect of relevant services[5] for the later of the two years ending immediately before the beginning of the liquidation in the case of a company in liquidation exceeded his exempt income level for that year; and
b one-quarter of any amount by which his income from the company in respect of relevant services for the earlier of those two years exceeded his exempt income level for that year.[6]

3 Exempt income level

The exempt income level of an intermediary of a company for any year is

---

1 A person acts as an intermediary of a company in relation to a long term contract if, otherwise than as an employee of the company,
a he invites any other person to take any step with a view to entering into a long term contract with the company;
b he introduces any other person to the company with a view to his entering into such a contract with the company; or
c he takes any other action with a view to securing that any other person will enter into such a contract with the company: ibid, s 19(8).

2 In this section 'long term contract' means a contract the effecting of which by a company constitutes the carrying on by the company of long term business in the United Kingdom, not being a contract of reinsurance: Policyholders Protection Act 1975, s 19(9). A long term contract is a 'relevant long term contract of a company' for the purposes of this section if it was effected within the period of 2 years mentioned in s 19(2): ibid, s 19(9).

3 Ibid, s 19(2).

4 Ibid, s 19(3). For the purposes of this subsection a contract is a contract of exclusive agency with a company in relation to the performance of any services under it if it provides that the person performing the services must not perform services of a like description for any other insurance company: ibid, s 19(3).

5 I e services in relation to 'any relevant long term contract' of the company. See footnote 2, ante.

6 Policyholders Protection Act 1975, s 19(4). In relation to any intermediary, his income liable to levy for either of those years or, where he had income liable to levy for each of those years, the aggregate of his income—liable for both of those years is referred to in the Act as income of the intermediary which is income liable to levy: ibid, s 19(4). As to 'exempt income level', see infra.

a where no other person is linked with the intermediary, £5,000; and
b in any other case, that proportion of £5,000 which is equal to the proportion which the intermediary's income from the company in respect of relevant services for the year in question bears to the total amount of the group's[7] income from the company in respect of such services of that year.[8]

The following persons are linked with an intermediary, whether the intermediary is a company or a person other than a company:

a any partner of the intermediary and any partnership of which the intermediary is a member;
b any company of which the intermediary is a director; and
c any director of any company which is linked with the intermediary.[9]

Where the intermediary in question is a company, the following are also persons linked with the intermediary:

a any person other than a company who has a controlling interest[10] in the intermediary, and any company other than the intermediary in which any such person also has a controlling interest;
b any company of which the intermediary is a subsidiary and any other subsidiary of any such company;
c any subsidiary of the intermediary; and
d any director of the intermediary.[11]

Where the intermediary in question is a person other than a company, the following are also persons linked with the intermediary:

a any company in which the intermediary has a controlling interest;[12]
b any company of which a company linked with the intermediary by virtue of s 20(3)(*b*) or s 20(5)(*a*) is a subsidiary and any other subsidiary of any such company;
c any subsidiary of any company linked with the intermediary by virtue of s 20(3)(*b*) or s 20(5)(*a*); and
d where the company is a partnership, each of its members.[13]

---

7 'Group' means the intermediary together with the person or (where there are more than one) all of the persons linked with the intermediary: Policyholders Protection Act 1975, s 20(2).

8 Ibid, s 20(1). Where in a case falling within s 20(1)(*b*) the income from the company in respect of relevant services for any year,

a of the intermediary; and
b of each person linked with the intermediary;

did not exceed £1,000, no account is taken of that income for the purpose of s 19: ibid, s 20(2).

9 Ibid, s 20(3).

10 A person other than a company is treated as having a controlling interest in a company if, but only if, that company would be a subsidiary of the person in question if that person were a company: ibid, s 20(6). In determining for the purposes of s 20(6) whether a company would be a subsidiary of any person other than a company, any shares held or power exercisable by either of two spouses or by both spouses jointly is treated as held or exercisable by each share: ibid, s 20(7).

11 Ibid, s 20(4).

12 For the meaning of controlling interest, see footnote 10, supra.

13 Policyholders Protection Act 1975, s 20(5).

4 Restriction on the imposition of the levy

No levy must be imposed in respect of any company

a after the end of the period of 2 years beginning with the beginning of the liquidation if the company is a company in liquidation; or
b after the end of the period of 2 years beginning with the relevant time[14] if the company is a company in financial difficulties.[15]

5 Rate of the levy

The rate of the levy imposed in respect of any company is:

a where the long term business expenditure incurred by the Board in relation to that company is less than the total amount of the income liable to levy, a percentage equal to the percentage of that amount which the expenditure represents; and
b in any other case, 100 per cent.[16]

Where a levy is imposed in respect of any company before the exact amount of the long term business expenditure of the Board in relation to that company is ascertained the above provision applies as if the Board's estimate of that expenditure were the expenditure actually incurred.[17]

6 Statement for the purposes of s 20[18]

The Board may by notice[19] in writing require any person who appears to them to be an intermediary of any company which is in liquidation or in financial difficulties to give them any information which appears to them to be necessary in order to determine what (if any) persons would be linked with that person if that person were an intermediary of that company.[20]

A person to whom a notice is sent must send to the Board within one month of the date of the notice a statement

a giving any of the information required by the notice which he is able to give; or
b informing the Board that he is unable to give any of the information required by the notice.[1]

Any person who causes or permits to be included in a statement sent to the Board information which he knows to be false in a material particular or

---

14 As defined by s 16(6).

15 Policyholders Protection Act 1975, Sch 2, para 1.

16 Ibid, Sch 2, para 2(1). 'The total amount of the income liable to levy' means, in relation to any company, the total amount of the income of all the persons who appear to the Board to be accountable intermediaries of that company which appears to the Board to be income liable to levy: ibid, Sch 2, para 2(3).

17 Ibid, Sch 2, para 2(2).

18 For s 20, see p 613, ante.

19 A notice may be sent by post, and a letter containing such a notice is deemed to be properly addressed if it is addressed to the person to whom it is sent at his last known place of business in the United Kingdom: Policyholders Protection Act 1975, Sch 2, para 7.

20 Ibid, Sch 2, para 3(1).

1 Ibid, Sch 2, para 3(2). Any person who makes default in complying with this provision is guilty of an offence and liable, on summary conviction, to a fine not exceeding level 5 on the standard scale: ibid, Sch 2, para 4(2); Criminal Justice Act 1982, ss 38, 46.

recklessly causes or permits to be so included any information which is false in a material particular is guilty of an offence and liable:

a on conviction on indictment, to imprisonment for a term not exceeding 2 years or to a fine, or to both;
b on summary conviction, to a fine not exceeding the prescribed sum[2] under the Magistrates' Courts Act 1980, s 32(2).[3]

7 Declaration and enforcement of the levy

On imposing a levy in respect of any company the Board must send notice[4] of the levy to every person who appears to the Board to be an accountable intermediary of that company.[5]

The notice must indicate:

a the name of the company in respect of which the levy is being imposed;
b the period covered, in the case of that company, by each of the 2 years mentioned in s 19(2);[6] and
c what in the view of the Board is the amount of the income of the intermediary in question which is income liable to levy;

and must specify the rate of the levy.[7]

An intermediary to whom notice of a levy is sent must pay to the Board within one month of the date of the notice the percentage specified in the notice of any income of the intermediary which is income liable to levy.[8]

Any sum due to the Board in respect of a levy is recoverable in any court of competent jurisdiction.[9]

8 Distribution of excess proceeds of levy

If the proceeds of any levy in respect of any company exceed the long term business expenditure incurred by the Board in relation to that company, the Board must distribute the excess among the accountable intermediaries of that company who have made any payments to the Board under the levy in proportion to the sums those intermediaries have respectively paid.[10]

H LEVIES ON AUTHORISED INSURANCE COMPANIES

The Board may from time to time for the purpose of financing general business

---

2 The 'prescribed sum' means £1,000 or such sum as is for the time being substituted in this definition by an order in force under the Magistrates' Courts Act 1980, s 143(1); Magistrates' Courts Act 1980, s 32(9).
3 Policyholders Protection Act 1975, Sch 2, para 4(1).
4 A notice may be sent by post and a letter containing such a notice is deemed to be properly addressed if it is addressed to the person to whom it is sent at his last known place of business in the United Kingdom: ibid, Sch 2, para 7.
5 Ibid, Sch 2, para 5(1).
6 See p 612, ante.
7 Policyholders Protection Act 1975, Sch 2, para 5(2).
8 Ibid, Sch 2, para 6(1).
9 Ibid, Sch 2, para 6(2).
10 Ibid, s 19(5).

expenditure,[11] impose a levy known as a 'general business levy' on authorised insurance companies carrying on general business in the United Kingdom.[12]

It may also from time to time for the purpose of financing long term business expenditure[13] impose a levy known as a 'long term business levy' on authorised insurance companies carrying on long term business in the United Kingdom.[14]

1 Net premium income

The amount each insurance company may be required to pay under general business levies imposed in any financial year must be calculated by reference to the net premium income for the year ending last before the beginning of that financial year in respect of general policies which were United Kingdom policies at the relevant time.[15]

The amount each insurance company may be required to pay under long term business levies imposed in any financial year is calculated by reference to the net premium income of the company for the year ending last before the beginning of that financial year in respect of long term policies which were United Kingdom policies at the relevant time.[16]

The net premium income of a company for any year in respect of policies of any description which were United Kingdom policies at the relevant time means the gross amounts recorded in the company's accounts during that year as paid or due to the company by way of premiums under policies of that description which were United Kingdom policies at the time when the amounts in question were so recorded, less any amounts deductible for that year in respect of policies of that description.[17]

In calculating a company's net premium income for any year in respect of any description, any rebates or refunds recorded in the company's accounts during that year as allowed or given in respect of any amounts so recorded during that or any previous year as paid or due to the company by way of premiums under policies of that description which were United Kingdom policies at the time when the rebates or refunds were so recorded must be deducted.[18]

In calculating a company's net premium income for any year in respect of general policies, any sums recorded in the company's accounts during that year as paid or due from the company by way of reinsuring its liabilities towards

---

11 'General business expenditure' means:
- a any expenditure of the Board under s 6, 7 or 8; and
- b any expenditure attributed by the Board under s 18(3) to general business expenditure: ibid, s 18(1).

12 Policyholders Protection Act 1975, s 21(1).

13 'Long term business expenditure' means:
- a any expenditure of the Board under s 10 or 11; and
- b any expenditure attributed by the Board under s 18(3) to long term business expenditure: ibid, s 18(2).

14 Ibid, s 21(2).

15 Ibid, s 21(3). Any such income is in the Act referred to, in relation to any company, as income of the company for the year in question which is income liable to the general business levy: ibid, s 21(3).

16 Ibid, s 21(4). Any such income is in the Act referred to any company, as income of the company for the year in question which is income liable to the long term business levy: ibid, s 21(4).

17 Ibid, s 21(5).

18 Ibid, s 21(6).

policyholders under general policies which were United Kingdom policies at the time when the sums in question were so recorded must be deducted.[19]

2 Application of proceeds

The proceeds of general business levies may be applied by the Board only on general business expenditure, and the proceeds of long term business levies may be applied by the Board only on long term business expenditure.[20]

3 Restrictions on the imposition of the levies

The amounts required to be paid by any company under general business levies imposed by the Board in any financial year must not exceed 1 per cent of any income of the company for the year ending last before the beginning of that financial year which is income liable to the general business levy.[1]

The amounts required to be paid by any company under long term business levies imposed by the Board in any financial year must not exceed 1 per cent of any income of the company for the year ending last before the beginning of that financial year which is income liable to the long term business levy.[2]

The Board may not impose a levy for the purpose of financing expenditure of any description unless:

- a the expenditure in question has already been incurred by the Board; or
- b it appears to the Board that the expenditure will be incurred within 12 months of the imposition of the levy.[3]

4 Statements of premium income

Every authorised insurance company must send to the Secretary of State before 1 March in any year a statement of any income of the company for the previous year which is income liable to the general business levy,[4] and a separate[5] statement of any income of the company which is income liable to the long term business levy.[6]

Any person who causes or permits to be included in a statement sent to the Secretary of State any information which he knows to be false in a material particular or recklessly causes or permits to be so included any information which is false in a material particular is guilty of an offence and liable

- a on conviction on indictment, to imprisonment for a term not exceeding 2 years or to a fine, or to both;
- b on summary conviction, to a fine not exceeding the prescribed sum[7] under the Magistrates' Courts Act 1980, s 32(2).[8]

---

19 Policyholders Protection Act 1975, s 21(7).
20 Ibid, s 21(8).
1 Ibid, Sch 3, para 2(1).
2 Ibid, Sch 3, para 2(2).
3 Ibid, Sch 3, para 2(2).
4 Ibid, Sch 3, para 4(1).
5 Ibid, Sch 3, para 4(3).
6 Ibid, Sch 3, para 4(2).
7 The 'prescribed sum' means £1,000 or such sum as is for the time being substituted in this definition by an order in force under the Magistrates' Courts Act 1980, s 143(1): Magistrates' Court Act 1980, s 32(9).
8 Policyholders Protection Act 1975, Sch 3, para 5(1).

Any company which makes default in complying with the obligation to send a statement to the Secretary of State is guilty of an offence and liable, on summary conviction, to a fine not exceeding level 5 on the standard scale.[9]

5 Declarations and enforcement of levies

Levies may be imposed by the Board at such times and at such rates in relation to income of authorised insurance companies liable to the general business levy or to the long term business levy as the Board may determine.[10]

On imposing a levy the Board must send a notice of the rate of levy to every authorised insurance company which may in the opinion of the Board have had income liable to the levy for the year ending last before the financial year in which the levy is imposed.[11]

An insurance company to which notice of the rate of a levy is sent must pay to the Board within one month of the date of the notice the percentage specified in the notice of any income of the company for the year ending last before the financial year in which the levy is imposed which is income liable to the levy in question.[12]

Any sum due to the Board in respect of a levy is recoverable in any court of competent jurisdiction.[13]

I MISCELLANEOUS

1 Provision for persons insured under contracts of insurance and not evidenced by policies

Where it appears to the Board:

a that a person is insured under a contract of insurance with an authorised insurance company which is not evidenced by any policy; and
b that if a policy evidencing the contract had been issued, the person in question would have been eligible as a policyholder in respect of that policy for the assistance or protection of any provision of ss 6 to 16,[14]

the Board may take such measures for the assistance or protection of the person in question as they would in their view have been required to take under the relevant provision if such a policy had been issued and the person in question had been the policyholder.[15]

---

9 Ibid, Sch 3, para 5(2); Criminal Justice Act 1982, ss 38, 46.

10 Policyholders Protection Act 1975, Sch 3, para 6(1).

11 Ibid, Sch 3, para 6(2). A notice under this sub-paragraph must indicate:
a whether the levy is a general business levy or a long term business levy;
b what description of income is liable to the levy in question; and
c the purpose for which the levy is being imposed;
and must specify the rate of the levy as a percentage of the income liable to the levy: ibid, Sch 3, para 6(3). The notice may be sent by post, and a letter containing such a notice is deemed to be properly addressed if it is addressed to the insurance company to which it is sent at its last known place of business in the United Kingdom: ibid, Sch 3, para 6(4).

12 Ibid, Sch 3, para 7(1).

13 Ibid, Sch 3, para 7(2).

14 See pp 601–610, ante.

15 Policyholders Protection Act 1975, s 23(1). For the purposes of s 18 any expenditure of the Board under s 23 is to be treated as expenditure under the relevant provision: ibid, s 23(2).

2 Application of general receipts by the Board

Subject to any arrangement made by the Board under s 13(6)[16] and to any regulations made by the Secretary of State under s 13(7),[17] any sums from time to time received by the Board in the course of or in connection with the exercise of their functions under the Act, otherwise than by virtue of any levy imposed under s 19[18] or s 21,[19] may be applied by the Board

a in so far as the sums are received in repayment or otherwise by virtue of any general business expenditure[20] incurred by the Board, on expenditure of that description only;

b in so far as the sums are received in repayment or otherwise by virtue of any long term business expenditure[1] by the Board, on expenditure of that description only.[2]

3 Application of surplus funds by the Board

If at any time the Secretary of State, after consultation with the Board, considers that the funds for the time being held by the Board exceed what is reasonably required for the purpose of exercising their functions under the Act, he may by order made by statutory instrument require the Board to distribute any of those funds appearing to him to be surplus to their requirements among authorised insurance companies carrying on business in the United Kingdom, in such manner and subject to such conditions as may be prescribed by the order.[3]

4 Overseas companies

Where it appears to the Secretary of State that any circumstances have occurred in relation to an overseas company[4] which are the equivalent under the law relating to companies in force in the country in which it is established of any of the events mentioned in s 5,[5] 15(1)[6] or 16,[7] the Secretary of State may

---

16 See p 606, ante.

17 See p 607, ante.

18 See p 611, ante.

19 See p 616, ante.

20 'General business expenditure' means:
a any expenditure of the Board under ss 6, 7 or 8; and
b any expenditure attributed by the Board under s 18(3) to general business expenditure: Policyholders Protection Act 1975, s 18(1).

1 'Long term business expenditure' means:
a any expenditure of the Board under s 10 or 11; and
b any expenditure attributed by the Board under s 18(3) to long term business expenditure: ibid, s 18(2).

2 Ibid, s 24.

3 Ibid, s 25(1). An order made under this section may make different provision for different circumstances and may be varied or revoked by a subsequent order so made: ibid, s 25(2). Any statutory instrument containing an order made under this section is subject to annulment in pursuance of a resolution of either House of Parliament: ibid, s 25(3).

4 'Overseas company' in this section means an authorised company established in a country outside the United Kingdom: ibid, s 16(1).

5 See p 601, ante.

6 See p 608, ante.

7 See p 609, ante.

refer[8] the company's case to the Board, in terms indicating whether it is to be treated as a company in liquidation for the purposes of the Act or solely as a company in provisional liquidation[9] or (as the case may be) as a company in financial difficulties.[10]

5 Disclosure of documents and information to the Board

Nothing in the Companies Act 1985 prevents the disclosure to the Board of any information obtained as mentioned in sub-s (1) of that section, if the disclosure is required for the purpose of facilitating the performance by the Board of any of their functions under the Policyholders Protection Act 1975.[11]

6 Statement by the Secretary of State in respect of the exercise of his powers

In the case of a company

a which is a company in liquidation; or
b which is a company in financial difficulties within the meaning of s 16[12] in relation to which the Board have exercised any of their powers under that section or s 15[13];

the Secretary must[14] before the end of the applicable period[15] lay before Parliament a statement with respect to the exercise of his powers under the Insurance Companies Act 1982 in relation to that company during the year ending immediately before the required time.[16]

The Secretary of State is not required to include in any statement any

---

8 Policyholders Protection Act 1975, s 26(2).

9 Within the meaning of s 15. See p 608, ante.

10 Within the meaning of s 16. See p 609, ante. The functions of the Board under the Act, or, as the case may be, under s 15 or 16 are exercisable in relation to a company whose case has been referred to the Board under s 26 in accordance with the terms of the reference: Policyholders Protection Act 1975, s 26(3). The provisions of the Act or as the case may be of section 15 or 16 apply in any such case subject to any modifications notified by the Secretary of State to the Board in connection with the reference: ibid, s 26(3). The modifications notified by the Secretary of State in connection with a reference are such only as appear to him to be necessary having regard to any differences between the law in force in the United Kingdom and the law for the time being in force in the country in which the overseas company in question is established: ibid, s 26(4).

11 Policyholders Protection Act 1975, s 27.

12 See p 609, ante.

13 See p 608, ante.

14 Policyholders Protection Act 1975, s 28(1).

15 The period applicable is:
a in a case falling within s 28(1)(*a*), the period of 6 months beginning with the beginning of the liquidation; and
b in a case falling within s 28(1)(*b*), the period of 6 months beginning with the date on which the Secretary of State receives written notification from the Board that they have exercised any of their powers under s 15 or 16 in relation to the company in question: ibid, s 28(2).
Where by virtue of s 28(1)(*a*) the Secretary of State is required to lay before Parliament a statement with respect of the exercise of his powers under the Insurance Companies Act 1982 in relation to any company, that subsection does not apply by virtue of para (*a*) thereof in the case of that company in the event of the company's going into liquidation: ibid, s 28(3).

16 The time referred to is the beginning of the liquidation in a case falling within s 28(1)(*a*) and the relevant time as defined by s 16(6) in a case falling within s 28(1)(*b*): ibid, s 28(1).

information which might in his view prejudice any criminal proceedings which have been or may be instituted against any person.[17]

7 Report by the Secretary of State with respect to the operation of the Act

Within the period of 6 months beginning with 1 January 1981, the Secretary of State must lay before Parliament a report reviewing the operation of the Act and its effectiveness as a method of protecting policyholders of authorised insurance companies carrying on business in the United Kingdom.[18]

8 Regulations

Any statutory instrument containing regulations made under any provision of the Act is subject to annulment in pursuance of a resolution of either House of Parliament.[19]

The power of the Secretary of State to make regulations under any provision of the Act includes power to make different provision for different circumstances but it is only exercisable after consultation with the Board.[20]

---

17 Policyholders Protection Act 1975, s 28(4).

18 Ibid, s 30. On 25 June 1981, the Secretary of State for Trade presented a 'Report on the Policyholders Protection Act 1975' (HC 363), which stated that it was intended to retain the Act in its present form. There was no present case for change in the scope of the Act and the level of protection should remain at 90 per cent. Legislation concerning the winding up of insurance companies would need to be reviewed when the EEC directive needed to be implemented. When an appropriate opportunity to enact legislation presented itself, changes might be made (i) to strengthen the powers of the Policyholders Protection Board (see p 596, ante); (ii) to clarify the role of the independent actuary under the Policyholders Protection Act 1975, s 12(1) (see p 604, ante) and s 17(4) (see p 611, ante); (iii) to revise the basis of calculating the levy (see p 611, ante); and to amend s 6 (see p 601, ante) so that any new compulsory scheme might be brought within the Act by order of the Secretary of State.

19 Policyholders Protection Act 1975, s 31(1).

20 Ibid, s 31(2).

CHAPTER 58

Compulsory insurance

Insurance is compulsory in the case of:

1 Motor vehicles.
2 Employers.
3 Solicitors.
4 Insurance brokers.
5 Estate agents.
6 Oil pollution.
7 Nuclear reactors.
8 Riding establishments.
9 Certain buildings.

1 Motor vehicles

It is not lawful for a person to use or to cause or permit any other person to use a motor vehicle on a road unless there is in force in relation to the use of the vehicle by that person or that other person, as the case may be, such a policy of insurance or such a security in respect of third party risks as complies with the requirements of Part VI of the Road Traffic Act 1972.[1]

2 Employers

The Employers' Liability (Compulsory Insurance) Act 1969, subject to certain exceptions, makes it compulsory for employers to insure against liability in respect of their employees.[2]

3 Solicitors

The Council of the Law Society, with the concurrence of the Master of the Rolls, may make rules concerning indemnity against loss arising from claims of any description of civil liability incurred:

- i by a solicitor in connection with his practice or with any trust of which he is or formerly was a trustee;
- ii by an employee or former employee of a solicitor or former solicitor in connection with that solicitor's practice or with any trust of which that solicitor or the employee is or formerly was a trustee.[3]

---

1 Road Traffic Act 1972, s 143(1). See Ivamy *Fire and Motor Insurance* (4th Edn, 1984) pp 299–325.
2 Employers' Liability (Compulsory Insurance) Act 1969, s 1(1). See Ivamy *Personal Accident, Life and Other Insurances* (2nd Edn, 1980) pp 292–296.
3 Solicitors Act 1974, s 37(1).

Such rules may,

a authorise or require the Society to establish and maintain a fund or funds;
b authorise or require the Society to take out and maintain insurance with authorised insurers;
c require solicitors or any specified class of solicitors to take out and maintain insurance with authorised insurers.[4]

4 Insurance brokers

The Insurance Brokers Registration Council may make rules for indemnifying:

i practising insurance brokers; and
ii enrolled bodies corporate and former enrolled bodies corporate,

against losses arising from claims in respect of any description of civil liability incurred by them or by employees of theirs in connection with their businesses.[5]

5 Estate agents

The Estate Agents Act 1979 provides that a person may not accept clients' money in the course of estate agency work unless there are in force authorised arrangements under which, in the event of his failing to account for such money to the person entitled to it, his liability will be made good by another.[6]

6 Oil Pollution

The Merchant Shipping (Oil Pollution) Act 1971 makes it necessary for certain ships to be insured in respect of liability for pollution by oil.[7]

7 Nuclear reactors

By the Nuclear Installations Act 1965 the licensee of a nuclear site must make such provision either by insurance or by some other means for sufficient funds to be available at all times to ensure that any claims which may be established against the licensee are satisfied up to the aggregate amount of £5m.[8]

8 Riding establishments

By the Riding Establishments Acts 1964 and 1970 every licence granted in respect of a riding establishment[9] is subject to the condition that the licence holder must hold a current insurance policy which insures him against liability for any injury sustained by:

---

4 Solicitors Act 1974, s 37(2). See Ivamy *Personal Accident, Life and Other Insurances* (2nd Edn, 1980) pp 278–279.
5 Insurance Brokers (Registration) Act 1977, s 12(1). See pp 573–575, ante.
6 Estate Agents Act 1979, s 16(1). See Ivamy *Personal Accident, Life and Other Insurances* (2nd Edn, 1980), pp 279–281. *Section 16 is not yet in force.*
8 Nuclear Installations Act 1965, s 19. See Ivamy *Personal Accident, Life and Other Insurances* (2nd Edn, 1980) pp 264–265.
9 'Riding establishment' refers to the carrying on of a business of keeping horses for the purpose of their being let out on hire for riding and/or for the purpose of their being used in providing, in return for payment, instruction in riding: Riding Establishments Act 1964, s 6(1).

i those who hire a horse from him for riding; and
ii those who use a horse in the course of receiving from him, in return for payment, instruction in riding

and arising out of such hire or use of a horse.[10]

The policy must insure such persons in respect of any liability which may be incurred by them in respect of injury to any person caused by, or arising out of, the hire or use of the horse.[11]

9 Certain buildings

It is the duty of the Parsonages Board to insure all parsonage houses in their diocese against all such risks as are included in the usual form of houseowner's policy relating to buildings.[12]

A tenant for life or other limited owner of land is required by various statutes[13] to insure and keep insured against fire, at his own expense, buildings which have been erected, improved or added to out of funds raised by means of charges on the settled land.

On the sale of a small holding under the Small Holdings and Allotments Act 1926 any dwelling house or other building erected on the holding is to be kept in repair and insured by the owner against fire to the satisfaction of the council.[14]

---

10 Riding Establishments Act 1964, s 1(4A); Riding Establishments Act 1970, s 2(1)(ii).

11 Riding Establishments Act 1964, s 2(4A): Riding Establishments Act 1970, s 2(1)(ii).

12 Repair of Benefice Buildings Measure 1972, s 12. See Ivamy *Fire and Motor Insurance* (4th Edn, 1984) pp 19–20.

13 I e Improvement of Land Act 1864, s 74, Limited Owners' Residences Act 1870, s 8, and Settled Land Act 1925, s 88. See Ivamy *Fire and Motor Insurance* (4th Edn, 1984) pp 20–21.

14 Small Holdings and Allotments Act 1926, s 6(1). See Ivamy *Fire and Motor Insurance* (4th Edn, 1984) p 21.

Appendices

APPENDIX I

Statutes

LIFE ASSURANCE ACT 1772[1]
(14 Geo 3 c 48)

An Act for regulating Insurances upon Lives, and for prohibiting all such Insurances except in cases where the Persons insuring shall have an Interest in the Life or Death of the Persons insured.

Whereas it hath been found by experience that the making insurances on lives or other events wherein the assured shall have no interest hath introduced a mischievous kind of gaming:

1. **No insurance to be made on lives, etc., by persons having no interest, etc.**—From and after the passing of this Act no insurance shall be made by any person or persons, bodies politick or corporate, on the life or lives of any person or persons, or on any other event or events whatsoever, wherein the person or persons for whose use, benefit, or on whose accounts such policy or policies shall be made, shall have no interest, or by way of gaming or wagering; and that every assurance made contrary to the true intent and meaning hereof shall be null and void to all intents and purposes whatsoever.

2. **No policies on lives without inserting the names of persons interested, etc.**—And . . . it shall not be lawful to make any policy or policies on the life or lives of any person or persons, or other event or events, without inserting in such policy or policies the person or person's name or names interested therein, or for whose use, benefit, or on whose account such policy is so made or underwrote.

3. **How much may be recovered where the insured hath interest in lives.**—And . . . in all cases where the insured hath interest in such life or lives, event or events, no greater sum shall be recovered or received from the insurer or insurers than the amount of value of the interest of the insured in such life or lives or other event or events.

4. **Not to extend to insurances on ships, goods, etc.**—Provided, always, that nothing herein contained shall extend or be construed to extend to insurances bona fide made by any person or persons on ships, goods, or merchandises, but every such insurance shall be as valid and effectual in the law as if this Act had not been made.

FIRES PREVENTION (METROPOLIS) ACT 1774
(14 Geo 3 c 78)

An Act . . . for the more effectually preventing Mischiefs by Fire within the Cities of London and Westminster and the Liberties thereof, and other the Parishes, Precincts, and Places within the Weekly Bills of Mortality, the Parishes of Saint Mary-le-bow, Paddington, Saint Pancras and Saint Luke at Chelsea, in the County of Middlesex . . .

---

[1] The Act is printed as amended.

83. Money insured on houses burnt, how to be applied.—And in order to deter and hinder ill-minded persons from wilfully setting their house or houses or other buildings on fire with a view of gaining to themselves the insurance money, whereby the lives and fortunes of many families may be lost or endangered: Be it further enacted by the authority aforesaid, that it shall and may be lawful to and for the respective governors or directors of the several insurance offices for insuring houses or other buildings against loss by fire, and they are hereby authorised and required, upon the request of any person or persons interested in or intitled unto any house or houses or other buildings which may hereafter be burnt down, demolished or damaged by fire, or upon any grounds of suspicion that the owner or owners, occupier or occupiers, or other person or persons who shall have insured such house or houses or other buildings have been guilty of fraud, or of wilfully setting their house or houses or other buildings on fire, to cause the insurance money to be laid out and expended, as far as the same will go, towards rebuilding, reinstating or repairing such house or houses or other buildings so burnt down, demolished or damaged by fire, unless the party or parties claiming such insurance money shall, within sixty days next after his, her or their claim is adjusted, give a sufficient security to the governors or directors of the insurance office where such house or houses or other buildings are insured, that the same insurance money shall be laid out and expended as aforesaid, or unless the said insurance money shall be in that time settled and disposed of to and amongst all the contending parties, to the satisfaction and approbation of such governors or directors of such insurance office respectively.

THE INSURANCE COMPANIES AMENDMENT ACT 1973

(1973 c 58)

50. Validation of certain group policies.—(1) Section 2 of the Life Assurance Act 1774 (policy on life or lives or other event or events not valid unless name or names of assured etc. inserted when policy is made) shall not invalidate a policy for the benefit of unnamed persons from time to time falling within a specified class or description if the class or description is stated in the policy with sufficient particularity to make it possible to establish the identity of all persons who at any given time are entitled to benefit under the policy.

(2) This section applies to policies effected before the passing of this Act as well as to policies effected thereafter.

POLICYHOLDERS PROTECTION ACT 1975[1]

(1975 c 75)

An Act to make provision for indemnifying (in whole or in part) or otherwise assisting or protecting policyholders and others who have been or may be prejudiced in consequence of the inability of authorised insurance companies carrying on business in the United Kingdom to meet their liabilities under policies issued or securities given by them, and for imposing levies on the insurance industry for the purpose; to authorise the disclosure of certain documents and information to persons appointed by the Secretary of State to advise him on the exercise of his powers under the Insurance Companies Act 1974; and for purposes connected with the matters aforesaid. [12 November 1975]

BE IT ENACTED by the Queen's most Excellent Majesty, by and with the advice and consent of the Lords Spiritual and Temporal, and Commons, in this present Parliament assembled, and by the authority of the same, as follows:—

---

[1] The Act is printed as amended.

The Policyholders Protection Board

1. The Policyholders Protection Board.—(1) There shall be a body corporate, to be called the Policyholders Protection Board (hereafter in this Act referred to as 'the Board').

(2) The functions of the Board shall be—

(a) to take the measures provided for by sections 6 to 16 below for the purpose of indemnifying (in whole or in part) or otherwise assisting or protecting policyholders and others who have been or may be prejudiced in consequence of the inability of insurance companies carrying on business in the United Kingdom to meet their liabilities under policies issued or securities given by them; and

(b) for the purpose of financing their expenditure on the performance of their functions under those sections, to impose levies, in accordance with sections 19, 20 and 21 below and Schedules 2 and 3 to this Act, on insurance companies and other persons engaged in the insurance industry in the United Kingdom;

and otherwise to do anything requisite for carrying out the provisions of this Act.

(3) Subject to subsection (4) below, the Board shall have power to borrow any sums they may from time to time require for performing any of their functions under this Act.

(4) The aggregate amount outstanding in respect of the principal of any money borrowed by the Board under subsection (3) above shall not exceed £10 million.

(5) Schedule 1 to this Act shall have effect with respect to the constitution of the Board and the other matters there mentioned.

2. Guidance to the Board by the Secretary of State.—(1) Subject to subsection (2) below, the Secretary of State may from time to time, after consultation with the Board, give guidance to the Board in writing with respect to the performance of any of their functions under this Act; and it shall be the duty of the Board to perform the functions in question in such a manner as they consider is in accordance with the guidance for the time being given to them in pursuance of this section.

(2) No guidance shall be given to the Board in pursuance of subsection (1) above unless a draft of the document containing it has been approved by a resolution of each House of Parliament.

General scope of the Board's functions under this Act

3. Authorised insurance companies.—(1) The functions of the Board under this Act shall be exercisable in relation to policyholders and others who have been or may be prejudiced in consequence of the inability of insurance companies to meet their liabilities under policies issued or securities given by them only in cases where the insurance companies in question are authorised insurance companies.

(2) An insurance company is an authorised insurance company for the purposes of this Act if it is authorised under section 3 or 4 of the Insurance Companies Act 1982 to carry on insurance business of any class in the United Kingdom.

4. Protection confined to United Kingdom policies.—(1) A policyholder is eligible for the assistance or protection of the Board in accordance with any provision of sections 6 to 16 below only in respect of a policy of insurance which was a United Kingdom policy for the purposes of this Act at the material time for the purposes of the provision in question.

(2) A policy of insurance is a United Kingdom policy for the purposes of this Act at any time when the performance by the insurer of any of his obligations under the contract evidenced by the policy would constitute the carrying on by the insurer of insurance business of any class in the United Kingdom.

Duties of the Board in case of companies in liquidation

5. Application of sections 6 to 11.—(1) Subject to the following provisions of this section, the functions of the Board under sections 6 to 11 below are exercisable where in the case of any authorised insurance company—

(a) a resolution has been passed, in accordance with the provisions of the Companies Act 1985 or (as the case may be) of the Companies Act (Northern Ireland) 1960 for the voluntary winding up of the company, otherwise than merely for the purpose of reconstruction of the company or of amalgamation with another insurance company; or
(b) without any such resolution having been passed beforehand, an order has been made for the winding up of the company by the court under either of those Acts.

(2) Sections 6 to 11 shall not apply in a case falling within subsection (1)(a) above (whether or not an order for the winding up of the company by or subject to the supervision of the court has been made since the resolution there mentioned was passed) unless the resolution was passed after 29 October 1974.

(3) Sections 6 to 11 shall not apply in a case falling within subsection (1)(b) above unless the petition for the winding up of the company by the court was presented after 29 October 1974.

(4) References in this Act to a company in liquidation are references to an authorised insurance company in whose case—

(a) a resolution has been passed as mentioned in subsection (1)(a) above after 29 October 1974; or
(b) an order has been made as mentioned in subsection (1)(b) above on a petition presented after that date.

(5) References in this Act, in relation to a company in liquidation, to the beginning of the liquidation, are references—

(a) in a case falling within subsection (1)(a) above, to the passing of the resolution; and
(b) in a case falling within subsection (1)(b) above, to the making of the order.

6. Compulsory insurance policies and securities.—(1) This section applies to any policy which satisfies the requirements of any of the following, that is to say—

(a) section 1(4A)(d) of the Riding Establishments Act 1964 or any corresponding enactment for the time being in force in Northern Ireland;
(b) section 1 of the Employers' Liability (Compulsory Insurance) Act 1969 or Article 5 of the Employers' Liability (Defective Equipment and Compulsory Insurance) (Northern Ireland) Order 1972; or
(c) Part VI of the Road Traffic Act 1972 or Part VIII of the Road Traffic Act (Northern Ireland) Order 1981;

and to any policy evidencing a contract of insurance effected for the purposes of section 19 of the Nuclear Installations Act 1965.

(2) This section applies to any security in respect of third-party risks given by an authorised insurance company which satisfies the requirements of Part VI of the Road Traffic Act 1972 or Part VIII of the Road Traffic Act (Northern Ireland) Order 1981.

(3) In this section 'a liability subject to compulsory insurance' means any liability required under any of the enactments mentioned in subsection (1) above to be covered by insurance or (as the case may be) by insurance or by some other provision for securing its discharge.

(4) Subject to sections 9, 13 and 14 below and the following provisions of this section, it shall be the duty of the Board to secure that a sum equal to the full amount of any liability

of a company in liquidation towards any policyholder or security holder under the terms of any policy or security to which this section applies is paid to the policyholder or security holder as soon as reasonably practicable after the beginning of the liquidation.

(5) Subsection (4) above does not apply by reference to any liability of a company in liquidation under the terms of a policy to which this section applies arising otherwise than in respect of a liability of the policyholder which is a liability subject to compulsory insurance.

(6) Subject to sections 9, 13 and 14 and subsection (8) below, it shall be the duty of the Board to secure that a sum equal to ninety per cent of the amount of any liability of a company in liquidation towards a private policyholder under the terms of any policy to which this section applies, being a liability arising otherwise than in respect of a liability of the policyholder which is a liability subject to compulsory insurance, is paid to the policyholder as soon as reasonably practicable after the beginning of the liquidation.

(7) In subsection (6) above 'private policyholder' means a policyholder who is either—

(a) an individual; or
(b) a partnership or other unincorporated body of persons all of whom are individuals.

(8) The duty of the Board under subsection (4) or (6) above shall not apply—

(a) in the case of any policy, unless it was a United Kingdom policy at the beginning of the liquidation; or
(b) in the case of any security in respect of third-party risks, unless it would have been a United Kingdom policy at the beginning of the liquidation if it had been an insurance policy and the contract governing the security had been a contract of insurance.

(9) References hereafter in this Act to policies which were United Kingdom policies at any time and to policyholders in respect of such policies shall be construed as including references to—

(a) securities to which this section applies which would have been United Kingdom policies at the time in question if they had been insurance policies and the contracts governing the securities had been contracts of insurance; and
(b) security holders in respect of such securities.

7. Third-party rights against insurance companies in road traffic cases.—Without prejudice to section 6 above, but subject to sections 9, 13 and 14 below, it shall be the duty of the Board to secure that a sum equal to the full amount of any liability of a company in liquidation in respect of a sum payable to a person entitled to the benefit of a judgment under—

(a) section 149 of the Road Traffic Act 1972 (duty of insurers to satisfy judgment against persons insured or secured against third-party risks); or
(b) Article 98 of the Road Traffic Act (Northern Ireland) Order 1981 (court orders for recovery from insurers of sums due under unsatisfied judgments against persons insured or secured by them);

is paid to that person as soon as reasonably practicable after the beginning of the liquidation.

8. General policies other than compulsory insurance policies.—(1) This section applies to any general policy other than a policy to which section 6 above applies.

(2) Subject to sections 9, 13 and 14 below, it shall be the duty of the Board to secure that a sum equal to ninety per cent of the amount of any liability of a company in liquidation towards a private policyholder under the terms of any policy to which this

section applies which was a United Kingdom policy at the beginning of the liquidation is paid to the policyholder as soon as reasonably practicable after the beginning of the liquidation.

(3) In subsection (2) above 'private policyholder' has the same meaning as in section 6(6) above.

(4) In this Act 'general policy' means any policy evidencing a contract the effecting of which constituted the carrying on of general business of any class other than class 5, 6, 7, 11 or 12, not being a contract of reinsurance.

9. Limits on the duties of the Board under sections 6 to 8.—(1) The Board shall not by virtue of any provision of sections 6 to 8 above be required to secure any sum for a policyholder in respect of a policy of a company in liquidation which was a United Kingdom policy at the beginning of the liquidation or (as the case may be) for a person entitled to the benefit of a judgment by reference to any liability (or any part of any liability) of a company in liquidation which is duplicated by the liability of any other authorised insurance company which is not a company in liquidation.

(2) A liability of a company towards a policyholder is duplicated by the liability of another company for the purposes of subsection (1) above in so far as that other company is also under a liability, under the terms of any general policy which was a United Kingdom policy at the beginning of the first-mentioned company's liquidation, to make any payment to or on behalf of the policyholder in respect of the matter to which the liability of the first-mentioned company relates.

(3) A liability of a company in respect of a sum payable under section 149 of the Road Traffic Act 1972 or Article 98 of the Road Traffic Act (Northern Ireland) Order 1981 to a person entitled to the benefit of a judgment is duplicated by the liability of another company for the purposes of subsection (1) above in so far as that other company is also liable under either of that section or that Article to pay any sum to that person in respect of the same judgment.

10. Long term policies.—(1) In this Act 'long term policy' means any policy evidencing a contract the effecting of which constituted the carrying on of long term business, . . . , not being a contract of reinsurance.

(2) Subject to sections 13 and 14 below, it shall be the duty of the Board to secure that a sum equal to ninety per cent of the amount of any liability of a company in liquidation towards any policyholder under the terms of a long term policy which was a United Kingdom policy at the beginning of the liquidation is paid to the policyholder as soon as reasonably practicable after the beginning of the liquidation.

11. Special provision for future benefits under long term policies.—(1) Subject to subsection (2) below, in this section 'future benefit', in relation to any long term policy of a company in liquidation, means any benefit provided for under the policy which has not fallen due to be paid by the company before the beginning of the liquidation.

(2) Any bonus provided for under a policy shall not by virtue of subsection (1) above be treated as a future benefit within the meaning of this section unless it was declared before the beginning of the liquidation.

(3) Subject to sections 13 and 14 below and to the following provisions of this section, it shall be the duty of the Board, as soon as reasonably practicable after the beginning of the liquidation, to make arrangements in pursuance of subsection (5) below for securing continuity of insurance for every policyholder of a company in liquidation who is a policyholder in respect of a long term policy which was a United Kingdom policy at the beginning of the liquidation.

(4) Subject to subsection (6) below, the duty of the Board under subsection (3) above to secure continuity of insurance for any policyholder extends only to securing that the policyholder will receive ninety per cent of any future benefit under his policy, subject to

and in accordance with terms corresponding so far as appears to the Board to be reasonable in the circumstances to the terms which would have applied under the policy.

(5) For the purpose of securing continuity of insurance for any policyholders of a company in liquidation in accordance with subsection (3) above, the Board may take such measures as appear to them to be appropriate—

(a) for securing or facilitating the transfer of the long term business of the company, or of any part of that business, to another authorised insurance company; or
(b) for securing the issue by another authorised insurance company to the policyholders in question of policies in substitution for their existing policies.

(6) Where a long term policy of a company in liquidation contains terms relating to matters other than future benefits under the policy the duty of the Board under subsection (3) above to secure continuity of insurance for the policyholder in question extends also to securing that the policy after any transfer of business in which it is included or (as the case may be) any policy issued in substitution for the policy in question contains terms relating to those matters which correspond so far as appears to the Board to be reasonable in the circumstances to the terms first mentioned above.

(7) During any period while the Board are seeking to make arrangements for securing continuity of insurance for any policyholders of a company in liquidation in accordance with subsection (3) above, it shall be the duty of the Board, subject to sections 13 and 14 and subsection (11) below, to secure that ninety per cent of any future benefit under a long term policy which would have fallen due to be paid to any of those policyholders during that period is paid to the policyholder in question as soon as reasonably practicable after the time when the benefit in question would have fallen due under the policy (but subject to and in accordance with any other terms which would have applied under the policy).

(8) Arrangements made by the Board in pursuance of subsection (5) above shall not be required to cover any future benefit under a policy in so far as any sums have been paid to the policyholder in pursuance of subsection (7) above by reference to that benefit.

(9) Where it appears to the Board that it is not reasonably practicable to secure continuity of insurance for any policyholder of a company in liquidation in accordance with subsection (3) above, it shall be the duty of the Board, subject to sections 13 and 14 and subsection (10) below, to pay to the policyholder a sum equal to ninety per cent of the value attributed to his policy for the purposes of any claim in respect of his policy in the winding up of the company, as soon as reasonably practicable after any such claim is admitted.

(10) The Secretary of State may by regulation made by statutory instrument—

(a) require the Board, in a case to which subsection (9) above applies, to pay to the policyholder at his option, instead of the sum there mentioned, a sum equal to ninety per cent of the value of the future benefits under his policy, or of such of those benefits as may be specified by the regulations, determined in such manner as the regulations may provide;
(b) make such provision as appears to him to be appropriate with respect to the time within which and the manner in which the Board are to perform any of their functions under this section (including any function conferred on them by virtue of paragraph (a) above).

(11) Any duty of the Board under subsection (3) or (7) above to take any measures for assisting a policyholder of a company in liquidation shall be subject to compliance on his part with any conditions imposed by the Board with respect to the payment, in any case or in any class or description of case, of sums which would have fallen due from policyholders of a company in liquidation by way of premiums under long term policies if the company had not gone into liquidation.

12. Disproportionate benefits under long term policies.—(1) If it appears to the Board, in the case of any long term policy of a company in liquidation which was a United Kingdom policy at the beginning of the liquidation, that the benefits provided for thereunder are or may be excessive in any respect, having regard to the premiums paid or payable and to any other terms of the policy, the Board shall refer the policy to an independent actuary.

(2) This subsection applies in any case where an actuary to whom a policy is referred under subsection (1) above makes to the Board a report in writing—

(a) stating, with respect to any of the benefits provided for under the policy, that in his view the benefit or benefits in question are excessive; and
(b) recommending, accordingly, that for the purposes of sections 10 and 11 above any liability of the company under the policy or any future benefit under the policy should be treated as reduced or (as the case may be) disregarded.

(3) In any case to which subsection (2) above applies the Board may determine in the light of any recommendation contained in the actuary's report that the liability or benefit to which that recommendation relates shall be treated as reduced or disregarded for the purposes of sections 10 and 11 above; and where the Board so determine the liability or benefit in question shall be treated as reduced or (as the case may be) disregarded accordingly for the purposes of the application of section 10, of any provision of subsections (3) to (7) of section 11, or of any provision of any regulations made under subsection (10) of section 11 above (as the case may require) in relation to the policy in question.

(4) This subsection applies in any case where—

(a) a claim has been admitted in the winding up of a company in respect of any policy which is the subject of a report by an actuary under subsection (2) above; and
(b) that report indicates, or the actuary makes to the Board a further report in writing indicating, what value would in his view have been attributed to the policy in the winding up if any future benefit under the policy to which any recommendation in the report under subsection (2) above relates had been treated as reduced or disregarded in accordance with the recommendation in determining the claim in respect of the policy in the winding up.

(5) In any case to which subsection (4) above applies the Board may determine in the light of the value indicated in the actuary's report that the value attributed to the policy in question for the purposes of the claim in respect of the policy in the winding up shall be treated as reduced for the purpose of calculating the sum payable to the policyholder in accordance with subsection (9) of section 11 above; and where the Board so determine the value so attributed to the policy shall be treated as reduced for that purpose accordingly.

(6) In this section 'future benefit' has the same meaning as in section 11 above.

General provisions with respect to the duties of the Board

13. General provisions with respect to the performance by the Board of their duties.—(1) Where it appears to the Board, in the case of any policy of a company in liquidation—

(a) that payment in respect of any sums falling due under the policy could have been made in accordance with the policy to a person other than the policyholder; or
(b) that any sums paid under the policy would have been subject to any trust, charge or other agreement binding on the policyholder;

the Board may secure the payment of any sum payable to the policyholder in accordance with any of the provisions of sections 6 to 10 or in accordance with section 11(7) above or pay any sum so payable in accordance with section 11(9) or (10) above (in whole or in part) to that other person or (as the case may be) to the person appearing to the Board to be entitled under the trust, charge or agreement in question, instead of to the policyholder.

Any payment made by virtue of this subsection to a person other than the policyholder shall be treated for the purposes of the provision in question as a payment to the policyholder and may be made on such conditions (with respect to the total or partial assignment to the Board of any rights of the recipient against the policyholder or any other person, or otherwise) as the Board think fit.

(2) The Board may secure the payment of any sum payable to a policyholder in accordance with any of the provisions of sections 6 to 10 or in accordance with section 11(7) above, or payable under section 7 above to a person entitled to the benefit of a judgment, and of any sum they are authorised to secure for a person other than the policyholder by virtue of subsection (1) above, by either or both of the following methods, that is to say—

(a) by themselves making payments in respect of the sum in question; or
(b) by securing by any measures appearing to them to be appropriate that such payments are made by any other person.

(3) Nothing in any provision of sections 6 to 11 above shall be construed as requiring the Board to make any payment or to incur any other expenditure thereunder at a time when it appears to the Board that the funds available to them for expenditure under that provision, together with any funds they may raise by means of a levy under section 19 or 21 below which might be applied on such expenditure, fall short of what they may require; and accordingly the Board may—

(a) postpone making any payment, or any part of any payment, they propose to make under any such provision; and
(b) postpone taking any measures under any such provision involving expenditure on their part;

from time to time, until it appears to them that their funds are adequate to meet the expenditure they propose to incur under the provision in question.

(4) Any duty of the Board to assist a policyholder of a company in liquidation by any of the measures provided for by sections 6 to 11 above shall be subject to compliance on his part with any conditions imposed by the Board with respect to the total or partial assignment to the Board of—

(a) his rights under or in respect of the policy;
(b) any rights he may have in respect of any payments made by him to the liquidator by way of premiums under the policy since the beginning of the liquidation; and
(c) any rights he may have against any other persons in respect of any event giving rise to any liability of the company under the policy.

(5) Any duty of the Board to secure the payment of any sum payable under section 7 above to a person entitled to the benefit of a judgment shall be subject to compliance on his part with any conditions imposed by the Board with respect to the total or partial assignment to the Board of any rights he may have against any other persons in respect of any event giving rise to the liability of the company in liquidation by reference to which that sum is so payable.

(6) In connection with imposing any conditions under any of the preceding provisions of this section with respect to the assignment to them of any rights the Board may make any arrangements which appears to them to be appropriate with any person on whom the conditions are imposed with respect to the manner in which they are to apply any sums they may receive by virtue of the rights in question.

(7) The Secretary of State may by regulations made by statutory instrument provide for the transfer to and the vesting in the Board by virtue of the regulations, in such circumstances as may be specified therein—

(a) of any such rights of a policyholder to whom the Board have given assistance by any of the measures provided for by sections 6 to 11 above as are mentioned in subsection (4) above;
(b) of any such rights of a person for whom the Board have secured any payment in accordance with section 7 above as are mentioned in subsection (5) above; and
(c) of any rights which a person to whom any payment has been made by virtue of subsection (1) above may have against the policyholder in respect of the policy or any sums falling due thereunder or against any other persons in respect of any event giving rise to any liability of the policyholder by virtue of which the payment in question was made;

and regulations made under this subsection may also provide for the manner in which the Board are to apply any sums received by them by virtue of any rights vested in them by the regulations.

14. Exclusion and modification of duties of the Board where payments are made by other persons, etc.—(1) Any payment made by any person other than the Board to the policyholder, to a person entitled to the benefit of a judgment, or to any other person, being a payment which is referable to any such liability of a company in liquidation as is mentioned in section 6, 7 or 8 above, shall be treated as reducing any sum payable to the policyholder or to the person entitled to the benefit of the judgment, in accordance with any provision of those sections, by reference to that liability.

(2) This subsection applies in any case where it appears to the Board, in respect of a long term policy of a company in liquidation—

(a) that any other person has made a payment to the policyholder or to any other person which is referable to any liability of the company under the policy which was outstanding at the beginning of the liquidation or which is otherwise required in accordance with subsection (3) below to be taken into account in relation to the policy; or
(b) that any other person has taken any other measures for assisting or protecting the policyholder (whether measures of a like description to those open to the Board under subsection (5) of section 11 above or otherwise) which ought to be taken into account for the purpose of excluding or modifying any of their duties towards the policyholder under sections 10 and 11 above.

(3) Any payments made—

(a) by reference to any valuation of a long term policy of a company in liquidation or of any of the benefits provided for under any such policy; or
(b) by reference to any future benefits under a long term policy of a company in liquidation;

shall be taken into account in relation to that policy for the purposes of subsection (2)(a) above (whether it was made to the policyholder or to any other person).

(4) Nothing in sections 10 and 11 above shall require the Board, in a case to which subsection (2) applies, to take any measures for assisting the policyholder in respect of the long term policy in question where it appears to the Board to be inappropriate to do so in view of any such payment or other measures of assistance or protection as are mentioned in that subsection.

(5) In any case to which subsection (2) above applies, other than one falling within subsection (4) above, the Board may treat any sum payable to the policyholder in accordance with section 10 or section 11(7), (9) or (10) above and any sum to be secured

for the policyholder by virtue of section 11(4) above as reduced to any extent appearing to them to be appropriate in the circumstances of the case.

(6) Any sums secured by the Board under subsection (7) of section 11 above for a policyholder of a company in liquidation or for any other person by reference to any future benefits under a long term policy shall be treated as reducing any sum payable to the policyholder in respect of that policy in accordance with subsection (9) or (10) of that section.

(7) The Board may postpone taking any of the measures provided for by sections 6 to 11 above in any case where it appears to the Board that, independently of any measures they may take, any other person (not being the liquidator) may make any payment or take any measures which would, by virtue of subsection (1), (4) or (5) above, affect any of their duties under those sections in relation to the case in question.

(8) A payment is referable to a liability of a company in liquidation for the purposes of this section if it has the effect of reducing or discharging, or is otherwise made by reference to, that liability or any liability of the policyholder or any other person from which that liability arises.

(9) In this section 'future benefit' has the same meaning as in section 11 above.

Powers of the Board to assist policyholders of companies in liquidation, etc.

15. Interim payments to policyholders of companies in liquidation, etc.—(1) An authorised insurance company, not being a company in liquidation, is a company in provisional liquidation for the purposes of this section if a provisional liquidator has been appointed in respect of the company under section 532 of the Companies Act 1985 or section 222 of the Companies Act (Northern Ireland) 1960, provided that the petition for the winding up of the company which led to his appointment was presented after 29 October 1974.

(2) A policyholder is eligible for assistance under this section—

(a) if he is a policyholder in respect of a general policy or a long term policy of a company in liquidation which was a United Kingdom policy at the beginning of the liquidation; or

(b) if he is a policyholder in respect of a general policy or a long term policy of a company in provisional liquidation which was a United Kingdom policy at the time when the provisional liquidator was appointed.

(3) In any case where it appears to the Board to be desirable to do so, the Board may—

(a) make payments to or on behalf of policyholders who are eligible for assistance under this section, on such terms (including any terms requiring repayment, in whole or in part) and on such conditions as the Board think fit; or

(b) secure that payments are made to or on behalf of any such policyholders by the liquidator or the provisional liquidator by giving him an indemnity covering any such payments or any class or description of such payments.

Powers of the Board to protect policyholders of companies in financial difficulties

16. Companies in financial difficulties: transfers of business, etc.—(1) An authorised insurance company, not being a company in liquidation, is a company in financial difficulties for the purposes of this section if—

(a) it is a company in provisional liquidation within the meaning of section 15 above;

(b) it has been proved, in any proceedings on a petition for the winding up of the company under the Companies Act 1985 or (as the case may be) the Companies Act (Northern Ireland) 1960, to be unable to pay its debts; or

(c) an application has been made to the court under section 425 of the Companies Act 1985 or section 197 of the Companies Act (Northern Ireland) 1960 for the sanctioning of a compromise or arrangement proposed between the company and its creditors or any class of them (whether or not any of its members are also parties thereto) and the terms of the compromise or arrangement provide for reducing the liabilities or the benefits provided for under any of the company's policies;

provided that, in a case falling within paragraph (b) above, the petition was presented after 29 October 1974, and in a case falling within paragraph (c) above, the application was made after that date.

(2) Subject to section 17 below and to the following provisions of this section, the Board may exercise any power conferred on them by subsection (3) or (4) below for the purpose of safeguarding policyholders of a company in financial difficulties who are eligible for protection under this section, or any class or description of such policyholders, to any extent appearing to the Board to be appropriate in any case or in any class or description of case, against loss arising from the financial difficulties of the company.

(3) Subject to section 17 below and to the following provisions of this section, the Board may take any measures appearing to them to be appropriate for securing or facilitating the transfer of all or any part of the insurance business carried on by a company in financial difficulties to another authorised insurance company, on terms (including terms reducing the liabilities or the benefits provided for under any policies) appearing to the Board to be appropriate in any case or in any class or description of case.

(4) Subject to section 17 below and to the following provisions of this section, in any case where it appears to the Board that it would be practicable to secure the purpose mentioned in subsection (2) above by giving assistance to the company in financial difficulties to enable it to continue to carry on insurance business, the Board may take such measures as appear to them to be appropriate for giving such assistance.

(5) Without prejudice to the generality of subsection (4) above, the Board may make the giving of any assistance to a company in financial difficulties under subsection (4) above conditional on the reduction of any liabilities or benefits provided for under any policies of the company to any extent appearing to them to be appropriate in any case or in any class or description of case.

(6) The Board shall not exercise any power conferred on them by subsection (3) or (4) above for the purpose of safeguarding any policyholders of a company in financial difficulties in any case where it appears to the Board that—

(a) persons who were members of the company at the relevant time; or
(b) persons who had any responsibility for or who may have profited from the circumstances giving rise to the company's financial difficulties;

would benefit to any material extent as a result of any measures the Board may take under either of those subsections.

In this subsection and in the following provisions of this section 'the relevant time' means—

(a) in a case falling within subsection (1)(a) above, the time when the provisional liquidator was appointed;
(b) in a case falling within subsection (1)(b) above, the time when the winding up petition was presented; and
(c) in a case falling within subsection (1)(c) above, the time when the application was made under section 425 of the Companies Act 1985 or (as the case may be) under section 197 of the Companies Act (Northern Ireland) 1960.

(7) The Board shall disregard for the purposes of subsection (6) above any benefit which may accrue to any such persons as are there mentioned who are policyholders of the company in financial difficulties in their capacity as such.

(8) The Board shall not take any measures in pursuance of subsection (3) or (4) above for the purpose of safeguarding any policyholders of a company in financial difficulties in any case where it appears to the Board that to take whatever measures may be required for the assistance of the policyholders in question under sections 6 to 11 above in the event of the company's going into liquidation would cost them less than to take the measures in question under subsection (3) or (4) above.

(9) A policyholder of a company in financial difficulties is eligible for protection under this section if he is a policyholder in respect of a general policy or a long term policy of the company which was a United Kingdom policy at the relevant time.

17. Special provision with respect to long term business of a company in financial difficulties.—(1) Without prejudice to subsection (8) of section 16 above, the Board shall not take any measures in pursuance of subsection (3) or (4) of that section for the purpose of safeguarding any policyholders of a company in financial difficulties in respect of long term policies of the company, other than measures allowed by subsection (2) below, in any case where it appears to the Board that to take those other measures would cost them more than to take measures allowed by subsection (2) below.

(2) The measures allowed by this subsection are any measures open to the Board under subsection (3) or (4) of section 16 above for the purpose of safeguarding policyholders of a company in financial difficulties which involve the imposition by the Board, as a prerequisite of their incurring any expenditure or liabilities for that purpose, of conditions requiring—

- (a) the reduction of all liabilities of the company under relevant long term policies and of all benefits provided for under any such policies which have not fallen due to be paid by the company before the time when the reduction is to take effect, to ninety per cent of the amount which would otherwise have been payable in accordance with the terms of the policies; and
- (b) the reduction of all premiums under any such policies which have not fallen due before that time to ninety per cent of the amount which would otherwise have been so payable.

A long term policy is a relevant long term policy for the purposes of this subsection if it is included in any transfer secured or facilitated by the Board under subsection (3) of section 16 or in any business continued by virtue of any assistance given by the Board under subsection (4) of that section.

(3) Without prejudice to the power of the Board to impose conditions in relation to taking any measures under subsection (3) or (4) of section 16 above with respect to matters other than those covered by the conditions mentioned in subsection (2) above, the benefits mentioned in paragraph (a) of subsection (2) shall not include any bonus provided for under a policy unless it was declared before the time when any such reduction of liabilities and benefits under that policy as is mentioned in that paragraph is to take effect.

(4) If it appears to the Board, in the case of any long term policy of a company in financial difficulties which was a United Kingdom policy at the relevant time as defined by section 16(6) above, that the benefits provided for thereunder are or may be excessive in any respect, having regard to the premiums paid or payable and to any other terms of the policy, the Board shall refer the policy to an independent actuary.

(5) Where an actuary to whom a policy of a company in financial difficulties is referred under subsection (4) above makes to the Board a report in writing—

- (a) stating, with respect to any of the benefits provided for under the policy, that in his view the benefit or benefits in question are excessive; and
- (b) recommending, accordingly, that for the purposes of any measures to be taken by the Board in pursuance of subsection (3) or (4) of section 16 above for safeguarding the policyholder in question against loss arising from the financial

difficulties of the company any such benefit should be treated as reduced or (as the case may be) disregarded;

the Board may determine in the light of any recommendation contained in the actuary's report that any benefit to which that recommendation relates shall be treated as reduced or disregarded for those purposes.

(6) Where in a case falling within subsection (5) above the Board determine that the benefit in question shall be disregarded for the purposes there mentioned, the conditions mentioned in subsection (2) above shall include conditions requiring the cancellation of that benefit or (as the case may be) of any liability representing that benefit.

(7) Where in a case falling within subsection (5) above the Board determine that the benefit in question shall be treated as reduced for the purposes there mentioned, subsection (2)(a) above shall apply in relation to the policy as if the amount of that benefit or (as the case may be) of any liability representing that benefit, as reduced in accordance with the Board's determination, were the amount which would otherwise have been payable in accordance with the terms of the policy.

(8) In this section 'company in financial difficulties' has the same meaning as in section 16 above.

Levies on the insurance industry to finance the performance by the Board of their functions

18. General business expenditure and long term business expenditure.—(1) In this Act 'general business expenditure' means—

(a) any expenditure of the Board under section 6, 7 or 8 above; and
(b) any expenditure attributed by the Board under subsection (3) below to general business expenditure.

(2) In this Act 'long term business expenditure' means—

(a) any expenditure of the Board under section 10 or 11 above; and
(b) any expenditure attributed by the Board under subsection (3) below to long term business expenditure.

(3) The Board may, in the case of—

(a) any expenditure under section 15 or 16 above;
(b) any expenditure in repaying or servicing any loans; and
(c) any expenditure on their administrative expenses in performing their functions under this Act;

attribute that expenditure to general business expenditure or to long term business expenditure, or partly to the one and partly to the other, in such manner as may appear to them to be reasonable in the circumstances of the case.

19. Levies on intermediaries.—(1) Where—

(a) the Board have incurred or propose to incur any long term business expenditure in relation to a company in liquidation or a company which is a company in financial difficulties within the meaning of section 16 above; and
(b) it appears to the Board that the company in question has accountable intermediaries;

it shall be the duty of the Board to impose a levy on those intermediaries in accordance with the following provisions of this section and Schedule 2 to this Act.

(2) Subject to section 20 and subsections (3) and (5) below, a person is an accountable intermediary of a company for the purposes of this section and Schedule 2 to this Act if—

(a) he has acted as an intermediary for the company in relation to any relevant long term contract of the company; and

(b) his income from the company in respect of his services (whether as an intermediary or otherwise) in relation to any such contracts (hereafter in this section and in section 20 below referred to as 'relevant services') for either or each of the two years comprised in the period of two years ending immediately before the time mentioned below in this subsection exceeded his exempt income level for the year in question.

The time referred to above is the beginning of the liquidation in the case of a company in liquidation and the relevant time as defined by section 16(6) above in the case of a company in financial difficulties within the meaning of that section.

(3) An individual shall not be an accountable intermediary of a company for the purposes of this section and Schedule 2 to this Act if the services in question under subsection (2)(b) above were performed in pursuance of a contract of exclusive agency with the company.

For the purposes of this subsection a contract is a contract of exclusive agency with a company in relation to the performance of any services thereunder if it provides that the person performing the services must not perform services of a like description for any other insurance company.

(4) Subject to section 20 and subsection (5) below, the income of an accountable intermediary of a company which is liable to levy under this section shall be—

(a) one-half of any amount by which his income from the company in respect of relevant services for the later of the two years mentioned in subsection (2) above exceeded his exempt income level for that year; and
(b) one-quarter of any amount by which his income from the company in respect of relevant services for the earlier of those two years exceeded his exempt income level for that year;

and in relation to any intermediary, his income liable to levy for either of those years or, where he had income liable to levy for each of those years, the aggregate of his income liable to levy for both of those years, is hereafter in this Act referred to as income of the intermediary which is income liable to levy.

(5) For the purposes of this section and section 20 below a person's income from a company in respect of relevant services for any year is the total amount of the sums paid or allowed to that person by the company in respect of relevant services which were recorded as debits in the company's accounts during that year; but no account shall be taken for those purposes of any sums recorded in a company's accounts at any time before 1 January 1976.

(6) If the proceeds of any levy imposed under this section in respect of any company exceed the long term business expenditure incurred by the Board in relation to that company the Board shall distribute the excess among the accountable intermediaries of that company who have made any payments to the Board under the levy in proportion to the sums those intermediaries have respectively paid thereunder.

(7) References in this section, in section 20 below and in Schedule 2 to this Act to an intermediary of a company are references to a person who has acted as an intermediary for the company in relation to any relevant long term contract of the company.

(8) For the purposes of this section a person acts as an intermediary for a company in relation to a long term contract if, otherwise than as an employee of the company—

(a) he invites any other person to take any step with a view to entering into a long term contract with the company;
(b) he introduces any other person to the company with a view to his entering into such a contract with the company; or
(c) he takes any other action with a view to securing that any other person will enter into such a contract with the company.

(9) In this section 'long term contract' means a contract the effecting of which by a

company constitutes the carrying on by the company of long term business . . . in the United Kingdom, not being a contract of reinsurance; and a long term contract is a relevant long term contract of a company for the purposes of this section if it was effected by the company within the period of two years mentioned in subsection (2) above.

(10) Schedule 2 to this Act shall have effect with respect to the imposition and enforcement of levies under this section.

20. The exempt income level for the purposes of section 19.—(1) For the purposes of section 19 above the exempt income level of an intermediary of a company for any year is—

(a) where no other person is linked with the intermediary, £5,000; and
(b) in any other case, that proportion of £5,000 which is equal to the proportion which the intermediary's income from the company in respect of relevant services for the year in question bears to the total amount of the group's income from the company in respect of such services for that year.

In paragraph (b) above 'the group' means the intermediary together with the person or (where there are more than one) all of the persons linked with the intermediary.

(2) Where in a case falling within subsection (1)(b) above the income from the company in respect of relevant services for any year—

(a) of the intermediary; and
(b) of each person linked with the intermediary;

did not exceed £1,000, no account shall be taken of that income for the purposes of section 19 above.

(3) The following are persons linked with an intermediary for the purposes of this section, whether the intermediary is a company or a person other than a company—

(a) any partner of the intermediary and any partnership of which the intermediary is a member;
(b) any company of which the intermediary is a director; and
(c) any director of any company which is linked with the intermediary.

(4) Where the intermediary in question is a company the following are also persons linked with the intermediary for the purposes of this section—

(a) any person other than a company who has a controlling interest in the intermediary, and any company other than the intermediary in which any such person also has a controlling interest;
(b) any company of which the intermediary is a subsidiary and any other subsidiary of any such company;
(c) any subsidiary of the intermediary; and
(d) any director of the intermediary.

(5) Where the intermediary in question is a person other than a company the following are also persons linked with the intermediary for the purposes of this section—

(a) any company in which the intermediary has a controlling interest;
(b) any company of which a company linked with the intermediary by virtue of subsection (3)(b) or paragraph (a) above is a subsidiary and any other subsidiary of any such company;
(c) any subsidiary of any company linked with the intermediary by virtue of subsection (3)(b) or paragraph (a) above; and
(d) where the intermediary is a partnership, each of its members.

(6) A person other than a company shall be treated as having a controlling interest in a company for the purposes of subsections (4)(a) and (5)(a) above if, but only if, that company would be a subsidiary of the person in question if that person were a company.

(7) In determining for the purposes of subsection (6) above whether a company would be a subsidiary of any person other than a company, any shares held or power exercisable by either of two spouses or by both spouses jointly shall be treated as held or exercisable by each spouse.

(8) In subsections (3) to (7) above 'company' includes any body corporate.

21. Levies on authorised insurance companies.—(1) Subject to the following provisions of this section and to Schedule 3 to this Act, the Board may from time to time, for the purpose of financing general business expenditure, impose a levy on authorised insurance companies carrying on general business in the United Kingdom (hereafter in this Act referred to as a 'general business levy').

(2) Subject to the following provisions of this section and to Schedule 3 to this Act, the Board may from time to time, for the purpose of financing long term business expenditure, impose a levy on authorised insurance companies carrying on long term business in the United Kingdom (hereafter in this Act referred to as a 'long term business levy').

(3) The amount each insurance company may be required to pay under general business levies imposed in any financial year shall be calculated by reference to the net premium income of the company for the year ending last before the beginning of that financial year in respect of general policies which were United Kingdom policies at the relevant time; and any such income is hereafter in this Act referred to, in relation to any company, as income of the company for the year in question which is income liable to the general business levy.

(4) The amount each insurance company may be required to pay under long term business levies imposed in any financial year shall be calculated by reference to the net premium income of the company for the year ending last before the beginning of that financial year in respect of long term policies effected after 31 December 1974 which were United Kingdom policies at the relevant time; and any such income is hereafter in this Act referred to, in relation to any company, as income of the company for the year in question which is income liable to the long term business levy.

(5) In subsections (3) and (4) above, the net premium income of a company for any year in respect of policies of any description which were United Kingdom policies at the relevant time means the gross amounts recorded in the company's accounts during that year as paid or due to the company by way of premiums under policies of that description which were United Kingdom policies at the time when the amounts in question were so recorded, less any amounts deductible for that year in respect of policies of that description in accordance with subsection (6) or (7) below.

(6) In calculating a company's net premium income for any year in respect of policies of any description, any rebates or refunds recorded in the company's accounts during that year as allowed or given in respect of any amounts so recorded during that or any previous year as paid or due to the company by way of premiums under policies of that description which were United Kingdom policies at the time when the rebates or refunds were so recorded shall be deductible.

(7) In calculating a company's net premium income for any year in respect of general policies, any sums recorded in the company's accounts during that year as paid by or due from the company by way of premiums for reinsuring its liabilities towards policyholders under general policies which were United Kingdom policies at the time when the sums in question were so recorded shall be deductible.

(8) The proceeds of general business levies may be applied by the Board only on general business expenditure, and the proceeds of long term business levies may be applied by the Board only on long term business expenditure.

(9) Schedule 3 to this Act shall have effect with respect to the imposition and enforcement of general business levies and long term business levies and the other matters there mentioned.

22. Treatment of business as, or as not being, long term business for the purposes of section 21 and Schedule 3.—(1) [*repealed*].

(2) [*repealed*].

Miscellaneous and supplementary

23. Special provision for persons insured under contracts of insurance not evidenced by policies.—(1) Where it appears to the Board—

(a) that a person is a person insured under a contract of insurance with an authorised insurance company which is not evidenced by any policy; and

(b) that if a policy evidencing the contract had been issued the person in question would have been eligible as a policyholder in respect of that policy for the assistance or protection of the Board under any provision of sections 6 to 16 above (hereafter in this section referred to as 'the relevant provision');

the Board may take such measures for the assistance or protection of the person in question as they would in their view have been required or authorised to take under the relevant provision if such a policy had been issued and the person in question had been the policyholder.

(2) For the purposes of section 18 above any expenditure of the Board under this section shall be treated as expenditure under the relevant provision.

24. Application of general receipts by the Board.—Subject to any arrangement made by the Board under subsection (6) of section 13 above and to any regulations made by the Secretary of State under subsection (7) of that section, any sums from time to time received by the Board in the course of or in connection with the exercise of any of their functions under this Act, but otherwise than by virtue of any levy imposed under section 19 or 21 above, may be applied by the Board—

(a) in so far as the sums are received in repayment or otherwise by virtue of any general business expenditure incurred by the Board, on expenditure of that description only;

(b) in so far as the sums are received in repayment or otherwise by virtue of any long term business expenditure incurred by the Board, on expenditure of that description only.

25. Application of surplus funds by the Board.—(1) If at any time the Secretary of State, after consultation with the Board, considers that the funds for the time being held by the Board exceed what is reasonably required for the purpose of exercising their functions under this Act, he may by order made by statutory instrument require the Board to distribute any of those funds appearing to him to be surplus to their requirements among authorised insurance companies carrying on business in the United Kingdom, in such manner and subject to such conditions as may be prescribed by the order.

(2) An order made under this section may make different provision for different circumstances and may be varied or revoked by a subsequent order so made.

(3) Any statutory instrument containing an order made under this section shall be subject to annulment in pursuance of a resolution of either House of Parliament.

26. Overseas companies.—(1) In this section 'overseas company' means an authorised insurance company established in a country outside the United Kingdom.

(2) Where it appears to the Secretary of State that any circumstances have occurred in relation to an overseas company which are the equivalent under the law relating to companies in force in the country in which it is established of any of the events mentioned in section 5, section 15(1) or section 16(1) above, the Secretary of State may refer the company's case to the Board, in terms indicating whether it is to be treated as a company

in liquidation for the purposes of this Act or solely as a company in provisional liquidation within the meaning of section 15 above or (as the case may be) as a company in financial difficulties for the purposes of section 16 above.

(3) The functions of the Board under this Act or, as the case may be, under section 15 or 16 above shall be exercisable in relation to a company whose case has been referred to the Board under this section in accordance with the terms of the reference; and the provisions of this Act or, as the case may be, of section 15 or 16 shall apply in any such case subject to any modifications notified by the Secretary of State to the Board in connection with the reference.

(4) The modifications notified by the Secretary of State to the Board in connection with a reference under this section shall be such only as appear to the Secretary of State to be necessary having regard to any differences between the law in force in the United Kingdom and the law for the time being in force in the country in which the overseas company in question is established.

27. Disclosure of documents and information to the Board.—Nothing in section 449 of the Companies Act 1985 or Article 109 of the Insurance Companies Act (Northern Ireland) Order 1978 (provision for security of information) shall prevent the disclosure to the Board of any information or document obtained as mentioned in subsection (1) of that section, if the disclosure is required for the purpose of facilitating the performance by the Board of any of their functions under this Act.

28. Statement by Secretary of State with respect to the exercise of his powers in relation to a company in liquidation, etc.—(1) Subject to the following provisions of this section, in the case of a company—

(a) which is a company in liquidation; or
(b) which is a company in financial difficulties within the meaning of section 16 above in relation to which the Board have exercised any of their powers under that section or under section 15 above;

the Secretary of State shall before the end of the period applicable by virtue of subsection (2) below lay before Parliament a statement with respect to the exercise of his powers under the Insurance Companies Act 1982 in relation to that company during the year ending immediately before the time mentioned below in this subsection.

The time referred to above is the beginning of the liquidation in a case falling within paragraph (a) above and the relevant time as defined by section 16(6) above in a case falling within paragraph (b) above.

(2) The period applicable by virtue of this subsection is—

(a) in a case falling within paragraph (a) of subsection (1) above, the period of six months beginning with the beginning of the liquidation; and
(b) in a case falling within paragraph (b) of that subsection, the period of six months beginning with the date on which the Secretary of State receives written notification from the Board that they have exercised any of their powers under section 15 or 16 above in relation to the company in question.

(3) Where by virtue of paragraph (b) of subsection (1) above the Secretary of State is required to lay before Parliament a statement with respect to the exercise of his powers under the Insurance Companies Act 1982 in relation to any company, that subsection shall not also apply by virtue of paragraph (a) thereof in the case of that company in the event of the company's going into liquidation.

(4) The Secretary of State shall not be required to include in any statement under this section any information which might in his view prejudice any criminal proceedings which have been or may be instituted against any person.

29. Disclosure of documents and information to insurance advisers appointed by the Secretary of State.—Nothing in section 425 of the Companies Act 1985 or Article 109 of the Companies (Northern Ireland) Order 1978 shall prevent the disclosure to any person appointed by the Secretary of State to advise him on the exercise of his powers under the Insurance Companies Act 1982, during the currency of that person's appointment, of any information or document obtained as mentioned in subsection (1) of that section if the disclosure is required for the purpose of enabling the Secretary of State to consult that person with respect to the exercise of any of his powers under the said Act of 1982.

30. Report by Secretary of State with respect to the operation of this Act.—Within the period of six months beginning with 1 January 1981 the Secretary of State shall lay before Parliament a report reviewing the operation of this Act and its effectiveness as a method of protecting policyholders of authorised insurance companies carrying on business in the United Kingdom.

31. Regulations.—(1) Any statutory instrument containing regulations made under any provision of this Act shall be subject to annulment in pursuance of a resolution of either House of Parliament.

(2) The power of the Secretary of State to make regulations under any provision of this Act includes power to make different provision for different circumstances, but shall only be exercisable after consultation with the Board.

32. Interpretation.—(1) In this Act—

'authorised insurance company' has the meaning given by section 3(2) above;
'the Board' has the meaning given by section 1(1) above;
'company in liquidation' has the meaning given by section 5(4) above;
'enactment' includes an enactment of the Parliament of Northern Ireland and a Measure of the Northern Ireland Assembly;
'financial year' means a period of twelve months ending with 31 March in any year;
'general business expenditure' has the meaning given by section 18(1) above;
'general business levy' has the meaning given by section 21(1) above;
'general policy' has the meaning given by section 8(4) above;
'long term business expenditure' has the meaning given by section 18(2) above;
'long term business levy' has the meaning given by section 21(2) above;
'long term policy' has the meaning given by section 10(1) above;

and references to United Kingdom policies shall be construed in accordance with section 4 above.

(2) Except as provided by subsection (1) above . . .

(a) expressions used in this Act have the same meaning as in the Insurance Companies Act 1982 . . .
(b) [*repealed*].

(3) [*repealed*]

(4) For the purposes of this Act, a liability of a company in liquidation towards a policyholder arising otherwise than under the terms of the policy shall be treated as a liability under the terms of the policy if the liability of the company arises from any failure on the part of the company to perform an obligation under the policy to provide any services or facilities on the occurrence of any event to which the risk under the policy relates.

(5) References in this Act to any other enactment include references to that enactment as amended or extended by or under any other enactment.

33. Short title and extent.—(1) This Act may be cited as the Policyholders Protection Act 1975.

(2) It is declared that this Act extends to Northern Ireland.

SCHEDULES

SCHEDULE 1
Section 1

ADDITIONAL PROVISIONS WITH RESPECT TO THE POLICYHOLDERS PROTECTION BOARD

Constitution of the Board

1.—(1) The Board shall consist of five persons appointed by the Secretary of State to be members of the Board, together with any persons appointed by the Secretary of State under sub-paragraph (3) below to be alternate members.

(2) Of the persons appointed to be members of the Board—

(a) at least three shall be persons who are directors, chief executives or managers of authorised insurance companies; and

(b) at least one shall be a person appearing to the Secretary of State to be qualified to represent the interests of policyholders of authorised insurance companies.

(3) The Secretary of State may appoint, in respect of each member of the Board, a person to perform his duties as a member in his absence, and a person so appointed shall be an alternate member of the Board and may take part in the proceedings of the Board in the absence of the member in respect of whom he was appointed or as provided by paragraph 4(4) below (but not otherwise).

(4) A person appointed as an alternate member of the Board in respect of a person who is a director, chief executive or manager of an authorised insurance company shall himself be such a director, chief executive or manager; and a person so appointed in respect of any such person as is mentioned in sub-paragraph (2)(b) above shall himself be a person appearing to the Secretary of State to be qualified as there mentioned.

(5) The Secretary of State shall consult persons appearing to him to be representative of the interests of authorised insurance companies before appointing a person who is a director, chief executive or manager of an authorised insurance company to be a member or alternate member of the Board.

Appointment and tenure of members, etc.

2.—(1) Any appointment made by the Secretary of State under paragraph 1 above shall be for a term not exceeding two years and the term of appointment of an alternate member shall not exceed the term, or the remainder of the term (as the case may be) of the member in respect of whom he is appointed.

(2) Nothing in sub-paragraph (1) above shall be taken as prejudicing the power of the Secretary of State to re-appoint a person as a member or alternate member of the Board on his ceasing to hold office in either capacity, or at any time thereafter.

3.—(1) The Secretary of State shall appoint one of the members of the Board to be the chairman of the Board.

(2) If the chairman ceases to be a member of the Board he shall cease to be the chairman.

4.—(1) Subject to the following provisions of this paragraph, the members and alternate members of the Board (including the chairman) shall hold and vacate office in accordance with the terms of their respective appointments.

(2) A person may at any time resign his office as a member, as an alternate member or as chairman by giving to the Secretary of State a notice in writing signed by that person and stating that he resigns that office.

(3) If the Secretary of State is satisfied that a member or an alternate member—

(a) is incapacitated by physical or mental illness; or
(b) is otherwise unable or unfit to discharge his functions as such;

the Secretary of State may by notice in writing given to the person in question remove him from office as member or (as the case may be) as alternate member; and his office shall thereupon become vacant.

(4) Where before the end of the term for which he was appointed a member dies or vacates office by virtue of sub-paragraph (2) or (3) above—

(a) the alternate member in respect of that member may act as member in his place until a person is appointed to fill his office as member; and
(b) the Secretary of State may vary the terms of appointment of the alternate member on appointing a person to fill the office vacated by the member in question.

Remuneration, etc. of members

5.—(1) Subject to sub-paragraph (2) below, the Board shall pay to each member or alternate member such remuneration and such travelling, subsistence or other allowances as the Board may determine.

(2) Any determination of the Board with respect to the remuneration to be paid to any member or alternate member shall be subject to the approval of the Secretary of State, and the Secretary of State shall not give his approval without the consent of the Minister for the Civil Service.

6. If a person ceases to be a member or an alternate member of the Board and it appears to the Secretary of State that there are special circumstances which make it right that that person should receive compensation, the Secretary of State may require the Board to pay to that person a sum of such amount as the Secretary of State may with the consent of the Minister for the Civil Service determine.

Powers and procedure, etc.

7.—(1) The Board may invest any funds held by them which appear to them to be surplus to their requirements for the time being—

(a) in any investment for the time being falling within Part I, Part II or Part III of Schedule 1 to the Trustee Investments Act 1961; or
(b) in any investment approved for the purpose by the Secretary of State.

(2) Subject to sub-paragraph (1) above, the Board shall have power to do anything incidental or conducive to the proper performance of their functions under this Act.

(3) Without prejudice to the generality of sub-paragraph (2) above, the measures open to the Board under any provision of this Act which authorises or requires the Board to take any measures appearing to them to be appropriate for any purpose include in particular—

(a) the making of payments to any person, on such terms (including terms requiring repayment, in whole or in part) and on such conditions as the Board think fit;
(b) the giving of guarantees or indemnities to or in favour of any person; and
(c) the making of any other agreement or arrangement with or for the benefit of any person.

8. Subject to the provisions of this Schedule, the Board shall have power to regulate their own procedure.

9.—(1) Subject to sub-paragraph (2) below, a member or an alternate member of the Board who is in any way directly or indirectly interested (whether as being a member or policyholder of an insurance company or in any other manner whatsoever) in any matter falling to be considered by the Board shall disclose the nature of his interest at a meeting of the Board and the disclosure shall be recorded in the minutes of the meeting; and the member or the alternate member in question shall not take part in any deliberation or decision of the Board with respect to that matter.

(2) Sub-paragraph (1) above shall not apply in relation to any interest of a member or alternate member arising from any connection with an insurance company where the only connection of the company in question with the matter under consideration arises from the fact that it has agreed or may agree to take a transfer of all or any part of the insurance business of a company in liquidation or of a company which is a company in financial difficulties within the meaning of section 16 above.

(3) A notice given by a member or alternate member at a meeting of the Board to the effect that he is a member or a policyholder of a specified insurance company and is to be regarded as interested in any matter affecting that company which falls to be considered by the Board after the date of the notice shall, for the purposes of sub-paragraph (1) above, be a sufficient disclosure of his interest in any such matter.

(4) A member or alternate member need not attend in person at a meeting of the Board in order to make a disclosure which he is required to make under this paragraph if he takes reasonable steps to secure that the disclosure is made by a notice which is taken into consideration and read at such a meeting.

10. The validity of any proceedings of the Board shall not be affected by any vacancy among the members or by any defect in the appointment of a member or of an alternate member or by any failure to comply with the requirements of paragraph 9 above.

Performance of functions

11. The Board may authorise any member or alternate member or any other person who is either an employee or an agent of theirs to perform on their behalf such of their functions (including the function conferred on them by this paragraph) as are specified in the authorisation.

Instruments and contracts

12. The fixing of the common seal of the Board shall be authenticated by the signature of the chairman of the Board or some other person authorised by the Board to act for that purpose.

13. A document purporting to be duly executed under the seal of the Board shall be received in evidence and shall unless the contrary is proved, be deemed to be so executed.

Accounts; audit and annual report

14.—(1) It shall be the duty of the Board—

(a) to keep proper accounts and proper records in relation to the accounts; and
(b) to prepare in respect of the period beginning with the date on which this Act is passed and ending with 31 March 1976 and in respect of each subsequent financial year a statement of accounts, in such form as the Secretary of State may direct, showing the state of affairs and income and expenditure of the Board.

(2) A statement of accounts prepared in accordance with sub-paragraph (1)(b) above shall be audited by auditors appointed by the Board.

(3) A person shall not be qualified to be appointed as auditor by the Board under sub-paragraph (2) above unless he is a member of one or more of the following bodies—

the Institute of Chartered Accountants in England and Wales;
the Institute of Chartered Accountants of Scotland;
the Association of Certified Accountants;
the Institute of Chartered Accountants in Ireland;
any other body of accountants established in the United Kingdom and for the time being recognised for the purposes of section 389(1)(a) of the Companies Act 1985 by the Secretary of State;

but a Scottish firm may be so appointed if each of the partners therein is qualified to be so appointed.

(4) It shall be the duty of the Board, as soon as possible after the end of the period mentioned in sub-paragraph (1)(b) above and each subsequent financial year, to prepare, in such manner as the Secretary of State may direct, a report on the performance of their functions during that period or (as the case may be) during that year.

(5) It shall be the duty of the Board to publish the statement of accounts prepared in accordance with sub-paragraph (1)(b) above and the report prepared in accordance with sub-paragraph (4) above in respect of the period mentioned in sub-paragraph (1)(b) above and any subsequent financial year at such time and in such manner as the Secretary of State may direct.

SCHEDULE 2
Section 19

Additional Provisions with respect to Levies on Intermediaries

Restriction on the imposition of the levy

1. No levy shall be imposed under section 19 above in respect of any company—

(a) after the end of the period of two years beginning with the beginning of the liquidation if the company is a company in liquidation; or
(b) after the end of the period of two years beginning with the relevant time as defined by section 16(6) above if the company is a company in financial difficulties within the meaning of that section.

The rate of the levy

2.—(1) Subject to sub-paragraph (2) below, the rate of a levy imposed under section 19 above in respect of any company shall be—

(a) where the long term business expenditure incurred by the Board in relation to that company is less than the total amount of the income liable to levy, a percentage equal to the percentage of that amount which that expenditure represents; and
(b) in any other case, one hundred per cent.

(2) Where a levy is imposed under section 19 above in respect of any company before the exact amount of the long term business expenditure of the Board in relation to that company is ascertained sub-paragraph (1)(a) above shall apply as if the Board's estimate of that expenditure were the expenditure actually incurred.

(3) In sub-paragraph (1) above 'the total amount of the income liable to levy' means, in relation to any company, the total amount of the income of all the persons who appear

to the Board to be accountable intermediaries of that company which appears to the Board to be income liable to levy.

Statements for the purposes of section 20

3.—(1) The Board may by notice in writing require any person who appears to them to be an intermediary of any such company as is mentioned in sub-paragraph (a) or (b) of paragraph 1 above to give to them any information which appears to them to be necessary in order to determine what (if any) persons would be linked with that person within the meaning of section 20 above if that person were an intermediary of that company.

(2) A person to whom a notice is sent under this paragraph shall send to the Board within one month of the date of the notice a statement—

(a) giving any of the information required by the notice which he is able to give; or
(b) informing the Board that he is unable to give any of the information required by the notice.

4.—(1) Any person who causes or permits to be included in a statement sent to the Board under paragraph 3 above any information which he knows to be false in a material particular or recklessly causes or permits to be so included any information which is false in a material particular shall be guilty of an offence and liable—

(a) on conviction on indictment, to imprisonment for a term not exceeding two years or to a fine, or to both;
(b) on summary conviction, to a fine not exceeding the prescribed sum under the Magistrates' Courts Act 1980, s 32(2).

(2) Any person who makes default in complying with paragraph 3 above shall be guilty of an offence and liable, on summary conviction, to a fine not exceeding level 5 on the standard scale.

Declaration and enforcement of the levy

5.—(1) On imposing a levy under section 19 above in respect of any company, the Board shall send notice of the levy to every person who appears to the Board to be an accountable intermediary of that company.

(2) A notice under sub-paragraph (1) above shall indicate—

(a) the name of the company in respect of which the levy is being imposed;
(b) the period covered, in the case of that company, by each of the two years mentioned in section 19(2) above; and
(c) what in the view of the Board is the amount of the income of the intermediary in question which is income liable to levy;

and shall specify the rate of the levy.

6.—(1) An intermediary to whom notice of a levy is sent under paragraph 5 above shall pay to the Board within one month of the date of the notice the percentage specified in the notice of any income of the intermediary which is income liable to levy.

(2) Any sum due to the Board in respect of a levy imposed under section 19 above shall be recoverable in any court of competent jurisdiction.

Notices under paragraphs 3 and 5

7. A notice under paragraph 3 or 5 above may be sent by post, and a letter containing such a notice shall be deemed to be properly addressed if it is addressed to the person to whom it is sent at his last known place of business in the United Kingdom.

SCHEDULE 3

Section 21

Additional Provisions with respect to Levies on Authorised Insurance Companies

Restrictions on the imposition of the levies

1. No levy may be imposed by the Board under section 21 above before the beginning of the financial year ending with 31 March 1977.

2.—(1) The amounts required to be paid by any company under general business levies imposed by the Board in any financial year shall not exceed one per cent of any income of the company for the year ending last before the beginning of that financial year which is income liable to the general business levy.

(2) The amounts required to be paid by any company under long term business levies imposed by the Board in any financial year shall not exceed one per cent of any income of the company for the year ending last before the beginning of that financial year which is income liable to the long term business levy.

3. The Board may not impose a levy for the purpose of financing expenditure of any description unless—

(a) the expenditure in question has already been incurred by the Board; or
(b) it appears to the Board that the expenditure will be incurred within twelve months of the imposition of the levy.

Statements of premium income

4.—(1) Every authorised insurance company shall send to the Secretary of State before 1 March 1976, and thereafter before 1 March in any subsequent year, a statement of any income of the company for the previous year which is income liable to the general business levy.

(2) Every authorised insurance company shall send to the Secretary of State before 1 March 1976, and thereafter before 1 March in any subsequent year, a statement of any income of the company for the previous year which is income liable to the long term business levy.

(3) Where an authorised insurance company is required under this paragraph to send a statement to the Secretary of State in respect of income of both descriptions mentioned in sub-paragraphs (1) and (2) above it shall send a separate statement in respect of income of each description.

5.—(1) Any person who causes or permits to be included in a statement sent to the Secretary of State under paragraph 4 above any information which he knows to be false in a material particular or recklessly causes or permits to be so included any information which is false in a material particular shall be guilty of an offence and liable—

(a) on conviction on indictment, to imprisonment for a term not exceeding two years or to a fine, or to both;
(b) on summary conviction, to a fine not exceeding the prescribed sum under the Magistrates' Courts Act 1980, s 32(2).

(2) Any insurance company which makes default in complying with paragraph 4 above shall be guilty of an offence and liable, on summary conviction, to a fine not exceeding level 5 on the standard scale.

(3) Sections 37(2)(b)(i) and 54(1)(b) of the Insurance Companies Act 1982 (failure to satisfy an obligation under that Act to be a ground for the exercise by the Secretary of State of certain powers in relation to an insurance company) shall have effect in relation to the obligation imposed on an insurance company by paragraph 4 above as they have effect in relation to obligations imposed on an insurance company under that Act.

(4) Sections 91 to 94 of the Insurance Companies Act 1982 shall apply in relation to an offence committed or alleged to have been committed under this paragraph as they apply in relation to an offence committed or alleged to have been committed under that Act.

(5) . . . [*repealed*].

Declaration and enforcement of levies

6.—(1) Subject to paragraphs 1 to 3 above, levies may be imposed by the Board under section 21 above at such times and at such rates in relation to income of authorised insurance companies liable to the general business levy or to the long term business levy as the Board may determine.

(2) On imposing a levy under section 21 above, the Board shall send notice of the rate of levy to every authorised insurance company which may in the opinion of the Board have had income liable to the levy for the year ending last before the financial year in which the levy is imposed.

(3) A notice under sub-paragraph (2) above shall indicate—

(a) whether the levy is a general business levy or a long term business levy;
(b) what description of income is income liable to the levy in question; and
(c) the purpose for which the levy is being imposed;

and shall specify the rate of the levy as a percentage of the income liable to the levy.

(4) A notice required to be sent by sub-paragraph (2) above may be sent by post, and a letter containing such a notice shall be deemed to be properly addressed if it is addressed to the insurance company to which it is sent at its last known place of business in the United Kingdom.

7.—(1) An insurance company to which notice of the rate of a levy is sent under paragraph 6 above shall pay to the Board within one month of the date of the notice the percentage specified in the notice of any income of the company for the year ending last before the financial year in which the levy is imposed which is income liable to the levy in question.

(2) Any sum due to the Board in respect of a levy imposed under section 21 above shall be recoverable in any court of competent jurisdiction.

INSURANCE BROKERS (REGISTRATION) ACT 1977[1]

(1977 c 46)

An Act to provide for the registration of insurance brokers and for the regulation of their professional standards; and for purposes connected therewith. [29 July 1977]

BE IT ENACTED by the Queen's most Excellent Majesty, by and with the advice and consent of the Lords Spiritual and Temporal, and Commons, in this present Parliament assembled, and by the authority of the same, as follows:—

The Insurance Brokers Registration Council

1. Establishment of Insurance Brokers Registration Council.—(1) There shall be established a body to be called the Insurance Brokers Registration Council (hereinafter referred to as 'the Council') which shall be a body corporate with perpetual succession and a common seal and shall have the general function of carrying out the powers and duties conferred on them by this Act.

(2) The Council shall be constituted in accordance with the Schedule to this Act and the supplementary provisions contained in that Schedule shall have effect with respect to the Council.

---

[1] The Act is printed as amended.

Registration and training of insurance brokers

2. The insurance brokers register.—The Council shall establish and maintain a register of insurance brokers (hereinafter referred to as 'the register') containing the names, addresses and qualifications, and such other particulars as may be prescribed, of all persons who are entitled under the provisions of this Act to be registered therein and apply in the prescribed manner to be so registered.

3. Qualifications for registration.—(1) Subject to subsection (2) below and to section 16 of this Act, a person shall be entitled to be registered in the register if he satisfies the Council—

(a) that he holds a qualification approved by the Council under section 6 of this Act, being a qualification granted to him after receiving instruction from an institution so approved; or
(b) that he holds a qualification recognised by the Council for the purposes of this paragraph, being a qualification granted outside the United Kingdom; or
(c) that he has carried on business as an insurance broker, or as a whole-time agent acting for two or more insurance companies in relation to insurance business, for a period of not less than five years; or
(d) that he holds a qualification recognised by the Council for the purposes of this paragraph and has carried on business as mentioned in paragraph (c) above for a period of not less than three years; or
(e) that he has been employed by a person carrying on business as mentioned in paragraph (c) above, or by an insurance company, for a period of not less than five years; or
(f) that he holds a qualification recognised by the Council for the purposes of this paragraph and has been employed by a person carrying on business as mentioned in paragraph (c) above, or by an insurance company, for a period of not less than three years; or
(g) that he has knowledge and practical experience of insurance business which is comparable to that of a person who has carried on business as an insurance broker for a period of five years; or
(h) that he holds a qualification recognised by the Council for the purposes of this paragraph and has knowledge and practical experience of insurance business which is comparable to that of a person who has carried on business as an insurance broker for a period of three years.

(2) A person shall not be entitled to be registered in the register by virtue of subsection (1) above unless he also satisfies the Council—

(a) as to his character and suitability to be a registered insurance broker; and
(b) in a case falling within paragraph (a), (b), (e) or (f) of subsection (1) above, that he has had adequate practical experience in the work of an insurance broker; and
(c) if he is carrying on business as an insurance broker at the time when the application is made, that he is complying with the requirements of rules under section 11(1) of this Act.

(3) Subject to section 16 of this Act, a person shall be entitled to be registered in the register if he satisfies the Council that he or a partnership of which he is a member is accepted as a Lloyd's broker by the Committee of Lloyd's.

(4) The Secretary of State may, after consulting the Council, by order provide that any of the paragraphs in subsection (1) or (2) above shall be omitted or shall have effect subject to such amendments as may be specified in the order.

4. List of bodies corporate carrying on business as insurance brokers.—(1) The Council shall establish and maintain a list of bodies corporate carrying on business as insurance brokers (hereinafter referred to as 'the list') containing the names, principal places of business and such other particulars as may be prescribed of all bodies corporate which are entitled under this section to be enrolled therein and apply in the prescribed manner to be so enrolled.

(2) Subject to subsection (3) below and to section 16 of this Act, a body corporate shall be entitled to be enrolled in the list if it satisfies the Council—

(a) that a majority of its directors are registered insurance brokers; or
(b) in the case of a body corporate having only one director, that he is a registered insurance broker; or
(c) in the case of a body corporate having only two directors, that one of them is a registered insurance broker and that the business is carried on under the management of that director.

(3) A body corporate shall not be entitled to be enrolled in the list by virtue of subsection (1) above unless it also satisfies the Council that it is complying with the requirements of rules under section 11(1) of this Act.

(4) Subject to section 16 of this Act, a body corporate shall be entitled to be enrolled in the list if it satisfies the Council that it is accepted as a Lloyd's broker by the Committee of Lloyd's.

5. Appeals against refusal to register or enrol.—(1) Before refusing an application for registration under section 3 of this Act or an application for enrolment under section 4 of this Act, the Council shall give the person by whom or the body corporate by which the application was made an opportunity of appearing before and being heard by a committee of the Council.

(2) Where the Council refuse any such application, the Council shall, if so required by the person by whom or the body corporate by which the application was made within seven days from notification of the decision, serve on that person or body a statement of the reasons therefor.

(3) A person or body corporate whose application is so refused may within twenty-eight days from—

(a) notification of the decision, or
(b) if a statement of reasons has been required under subsection (2) above, service of the statement,

appeal against the refusal to the Court.

(4) The Council may appear as respondent on any such appeal and for the purpose of enabling directions to be given as to the costs of any such appeal the Council shall be deemed to be a party thereto, whether they appear on the hearing of the appeal or not.

(5) On the hearing of any such appeal the Court may make such order as it thinks fit and its order shall be final.

6. Approval of educational institutions and qualifications.—(1) The Council may approve for the purposes of this Act any institution (hereinafter referred to as 'an approved educational institution') where the instruction given to persons being educated as insurance brokers appears to the Council to be such as to secure to them adequate knowledge and skill for the practice of their profession.

(2) The Council may approve for the purposes of this Act any qualification (hereinafter referred to as 'an approved qualification') which appears to the Council to be granted to candidates who reach such a standard of proficiency at a qualifying examination as to secure to them adequate knowledge and skill for the practice of their profession.

(3) Where the Council have refused to approve an institution or qualification under this section as suitable for any purpose, the Secretary of State, on representations being made to him within one month of the refusal, may, if he thinks fit, after considering the

representations and after consulting the Council, order the Council to approve the institution or qualification as suitable for that purpose.

(4) The Council shall publish before the day appointed for the coming into operation of section 3(1)(a) of this Act, and from time to time thereafter, a list of approved educational institutions and approved qualifications.

7. Supervision of educational institutions and qualifying examinations.—(1) It shall be the duty of the Council to keep themselves informed of the nature of the instruction given by any approved educational institution to persons being educated as insurance brokers and of the examinations on the results of which approved qualifications are granted.

(2) For the purposes of their duty under subsection (1) above the Council may appoint persons to visit approved educational institutions and to attend at the examinations held by the bodies which grant approved qualifications.

(3) It shall be the duty of visitors appointed under subsection (2) above to report to the Council as to the sufficiency of the instruction given by the institutions visited by them, or of the examinations attended by them, and as to any other matters relating thereto which may be specified by the Council either generally or in any particular case, but no visitor shall interfere with the giving of any instruction or the holding of any examination.

(4) Where it appears to the Council (as a result of a report under subsection (3) above or otherwise),—

(a) that the instruction given by any approved educational institution to persons being educated as insurance brokers or the examinations taken by such persons are not such as to secure the possession by them of adequate knowledge and skill for the practice of their profession; and

(b) that by reason thereof the approval of the institution or qualification in question should be withdrawn,

the Council shall give notice in writing to the institution or body of their opinion, sending therewith a copy of any report on which their opinion is based.

(5) On the receipt of the notice the institution or body may, within such period (not being less than one month) as the Council may have specified in the notice, make to the Council observations on the notice and any report sent therewith or objections to the notice and report.

(6) As soon as may be after the expiration of the period specified in the notice under subsection (4) above the Council shall determine whether or not to withdraw their approval of the institution or qualification, as the case may be, taking into account any observations or objections duly made under subsection (5) above.

(7) The Council shall give notice in writing of any decision under this section to withdraw approval of an institution or qualification to the institution or body concerned and the decision shall not take effect until the expiration of one month from the date of the giving of the notice or, if during that time the institution or body makes representations with respect to the decision to the Secretary of State, until the representations are finally dealt with.

(8) Where the Council have decided to withdraw approval of an institution or qualification, the Secretary of State, on representations being made to him within one month from the giving of notice of the decision, may, if he thinks fit, after considering the representations and after consulting the Council order the Council to annul the withdrawal of approval.

(9) The Council may pay to visitors appointed under this section such fees and such travelling and subsistence allowances as the Council may determine.

8. Supplementary provisions as to the register and list.—(1) The register and list shall be kept by the registrar of the Council who shall be appointed by the Council.

(2) The Council may make rules with respect to the form and keeping of the register and list and the making of entries and alterations therein and, in particular—

- (a) regulating the making of applications for registration or enrolment and providing for the evidence to be produced in support of any such applications;
- (b) providing for the notification to the registrar of any change in the particulars required to be entered in the register or list;
- (c) prescribing a fee to be charged on the entry of a name in, or the restoration of a name to, the register or list;
- (d) prescribing a fee to be charged in respect of the retention in the register or list of any name in any year subsequent to the year in which that name was first entered in the register or list;
- (e) providing for the entry in the register of qualifications (whether approved qualifications or not) possessed by persons whose names are registered therein and for the removal of such qualifications from the register, and prescribing a fee to be charged in respect of the entry;
- (f) authorising the registrar to refuse to enter a name in, or restore it to, the register or list until a fee prescribed for the entry or restoration has been paid and to erase from the register or list the name of a person who or body corporate which, after the prescribed notices and warnings, fails to pay the fee prescribed in respect of the retention of that name in the register or list;
- (g) authorising the registrar to erase from the register or list the name of a person who or body corporate which, after the prescribed notices and warnings, fails to supply information required by the registrar with a view to ensuring that the particulars entered in the register or list are correct;
- (h) prescribing anything required or authorised to be prescribed by the provisions of this Act relating to the register or list.

(3) Rules under this section which provide for the erasure of a name from the register or list on failure to pay a fee shall provide for its restoration thereto on the making of the prescribed application in that behalf and on payment of that fee and any additional fee prescribed in respect of the restoration.

(4) Rules under this section prescribing fees may provide for the charging of different fees in different classes of cases and for the making of arrangements for the collection of fees with such body or bodies as may be prescribed.

9. Publication of register and list.—(1) The Council shall cause the register and list to be printed and published within one year of the establishment of the Council and as often thereafter as they think fit.

(2) Where the register or list is not published in any year after the first publication thereof, the Council shall cause any alterations in the entries in the register or list which have been made since the last publication thereof to be printed and published within that year.

(3) A copy of the register or list purporting to be printed and published by the Council, shall, as altered by any alterations purporting to be printed and published by the Council, be evidence in all proceedings that the individuals specified in the register are registered therein or, as the case may be, that the bodies corporate specified in the list are enrolled therein; and the absence of the name of any individual or body corporate from any such copy of the register or list shall be evidence, until the contrary is shown, that he is not registered or, as the case may be, that it is not enrolled therein.

(4) In the case of an individual whose name or a body corporate the name of which does not appear in any such copy of the register or list as altered as aforesaid, a certified copy, under the hand of the registrar, of the entry relating to that individual or body corporate in the register or list shall be evidence of the entry.

Regulation of conduct

10. Code of conduct.—(1) The Council shall draw up and may from time to time revise a statement of the acts and omissions which, if done or made by registered insurance brokers or enrolled bodies corporate, or by registered insurance brokers or enrolled bodies corporate in particular circumstances, constitute in the opinion of the Council unprofessional conduct.

(2) The statement shall serve as a guide to registered insurance brokers and enrolled bodies corporate and persons concerned with the conduct of registered insurance brokers and enrolled bodies corporate, but the mention or lack of mention in it of a particular act or omission shall not be taken as conclusive of any question of professional conduct.

11. Requirements for carrying on business.—(1) The Council shall make rules requiring registered insurance brokers who are carrying on business as insurance brokers (hereinafter referred to as 'practising insurance brokers') and enrolled bodies corporate to ensure—

(a) that their businesses have working capital of not less than such amount as may be prescribed;
(b) that the value of the assets of their businesses exceeds the amount of the liabilities of their businesses by not less than such amount as may be prescribed; and
(c) that the number of insurance companies with which they place insurance business, and the amount of insurance business which they place with each insurance company, is such as to prevent their businesses from becoming unduly dependent on any particular insurance company.

(2) The Council shall also make rules requiring practising insurance brokers and enrolled bodies corporate—

(a) to open and keep accounts at banks for money received by them from persons with whom they do business;
(b) to hold money so received in such manner as may be prescribed;
(c) to keep such accounting records showing and explaining the transactions of their businesses as may be prescribed; and
(d) to prepare and submit to the Council at such intervals as may be prescribed balance sheets and profit and loss accounts containing such information as may be prescribed for the purpose of giving a true and fair view of the state of their businesses.

(3) Without prejudice to the generality of subsections (1) and (2) above, rules under this section may empower the Council—

(a) to require practising insurance brokers and enrolled bodies corporate to deliver at such intervals as may be prescribed reports given by qualified accountants and containing such information as may be prescribed for the purpose of ascertaining whether or not the rules have been complied with;
(b) to require practising insurance brokers and enrolled bodies corporate to deliver at such intervals as may be prescribed statements made by them and containing such information as may be prescribed for the purpose of ascertaining whether or not the rules are being complied with; and
(c) to take such other steps as they consider necessary or expedient for the purpose of ascertaining whether or not the rules are being complied with.

(4) Subject to subsections (5) and (6) below, an accountant is qualified to give reports for the purposes of the rules if he is a member of a recognised body of accountants or is for the time being authorised by the Secretary or State under section 389(1)(b) of the

Companies Act 1985 or, in Northern Ireland, by the Department of Commerce for Northern Ireland under section 155(1)(b) of the Companies Act (Northern Ireland) 1960.

(5) An accountant shall not be qualified to give such reports—

(a) in relation to a practising insurance broker, if he is an employee or partner of, or an employee of a partner of, the practising insurance broker;
(b) in relation to an enrolled body corporate, if he is not qualified for appointment as auditor of the enrolled body corporate.

(6) A Scottish firm of accountants shall be qualified to give such reports if, but only if, all the partners are so qualified.

(7) Rules under this section may make different provision for different circumstances, and may specify circumstances in which persons are exempt from any of the requirements of the rules.

12. Professional indemnity, etc.—(1) The Council shall make rules for indemnifying—

(a) practising insurance brokers and former practising insurance brokers, and
(b) enrolled bodies corporate and former enrolled bodies corporate,

against losses arising from claims in respect of any description of civil liability incurred by them, or by employees or former employees of theirs, in connection with their businesses.

(2) The Council shall also make rules for the making of grants or other payments for the purpose of relieving or mitigating losses suffered by persons in consequence of—

(a) negligence or fraud or other dishonesty on the part of practising insurance brokers or enrolled bodies corporate, or of employees of theirs, in connection with their businesses; or
(b) failure on the part of practising insurance brokers or enrolled bodies corporate to account for money received by them in connection with their businesses.

(3) For the purpose of providing such indemnity and of enabling such grants or other payments to be made, rules under this section—

(a) may authorise or require the Council to establish and maintain a fund or funds;
(b) may authorise or require the Council to take out and maintain insurance with authorised insurers;
(c) may require practising insurance brokers or enrolled bodies corporate or any specified description of practising insurance brokers or enrolled bodies corporate to take out and maintain insurance with authorised insurers.

(4) Without prejudice to the generality of the preceding subsections, rules under this section—

(a) may specify the terms and conditions on which indemnity or a grant or other payment is to be available, and any circumstances in which the right to it is to be excluded or modified;
(b) may provide for the management, administration and protection of any fund maintained by virtue of subsection (3)(a) above and require practising insurance brokers or enrolled bodies corporate or any description of practising insurance brokers or enrolled bodies corporate to make payments to any such fund;
(c) may require practising insurance brokers or enrolled bodies corporate or any description of practising insurance brokers or enrolled bodies corporate to make payments by way of premium on any insurance policy maintained by the Council by virtue of subsection (3)(b) above;

(d) may prescribe the conditions which an insurance policy must satisfy for the purposes of subsection (3)(c) above;
(e) may authorise the Council to determine the amount of any payments required by the rules, subject to such limits, or in accordance with such provisions, as may be prescribed;
(f) may specify circumstances in which, where a registered insurance broker or an enrolled body corporate for whom indemnity is provided has failed to comply with the rules, the Council or insurers may take proceedings against him or it in respect of sums paid by way of indemnity in connection with a matter in relation to which there has been a failure to comply with the rules;
(g) may specify circumstances in which, where a grant or other payment is made in consequence of the act or omission of a practising insurance broker or enrolled body corporate, the Council or insurers may take proceedings against him or it in respect of the sum so paid;
(h) may make different provision for different circumstances, and may specify circumstances in which practising insurance brokers or enrolled bodies corporate are exempt from any of the rules;
(i) may empower the Council to take such steps as they consider necessary or expedient to ascertain whether or not the rules are being complied with; and
(j) may contain incidental, procedural or supplementary provisions.

Disciplinary proceedings

13. Preliminary investigation of disciplinary cases.—(1) The Council shall set up a committee, to be known as the Investigating Committee, for the preliminary investigation of cases in which—

(a) it is alleged that a registered insurance broker or enrolled body corporate is liable to have his or its name erased from the register or list on any ground specified in section 15 of this Act; or
(b) a complaint is made to the Council by or on behalf of a member of the public about a registered insurance broker or an enrolled body corporate or an employee of a registered insurance broker or an enrolled body corporate.

Any such case is hereinafter referred to as 'a disciplinary case'.

(2) A disciplinary case shall be referred to the Investigating Committee who shall carry out a preliminary investigation of it and, unless they are satisfied that there is insufficient evidence to support a finding that the registered insurance broker or enrolled body corporate is liable to have his or its name erased from the register or list, the Committee shall refer the case, with the results of their investigation, to the Disciplinary Committee set up under the next following section.

(3) The Council shall make rules as to the constitution of the Investigating Committee.

14. The Disciplinary Committee.—(1) The Council shall set up a committee, to be known as the Disciplinary Committee, for the consideration and determination of discplinary cases referred to them under the last foregoing section and of any other cases of which they have cognizance under the following provisions of this Act.

(2) The Council shall make rules as to the constitution of the Disciplinary Committee, the times and places of the meetings of the Committee, the quorum and the mode of summoning the members thereof.

(3) Rules under this section shall secure that a person, other than the Chairman of the Council, who has acted in relation to any disciplinary case as a member of the Investigating Committee does not act in relation to that case as a member of the Disciplinary Committee.

15. Erasure from the register and list for crime, unprofessional conduct, etc.—(1) If a registered insurance broker or enrolled body corporate—

(a) is convicted by any court in the United Kingdom of any criminal offence, not being an offence which, owing to its trivial nature or the circumstances under which it was committed, does not render him or it unfit to have his or its name on the register or list, or

(b) is judged by the Disciplinary Committee to have been guilty of unprofessional conduct,

the Disciplinary Committee may, if they think fit, direct that the name of the insurance broker or body corporate shall be erased from the register or list.

(2) If it appears to the Disciplinary Committee that a registered insurance broker or an enrolled body corporate has contravened or failed to comply with any rules made under section 11 or section 12 of this Act and that the contravention or failure is such as to render the insurance broker unfit to have his name on the register or the body corporate unfit to have its name on the list, the Disciplinary Committee may, if they think fit, direct that the name of the insurance broker or body corporate shall be erased from the register or list.

(3) Where—

(a) the name of a director of an enrolled body corporate is erased from the register under subsection (1) above, or

(b) a director of any such body corporate is convicted of an offence under this Act, or

(c) the name of a registered insurance broker employed by any such body corporate is erased from the register under subsection (1) above and the act or omission constituting the ground on which it was erased was instigated or connived at by a director of the body corporate, or, if the act or omission was a continuing act or omission, a director of the body corporate had or reasonably ought to have had knowledge of the continuance thereof,

the Disciplinary Committee may, if they think fit, direct that the name of the body corporate shall be erased from the list:

Provided that the Disciplinary Committee shall not take a case into consideration during any period within which proceedings by way of appeal may be brought which may result in this subsection being rendered inapplicable in that case or while any such proceedings are pending.

(4) If the Disciplinary Committee are of opinion as respects an enrolled body corporate that the conditions for enrolment in section 4 of this Act are no longer satisfied, the Disciplinary Committee may, if they think fit, direct that the name of the body corporate shall be erased from the list.

(5) Where a registered insurance broker dies while he is a director of an enrolled body corporate, he shall be deemed for the purposes of subsection (4) above to have continued to be a director of that body until the expiration of a period of six months beginning with the date of his death or until a director is appointed in his place, whichever first occurs.

(6) When the Disciplinary Committee direct that the name of an individual or body corporate shall be erased from the register or list, the registrar shall serve on that individual or body a notification of the direction and a statement of the Committee's reasons therefor.

16. Restoration of names erased as result of disciplinary cases, etc.—(1) Where the name of an individual or body corporate has been erased from the register or list in pursuance of a direction under the last foregoing section, the name of that individual or body corporate shall not again be entered in the register or list unless the Disciplinary Committee on application made to them in that behalf otherwise direct.

(2) An application under subsection (1) above for the restoration of a name to the register or list shall not be made to the Disciplinary Committee—

(a) within ten months of the date of erasure; or
(b) within ten months of a previous application thereunder.

17. Erasure from register and list on grounds of fraud or error.—(1) If it is proved to the satisfaction of the Disciplinary Committee that any entry in the register or list has been fraudulently or incorrectly made, the Disciplinary Committee may, if they think fit, direct that the entry shall be erased from the register or list.

(2) An individual may be registered or a body corporate enrolled in pursuance of this Act notwithstanding that his or its name has been erased under this section, but if it was so erased on the ground of fraud, that individual or body corporate shall not be registered or enrolled except on an application in that behalf to the Disciplinary Committee; and on any such application the Disciplinary Committee may, if they think fit, direct that the individual or body corporate shall not be registered or enrolled, or shall not be registered or enrolled until the expiration of such period as may be specified in the direction.

(3) Where the Disciplinary Committee direct that the name of an individual or body corporate shall be erased from the register or list under this section, the registrar shall serve on that individual or body a notification of the direction and a statement of the Committee's reasons therefor.

18. Appeals in disciplinary and other cases.—(1) At any time within twenty-eight days from the service of a notification that the Disciplinary Committee have under section 15 or section 17 of this Act directed that the name of an individual or a body corporate be erased from the register or list that individual or body corporate may appeal to the Court.

(2) The Council may appear as respondent on any such appeal and for the purpose of enabling directions to be given as to the costs of any such appeal the Council shall be deemed to be a party thereto, whether they appear on the hearing of the appeal or not.

(3) Where no appeal is brought against a direction under section 15 or section 17 of this Act or where such an appeal is brought but withdrawn or struck out for want of prosecution, the direction shall take effect on the expiration of the time for appealing or, as the case may be, on the withdrawal or striking out of the appeal.

(4) Subject as aforesaid, where an appeal is brought against a direction under either of those sections, the direction shall take effect if and when the appeal is dismissed and not otherwise.

19. Procedure of Disciplinary Committee.—(1) For the purpose of any proceedings before the Disciplinary Committee in England or Wales or Northern Ireland the Disciplinary Committee may administer oaths, and any party to the proceedings may sue out writs of subpoena ad testificandum and duces tecum, but no person shall be compelled under any such writ to produce any document which he could not be compelled to produce on the trial of an action.

(2) The provisions of section 36 of the Supreme Court Act 1981 or of the Attendance of Witnesses Act 1854 (which provide a special procedure for the issue of such writs so as to be in force throughout the United Kingdom) shall apply in relation to any proceedings before the Disciplinary Committee in England or Wales or, as the case may be, in Northern Ireland as they apply in relation to causes or matters in the High Court or actions or suits pending in the High Court of Justice in Northern Ireland.

(3) For the purpose of any proceedings before the Disciplinary Committee in Scotland, the Disciplinary Committee may administer oaths and the Court of Session shall on the application of any party to the proceedings have the like power as in any action in that Court—

(a) to grant warrant for the citation of witnesses and havers to give evidence or to produce documents before the Disciplinary Committee, and for the issue of letters of second diligence against any witness or haver failing to appear after due citation,
(b) to grant warrant for the recovery of documents, and
(c) to grant commissions to persons to take the evidence of witnesses or to examine havers and receive their exhibits and productions.

(4) The Council shall make rules as to the procedure to be followed and the rules of evidence to be observed in proceedings before the Disciplinary Committee; and in particular—

(a) for securing that notice that the proceedings are to be brought shall be given, at such time and in such manner as may be specified in the rules, to the individual or body corporate alleged to be liable to have his or its name erased from the register or list;
(b) for securing that any party to the proceedings shall, if he so requires, be entitled to be heard by the Disciplinary Committee;
(c) for enabling any party to the proceedings to be represented by counsel or solicitor or (if the rules so provide and the party so elects) by a person of such other description as may be specified in the rules;
(d) for requiring proceedings before the Disciplinary Committee to be held in public except in so far as may be provided by the rules;
(e) for requiring, in cases where it is alleged that a registered insurance broker or enrolled body corporate has been guilty of unprofessional conduct, that where the Disciplinary Committee judge that the allegation has not been proved they shall record a finding that the insurance broker or body corporate is not guilty of such conduct in respect of the matters to which the allegation relates;
(f) for requiring, in cases where it is alleged that a registered insurance broker or enrolled body corporate is liable to have his or its name erased from the register or list under section 15(2) of this Act, that where the Disciplinary Committee judge that the allegation has not been proved they shall record a finding that the insurance broker or body corporate is not guilty of the matters alleged.

(5) Before making rules under this section the Council shall consult such organisations representing the interests of insurance brokers and bodies corporate carrying on business as insurance brokers as appear to the Council requisite to be consulted.

(6) In this section and in section 20 of this Act 'proceedings' means proceedings under this Act, whether relating to disciplinary cases or otherwise.

20. Assessors to Disciplinary Committee.—(1) For the purpose of advising the Disciplinary Committee on questions of law arising in proceedings before them there shall in all such proceedings be an assessor to the Disciplinary Committee who shall be a barrister, advocate or solicitor of not less than ten years' standing.

(2) The power of appointing assessors under this section shall be exercisable by the Council, but if no assessor appointed by them is available to act at any particular proceedings the Disciplinary Committee may appoint an assessor under this section to act at those proceedings.

(3) The Lord Chancellor or, in Scotland, the Lord Advocate may make rules as to the functions of assessors appointed under this section, and, in particular, rules under this subsection may contain such provisions for securing—

(a) that where an assessor advises the Disciplinary Committee on any question of law as to evidence, procedure or any other matters specified in the rules, he shall do so in the presence of every party, or person representing a party, to the proceedings who appears thereat or, if the advice is tendered after the Disciplinary Committee have begun to deliberate as to their findings, that every such party or person as aforesaid shall be informed what advice the assessor has tendered;

(b) that every such party or person as aforesaid shall be informed if in any case the Disciplinary Committee do not accept the advice of the assessor on any such question as aforesaid,

and such incidental and supplementary provisions, as appear to the Lord Chancellor or the Lord Advocate expedient.

(4) Subject to the provisions of this section, an assessor under this section may be appointed either generally or for any particular proceedings or class of proceedings, and shall hold and vacate office in accordance with the terms of the instrument under which he is appointed.

(5) Any remuneration paid by the Council to persons appointed to act as assessors shall be at such rates as the Council may determine.

(6) The power to make rules conferred by this section shall be exercisable by statutory instrument.

Committees of the Council

21. General power to appoint committees.—(1) The Council may set up a committee for any purpose (other than a purpose for which the Council are required to set up a committee under this Act) and may delegate to a committee set up under this section, with or without restrictions or conditions, as they think fit, any functions exercisable by them except the following—

(a) the power to make rules under this Act,

(b) any functions expressly conferred by this Act on any committee set up under any of the foregoing provisions of this Act, and

(c) subject to any express provision for delegation in the rules, any functions expressly conferred on the Council by rules under this Act.

(2) The number of members of a committee set up under this section and their term of office shall be fixed by the Council.

(3) A committee set up under this Act may include persons who are not members of the Council, but at least two-thirds of the members of every such committee shall be members of the Council.

(4) Every member of a committee set up under this Act who at the time of his appointment was a member of the Council shall, upon ceasing to be a member of the Council, also cease to be a member of the committee:

Provided that for the purposes of this subsection a member of the Council shall not be deemed to have ceased by reason of retirement to be a member thereof if he has again been nominated or elected a member thereof not later than the day of his retirement.

Restriction on use of titles and descriptions

22. Penalty for pretending to be registered, etc—(1) Any individual who wilfully—

(a) takes or uses any style, title or description which consists of or includes the expression 'insurance broker' when he is not registered in the register, or

(b) takes or uses any name, title, addition or description falsely implying, or otherwise pretends, that he is registered in the register,

shall be liable on summary conviction to a fine not exceeding the prescribed sum under the Magistrates' Courts Act 1980, s 32(2), or on conviction on indictment to a fine.

(2) Any body corporate which wilfully—

(a) takes or uses any style, title or description which consists of or includes the expression 'insurance broker' when it is not enrolled in the list, or

(b) takes or uses any name, title, addition or description falsely implying, or otherwise pretends, that it is enrolled in the list,

shall be liable on summary conviction to a fine not exceeding the prescribed sum under the Magistrates' Courts Act 1980, s 32(2), or on conviction on indictment to a fine.

(3) References in this section to the expression 'insurance broker' include references to the following related expressions, that is to say 'assurance broker', 'reinsurance broker' and 'reassurance broker'.

23. Exceptions from s 22.—(1) Where a practising insurance broker dies, then, during the period of three months beginning with his death or such longer period as the Council may in any particular case allow, the last foregoing section shall not operate to prevent his personal representatives, his surviving spouse or any of his children or trustees on behalf of his surviving spouse or any of his children from taking or using in relation to his business, but in conjunction with the name in which he carried it on, any title which he was entitled to take or use immediately before his death.

(2) Where a practising insurance broker becomes bankrupt, then, during the period of three months beginning with the bankruptcy or such longer period as the Council may in any particular case allow, the last foregoing section shall not operate to prevent his trustee in bankruptcy or, in Northern Ireland, the assignee in bankruptcy, from taking or using in relation to his business, but in conjunction with the name in which he carried it on, any title which he was entitled to take or use immediately before the bankruptcy.

24. Offences by bodies corporate. Where an offence under this Act which has been committed by a body corporate is proved to have been committed with the consent or connivance of, or to be attributable to any neglect on the part of, any director, manager, secretary or other similar officer of the body corporate, or any person purporting to act in any such capacity, he as well as the body corporate shall be guilty of that offence and shall be liable to be proceeded against and punished accordingly.

Miscellaneous

25. Accounts of Council.—(1) The Council shall keep proper accounts of all sums received or paid by them and proper records in relation to those accounts.

(2) The Council shall appoint auditors to the Council who shall be members of a recognised body of accountants.

(3) The Council shall cause their accounts to be audited annually by the auditors to the Council and as soon as is practicable after the accounts for any period have been audited the Council shall cause them to be published and shall send a copy of them to the Secretary of State together with a copy of any report of the auditors thereon.

26. Service of documents. Any notice or other document authorised or required to be given under this Act may, without prejudice to any other method of service but subject to any provision to the contrary in rules under this Act, be served by post; and for the purpose of the application to this section of section 26 of the Interpretation Act 1889 (which relates to service by post) the proper address of a person or body corporate to whose registration or enrolment such a document relates shall be his or its address in the register or list.

27. Rules etc. made by Council.—(1) Rules made by the Council under sections 8, 11, 12, 13, 14 or 19 of this Act, the statement drawn up by the Council under section 10 of this Act or any revision of that statement made by the Council under that section shall not come into operation until approved by order of the Secretary of State.

(2) The Secretary of State may approve rules made under section 19 of this Act either as submitted to him or subject to such modifications as he thinks fit; but where the Secretary of State proposes to approve any such rules subject to modifications he shall

notify the modifications to the Council and consider any observations of the Council thereon.

(3) The Secretary of State may, after consulting the Council, by order vary or revoke any rules made under sections 8, 11 or 12 of this Act or revise the statement under section 10 of this Act.

28. Orders.—(1) The power to make orders under this Act shall be exercisable by statutory instrument; and any order made under this Act may be varied or revoked by a subsequent order so made.

(2) Any statutory instrument by which that power is exercised, except one containing an order under section 30(3) of this Act or any such order as is mentioned in subsection (3) below, shall be subject to annulment in pursuance of a resolution of either House of Parliament.

(3) An order under section 3(4) or section 27(3) of this Act, an order under paragraph 2 of the Schedule to this Act approving a scheme subject to modifications or an order under paragraph 10 of that Schedule shall not be made unless a draft of the order has been approved by resolution of each House of Parliament.

29. Interpretation.—(1) In this Act, unless the context otherwise requires—

'approved qualification' and 'approved educational institution' have the meanings respectively assigned to them by section 6 of this Act;

'authorised insurers' means a person permitted under the Insurance Companies Act 1982 to carry on insurance business of class 13 or of classes 1, 2, 14, 15, 16 and 17 in Schedule 2 to the Insurance Companies Act 1982;

'the Council' means the Insurance Brokers Registration Council established pursuant to section 1 of this Act;

'the Court' means the High Court or, in relation to Scotland, the Court of Session or, in relation to Northern Ireland, a judge of the High Court of Justice in Northern Ireland;

'disciplinary case' has the meaning assigned to it by section 13 of this Act;

'employee', in relation to a body corporate, includes a director of the body corporate and 'employed' shall be construed accordingly;

'enrolled' means enrolled in the list and 'enrolment' shall be construed accordingly;

'functions' includes powers and duties;

'insurance business' means insurance business other than industrial assurance business (within the meaning of section 1(2) of the Industrial Assurance Act 1923 or Articles 2(2) and 3(1) of the Industrial Assurance (Northern Ireland) Order 1979), and 'insurance broker' shall be construed accordingly;

'insurance company' means a person or body of persons (whether incorporated or not) carrying on insurance business;

'list' means the list of bodies corporate carrying on business as insurance brokers;

'practising insurance broker' means a registered insurance broker who is carrying on business as an insurance broker;

'prescribed' means prescribed by rules under this Act;

'recognised body of accountants' means any one of the following, namely—

the Institute of Chartered Accountants in England and Wales;
the Institute of Chartered Accountants of Scotland;
the Association of Certified Accountants;
the Institute of Chartered Accountants in Ireland;
any other body of accountants established in the United Kingdom and for the time being recognised for the purposes of section 389(1)(a) of the Companies Act 1985 by the Secretary of State;

'register' means the register of insurance brokers and 'registered' and 'registration' shall be construed accordingly;

'registered insurance broker' means a person who is registered in the register;
'the registrar' means the registrar of the Council appointed under section 8(1) of this Act.

(2) References in this Act to any other enactment (including an enactment of the Parliament of Northern Ireland and an Order in Council under the Northern Ireland Act 1974) shall be construed as references thereto, as amended, and as including references thereto as extended, by or under any subsequent enactment.

30. Short title, extent and commencement.—(1) This Act may be cited as the Insurance Brokers (Registration) Act 1977.

(2) This Act extends to Northern Ireland.

(3) Subject to subsection (4) below, this Act shall come into operation on such date as the Secretary of State may by order appoint and different dates may be appointed for different provisions and for different purposes.

(4) The day appointed for the coming into operation of section 22 of this Act shalt not be earlier than the expiration of a period of two years beginning with the day appointed for the coming into operation of section 1 of this Act.

SCHEDULE

Constitution, etc, of Insurance Brokers Registration Council

1. The Council shall consist of—

(a) twelve persons chosen to represent registered insurance brokers of whom one shall be Chairman of the Council;

(b) five persons nominated by the Secretary of State of whom one shall be a barrister, advocate or solicitor, another shall be a member of a recognised body of accountants and a third shall be a person appearing to the Secretary of State to represent the interests of persons who are or may become policyholders of insurance companies.

2.—(1) The persons chosen to represent registered insurance brokers in the first instance shall be nominated by the British Insurance Brokers' Association.

(2) The persons chosen to represent registered insurance brokers after the retirement of those nominated under sub-paragraph (1) above shall be elected by registered insurance brokers in accordance with a scheme which—

(a) shall be made by the Council;

(b) shall not come into operation until approved by order of the Secretary of State; and

(c) may be varied or revoked by a subsequent scheme so made and so approved.

(3) The Secretary of State may approve a scheme either as submitted to him or subject to such modifications as he thinks fit; but where the Secretary of State proposes to approve a scheme subject to modifications he shall notify the modifications to the Council and consider any observations of the Council thereon.

(4) The Council shall submit a scheme to the Secretary of State for approval before the expiration of a period of two years beginning with the day appointed for the coming into operation of section 1 of this Act.

(5) In the exercise of any functions under this paragraph due regard shall be had to the desirability of securing that the Council includes persons representative of all parts of the United Kingdom.

3. Nominations of the first members of the Council shall so far as practicable be made before the day appointed for the establishment of the Council in time to enable the persons nominated to assume membership on its establishment.

4.—(1) The term of office of—

(a) members nominated by the British Insurance Brokers' Association shall be such period, not exceeding four years, as may be fixed by the scheme;
(b) members elected by registered insurance brokers shall be such period as may be fixed by the scheme;
(c) members nominated by the Secretary of State shall be such period, not exceeding three years, as may be fixed by the Secretary of State.

(2) In this paragraph 'the scheme' means the scheme or schemes under paragraph 2 above which are for the time being in operation.

5. A member of the Council may at any time, by notice in writing addressed to the registrar, resign his office.

6.—(1) A person nominated or elected to fill a casual vacancy among the members of the Council shall hold office during the remainder of the term of office of the person whose vacancy he has filled.
(2) Any vacancy other than a casual vacancy in the membership of the Council shall be filled before the date on which the vacancy occurs.

7. A person ceasing to be a member of the Council shall be eligible to be again nominated or elected a member.

8.—(1) The Council shall have power to do anything which in their opinion is calculated to facilitate the proper discharge of their functions.
(2) The Council shall, in particular, have power—

(a) to appoint, in addition to a registrar, such officers and servants as the Council may determine;
(b) to pay to the members of the Council or their committees such fees for attendance at meetings of the Council or their committees and such travelling and subsistence allowances while attending such meetings or while on any other business of the Council as the Council may determine;
(c) to pay to their officers and servants such remuneration as the Council may determine;
(d) as regards any officers or servants in whose case they may determine to do so, to pay to, or in respect of them, such pensions and gratuities, or provide and maintain for them such superannuation schemes (whether contributory or not), as the Council may determine;
(e) subject to the provisions of section 1 of the Borrowing (Control and Guarantees) Act 1946 or, in Northern Ireland, of section 2 of the Loans Guarantee and Borrowing Regulation Act (Northern Ireland) 1946 and of any order under those provisions for the time being in force, to borrow such sums as the Council may from time to time require for performing any of their functions under this Act.

(3) The powers of the Council and any of its committees may be exercised notwithstanding any vacancy, and no proceedings of the Council or of any of its committees shall be invalidated by any defect in the nomination or election of a member.

9. The Council may make standing orders for regulating the proceedings (including quorum) of the Council and of any committee thereof:

Provided that orders shall not be made under this paragraph with respect to the proceedings of the Disciplinary Committee.

10. The Secretary of State may after consulting the Council, by order so amend the provisions of this Schedule as to vary the number of members and the manner in which they are chosen or appointed.

INSURANCE COMPANIES ACT 1982[1]

1982 c 50

An Act to consolidate the Insurance Companies Acts 1974 and 1981

PART I

RESTRICTION ON CARRYING ON INSURANCE BUSINESS

Preliminary

1. Classification.—(1) For the purposes of this Act insurance business is divided into long term business and general business; and—

'long term business' means insurance business of any of the classes specified in Schedule 1 to this Act, and

'general business' means insurance business of any of the classes specified in Part I of Schedule 2 to this Act.

(2) For the purposes of this Act the effecting and carrying out of a contract whose principal object is within one class of insurance business, but which contains related and subsidiary provisions within another class or classes, shall be taken to constitute the carrying on of insurance business of the first-mentioned class, and no other, if subsection (3) or (4) below applies to the contract.

(3) This subsection applies to a contract whose principal object is within any class of long term business but which contains subsidiary provisions within general business class 1 or 2 if the insurer is authorised under section 3 or 4 below to carry on long term business class 1.

(4) This subsection applies to a contract whose principal object is within one of the classes of general business but which contains subsidiary provisions within another of those classes, not being class 14 or 15.

2. Restriction on carrying on insurance business.—(1) Subject to the following provisions of this section, no person shall carry on any insurance business in the United Kingdom unless authorised to do so under section 3 or 4 below.

(2) Subsection (1) above shall not apply to insurance business (other than industrial assurance business) carried on—

(*a*) by a member of Lloyd's; or
(*b*) by a body registered under the enactments relating to friendly societies; or
(*c*) by a trade union or employer's association where the insurance business carried on by the union or association is limited to the provision for its members of provident benefits or strike benefits.

In this subsection 'trade union' and 'employers' association' have (throughout the United Kingdom) the meanings assigned to them by section 28 of the Trade Union and Labour Relations Act 1974.

(3) Subsection (1) above shall not apply to industrial assurance business carried on by a friendly society registered under the enactments relating to such societies.

---

[1] The Act is printed as amended.

(4) Subsection (1) above shall not apply to general business of class 14, 15, 16 or 17 if it is carried on solely in the course of carrying on, and for the purposes of, banking business.

(5) Subsection (1) above shall not apply to general business consisting in the effecting and carrying out, by an insurance company that carries on no other insurance business, of contracts of such descriptions as may be prescribed, being contracts under which the benefits provided by the insurer are exclusively or primarily benefits in kind.

Authorised insurance companies

3. Authorisation by Secretary of State.—(1) The Secretary of State may authorise a body to carry on in the United Kingdom such of the classes of insurance business specified in Schedule 1 or 2 to this Act, or such parts of those classes, as may be specified in the authorisation.

(2) An authorisation under this section may be restricted to industrial assurance business or to reinsurance business; and a body may not carry on industrial assurance business by virtue of an authorisation under this section unless the authorisation expressly extends to such business.

(3) An authorisation under this section may identify classes or parts of classes of general business by referring to the appropriate groups specified in Part II of Schedule 2 to this Act.

(4) On the issue to a body of an authorisation under this section, any previous authorisation of that body under this section or section 4 below shall lapse.

4. Existing insurance companies.—(1) A body that was, immediately before the commencement of this Act, authorised under section 3 or 4 of the Insurance Companies Act 1981 to carry on in the United Kingdom insurance business of a class specified in Schedule 1 or 2 to that Act (or a part of such a class) is authorised to carry on there insurance business of the class identified by the same number in Schedule 1 or 2 to this Act (or that part of such a class).

(2) A body may not carry on industrial assurance business by virtue of this section unless—

(*a*) it was carrying on such business immediately before 1 January 1982, or
(*b*) it was immediately before the commencement of this Act authorised to carry on such business under section 3 of the Insurance Companies Act 1981.

Applications for authorisation

5. Submission of proposals, etc.—(1) The Secretary of State shall not issue an authorisation under section 3 above unless—

(*a*) the applicant has submitted to him such proposals as to the manner in which it proposes to carry on business, such financial forecasts and such other information as may be required by or in accordance with regulations under this Act, and
(*b*) he is satisfied on the basis of that and any other information received by him that the application ought to be granted.

(2) The Secretary of State shall decide an application for an authorisation under section 3 above within six months of receiving the information referred to in subsection (1)(*a*) above; and if he refuses to issue the authorisation he shall inform the applicant in writing of the reasons for the refusal.

6. Combination of long term and general business.—The Secretary of State shall not under section 3 above authorise a body to carry on both long term business and general business unless—

(*a*) the long term business is restricted to reinsurance, or (*b*) the body is at the time the authorisation is issued already lawfully carrying on in the United Kingdom both long term business and general business (in neither case restricted to reinsurance).

7. United Kingdom applicants.—(1) The Secretary of State shall not issue an authorisation under section 3 above to an applicant whose head office is in the United Kingdom unless the applicant is—

(*a*) a company as defined in section 735 of the Companies Act or section 399 of the Companies Act (Northern Ireland) 1960, or
(*b*) a registered society, or
(*c*) a body corporate established by royal charter or Act of Parliament and already authorised under section 3 or 4 above to carry on insurance business (though not to the extent proposed in the application).

(2) The Secretary of State shall not issue an authorisation under section 3 above to an applicant whose head office is in the United Kingdom if it has an issued share capital any part of which was issued after the commencement of this section but is not fully paid up.

(3) The Secretary of State shall not issue an authorisation under section 3 above to an applicant whose head office is in the United Kingdom if it appears to the Secretary of State that any director, controller, manager or main agent of the applicant is not a fit and proper person to hold the position held by him.

(4) In this section 'controller', in relation to the applicant, means—

(*a*) a managing director of the applicant or of a body corporate of which the applicant is a subsidiary;
(*b*) a chief executive of the applicant or of a body corporate, being an insurance company, of which the applicant is a subsidiary;
(*c*) a person—
  (i) in accordance with whose directions or instructions the directors of the applicant or of a body corporate of which it is a subsidiary are accustomed to act, or
  (ii) who either alone or with any associate or associates is entitled to exercise, or control the exercise of, one-third or more of the voting power at any general meeting of the applicant or of a body corporate of which it is a subsidiary.

(5) In this section 'manager', in relation to the applicant, means an employee of the applicant (other than a chief executive) who, under the immediate authority of a director or chief executive of the applicant—

(*a*) exercises managerial functions, or
(*b*) is responsible for maintaining accounts or other records of the applicant,

not being a person whose functions relate exclusively to business conducted from a place of business outside the United Kingdom.

(6) In this section 'main agent', in relation to the applicant, means, subject to such exceptions as may be prescribed, a person appointed by the applicant to be its agent in respect of general business in the United Kingdom, with authority to enter into contracts on behalf of the applicant in any financial year—

(*a*) without limit on the aggregate amount of premiums; or
(*b*) with a limit in excess of 10 per cent of the premium limit as determined in accordance with Schedule 3 to this Act.

(7) In this section 'chief executive', in relation to the applicant or a body corporate of which it is a subsidiary, means an employee of the applicant or that body corporate, who, either alone or jointly with others, is responsible under the immediate authority of the directors for the conduct of the whole of the insurance business of the applicant or that body corporate.

(8) In this section 'associate', in relation to any person, means—

(*a*) the wife or husband or minor son or daughter of that person;
(*b*) any company of which that person is a director;
(*c*) any person who is an employee or partner of that person;
(*d*) if that person is a company—

(i) any director of that company;
(ii) any subsidiary of that company;
(iii) any director or employee of any such subsidiary;

and for the purposes of this subsection 'son' includes step-son, 'daughter' includes step-daughter and 'minor', in relation to Scotland, includes pupil.

8. Applicants from other member States.—(1) The Secretary of State shall not issue an authorisation under section 3 above to an applicant whose head office is in a member State other than the United Kingdom unless the applicant has a representative fulfilling the requirements of section 10 below.

(2) The Secretary of State shall not issue an authorisation under section 3 above to an applicant whose head office is in a member State other than the United Kingdom if it appears to the Secretary of State that any relevant executive or main agent of the applicant is not a fit and proper person to hold the position held by him.

(3) Where an applicant whose head office is in a member State other than the United Kingdom seeks an authorisation under section 3 above restricted to reinsurance business—

(*a*) the Secretary of State shall not issue the authorisation unless he is satisfied that the applicant is a body corporate entitled under the law of that State to carry on insurance business there; and
(*b*) subsection (2) above shall have effect as if the reference to any relevant executive were a reference to any person who is a director, controller or manager of the applicant or a person within paragraph (*a*) or (*b*) of subsection (4) below.

(4) In this section 'relevant executive' in relation to the applicant means a person who is—

(*a*) the representative referred to in subsection (1) above or the individual representative referred to in section 10(5) below;
(*b*) an officer or employee of the applicant who, either alone or jointly with others, is responsible for the conduct of the whole of the insurance business carried on by the applicant in the United Kingdom, not being a person who—

(i) is also responsible for the conduct of insurance business carried on by the applicant elsewhere, and
(ii) has a subordinate who is responsible for the whole of the insurance business carried on by the applicant in the United Kingdom; or

(*c*) an employee of the applicant who, under the immediate authority of a director or of an officer or employee within paragraph (*b*) above,—

(i) exercises managerial functions, or
(ii) is responsible for maintaining accounts or other records of the applicant,
not being a person whose functions relate exclusively to business conducted from a place of business outside the United Kingdom;

and 'controller', 'manager' and 'main agent' have the same meanings as in section 7 above.

9. Applicants from outside the Community.—(1) The Secretary of State shall not issue an authorisation under section 3 above in respect of long term or general business to an applicant whose head office is not in a member State unless he is satisfied—

(*a*) that the applicant is a body corporate entitled under the law of the place where its head office is situated to carry on long term or, as the case may be, general business there;
(*b*) that the applicant has in the United Kingdom assets of such value as may be prescribed; and
(*c*) that the applicant has made a deposit of such amount and with such person as may be prescribed;

but subject to subsections (2) and (3) below.

(2) Where the applicant seeks to carry on insurance business in the United Kingdom and one or more other member States, the Secretary of State and the supervisory authority in the other State or States concerned may agree that this subsection shall apply to the applicant; and in that event—

(*a*) paragraph (*b*) of subsection (1) above shall have effect as if the reference to the United Kingdom were a reference to the member States concerned taken together; and
(*b*) paragraph (*c*) of that subsection shall have effect as if the reference to such person as may be prescribed were a reference to such person as may be agreed between the Secretary of State and the other supervisory authority or authorities concerned.

(3) Paragraph (*c*) of subsection (1) above shall not apply where the authorisation sought is one restricted to reinsurance.

(4) The Secretary of State shall not issue an authorisation under section 3 above to an applicant whose head office is not in a member State unless the applicant has a representative fulfilling the requirements of section 10 below.

(5) The Secretary of State shall not issue an authorisation under section 3 above to an applicant whose head office is not in a member State if it appears to the Secretary of State that—

(*a*) the representative of the applicant referred to in subsection (4) above or the individual representative referred to in section 10(5) below, or
(*b*) any director, controller or manager of the applicant, or
(*c*) a main agent of the applicant,

is not a fit and proper person to hold the position held by him.

(6) In this section 'controller', 'manager' and 'main agent' have the same meanings as in section 7 above, except that for the purposes of this section the controllers of the applicant shall be taken to include any officer or employee who, either alone or jointly with others, is responsible for the conduct of the whole of the insurance business carried on by the applicant in the United Kingdom, not being a person who—

(*a*) is also responsible for the conduct of insurance business carried on by it elsewhere; and
(*b*) has a subordinate who is responsible for the whole of the insurance business carried on by the applicant in the United Kingdom.

(7) Regulations under this Act may make such provision as to deposits under this section as appears to the Secretary of State to be necessary or expedient, including provision for the deposit of securities instead of money, and, in relation to deposits with the Accountant General of the Supreme Court, provision applying (with or without modification) any of the provisions of the rules for the time being in force under section 38(7) of the Administration of Justice Act 1982.

10. General representatives.—(1) The requirements referred to in sections 8(1) and 9(4) above are those set out in the following provisions of this section.

(2) The representative must be a person resident in the United Kingdom who has been designated as the applicant's representative for the purposes of this section.

(3) The representative must be authorised to act generally, and to accept service of any document, on behalf of the applicant.

(4) The representative must not be an auditor, or a partner or employee of an auditor, of the accounts of any business carried on by the applicant.

(5) If the representative is not an individual, it must be a company as defined in section 735 of the Companies Act or section 399 of the Companies Act (Northern Ireland) 1960 with its head office in the United Kingdom and must itself have an individual representative resident in the United Kingdom who is authorised to act generally, and to accept service of any document, on behalf of the company in its capacity as representative of the applicant.

Withdrawal of authorisation

11. Withdrawal of authorisation in respect of new business.—(1) The Secretary of State may, at the request of the company or on any grounds set out in subsection (2) below, direct that an insurance company authorised under section 3 or 4 above to carry on insurance business shall cease to be authorised to effect contracts of insurance, or contracts of any description specified in the direction.

(2) The grounds referred to in subsection (1) above are—

- (*a*) that it appears to the Secretary of State that the company has failed to satisfy an obligation to which it is subject by virtue of this Act;
- (*b*) that there exists a ground on which he would be prohibited by section 7, 8 or 9 above from issuing an authorisation to the company;
- (*c*) that the company has ceased to be authorised to effect contracts of insurance, or contracts of a particular description, in a member State where it has its head office or where it has in accordance with section 9(2) above made a deposit.

(3) After giving a direction under this section otherwise than at the request of the company concerned the Secretary of State shall inform the company in writing of his reasons for giving the direction.

(4) A direction under this section shall not prevent a company from effecting a contract of insurance in pursuance of a term of a subsisting contract of insurance.

(5) Where a direction under this section has been given in respect of a company which has its head office, or has in accordance with section 9(2) above made a deposit, in a member State other than the United Kingdom, the Secretary of State may revoke or vary the direction if after consultation with the supervisory authority in that member State he considers it appropriate to do so.

(6) Subject to subsection (5) above a direction given under this section in respect of any insurance company may not be revoked or varied; but if the Secretary of State subsequently issues to the company under section 3 above an authorisation to carry on insurance business of a class to which the direction relates, the direction shall cease to have effect in relation to such business.

12. Notices of withdrawal under section 11.—(1) Before giving a direction under section 11 above otherwise than at the request of the company concerned the Secretary of State shall serve on the company a written notice stating—

- (*a*) that he is considering giving a direction and the ground on which he is considering it; and
- (*b*) that the company may, within the period of one month from the date of service of the notice, make written representations to the Secretary of State and, if the

company so requests, oral representations to an officer of the Department of Trade appointed for the purpose by the Secretary of State.

(2) Before giving a direction under section 11 above in respect of a company on the ground that he would be prohibited by section 7(3), 8(2) or 9(5) from issuing an authorisation to the company, the Secretary of State shall serve on the person whose fitness is in question a written notice stating—

(*a*) that he is considering giving a direction on that ground; and

(*b*) that the person on whom the notice is served may, within the period of one month from the date of service of the notice, make written representations to the Secretary of State and, if that person so requests, oral representations to an officer of the Department of Trade appointed for the purpose by the Secretary of State.

(3) Subject to subsection (4) below, the Secretary of State shall consider any representations made in response to a notice under subsection (2) above before serving a notice under subsection (1) above.

(4) Subsection (3) above shall not apply where the position held by the person on whom the notice under subsection (2) above is served, and whose fitness for that position is in question, is controller of a company.

(5) A notice under subsection (1) or (2) above shall give particulars of the ground on which the Secretary of State is considering giving a direction.

(6) Where representations are made in response to a notice under subsection (1) or (2) above, the Secretary of State shall take them into consideration before giving a direction.

(7) Any notice to be served on a person under subsection (1) or (2) above may be served by post, and a letter containing the notice shall be deemed to be properly addressed if it is addressed to that person at his last known residence or last known place of business in the United Kingdom.

(8) After giving a direction under section 11 above the Secretary of State shall publish notice of it in the London, Edinburgh and Belfast Gazettes and in such other ways as appear to him expedient for notifying the public.

13. Final withdrawal of authorisation.—(1) Where an insurance company ceases to carry on in the United Kingdom any insurance business, or insurance business of any class, the Secretary of State may direct that it shall cease to be authorised under section 3 or 4 above to carry on insurance business, or insurance business of that class.

(2) If a body authorised under section 3 above to carry on insurance business of any class has not at any time carried on business of that class, and at least twelve months have elapsed since the issue of the authorisation, the Secretary of State may direct that it shall cease to be authorised to carry on business of that class.

(3) A direction under this section is without prejudice to the subsequent issue of an authorisation to carry on insurance business of a class to which the direction relates.

Offences

14. Offences under Part I.—(1) A person who carries on business in contravention of this Part of this Act shall be guilty of an offence.

(2) A person who for the purpose of obtaining the issue of an authorisation furnishes information which he knows to be false in a material particular or recklessly furnishes information which is false in a material particular shall be guilty of an offence.

(3) A person guilty of an offence under this section shall be liable—

(*a*) on conviction on indictment, to imprisonment for a term not exceeding two years, or to a fine, or to both;

(*b*) on summary conviction—

(i) in England and Wales . . ., to a fine not exceeding £1,000 or, if it is greater, the prescribed sum within the meaning of section 32 of the Magistrates' Courts Act 1980;

(ii) in Scotland, to a fine not exceeding £1,000 or, if it is greater, the prescribed sum within the meaning of section 289B of the Criminal Procedure (Scotland) Act 1975;

(iii) in Northern Ireland, to a fine not exceeding £2,000 or, if it is greater, the prescribed sum within the meaning of Article 4 of the Fines and Penalties (Northern Ireland) Order 1984.

PART II

Regulation of Insurance Companies

Preliminary

15. Insurance companies to which Part II applies.—(1) Subject to the provisions of this section, this Part of this Act applies to all insurance companies, whether established within or outside the United Kingdom, which carry on insurance business within the United Kingdom.

(2) This Part of this Act does not apply to any insurance company which is registered under the enactments relating to friendly societies.

(3) Where a trade union or an employers' association carries on insurance business, this Part of this Act does not apply to it as an insurance company if the insurance business is limited to the provision for its members of provident benefits or strike benefits.

In this subsection 'trade union' and 'employers' association' have (throughout the United Kingdom) the meanings assigned to them by section 28 of the Trade Union and Labour Relations Act 1974.

(4) This Part of this Act does not apply to a member of Lloyd's who carries on insurance business of any class provided that he complies with the requirements set out in section 83 below and applicable to business of that class.

(5) This Part of this Act does not apply to a person by reason only that he carries on general business of class 14, 15, 16 or 17 in the course of carrying on, and for the purposes of, banking business.

(6) This Part of this Act does not apply to an insurance company whose insurance business is restricted to general business consisting in the effecting and carrying out of contracts of such descriptions as may be prescribed, being contracts under which the benefits provided by the insurer are exclusively or primarily benefits in kind.

16. Restriction of business to insurance.—(1) an insurance company to which this Part of this Act applies shall not carry on any activities, in the United Kingdom or elsewhere, otherwise than in connection with or for the purposes of its insurance business.

(2) For the purposes of subsection (1) above any activities of an insurance company that are excluded from the definition of insurance business by section 95(c)(ii) below shall be treated as carried on in connection with its insurance business.

Accounts and statements

17. Annual accounts and balance sheets.—(1) Every insurance company to which this Part of this Act applies shall, with respect to each financial year of the company, prepare a revenue account for the year, a balance sheet as at the end of the year and a profit and loss account for the year or, in the case of a company not trading for profit, an income and expenditure account for the year.

(2) The contents of the documents required by subsection (1) above to be prepared shall be such as may be prescribed, but regulations may provide for enabling information required to be given by such documents to be given instead in a note thereon or statement or report annexed thereto or may require there to be given in such a note, statement or report such information in addition to that given in the documents as may be prescribed.

(3) Regulations may, as respects such matters stated in such documents as aforesaid or in statements or reports annexed thereto as may be prescribed, require there to be given by such persons as may be prescribed and to be annexed to the documents certificates of such matters as may be prescribed.

(4) If a form is prescribed—

(*a*) for any such document as aforesaid or,
(*b*) as that in which information authorised or required to be given in a statement or report annexed to any such document is to be given or,
(*c*) for a certificate to be so annexed,

the document shall be prepared, the information shall be given or, as the case may be, the certificate shall be framed, in that form.

18. Periodic actuarial investigation of company with long term business.—(1) Every insurance company to which this Part of this Act applies which carries on long term business—

(*a*) shall, once in every period of twelve months, cause an investigation to be made into its financial condition in respect of that business by the person who for the time being is its actuary under section 19(1) below or any corresponding enactment previously in force; and
(*b*) when such an investigation has been made, or when at any other time an investigation into the financial condition of the company in respect of its long term business has been made with a view to the distribution of profits, or the results of which are made public, shall cause an abstract of the actuary's report of the investigation to be made.

(2) An investigation to which subsection (1)(*b*) above relates shall include—

(*a*) a valuation of the liabilities of the company attributable to its long term business; and
(*b*) a determination of any excess over those liabilities of the assets representing the fund or funds maintained by the company in respect of that business and, where any rights of any long term policy holders to participate in profits relate to particular parts of such a fund, a determination of any excess of assets over liabilities in respect of each of those parts.

(3) At least once in every period of five years an insurance company to which subsection (1) above applies shall prepare a statement of its long term business at the date to which the accounts of the company are made up for the purposes of an investigation in pursuance of paragraph (*a*) of that subsection.

(4) For the purposes of any investigation to which this section applies the value of any assets and the amount of any liabilities shall be determined in accordance with any applicable valuation regulations.

(5) The form and contents of any abstract or statement under this section shall be such as may be prescribed.

19. Appointment of actuary by company with long term business.—(1) Every insurance company to which this Part of this Act applies shall within one month of beginning to carry on long term business appoint an actuary as actuary to the company; and whenever an appointment under this section or any corresponding enactment previously in force comes to an end the company shall as soon as practicable make a fresh appointment.

(2) A company making an appointment under this section shall within fourteen days serve on the Secretary of State a written notice stating that fact and the name and qualifications of the person appointed; and if an appointment under this section or any corresponding enactment previously in force comes to an end the company shall within fourteen days serve on the Secretary of State a written notice stating that fact and the name of the person concerned.

20. Annual statements by company with prescribed class of insurance business.—Classes of insurance business may be prescribed for the purposes of this section, and every insurance company to which this Part of this Act applies which carries on such business of a prescribed class shall annually prepare the prescribed statement of business of that class, being, if a form is prescribed for the statement, a statement in the prescribed form.

21. Audit of accounts.—(1) The accounts and balance sheets of every insurance company to which this Part of this Act applies shall be audited in the prescribed manner by a person of the prescribed description, and regulations made for the purposes of this section may apply to such companies the provisions of the Companies Act relating to audit, subject to such adaptations and modifications as may appear necessary or expedient.

(2) In subsection (1) above the reference to accounts and balance sheets shall include a reference to any statement or report annexed thereto giving information authorised or required by virtue of section 17(2) above to be given in a statement or report so annexed.

22. Deposit of accounts etc with Secretary of State.—(1) Every account, balance sheet, abstract or statement required by sections 17, 18 and 20 above and any report of the auditor of the company made in pursuance of section 21 above shall be printed, and five copies shall be deposited with the Secretary of State within six months after the close of the period to which the account, balance sheet, abstract, statement or report relates; but if in any case it is made to appear to the Secretary of State that the circumstances are such that a longer period than six months should be allowed, the Secretary of State may extend that period by such period not exceeding three months as he thinks fit.

(2) There shall be deposited with the Secretary of State, at the same time as the documents mentioned in subsection (1) above, five printed copies of a statement of the names and the connection with the company of any persons who, during the period to which those documents relate—

(*a*) were authorised by the company to issue, or to the knowledge of the company have issued, any such invitation in relation to the company as is mentioned in subsection (1)(*a*) of section 74 below; and

(*b*) were connected with the company as provided by regulations under that section.

(3) One of the copies of any document deposited under subsection (1) or (2) above except an auditor's report shall be a copy signed by such persons as may be prescribed.

(4) One of the copies of any auditor's report deposited under subsection (1) above shall be a copy signed by the auditor.

(5) The Secretary of State shall consider the documents deposited under subsections (1) and (2) above, and if any such document appears to him to be inaccurate or incomplete in any respect he shall communicate with the company with a view to the correction of any inaccuracies and the supply of deficiencies.

(6) There shall be deposited with every revenue account and balance sheet of a company any report on the affairs of the company submitted to the shareholders or policy holders of the company in respect of the financial year to which the account and balance sheet relate.

(7) In this section any reference to an account or balance sheet includes a reference to any statement or report annexed thereto giving information authorised or required by virtue of subsection (2) of section 17 above to be so given and any certificate so annexed by virtue of subsection (3) of that section.

23. Right of shareholders and policy holders to receive copies of deposited documents.—(1) Subject to subsection (2) below, an insurance company shall forward by post or otherwise to any shareholder or policy holder who applies for one—

(*a*) a printed copy of any of the documents last deposited by the company under subsection (1) or (2) of section 22 above;
(*b*) a copy of any document supplied to the Secretary of State under subsection (5) of that section which relates to any of those documents;
(*c*) a copy of any report deposited with any of those documents under subsection (6) of that section.

(2) If, in the opinion of the Secretary of State, the disclosure of information contained in—

(*a*) a statement or report annexed to a document prepared in pursuance of section 17(1) above by an insurance company; or
(*b*) a statement prepared in pursuance of section 20 above by such a company

would be harmful to the business of the company or of any of its subsidiaries, the Secretary of State may dispense the company from complying with the obligation imposed by subsection (1) above to forward a copy of the document containing the information to a shareholder or policy holder who applies for it.

24. Deposit of accounts etc by registered society.—(1) A registered society shall, in addition to depositing with the Secretary of State, as required by section 22 above, five copies of each document to which subsections (1) and (2) of that section apply, deposit, within the time limited by virtue of that section for depositing them, a copy with the appropriate registrar in the case of a society registered in Great Britain or with the registrar in the case of a society registered in Northern Ireland, being a copy signed by the like persons as those by whom the copies deposited under that section are required to be signed.

(2) Subsection (6) of the said section 22 shall have effect in relation to the deposit by virtue of this section of accounts and balance sheets as it has effect in relation to the deposit by virtue of that section of accounts and balance sheets.

(3) Section 71(1) of the Industrial and Provident Societies Act 1965 (which empowers the Treasury to make regulations respecting, among other things, the inspection of documents kept by the appropriate registrar under that Act) and section 97(1) of the Industrial and Provident Societies Act (Northern Ireland) 1969 (which confers corresponding powers on the Department of Commerce for Northern Ireland) shall have effect as if the reference to documents kept by the appropriate registrar under that Act of 1965 or, as the case may be, by the registrar under that Act of 1969 included a reference to documents deposited in pursuance of this section.

(4) In this section "appropriate registrar" has the meaning given in section 73(1) of the said Act of 1965 and "registrar" has the meaning given by section 101(1) of the said Act of 1969.

25. Periodic statements by company with prescribed class of business.—(1) Every insurance company to which this Part of this Act applies which carries on business of a class or description prescribed for the purposes of this section shall prepare, at such intervals and for such periods as may be prescribed, a statement of its business of that class or description.

(2) The form and contents of any statement under this section shall be such as may be prescribed.

(3) Regulations may, as respects such matters contained in a statement under this section as may be prescribed, require there to be given by such persons as may be prescribed and to be annexed to the statement certificates of such matters and in such form as may be prescribed.

(4) Five copies of any statement made under this section (with any certificate annexed thereto in pursuance of subsection (3) above) shall be deposited by the company with the

Secretary of State within such period as may be prescribed, and one of those copies shall be a copy signed by the persons required to sign copies of statements made under section 20 above which are deposited under section 22 above.

(5) The whole or any part of any document deposited under subsection (4) above may be deposited by the Secretary of State with the registrar of companies or with the registrar of companies in Northern Ireland or with both and may be published by the Secretary of State in such ways as he thinks appropriate.

26. Statements of transactions of prescribed class or prescription.—(1) Classes or descriptions of agreements or arrangements appearing to the Secretary of State as likely to be undesirable in the interests of policy holders may be prescribed for the purposes of this section, and every insurance company to which this Part of this Act applies or subordinate company within the meaning of section 31 below of any such company which enters into an agreement or arrangement of a class or description so prescribed shall, within such period as may be prescribed, furnish the Secretary of State with a statement containing such particulars of that agreement or arrangement as may be prescribed.

(2) Different classes or descriptions of agreements or arrangements may be prescribed for the purposes of this section in relation to companies of different classes or descriptions.

(3) The whole or any part of any statement furnished to the Secretary of State under this section may be deposited by him with the registrar of companies or with the registrar of companies in Northern Ireland or with both and may be published by the Secretary of State in such ways as he thinks appropriate.

27. Companies from outside the Community.—An insurance company to which this Part of this Act applies whose head office is not in a member State shall keep in the United Kingdom proper accounts and records in respect of insurance business carried on in the United Kingdom.

Assets and liabilities attributable to long term business

28. Separation of assets and liabilities attributable to long term business.—(1) Where an insurance company to which this Part of this Act applies carries on ordinary long-term insurance business or industrial assurance business or both of those kinds of insurance business—

(*a*) the company shall maintain an account in respect of that business or, as the case may be, each of those kinds of business; and
(*b*) the receipts of that business or, as the case may be, of each of those kinds of business shall be entered in the account maintained for that business and shall be carried to and form a separate insurance fund with an appropriate name.

(2) An insurance company to which this Part of this Act applies which carries on ordinary long-term insurance business or industrial assurance business or both of those kinds of business shall maintain such accounting and other records as are necessary for identifying—

(*a*) the assets representing the fund or funds maintained by the company under subsection (1)(*b*) above (but without necessarily distinguishing between the funds if more than one); and
(*b*) the liabilities attributable to that business or, as the case may be, each of those kinds of business.

29. Application of assets of company with long term business.—(1) Subject to subsections (2) and (4) and section 55(3) below, the assets representing the fund or funds maintained by an insurance company in respect of its long term business—

(*a*) shall be applicable only for the purposes of that business, and
(*b*) shall not be transferred so as to be available for other purposes of the company except where the transfer constitutes reimbursement of expenditure borne by other assets (in the same or the last preceding financial year) in discharging liabilities wholly or partly attributable to long term business.

(2) Where the value of the assets mentioned in subsection (1) above is shown, by an investigation to which section 18 above applies or which is made in pursuance of a requirement imposed under section 42 below, to exceed the amount of the liabilities attributable to the company's long term business the restriction imposed by that subsection shall not apply to so much of those assets as represents the excess.

(3) Subsection (2) above shall not authorise a transfer or other application of assets by reference to an actuarial investigation at any time after the date when the abstract of the actuary's report of the investigation has been deposited with the Secretary of State in accordance with section 22(1) above or section 42(4) below.

(4) Nothing in subsection (1) above shall preclude an insurance company from exchanging, at fair market value, assets representing a fund maintained by the company in respect of its long term business for other assets of the company.

(5) Any mortgage or charge (including—

(*a*) a charge imposed by a court on the application of a judgment creditor,
(*b*) in Scotland, a charge imposed by way of diligence, and
(*c*) a charge imposed by the Enforcement of Judgments Office in Northern Ireland)

shall be void to the extent to which it contravenes subsection (1) above.

(6) Money from a fund maintained by a company in respect of its long term business may not be used for the purposes of any other business of the company notwithstanding any arrangement for its subsequent repayment out of the receipts of that other business.

(7) No insurance company to which this Part of this Act applies, and no company of which any such insurance company is a subsidiary, shall declare a dividend at any time when the value of the assets representing the fund or funds maintained by the insurance company in respect of its long term business, as determined in accordance with any applicable valuation regulations, is less than the amount of the liabilities attributable to that business as so determined.

30. Allocations to policy holders.—(1) Where in the case of an insurance company to which this Part of this Act applies—

(*a*) there is an established surplus in which long term policy holders of any category are eligible to participate, and
(*b*) an amount has been allocated to policy holders of that category in respect of a previously established surplus in which policy holders of that category were eligible to participate,

the company shall not by virtue of section 29(2) above transfer or otherwise apply assets representing any part of the surplus mentioned in paragraph (*a*) above unless the company has either allocated to policy holders of that category in respect of that surplus an amount not less than the relevant minimum, or complied with the requirements of subsection (3) below and made to those policy holders any allocation of which notice is given under paragraph (*a*) of that subsection.

(2) Subject to subsections (6) and (7) below, the relevant minimum is the amount represented by the formula

$$\frac{b \times c}{a} - \frac{c}{200}$$

where—

a is the last previously established surplus in respect of which an amount was allocated to policy holders of the category in question;
b is the amount so allocated; and
c is the surplus referred to in subsection (1)(*a*).

(3) The requirements of this subsection are that the company—

(*a*) has served on the Secretary of State a written notice stating that it proposes to make no allocation or an allocation of an amount (specifying it) which is smaller than the relevant minimum; and
(*b*) has published a statement approved by the Secretary of State in the London, Edinburgh and Belfast Gazettes and in such other ways as he may have directed,

and that a period of not less than fifty-six days has elapsed since the date, or the last date, on which the company has published the statement mentioned in paragraph (*b*) above as required by or under that paragraph.

(4) In this section 'established surplus' means an excess of assets representing the whole or a particular part of the fund or funds maintained by the company in respect of its long term business over the liabilities, or a particular part of the liabilities, of the company attributable to that business as shown by an investigation to which section 18 above applies or which is made in pursuance of a requirement imposed under section 42 below.

(5) For the purposes of this section an amount is allocated to policy holders if, and only if—

(*a*) bonus payments are made to them; or
(*b*) reversionary bonuses are declared in their favour or a reduction is made in the premiums payable by them;

and the amount of the allocation is, in a case within paragraph (*a*) above, the amount of the payments and, in a case within paragraph (*b*) above, the amount of the liabilities assumed by the company in consequence of the declaration or reduction.

(6) For the purposes of this section the amount of any bonus payments made in anticipation of an established surplus shall be treated as an amount allocated in respect of the next established surplus in respect of which an amount is allocated to eligible policy holders generally; and for the purposes of subsection (2) above the amount of any surplus in respect of which such an allocation is made shall be treated as increased by the amount of any such payments.

(7) Subsection (1) above shall not authorise the application for purposes other than those mentioned in section 29(1) above of assets representing any part of the surplus mentioned in subsection (1)(*a*) above which the company has decided to carry forward unappropriated; and for the purposes of subsection (2) above the amount of any surplus shall be treated as reduced by any part thereof which the company has decided to carry forward as aforesaid.

(8) For the purposes of subsection (1) above policy holders shall be taken to be eligible to participate in an established surplus in any case where they would be eligible to participate in a later established surplus representing it if it were carried forward unappropriated.

31. Restriction on transactions with connected persons.—(1) Neither an insurance company to which this Part of this Act applies which carries on long term business nor a subordinate company of any such insurance company shall enter into a transaction to which this section applies—

(*a*) at a time when the aggregate of the value of the assets and the amount of the liabilities attributable to such transactions already entered into by the insurance company and its subordinate companies exceeds the prescribed percentage of the total amount standing to the credit of the insurance company's long term funds; or

(*b*) at any other time when the aggregate of the value of those assets and the amount of those liabilities would exceed that percentage if the transaction were entered into.

(2) This section applies to any transaction entered into by any such insurance company as is mentioned in subsection (1) above (whether or not itself a subordinate company of another company), being a transaction under which—

(*a*) a person connected with the insurance company will owe it money; or
(*b*) the insurance company acquires shares in a company which is a person connected with it; or
(*c*) the insurance company undertakes a liability to meet an obligation of a person connected with it or to help such a person to meet an obligation,

if the right to receive the money would constitute a long term asset of the insurance company, the acquisition is made out of its long term funds or the liability would fall to be discharged out of those funds, as the case may be.

(3) Without prejudice to subsection (2) above, this section applies to any transaction entered into by a subordinate company of any such insurance company as is mentioned in subsection (1) above, being a transaction under which—

(*a*) the insurance company or a person connected with it will owe money to the subordinate company (not being money owed by the insurance company which can be properly paid out of its long term funds); or
(*b*) the subordinate company acquires shares in the insurance company or in a company which is a person connected with the insurance company; or
(*c*) the subordinate company undertakes a liability to meet an obligation of the insurance company or of a person connected with that company or to help the insurance company or such a person to meet an obligation;

but where the subordinate company is itself such an insurance company as is mentioned in subsection (1) above this section shall not by virtue of this subsection apply to any such transaction if the right to receive the money would constitute a long term asset of the subordinate company, the acquisition is made out of its long term funds or the liability would fall to be discharged out of those funds, as the case may be.

(4) In this section 'subordinate company', in relation to any such insurance company as is mentioned in subsection (1) above, means—

(*a*) a company having equity share capital some or all of which is held by the insurance company as part of its long term assets where the share capital so held by the insurance company—

  (i) amounts to more than half in nominal value of that share capital; and
  (ii) confers on the insurance company the power to appoint or remove the holders of all or a majority of the directorships of the company whose share capital is held and more than one-half of the voting power at any general meeting of that company;

(*b*) a company having equity share capital some or all of which is held by another company which is itself a subordinate company of the insurance company where the share capital held by that other company—

  (i) amounts to more than half in nominal value of that share capital; and
  (ii) confers on that other company the power to appoint or remove the holders of all or a majority of the directorships of the company whose share capital is held and more than one-half of the voting power at any general meeting of that company;

and for the purposes of this subsection share capital held for any person by a nominee shall (except where that person is concerned only in a fiduciary capacity) be treated as held by that person, and share capital held by a person in a fiduciary capacity or by way of security shall be treated as not held by that person.

(5) For the purposes of this section a person is connected with any such insurance company as is mentioned in subsection (1) above if that person is not a subordinate company of the insurance company but—

(*a*) controls, or is a partner of a person who controls, the insurance company; or
(*b*) being a company, is controlled by the insurance company or by another person who also controls the insurance company; or
(*c*) is a director of the insurance company or the wife or husband or a minor son or daughter of such a director;

and for the purposes of this subsection a person controls a company if he is a controller of it within the meaning of section 7(4)(*c*) above.

(6) For the purposes of this section the value of any assets and the amount of any liabilities shall be determined in accordance with any applicable valuation regulations.

(7) In this section—

'company' (except in the expression 'insurance company') includes any body corporate;
'equity share capital' means, in relation to a company, its issued share capital excluding any part thereof which, neither as respects dividends nor as respects capital, carries any right to participate beyond a specified amount in a distribution;
'liability' includes a contingent liability;
'long term assets' and 'long term funds', in relation to an insurance company, mean respectively assets representing the fund or funds maintained by the company in respect of its long term business and that fund or those funds;
'the prescribed percentage' means 5 per cent, or such greater percentage as may from time to time be prescribed for the purposes of this section by regulations;
'share' has the same meaning as in the Companies Act 1985 or the Companies Act (Northern Ireland) 1960;
'son' includes step-son, 'daughter' includes step-daughter, and 'minor', in relation to Scotland, includes pupil and, (without prejudice to section 39(6) of the Adoption Act 1976 and section 39(4) of the Adoption (Scotland) Act 1978) in relation to Northern Ireland, 'son' includes step-son and adopted son and 'daughter' includes step-daughter and adopted daughter.

(8) This section shall not be construed as making any transaction unenforceable as between the parties thereto or as otherwise making unenforceable any rights or liabilities in respect of property.

Financial resources

32. Margins of solvency.—(1) Every insurance company to which this Part of this Act applies—

(*a*) whose head office is in the United Kingdom, or
(*b*) whose business in the United Kingdom is restricted to reinsurance,

shall maintain a margin of solvency of such amount as may be prescribed by or determined in accordance with regulations made for the purposes of this section.

(2) Subject to subsection (3) below, every insurance company to which this Part of this Act applies whose head office is not in a member State shall maintain—

(*a*) a margin of solvency, and
(*b*) a United Kingdom margin of solvency,

of such amounts as may be prescribed by or determined in accordance with regulations made for the purposes of this section.

(3) Subsection (2) above shall not apply to an insurance company if its business in the United Kingdom is restricted to reinsurance or if section 9(2) above applies to it; but an insurance company that has made a deposit in the United Kingdom in accordance with section 9(2)(*b*) above shall maintain—

(*a*) a margin of solvency, and
(*b*) a Community margin of solvency,

of such amounts as may be prescribed by or determined in accordance with regulations made for the purposes of this section.

(4) An insurance company that fails to comply with subsection (1), (2) or (3) above—

(*a*) shall at the request of the Secretary of State submit to him a plan for the restoration of a sound financial position;
(*b*) shall propose modifications to the plan (or the plan as previously modified) if the Secretary of State considers it inadequate;
(*c*) shall give effect to any plan accepted by the Secretary of State as adequate.

(5) For the purposes of this Act—

(*a*) the margin of solvency of an insurance company is the excess of the value of its assets over the amount of its liabilities, that value and amount being determined in accordance with any applicable valuation regulations;
(*b*) the United Kingdom margin of solvency of an insurance company is its margin of solvency computed by reference to the assets and liabilities of the business carried on by the company in the United Kingdom;
(*c*) the Community margin of solvency of an insurance company is its margin of solvency computed by reference to the assets and liabilities of the business carried on by the company in member States (taken together).

(6) In the case of an insurance company that carries on both long term and general business, subsections (1), (2) and (3) above shall have effect as if—

(*a*) the requirements to maintain a margin of solvency, and
(*b*) where the company carries on both kinds of business in the United Kingdom, the requirement to maintain a United Kingdom margin of solvency, and
(*c*) where the company carries on both kinds of business in member States (taken together), the requirement to maintain a Community margin of solvency,

were requirements to maintain separate margins in respect of the two kinds of business (and accordingly as if the references in subsection (5) to assets and liabilities were references to assets and liabilities relating to the kind of business in question).

33. Failure to maintain minimum margin.—(1) If—

(*a*) the margin of solvency of an insurance company to which section 32(1) above applies, or
(*b*) the margin of solvency or United Kingdom margin of solvency of an insurance company to which section 32(2) above applies, or
(*c*) the margin of solvency or Community margin of solvency of an insurance company to which section 32(3) above applies,

falls below such amount as may be prescribed by or determined in accordance with regulations made for the purposes of this section, the company shall at the request of the Secretary of State submit to him a short-term financial scheme.

(2) An insurance company that has submitted a scheme to the Secretary of State under subsection (1) above shall propose modifications to the scheme (or the scheme as previously modified) if the Secretary of State considers it inadequate, and shall give effect to any scheme accepted by him as adequate.

(3) Where a company is required by virtue of section 32(6) above to maintain

separate margins in respect of long term and general business, subsection (1) above shall have effect as if any reference to the margin of solvency, the United Kingdom margin of solvency or the Community margin of solvency of the company were a reference to the margin in respect of either of the two kinds of business.

34. Companies supervised in other member States.—(1) An insurance company to which this Part of this Act applies—

(*a*) whose head office is in a member State other than the United Kingdom, or
(*b*) which has in accordance with section 9(2) above made a deposit in such a member State,

shall secure that the value of the assets of the business carried on by it in the United Kingdom does not fall below the amount of the liabilities of that business, that value and amount being determined in accordance with any applicable valuation regulations.

(2) In the case of a company that carries on in the United Kingdom both long term and general business subsection (1) above shall have effect separately in relation to the assets and liabilities of the two kinds of business.

35. Form and situation of assets.—(1) Regulations may make provision for securing that, in such circumstances and to such extent as may be prescribed, the assets of an insurance company to which this Part of this Act applies are maintained in such places as may be prescribed and the nature of the assets is appropriate in relation to the currency in which the liabilities of the company are or may be required to be met.

(2) Regulations made for the purposes specified in subsection (1) above shall not have effect in relation to the assets of an insurance company whose head office is in a member State so far as their value exceeds the amount of the liabilities of the business carried on by the company in the United Kingdom, that value and amount being determined in accordance with any applicable valuation regulations.

Liabilities of unlimited amount

36. Avoidance of contracts for unlimited amounts.—A contract entered into after the coming into force of this section by an insurance company to which this Part of this Act applies shall be void if—

(*a*) it is a contract under which the company undertakes a liability the amount, or maximum amount, of which is uncertain at the time when the contract is entered into; and
(*b*) it is not a contract of insurance or a contract of a class or description exempted by regulations from the operation of this section.

Powers of intervention

37. Grounds on which powers are exercisable.—(1) The powers conferred on the Secretary of State by sections 38 to 45 below shall be exercisable in relation to any insurance company to which this Part of this Act applies and shall be exercisable in accordance with the following provisions of this section.

(2) The powers conferred by sections 38 and 41 to 45 below shall be exercisable on any of the following grounds—

(*a*) that the Secretary of State considers the exercise of the power to be desirable for protecting policy holders or potential policy holders of the company against the risk that the company may be unable to meet its liabilities or, in the case of long term business, to fulfil the reasonable expectations of policy holders or potential policy holders;
(*b*) that it appears to him—

(i) that the company has failed to satisfy an obligation to which it is or was subject by virtue of this Act or any enactment repealed by this Act or by the Insurance Companies Act 1974;

(ii) that a company of which it is a subsidiary has failed to satisfy an obligation to which it is or was subject by virtue of section 29(7) above or section 24(6) of the Insurance Companies Act 1974 or section 8(6) of the Insurance Companies Amendment Act 1973; or

(iii) that a subordinate company within the meaning of section 31 above of the company has failed to satisfy an obligation to which it is or was subject by virtue of that section or section 26 above or section 22 or 26 of the Insurance Companies Act 1974 or of section 6 or 10 of the said Act of 1973;

(*c*) that it appears to him that the company has furnished misleading or inaccurate information to the Secretary of State under or for the purposes of any provision of this Act or any enactment repealed by this Act or by the Insurance Companies Act 1974;

(*d*) that he is not satisfied that adequate arrangements are in force or will be made for the reinsurance of risks against which persons are insured by the company in the course of carrying on business, being risks of a class in the case of which he considers that such arrangements are required;

(*e*) that there exists a ground on which he would be prohibited, by section 7, 8 or 9 above, from issuing an authorisation with respect to the company if it were applied for;

(*f*) that it appears to him that there has been a substantial departure from any proposal or forecast submitted to him by the company in accordance with section 5 above;

(*g*) that the company has ceased to be authorised to effect contracts of insurance, or contracts of a particular description, in a member State where it has its head office or has in accordance with section 9(2) above made a deposit.

(3) The powers conferred on the Secretary of State by sections 39 and 40 below shall not be exercisable in relation to an insurance company except—

(*a*) where the Secretary of State has given (and not revoked) a direction in respect of the company under section 11 above or section 11 of the Insurance Companies Act 1981; or

(*b*) on the ground that it appears to the Secretary of State that the company has failed to satisfy an obligation to which it is or was subject by virtue of section 33, 34 or 35 above or section 26B, 26C or 26D of the Insurance Companies Act 1974; or

(*c*) on the ground that a submission by the company to the Secretary of State of an account or statement specifies, as the amount of any liabilities of the company, an amount appearing to the Secretary of State to have been determined otherwise than in accordance with valuation regulations or, where no such regulations are applicable, generally accepted accounting concepts, bases and policies or other generally accepted methods appropriate for insurance companies.

(4) The power conferred on the Secretary of State by subsections (2) to (4) of section 44 below shall also be exercisable on the ground that he considers the exercise of that power to be desirable in the general interests of persons who are or may become policy holders of insurance companies to which this Part of this Act applies, and references in those subsections to a company include references to any body (whether incorporated or not) which appears to the Secretary of State to be an insurance company to which this Part of this Act applies.

(5) Any power conferred on the Secretary of State by section 38, 41, 42, 44(1) or 45 below shall also be exercisable, whether or not any of the grounds specified in subsections

(2) and (4) above exists, in relation to—

(*a*) any body in respect of which the Secretary of State has issued an authorisation;
(*b*) any insurance company to which this Part of this Act applies in the case of which a person has become a controller within the meaning of section 7(4)(*c*) above,

if that power is exercised before the expiration of the period of five years beginning with the date on which the authorisation was issued or that person became such a controller, as the case may be; but no requirement imposed by virtue of this subsection shall continue in force after the expiration of the period of ten years beginning with that date.

(6) The power conferred on the Secretary of State be section 45 below shall not be exercisable except in a case in which he considers that the purpose mentioned in that section cannot be appropriately achieved by the exercise of the powers conferred by sections 38 to 44 below or by the exercise of those powers alone.

(7) The Secretary of State shall, when exercising any power conferred by sections 38 to 45 below, state the ground on which he is exercising it or, if he is exercising it by virtue of subsection (5) above, that he is so exercising it; but this subsection shall not apply where the Secretary of State has given notice under section 46 below of the proposed exercise of the power.

(8) The grounds specified in subsections (2)(*b*) to (*g*) and (4) above are without prejudice to the ground specified in subsection (2)(*a*) above.

38. Requirements about investments.—(1) The Secretary of State may require a company—

(*a*) not to make investments of a specified class or description;
(*b*) to realise, before the expiration of a specified period (or such longer period as the Secretary of State may allow), the whole or a specified proportion of investments of a specified class or description held by the company when the requirement is imposed.

(2) A requirement under this section may be framed so as to apply only to investments which are (or, if made, would be) assets representing a fund or funds maintained by the company in respect of its long term business or so as to apply only to other investments.

(3) A requirement under this section shall not apply to the assets of a company so far as their value exceeds—

(*a*) in the case of a company whose head office is in a member State other than the United Kingdom, or which has in accordance with section 9(2) above made a deposit in such a member State, the amount of the liabilities of the business carried on by the company in the United Kingdom;
(*b*) in any other case, the amount of the liabilities of the company;

that value and amount being determined in accordance with any applicable valuation regulations.

39. Maintenance of assets in the United Kingdom.—(1) The Secretary of State may require that assets of a company of a value which at any time is equal to the whole or a specified proportion of the amount of its domestic liabilities shall be maintained in the United Kingdom.

(2) The Secretary of State may direct that for the purposes of any requirement under this section assets of a specified class or description shall or shall not be treated as assets maintained in the United Kingdom.

(3) The Secretary of State may direct that for the purposes of any requirement under this section the domestic liabilities of a company, or such liabilities of any class or description, shall be taken to be the net liabilities after deducting any part of them which is reinsured.

(4) A requirement imposed under this section may be framed so as to come into effect immediately after the day on which it is imposed or so as to come into effect after the expiration of a specified period (or such longer period as the Secretary of State may allow).

(5) In this section any reference to a domestic liability is a reference to a liability of the business carried on by the company in the United Kingdom.

(6) Subject to subsection (7) below, in computing the amount of any liabilities for the purposes of this section all contingent and prospective liabilities shall be taken into account but not liabilities in respect of share capital.

(7) For the purposes of this section the value of any assets and the amount of any liabilities shall be determined in accordance with any applicable valuation regulations; and subsection (6) above shall have effect subject to any such regulations made by virtue of section 90(2) below.

40. Custody of assets.—(1) The Secretary of State may, in the case of a company on which a requirement has been imposed under section 39 above or under section 31 of the Insurance Companies Act 1974, impose an additional requirement that the whole or a specified proportion of the assets to which the requirement under that section applies shall be held by a person approved by him for the purposes of the requirement under this section as trustee for the company.

(2) Section 39(4) above shall apply also to a requirement under this section.

(3) Assets of a company held by a person as trustee for a company shall be taken to be held by him in compliance with a requirement imposed under this section if, and only if, they are assets in whose case the company has given him written notice that they are to be held by him in compliance with such a requirement or they are assets into which assets in whose case the company has given him such written notice have, by any transaction or series of transactions, been transposed by him on the instructions of the company.

(4) No assets held by a person as trustee for a company in compliance with a requirement imposed under this section shall, so long as the requirement is in force, be released except with the consent of the Secretary of State.

(5) If a mortgage or charge is created by a company at a time when there is in force a requirement imposed on the company by virtue of this section, being a mortgage or charge conferring a security on any assets which are held by a person as trustee for the company in compliance with the requirement, the mortgage or charge shall, to the extent that it confers such a security, be void against the liquidator and any creditor of the company.

41. Limitation of premium income.—(1) The Secretary of State may require a company to take all such steps as are requisite to secure that the aggregate of the premiums—

(*a*) to be received by the company in consideration of the undertaking by it during a specified period of liabilities in the course of carrying on general business or any specified part of such business; or

(*b*) to be received by it in a specified period in consideration of the undertaking by the company during that period of liabilities in the course of carrying on long term business or any specified part of such business,

shall not exceed a specified amount.

(2) A requirement under this section may apply either to the aggregate premiums to be received as mentioned in subsection (1) above or to the aggregate of those premiums after deducting any premiums payable by the company for reinsuring the liabilities in consideration of which the first-mentioned premiums are receivable.

42. Actuarial investigations.—(1) The Secretary of State may require a company which carries on long term business—

(*a*) to cause the person who for the time being is its actuary under section 19(1) above or any corresponding enactment previously in force to make an investigation into its financial condition in respect of that business, or any specified part of that business, as at a specified date;
(*b*) to cause an abstract of that person's report of the investigation to be made; and
(*c*) to prepare a statement of its long term business or of that part thereof as at that date.

(2) For the purposes of any investigation made in pursuance of a requirement under this section the value of any assets and the amount of any liabilities shall be determined in accordance with any applicable valuation regulations.

(3) The form and contents of any abstract or statement made in pursuance of a requirement under this section shall be the same as for an abstract or statement made under section 18 above and subsection (2) of that section shall apply to an investigation made in pursuance of this section as it applies to an investigation to which subsection (1)(*b*) of that section relates.

(4) Five copies of any abstract or statement made in pursuance of a requirement under this section shall be deposited by the company with the Secretary of State on or before such date as he may specify, and one of those copies shall be a copy signed by the persons required to sign copies of abstracts or statements made under the said section 18 which are deposited under section 22 above.

43. Acceleration of information required by accounting provisions.—(1) The Secretary of State may require any documents which under section 22 above are required to be deposited with him by a company within the period specified in that section to be deposited with him on or before a specified date before the end of that period, being a date not earlier than three months before the end of that period and not earlier than one month after the date on which the requirement is imposed.

(2) The Secretary of State may require any statement which under section 25 above is required to be deposited with him by a company within a period prescribed under that section to be deposited with him on or before a specified date before the end of that period.

44. Power to obtain information and require production of documents.—(1) The Secretary of State may require a company to furnish him, at specified times or intervals, with information about specified matters being, if he so requires, information verified in a specified manner.

(2) The Secretary of State may—

(*a*) require a company to produce, at such time and place as he may specify, such books or papers as he may specify; or
(*b*) authorise any person, on producing (if required so to do) evidence of his authority, to require a company to produce to him forthwith any books or papers which that person may specify.

(3) Where by virtue of subsection (2) above the Secretary of State or a person authorised by him has power to require the production of any books or papers from any company, the Secretary of State or that person shall have the like power to require production of those books or papers from any person who appears to him to be in possession of them, but where any person from whom such production is required claims a lien on books or papers produced by him, the production shall be without prejudice to the lien.

(4) Any power conferred by or by virtue of subsections (2) and (3) above to require a company or other person to produce books or papers shall include power—

(*a*) if the books or papers are produced—

(i) to take copies of them or extracts from them; and
(ii) to require that person, or any other person who is a present or past director, controller or auditor of, or is or was at any time employed by, the company in question, to provide an explanation of any of them;

(*b*) if the books or papers are not produced, to require the person who was required to produce them to state, to the best of his knowledge and belief, where they are.

(5) A statement made by a person in compliance with a requirement imposed by virtue of this section may be used in evidence against him.

(6) In this section "books or papers" includes accounts, deeds, writings and documents.

45. Residual power to impose requirements for protection of policy holders.—(1) The Secretary of State may require a company to take such action as appears to him to be appropriate for the purpose of protecting policy holders or potential policy holders of the company against the risk that the company may be unable to meet its liabilities or, in the case of long term business, to fulfil the reasonable expectations of policy holders or potential policy holders.

(2) The power conferred by this section shall not be exercised in such a way as to restrict the company's freedom to dispose of its assets except where it is exercised—

(*a*) after the Secretary of State has given a direction under section 11 above or section 11 of the Insurance Companies Act 1981; or
(*b*) on the ground that it appears to the Secretary of State that the company has failed to satisfy an obligation to which it is or was subject by virtue of sections 33, 34 or 35 above or sections 26B, 26C or 26D of the Insurance Companies Act 1974; or
(*c*) where the ground for intervention arises out of the submission by the company to the Secretary of State of an account or statement specifying, as the amount of any liabilities of the company, an amount appearing to the Secretary of State to have been determined otherwise than in accordance with valuation regulations or, where no such regulations are applicable, generally accepted accounting concepts, bases and policies or other generally accepted methods appropriate for insurance companies.

46. Notice of proposed exercise of powers on ground of unfitness of certain persons.—(1) Before exercising with respect to a company any power or powers conferred by sections 38 to 45 above on the ground that he would be prohibited from issuing an authorisation to the company because of the unfitness of a person for the position held by him (not being that of controller of the company), the Secretary of State shall serve on that person a written notice stating—

(*a*) that the Secretary of State is considering exercising a power or powers conferred by those sections and the ground on which he is considering the exercise of the power or powers; and
(*b*) that the person on whom the notice is served may, within the period of one month from the date of service of the notice, make written representations to the Secretary of State and, if that person so requests, oral representations to an officer of the Department of Trade appointed for the purpose by the Secretary of State.

(2) Unless the Secretary of State, after considering any representations made in accordance with subsection (1) above by the person served with a notice under that subsection, decides not to exercise the power or powers in relation to which the notice was served, he shall before exercising the power or powers serve on the company a written notice—

(*a*) containing the matters mentioned in paragraphs (*a*) and (*b*) of that subsection, taking references to the person there mentioned as references to the company; and

(*b*) specifying the power or powers which he proposes to exercise and, if the power or one of them is that conferred by section 45 above, specifying the manner of its proposed exercise.

(3) A notice under this section shall give particulars of the ground on which the Secretary of State is considering the exercise of the power or powers in question.

(4) Where representations are made in accordance with this section the Secretary of State shall take them into consideration before exercising the power or powers in question.

(5) A requirement imposed on a company in the exercise of any power or powers to which this section applies may be framed so as to come into effect after the expiration of a specified period (or such longer period as the Secretary of State may allow) unless before the expiration of that period the person whose fitness is in question has ceased to hold the position concerned.

47. Rescission, variation and publication of requirements.—(1) The Secretary of State may rescind a requirement imposed under sections 38 to 45 above if it appears to him that it is no longer necessary for the requirement to continue in force, and may from time to time vary any such requirement.

(2) No requirement imposed by virtue of subsection (5) of section 37 above shall be varied after the expiration of the period of five years mentioned in that subsection except in a manner which relaxes that requirement.

(3) Where a requirement is imposed under section 40 above or any such requirement is rescinded or varied the Secretary of State shall forthwith serve—

(*a*) except where paragraph (*b*) below applies, on the Registrar of Companies or on the Registrar of Companies in Northern Ireland or on both;

(*b*) if the requirement is imposed on a registered society, on the appropriate registrar as defined by section 73(1) of the Industrial and Provident Societies Act 1965 in the case of a society registered in Great Britain or on the registrar as defined by section 101(1) of the Industrial and Provident Societies Act (Northern Ireland) 1969 in the case of a society registered in Northern Ireland;

a written notice stating that fact and, in the case of a notice of the imposition of a requirement, setting out the terms of the requirement, in the case of a notice of the rescission of a requirement, identifying the requirement and, in the case of a notice of a variation of a requirement, identifying the requirement and setting out the terms of the variation.

(4) A notice served in pursuance of subsection (3) above on the Registrar of Companies or the Registrar of Companies in Northern Ireland shall be open to inspection, and a copy thereof may be procured by any person on payment of such fee as the Secretary of State or, in the case of a notice served on the Registrar of Companies in Northern Ireland, the Department of Commerce for Northern Ireland may direct; and every document purporting to be certified by the Registrar of Companies or the Registrar of Companies in Northern Ireland to be a copy of such a notice shall be deemed to be a copy of that notice and shall be received in evidence as if it were the original notice unless some variation between it and the original is proved.

(5) Section 71(1) of the said Act of 1965 (which empowers the Treasury to make regulations respecting, among other things, the inspection of documents kept by the appropriate registrar under that Act) and section 97(1) of the said Act of 1969 (which confers corresponding powers on the Department of Commerce for Northern Ireland) shall have effect as if the reference to documents so kept included a reference to notices served in pursuance of subsection (3) above on the appropriate registrar or, as the case may be, on the registrar.

47A. Security of information.—(1) No information or document relating to a body which has been obtained under section 44(2) to (4) shall, without the previous consent in writing of that body, be published or disclosed, except to a competent authority, unless the publication or disclosure is required for the purposes specified in section 449(1)(*a*) to (*e*) of the Companies Act.

(2) The competent authorities for the purposes of this section are the same as those specified in section 449 of that Act.

(3) This section does not extend to Northern Ireland.

47B. Privilege from disclosure.—(1) A requirement imposed under section 44(2) to (4) above shall not compel the production by any person of a document which he would in an action in the High Court or, in Scotland, in the Court of Session be entitled to refuse to produce on grounds of legal professional privilege or authorise the taking of possession of any such document which is in his possession.

(2) This section does not extend to Northern Ireland.

48. Power of Secretary of State to bring civil proceedings on behalf of insurance company.—(1) Section 438(1) of the Companies Act (power of Secretary of State to bring civil proceedings on behalf of body corporate) shall have effect in relation to an insurance company to which this Part of this Act applies (whether or not a body corporate) as if the reference to any information or document obtained under the provisions there mentioned included a reference to any information or document obtained under this Act or any enactment repealed by this Act or by the Insurance Companies Act 1974.

(2) The Secretary of State may bring civil proceedings in the name and on behalf of an insurance company to which this Part of this Act applies (whether or not a body corporate) under subsection (1) of section 163 of the Companies Act (Northern Ireland) 1960 and that subsection shall have effect in relation to such an insurance company as if the reference to any information or document obtained under the provisions there mentioned included a reference to any information or document obtained under this Act or any enactment repealed by this Act or by the Insurance Companies Act 1980 and any reference to the Department of Commerce for Northern Ireland were a reference to the Secretary of State.

(3) Where under a judgment given or decree pronounced in proceedings brought by virtue of section 438(1) of the Companies Act or section 163(1) of the said Act of 1960 on behalf of an insurance company a sum is recovered in respect of a loss of assets representing a fund or funds maintained by the company in respect of its long term business the court shall direct that the sum shall be treated for the purposes of this Act as assets of that fund or those funds and this Act shall have effect accordingly.

Transfers of long term business

49. Sanction of court for transfer of long term business.—(1) Where it is proposed to carry out a scheme under which the whole or part of the long term business carried on in the United Kingdom by an insurance company to which this Part of this Act applies ('the transferor company') is to be transferred to another body whether incorporated or not ('the transferee company') the transferor company or transferee company may apply to the court, by petition, for an order sanctioning the scheme.

(2) The court shall not determine an application under this section unless the petition is accompanied by a report on the terms of the scheme by an independent actuary and the court is satisfied that the requirements of subsection (3) below have been complied with.

(3) The said requirements are—

(*a*) that a notice has been published in the London, Edinburgh and Belfast Gazettes and, except where the court has otherwise directed, in two national newspapers stating that the application has been made and giving the address of the offices at which, and the period for which, copies of the documents mentioned in paragraph (*d*) below will be available as required by that paragraph;

(*b*) except where the court has otherwise directed, that a statement—

(i) setting out the terms of the scheme; and

(ii) containing a summary of the report mentioned in subsection (2) above sufficient to indicate the opinion of the actuary on the likely effects of the scheme on the long term policy holders of the companies concerned,

has been sent to each of those policy holders and to every member of those companies;

(*c*) that a copy of the petition, of the report mentioned in subsection (2) above and of any statement sent out under paragraph (*b*) above has been served on the Secretary of State and that a period of not less than twenty-one days has elapsed since the date of service;

(*d*) that copies of the petition and of the report mentioned in subsection (2) above have been open to inspection at offices in the United Kingdom of the companies concerned for a period of not less than twenty-one days beginning with the date of the first publication of a notice in accordance with paragraph (*a*) above.

(4) Each of the companies concerned shall, on payment of such fee as may be prescribed by rules of court, furnish a copy of the petition and of the report mentioned in subsection (2) above to any person who asks for one at any time before an order sanctioning the scheme is made on the petition.

(5) On any petition under this section—

(*a*) the Secretary of State, and

(*b*) any person (including any employee of the transferor company or the transferee company) who alleges that he would be adversely affected by the carrying out of the scheme,

shall be entitled to be heard.

(6) The court shall not make an order sanctioning the scheme unless it is satisfied that the transferee company is, or immediately after the making of the order will be, authorised under section 3 or 4 above to carry on long term business of the class or classes to be transferred under the scheme.

(7) No such transfer as is mentioned in subsection (1) above shall be carried out unless the scheme relating to the transfer has been sanctioned by the court in accordance with this section; and no order shall be made under section 425 or 427 of the Companies Act or section 197 or section 199 of the Companies Act (Northern Ireland) 1960 (compromises and arrangements between a company and its creditors or members) in respect of so much of any compromise or arrangement as involves any such transfer.

(8) In this section "the court" means the High Court of Justice in England except that it means—

(*a*) the Court of Session if the transferor company and the transferee company are both registered or both have their head offices in Scotland; and

(*b*) the High Court of Justice in Northern Ireland if the transferor company and the transferee company are both registered or both have their head offices in Northern Ireland; and

(*c*) either the High Court of Justice in England or the Court of Session if either the transferor company or the transferee company is registered or has its head office in Scotland; and

(*d*) either the High Court of Justice in England or the High Court of Justice in Northern Ireland if either the transferor company or the transferee company is registered or has its head office in Northern Ireland; and (*e*) either the Court of Session or the High Court of Justice in Northern Ireland if the transferor company or the transferee company is registered or has its head office in Scotland and the other such company is registered or has its head office in Northern Ireland.

50. Provisions supplementary to section 49.—(1) Where the court makes an order under section 49 above sanctioning a scheme the court may, either by that order or by any subsequent order, make provision for all or any of the following matters—

(*a*) the transfer to the transferee company of the whole or any part of the undertaking and of the property or liabilities of the transfer company;
(*b*) the allotting or appropriation by the transferee company of any shares, debentures, policies or other like interests in that company which under the scheme are to be allotted or appropriated by that company to or for any person;
(*c*) the continuation by or against the transferee company of any legal proceedings pending by or against the transferor company;
(*d*) the dissolution, without winding up, of the transferor company;
(*e*) such incidental, consequential and supplementary matters as are necessary to secure that the scheme shall be fully and effectively carried out.

(2) Where any such order provides for the transfer of property or liabilities, that property shall, by virtue of the order, be transferred to and vest in, and those liabilities shall, by virtue of the order, be transferred to and become the liabilities of, the transferee company, and in the case of any property, if the order so directs, freed from any mortgage or charge which is by virtue of the scheme to cease to have effect.

(3) For the purposes of any provision requiring the delivery of an instrument of transfer as a condition for the registration of a transfer of any property (including in particular section 183(1) of the Companies Act, section 56(4) of the Finance Act 1946, section 75 of the Companies Act (Northern Ireland) 1960 and section 27(4) of the Finance (No. 2) Act (Northern Ireland) 1946) an order which by virtue of this section operates to transfer any property shall be treated as an instrument of transfer.

(4) Where a scheme is sanctioned by an order of the court under section 49 above the transferee company shall, within ten days from the date on which the order is made or such longer period as the Secretary of State may allow, deposit two office copies of the order with the Secretary of State.

(5) In this section "property" includes property, rights and powers of every description, "liabilities" includes duties and "shares" and "debentures" have the same meaning as in the Companies Act 1948 or the Companies Act (Northern Ireland) 1960.

Transfers of general business

51. Approval of transfers of general business.—(1) Where it is proposed to execute an instrument by which an insurance company to which this Part of this Act applies ('the transferor') is to transfer to another body ('the transferee') all its rights and obligations under such general policies, or general policies of such descriptions, as may be specified in the instrument, the transferor may apply to the Secretary of State for his approval of the transfer.

(2) The Secretary of State shall not determine an application made under subsection (1) above unless he is satisfied that—

(*a*) a notice approved by him for the purpose has been published in the London, Edinburgh and Belfast Gazettes and, if he thinks fit, in two national newspapers which have been so approved; and
(*b*) except in so far as he has otherwise directed, a copy of the notice has been sent to every affected policy holder and every other person who claims an interest in a policy included in the transfer and has given written notice of his claim to the transferor; and

(*c*) copies of a statement setting out particulars of the transfer and approved by him for the purpose have been available for inspection at one or more places in the United Kingdom for a period of not less than thirty days beginning with the date of the first publication of the notice in accordance with paragraph (*a*) above.

(3) The notice referred to in subsection (2) above shall include a statement that written representations concerning the transfer may be sent to the Secretary of State before a specified day, which shall not be earlier than sixty days after the day of the first publication of the notice in accordance with paragraph (*a*) above; and the Secretary of State shall not determine the application until after considering any representations made to him before the specified day.

(4) The Secretary of State shall not approve a transfer on application under subsection (1) above unless he is satisfied that—

(*a*) every policy included in the transfer evidences a contract which—

(i) was entered into before the date of the application; and
(ii) imposes on the insurer obligations the performance of which will constitute the carrying on of insurance business in the United Kingdom; and

(*b*) the transferee is, or immediately after the approval will be, authorised under section 3 or 4 above to carry on in the United Kingdom insurance business of the appropriate class or classes;

and unless in his opinion the transferee's financial resources and the other circumstances of the case justify the giving of his approval.

(5) On determining an application made under subsection (1) above, the Secretary of State shall—

(*a*) publish a notice of his decision in the London, Edinburgh and Belfast Gazettes and in such other manner as he may think fit, and
(*b*) send a copy of that notice to the transferor, the transferee and every person who made representations in accordance with the notice referred to in subsection (2) above;

and if he refuses the application he shall inform the transferor and the transferee in writing of the reasons for his refusal.

(6) Any notice or other document authorised or required to be given or served under this section or section 52 below may, without prejudice to any other method of service, be served by post; and a letter containing the notice or other document shall be deemed to be properly addressed if it is addressed to that person at his last known residence or last known place of business in the United Kingdom.

(7) In this section "general policy" means a policy evidencing a contract the effecting of which constituted the carrying on of general business; and for the purposes of this section a policy holder is an "affected policy holder" in relation to a proposed transfer if—

(*a*) his policy is included in the transfer, or
(*b*) his policy is with the transferor and the Secretary of State has certified, after consulting the transferor, that in the opinion of the Secretary of State the policy holder's rights and obligations under the policy will or may be materially affected by the transfer.

52. Effect of approval under section 51.—(1) Subject to subsection (2) below, an instrument giving effect to a transfer approved by the Secretary of State under section 51 above shall be effectual in law—

(*a*) to transfer to the transferee all the transferor's rights and obligations under the policies included in the instrument, and (*b*) if the instrument so provides, to secure the continuation by or against the transferee of any legal proceedings by or against the transferor which relate to those rights or obligations,

notwithstanding the absence of any agreements or consents which would otherwise be necessary for it to be effectual in law for those purposes.

(2) Except in so far as the Secretary of State may otherwise direct, a policy holder whose policy is included in such an instrument shall not be bound by it unless he has been given written notice of its execution by the transferor or the transferee.

Winding up

53. Winding up of insurance companies under Companies Acts.—The court may order the winding up, in accordance with the Companies Act or, as the case may be, the Companies Act (Northern Ireland) 1960, of an insurance company to which this Part of this Act applies and the provisions of the Companies Act or, as the case may be, that Act of 1960 shall apply accordingly subject to the modification that the company may be ordered to be wound up on the petition of ten or more policy holders owning policies of an aggregate value of not less than £10,000.

Such a petition shall not be presented except by leave of the court, and leave shall not be granted until a prima facie case has been established to the satisfaction of the court and until security for costs for such amount as the court may think reasonable has been given.

54. Winding up on petition of Secretary of State.—(1) The Secretary of State may present a petition for the winding up, in accordance with the Companies Act, of an insurance company to which this Part of this Act applies, being a company which may be wound up by the court under the provisions of that Act, on the ground—

(*a*) that the company is unable to pay its debts within the meaning of section 518 or sections 667 to 669 of that Act;
(*b*) that the company has failed to satisfy an obligation to which it is or was subject by virtue of this Act or any enactment repealed by this Act or by the Insurance Companies Act 1974; or
(*c*) that the company, being under the obligation imposed by sections 221 and 222 of the Companies Act with respect to the keeping of accounting records, has failed to satisfy that obligation or to produce records kept in satisfaction of that obligation and that the Secretary of State is unable to ascertain its financial position.

(2) The Secretary of State may present a petition for the winding up, in accordance with the Companies Act (Northern Ireland) 1960, of an insurance company to which this Part of this Act applies, being a company which may be wound up by the court under the provisions of that Act, on the ground—

(*a*) that the company is unable to pay its debts within the meaning of sections 210 and 211 or section 349 of that Act;
(*b*) that the company has failed to satisfy an obligation to which it is or was subject by virtue of this Act or any enactment repealed by this Act or by the Insurance Companies Act 1980; or
(*c*) that the company, being under an obligation imposed by Article 25 of the Companies (Northern Ireland) Order 1978 with respect to the keeping of accounting records, has failed to satisfy that obligation or to produce records kept in satisfaction of that obligation and that the Secretary of State is unable to ascertain its financial position;

and subsection (3) of section 163 of the said Act of 1960 shall have effect in relation to such an insurance company as if any reference to the Department of Commerce for Northern Ireland were a reference to the Secretary of State.

(3) In any proceedings on a petition to wind up an insurance company presented by the Secretary of State under subsection (1) or (2) above, evidence that the company was insolvent—

(*a*) at the close of the period to which—

(i) the accounts and balance sheet of the company last deposited under section 22 above; or

(ii) any statement of the company last deposited under section 25 above, relate; or

(*b*) at any date or time specified in a requirement under section 42 or 44 above,

shall be evidence that the company continues to be unable to pay its debts, unless the contrary is proved.

(4) If, in the case of an insurance company to which this Part of this Act applies, being a company which may be wound up by the court under the provisions of the Companies Act or, as the case may be, the Companies Act (Northern Ireland) 1960, it appears to the Secretary of State that it is expedient in the public interest that the company should be wound up, he may, unless the company is already being wound up by the court, present a petition for it to be so wound up if the court thinks it just and equitable for it to be so wound up.

(5) Where a petition for the winding up of an insurance company to which this Part of this Act applies is presented by a person other than the Secretary of State, a copy of the petition shall be served on him and he shall be entitled to be heard on the petition.

55. Winding up of insurance companies with long term business.—(1) No insurance company to which this Part of this Act applies which is an unincorporated body and carries on long term business shall be made the subject of bankruptcy proceedings or, in Scotland, sequestration proceedings.

(2) No insurance company to which this Part of this Act applies which carries on long term business shall be wound up voluntarily.

(3) Section 29(1) above shall not have effect in relation to the winding up of a company to which section 28(1) above applies but, subject to subsection (4) below and to rules made by virtue of section 59(2) below, in any such winding up—

(*a*) the assets representing the fund or funds maintained by the company in respect of its long term business shall be available only for meeting the liabilities of the company attributable to that business;

(*b*) the other assets of the company shall be available only for meeting the liabilities of the company attributable to its other business.

(4) Where the value of the assets mentioned in either paragraph of subsection (3) above exceeds the amount of the liabilities mentioned in that paragraph the restriction imposed by that subsection shall not apply to so much of those assets as represents the excess.

(5) In relation to the assets falling within either paragraph of subsection (3) above the creditors mentioned in subsections (1) to (3) of section 540 of the Companies Act or, as the case may be, paragraphs (1) and (2) of Article 73 of the Companies (Northern Ireland) Order 1978 shall be only those who are creditors in respect of liabilities falling within that paragraph; and any general meetings of creditors summoned for the purposes of that section shall accordingly be separate general meetings of the creditors in respect of the liabilities falling within each paragraph.

(6) Where under section 631 of the Companies Act or section 299(1) of the Companies Act (Northern Ireland) 1960 (defalcations of directors etc. disclosed in course of winding up) a court orders any money or property to be repaid or restored to a company or any

sum to be contributed to its assets then, if and so far as the wrongful act which is the reason for the making of the order related to assets representing a fund or funds maintained by the company in respect of its long term business, the court shall include in the order a direction that the money, property or contribution shall be treated for the purposes of this Act as assets of that fund or those funds and this Act shall have effect accordingly.

56. Continuation of long term business of insurance companies in liquidation.—(1) This section has effect in relation to the winding up of an insurance company to which this Part of this Act applies, being a company carrying on long term business.

(2) The liquidator shall, unless the court otherwise orders, carry on the long term business of the company with a view to its being transferred as a going concern to another insurance company, whether an existing company or a company formed for that purpose; and, in carrying on that business as aforesaid, the liquidator may agree to the variation of any contracts of insurance in existence when the winding up order is made but shall not effect any new contracts of insurance.

(3) If the liquidator is satisfied that the interests of the creditors in respect of liabilities of the company attributable to its long term business require the appointment of a special manager of the company's long term business, he may apply to the court, and the court may on such application appoint a special manager of that business to act during such time as the court may direct, with such powers, including any of the powers of a receiver or manager, as may be entrusted to him by the court.

(4) Section 556(3) of the Companies Act or, in the case of a special manager appointed in proceedings in Northern Ireland, subsections (2) and (3) of section 236A of the Companies Act (Northern Ireland) 1960 (special manager to give security and receive remuneration) shall apply to a special manager appointed under subsection (3) above as they apply to a special manager appointed under section 556 of the Companies Act or, as the case may be, section 236A of the said Act of 1960.

(5) The court may, if it thinks fit and subject to such conditions (if any) as it may determine, reduce the amount of the contracts made by the company in the course of carrying on its long term business.

(6) The court may, on the application of the liquidator, a special manager appointed under subsection (3) above or the Secretary of State, appoint an independent actuary to investigate the long term business of the company and to report to the liquidator, the special manager or the Secretary of State, as the case may be, on the desirability or otherwise of that business being continued and on any reduction in the contracts made in the course of carrying on that business that may be necessary for its successful continuation.

(7) Notwithstanding section 539(1) of the Companies Act or, as the case may be, section 227(1) of the said Act of 1960 (which requires a liquidator to obtain the sanction of the court or committee of inspection for the bringing of legal proceedings in the name of and on behalf of the company) the liquidator may without any such sanction make an application in the name of and on behalf of the company under section 49 above.

(8) In this section 'the court' means the court having jurisdiction to wind up the company.

57. Subsidiary companies.—(1) Where the insurance business or any part of the insurance business of an insurance company has been transferred to an insurance company to which this Part of this Act applies under an arrangement in pursuance of which the first-mentioned company (in this section called 'the subsidiary company') or the creditors thereof has or have claims against the company to which the transfer was made (in this section called 'the principal company'), then, if the principal company is being wound up by or under the supervision of the court, the court shall, subject to the provisions of this section, order the subsidiary company to be wound up in conjunction with the principal company, and may by the same or any subsequent order appoint the same person to be liquidator for the two companies, and make provision for such other matters as may seem to the court necessary, with a view to the companies being wound up as if they were one company.

(2) The commencement of the winding up of the principal company shall, save as otherwise ordered by the court, be the commencement of the winding up of the subsidiary company.

(3) In adjusting the rights and liabilities of the members of the several companies between themselves, the court shall have regard to the constitution of the companies, and to the arrangements entered into between the companies, in the same manner as the court has regard to the rights and liabilities of different classes of contributories in the case of the winding up of a single company, or as near thereto as circumstances admit.

(4) Where any company alleged to be subsidiary is not in process of being wound up at the same time as the principal company to which it is subsidiary, the court shall not direct the subsidiary company to be wound up unless, after hearing all objections (if any) that may be urged by or on behalf of the company against its being wound up, the court is of the opinion that the company is subsidiary to the principal company, and that the winding up of the company in conjunction with the principal company is just and equitable.

(5) An application may be made in relation to the winding up of any subsidiary company in conjunction with a principal company by any creditor of, or person interested in, the principal or subsidiary company.

(6) Where a company stands in the relation of a principal company to one company, and in the relation of a subsidiary company to some other company, or where there are several companies standing in the relation of subsidiary companies to one principal company, the court may deal with any number of such companies together or in separate groups, as it thinks most expedient, upon the principles laid down in this section.

58. Reduction of contracts as alternative to winding up.—In the case of an insurance company which has been proved to be unable to pay its debts, the court may, if it thinks fit, reduce the amount of the contracts of the company on such terms and subject to such conditions as the court thinks just, in place of making a winding up order.

59. Winding up rules.—(1) Rules may be made under section 663 of the Companies Act or section 317 of the Companies Act (Northern Ireland) 1960 (general rules about winding up) for determining the amount of the liabilities of an insurance company to policy holders of any class or description for the purpose of proof in a winding up and generally for carrying into effect the provisions of this Part of this Act with respect to the winding up of insurance companies.

(2) Without prejudice to the generality of subsection (1) above, rules under section 663 of the Companies Act or, as the case may be, section 317 of the said Act of 1960 may make provision for all or any of the following matters—

(*a*) the identification of the assets and liabilities falling within either paragraph of subsection (3) of section 55 above;

(*b*) the apportionment between the assets falling within paragraphs (*a*) and (*b*) of that subsection of the costs, charges and expenses of the winding up and of any debts of the company having priority under section 614 of, and Schedule 19, to the Companies Act, or, as the case may be, section 287 of the said Act of 1960;

(*c*) the determination of the amount of liabilities of any description falling within either paragraph of that subsection for the purpose of establishing whether or not there is any such excess in respect of that paragraph as is mentioned in subsection (4) of section 55 above;

(*d*) the application of assets within paragraph (*a*) of the said subsection (3) for meeting the liabilities within that paragraph;

(*e*) the application of assets representing any such excess as is mentioned in the said subsection (4).

Changes of director, controller or manager etc

60. Approval of proposed managing director or chief executive of insurance company.—(1) No insurance company to which this Part of this Act applies shall appoint a person as managing director or chief executive of the company unless—

(*a*) the company has served on the Secretary of State a written notice stating that it proposes to appoint that person to that position and containing such particulars as may be prescribed; and

(*b*) either the Secretary of State has, before the expiration of the period of three months beginning with the date of service of that notice, notified the company in writing that there is no objection to that person being appointed to that position or that period has elapsed without the Secretary of State having served on the company a written notice of objection.

(2) A notice served by a company under subsection (1)(*a*) above shall contain a statement signed by the person proposed to be appointed that it is served with his knowledge and consent.

(3) The Secretary of State may serve a notice of objection under subsection (1) above on the ground that it appears to him that the person proposed to be appointed is not a fit and proper person to be appointed to the position in question, but before serving such a notice the Secretary of State shall serve on the company and on that person a preliminary written notice stating—

(*a*) that the Secretary of State is considering the service on the company of a notice of objection on that ground; and

(*b*) that the company and that person may, within the period of one month from the date of service of the preliminary notice, make written representations to the Secretary of State and, if the company or that person so requests, oral representations to an officer of the Department of Trade appointed for the purpose by the Secretary of State.

(4) The Secretary of State shall not be obliged to disclose to the company or to the person proposed to be appointed any particulars of the ground on which he is considering the service on the company of a notice of objection.

(5) Where representations are made in accordance with this section the Secretary of State shall take them into consideration before serving the notice of objection.

61. Approval of person proposing to become controller of insurance company where section 60 does not apply.—(1) No person shall become a controller of an insurance company to which this Part of this Act applies otherwise than by virtue of an appointment in relation to which section 60 above has effect unless—

(*a*) he has served on the Secretary of State a written notice stating that he intends to become a controller of that company and containing such particulars as may be prescribed; and

(*b*) either the Secretary of State has, before the expiration of the period of three months beginning with the date of service of that notice, notified him in writing that there is no objection to his becoming a controller of the company or that period has elapsed without the Secretary of State having served on him a written notice of objection.

(2) The Secretary of State may serve a notice of objection under subsection (1) above on the ground that it appears to him that the person concerned is not a fit and proper person to be a controller of the company, but before serving such a notice the Secretary of State shall serve on that person a preliminary written notice stating—

(*a*) that the Secretary of State is considering the service on him of a notice of objection on that ground; and
(*b*) that that person may, within the period of one month from the date of service of the preliminary notice, make written representations to the Secretary of State and, if that person so requests, oral representations to an officer of the Department of Trade appointed for the purpose by the Secretary of State.

(3) The Secretary of State shall not be obliged to disclose to any person any particulars of the ground on which he is considering the service on him of a notice of objection.

(4) Where representations are made in accordance with this section the Secretary of State shall take them into consideration before serving the notice of objection.

62. Duty to notify change of director, controller or manager.—(1) A person who becomes or ceases to be a controller of an insurance company to which this Part of this Act applies shall, before the expiration of the period of seven days beginning with the day next following that on which he does so, notify the insurance company in writing of that fact and of such other matters as may be prescribed; and a person who becomes a director or manager of any such insurance company shall, before the expiration of the period of seven days beginning with the day next following that on which he does so, notify the insurance company in writing of such matters as may be prescribed.

(2) An insurance company to which this Part of this Act applies shall give written notice to the Secretary of State of the fact that any person has become or ceased to be a director, controller or manager of the company and of any matter of which any such person is required to notify the company under subsection (1) above; and that notice shall be given before the expiration of the period of fourteen days beginning with the day next following that on which that fact or matter comes to the company's knowledge.

63. Change of manager etc of company from outside United Kingdom.—(1) In relation to an insurance company whose head office is in a member State other than the United Kingdom, excluding a company whose business in the United Kingdom is restricted to reinsurance,—

(*a*) section 60 above shall have effect as if the references to a managing director or chief executive were references to a principal United Kingdom executive;
(*b*) section 61 above shall not apply;
(*c*) section 62 above shall have effect as if references to a director or manager were references to a principal United Kingdom executive, an employee within section 8(4)(*c*) above or an authorised United Kingdom representative.

(2) In relation to any other insurance company whose head office is outside the United Kingdom—

(*a*) section 60 above shall have effect as if the references to a chief executive included references to a principal United Kingdom executive; and
(*b*) section 62 above shall have effect as if the references to a director included references to a principal United Kingdom executive and to an authorised United Kingdom representative.

(3) In this section—

'principal United Kingdom executive' means an officer or employee within section 8(4)(*b*) or 9(6) above; and 'authorised United Kingdom representative' means a representative fulfilling the requirements of section 10 above or an individual representative of the kind described in subsection (5) of that section.

64. Duty to notify change of main agent.—(1) An insurance company to which this Part of this Act applies shall give written notice to the Secretary of State of the fact that any person has become or ceased to be a main agent of the company and, if a main agent is a body corporate or a firm, of the fact that any person has become or ceased to be director of the body or partner of the firm.

(2) A notice under this section shall be given before the expiration of the period of fourteen days beginning with the day next following that on which the change comes to the knowledge of the insurance company.

Miscellaneous

65. Documents deposited with Secretary of State.—(1) The Secretary of State shall deposit with the Registrar of Companies one copy of—

(*a*) any document deposited with the Secretary of State under section 22 above, including any document obtained under subsection (5) of that section;
(*b*) any document deposited with him under section 42(4) or 50(4) above.

(2) Subject to subsection (3) below, any document deposited under this section or section 25(5) or 26(3) above with the Registrar of Companies shall be open to inspection and copies thereof may be procured by any person on payment of such fees as the Secretary of State may direct.

(3) Subsection (2) above shall not apply to any document if it is a copy of a document in respect of which a dispensation has been granted under section 23(2) above.

(4) Every document deposited with the Secretary of State under this Part of this Act and certified by the Registrar of Companies to be a document so deposited shall be deemed to be a document so deposited; and every document purporting to be certified by the Registrar of Companies to be a copy of a document so deposited shall be deemed to be a copy of that document and shall be received in evidence as if it were the original document unless some variation between it and the original is proved.

66. Documents deposited in Northern Ireland.—Any insurance company which is required to prepare and deliver accounts under Article 3 or 11 of the Companies (Northern Ireland) Order 1978 shall deposit with the Registrar of Companies in Northern Ireland one copy of—

(*a*) any document deposited with the Secretary of State under section 22(1), 22(2), 22(6), 42(4) or 50(4) above;
(*b*) any document supplied by the company to the Secretary of State under section 22(5) above.

67. Power to treat certain business as or as not being ordinary long-term insurance business.—(1) The Secretary of State may, on the application or with the consent of an insurance company to which this Part of this Act applies, by order direct that for the purposes of the application to the company of all or any of the provisions to which this section applies—

(*a*) business of a kind specified in the order, not being ordinary long-term insurance business, shall be treated as being such business; or
(*b*) ordinary long-term insurance business of a kind so specified shall be treated as not being such business.

(2) An order under subsection (1)(*b*) above may direct that the business specified in the order shall be treated as falling within a specified class of business.

(3) An order under this section may be subject to conditions and may be varied or revoked at any time by the Secretary of State.

(4) The provisions to which this section applies are sections 17 to 20, 25, 28 to 31, 42, 55, 56 and 59(2) of this Act and section 21 of the Policyholders Protection Act 1975 and Schedule 3 to that Act.

68. Power to modify Part II in relation to particular companies.—(1) The Secretary of State may, on the application or with the consent of an insurance company to which this Part of this Act applies, by order direct that all or any of the provisions to which this section applies shall not apply to the company or shall apply to it with such modifications as may be specified in the order.

(2) An order under this section may be subject to conditions.

(3) An order under this section may be revoked at any time by the Secretary of State; and the Secretary of State may at any time vary any such order on the application or with the consent of the company to which it applies.

(4) The provisions to which this section applies are sections 16 to 22, 23(1) and 25 to 36 of this Act, the provisions of regulations made for the purposes of any of those sections and the provisions of any valuation regulations.

(5) In relation to section 31 above, subsection (1) above shall have effect as if the reference to an insurance company to which this Part of this Act applies included a reference to any subordinate company within the meaning of that section of any such insurance company.

69. Power to alter insurance company's financial year.—The Secretary of State may extend or shorten, for the purposes of this Part of this Act, the duration of any financial year of an insurance company to which this Part of this Act applies.

70. Service of notices.—(1) Any notice which is by this Part of this Act required to be sent to any policy holder may be addressed and sent to the person to whom notices respecting that policy are usually sent, and any notice so addressed and sent shall be deemed to be notice to the holder of the policy.

(2) Where any person claiming to be interested in a policy has given to the company notice in writing of his interest, any notice which is by this Part of this Act required to be sent to policy holders shall also be sent to that person at the address specified by him in his notice.

(3) Any notice to be served on any person by the Secretary of State under section 46, 60 or 61 above may be served by post, and a letter containing that notice shall be deemed to be properly addressed if it is addressed to that person at his last known residence or last known place of business in the United Kingdom.

71. Offences under Part II.—(1) Any person who—

(*a*) makes default in complying with sections 28 to 30 or 62(1) above; or

(*b*) in purported compliance with a requirement imposed under section 44 above furnishes information which he knows to be false in a material particular or recklessly furnishes information which is false in a material particular; or

(*c*) causes or permits to be included in—

(i) any document copies of which are, by section 22 of this Act, required to be deposited with the Secretary of State;

(ii) any notice, statement or certificate served or furnished under or by virtue of section 19(2) or 26(1) above;

(iii) any document deposited with the Secretary of State under section 25(4) or 42(4) above;
(iv) any statement sent out under section 49(3)(*b*) above or made available under section 51(2)(*c*) above,

a statement which he knows to be false in a material particular or recklessly causes or permits to be so included any statement which is false in a material particular,

shall be guilty of an offence.

(2) Any person guilty of an offence under subsection (1) above shall be liable—

(*a*) on conviction on indictment, to imprisonment for a term not exceeding two years, or to a fine, or to both;
(*b*) on summary conviction—

(i) in England and Wales . . ., to a fine not exceeding £1,000 or, if it is greater, the prescribed sum within the meaning of section 32 of the Magistrates' Courts Act 1980;
(ii) in Scotland, to a fine not exceeding £1,000 or, if it is greater, the prescribed sum within the meaning of section 289B of the Criminal Procedure (Scotland) Act 1975;
(iii) in Northern Ireland, to a fine not exceeding £2,000 or, if it is greater, the prescribed sum within the meaning of Article 4 of the Fines and Penalties (Northern Ireland) Order 1984.

(3) Subject to the following provisions of this section—

(*a*) any insurance company which makes default in complying with, or with a requirement imposed under, any provision of this Part of this Act, being a default for which no penalty is provided by the foregoing provisions of this section; and
(*b*) any other person who makes default in complying with, or with a requirement imposed under, section 26, 29(7), 31, 38, 39, 40, 41, 44, 45, 49(4), 50(4) or 61(1) above,

shall be guilty of an offence and liable, on summary conviction in England and Wales and Scotland to a fine not exceeding level 5 on the standard scale and, on summary conviction in Northern Ireland, to a fine not exceeding £400.

(4) Where a person continues to make default in complying with—

(*a*) section 22(1) or (2), 24(1), 25(4) or 42(4) above; or
(*b*) a requirement imposed under section 43 or 44(1) above, after being convicted of that default he shall be guilty of a further offence and liable on summary conviction to a fine not exceeding £40 for each day on which the default so continues.

(4A) A person who publishes or discloses any information or document in contravention of section 47A above shall be guilty of an offence under section 449 of the Companies Act and liable accordingly.

(5) A person shall not be guilty of an offence by reason of his default in complying with section 61 or 62(1) above if he proves that he did not know that the acts or circumstances by virtue of which he became or ceased to be a controller of the body in question were such as to have that effect.

(6) Where a person is charged with an offence in respect of his default in complying with a requirement imposed under section 44(2) or (3) above to produce any books or papers it shall be a defence to prove that they were not in his possession or control and that it was not reasonably practicable for him to comply with the requirement.

(7) An insurance company shall not be guilty of an offence by reason of its defaults in complying with section 16 or 51 (other than subsection (2)(*c*) above.)

PART III

CONDUCT OF INSURANCE BUSINESS

72. Insurance advertisements.—(1) Regulations may be made as to the form and contents of insurance advertisements.

(2) Regulations under this section may make different provision in relation to insurance advertisements of different classes or descriptions.

(3) Subject to subsection (4) below, any person who issues an insurance advertisement which contravenes regulations under this section shall be guilty of an offence.

(4) A person who in the ordinary course of his business issues an advertisement to the order of another person, being an advertisement the issue of which by that other person constitutes an offence under subsection (3) above, shall not himself be guilty of the offence if he proves that the matters contained in the advertisement were not (wholly or in part) devised or selected by him or by any person under his direction or control.

(5) In this section 'insurance advertisement' means an advertisement inviting persons to enter into or to offer to enter into contracts of insurance, and an advertisement which contains information calculated to lead directly or indirectly to persons entering into or offering to enter into such contracts shall be treated as an advertisement inviting them to do so.

(6) In this section 'advertisement' includes every form of advertising, whether in a publication or by the display of notices or by means of circulars or other documents or by an exhibition of photographs or cinematograph films or by way of sound broadcasting or television or by inclusion in a cable programme service, and references to the issue of an advertisement shall be construed accordingly.

(7) For the purposes of this section an advertisement issued by any person on behalf of or to the order of another person shall be treated as an advertisement issued by that other person; and for the purposes of any proceedings under this section an advertisement inviting persons to enter into or to offer to enter into contracts with a person specified in the advertisement shall be presumed, unless the contrary is proved, to have been issued by that person.

73. Misleading statements, etc inducing persons to enter into contracts of insurance.—Any person who, by any statement, promise or forecast which he knows to be misleading, false or deceptive, or by any dishonest concealment of material facts, or by the reckless making (dishonestly or otherwise) of any statement, promise or forecast which is misleading, false or deceptive, induces or attempts to induce another person to enter into or offer to enter into any contract of insurance with an insurance company shall be guilty of an offence.

74. Intermediaries in insurance transactions.—(1) Regulations may be made for requiring any person who—

(*a*) invites another person to make an offer or proposal or to take any other step with a view to entering into a contract of insurance with an insurance company; and

(*b*) is connected with that company provided in the regulations,

to give the prescribed information with respect to his connection with the company to the person to whom the invitation is issued.

(2) Regulations may be made for requiring any person who, in the course of carrying on any business or profession, issues any such invitation as is mentioned in subsection (1)(*a*) above in relation to an insurance company which is not an authorised insurer in respect of the contract in question to inform the person to whom the invitation is issued that the company is not such an insurer as aforesaid.

In this subsection 'authorised insurer', in relation to a contract of any description, means a person entitled to carry on in the United Kingdom insurance business of a class comprising the effecting of contracts of that description.

(3) Any person who contravenes regulations under this section shall be guilty of an offence.

75. Statutory notice by insurer in relation to long term policy.—(1) Subject to subsection (5) below, no insurance company to which Part II of this Act applies and no member of Lloyd's shall enter into a contract the effecting of which constitutes the carrying on of ordinary long-term insurance business unless that company or member ('the insurer') either—

(*a*) has sent by post to the other party to the contract a statutory notice in relation to that contract; or

(*b*) does so at the time when the contract is entered into.

(2) For the purposes of this section a statutory notice is a notice which—

(*a*) contains such matters (and no others) and is in such form as may be prescribed for the purposes of this section and complies with such requirements (whether as to type, size, colour or disposition of lettering, quality or colour of paper, or otherwise) as may be prescribed for securing that the notice is easily legible; and

(*b*) has annexed to it a form of notice of cancellation of the prescribed description for use under section 76 below.

(3) The Secretary of State may, on the application of any insurer, alter the requirements of any regulations made for the purposes of subsection (2)(*a*) above so as to adapt those requirement to the circumstances of that insurer or to any particular kind of contract proposed to be entered into by that insurer.

(4) Any insurer who contravenes this section shall be guilty of an offence but, without prejudice to section 76(2) below, no contract shall be invalidated by reason of the fact that the insurer has contravened this section in relation to that contract.

(5) Subsection (1) of this section does not apply to any contract the effecting of which by the insurer constitutes the carrying on of industrial assurance business; and regulations may exempt from that subsection contracts of any other class or description.

(6) In sections 76 and 77 below 'insurer' and 'statutory notice' have the same meaning as in this section.

76. Right to withdraw from transaction in respect of long term policy.—(1) A person who has received a statutory notice from an insurer in relation to any contract to which section 75(1) above applies may before the expiration of—

(*a*) the tenth day after that on which he received the notice, or

(*b*) the earliest day on which he knows both that the contract has been entered into and that the first or only premium has been paid,

whichever is the later, serve a notice of cancellation on the insurer.

(2) A person to whom an insurer ought to have, but has not, sent a statutory notice in relation to any such contract as aforesaid may serve a notice of cancellation on the insurer; but if the insurer sends him a statutory notice in relation to that contract before he has served a notice of cancellation under this subsection, then, without prejudice to his right to serve a notice of cancellation under subsection (1) above, his right to do so under this subsection shall cease.

(3) A notice of cancellation may, but need not, be in the form annexed to the statutory notice and shall have effect if, however expressed, it indicates the intention of the person serving it to withdraw from the transaction in relation to which the statutory notice was or ought to have been sent.

(4) Where a person serves a notice of cancellation, then—

(*a*) if at the time when the notice is served the contract has been entered into, the notice shall operate so as to rescind the contract;
(*b*) in any other case, the service of the notice shall operate as a withdrawal of any offer to enter into the contract which is contained in, or implied by, any proposal made to the insurer by the person serving the notice of cancellation and as notice to the insurer that any such offer is withdrawn.

(5) Where a notice of cancellation operates to rescind a contract or as the withdrawal of an offer to enter into a contract—

(*a*) any sum which the person serving the notice has paid in connection with the contract (whether by way of premium or otherwise and whether to the insurer or to a person who is the agent of the insurer for the purpose of receiving that sum) shall be recoverable from the insurer by the person serving the notice;
(*b*) any sum which the insurer has paid under the contract shall be recoverable by him from the person serving the notice.

(6) Any sum recoverable under subsection (5) above shall be recoverable as a simple contract debt in any court of competent jurisdiction.

77. Service of notice of cancellation.—(1) For the purposes of section 76 above a notice of cancellation—

(*a*) shall be deemed to be served on the insurer if it is sent by post addressed to any person specified in the statutory notice as a person to whom a notice of cancellation may be sent, and is addressed to that person at an address so specified; and
(*b*) where paragraph (*a*) above applies, shall be deemed to be served on the insurer at the time when it is posted.

(2) Subsection (1) above shall have effect without prejudice to the service of a notice of cancellation (whether by post or otherwise) in any way in which the notice could be served apart from that subsection, whether the notice is served on the insurer or on a person who is the agent of the insurer for the purpose of receiving such a notice.

(3) A notice of cancellation which is sent by post to a person at his proper address, otherwise than in accordance with subsection (1) above, shall be deemed to be served on him at the time when it is posted.

(4) So much of section 7 of the Interpretation Act 1978 as relates to the time when service is deemed to have been effected shall not apply to a notice of cancellation.

78. Linked long term policies.—(1) Regulations may be made, as respects the matters specified in subsection (2) below, in relation to contracts the effecting of which constitutes the carrying on of ordinary long-term insurance business and which—

(*a*) are entered into by insurance companies to which Part II of this Act applies or by members of Lloyd's; and
(*b*) are contracts under which the benefits payable to the policy holder are wholly or partly to be determined by reference to the value of, or the income from, property of any description (whether or not specified in the contract) or by reference to fluctuations in, or in an index of, the value of property of any description (whether or not so specified).

(2) Regulations under this section may make provision for—

(*a*) restricting the descriptions of property or the indices of the value of property by reference to which benefits under the contracts may be determined;
(*b*) regulating the manner in which and the frequency with which property of any

description is to be valued for the purpose of determining such benefits and the times at which reference is to be made for that purpose to any index of the value of property;

(*c*) requiring insurers under the contracts to appoint valuers for carrying out valuations of property of any description for the purpose of determining such benefits (being valuers who comply with the prescribed requirements as to qualifications and independence from the insurer) and to furnish the Secretary of State with the prescribed information in relation to such appointments;

(*d*) requiring insurers under the contracts to furnish, in such manner and at such times or intervals as may be prescribed, such information relating to the value of the benefits under the contracts as may be prescribed, whether by sending notices to policy holders, depositing statements with the Secretary of State or the Registrar of Companies or the Registrar of Companies in Northern Ireland or with both such registrars, publication in the press or otherwise;

(*e*) requiring insurers under the contracts to furnish to the Secretary of State, in such manner and at such times or intervals as may be prescribed, such information certified in such manner as may be prescribed with respect to so much of their business as is concerned with the contracts or with any class or description of the contracts, and enabling the Secretary of State to publish such information in such ways as he thinks appropriate.

(3) Regulations made for the purposes of subsection (2)(*d*) above may, in relation to notices required to be sent to policy holders, impose requirements (whether as to type, size, colour or disposition of lettering, quality or colour of paper, or otherwise) for securing that such notices are easily legible.

(4) The Secretary of State may, on the application of any insurer, alter the requirements of any regulations under this section so as to adapt those requirements to the circumstances of that insurer or to any particular kind of contract entered into or proposed to be entered into by that insurer.

(5) Regulations under this section may, to such extent as may be specified therein, apply in relation to contracts entered into before the coming into operation of the regulations, including contracts entered into before the passing of this Act.

(6) Regulations under this section shall apply in relation to any contract the effecting of which by the insurer constitutes the carrying on of industrial assurance business or to any contract entered into by an insurance company to which Part II of this Act applies by reason only that the policy holder is eligible to participate in any established surplus as defined in section 30(4) above.

79. Scope of Prevention of Fraud (Investments) Acts.—The agreements and arrangements mentioned in section 13(1) of the Prevention of Fraud (Investments) Act 1958 and section 12(1) of the Prevention of Fraud (Investments) Act (Northern Ireland) 1940 (misleading statements etc. inducing persons to invest money) and in the definition of 'dealing in securities' in section 26(1) of that Act of 1958 and section 22(1) of that Act of 1940 shall not include contracts of insurance.

80. Capital redemption business.—Where an insurance company to which Part II of this Act applies carries on capital redemption business in the case of which the premiums in return for which a contract is effected are payable at intervals of less than six months, the company shall not give the holder of any policy issued after 2nd December 1909 any advantage dependent on lot or chance.

This section shall not be construed as in any way prejudicing any question as to the application to any such transaction, whether in respect of a policy issued before, on or after that date, of the law relating to lotteries.

81. Penalties and offences under Part III.—(1) Any person guilty of an offence under section 72, 73 or 74 above shall be liable—

(*a*) on conviction on indictment, to imprisonment for a term not exceeding two years or to a fine, or to both;

(*b*) on summary conviction—

(i) in England and Wales and Northern Ireland, to a fine not exceeding £1,000 or, if it is greater, the prescribed sum within the meaning of section 32 of the Magistrates' Courts Act 1980;

(ii) in Scotland, to a fine not exceeding £1,000 or, if it is greater, the prescribed sum within the meaning of section 289B of the Criminal Procedure (Scotland) Act 1975;

(iii) in Northern Ireland, to a fine not exceeding £2,000 or, if it is greater, the prescribed sum within the meaning of Article 4 of the Fines and Penalties (Northern Ireland) Order 1984.

(2) Any person who makes default in complying with, or with a requirement imposed under, any other provision of this Part of this Act shall be guilty of an offence and liable on summary conviction in England and Wales and Scotland, to a fine not exceeding level 5 on the standard scale and, on summary conviction in Northern Ireland, to a fine not exceeding £400.

PART IV

Special Classes of Insurers

82. Industrial assurance business.—(1) In its application to industrial assurance business this Act shall have effect subject to the modifications specified in this section.

(2) Where an insurance company carries on any industrial assurance business, the company shall deposit with the Industrial Assurance Commissioner and the Industrial Assurance Commissioner for Northern Ireland a copy of any document which relates to industrial assurance business and which is deposited with the Secretary of State under section 22(1), (2) and (6) above or which is supplied by the company to the Secretary of State under section 22(5) above.

(3) The provisions of sections 22 and 23(1) above shall have effect in relation to any document mentioned in subsection (2) above as if references in those provisions to the Secretary of State included references to the Commissioner and the Commissioner for Northern Ireland.

(4) Where any document required to be deposited by a company under subsection (4) of section 42 above relates to industrial assurance business the company shall also, within the time required under that subsection, deposit one copy of that document with the Commissioner and the Commissioner for Northern Ireland, and section 71(4) above shall have effect in relation to this subsection as it has effect in relation to that subsection.

(5) Where any business proposed to be transferred as mentioned in section 49 above is or includes industrial assurance business that section and section 50(4) above shall have effect as if references to the Secretary of State included references to the Commissioner and the Commissioner for Northern Ireland.

(6) Where any apportionment is made between the industrial assurance business and any other business carried on by the company in respect of management expenses, income from investments, gains or losses on the disposal of investments, appreciation or depreciation in the value of investments, or taxation, the auditor shall include in his report a special report as to the propriety or otherwise of the apportionment; and a copy of every report of the auditor shall be furnished to the Commissioner and the Commissioner for Northern Ireland.

(7) The provisions of this Act relating to industrial assurance business shall have effect notwithstanding anything in the memorandum or articles of association or rules or special Act of any insurance company carrying on such business; but nothing in this Act

shall affect the liability of the industrial assurance fund or of the ordinary long-term insurance fund, in the case of a company established in Great Britain before 1 January 1924 or in Northern Ireland before 1 January 1925, to the prejudice of persons interested in contracts entered into by the company before that date.

(8) The Commissioner shall include in his annual report under section 44 of the Industrial Assurance Act 1923 a report on his proceedings under this Act, and that section shall have effect accordingly.

83. Requirements to be complied with by Lloyd's underwriters.—(1) The requirements referred to in section 15(4) above are as follows.

(2) Every underwriter shall, in accordance with the provisions of a trust deed approved by the Secretary of State, carry to a trust fund all premiums received by him or on his behalf in respect of any insurance business.

(3) Premiums received in respect of long term business shall in no case be carried to the same trust fund under this section as premiums received in respect of general business, but the trust deed may provide for carrying the premiums received in respect of all or any classes of long term business and all or any classes of general business either to a common fund or to any number of separate funds.

(4) The accounts of every underwriter shall be audited annually by an accountant approved by the Committee of Lloyd's and the auditor shall furnish a certificate in the prescribed form to the Committee and the Secretary of State.

(5) The said certificate shall in particular state whether in the opinion of the auditor the value of the assets available to meet the underwriter's liabilities in respect of insurance business is correctly shown in the accounts, and whether or not that value is sufficient to meet the liabilities calculated—

(*a*) in the case of liabilities in respect of long term business, by an actuary; and
(*b*) in the case of other liabilities, by the auditor on a basis approved by the Secretary of State.

(6) Where any liabilities of an underwriter are calculated by an actuary under subsection (5) above, he shall furnish a certificate of the amount thereof to the Committee of Lloyd's and to the Secretary of State, and shall state in his certificate on what basis the calculation is made; and a copy of his certificate shall be annexed to the auditor's certificate.

(7) The underwriter shall, when required by the Committee of Lloyd's, furnish to them such information as they may require for the purpose of preparing the statement of business which is to be deposited with the Secretary of State under section 86 below.

84. Lloyd's underwriters – financial resources.—(1) Subject to such modifications as may be prescribed and to any determination made by the Secretary of State in accordance with regulations, section 32, 33 and 35 above shall apply to the members of Lloyd's taken together as they apply to an insurance company to which Part II of this Act applies and whose head office is in the United Kingdom.

(2) The powers conferred on the Secretary of State by sections 38 to 41, 44 and 45 above shall be exercisable in relation to the members of Lloyd's if there is a breach of an obligation imposed by virtue of subsection (1) above.

85. Lloyd's underwriters – transfer of business.—(1) Sections 49 to 52 above shall apply in relation to transfers to and from members of Lloyd's if, and only if, the conditions specified in subsection (2) below are satisfied.

(2) The conditions referred to in subsection (1) above are—

(*a*) that the transfer is not one where both the transferor and the transferee are members of Lloyd's;
(*b*) that the Committee of Lloyd's have by resolution authorised one person to act

in connection with the transfer for the members concerned as transferor or transferee;

(*c*) that the copy of the resolution has been given to the Secretary of State.

(3) Where sections 49 and 50 or sections 51 and 52 above apply in relation to a transfer to or from members of Lloyd's they shall apply as if—

(*a*) references to insurance companies to which Part II of this Act applies, or to persons authorised under section 3 or 4 of this Act, included references to members of Lloyd's; and

(*b*) anything done in connection with the transfer by the person authorised in accordance with subsection (2)(*b*) above had been done by the members for whom he acted.

86. Statement of business by Committee of Lloyd's.—(1) The Committee of Lloyd's shall deposit every year with the Secretary of State a statement in the prescribed form summarising the extent and character of the insurance business done by the members of Lloyd's in the twelve months to which the statement relates.

(2) Regulations made for the purposes of this section may require the statement to deal separately with such classes or descriptions of business as may be specified in the regulations.

87. Companies established outside the United Kingdom.—(1) The provisions specified in subsection (2) below, if, apart from this section they would not so apply, shall apply in relation to an insurance company incorporated outside the United Kingdom which carries on insurance business within Great Britain or, as the case may be, Northern Ireland as they apply in relation to oversea companies within the meaning of the Companies Act or, as the case may be, companies to which Part X of the Companies Act (Northern Ireland) 1960 applies.

(2) The provisions referred to in subsection (1) above are—

(*a*) sections 691 to 693, 695 to 698, 700 to 703 of the Companies Act

(*b*) . . . [*repealed*].

(*c*) sections 356, 358 to 364 and 373 of the Companies Act (Northern Ireland) 1960, and

(*d*) Articles 11 to 13 of the Companies (Northern Ireland) Order 1978.

88. Unregistered companies.—(1) Every insurance company to which Part II of this Act applies, being a company which is not registered under the Companies Act 1948, under the Companies Act (Northern Ireland) 1960 or under the former Companies Acts—

(*a*) if it has not incorporated in its deed of settlement section 10 of the Companies Clauses Consolidation Act 1845, shall keep a shareholders address book in accordance with the provisions of that section and shall, on the application of any shareholder or policy holder of the company, furnish to him a copy of the book on payment of a sum not exceeding 2½p for every hundred words required to be copied;

(*b*) shall cause a sufficient number of copies of its deed of settlement to be printed and shall, on the application of any shareholder or policy holder of the company, furnish to him one of those copies on payment of a sum not exceeding 5p.

(2) Any insurance company which makes default in complying with this section shall be guilty of an offence and liable on summary conviction in England and Wales and Scotland, to a fine not exceeding level 5 on the standard scale and, on summary conviction in Northern Ireland, to a fine not exceeding £400.

89. Insurance companies formed before 1967 in contravention of section 434 of the Companies Act 1948.—(1) Section 716 of the Companies Act (which in certain cases forbids the formation otherwise than under that Act of a company, association or partnership consisting of more than twenty persons) shall be deemed not to have invalidated the formation of any insurance company which immediately before 3 November 1966 was carrying on in Great Britain insurance business of any class relevant for the purposes of Part I of the Insurance Companies Act 1974 and was carrying on business of that class on 25 July 1973.

(2) In subsection (1) above the reference to the said section 716 includes a reference to any corresponding enactment previously in force.

PART V

Supplementary Provisions

Valuation regulations

90. Power to make valuation regulations.—(1) Regulations may be made with respect to the determination of the value of assets and the amount of liabilities in any case in which the value or amount is required by any provision of this Act to be determined in accordance with valuation regulations.

(2) Without prejudice to the generality of subsection (1) above, regulations under this section may provide that, for any specified purpose, assets or liabilities of any specified class or description shall be left out of account or shall be taken into account only to a specified extent.

(3) Regulations under this section may make different provision in relation to different cases or circumstances and for the purposes of different enactments.

Criminal proceedings

91. Criminal liability of directors.—(1) Where an offence under this Act committed by a body corporate is proved to have been committed with the consent or connivance of, or to be attributable to any neglect on the part of, any director, chief executive, manager, secretary or other similar officer of the body corporate or any person who was purporting to act in any such capacity, he, as well as the body corporate, shall be guilty of that offence and liable to be proceeded against and punished accordingly.

(2) For the purposes of this section a person shall be deemed to be a director of a body corporate if he is a person in accordance with whose directions or instructions the directors of the body corporate or any of them act.

92. Criminal proceedings against unincorporated bodies.—(1) Proceedings for an offence alleged to have been committed under this Act by an unincorporated body shall be brought in the name of that body (and not in that of any of its members) and, for the purposes of any such proceedings, any rules of court relating to the service of documents shall have effect as if that body were a corporation.

(2) A fine imposed on an unincorporated body on its conviction of an offence under this Act shall be paid out of the funds of that body.

(3) In a case in which an unincorporated body is charged with an offence under this Act—

(*a*) in England or Wales, section 33 of the Criminal Justice Act 1925 and Schedule 3 to the Magistrates' Courts Act 1980 (procedure on charge of offence against a corporation);

(*b*) in Northern Ireland, section 18 of the Criminal Justice Act (Northern Ireland) 1945 and Schedule 4 to the Magistrates' Courts (Northern Ireland) Order 1981 (procedure on charge of offence against a corporation) shall have effect in like manner as they have effect in the case of a corporation so charged.

(4) In relation to any proceedings on indictment in Scotland for an offence alleged to have been committed under this Act by an unincorporated body, section 74 of the Criminal Procedure (Scotland) Act 1975 (proceedings on indictment against bodies corporate) shall have effect as if that body were a body corporate.

93. Restriction on institution of prosecutions.—Proceedings in respect of an offence under this Act shall not be instituted—

(*a*) in England or Wales, except by or with the consent of the Secretary of State, the Industrial Assurance Commissioner or the Director of Public Prosecutions,

(*b*) in Northern Ireland, except by or with the consent of the Secretary of State, the Department of Commerce for Northern Ireland or the Director of Public Prosecutions for Northern Ireland.

94. Summary proceedings.—(1) Summary proceedings for any offence under this Act may (without prejudice to any jurisdiction exercisable apart from this subsection) be taken against a body corporate at any place at which the body has a place of business, and against any other person at any place at which he is for the time being.

(2) Notwithstanding anything in section 127 of the Magistrates' Courts Act 1980, an information relating to an offence under this Act which is triable by a magistrates' court in England and Wales may be so tried if it is laid at any time within three years after the commission of the offence and within twelve months after the date on which evidence sufficient in the opinion of the Director of Public Prosecutions, the Secretary of State or the Industrial Assurance Commissioner, as the case may be, to justify the proceedings comes to his knowledge.

(3) Summary proceedings in Scotland for an offence under this Act shall not be commenced after the expiration of three years from the commission of the offence.

(4) Subject to the limitation in subsection (3) above and notwithstanding anything in section 331 of the Criminal Procedure (Scotland) Act 1975, the proceedings referred to in that subsection may be commenced at any time within twelve months after the date on which evidence sufficient in the opinion of the Lord Advocate to justify the proceedings comes to his knowledge, or where such evidence was reported to him by the Secretary of State or the Industrial Assurance Commissioner, within twelve months after the date on which it came to the knowledge of the Secretary of State or Commissioner.

(5) Subsection (3) of section 331 of the said Act of 1975 shall apply for the purposes of subsections (3) and (4) above as it applies for the purposes of that section.

(6) Notwithstanding anything in Article 19(1) of the Magistrates' Courts (Northern Ireland) Order 1981, a complaint relating to an offence under this Act which is triable by a court of summary jurisdiction in Northern Ireland may be so tried if it is made at any time within three years after the commission of the offence and within twelve months after the date on which evidence sufficient, in the opinion of the Director of Public Prosecutions for Northern Ireland, the Secretary of State or the Department of Commerce for Northern Ireland, as the case may be, to justify the proceedings comes to his or that Department's knowledge.

(7) For the purposes of this section a certificate of the Director of Public Prosecutions, the Lord Advocate, the Director of Public Prosecutions for Northern Ireland, the Secretary of State, the Department of Commerce for Northern Ireland or the Industrial Assurance Commissioner, as the case may be, as to the date on which such evidence as aforesaid came to his, or that Department's, knowledge shall be conclusive evidence.

94A. Fees.—(1) When documents are deposited under section 22(1) above the company concerned shall pay to the Secretary of State such fee as may be prescribed.

(2) In the case of a company for which a fee is prescribed, documents shall not be taken to have been deposited under section 22(1) until the company has paid the fee.

(3) When a statement is deposited under section 86(1) above the Council of Lloyd's shall pay to the Secretary of State such fee as may be prescribed.

(4) In making regulations for the purposes of subsections (1) and (3) above the Secretary of State shall have regard to the object of securing (so far as practicable) that the amount of the fees payable in any relevant period by insurance companies and the Council of Lloyd's is equal to the cost incurred, or likely to be incurred, in the period by the Secretary of State in exercising relevant functions.

(5) This section does not apply where documents are, or a statement is, deposited before 1 April 1986, and in subsection (4) above "relevant period" means the period of twelve months beginning with 1 April 1986 and each successive period of twelve months beginning with 1 April.

(6) In subsection (4) above "relevant functions" means such functions of the Secretary of State in relation to insurance companies and the members of Lloyd's as may be prescribed.

(7) Sums received by the Secretary of State under this section shall be paid into the Consolidated Fund.

Interpretation

95. Insurance business.—For the purposes of this Act "insurance business" includes—

(*a*) the effecting and carrying out, by a person not carrying on a banking business, of contracts for fidelity bonds, performance bonds, administration bonds, bail bonds or customs bonds or similar contracts of guarantee, being contracts effected by way of business (and not merely incidentally to some other business carried on by the person effecting them) in return for the payment of one or more premiums;

(*b*) the effecting and carrying out of tontines;

(*c*) the effecting and carrying out, by a body (not being a body carrying on a banking business) that carries on business which is insurance business apart from this paragraph, of—

(i) capital redemption contracts;

(ii) contracts to manager the investments of pension funds (other than funds solely for the benefit of its own officers or employees and their dependants or, in the case of a company, partly for the benefit of officers or employees and their dependants of its subsidiary or holding company or a subsidiary of its holding company);

(*d*) the effecting and carrying out of contracts to pay annuities on human life.

96. General interpretation.—(1) In this Act, unless the context otherwise requires—

"actuary" means an actuary possessing the prescribed qualifications;

"annuities on human life" does not include superannuation allowances and annuities payable out of any fund applicable solely to the relief and maintenance of persons engaged or who have been engaged in any particular profession, trade or employment, or of the dependants of such persons;

"body corporate" does not include a corporation sole or a Scottish firm but includes a body incorporated outside the United Kingdom;

"chief executive" has the meaning given in section 7 above;

"Companies Act" means the Companies Act 1985;

"contract of insurance" includes any contract the effecting of which constitutes the carrying on of insurance business by virtue of section 95 above;

"controller" has the meaning given in section 7 above;

"court" means the High Court of Justice in England or, in the case of an insurance company registered or having its head office in Scotland, the Court of Session or, in the case of an insurance company registered or having its head office in Northern Ireland, the High Court of Justice in Northern Ireland;

"deed of settlement", in relation to an insurance company, includes any instrument constituting the company;

"director" includes any person occupying the position of director by whatever name called;

"enactment" includes an enactment of the Parliament of Northern Ireland and a Measure of the Northern Ireland Assembly;

"financial year" means, subject to section 69 above, each period of twelve months at the end of which the balance of the accounts of the insurance company is struck or, if no such balance is struck, the calendar year;

"former Companies Acts" means the Companies Act 1929 or the Companies Act (Northern Ireland) 1932 and any enactment repealed by that Act of 1929 or, as the case may be, that Act of 1932 or by the Companies (Consolidation) Act 1908 and the Companies Acts 1948 to 1983;

"general business' has the meaning given in section 1 above;

"holding company" shall be construed in accordance with section 736 of the Companies Act or section 148 of the Companies Act (Northern Ireland) 1960;

"industrial assurance business' has the meaning given in section 1(2) of the Industrial Assurance Act 1923 or Articles 2(2) and 3(1) of the Industrial Assurance (Northern Ireland) Order 1979;

"insolvent" means in relation to an insurance company at any relevant date, that if proceedings had been taken for the winding up of the company the court could, in accordance with the provisions of sections 517 and 518 or section 666 of the Companies Act or, as the case may be, sections 210 and 211 or section 349 of the Companies Act (Northern Ireland) 1960, hold or have held that the company was at that date unable to pay its debts;

"insurance company" means a person or body of persons (whether incorporated or not) carrying on insurance business;

"life policy" means any instrument by which the payment of money is assured on death (except death by accident only) or the happening of any contingency dependent on human life, or any instrument evidencing a contract which is subject to payment of premiums for a term dependent on human life;

"long term business' has the meaning given in section 1 above;

"long term policy holder" means a policy holder in respect of a policy the effecting of which by the insurer constituted the carrying on of long term business;

"main agent" has the meaning given in section 7 above;

"manager", except in section 56, has the meaning given in section 7 above;

"margin of solvency", "United Kingdom margin of solvency" and "Community margin of solvency" shall be construed in accordance with section 32 above;

"mortgage", in relation to Scotland, means a heritable security within the meaning of section 9(8) of the Conveyancing and Feudal Reform (Scotland) Act 1970;

"ordinary long-term insurance business" means long term business that is not industrial assurance business;

"policy"—

(*a*) in relation to ordinary long-term insurance business and industrial assurance business, includes an instrument evidencing a contract to pay an annuity upon human life;

(*b*) in relation to insurance business of any other class includes any policy under which there is for the time being an existing liability already accrued or under which a liability may accrue; and (*c*) in relation to capital redemption business, includes any policy, bond, certificate, receipt or other instrument evidencing the contract with the company;

"policy holder" means the person who for the time being is the legal holder of the policy for securing the contract with the insurance company or, in relation to capital redemption business, means the person who for the time being is the legal holder of the policy, bond, certificate, receipt or other instrument evidencing the contract with the company, and—

(*a*) in relation to such ordinary long-term insurance business or industrial assurance business as consists in the granting of annuities upon human life, includes an annuitant; and

(*b*) in relation to insurance business of any kind other than such as is mentioned in the foregoing paragraph or capital redemption business, includes a person to whom, under a policy, a sum is due or a periodic payment is payable;

"prescribed" means prescribed by regulations under this Act;

"registered society" means a society registered or deemed to be registered under the Industrial and Provident Societies Act 1965 or the Industrial and Provident Societies Act (Northern Ireland) 1969;

"registrar of companies" has the same meaning as in the Companies Act 1948 and "registrar of companies in Northern Ireland" means the Registrar of Companies within the meaning of section 399(1) of the Companies Act (Northern Ireland) 1960;

"subsidiary", except in section 57, shall be construed in accordance with section 736 of the Companies Act or section 148 of the Companies Act (Northern Ireland) 1960;

"supervisory authority", in relation to a member State other than the United Kingdom, means the authority responsible in that State for supervising insurance companies;

"underwriter" includes any person named in a policy or other contract of insurance as liable to pay or contribute towards the payment of the sum secured by the policy or contract;

"valuation regulations" means regulations under section 90 above;

"vessel" includes hovercraft.

(2) References in this Act to a fund or funds maintained in respect of long term business are references to a fund or funds maintained under section 28(1)(*b*) above and in sections 48(3) and 55(6) above include references to a fund or funds maintained under section 3(1) of the Insurance Companies Act 1958 or section 14(1) of the Insurance Companies Act (Northern Ireland) 1968.

(3) A person shall not be deemed to be within the meaning of any provision of this Act a person in accordance with whose directions or instructions the directors of a company or other body corporate or any of them are accustomed to act by reason only that the directors of the company or body act on advice given by him in a professional capacity.

(4) Any reference in this Act to an enactment of the Parliament of Northern Ireland or a Measure of the Northern Ireland Assembly shall include a reference to any enactment re-enacting it with or without modifications.

Supplementary

97. Regulations and orders.—(1) The Secretary of State may make regulations under this Act for any purpose for which regulations are authorised or required to be made thereunder.

(2) Regulations under this Act may make different provision for cases of different descriptions.

(3) Any power conferred by this Act to make regulations shall be exercisable by statutory instrument.

(4) Any statutory instrument containing regulations under this Act shall be subject to annulment in pursuance of a resolution of either House of Parliament.

98. Annual report by Secretary of State.—The Secretary of State shall cause a general annual report of matters within this Act to be laid before Parliament.

99. Savings, transitionals, consequential amendments and repeals.—(1) The saving and transitional provisions specified in Schedule 4 to this Act shall have effect.

(2) The enactments mentioned in Schedule 5 to this Act shall have effect subject to the amendments there specified, being amendments consequential on the provisions of this Act.

(3) The enactments mentioned in Schedule 6 to this Act are hereby repealed to the extent specified in the third column of that Schedule.

100. Short title, commencement and extent.—(1) This Act may be cited as the Insurance Companies Act 1982.

(2) Subject to Schedule 4 to this Act, this Act shall come into force at the expiration of the period of three months beginning with the date on which it is passed.

(3) This Act except sections 47A, 47B and 71(4A) extends to Northern Ireland.

SCHEDULES

SCHEDULE 1

Section 1

Classes of Long Term Business

Number	Description	Nature of business
I	Life and annuity.	Effecting and carrying out contracts of insurance on human life or contracts to pay annuities on human life, but excluding (in each case) contracts within Class III below.
II	Marriage and birth.	Effecting and carrying out contracts of insurance to provide a sum on marriage or on the birth of a child, being contracts expressed to be in effect for a period of more than one year.
III	Linked long term.	Effecting and carrying out contracts of insurance on human life or contracts to pay annuities on human life where the benefits are wholly or partly to be determined by reference to the value of, or the income from, property of any description (whether or not specified in the contracts) or by reference to fluctuations in, or in an index of, the value of property of any description (whether or not so specified).
IV	Permanent health.	Effecting and carrying out contracts of insurance providing specified benefits against risks of persons becoming incapacitated in consequence of sustaining injury as a result of an accident or of accident of a specified class or of sickness or infirmity, being contracts that—

Number	Description	Nature of business
		(*a*) are expressed to be in effect for a period of not less than five years, or until the normal retirement age for the persons concerned, or without limit of time, and (*b*) either are not expressed to be terminable by the insurer, or are expressed to be so terminable only in special circumstances mentioned in the contract.
V	Tontines.	Effecting and carrying out tontines.
VI	Capital redemption.	Effecting and carrying out capital redemption contracts.
VII	Pension fund management.	Effecting and carrying out— (*a*) contracts to manage the investments of pension funds, or (*b*) contracts of the kind mentioned in paragraph (*a*) above that are combined with contracts of insurance covering either conservation of capital or payment of a minimum interest.

SCHEDULE 2

Sections 1, 3

GENERAL BUSINESS

PART I

CLASSES

Number	Description	Nature of business
1	Accident.	Effecting and carrying out contracts of insurance providing fixed pecuniary benefits or benefits in the nature of indemnity (or a combination of both) against risks of the person insured or, in the case of a contract made by virtue of section 140, 140A or 140B of the Local Government Act 1972, a person for whose benefit the contract is made— (*a*) sustaining injury as the result of an accident or of an accident of a specified class, or (*b*) dying as the result of an accident or of an accident of a specified class, or (*c*) becoming incapacitated in consequence of disease or of disease of a specified class, inclusive of contracts relating to industrial injury and occupational disease but exclusive of contracts falling within class 2 below or within class IV in Schedule 1 to this Act (permanent health).

Number	Description	Nature of business
2	Sickness.	Effecting and carrying out contracts of insurance providing fixed pecuniary benefits or benefits in the nature of indemnity (or a combination of the two) against risks of loss to the persons insured attributable to sickness or infirmity, but exclusive of contracts falling within class IV in Schedule 1 to this Act.
3	Land vehicles.	Effecting and carrying out contracts of insurance against loss of or damage to vehicles used on land, including motor vehicles but excluding railway rolling stock.
4	Railway rolling stock.	Effecting and carrying out contracts of insurance against loss of or damage to railway rolling stock.
5	Aircraft.	Effecting and carrying out contracts of insurance upon aircraft or upon the machinery, tackle, furniture or equipment of aircraft.
6	Ships.	Effecting and carrying out contracts of insurance upon vessels used on the sea or on inland water, or upon the machinery, tackle, furniture or equipment of such vessels.
7	Goods in transit.	Effecting and carrying out contracts of insurance against loss of or damage to merchandise, baggage and all other goods in transit, irrespective of the form of transport.
8	Fire and natural forces.	Effecting and carrying out contracts of insurance against loss of or damage to property (other than property to which classes 3 to 7 above relate) due to fire, explosion, storm, natural forces other than storm, nuclear energy or land subsidence.
9	Damage to property.	Effecting and carrying out contracts of insurance against loss of or damage to property (other than property to which classes 3 to 7 above relate) due to hail or frost or to any event (such as theft) other than those mentioned in class 8 above.
10	Motor vehicle liability.	Effecting and carrying out contracts of insurance against damage arising out of or in connection with the use of motor vehicles on land, including third-party risks and carrier's liability.
11	Aircraft liability.	Effecting and carrying out contracts of insurance against damage arising out of or in connection with the use of aircraft, including third-party risks and carrier's liability.
12	Liability for ships.	Effecting and carrying out contracts of insurance against damage arising out of or in connection with the use of vessels on the sea or on inland water, including third-party risks and carrier's liability.

Number	Description	Nature of business
13	General liability.	Effecting and carrying out contracts of insurance against risks of the persons insured incurring liabilities to third parties, the risks in question not being risks to which class 10, 11 or 12 above relates.
14	Credit.	Effecting and carrying out contracts of insurance against risks of loss to the persons insured arising from the insolvency of debtors of theirs or from the failure (otherwise than through insolvency) of debtors of theirs to pay their debts when due.
15	Suretyship.	Effecting and carrying out— (*a*) contracts of insurance against risks of loss to the persons insured arising from their having to perform contracts of guarantee entered into by them; (*b*) contracts for fidelity bonds, performance bonds, administration bonds, bail bonds or customs bonds or similar contracts of guarantee.
16	Miscellaneous financial loss.	Effecting and carrying out contracts of insurance against any of the following risks, namely— (*a*) risks of loss to the persons insured attributable to interruptions of the carrying on of business carried on by them or to reduction of the scope of business so carried on; (*b*) risks of loss to the persons insured attributable to their incurring unforeseen expense; (*c*) risks neither falling within paragraph (*a*) or (*b*) above nor being of a kind such that the carrying on of the business of effecting and carrying out contracts of insurance against them constitutes the carrying on of insurance business of some other class.
17	Legal expenses.	Effecting and carrying out contracts of insurance against risks of loss to the persons insured attributable to their incurring legal expenses (including costs of litigation).

PART II

GROUPS OF CLASSES

Number	Description	Composition
1	Accident and health.	Classes 1 and 2.
2	Motor.	Class 1 (to the extent that the relevant risks are risks of the person insured sustaining injury, or dying, as the result of travelling as a passenger) and classes 3, 7 and 10.
3	Marine and transport.	Class 1 (to the said extent) and classes 4, 6, 7 and 12.
4	Aviation.	Class 1 (to the said extent) and classes 5, 7 and 11.
5	Fire and other damage to property.	Classes 8 and 9.
6	Liability.	Classes 10, 11, 12 and 13.
7	Credit and suretyship.	Classes 14 and 15.
8	General.	All classes.

SCHEDULE 3

Section 7

DETERMINATION OF PREMIUM LIMIT

1. Subject to the following provisions of this Schedule, the premium limit for the purposes of section 7(6) above is the aggregate of the accounts of gross premiums shown in the annual accounts relating to the business of the applicant in the United Kingdom last deposited under section 22 above as receivable in respect of general business in the financial year to which the accounts relate.

2. If the accounts so deposited relate to a financial year which is not a period of 12 months, the aggregate of the amounts of gross premiums shown in the accounts as receivable in that financial year shall be divided by the number of months in that financial year and multiplied by twelve.

3. If no accounts have been deposited under section 22 above the aggregate amount of gross premiums shall be the amount or, if more than one amount, the lower or lowest amount, shown in respect of gross premiums relating to the business of the applicant in the United Kingdom in the financial forecast last submitted by the applicant in accordance with regulations made for the purposes of section 5(1)(*a*) above.

SCHEDULE 4

Section 99(1)

SAVING AND TRANSITIONAL PROVISIONS

Saving for requirements, directions and powers under the Companies Act 1967

1. The repeal by the Insurance Companies Amendment Act 1973 of sections 65, 68 and 80 and subsection (1)(*f*) of section 109 of the Companies Act 1967 shall not affect—

(*a*) any requirement or direction imposed or given under any of those sections before 25th July 1973;

(*b*) the giving of a direction under the said section 68 in any case in which a notice has been served under subsection (3) of that section before that date; or (*c*) the exercise by an officer of any powers under the said section 109 in a case in which he has been authorised before that date to exercise them;

and the said Act of 1967 shall have effect in relation to any such requirement, direction or powers as if the said Act of 1973, the Insurance Companies Act 1974 and this Act had not been passed.

Periodic actuarial investigations under section 18 above in relation to any period of twelve months beginning before 1st October 1982

2. In relation to any period of twelve months beginning before 1 October 1982, section 18 of this Act shall have effect as if—

(*a*) for subsection (1)(*a*) there were substituted—
"(*a*) shall, once in every three years or at such shorter intervals as may be prescribed by the deed of settlement of the company or by its regulations or byelaws, cause an investigation to be made into its financial condition in respect of that business, including a valuation of its liabilities in respect thereof, by the person who for the time being is its actuary under section 19(1) below or any corresponding enactment previously in force; and";
(*b*) subsection (2) were omitted.

Adjustments of established surplus for purposes of section 30(1) above

3. For the purposes of section 30(1) of this Act, where an established surplus corresponds partly but not wholly with a previously established surplus which was the latest to be established before 1 January 1982—

(*a*) an adjustment shall be made to that previously established surplus so as to make it as nearly as may be comparable with the first-mentioned surplus, and
(*b*) the relevant minimum shall be determined on the basis of that adjustment and an analogous adjustment of the allocation from that previously established surplus.

Margins of solvency

4. The requirements of sections 32 and 33 of this Act (or of regulations made for the purposes of those sections) shall not apply until 15 March 1984 in relation to long term business if the company concerned—

(*a*) was carrying on long term business in the United Kingdom immediately before 1 January 1982, and
(*b*) has not after that date obtained an authorisation under the Insurance Companies Act 1981 for a class of long term business for which on 1 January 1982 it was not authorised under that Act, and
(*c*) does not after the commencement of this Act obtain an authorisation under this Act for a class of long term business for which on 1 January 1982 it was not authorised under the Insurance Companies Act 1981.

5. So long as paragraph 4 above applies to a company and a class of long term business carried on by it, then, in relation to that company and that business, the grounds for withdrawal of authorisation set out in section 11(2) of this Act shall be deemed to include the grounds set out in section 28(1)(*a*) and (2) of the Insurance Companies Act 1974 as in force immediately before 1 January 1982.

Postponement of coming into force of section 36 above

6. If no regulations under section 27 of the Insurance Companies Act 1974 have come into operation before the expiration of the period mentioned in section 100(2) above

section 36 of this Act shall not take effect until the first regulations under the said section 27 or 36 come into operation.

Saving for schemes of operation submitted under Insurance Companies (Authorisation and Accounts: General Business) Regulations

7. For the purposes of section 37(2)(*f*) of this Act, a scheme of operations submitted pursuant to regulation 5 of the Insurance Companies (Authorisation and Accounts: General Business) Regulations 1978 shall be regarded as a proposal or forecast submitted in accordance with section 5 of this Act.

Saving for requirements under section 29 of the Insurance Companies Act 1974

8. Where a requirement under section 29 of the Insurance Companies Act 1974 was in force immediately before 1 January 1982—

(*a*) that requirement shall continue in force,
(*b*) any requirement imposed under sections 30 to 37 of that Act on the company concerned, if it was in force immediately before that day, shall continue in force, and
(*c*) section 47(1) of this Act shall apply to any requirement that continues in force under sub-paragraph (*a*) or (*b*) above.

Postponement of effect of sections 37(3) and 38(3) above in respect of long term business

9. Until 15 March 1984, sections 37(3) and 38(3) of this Act shall not affect requirements imposed on companies before 1 January 1982 in respect of long term business.

Deposits made with Accountant General before 1 January 1982

10. A deposit made under regulation 6 of the Insurance Companies (Solvency: General Business) Regulations 1977 shall, in so far as it remained with the Accountant General of the Supreme Court immediately before 1 January 1982, be regarded as having been made under section 9(1)(*c*) of this Act.

Continuation of business where contract made before 1 January 1982

11. Where—

(*a*) as a result of the repeal of section 83(2)(*b*) of the Insurance Companies Act 1974 any particular kind of ordinary long term insurance business has become general business, and
(*b*) an insurance company was immediately before 1 January 1982 lawfully carrying on that particular kind of business in the United Kingdom,

then, notwithstanding the lack of an authorisation to carry on general business, the company may continue to carry out any contract of insurance relating to that particular kind of business if the contract was made before 1 January 1982.

Applications for approval of transfer made before 1 January 1982

12. Where an application to the Secretary of State under the Insurance (Transfer of General Business) Regulations 1980 for approval of a transfer has been made before 1 January 1982 and not determined before the commencement of this Act, the application shall be determined in accordance with the law in force immediately before 1 January 1982.

Saving for section 42 of the Insurance Companies Act 1974

13. Section 42 of the Insurance Companies Act 1974 shall continue to have effect in

relation to an application made to the court under that section before 1 January 1982 as if this Act and section 27 of the Insurance Companies Act 1981 had not been enacted and section 50 of this Act shall apply to an order made by virtue of this paragraph as if it were an order made under section 49 of this Act.

Postponement of effect of section 54(1)(c) of this Act in relation to unregistered companies

14. Until the coming into force of section 12 of the Companies Act 1976 in relation to unregistered companies to which section 147 of the Companies Act 1948 applies by virtue of section 435 of the said Act of 1948, section 54(1)(*c*) of this Act shall have effect in relation to such companies as if—

(*a*) for the reference to section 12 of the Companies Act 1976 there were substituted a reference to section 147 of the Companies Act 1948;
(*b*) for the reference to accounting records there were substituted a reference to proper books of account;
(*c*) for the reference to records there were substituted a reference to books.

Saving for winding up commenced before rules made under section 365 of the Companies Act 1948 or section 317 of the Companies Act (Northern Ireland) 1960

15. The provisions of this Act, so far as re-enacting provisions of the Insurance Companies Act 1974 which repealed and re-enacted provisions of the Insurance Companies Amendment Act 1973 relating to winding up, shall not affect any winding up commenced before the date on which the first rules made under section 365 of the Companies Act 1948 or, as the case may be, section 317 of the Companies Act (Northern Ireland) 1960 by virtue of section 51(2) of the said Act of 1974 or section 59(2) above come into operation.

Saving for repeal of section 17(2) and (3) of, and Schedules 3 and 4 to, the Insurance Companies Act 1958

16. If no rules under section 51(2) of the Insurance Companies Act 1974 have come into operation before the commencement of this Act the repeal of section 17(2) and (3) of, and Schedules 3 and 4 to, the Insurance Companies Act 1958 shall not take effect until the first rules made under section 365 of the Companies Act 1948 or, as the case may be, section 317 of the Companies Act (Northern Ireland) 1960 by virtue of the said section 51(2) or section 59(2) above come into operation.

Northern Ireland

17. Section 17(2)(*a*) of the Interpretation Act 1978 shall not apply to the reference to the Insurance Companies Act 1974 in paragraph 2 of Schedule 4 to the Insurance Companies Act 1980.

18. Until Articles 3, 11, 13 and 25 of the Companies (Northern Ireland) Order 1978 come into operation the following provisions of this Act shall have effect subject to the following modifications—

(*a*) in section 54(2)(*c*) for the reference to Article 25 of that Order there shall be substituted a reference to sections 141 and 297 of the Companies Act (Northern Ireland) 1960;
(*b*) in section 66 for the reference to Article 3 or 11 of that Order there shall be substituted a reference to section 122, 142 or 359 of that Act;
(*c*) in section 87(2)(*d*) for the reference to Articles 11 to 13 of that Order there shall be substituted a reference to sections 359 and 363 of that Act.

Continuing offences

19. Where an offence for the continuance of which a penalty was provided has been

committed under any enactment repealed by this Act proceedings may be taken under this Act in respect of the continuance of the offence after the commencement of this Act in the like manner as if the offence had been committed under the corresponding provision of this Act.

Transitional provisions relating to sections 9(7), 71(3), 81(2) and 88(2) of this Act

20. Until the coming into force of paragraph (*g*) of subsection (2) of section 46 of the Administration of Justice Act 1982, the reference in section 9(7) of this Act to section 38(7) of that Act shall be construed as a reference to section 7 of the Administration of Justice Act 1965.

21. In relation to offences under this Act committed in England and Wales before the coming into force of section 38 of the Criminal Justice Act 1982 or in Scotland before the coming into force of section 53 of that Act the reference in each of the following provisions of this Act, namely—

(*a*) section 71(3)
(*b*) section 81(2), and
(*c*) section 88(2)

to level 5 on the standard scale shall have effect as a reference to £400.

General

22. Subject to paragraph 17 above and without prejudice to any express amendment made by this Act, any enactment or other document whatsoever referring to any enactment repealed by this Act shall, unless the context otherwise requires, be construed as referring (or as including a reference) to the corresponding enactment in this Act.

23. Without prejudice to paragraph 20 above, any enactment whatsoever referring to an assurance company within the meaning of the Assurance Companies Act 1909 shall be construed as referring (or as including a reference) to an insurance company to which Part II of this Act applies.

24. Where a period of time specified in any enactment repealed by this Act is current at the commencement of this Act, this Act has effect as if the corresponding provision of this Act had been in force when that period began to run.

SCHEDULE 5

Section 99(2)

Consequential Amendments

. . .

SCHEDULE 6

Section 99(3)

Repeals

. . .

APPENDIX II

Statutory instruments
(A) Insurance companies

INSURANCE COMPANIES REGULATIONS 1981[1]

(SI 1981/1654)

Part I

Preliminary

Citation and commencement

1.—These Regulations may be cited as the Insurance Companies Regulations 1981 and shall come into operation—

(*a*) except for regulations 24 to 27 and 54 to 64, on 1st January 1982,
(*b*) as respects regulations 24 to 27, on 1st April 1982, and
(*c*) as respects regulations 54 to 64, on 1st October 1982.

Interpretation: general

2.—(1) In these Regulations, unless the context otherwise requires—

'the 1974 Act' means the Insurance Companies Act 1974;

'the 1981 Act' means the Insurance Companies Act 1981;

'cede' and 'cession', in relation to reinsurance, include retrocede and retrocession;

'deposit back arrangement', in relation to any contract of reinsurance, means an arrangement whereby an amount is deposited by the reinsurer with the cedant;

'external company' means an insurance company whose head office is not in a member State;

'guarantee fund' has the meaning given in regulation 9(1) below;

'holding company' has the meaning given by section 154 of the Companies Act 1948 or section 148 of the Companies Act (Northern Ireland) 1960;

'linked long term contract' means a contract of the kind described in section 68(1) of the 1974 Act;

'mathematical reserves' means the provision made by an insurer to cover liabilities (excluding liabilities which have fallen due and liabilities arising from deposit back arrangements) arising under or in connection with contracts for long term business;

'minimum guarantee fund' has the meaning given in regulation 9(2) below;

'mutual' means an insurance company which is—

(*a*) a body corporate having no share capital (except a wholly owned subsidiary with no share capital but limited by guarantee), or
(*b*) a registered society;

'pure reinsurer' means an insurance company whose authorisation to carry on business in the United Kingdom is restricted to reinsurance;

'Schedule' means Schedule to these Regulations;

[1] The regulations are printed as amended.

'subsidiary' has the meaning given by section 154 of the Companies Act 1948 or section 148 of the Companies Act (Northern Ireland) 1960;

'United Kingdom company' means an insurance company whose head office is in the United Kingdom.

(2) For the purposes of these Regulations—

(*a*) a unit of account is the unit of account known as the ECU and defined in Council Regulation (EEC) No. 3180/78 (which changed the value of the unit of account used by the European Monetary Co-operation Fund), and

(*b*) the rate of conversion from the ECU to pounds sterling for each year beginning on 31st December shall, subject to a minimum of 41.66 pence per unit, be the rate published in the Official Journal of the Communities on the last day of the preceding October for which ECU conversion rates were so published for the currencies of all States that were then member States.

PART II

MARGINS OF SOLVENCY

Interpretation: Part II

3.—In this Part of these Regulations—

'first calculation' and 'second calculation' have the meaning given in regulation 5(1) to (3) below;

'implicit items' has the meaning given by regulation 10(4) below and 'implicit item' shall be construed accordingly;

'required margin of solvency' means a margin of solvency required by section 26A of the 1974 Act;

'zillmerising' means the method known by that name for modifying the net premium reserve method of valuing a long term policy by increasing the part of the future premiums for which credit is taken so as to allow for initial expenses.

Margins of solvency: determination

4.—(1) Subject to paragraphs (2) to (5) below, the margin of solvency to be maintained by an insurance company to which Part II of the 1974 Act applies shall be determined—

(*a*) as regards long term business, in accordance with regulations 5 to 8 below, and

(*b*) as regards general business, by taking the greater of the two sums resulting from the application of the two methods of calculation set out in Schedules 1 and 2 respectively.

(2) Where an insurance company is required to maintain a United Kingdom margin of solvency or a Community margin of solvency—

(*a*) the United Kingdom margin of solvency shall be determined by applying paragraph (1) above, but only to business carried on in the United Kingdom, and

(*b*) the Community margin of solvency shall be determined by applying paragraph (1) above, but only to business carried on in the member States taken together.

(3) For a contract to which section 1(3) of the 1981 Act applies, the required margin of solvency shall be determined by taking the aggregate of the results arrived at by applying—

(*a*) in the case of so much of the contract as is within any class of long term business, the appropriate method prescribed by this Part of these Regulations for that class, and

(*b*) in the case of so much of the contract as is within general business class 1 or 2, the method of calculation set out in Schedule 1 (excluding paragraphs 7, 8 and 9).

(4) Where an insurance company carries on long term business and owing to the nature of that business more than one margin of solvency is produced in respect of that business by the operation of this Part of these Regulations, the margins in question shall be aggregated as regards the company in order to arrive at the company's required margin of solvency for long term business.

(5) Where an insurance company carries on both long term and general business and is accordingly required to maintain separate margins of solvency in respect of the two kinds of business—

(*a*) these Regulations shall apply for determining the margin of solvency for each kind of business separately, and

(*b*) assets other than those representing the fund or funds maintained by the company in respect of its long term business, if they are not included among the assets covering the liabilities and the margin of solvency relating to the company's general business, may be included among the assets taken into account in covering the liabilities and the margin of solvency for the company's long term business.

Long term classes I and II

5.—(1) For long term business of class I or II the required margin of solvency shall be determined by taking the aggregate of the results arrived at by applying the calculation described in paragraph (2) below ('the first calculation') and the calculation described in paragraphs (3), (4), (5) and (5A) below ('the second calculation').

(2) For the first calculation—

(*a*) there shall be taken a sum equal to 4 per cent of the mathematical reserves for direct business and reinsurance acceptances without any deduction for reinsurance cessions,

(*b*) the amount of the mathematical reserves at the end of the last preceding financial year after the deduction of reinsurance cessions shall be expressed as a percentage of the amount of those mathematical reserves before any such deduction, and

(*c*) the sum mentioned in sub-paragraph (*a*) above shall be multiplied—

(i) where the percentage arrived at under sub-paragraph (*b*) above is greater than 85 per cent (or, in the case of a pure reinsurer, 50 per cent), by that greater percentage, and

(ii) in any other case, by 85 per cent (or, in the case of a pure reinsurer, 50 per cent).

(3) For the second calculation—

(*a*) there shall be taken, subject to paragraphs (4), (5) and (5A) below, a sum equal to 0.3 per cent of the capital at risk for contracts on which the capital at risk is not a negative figure,

(*b*) the amount of the capital at risk at the end of the last preceding financial year for contracts on which the capital at risk is not a negative figure, after the deduction of reinsurance cessions, shall be expressed as a percentage of the amount of that capital at risk before any such deduction, and

(*c*) the sum arrived at under sub-paragraph (*a*) above shall be multiplied—

(i) where the percentage arrived at under sub-paragraph (*b*) above is greater than 50 per cent, by that greater percentage, and

(ii) in any other case, by 50 per cent.

(4) Where, in a case other than that of a pure reinsurer, a contract provides for benefits payable only on death within a specified period and is valid for a period of not more than three years from the date when the contract was first made, the percentage to

be taken for the purposes of paragraph (3)(*a*) above shall be 0.1 per cent; and where the period of validity from that date is more than three years but not more than five years, the percentage to be so taken shall be 0.15 per cent.

(5) For the purposes of paragraph (4) above, the period of validity of the contract evidencing a group policy is the period from the date when the premium rates under the contract were last reviewed for which the premium rates are guaranteed.

(5A) In the case of pure reinsurers, the percentage to be taken for the purposes of paragraph (3)(*a*) above shall be 0.1 per cent.

(6) For the purposes of the second calculation, the capital at risk is—

(*a*) in any case in which an amount is payable in consequence of death other than a case falling within sub-paragraph (*b*) below, the amount payable on death, and

(*b*) in any case in which the benefit under the contract in question consists of the making, in consequence of death, of the payment of an annuity, payment of a sum by instalments or any other kind of periodic payments, the present value of that benefit,

less in either case the mathematical reserves in respect of the relevant contracts.

(7) When the amount of the mathematical reserves referred to in paragraph (2)(*a*) above, or the amount of the capital at risk referred to in paragraph (3)(*a*) above, is to be calculated for the purposes of determining the required margin of solvency, the day as on which that amount is calculated shall be the same as that as on which the margin of solvency is determined; and the mathematical reserves referred to in paragraph (6) above shall also be calculated on that day when the capital at risk in question is that referred to in paragraph (3)(*a*) above, but shall be calculated as at the end of the last preceding financial year when the capital at risk in question is that referred to in paragraph (3)(*b*) above.

Long term classes III and VII

6.—(1) For long term business of class III or VII the required margin of solvency shall be determined in accordance with paragraphs (2) to (5) below.

(2) In so far as an insurance company bears an investment risk, the first calculation shall be applied.

(3) In so far as—

(*a*) an insurance company bears no investment risk, and

(*b*) the total expired and unexpired term of the relevant contract exceeds five years, and

(*c*) the allocation to cover management expenses in the relevant contract has a fixed upper limit which is effective as a limit for a period exceeding five years,

the first calculation shall be applied, but as if regulation 5(2)(*a*) above contained a reference to 1 per cent instead of 4 per cent.

(4) If neither paragraph (2) nor paragraph (3) above applies, then, subject to paragraph (5) below, the required margin of solvency is zero.

(5) Where an insurance company covers a death risk, a sum arrived at by applying the second calculation (regulation 5(4) and (5) above being disregarded) shall be added to any required margin of solvency, including a required margin of solvency of zero, arrived at under paragraph (2), (3) or (4) above.

Long term classes IV and VI

7.—For long term business of class IV or VI the required margin of solvency shall be determined by applying the first calculation.

Long term class V

8.—For long term business of class V the required margin of solvency shall be equal to 1 per cent of the assets of the relevant tontine.

Guarantee fund and minimum guarantee fund

9.—(1) Subject to paragraphs (2) and (3) below, one-third of a required margin of solvency (being, in the case of long term business, the required margin of solvency arrived at in accordance with regulation 4(4) above) shall constitute the amount ('the guarantee fund') to be prescribed or determined for the purposes of section 26B of the 1974 Act.

(2) The guarantee fund shall not be less than an amount ('the minimum guarantee fund') arrived at in accordance with Schedule 3 whether the required margin of solvency is greater or lesser than that amount.

(3) In the case of long term business, items that are not implicit items must be at least large enough to cover either the minimum guarantee fund or 50 per cent of the guarantee fund, whichever is the greater.

Valuation

10.—(1) Where an insurance company has assets equal to or in excess of its liabilities, then, in addition to any other applicable valuation regulations, paragraphs (2) to (4) below shall have effect for determining the extent to which the value of the assets exceeds the amount of liabilities in connection with the required margin of solvency, the guarantee fund and the minimum guarantee fund.

(2) Where—

(*a*) a company has issued shares some or all of which are not fully paid and the total paid-up value of all the shares is equal to or greater than one quarter of their nominal value or, in the case of shares issued at a premium, of the aggregate of their nominal value and the premium, or

(*b*) at least one quarter of the fund of a mutual is paid up,

an amount not greater than half the total value of the amounts unpaid may be taken into account as an asset and for the purposes of this paragraph a share shall not be regarded as fully paid if there are any amounts due but unpaid thereon.

(3) In the case of a mutual carrying on general business, any claim which the mutual has against its members by way of a call for supplementary contributions for a financial year shall have its full value for that financial year, subject to the limitation that the value shall not exceed—

(*a*) 50 per cent of the difference between the maximum contributions and the contributions called in, or

(*b*) 50 per cent of the required margin of solvency.

(4) The items mentioned in regulations 11 to 13 below (which relate to future profits, zillmerising and hidden reserves and shall be known as 'implicit items') shall have no value except in pursuance of an order under section 57 of the 1974 Act; but in pursuance of such an order—

(*a*) any of the implicit items may be valued in accordance with the said regulations 11 to 13 as respects long term business, and

(*b*) the implicit item relating to hidden reserves may be valued in accordance with regulation 13 below as respects general business.

Implicit items: future profits

11.—(1) The implicit item relating to future profits may be valued at not more than 50 per cent of the full amount of future profits.

(2) For the purposes of paragraph (1) above, the full amount of future profits shall be obtained by multiplying the estimated annual profit by a factor which shall as nearly as may be represent the average number of years remaining to run on policies but shall, if it exceeds 10, be reduced to 10.

(3) For the purposes of paragraph (2) above—

(*a*) the estimated annual profit shall be taken to be one-fifth of the profits made in long term business over a period of five years ('the relevant period') ending on the last day of the most recent financial year for which a valuation under section 18 of the Insurance Companies Act 1982 has been carried out, substantial items of an exceptions nature being excluded, and

(*b*) the average number of years remaining to run on policies shall be calculated—

(i) by multiplying the number of years to run on each policy by the actuarial value of the benefits payable under the policy, adding together the products so obtained and dividing the total by the aggregate of the actuarial values of the benefits payable under all the policies, or

(ii) by an approximation to this method of calculation suitable to the circumstances of the case, including, where appropriate, an approximation involving the grouping of contracts,

appropriate allowance being made in either case for premature termination of contracts.

(4) For the purposes of paragraph (3) above—

(*a*) where a valuation under section 14 of the 1974 Act has been carried out annually in relation to the relevant period, the profits made in long term business for any particular year of the relevant period shall be taken to be the surplus (if any) arising in the long term fund since the last such valuation, and the profits so made for that period shall be taken to be the aggregate of those surpluses less any deficiencies in the long term fund during that period;

(*b*) where an insurance company has carried on long term business throughout the relevant period but valuations under section 14 of the 1974 Act have not been made annually in that period, the profits so made for that period shall be taken to be the aggregate of surpluses arising in the long term fund since the last valuation preceding the relevant period less any deficiencies in the long term fund since that last valuation, except that the surplus or deficiency arising in the period ending with the first valuation within the relevant period shall be proportionately reduced to allow for any period of time falling outside the relevant period;

(*c*) where an insurance company has not carried on long term business throughout the relevant period, the profits made in long term business for the relevant period shall be taken to be the aggregate of any surpluses arising in the long term fund during that part of the relevant period for which long term business was carried on less any deficiencies in the long term fund during that part of that period.

Implicit items: zillmerising

12.—(1) Where zillmerising is appropriate but either is not practised or is at a rate less than the loading for acquisition costs included in the premium, then, subject to paragraph (6) below, the implicit item relating to zillmerising may be valued at an amount not exceeding the difference between—

(*a*) the non-zillmerised or partially zillmerised figure for mathematical reserves maintained by the company concerned, and

(*b*) a figure for mathematical reserves (not less than those required by Part VI of these Regulations) zillmerised at a rate equal to the loading for acquisition costs included or allowed for in the premium.

(2) Where zillmerising is not practised, then, subject to paragraph (6) below, the value given by paragraph (1) above (less any amount relating to temporary assurances) shall not exceed 3.5 per cent of the aggregate of the difference between—

(*a*) the relevant capital sums for long term business activities, and

(*b*) the mathematical reserves (excluding mathematical reserves for temporary assurances).

(3) Where zillmerising is practised but is at a rate less than the loading for acquisition costs, then, subject to paragraph (6) below, the value given by paragraph (1) above (less

any amount relating to temporary assurances) together with the difference between the partially zillmerised mathematical reserves and the non-zillmerised mathematical reserves shall not exceed 3.5 per cent of the aggregate of the difference between—

(*a*) the relevant capital sums of long term business activities, and

(*b*) the mathematical reserves (excluding mathematical reserves for temporary assurances).

(4) In paragraphs (2) and (3) above 'relevant capital sums' means—

(*a*) for whole life assurances, the sum assured,

(*b*) for policies where a sum is payable on maturity (including policies where a sum is also payable on earlier death), the sum payable on maturity,

(*c*) for deferred annuities, the capitalised value of the annuity at the vesting date (or the cash option if it is greater),

(*d*) for capital redemption contracts, the sums payable at the end of the contract period, and

(*e*) for linked long term contracts, notwithstanding sub-paragraphs (*a*) to (*d*) above, the lesser of—

(i) the amount for the time being payable on death, and

(ii) the aggregate of the value for the time being of the units allocated to the contract (or, where entitlement is not denoted by means of units, the value for the time being of any other measure of entitlement under the contract equivalent to units) and the total amount of the premiums remaining to be paid during such of the term of the contract as is appropriate for zillmerising or, if such premiums are payable beyond the age of seventy-five, until that age,

excluding in all cases any vested reversionary bonus and any capital sums for temporary assurances.

(5) Where, under the contract relating to any such business as is mentioned in paragraph (4) above, the payment of premiums is to stop before the sum assured becomes due, then, notwithstanding the said paragraph (4), 'relevant capital sums' in paragraphs (1) to (3) above shall be taken to mean the mathematical reserves appropriate for that contract at the end of the premium-paying term.

(6) For the purposes of this regulation—

(*a*) reserves for vested reversionary bonuses shall not be regarded as mathematical reserves, and

(*b*) the result given by paragraph (1), (2) or (3) above shall be reduced by the amount of any undepreciated acquisition costs brought into account as an asset.

Implicit items: hidden reserves

13.—The implicit item relating to hidden reserves, if it consists of hidden reserves resulting from the underestimation of assets and overestimation of liabilities (other than mathematical reserves), may, in so far as the hidden reserves in question are not of an exceptional nature, be given its full value.

Part III

Deposits

Interpretation: Part III

14.—In this Part of these Regulations—

'Accountant General' means the Accountant General of the Supreme Court;

'deposit' means the deposit mentioned in section 9(1)(*c*) of the 1981 Act and 'depositor' means an insurance company making (or intending to make) such a deposit;

'the minimum', in relation to a deposit, means one-half of the minimum guarantee fund appropriate to the margin of solvency which the depositor is required to maintain under section 32(2)(*b*) of the Insurance Companies Act 1982.

'permitted securities' means securities in which cash under the control of or subject to the order of the Supreme Court may be invested pursuant to Order 22, rule 13, of the Rules of the Supreme Court 1965.

Making and amount of deposit

15.—Every deposit made pursuant to section 9(1)(*c*) of the 1981 Act shall (subject to section 9(2)(*b*) of that Act) be made with the Accountant General and shall be maintained by the depositor at a level equal to at least the minimum.

Direction etc by the Secretary of State

16.—(1) The Secretary of State, where he is satisfied that a deposit is required to be made with the Accountant General pursuant to regulation 15 above or under an agreement of the kind mentioned in section 9(2)(*b*) of the 1981 Act, may (and on the application of the depositor shall)—

(*a*) certify the fact of the requirement,
(*b*) specify the minimum in pounds sterling, and
(*c*) direct the Accountant General to receive the deposit.

(2) Where the minimum changes, the Secretary of State may (and on the application of the depositor shall)—

(*a*) certify the fact of the change
(*b*) specify the changed minimum in pounds sterling, and
(*c*) direct the Accountant General to receive any additional sum required to ensure that the deposit is maintained in accordance with regulation 15 above.

Permitted securities

17.—(1) Subject to paragraph (2) below, any payment to be made by the depositor to the Accountant General in respect of the deposit may be partly or wholly effected by the lodgment of permitted securities instead of cash.

(2) Paragraph (1) above shall not apply unless the depositor gives to the Accountant General—

(*a*) a valuation of the securities as on a day not more than two days before that on which the Accountant General receives the request for such a lodgment to be effected, and
(*b*) a report by a duly authorised person stating that in his opinion the valuation has been made in accordance with Part V of these Regulations.

(3) in paragraph (2) above 'duly authorised person' means a member of the Stock Exchange or a person qualified by virtue of section 161(1)(*a*) or (*b*) of the Companies Act 1948 to be auditor of a company.

Investment

18.—(1) Subject to paragraph (2) below, the Accountant General may on the application of a depositor—

(*a*) invest in permitted securities (to be specified by the applicant) any cash which constitutes or forms part of the deposit or will do so on the maturity of any security, or
(*b*) realise any securities (to be specified by the applicant) constituting or forming part of the deposit and either reinvest the net proceeds in permitted securities (to be specified by the applicant) or retain the net proceeds as cash.

(2) No application may be made under paragraph (1) above unless at least twenty-eight days have elapsed since any previous application under that paragraph.

Disposal of securities

19.—(1) Subject to paragraphs (2) and (3) below, the Secretary of State on the application of a depositor may direct the Accountant General—

(*a*) to transfer to the depositor any of the securities constituting or forming part of the deposit, or

(*b*) to realise any of the securities constituting or forming part of the deposit and to pay the net proceeds to the depositor, or

(*c*) to pay to the depositor any cash which constitutes or forms part of the deposit (or will do so on the maturity of any security).

(2) The Secretary of State shall not give a direction under paragraph (1) above unless it appears to him that the remaining cash and securities constituting the deposit after the dealing specified in the direction has been carried out will, if valued in accordance with Part V of these Regulations as on the day before the direction is given, be equal in value to at least the minimum.

(3) Nothing in paragraph (1) or (2) above shall relieve the depositor of the obligation imposed on him by regulation 15 above to maintain the deposit at a level equal to at least the minimum.

Cessation of business etc

20.—(1) Where the depositor has ceased to carry on in the United Kingdom the business in respect of which the deposit was made or has ceased to be an external company, then, except in a case where paragraph (2) below applies, the depositor or any other person who is entitled to give a good discharge for the funds representing the deposit may apply to the Secretary of State for those funds to be released to the depositor or to that other person, as the case may be.

(2) In the event of the depositor becoming bankrupt, the amount of the deposit shall be paid to the trustee or assignees in bankruptcy; and if, in a case where the depositor is a corporation, the corporation is ordered to be wound up by or under the supervision of the court, the amount of the deposit shall be repaid to the corporation.

(3) The Secretary of State, on receipt of an application under paragraph (1) above accompanied by the appropriate declaration, may in relation to any cash or securities constituting the deposit or part of the deposit direct the Accountant General that—

(*a*) the cash shall be paid to the applicant, or

(*b*) the securities shall be realised and the net proceeds shall be paid to the applicant, or

(*c*) the securities shall be transferred to the applicant.

(4) In paragraph (3) above 'the appropriate declaration' means a statutory declaration by the applicant—

(*a*) declaring that the applicant knows of no other person who has made or is entitled to make any claim to or on the relevant funds, and

(*b*) if the applicant is not the depositor—

(i) declaring that the applicant is entitled to give a good discharge for the relevant funds, and

(ii) stating the circumstances in which the applicant is so entitled.

Effect of direction etc

21.—(1) A direction given by the Secretary of State pursuant to this Part of these Regulations shall be sufficient authority for the Accountant General to comply with it; and it shall be the duty of the Accountant General to act accordingly.

(2) A direction given under regulation 16(1) or (2) above shall be construed as authorising the Accountant General to receive any amount necessary to ensure the maintenance of the deposit at a level equal to at least the minimum or the changed minimum, as the case may be.

(3) The Secretary of State (without prejudice to his power to give a direction under regulation 16(1) or (2) above) may give a direction authorising the Accountant General to receive an amount which, either alone or when aggregated with sums already deposited, is less than the minimum or the changed minimum, as the case may be.

Application of rules under s 7 of the Administration of Justice Act 1965

22.—(1) The funds rules (except in so far as they may be inconsistent with this Part of these Regulations) shall apply for the purposes of this Part of these Regulations, subject to the modification in paragraph (2) below.

(2) Any reference in the funds rules to cash, securities or funds lodged in court shall be taken to include any cash or securities deposited with the Accountant General pursuant to the 1981 Act and this Part of these Regulations.

(3) In paragraphs (1) and (2) above 'the funds rules' means any rules for the time being in force under section 7 of the Administration of Justice Act 1965.

Part IV

Benefits in Kind, Main Agents, Matching, Localisation, Authorisation and Change of Control

Benefits in kind

23.—(1) For the purposes of sections 2(5) and 16 of the 1981 Act, there is hereby prescribed any contract of insurance which—

(*a*) is a contract under which the benefits provided by the insurer are exclusively or primarily benefits in kind in the event of accident to or breakdown of a vehicle, and

(*b*) contains the terms specified in paragraph (2) below.

(2) The terms referred to in paragraph (1) above are—

(*a*) that, subject to such restrictions as may be set out in the contract, the assistance shall normally be available on demand at least throughout the mainland of Great Britain;

(*b*) that the assistance shall normally be provided by the insurer's servants or exceptionally by garages acting as the insurer's agents or appointed by the insurer;

(*c*) that the assistance may take one or more of the following forms—

(i) repairs to the relevant vehicle at the roadside;

(ii) removal of the relevant vehicle to another place;

(iii) conveyance of the relevant vehicle's occupants to another place;

(iv) delivery of parts, fuel, oil, water or keys to the relevant vehicle;

(v) reimbursement of the policy holder for all or part of any sums paid by him in respect of the assistance either because he failed to identify himself as the policy holder or because he was unable to get in touch with the insurer in order to claim the assistance.

(3) In this regulation—

'the assistance' means the benefits to be provided under a contract of the kind prescribed in paragraph (1) above;

'breakdown' means an event—

(*a*) which causes the driver of the relevant vehicle involuntarily to bring the vehicle to a halt on a journey because of some malfunction of the vehicle or failure of it to function, and

(*b*) after which the journey cannot reasonably be continued in the relevant vehicle;

'the insurer' means the insurance company providing the assistance;

'the policy holder' means the person entitled to the assistance;

'the relevant vehicle' means the vehicle (including a trailer or caravan) in respect of which the assistance is required.

Main agents: exceptions

24.—(1) An unlimited agent shall not be regarded as a main agent of an applicant for the purposes of section 7 of the 1981 Act if—

(*a*) he was appointed before 1st April 1982, and

(*b*) for the base period and for every subsequent year of account the value of the agent's business has been not more than 10 per cent of the value of the applicant's business.

(2) In this regulation—

'the base period' means the financial year covered by the last set of annual accounts deposited by the applicant under section 18 of the 1974 Act before 1st April 1982;

'unlimited agent' means a person appointed by an applicant to be the applicant's agent in respect of general business in the United Kingdom with authority to enter into contracts on behalf of the applicant without limit on the aggregate amount of premiums;

'the value of the agent's business' means the aggregate of the amounts of gross premiums receivable by the applicant in respect of general business in the United Kingdom under contracts entered into by the agent on the applicant's behalf;

'the value of the applicant's business' means the aggregate of the amounts of gross premiums receivable by the applicant in respect of general business in the United Kingdom;

'year of account' means a financial year for which a set of annual accounts has been deposited by the applicant under section 18 of the 1974 Act.

Matching

25.—(1) Where the liabilities of an insurance company in any particular currency exceed 5 per cent of the company's total liabilities, then, subject to paragraphs (2) and (3) below, the company shall hold sufficient assets expressed in or capable of being realised without exchange risk into that currency to cover at least 80 per cent of the company's liabilities in that currency.

(2) In so far as the liabilities for property linked benefits are covered by assets which determine the benefits payable under a linked long term contract, paragraph (1) above shall not apply.

(3) In so far as the liabilities for property linked benefits are determined by reference to assets expressed in or capable of being realised without exchange risk into a currency other than the currency in which the insurer's obligations to the policy holder are expressed, those liabilities shall for the purposes of paragraph (1) above be deemed to be liabilities in the first-mentioned currency.

(4) Where an insurance company carries on both long term and general business, the requirement of paragraph (1) above shall apply to the assets and liabilities of each kind of business separately.

(5) For the purposes of paragraphs (1) and (3) above, an asset is capable of being realised without exchange risk into a currency if it is reasonably capable of being realised into that currency without risk that changes in exchange rates would reduce the cover of liabilities in that currency.

(6) In this regulation—

'assets', except in the case of assets of the kind referred to in regulation 38(2) below, means assets valued in accordance with Part V of these Regulations;

'liabilities' means provision by an insurer to cover liabilities arising under or in connection with contracts of insurance (not being liabilities relating to insurance business excluded by regulation 27 below);

'property linked benefits' has the meaning given by regulation 37(1) below.

Localisation

26.—(1) Assets held pursuant to regulation 25 above shall be held—

(*a*) if they cover liabilities in sterling, in the United Kingdom;

(*b*) if they cover liabilities in any other currency, in the United Kingdom or in the country of that currency;

(*c*) in the case of a relevant co-insurance operation and a relevant company, in the United Kingdom or in the member State where the head office, branch or agency is established through which the leading insurer participates in the operation.

(2) For the purpose of applying paragraph (1) above to tangible assets and assets consisting of a claim against a debtor or a listed or unlisted investment, the following provisions shall have effect—

(*a*) a tangible asset shall be regarded as held in the place where it is situated;

(*b*) an asset consisting of a claim against a debtor shall be regarded as held in any place where it can be enforced by legal action;

(*c*) an asset consisting of a listed investment shall be regarded as held in any place where—

(i) there is a stock exchange (of the kind described in paragraph (*a*) or (*b*) of the definition of 'listed' in regulation 37(1) below) where it is listed, or

(ii) there is a securities market (of the kind described in paragraph (*c*) of that definition) where it is dealt in;

(*d*) an asset consisting of an unlisted investment issued by an incorporated company shall be regarded as held in the place where the head office of that company is situated.

(3) In this regulation—

'assets' and 'liabilities' have the same meaning as in regulation 25 above;

'leading insurer', 'relevant co-insurance operation' and 'relevant company' have the same meaning as in regulation 53 below;

'listed' and 'unlisted' have the same meaning given in regulation 37(1) below.

Exclusions from regulations 25 and 26

27.—Nothing in regulation 25 or 26 above shall apply to—

(*a*) insurance business carried on outside the United Kingdom, or

(*b*) insurance business of groups 3 and 4 (within the meaning of Part II of Schedule 2 to the 1981 Act), or

(*c*) reinsurance business (unless it is facultative reinsurance written by an insurer who also carries on insurance business that is not reinsurance).

Margin of solvency of external company: location of assets

28.—Without prejudice to regulation 26 above—

(*a*) the assets representing a United Kingdom margin of solvency maintained by an external company under section 26A(2)(*b*) of the 1974 Act shall be kept—

(i) up to an amount at least equal to the appropriate guarantee fund or minimum guarantee fund (whichever is the greater), within the United Kingdom, and

(ii) as to the remainder, within the United Kingdom and the other member States, and

(*b*) the assets representing a Community margin of solvency maintained by an external company under section 26A(3)(*b*) of the 1974 Act shall be kept—

(i) up to an amount at least equal to the appropriate guarantee fund or minimum guarantee fund (whichever is the greater), within the member States where the company carries on business (or in any one or more of them), and

(ii) as to the remainder, within the United Kingdom and the other member States.

Authorisation: submission of information

29.—(1) The information to be submitted pursuant to section 5(1) of the 1981 Act shall be—

(*a*) for long term business, the information specified in the appropriate Part of Schedule 4, and

(*b*) for general business, the information specified in the appropriate Part of Schedule 5.

(2) In Schedules 4 and 5 (subject to the notes at the beginning of each Schedule)—

(*a*) Part I is appropriate for United Kingdom companies in respect of direct business and reinsurance,

(*b*) Part II is appropriate for non-UK Community companies in respect of—

(i) direct business, or

(ii) both direct business and reinsurance.

(*c*) Part III is appropriate for external companies in respect of—

(i) direct business, or

(ii) both direct business and reinsurance, and

(*d*) Part IV is appropriate for non-UK Community companies and external companies in respect of reinsurance only.

(3) For the purposes of this regulation—

'the Asset Valuation Regulations', in Schedules 4 and 5, means Part V of these Regulations;

'the Change of Control Regulations', in Schedules 4 and 5, means regulations 31 to 36 below;

'classes of insurance business', in Schedules 4 and 5, means the classes of insurance business specified in Schedules 1 and 2 to the 1981 Act;

'the company', in Schedules 4 and 5, means an insurance company and includes a body that seeks to become an insurance company after authorisation;

'direct business', in paragraph (2) above and in Schedules 4 and 5, means insurance business that is not reinsurance;

'information', in paragraph (1) above and in Schedules 4 and 5, includes proposal and financial forecast;

'non-UK Community company', in paragraph (2) and in Schedules 4 and 5, means an insurance company whose head office is in a member State other than the United Kingdom.

Authorisation: UK assets of external company

30.—For the purposes of section 9(1)(*b*) of the 1981 Act (which provides that the Secretary of State shall not issue an authorisation under section 3 of that Act in respect of long term or general business to an applicant whose head office is not in a member State unless he is satisfied that the applicant has in the United Kingdom assets of such value as may be prescribed) there is hereby prescribed—

(*a*) a value at least equal to the minimum guarantee fund appropriate to the United Kingdom margin of solvency required by section 26A(2)(*b*) of the 1974 Act, or

(*b*) where in relation to an applicant seeking to carry on insurance business in the United Kingdom and one or more other member States the said section 9(1)(*b*) is (by virtue of section 9(2)(*a*) of the 1981 Act) to have effect as if the reference to the United Kingdom were a reference to the member States concerned taken together, a value at least equal to—

(i) the minimum guarantee fund appropriate to the Community margin of solvency required by section 26A(3)(*b*) of the 1974 Act, or

(ii) if the deposit is not made in the United Kingdom, half the minimum guarantee fund specified in paragraphs 1 to 8 of Schedule 3 as appropriate to the type of business to be carried on by the applicant.

Particulars of proposed managing director, chief executive or principal UK executive

31.—A notice served on the Secretary of State pursuant to section 52(1)(*a*) of the 1974 Act shall contain—

(*a*) where the person proposed to be appointed managing director, chief executive or principal United Kingdom executive is—

(i) an individual, the particulars in Form A in Schedule 6;

(ii) a body corporate, the particulars in Form C in Schedule 6; and

(*b*) where a partnership is proposed to be appointed chief executive or principal United Kingdom executive—

(i) the particulars in Form A in Schedule 6 in respect of each partner who is an individual;

(ii) the particulars in Form C in Schedule 6 in respect of each partner which is a body corporate.

Particulars of persons proposing to become controller

32.—A notice served on the Secretary of State pursuant to section 53(1)(*a*) of the 1974 Act shall contain, where the person proposing to become a controller (not being a person in respect of whom particulars have been supplied under regulation 31 above) is—

(*a*) an individual, the particulars prescribed in Form B in Schedule 6;

(*b*) a body corporate, the particulars prescribed in Form C in Schedule 6.

Notification by person becoming or ceasing to be controller

33.—A person who notifies an insurance company of the fact that he has become or has ceased to be a controller of that company shall, pursuant to section 54(1) of the 1974 Act, at the same time notify the company in writing of the matters prescribed in Form D in Schedule 6.

Notification by person becoming principal UK executive

34.—A person who becomes principal United Kingdom executive of an insurance company shall, pursuant to section 54(1) of the 1974 Act, notify the company in writing of the matters prescribed in Form D in Schedule 6.

Notification by person becoming director or authorised UK representative

35.—A person who becomes a director of an insurance company or becomes its authorised United Kingdom representative shall, pursuant to section 54(1) of the 1974 Act, notify the company in writing—

(*a*) where that person is an individual, of the matters prescribed in Form B in Schedule 6;

(*b*) where that person is a body corporate, of the matters prescribed in Form C in Schedule 6.

Notification by person becoming manager or employee within s 8(4)(c) of the 1981 Act

36.—A person who becomes a manager of an insurance company or becomes an employee of an insurance company within the meaning of section 8(4)(*c*) of the 1981 Act shall, pursuant to section 54(1) of the 1974 Act, notify the company in writing—

(*a*) where that person is an individual, of the matters prescribed in Form B in Schedule 6;

(*b*) where that person is a body corporate, of the matters prescribed in Form C in Schedule 6; and

(*c*) where that person is a partnership—
 (i) of the matters prescribed in Form B in Schedule 6 in respect of each partner who is an individual;
 (ii) of the matters prescribed in Form C in Schedule 6 in respect of each partner which is a body corporate.

Part V

Valuation of assets

Interpretation: Part V

37.—(1) In this Part of these Regulations, unless the context otherwise requires—

'approved financial institution' means any of the following—

(*a*) the Bank of England,
(*b*) the National Savings Bank,
(*c*) a trustee savings bank within the meaning of the Trustee Savings Banks Act 1976,
(*d*) a recognised bank or a licensed deposit-taking institution within the meaning of the Banking Act 1979,
(*e*) a person duly authorised by the Treasury to act for the purposes of the Exchange Control Act 1947 as an authorised dealer in relation to any foreign currency,
(*f*) Investors in Industry Group Public Limited Company,
the International Bank for Reconstruction and Development,
the Inter-American Development Bank,
the African Development Bank,
the Asian Development Bank,
the Caribbean Development Bank,
the European Investment Bank,
the Commission of the European Communities, and
the European Coal and Steel Community,
(*g*) the Post Office in the exercise of its powers to provide banking services, and
(*h*) a building society;

'approved securities' means any of the following—

(*a*) securities issued by Her Majesty's Government in the United Kingdom or the Government of Northern Ireland, being securities registered in the United Kingdom, Treasury Bills, Tax Reserve Certificates or Certificates of Tax Deposit;
(*b*) securities the repayment of the principal of which, or the payment of interest on which, is guaranteed by Her Majesty's Government in the United Kingdom or the Government of Northern Ireland;
(*c*) fixed interest securities issued in the United Kingdom by any public authority or nationalised industry or undertaking in the United Kingdom;
(*d*) debentures issued by the Agricultural Mortgage Corporation Limited or the Scottish Agricultural Securities Corporation Limited;
(*e*) loans to any authority to which this paragraph applies charged on all or any of the revenues of the authority or on a fund into which all or any of those revenues are payable, any fixed interest securities issued in the United Kingdom by any such authority for the purpose of borrowing money so charged, and deposits with any such authority by way of temporary loan made on the giving of a receipt for the loan by the treasurer or other similar officer of the authority and on the giving of an undertaking by the authority that, if requested to charge the loan as aforesaid, it will either comply with the request or repay the loan:
The authorities to which this paragraph applies are—
 (i) any local authority in the United Kingdom;

(ii) any authority all the members of which are appointed or elected by one or more local authorities in the United Kingdom;

(iii) any authority the majority of the members of which are appointed or elected by one or more local authorities in the United Kingdom, being an authority which by virtue of any enactment has power to issue a precept to a local authority in England and Wales, or a requisition to a local authority in Scotland, or to the expenses of which, by virtue of any enactment, a local authority in the United Kingdom is or can be required to contribute;

(iv) the Receiver for the Metropolitan Police District or a combined police authority (within the meaning of the Police Act 1964);

(v) any water authority established under the Water Act 1973 and any water authority as defined in section 148 of the Local Government (Scotland) Act 1973;

(*f*) any loan to, or deposit with, an approved financial institution; and

(*g*) any securities issued or guaranteed by, and any deposits of cash with, any government, public or local authority or nationalised industry or undertaking outside the United Kingdom;

'asset' includes part of an asset;

'associate' has the same meaning as in section 7(8) of the 1981 Act;

'building society' means a building society within the meaning of the Building Societies Act 1962 or the Building Societies Act (Northern Ireland) 1967;

'company' includes any body corporate;

'computer equipment' means the electro-mechanical and electronic units which make up a computer configuration;

'debenture' includes debenture stock and bonds, whether constituting a charge on assets or not, and loan stock or notes;

'debenture option' means a right exercisable within a specified period, at the option of the holder of the right, to acquire or dispose of any debenture at a specified price;

'debt' includes an obligation to pay a sum of money under a negotiable instrument;

'enactment' includes an enactment of the Parliament of Northern Ireland;

'equity share' means a share of equity share capital;

'equity share capital', in relation to a company, means its issued share capital excluding any part thereof which, neither as respects dividends nor as respects capital, carries any right to participate beyond a specified amount in a distribution;

'fixed interest securities' means securities which under their terms of issue provide for fixed amounts of interest;

'general business amount' has the meaning assigned to it in regulation 49(2) below;

'general business assets' and 'general business liabilities' mean respectively assets and liabilities of an insurance company which are not long term business assets or long term business liabilities;

'general premium income' means, in relation to any body in any year, the net amount, after deduction of any premiums payable for reinsurance, of the premiums receivable by the body in that year in respect of all insurance business other than long term business;

'industrial and provident society' means any society registered (or deemed to be registered) under the Industrial and Provident Societies Act 1965 or the Industrial and Provident Societies Act (Northern Ireland) 1969;

'insurance liabilities' means, in relation to an insurance company, any debt due from or other liabilities of the company under any contract of insurance to which it is a party;

'intermediary' means a person who in the course of any business or profession invites other persons to make offers or proposals or to take other steps with a view to entering into contracts of insurance with an insurance company, other than a person who only publishes such invitations on behalf of, or to the order of, some other person;

'linked assets' means, in relation to an insurance company, long term business assets of the company which are, for the time being, identified in the records of the company as being assets by reference to the value of which property linked benefits are to be determined;

'listed' means, in relation to an investment—

(*a*) that there has been granted and not withdrawn a listing in respect of that investment on a stock exchange within the meaning of the Companies Act 1948 or the Companies Act (Northern Ireland) 1960, or

(*b*) that there has been granted and not withdrawn such a listing on any stock exchange of repute outside the United Kingdom; or

(*c*) that dealings in that investment are effected in a securities market of repute outside the United Kingdom being a market in which prices of all securities in which there are dealings are publicly listed and which are supervised by a public body;

and 'unlisted' shall be construed accordingly;

'local authority' in relation to the United Kingdom means any of the following authorities—

(*a*) in England and Wales, a local authority within the meaning of the Local Government Act 1972, the Common Council of the City of London, the Greater London Council and the Council of the Isles of Scilly;

(*b*) in Scotland, a local authority within the meaning of the Local Government (Scotland) Act 1973;

(*c*) in Northern Ireland, any district council;

'long term business amount' has the meaning assigned to it in regulation 49(2) below;

'long term business assets' and 'long term business liabilities' mean respectively assets of an insurance company which are, for the time being, identified as representing the long term fund or funds maintained by the company in respect of its long term business and liabilities of the company which are attributable to its long term business;

'middle market quotation' means—

(*a*) in relation to an investment for which two prices are quoted in the official list published for the relevant market, the average of the two prices so quoted for the relevant date or, if no official list has been published for that day, for the most recent day prior to that day for which the official list has been published; and

(*b*) in relation to an investment for which one price is quoted in the official list published for the relevant market, the price so quoted for the relevant date or, if no official list has been published for that day, for the most recent day prior to that day for which the official list has been published; and

(*c*) in any other case, the nearest equivalent to the average referred to in paragraph (*a*) above which is published or can be reasonably ascertained from information which is published;

'price earnings ratio' means the price earnings ratio (net) estimated in respect of the Industrial Group index of the Financial Times Actuaries Share Indices jointly compiled by the Financial Times, the Institute of Actuaries and the Faculty of Actuaries;

'proper valuation' means, in relation to land, a valuation made by a qualified valuer not more than three years before the relevant date which determined the amount which would be realised at the time of the valuation on an open market sale of the land free from any mortgage or charge;

'property linked benefits' means benefits—

(*a*) provided for under any contract the effecting of which constitutes the carrying on of ordinary long-term insurance business, and

(*b*) determined by reference to the value of property of any description (whether specified in the contract or not);

'qualified valuer', in relation to any particular type of land in any particular area, means—

(*a*) a person who is a fellow or professional associate of the Royal Institution of Chartered Surveyors or a fellow or associate of the Incorporated Society of Valuers and Auctioneers or a fellow or associate of the Rating and Valuation Association and either—

(i) has knowledge of and experience in the valuation of that particular type of land in that particular area, or

(ii) has knowledge of and experience in the valuation of land and has taken advice from a valuer who he is satisfied has knowledge of and experience in the valuation of that particular type of land in that particular area, or

(*b*) a person who conforms with paragraph (*a*)(i) or (ii) above and immediately before 15th June 1981 was recognised as a qualified valuer by virtue of an approval by the Secretary of State under the Insurance Companies (Valuation of Assets) Regulations 1976 (and for these purposes an approval given under the Insurance Companies (Valuation of Assets) Regulations 1974 shall be deemed to have been given under the said Regulations of 1976);

'related company' means, in relation to an insurance company—

(*a*) a dependant of the insurance company, or
(*b*) a company of which the insurance company is a dependant, or
(*c*) a dependant of a company of which the insurance company is a dependant;

'relevant date' means, in relation to the valuation of any asset for any purpose for which this Part of these Regulations applies, the date when the asset falls to be valued for that purpose;

'salvage right' means any right of an insurance company under a contract of insurance to take possession of and to dispose of property by virtue of the fact that the company has made a payment or has become liable to make a payment in respect of a loss thereof;

'securities' includes shares, debentures, Treasury Bills, Tax Reserve Certificates and Certificates of Tax Deposit;

'share' includes stock;

'share option' means a right exercisable within a specified period, at the option of the holder of the right, to acquire or dispose of any share at a specified price;

'traded option' means a share or debenture option in respect of which permission to deal has been granted on the trade option market of a recognised stock exchange within the meaning of the Companies Act 1948 or the Companies Act (Northern Ireland) 1960 or a stock or options exchange of repute outside the United Kingdom;

'Treasury Bills' includes bills issued by Her Majesty's Government in the United Kingdom and Northern Ireland Treasury Bills.

(2) For the purposes of these Regulations, a company is a dependant of another company if—

(*a*) that other company, either alone or with any associate or associates, is entitled to exercise, or control the exercise of one-third or more of the voting power at any general meeting of the first-mentioned company, or
(*b*) the first-mentioned company is a dependant of any company which is that other company's dependant.

Application: Part V

38.—(1) Subject to paragraph (2) below, this Part of these Regulations applies with respect to the determination of the value of assets of insurance companies for the purposes of—

(*a*) sections 24(6), 26, 26A, 26C, 26D, 30, 31 and 37 of the 1974 Act,
(*b*) any investigation to which section 14 of the 1974 Act applies, and
(*c*) any investigation made in pursuance of a requirement under section 34 of the 1974 Act.

(2) Where an insurance company has entered into any contracts providing for the payment of property linked benefits, this Part of these Regulations shall not apply with respect to the determination of the value of the linked assets by reference to the value of which those benefits are to be determined.

(3) Any asset to which this Part of these Regulations applies (other than cash) for the valuation of which no provision is made in this Part of these Regulations shall be left out of account for the purposes specified in paragraph (1) above.

(4) Where in accordance with this Part of these Regulations the value of any asset is to be not greater than any specified amount and, in all the circumstances of the case, it

appears that the asset is of a lesser value than that amount, such lesser value shall be the value of the asset.

(5) Notwithstanding paragraph (1) above (but subject to the conditions set out in paragraph (6) below), an insurance company may, for the purposes of an investigation to which section 14 of the 1974 Act applies or an investigation made in pursuance of a requirement under section 34 of the 1974 Act, elect to assign to any of its assets the value given to the asset in question in the books or other records of the company.

(6) The conditions referred to in paragraph (5) above are—

(*a*) that the election shall not enable the company to bring into account any asset for the valuation of which no provision is made in this Part of these Regulations;

(*b*) that the value assigned to the aggregate of the assets shall not be higher than the aggregate of the value of those assets as determined in accordance with regulations 39 to 49 of these Regulations.

Shares in and debts due or to become due from dependants

39.—(1) The value of any share in a dependant of an insurance company shall be not greater than that part of the net asset value of the dependant which would be payable in respect of the share if the dependant were in liquidation and the net asset value were the amount distributable to the shareholders in the winding up.

(2) In this regulation, 'net asset value' means, in relation to a dependant, the amount by which the value of its assets, as determined in accordance with regulation 40 below, exceeds the amount of its liabilities as determined in the case of a dependant which is an insurance company, in accordance with the said regulation 40.

(3) The value of any debt due, or to become due, to an insurance company from a dependant (other than a debt to which regulation 41(2) or (3) below applies) shall be the amount which would reasonably be expected to be recovered in respect of that debt (due account being taken of any security held in respect thereof) if the dependant were in liquidation and—

(*a*) in the case of a dependant which is an insurance company, the amount realised from its assets and the amount of its liabilities in the liquidation were equal to the value of those assets and the amount of those liabilities, as determined in accordance with regulation 40 below, and

(*b*) in the case of a dependant which is not an insurance company, the amount realised from its assets in the liquidation were equal to the value of those assets, as determined in accordance with the said regulation 40.

(4) Any share in a dependant—

(*a*) in which there is no excess of assets over liabilities as is mentioned in paragraph (2) above, or

(*b*) in relation to which an insurance company cannot reasonably ascertain the amount of the liabilities of the dependant for the purposes of the said paragraph (2),

shall be left out of account for the purposes for which this Part of these Regulations applies.

(5) Where an insurance company is unable to determine the value of any debt due or to become due to the company from a dependant because it cannot reasonably ascertain the amount of the liabilities of the dependant for the purpose of ascertaining what would reasonably be expected to be recovered in respect of that debt in accordance with paragraph (3) above, the debt shall be left out of account for the purposes for which this Part of these Regulations applies.

Valuation of assets and liabilities of dependants for the purposes of regulation 39

40.—(1) This regulation shall apply with respect to the determination of the value of the assets and the amount of the liabilities of a dependant for the purposes of regulation 39 above.

(2) In the case of a dependant which is an insurance company, whether or not it is a company to which Part II of the 1974 Act applies—

(*a*) subject to paragraph (4) below and paragraph 3 of Schedule 7, the value of its assets shall be determined in accordance with this Part of these regulations;

(*b*) subject to paragraphs (*c*), (*d*), (*e*) and (*f*) below, the amount of its liabilities shall be determined in accordance with Part VI of these Regulations;

(*c*) where the dependant carries on general business, its general business liabilities shall be deemed to include an amount equal to whichever is the greater of 400,000 units of account or 20 per cent of the general premium income;

(*d*) where the dependant carries on long term business, its long term business liabilities shall from 15th March 1984 be deemed to include whichever is the greatest of the following three amounts—

(i) an amount ('the first amount') which is one-sixth of the margin of solvency that would be arrived at by regarding the dependant as having its head office in the United Kingdom (whether it has or not) and applying regulations 5 to 8 above;

(ii) an amount which is six times the first amount, reduced by the implicit figure within the meaning of sub-paragraph (*e*) below;

(iii) 800,000 units of account or, in the case described in paragraph 1(*a*) of Schedule 3, 200,000 units of account;

(*e*) for the purposes of sub-paragraph (*d*)(ii) above the implicit figure is—

(i) in the case of a dependant having its head office in the United Kingdom, the amount of any implicit items relating to future profits, zillmerising or hidden reserves which the dependant is permitted to count by virtue of an order under section 57 of the 1974 Act of the kind mentioned in regulation 10(4) above and the application of regulations 10(4), 11, 12 and 13 above, and

(ii) in the case of a dependant having its head office elsewhere than in the United Kingdom, the amount of any implicit items relating to future profits or zillmerising which would be arrived at by regarding the dependant as having its head office in the United Kingdom and as having received an order under section 57 of the 1974 Act of the kind mentioned in regulation 10(4) above and by applying regulations 10(4), 11, and 12 above accordingly;

(*f*) in any case where the dependant is required to establish a long term business fund or funds under section 23 of the 1974 Act, its long term business liabilities shall be deemed to be not less than the value of the assets representing that fund or funds.

(3) In the case of a dependant which is not an insurance company—

(*a*) the value of its assets shall be determined in accordance with this Part of these Regulations, subject to the provisions of and the modifications provided for in paragraphs 3 and 4 of Schedule 7;

(*b*) subject to paragraph (4) below, assets of the dependant which are of a relevant description shall be taken into account only to the extent that their value does not exceed the permitted limit applicable to the dependant in relation to those assets; and

(*c*) any equipment leased by the dependant exclusively to any person other than its subsidiary or holding company or a subsidiary of its holding company shall be valued as a debt for the purposes of this Part of these Regulations.

(4) Where—

(*a*) the dependant is an insurance company and has general business assets of a relevant description or is not an insurance company and has assets of a relevant description,

(*b*) the value of such assets exceeds the permitted limit applicable to the dependant in relation to those assets, and (*c*) the insurance company has no assets of the same description of the relevant class, or has assets of the same description of the relevant class and their value is less than the permitted limit applicable to the insurance company in relation to those assets,

then, for the purpose of determining the value of the assets of the dependant, there shall be added to the permitted limit applicable to the dependant in relation to the assets referred to in sub-paragraph (*a*) above an amount equal to the supplementary amount determined in accordance with Part I of Schedule 7.

(5) In this regulation and Schedule 7—

'assets of a relevant description' means assets of a description specified in Part I of Schedule 8 or, in the case of a dependant which is not an insurance company, assets which would be of such a description if it were an insurance company;

'the insurance company' means the company the value of whose shares in or debt due or to become due from the dependant is being determined in accordance with regulation 39 above;

'permitted limit' means, in relation to assets of a relevant description—

(*a*) in the case of the insurance company, or a dependant which is an insurance company, an amount equal to the percentage of the general business amount or, as the case may be, the long term business amount applicable in relation to assets of that description in accordance with regulation 49 below (as applied in the case of a dependant pursuant to paragraph (2) above); and

(*b*) in the case of a dependant which is not an insurance company, an amount equal to the percentage specified in Schedule 8, with respect to assets of that description, of the liabilities of the dependant, other than liabilities to the insurance company or any other related company of the insurance company;

and references to assets held by any company being of the same description as assets held by a dependant mean—

(i) in relation to land of the dependant of a description specified in paragraph 1 of Schedule 8, any interest of that other company in that land,

(ii) in relation to assets of the dependant of a description specified in paragraph 2 of Schedule 8, any debt due or to become due to that other company which is secured on the land on which the debt due or to become due to the dependant is secured, and

(iii) in relation to assets of the dependant of a description specified in paragraphs 3 to 13 of Schedule 8, assets of that other company which, if held by the dependant, would be assets of that description.

(6) Save as otherwise provided in paragraph 3(5) of Schedule 7, references in this regulation and in Schedule 7 to assets of the insurance company being of a relevant class mean—

(*a*) where this regulation and Schedule 7 are being applied for the purpose of determining the value of a long term business asset of the insurance company, assets of the insurance company which are long term business assets, and

(*b*) in any other case, assets of the insurance company which are general business assets.

(7) Where the insurance company cannot reasonably ascertain in accordance with the provisions of this regulation—

(*a*) the value of any asset of the dependant, or

(*b*) the amount of the permitted limit applicable in relation to any asset of the dependant,

that asset shall be left out of account in determining the value of the assets of the dependant under this regulation.

Debts and other rights

41.—(1) The value of any debt due, or to become due, to an insurance company, other than a debt to which regulation 39(3) above, paragraph (2), (3) or (4) of this regulation or regulation 46 or 48 below applies, shall be—

(*a*) in the case of any such debt which is due, or will become due, within twelve months of the relevant date (including any debt which would become due within that period if the company were to exercise any right to which it is entitled to require payment of the same), the amount which can reasonably be expected to be recovered in respect of that debt (due account being taken of any security being held in respect thereof); and

(*b*) in the case of any other such debt, the amount which would reasonably be paid by way of consideration for an immediate assignment of the debt together with the benefit of any security held in respect thereof.

Provided that in determining the amounts referred to in sub-paragraphs (*a*) and (*b*) above, no account shall be taken of any letter of credit.

(2) The value of any debt due, or to become due, to the company which is secured on a policy of insurance by the company and which (together with any other debt secured on that policy) does not exceed the amount payable on a surrender of that policy at the relevant date shall be the amount of that debt.

(3) Any debt due or to become due to the company—

(*a*) from an intermediary in respect of money advanced on account of commission to which that intermediary is not absolutely entitled at the relevant date, or

(*b*) in respect of unpaid share capital of the company, or

(*c*) under a letter of credit,

shall be left out of account for the purposes for which this Part of these Regulations applies.

(4) The value of any debt due to, or other rights of, the company under any contract of reinsurance to which the company is a party (other than a debt to which regulation 39(3) above applies) shall be the amount which can reasonably be expected to be recovered in respect of that debt or right.

(5) The value of any salvage right of the company shall be the amount which can reasonably be expected to be recovered by virtue of the exercise of that right.

Land

42.—The value of any land of an insurance company (other than land held by the company as security for a debt or to which regulation 47 below applies) shall be not greater than the amount which (after deduction of the reasonable expenses of sale) would be realised if the land were sold at a price equal to the most recent proper valuation of that land which has been provided to the company and any such land of which there is no proper valuation shall be left out of account for the purposes for which this Part of these Regulations applies.

Equipment

43.—(1) The value of any computer equipment of an insurance company—

(*a*) in the financial year of the company in which it is purchased, shall be not greater than three-quarters of the cost thereof to the company;

(*b*) in the first financial year thereafter, shall be not greater than one-half of that cost;

(*c*) in the second financial year thereafter, shall be not greater than one-quarter of that cost; and

(*d*) in any subsequent financial year, shall be left out of account for the purposes for which this Part of these Regulations applies.

(2) The value of any office machinery (other than computer equipment), furniture, motor vehicles and other equipment of an insurance company, shall be, in the financial year of the company in which it is purchased, not greater than one-half of the cost thereof and shall be, in any subsequent financial year, left out of account for the purposes for which this Part of these Regulations applies.

Unlisted securities

44.—(1) This regulation does not apply to the valuation of shares in a dependant of an insurance company.

(2) The value of an unlisted security which is dealt in on a recognised stock exchange within the meaning of the Companies Act 1948 or the Companies Act (Northern Ireland) 1960 or on a stock exchange of repute outside the United Kingdom shall be an amount not greater than the middle market quotation.

(3) The value of any unlisted equity share, other than a share to which paragraph (2) above applies, shall be not greater than—

(*a*) where the company in which the share is held has been carrying on business for more than three financial years, the multiple of the price earnings ratio for the relevant date (or, if no price earnings ratio has been published for that date, for the most recent date prior to that date for which a price earnings ratio has been published) and the proportionate amount attributable to that share of the average amount of the profits of the company for the last three financial years; and

(*b*) where the company has been carrying on business for less than three but more than one financial year, the multiple of such price earnings ratio and the proportionate amount attributable to that share of the average amount of the profits of the company for its two financial years or the profits of the company in its only financial year (as the case may be).

(4) For the purposes of this regulation, the average amount of the profits of a company for any specified years shall be the amount represented by the formula—

$$\frac{P-L}{Y}$$

where—

(*a*) P is the aggregate amount of the profits of the company after provision for taxation in each of the specified years,

(*b*) L is the aggregate amount of any losses made by the company after provision for taxation in any of the specified years in which there were no profits, and

(*c*) Y is the number of years specified,

no account being taken of any profit or loss brought forward from any year preceding the specified years.

(5) In this regulation, the proportionate amount attributable to any share of the average amount or the amount of any profits of the company in which the share is held for any specified years shall be the amount which could reasonably be expected to be received in respect of that share if the average amount or the amount (as the case may be) of the profits in question were available for distribution by the company among its shareholders.

(6) Where the value of any share would otherwise be determined in accordance with the provisions of paragraph (3) above but cannot be so determined because the amount of the profits of, or the amount of losses incurred by, the company in the last financial year cannot be reasonably ascertained, then the value of that share shall be determined—

(*a*) in the case of a company which has been carrying on business for not less than four financial years, by reference to the average amount of the profits of the company for the three financial years preceding the last financial year; and

(*b*) in the case of a company which has been carrying on business for less than four but more than two financial years, by reference to the average amount or the amount (as the case may be) of the profits of the company in any specified years other than the last financial year.

(7) Any share to be valued in accordance with paragraphs (3) to (6) above shall be left out of account for the purposes for which this Part of these Regulations applies if—

(*a*) no amount is attributable thereto in accordance with paragraph (3) above;
(*b*) the company in which the share is held has been carrying on business for less than one financial year; or
(*c*) the value of the share cannot be ascertained in accordance with paragraphs (3) to (6) above because the amount of the profits of, or the amount of the losses incurred by, the company in any of the specified years cannot reasonably be ascertained and no provision is made for its valuation in paragraph (6) above.

(8) The value of any unlisted share other than one to which paragraph (2) or (3) above applies shall be the amount which would reasonably be paid by way of consideration for an immediate transfer of that share.

Unit trusts

45.—The value of any holding of units, or other beneficial interest, under a unit trust scheme authorised for the purposes of the Prevention of Fraud (Investments) Act 1958 or the Prevention of Fraud (Investments) Act (Northern Ireland) 1940 shall be the price at which the managers under the unit trust scheme would purchase the holding of units or other beneficial interest if required to do so.

Listed investments

46.—(1) The value of any listed debenture which is not a debenture issued by a dependant of the insurance company, and of any listed share which is not a share in such a dependant nor a share in any body specified in regulation 48(2)(*a*) below, shall be the middle market quotation.

(2) Where the listing of any listed debenture or listed share, the value of which falls to be determined in accordance with this regulation, was suspended at a relevant date, then for the purpose or purposes for which that date was the relevant date—
(*a*) if that suspension was in force for a period in excess of ten days, that debenture or share shall be left out of account, and
(*b*) if that suspension was in force for a period not exceeding ten days, the value of that debenture or share shall be the lower of—
(i) the middle market quotation on the day before the day the suspension came into force, and
(ii) the middle market quotation on the day after the day the suspension was terminated.

(3) For the purposes of paragraph (2) above, a day which is a Saturday or a Sunday or a bank holiday in any part of the United Kingdom shall be disregarded.

Life interests, reversionary interests etc

47.—The value of any asset consisting of an interest in property which—
(*a*) is determinable upon the death of any person or upon the happening of some other future event or at some future time or is a remainder, reversionary interest, right of fee subject to a life rent or other future interest, whether vested or contingent, and
(*b*) is not a lease or reversionary interest expectant upon the determination of a lease,
shall be the amount which would reasonably be paid by way of consideration for an immediate transfer or assignment thereof.

Other assets

48.—(1) The value of any approved securities shall be—
(*a*) in the case of listed securities, the middle market quotation;
(*b*) in the case of securities which are not transferable, the amount payable on a

surrender or redemption of such securities at the relevant date; and

(*c*) in any other case, the amount which would reasonably be paid by way of consideration for an immediate transfer or assignment thereof.

(2) The value of—

(*a*) shares in any building society or industrial and provident society, and

(*b*) share options and debenture options, not being traded options,

shall be the amount which would reasonably be paid by way of consideration for an immediate transfer or assignment thereof.

(3) The value of traded options shall be the middle market quotation.

Assets to be taken into account only to a specified extent

49.—(1) Assets of an insurance company of any of the descriptions specified in Schedule 8 shall be taken into account only to the extent that the value of those assets does not exceed—

(*a*) for a company carrying on general business, whether or not also carrying on long term business, in the case of general business assets of a description specified in Part I of Schedule 8, an amount equal to the percentage of the general business amount specified in Schedule 8 for assets of that description;

(*b*) for a company carrying on only long term business, for all assets of a description specified in Part I of Schedule 8, an amount equal to the percentage of the long term business amount specified in Schedule 8 for assets of that description;

(*c*) for a company carrying on general business and long term business, in the case of long term business assets of a description specified in Part I of Schedule 8, an amount equal to the percentage of the long term business amount specified in Schedule 8 for assets of that description;

(*d*) for a company carrying on general business, whether or not also carrying on long term business, in the case of general business assets of the description specified in Part II of Schedule 8, an amount equal to the percentage specified in Schedule 8 of the net premium income of the company in respect of general business (other than premium income in respect of treaty reinsurance accepted) for the twelve months preceding the relevant date;

(*e*) for a company carrying on only long term business, for all assets of the description specified in Part II of Schedule 8, an amount equal to the percentage so specified of the net premium income of the company in respect of long term business (other than premium income in respect of treaty reinsurance accepted) for the twelve months preceding the relevant date; and

(*f*) for a company carrying on general business and long term business, in the case of long term business assets of the description specified in Part II of Schedule 8, an amount equal to the percentage so specified of the net premium income of the company in respect of long term business (other than premium income in respect of treaty reinsurance accepted) for the twelve months preceding the relevant date.

(2) In this regulation—

'general business amount' means the aggregate of the company's general business liabilities and in the case of a company which carries on general business an amount equal to whichever is the greater of 400,000 units of account or 20 per cent of the general premium income less the amount of the deduction specified in paragraph (3) below;

'long term business amount' means the aggregate of the company's long term business liabilities and (from 15th March 1984) whichever is the greater of—

(*a*) one-sixth of the margin of solvency which the company—

(i) if its head office is in the United Kingdom, is required to maintain, or

(ii) if its head office is elsewhere, would be required to maintain if its head office were in the United Kingdom, and (*b*) 800,000 units of account or, in the case described in paragraph 1(*a*) of Schedule 3, 200,000 units of account,

less the amount of the deduction specified in paragraph (3) below;

'the net premium income' of a company for any specified period means the gross amounts first recorded in the company's books during that period as paid or due to the company by way of premiums, less any rebates, refunds and commission so recorded during that period as allowed or paid on those gross amounts or on any such gross amounts so recorded in any previous period.

(3) The deduction to be made in determining the general business amount or the long term business amount in accordance with paragraph (2) above shall be the aggregate of the following—

(*a*) the amount of any general business or, as the case may be, long term business liabilities of the company to related companies, other than insurance liabilities, and

(*b*) the value of the debts due or become due to and other rights of the company under contracts of reinsurance ceded by it (but excluding any rights of recovery in respect of insurance liabilities already discharged by the company) which are general business or, as the case may be, long term business assets of the company, and

(*c*) in the case of the long term business amount, the amount of any liabilities of the company in respect of property linked benefits.

(4) Where—

(*a*) an asset (or a group of assets) of a company carrying on only long term business is attributed by the company partly to its long term business assets and partly to its other assets, and

(*b*) by virtue of paragraph (1)(*b*) above there is a reduction in the extent to which that asset or group of assets is to be taken into account,

the reduction shall be in the same proportion as the attribution.

(5) For the purposes of this regulation, the amount of the liabilities of an insurance company shall be determined in accordance with Part VI of these Regulations.

(6) This regulation shall not apply to any approved securities or to any interest accrued thereon.

Part VI

Determination of Liabilities

Interpretation: Part VI

50.—In this Part of these Regulations—

'long term liabilities' means liabilities of an insurance company arising under or in connection with contracts for long term business including liabilities arising from deposit back arrangements;

'the valuation date', in relation to an actuarial investigation, means the date to which the investigation relates.

Application: Part VI

51.—This Part of these Regulations applies with respect to the determination of the amount of liabilities of insurance companies for the purposes of—

(*a*) sections 24(6), 26, 26A, 26C, 26D, 30, 31 and 37 of the 1974 Act,

(*b*) section 22 of the 1981 Act,

(*c*) any investigation to which section 14 of the 1974 Act applies, and

(*d*) any investigation made in pursuance of a requirement under section 34 of the 1974 Act.

Long term and general business

52.—(1) Subject to this Part of these Regulations, the amount of liabilities of an insurance company in respect of long term and general business shall be determined in accordance with generally accepted methods appropriate for insurance companies.

(2) In determining under paragraph (1) above the amount of liabilities of an insurance company, all contingent and prospective liabilities shall be taken into account but not liabilities in respect of share capital.

Relevant co-insurance operations: general business

53.—(1) Where a relevant company determines the amount of a liability in order to make provision for outstanding claims arising under a relevant co-insurance operation, then, if the leading insurer has informed the company of the amount of the provision made by the leading insurer for such claims, the amount determined by the company—

(*a*) shall be at least as great as the amount of the provision made by the leading insurer, or

(*b*) in a case where it is not the practice in the United Kingdom to make such provision separately, shall be sufficient, when all liabilities are taken into account, to include provision at least as great as that made by the leading insurer for such claims,

due regard being had in either case to the proportion of the risk covered by the company and by the leading insurer respectively.

(2) In paragraph (1) above—

'leading insurer', in relation to a relevant co-insurance operation, means an insurer who—

(*a*) is recognised as the leading insurer by the other insurers involved in the operation, and

(*b*) determines the terms and conditions of insurance for the operation;

'relevant co-insurance operation' has the meaning given by Schedule 9;

'relevant company', in relation to a relevant co-insurance operation, means an insurer carrying on insurance business in the United Kingdom who is concerned in the operation but is not the leading insurer or a member of Lloyd's.

Long term liabilities

54.—The determination of the amount of long term liabilities (other than liabilities which have fallen due for payment before the valuation date) shall be made on actuarial principles and shall make proper provision for all liabilities on prudent assumptions in regard to the relevant factors; and that amount shall in the aggregate not in any case be less than the amount calculated in accordance with regulations 55 to 64 below (which shall apply only to long term liabilities).

Nature and term of assets

55.—The determination of the amount of long term liabilities shall take into account the nature and term of the assets representing the long term fund and the value placed upon them and shall include appropriate provision against the effects of possible future changes in the value of the assets on their adequacy to meet the liabilities.

Avoidance of future valuation strain

56.—The amount of the liability determined in respect of a group of contracts shall not be less than such amount as, if the assumptions adopted for the valuation were to remain unaltered and were fulfilled in practice, would enable liabilities similarly determined at all times in the future to be covered from resources arising solely from the contracts and the assets covering the amount of the liability determined at the current valuation.

Valuation of future premiums

57.—(1) Where further specified premiums are payable by the policy holder under a contract (not being a linked long term contract) under which benefits (other than benefits arising from a distribution of profits) are determined from the outset in relation to the total premiums payable thereunder, then, subject to regulation 58 below—

(*a*) where the premiums under the contract are at a uniform rate throughout the period for which they are payable, the premiums to be valued shall be not greater than such level premiums as, if payable for the same period as the actual premiums under the contract and calculated according to the rates of interest and rates of mortality or disability which are to be employed in calculating the liability under the contract, would have been sufficient at the outset to provide for the benefits under the contract according to the contingencies upon which they are payable, exclusive of any additions for profits, expenses or other charges;

(*b*) where the premiums under the contract are not at a uniform rate throughout the period for which they are payable, the premiums to be valued shall be not greater than such premiums as would be determined on the principles set out in sub-paragraph (*a*) above modified as appropriate to take account of the variations in the premiums payable by the policy holder in each year;

save that a premium to be valued shall in no year be greater than the amount of the premium payable by the policy holder.

(2) Where the terms of the contract have changed since the contract was first made (the terms of the contract being taken to change for the purposes of this paragraph if the change is indicated in an indorsement on the policy but not if a new policy is issued), then, for the purposes of paragraph (1) above it shall be assumed that those changes from the time they occurred were provided for in the contract at the time it was made.

(3) Where under a contract (not being a linked long term contract)—

(*a*) each premium paid increases the benefits (other than benefits arising from a distribution of profits) provided under the contract, or

(*b*) the amount of a premium payable in future is not determinable until it comes to be paid,

future premiums and the corresponding liability may be left out of account so long as adequate provision is made against any risk that the increase in the liabilities of the company resulting from the payment of future premiums might exceed the amount of the premiums.

Acquisition expenses

58.—(1) In order to take account of acquisition expenses, the maximum annual premium to be valued under regulation 57 above may (subject to paragraph (2) below) be increased by an amount not greater than the equivalent, taken over the whole period of premium payments and calculated according to the rates of interest and rate of mortality or disability employed in valuing the contract, of 3.5 per cent (or the defined percentage, if it is lower than 3.5 per cent) of the relevant capital sum under the contract.

(2) For the purposes of paragraph (1) above 'the defined percentage' is the percentage arrived at by taking (for all contracts of the same type as the contract in question for which an adjustment is made) the average of the percentages of the relevant capital sum under each such contract that represent the acquisition costs for which, after allowing for the effects of taxation, allowance is made in the premiums.

(3) The increase permitted by paragraph (1) above shall be subject to the limitation that the amount of a future premium valued shall not in any event be greater than the amount of the premium actually payable by the policy holder.

(4) For the purposes of this regulation—

(*a*) for contracts other than temporary assurances, the relevant capital sum under a contract shall be arrived at in accordance with regulation 12(4) above, and

(*b*) for temporary assurances, the relevant capital sum shall be the sum assured on the valuation date.

Rates of interest

59.—(1) In determining the rates of interest to be used in calculating the present value of future payments by or to an insurance company, regard shall be had to the yields on the existing assets attributed to the long term business and, to the extent appropriate, to the yield which it is expected will be obtained on sums to be invested in the future.

(2) For the purposes of paragraph (1) above, the assumed yield on an asset attributed to the long term business, before any adjustment to take account of the effect of taxation, shall not exceed the yield on that asset calculated in accordance with paragraphs (3) to (6) below, reduced by 7.5 per cent of that yield.

(3) For the purpose of calculating the yield on an asset—

(*a*) the asset shall be valued in accordance with Part V of these Regulations, excluding any provision under which assets may be taken at lower book values for the purposes of any investigation to which section 14 of the 1974 Act applies or any investigation made in pursuance of a requirement under section 34 of the 1974 Act, and

(*b*) where a particular asset is required to be taken into account only to a specified extent by the operation of regulation 49 above, the future income to be taken into account (whether interest, dividends or repayments of capital) shall be correspondingly reduced.

(4) For fixed interest investments (that is to say, investments which are fixed interest securities as defined in regulation 37(1) above) the yield on an asset, subject to paragraph (6) below, shall be that annual rate of interest which, if used to calculate the present value of future payments of interest before the deduction of tax and the present value of repayments of capital, would result in the sum of those amounts being equal to the value of the asset.

(5) For variable interest investments (that is to say, investments which are not fixed interest securities as defined in regulation 37(1) above) the yield on an asset, subject to paragraph (6) below, shall be the ratio to the value of the asset of the income before deduction of tax which would be received in the period of twelve months following the valuation date on the assumption that the asset will be held throughout that period and that the factors which affect income will remain unchanged, so however that account shall be taken of any changes in those factors known to have occurred by the valuation date and in particular, without prejudice to the generality of the foregoing, of—

(*a*) any known changes in the rental income from property or in dividends on equity shares,

(*b*) any forecast changes in dividends which have been publicly announced by the valuation date,

(*c*) the effect of any alterations in capital structure, and

(*d*) the value (at the most recent date for which it is known at the valuation date) of any determinant of the amount of any future interest payment, the said value being deemed to remain unaltered for all subsequent dates.

(6) In calculating the yield on an asset under this regulation—

(*a*) if the asset does not consist of equity shares or land—

(i) an adjustment shall be made to exclude that part of the yield estimated to represent compensation for the risk that the income from the asset might not be maintained or that capital repayments might not be received as they fall due, and

(ii) in making that adjustment, regard shall be had wherever possible to the yields on risk-free investments of a similar term in the same currency;

(*b*) for assets which are equity shares or land, adjustments to yields shall be made as appropriate to exclude that part, if any, of the total yield from those assets, taken together, that is needed to compensate for the risk that the aggregate income from those assets taking one year with another might not be maintained, so however that the yield assumed on an asset shall not be greater than that on British Government $2\frac{1}{2}$ per cent Consolidated Stock on the valuation date.

(7) To the extent that it is necessary to make an assumption about the yields which will be obtained on sums to be invested in future, the yield assumed on any investment to be made more than three years after the valuation date shall not exceed 7.2 per cent per annum before any adjustment to take account of the effect of taxation.

(8) In no case shall a rate of interest determined for the purposes of paragraph (1) above exceed the adjusted overall yield on assets calculated as the weighted average of the reduced yields on the individual assets arrived at under paragraph (2) above; and when that weighted average is calculated—

(*a*) the weight given to each investment shall be its value as an asset determined in accordance with Part V of these Regulations, excluding any provision under which assets may be taken at lower book values for the purposes of any investigation to which section 14 of the 1974 Act applies or any investigation made in pursuance of a requirement under section 34 of the 1974 Act, and

(*b*) except in relation to the rate of interest used in valuing payments of property linked benefits (as defined in regulation 37(1) above), both the yield and the value of any linked assets (as so defined) shall be omitted from the calculation.

For the purpose of determining the rates of interest to be used in valuing a particular category of contracts the assets may, where appropriate, be notionally apportioned between different categories of contracts and in such cases the limit under paragraph (8) above shall be applied on the basis of the overall yield on the assets apportioned to the contracts in question.

Rates of mortality and disability

60.—The amount of the liability in respect of any category of contract shall, where relevant, be determined on the basis of appropriate rates of mortality and disability that take into account—

(*a*) relevant published tables of rates of mortality and disability, and

(*b*) the rates of mortality and disability experienced in connection with any similar contracts issued by the company in the past.

Expenses

61.—(1) Provision shall be made for meeting the expenses likely to be incurred in future in fulfilling the existing contracts, taking account of the effect of taxation as appropriate, but credit may be taken to the extent appropriate for the fractions of future premiums left out of account pursuant to regulation 57(1) above.

(2) The provision mentioned in paragraph (1) above shall have regard to, among other things, the company's actual expenses in the last twelve months before the valuation date and the contingency that the company may cease to transact new business.

Options

62.—(1) Provision shall be made to cover any increase in liabilities caused by policy holders exercising options under their contracts.

(2) Where a contract includes an option whereby the policy holder could secure a guaranteed cash payment within twelve months following the valuation date, the provision for that option shall be such as to ensure that the value placed on the contract is not less than the amount required to provide for the payments that would have to be made if the option were exercised.

Contracts not to be treated as assets

63.—No contract for long term business shall be treated as an asset.

No credit for profits from voluntary discontinuance

64.—Allowance shall not be made in the valuation for the voluntary discontinuance of any contract if the amount of the liability so determined would thereby be reduced.

Part VII

Advertisements, Intermediaries, Notices of Long Term Policies, Linked Contracts and Revocations

'*Interpretation of regulations 65A to 65C*

65.—(1) For the purposes of regulations 65A to 65C below—

(*a*) 'authorised' in relation to an insurer, means authorised to carry on long term business in the United Kingdom by or under section 3 or 4 of the Insurance Companies Act 1982;

(*b*) 'insurance advertisement' means an insurance advertisement which invites any person to enter into or to offer to enter into, or which contains information calculated to lead directly or indirectly to any person entering or offering to enter into, any contract of insurance (other than a contract of reinsurance) the effecting of which would constitute the carrying on of ordinary long-term insurance business;

(*c*) 'permitted', in relation to an insurer, means permitted to carry on long term business in the United Kingdom otherwise than by virtue of section 3 or 4 of the Insurance Companies Act 1982.

(2) For the purposes of regulations 65A to 65C below, an insurance advertisement shall be taken to refer to an insurer—

(*a*) if the insurer is named in the advertisement; or

(*b*) if the insurer is identifiable from information contained in the advertisement; or

(*c*) if particulars of any of the terms upon which the insurer may be prepared to effect contracts of insurance or of any of the benefits which may accrue to the insured under a contract of insurance are contained in the advertisement.

Contents of advertisements (non-specific)

65A.—(1) This regulation applies to every insurance advertisement unless—

(*a*) an insurer is named in the advertisement (whether by his full name or by a name under which he ordinarily carries on business), and

(*b*) the advertisement is issued at a time when the insurer named in the advertisement is an authorised or permitted insurer.

but does not apply to an advertisement to which regulation 65B below applies.

(2) An advertisement to which this regulation applies and which relates to a contract of insurance with an insurer who, at the time when the advertisement is issued, is not an authorised or permitted insurer but does not refer to an insurer shall include the following matters, that is to say—

(*a*) the words 'This advertisement relates to an insurance company which does not, and is not authorised to, carry on in any part of the United Kingdom business of the class to which this advertisement relates. This means that the management and solvency of the company are not supervised by a United Kingdom Government Department. Holders of policies issued by the company will not be protected by the Policyholders Protection Act 1975 if the company should become unable to meet its liabilities to them'; and

(*b*) if it be the case, a statement—

(i) that the advertisement is also about securities; or

(ii) that the advertisement is also about securities or other investments, being securities or investments of a kind specified in the advertisement.

(3) Every insurance advertisement to which this regulation applies (other than an advertisement within paragraph (2) above) shall include, as may be appropriate, a statement—

(*a*) that the advertisement is about insurance; or

(*b*) that the advertisement is about insurance and securities; or

(*c*) that the advertisement is about insurance and securities or other investments, being securities or investments of a kind specified in the advertisement.

Contents of advertisements (overseas insurers)

65B.—(1) This regulation applies to any insurance advertisement which—

(*a*) relates to a contract of insurance with an insurer referred to in the advertisement, and

(*b*) is issued at a time when the insurer referred to in the advertisement is not an authorised or permitted insurer.

(2) Where an insurer referred to in an advertisement to which this regulation applies does not have his head office in a member State and either—

(*a*) he is not permitted under the laws of a member State to carry on business of a description similar to long term business, or

(*b*) he proposes to effect a contract of insurance to which the advertisement relates otherwise than through a branch or agency in a member State,

the advertisement shall contain the matters specified in paragraph (3) below.

(3) The matters referred to in paragraph (2) above are—

(*a*) the full name of the insurer and the country where the insurer is registered and the country where his principal office is situated (if different);

(*b*) the full name of any trustee of property of any description maintained by the insurer in respect of contracts of insurance to which the advertisement relates;

(*c*) an indication whether the investment of such property (or any part of it) is managed by the insurer (or his employee) or by another person and, where such investment is managed by such another person, the full name of every such investment manager;

(*d*) the registered office of any such trustee and of any such investment manager, and of his principal office (if different);

(*e*) where any person in the United Kingdom is to, or may, take any steps on behalf of the insurer with a view to the entering into of contracts of insurance to which the advertisement relates, the full name of, and the registered or principal office in the United Kingdom of, such United Kingdom agent or, if there is more than one, of a principal or main United Kingdom agent; and

(*f*) the words 'An insurance company which does not, and is not authorised to, carry on in any part of the United Kingdom business of the class to which this advertisement relates. This means that the management and solvency of the company are not supervised by a United Kingdom Government Department. Holders of policies issued by the company will not be protected by the Policyholders Protection Act 1975 if the company should become unable to meet its liabilities to them.'

(4) Every insurance advertisement to which this regulation applies (other than an advertisement within paragraph (2) above) shall include—

(*a*) the full name of the insurer and the country where the insurer is registered and the country where his principal office is situated (if different); and

(*b*) the words 'Holders of policies issued by the company will not be protected by the Policyholders Protection Act 1975 if the company should become unable to meet its liabilities to them'.

Provisions supplemental to regulations 65A and 65B

65C.—(1) The matters required to be included in an advertisement pursuant to regulation 65A or 65B above shall be shown prominently, clearly and legibly.

(2) The words specified in regulation 65B(3)(*f*) or (4)(*b*) above shall appear prominently—

(*a*) immediately after or alongside the statement of the full name of the insurer, or

(*b*) if the name (whether the full name or any other name) of the insurer is stated more than once in the advertisement, immediately after or alongside the most prominent of the statements of the name; and, for this purpose, if two or more statements of the name are equally prominent that which appears first in the advertisement shall be treated as the most prominent.

(3) An insurance advertisement to which regulation 65B above applies, if it states the name of any trustee, investment manager or United Kingdom agent of the insurer referred to in the advertisement and that trustee, investment manager or United Kingdom agent is not independent of the insurer referred to in the advertisement, shall contain a statement naming the insurer and stating that the trustee, investment manager or United Kingdom agent, as the case may require, is a person who is not independent of the insurer, and that statement shall appear prominently—

(*a*) immediately after or alongside the statement of the full name of the trustee, investment manager or United Kingdom agent, as the case may be, or

(*b*) if the name (whether the full name or any other name) of the trustee, investment manager or United Kingdom agent, as the case may be, of the insurer is stated more than once in the advertisement, immediately after or alongside the most prominent of the statements of the name; and, for this purpose, if two or more statements of a name are equally prominent that which appears first in the advertisement shall be treated as the most prominent.

(4) For the purposes of paragraph (3) above, a trustee, investment manager or United Kingdom agent of an insurer shall be regarded as not independent of the insurer at a particular time if, at that time—

(*a*) the person in question, his spouse or any partner, director, controller or manager of his is a partner, director, controller or manager of the insurer,

(*b*) the insurer or any partner, director, controller or manager of the insurer is the spouse or a partner, director, controller or manager of that person,

(*c*) that person is a body corporate and the insurer has any interest in any shares or debentures of it, or

(*d*) the insurer is a body corporate and that person, his spouse or any partner, director, controller or manager of his has any interest in any of the shares or debentures of the insurer,

and for this purpose a person shall be deemed to be interested in shares or debentures of a body corporate if he is interested in them according to the rules set out in section 28 of the Companies Act 1967 with the addition, in sub-section (9) of that section of a reference to a scheme made under section 20 of the Charities Act (Northern Ireland) 1964 and to an authorised unit trust scheme within the meaning of the Prevention of Fraud (Investments) Act (Northern Ireland) 1940.

(5) In regulations 65A and 65B above and this regulation, 'full name' means—

(*a*) in the case of a body corporate, its corporate name, and

(*b*) in the case of an individual or an unincorporated body, the name under which the individual or body lawfully carries on business.

Contents of advertisements: statements of capital

66.—Any insurance advertisement which contains the name of an insurance company to which Part II of the 1974 Act applies, being a company incorporated with a share capital, and which states the amount of the authorised capital of the company shall also state the amount of that capital which has been subscribed and the amount thereof which has been paid up at the time the advertisement is issued.

Intermediaries: connected persons

67.—(1) For the purposes of regulation 68 below a person is connected with an insurance company if—

(*a*) that person, or any partner, director, controller or manager of that person, is a partner, director, controller or manager of the insurance company or of any controller thereof;

(*b*) the insurance company, or any partner, director, controller or manager of the insurance company, is a partner, director, controller or manager of that person or of any controller thereof;

(*c*) that person or any controller thereof has a significant interest in shares of the insurance company or of any controller thereof;

(*d*) the insurance company or any controller thereof has a significant interest in shares of that person or of any controller thereof;

(*e*) that person, under any contract, not being a contract of employment, or under any other arrangement (whether legally enforceable or not) with the insurance company or with any associated company, undertakes not to perform any services relating to any class of insurance business (or any category thereof) for any insurance company other than the insurance company and, where the undertaking also relates to any associated company, the associated company:

Provided that an individual who gives an undertaking of the kind referred to above to any registered society shall not, by virtue of such undertaking, be a person connected with the society or with any company which is, within the meaning of section 150 of the Companies Act 1948 or section 144 of the Companies Act (Northern Ireland) 1960, a wholly owned subsidiary of the society.

(2) For the purposes of paragraph (1)(*c*) and (*d*) above, a person shall be treated as having an interest in shares of a company if, by virtue of section 28 (other than subsection (3)(*b*)) of the Companies Act 1967, he would be so treated for the purposes of section 27 of that Act; and the interest shall be treated as significant if it is such that notification of it would be required under section 33 of that Act.

(3) A person who issues an invitation of the kind mentioned in regulation 68(1) below in respect of a contract of insurance which will be underwritten at Lloyd's shall, in respect of that contract of insurance, be connected with the insurance company to which that contract relates if that person or any partner, director, controller or manager of that person will take a share in the contract as a member of Lloyd's.

(4) In this regulation—

'associated company', in relation to a body corporate means a subsidiary or holding company or subsidiary of the holding company of that body;

'controller', in relation to a body corporate which is not an insurance company, means a person who is or would be, if he were a company, a holding company of that body;

'manager', in relation to a body corporate which is not an insurance company, means a person who directly or indirectly takes part in or is concerned in the management of the affairs of that body.

Invitation by connected person

68.—(1) Subject to regulation 69 below, any person who invites another person who is ordinarily resident in the United Kingdom to make an offer or proposal or to take any other step with a view to entering into a contract of insurance with an insurance company shall, if he is connected with that company at the time the invitation is issued, provide the person to whom the invitation is issued, in the manner specified in paragraph (3) below, with information indicating the circumstances of his connection with that company.

(2) Subject to regulation 69 below, any person who, in the course of carrying on any business or profession invites another person who is ordinarily resident in the United Kingdom to make an offer or proposal or to take any other step with a view to entering into a contract of insurance with an insurance company which is not an authorised insurer shall provide the person to whom the invitation is issued, in the manner specified in paragraph (3) below, with information indicating that the insurance company to which the invitation relates is not an authorised insurer in respect of the contract in question.

(3) An intermediary shall provide the information required under paragraph (1) or (2) above in the following manner—

(*a*) where the invitation is issued in writing and is sent or delivered, by sending or (as the case may be) by delivering with the invitation a written statement containing that information;

(*b*) where the invitation is issued orally, by supplying that person with the information orally, and—

(i) if the person is present when the invitation is issued, by delivering to him immediately thereafter a written statement containing that information; or

(ii) if the person is not so present, by sending by post or causing to be delivered to him as soon as reasonably practicable, at the address supplied by him for the purpose or at his last known address, a written statement containing that information.

(4) The requirement of the written statement referred to in paragraph (3) above shall be deemed to have been complied with where the invitation issued by the intermediary under paragraph (1) above is issued on stationery having printed upon it, in prominent positions, on the side on which the invitation is contained, the name of the intermediary, the name of the insurance company and a clear statement of the relationship between them and which contains in the body of the invitation a clear indication of the name of the insurance company to which the invitation relates, expressed in the same style as in the printed statement:

Provided that where the intermediary is a Lloyd's broker or a member of Lloyd's and it is clearly indicated in the invitation that the contract will be underwritten at Lloyd's there may be inserted, in place of the statement of relationship referred to above, the expression 'Lloyd's Brokers' or (as the case may be) 'Mr. . . . . is a member of Lloyd's' without a reference to the name of the underwriters concerned.

(5) In this regulation—

'contract of insurance' does not include a contract of reinsurance or a contract of insurance the effecting and carrying out of which constitutes the carrying on of industrial assurance business or insurance business of groups 3 and 4 as specified in Part II of Schedule 2 to the 1981 Act;

'intermediary' means a person to whom the requirements of paragraph (1) or (2) above apply in respect of an invitation issued by him.

Cases excepted from regulation 68

69.—(1) Regulation 68 above shall not apply to—

(*a*) an invitation for the renewal or amendment of the terms of any contract of insurance effected before 11th October 1976;

(*b*) an invitation for the renewal or amendment of the terms of a contract of insurance effected as a result of an invitation issued by an intermediary in accordance with regulation 68 above where there has been no significant change in the circumstances relevant to the information provided when the contract was first effected;

(*c*) an amendment of an invitation issued by an intermediary in accordance with regulation 68 above where there has been no significant change in the circumstances relevant to the information provided when the invitation was first issued;

(*d*) an invitation for the effecting of a contract of insurance in respect of general business where—

(i) the contract relates to business of group 2 or 5 as specified in Part II of Schedule 2 to the 1981 Act and the initial premium to be paid in respect of that contract exceeds £5,000; or where the person to whom the invitation is made has, through the intermediary, prior to that invitation entered into other contracts of insurance of the class to which the contract relates and has paid premiums in respect thereof which in the aggregate either exceed £5,000 in the previous calendar year or exceed that figure in the calendar year during which the invitation in question is made; or

(ii) the contract relates to any other class of insurance business and the initial premium to be paid exceeds £1,000; or where the person to whom the invitation is made has, through the intermediary, prior to that invitation entered into contracts of insurance of the class to which the contract relates and has paid premiums in respect thereof which in the aggregate either exceed £1,000 in the previous calendar year or exceed that figure in the calendar year during which the invitation is made;

(*e*) an invitation for the effecting of a contract of insurance with such persons as are mentioned in section 2(2)(*b*) or (*c*) of the 1981 Act.

(2) Regulation 68(1) above shall not apply to an invitation for the effecting of a contract of insurance the carrying out of which is to be shared between two or more insurance companies where the share to be taken by any company, or the share in the aggregate to be taken by two or more companies, with which the intermediary is connected, does not exceed one-quarter of the total.

(3) Regulation 68(2) above shall not apply to an invitation for the effecting of a contract of insurance the carrying out of which is to be shared between two or more insurance companies where the share to be taken by any company which is not an authorised insurer, or the share in the aggregate to be taken by two or more companies which are not authorised insurers, does not exceed one-quarter of the total.

(4) In this regulation 'contract of insurance' and 'intermediary' have the same meaning as in regulation 68 above.

Notice of long-term contract

70.—(1) Subject to the following provisions of this regulation—

(*a*) a statutory notice in relation to an ordinary long-term contract which is not a linked long-term contract shall have the contents and be in the form set out in Schedule 10;

(*b*) a statutory notice in relation to an ordinary long-term contract which is a linked long-term contract shall have the contents and be in the form set out in Schedule 11;

(*c*) the notice of cancellation annexed to a statutory notice shall be a tear-off slip and shall have the contents and be in the form set out in Schedule 12.

(2) A statutory notice shall be printed on a single sheet of paper, and—

(*a*) if the notice is so printed that its text is continued on the back of the paper, the symbol and word '/over' shall be printed below that part of the text which appears on the front of the paper; and

(*b*) if the notice is so printed that its text appears entirely on one side of the paper, the notice of cancellation annexed thereto shall be so printed that not more than the last two lines of the text of that notice appears on the other side of the paper.

(3) The lettering of statutory notices and notices of cancellation shall be easily legible and of a colour which is readily distinguishable from the colour of the paper; and capital letters and figures shall be used in all the places in which they are shown in the form as set out in each Schedule.

(4) Except as provided in paragraph (5) below, no capital letter or figure in a statutory notice or a notice of cancellation shall be less than 2 millimetres high with lower case letters in proportion.

(5) The provisions of paragraph (4) above shall not apply to the lettering of the following items in a statutory notice which shall be smaller than all other lettering—

(*a*) the statement in brackets appearing beneath the words 'STATUTORY NOTICE RELATING TO LONG-TERM INSURANCE CONTRACT', and

(*b*) the two foot-notes.

(6) In statutory notices the lettering of the words 'IMPORTANT—YOU SHOULD READ THIS CAREFULLY' shall be set out in larger printing than all other lettering and in bolder printing than all other lettering except that of main headings and sub-headings.

(7) In statutory notices and notices of cancellation the lettering of all main headings and sub-headings shall be set out in bolder printing than all other lettering except (in the case of a statutory notice) that of the words 'IMPORTANT—YOU SHOULD READ THIS CAREFULLY'.

(8) In statutory notice and notices of cancellation there shall be substituted for words contained within square brackets in the appropriate Schedule and for the square brackets containing them the information or wording which, as indicated by those words, should be inserted there.

(9) Statutory notices and notices of cancellation shall be printed in roman or upright sanserif lettering, but the information or wording referred to in paragraph (8) above may be inserted in manuscript or otherwise after a notice has been printed.

(10) For the purposes of this regulation and Schedules 10, 11 and 12—

'notice of cancellation' means a notice of the kind mentioned in section 65(2)(*b*) of the 1974 Act;

'ordinary long-term contract' means (subject to regulation 71(*b*) below) a contract for ordinary long-term insurance business;

'statutory notice' means a notice of the kind mentioned in section 65(2) of the 1974 Act;

and in paragraphs 4 and 5 of the form set out in Schedule 10 and in paragraphs 5 and 6 of the form set out in Schedule 11, the reference to a name shall be deemed to include a reference to the description or title of the person concerned.

Exemptions from regulation 70

71.—Regulation 70 above shall not apply to—

(*a*) contracts which, by virtue of section 4(2) of the Policyholders Protection Act 1975, would not be regarded as United Kingdom contracts for the purposes of that Act;

(*b*) contracts for long term business of class IV in Schedule 1 to the 1981 Act;

(*c*) contracts for which the proposer is not an individual;

(*d*) contracts which form part of a retirement benefits scheme approved by the Board of Inland Revenue under section 19 or 20 of the Finance Act 1970 as amended by section 21 of the Finance Act 1971;

(*e*) contracts approved by the Board of Inland Revenue of the kind described in sections 226(13) and 226A(1) of the Income and Corporation Taxes Act 1970 as amended by Schedule 2 to the Finance Act 1971;

(*f*) contracts for which the proposer or, if there is more than one proposer, at least one of the proposers is neither a person on whose life the contract is made nor the spouse of such a person;

(*g*) contracts of term assurance, other than convertible term assurance, effected for periods of seven years or less;

(*h*) contracts into which the proposer is required to enter in order to obtain credit under a personal credit agreement of the kind mentioned in section 8(1) of the Consumer Credit Act 1974;

(*i*) contracts under which the benefits payable are secured by payment of a single premium.

Linked contracts

72.—(1) Benefits payable under any contract to which this regulation applies shall not be determined, either wholly or partly, by reference to the value of, or the income from, or fluctuations in the value of, property of any description other than—

(*a*) property of any of the descriptions specified in Part I of Schedule 13, or

(*b*) property which was property of any of the descriptions specified in paragraphs 1 to 7 of Part I of Schedule 13 when it first became a property by reference to which benefits under that contract, or under any contract of a similar description to that contract, were to be determined, and which ceased to conform with that description not more than fifteen months previously.

(2) Benefits payable under any contract to which this regulation applies shall not be determined, either wholly or partly, by reference to fluctuations in any index of the value of property other than an index described in Part II of Schedule 13.

(3) This regulation applies to ordinary long-term contracts which—

(*a*) are entered into by insurance companies to which Part II of the 1974 Act applies or by members of Lloyd's or have been entered into by any such insurance company or other person at any time before 1st July 1975 and are still in force;

(*b*) are contracts under which the benefits payable to the policy holder are wholly or partly to be determined by reference to the value of, or the income from, property of any description (whether or not specified in the contract) or by reference to fluctuations in, or in an index of, the value of property of any description (whether or not so specified); and

(*c*) are not contracts specified in paragraph (4) below as being contracts to which this regulation does not apply.

(4) The contracts referred to in paragraph 3(*c*) above to which this regulation does not apply are—

(*a*) contracts entered into before 2nd June 1975 providing for benefits which would, if they had become due for payment on that date, have been wholly or partly determined either—

(i) by reference to the value of, or the income from or fluctuations in the value of, property of any description other than a description specified in Part I of Schedule 13, or

(ii) by reference to fluctuations in an index of the value of property other than an index specified in Part II of Schedule 13;

(*b*) contracts entered into after 2nd June 1975 but before 1st September 1976, which are contracts of a similar description to any contract falling within sub-paragraph (*a*) above;

(*c*) contracts with any policy holder who is a person not ordinarily resident in the United Kingdom;

(*d*) contracts the effecting of which by the insurer constitutes the carrying on of industrial assurance business;

(*e*) contracts entered into by an insurance company to which Part II of the 1974 Act applies by reason only that the policy holder is eligible to participate in any established surplus as defined in section 25(4) of the 1974 Act;

(*f*) contracts under or relating to a retirement benefits scheme (whether evidenced by deed, agreement or series of agreements or other arrangement) not being a scheme whereby—

(i) the benefit is assured by means of one or more contracts;

(ii) each contract provides in respect of each member of the scheme separate assurance, the proceeds of which are to go to that member at least to the extent that they are not greater than the benefits to which he is entitled at normal pension age;

(iii) the premium payable under each contract in respect of each member is payable at least annually; and

(iv) the amount of the premium (expressed as an annual rate) remains unchanged except in consequence of the declaration of a bonus or a change in the premium rate of the insurer.

(5) In this regulation—

'ordinary long-term contract' means a contract for ordinary long-term insurance business;

'retirement benefits scheme' means a scheme for the provision to a member of the scheme or to his wife or widow, children, dependants or personal representatives of any pension, annuity, lump sum, gratuity or other like benefit given or to be given on retirement or on death, or in anticipation of retirement, or, in connection with past service, after retirement or death, except that it does not include any benefit which is to be afforded solely by reason of the disablement by accident of a member occurring during his service or of his death by accident so occurring and for no other reason.

(6) Any reference in this regulation to contracts of a similar description to any specified contract is a reference to contracts which correspond with that contract in both the following respects—

(*a*) the provisions defining the descriptions of property or indices by reference to which the benefits payable thereunder are to be determined are the same as in that contract; and

(*b*) the insurance company or other person undertaking to pay the benefits provided for thereunder is the same as in that contract.

Revocations

73.—The regulations mentioned in Schedule 14 are hereby revoked.

SCHEDULES

SCHEDULE 1

Regulation 4

GENERAL BUSINESS SOLVENCY MARGIN: FIRST METHOD OF CALCULATION (PREMIUM BASIS)

1. In this Schedule—

'net premiums'—

(*a*) means premiums after deduction of discounts, refunds and rebates of premium, and

(*b*) includes premiums receivable under reinsurance contracts accepted (there being no deduction of premiums for reinsurance ceded).

'receivable', in relation to an insurance company, a financial year and a premium, means recorded in the company's books as due to the company in respect of—

(*a*) a contract commencing in that year, or

(*b*) a contract not accounted for in an annual revenue account of the company prior to that year, even though the contract commenced in an earlier financial year,

whether or not the company has received the premium;

'recoverable', in relation to an insurance company and a financial year, means recorded in the company's books as due in that year, whether or not the company has received any payment.

2. The net premiums receivable by members of Lloyd's for the last preceding

financial year in respect of general business shall be aggregated; and the resulting figure shall be multiplied by a flat-rate percentage determined for that year by the Secretary of State in the light of the most recent statistical data on commissions paid.

3. From the amount arrived at under paragraph 2 above there shall be deducted—

(*a*) any taxes included in the premiums mentioned in paragraph 2 above, and

(*b*) any levies that are related to premiums and are recorded in the company's books as payable in the last preceding financial year in respect of general business.

4. The amount arrived at under paragraph 3 above shall be multiplied by twelve and divided by the number of months in the financial year.

5. If the amount arrived at under paragraph 4 above is more than 10 million units of account, it shall be divided into two portions, the former consisting of 10 million units of account and the latter comprising the excess.

6. Where there has been a division into two portions pursuant to paragraph 5 above, there shall be calculated and added together 18 per cent and 16 per cent of the two portions respectively; and where there has been no such division, there shall be calculated 18 per cent of the amount arrived at under paragraph 4 above.

7. In the case of general business consisting of health insurance based on actuarial principles, paragraph 6 above shall apply with the substitution of '6 per cent' for 18 per cent' and '$5\frac{1}{3}$ per cent' for '16 per cent', but only if all the necessary conditions are satisfied.

8. For the purposes of paragraph 7 above, the necessary conditions are as follows, that is to say—

(*a*) the gross premiums receivable shall be calculated on the basis of sickness tables appropriate to insurance business;

(*b*) the reserves shall include provision for increasing age;

(*c*) an additional premium shall be collected in order to set up a safety margin of an appropriate amount;

(*d*) it shall not be possible for the insurer to cancel the contract after the end of the third year of insurance;

(*e*) the contract shall provide for the possibility of increasing premiums or reducing payments during its currency.

9. Where paragraph 7 above applies to a company whose general business consists partly of health insurance based on actuarial principles and partly of other business, the procedure provided in paragraphs 2 to 7 above shall operate separately for each part of the general business, so as to produce a sum under paragraph 7 above for the health insurance and a sum under paragraph 6 above for the other business.

10.—(1) If the provision for claims outstanding at the end of the last preceding financial year exceeds the provision for claims outstanding at the beginning of that year, the amount of the excess shall be added to the amount of claims paid in the last preceding financial year.

(2) If the provision for claims outstanding at the beginning of the last preceding financial year exceeds the provision for claims outstanding at the end of that year, the amount of the excess shall be deducted from the amount of claims paid in the last preceding financial year.

11.—(1) For the purposes of paragraph 10 above, the amount of claims paid, in relation to an insurance company and a financial year, is the amount that is recorded in the company's books as at the end of the financial year as paid by it (whether or not payment has been effected in that year) in full or partial settlement of—

(*a*) the claims described in sub-paragraph (2) below, and

(*b*) the expenses described in sub-paragraph (3) below,

less any recoverable amounts within the meaning of sub-paragraph (4) below.

(2) The claims mentioned in sub-paragraph (1) above are claims under contracts of insurance (and under contracts of reinsurance accepted by the company) including claims relating to business accounted for over a longer period than a financial year.

(3) The expenses mentioned in sub-paragraph (1) above are expenses (such as, for example, legal, medical, surveying or engineering costs) which are incurred by the company, whether through the employment of its own staff or otherwise, and are directly attributable to the settlement of individual claims, whether or not the individual claims in question are those mentioned in sub-paragraph (1) above.

(4) Recoverable amounts for the purposes of sub-paragraph (1) above are amounts recoverable by the company in respect of the claims mentioned in that sub-paragraph or other claims, including amounts recoverable by way of salvage, amounts recoverable from third parties and amounts recoverable from other insurers but excluding amounts recoverable in respect of reinsurance ceded by the company.

12.—(1) For the purposes of paragraph 10 above, the provision for claims outstanding, in relation to an insurance company and a financial year, is (subject to any applicable valuation regulations) the amount set aside by the company as at the beginning or end of the financial year as being an amount likely to be sufficient to meet—

(*a*) the claims described in sub-paragraph (2) below, and
(*b*) the expenses described in sub-paragraph (3) below,

less any recoverable amounts within the meaning of sub-paragraph (4) below.

(2) The claims mentioned in sub-paragraph (1) above are claims under contracts of insurance (and under contracts of reinsurance accepted by the company) in respect of incidents occurring—

(*a*) in the case of an amount set aside as at the beginning of the financial year, before the beginning of that year, and
(*b*) in the case of an amount set aside as at the end of a financial year, before the end of that year,

being claims which have not been treated as claims paid and including claims relating to business accounted for over a longer period than a financial year, claims the amounts of which have not been determined and claims arising out of incidents that have not been notified to the company.

(3) The expenses mentioned in sub-paragraph (1) above are expenses (such as, for example, legal, medical, surveying or engineering costs) which are likely to be incurred by the company, whether through the employment of its own staff or otherwise, and are directly attributable to the settlement of individual claims, whether or not the individual claims in question are those mentioned in sub-paragraph (1) above.

(4) Recoverable amounts for the purposes of sub-paragraph (1) above are amounts estimated by the company to be recoverable by it in respect of the claims mentioned in that sub-paragraph, including amounts recoverable by way of salvage, amounts recoverable from third parties and amounts recoverable from other insurers but excluding amounts recoverable in respect of reinsurance ceded by the company.

13. From the amount determined under paragraph 10(1) or (2) above there shall be deducted the total sum recoverable in respect of that amount under reinsurance contracts ceded.

14. The amount determined under paragraph 13 above shall be expressed as a percentage of the amount determined under paragraph 10(1) or (2) above.

15. The sum arrived at under paragraph 6 or 7 above or the aggregate of the sums arrived at under those paragraphs, as the case may be, shall be multiplied—

(*a*) where the percentage at under paragraph 14 above is greater than 50 per cent but not greater than 100 per cent, by the percentage so arrived at,
(*b*) where the percentage so arrived at is greater than 100 per cent, by 100 per cent, and
(*c*) in any other case, by 50 per cent.

SCHEDULE 2

Regulation 4

GENERAL BUSINESS SOLVENCY MARGIN: SECOND METHOD OF CALCULATION (CLAIMS BASIS)

1. In this Schedule 'reference period', in relation to an insurance company, means either—
   (*a*) the three last preceding financial years, or
   (*b*) the seven last preceding financial years if more than one-half of the gross premiums receivable (as defined in Schedule 1) in that period were in respect of all or any of the following, namely, storm (as included in general business class 8), hail (as included in general business class 9) and frost (as included in general business class 9).

2. If a company has not been in existence long enough to acquire a reference period, this Schedule shall be deemed to give a lower result than that given by Schedule 1 and shall otherwise not apply to the company.

3.—(1) If the provision for claims outstanding at the end of the reference period exceeds the provision for claims outstanding at the beginning of the reference period, the amount of the excess shall be added to the amount of claims paid in the reference period.

(2) If the provision for claims outstanding at the beginning of the reference period exceeds the provision for claims outstanding at the end of the reference period, the amount of the excess shall be deducted from the amount of claims paid in the reference period.

(3) For the purposes of this paragraph the expressions 'amount of claims paid' and 'provision for claims outstanding' have, in relation to a reference period, the same meaning as they have in paragraph 10 of Schedule 1 in relation to a financial year.

4. The aggregate obtained under paragraph 3(1) or (2) above shall be divided by the number of months in the reference period and multiplied by twelve.

5. If the amount arrived at under paragraph 4 above is more than 7 million units of account, it shall be divided into two portions, the former consisting of 7 million units of account and the latter comprising the excess.

6. Where there has been a division into two portions pursuant to paragraph 5 above, there shall be calculated and added together 26 per cent and 23 per cent of the two portions respectively; and where there has been no such division, there shall be calculated 26 per cent of the amount arrived at under paragraph 4 above.

7. In the case of general business consisting of health insurance based on actuarial principles, paragraph 6 above shall apply with the substitution of '$8\frac{2}{3}$ per cent' for '26 per cent' and '$7\frac{2}{3}$ per cent' for '23 per cent', but only if all the necessary conditions are satisfied.

8. The necessary conditions for the purposes of paragraph 7 above are the same as those set out in paragraph 8 of Schedule 1.

9. In a case of the kind mentioned in paragraph 9 of Schedule 1, that paragraph shall apply (with the necessary modifications) so as to produce separate sums under paragraphs 6 and 7 above.

10. The sum arrived at under paragraph 6 or 7 above or the aggregate of the sums arrived at under those paragraphs, as the case may be, shall be multiplied by the same percentage as is applicable for the purposes of paragraph 15 of Schedule 1.

SCHEDULE 3

Regulation 9(2)

MINIMUM GUARANTEE FUND

Long term business

1. Subject to paragraph 9 below, the minimum guarantee fund for long term business shall be—
   (*a*) in the case of a pure reinsurer which—
      (i) is the wholly-owned subsidiary of an insurance company carrying on long term business, and
      (ii) carries on only such reinsurance business as is ceded to it by that company,

200,000 units of account,
   (*b*) in the case of a mutual, 600,000 units of account, and
   (*c*) in any other case, 800,000 units of account.

2. [*repealed*].

3. [*repealed*].

4. [*repealed*].

5. [*repealed*].

General business

6. Subject to paragraphs 7, 8 and 9 below, the minimum guarantee fund for general business shall be the amount shown in the table below as applicable to the general business class for which the relevant company is authorised (or the highest such amount if the company is authorised for more than one class).

GENERAL BUSINESS CLASS	AMOUNT
Class 10, 11, 12, 13, 14 or 15	400,000 units of account
Class 1, 2, 3, 4, 5, 6, 7, 8 or 16	300,000 units of account
Class 9 or 17	200,000 units of account

7. A company authorised for part of a class shall, for the purposes of paragraph 6 above, be regarded as authorised for the whole of the class.

8. In the case of a mutual, the minimum guarantee fund required by paragraphs 6 and 7 above shall be reduced by 25 per cent.

Long term and general business.

9. In relation to a United Kingdom or Community margin of solvency maintained under section 26A(2)(*b*) or (3)(*b*) of the 1974 Act, the minimum guarantee fund for long term business or general business shall be one-half of the amount arrived at by applying the foregoing provisions of this Schedule.

SCHEDULE 4

Regulation 29

INFORMATION TO BE SUBMITTED: LONG TERM BUSINESS

PART I

UNITED KINGDOM COMPANIES (DIRECT BUSINESS AND REINSURANCE)

The company

1. *Date of incorporation and registered number.

2. *Brief summary of the objects of the company.

3. A statement showing the amount by which the assets are expected to exceed liabilities at the date of authorisation (after application of valuation regulations) and how calculated.

4. *Date on which the company's financial year will end.

5. *Name and address of the auditors of the company.

6. *Names and addresses of the company's principal bankers.

7. Names of the persons who will be directors, controllers or managers of the company. The appropriate form prescribed in the Change of Control Regulations shall be completed for each person listed.

8. Particulars of any association which exists or which is proposed to exist between the directors or controllers of the company and any person who acts or will act as an insurance broker, agent, loss adjuster or reinsurer for the company.

Authorisations to be continued

9. Particulars of classes of insurance business for which the company is already authorised in the United Kingdom and which it wishes to be included in the new authorisation.

Scheme of operations

10. **The sources of business (for example, insurance brokers, agents, own employees or direct selling), and the approximate percentage expected from each source.

11. **The nature of the commitments which the company proposes to take on and the general and special policy or treaty conditions which it proposes to use.

12. **A statement showing for each of the first three financial years following authorisation for each type of contract or treaty, on both optimistic and pessimistic bases and broken down between the United Kingdom, other member States and elsewhere—
   (*a*) the number of contracts or treaties expected to be issued,
   (*b*) the total premium income both gross and net of reinsurance, and
   (*c*) the total sums assured or amounts of annuity per annum.

13. **The technical bases that the actuary who will be appointed for the purposes of

section 15 of the 1974 Act proposes to employ for each class of business, including the bases needed for calculating premium rates and mathematical reserves.

14. **The guiding principles as to reinsurance including the company's maximum retention per risk or event after all reinsurance ceded and the names of the principal reinsurers.

15. *The assets which represent or will represent the minimum guarantee fund being assets admissible under and valued in accordance with the Asset Valuation Regulations and the names of the principal insurers.

16. **The estimated costs of installing the administrative services and organisation for securing business, and the financial resources intended to cover those costs.

Projections

17. For each of the first three financial years following authorisation—
(*a*) a forecast balance sheet (on both optimistic and pessimistic bases),
(*b*) a plan (on both optimistic and pessimistic bases) setting out detailed estimates of income and expenditure in respect of direct business, reinsurance acceptances and reinsurance cessions, and
(*c*) estimates relating to the financial resources intended to cover underwriting liabilities and the margin of solvency.

17A. The technical bases used to calculate the forecast and estimates specified in paragraph 17 above and the factors used to determine the level of the required margin of solvency assumed for the purposes of paragraph 17(*c*) above.

Other information, agreements, treaties and certificates required

18. A statement showing the types of investments which are expected to represent the insurance funds and the estimated proportion which will be represented by each type of investment.

19. **Copies or drafts of reinsurance treaties.

20. **Copies or drafts of any standard agreements with brokers or agents.

21. **Copies or drafts of any agreements with persons (other than employees of the company) who will manage the business of the company.

22. **A certificate by the actuary who will be appointed for the purposes of section 15 of the 1974 Act that—
(*a*) he considers the premium rates to be suitable,
(*b*) he considers the financing of the company to be sufficient to cover both technical reserves and the required margin of solvency during the first three financial years following authorisation, and
(*c*) he agrees with the information provided under paragraphs 11, 14 and 17 above.

NOTES

*This information is not required from applicants already authorised to carry on insurance business in the United Kingdom.

**This information is required only in respect of the classes of insurance business for which new authorisation is being sought.

PART II

NON-UK COMMUNITY COMPANIES (DIRECT BUSINESS OR BOTH DIRECT BUSINESS AND REINSURANCE)

The company

1. *Date of incorporation, place of incorporation and registered number.

2. *Copies of the memorandum and articles of association of the company (or their equivalent
3. *Name and address of the auditors of the company in the United Kingdom.
4. *Names and addresses of the company's principal bankers in the United Kingdom.
5. Names of the directors and managers of the company.
6. Names of the persons who will be the principal United Kingdom executive, the authorised United Kingdom representative or an employee within section 8(4)(*c*) of the 1981 Act. The appropriate form prescribed in the Change of Control Regulations shall be completed for each person listed.
7. Particulars of any association which exists or which is proposed to exist between the directors or controllers of the company and any person who acts or will act as an insurance broker, agent, loss adjuster or reinsurer for the company in the United Kingdom.

Statement from head office supervisor

8. A statement from the supervisory authority of the member State in which the company has its head office stating the classes of insurance business which the company is authorised to carry on in that member State, specifying the risks covered there, declaring that the company has the required margin of solvency or minimum guarantee fund and specifying the financial resources from which the costs referred to in paragraph 16 below will be met.

Authorisations to be continued

9. Particulars of classes of insurance business for which the company is already authorised in the United Kingdom and which it wishes to be included in the new authorisation.

Scheme of operations for the United Kingdom

10. **The sources of business in the United Kingdom (for example, insurance brokers, agents, own employees or direct selling) with the approximate percentage expected from each source.
11. **The nature of the commitments which the company proposes to take on in the United Kingdom and the general and special policy or treaty conditions which it proposes to use.
12. **A statement in respect of the United Kingdom business showing for each of the first three financial years following authorisation and for each type of contract or treaty, on both optimistic and pessimistic bases—

(*a*) the number of contracts or treaties expected to be issued,
(*b*) the total premium income both gross and net of reinsurance ceded, and
(*c*) the total sums assured or amounts of annuity per annum.

13. **The technical bases that the actuary who will be appointed for the purposes of section 15 of the 1974 Act proposes to employ for each class of business in the United Kingdom, including the bases needed for calculating premium rates including mathematical reserves.
14. **The guiding principles as to reinsurance of business written in the United Kingdom including the maximum retention per risk or event after all reinsurance ceded and the names of the principal reinsurers.
15. A statement showing the current margin of solvency of the company, the margin of solvency required and how both have been calculated and the names of the principal reinsurers.
16. **The estimated costs of installing the administrative services and organisation for securing business in the United Kingdom and the financial resources intended to cover those costs.

Projections for the United Kingdom

17. For each of the first three financial years following authorisation, on both optimistic and pessimistic bases—

(*a*) a forecast balance sheet for the proposed agency or branch, and

(*b*) a plan setting out detailed estimates of income and expenditure in respect of direct business, reinsurance acceptances and reinsurance cessions of the proposed agency or branch.

17A. The technical bases used to calculate the forecast and estimates specified in paragraph 17 above.

Accounts, agreements, treaties and certificates required

18. *Balance sheets and profit and loss accounts of the company for each of the last three financial years or, if the company has not been in business for three financial years, for each of the financial years for which it has been in business.

19. A statement showing the types of investments which are expected to represent the insurance funds in the United Kingdom and the estimated proportion which will be represented by each type of investment.

20. **Copies or drafts of any separate reinsurance treaties covering business written in the United Kingdom.

21. **Copies or drafts of any standard agreements which the company will have with brokers or agents in the United Kingdom.

22. **Copies or drafts of any agreement which the company will have with persons (other than employees of the company) who will manage the business of the proposed branch.

23. **A certificate by the actuary who will be appointed for the purposes of section 15 of the 1974 Act indicating the sums he considers it will be necessary to transfer from the company's head office in each of the first three years after authorisation to provide adequate technical reserves in the United Kingdom and stating that—

(*a*) he considers the premium rates which will be used in the United Kingdom are suitable, and

(*b*) he agrees with the information provided under paragraphs 11, 14 and 17 above.

NOTES

*This information is not required from applicants already authorised to carry on insurance business in the United Kingdom.

**This information is required only in respect of the classes of insurance business for which new authorisation is being sought.

PART III

EXTERNAL COMPANIES (DIRECT BUSINESS OR BOTH DIRECT BUSINESS AND REINSURANCE)

The company

1. *Date of incorporation, place of incorporation and registered number.

2. *Brief summary of the objects of the company.

3. A statement of the classes of insurance business which the company is authorised to carry on in the country in which its head office is situated.

4. The assets which represent or will represent the minimum guarantee fund in the United Kingdom being assets admissible under and valued in accordance with the Asset Valuation Regulations.

5. *Name and address of the auditors of the company in the United Kingdom.

6. *Names and addresses of the company's principal bankers in the United Kingdom.

7. Names of the persons who will be directors, controllers or managers of the company, its principal United Kingdom executive, or its authorised United Kingdom

representative. The appropriate form prescribed in the Change of Control Regulations shall be completed for each person listed.

8. Particulars of any association which exists or which is proposed to exist between the directors or controllers of the company and any person who acts or will act as an insurance broker, agent or loss adjuster for the company in the United Kingdom or a reinsurer of the company.

Authorisations to be continued

9. Particulars of classes of insurance business for which the company is already authorised in the United Kingdom and which it wishes to be included in the new authorisation.

Scheme of operations for the United Kingdom

10. **The sources of business in the United Kingdom (for example, insurance brokers, agents, own employees or direct selling) and the approximate percentage expected from each source.

11. **The nature of the commitments which the company proposes to take on in the United Kingdom and the general and special policy or treaty conditions which it proposes to use.

12. **A statement in respect of United Kingdom business showing for each of the first three financial years following authorisation and for each type of contract or treaty, on both optimistic and pessimistic bases—

(*a*) the number of contracts or treaties expected to be issued,
(*b*) the total premium income both gross and net of reinsurance ceded, and
(*c*) the total sums assured or amounts of annuity per annum.

13. **The technical bases that the actuary who will be appointed for the purposes of section 15 of the 1974 Act proposes to employ for each class of business carried on in the United Kingdom including the bases needed for calculating premium rates and mathematical reserves.

14. **The guiding principles as to reinsurance of business written in the United Kingdom including the company's maximum retention per risk or event after all reinsurance ceded and the names of the principal reinsurers.

15. A statement showing the current margin of solvency of the company (after application of valuation regulations), the margin of solvency required and how both have been calculated and the names of the principal reinsurers.

16. **The estimated costs of installing the administrative services and organisation for securing business in the United Kingdom, and the financial resources intended to cover those costs.

Projections for the United Kingdom

17. For each of the first three financial years following authorisation, on both optimistic and pessimistic bases—

(*a*) a forecast balance sheet for the proposed agency or branch, and
(*b*) a plan setting out detailed estimates of income and expenditure in respect of direct business, reinsurance acceptances and reinsurance cessions of the proposed agency or branch.

17A. The technical bases used to calculate the forecast and estimates specified in paragraph 17 above.

Other information, accounts, agreements, treaties and certificates required

18. *Balance sheets and profit and loss accounts of the company for each of the last three financial years or, if the company has not been in business for three financial years, for each of the financial years for which it has been in business.

19. A statement showing the types of investments which are expected to represent the

insurance funds in the United Kingdom and the estimated proportion which would be represented by each type of investment.

19A. The technical bases used to calculate the forecasts and estimates specified in paragraph 19 above.

20. For each of the first three financial years following authorisation, the estimated world-wide premium income of the company both gross and net of reinsurance ceded and broken down between the United Kingdom, other member States and elsewhere.

21. A brief description of the risks the company will underwrite outside the United Kingdom.

22. A brief summary of the reinsurance arrangements for the business of the company outside the United Kingdom including the company's maximum retention per risk or event after all reinsurance ceded and the names of the principal reinsurers.

23. Estimated capital expenditure in respect of operations outside the United Kingdom during each of the first three financial years following authorisation.

24. **Copies or drafts of any separate reinsurance treaties covering business written in the United Kingdom.

25. **Copies or drafts of any standard agreements which the company will have with brokers or agents in the United Kingdom.

26. **Copies or drafts of any agreements which the company will have with persons (other than employees of the company) who will manage the business of the proposed branch.

27. **A certificate by the actuary who will be appointed for the purposes of section 15 of the 1974 Act stating that the premium rates which will be used in the United Kingdom are suitable and that he agrees with the information provided under paragraphs 11, 14 and 17 above.

28. A certificate by the actuary of the company stating that he considers the finances of the company are sufficient—

(*a*) to meet the required technical reserves for its total business on both optimistic and pessimistic bases in the first three financial years following authorisation, and

(*b*) to provide the required margin of solvency.

NOTES

*This information is not required from applicants already authorised to carry on insurance business in the United Kingdom.

**This information is required only in respect of the classes of insurance business for which new authorisation is being sought.

PART IV

NON-UK COMMUNITY COMPANIES AND EXTERNAL COMPANIES (REINSURANCE ONLY)

The company

1. *Date of incorporation, place of incorporation and registered number.

2. *A brief summary of the objects of the company.

3. A statement showing the classes of insurance business which the company is authorised to carry on in the country in which its head office is situated and particulars of any limitations.

4. *Balance sheets and profit and loss accounts of the company for each of the last three financial years or, if the company has not been in business for three financial years, for each of the financial years for which it has been in business.

5. A statement showing the current margin of solvency of the company (after application of valuation regulations), the margin of solvency required and how both have been calculated.

6. *Name and address of the auditors of the company in the United Kingdom.

7. *Names and addresses of the company's principal bankers in the United Kingdom.

8. Names of the persons who will be directors, controllers or managers of the company, its principal United Kingdom executive or its authorised United Kingdom representative. The appropriate form prescribed in the Change of Control Regulations shall be completed for each person listed.

9. Particulars of any association which exists or which is proposed to exist between the directors or controllers of the company and any person who acts or will act as the company's insurance broker, agent or loss adjuster in the United Kingdom or a retrocessionaire of the company.

Authorisations to be continued

10. Particulars of classes of insurance business for which the company is already authorised in the United Kingdom and which it wishes to be included in the new authorisation.

Scheme of operations for the United Kingdom

11. *The sources of business in the United Kingdom (for example, insurance brokers or direct selling) and the approximate percentage expected from each source.

12. **The nature of the commitments which the company proposes to take on in the United Kingdom and the general and special contracts or treaties which it proposes to use.

13. **The technical bases which the actuary who will be appointed for the purposes of section 15 of the 1974 Act proposes to employ for each business carried on in the United Kingdom, including the bases needed for calculating premium rates and mathematical reserves.

14. **A statement in respect of the United Kingdom business showing for each of the first three financial years following authorisation and for each type of contract or treaty, on both optimistic and pessimistic bases—

(*a*) the number of contracts or treaties expected to be issued,
(*b*) the total premium income both gross and net of reinsurance, and
(*c*) total sums assured or amounts of annuity per annum.

15. **The guiding principles as to reinsurance of business written in the United Kingdom including the company's maximum retention per risk or event after all retrocessions and the names of the principal retrocessionaires.

16. **The estimated costs of installing the administrative services and organisation for securing business in the United Kingdom and the financial resources intended to cover those costs.

Other information, agreements, treaties and certificates required

17. A brief description of the risks underwritten by the company outside the United Kingdom.

18. A brief summary of the retrocession arrangements for the business written outside the United Kingdom including the company's maximum retention per risk or event after all retrocessions and the names of the principal retrocessionaires.

19. For each of the first three financial years following authorisation, on both optimistic and pessimistic bases—

(*a*) a forecast balance sheet, and
(*b*) a plan setting out detailed estimates of income and expenditure in respect of business accepted and reinsurance cessions broken down between the United Kingdom, other member States and elsewhere.

20. A statement of the types of investments which are expected to represent the insurance funds and the estimated proportion which will be represented by each type of investment.

21. **Copies or drafts of any separate reinsurance treaties covering business written in the United Kingdom.

22. **Copies or drafts of any agreements which the company will have with persons (other than employees of the company) who will manage the business of the proposed branch.

23. **Copies or drafts of any standard agreements which the company will have with reinsurance brokers or agents in the United Kingdom.

24. **A certificate by the actuary who will be appointed for the purposes of section 15 of the 1974 Act stating that the premium rates which will be used in the United Kingdom are suitable and that he agrees with the information provided under paragraphs 12, 15 and 19 above.

25. A certificate by the actuary of the company stating that he considers the finances of the company are sufficient—

(*a*) to meet the required technical reserves for its total business on both optimistic and pessimistic bases in the first three financial years following authorisation, and

(*b*) to provide the required margin of solvency.

NOTES

*This information is not required from applicants already authorised to carry on insurance business in the United Kingdom.

**This information is required only in respect of the classes of insurance business for which new authorisation is being sought.

SCHEDULE 5

Regulation 29

INFORMATION TO BE SUBMITTED: GENERAL BUSINESS

PART I
UNITED KINGDOM COMPANIES (DIRECT BUSINESS AND REINSURANCE)

The company

1. *Date of incorporation, place of incorporation and registered number.

2. *Brief summary of the objects of the company.

3. A statement showing the amount by which assets are expected to exceed liabilities at the date of authorisation (after application of valuation regulations) and how calculated.

4. *Date on which the company's financial year will end.

5. *Name and address of the auditors of the company.

6. *Names and addresses of the company's principal bankers.

7. Names of the persons who will be directors, controllers or managers of the company. The appropriate form prescribed in the Change of Control Regulations shall be completed for each person listed.

8. Names of main agents in the United Kingdom.

9. Particulars of any association which exists or which is proposed to exist between the directors and controllers of the company and any person who acts or will act as an insurance broker, agent, loss adjuster or reinsurer for the company.

Authorisations to be continued

10. Particulars of classes of insurance business for which the company is already authorised in the United Kingdom and which it wishes to be included in the new authorisation.

Scheme of operations

11. **The sources of business (for example, insurance brokers, agents, own employees or direct selling) and the approximate percentage expected from each source.

12. **The nature of the commitments which the company proposes to take on and the general and special policy or treaty conditions which it proposes to use.

13. **The tariffs which the company proposes to apply for each category of business.

14. **Notwithstanding paragraph 12 or 13 above—

(*a*) the particulars mentioned in paragraph 12 and 13 above may be omitted in relation to general business class 4, 5, 6, 7 or 12, and

(*b*) the particulars mentioned in paragraph 13 above may be omitted in relation to general business class 14 or 15.

15. **The guiding principles as to reinsurance including the company's maximum retention per risk or event after all reinsurance ceded.

16. *The assets which represent or will represent the minimum guarantee fund being assets admissible under and valued in accordance with the Asset Valuation Regulations.

17. **The estimated costs of installing the administrative services and organisation for securing business, and the financial resources intended to cover those costs.

Projections

18. For each of the first three financial years following authorisation—

(*a*) estimates relating to expenses of management (other than costs of installation) and in particular to current general expenses and commissions,

(*b*) ***estimates relating to premiums or contributions both gross and net of reinsurance and broken down between the United Kingdom, other member States and elsewhere and to claims (after all reinsurance recoveries),

(*c*) a forecast balance sheet, and

(*d*) estimates relating to the financial resources intended to cover underwriting liabilities and the margin of solvency.

Other information, agreements and treaties required

19. A statement showing the types of the investments which are expected to represent the insurance funds and the estimated proportion which will be represented by each type of investment.

20. **Copies or drafts of reinsurance treaties.

21. **Copies or drafts of any agreements which the company will have with persons (other than employees of the company) who will manage the business of the company.

22. **Copies or drafts of any standard agreements which the company will have with brokers or agents.

23. **Copies or drafts of agreements which the company will have with main agents.

NOTES

*This information is not required from applicants already authorised to carry on insurance business in the United Kingdom.

**This information is required only in respect of the classes of insurance business for which new authorisation is being sought.

***Premiums, contributions and claims should be shown under the accounting classes specified in paragraph 5 of Schedule 2 to the Insurance Companies (Accounts and Statements) Regulations 1980.

PART II

NON-UK COMMUNITY COMPANIES (DIRECT BUSINESS OR BOTH DIRECT BUSINESS AND REINSURANCE)

The company

1. *Date of incorporation, place of incorporation and registered number.

2. *Copies of the memorandum and articles of association of the company (or their equivalent).

3. *Name and address of the auditors of the company in the United Kingdom.

4. *Names and addresses of the company's principal bankers in the United Kingdom.

5. Names of the directors and managers of the company.

6. Names of the persons who will be the principal United Kingdom executive, the authorised United Kingdom representative or an employee within section 8(4)(*c*) of the 1981 Act. The appropriate form prescribed in the Change of Control Regulations shall be completed for each person listed.

7. Names of main agents in the United Kingdom.

8. Particulars of any association which exists or which is proposed to exist between the directors or controllers of the company and any person who acts or will act as an insurance broker, agent, loss adjuster or reinsurer for the company in the United Kingdom.

Statement from head office supervisor

9. A statement from the supervisory authority in the member State in which the company has its head office stating the classes of insurance business which the company is authorised to carry on in the member State, specifying the risks covered there, declaring that the company has the required solvency margin or minimum guarantee fund and specifying the financial resources from which the costs referred to in paragraph 17 below will be met.

Authorisations to be continued

10. Particulars of classes of insurance business for which the company is already authorised in the United Kingdom and which it wishes to be included in the new authorisation.

Scheme of operations for the United Kingdom

11. **The sources of business in the United Kingdom (for example, insurance brokers, agents, own employees or direct selling) and the approximate percentage expected from each source.

12. **The nature of the commitments which the company proposes to take on in the United Kingdom and the general and special policy or treaty conditions which it proposes to use.

13. **The tariffs which the company proposes to apply for each category of business.

14. **Notwithstanding paragraph 12 or 13 above—

(*a*) the particulars mentioned in paragraphs 12 and 13 above may be omitted in relation to general business class 4, 5, 6, 7, or 12, and

(*b*) the particulars mentioned in paragraph 13 above may be omitted in relation to general business class 14 or 15.

15. **The guiding principles as to reinsurance of business written in the United Kingdom including the company's maximum retention per risk or event after all reinsurance ceded.

16. A statement showing the current margin of solvency of the company, the margin of solvency required and how both have been calculated.

17. **The estimated cost of installing the administrative services and organisation for securing business in the United Kingdom and the financial resources intended to cover those costs.

Projections for the United Kingdom

18. For each of the first three financial years following authorisation, in relation to the business to be carried on in the United Kingdom—

(*a*) estimates relating to expenses of management (other than costs of installation) and in particular to current general expenses and commissions,
(*b*) *** estimates relating to premiums or contributions (both gross and net of all reinsurance ceded) and to claims (after all reinsurance recoveries),
(*c*) a forecast balance sheet for the proposed agency or branch, and
(*d*) the source and nature of the assets which will be used to cover any deficit shown in the forecast balance sheet.

Other information, accounts, agreements and treaties required

19. *Balance sheets and profit and loss accounts of the company for each of the last three financial years or, if the company has not been in business for three financial years, for each of the financial years for which it has been in business.

20. A statement showing the types of investments which are expected to represent the insurance funds in the United Kingdom and the estimated proportion which will be represented by each type of investment.

21. **Copies or drafts of any separate reinsurance treaties covering business written in the United Kingdom.

22. **Copies or drafts of any standard agreements which the company will have with brokers or agents in the United Kingdom.

23. **Copies or drafts of any agreements which the company will have with persons (other than employees of the company) who will manage the business of the proposed branch.

24. **Copies or drafts of any agreements which the company will have with main agents in the United Kingdom.

NOTES

*This information is not required from applicants already authorised to carry on insurance business in the United Kingdom.

**This information is required only in respect of the classes of insurance business for which new authorisation is being sought.

***Premiums, contributions and claims should be shown under the accounting classes specified in paragraph 5 of Schedule 2 to the Insurance Companies (Accounts and Statements) Regulations 1980.

PART III

EXTERNAL COMPANIES (DIRECT BUSINESS OR BOTH DIRECT BUSINESS AND REINSURANCE)

The company

1. *Date of incorporation, place of incorporation and registered number.

2. *Brief summary of the objects of the company.

3. A statement of the classes of insurance business which the company is authorised to carry on in the country in which its head office is situated.

4. The assets which represent or will represent the minimum guarantee fund in the United Kingdom being assets admissible under and valued in accordance with the Asset Valuation Regulations.

5. *Name and address of the auditors of the company in the United Kingdom.

6. *Names and addresses of the company's principal bankers in the United Kingdom.

7. Names of the persons who will be directors, controllers or managers of the company, its principal United Kingdom executive or its authorised United Kingdom representative. The appropriate form prescribed in the Change of Control Regulations shall be completed for each person listed.

8. Particulars of any association which exists or which is proposed to exist between the directors or controllers of the company and any person who acts or will act as an insurance broker, agent, or loss adjuster for the company in the United Kingdom or a reinsurer of the company.

9. Names of main agents in the United Kingdom.

Authorisations to be continued

10. Particulars of classes of insurance business for which the company is already authorised in the United Kingdom and which it wishes to be included in the new authorisation.

Scheme of operations for the United Kingdom

11. **The sources of business in the United Kingdom (for example, insurance brokers, agents, own employees or direct selling) and the approximate percentage expected from each source.

12. **The nature of the commitments which the company proposes to take on in the United Kingdom and the general and special policy or treaty conditions which it proposes to use.

13. **The tariffs which the company proposes to apply for each category of business in the United Kingdom.

14. **Notwithstanding paragraph 12 or 13 above—

(*a*) the particulars mentioned in paragraphs 12 and 13 above may be omitted in relation to general business class 4, 5, 6, 7, or 12, and

(*b*) the particulars mentioned in paragraph 13 above may be omitted in relation to general business class 14 or 15.

15. **The guiding principles as to reinsurance of business written in the United Kingdom including the company's maximum retention per risk or event after all reinsurance ceded.

Projections for the United Kingdom

16. For each of the first three financial years following authorisation, in relation to the business to be carried on in the United Kingdom—

(*a*) estimates relating to expenses of management (other than costs of installation) and in particular to current general expenses and commissions,

(*b*) ***estimates relating to premiums or contributions (both gross and net of all reinsurance ceded) and to claims (after all reinsurance recoveries), and

(*c*) a forecast balance sheet for the proposed agency or branch.

Other information, accounts, agreements and treaties required

17. ***Estimates of world-wide premium income both gross and net of reinsurance ceded in each of the first three financial years following authorisation and broken down between the United Kingdom, other member States and elsewhere.

18. Brief description of the risks the company will underwrite outside the United Kingdom.

19. Brief summary of the reinsurance arrangements for the business of the company written outside the United Kingdom including the company's maximum retention per risk or event after all reinsurance ceded and the names of the principal reinsurers.

20. Estimated capital expenditure in respect of operations outside the United Kingdom during each of the first three financial years after authorisation.

21. A statement showing the current margin of solvency of the company (after application of valuation regulations), the margin of solvency required and how both have been calculated.

22. **The estimated costs of installing the administrative services and organisation for securing business in the United Kingdom and the financial resources intended to cover those costs.

23. *Balance sheets and profit and loss accounts of the company for each of the last three financial years or, if the company has not been in business for three financial years, for each of the financial years for which it has been in business.

24. A statement showing the types of the investments which are expected to represent the insurance funds in the United Kingdom and the estimated proportion which will be represented by each type of investment.

25. **Copies or drafts of any separate reinsurance treaties covering business written in the United Kingdom.

26. **Copies or drafts of any standard agreements which the company will have with brokers or agents in the United Kingdom.

27. **Copies or drafts of any agreements which the company will have with persons (other than employees of the company) who will manage the business of the proposed branch.

28. **Copies or drafts of any agreements which the company will have with main agents in the United Kingdom.

NOTES

*This information is not required from applicants already authorised to carry on insurance business in the United Kingdom.

**This information is required only in respect of the classes of insurance business for which new authorisation is being sought.

***Premiums, contributions and claims should be shown under the accounting classes specified in paragraph 5 of Schedule 2 to the Insurance Companies (Accounts and Statements) Regulations 1980.

PART IV

NON-UK COMMUNITY COMPANIES AND EXTERNAL COMPANIES (REINSURANCE ONLY)

The company

1. *Date of incorporation, place of incorporation and registered number.
2. *A brief summary of the objects of the company.
3. A statement showing the classes of insurance business which the company is authorised to carry on in the country in which its head office is situated and particulars of any limitation.
4. *Balance sheets and profit and loss accounts of the company for each of the last three financial years or, if the company has not been in business for three financial years, for each of the financial years for which it has been in business.
5. A statement showing the current margin of solvency of the company (after application of valuation regulations), the margin of solvency required and how both have been calculated.
6. *Name and address of the auditors of the company in the United Kingdom.
7. *Names and addresses of the company's principal bankers in the United Kingdom.
8. Names of the persons who will be directors, controllers or managers of the company, its principal United Kingdom executive or its authorised United Kingdom representative. The appropriate form prescribed in the Change of Control Regulations shall be completed for each person listed.
9. Names of main agents in the United Kingdom.
10. Particulars of any association which exists or which is proposed to exist between the directors or controllers of the company and any person who acts or will act as an

insurance broker, agent or loss adjuster for the company in the United Kingdom or a retrocessionaire of the company.

Authorisations to be continued

11. Particulars of classes of insurance business for which the company is already authorised in the United Kingdom and which it wishes to be included in the new authorisation.

Scheme of operations for the United Kingdom

12. **The sources of business in the United Kingdom (for example, insurance brokers or direct selling) and the approximate percentage expected from each source.

13. **The nature of the commitments which the company proposes to take on in the United Kingdom and the general and special contracts or treaties which it proposes to use.

14. **The guiding principles as to reinsurance of business written in the United Kingdom including the company's maximum retention per risk or event after all retrocessions and the names of the principal retrocessionaires.

15. **/***Estimates of the premium income (both gross and net of reinsurance) in the United Kingdom in each of the first three financial years following authorisation.

16. The estimated costs of installing the administrative services and the organisation for securing business in the United Kingdom and the financial resources intended to cover those costs.

Other information, agreements and treaties required

17. Brief description of risks underwritten by the company outside the United Kingdom.

18. Brief summary of the retrocession arrangements for the business of the company written outside the United Kingdom including the company's maximum retention per risk or event after all retrocessions and the names of the principal retrocessionaires.

19. For each of the first three financial years following authorisation—

(*a*) estimates relating to expenses of management (other than costs of installation) and in particular to current general expenses and commissions,

(*b*) ***estimates relating to premiums or contributions (both gross and net of retrocessions) and broken down between the United Kingdom, other member States and elsewhere,

(*c*) ***estimates relating to claims (after all reinsurance recoveries),

(*d*) a forecast balance sheet, and

(*e*) estimates relating to the financial resources intended to cover underwriting liabilities and the margin of solvency.

20. A statement showing the types of investments which are expected to represent the insurance funds and the estimated proportion which will be represented by each type of investment.

21. **Copies or drafts of any separate reinsurance treaties covering business written in the United Kingdom.

22. **Copies or drafts of any standard agreements which the company will have with reinsurance brokers or agents in the United Kingdom.

23. **Copies or drafts of any agreements which the company will have with persons (other than employees of the company) who will manage the business of the proposed branch.

24. **Copies or drafts of any agreements which the company will have with main agents in the United Kingdom.

NOTES

*This information is not required from applicants already authorised to carry on insurance business in the United Kingdom.

**This information is required only in respect of the classes of insurance business for which new authorisation is being sought.

***Premiums, contributions and claims should be shown under the accounting classes specified in paragraph 5 of Schedule 2 to the Insurance Companies (Accounts and Statements) Regulations 1980.

SCHEDULE 6

Regulations 31 to 36

FORMS (CHANGE OF CONTROL ETC)

FORM A

INSURANCE COMPANIES ACT 1974: SECTION 52

*Particulars of proposed Managing Director, Chief Executive or principal United Kingdom executive or of a partner in a partnership which is a proposed Chief Executive or principal United Kingdom executive***

The (INSERT NAME OF INSURANCE COMPANY) .... proposes to appoint—

*(*a*) (INSERT NAME OF INDIVIDUAL TO WHOM PARTICULARS RELATE) .... as Managing Director*/Chief Executive*/principal United Kingdom executive*

*(*b*) (INSERT NAME OF PARTNERSHIP) .... of which (INSERT NAME OF INDIVIDUAL TO WHOM PARTICULARS RELATE) .... is a partner, as Chief Executive*/principal United Kingdom executive

and the said (INSERT NAME OF INDIVIDUAL TO WHOM PARTICULARS RELATE) .... has supplied the following particulars—

1. Surname Forename(s)

....

Any previous name(s) by which he has been known

....

2. Private address.

2A. If the answer to question 2 is an address in the United Kingdom and he has at any time during the last five years been resident outside the United Kingdom, his last private address outside the United Kingdom.

3. Date of birth.

3A. Place of birth (including borough, town or city; if London, state borough).

4. Nationality, including a statement as to whether it was acquired by birth or naturalisation.

5. Qualifications and experience, including those relating to insurance and allied matters.

6. Present occupation or employment and occupations and employment during the last ten years, including the name of the employer, the nature of the business, the position held and relevant dates.

7. Has he at any time been convicted of any offence (other than an offence committed when he was of or under the age of 17 years *unless* the same was committed within the last ten years) by any court, whether civil or military, in the United Kingdom or elsewhere? If so, give full particulars of the court by which he was convicted, the offence and the penalty imposed and the date of the conviction.

(*Note: By virtue of Article 3(a)(iii) of the Rehabilitation of Offenders Act 1974 (Exceptions) Order 1975, spent convictions are to be disclosed.*)

8. Has he in the last ten years, in the United Kingdom or elsewhere, been censured, disciplined or publicly criticised by any professional body to which he belongs or belonged or been dismissed from any office or employment or refused entry to any profession or occupation? If so, give full particulars.

9. Has he in the last ten years been adjudicated bankrupt by a court in the United Kingdom or elsewhere? If so, give full particulars.

10. Has he at any time failed to satisfy any debt adjudged due and payable by him as a judgment-debtor under an order of a court in the United Kingdom or elsewhere? If so, give full particulars.

11. Has he, in connection with the formation or management of any body corporate or insurance company, been adjudged by a court in the United Kingdom or elsewhere civilly liable for any fraud, misfeasance or other misconduct by him towards such a body or company or towards any members thereof? If so, give full particulars.

12. Has any body corporate or insurance company with which he was associated as a director or a controller in the last ten years, in the United Kingdom or elsewhere, been compulsorily wound up or made any compromise or arrangement with its creditors or ceased trading in circumstances where its creditors did not receive or have not yet received full settlement of their claims, either whilst he was associated with it or within one year after he ceased to be associated with it? If so, give full particulars.

(Note: In relation to a body corporate which is not an insurance company 'controller' is to be construed as a reference to a person who would, if he were a company, be a holding company of that body in accordance with section 154 of the Companies Act 1948 or section 148 of the Companies Act (Northern Ireland) 1960.)

13. Of what bodies corporate or insurance companies is he now a director?

14. Of what other bodies corporate or insurance companies has he been a director at any time during the last ten years?

I (INSERT NAME OF INDIVIDUAL TO WHOM PARTICULARS RELATE) .... certify that I have supplied the above information and to the best of my knowledge and belief the information is true and complete.**

Date........................ Signed........................

I certify that (INSERT NAME OF INDIVIDUAL TO WHOM PARTICULARS RELATE) .... has supplied the above information and signed the above certificate in my presence.

Date........................ Signed........................

(Director*/Secretary* of the insurance company)
*Delete as necessary.

**Note: The notice by the insurance company must contain, pursuant to section 52(2) of the 1974 Act, a statement signed by the person proposed to be appointed that the notice is served with his knowledge and consent. The statement may be included at the end of the certificate (to be signed by the person proposed to be appointed) by the addition of the words 'and I certify that this notice is served with my knowledge and consent'.

FORM B

INSURANCE COMPANIES ACT 1974: SECTIONS 53 AND 54

Particulars of proposed Controller, newly appointed Director or Manager, partner in a partnership which is newly appointed Manager, newly appointed authorised United Kingdom representative, newly appointed employee within s. 8(4)(c) of the 1981 Act or a partner in a partnership which is a newly appointed employee within s. 8(4)(c) of the 1981 Act.

1. Surname........................

Forename(s)........................

Any previous name(s) by which you have been known

....

2. Private address.

2A. If the answer to question 2 is an address in the United Kingdom and you have at any time during the last five years been resident outside the United Kingdom, your last private address outside the United Kingdom.

3. Date of birth.

3A. Place of birth (including borough, town or city; if London, state borough).

4. Nationality, including a statement as to whether it was acquired by birth or naturalisation.

***5. Qualifications and experience, including those relating to insurance and allied matters.

6. Present occupation or employment and occupations and employment during the last ten years, including the name of the employer, the nature of the business, the position held and relevant dates.

7. Have you at any time been convicted of any offence (other than an offence committed when you were of or under the age of 17 years *unless* the same was committed within the last ten years) by any court, whether civil or military, in the United Kingdom or elsewhere? If so, give full particulars of the court by which you were convicted, the offence and the penalty imposed and the date of the conviction.

(Note: By virtue of Article 3(a)(iii) of the Rehabilitation of Offenders Act 1974 (Exceptions) Order 1975, spent convictions are to be disclosed.)

8. Have you in the last ten years, in the United Kingdom or elsewhere, been censured, disciplined or publicly criticised by any professional body to which you belong or belonged or been dismissed from any office or employment or refused entry to any profession or occupation? If so, give full particulars.

**9. Have you in the last ten years been adjudicated bankrupt by a court in the United Kingdom or elsewhere? If so, give full particulars.

10. Have you at any time failed to satisfy any debt adjudged due and payable by you as a judgment-debtor under an order of a court in the United Kingdom or elsewhere? If so, give full particulars.

11. Have you, in connection with the formation or management of any body corporate or insurance company, been adjudged by a court in the United Kingdom or elsewhere civilly liable for any fraud, misfeasance or other misconduct by you towards such a body or company or towards any members thereof? If so, give full particulars.

**12. Has any body corporate or insurance company with which you were associated as a director or controller in the last ten years, in the United Kingdom or elsewhere, been compulsorily wound up or made any compromise or arrangement with its creditors or ceased trading in circumstances where its creditors did not receive or have not yet received full settlement of their claims, either whilst you were associated with it or within one year after you ceased to be associated with it? If so, give particulars.

(Note: In relation to a body corporate which is not an insurance company 'controller' is to be construed as a reference to a person who would, if he were a company, be a holding company of that body in accordance with section 154 of the Companies Act 1948 or section 148 of the Companies Act (Northern Ireland) 1960.)

**13. Of what bodies corporate or insurance companies are you now a director?

**13A. Of what other bodies corporate or insurance companies have you been a director at any time during the last ten years?

*14. Give particulars of the circumstances (by reference to section 7(4)(*c*) of the 1981 Act) by virtue of which you will become a controller of (INSERT NAME OF INSURANCE COMPANY) ....

I certify that the above information is complete and correct to the best of my knowledge and belief and that

*(*a*) I propose to become a controller of (INSERT NAME OF INSURANCE COMPANY) ....

*(*b*) I became a director/manager/authorised United Kingdom representative/an employee within the meaning of section 8(4)(*c*) of the 1981 Act of (INSERT NAME OF INSURANCE COMPANY) .... on .... (date)

*(*c*) I am a partner of (INSERT NAME OF PARTNERSHIP) .... which became a manager */an employee* within the meaning of section 8(4)(*c*) of the 1981 Act of (INSERT NAME OF INSURANCE COMPANY) .... on .... (date)

Date........................ Signed........................

***To be answered by proposed controllers, by managers and by employees within s. 8(4)(*c*) of the 1981 Act.

**To be answered by proposed controllers, by directors and by authorised United Kingdom representatives.

*Delete as necessary.

Form C

Insurance Companies Act 1974: Sections 52, 53 and 54

*Particulars of body corporate proposing to become Managing Director, Chief Executive or Controller or which is a newly appointed Director or Manager or is a partner in a partnership which is a proposed Chief Executive or a newly appointed Manager and particulars of a proposed principal United Kingdom executive, a newly appointed authorised United Kingdom representative, a newly appointed employee within s. 8(4)(c) of the 1981 Act, a partner in a partnership which it is proposed should become a principal United Kingdom executive and a partner in a partnership newly appointed as an employee within s. 8(4)(c) of the 1981 Act***.

1. Name and address of body corporate and address of registered office (where different).

2. Address of principal place of business established in the United Kingdom.

3. Date and place of incorporation.

4. Registered number.

5. Full name of every director and every controller.

(Note: In relation to a body corporate which is not an insurance company 'controller' is to be construed as a reference to a person who would, if he were a company, be a holding company of that body in accordance with section 154 of the Companies Act 1948 or section 148 of the Companies Act (Northern Ireland) 1960.)

6. Name and address of main bank.

7. Accounts for last three completed financial years and particulars of any reports, resolutions and other circulars issued to shareholders during the last four years.

*8. In the case of an oversea company within the meaning of section 406 of the Companies Act 1948 or section 355 of the Companies Act (Northern Ireland) 1960—

(*a*) Name(s) and address(es) of any person(s) resident in the United Kingdom authorised to accept on behalf of the company service of process and any notices.

(*b*) Date of registration under Part X of the Companies Act 1948 or under Part X of the Companies Act (Northern Ireland) 1960.

*9. Particulars of circumstances (by reference to section 7(4)(*c*) of the 1981 Act) by virtue of which the above-named body will become a controller (other than managing director or chief executive) of (INSERT NAME OF INSURANCE COMPANY)........................

*10. The above-named body—

(i) proposes to become a controller/principal United Kingdom executive* of (INSERT NAME OF INSURANCE COMPANY) ....

(ii) became a director/manager*/authorised United Kingdom representative*/an employee within the meaning of section 8(4)(*c*) of the 1981 Act* of (INSERT NAME OF INSURANCE COMPANY) .... on .... (date);

(iii) is a partner of (INSERT NAME OF PARTNERSHIP) .... which became a manager/an employee* within the meaning of section 8(4)(*c*) of the 1981 Act* of (INSERT NAME OF INSURANCE COMPANY) .... on .... (date)/ which it is proposed should become principal United Kingdom executive of (INSERT NAME OF INSURANCE COMPANY) ....*

I certify that the above information is complete and correct to the best of my knowledge and belief**.

Date........................ Signed........................

(Director/Secretary* of body corporate).

*I certify that the above particulars have been supplied by the above-named body and that the (INSERT NAME OF INSURANCE COMPANY) .... proposes to appoint—

*(*a*) the above-named body as managing director*/chief executive*/principal United Kingdom executive*;

*(*b*) (INSERT NAME OF PARTNERSHIP) .... of which the above-named body is a partner as chief executive*/principal United Kingdom executive*

Date........................ Signed........................

(Director/Secretary* of the insurance company).

*Delete as necessary.

**Note: In the case of the proposed appointment of a body corporate as managing director or chief executive (or the proposed appointment as chief executive of a partnership of which the body corporate is a partner) the notice by the insurance company must contain, pursuant to section 52(2) of the 1974 Act, a statement signed on behalf of the body corporate that the notice is served with its knowledge and consent. The statement may be included at the end of the certificate (to be signed on behalf of the body corporate) by the addition of the words 'and I certify that this notice is served with the knowledge and consent of the above-named body corporate'.

FORM D

INSURANCE COMPANIES ACT 1974: SECTION 54

Particulars of persons becoming or ceasing to be Managing Director, Chief Executive, or Controller and persons becoming principal United Kingdom executive

1. Name of person.***

2. Name of insurance company of which person has become/ceased to be* controller*/managing director*/chief executive* or has become principal United Kingdom executive*.

3. Date on which person became/ceased to be* controller*/managing director*/chief executive* or became principal United Kingdom executive*.

**4. Circumstances by virtue of which person became controller, e.g. appointment as managing director or chief executive or, in any other case, full particulars of circumstances (by reference to section 7(4) of the 1981 Act) which rendered the person a controller.

**5. Confirmation that section 53(1) of the 1974 Act has been complied with and that no notice of objection has been served, under section 53(2) of the 1974 Act, on the person becoming controller.

**6. Reason for ceasing to be controller*/managing director*/chief executive.*

Date........................ Signed........................

**(Director/Secretary*)

***Insert name of individual or body corporate.

*Delete as necessary.
**Delete if inapplicable.

SCHEDULE 7

Regulation 40

VALUE OF DEPENDANTS

PART I

THE SUPPLEMENTARY AMOUNT

1. Subject to paragraph 2(1) below, the supplementary amount in relation to assets of a relevant description held by a dependant of the insurance company shall be determined in accordance with the following formula—

$$A = \frac{B}{C} \times D$$

in which—

A is the supplementary amount;
B is the amount by which the value of assets of that description held by the dependant, excluding any long term business assets of the dependant if it is an insurance company, exceeds the permitted limit applicable to the dependant in relation to those assets;
C is the aggregate of the amount specified in B above and of the amounts by which the value of assets of the same description held by other relevant dependants, excluding any long term business assets of a dependant which is an insurance company, exceeds respectively the permitted limits applicable to such other relevant dependants in relation to those assets;

D is—

(*a*) where the insurance company holds no assets of the same description of the relevant class, the amount of the permitted limit that would be applicable to the insurance company in relation to such assets were it to hold them; and

(*b*) where the insurance company holds assets of the same description of the relevant class, the amount by which the permitted limit applicable to the insurance company in relation to those assets exceeds the value of those assets.

2.—(1) Where for the purpose of determining any supplementary amount in accordance with paragraph 1 above the insurance company cannot reasonably ascertain—

(*a*) the value of any asset of a relevant dependant, or

(*b*) the amount of the permitted limit applicable in relation to any asset of a relevant dependant,

the asset in question shall be left out of account for that purpose.

(2) In this Part of this Schedule—

'relevant dependant' means—

(*a*) where this Schedule is being applied in relation to the determination of the value of a share in, or debt due to or to become due from, a dependant of the insurance company which is a long term business asset of the insurance company, any dependant of the insurance company—

(i) a share in which, or in any company of which it is a dependant, is a long term business asset of the insurance company, or

(ii) from which a debt is due, or will become due, to the insurance company which is a long term business asset of that company; and

(*b*) in any other case, any dependant of the insurance company—

(i) a share in which, or in any company of which it is a dependant, is a general business asset of the insurance company, or

(ii) from which a debt is due, or will become due, to the insurance company which is a general business asset of that company.

Part II

Further Provisions and Modifications of the Regulations Applicable with Respect to the Determination of the Value of Dependants

3.—(1) This paragraph applies where, for the purpose of ascertaining the value of the assets of the subject company under regulation 40 above, any determination falls to be made in accordance with the said regulation 40 of the value of the assets of a dependant of the insurance company, a share in which, or a debt due or to become due from which, is an asset of the subject company; and references herein to a determination of the value of assets of a dependant to which this paragraph applies are references to any such determination.

(2) Regulation 40(4) shall not apply with respect to a determination of the value of assets of a dependant to which this paragraph applies.

(3) Where, in the case of a determination of the value of assets of a dependant to which this paragraph applies—

(*a*) the dependant is an insurance company and has general business assets of a relevant description or is not an insurance company and has assets of a relevant description,

(*b*) the value of such assets exceeds the permitted limit applicable to the dependant in relation to those assets, and

(*c*) any controller of the dependant has no assets of the same description of the relevant class, or has assets of the same description of the relevant class and their value is less than the permitted limit applicable to that controller in relation to those assets;

then, for the purposes of such determination, there shall be added to the permitted limit applicable to the dependant in relation to the assets referred to in sub-paragraph (*a*) above an amount equal to the supplementary amount or, if there is more than one such controller, to the aggregate of the supplementary amounts, determined with respect to any such controller in accordance with Part I of this Schedule, subject, where the controller is not the insurance company, to the modifications specified in sub-paragraph (5) below.

(4) In this paragraph, 'a controller' means, in relation to a dependant—

(*a*) the insurance company,
(*b*) the subject company, if it is an insurance company, and
(*c*) a dependant of the insurance company which is an insurance company and of which the subject company is a dependant.

(5) Where sub-paragraph (3) above is being applied in relation to a controller, other than the insurance company—

(*a*) Part I of this Schedule, as applied in accordance with the said sub-paragraph (3), shall have effect as if, for the reference to the insurance company, there were substituted references to the controller, and
(*b*) the references to assets being of a relevant class in the said sub-paragraph (3) and in Part I of this Schedule, as so applied, shall be construed as referring to long term business assets of the controller, if the said sub-paragraph (3) is being applied in connection with the determination of the value of a long term business asset of the controller, and to general business assets of the controller, in any other case.

4. The modifications of these Regulations applicable (in addition to that specified in paragraph 3(2) above) with respect to the determination of the value of the assets of the subject company where it is not an insurance company are as follows—

(*a*) these Regulations shall apply to the subject company as if it were an insurance company and its assets were being valued for the purpose specified in regulation 38(1);
(*b*) regulation 38(2) shall not apply; and
(*c*) regulation 49 shall not apply.

5. In this Schedule, 'subject company' means the dependant of the insurance company the value of whose assets is being determined in accordance with regulation 40(2) or (3) (as the case may be).

SCHEDULE 8

Regulation 49

Assets to be taken into Account only to a Specified Extent

Part I

Description of Asset	Percentage of general business or long term business amount
1. A piece of land (not being land held as a security for a debt) or a number of pieces of such land to which in the most recent proper valuation of such pieces of land an aggregate value is ascribed which is greater than the aggregate of the value of each of such pieces of land valued separately	5%

Description of Asset	Percentage of general business or long term business amount
2. A debt (other than a listed debenture) due or to become due to the insurance company from any person (not being an individual nor a dependant of the insurance company) which is fully secured on land or a number of such debts all of which are secured on the same land	5%
3. Debts (other than listed debentures, debts to which regulation 41(2), (3) or (4) above applies, and debts of the descriptions specified in paragraph 2 above or paragraph 14 below) which are due or will become due to the insurance company within twelve months of the relevant date (including debts which would become due within that period if the company were to exercise any right to which it is entitled to require payment or repayment of the same) from—	
(*a*) any one company and any of its connected companies (not being a dependant of the insurance company)	$2\frac{1}{2}$%
(*b*) any one unincorporated body of persons	$2\frac{1}{2}$%
not being moneys due from the Crown or any public body	
4. Debts (other than listed debentures, debts to which regulation 41(2), (3) or (4) above applies and debts of the descriptions specified in paragraph 2 or 3 above or paragraph 14 below) which will become due to the insurance company from—	
(*a*) any one company and any of its connected companies (not being a dependant of the insurance company)	1%
(*b*) any one unincorporated body of persons	1%
not being moneys due from the Crown or any public body	
5. Listed equity shares in any one company and any of its connected companies (not being a dependant of the insurance company)	$2\frac{1}{2}$%
6. Listed shares (including listed equity shares but only to the extent that such shares may be taken into account in accordance with paragraph 5 above) and listed debentures in any one company and any of its connected companies (not being a dependant of the insurance company)	5%
7. Unlisted shares in any one company and any of its connected companies (not being a dependant of the insurance company)	1%
8. Debenture options and share options (including traded options) in any one company and any of its connected companies (not being a dependant of the insurance company)	1/10%
9. Options of the description specified in paragraph 8 above and debts and shares of the descriptions specified in paragraphs 3, 4, 5, 6 and 7 above due or to become due from or held in any one company and any of its connected companies to the extent that such debts and shares and options may be taken into account in accordance with the provisions of those paragraphs	$7\frac{1}{2}$%

Description of Asset	Percentage of general business or long term business amount
10. Debts due or to become due to the insurance company from an individual (other than debts of the descriptions specified in regulation 41(2) above or paragraph 3(*b*) or 4(*b*) above or paragraphs 11 and 14 below)	¼%
11. Debts due or to become due to the insurance company from an individual (other than an individual who is connected with the insurance company as mentioned in section 26(5) of the 1974 Act), being debts which are fully secured on any dwelling or any land appurtenant thereto owned or to be purchased by the individual and used or to be used by him for his own residence	1%
12. Computer equipment	5%
13. Office machinery (other than computer equipment), furniture, motor vehicles and other equipment	2½%

PART II

14. Amounts recorded in the insurance company's books as due in respect of premiums (other than premiums in respect of treaty reinsurance accepted) which either— (*a*) have not been paid, or (*b*) have been received by an intermediary on behalf of the company, but have not been paid to the company by the intermediary, less any rebates, refunds and commission recorded in the company's books as allowable or payable in respect of any such amounts	30%

PART III

15. In this Schedule, a company is a connected company of another company if it is—
(*a*) a subsidiary of that other company, or
(*b*) the holding company of that other company, or
(*c*) a subsidiary of the holding company of that other company.

16. In this Schedule, a debt is fully secured on land if the amount that would be realised on the sale of that land at a price equal to the most recent proper valuation of that land would (after deducting the reasonable expenses of sale) be sufficient to enable that debt (and any other obligation secured on that land which has priority to or ranks equally with that debt) to be discharged in full.

SCHEDULE 9

Regulation 53

RELEVANT CO-INSURANCE OPERATIONS

1. An insurance operation is a relevant co-insurance operation for the purposes of regulation 53 above if—

(*a*) it is not a reinsurance acceptance, and
(*b*) it relates to any of the classes specified in paragraph 2 below, and
(*c*) it satisfies all the conditions specified in paragraph 3 below.

2. The classes referred to in paragraph 1(*b*) above are—
   class 4 (railway rolling stock),
   class 5 (aircraft),
   class 6 (ships),
   class 7 (goods in transit),
   class 8 (fire and natural forces),
   class 9 (damage to property),
   class 11 (aircraft liability),
   class 12 (liability for ships),
   class 13 (general liability), excluding risks which concern damage arising from nuclear sources or from medicinal products, and
   class 16 (miscellaneous financial loss),

as specified in Part I of Schedule 2 to the 1981 Act.

3. The conditions referred to in paragraph 1(*c*) above are—
   (*a*) that the risk is covered by a single contract at an overall premium and for the same period by two or more insurers, each for his own part;
   (*b*) that the risk is situated (within the meaning of paragraph 4 below) within a member State;
   (*c*) that at least one of the insurers participating in the operation does so through a head office, agency or branch established in a member State other than that in which the leading insurer's head office (or if the leading insurer is participating through an agency or branch, that agency or branch) is established.

4. For the purposes of paragraph 3(*b*) above, a risk is situated in a member State—
   (*a*) in the case of insurance relating to immovable property, if the property is situated in a member State,
   (*b*) in the case of insurance relating to a registered vessel, aircraft or vehicle (including railway rolling stock) if the vessel, aircraft or vehicle is registered in a member State, and
   (*c*) in any other case, if the policy holder is incorporated or has his habitual residence in a member State.

SCHEDULE 10

Regulation 70

STATUTORY NOTICE (NON-LINKED CONTRACTS)

Form 1

IMPORTANT—YOU SHOULD READ THIS CAREFULLY

STATUTORY NOTICE* RELATING TO LONG-TERM INSURANCE CONTRACT

(This notice does not form part of the contract to which it relates. The terms and conditions of the contract will be set out in the policy document.)

YOUR RIGHT TO CHANGE YOUR MIND

1 You have proposed entering into a long-term insurance contract with [name of the insurer with whom the contract is being entered into]. In entering into this contract you are undertaking to pay premiums in return for which you, or other persons chosen by you, will become entitled to receive benefits, payable in circumstances set out in the policy. It is therefore, important for you to be sure that the contract meets your needs. The law** gives you 10 days from the day on which you receive this notice (or in some cases longer—see paragraph 5) to consider the matter again and, if you so wish, to withdraw from the transaction. Some of the points you should consider in deciding whether the contract meets your needs are set out in paragraphs 2 and 3.

POINTS YOU SHOULD CONSIDER

2 Premiums and benefits

(*a*) How much are you undertaking to pay by way of premiums, at what intervals, and over what period?

(*b*) What benefits is the insurer promising to pay when you die (or when your wife or husband dies)?

(*c*) Is the insurer promising to pay benefits at any time *before* you die? If so, what are they? In what circumstances will they be paid?

(*d*) Are the benefits limited to the amounts specified in the contract or does the contract provide for entitlement to additional benefits in the form of a share in future profits of the insurer?

3 Stopping the payment of premiums In case you later wish to discontinue payment of premiums, you should consider what the entitlement to benefits would be in those circumstances. Possibilities are:—

(i) **Paid-up Policy** In some cases—normally savings-type policies—the insurer may agree to convert your policy into a 'paid-up' policy, provided that a certain number of years' premiums have been paid. This means that, although you would pay no more premiums, the policy would remain in force but the benefits would be reduced. Some policies give a right to conversion to a 'paid-up' policy, but unless your policy does so it will be for the insurer to decide whether or not he agrees to convert it and, if so, on what terms. Some policies cannot in any circumstances be converted in this way.

(ii) **Surrender** As an alternative to a 'paid-up' policy you might prefer to ask for a cash sum in return for surrendering the policy. This cash sum is known as the 'surrender value'. Unless it is guaranteed in the policy it will be for the insurer to decide whether such a sum is payable, and how much it will be. The surrender value may well be less than the total of premiums paid by you up to the date of surrender, particularly in the early years in which the policy is in force, when no sum may be payable at all. Some policies do not in any circumstances have a surrender value.

4 Further information If you need further information about the contract you should get in touch as soon as possible either with the person who arranged the insurance for you or with [name, address, telephone number of appropriate contact]. If you are not satisfied with the information you get within 10 days of receiving this notice you may wish to exercise your right to withdraw from the transaction.

RIGHT TO WITHDRAW FROM THE TRANSACTION

5 If you wish to go ahead with the transaction you should do nothing with the attached cancellation notice. But if you wish to withdraw and to have back any money you have paid to the insurer or his agent in connection with the contract, you should send notice of cancellation (either on the form attached to this document or otherwise in writing to the same effect) to [insert either the name and address of the person to whom a notice of cancellation may be sent or, if that person is the same as that named in the preceding paragraph, the words 'the person whose name and address are given in the preceding

paragraph'], and you must post it before the end of—

—the tenth day after the day on which you received this notice; or

—the earliest day on which you know both that the contract has been entered into and that the first premium has been paid,

whichever is the later.

This notice relates to insurance contract reference [contract reference number or code]. Please quote this reference in any correspondence.

*This notice is issued in compliance with the requirements of regulations made under section 65 of the Insurance Companies Act 1974.
**Section 66 of the Insurance Companies Act 1974.

SCHEDULE 11

Regulation 70

STATUTORY NOTICE (LINKED CONTRACTS)

Form 2

IMPORTANT—YOU SHOULD READ THIS CAREFULLY

STATUTORY NOTICE* RELATING TO LONG-TERM INSURANCE CONTRACT

(This notice does not form part of the contract to which it relates. The terms and conditions of the contract will be set out in the policy document.)

YOUR RIGHT TO CHANGE YOUR MIND

1 You have proposed entering into a long-term insurance contract with [name of the insurer with whom the contract is being entered into]. In entering into this contract you are undertaking to pay premiums in return for which you, or other persons chosen by you, will become entitled to receive benefits, payable in circumstances set out in the policy. It is, therefore, important for you to be sure that the contract meets your needs. The law** gives you 10 days from the day on which you receive this notice (or in some cases longer—see paragraph 6) to consider the matter again and, if you so wish, to withdraw from the transaction. Some of the points you should consider in deciding whether the contract meets your needs are set out in paragraphs 2 to 4.

POINTS YOU SHOULD CONSIDER

2 Premiums and fixed benefits

(*a*) How much are you undertaking to pay by way of premiums, at what intervals, and over what period?

(*b*) Is the insurer promising to pay any benefits of fixed amount when you die (or when your wife or husband dies)? If so, what are they?

(*c*) Is the insurer promising to pay benefits of fixed amount at any time *before* you die? If so, what are they? In what circumstances will they be paid?

3 Variable ('linked') benefits The contract is a linked life assurance contract. Briefly, this means that some or all of the benefits the insurer promises to pay are not fixed sums of money. The value of these benefits will depend, for example, on the value of certain assets—or on the level of an index of asset values—when the time comes for the insurer to pay them; and the amount to be paid will be calculated according to a formula laid down in the policy. As the value of most assets can go up or down, so the amount of benefits at the time they are paid may be more or less than if the calculation were made now. You should also remember that, although the benefits may be related to the value of particular assets, those assets do not belong to you: the premiums you pay are for entitlement to the benefits under the contract. Here, then, are some other points you should consider:—

(*a*) How much of the premiums will go towards providing linked benefits?
(*b*) In what circumstances is the insurer promising to pay linked benefits?
(*c*) To what asset values or indices will the benefits be linked? How will the benefits be calculated? How far will the benefits be affected by the income the insurer receives from the linked assets or by his tax liability in respect of them?
(*d*) If the benefits are to be calculated wholly or partly on the basis of units in an investment fund owned or managed by the insurer—what is the name of the fund? in what types of asset may the fund be invested? how far may the insurer's management or other expenses be met from the fund? is there any provision allowing the insurer to postpone payment of the benefits?

4 Stopping the payment of premiums In case you later wish to discontinue payment of premiums, you should consider what the entitlement to benefits would be in those circumstances. Possibilities are:—

(i) **Paid-up Policy** The insurer may agree to convert your policy into a 'paid-up' policy. This means that, although you would pay no more premiums, the policy would remain in force but the benefits would be reduced. Some policies give a right to conversion to a 'paid-up' policy, but unless your policy does so it will be for the insurer to decide whether or not he agrees to convert it and, if so, on what terms.
(ii) **Surrender** As an alternative to a 'paid-up' policy you might prefer to ask for a cash sum in return for surrendering the policy. This cash sum is known as the 'surrender value'. It may well be less than the total of premiums paid by you up to the date of surrender, particularly in the early years in which the policy is in force; indeed, some policies have no surrender values in the first 2 years or so.

5 Further information If you need further information about the contract you should get in touch as soon as possible either with the person who arranged the insurance for you or with [name, address, telephone number of appropriate contact]. If you are not satisfied with the information you get within 10 days of receiving this notice you may wish to exercise your right to withdraw from the transaction.

RIGHT TO WITHDRAW FROM THE TRANSACTION

6 If you wish to go ahead with the transaction you should do nothing with the attached cancellation notice. But if you wish to withdraw and to have back any money you have paid to the insurer or his agent in connection with the contract, you should send notice of cancellation (either on the form attached to this document or otherwise in writing to the same effect) to [insert either the name and address of the person to whom a notice of cancellation may be sent or, if that person is the same as that named in the preceding paragraph, the words 'the person whose name and address are given in the preceding paragraph'], and you must post it before the end of—

—the tenth day after the day on which you received this notice; or
—the earliest day on which you know both that the contract has been entered into and that the first premium has been paid,

whichever is the later.

This notice relates to insurance contract reference [contract reference number or code]. Please quote this reference in any correspondence.

*The notice is issued in compliance with the requirements of regulations made under section 65 of the Insurance Companies Act 1974.

**Section 66 of the Insurance Companies Act 1974.

SCHEDULE 12

Regulation 70

NOTICE OF CANCELLATION

NOTICE OF CANCELLATION

(To be returned only if you wish to cancel the contract)

To [name of insurer]........................

I hereby give notice that I have decided not to proceed with this insurance contract; and I require the return of any money paid to you or your agent in connection with it.

Signed........................

Date........................

[Name and address of the person to whom the Statutory Notice is being sent]

This notice relates to insurance contract reference [contract reference number or code].

SCHEDULE 13

Regulation 72

PERMITTED LINKS

PART I

DESCRIPTIONS OF PROPERTY BY REFERENCE TO WHICH BENEFITS MAY BE DETERMINED

1. Securities (other than traded options) listed on any recognised stock exchange specified in paragraph 13 of this Schedule.

1A (*a*) Securities of a company which has been accorded facilities for dealings in those securities on the Stock Exchange (otherwise than as listed securities) without prior permission for individual transactions from the Council of The Stock Exchange and without limit as to the time during which those facilities are to be available.

(*b*) Securities traded on the over-the-counter market in the United States of America regulated by the National Association of Securities Dealers.

1B. Securities of the following governments: the government of Canada or of any province of Canada; the government of the United States of America or of any state of the United States of America.

2. Land (including any interest in land) in Australia, Belgium, Canada, the Channel Islands, Denmark, the Federal Republic of Germany, France, Gibraltar, Greece, Hong Kong, the Republic of Ireland, Italy, the Isle of Man, Luxembourg, the Netherlands, New Zealand, Portugal, the Republic of South Africa, Singapore, Spain, the United Kingdom and the United States of America.

3. Loans—

(*a*) which are fully secured by mortgage or charge on land (or any interest in land) which—

(i) is situated in any of the countries specified in paragraph 2 above, and

(ii) in the case of a loan made to a person other than a body corporate, is not used wholly or mainly for domestic purposes, and

(*b*) of which the rate of interest and the due dates for the payment of interest and the repayment of principal can be fully ascertained from the terms of any agreement relating to the loan.

4. Units in an authorised unit trust scheme within the meaning of the Prevention of Fraud (Investments) Act 1958 or the Prevention of Fraud (Investments) Act (Northern Ireland) 1940.

5. (*a*) Shares in, and deposits with, a building society within the meaning of the Building Societies Act 1962 or the Building Societies Act (Northern Ireland) 1967.

(*b*) Loans to a building society designated under section 1 of the House Purchase and Housing Act 1959.

6. Loans to or deposits with Her Majesty's Government in the United Kingdom or any public or local authority or nationalised industry or undertaking in the United Kingdom.

7. Loans to, deposit with (including certificates of deposits issued by), amounts standing to the credit of any account with, and bills of exchange accepted by, any of the following being, in any case, in the currency of any country,—

The Bank of England;
The National Savings Bank;
The Post Office in the exercise of its powers to provide banking services;
A trustee savings bank within the meaning of the Trustee Savings Bank Act 1981;
A bank which is a recognised bank for the purposes of the Banking Act 1979 or a licensed institution within the meaning of that Act;
Finance for Industry Limited;
The International Bank for Reconstruction and Development;
The Inter-American Development Bank;
The African Development Bank;
The Asian Development Bank;
The Caribbean Development Bank;
The European Investment Bank;
The Commission of the European Communities.

8. . . .

9. Income due or to become due in respect of property of any of the descriptions specified in the foregoing paragraphs of this Schedule.

10. Cash . . .

PART II

INDICES BY REFERENCE TO WHICH BENEFITS MAY BE DETERMINED

11. The Financial Times Industrial Ordinary Stock Index.

12. The Financial Times Actuaries Share Indices jointly compiled by the Financial Times, the Institute of Actuaries and the Faculty of Actuaries.

12A. The Financial Times–Stock Exchange 100 Share Index.

PART III

13. In this Schedule 'recognised stock exchange' means any of the following—

(*a*) any stock exchange in any of the countries specified below which is a stock exchange within the meaning of the law of that country relating to stock exchanges—

[Austria; Belgium; Brazil; Greece; Republic of Ireland; Italy; Japan; Luxembourg; Mexico; Netherlands; New Zealand; Norway; Portugal; Spain; Sweden; Switzerland.]

(*b*) the Stock Exchange; the Copenhagen Stock Exchange; the Helsinki Stock Exchange; the Johannesburg Stock Exchange; the Kuala Lumpur Stock Exchange; the Singapore Stock Exchange.

(*c*) any stock exchange in Australia which is a member of the Australian Associated Stock Exchanges, being a prescribed stock exchange within the meaning of Australian law relating to stock exchanges;

(*d*) any stock exchange prescribed for the purposes of the Canadian Income Tax Act;

(*e*) any stock exchange approved under the laws relating to stock exchanges in the Federal Republic of Germany;

(*f*) any stock exchange set up in France in accordance with the French legislation;

(*g*) any stock exchange in Hong Kong which is recognised under the laws of Hong Kong;

(*h*) any exchange registered with the Securities and Exchange Commission of the United States as a national securities exchange.

14. For the purposes of this Schedule the expression 'traded option' does not include an option granted by the company to the securities of which the option relates, but otherwise means any traded option, whether within the meaning of regulation 37(1) above or not.

INSURANCE COMPANIES (ACCOUNTS AND STATEMENTS) REGULATIONS 1983

(SI 1983/1811)

Citation and commencement

1. These Regulations may be cited as the Insurance Companies (Accounts and Statements) Regulations 1983 and shall come into operation on 15th March 1984.

Application

2.—(1) These Regulations apply to the accounts and statements (as hereinafter specified) of every company to which Part II of the Act applies in respect of any financial year of the company ending on or after 15th March 1984.

(2) These Regulations do not apply to a Community company (other than a United Kingdom company or a pure reinsurer) or to a Community deposit company, in relation to long term business or general business carried on by it outside the United Kingdom.

Interpretation

3.—(1) In these Regulations, unless the context otherwise requires,—

'accounting class' means an accounting class set out in the following table—

Accounting class	*Corresponding classes of general business*
1 Accident and health	1, 2
2 Motor vehicle (including damage to other land vehicles), damage and liability	3, 10
3 Aircraft, damage and liability	5, 11
4 Ships, damage and liability	6, 12
5 Goods in transit	7
6 Property damage	4, 8, 9
7 General liability	13
8 Pecuniary loss	14, 15, 16, 17
9 Non-proportional treaty reinsurance	—
10 Proportional treaty reinsurance	—

'the Act' means the Insurance Companies Act 1982;

'additional amount for unexpired risks' means the amount set aside by a company at the end of its financial year, in addition to any unearned premiums, which is considered necessary to meet the cost of claims and expenses of settlement arising from risks to be borne by the company after the end of the financial year under contracts of insurance entered into before the end of that year;

'admissible asset' means an asset which is not required by Regulation 38(3) of the Insurance Companies Regulations to be left out of account for the purposes specified in Regulation 38(1) of those Regulations;

'appointed actuary' means the person appointed as actuary to a company under section 19 of the Act or under any corresponding enactment previously in force;

'authorised unit trust scheme' means a scheme authorised under the Prevention of Fraud (Investments) Act 1958 or the Prevention of Fraud (Investments) Act (Northern Ireland) 1940;

'charges for management' means amounts chargeable in respect of the management of an internal linked fund in accordance with the conditions of those contracts of insurance under which property linked benefits are linked to the value of the fund or units of the fund;

'claim' means a claim against a company under a contract of insurance;

'claims equalisation' means the amount set aside by a company as at the end of its financial year for the purpose of being used to prevent exceptional fluctuations in the amounts charged to revenue in subsequent financial years in respect of claims arising due to the occurrence of events of an exceptional nature, that is to say, events not normally occurring every year;

'claims outstanding' means, unless otherwise specified, the amount set aside by a company as at the beginning or end of its financial year as being an amount likely to be sufficient to meet—

(*a*) claims in respect of incidents occurring—
  (i) in the case of an amount set aside as at the beginning of the financial year, before the beginning of that year, and
  (ii) in the case of an amount set aside as at the end of the financial year, before the end of that year,

being claims which have not been treated as claims paid and including claims relating to business accounted for over a period longer than a financial year, claims the amounts of which have not been determined and claims arising out of incidents that have not been notified to the company, and

(*b*) expenses (such as, for example, legal, medical, surveying or engineering costs) which have been incurred but not yet recorded as paid or which are likely to be incurred by the company, whether through the employment of its own staff or otherwise, and are directly attributable to the settlement of individual claims which relate to incidents occurring before the beginning or the end of the financial year (as the case may be), whether or not the individual claims in question are those mentioned above,

less any recoverable amounts;

'claims paid', in relation to general business, means unless otherwise specified the amount that is recorded in a company's books as at the end of its financial year as paid by it (whether or not payment has been effected in that year) in full or partial settlement of—

(*a*) claims, including claims relating to business accounted for over a period longer than a financial year, and

(*b*) expenses (such as, for example, legal, medical, surveying or engineering costs) which are incurred by the company, whether through the employment of its own staff or otherwise, and are directly attributable to the settlement of individual claims, whether or not the individual claims in question are those mentioned above,

less any recoverable amounts;

'claims payable', in relation to long term business, means the amount due to be paid by a company during a financial year in respect of claims whether or not paid during that year;

'commission payable' means, in relation to a financial year of a company, the amounts, whether or not paid during that year, which are recorded during that year as due to intermediaries and cedants in respect of the inception, amendment or renewal of contracts of insurance;

'Community company' means a company whose head office is in a member State;

'Community deposit company' means a company (other than a pure reinsurer) whose head office is not in a member State and which has made a deposit in a member State other than the United Kingdom in accordance with section 9(2)(*b*) of the Act;

'company' means an insurance company;

'contract of insurance' includes a contract of reinsurance;

'direct and facultative' refers to direct insurance business and inwards facultative reinsurance business;

'expenses for settling claims' means that part of a company's expenses which has been incurred in respect of general business in the settlement of claims other than expenditure which falls to be included under claims paid;

'expenses for settling claims outstanding' means the amount set aside by a company at the end of its financial year as being an amount likely to be sufficient to meet that part of the company's expenses which is likely to be incurred in respect of general business in the settlement of claims in respect of incidents occurring before the end of that year other than expenses which fall to be included under claims outstanding;

'external company' means a company, other than a company to which section 9(2) of the Act applies, whose head office is not in a member State;

'fund' in relation to general business recorded as commencing in any financial year of a company but accounted for over a period longer than that financial year, means, during such period, an amount not less than the aggregate amount of the premiums receivable during that period (net of reinsurance premiums payable) reduced by the aggregate amount of the claims paid (net of reinsurance recoveries), expenses for settling claims, commission (net of reinsurance commission receivable) and premium taxes in respect of that business and any management expenses attributable to the management of the fund and, after the end of such period, means such amount as is considered necessary to discharge the remaining obligations (net of reinsurance) in respect of that business;

'gross premiums', in relation to a financial year—

(*a*) means premiums after deduction of discounts, refunds and rebates of premium but before deduction of premiums for reinsurance ceded and of commission payable by the company, and

(*b*) includes premiums receivable by the company under reinsurance contracts accepted by the company;

'guarantee fund' has the same meaning as in the Insurance Companies Regulations;

'home foreign business' means general insurance business written in the United Kingdom primarily relating to risks situated outside the United Kingdom but excluding business in accounting classes 3, 4 or 5 and business where the risk commences in the United Kingdom;

'incepted' refers to the time when the liability to risk of an insurer under a contract of insurance commenced and, for this purpose, a contract providing permanent open cover shall be deemed to commence on each anniversary date of the contract, 'inception' and 'incepting' shall be construed accordingly;

'industrial assurance company' means an insurance company to which Part II of the Act applies and which carries on industrial assurance business;

'Insurance Companies Regulations' means the Insurance Companies Regulations 1981;[1]

---

[1] See p 727, ante.

'intermediary' means a person who in the course of any business or profession invites other persons to make offers or proposals or to take other steps with a view to entering into contracts of insurance with a company, other than a person who only publishes such invitations on behalf of, or to the order of, some other person;

'internal linked fund' means an account to which a company appropriates certain linked assets and which may be sub-divided into units the value of which is determined by the company by reference to the value of those linked assets;

'linked assets' means long term business assets of a company which are, for the time being, identified in the records of the company as being assets by reference to the value of which property linked benefits are to be determined;

'linked contract' means a contract falling within class III of long term business as specified in Schedule I to the Act and 'non-linked contract' shall be construed accordingly;

'loss portfolio' means an amount payable by a reinsurer to a cedant in consideration of the release of the reinsurer from all or part of the liability arising under a contract of reinsurance in respect of claims incurred prior to a fixed date; and for the purposes of these Regulations a loss portfolio shall, unless otherwise specified, be treated by the reinsurer as a refund of premiums receivable and shall be treated by the cedant as a refund or reinsurance premiums payable;

'management expenses' means expenses incurred in the administration of a company or its business which are not commission payable and, in the case of general business, are not included in claims paid, claims outstanding, expenses for settling claims and expenses for settling claims outstanding;

'mathematical reserves' has the same meaning as in the Insurance Companies Regulations;

'minimum guarantee fund' has the same meaning as in the Insurance Companies Regulations;

'non-proportional reinsurance treaty' means a reinsurance treaty which is not a proportional reinsurance treaty;

'outstanding claims portfolio' means an amount payable by a cedant to a reinsurer in consideration of the reinsurer accepting liability arising under a contract of reinsurance in respect of all or part of reinsurance claims incurred and arising prior to a fixed date; and for the purposes of these Regulations an outstanding claims portfolio shall, unless otherwise specified, be treated by the cedant as reinsurance premiums payable and shall be treated by the reinsurer as premiums receivable;

'period of risk' means the period for which a contract of insurance provides cover;

'permanent health contracts' means contracts falling within class IV of long term business as specified in Schedule I to the Act;

'premiums' includes the consideration for the granting of an annuity;

'premium portfolio' means an amount payable by a reinsurer to a cedant in consideration of the release of the reinsurer from all or part of the liability arising under a contract of reinsurance for claims occurring after a fixed date under all or certain underlying contracts incepting prior to that date; and for the purposes of these Regulations a premium portfolio shall, unless otherwise specified, be treated by the reinsurer as a refund of premiums receivable and shall be treated by the cedant as a refund of reinsurance premiums payable;

'premiums receivable' means—

(*a*) in the case of a linked contract the liability under which has been valued on the basis of premiums actually received by the company in a financial year, the amount of premiums received in respect of that contract, and

(*b*) in any other case, the premiums recorded in the company's books in respect of a financial year as due to it in respect of contracts commencing in that year or contracts commencing in earlier financial years but not accounted for in the company's revenue account prior to that financial year, whether or not received by the company during that financial year, after deducting discounts, refunds and rebates of premiums as recorded in respect of the same period; and for the purpose of determining whether a premium is due no account shall be taken of any credit arrangements made in respect thereof;

'profit and loss account', in relation to a company not trading for profit, means an income and expenditure account;

'property linked benefits' means benefits provided for under any contract the effecting of which constitutes the carrying on of long term insurance business, and which are determined by reference to the value of, or the income from, property of any description (whether or not specified in the contract) or by reference to fluctuations in, or an index of, the value of property of any description (whether or not specified in the contract);

'proportional reinsurance treaty' means a reinsurance treaty under which a pre-determined proportion of each claim payment by the cedant under policies subject to the treaty is recoverable from the reinsurer;

'pure reinsurer' means a company whose authorisation to carry on business in the United Kingdom is restricted to reinsurance;

'receivable', in relation to income during a financial year, means, unless otherwise specified, such amounts as become due to the company, whether or not received by the company during that year, including (where appropriate) income which has accrued;

'recoverable amounts' means, for the purposes of claims outstanding and claims paid, the amounts recoverable by a company (whether or not received) in respect of the claims mentioned under those expressions or other claims, including amounts recoverable by way of salvage, amounts recoverable from third parties and amounts recoverable from other insurers but excluding amounts recoverable in respect of reinsurance ceded by the company;

'reinsurance' and 'reinsurer' include retrocession and retrocessionaire, respectively;

'reinsurance commission receivable' means amounts due to a company during a financial year from reinsurers, whether or not received by the company during that year, in respect of reinsurance premiums payable by the company;

'reinsurance premiums payable'—

(*a*) means the premiums recorded in a company's books during a financial year as due by it to reinsurers in respect of reinsurance contracts commencing in that year or reinsurance contracts commencing in earlier financial years but not accounted for in the company's revenue account prior to that financial year, whether or not paid by the company during that financial year, after deducting discounts, refunds and rebates of premiums as recorded in the same period, and for the purpose of determining whether a premium is due no account shall be taken of any credit arrangements made in respect thereof, and

(*b*) in the case of general business, includes, unless otherwise specified, unearned premium portfolios and outstanding claims portfolios payable by the company under reinsurance contracts ceded by the company, after deduction of any premium portfolios or loss portfolios refunded to the company by reinsurers;

'related company' has the same meaning as in Part V of the Insurance Companies Regulations;

'required margin of solvency' has the same meaning as in Part II of the Insurance Companies Regulations;

'required minimum margin' means the greater of the appropriate required margin of solvency and the amount of the appropriate minimum guarantee fund and 'required Community minimum margin' and 'required United Kingdom minimum margin' shall be construed accordingly;

'subordinated', in relation to a loan to a company, means a loan which in the event of the winding up of the company is repayable by the company only after all other liabilities of the company, other than those in respect of share capital and amounts which the company may be liable to pay by virtue of section 59(4) of the Companies Act 1981, have been paid in full;

'unearned premiums' means the amount set aside by a company at the end of its financial year out of premiums in respect of risks to be borne by the company after the end of the financial year under contracts of insurance entered into before the end of that year;

'unearned premium portfolio' means an amount payable by a cedant to a reinsurer in consideration of the reinsurer accepting liability for all or part of the liability arising under a contract of reinsurance for claims occurring after a fixed date under all or certain underlying contracts incepting prior to that date; and for the purposes of these Regulations an unearned premium portfolio shall, unless otherwise specified, be treated by the cedant as reinsurance premiums payable and shall be treated by the reinsurer as premiums receivable;

'United Kingdom company' means a company whose head office is in the United Kingdom;

'United Kingdom deposit company' means a company (other than a pure reinsurer) whose head office is not in a member State and which has made a deposit in the United Kingdom in accordance with section 9(2)(*b*) of the Act;

'zillmerising' has the same meaning as in Part II of the Insurance Companies Regulations.

(2) For the purposes of supplying any information under any Schedule to these Regulations (or in any Form therein) required to be supplied by reference to valuation regulations, words and expressions used in any such Schedule (or in any Form therein) shall, unless otherwise specified, have the meanings assigned to them in such valuation regulations.

(3) In these Regulations, any reference to long term business or general business shall, in relation to a Community company (other than a United Kingdom company or a pure reinsurer) and a Community deposit company, be taken to refer to long term or general business carried on by it through an agency or branch in the United Kingdom; and accordingly, any reference to, or requirement imposed in respect of, the accounts and balance sheet (including any notes, statements, reports and certificates annexed thereto) shall be taken as referring to, or imposing the requirement in respect of, business carried on through that agency or, as the case may be, that branch.

(4) In these Regulations, any reference to long term business or to general business shall,—

(*a*) in relation to an external company (other than a pure reinsurer), be taken to refer to its entire long term business or to its entire general business and to any long term business or general business carried on by it through an agency or branch in the United Kingdom; and

(*b*) in relation to a United Kingdom deposit company, be taken to refer to its entire long term business or entire general business and to any long term business or general business carried on by it through an agency or branch in any member State;

and accordingly any reference to, or requirement imposed in respect of, the accounts and balance sheet (including any notes, statements reports and certificates annexed thereto) relevant to long term business or to general business shall be taken as referring to or, as the case may be, imposing the requirement in respect of,—

(i) accounts prepared in respect of its entire long term business or entire general business, and

(ii) accounts prepared in respect of the long term business or the general business carried on, in the case of an external company, by the agency or branch in the United Kingdom and, in the case of a United Kingdom deposit company, by the agencies or branches in question in the member States taken together.

(5) Regulation 2(2) of the Insurance Companies Regulations shall have effect for the purposes of these Regulations as it has effect for the purpose of those Regulations and 'ECU' shall be construed accordingly.

(6) In these Regulations—

(*a*) any reference to a numbered Form is a reference to the Form so numbered in Schedules 1 to 5 below; and

(*b*) references to a numbered class of general business are references to the class so numbered in Part I of Schedule 2 to the Act.

Value of assets and amount of liabilities

4. Unless otherwise provided in these Regulations, in the documents which a company is required to prepare in accordance with these Regulations,—

(*a*) the value or amount given for an assset or a liability of the company shall be the value or amount of that asset or liability as determined in accordance with any applicable valuation regulations;

(*b*) where there are no applicable valuation regulations, then,

(i) in the case of an asset of the company other than a linked asset, the value given shall be the value which that asset would have if valuation regulations were applicable, and

(ii) in the case of a linked asset of the company, the value given shall be the value of that asset as determined in accordance with generally accepted accounting concepts, bases and policies or other generally accepted methods appropriate for insurance companies.

Contents and form of accounts

5. Every account, balance sheet, note, statement, report and certificate required to be prepared by a company pursuant to section 17(1), (2) and (3) of the Act shall be prepared in the manner hereinafter specified and shall fairly state the information provided on the basis required by these Regulations.

Balance sheet

6.—(1) The balance sheet required to be prepared by every company under section 17(1) of the Act shall comply with the requirements of Schedule 1 below and shall be in Forms 9 to 15 completed (as may be appropriate) as specified in paragraphs (2) to (7) below.

(2) Form 9 shall be completed by every United Kingdom company, external company, United Kingdom deposit company and pure reinsurer.

(3) Form 10 shall be completed by every company.

(4) Forms 11 and 12 shall be completed by every United Kingdom company, external company, United Kingdom deposit company and pure reinsurer which carries on general business.

(5) Form 13 shall be completed (as appropriate)—

(*a*) by every United Kingdom company, external company, United Kingdom deposit company and pure reinsurer which carries on long term business in respect of—

(i) the total assets representing the fund or funds maintained by it in accordance with section 28 of the Act; and

(ii) the assets appropriated by it in respect of each separate long term business fund or group of funds for which separate assets have been appropriated;

(*b*) by every Community company (other than a United Kingdom company or a pure reinsurer) and every Community deposit company in respect of long term business carried on by it through an agency or branch in the United Kingdom in respect of—

(i) the assets of the company relating to that business representing the fund or funds maintained by it in accordance with section 28 of the Act, and

(ii) the assets of the company relating to that business appropriated by it in respect of each long term business fund or group of funds for which separate assets have been appropriated;

(*c*) by every United Kingdom company, external company, United Kingdom deposit company and pure reinsurer in respect of its total assets other than long term business assets;

(*d*) by every Community company (other than a United Kingdom company or a pure reinsurer) and every Community deposit company in respect of general business carried on by it through an agency or branch in the United Kingdom in respect of the assets, other than long term business assets, of the company relating to that business;

(*e*) by every external company (other than a pure reinsurer) in respect of long term or general business carried on by it through an agency or branch in the United Kingdom in respect of those assets which are—

(i) deposited with the Accountant General,

(ii) maintained in the United Kingdom, and

(iii) maintained in the United Kingdom and other member States; and

(*f*) by every United Kingdom deposit company in respect of long term or general business carried on by it through agencies or branches in the member States concerned in respect of those assets which are—

(i) deposited with the Accountant General,

(ii) maintained in the United Kingdom and such other member States where business is carried on, and

(iii) maintained in the United Kingdom and the other member States.

(6) Form 14 shall be completed by every company which carries on long term business.

(7) Form 15 shall be completed by every company except a company not trading for profit which carries on only long term business.

Profit and loss account

7. The profit and loss account required to be prepared by every company under section 17(1) of the Act shall comply with the requirements of Schedule 1 below and shall be prepared in Form 16.

Revenue account

8. The revenue account required to be prepared by every company under section 17(1) of the Act—

(*a*) in the case of a company carrying on general business, shall comply with the requirements of Schedule 2 below and shall be in Form 20 so, however, that every such company shall prepare a separate account in Form 20 in respect of each accounting class and a summary account in that Form in respect of the whole of the general business carried on by it;

(*b*) in the case of a company carrying on long term business, shall comply with the requirements of Schedule 3 below and shall be in Form 40 so, however, that—

(i) every such company shall prepare a separate account in Form 40 in respect of each long term business fund maintained by it, and

(ii) where there is more than one fund for ordinary long term insurance business or for industrial assurance business, the company shall also prepare a summary form for ordinary long term insurance business or for industrial assurance business, as the case may require.

Additional information on general business (accounting classes)

9. Every company which carries on general business shall, in respect of each financial year and in accordance with the requirements of Schedule 2 below, prepare—

(*a*) Forms 21, 22 and 23 in respect of each of the accounting classes 1 to 8 save that where, in respect of any of the accounting classes 3, 4 and 5, the company elects to account for any business on a three-year basis it shall prepare Forms 24 and 25 instead of Forms 21, 22 and 23 in respect of that business;

(*b*) Forms 24, 25 and 26 in respect of accounting class 9; and

(*c*) Forms 27 and 28 in respect of accounting class 10.

Risk groups for general business

10.—(1) Every company which carries on general business shall, in the manner provided in paragraph (2) below and for the purpose of completing the forms specified in Regulation 11 below, classify the business carried on by it in each country into risk groups by reference to accounting classes 1 to 8 as appropriate but excluding, for that purpose, any risks relevant to treaty reinsurance business under accounting classes 3, 4 and 5.

(2) Each risk group classified for the purposes of this Regulation shall comprise risks within an accounting class insured by the company in each country which, in the opinion of the directors, are not significantly dissimilar either by reference to the nature of the objects exposed to such risks or by reference to the nature of the cover against such risks given by the company so however that—

(*a*) if the company carries on private motor vehicle insurance business it shall, in relation to accounting class 2 and in such manner as it considers appropriate, so classify its risks that—

(i) policies in respect of private motor car risks are not included in the same risk group as policies in respect of other risks, and

(ii) policies in respect of comprehensive private motor car risks are not included in the same risk group as policies in respect of non-comprehensive private motor car risks;

(*b*) subject to sub-paragraph (*a*) above, if the directors are of the opinion that the risks insured by the company within an accounting class in any one country are not significantly dissimilar in the manner aforesaid, there shall be only one risk group for those risks:

Provided that if there is only one risk group for an accounting class, it shall be classified by reference to the particular type of business within the accounting class which is carried on by the company.

(3) For the purposes of this Regulation and Regulations 11 and 12 below, home foreign business shall be treated as though it was carried on in a different country from other business carried on in the United Kingdom.

Additional information on general business (risk groups)

11. Subject to Regulation 12 below, every company which carries on general business shall, with respect to each financial year and in relation to each country, each year of origin and each risk group (as classified by it under Regulation 10 above), prepare in accordance with the requirements of Schedule 2 below—

(*a*) Forms 31 and 33 in respect of accounting classes 1 to 8 save that where, in respect of any of the accounting classes 3, 4 and 5, the company elects to account for any business on a three-year basis it shall prepare Forms 34 and 35 instead of Forms 31 and 33 in respect of that business;

(*b*) Form 32 in respect of accounting class 2:

Provided that where any form referred to above has been prepared in respect of the entire business of a company, no separate forms need be prepared—

(i) in the case of an external company, in respect of the business carried on by it through any agency or branch situated in the United Kingdom, and

(ii) in the case of a United Kingdom deposit company in respect of the businesss carried on by it through any agency or branch in any member State where business is carried on.

Provisions supplemental to Regulation 11

12.—(1) No Forms need be prepared under Regulation 11 above with respect to any financial year of a company—

(*a*) in relation to any country, if the aggregate of the company's gross premiums for that year in respect of general business (direct and facultative) carried on by it in that country was less than $2\frac{1}{2}$ per cent of the aggregate of its gross premiums for the year in respect of general business (including inwards reinsurance treaties) carried on by it in all parts of the world (including that country);

(*b*) in relation to any accounting class of business carried on in any country, if the aggregate of the company's gross premiums for that year in respect of that class (direct and facultative) carried on in that country was less than £100,000;

(*c*) if the aggregate of the company's gross premiums for that year in respect of its general business (direct and facultative) carried on in the United Kingdom was less than £100,000:

Provided that—

(i) sub-paragraphs (*a*) and (*b*) above shall not apply to general business carried on through an agency or branch in the United Kingdom by a Community company having its head office in a member State other than the United Kingdom or by an external company nor, in the case of a United Kingdom deposit company or a Community deposit company, shall they apply to general business carried on through an agency or branch in the member State concerned;

(ii) where a company has prepared any Forms pursuant to Regulation 11 above with respect to any financial year in relation to a country, year of origin and risk group it shall, notwithstanding the provisions of this paragraph, prepare in respect of each subsequent financial year during which there are any liabilities relevant to the business to which the forms relate Forms 33, 34 and 35 (as appropriate) in accordance with the requirements of Schedule 2 below in respect of that business.

(2) A company which, by virtue of paragraph (1) above, has not prepared forms under Regulation 11 in respect of any of its general business (direct and facultative) shall, in accordance with the requirements of Schedule 2 below, prepare in respect of any such business carried on in the United Kingdom and prepare separately in respect of any such business carried on elsewhere Forms 31 and 33 in respect of each of accounting classes 1 to 8 save that where, in respect of any of the accounting classes 3, 4 and 5, the company elects to account for any business on a three-year basis it shall prepare Forms 34 and 35 instead of Forms 31 and 33 in respect of that business.

Currencies other than sterling

13. Every company which prepares any Forms under Regulation 11 above or 21 or 22 below in respect of a financial year which contain figures in a currency other than sterling shall prepare Form 36 in accordance with the requirements of Schedule 2 below.

Additional information on general business (co-insurance)

14. Every relevant company (as defined in Regulation 53 of the Insurance Companies Regulations) which has participated in a relevant co-insurance operation (as so defined) in any financial year shall prepare Form 37 in accordance with the requirements of Schedule 2 below.

Additional information on long term business

15. Every company which carries on long term business shall, in respect of each financial year and in accordance with the requirements of Schedule 3 below, prepare—

(*a*) in respect of ordinary long-term insurance business—

(i) Forms 41 to 43 and 44, and

(ii) such of Forms 45 to 51 as are appropriate; and

(*b*) in respect of industrial assurance business—

(i) Forms 41, 42, 43A, 44A, 45 and 46, and

(ii) such of Forms 47 to 51 as are appropriate.

Forms prepared pursuant to Regulations 9 and 11 to 15

16. The Forms prepared pursuant to Regulations 9 and 11 to 15 above shall be annexed to the documents referred to in Regulations 6, 7 and 8 above.

Additional information on general business ceded under reinsurance treaties

17.—(1) Subject to the provisions of Regulation 20 below, a company which carries on general business in a financial year shall annex to the documents referred to in Regulations 6, 7 and 8 above and relating to that financial year a statement of—

(*a*) the full name of each of its major reinsurers and the address of the registered office or of the principal office in the country where it is incorporated (or, in the case of an unincorporated body, of the principal office) of each such reinsurer;

(*b*) whether (and, if so, how) the company was at any time in the financial year connected with any such reinsurer; and

(*c*) the amount—

(i) of the reinsurance premiums payable in the financial year to each major reinsurer in respect of general business ceded under reinsurance treaties, and

(ii) of any debt of the reinsurer to the company in respect of general business ceded under reinsurance treaties at the end of the financial year included at line 53 of Form 13,

or a statement that it has no major reinsurer.

(2) For the purposes of this Regulation, a major reinsurer of a company is another insurance company to which (whether alone or with any body corporate which is connected with such other company) the company has ceded general business reinsurance under one or more reinsurance treaties—

(*a*) in the case of proportional reinsurance, for which the total amount of the reinsurance premiums payable is equal to not less than 2 per cent of the gross premiums receivable by the company in respect of general business, or

(*b*) in the case of other reinsurance, for which the total amount of the reinsurance premiums payable is equal to not less than 5 per cent of the total premiums payable by the company in respect of all such other reinsurance,

in the financial year in question or in any of the five immediately preceding financial years of the company (not being a financial year ended before 23rd December 1982).

Additional information on general business ceded under facultative reinsurance contracts

18. Subject to the provisions of Regulation 20 below, a company which carries on general business shall annex to the documents referred to in Regulations 6, 7 and 8 above and relating to each financial year of the company a statement of—

(*a*) the full name of each reinsurer under a facultative reinsurance contract included in the number inserted in column 7 or in column 9 of Form 30 and the address of the registered office or of the principal office in the country where it is incorporated (or, in the case of an unincorporated body, of the principal office) of each such reinsurer,

(*b*) whether (and, if so, how) the company was at any time in the financial year connected with any such reinsurer; and

(*c*) the amount of the total premiums payable in the financial year to each such reinsurer in respect of general business ceded under facultative reinsurance contracts and included in column 8 or column 10, as the case may be, of that Form.

Information on major general business reinsurance cedants

19.—(1) Subject to the provisions of Regulation 20 below, a company which carries on general business shall annex to the documents referred to in Regulations 6, 7 and 8 above and relating to each financial year of the company a statement of—

(*a*) the full name of each of its major cedants and the address of the registered office or of the principal office in the country where it is incorporated (or, in the case of an unincorporated body, of the principal office) of each such cedant;

(*b*) whether (and, if so, how) the company was at any time in the financial year connected with any such cedant; and

(*c*) the amount of the total of the gross premiums receivable by the company from each such cedant in respect of general business treaty reinsurance accepted in the financial year to which the return relates,

or a statement that it has no such cedant.

(2) For the purposes of this Regulation, a major cedant of a company is another insurance company from which (whether from that company alone or from that company and any body corporate which is connected with that company) the company has accepted general business treaty reinsurance in respect of which the gross premiums receivable exceed the greater of—

(*a*) 5 per cent of the gross premiums receivable by the company in respect of general business treaty reinsurance, and

(*b*) 2 per cent of the gross premiums receivable by the company in respect of general business,

in the financial year in question or in any of the three immediately preceding financial years of the company (being a financial year beginning after 31st December 1982).

Provisions supplemental to Regulations 17, 18 and 19

20.—(1) Subject to the provisions of this Regulation, for the purposes of Regulations 17(1)(*b*) and (2), 18(*b*) and 19(1)(*b*) and (2) above, a body corporate and another person are connected with each other if—

(*a*) the other person is—

(i) a subsidiary of the body corporate;

(ii) a holding company of the body corporate; or

(iii) a subsidiary of the holding company of the body corporate; or

(*b*) one of them is controlled by the other or both are controlled by the same person,

but a body corporate shall not be taken to be connected with another person if the company furnishing the statement does not know and could not upon reasonable enquiry be expected to find that it is so connected with the other person.

(2) Except as provided in paragraph (3) below, for the purposes of paragraph (1)(*b*) above, a person shall be taken to control a body corporate if he is a person—

(*a*) in accordance with whose directions or instructions the directors of that body corporate or of a body corporate of which it is a subsidiary are accustomed to act, or

(*b*) who, either alone or with any other person who in accordance with paragraph (4)(*b*) below is to be treated as one with that person, is entitled to exercise, or control the exercise of, one-third or more of the voting power at any general meeting of the body corporate or of a body corporate of which it is a subsidiary.

(3) In relation to a company—

(*a*) making a statement pursuant to Regulation 17 above, a reinsurer shall not be taken by virtue of paragraph (2) above to be connected with another reinsurer, or

(*b*) making a statement pursuant to Regulation 19 above, a cedant shall not be taken by virtue of paragraph (2) above to be connected with another cedant,

for the purposes of paragraph (2) of the said Regulations 17 or 19, as the case may be, unless it is also connected by virtue of paragraph (1) above with the company making the statement.

(4) In Regulations 17, 18 and 19 above and this Regulation—

(*a*) 'full name' means—

(i) in the case of a body corporate, its corporate name, and

(ii) in the case of an individual or any unincorporated body, the name under which the individual or body lawfully carries on business; and

(*b*) the following persons shall be treated as one, that is to say,—

(i) an individual and his wife and minor child (including step-child and, in relation to Scotland, a pupil); and

(ii) an individual and any body corporate of which the individual is a director.

(5) The following provisions of Schedule 1 below shall apply for the purposes of Regulations 17(1)(*c*) and (2), 18 and 19 above—

(*a*) paragraphs 4 and 5 (which relate to currencies other than sterling); and

(*b*) sub-paragraphs (1) and (2) of paragraph 8 (which, among other things, relate to amounts due to the company) with the substitution in sub-paragraph (1) for the words 'sub-paragraphs (2) and (3)' of the words 'sub-paragraph (2)'.

(6) Regulations 17(2), 18(a) to (c) and 19 above shall apply to the members of Lloyd's taken together as they apply to an insurance company and the foregoing provisions of this Regulation (other than paragraph (5)) shall not have effect.

Additional information on general business accepted under reinsurance treaties (proportional and non-proportional)

21.—(1) Every company which carries on general business shall, for the purposes of this Regulation, allocate its general business treaty reinsurance accepted (but, in the case of proportional reinsurance business, only in respect of classes 5, 6 and 12 and, if accounted for on a three-year basis, class 7) to separate categories including—

(*a*) casualty (including classes 1, 2 and 13);

(*b*) property (including classes 4, 8 and 9);

(*c*) aviation (including classes 5 and 11); and

(*d*) marine (including classes 6 and 12);

and shall, in respect of each financial year and in accordance with the requirements of Schedule 2 below prepare Form 29 (which shall be annexed to the documents referred to in Regulations 6, 7 and 8 above) showing the information specified in respect of each such category of reinsurance business accepted:

Provided that—

(i) instead of allocating business within a class or classes referred to in any one of sub-paragraphs (*a*) to (*d*) above to a category therein mentioned, a company may allocate all its reinsurance business within that class or those classes to a separate category comprising only that class or those classes; and

(ii) the number of categories to which business is allocated in accordance with this paragraph shall not exceed ten.

(2) For the purposes of paragraph (1) above—

(*a*) acceptance of proportional retrocessions of non-proportional treaty reinsurance business shall be treated as non-proportional treaty reinsurance business unless—

(i) the company is unable to show information relating to it on Form 29, and

(ii) the information is shown on Form 27 in respect of all such business as a single category separate from other categories and an explanation is given in a note annexed to the form of why the information is so given; and

(*b*) all reinsurance treaties accepted, other than those included in the categories mentioned in sub-paragraphs (*a*) to (*d*) of paragraph (1) above, under which it may reasonably be foreseen that a substantial proportion of claims will be settled more than ten years after the inception of the business shall be allocated to one or more separate categories including only such treaties.

(3) Information relating to reinsurance treaties accepted which fall within more than one category for the purposes of paragraph (1) above shall be shown—

(*a*) in respect of each such category (amounts being apportioned as necessary), or

(*b*) in the category within which the greater part of the business to which the treaty relates falls,

and an explanation shall be given in a note annexed to the form of the method used in any such apportionment or of the business to which it relates falling outside the category within which it is included, as the case may require.

(4) Unless an explanation is given in a note annexed to Form 29 for allocation of the information in question to a different category—

(*a*) where information relating to an underwriting year of a reinsurance treaty accepted has been shown in a return in respect of a financial year, information relating to that underwriting year of the treaty shall be included in the same category in each relevant later financial year; and

(*b*) where a reinsurance treaty accepted relates to risks which are of a description similar to those to which an earlier treaty (in relation to which information has been given in respect of an earlier financial year) related and covers those descriptions of risk in similar proportions, information relating to that reinsurance treaty shall be included in the same category as information relating to the earlier treaty.

(5) Subject to paragraph (7) below, where the gross premiums receivable by a company in a financial year in respect of general business reinsurance treaties do not exceed $2\frac{1}{2}$ per cent of the gross premiums receivable by the company in that year in respect of general business, no information shall be shown on Form 29 relating to reinsurance treaties.

(6) Subject to paragraph (7) below, where the gross premiums receivable by a company in a financial year in respect of general business reinsurance treaties falling within a category in respect of which information is required to be shown on Form 29 do not exceed the lesser of £100,000 and $2\frac{1}{2}$ per cent of the gross premiums receivable by the company in that year in respect of general business treaty reinsurance accepted in that year, no information shall be shown on Form 29 relating to reinsurance treaties included in any such category.

(7) Where a company has, in respect of any financial year, shown information on

Form 29 relating to any reinsurance business then, notwithstanding the provisions of paragraph (5) or paragraph (6) above, as the case may be, information relating to that business shall be shown on Form 29 in respect of each relevant later financial year.

(8) Where information is shown on Form 29 in relation to a reinsurance treaty before the first financial year of the company in respect of which Form 29 is required to be prepared, information relating to that treaty in respect of business incepted in earlier financial years—

(*a*) may be aggregated instead of being shown separately in respect of each such financial year, and

(*b*) may, in the case of business incepted before 1st January 1983 for which the information is not available, be shown as an estimate.

Additional information on general business accepted under reinsurance treaties (proportional)

22.—(1) Without prejudice to Regulation 9 above, this Regulation has effect in relation to all proportional treaty reinsurance business accepted in respect of which, in relation to a financial year of a company, information is not shown on Form 29 pursuant to Regulation 21 above.

(2) Every company which carries on general business shall, for the purposes of this Regulation, allocate its general business proportional treaty reinsurance accepted to separate categories including—

(*a*) casualty (including classes 1, 2 and 13); and

(*b*) property (including classes 4, 8 and 9),

and shall, in respect of each financial year and in accordance with the requirements of Schedule 2 below prepare Form 27 (which shall be annexed to the documents referred to in Regulations 6, 7 and 8 above) showing the information specified in respect of each such category of proportional reinsurance business:

Provided that—

(i) instead of allocating business within a class or classes referred to in either of sub-paragraphs (*a*) and (*b*) above to a category therein mentioned, a company may allocate all its reinsurance business within that class or those classes to a separate category comprising only that class or those classes; and

(ii) the number of categories to which business is allocated in accordance with this paragraph shall not exceed ten.

(3) For the purposes of paragraph (2) above, all reinsurance treaties accepted, other than those included in the categories mentioned in sub-paragraphs (*a*) and (*b*) of that paragraph, under which it may reasonably be foreseen that a substantial proportion of claims will be settled more than ten years after the inception of the business shall be allocated to one or more separate categories including only such treaties.

(4) Paragraphs (3) to (7) of Regulation 21 above shall have effect for the purposes of this Regulation as they have effect for the purposes of that Regulation with the substitution for references to Form 29 of references to Form 27.

Prescribed class of general business

23. General business is hereby prescribed as a class of insurance business for the purposes of section 20 of the Act and every company which carries on such business shall, in respect of each financial year and in accordance with the requirements of Schedule 2 below, prepare a statement of business of that class in Form 30.

Periodic actuarial investigation

24. Save in relation to sub-paragraph (*a*)(ii) below, for the purposes of section 18 of the Act, ordinary long-term insurance business and industrial assurance business shall be treated separately and—

(*a*) the abstract of the report of the actuary on long term business—
(i) shall comply with the requirements of Schedule 4 below and shall contain the information (together with such of Forms 55 to 58 as may be appropriate) specified in that Schedule, and
(ii) except in the case of a Community company (other than a United Kingdom company or a pure reinsurer) and a Community deposit company, shall also include Form 60 and, where appropriate, Form 61; and
(*b*) the statement of long term business shall comply with the requirements of Schedule 5 below and shall contain the information (together with Forms 65 to 78) specified in that Schedule.

Signature of documents

25.—(1) In respect of any document relating to the business of a company wherever it may be carried on, the persons prescribed for the purposes of section 22(3) of the Act are—
(*a*) in any case—
(i) where there are more than two directors of the company, at least two of those directors and, where there are not more than two directors, all the directors; and
(ii) a chief executive, if any, of the company or (if there is no chief executive) the secretary, if any; and
(*b*) in the case of an abstract or statement under section 18 of the Act, the actuary who made the investigation to which the abstract relates or by reference to which the statement was prepared.

(2) In respect of any document relating to business carried on through an agency or branch in the United Kingdom by a Community company, Community deposit company or an external company or through agencies or branches in any member States taken together by a United Kingdom deposit company, the persons prescribed for the purposes of section 22(3) of the Act are—
(*a*) in any case—
(i) the representative referred to in sections 8(1) or 9(4) of the Act or, where the representative is a body corporate, the individual representative referred to in section 10(5) of the Act; and
(ii) an officer or employee of the description specified in section 8(4)(*b*) of the Act or, if there is no such officer or employee or he is also the representative or individual representative referred to above, an employee of the description specified in section 8(4)(*c*) of the Act; and
(*b*) in the case of an abstract or statement under section 18 of the Act, the actuary who made the investigation to which the abstract relates or by reference to which the statement was prepared.

Certificates

26. There shall be annexed to the documents referred to in Regulations 6, 7 and 8 above—
(*a*) a certificate in accordance with the requirements of Part I of Schedule 6 below which shall be signed by the persons required by Regulation 25 above to sign the documents to which the certificate relates; and
(*b*) in the case of a company which has at any time during the financial year carried on long term business a certificate in accordance with the requirements of Part II of Schedule 6 below which shall be signed by the appointed actuary.

Audit and auditors' report

27.—(1) The documents referred to in Regulations 6, 7 and 8 above, and every statement, analysis, report or certificate annexed thereto pursuant to Regulations 16, 17, 19, 21, 22 and 26(*a*) above, shall be audited by a person of the description prescribed under Regulation 30 below who shall make and annex to the documents aforesaid a report in accordance with the requirements of Part III of Schedule 6 below.

(2) For the purposes of these Regulations—

(*a*) section 14(4), (5) and (6) of the Companies Act 1967 shall apply as if—

(i) in sub-section (4) of that section the words '(unless it is framed as a consolidated profit and loss account)' wherever they occur therein were omitted and as if the references to the profit and loss account included references to the revenue account, and

(ii) the auditors of a company were not under a duty for the purposes of preparing their report to carry out any investigation into information given in Forms 33 and 35 relating wholly or partly to the number of claims notified or the amount of payments made prior to the financial year of the company to which the Insurance Companies (Accounts and Statements) Regulations 1980 first applied; and

(*b*) section 18(1) of the Companies Act 1976 shall apply as if the reference therein to 'the holding company' were a reference to the insurance company.

Qualifications of actuary

28.—(1) For the purposes of the definition of 'actuary' in section 96(1) of the Act, it is hereby prescribed that a person qualified for appointment as an actuary under section 19 of the Act shall be a Fellow of the Institute of Actuaries or of the Faculty of Actuaries and shall have attained the age of 30 years.

(2) Any person who, immediately before 1st January 1981, held an appointment as actuary to a company by virtue of Regulation 15 of the Insurance Companies (Accounts and Forms) Regulations 1968 shall, notwithstanding paragraph (1) above, be deemed for the purposes of these Regulations and for the period during which he continues to hold that appointment to be qualified to hold that appointment.

Information on appointed actuary

29.—(1) Subject to the provisions of this Regulation, a company shall annex to the documents referred to in Regulations 6, 7 and 8 above and relating to each financial year of the company as respects every person who, at any time during the year, was the appointed actuary to the company, a statement of the following information, that is to say,—

(*a*) particulars of any shares in, or debentures of, the company in which the actuary was interested at any time during that year;

(*b*) particulars of any pecuniary interest of the actuary in any transaction between the actuary and the company and subsisting at any time during that year or, in the case of transactions of a minor character, a general description of such interests;

(*c*) the aggregate amount of—

(i) any remuneration and the value of any other benefits (other than a pension or other future or contingent benefit) under any contract of service of the actuary with, or contract for services by the actuary to, the company, and

(ii) any emoluments, pensions or compensation as director of the company which are required by section 196 of the Companies Act 1948 to be included in a note to the accounts of the company under section 1 of the Companies Act 1976, receivable by the actuary in respect of any period in that year; and

(*d*) a general description of any other pecuniary benefit (including any pension and other future or contingent benefit) received by the actuary from the company in that year or receivable by him from the company,

together with the statement specified in paragraph (2) below.

(2) The statement last referred to in paragraph (1) above is a statement that the company has made a request to the actuary to furnish to it the particulars specified in that paragraph and identifying any particulars furnished pursuant to that request.

(3) For the purposes of sub-paragraphs (*a*) to (*d*) of paragraph (1) above—

(*a*) references to the actuary include reference to—

(i) the spouse and minor child (including step-child and, in relation to Scotland, a pupil) of the actuary;

(ii) any person who is a partner of the actuary;

(iii) any person (other than the company) of which the actuary is an employee; and

(iv) any body corporate (other than the company) of which the actuary is a director or which is controlled by him;

(*b*) a person shall be deemed to be interested in shares or debentures of a body corporate if he is interested in them according to the rules set out in section 28 of the Companies Act 1967 with the addition, in subsection (9) of that section, of a reference to a scheme under section 20 of the Charities Act (Northern Ireland) 1964 and to an authorised unit trust scheme within the meaning of the Prevention of Fraud (Investments) Act (Northern Ireland) 1940; and

(*c*) a person shall be deemed to have any interest or benefit if he has a beneficial interest in it.

(4) For the purposes of sub-paragraphs (*a*) to (*d*) of paragraph (1) above and of paragraph (3)(*a*) above, references to a company include references to any body corporate which is the company's subsidiary or holding company and to any other subsidiary of its holding company.

(5) For the purposes of paragraph (3) above, a person shall be taken to control a body corporate if he is a person—

(*a*) in accordance with whose directions or instructions the directors of that body corporate or of a body corporate of which it is a subsidiary are accustomed to act, or

(*b*) who, either alone or with any other person falling within sub-paragraph (*a*) of that paragraph, is entitled to exercise, or control the exercise of, one-third or more of the voting power at any general meeting of the body corporate or of a body corporate of which it is a subsidiary.

Qualifications of auditor

30. For the purposes of section 21 of the Act, it is hereby prescribed that the description of the person qualified to audit the accounts and statements of a company under Regulation 27 above shall be a person who would be qualified to audit them (otherwise than by virtue of section 13 of the Companies Act 1967) if they were the accounts of a company within the meaning of the Companies Acts 1948 to 1981 prepared under section 1 of the Companies Act 1976.

Transitional provisions

31.—(1) Every document submitted to the Secretary of State pursuant to section 22 of the Act in respect of a financial year of a company preceding that financial year of the company to which these Regulations first apply shall be in the form in which it would have been and have the contents which it would have had if these Regulations had not been made; and Regulation 32 below shall be construed accordingly.

(2) A company shall not be required to include in any account or balance sheet prepared in accordance with these Regulations any information relating to the financial year of the company immediately preceding that financial year of the company to which the Insurance Companies (Accounts and Statements) Regulations 1980 first applied by virtue of Regulation 2(1) thereof.

(3) Any reference in any provision of these Regulations to a document submitted to the Secretary of State or prepared in respect of a financial year of a company which is a financial year of the company preceding that to which these Regulations first apply shall be construed as a reference to the document so submitted or prepared in accordance with the corresponding provisions of the Regulations hereby revoked.

Revocations

32. The Regulations specified in Schedule 7 below are hereby revoked.

SCHEDULE 1

Regulations 6 and 7

Balance Sheet and Profit and Loss Account
(Forms 9 to 16)

1. All the Forms included in the part of the return to which this Schedule relates (Forms 9 to 16) are to be laid out as shown in this Schedule.

Completion of Forms

2. Where 'source' appears at the head of a column on a Form, the information to be included in the preceding columns of a particular line is to be taken from those items in the returns to which reference is made on that line in the column headed 'source'. No entries are to be made in the column headed 'source'.

3.—(1) The company registration number to be entered on every Form shall be whichever is first applicable of the following—

(*a*) in the case of a company incorporated in the United Kingdom, the registration number allocated by the appropriate Registrar;

(*b*) in the case of an overseas company with an established place of business within Great Britain, the number allocated by the appropriate Registrar of Companies on the registration of its documents under Part X of the Companies Act 1948;

(*c*) in any other case, such number as may be agreed between the company and the Secretary of State.

(2) Boxes marked 'Global/UK/CM' or Global/UK' shall be completed by inserting—

(*a*) 'UK' in the case of a Form which is part of the returns prepared by a Community company (other than a United Kingdom company or a pure reinsurer) or a Community deposit company in respect of long term or general business carried on through an agency or branch in the United Kingdom or in respect of returns prepared by an external company (other than a pure reinsurer) in respect of long term or general business carried on through an agency or branch in the United Kingdom; or

(*b*) 'CM' in the case of a Form which is part of the returns prepared by a United Kingdom deposit company in respect of long term or general business carried on through agencies or branches in the member States concerned; or

(*c*) 'GL' in any other case.

(3) Boxes marked 'Period ended' should be completed so as to show, in numerals, the date of the last day of the financial year to which the returns relate.

(4) No entry should be made in a box which is shaded, is labelled 'For official use', or is not labelled.

Currency

4. Except as provided in paragraph 5 of this Schedule, the following shall be expressed in sterling as if conversion had taken place at the closing middle rate on the last day for which the appropriate rate is available in the financial year to which the figures relate—

(*a*) the value of any asset or liability expressed in a currency other than sterling;
(*b*) amounts of premiums and other income receivable in a currency other than sterling;
(*c*) amounts of claims and other expenditure payable in a currency other than sterling.

5. Notwithstanding the provisions of paragraph 4 of this Schedule, amounts of income and expenditure in currencies other than sterling relating to business which is—

(*a*) long term business, or
(*b*) general business carried on in the United Kingdom in accounting classes 3, 4, 5, 9 or 10, or
(*c*) home foreign business,

may be expressed in sterling using other bases of conversion provided that a note is included in the returns stating the bases employed.

Presentation of amounts

6. Negative amounts shall be shown between round brackets.

7. Where any amount which is shown as brought forward from a previous year differs from the corresponding amount shown as carried forward from that year and the difference is not due solely to the fact that a different rate has been used to express other currencies in sterling, a note of explanation shall be included in the return.

8.—(1) Except to the extent permitted by sub-paragraphs (2) and (3) of this paragraph amounts due to or from the company shall be shown as gross amounts.

(2) In calculating amounts due to the company, amounts due from any one person may be included net of amounts due to that person and, in calculating amounts due from the company, amounts due to any one person may be included net of amounts due from that person.

(3) For the purposes of sub-paragraph (2) above amounts due from or to any person through an intermediary may be regarded as due from or to that intermediary.

(4) If amounts shown include amounts calculated on the basis set out in sub-paragraphs (2) and (3) above, a note to that effect shall be included and if more than 25 per cent of any such amount shown as due to the company is due from or through any one intermediary, or from or through any one intermediary and any of its connected companies, a note shall also be included to that effect.

(5) In this paragraph 'connected company' means a company which is a connected company within the meaning of Part III of Schedule 8 to the Insurance Companies Regulations.

9. All amounts are to be shown to the nearer £1,000.

Contingent liabilities

10.—(1) Contingent liabilities are normally to be included under the appropriate headings in Form 14 in respect of long term business and Form 15 in respect of other business.

(2) The matters referred to in the following sub-paragraphs are to be stated by way of a note to Forms 14 or 15—

(*a*) particulars of any charge on the assets of the company to secure the liabilities of any other person (other than liabilities arising under a contract of insurance) including, where practicable, the amount secured;

(*b*) whether any provision has been made for any liability to tax on capital gains which might arise if the company disposed of its assets and, if so, the amount of the provision;

(*c*) the general nature of any other contingent liabilities not included in the manner specified in sub-paragraph (1) of this paragraph (other than a liability arising under a contract of insurance) and, where practicable, the amounts or estimated amounts of those liabilities.

Returns under Insurance Companies Legislation

Form 9
(Sheet 1)

Statement of solvency

Name of Company

Global business/UK branch business/Community branch business

Financial year ended

	Company registration number	Global/ UK/CM	Period ended day	month	year	Units	For official use
F9					19	£000	

		As at the end of the financial year 1	As at the end of the previous year 2	Source Form / Line / Column
GENERAL BUSINESS				
Available assets				
Other than long term business assets allocated towards general business required minimum margin	11			See instructions 1 and 2 below
Required minimum margin				
Required minimum margin for general business	12			12.49
Excess (deficiency) of available assets over the required minimum margin (11 – 12)	13			
Implicit items admitted under regulation 10(4) of the Insurance Companies Regulations 1981	14			
LONG TERM BUSINESS				
Available assets				
Long term business admissible assets	21			10.11
Other than long term business assets allocated towards long term business required minimum margin	22			See instructions 1 and 3 below
Total mathematical reserves (after distribution of surplus)	23			See Instruction 4 below
Other insurance and non-insurance liabilities	24			See instruction 5 below
Available assets for long term business required minimum margin (21 + 22 – 23 – 24)	25			
Implicit items admitted under regulation 10(4) of the Insurance Companies Regulations 1981				
Future profits	31			
Zillmerising	32			
Hidden reserves	33			
Total of available assets and implicit items (25 + 31 + 32 + 33)	34			
Required minimum margin				
Required minimum margin for long term business	41			60.13
Explicit required minimum margin (1/6 x 41, or minimum guarantee fund if greater)	42			
Excess (deficiency) of available assets over explicit required minimum margin (25 – 42)	43			
Excess (deficiency) of available assets and implicit items over the required minimum margin (34 – 41)	44			

Form 9

(Sheet 2)

Returns under Insurance Companies Legislation

Statement of solvency

Name of Company Global business/UK branch business/Community branch business		Company registration number	Global/UK/CM	Period ended day	month	year	Units	For official use
Financial year ended	F9					19	£000	

		As at the end of the financial year 1	As at the end of the previous year 2	Source Form / Line / Column
ALLOCATION OF OTHER THAN LONG TERM BUSINESS ASSETS				
Other than long term business assets allocated towards general business required minimum margin	51			
Other than long term business assets allocated towards long term business required minimum margin	52			
Net other than long term business assets (51 + 52)	53			10.29
CONTINGENT LIABILITIES				
Quantifiable contingent liabilities in respect of other than long term business as shown in a supplementary note to Form 15	60			See Instruction 6 below
Quantifiable contingent liabilities in respect of long term business as shown in a supplementary note to Form 14	61			See Instruction 6 below

Instructions

(1) For a composite company, the whole Form shall be completed, with the entries at lines 11 and 22 being equal to the entries at lines 51 and 52 respectively.

(2) For a company transacting only general business, only lines 11 to 14 and line 60 shall be completed, with the entry at line 11 being equal to the entry at Form 10 line 29.

(3) For a company transacting only long term business, only lines 21 to 44 and lines 60 and 61 shall be completed, with the entry at line 22 being equal to the entry at Form 10 line 29.

(4) The entry at line 23 shall be equal to the sum of lines 11 and 15 in Form 14 and the amount (if any) stated in a note to that Form in accordance with Instruction 3 to that Form.

(5) The entry at line 24 shall be equal to the total of lines 21 to 47 in Form 14 and the amount of any cash bonuses stated in a note to that Form in accordance with Instruction 2 to that Form.

(6) The entries at lines 60 and 61 shall not include provision for any liability to tax on capital gains referred to in paragraph 10(2) (b) of Schedule 1.

Form 10

Returns under Insurance Companies Legislation

Statement of net assets

Name of Company

Global business/UK branch business/Community branch business

Financial year ended

	Company registration number	Global/ UK/CM	Period ended day	month	year	Units	For official use
F10					19	£000	

		As at the end of the financial year 1	As at the end of the previous year 2	Source Form / Line / Column
Long Term business-admissible assets	11			13.93
Long Term business-liabilities and margins	12			14.59
Other than Long Term business-admissible assets	21			13.93
Other than Long Term business-liabilities	22			15.59
Net admissible assets (21-22)	27			
Unpaid capital — as per line 53	28			
Net assets (27 + 28)	29			
Authorised share capital	41			
Paid up share capital	51			
Share premium account	52			
Unpaid amounts (including share premium) on partly paid shares within the limits allowed by Regulation 10 of the Insurance Companies Regulations 1981	53			
Amounts representing the balance of net assets	54			
Total (51 to 54) and equal to line 29 above	59			

Returns under Insurance Companies Legislation

Form 11

General business: Calculation of required margin of solvency – first method

Name of Company

Global business/UK branch business/Community branch business

Financial year ended

	Company registration number	Global/ UK/CM	Period ended day	month	year	Units	For official use
F11					19	£000	

				The financial year 1	Previous year 2	Source Form / Line / Column
Gross premiums receivable			11			See Note below
Premium taxes and levies (included in line 11)			12			
Sub-total A (11–12)			13			
Adjusted Sub-total A if financial year is not a 12 month period to produce an annual figure			14			
Division of Sub-total A (or adjusted Sub-total A if appropriate)	Other than health insurance	Up to and including sterling equivalent of 10M ECU × 18/100	15			
		Excess (if any) over 10M ECU × 16/100	16			
	Health insurance	Up to and including sterling equivalent of 10M ECU × 6/100	17			
		Excess (if any) over 10M ECU × 16/300	18			
Sub-total B (15 + 16 + 17 + 18)			19			
Claims paid			21			
Claims outstanding carried forward at the end of the financial year		For business not accounted for on a one-year basis	22			
		For business accounted for on a one-year basis	23			
Claims outstanding brought forward at the beginning of the financial year		For business not accounted for on a one-year basis	24			
		For business accounted for on a one-year basis	25			
Sub-total C (21 + 22 + 23 – (24 + 25))			29			
Amounts recoverable from reinsurers in respect of claims included in Sub-total C			30			
Sub-total D (29–30)			39			
First result Sub-total B × $\frac{\text{Sub-total D}}{\text{Sub-total C}}$ (or, if $\frac{1}{2}$ is a greater fraction, × $\frac{1}{2}$)			41			

Note
The amount to be entered at line 11.11.1 is the sum of 21.41.1 (all appropriate accounting classes), 25.71.5 and 25.72.5 for all appropriate accounting classes except class 9 (or 24.11.5 and 24.12.5 where grossing up has not been required), 26.19.5 and 26.49.5 for non-proportional treaty reinsurance, and 28.19.3 and 28.49.3 for proportional treaty reinsurance.

Returns under Insurance Companies Legislation

Form 12

General business: Calculation of required margin of solvency — second method, and statement of required minimum margin

Name of Company

Global business/UK branch business/Community branch business

Financial year ended

	Company registration number	Global/UK/CM	Period ended day	month	year	Units	For official use
F12					19	£000	

			Line	The financial year 1	Previous year 2	Source: Form	Line	Column
Reference period (No. of financial years) Insert "3" or "7" here			11			See note		
Claims paid in reference period			21					
Claims outstanding carried forward at the end of the reference period	For business not accounted for on a one-year basis		22					
	For business accounted for on a one-year basis		23					
Claims outstanding brought forward at the beginning of the reference period	For business not accounted for on a one-year basis		24					
	For business accounted for on a one-year basis		25					
Sub-total E (21 + 22 + 23 – (24 + 25))			29					
Sub-total F – Conversion of Sub-total E to annual figure (Multiply by 12 and divide by number of months in reference period)			31					
Division of Sub-total F	Other than health insurance	Up to and including sterling equivalent of 7M ECU x 26/100	32					
		Excess (if any) over 7M ECU x 23/100	33					
	Health insurance	Up to and including sterling equivalent of 7M ECU x 26/300	34					
		Excess (if any) over 7M ECU x 23/300	35					
Sub-total G (32 + 33 + 34 + 35)			39					
Second result Sub total G x **Sub-total D** / Sub-total C (or, if ½ is a greater fraction, x ½)			41					

	Line			Source
First result	42			11.41
Required margin of solvency (the higher of lines 41 and 42)	43			

	Line			
Minimum guarantee fund	44			

	Line			
Required minimum margin (the higher of lines 43 and 44)	49			

Note

If the company has not been in existence long enough to acquire a reference period, this shall be stated and lines 11 to 41 ignored.

Returns under Insurance Companies Legislation

Form 13
(Sheet 1)

Analysis of admissible assets

Name of Company

Global business/UK branch business/Community branch business

Business: Long Term/Other than Long Term

Financial year ended

Category of Assets

	Company registration number	Global/ UK/CM	Period ended day	month	year	Units	Category of assets	For official use
F13					19	£000		

Admissible assets				As at the end of the financial year 1	As at the end of the previous year 2
Land			11		
Fixed interest securities	Issued by, or guaranteed by, any government or public authority		12		
	Other fixed interest securities except those in dependants which must be included in lines 29 to 34 and any to be included in lines 61 or 62	listed	13		
		unlisted debentures	14		
		other unlisted	15		
Variable interest securities except those included at lines 21 to 34	Issued by, or guaranteed by, any government or public authority, except those included at line 17		16		
	Issued by, or guaranteed by, any government or public authority, where the capital value or interest is determined by an index of prices		17		
	Other		18		
Other variable interest investments	Equity shares except those in dependants which must be included in lines 29, 31 or 33	listed	21		
		unlisted	22		
	Holdings in authorised unit trust schemes		23		
Investments in dependants	Companies authorised to transact insurance business in the United Kingdom	Value of any shares held	29		
		Debts, other than amounts which must be included in lines 41 or 51 to 54	30		
	Other insurance companies	Value of any shares held	31		
		Debts, other than amounts which must be included in lines 41 or 51 to 54	32		
	Non-insurance companies	Value of any shares held	33		
		Debts, other than amounts which must be included in lines 41 or 51 to 54	34		
Share options and debenture options			35		
Total (11 to 35)					

(Sheet 2)

Analysis of admissible assets

Name of Company

Global business/UK branch business/Community branch business

Business: Long Term/Other than Long Term

Financial year ended

Category of Assets

	Company registration number	Global/ UK/CM	Period ended day	month	year	Units	Category of assets	For official use
F13					19	£000		

Admissible assets				As at the end of the financial year 1	As at the end of the previous year 2
Loans secured by policies of insurance issued by the company			41		
Tax recoveries due from taxation authorities			42		
Deposit and current accounts with approved financial institutions, and deposits with local authorities and Building Societies	Current accounts and amounts on deposit for a fixed term of, or on deposit and withdrawable after giving notice of, 12 months or less after the end of the financial year, and certificates of deposit maturing during that period		43		
	Other		44		
Insurance debts including those due from dependants and individuals	Premium income in respect of direct insurance and facultative reinsurance contracts accepted not yet paid to the company less commission payable thereon		51		
	Amounts due from ceding insurers and intermediaries under reinsurance treaties accepted		52		
	Amounts due from reinsurers and intermediaries under reinsurance contracts ceded		53		
	Recoveries due by way of salvage or from other insurers in respect of claims paid other than recoveries under reinsurance contracts ceded		54		
Debts fully secured on land except listed debentures (which must be included in line 13), debts due from dependants (which must be included in lines 30, 32 or 34), and debts due from individuals (which must be included in lines 64 or 66)		due more than 12 months after the end of the financial year	61		
		due in 12 months or less after the end of the financial year, or which would become due if the company exercised any right to require repayment within that period	62		
Debts except those which must be included in other lines	due more than 12 months after the end of the financial year	due from companies and unincorporated bodies of persons	63		
		due from individuals	64		
	due in 12 months or less after the end of the financial year, or which would become due if the company exercised any right to require repayment within that period	due from companies and unincorporated bodies of persons	65		
		due from individuals	66		
Total (41 to 66)			69		

Returns under Insurance Companies Legislation

Form 13
(Sheet 3)

Analysis of admissible assets

Name of Company

Global business/UK branch business/Community branch business

Business: Long Term/Other than Long Term

Financial year ended

Category of Assets

	Company registration number	Global/ UK/CM	Period ended day	month	year	Units	Category of assets	For official use
F13					19	£000		

Admissible assets			As at the end of the financial year 1	As at the end of the previous year 2
Shares in Building Societies and Industrial and Provident Societies		71		
Cash		72		
Computer equipment		81		
Other office machinery, furniture, motor vehicles and other equipment		82		
Life interests, reversionary interests and similar interests in property		83		
Linked assets	linked assets in internal linked funds (as shown in line 12 on Form 49)	85		
	other linked assets	86		
		87		
Total of Sheet 1 (13.39)		91		
Total of Sheet 2 (13.69)		92		
Gross Total of admissible assets (71 to 92)		93		

Total of assets valued in accordance with valuation regulations which would have been included in one of the headings above but for the admissibility limits applied by which certain assets are required to be taken into account only to a specified extent	94		
Amount included in line 93 attributable to debts due from related companies, other than those under contracts of insurance or reinsurance	95		

Instructions for Completion of Form 13

1 Long-term business: Form 13 shall be completed for the total long-term business assets of the company or branch and for each fund or group of funds for which separate assets are appropriated. The word "Total" or the name of the fund shall be shown against the heading "Category of Assets". The corresponding code box shall contain "10" for the total assets and, in the case of separate funds, code numbers allocated sequentially beginning with code "11".

2 Other than long-term business: Form 13 shall be completed in respect of the total assets of the company or branch (other than any long-term business assets) and code "1" entered in the code box "Category of Assets".

3 (a) In the case of the United Kingdom branch return of an external company (other than a pure reinsurer) Form 13 shall be completed for the following categories of assets —

Category	Code
Assets deposited with the Accountant General	2
Assets maintained in the United Kingdom	3
Assets maintained in the United Kingdom and the other member States	4

(b) In the case of a Community branch return of a United Kingdom deposit company, Form 13 shall be completed for the following categories of assets —

Category	Code
Assets deposited with the Accountant General	2
Assets maintained in the United Kingdom and the other member States where business is carried on	5
Assets maintained in the United Kingdom and the other member States	4

4 Linked assets shall be included in lines 85 and 86 wherever appropriate and not in lines 11 to 83.

5 In line 83 "life interests, reversionary interests and similar interests in property" means those interests of the kind described in Regulation 47 of the Insurance Companies Regulations 1981.

Returns under Insurance Companies Legislation

Form

Long Term business liabilities and margins

Name of Company

Global business/UK branch business/Community branch business

Financial year ended

	Company registration number	Global/ UK/CM	Period ended day	month	year	Units	For official use
F14					19	£000	

<table>
<tr><th colspan="2"></th><th></th><th>As at the end of the financial year
1</th><th>As at the end of the previous year
2</th><th>Source (Form / Line / Col)</th></tr>
<tr><td rowspan="4">Ordinary Long Term Business (all funds)</td><td>Mathematical reserves as shown in Schedule 4, after distribution of surplus</td><td>11</td><td></td><td></td><td>See Instructions 1 below</td></tr>
<tr><td>Balance of long term business funds</td><td>12</td><td></td><td></td><td>See Instructions 2 below</td></tr>
<tr><td>Ordinary long term business funds (11 + 12)</td><td>13</td><td></td><td></td><td>40 . 16</td></tr>
<tr><td>Valuation deficiencies</td><td>14</td><td></td><td></td><td></td></tr>
<tr><td rowspan="4">Industrial Assurance Business</td><td>Mathematical reserves as shown in Schedule 4, after distribution of surplus</td><td>15</td><td></td><td></td><td>See Instructions 1 below</td></tr>
<tr><td>Balance of long term business funds</td><td>16</td><td></td><td></td><td>See Instructions 2 below</td></tr>
<tr><td>Industrial long term business funds (15 + 16)</td><td>17</td><td></td><td></td><td>40 . 16</td></tr>
<tr><td>Valuation deficiencies</td><td>18</td><td></td><td></td><td></td></tr>
<tr><td rowspan="4">Other Insurance Liabilities</td><td>Claims admitted but not paid</td><td>21</td><td></td><td></td><td></td></tr>
<tr><td>Amounts due in respect of direct insurance and facultative reinsurance contracts accepted except amounts which must be included in line 21</td><td>31</td><td></td><td></td><td></td></tr>
<tr><td>Amounts due to ceding insurers and intermediaries under reinsurance treaties accepted except amounts which must be included in line 21</td><td>32</td><td></td><td></td><td></td></tr>
<tr><td>Amounts due to reinsurers and intermediaries under reinsurance contracts ceded</td><td>33</td><td></td><td></td><td></td></tr>
<tr><td rowspan="4">Other Liabilities</td><td>Loans secured</td><td>41</td><td></td><td></td><td></td></tr>
<tr><td>Loans unsecured</td><td>42</td><td></td><td></td><td></td></tr>
<tr><td>Taxation</td><td>44</td><td></td><td></td><td></td></tr>
<tr><td>Other creditors</td><td>47</td><td></td><td></td><td></td></tr>
<tr><td colspan="2">Excess of the value of admissible assets representing the long term business funds over the amount of those funds</td><td>51</td><td></td><td></td><td>See Instructions 3 below</td></tr>
<tr><td colspan="2">Total (13 + 14 + 17 to 51)</td><td>59</td><td></td><td></td><td></td></tr>
<tr><td colspan="2">Amount included in line 59 attributable to liabilities to related companies, other than those under contracts of insurance or reinsurance</td><td>61</td><td></td><td></td><td></td></tr>
<tr><td colspan="2">Amount included in line 59 attributable to liabilities in respect of property linked benefits</td><td>62</td><td></td><td></td><td></td></tr>
</table>

Instructions:

1 The entries at 14.11 and 14.15 shall equal the sum of lines 9, 19, 20 and 21 of the appropriate Form 58.

2 The amount of any cash bonuses allocated but not yet paid to policy holders, as shown in 58.18, (which together with 58.25 constitutes the balance of the long-term business funds) shall be stated in a note.

3 The value of admissible assets representing the long term business funds is determined by deducting from the total value of the admissible assets an amount equal to the liabilities itemised in lines 21 to 47. The amount of any additional mathematical reserves included in line 51 which have been taken into account in the actuary's certificate because the amount of the mathematical reserves determined in Schedule 4 was not calculated in all respects in relation to assets valued in accordance with Part V of the Insurance Companies Regulations 1981, as shown in Form 13, shall be stated in a note.

Returns under Insurance Companies Legislation

Form 15

Liabilities (other than Long Term business)

Name of Company

Global business/UK branch business/Community branch business

Financial year ended

	Company registration number	Global/ UK/CM	Period ended day	month	year	Units	For official use
F15					19	£000	

				As at the end of the financial year 1	As at the end of the previous year 2	Source Form / Line / Column
General business technical reserves	Unearned premiums		21			See Note below
	Additional amount for unexpired risks		22			
	Claims outstanding (less amounts recoverable from reinsurers)	Reported claims	23			
		Claims incurred but not reported	24			
	Expenses for settling claims outstanding		25			
	Funds		26			
	Claims equalisation		27			
	Other		28			
	Total (21 to 28)		29			
Other insurance liabilities	Amounts due in respect of direct insurance and facultative reinsurance contracts accepted except amounts which must be included in line 29		31			
	Amounts due to ceding insurers and intermediaries under reinsurance treaties accepted except amounts which must be included in line 29		32			
	Amounts due to reinsurers and intermediaries under reinsurance contracts ceded		33			
Other liabilities	Loans secured		41			
	Loans unsecured		42			
	Subordinated loan stock		43			
	Taxation		44			
	Recommended dividend		45			
	Cumulative preference share dividend accrued		46			
	Other creditors		47			
Total (29 to 47)			59			

Amounts included in line 59 attributable to liabilities to related companies, other than those under contracts of insurance or reinsurance	61			

Note

The sources are as follows:

Line 21 All forms 21.29.6 + 21.31.6 —(22.23.3 + 22.24.3 — 22.25.3)
Line 22 Summary form 20.23
Line 23 All forms 22.31.3 + 22.41.3
Line 24 All forms 22.32.3 + 22.42.3
Line 25 All forms 22.21.3 + 22.22.3
Line 26 All forms 24.42.5 + 27.46.3

Returns under Insurance Companies Legislation

Form 16

Statement of other income and expenditure

Name of Company

Global business/UK branch business/Community branch business

Financial year ended

	Company registration number	Global/ UK/CM	Period ended day	month	year	Units	For official use
F16					**19**	**£000**	

		The financial year 1	Previous year 2	Source Form / Line / Column
Transfer from (to) Long Term Business Revenue Account	**11**			
Transfer from (to) General Business Revenue Account Summary	**12**			20 . 79
Investment income receivable, before deduction of tax	**13**			See Note below
Other income	**14**			See Note below
Total (11 to 14)	**19**			
Management expenses	**21**			See Note below
Interest payable, before deduction of tax	**22**			
Taxation, other than that applicable to long term business	**23**			
Dividends paid and/or recommended	**24**			
Other expenditure	**25**			See Note below
Total (21 to 25)	**29**			
Excess of income over expenditure (19-29)	**39**			

Note
The amounts at lines 13, 14, 21 and 25 exclude any amounts included elsewhere in the returns.

SCHEDULE 2

Regulations 8, 9, 11, 12, 13, 14, 21, 22 and 23

GENERAL BUSINESS: REVENUE ACCOUNT AND ADDITIONAL INFORMATION
(Forms 20 to 37)

1. All the Forms included in the part of the return to which this Schedule relates (Forms 20 to 37) are to be laid out as shown in the Schedule except that Forms 29 and 30 need only be in the general form shown.

2. The provisions of paragraphs 2 to 7 of Schedule 1 above shall, unless otherwise provided, also apply for the purposes of this Schedule.

Currency

3. Notwithstanding the provisions of paragraph 2 of this Schedule, amounts on Form 29 submitted in accordance with Regulation 21 and on Forms 31, 33, 34 and 35 submitted in accordance with Regulation 11 in respect of business carried on in any country other than the United Kingdom shall be shown in the currency of the country concerned, except that figures shall be shown in sterling in those columns and lines which the Forms indicate are always to contain figures expressed in sterling. For every currency other than sterling in which amounts are shown on these Forms an entry shall be made on Form 36 to show the rate used to convert those amounts to sterling for inclusion elsewhere in the returns.

4. All amounts shown in sterling shall be shown to the nearer £1,000. Amounts in any other currency on Forms 29, 31, 33, 34 and 35 shall be shown to the nearer 1,000 principal monetary units of that currency except that, where the rate of exchange of the currency in relation to sterling on the last day of the company's financial year exceeded 1,000 principal monetary units of that currency, the amounts shall be shown to the nearer 1,000,000 principal monetary units and the fact that this has been done shall be indicated by inserting '000,000' in the box labelled 'Monetary units'. In other cases, this box shall be completed by inserting '000'.

5.—(1) Where premiums are receivable by a company or claims are paid by it under a reinsurance treaty,—

(*a*) notwithstanding paragraphs 2 to 4 above, amounts shown on Form 29 may be shown in sterling or in United States dollars or in Canadian dollars or in an appropriately weighted average of European currencies; and

(*b*) if in a financial year the proportion of gross premiums receivable, or of claims paid by the company or outstanding from the company, in any one currency other than sterling, United States dollars or Canadian dollars exceeds ten per cent of such premiums or claims under all such treaties, Form 29 may be prepared in that currency,

and where the provisions of this sub-paragraph have been applied in respect of a reinsurance treaty in relation to a financial year, those provisions shall be applied in the same manner in respect of that treaty in relation to any later financial year.

(2) An explanation in a note annexed to the Form shall be given of the method by which the said average has been determined and of any change from the manner in which Form 29 was prepared in respect of the preceding financial year.

Accounting classes

6.—(1) Direct insurance and facultative reinsurance shall be included in the returns in accordance with the accounting classes save that—

(*a*) where a company undertakes business in accounting class 4 only in respect of risks relating to hovercraft, it may account for such business in accounting class 3 if it also undertakes business in that class; and

(*b*) a company may include in accounting class 5 business covering liability for loss or damage to or of goods in transit which would otherwise be included in accounting class 2 provided that the policy does not cover damage to vehicles except as a related and subsidiary provision within the meaning of section 1(2) and (4) of the Act.

(2) Treaty reinsurance within accounting classes 3, 4 and 5, when accounted for on a three-year basis, shall also be included in the returns in the appropriate class.

(3) Treaty reinsurance business other than that for which provision is made in accounting classes 3, 4 and 5 shall be included in accounting classes 9 or 10.

7. Boxes marked 'Accounting class' or 'Accounting class code' shall be completed so as to show the number of the accounting class. '99' shall be shown in the case of the summary account in Form 20.

UK and overseas premiums

8. For the purpose of this Schedule a premium receivable shall be shown or included as a UK premium if, in the case of direct insurance or inwards facultative reinsurance, the contract of insurance was made in the United Kingdom or if, in the case of a reinsurance treaty, the cedant was a company having its head office in the United Kingdom or was a member of Lloyd's; and 'overseas premium' shall be construed accordingly.

Premiums and claims: one-year business

9. In Forms 20, 21 and 31 the amounts of premiums receivable shall be recorded in relation to the date on which the contract of insurance was incepted. However, in relation to business which is included in the reconciliation return in Form 31 or which is obtained through an agent of the company in an overseas territory (and not directly by the company or a branch of the company), the amounts in Forms 20, 21 and 31 may be shown by reference to a date later than that on which the contract was incepted but not later than the date on which the company or a branch of the company recorded that the risk had been accepted.

10. In Forms 20, 22, 23 and 33 where an amount or a number is required to be shown in respect of claims arising from incidents occurring in a specified period or attributed to a specified year of origin, the incidents which shall be included shall be determined by the date on which the incident giving rise to the claim occurred (or is believed by the company to have occurred). However claims included in the reconciliation return in Form 33 may be regarded, for the purposes of completing Forms 20 and 22, as though they all resulted from incidents occurring in the financial year to which the returns relate.

Premiums and claims: three-year business

11. In Forms 24, 25, 26, 34 and 35 where an amount is required to be shown in respect of insurance business incepted in a year or in respect of treaties commencing in a year, or in respect of claims attributable to a year of origin, the allocation of business to the year shall be determined in each case by the date on which the contract commenced, and 'underwriting year' shall have the same meaning. However in respect of accounting classes 3, 4 and 5 the year may be determined by a date later than that on which the contract commenced but not later than that on which the policy was issued and if this is done a note shall be included in the return stating the basis on which the year has been determined.

Premiums and claims: proportional treaty reinsurance business

12. In Forms 27 and 28 where an amount is required to be shown by reference to the financial year in which insurance business written under a treaty is closed, the year of closing shall be determined by the date on which all relevant accounting information is advised by the cedant to the reinsurer. Business may also be regarded as closed in a financial year if—

(*a*) the relevant information has been advised by the cedant after the end of the financial year but before the returns are prepared, or

(*b*) the relevant information has not been advised by the cedant but the business relates to a treaty having an effective date of commencement or renewal prior to the beginning of the financial year.

Reconciliation of returns: general business reinsurance

13. An explanation shall be given—

(*a*) in a note annexed to Form 27 prepared pursuant to Regulation 9 above reconciling all amounts shown on that Form with amounts shown on each Form 27 prepared pursuant to Regulation 22 above and with amounts shown on each Form 29, and

(*b*) in a note annexed to Form 29 reconciling all amounts (in whatever currency) shown on that Form with amounts shown on each Form 29 prepared pursuant to Regulation 21 above and with amounts shown on each Form 24 and each Form 27.

Commission

14. In Form 21, amounts of premiums receivable are to be shown gross of commission. If, because of market practice, it is customary for a company to account for business net of commission, an estimated gross figure must be shown and the amount recorded as commission payable on Form 22 shall include the difference between the net figure and the estimated gross figure. Where an estimated figure is used an explanation of the basis on which the estimate has been calculated shall be included in a note.

15. In Form 24, the amounts of premium shown at lines 11, 12, 13, 14 and 19 (and accordingly also at lines 1, 2 and 4 of Form 29) are normally to be shown gross of commission. If, because of market practice, it is customary for a company to account for business net of commission, the amount shown in those lines may be net of the commission which would have appeared in line 32. Where premiums are shown net of commission in Form 24 the premium income concerned shall be grossed up by an appropriate amount and shown in lines 71 to 79 on Form 25.

Unearned premiums

16. In Form 21 the basis on which the unearned premiums are calculated shall be stated by way of a supplementary note. If the basis is less accurate than the twenty-fourths method the reason for its adoption shall be included in the note.

Reconciliation returns

17.—(1) In this Schedule 'reconciliation return' means the abbreviated returns in Forms 31, 33, 34 and 35 which are prepared under Regulation 12(2) above in respect of business which is excluded from the full requirements of Regulation 11 above.

(2) The headings of the reconciliation return shall be completed so as to show against 'Country'—

(*a*) 'UK Reconciliation' in the case of a Form completed in respect of business carried on in the United Kingdom;

(*b*) 'Overseas Reconciliation' in any other case.

(3) All amounts in the reconciliation return shall be shown in sterling.

(4) The reconciliation return in Form 31 shall include only premiums receivable in the financial year.

Returns under Insurance Companies Legislation

Form 20

General business: Revenue account

Name of Company

Global business/UK branch business/Community branch business

Financial year ended

Accounting class/Summary

	Company registration number	Global/ UK/CM	Period ended day	month	year	Units	Accounting class/ summary	For official use
F20					19	£000		

Items to be shown net of outwards reinsurance

			The financial year 1	Previous year 2	Source Form . Line . Column
Underwriting income	Unearned premiums brought forward from previous years and earned in the financial year	**11**			21 . 31 . 5
	Premiums receivable earned in the financial year	**12**			21 . 29 . 5
	Additional amount for unexpired risks brought forward	**13**			
	Total (11 + 12 + 13)	**19**			
Underwriting expenditure	Claims paid and outstanding arising from incidents occurring in the financial year	**21**			22 . 16 . 4
	Expenses incurred in respect of the financial year	**22**			22 . 26 . 4
	Additional amount for unexpired risks carried forward	**23**			
	Total (21 + 22 + 23)	**29**			
Balance of year's underwriting (19-29)		**39**			
Other underwriting adjustments	Premiums receivable but earned in previous financial years	**41**			21 . 11 . 5
	Increase (decrease) in the financial year in the estimated cost of claims arising from incidents occurring in previous financial years	**42**			22 . 13 . 4
	Increase (decrease) in the financial year in expenses for settling claims outstanding at the end of the previous financial year	**43**			22 . 21 . 4
	Balance (41–42–43)	**49**			
Funded business	Premiums receivable	**51**			24 . 19 . 5 27 . 19 . 3
	Claims paid	**52**			24 . 29 . 5 27 . 29 . 3
	Total expenses	**53**			24 . 39 . 5 27 . 39 . 3
	Increase (decrease) in funds in the financial year	**54**			24 . 49 . 5 27 . 49 . 3
	Balance (51–52–53–54)	**59**			
Balance of all years' underwriting (39 + 49 + 59)		**69**			
Other attributed income and expenditure	Investment income receivable before deduction of tax	**71**			
	Other expenditure	**72**			
Transfer to (from) statement of other income and expenditure (69 + 71–72)		**79**			

Returns under Insurance Companies Legislation

Form 21
(Sheet 1)

General business: Analysis of premiums for direct insurance and facultative reinsurance business

Name of Company

Global business/UK branch business/Community branch business

Financial year ended

Accounting class

	Company registration number	Global/ UK/CM	Period ended day	month	year	Units	Accounting class	For official use
F21					19	£000		

Premiums receivable (less rebates and refunds) in the financial year				Gross		Reinsurance premiums payable		Net of reinsurance	
				Earned in previous financial years 1		Earned in previous financial years 3		Earned in previous financial years 5	
in respect of risks incepted in previous financial years			11						
				Earned in the financial year 1	Unearned at end of the financial year 2	Earned in the financial year 3	Unearned at end of the financial year 4	Earned in the financial year 5	Unearned at end of the financial year 6
in respect of risks incepted in previous financial years			12						
in respect of risks incepted in the financial year for periods of less than 12 months	expiring by the end of the financial year		13						
	expiring after the end of the financial year		14						
in respect of risks incepted in the financial year for periods of 12 months	commencing prior to the last 12 months of the financial year		15						
	commencing in each of the last 12 months of the financial year	Month 1	16						
		Month 2	17						
		Month 3	18						
		Month 4	19						
		Month 5	20						
		Month 6	21						
		Month 7	22						

Note

- for the normal financial year of 12 months, the amounts for each month are entered at lines 16 to 27, commencing with the first month at line 16

- when there are more than twelve months in the financial year, the total amounts for the months before the last 12 months in the financial year are entered at line 15, the amounts for each of the last 12 months are

- when there are less than 12 months in the financial year, amounts shall be entered for each month with the amounts for the last month of the financial year at line 27, with preceding months at lines 26, 25 etc.

(Sheet 2)

General business: Analysis of premiums for direct insurance and facultative reinsurance business

Name of Company

Global business/UK branch business/Community branch business

Financial year ended

Accounting class

	Company registration number	Global/ UK/CM	Period ended day	month	year	Units	Accounting class	For official use
F21					19	£000		

Premiums receivable (less rebates and refunds) in the financial year				Gross: Earned in the financial year 1	Gross: Unearned at end of the financial year 2	Reinsurance premiums payable: Earned in the financial year 3	Reinsurance premiums payable: Unearned at end of the financial year 4	Net of reinsurance: Earned in the financial year 5	Net of reinsurance: Unearned at end of the financial year 6
in respect of risks incepted in the financial year for periods of 12 months	commencing in each of the last 12 months of the financial year	Month 8	23						
		Month 9	24						
		Month 10	25						
		Month 11	26						
		Month 12	27						
in respect of risks incepted in the financial year for periods of more than 12 months			28						
Total (12 to 28)			29						
Premiums receivable (less rebates and refunds) in previous financial years not earned in those years and brought forward to the financial year			31						

			Gross 1		Reinsurance premiums payable 3		Net of reinsurance 5		Amount included in col 1 of premiums which have not been analysed by date of inception of risk 7
Total premiums receivable (less rebates and refunds) in the financial year		41							
Total premiums at Line 41 attributable to	UK	42							
	Overseas	43							

Note
41.1 is 11.1 + 29.1 − 29.2 41.3 is 11.3 + 29.3 + 29.4 41.5 is 11.5 + 29.5 + 29.6

Returns under Insurance Companies Legislation **Form 22**

General business: Analysis of claims and expenses for direct insurance and facultative reinsurance business

Name of Company

Global business/UK branch business/Community branch business

Financial year ended

Accounting class

	Company registration number	Global/UK/CM	Period ended day	month	year	Units	Accounting class	For official use
F 22					19	£000		

			Amount brought forward from previous financial year 1	Amount payable/receivable in the financial year 2	Amount carried forward to next financial year 3	Amount attributable to the financial year 4
Claims arising from incidents occurring in previous financial years	gross	11				
	recoverable from reinsurers	12				
	net (11–12)	13				
Claims arising from incidents occurring in the financial year (including claims reported in the reconciliation return on Form 33)	gross	14				
	recoverable from reinsurers	15				
	net (14–15)	16				
Expenses	expenses for settling claims arising from incidents occurring in previous financial years	21				
	expenses for settling claims arising from incidents occurring in the financial year (including claims reported in the reconciliation return on Form 33)	22				
	management expenses	23				
	commission payable	24				
	reinsurance commission receivable	25				
	expenses in respect of the financial year (22+23+24 - 25)	26				
	total (21+26)	29				

Amount included in line 13 attributable to	reported claims	31				
	claims incurred but not reported	32				
Amount included in line 16 attributable to	reported claims	41				
	claims incurred but not reported	42				

Notes

1 Any amounts included in 14.1, 15.1, 16.1 and 22.1 relate only to claims included in the reconciliation return on Form 33

2 The values in column 4 are calculated as follows:
for lines 11 to 22, values in columns 2+3−1
for lines 23 to 25, values in columns 1+2−3

Returns under Insurance Companies Legislation

Form 23

General business: Analysis of claims outstanding net of reinsurance recoveries for direct insurance and facultative reinsurance business

Name of Company

Global business/UK branch business /Community branch business

Financial year ended

	Company registration number	Global/ UK/CM	Period ended day	month	year	Units	For official use
F23					19	£000	

Year of origin ended month	year	Accounting class code		Claims outstanding (net) as at end of year of origin 1	Total claims paid (net) in all years since year of origin 2	Claims outstanding (net) at end of financial year 3

Accounting class

month	year	Accounting class code	Line	1	2	3
	19		11			
	19		12			
	19		13			
	19		14			
	19		15			
	19		16			
	19		17			
Previous years			18			
Reconciliation			19			
Total			29			

Accounting class

month	year	Accounting class code	Line	1	2	3
	19		11			
	19		12			
	19		13			
	19		14			
	19		15			
	19		16			
	19		17			
Previous years			18			
Reconciliation			19			
Total			29			

Notes

1 All figures are net of reinsurance recoveries

2 Line 19 relates to claims reported in the reconciliation return on Form 33. These claims are not included in lines 11 to 18.

3 23.29.3=22.13.3+22.16.3

Instructions for Completion of Form 23

1 Line 11 shall be completed in respect of the financial year to which the return relates. Columns 1 and 3 will be the same as each other; column 2 will be blank.

2 Lines 12 to 17 shall be completed in respect of the preceding 6 years of origin beginning with the most recent. Years of origin commencing before 1 January 1981 shall not, however, be included.

3 Line 18 will show, in the first financial year for which this form is prepared, a figure in columns 1 and 3 which represents the total claims outstanding at the end of *that financial year* in respect of all years of origin commencing before 1 January 1981. Column 2 will be blank for the first year. In subsequent financial years the figure at column 1 will remain the same, subject to instruction 4, and column 2 will show the claims paid since the end of the first financial year. When there are no longer any claims outstanding in respect of any year of origin commencing prior to 1 January 1981 information in respect of those years shall cease to be included in line 18.

4 If any claims remain outstanding in respect of a year of origin commencing on or after 1 January 1981 for more than 6 years after the end of that year, information in respect of the year shall be added to any other information included in line 18 until such time as there are no longer any claims outstanding in respect of that year.

Returns under Insurance Companies Legislation **Form 24**

General business (three year accounting): Analysis of premiums, claims, expenses and funds

Name of Company

Global business/UK branch business/Community branch business

Financial year ended

Accounting class

	Company registration number	Global/ UK/CM	Period ended day	month	year	Units	Accounting class	For official use
F24					19	£000		

Amounts receivable or payable in the financial year				**Insurance business incepted in:** All years prior to the second year preceding the financial year 1	Second year preceding the financial year 2	First year preceding the financial year 3	The financial year 4	Total (1 + 2 + 3 + 4) 5
Premiums	receivable under direct insurance and facultative reinsurance contracts		**11**					
	receivable under reinsurance treaties accepted		**12**					
	payable to reinsurers to reinsure business of a kind shown at line 11		**13**					
	payable to retrocessionaires to reinsure business of a kind shown at line 12		**14**					
	amounts receivable net of retrocessions in respect of outstanding claims and loss portfolios		**15**					
	receivable net (11 + 12 − 13 − 14 + 15)		**19**					
Claims	paid under contracts of a kind shown at	line 11	**21**					
		line 12	**22**					
	recoverable from reinsurers under contracts of a kind shown at	line 13	**23**					
		line 14	**24**					
	paid net (21 + 22 − 23 − 24)		**29**					
Expenses	management expenses and expenses for settling claims		**31**					
	commission payable		**32**					
	reinsurance commission receivable		**33**					
	total (31 + 32 − 33)		**39**					
Funds	brought forward		**41**					
	carried forward		**42**					
	increase (decrease) in the financial year (42 − 41)		**49**					
Balance on each underwriting year (19 − 29 − 39 − 49)			**51**					

Note
The references to reinsurers and reinsurance in lines 13, 23 and 33 include retrocessionaires and retrocession.

Instructions for Completion of Form 24

1 (i) When the form is used in respect of accounting classes 3, 4 or 5 premiums receivable shown at line 12 shall include unearned premium portfolios less premium portfolios, and outstanding claims portfolios less loss portfolios.

(ii) When the form is used in respect of accounting class 9 (non-proportional treaty reinsurance) premiums receivable shown at line 12 shall include unearned premium portfolios less premium portfolios, whilst outstanding claims portfolios less loss portfolios shall be part of the constituents of line 15.

2 In the case of accounting class 9 the figures in lines 12, 14 and 15 shall equal respectively those in lines 19, 29 and 61 of Form 26.

3 For business closed through the Institute of London Underwriters, amounts paid shall include amounts agreed for settlement but not yet paid.

Returns under Insurance Companies Legislation **Form 25**

General business (three year accounting): Additional information relating to premiums

Name of Company

Global business/UK branch business/Community branch business

Financial year ended

Accounting class

	Company registration number	Global/ UK/CM	Period ended day	month	year	Units	Accounting class	For official use
Division of premiums between UK and overseas F 25					19	£000		

	Premiums on Form 24 attributed to		UK 6	Overseas 7
Premiums	receivable under direct insurance and facultative reinsurance contracts	11		
	receivable under reinsurance treaties accepted	12		
	payable to reinsurers and retrocessionaires to reinsure business of a kind shown at line 11	13		
	payable to retrocessionaires to reinsure business of a kind shown at line 12	14		
	amounts receivable net of retrocessions in respect of outstanding claims and loss portfolios	15		
	receivable net (11+12−13−14+15)	19		

Note 25.19.6 + 25.19.7 = 24.19.5

Grossed-up premiums (only to be completed if values in the first part of the form are net of commission)

Grossed up values of entries shown at lines 11 to 14 on Form 24			**Insurance business incepted in:** All years prior to the second year preceding the financial year 1	Second year preceding the financial year 2	First year preceding the financial year 3	The financial year 4	Total (1+2+3+4) 5
Premiums	receivable under direct insurance and facultative reinsurance contracts	71					
	receivable under reinsurance treaties accepted	72					
	payable to reinsurers and retrocessionaires to reinsure business of a kind shown at line 71	73					
	payable to retrocessionaires to reinsure business of a kind shown at line 72	74					
	Balance (71+72−73−74)	79					

Returns under Insurance Companies Legislation **Form 26**

General business: Analysis of premiums for non-proportional treaty reinsurance business

Name of Company

Global business/UK branch business/Community branch business

Financial year ended

	Company registration number	Global/ UK/CM	Period ended day	month	year	Units	Accounting class	For official use
F26					19	£000		

Amounts receivable or payable in the financial year		In respect of treaties commencing in: All years prior to the second year preceding the financial year 1	Second year preceding the financial year 2	First year preceding the financial year 3	The financial year 4	Total (1 + 2 + 3 + 4) 5
Premiums receivable (other than to assume portfolios)	11					
Premiums receivable to assume unearned premium portfolios	12					
Premium portfolios payable to cedants	13					
Total premiums receivable (11 + 12 – 13)	19					
Premiums payable to retrocessionaires (other than to assume portfolios)	21					
Premiums payable to retrocessionaires to assume unearned premium portfolios	22					
Premium portfolios receivable from retrocessionaires	23					
Total premiums payable to retrocesssionaires (21 + 22 – 23)	29					
Net premiums receivable (19–29)	31					

Amounts receivable to assume outstanding claims portfolios	41					
Loss portfolios payable to cedants	42					
Net amounts receivable from cedants in respect of outstanding claims and loss portfolios (41–42)	49					
Amounts payable to retrocessionaires to assume outstanding claims portfolios	51					
Loss portfolios receivable from retrocessionaires	52					
Net amounts payable to retrocessionaires in respect of outstanding claims and loss portfolios (51–52)	59					
Amounts receivable net of retrocessions in respect of outstanding claims and loss portfolios (49–59)	61					

Note
The amounts shown in lines 19, 29 and 61 are carried forward to Form 24

Returns under Insurance Companies Legislation

Form 27

General business: Revenue analysis of proportional treaty reinsurance business

Name of Company

Global business/UK branch business / Community branch business

Financial year ended

Total/Category (to be specified)

	Company registration number	Global/ UK/CM	Period ended day	month	year	Units	Accounting class	For official use
F27					19	£000	10	

Amounts receivable or payable in the financial year			Insurance business written under treaties: closed in the financial year ('closed treaty year') 1	Insurance business written under treaties: to be closed in the next financial year ('open treaty year') 2	Total (1 + 2) 3	Source Form . Line
Premiums	receivable under reinsurance treaties accepted	12				28 . 19
	payable to retrocessionaires to reinsure business of a kind shown at line 12	14				28 . 29
	amounts receivable net of retrocessions in respect of outstanding claims and loss portfolios	15				28 . 61
	receivable net (12–14 + 15)	19				
Claims	paid under contracts of a kind shown at line 12	22				
	recoverable from retrocessionaires under contracts of a kind shown at line 14	24				
	paid net (22–24)	29				
Expenses	management expenses and expenses for settling claims	31				
	commission payable	32				
	reinsurance commission receivable from retrocessionaires	33				
	total (31 + 32–33)	39				
Funds and other amounts set aside for unearned premiums and outstanding claims	fund brought forward from previous financial year	41				
	unearned premiums carried over to 'open treaty year'	42				
	unearned premiums brought forward from 'closed treaty year'	43				27 . 42
	claims outstanding carried over to 'open treaty year'	44				
	claims outstanding brought forward from 'closed treaty year'	45				27 . 44
	fund carried forward to next financial year	46				
	increase (decrease) in the financial year (42 + 44 + 46–41–43–45)	49				
Balance on each treaty year (19–29–39–49)		51				

Returns under Insurance Companies Legislation **Form 28**

General business: Analysis of premiums for proportional treaty reinsurance business

Name of Company

Global business/UK branch business/Community branch business

Financial year ended

	Company registration number	Global/ UK/CM	Period ended day	month	year	Units	Accounting class	For official use
F28					19	£000	10	

Amounts receivable or payable in the financial year		Insurance business written under treaties: closed in the financial year ('closed treaty year') 1	to be closed in the next financial year ('open treaty year') 2	Total (1+2) 3
Premiums receivable (other than to assume portfolios)	11			
Premiums receivable to assume unearned premium portfolios	12			
Premium portfolios payable to cedants	13			
Total premiums receivable (11 + 12−13)	19			
Premiums payable to retrocessionaires (other than to assume portfolios)	21			
Premiums payable to retrocessionaires to assume unearned premium portfolios	22			
Premium portfolios receivable from retrocessionaires	23			
Total premiums payable to retrocessionaires (21 + 22−23)	29			
Net premiums receivable (19–29)	31			

Amounts receivable to assume outstanding claims portfolios	41			
Loss portfolios payable to cedants	42			
Net amounts receivable from cedants in respect of outstanding claims and loss portfolios (41–42)	49			
Amounts payable to retrocessionaires to assume outstanding claims portfolios	51			
Loss portfolios receivable from retrocessionaires	52			
Net amounts payable to retrocessionaires in respect of outstanding claims and loss portfolios (51–52)	59			
Amounts receivable net of retrocessions in respect of outstanding claims and loss portfolios (49-59)	61			

Division of premiums between UK and overseas

	Premiums on Form 27 attributed to		UK 4	Overseas 5
Premiums	receivable under reinsurance treaties accepted	72		
	payable to retrocessionaires to reinsure business of a kind shown at line 72	74		
	amounts receivable net of retrocessions in respect of outstanding claims and loss portfolios	75		
	receivable net (72−74 + 75)	79		

Note 28.79.4 + 28.79.5 = 27.19.3

Returns under Insurance Companies Legislation

Form 29

General business (reinsurance accepted): Analysis in respect of non-proportional and certain proportional general business treaty reinsurance

Name of Company

Global business/UK branch business/Community branch business

Financial year ended

Category

Currency

Amounts receivable or payable in the financial year in respect of treaties incepted in			Each year before the financial year	The financial year	Total
Premiums	Receivable under reinsurance treaties accepted	1			
	Payable to retrocessionaires	2			
	Amounts receivable net of retrocessions in respect of outstanding claims and loss portfolios	3			
	Receivable net (1−2 + 3)	4			
Claims	Paid under reinsurance treaties accepted	5			
	Recoverable from retrocessionaires	6			
	Paid net (5 − 6)	7			
Expenses	Expenses and commissions (net)	8			
Funds	Brought forward	9			
	Carried forward	10			
	Increase (decrease) in the financial year (10 − 9)	11			
	Balance on each underwriting year (4 − 7 − 8 − 11)	12			

Note

Information is to be shown separately in respect of each year before the financial year (but see Regulation 21(8)).

Returns under Insurance Companies Legislation

Form 30

General business: Summary of reinsurance business ceded

Name of Company

Global business/UK branch business/Community branch business

Financial year ended

Accounting class/ risk group	Type of reinsurance cover	Period covered (where different from the ceding company's financial year)	Ceding company's maximum net retention or probable maximum loss in respect of		Reinsurers' potential liability under contract	Cessions to				Remarks
						Reinsurers permitted to carry on business in the UK		Other reinsurers		
			any one risk	any one event		Number of reinsurers	Premiums payable	Number of reinsurers	Premiums payable	
1	2	3	4	5	6	7	8	9	10	11
			£000	£000	£000		£000		£000	

Reconciliation with Forms 21, 24 and 27

	£000
Aggregate of columns 8 and 10 above	
Total reinsurance premiums payable shown on Forms 21, 24 and 27	
Balance	

Instructions for Completion of Form 30

1 The form shall show all reinsurance arrangements for which premiums were payable in respect of the financial year to which the return relates. Separate entries shall be made for each accounting class (ie of business accepted). Where reinsurance has been arranged separately for risk groups within an accounting class, separate entries shall be made for the risk groups.

2 For each accounting class or risk group, the types of reinsurance cover obtained shall be entered in column 2. The entries here shall specify whether the reinsurance cover has been arranged on a facultative or treaty basis, and, where it is the latter, shall also state the nature of the treaty eg quota share.

3 The information given in column 6 shall include, in the case of surplus treaties, the number of lines accepted by the reinsurer. For treaties providing excess of loss cover, it shall include the layers of the treaty, ie the level at which each layer takes effect, and also the reinsurers' potential liability under it.

4 The combined aggregate of amounts entered in columns 8 and 10 shall be reconciled in total with the reinsurance premiums payable shown in Forms 21, 24 and 27.

5 In the case of facultative reinsurance cover, —

(a) only one entry is required for each accounting class; the word "facultative" shall be recorded in column 2, the word "variable" may be used in column 3, and columns 4, 5 and 6 need not be completed;

(b) columns 7 to 10 need only be completed for a class if the total number of facultative reinsurers for that class is ten or less or if the total premiums payable for facultative cover for that class are more than 30 per cent of the gross premiums receivable for the class; if these columns are not separately completed for a class the reason shall be stated together with the total amount of facultative premiums ceded for the class; and

(c) column 11 shall include a note of the number of reinsurers who are not permitted to carry on business in the UK and who each receive premiums in respect of facultative cover which amount to more than 5 per cent of the gross premiums receivable for the class.

6 Remarks in column 11 shall include details of reinsurance ceded to related companies.

Returns under Insurance Companies Legislation

Form 31

General business: Analysis of exposure to risk measured by premiums

Name of Company

Financial year ended

Country

Currency

Accounting class

	Company registration number	Period ended day	month	year	Monetary units	Country	Accounting class	For official use
F31				19				

Gross premiums receivable (less rebates and refunds) on direct insurance and facultative reinsurance business				Additional exposure attributable to previous financial years 1	Exposure in the financial year 2	Exposure carried forward to following financial years 3	Total gross premiums (1+2+3) 4	Total gross premiums expressed in sterling (£000) 5
Risk group								
in previous financial years			11					
in the financial year in respect of risks incepted in	previous financial years		12					
	the financial year		13					
Total (11+12+13)			19					
Risk group								
in previous financial years			11					
in the financial year in respect of risks incepted in	previous financial years		12					
	the financial year		13					
Total (11+12+13)			19					
Risk group								
in previous financial years			11					
in the financial year in respect of risks incepted in	previous financial years		12					
	the financial year		13					
Total (11+12+13)			19					
Risk group								
in previous financial years			11					
in the financial year in respect of risks incepted in	previous financial years		12					
	the financial year		13					
Total (11+12+13)			19					

Instructions for Completion of Form 31

1 For business other than proportional and non-proportional treaty reinsurance business, and business to be included in Forms 34 and 35 (that is, accounted for on a three-year basis) forms shall be completed as indicated below:

		Coverage	Country code
(a)	for each country not exempted by Regulation 12(1)	one or more forms for each accounting class with a section completed for each risk group carried on in the country	the code for the country
(b)	for UK business not returned under *(a)*	box 19.5 only of one section of one form for each accounting class	AZ
(c)	for all other business not returned under *(a)* or *(b)*	box 19.5 only of one section of one form for each accounting class	YZ

2 If the amounts shown at 31.12.4 and 31.13.4 are in sterling then the same amounts shall be shown also at 31.12.5 and 31.13.5 respectively.

3 The aggregate of the amounts shown at 31.19.5 for all forms within an accounting class shall be the amount shown at 21.41.1 for that accounting class.

Returns under Insurance Companies Legislation **Form 32**

General business: Analysis of exposure to risk measured by vehicle years

Name of Company

Financial year ended

Country

Accounting class Motor vehicle

	Company registration number	Period ended day	month	year	Country	Accounting class	For official use
F32				19		2	

Number of units of exposure in vehicle years corresponding to premiums recorded on Form 31		Additional exposure attributable to previous financial years 1	Exposure in the financial year 2	Exposure carried forward to following financial years 3	Total vehicle years (1+2+3) 4	Claim frequency in the financial year % 5

Risk group

			1	2	3	4	5
in previous financial years		11					
in the financial year in respect of risks incepted in	previous financial years	12					
	the financial year	13					
Total for columns 1 to 4 (11+12+13)		19					

Risk group

			1	2	3	4	5
in previous financial years		11					
in the financial year in respect of risks incepted in	previous financial years	12					
	the financial year	13					
Total for columns 1 to 4 (11+12+13)		19					

Risk group

			1	2	3	4	5
in previous financial years		11					
in the financial year in respect of risks incepted in	previous financial years	12					
	the financial year	13					
Total for columns 1 to 4 (11+12+13)		19					

Risk group

			1	2	3	4	5
in previous financial years		11					
in the financial year in respect of risks incepted in	previous financial years	12					
	the financial year	13					
Total for columns 1 to 4 (11+12+13)		19					

Note
The figure at 32.19.5 is the number of claims (shown at 33.19.1 for the corresponding year of origin) as a percentage of the number of vehicle years (32.19.2)

Instructions for Completion of Form 32

1 Form 32 shall be completed only in respect of accounting class 2 (Motor Vehicle).

2 Forms shall be completed as required under Instruction 1(a) to Form 31.

3 The number of vehicle years insured under any insurance contract is the product of the period (expressed in years and parts of years) for which the contract is in force and the number of vehicles insured under the contract; (eg two vehicles insured for six months and one vehicle insured for one year each to be regarded as one vehicle year). Figures entered on the form are to be rounded to the nearest vehicle year only after aggregating the component figures.

4 Figures at 32.19.5 shall be expressed as percentages to one place of decimals.

Returns under Insurance Companies Legislation

Form 33

General business: Analysis of claims by number and cost

Name of Company

Financial year ended

Country

Currency

Accounting class

Risk group

	Company registration number	Period ended day	month	year	Monetary units	Country	Accounting class	For official use	
F33				19					

For direct insurance and facultative reinsurance business

Claims attributable to year of origin ended		month	year 19	Number of claims 1	Amounts of payments made in the financial year 2	Amounts of payments made in previous financial years relating to claims in column 1 3	Estimates of payments remaining to be made 4	Total gross amount paid and outstanding (2+3+4) 5
Claims closed in the financial year	at no cost (other than reopened claims)	11						
	at some cost (other than reopened claims)	12						
	reopened claims	13						
Claims outstanding at the end of the financial year	reported (other than reopened claims)	14						
	incurred but not reported (IBNR)	15						
	reopened claims	16						
Claims closed in previous financial years (excluding those reopened claims shown at lines 13 and 16)		17						
Total claims attributable to the year of origin (11 to 17)		19						
Line 19 expressed in sterling (£000)		29						

Year of origin ended		month	year 19					
Claims closed in the financial year	at no cost (other than reopened claims)	11						
	at some cost (other than reopened claims)	12						
	reopened claims	13						
Claims outstanding at the end of the financial year	reported (other than reopened claims)	14						
	incurred but not reported (IBNR)	15						
	reopened claims	16						
Claims closed in previous financial years (excluding those reopened claims shown at lines 13 and 16)		17						
Total claims attributable to the year of origin (11 to 17)		19						
Line 19 expressed in sterling (£000)		29						

Instructions for Completion of Form 33

1 For business other than proportional and non-proportional treaty reinsurance business, and business to be included in Forms 34 and 35 (that is, accounted for on a three-year basis), forms shall be completed as indicated below:

		Coverage	Country code	Year of origin	
				Month	Year
(a)	for each country not exempted by Regulation 12(1)	one or more forms for each risk group carried on in the country, with a section completed for each year of origin	the code for the country	the last month (eg 6)	the year of the last month (eg 1981)
(b)	for UK business not returned under *(a)*	one form for each accounting class with boxes 29.2 and 29.4 of one section completed for claims originating in all years of origin	AZ	XX	19XX
(c)	for all other business not returned under *(a)* or *(b)*	one form for each accounting class with boxes 29.2 and 29.4 of one section completed for claims originating in all years of origin	YZ	XX	19XX

2 Under 1(a) a form is required for a year of origin commencing before 1 January 1981 only if that year of origin was required to be reported under the Insurance Companies (Accounts and Forms) Regulations 1968.

3 Lines 13 and 16 need not be completed for a year of origin commencing before 1 January 1981. If they are not completed, reopened claims shall be included in lines 11, 12 and 14 as appropriate.

4 If the amounts shown at 33.19.2 and 33.19.4 are in sterling then the same amounts shall be shown also at 33.29.2 and 33.29.4 respectively.

5 Expenses incurred by the company for legal, medical, surveying, engineering and other technical services which are directly attributable to individual claims shall be included as part of the cost of that claim. General administrative expenses are not to be included as part of the cost of the claim and if only such expenses are incurred the claim is to be regarded as settled at no cost.

6 For the purpose of line 11 a claim is *not* to be regarded as settled at no cost (before deduction of reinsurance recoveries) if any cost of a kind described in the first sentence of Instruction 5 has been incurred by the company specifically in connection with consideration of the claim.

7 A reopened claim is a claim which had been closed in a previous financial year and has been reopened in a different financial year.

8 The aggregate of the amounts shown at 33.29.2 for all forms within an accounting class shall be the sum of the amounts shown at 22.11.2 and 22.14.2 for that accounting class. The aggregate of the amounts shown at 33.29.4 for all forms within an accounting class shall be the sum of the amounts shown at 22.11.3 and 22.14.3 for that accounting class.

Returns under Insurance Companies Legislation

Form 34

General business (three year accounting): Analysis of premiums

Name of Company

Financial year ended

Country

Currency

	Company registration number	Period ended day	month	year	Monetary units	Country	For official use
F34				19			

	Gross premiums receivable (less rebates and refunds) on direct insurance and facultative reinsurance business in the financial year for			Insurance business incepted in:					
	Names of accounting class/risk group	Accounting class code		All years prior to the second year preceding the financial year 1	Second year preceding the financial year 2	First year preceding the financial year 3	The financial year 4	Total (1+2+3+4) 5	Column 5 expressed in sterling (£000) 6
C			11						
RG									
C			11						
RG									
C			11						
RG									
C			11						
RG									
C			11						
RG									
C			11						
RG									

structions for Completion of Form 34

For business other than proportional and non-proportional treaty reinsurance business, and business to be included in Forms 31 and 33 (that is, accounted for on a one-year basis), forms shall be completed as indicated below:

		Coverage	Country code
(a)	for each country not exempted by Regulation 12(1)	one section of a form for each risk group carried on in the country	the code for the country
(b)	for UK business not returned under *(a)*	one section of a form for each accounting class	AZ
(c)	for all other business not returned under *(a)* or *(b)*	one section of a form for each accounting class	YZ

If the amount shown at 34.11.5 is in sterling then the same amount shall be shown also at 34.11.6.

The aggregate of the amounts shown at 34.11.6 for all sections relating to one accounting class shall be the amount shown at 24.11.5 for that accounting class.

Returns under Insurance Companies Legislation

Form 35

General business (three year accounting): Analysis of claims by cost

Name of Company

Financial year ended

Risk group

Country

Currency

Accounting class

For direct insurance and facultative reinsurance business

	Company registration number	Period ended day	Period ended month	Period ended year	Monetary units	Country	Accounting class	For official use	
F35				19					

Year of origin ended month	year		Amount of payments made in the financial year 1	Estimate of payments remaining to be made 2	Latest estimated total of amounts paid and outstanding (columns 1 + 2 plus amount of payments made in previous financial years) 3	Column 1 expressed in sterling (£000) 4	Column 2 expressed in sterling (£000) 5
	19	11					
	19	11					
	19	11					
	19	11					
	19	11					
	19	11					
	19	11					
	19	11					
	19	11					
	19	11					
	19	11					
	19	11					
	19	11					
	19	11					
	19	11					
	19	11					
	19	11					
	19	11					
	19	11					
	19	11					
	19	11					

Instructions for Completion of Form 35

1 For business other than proportional and non-proportional treaty reinsurance business, and business to be included in Forms 31 and 33 (that is, accounted for on a one-year basis), forms shall be completed as indicated below:

		Coverage		Country Code	Year of origin Month	Year
(a)	for each country not exempted by Regulation 12(1)	one form for each risk group with one line for each year of origin		the code for the country	the last month (eg 6)	the year of the last month (eg 1981)
(b)	for UK business not returned under *(a)*	one form for each accounting class (with column 4 only completed)	(i) one line for each of the years of origin identified in columns 2, 3 and 4 on the corresponding Form 34	AZ	the last month	the year of the last month
			(ii) one line for the years of origin identified in column 1 on the corresponding Form 34	AZ	PR	19
(c)	for all other business not returned under *(a)* or *(b)*	one form for each accounting class (with column 4 only completed)	as *(b)* (i)	YZ	the last month	the year of the last month
			as *(b)*(ii)	YZ	PR	19

2 (i) Under 1*(a)* a line is required for a year of origin commencing before 1 January 1981 only if that year of origin was required to be reported under the Insurance Companies (Accounts and Forms) Regulations 1968.

(ii) For marine hull and aviation hull business, lines on forms completed under 1*(a)* relating to years of origin commencing before 1 January 1981 may be limited to payments on major claims if the returns were so prepared in previous financial years.

(iii) Forms completed under 1*(b)* and *(c)* shall include any payments not reported under 1*(a)* because of the operation of instruction 2(ii).

3 The amounts shown in column 2 shall be in respect of risks for which premiums are required to be shown in Form 34.

4 If the amounts shown at 35.11.1 and 35.11.2 are in sterling then the same amounts shall be shown also at 35.11.4 and 35.11.5 respectively.

5 Expenses incurred by the company for legal, medical, surveying, engineering and other technical services which are directly attributable to individual claims shall be included as part of the cost of that claim. General administrative expenses are not to be included as part of the cost of the claim and if only such expenses are incurred the claim is to be regarded as settled at no cost.

6 The aggregate of the amounts shown at 35.11.4 for all forms relating to one accounting class shall be the amount shown at 24.21.5 for that accounting class.

Returns under Insurance Companies Legislation

Form 36

Currency rates

Name of Company

Financial year ended

	Company registration number	Period ended day	month	year		For official use
F36				19		

Name of Country	Country code		No. of units to £ Sterling 1
		11	
		11	
		11	
		11	
		11	
		11	
		11	
		11	
		11	
		11	
		11	
		11	
		11	
		11	
		11	
		11	
		11	
		11	
		11	
		11	
		11	
		11	
		11	
		11	

General business: Analysis of gross premiums receivable through participation in Community co-insurance operations

Name of Company

Global business/UK branch business/Community branch business

Financial year ended

	Company registration number	Global/ UK/CM	Period ended day	month	year	Units	For official use
F37					19	£000	

Country of Risk	Country Code		Gross premiums receivable (less rebates and refunds) on Community co-insurance operations in the financial year in accounting class: Aircraft (accounting class 3) 1	Ships (accounting class 4) and Goods in transit (accounting class 5) 2 (see note 2)	Property damage (accounting class 6) 3 (see note 2)	General liability (accounting class 7) 4	Pecuniary loss (accounting class 8) 5	TOTAL (1 + 2 + 3 + 4 + 5) 6
		11						
		12						
		13						
		14						
		15						
		16						
		17						
		18						
		19						
		20						
		21						
		22						
		23						
Total		29						

Notes;

1 The figures in this form relate only to participation in Community co-insurance operations from a Head Office, Branch or Agency in the United Kingdom where the risk is situated in another member State.

2 Any business of accounting class 6 which consists of the insurance of railway rolling stock shall be included in column 2 and not column 3.

SCHEDULE 3

Regulations 8 and 15

LONG TERM BUSINESS: REVENUE ACCOUNT AND ADDITIONAL INFORMATION
(Forms 40 to 51)

1. Information on long term business is to be given in the form set out in Forms 40 to 51.

2. All amounts shall be shown in sterling. In Forms 40 to 42 amounts shall be shown to the nearer £1,000. In Forms 43 to 51 amounts may be shown to the nearer £1,000. Amounts in currencies other than sterling should be converted in accordance with the provisions of paragraphs 4 and 5 of Schedule 1 above.

3. For the purposes of this Schedule a contract shall be regarded as a UK contract if, in the case of direct insurance or facultative reinsurance, the contract was made in the United Kingdom or if, in the case of a reinsurance treaty, the cedant was a company having its head office in the United Kingdom or was a member of Lloyd's; and 'overseas contracts' shall be construed accordingly.

4.—(1) Where a company maintains more than one long term business fund, a statement shall be annexed to Form 40 giving the principles and methods applied to apportioning the investment income, increase or decrease in the value of assets brought into account, expenses and taxation between the different funds.

(2) The box marked 'No of Fund/Summary' in Forms 40, 41 and 42 shall be completed by the inclusion of a discrete number to identify each fund or, if the Form relates to a part of the fund, the fund of which it is part. Where there is only one fund for ordinary long-term insurance business or for industrial assurance business, as the case may be, the number '1' shall be shown in the box marked 'No of Fund/Summary'. Where the Form is a summary Form, the number '99' shall be inserted in that box. The box marked 'No. of part of fund' shall show a discrete number for each part of a fund or the figure '0' if the Form is a statement of the whole fund.

5. Where arrangements have been made for the provision of management services to a company by another company (whether an insurance company or not)—

(*a*) the first mentioned company shall annex to Form 40 relating to the financial year of the company during any part of which those arrangements are in force, and

(*b*) the other company (being an insurance company) shall annex to Form 40 relating to the financial year of that insurance company during any part of which those arrangements are in force,

a statement that the arrangements have been so in force in the financial year and naming the parties to them.

6. Forms of return as set out in Forms 41 and 42 are to be completed separately in respect of each fund in respect of which a separate revenue account is required to be prepared in Form 40.

7. Information is to be given in the form set out in Form 43 for all non-group contracts and is to be gross of reinsurance ceded. Separate statements are to be given for United Kingdom business and overseas business and in each case for non-linked contracts and linked contracts. For group contracts only the number of contracts in force at the end of the year and the estimated number of persons covered thereunder are to be given in a note to the appropriate statement.

8.—(1) Separate statements are to be given in the form set out in Form 44 for United Kingdom business and overseas business and the information on each statement is to be totalled except for columns 4 and 7. The amounts are to be given gross of reinsurance ceded.

(2) The information is to be analysed and sub-totalled within each type of business in the sequence specified below—

(i) life assurance business
(ii) general annuity business
(iii) pension business
(iv) permanent health business
(v) capital redemption business.

(3) The information is to be further analysed and sub-totalled within each basis of participation in profits in the sequence specified below—

(i) non-linked contracts: with participation in profits
(ii) non-linked contracts: without participation in profits
(iii) linked contracts.

(4) Within each sub-division required under sub-paragraphs (2) and (3) of this paragraph the appropriate types of insurance from the following list are to be shown separately—

(i) whole life assurance
(ii) endowment assurance
(iii) pure endowment assurance
(iv) term assurance
(v) other assurance (to be specified)
(vi) deferred annuity
(vii) annuity in payment
(viii) other annuity (to be specified)
(ix) group pension
(x) group life
(xi) other group (to be specified)
(xii) permanent health insurance
(xiii) capital redemption assurance
(xiv) annuity certain.

(5) In the case of group contracts the information to be given is to relate only to new contracts and is to be exclusive of increments under existing contracts.

9. Separate statements of the expected income from non-linked assets are to be given in the forms set out in Forms 45 and 46 in respect of each fund or group of funds for which separate assets are appropriated. If a company carrying on both industrial assurance business and ordinary long-term insurance business does not separately identify the assets representing the industrial assurance business, Forms 45 and 46 shall be prepared in respect of all the company's long term business.

10. Forms of return as set out in Forms 47 and 48 are to be completed in respect of assets matching liabilities in respect of property linked benefits other than holdings in internal linked funds. The information in Form 48 is to be sub-divided and totalled according to the names of the categories of linked contract under which the liabilities in respect of property linked benefits are matched by such assets. The basis on which the assets have been valued is to be stated in a note to the Forms.

11. Forms of return as set out in Forms 49, 50 and 51 are to be completed in respect of internal linked funds operated by the company. The basis on which the assets have been valued and the total amount of unrealised capital gain or loss relating to each internal linked fund are to be given in a separate statement.

Form 40

Returns under Insurance Companies Legislation

Long Term business: Revenue account

Name of Company

Global business/UK branch business/Community branch business

Financial year ended

Name and number of Fund/Summary

	Company registration number	Global/ UK/CM	Period ended day	month	year	Units	OB/IB	No. of Fund/ Summary	No. of part of Fund	For official use
F40					19	£000				

Items to be shown net of reinsurance ceded		The financial year 1	Previous financial year 2
Premiums receivable (less rebates and refunds)	1		
Investment income receivable before deduction of tax	2		
Increase (decrease) in the value of non-linked assets brought into account	3		
Increase (decrease) in the value of linked assets	4		
Other income (particulars to be specified)	5		
Total income (1 to 5)	6		
Claims payable	7		
Expenses payable	8		
Interest payable before deduction of tax	9		
Taxation	10		
Other expenditure (particulars to be specified)	11		
Transfer to (from) statement of other income and expenditure	12		
Total expenditure (7 to 12)	13		
Increase (decrease) in fund in financial year (6–13)	14		
Fund brought forward	15		
Fund carried forward (14 + 15)	16		

Instructions for Completion of Form 40

1 The entry at 40.1.1 shall be equal to 41.9.3,
the entry at 40.7.1 shall be equal to 42.21.3 and
the entry at 40.8.1 shall be equal to 41.16.3.

2 Where a company decides to allocate to the long term business the whole or any part of investment income and/or net capital gains arising from assets not attributable to its long term business, the amounts in question shall be shown as a transfer in line 12.

3 Where a transfer is made to the statement of other income and expenditure, the entry at 40.12.1 will show amounts which have been included in line 23 of Form 58. Transfers from or to other funds shall be included in line 5 or 11, with transfers to reserves associated with a transfer of contracts from one fund to another distinguished from other transfers.

Returns under Insurance Companies Legislation

Form 41

Long Term business: Analysis of premiums and expenses

Name of Company

Global business/UK branch business/Community branch business

Financial year ended

Name and number of Fund/Summary

	Company registration number	Global/ UK/CM	Period ended day	month	year	Units	OB/IB	No of Fund/ Summary	No of part of Fund	For official use
F41					19	£000				

				Gross	Payable to or recoverable from reinsurers	Net of reinsurance (1–2)
				1	2	3
Premiums receivable (less rebates and refunds) in the financial year	life assurance contracts	single premium	1			
		regular premiums	2			
	general annuity contracts	single premium	3			
		regular premiums	4			
	pension ~~business~~ contracts	single premium	5			
		regular premiums	6			
	permanent health contracts		7			
	capital redemption contracts		8			
	total premiums (1 to 8)		9			
	total premiums at line 9 attributable to	UK contracts	10			
		Overseas contracts	11			
Expenses payable in the financial year	commission payable in connection with acquisition of business		12			
	other commission payable		13			
	management expenses in connection with acquisition of business		14			
	other management expenses		15			
	total expenses (12 to 15)		16			
	total expenses at line 16 attributable to	UK contracts	17			
		Overseas contracts	18			

Returns under Insurance Companies Legislation

Form 42

Long Term business: Analysis of claims

Name of Company

Global business/UK branch business/Community branch business

Financial year ended

Name and number of Fund/Summary

	Company registration number	Global/ UK/CM	Period ended day	month	year	Units	OB/IB	No. of Fund/ Summary	No. of part of Fund	For official use
F42					19	£000				

Claims payable in the financial year			Gross 1	Recoverable from re-insurers 2	Net of re-insurance (1−2) 3
Life assurance contracts	on death	1			
	on maturity	2			
	on surrender or partial surrender	3			
	total life assurance claims (1 to 3)	4			
General annuity contracts	on death	5			
	by way of lump sums on maturity	6			
	by way of periodical payments	7			
	on surrender or partial surrender	8			
	total general annuity claims (5 to 8)	9			
Pension business	on death	10			
	by way of lump sums on maturity	11			
	by way of periodical payments	12			
	on surrender or partial surrender	13			
	total pension business claims (10 to 13)	14			
Permanent health contracts	by way of lump sums	15			
	by way of periodical payments	16			
	total permanent health claims (15 + 16)	17			
Capital redemption contracts	by way of lump sums	18			
	by way of periodical payments	19			
	total capital redemption claims (18 + 19)	20			
Total claims (4 + 9 + 14 + 17 + 20)		21			
Total claims at line 21 attributable to	UK contracts	22			
	Overseas contracts	23			

Instructions for Completion of Form 42

In the case of industrial assurance, claims payable on survival in respect of periodical endowment benefits shall be shown separately from other claims payable on the maturity of contracts of industrial assurance.

Returns under Insurance Companies Legislation

Form 43

Long Term business: Summary of changes in ordinary long term business

Name of Company

Global business/UK branch business/Community branch business

United Kingdom/Overseas

Financial year ended

Non-linked/Linked

		Life assurance		General annuity		Pension business		Permanent health		Capital redemption	
		No of contracts 1	Annual premiums 2	No of contracts 3	Annual premiums 4	No of contracts 5	Annual premiums 6	No of contracts 7	Annual premiums 8	No of contracts 9	Annual premiums 10
In force at beginning of year	1										
New business	2										
Net transfers and other alterations 'on'	3										
Total 'on' (2 + 3)	4										
Deaths	5										
Maturities	6										
Surrenders	7										
Forfeitures	8										
Conversions to paid-up policies for reduced benefits	9										
Net transfers, expiries and other alterations 'off'	10										
Total 'off' (5 to 10)	11										
In force at end of year (1 + 4 – 11)	12										

Form 43A

Returns under Insurance Companies Legislation

Long Term business: Summary of changes in industrial assurance business

Name of Company

Global business/UK branch business/Community branch business

Financial year ended

	Paying		Paid-up
	No of policies	Annual premiums	No of policies
In force at beginning of year			
Taken up during year - Weekly business			–
Monthly business			–
Converted to paid-up policies during year	–	–	
Total "on"			
Discontinued during year by –			
(a) Deaths		–	
(b) Maturities		–	
(c) Surrenders for cash		–	
(d) Terminations by return of premiums		–	
(e) Conversions to paid-up policies for full sums assured		–	–
(f) Conversions to paid-up policies for reduced sums assured		–	–
(g) Forfeitures without grant of paid-up policy or cash surrender		–	–
Total "off"		–	
In force at end of year			

Notes: (1) Separate forms shall be prepared in respect of business carried on in the United Kingdom and in Northern Ireland, but information about the numbers of policies in force at the beginning and at the end of the year need not be given in respect of business carried on in Northern Ireland.

(2) Policies discontinued by return of premiums on death of assured shall be included in class (a) and not in class (d).

(3) Paid-up policies which are written off shall be included in class (a) in the case of whole life policies and class (b) in the case of endowments.

Returns under Insurance Companies Legislation

Fo

Long Term business: Analysis of new ordinary long term business

Name of Company

United Kingdom/O

Global business/UK branch business/Community branch business

Financial year ended

Type of insurance	Single premium contracts			Regular premium contracts		
	No. of contracts	Premiums	Sums assured, annuities per annum or other measure of benefits	No. of contracts	Annual premiums	Sums as annuitie annum c measure benefits
1	2	3	4	5	6	7

Returns under Insurance Companies Legislation

Form 44A

Long Term business: Analysis of new industrial assurance business

Name of Company

Global business/UK branch business/Community branch business

Financial year ended

	Whole life (including joint life) 1	Endowment assurance (including joint life) 2	(See note) 3	Other tables 4
Number of New Assurances Weekly business Monthly business				
Sums Assured Weekly business Monthly business	£	£	£	£
Annual Premiums Weekly business Monthly business	£	£	£	£

Notes

(1) Separate forms shall be prepared in respect of business carried on in the United Kingdom and in Northern Ireland.

(2) If any table other than those shown in columns 1 and 2 (eg a table providing for recurring payments) is of significant amount details shall be given in column 3 with an appropriate heading. In the case of a table including a recurring payment, the sum assured on death before the date of the first recurring payment shall be shown against 'Sums Assured' above and the amount of the recurring payment shall be shown separately in brackets.

Returns under Insurance Companies Legislation

Form 45

Long Term business: Expected income from admissible non-linked assets

Name of Company

Global business/UK branch business/Community branch business

OB/IB

Financial year ended

Fund

Type of asset			Value of admissible assets as shown on Form 13	Expected income from admissible assets	Yield %
			1	2	3
Land		1			
Fixed interest securities	issued by, or guaranteed by, any government or public authority	2			
	other	3			
Variable interest securities excluding equity shares	issued by, or guaranteed by, any government or public authority except those included at line 5	4			
	issued by, or guaranteed by, any government or public authority where the capital value or interest is determined by an index of prices	5			
	other	6			
Equity shares		7			
Debts fully secured on land	due more than 12 months after the end of the financial year	8			
	due in 12 months or less after the end of the financial year	9			
All other assets	producing income	10			
	not producing income	11			
Total		12			

Instructions

1. Where Form 13 is for the same fund or group of funds:—

The entry at 45.1.1 shall be equal to 13.11.1
the entry at 45.2.1 shall be equal to 13.12.1
the entry at 45.3.1 shall be equal to 13.13.1 + 13.14.1 + 13.15.1
the entry at 45.4.1 shall be equal to 13.16.1
the entry at 45.5.1 shall be equal to 13.17.1
the entry at 45.6.1 shall be equal to 13.18.1
the entry at 45.7.1 shall be equal to 13.21.1 + 13.22 + 13.23.1
the entry at 45.8.1 shall be equal to 13.61.1 + part of 13.64.1
the entry at 45.9.1 shall be equal to 13.62.1 + part of 13.66.1 and
the entry at 45.12.1 shall be equal to 13.93.1 – (13.85.1 + 13.86.1).

2 The expected income is to be given as the amounts before deduction of tax which would be received in the next financial year on the assumptions that the assets will be held throughout that year and that the factors which affect income will remain unchanged but account shall be taken of any changes in those factors known to have occurred by the valuation date (in particular changes of the type *(a)*, *(b)*, *(c)* or *(d)* denoted in Regulation 59(5) of the Insurance Companies Regulations 1981). The figures shown in this Form shall be those determined before any adjustments considered necessary because of Regulation 59(6).

3 Where a particular asset is required to be taken into account only to a specified extent by the application of the admissibility limits the expected income from that asset shall be included only to the same extent.

4 The treatment of the expected income from any asset where the payment of interest is in default and the amount of interest involved shall be stated.

5 The entries at 45.2.3 and 45.3.3 shall be equal to 46.9.4 and 46.18.4 respectively; the yields to be inserted in column 3 for other categories of asset shall be the running yields. The entry at 45.12.3 shall be the weighted average of the yields in column 3, where the weight given to each asset is the value of that asset applicable for entry into column 1; assets not producing income shall be included in the calculation.

Returns under Insurance Companies Legislation

Form 46

Long Term business: Analysis of admissible non-linked fixed interest securities

Name of Company

Global business/UK branch business/Community branch business

OB/IB

Financial year ended

Fund

Redemption period in years			Value of admissible assets as shown on Form 13 1	Expected income from admissible assets 2	Amount payable on redemption 3	Gross redemption yield % 4
Issued or guaranteed by any government or public authority	one year or less	1				
	more than one year but not more than five years	2				
	more than five years but not more than ten years	3				
	more than ten years but not more than fifteen years	4				
	more than fifteen years but not more than twenty years	5				
	more than twenty years but not more than twenty five years	6				
	more than twenty five years	7				
	irredeemable	8				
	total (1 to 8)	9				
Other	one year or less	10				
	more than one year but not more than five years	11				
	more than five years but not more than ten years	12				
	more than ten years but not more than fifteen years	13				
	more than fifteen years but not more than twenty years	14				
	more than twenty years but not more than twenty five years	15				
	more than twenty five years	16				
	irredeemable	17				
	total (10 to 17)	18				

Instructions

1 The gross redemption yield for each asset shall be calculated as in Regulation 59(3) and (4) of the Insurance Companies Regulations 1981, leaving out of account any adjustment considered necessary because of Regulation 59(6). Where a number of assets with different gross redemption yields are held, the weighted average gross redemption yield shall be calculated using as weights the value of the asset applicable for entry into column 1.

2 Where securities may be redeemed over a period at the option of the guarantor or issuer, they shall be classified on the assumption that they will be redeemed at the latest possible date or, if it is assumed that they will be redeemed at any earlier date, a note shall be provided explaining what assumption has been made.

3 46.9.1, 46.9.2, 46.18.1 and 46.18.2 shall be equal to the values at 45.2.1, 45.2.2, 45.3.1 and 45.3.2 respectively.

4 The entries at 46.9.4 and 46.18.4 shall be the weighted average of the yields in column 4 for lines 1 to 8 and 10 to 17 respectively, where the weight given to each yield is the value shown in column 1.

Returns under Insurance Companies Legislation

Form 47

Long Term business: Analysis of holdings in authorised unit trusts directly matching liabilities in respect of property linked benefits

Name of Company

Global business/UK branch business/Community branch business

OB/IB

Financial year ended

Name of unit trust 1	Number of units held 2	Valuation price per unit 3	Value of units held 4
Total			

Returns under Insurance Companies Legislation **Form 48**

Long Term business: Analysis of assets which are matching liabilities in respect of property linked benefits other than holdings in authorised unit trusts or internal linked funds

Name of Company

Global business/UK branch business/Community branch business OB/IB

Financial year ended

Name of contract / Type of asset	Value of assets				
	1	2	3	etc	Total
Total					

Returns under Insurance Companies Legislation **Form 49**

Long Term business: Balance sheet for internal linked funds

Name of Company

Global business/UK branch business/Community branch business **OB/IB**

Financial year ended

Type of asset \ Names of funds			A	B	etc	Total
Land		1				
Fixed interest securities	Government or public authority	2				
	Other	3				
Variable interest securities		4				
Unit Trusts		5				
Mortgages on land		6				
Building Society shares and deposits		7				
Deposits and loans		8				
Income due or accrued		9				
Cash		10				
Other assets (particulars to be specified)		11				
Total (1 to 11)		12				
Total investment in other internal linked funds of the company		13				
Total assets (12 + 13)		14				
Amount set aside for tax on capital gains not yet realised		15				
Secured loans		16				
Unsecured loans		17				
Other liabilities (particulars to be specified)		18				
Total liabilities (15 to 18)		19				
Net asset value (14 – 19)		20				

Instructions

1 The entries at line 20 shall be the same as those at line 15 on Form 51.

2 The entry at line 12 in the Total column shall be equal to line 85 on Form 13.

Returns under Insurance Companies Legislation **Form 50**

Long Term business: Analysis of units in internal linked funds

Name of Company

Global business/UK branch business/Community branch business **OB/IB**

Financial year ended

Name of internal linked fund in which invested	Name of unit link	Valuation price per unit	Total number of units in force	Value of total units in force	Value of units held by each internal linked fund in each unit link of other internal linked funds				Value of units in force excluding those held by other internal linked funds (5–9)
					A	B	etc	Total	
1	**2**	**3**	**4**	**5**	**6**	**7**	**8**	**9**	**10**
A	Link 1								
	etc								
	Total								
B	Link 1								
	etc								
	Total								
etc									
Total									

Instructions

1 The entries in column 5 for the total values of all units in force in each internal linked fund shall equal the entries in line 20 on Form 49.

2 The totals of columns 6, 7 etc shall equal the entries in line 13 on Form 49.

Returns under Insurance Companies Legislation

Form 51

Long Term business: Revenue account for internal linked funds

Name of Company

Global business/UK branch business/Community branch business **OB/IB**

Financial year ended

Names of funds		A	B	C	D	E	etc
Value of net creation of units	1						
Investment income attributable to the fund before deduction of tax	2						
Increase (decrease) in the value of investments in financial year	3						
Other income (particulars to be specified)	4						
Total income (1 to 4)	5						
Value of net cancellation of units	6						
Charges for management	7						
Charges in respect of tax on investment income	8						
Taxation on realised capital gains	9						
Increase (decrease) in amount set aside for tax on capital gains not yet realised	10						
Other expenditure (particulars to be specified)	11						
Total expenditure (6 to 11)	12						
Increase (decrease) in fund in the financial year (5–12)	13						
Internal linked fund brought forward	14						
Internal linked fund carried forward	15						

Instruction

Funds shall be entered in the same column positions on this form and on Form 49.

SCHEDULE 4

Regulation 24

ABSTRACT OF VALUATION REPORT PREPARED BY THE APPOINTED ACTUARY
(Forms 55 to 61)

The abstract shall state that the valuation has been made in conformity with Regulation 54 of the Insurance Companies Regulations.

The following information shall be given, the answers being numbered to accord with the numbers of corresponding paragraphs of this Schedule and any monetary amounts being shown in sterling (converted from other currencies, where necessary, at the latest closing middle rate available on the date to which the investigation relates)—

1. The date to which the investigation relates.

2. The date to which the latest previous investigation under section 18 of the Act related.

3. For each category of non-linked contract, other than those fully described by the entry in column 1 of Form 55, a full description of the benefits including any premium rate guarantees and options.

4.—(1) For each category of linked contract—

(*a*) a full description of the benefits including any guarantees and options;

(*b*) the percentage of premiums invested (deemed or actual) for specimen ages and terms;

(*c*) a list of the internal linked funds to which benefits under the contract may be linked, with details of the type of unit allocated where the fund is divided into more than one type;

(*d*) a list of the authorised unit trusts to which benefits under the contract may be linked.

(2) For each internal linked fund—

(*a*) the general nature of the investments of the fund and the charges that are made to the fund in respect of investment expenses;

(*b*) for each type of unit based on that fund, the initial and periodic charges made, and the nature of any other pricing adjustments.

(3) For each authorised unit trust, the rate of discount, commission or other allowance made to the insurance company on the purchase or sale of units.

(NB: It shall be sufficient, instead of giving the full information required by paragraphs 3 and 4, to refer to the previous abstract when full information in respect of the category of contract was last given, if full information in respect of every category of contract is given in the abstract when a statement of long term business is also prepared.)

5.—(1) The general principles and methods adopted in the valuation including specific reference to the following—

(*a*) the basis of the provision made for any mismatching between the nature (including currency) and term of the assets held and the liabilities valued;

(*b*) where the net premium method has been used, whether and to what extent it has been modified and for what purposes the modification has been made and whether any modifications on account of zillmerising conform to Regulation 58 of the Insurance Companies Regulations;

(*c*) whether any negative reserves arose and the steps taken to ensure that no contract of insurance was treated as an asset;

(*d*) whether any specific reserve has been made for future bonus and, if so, at what rate or rates;

(*e*) the basis of the provision made for any prospective liability for tax on unrealised capital gains;

(*f*) in the case of linked contracts and deposit administration contracts, the basis of the provision made for any investment performance guarantees;

(*g*) the basis of the provision made for any guarantees and options (other than investment performance guarantees).

(2) For the purposes of this paragraph—

(*a*) where, in determining the provisions referred to in sub-paragraphs (*a*) and (*e*) above, account has been taken of that fact that the fund has been brought into Form 58 at book value in accordance with Regulation 38(5) of the Insurance Companies Regulations, that fact should be stated; and

(*b*) it shall be sufficient, instead of giving the full information required by this paragraph, to state whether changes have been made since the previous abstract when full information was last given, if full information of the general principles and methods adopted in the valuation is given in the abstract when a statement of long term business is also prepared.

6.—(1) Where applicable, the rates of interest and tables of mortality and disability assumed in the valuation of the various categories of contracts (to be shown in Forms 55 and 56).

(2) If the tables used have not been published, full details of the rates of mortality or disability used.

7. In respect of non-linked contracts—

(*a*) where appropriate, the proportion of the office premiums explicitly or implicitly reserved for expenses and profits for each type of insurance (to be shown in column 8 of Form 55);

(*b*) the method by which provision is made for expenses after premiums have ceased or where no future premiums are payable or where the method of valuation does not take credit for future premiums as an asset;

(*c*) where a prospective method of valuation has not been used, details of the tests of the adequacy of the method used;

(*d*) where, in valuing contracts falling within the circumstances described in Regulation 57(1) of the Insurance Companies Regulations, future premiums brought into account are not in accordance with that Regulation, such additional information as is necessary to demonstrate whether the mathematical reserves determined in the aggregate for each of the main categories of contract are greater than an amount for each such category calculated in accordance with Regulations 55 to 64 of those Regulations:

Provided that where the mathematical reserves (after deduction of reinsurance cessions) determined in the aggregate for all categories of contracts referred to in sub-paragraph (*d*) above represent less than 5 per cent of the total mathematical reserves (after deduction of reinsurance cessions) for all non-linked contracts, it shall be sufficient for the actuary to state that the mathematical reserves for each such category of contracts are not less than the mathematical reserves that would be determined on a net premium reserving basis which shall be specified by the actuary in the abstract.

8. For each category of linked contract,—

(*a*) all assumptions made in calculating the valuation net liability in columns 11 and 12 of Form 56; and

(*b*) where explicit provision has not been made for meeting the expenses likely to be incurred in future in fulfilling the existing contracts on the basis of specific assumptions in regard to the relevant factors, details of the basis used in testing the adequacy of the reserves to satisfy Regulation 61(1) of the Insurance Companies Regulations.

9. The proportion of the total mathematical reserves (other than liabilities for property linked benefits under linked contracts) as shown in Forms 55 and 56 not matched by assets in the same currency.

10.—(1) For reinsurance ceded on a facultative basis to a reinsurer who is not authorised to carry on insurance business in the United Kingdom at any time during the period since the date to which the last investigation related—

(*a*) the aggregate of premiums payable by the company to all such reinsurers (sub-divided according to accounting periods if appropriate) and the aggregate amount deposited at the date to which the valuation relates under any deposit back arrangement; and

(*b*) the amount of any such premiums payable by the company to a reinsurer with whom the company is connected and the aggregate of such amounts deposited at that date under deposit back arrangements with all such reinsurers.

(2) For each reinsurance treaty where the company is the cedant and under which business is in force at the date to which the valuation relates—

(*a*) whether the reinsurer is authorised to carry on insurance business in the United Kingdom;

(*b*) whether the company and the reinsurer are connected;

(*c*) an indication of the nature and extent of the cover given under the treaty;

(*d*) the premiums payable by the company under the treaty during the period since the date to which the last valuation report related;

(*e*) the amount deposited at that date in respect of the treaty under any deposit back arrangements;

(*f*) the extent to which provision has been made for any liability of the company to refund any amounts of reinsurance commission in the event of lapses or surrender of the contract; and

(*g*) whether the treaty is closed to new business.

(3) In this paragraph—

(*a*) 'deposit back arrangement', in relation to any contract of reinsurance, means an arrangement whereby an amount is deposited by the reinsurer with the cedant; and

(*b*) paragraphs (1), (2) and (3)(*a*) of Regulation 20 above (which relate to connected persons) shall have effect for the purposes of this paragraph as they have effect for the purposes of the Regulations therein mentioned.

11. Where any rights of any policyholders to participate in profits relate to profits from particular parts of a long term business fund—

(*a*) a revenue account in the format of Form 40 for each such part except where such information is provided elsewhere;

(*b*) the principles and methods applied in apportioning the investment income, increase or decrease in the value of assets brought into account, expenses and taxation between each part, where these particulars are not provided elsewhere.

12. Whether there is any reference to the principles on which the distribution of profits among policyholders and shareholders is made in the constitution of the company or in provisions made thereunder, in any policy issued by the company or in any advertisement by the company and, if so, a description of the principles and a reference to the document in which they are expressed.

13. Particulars of the bonus allocated to each category of contract, including the basis of calculation and the circumstances and the form in which the bonus is payable.

(NB: Wherever appropriate, rates of bonus are to be expressed as a fraction of the attribute of the contract to which they are related, e g as rates per £1,000 of the sum assured and existing bonuses.)

14. Where the rates of bonus allocated depend on the original term of the contract or on the period of years a contract has been in force or on the age of the life assured, specimen rates at 5-year intervals of original term or duration or at 10-year intervals of age, as the case may be.

(NB: Where the rates of bonus allocated depend on a formula or a series of formulae, then the formula or formulae should be listed instead of the specimen rates.)

15. Where any conditions attach to the allocation of bonus to any category of contract concerning the number of years premiums to be paid before a bonus vests or otherwise, particulars of such conditions in relation to each category of contract.

16. A statement of the practice regarding any bonus payments (in addition to those for which the company had become contractually liable) to be made on claims arising in the period up to the next investigation together with the rates at which such bonus payments are to be determined.

17. Separate valuation summaries in the forms set out in Forms 55 and 56 and separate analyses of unit liabilities in the form set out in Form 57 in respect of each separate fund or part of a fund for which a surplus is determined under section 18 of the Act for—

(i) direct business and reinsurance accepted;
(ii) reinsurance ceded.

18. Separate statements of the results of the valuation in the form set out in Form 58 in respect of each separate fund or part of a fund for which a surplus is determined under section 18 of the Act.

19. Separate statements of the required minimum margin for long term business in the form set out in Form 60, and of the required margin of solvency for Supplementary Accident and Sickness Insurance in the form set out in Form 61.

(N.B. If the gross annual office premiums for Supplementary Accident and Sickness Insurance in force on the valuation date do not exceed 1 per cent of the gross annual office premiums in force on that date for all long term business, Form 61 need not be completed provided it can be stated that the entry in line 10 of Form 60 exceeds the amount that would be obtained if Form 61 were to be completed. In this circumstance, the method of estimating the entry in line 10 of Form 60, together with a statement of the gross annual office premiums in force at the valuation date in respect of Supplementary Accident and Sickness Insurance, should be given.)

Global business/UK branch business/Community branch business **OB/IB**

Fund/Part of Fund

Type of insurance	Valuation basis		Number of contracts	Amount of sums assured or annuities per annum, including vested reversionary bonuses	Amount of annual premiums		Proportion of office premiums reserved for expenses and profits	Value of sums assured or annuities per annum, including vested reversionary bonuses	Value of annual premiums		Amount of mathematical reserves
	Rate of interest	Mortality or disability table			Office premiums	Net premiums			Office premiums	Net premiums	
1	2	3	4	5	6	7	8	9	10	11	12

Form 56

OB/IB

Valuation summary of linked contracts

Global business/UK branch business/Community branch business

Fund/Part of Fund

Name of contract	Valuation basis		Number of contracts	Amount of sums assured, annuities per annum, or other measure of benefit, including vested reversionary bonuses			Amount of annual premiums		Category of unit link	Unit liability	Non-unit liabilities		Amount of mathematical reserves
	Rate of interest	Mortality table		Guaranteed on death	Current on death	Guaranteed on maturity	Office premiums	Net premiums			Mortality and expenses	Options and guarantees other than investment performance guarantees	
1	2	3	4	5	6	7	8	9	10	11	12	13	14

Instructions for Completion of Forms 55 and 56

1 Information shall be shown separately and totalled within each section in the sequence specified below:

(i) United Kingdom business

(ii) overseas business.

The totals net of reinsurance ceded of United Kingdom business and overseas business are also to be shown together with a summary of global net total business.

Separate totals for column 5 on Form 55 and columns 5, 6 and 7 on Form 56 shall be shown for sums insured, for annuities per annum and for other measures of benefit.

2 The information shall be analysed and sub-totalled within each type of business in the sequence specified below:

(i) life assurance business

(ii) general annuity business

(iii) pension business

(iv) permanent health business

(v) capital redemption business.

3 The information shall be further analysed and sub-totalled within each basis of participation in profits in the sequence specified below:

(i) with participation in profits

(ii) without participation in profits.

4 Within each subdivision required under paragraphs 2 and 3 above the appropriate types of insurance from the following list shall be shown separately:

(i) whole life assurance

(ii) endowment assurance

(iii) pure endowment assurance

(iv) term assurance

(v) other assurance (to be specified)

(vi) miscellaneous assurance

(vii) deferred annuity

(viii) annuity in payment

(ix) other annuity (to be specified)

(x) miscellaneous annuity

(xi) group pension

(xii) group life

(xiii) other group (to be specified)

(xiv) permanent health insurance

(xv) capital redemption assurance

(xvi) annuity certain.

And particulars shall also be shown of any subsidiary provisions within general business class 1 or 2 which, by virtue of section 1(2) and (3) of the Insurance Companies Act 1982 are to be taken to be included in long term business of any class (Supplementary Accident and Sickness Insurance – see Form 61).

5 A further subdivision into each separate category of contract is required as follows:

Form 55 – each category of contract which is valued on a different valuation basis;

Form 56 – each category of contract which provides different guarantees or options, and each category of unit link. For the purpose of determining the category of the unit link, all authorised unit trusts may be considered to be one category and all internal linked funds may be considered to be one category.

Reserves for tax on capital gains or for investment performance guarantees may be shown on separate lines in the mathematical reserves column, where they are calculated on an aggregate basis, or in additional columns of non-unit liabilities, where they are calculated on an individual basis.

6 Special reserves (including reserves calculated on an aggregate basis for tax on capital gains and investment performance guarantees) or adjustments shall be shown on separate lines in the mathematical reserves column and the particulars of such reserves or adjustments shall be specified.

7 Any contract which consists of a combination of different types of insurance shall be treated as a number of separate contracts each dealing with one of the different types of insurance so combined and the amount by which the total number of contracts shown in column 4 of any valuation summary exceeds the actual number of contracts to which that valuation summary relates shall be stated:

Provided that, in relation to any category of such combined contract, any types of insurance included in the combination which in the aggregate account for less than 10 per cent of the total mathematical reserves under that category of contract need not be separately distinguished.

8 Non-linked contracts the nature of which or the method of valuation of which makes it impossible or inappropriate to give the information required in columns 7 to 11 of Form 55 shall be shown separately and the reason for the impossibility or the inappropriateness stated.

9 Linked contracts the nature of which or the method of valuation of which makes it impossible or inappropriate to give the information in the exact form required by Form 56 shall be shown on a separate valuation summary with appropriately modified column headings and the reason for the modification stated.

10 Contracts of any description may be grouped together under any 'miscellaneous' heading provided that mathematical reserves for business shown under all such headings in any one valuation summary do not exceed 5 per cent of the total mathematical reserves for all business shown in that valuation summary.

11 Contracts with deferred participation in profits and contracts with an option to convert to another category of contract shall be included in the category in which they fall at the date to which the investigation relates.

12 Contracts on more than one life may be included with single life contracts.

13 Contracts subject to limited premiums may be included with contracts under which premiums are payable throughout.

14 Life annuities guaranteed for a term certain or which provide for a refund of the balance of the purchase money on early death may be included with other life annuities.

15 In the case of contracts with variable benefits the benefits shall be taken as at the date to which the investigation relates and, where such benefits are included as approximate amounts only, that fact shall be stated.

16 In relation to group deferred annuity contracts under which premiums have not ceased, a statement of how the amount of annual office premiums has been arrived at shall be given.

17 Where for group life and pension schemes the mathematical reserves at the valuation date are based on those in respect of the business in force at the last scheme revision date, any adjustment on account of changes after that date shall be shown separately.

18 It is to be stated in relation to each category of contract where it is appropriate, whether the amount of the sum assured or deferred annuity shown in the valuation summary is the full sum assured or annuity which would come into payment on the maturity date or the amount accrued or actually purchased at the date to which the investigation relates and, where it is the amount accrued or actually purchased at the date, an estimate of the full prospective sum assured or annuity for that category shall be given.

Form 57

Analysis of unit liabilities

Global business/UK branch business/Community branch business

OB/IB

Fund / Part of Fund

Name of unit link **1**	Valuation price per unit **2**	Number of units deemed allocated to contracts **3**	Unit liability **4**
Total			

Instructions

1 The total of column 4 shall equal the total of column 11 on Form 56.

2 A separate line shall be used for each authorised unit trust and each different type of unit of each internal linked fund.

Valuation result and distribution of surplus **Form 58**

Global business/UK branch business/Community branch business
Fund/Part of Fund

OB

Valuation result	Fund carried forward		1	
	Bonus payments made to policyholders in anticipation of a surplus		2	
	Transfers out of Fund/Part of Fund	Net transfer to (from) statement of other income and expenditure	3	
		Net transfer to (from) other Funds/Parts of Funds	4	
	Net transfer out of Fund/Part of Fund (3 + 4)		5	
	Total (1 + 2 + 5)		6	
	Mathematical reserves for non-linked contracts		7	
	Mathematical reserves for linked contracts		8	
	Total (7 + 8)		9	
	Surplus including contingency and other reserves held towards the solvency margin (deficiency) (6 – 9)		10	
Composition of surplus	Balance of surplus brought forward unappropriated from last valuation		11	
	Transfers into Fund/Part of Fund	Net transfer from (to) statement of other income and expenditure	12	
		Net transfer from (to) other Funds/Parts of Funds	13	
	Net transfer into Fund/Part of Fund (12 + 13)		14	
	Surplus arising since the last valuation		15	
	Total (11 + 14 + 15) (= 10)		16	
Distribution of surplus	Bonus payments made to policyholders in anticipation of a surplus		17	
	Allocated to policyholders by way of	cash bonuses	18	
		reversionary bonuses	19	
		other bonuses	20	
		premium reductions	21	
	Total allocated to policyholders (17 to 21)		22	
	Net transfer out of Fund/Part of Fund (= 5)		23	
	Total distributed surplus (22 + 23)		24	
	Balance of surplus (including contingency and other reserves held towards the solvency margin) carried forward unappropriated		25	
	Total (24 + 25) (= 10)		26	
Percentage of distributed surplus allocated to policyholders of Fund/Part of Fund			27	
Corresponding percentage at three immediately previous valuations	latest (date of valuation)		28	
	earlier (date of valuation)		29	
	earliest (date of valuation)		30	

Instructions for Completion of Form 58

1 The entry at line 1 shall be equal to the entry at line 16 in the revenue account for the relevant fund/part of fund.

2 Where interim, mortuary or terminal bonuses are determined in advance of a valuation and are paid in anticipation of surplus arising at the valuation, the amounts of such bonus actually paid in the period up to the valuation date shall be entered in lines 2 and 17. To the extent that it is the practice of the company to make specific provision for the cost of such bonuses payable on future claims out of surplus arising at a valuation, such amounts shall be treated as amounts allocated to policyholders at the valuation in question and included in line 20, and the actual amounts paid shall not appear at lines 2 and 17 at future valuations. An appropriate note shall be appended identifying the various items where necessary.

3 Where policies have been transferred from one fund/part of fund to another, the associated transfer of reserves shall not be included as a "transfer" in this Form. Where any other transfer has been made, only one positive figure shall be inserted in either line 5 or line 14 (depending on the direction of the net transfer) leaving the other line blank. Corresponding entries shall be made in either the block comprising lines 3 and 4 or the block comprising lines 12 and 13, as applicable.

4 Where the entry in line 4 or line 13 represents more than one transaction, each transfer shall be separately identified in the form or in a note.

5 In the case of a company which makes allocations to eligible policyholders generally at intervals of more than one year, bonus payments made to policyholders in anticipation of a surplus, transfers to or from other income and expenditure or to or from other funds or parts of funds shall include the amounts of all such bonus payments and transfers made since the date of the last general allocation. In that case the word "valuation" in lines 11 and 15 shall be replaced by "general allocation", and line 11 shall show the balance of the surplus brought forward unappropriated from the date of the last general allocation and line 15 shall show the total amount of the surplus arising since that date. When the bonus payments or transfers relate to a period of more than one year that fact shall be stated in a note.

6 Line 27 is line 22 as a percentage of line 24. Line 27 shall not be completed in years where there is no general allocation.

Returns under Insurance Companies Legislation
Global business/UK branch business/Community branch business

Required minimum margin – Long Term business

Form 60

CLASS	Classes I and II	Class III business with relevant factor of				Classes IV and VI	Class VII business with relevant factor of				Unallocated additional mathematical reserves with relevant factor of		Total for all classes	
Relevant factor (Note 5)	4%	4%	1%	Nil	Total	4%	4%	1%	Nil	Total	4%	1%	The financial year	The previous year
1 Mathematical reserves before deduction for reinsurance: (a) Reserves before distribution of surplus (b) Reserves for bonus allocated to policyholders (c) Reserves after distribution of surplus														
2 Mathematical reserves after deduction for reinsurance: (a) Reserves before distribution of surplus (b) Reserves for bonus allocated to policyholders (c) Reserves after distribution of surplus														
3 Ratio of 2 (c) to 1 (c), or 0.85 if greater (see Note 1)														
4 Required margin of solvency – first result = 1 (c) x 3 x relevant factor														
5 Non negative capital at risk before reinsurance: (see Note 2) (a) Temporary assurances with required margin of solvency of .001 (b) Temporary assurances with required margin of solvency of .0015 (c) All other contracts with required margin of solvency of .003 (d) Total for (a) + (b) + (c)														
6 Non negative capital at risk after reinsurance (all contracts): (see Note 2)														
7 Ratio of 6 to 5 (d), or 0.50 if greater														
8 Required margin of solvency · second result (see Note 3)														
9 Sum of first and second result = 4 + 8														
10 Required margin of solvency for Supplementary, Accident and Sickness Insurance														
11 Total required margin of solvency for long term business = 9 + 10														
12 Minimum guarantee fund														
13 Required minimum margin (greater of 11 and 12)														

NOTES

1 For a pure reinsurer, the factor of 0.85 shall be replaced by 0.50

4 Any additional mathematical reserves referred to in the note to Form 14 shall be included on this Form.

Returns under Insurance Companies Legislation

Form 61

Supplementary Accident and Sickness Insurance

Calculation of required margin of solvency

Global business/UK branch business/Community branch business

			The financial year 1	The previous year 2
Gross premiums receivable		1		
Premium taxes and levies (included in line 1)		2		
Sub-total A (1–2)		3		
Adjusted sub-total A if financial year is not a 12 month period to produce an annual figure		4		
Division of sub-total A (or adjusted sub-total A if appropriate)	Up to and including sterling equivalent of 10M ECU x 18/100	5		
	Excess (if any) over 10M ECU x 16/100	6		
Sub-total B (5 + 6)		7		
Claims paid		8		
Claims outstanding carried forward at end of financial year		9		
Claims outstanding brought forward at beginning of financial year		10		
Sub-total C (8 + 9 – 10)		11		
Amounts recoverable from reinsurers in respect of claims included in sub-total C		12		
Sub-total D (11–12)		13		
Required margin of solvency for Supplementary Accident and Sickness Insurance:- Sub-total B x sub-total D / sub-total C (or, if ½ is a greater fraction, x ½)		14		

Note

"Supplementary Accident and Sickness Insurance" means insurance falling within Class 1 (Accident) and Class 2 (Sickness) of general business included in contracts to which section 1(2) and (3) of the Insurance Companies Act 1982 applies.

SCHEDULE 5

Regulation 24

STATEMENT OF LONG TERM BUSINESS BY THE APPOINTED ACTUARY
(Forms 65 to 78)

1. The date at which the valuation is made shall be stated.

2.—(1) A statement for each category of non-linked contract which is separately distinguished in Form 55 is to be given in such one of the forms set out in Forms 65 to 70 as is appropriate to that category of contract, or, in the case of a category of contract to which none of these forms is appropriate, in such form and containing such particulars as are sufficient to enable an independent assessment of the liabilities of the company's long term business to be made. As far as possible, the order in which the statements appear in this Schedule shall follow the order in which the categories of contract appear in Form 55.

(2) A statement for each category of linked contract which is separately distinguished in Form 56 is to be given in such one of the forms set out in Forms 72 to 77 as is appropriate to that category of contract, or, in the case of a category of contract to which none of these forms is appropriate, in such form and containing such particulars as are sufficient to enable an independent assessment of the liabilities of the company's long term business to be made. As far as possible, the order in which the statements appear in this Schedule shall follow the order in which the categories of contract appear in Form 56. The amounts shall be expressed in terms of currency or units as appropriate. In the case of contracts expressed in non-monetary units, the sterling values of the bid and offer prices of the units at 3-monthly intervals since the date of the previous statement prepared under section 18(2) of the Act are to be given in a supplement.

(3) Where contracts are written in currencies other than sterling, amounts in such currencies may be distinguished in the statements referred to above and expressed in those currencies, provided that the 'total' items in each statement are also given in sterling for each currency at the rate of exchange for that currency used for the purpose of preparing the valuation summary.

(4) A separate statement is to be given in respect of each category of contract for—

(i) direct business and reinsurance accepted; and

(ii) reinsurance ceded.

(5) In the case of a category of contract subject to premiums payable only for a limited term, the premiums are to be classified either—

(*a*) according to age, or

(*b*) according to the number of annual payments remaining to be made,

but if the premiums are classified under (*a*) there is to be appended to the form either a statement of the corresponding valuation factors required in calculating the value of future premiums or a statement of the average future period of payment of the premiums at each age.

3.—(1) In the case of a category of linked contract being a single premium whole life assurance where the death benefit is a function of the age at death and has been calculated to be equivalent to the valuation mortality rate, so as to make the value of the death benefit liability independent of age, it is sufficient for that fact to be stated and for the information to be given for all ages combined rather than analysed by age groups as required by paragraph 2(2) above.

(2) In the case of a category of linked contract where the non-unit liability is less than 1 per cent of the unit liability for that category of contract, it will be sufficient for that fact to be stated and for the information to be given for all ages combined rather than analysed by age groups as required by paragraph 2(2) above—

Provided that if the category of contract contains an investment performance guarantee or if the valuation method requires the discounting of the value of units, no advantage may be taken of this sub-paragraph.

4. In the case of those categories of contract which are shown in Forms 55 and 56 under a heading of 'miscellaneous', statements may be prepared in the form set out in Forms 71 and 78 respectively, and, if this be done, no statement need be prepared in pursuance of paragraph 2 above for those categories of contract.

5.—(1) For all contracts other than those included under the description 'miscellaneous' in Forms 55 and 56 particulars are to be given of the methods and bases employed in calculating any minimum surrender values and paid-up amounts guaranteed in the contracts with examples of the application of the method to contracts which have been in force for 1, 2, 3, 4, 5, 10, 15 and 20 years taken out at each of the ages 25, 40 and 55 or for original terms of 10, 20 and 30 years maturing at age 60, as appropriate.

(2) For those contracts where there are no minimum values or amounts guaranteed, particulars and examples of the values and amounts currently allowed are to be given as under sub-paragraph (1) of this paragraph but only in respect of standard types of insurance.

(3) In the case of linked contracts where full information has been given under paragraph (4)(1)(*a*) of Schedule 4 above no information in respect of surrender values and paid-up amounts need be given under this paragraph.

(4) Where any of the surrender values or paid-up amounts referred to in this paragraph in relation to industrial assurance business are the minimum amounts prescribed under the Industrial Assurance Act 1923 or under the Industrial Assurance and Friendly Societies Act 1929, or under the Industrial Assurance (Northern Ireland) Order 1979, this fact is to be stated.

Whole life assurances **Form 65**

OB/IB

Global business/UK branch business/Community branch business

Age (starting with the youngest) 1	Sums assured 2	Reversionary bonuses 3	Annual office premiums 4
Total			

Instructions

1 The information may be given for 5-year age groups.

2 The basis on which the age has been assessed shall be stated.

Form 66

Endowment assurances

Global business/UK branch business/Community branch business OB/IB

Year of maturity (starting with the nearest) 1	Sums assured 2	Reversionary bonuses 3	Annual office premiums 4
Total			

Instruction

The information may be given for 5-year groups of year of maturity for contracts maturing more than 15 years after the valuation date.

Form 67

Deferred annuities with guaranteed cash options

Global business/UK branch business/Community branch business OB/IB

Year in which payment of annuity is due to commence (starting with the nearest) 1	Cash option in lieu of annuity (excluding bonus) 2	Cash option in lieu of bonus additions 3	Annual office premiums 4
Total			
	Total annuity per annum corresponding to total cash options in		
	Column 2	Column 3	

Instructions

1 An explanation shall be given of the criteria adopted for deciding whether to value the cash option or the deferred annuity payments under such contracts.

2 For any contracts which have been valued by discounting the deferred annuity payments instead of the cash option, a separate table shall be given in the form of Form 68.

3 The information may be given for 5-year groups of year of commencement of annuity for annuities due to commence more than 15 years after the valuation date.

4 For deferred annuities secured under group or master contracts, under which premiums have not ceased but which have been valued on the basis that no future premiums will be payable, the cash options and annuity shown shall be those secured by the premiums already paid and no office premiums shall be given.

5 Separate tables shall be given in respect of business with a return of premiums on death before payment of the annuity is due to commence and in respect of business with no such benefit provided that one table only need be given for both these categories if that table contains sufficient additional information to enable the actuarial value of the death benefit to be estimated.

6 When the date on which the annuity was due to commence has passed but the annuity has not commenced and the cash option has not been taken, the basis on which the cash option and annuity have been included shall be stated.

Form 68

Deferred annuities without guaranteed cash options

Global business/UK branch business/Community branch business **OB/IB**

Year in which payment of annuity is due to commence (starting with the nearest)	Men			Women		
	Annual amount of annuities (excluding bonus)	Amount of bonus additions per annum	Annual office premiums	Annual amount of annuities (excluding bonus)	Amount of bonus additions per annum	Annual office premiums
1	2	3	4	5	6	7
Total						

Instructions

1 The information may be given for 5-year groups of year of commencement of annuity for annuities due to commence more than 15 years after the valuation date.

2 For deferred annuities secured under group or master contracts under which premiums have not ceased but which have been valued on the basis that no future premiums will be payable, the annuity shown shall be that secured by the premiums already paid and no office annual premiums shall be given.

3 Separate tables shall be given in respect of business with a return of premiums on death before payment of the annuity is due to commence and in respect of business with no such benefit, provided that one table only need be given for both these categories if that table contains sufficient additional information to enable the actuarial value of the death benefit to be estimated.

4 Where separate tables are not given for each age at which annuities are due to commence, the average age of commencement shall be stated, for each sex separately.

5 Where the date on which the annuity was due to commence has passed but the annuity has not commenced, the basis on which the annuity has been included (and the value of it, if shown) shall be stated.

Form 69

Annuities in payment: Payable for life including those guaranteed for a minimum term certain

Global business/UK branch business/Community branch business **OB/IB**

Age (starting with the youngest) 1	Amount in payment per annum	
	Men 2	Women 3
Total		

Instructions

1 For ages under 60 the information may be given for 5-year age groups.

2 The basis on which the age has been assessed shall be stated.

3 Deferred annuities where the date on which the annuity was due to commence has passed but the annuity has not commenced, and any cash option has not been taken, shall be included in Form 67 or Form 68 as appropriate.

Form 70

Annuities in payment: Payable for a temporary period, including those payable for a term certain

Global business/UK branch business/Community branch business **OB/IB**

Year in which the term ends (starting with the nearest) **1**	Amount in payment per annum **2**
Total	

Form 71

Miscellaneous non-linked contracts

Global business/UK branch business/Community branch business **OB/IB**

Type of insurance 1	Number of contracts 2	Amount of sums assured or annual amounts of annuity 3	Amount of reversionary bonuses 4	Amount of annual office premiums 5	Amount of mathematical reserves 6
Total					

Form 72

Linked single premium assurances

Global business/UK branch business/Community branch business

OB/IB

Age (starting with the youngest) 1	Current sums assured 2	Guaranteed minimum sums assured 3	Number of units allocated at valuation date 4
Total			

Instructions

1 The information may be given for 5-year age groups.

2 The basis on which the age has been assessed shall be stated.

3 A separate column 4 shall be provided for each different unit link to which a category of contract is linked.

4 If there are any monetary guarantees on surrender the contracts shall be classified by term to the next guarantee date rather than by age and an additional column showing the mean age shall be given.

Form 73

Linked regular premium assurances without monetary guarantees on survival: Unit liability not discounted

Global business/UK branch business/Community branch business OB/IB

Age (starting with the youngest) 1	Current sums assured 2	Guaranteed minimum sums assured 3	Number of units allocated at valuation date 4	Annual office premiums 5	Annual amount deemed invested in units in future 6
Total					

Instructions

1 The information may be given for 5-year age groups.

2 The basis on which the age has been assessed shall be stated.

3 A separate column 4 shall be provided for each different unit link to which a category of contract is linked.

4 Where the annual amount invested in units in future is not constant this shall be stated and additional information given.

Form 74

Linked regular premium assurances with monetary guarantees on survival: Unit liability not discounted

Global business/UK branch business/Community branch business OB/IB

Year of maturity (starting with the nearest)	Current sums assured on death	Guaranteed minimum sums assured on death	Guaranteed minimum sums assured on maturity or surrender	Number of units allocated at valuation date	Annual office premiums	Annual amount deemed invested in units in future
1	2	3	4	5	6	7
Total						

Instructions

1 The information may be given for 5-year groups of year of maturity for contracts maturing more than 15 years after the valuation date.

2 A separate column 5 shall be provided for each different unit link to which a category of contract is linked.

3 Where the annual amount invested in units in future is not constant this shall be stated and additional information given.

4 For contracts with monetary guarantees on surrender rather than on maturity the year shown in column 1 shall be the year of the next such guarantee.

Form 75

Linked regular premium assurances with or without monetary guarantees on survival: Unit liability partially or wholly discounted

Global business/UK branch business/Community branch business — **OB/IB**

Year of maturity (starting with the nearest) 1	Current sums assured on death 2	Guaranteed minimum sums assured on death 3	Guaranteed minimum sums assured on maturity 4	Number of units allocated at valuation date 5	Annual office premiums 6	Annual amount deemed invested in units in future 7
Total						

Instructions

1 The information may be given for 5-year groups of year of maturity for contracts maturing more than 15 years after the valuation date.

2 A separate column 5 shall be provided for each different unit link to which a category of contract is linked.

3 Where the annual amount invested in units in future is not constant this shall be stated and additional information given.

Form 76

Linked deferred annuities

Global business/UK branch business/Community branch business

OB/IB

Year in which payment of annuity is due to commence (starting with the nearest) **1**	Number of units allocated at valuation date **2**
Total	

Instructions

1 The information may be given for 5-year groups of year of commencement of annuity for annuities due to commence more than 15 years after the valuation date.

2 A separate column 2 shall be provided for each different unit link to which a category of contract is linked.

3 Separate tables shall be given in respect of business with a return of premiums on death before payment of the annuity is due to commence and in respect of business with no such benefit, provided that one table only need be given for both these categories if that table contains sufficient additional information to enable the actuarial value of the death benefit to be estimated.

Form 77

Linked annuities in payment

Global business/UK branch business/Community branch business OB/IB

Age (starting with the youngest)	Men		Women	
	Number of units in payment per annum	Number of annuity units deemed allocated	Number of units in payment per annum	Number of annuity units deemed allocated
1	2	3	4	5
Total				

Instructions

1 For ages under 60 the information may be given for 5-year age groups.

2 The basis on which the age has been assessed shall be stated.

3 Columns 2 and 4 shall be completed only for those categories of contract where the company bears the mortality risk. Columns 3 and 5 shall be completed for those categories of contract where the policyholders bear the mortality risks.

4 A separate form shall be provided for each different unit link to which a category of contract is linked.

Form 78

Miscellaneous linked contracts

Global business/UK branch business/Community branch business

OB/IB

Name of contract 1	Number of contracts 2	Amount of sums assured or annual amounts of annuity, including bonuses 3	Amount of annual office premiums 4	Name of unit link 5	Number of units deemed allocated 6	Unit liability 7	Non-unit liability 8
Total							

Instruction

Where a category of contract has more than one unit link, a sub-division into each different unit link is required in columns 5, 6 and 7. Columns 6 and 7 shall be totalled in respect of each different unit link.

SCHEDULE 6

Regulations 26 and 27

PART 1

Certificate by directors etc.

1. Subject to paragraph 8 below, the certificate required by Regulation 26(*a*) above shall state, in relation to the part of the return comprising Forms 9 to 16, 20 to 29, 31 to 37 and 40 to 51,—

(*a*) that for the purposes of preparing the return—

(i) proper accounts and records have been maintained and adequate information has been obtained by the company, and

(ii) an appropriate system of control has been established and maintained by the company over its transactions and records;

(*b*) that the value shown for each category of asset has been determined in conformity with Regulation 4 above and includes the value of only such assets or such parts thereof as are permitted to be taken into account;

(*c*) that the amount shown for each category of liability (including contingent and prospective liabilities) has been determined in conformity with Regulation 4 above; and

(*d*) that in respect of the company's business which is not excluded by Regulation 27 of the Insurance Companies Regulations, the assets held at the end of the financial year enabled the company to comply with Regulations 25 and 26 (matching and localisation) of those Regulations.

2. Subject to paragraph 8 below, the certificate required by Regulation 26(*a*) above shall state in relation to the part of the return comprising a statement required by Regulations 17, 18 or 19 above that, for the purposes of preparing the statement,—

(*a*) proper accounts and records have been maintained and, as necessary, reasonable enquiries have been made by the company for the purpose of finding whether any person and any body corporate are connected for the purposes of Regulations 17(1)(*b*) and (2), 18(*b*) and 19(1)(*b*) and (2) above, and

(*b*) an appropriate system of control has been established and maintained by the company over its transactions and records.

3. Subject to paragraph 8 below, the certificate required by Regulation 26(*a*) above shall state, in relation to the statement required by Regulation 29 above,—

(*a*) that for the purpose of preparing the statement, proper accounts and records have been maintained; and

(*b*) that the information given has been ascertained in conformity with that Regulation.

4. Subject to paragraph 8 below the certificate required by Regulation 26(*a*) above shall state separately in respect of long term business and of general business,—

(*a*) in the case of a United Kingdom company, a pure reinsurer or (in respect of its global business) a United Kingdom deposit company or external company, that—

(i) immediately following the end of the financial year the amount of the company's required minimum margin was as shown in Form 9; and

(ii) at the end of the financial year the amount of the company's available assets and quantifiable contingent liabilities (other than those included in Form 14 or Form 15 in accordance with paragraph 10(1) of Schedule 1 above) and the identity and value of items admitted as implicit items in accordance with Regulation 10(4) of the Insurance Companies Regulations were as shown in Form 9;

(*b*) in the case of a Community company (other than a United Kingdom company or a pure reinsurer) and of a Community deposit company, that the value of the admissible assets of the long term business or of the general business carried on by the company through an agency or branch in the United Kingdom was maintained at not less than the amount of the liabilities of that business;

(*c*) in the case of an external company (other than a pure reinsurer),—

(i) in relation to the long term business or to the general business carried on by the company through an agency or branch in the United Kingdom that—

(*aa*) immediately following the end of the financial year the amount of the company's required United Kingdom minimum margin was as shown in Form 9; and

(*bb*) at the end of the financial year the amount of the company's available assets and quantifiable contingent liabilities (other than those included in Form 14 or in Form 15 in accordance with paragraph 10(1) of Schedule 1 above) and the identity and value of items admitted as implicit items in accordance with Regulation 10(4) of the Insurance Companies Regulations were as shown in Form 9;

(ii) that the company has kept admissible assets representing the required United Kingdom minimum margin of an amount at least equal to the appropriate guarantee fund or minimum guarantee fund, whichever was the greater, within the United Kingdom and has kept admissible assets representing the remainder of that minimum margin within the United Kingdom and the other member States; and

(iii) that the deposit made in accordance with section 9(1)(*c*) of the Act has been maintained at a level equal to at least the minimum as defined in Regulation 14 of the Insurance Companies Regulations;

(*d*) in the case of a United Kingdom deposit company,—

(i) in relation to the long term business or to the general business carried on by the company through agencies and branches in the member States concerned that—

(*aa*) immediately following the end of the financial year the amount of the company's required Community minimum margin was as shown in Form 9; and

(*bb*) at the end of the financial year the amount of the company's available assets and quantifiable contingent liabilities (other than those included in Form 14 or in Form 15 in accordance with paragraph 10(1) of Schedule 1 above) and the identity and value of items admitted as implicit items in accordance with Regulation 10(4) of the Insurance Companies Regulations were as shown in Form 9;

(ii) that the company has kept admissible assets representing the required Community minimum margin of an amount at least equal to the appropriate guarantee fund or minimum guarantee fund, whichever was the greater, within the member States concerned and has kept admissible assets representing the remainder of that minimum margin within the member States concerned and the other member States; and

(iii) that the deposit made in accordance with section 9(2) of the Act has been maintained at a level equal to at least the minimum as defined in Regulation 14 of the Insurance Companies Regulations.

5.—(1) If a company accounts for any of its general business over periods longer than twelve months, subject to paragraph 8 below, the certificate required by Regulation 26(*a*) above shall state that all premiums and considerations receivable in respect of any such business so accounted for (and in relation to which separate provision is not made for unearned premiums and claims outstanding) have been retained in the fund or funds of the account subject only to—

(*a*) the discharge of liabilities (including expenses) proper to the execution of that business, and

(*b*) the transfer of any profits after the closing of the account at the end of the appropriate accounting period.

(2) A certificate under paragraph (1) above shall state that any shortfall of any fund which is referred to therein below the amount which is estimated to be required to meet outstanding liabilities (net of reinsurance and other recoveries) has been made good by transfers into that fund.

6. If a company carries on long term business the certificate required by Regulation 26(*a*) above shall also state, subject to paragraph 8 below,—

(*a*) except in the case of a company which has no shareholders and carries on no business whatsoever other than long term business, that the requirements of sections 28 to 31 of the Act have been fully complied with and in particular that, subject to the provisions of section 29(2) to (4) and section 30 of the Act, assets attributable to long term business, the income arising therefrom, the proceeds of any realisation of such assets and any other income or proceeds allocated to the long term business fund or funds have not been applied otherwise than for the purpose of the long term business;

(*b*) that any amount payable from or receivable by the long term business fund or funds in respect of services rendered by or to any other business carried on by the company or by a person who, for the purposes of section 31 of the Act, is connected with it or is a subordinate company of it has been determined and where appropriate apportioned on terms which are believed to be no less than fair to that fund or those funds, and any exchange of assets representing such fund or funds for other assets of the company has been made at fair market value;

(*c*) that all guarantees given by the company of the performance by a related company of a contract binding on the related company which would fall to be met by any long term business fund have been disclosed in the return, and that the fund or funds on which each such guarantee would fall has been identified therein; and

(*d*) in the case of a United Kingdom company, pure reinsurer, United Kingdom deposit company or external company which has financial, commercial or administrative links with any other company carrying on insurance business, that the returns in respect of long term business are not distorted by agreements between the companies concerned or by any arrangements which could affect the apportionment of expenses and income.

7. Except in the case of a Community company, the certificate required by Regulation 26(*a*) above shall also state, subject to paragraph 8 below, that proper accounts and records have been maintained in the United Kingdom in respect of business carried on through an agency or branch in the United Kingdom.

8.—(1) Where, in the opinion of those signing the certificate, the circumstances are such that any of the statements required by paragraphs 1 to 7 above (other than sub-paragraphs (*a*), (*c*)(i) and (*d*)(i) of paragraph 4) cannot truthfully be made, the relevant statements shall be omitted.

(2) Where, by virtue of sub-paragraph (1) of this paragraph, any statements have been omitted from the certificate, this fact shall be stated in a note.

Part II

Certificate by appointed actuary

9. The certificate required by Regulation 26(*b*) above to be signed by the appointed actuary—

(*a*) shall state, if such be the case,—

(i) that in his opinion proper records have been kept by the company adequate for the purpose of the valuation of the liabilities of its long term business;

(ii) that the mathematical reserves as shown in Form 14, together, if the case so require, with an amount specified in the certificate (being part of the excess of the value of the admissible assets representing the long term business funds over the amount of those funds shown in Form 14) constitute proper provision at the end of the financial year for the liabilities (other than liabilities which had fallen due before the end of the financial year) arising under or in connection with contracts for long term business including any increase in those liabilities arising from a distribution of surplus as a result of an investigation as at that date into the financial condition of the long term business; and

(iii) that for the purposes of sub-paragraph (ii) above the liabilities have been assessed in accordance with Part VI of the Insurance Companies Regulations in the context of assets valued in accordance with Part V of those Regulations, as shown in Form 13; and

(*b*) shall state the amount of the required minimum margin, required Community minimum margin or required United Kingdom minimum margin, as the case may be, applicable to the company's long term business immediately following the end of the financial year (including any amounts resulting from any increase in liabilities arising from a distribution of surplus as a result of the investigation into the financial condition of the long term business).

10. If he considers it necessary, the appointed actuary shall add to the certificate such qualification, amplification or explanation as may be appropriate.

Part III

Auditors' report

11. The report required by Regulation 27 above shall, in addition to any statement required by section 14(4) and (6) of the Companies Act 1967 as applied by the said Regulation 27, state,—

(*a*) in the auditors' opinion, whether the parts of the return required to be audited (that is Forms 9 to 16, 20 to 29, 31 to 37 and 40 to 51 and information furnished pursuant to Regulations 17 and 19 above) have been properly prepared in accordance with the provisions of these Regulations;

(*b*) in the auditors' opinion and according to the information and explanations they have received,—

(i) whether the certificate required to be signed in accordance with Regulation 26(*a*) above (other than so much of it as relates to paragraph 3 above) has been properly prepared in accordance with these Regulations; and

(ii) whether it was reasonable for the persons giving the certificate to have made the statements therein,

but, in so far as the certificate is given pursuant to paragraph 2 above only to the extent that it applies to information required by Regulations 17 and 19 above; and

(*c*) that in giving their opinion the auditors have relied,—

(i) in the case of a company carrying on long term business, on the certificate of the actuary given in accordance with the requirements of Part II of this Schedule with respect to the mathematical reserves and required minimum margin, required Community minimum margin or required United Kingdom minimum margin, as the case may be, of the company; and

(ii) in the case of a company carrying on long term or general business, on the identity and value of any implicit items as they have been admitted in accordance with Regulation 10(4) of the Insurance Companies Regulations.

SCHEDULE 7

Regulation 32

REGULATIONS REVOKED

Number	*Title*
SI 1980/6	The Insurance Companies (Accounts and Statements) Regulations 1980
SI 1980/1129	The Insurance Companies (Accounts and Statements) (Northern Ireland) Regulations 1980
SI 1980/1820	The Industrial Assurance Companies (Accounts and Statements) Regulations 1980
SI 1981/1656	The Insurance Companies (Accounts and Statements) (Amendment) Regulations 1981
SI 1982/305	The Insurance Companies (Accounts and Statements) (Amendment) Regulations 1982
SI 1982/1795	The Insurance Companies (Accounts and Statements) (Amendment) (No 2) Regulations 1982
SI 1983/469	The Insurance Companies (Accounts and Statements) (Amendment) (General Business Reinsurance) Regulations 1983
SI 1983/1192	The Insurance Companies (Accounts and Statements) (Amendment) Regulations 1983

INSURANCE COMPANIES (WINDING-UP) RULES 1985

(SI 1985/95)

Citation and commencement

1. These Rules may be cited as the Insurance Companies (Winding-Up) Rules 1985 and shall come into operation on 1st March 1985.

Interpretation

2.—(1) In these Rules, unless the context or subject-matter otherwise requires:
'the Act of 1923' means the Industrial Assurance Act 1923;
'the Act of 1948' means the Companies Act 1948;
'the Act of 1982' means the Insurance Companies Act 1982;
'company' means an insurance company which is being wound up;

'excess of the long term business assets' means the amount, if any, by which the value as at the date of the winding-up order of the assets representing the fund or funds maintained by the company in respect of its long term business exceeds the value as at that date of the liabilities of the company attributable to that business;

'excess of the other business assets' means the amount, if any, by which the value as at the date of the winding-up order of the assets of the company which do not represent the fund or funds maintained by the company in respect of its long term business exceeds the value as at that date of the liabilities of the company (other than liabilities in respect of share capital) which are not attributable to that business;

'general business policy' means a policy the effecting of which by the company constitutes the carrying on of general business;

'the Industrial Assurance Acts' means the Act of 1923 and the Industrial Assurance and Friendly Societies Act 1929;

'insurance company' means an insurance company to which Part II of the Act of 1982 applies;

'linked liability' means any liability under a policy the effecting of which constitutes the carrying on of long term insurance business the amount of which is determined by reference to:

(*a*) the value of property of any description (whether or not specified in the policy),

(*b*) fluctuations in the value of such property,

(*c*) income from any such property, or

(*d*) fluctuations in an index of the value of such property;

'linked policy' means a policy which provides for linked liabilities and a policy which when made provided for linked liabilities shall be deemed to be a linked policy even if the policy holder has elected to convert his rights under the policy so that at the date of the winding-up order there are no longer linked liabilities under the policy;

'long term policy' means a policy the effecting of which by the company constitutes the carrying on of long term business;

'non-linked policy' means a policy which is not a linked policy;

'other business', in relation to a company carrying on long term business, means such of the business of the company as is not long term business;

'the principal Rules' means the Companies (Winding-up) Rules 1949, as amended;

'stop order' in relation to a company means an order of the court, made under section 56(2) of the Act of 1982, ordering the liquidator to stop carrying on the long term business of the company;

'unit' in relation to a linked policy means any unit (whether or not described as a unit in the policy) by reference to the numbers and value of which the amount of the linked liabilities under the policy at any time is measured.

(2) Unless the context otherwise requires words or expressions contained in these Rules bear the same meaning as in the principal Rules, the Act of 1948, the Act of 1982, or any statutory modification thereof respectively.

Application

3.—(1) These Rules apply to proceedings for the winding-up of an insurance company which commence on or after the date on which these Rules come into operation.

(2) These Rules supplement the principal Rules which continue to apply to the proceedings in the winding-up of an insurance company under the Act of 1948 as they apply to proceedings in the winding-up of any company under that Act but in the event of conflict between these Rules and the principal Rules these Rules prevail.

Appointment of liquidator

4. Upon the consideration of the resolutions and determinations of the first meetings of creditors and contributories the court, as well as hearing the Official Receiver and any creditor or contributory in accordance with Rule 58(4) of the principal Rules, shall also hear the Policyholders Protection Board.

Separation of long term and other business in winding-up

5.—(1) This Rule applies in the case of a company carrying on long term business.

(2) The assets of the company which in accordance with sections 55(3) and (4) of the Act of 1982 are available for meeting the liabilities of the company attributable to its long term business shall, in pursuance of section 257 of the Act of 1948, be applied in discharge of those liabilities as though those assets and those liabilities were the assets and liabilities of a separate company.

(3) The assets of the company which in accordance with sections 55(3) and (4) of the Act of 1982 are available for meeting the liabilities of the company attributable to its other business shall, in pursuance of section 257 of the Act of 1948, be applied in discharge of those liabilities as though those assets and those liabilities were the assets and liabilities of a separate company.

Valuation of general business policies

6. Except in relation to amounts which have fallen due for payment before the date of the winding-up order, the holder of a general business policy shall be admitted as a creditor in relation to his policy without proof for an amount equal to the value of the policy and for this purpose the value of a policy shall be determined in accordance with Schedule 1.

Valuation of long term policies

7.—(1) This Rule applies in relation to a company's long term business where no stop order has been made.

(2) In relation to a claim under a policy which has fallen due for payment before the date of the winding-up order, a policy holder shall be admitted as a creditor without proof for such amount as appears from the records of the company to be due in respect of that claim.

(3) In all other respects a policy holder shall be admitted as a creditor in relation to his policy without proof for an amount equal to the value of the policy and for this purpose the value of a policy of any class shall be determined in the manner applicable to policies of that class provided by Schedules 2, 3 and 4.

(4) This Rule applies in relation to a person entitled to apply for a free paid-up policy under section 24 of the Act of 1923 and to whom no such policy has been issued before the date of the winding-up order (whether or not it was applied for) as if such policy had been issued immediately before the date of the winding-up order—

(*a*) for the minimum amount determined in accordance with section 24(2) of the Act of 1923, or

(*b*) if the liquidator is satisfied that it was the practice of the company during the five years immediately before the date of the winding-up order to issue policies under the said section 24 in excess of the minimum amounts so determined, for the amount determined in accordance with that practice.

8.—(1) This Rule applies in relation to a company's long term business where a stop order has been made.

(2) In relation to a claim under a policy which has fallen due for payment on or after the date of the winding-up order and before the date of the stop order, a policy holder shall be admitted as a creditor without proof for such amount as appears from the records of the company and of the liquidator to be due in respect of that claim.

(3) In all other respects a policy holder shall be admitted as a creditor in relation to

his policy without proof for an amount equal to the value of the policy and for this purpose the value of a policy of any class shall be determined in the manner applicable to policies of that class provided by Schedule 5.

(4) Paragraph (4) of Rule 7 applies for the purposes of this Rule as if references to the date of the winding-up order (other than that in sub-paragraph (*b*) of that paragraph) were references to the date of the stop order.

Attribution of assets and liabilities to the long term business

9.—(1) This Rule applies in the case of a company carrying on long term business if at the date of the winding-up order there are liabilities of the company in respect of which it is not clear from the accounting and other records of the company whether they are or are not attributable to the company's long term business.

(2) The liquidator shall, in such manner and according to such accounting principles as he shall determine, identify the liabilities referred to in paragraph (1) as attributable or not attributable to a company's long term business and those liabilities shall for the purposes of the winding-up be deemed as at the date of the winding-up order to be so attributable or not as the case may be.

(3) In making his determination under this Rule the liquidator may determine that some liabilities are attributable to the company's long term business and that others are not or he may determine that a part of a liability is attributable to the company's long term business and that the remainder of that liability is not and he may use one method for some of the liabilities and the other method for the remainder of them.

10.—(1) This Rule applies in the case of a company carrying on long term business if at the date of the winding-up order there are assets of the company in respect of which—

(*a*) it is not clear from the accounting and other records of the company whether they do or do not represent the fund or funds maintained by the company in respect of its long term business, and

(*b*) it cannot be inferred from the source of the income out of which those assets were provided whether they do or do not represent those funds.

(2) Subject to paragraph (6) the liquidator shall determine which (if any) of the assets referred to in paragraph (1) are attributable to those funds and which (if any) are not and those assets shall, for the purposes of the winding-up, be deemed as at the date of the winding-up order to represent those funds or not in accordance with the liquidator's determination.

(3) For the purposes of paragraph (2) the liquidator may:—

(*a*) determine that some of those assets shall be attributable to those funds and that others of them shall not (the first method); or

(*b*) determine that a part of the value of one of those assets shall be attributable to those funds and that the remainder of that value shall not (the second method),

and he may use the first method for some of those assets and the second method for others of them.

(4) (*a*) In making the attribution the liquidator's objective shall in the first instance be so far as possible to reduce any deficit that may exist, at the date of the winding-up order and before any attribution is made, either in the company's long term business or in its other business.

(*b*) If there is a deficit in both the company's long term business and its other business the attribution shall be in the ratio that the amount of the one deficit bears to the amount of the other until the deficits are eliminated.

(*c*) Thereafter the attribution shall be in the ratio which the aggregate amount of the liabilities attributable to the company's long term business bears to the aggregate amount of the liabilities not so attributable.

(5) For the purpose of paragraph (4) the value of a liability of the company shall, if it falls to be valued under Rule 6 or 7, have the same value as it has under that Rule but otherwise it shall have such value as would have been included in relation to it in a balance sheet of the company prepared in pursuance of section 17 of the Act of 1982 as at the date of the winding-up order and, for the purpose of determining the ratio referred to in paragraph (4) but not for the purpose of determining the amount of any deficit therein referred to, the net balance of shareholders' funds shall be included in the liabilities not attributable to the company's long term business.

(6) Notwithstanding anything in the preceding paragraphs of this Rule the court may order that the determination of which (if any) of the assets referred to in paragraph (1) are attributable to the fund or funds maintained by the company in respect of its long term business and which (if any) are not shall be made in such manner and by such methods as the court may direct or the court may itself make the determination.

Excess of long term business assets

11. Where the company is one carrying on long term business, for the purpose of determining the amount, if any, of the excess of the long term business assets, there shall be included amongst the liabilities of the company attributable to its long term business an amount determined by the liquidator in respect of liabilities and expenses likely to be incurred in connection with the transfer of the company's long term business as a going concern to another insurance company being liabilities not included in the valuation of the long term policies made in pursuance of Rule 7.

Actuarial advice

12.—(1) Before determining the value of a policy in accordance with Schedules 1 to 5 (other than paragraph 2 of Schedule 1), before identifying long term assets and liabilities in accordance with Rules 9 and 10 and before determining the amount (if any) of the excess of the long term business assets in accordance with Rule 11, and before determining the terms on which he will accept payment of overdue premiums under Rule 22(1) and the amount and nature of any compensation under Rule 22(2), the liquidator shall obtain and consider advice thereon (including an estimate of any value or amount required to be determined) from an actuary.

(2) Before seeking, for the purpose of valuing a policy, the direction of the court as to the assumption of a particular rate of interest or the employment of any rates of mortality or disability, the liquidator shall obtain and consider advice thereon from an actuary.

Utilisation of excess of assets

13.—(1) Except at the direction of the court

(*a*) no distribution may be made out of and no transfer to another insurance company may be made of any part of the excess of the long term business assets which has been transferred to the other business, and

(*b*) no distribution may be made out of and no transfer to another insurance company may be made of any part of the excess of the other business assets which has been transferred to the long term business.

(2) Before giving a direction under paragraph (1) the court may require the liquidator to advertise the proposal to make a distribution or a transfer in such manner as the court shall direct.

Special bank account

14.—(1) In the case of a company carrying on long term business, in whose case no stop order has been made, Rule 170 of the principal Rules applies only in relation to the company's other business.

(2) The liquidator of such a company may open any special bank account which he is authorised to open by the Secretary of State and he may pay into such an account any moneys which form part of the assets representing the fund or funds maintained by the company in respect of its long term business.

(3) All payments out of any such special bank account shall be made by cheque payable to order and every cheque shall have marked or written on the face of it the name of the company and shall be signed by the liquidator or by any special manager appointed under section 56(3) of the Act of 1982 and, if it is for a sum greater than an amount to be determined for this purpose by the Committee of Inspection, it shall be countersigned by a person nominated by the Committee of Inspection.

Custody of assets

15.—(1) The Secretary of State may, in the case of a company carrying on long term business in whose case no stop order has been made, require that the whole or a specified proportion of the assets representing the fund or funds maintained by the company in respect of its long term business shall be held by a person approved by him for the purpose as trustee for the company.

(2) No assets held by a person as trustee for a company in compliance with a requirement imposed under this Rule shall, so long as the requirement is in force, be released except with the consent of the Secretary of State but they may be transposed by the trustee into other assets by any transaction or series of transactions on the written instructions of the liquidator.

(3) The liquidator may not grant any mortgage or charge of assets which are held by a person as trustee for the company in compliance with a requirement imposed under this Rule except with the consent of the Secretary of State.

Maintenance of accounting, valuation and other records

16.—(1) In the case of a company carrying on long term business, in whose case no stop order has been made, Rule 172 of the principal Rules applies only in relation to the company's other business.

(2) The liquidator of such a company shall, with a view to the long term business of the company being transferred to another insurance company, maintain such minute books and accounting, valuation and other records as will enable such other insurance company upon the transfer being effected to comply with the requirements of the provisions of the Act of 1982 relating to accounts and statements of insurance companies.

Additional powers in relation to the long term business

17.—(1) In case of a company carrying on long term business, in whose case no stop order has been made, Rule 173 of the principal Rules applies only in relation to the company's other business.

(2) The liquidator of a company carrying on long term business shall, so long as no stop order has been made, have power to do all such things as may be necessary to the performance of his duties under section 56(2) of the Act of 1982 but the Secretary of State may require him—

(*a*) not to make investments of a specified class or description,

(*b*) to realise, before the expiration of a specified period (or such longer period as the Secretary of State may allow), the whole or a specified proportion of investments of a specified class or description held by the liquidator when the requirement is imposed.

Accounts and audit

18.—(1) In the case of a company carrying on long term business, in whose case no stop order has been made, Rules 174 to 179 of the principal Rules apply only in relation to the company's other business.

(2) The liquidator of such a company shall supply the Secretary of State, at such times or intervals as he shall specify, with such accounts as he may specify and audited in such manner as he may require and with such information about specified matters and verified in such specified manner as he may require.

(3) The liquidator of such a company shall, if required to do so by the Secretary of State, instruct an actuary to investigate the financial condition of the company's long term business and to report thereon in such manner as the Secretary of State may specify.

(4) The liquidator of such a company shall, at the expiration of six months from the date of the winding-up order and at the expiration of every six months thereafter, prepare a summary of his receipts and payments in the course of carrying on the long term business of the company during that period, procure that the summary be examined and verified by a person qualified under section 161 of the Act of 1948 to audit the accounts of companies and transmit to the Secretary of State two copies of the summary verified as aforesaid.

(5) The Secretary of State shall file one of these copies with the Registrar and that copy shall be open to the inspection of any person on payment of the same fee as is payable with respect to the inspection of the file of proceedings under Rule 19 of the principal Rules.

Special Manager

19. Rules 50, 51, 59 and 60 of the principal Rules apply to the appointment of a special manager under section 56(3) of the Act of 1982 as they apply to the appointment of a special manager under the Act of 1948 but as though for the references to the Official Receiver in Rules 50 and 51 there were substituted references to the liquidator.

Security by liquidator and special manager

20. In the case of a company carrying on long term business, in whose case no stop order has been made, Rule 59 of the principal Rules applies separately to the company's long term business and to its other business.

Proof of debts

21.—(1) This Rule applies in the case of a company carrying on long term business.

(2) The liquidator may in relation to the company's long term business and to its other business fix different days on or before which the creditors of the company who are required to prove their debts or claims are to prove their debts or claims and he may fix one of those days without at the same time fixing the other.

(3) In submitting a proof of any debt a creditor may claim the whole or any part of such debt as attributable to the company's long term business or to its other business or he may make no such attribution.

(4) When he admits any debt in whole or in part the liquidator shall state in writing how much of what he admits is attributable to the company's long term business and how much to the company's other business.

Failure to pay premiums

22.—(1) The liquidator may in the course of carrying on the company's long term business and on such terms as he thinks fit accept payment of a premium even though the payment is tendered after the date on which under the terms of the policy it was finally due to be paid.

(2) The liquidator may in the course of carrying on the company's long term business, and having regard to the general practice of insurers, compensate a policy

holder whose policy has lapsed in consequence of a failure to pay any premium by issuing a free paid-up policy for reduced benefits or otherwise as the liquidator thinks fit.

Notice of valuation of policy

23.—(1) The liquidator shall give notice of the value of each general business policy, as determined by him in accordance with Rule 6, to the persons appearing from the records of the company or otherwise to be entitled to an interest in that policy and he shall do so in such manner as the court may direct.

(2) In the case of a company carrying on long term business, if the liquidator, before a stop order is made in relation to the company, summons a separate general meeting of creditors in respect of liabilities of the company attributable to its long term business in pursuance of section 246 of the Act of 1948 as that section has effect by virtue of section 55(5) of the Act of 1982, he shall give notice in Form No. 1 set out in Schedule 6 to the persons appearing from the records of the company or otherwise to be entitled to a payment under or to an interest in a long term policy of the amount of that payment or the value of that policy as determined by him in accordance with Rules 7(2) or (3) as the case may be and he shall give that notice with the notice summoning the meeting.

(3) If a stop order is made in relation to the company the liquidator shall give notice to all the persons appearing from the records of the company or otherwise to be entitled to a payment under or to an interest in a long term policy of the amount of that payment or the value of that policy as determined by him in accordance with Rules 8(2) or (3) as the case may be and he shall give that notice in such manner as the court may direct.

(4) Any person to whom notice is so given shall be bound by the value so determined unless and until the court otherwise orders.

(5) Paragraphs (2) and (3) of this Rule have effect as though references therein to persons appearing to be entitled to an interest in a long term policy and to the value of that policy included respectively references to persons appearing to be entitled to apply for a free paid-up policy under section 24 of the Act of 1923 and to the value of that entitlement under Rule 7 (in the case of paragraph (2) of this Rule) or under Rule 8 (in the case of paragraph (3) of this Rule).

Dividends to creditors

24.—(1) This Rule applies in the case of a company carrying on long term business.

(2) Rule 119 of the principal Rules applies separately in relation to the two separate companies assumed for the purposes of Rule 5.

(3) The court may, at any time before the making of a stop order, permit a dividend to be declared and paid on such terms as it thinks fit in respect only of debts which fell due for payment before the date of the winding-up order or, in the case of claims under long term policies, which have fallen due for payment on or after the date of the winding-up order.

Meetings of creditors

25.—(1) In the case of a company carrying on long term business, Rules 127 to 156 of the principal Rules apply to each separate general meeting of the creditors summoned under section 246 of the Act of 1948 as that section has effect by virtue of section 55(5) of the Act of 1982.

(2) In relation to any such separate meeting:—

(*a*) Rule 132(2) of the principal Rules has effect as if the reference therein to assets of the company were a reference to the assets available under section 55 of the Act of 1982 for meeting the liabilities of the company owed to the creditors summoned to the meeting, and

(*b*) Rule 134 of the principal Rules applies as if the reference therein to value in relation to a creditor who is not, by virtue of Rule 6, 7 or 8 required to prove his debt, were a reference to the value most recently notified to him under Rule 23 or, if the court has determined a different value in accordance with Rule 23(4), as if it were a reference to that different value.

Remuneration of liquidator carrying on long term business

26. So long as no stop order has been made in relation to the company paragraph (1) of Rule 159 of the principal Rules applies in relation to the carrying on of that business as if for the words from 'be in the nature of' to the end of the paragraph there were substituted the words 'be on a time and rate basis'.

Apportionment of costs payable out of the assets

27.—(1) Rule 195(1) of the principal Rules applies separately to the assets of the company's long term business and to the assets of the company's other business.

(2) But where any fee, expense, cost, charge, disbursement or remuneration does not relate exclusively to the assets of the company's long term business or to the assets of the company's other business the liquidator shall apportion it amongst those assets in such manner as he shall determine.

Notice of stop order.

28.—(1) When a stop order has been made in relation to the company the Registrar shall, on the same day, send to the Official Receiver a notice informing him that the stop order has been pronounced.

(2) The notice shall be in Form No 2 set out in Schedule 6 with such variation as circumstances may require.

(3) Three copies of the stop order sealed with the seal of the court shall forthwith be sent by post or otherwise by the Registrar to the Official Receiver.

(4) The Official Receiver shall cause a sealed copy of the order to be served upon the liquidator by prepaid letter or upon such other person or persons, or in such other manner as the court may direct, and shall forward a copy of the order to the Registrar of Companies.

(5) The Official Receiver shall forthwith give notice of the order in Form No. 3 set out in Schedule 6 to the Department of Trade and Industry, who shall cause the notice to be gazetted.

(6) The Official Receiver shall forthwith send notice of the order in Form No. 4 set out in Schedule 6 to such local paper as the Department of Trade and Industry may from time to time direct, or, in default of such direction, as he may select.

SCHEDULE 1

General business policies

1.—(1) This paragraph applies in relation to periodic payments under a general business policy which fall due for payment after the date of the winding-up order where the event giving rise to the liability to make the payments occurred before the date of the winding-up order.

(2) The value to be attributed to such periodic payments shall be determined on such actuarial principles and assumptions in regard to all relevant factors as the court shall direct.

2.—(1) This paragraph applies in relation to liabilities under a general business policy not dealt with by paragraph 1.

(2) The value to be attributed to those liabilities shall:—

(*a*) if the terms of the policy for a repayment of premium upon the early termination of the policy or the policy is expressed to run from one definite date to another or the policy may be terminated by any of the parties with effect from a definite date, be the greater of the following two amounts:—

(i) the amount (if any) which under the terms of the policy would have been repayable on early termination of the policy had the policy terminated on the date of the winding-up order, and

(ii) where the policy is expressed to run from one definite date to another or may be terminated by any of the parties with effect from a definite date, such proportion of the last premium paid as is proportionate to the unexpired portion of the period in respect of which that premium was paid; and

(*b*) in any other case, be a just estimate of that value.

SCHEDULE 2

Rules for valuing non-linked life policies, non-linked deferred annuity policies, non-linked annuities in payment and capital redemption policies

General

1.—(1) In valuing a policy:—

(*a*) where it is necessary to calculate the present value of future payments by or to the company interest shall be assumed at such rate or rates as the court may direct;

(*b*) where relevant the rates of mortality and the rates of disability to be employed shall be such rates as the court may consider appropriate after taking into account:—

(i) relevant published tables of rates of mortality and rates of disability, and

(ii) the rates of mortality and the rates of disability experienced in connection with similar policies issued by the company;

(*c*) there shall be determined:—

(i) the present value of the ordinary benefits,

(ii) a reserve for options,

(iii) a reserve for expenses, and

(iv) if further fixed premiums fall due to be paid under the policy on or after the date of the winding-up order, the present value of the modified net premiums;

and for the purpose of this Schedule a premium is a fixed premium if the amount of it is determined by the terms of the policy and it cannot be varied.

(2) Where under the terms of the policy or on the basis of the company's established practice the policy holder has a right to receive or an expectation of receiving benefits additional to the minimum benefits guaranteed under those terms the court shall determine rates of interest, mortality and disability under paragraph (1) which will result in the inclusion in the present value of the ordinary benefits and in the present value of the modified net premiums of such margin (if any) as the court may consider appropriate to provide for that right or expectation in respect of the period after the date of the winding-up order.

Present value of the ordinary benefits

2.—(1) Ordinary benefits are the benefits which will become payable to the policy holder on or after the date of the winding-up order without his having to exercise any option under the policy (including any bonus or addition to the sum assured or the amount of annuity declared before the date of the winding-up order) and for this purpose 'option' includes a right to surrender the policy.

(2) The present value of the ordinary benefits shall be the value at the date of the winding-up order of the reversion in the ordinary benefits according to the contingency

upon which those benefits are payable calculated on the basis of the rates of interest, mortality and disability referred to in paragraph 1.

Reserve for options

3. The amount of the reserve for options shall be the amount which, in the opinion of the liquidator, arrived at on appropriate assumptions in regard to all relevant factors, is necessary to be provided at the date of the winding-up order (in addition to the amount of the present value of the ordinary benefits) to cover the additional liabilities likely to arise upon the exercise on or after that date by the policy holder of any option conferred upon him by the terms of the policy or, in the case of an industrial assurance policy, by the Industrial Assurance Acts other than an option whereby the policy holder can secure a guaranteed cash payment within the period of 12 months beginning with that date.

Reserve for expenses

4.—(1) The amount of the reserve for expenses is the amount which, in the opinion of the liquidator, is necessary to be provided at the date of the winding-up order for meeting future expenses.

(2) In this paragraph 'future expenses' means such part of the expenses likely to be incurred after that date in the fulfilling by the liquidator or by any transferee from the liquidator of the company's long term business of the obligations of that business as is appropriate to the policy and which cannot be met out of the amounts (if any) by which the actual premiums payable under that policy after that date exceed the amounts of the modified net premiums which correspond to those actual premiums.

Net premiums

5.—(1) For the purpose of determining the present value of the modified net premiums a net premium shall be determined in relation to each actual premium paid or payable under the policy in such a way that:—

(*a*) the net premiums, if they had been payable when the corresponding actual premiums were or are payable, would, on the basis of the rates of interest, mortality and disability referred to in paragraph 1, have been sufficient when the policy was issued to provide for the benefits under the policy according to the contingencies on which they are payable, exclusive of any addition for profits, expenses or other charges, and

(*b*) the ratio between the amounts of any two net premiums is the same as the ratio between the amounts of the two actual premiums to which they correspond (any actual premium which includes a loading for unusual risks assumed by the company in respect of part only of the term of the policy being treated for this purpose as if it did not include that loading).

(2) For the purposes of this paragraph, where at any time after the policy was issued the terms of the policy have been varied (otherwise than by the surrender of the policy in consideration of the issue of a new policy), it shall be assumed that the policy when it was issued provided for those variations to take effect at the time when they did in fact take effect.

Modified net premiums

6.—(1) A modified net premium shall be determined in relation to each net premium by making an addition to each net premium such that:—

(*a*) the additions, if each was payable when the corresponding actual premium was or is payable, would, on the basis of the rates of interest, mortality and disability referred to in paragraph 1, have been sufficient to compensate for the acquisition expenses relating to the policy, and (*b*) the ratio between the amounts of any two modified net premiums is the same as the ratio between the amounts of the two net premiums to which they correspond.

(2) For this purpose the acquisition expenses relating to the policy shall be taken to be 3.5 per cent (or the defined percentage if it be lower than 3.5 per cent) of the relevant capital sum under the contract and for this purpose:—

(*a*) 'the defined percentage' is the percentage arrived at by taking (for all policies which in the opinion of the liquidator have the same or similar characteristics to the policy in question, and which he considers appropriate to be taken notice of for this purpose), the average of the percentages of the relevant capital sums under those policies that represent the acquisition expenses for which, after allowing for the effects of taxation, allowance is made in the premiums actually payable; and

(*b*) 'the relevant capital sum' in relation to any policy is:—

(i) for whole life assurances, the sum assured,

(ii) for policies where a sum is payable on maturity (including policies where a sum is also payable on earlier death), the sum payable on maturity,

(iii) for temporary assurances, the sum assured on the date of the winding-up order,

(iv) for deferred annuity policies, the capitalised value on the date on which the first payment is due to be made of the payments due to be made under the policy calculated on the basis of the rates of interest, mortality and disability referred to in paragraph 1 or, if the terms of the policy include a right on the part of the policy holder to surrender the policy on that date for a cash payment greater than the said capitalised value, the amount of that cash payment, and

(v) for capital redemption policies, the sum payable at the end of the contract period.

(3) Where the amount of a modified net premium calculated in accordance with sub-paragraphs (1) and (2) is greater than the amount of the actual premium to which it corresponds then the amount of that modified net premium shall be the amount of that actual premium and not the amount calculated in accordance with sub-paragraphs (1) and (2).

Present value of the modified net premiums

7. The present value of the modified net premiums shall be the value as at the date of the winding-up order, calculated on the basis of the rates of interest, mortality and disability referred to in paragraph 1, of the modified net premiums payable after that date on the assumption that they are payable as and when the corresponding actual premiums are payable.

Value of the policy

8.—(1) Subject to sub-paragraph (2):—

(*a*) if no further fixed premiums fall due to be paid under the policy on or after the date of the winding-up order, the value of the policy shall be the aggregate of:—

(i) the present value of the ordinary benefits,

(ii) the reserve for options,

(iii) the reserve for expenses, and

(iv) where under the terms of the policy or on the basis of the company's established practice the policy holder has a right to receive or an expectation of receiving benefits additional to the ordinary benefits, such amount (if any) as the court may determine to reflect that right or expectation in respect of the period ending with the date of the winding-up order;

(*b*) if further fixed premiums fall due to be so paid and the aggregate value referred to in sub-paragraph (*a*) exceeds the present value of the modified net premiums, the value of the policy shall be the amount of that excess; and

(*c*) if further fixed premiums fall due to be so paid and that aggregate does not exceed the present value of the modified net premiums, the policy shall have no value.

(2) Where the policy holder has a right conferred upon him by the terms of the policy or by the Industrial Assurance Acts whereby the policy holder can secure a guaranteed cash payment within the period of 12 months beginning with the date of the winding-up order, the liquidator shall determine the amount which in his opinion it is necessary to provide at that date to cover the liabilities which will accrue when that option is exercised (on the assumption that it will be exercised) and the value of the policy shall be that amount if it exceeds the value of the policy (if any) determined in accordance with sub-paragraph (1).

SCHEDULE 3

Rules for valuing life policies and deferred annuity policies which are linked policies

1.—(1) Subject to sub-paragraph (2) the value of the policy shall be the aggregate of the value of the linked liabilities (calculated in accordance with paragraph 2 or 4) and the value of other than linked liabilities (calculated in accordance with paragraph 5) except where that aggregate is a negative amount in which case the policy shall have no value.

(2) Where the terms of the policy include a right whereby the policy holder can secure a guaranteed cash payment within the period of 12 months beginning with the date of the winding-up order then, if the amount which in the opinion of the liquidator is necessary to be provided at that date to cover any liabilities which will accrue when that option is exercised (on the assumption that it will be exercised) is greater than the value determined under sub-paragraph (1) of this paragraph, the value of the policy shall be that greater amount.

2.—(1) Where the linked liabilities are expressed in terms of units the value of those liabilities shall, subject to paragraph 3, be the amount arrived at by taking the product of the number of units of each class of units allocated to the policy on the date of the winding-up order and the value of each such unit on that date and then adding those products.

(2) For the purposes of sub-paragraph (1):—

(i) where under the terms of the policy the value of a unit at any time falls to be determined by reference to the value at that time of the assets of a particular fund maintained by the company in relation to that and other policies, the value of a unit on the date of the winding-up order shall be determined by reference to the net realisable value of the assets credited to that fund on that date (after taking account of disposal costs, any tax liabilities resulting from the disposal of assets in so far as they have not already been provided for by the company and any other amounts which under the terms of those policies are chargeable to the fund), and

(ii) in any other case, the value of a unit on the date of the winding-up order shall be the value which would have been ascribed to each unit credited to the policy holder, after any deductions which may be made under the terms of the policy, for the purpose of determining the benefits payable under the policy on the date of the winding-up order had the policy matured on that date.

3.—(1) This paragraph applies where—

(*a*) paragraph 2(2)(i) applies and the company has a right under the terms of the policy either to make periodic withdrawals from the fund referred to in that paragraph or to retain any part of the income accruing in respect of the assets of that fund, or

(*b*) paragraph 2(2)(ii) applies and the company has a right under the terms of the policy to receive the whole or any part of any distributions made in respect of the units referred to in that paragraph, or

(*c*) paragraph 2(2)(i) or paragraph 2(2)(ii) applies and the company has a right under the terms of the policy to make periodic cancellations of a proportion of the number of units credited to the policy.

(2) Where this paragraph applies the value of the linked liabilities calculated in accordance with paragraph 2(1) shall be reduced by an amount calculated in accordance with sub-paragraph (3) of this paragraph.

(3) The said amount is—

(*a*) where this paragraph applies by virtue of head (*a*) or (*b*) of sub-paragraph (1), the value as at the date of the winding up order, calculated on actuarial principles, of the future income of the company in respect of the units in question arising from the rights referred to in head (*a*) or (*b*) of sub-paragraph (1) as the case may be, or

(*b*) where this paragraph applies by virtue of head (*c*) of sub-paragraph (1), the value as at the date of the winding up order, calculated on actuarial principles, of the liabilities of the company in respect of the units which fall to be cancelled in the future under the right referred to in head (*c*) of sub-paragraph (1).

(4) In calculating any amount in accordance with sub-paragraph (3) there shall be disregarded:—

(*a*) such part of the rights referred to in the relevant head of sub-paragraph (1) which in the opinion of the liquidator constitutes provision for future expenses and mortality risks, and

(*b*) such part of those rights (if any) which the court considers to constitute appropriate provision for any right or expectation of the policyholder to receive benefits additional to the benefits guaranteed under the terms of the policy.

(5) In determining the said amount:—

(*a*) interest shall be assumed at such rate or rates as the court may direct, and

(*b*) where relevant the rates of mortality and the rates of disability to be employed shall be such rates as the court may consider appropriate after taking into account:—

(i) relevant published tables of rates of mortality and rates of disability, and

(ii) the rates of mortality and the rates of disability experienced in connection with similar policies issued by the company,

4. Where the linked liabilities are not expressed in terms of units the value of those liabilities shall be the value which would have been ascribed to those liabilities had the policy matured on the date of the winding-up order.

5.—(1) The value of any liabilities other than linked liabilities including reserves for future expenses, options and guarantees shall be determined on actuarial principles and appropriate assumptions in regard to all relevant factors including the assumption of such rate or rates of interest, mortality and disability as the court may direct.

(2) In valuing liabilities under this paragraph credit shall be taken for those parts of future premiums which do not fall to be applied in the allocation of further units to the policy and for any rights of the company which have been disregarded under paragraph 3(4)(*a*) in valuing the linked liabilities.

SCHEDULE 4

Rules for valuing long term policies which are not dealt with in Schedules 2 and 3

The value of a long term policy not covered by Schedule 2 or 3 shall be determined on such actuarial principles and assumptions in regard to all relevant factors as the court shall determine.

SCHEDULE 5

Rules for valuing long term policies where a stop order has been made

1. Subject to paragraphs 2 and 3, in valuing a policy Schedules 2, 3 or 4 shall apply according to the class of that policy as if those Schedules were herein repeated but with a view to a fresh valuation of each policy on appropriate assumptions in regard to all relevant factors and subject to the following modifications:—

(*a*) references to the stop order shall be substituted for references to the winding-up order,

(*b*) in paragraph 3 of Schedule 2 for the words 'whereby the policy holder can secure a guaranteed cash payment within the period of 12 months beginning with that date' there shall be substituted the words 'to surrender the policy which can be exercised on that date',

(*c*) in paragraph 4(2) of Schedule 2 for the words 'likely to be incurred' there shall be substituted the words 'which were likely to have been incurred' and for the words 'cannot be met' there shall be substituted the words 'could not have been met'.

(*d*) paragraph 8(2) of Schedule 2 shall be deleted, and

(*e*) paragraph 1(2) of Schedule 3 shall be deleted.

2.—(1) This paragraph applies where the policy holder has a right conferred upon him under the terms of the policy or by the Industrial Assurance Acts to surrender the policy and that right is exercisable on the date of the stop order.

(2) Where this paragraph applies and the amount required at the date of the stop order to provide for the benefits payable upon surrender of the policy on the assumption that the policy is surrendered on the date of the stop order is greater than the value of the policy determined in accordance with paragraph 1 the value of the policy shall, subject to paragraph 3, be the said amount so required.

(3) Where any part of the surrender value is payable after the date of the stop order sub-paragraph (2) shall apply but the value therein referred to shall be discounted at such rate of interest as the court may direct.

3.—(1) This paragraph applies in the case of a linked policy where:—

(*a*) the terms of the policy include a guarantee that the amount assured will on maturity of the policy be worth a minimum amount calculable in money terms, or

(*b*) the terms of the policy include a right on the part of the policy holder to surrender the policy and a guarantee that the payment on surrender will be worth a minimum amount calculable in money terms and that right is exercisable on or after the date of the stop order.

(2) Where this paragraph applies the value of the policy shall be the greater of the following two amounts:—

(*a*) the value the policy would have had at the date of the stop order had the policy been a non-linked policy, that is to say, had the linked liabilities provided by the policy not been so provided but the policy had otherwise been on the same terms, and

(*b*) the value the policy would have had at the date of the stop order had the policy not included any guarantees of payments on maturity or surrender worth a minimum amount calculable in money terms.

SCHEDULE 6

Form No. 1

NOTICE OF MEETING OF LONG TERM BUSINESS CREDITORS

(Title)

Take notice that a meeting of creditors of the company's long term business will be held at on the day of 19 , at o'clock in the noon.

For the purpose of voting at this meeting [your claim has been valued at £ . .] [your policy has been valued at £ . .]

NOTE: The valuation of your policy is for the purpose of voting only and a different value may be attributed to your policy for other purposes.

Agenda

[Here insert purpose for which meeting is called]

Dated this day of 19 .

(Signed) [*'Liquidator' or 'Official Receiver'*]

Forms of general and special proxies are enclosed herewith. Proxies to be used at the meeting must be lodged with at , in the County of , not later than o'clock on the day of 19 .

Form No. 2

NOTIFICATION TO OFFICIAL RECEIVER OF ORDER PRONOUNCED UNDER SECTION 56(2) OF THE INSURANCE COMPANIES ACT 1982

(Title)

To the Official Receiver of the Court

(Address)

Order pronounced this day by the Honourable Mr Justice [*or, as the case may be*] that the Liquidator of [*insert name of company*] shall not carry on the long term business of the company.

Form No 3

NOTICE FOR LONDON GAZETTE

NOTICE OF ORDER PRONOUNCED UNDER SECTION 56(2) OF THE INSURANCE COMPANIES ACT 1982 FOR CESSATION OF LONG TERM BUSINESS

Name of Company Address of Registered Office

Court Number of Matter Date of Order

Date of Winding-up Order

Form No. 4

NOTICE FOR NEWSPAPER

NOTICE OF ORDER PRONOUNCED UNDER SECTION 56(2) OF THE INSURANCE COMPANIES ACT 1982 FOR CESSATION OF LONG TERM BUSINESS

Name of Company

Date of Winding-up Order

Date of Order

Official Receiver.

(B) LLOYD'S

INSURANCE (LLOYD'S) REGULATIONS 1983

(SI 1983/224)

Citation, commencement and revocation

1.—(1) These Regulations may be cited as the Insurance (Lloyd's) Regulations 1983 and shall come into operation on 22nd March 1983.

(2) The Assurance Companies Rules 1950, the Lloyd's (Financial Resources) Regulations 1981 and the Lloyd's (Audit Certificate) Regulations 1982 are hereby revoked.

Interpretation

2.—(1) In these Regulations—

'the Act' means the Insurance Companies Act 1982;

'minimum guarantee fund' means the amount determined under regulation 9(2) of the Insurance Companies Regulations 1981 for the purposes of section 33 of the Act;

'reinsurance' includes both reinsurance ceded and reinsurance retroceded;

'required margin of solvency' has the same meaning as in Part II of the Insurance Companies Regulations 1981;

'required minimum margin' means the greater of the required margin of solvency and the minimum guarantee fund,

and references to a numbered form are references to the Form so numbered in Schedule 3 below.

(2) Regulation 2(2) of the Insurance Companies Regulations 1981 shall have effect for the purposes of these Regulations as it has effect for the purposes of those Regulations and 'ECU' shall be construed accordingly.

Financial resources

3.—(1) In the application to the members of Lloyd's taken together of sections 32 and 33 of the Act (which relate to margins of solvency) and of regulations made for the purposes of those sections—

(*a*) no valuation regulations (other than regulation 53 of, and Schedule 9 to, the Insurance Companies Regulations 1981 and which relate to co-insurance) shall be applicable; and

(*b*) the following items shall have no value except in pursuance of a determination made by the Secretary of State pursuant to section 84(1) of the Act, that is to say,—

(i) those relating to future profits;

(ii) those relating to zillmerising, that is to say the method known by that name for modifying the net premium reserve method of valuing a long term policy by increasing the part of the future premiums for which credit is taken so as to allow for initial expenses; and

(iii) those relating to hidden reserves resulting from the under-estimation of assets and the over-estimation of liabilities (other than mathematical reserves),

and accordingly, in the definition of 'relevant company' in paragraph (2) of the said regulation 53, the words 'or a member of Lloyd's' shall be omitted.

(2) In arriving at the margin of solvency to be maintained pursuant to sections 32 and 33 of the Act by the members of Lloyd's taken together—

(*a*) account shall be taken of the assets and liabilities of Lloyd's in addition to the assets and liabilities of the members; and

(*b*) Schedules 1 and 2 to the Insurance Companies Regulations 1981 (which relate to general business margins of solvency) shall be modified in the manner set out in Schedule 1 below.

(3) In the application to the members of Lloyd's taken together of section 35 of the Act (form and situation of assets) and of regulations made for the purposes of that section, all insurance business carried on by members of Lloyd's as such members shall be treated as carried on in the United Kingdom except business carried on in accordance with an authority or permission under the laws of another country and included in a return to a supervisory authority in that country.

Audit

4.—(1) The certificate mentioned in section 83(4) of the Act (which requires the accounts of every underwriting member of Lloyd's to be audited annually by an accountant approved by the Council of Lloyd's) shall, in relation to the twelve months ending on 31st December in the year 1982 and in each subsequent year, be in the form set out in Schedule 2 below.

(2) A person performing the functions of an actuary for the purpose of section 83 of the Act shall be a Fellow of the Institute of Actuaries or a Fellow of the Faculty of Actuaries and shall have attained the age of thirty years.

Statement of business

5.—(1) Subject to the provisions of this regulation, the statement mentioned in section 86(1) of the Act (being the statement in respect of the twelve months ending on 31st December in the year 1982 or in any subsequent year) shall be in the form set out in Schedule 3 below to which shall be annexed forms (as set out in that Schedule) containing the information therein specified except, in the case of Forms 6 and 8, information relating to long term business at any date before 1st January 1984.

(2) Form 1 (three-year revenue accounts) shall show the information therein specified—

(*a*) for each of the accounting classes for general business specified in paragraph (3) below;

(*b*) for long term business; and

(*c*) for all insurance business.

(3) The accounting classes for general business referred to in paragraph (2)(*a*) above are set out in column 1 of the following table and consist in each case of the corresponding class or classes of general business referred to in column 2 of that table.

Column 1 *Accounting Class*	Column 2 *Corresponding classes of general business*
1. Accident and health	1 and 2
2. Motor vehicle (including damage to other land vehicles), damage and liability	3 and 10
3. Aircraft, damage and liability	5 and 11
4. Ships, damage and liability	6 and 12
5. Goods in transit	7
6. Property damage	4, 8 and 9
7. General liability	13
8. Pecuniary loss	14, 15, 16 and 17

SCHEDULE 1

(Regulation 3(2)(*b*))

MODIFICATIONS OF SCHEDULES 1 AND 2 TO THE INSURANCE COMPANIES REGULATIONS 1981

1. *(amends Insurance Companies Regulations 1981, Sch 1, para 1).*

2. *(amends Insurance Companies Regulations 1981, Sch 1, para 2).*

3. *(amends Insurance Companies Regulations 1981, Sch 1, para 3).*

4. Paragraphs 7 to 9 of the said Schedule 1 shall not apply; and in paragraph 15 of the said Schedule 1 the references to paragraph 7 of that Schedule shall be disregarded.

5. Paragraphs 7 to 9 of Schedule 2 to the Insurance Companies Regulations 1981 shall not apply; and in paragraph 10 of the said Schedule 2 the references to paragraph 7 of that Schedule shall be disregarded.

SCHEDULE 2

(Regulation 4(1))

AUDIT CERTIFICATE

UNDERWRITING ACCOUNTS IN THE NAMES OF

Through the Agency of

To the Council of Lloyd's and to the Secretary of State

INSURANCE COMPANIES ACT 1982

We have examined the accounts relating to the insurance business carried on by the above-mentioned underwriting members through the above-named Agency during the year ended 31st December 19 , in accordance with the current Instructions for the guidance of Lloyd's auditors drawn up by the Council of Lloyd's and approved by the Secretary of State.

In connection with our examination, we have relied upon a report in respect of the underwriting accounts from accountants approved by the Council of Lloyd's acting as auditors of each syndicate in which each underwriting member has participated during that year stating that in their opinion all assets have been valued and all liabilities have been calculated in accordance with the said Instructions (liabilities in respect of long term business having been calculated by an actuary) and that the profits or losses arising on the closed accounts and the surpluses or deficiencies arising on the open accounts have been allocated to each underwriting member in accordance with the arrangements for his participation in each such account.

In our opinion, the value of the assets, valued in accordance with the said Instructions (in the case of each underwriting member's Lloyd's Deposit, as certified by the Council of Lloyd's), available to meet each underwriting member's liabilities, calculated in accordance with the said Instructions, in respect of his insurance business is correctly shown in the accounts and is sufficient to meet his liabilities in respect of that business.

Dated this day of 19 .

Accountants approved by the
Council of Lloyd's.

SCHEDULE 3

(Regulation 5)

STATEMENT OF BUSINESS BY COUNCIL OF LLOYD'S
pursuant to Section 86(1) of the Insurance Companies Act 1982

19 , 19 , 19 years of account

The information set out in the annexed forms relates to insurance business transacted—

by [insert number] underwriting members of Lloyd's in the
19 year of account,

by [insert number] underwriting members of Lloyd's in the
19 year of account,

by [insert number] underwriting members of Lloyd's in the
19 year of account,

We certify that

1. The information set out in the annexed forms has been properly prepared in accordance with information received by the Council of Lloyd's.

2. In accordance with the requirements of the Insurance Companies Act 1982 all liabilities attaching to such insurance business have been calculated,—

(*a*) in the case of long term business, by an actuary, and

(*b*) in the case of general business, on a basis approved by the Secretary of State.

3. A certificate complying with subsection (5) of section 83 of the Insurance Companies Act 1982 has been furnished to the Council of Lloyd's and the Secretary of State pursuant to subsection (4) of that section in respect of every underwriting member of Lloyd's.

4. In respect of the business to which regulations 25 and 26 of the Insurance Companies Regulations 1981 (matching and localisation) apply, the assets held by Lloyd's and by or in trust for the underwriting members of Lloyd's enabled the members of Lloyd's taken together at 31 December 19 to comply with those Regulations (having effect as modified by regulation 3(3) of the Insurance (Lloyd's) Regulations 1983).

5. A report by an accountant approved by the Council of Lloyd's has been furnished to the Council in respect of every member of Lloyd's that he has complied with

regulation 53 (which relates to co-insurance) of the Insurance Companies Regulations 1981 (as amended by regulation 3(1) of the Insurance (Lloyd's) Regulations 1983).

Dated 19 . Chairman of Lloyd's

Deputy Chairman of Lloyd's

Secretary General of Lloyd's

FORM 1 – THREE YEAR REVENUE ACCOUNTS TO 31 DECEMBER 19. . . .

INSURANCE BUSINESS TRANSACTED BY UNDERWRITING MEMBERS OF LLOYD'S

GENERAL BUSINESS ACCOUNTING CLASS (insert description)/LONG TERM BUSINESS/ALL BUSINESS

		Business transacted for the 19........ account				Business transacted for the 19......account			Business transacted for the 19....... account	Income and expenditure in 19...... (ie the financial year)
		Income and expenditure in 19......(ie the second year preceding the financial year)	Income and expenditure in 19......(ie the first year preceding the financial year)	Income and expenditure in 19......(ie the financial year)	Total of columns 1,2 and 3	Income and expenditure in 19......(ie the first year preceding the financial year)	Income and expenditure in 19......(ie the financial year)	Total of columns 5 and 6	Income and expenditure in 19..... (ie the financial year)	Total of columns 3, 6 and 8
		1	2	3	4	5	6	7	8	9
INCOME		£000	£000	£000	£000	£000	£000	£000	£000	£000
Balance brought forward	1								–	
Reinsurance premiums received and amounts placed to reserve in repect of estimated liabilities from previous accounts	2									
Premiums (*net* of brokerage, discount, commission, refunds, rebates, taxes, levies and premiums for reinsurance ceded)	3									
Net income on syndicate funds	4									
Other income (particulars to be specified)	5									
Loss	6									
Total (1 to 6)	7									
EXPENDITURE										
Reinsurance premiums paid and amounts placed to reserve in respect of estimated liabilities at close of account	8	–	–			–	–	–	–	
Claims, including all expenses directly incurred in settling claims, less refunds and reinsurance recoveries	9									
Expenses of management	10									
Other expenditure (particulars to be specified)	11									
Balance carried forward	12									
Profit	13	–	–			–	–	–	–	
Total (8 to 13)	14									

FORM 2 – REVENUE ACCOUNTS FOR THE YEAR ENDED 31 DECEMBER 19 ....

INSURANCE BUSINESS TRANSACTED BY UNDERWRITING MEMBERS OF LLOYD'S

		GENERAL BUSINESS ACCOUNTING CLASS								GENERAL BUSINESS Total	LONG TERM BUSINESS	ALL BUSINESS Total
		Accident and health	Motor vehicle damage and liability	Aircraft damage and liability	Ships damage and liability	Goods in transit	Property damage	General liability	Pecuniary loss			
		1	2	3	4	5	6	7	8	9	10	11
INCOME		£000	£000	£000	£000	£000	£000	£000	£000	£000	£000	£000
Balance brought forward	1											
Reinsurance premiums received and amounts placed to reserve in respect of estimated liabilities from previous accounts	2											
Premiums (*net* of brokerage, discount, commission, refunds, rebates, taxes, levies and premiums for reinsurance ceded)	3											
Net income on syndicate funds	4											
Other income (particulars to be specified)	5											
Loss	6											
Total (1 to 6)	7											
EXPENDITURE												
Reinsurance premiums paid and amounts placed to reserve in respect of estimated liabilities at close of account	8											
Claims, including all expenses directly incurred in settling claims, less refunds and reinsurance recoveries	9											
Expenses of management	10											
Other expenditure (particulars to be specified)	11											
Balance carried forward	12											
Profit	13											
Total (8 to 13)	14											

The entries in columns 1 to 8 and 10 are to be the same as entries in column 9 of Form 1 relating to the corresponding kind of business

FORM 3 – PREMIUM ANALYSIS FOR THE YEAR ENDED 31 DECEMBER 19 . . . . . .

INSURANCE BUSINESS TRANSACTED BY UNDERWRITING MEMBERS OF LLOYD'S

PREMIUMS (gross of reinsurance ceded)		GENERAL BUSINESS ACCOUNTING CLASS								GENERAL BUSINESS	LONG TERM BUSINESS	ALL BUSINESS
		Accident and health	Motor vehicle damage and liability	Aircraft damage and liability	Ships damage and liability	Goods in transit	Property damage	General liability	Pecuniary loss	Total		Total
		1	2	3	4	5	6	7	8	9	10	11
		£000	£000	£000	£000	£000	£000	£000	£000	£000	£000	£000
UK direct and facultative business	1											
UK reinsurance business other than facultative business	2											
Overseas direct and facultative business	3											
Overseas reinsurance business other than facultative business	4											
Treaty reinsurance business in which UK and overseas components cannot be distinguished	5											
Total (1 to 5)	6											

Premiums are net of brokerage, discount, commission, refunds, rebates, taxes and levies.

FORM 4 – ANALYSIS OF GENERAL BUSINESS PREMIUMS RECEIVABLE BY UNDERWRITING MEMBERS OF LLOYD'S THROUGH PARTICIPATION IN COMMUNITY CO–INSURANCE OPERATIONS IN THE YEAR ENDED 31 DECEMBER 19 . . . . . .

COUNTRY OF RISK		Premiums receivable (less rebates and refunds) on Community co-insurance operations					
		Aircraft (accounting class 3)	Ships (accounting class 4) and Goods in transit) (accounting class 5) (see note 2)	Property damage (accounting class 6) (see note 2)	General liability (accounting class 7)	Pecuniary loss (accounting class 8)	Total (1 + 2 + 3 + 4 + 5)
		1	2	3	4	5	6
		£000	£000	£000	£000	£000	£000
	1						
	2						
	3						
	4						
	5						
	6						
	7						
	8						
	9						
	10						
	11						
	12						
	13						
Total (all lines)	14						

Notes:

1 The figures in this form relate only to participation in Community co-insurance operations from the United Kingdom where the risk is situated in another member State.

2 Any business of accounting class 6 which consists of the insurance of railway rolling stock will be included in column 2 and not column 3.

FORM 5 – SUMMARY AND VALUATION AS AT 31 DECEMBER 19. . . . . OF POLICIES ISSUED BY UNDERWRITING MEMBERS OF LLOYD'S IN THE COURSE OF CARRYING ON LONG TERM INSURANCE BUSINESS

TYPE OF INSURANCE		Number of contracts	Amount of sums assured	Amount of annual premiums	Value of sums assured	Value of future annual premiums	Amount of mathematical reserves
		1	2	3	4	5	6
			£000	£000	£000	£000	£000
Direct Business and Reinsurance accepted							
Term assurance							
(i) by single premium	1						
(ii) by annual premium	2						
Group life assurance	3						
Other reserves	4	–					
Total (1 + 2 + 3 + 4)	5	–					
Reinsurance ceded							
Term assurance							
(i) by single premium	6						
(ii) by annual premium	7						
Group life assurance	8						
Total (6 + 7 + 8)	9	–					
Net amount of insurance (5 – 9)	10	–					
Adjustments, if any (to be separately identified)	11	–					
Total of the results (10 + 11)	12	–					

FORM 6 – STATEMENT OF SOLVENCY OF UNDERWRITING MEMBERS OF LLOYD'S

		As at 31 December 19 . . . . £000	As at 31 December 19 . . . . (the preceding year) £000
GENERAL BUSINESS			
Amount of the required minimum margin (Form 7, line 43)	1		
Net assets available within General Business Underwriting Accounts to meet the required minimum margin (Form 9, line 6)	2		
Other assets treated as available to meet the required minimum margin (Note 1)	3		
Implicit items (Note 2)	4		
Total of assets available to meet the required minimum margin (lines 2 + 3 + 4)	5		
LONG TERM BUSINESS			
Amount of the required minimum margin (Form 8, line 14)	6		
Net assets available within Long Term Business Underwriting Accounts to meet the required minimum margin (Form 9, line 12)	7		
Other assets treated as available to meet the required minimum margin (Note 1)	8		
Implicit items (Note 2)	9		
Total of assets available to meet the required minimum margin (lines 7 + 8 + 9)	10		

Notes: 1 Line 3 plus line 8 are to equal Form 9 line 16

2 No amount shall be shown in line 4 or line 9 (implicit items) except in accordance with a determination by the Secretary of State under the Insurance (Lloyd's) Regulations 1983.

FORM 7 (sheet 1) – CALCULATION OF REQUIRED MINIMUM MARGIN FOR GENERAL BUSINESS CARRIED ON BY UNDERWRITING MEMBERS OF LLOYD'S

FIRST METHOD			Year ended 31 December 19.. £000	The preceding year £000
Premiums receivable, including premiums receivable under reinsurance contracts accepted (gross of reinsurance ceded, but net of commissions payable, discounts, refunds, rebates, taxes and levies)		1		
Percentage determined by Secretary of State in accordance with paragraph 2 of Schedule 1 to the Insurance (Lloyd's) Regulations 1983	Latest year / Preceding year	2	–	–
SUB-TOTAL A (1 multiplied by percentage at 2)		3		
Adjusted SUB-TOTAL A (if financial year is not a 12 month period) to produce an annual figure		4		
Division of sub-total A (or adjusted sub-total A if appropriate)	Up to and including sterling equivalent of 10 million ECU x 18/100	5		
	Excess (if any) over 10 million ECU x 16/100	6		
SUB-TOTAL B (5 + 6)		7		
Claims paid (gross of reinsurance recoverable)		8		
Outstanding claims (gross of anticipated reinsurance recoveries) carried forward at the end of the financial year	For business not accounted for on a one-year basis	9		
	For business accounted for on a one-year basis	10		
Outstanding claims (gross of anticipated reinsurance recoveries) brought forward at the beginning of the financial year	For business not accounted for on a one-year basis	11		
	For business accounted for on a one-year basis	12		
SUB-TOTAL C (8 + 9 + 10 – (11 + 12))		13		
Amounts recoverable from reinsurers in respect of claims included in Sub-total C		14		
SUB-TOTAL D (13 – 14)		15		
FIRST RESULT Sub-total B x $\frac{\text{Sub-total D}}{\text{Sub-total C}}$ (or, if ½ is greater fraction, x ½)		16		

Line 1 equals Form 3, line 6, column 9.

FORM 7 (sheet 2) – CALCULATION OF REQUIRED MINIMUM MARGIN FOR GENERAL BUSINESS CARRIED ON BY UNDERWRITING MEMBERS OF LLOYD'S

SECOND METHOD			Year ended 31 December 19... £000	The preceding year £000
Reference period (no. of financial years)	Insert "3" or "7" here	21	–	–
Claims paid in reference period (gross of reinsurance recoverable)		22		
Outstanding claims (gross of anticipated reinsurance recoveries) carried forward at the end of the reference period	For business not accounted for on a one-year basis	23		
	For business accounted for on a one-year basis	24		
Outstanding claims (gross of anticipated reinsurance recoveries) brought forward at the beginning of the reference period	For business not accounted for on a one-year basis	25		
	For business accounted for on a one-year basis	26		
SUB-TOTAL E (22 + 23 +24 - (25 + 26))		27		
SUB-TOTAL F Conversion of Sub-total E to annual figure (Multiply by 12 and divide by number of months in reference period)		28		
Division of Sub-total F	Up to and including sterling equivalent of 7 million ECU x 26/100	29		
	Excess (if any) over 7 million ECU x 23/100	30		
SUB-TOTAL G (29 + 30)		31		
SECOND RESULT Sub-total G x $\frac{\text{Sub-total D}}{\text{Sub-total C}}$ (or, if ½ is a greater fraction, x ½)		32		

SUMMARY			
REQUIRED MARGIN OF SOLVENCY (the higher of lines 16 and 32)	41		
MINIMUM GUARANTEE FUND	42		
REQUIRED MINIMUM MARGIN (the higher of lines 41 and 42)	43		

FORM 8 CALCULATION OF REQUIRED MINIMUM MARGIN FOR LONG TERM BUSINESS CARRIED ON BY UNDERWRITING MEMBERS OF LLOYD'S

		As at 31 December 19 ... £000	As at 31 December 19 ... (the preceding year) £000
Mathematical reserves before deduction for reinsurance	1		
Mathematical reserves after deduction for reinsurance	2		
Ratio of line 2 to line 1, or 0.85 if greater	3		
FIRST RESULT = line 1 x line 3 x 0.04	4		
Non-negative capital at risk before reinsurance (a) Temporary assurance with solvency margin of 0.001	5		
(b) Temporary assurances with solvency margin of 0.0015	6		
(c) Temporary assurance with solvency margin of 0.003	7		
Total (lines 5 + 6 + 7)	8		
Non-negative capital at risk after reinsurance (all contracts)	9		
Ratio of line 9 to line 8 or 0.50 if greater	10		
SECOND RESULT = (0.001 x line 5 + 0.0015 x line 6 + 0.003 x line 7) x line 10	11		

SUMMARY

REQUIRED MARGIN OF SOLVENCY (line 4 + line 11)	12		
MINIMUM GUARANTEE FUND	13		
REQUIRED MINIMUM MARGIN (greater of lines 12 and 13)	14		

FORM 9 – CONSOLIDATED STATEMENT OF ASSETS AND LIABILITIES OF UNDERWRITING MEMBERS OF LLOYD'S

		As at 31 December 19 . . . . £000	As at 31 December 19 . . . . (the preceding year) £000
UNDERWRITING ACCOUNTS (GENERAL BUSINESS) Assets held in premium trust funds plus amounts due from Lloyd's brokers (Note 1)	1		
Provision for estimated future liabilities	2		
Sub-total (1 - 2)	3		
Lloyd's Deposits (general business) (Note 2)	4		
Lloyd's Special Reserve Funds (excluding any amount shown at line 11) (Note 3)	5		
Total (3 + 4 + 5)	6		
UNDERWRITING ACCOUNTS (LONG TERM BUSINESS) Assets held in premium trust funds plus amounts due from Lloyd's brokers (Note 1)	7		
Provision for estimated future liabilities	8		
Sub-total (7 - 8)	9		
Lloyd's Deposits (long-term business) (Note 2)	10		
Lloyd's Special Reserve Funds applied to long term business (Note 3)	11		
Total (9 + 10 + 11)	12		
OTHER ASSETS Underwriting members' qualifying assets (Note 4)	13		
Lloyd's Central Fund (Note 5)	14		
Corporation of Lloyd's: total net assets (Note 6)	15		
Total (13 + 14 + 15)	16		
GRAND TOTAL (6 + 12 + 16)	17		

Notes

1. A premium trust fund is a fund to which, in accordance with the provisions of a trust deed approved by the Secretary of State under section 83(2) of the Insurance Companies Act 1982, are carried all premiums received by, or on behalf of an underwriting member in respect of any insurance business.

2. A Lloyd's Deposit is a deposit made by an underwriting member and held in trust by Lloyd's by way of security for the member's underwriting obligations.

3. A Lloyd's Special Reserve Fund is a fund maintained under arrangements to which Schedule 10 to the Income and Corporation Taxes Act 1970 applies.

4. Underwriting members' qualifying assets have been assessed by reference to the Lloyd's means test applicable to individual members' level of underwriting.

5. The Lloyd's Central Fund is a fund to which underwriting members contribute and which is held on trust by Lloyd's to be applied in or towards paying and making good or purchasing such of the claims and returns on contracts of insurance and guarantee underwritten by members of Lloyd's in respect of which they have been declared by the Council of Lloyd's to have made default.

6. The total net assets of the Corporation of Lloyd's are as shown by the audited accounts of the Corporation.

FORM 10 – ANALYSIS OF ASSETS REPRESENTING THE LLOYD'S DEPOSITS AND SPECIAL RESERVE FUNDS OF UNDERWRITING MEMBERS OF LLOYD'S

				As at 31 December 19 ...... £000	As at 31 December 19 .... (the preceding year) £000
Fixed interest irredeemable investments	Issued or guaranteed by a British Government authority		1		
	Issued or guaranteed by a Government or public authority or local authority not being a British Government authority		2		
	Others	Listed	3		
		Unlisted	4		
Fixed interest redeemable investments (other than those redeemable within one year after the end of the financial year)	Issued or guaranteed by a British Government authority		5		
	Issued or guaranteed by a Government or public authority or local authority not being a British Government authority		6		
	Others	Listed	7		
		Unlisted	8		
Variable interest investments (other than those redeemable within one year after the end of the financial year)	Listed		9		
	Unlisted		10		
Investment mortgages and loans which must be redeemed within one year after the end of the financial year	Investments		11		
	Mortgages and loans		12		
Deposits withdrawable after more than 7 days notice			13		
Deposits withdrawable at call or at notice of not more than 7 days			14		
Other assets (to be specified):			15		
			16		
			17		
			18		
Total (1 to 18) (= Form 9, lines 4 + 5 + 10 + 11)			19		

Lloyd's Deposits and Special Reserve Funds are described in Notes 2 and 3 to Form 9

(C) INSURANCE BROKERS

INSURANCE BROKERS REGISTRATION COUNCIL (CODE OF CONDUCT) APPROVAL ORDER 1978

(SI 1978/1394)

1. This Order may be cited as the Insurance Brokers Registration Council (Code of Conduct) Approval Order 1978 and shall come into operation on 20th October 1978.

2. The Code of Conduct drawn up by the Insurance Brokers Registration Council pursuant to section 10 of the Insurance Brokers (Registration) Act 1977 is hereby approved as set out in the Schedule to this Order.

SCHEDULE

CODE OF CONDUCT DRAWN UP BY THE INSURANCE BROKERS REGISTRATION COUNCIL PURSUANT TO SECTION 10 OF THE INSURANCE BROKERS (REGISTRATION) ACT 1977

Words and expressions used in this Code of Conduct shall have the same meaning as are ascribed to them in the Act except that:

'insurance broker' means registered insurance broker and enrolled body corporate;

'insurer' means a person or body of persons carrying on insurance business;

'advertisements' or 'advertising' means canvassing, the offer of services or other methods whereby business is sought by insurance brokers.

1. This Code of Conduct shall serve as a guide to insurance brokers and other persons concerned with their conduct but the mention or lack of mention in it of a particular act or omission shall not be taken as conclusive of any question of professional conduct.

In the opinion of the Council the objective of the Code is to assist in establishing a recognised standard of professional conduct required of all insurance brokers who should, in the interests of the public and in the performance of their duties, bear in mind both this objective and the underlying spirit of this Code.

Matters which might relate to acts or omissions amounting to negligence will be dealt with, if necessary, by the Courts but the Council acknowledges that gross negligence *or* repeated cases of negligence may amount to unprofessional conduct.

2. The following are, in the opinion of the Council, the acts and omissions which, if done or made by registered insurance brokers or enrolled bodies corporate constitute unprofessional conduct: namely any acts or omissions that breach the fundamental principles governing the professional conduct of insurance brokers set out in paragraph 3 below.

3. The principles mentioned in paragraph 2 above are as follows:—

A. *Insurance brokers shall at all times conduct their business with utmost good faith and integrity.*

B. *Insurance brokers shall do everything possible to satisfy the insurance requirements of their clients and shall place the interests of those clients before all other considerations. Subject to these requirements and interests, insurance brokers shall have proper regard for others.*

C. *Statements made by or on behalf of insurance brokers when advertising shall not be misleading or extravagant.*

The following are some specific examples of the application of these principles:

(1) In the conduct of their business insurance brokers shall provide advice objectively and independently.

(2) Insurance brokers shall only use or permit the use of the description 'insurance broker' in connection with a business provided that business is carried on in accordance

with the requirements of the Rules made by the Council under sections 11 and 12 of the Act.

(3) Insurance brokers shall ensure that all work carried out in connection with their insurance broking business shall be under the control and day-to-day supervision of a registered insurance broker and they shall do everything possible to ensure that their employees are made aware of this Code.

(4) Insurance brokers shall on request from the client explain the differences in, and the relative costs of, the principal types of insurance which in the opinion of the insurance broker might suit a client's needs.

(5) Insurance brokers shall ensure the use of a sufficient number of insurers to satisfy the insurance requirements of their clients.

(6) Insurance brokers shall, upon request, disclose to any client who is an individual and who is, or is contemplating becoming, the holder of a United Kingdom policy of insurance the amount of commission paid by the insurer under any relevant policy of insurance.

(7) Although the choice of an insurer can only be a matter of judgment, insurance brokers shall use their skill objectively in the best interests of their client.

(8) Insurance brokers shall not withhold from the policyholder any written evidence or documentation relating to the contract of insurance without adequate and justifiable reasons being disclosed in writing and without delay to the policyholder. If an insurance broker withholds a document from a policyholder by way of a lien for monies due from that policyholder he shall provide the reason in the manner required above.

(9) Insurance brokers shall inform a client of the name of all insurers with whom a contract of insurance is placed. This information shall be given at the inception of the contract and any charges thereafter shall be advised at the earliest opportunity to the client.

(10) Before any work involving a charge is undertaken or an agreement to carry out business is concluded, insurance brokers shall disclose and identify any amount they propose to charge to the client or policyholder which will be in addition to the premium payable to the insurer.

(11) Insurance holders shall disclose to a client any payment which they receive as a result of securing on behalf of that client any service additional to the arrangement of a contract of insurance.

(12) Insurance brokers shall have proper regard for the wishes of a policyholder or client who seeks to terminate any agreement with them to carry out business.

(13) Any information acquired by an insurance broker from his client shall not be used or disclosed except in the normal course of negotiating, maintaining, or renewing a contract of insurance for that client or unless the consent of the client has been obtained or the information is required by a court of competent jurisdiction.

(14) In the completion of the proposal form, claim form, or any other material document, insurance brokers shall make it clear that all the answers or statements are the client's own responsibility. The client should always be asked to check the details and told that the inclusion of incorrect information may result in a claim being repudiated.

(15) Advertisements made by or on behalf of insurance brokers shall comply with the applicable parts of the Code of Advertising Practice published by the Advertising Standards Authority and for this purpose the Code of Advertising Practice shall be deemed to form part of this Code of Conduct.

(16) Advertisements made by or on behalf of insurance brokers shall distinguish between contractual benefits, that is those that the contract of insurance is bound to provide, and non-contractual benefits, that is the amount of benefit which it might provide assuming the insurer's particular forecast is correct. Where such advertisements include a forecast of non-contractual benefits, insurance brokers shall restrict the forecast to that provided by the insurer concerned.

(17) Advertisements made by or on behalf of insurance brokers shall not be restricted to the policies of one insurer except where the reasons for such restriction are fully

explained in the advertisement, the insurer named therein, and the prior approval of that insurer obtained.

(18) When advertising their services directly or indirectly either in person or in writing insurance brokers shall disclose their identity, occupation and purpose before seeking information or before giving advice.

(19) Insurance brokers shall display in any office where they are carrying on business and to which the public have access a notice to the effect that a copy of the Code of Conduct is available upon request and that if a member of the public wishes to make a complaint or requires the assistance of the Council in resolving a dispute, he may write to the Insurance Brokers Registration Council at its offices at 15 St. Helen's Place, London EC3A 6DS.

INSURANCE BROKERS REGISTRATION COUNCIL (REGISTRATION AND ENROLMENT) RULES APPROVAL ORDER 1978

(SI 1978/1395)

1. This Order may be cited as the Insurance Brokers Registration Council (Registration and Enrolment) Rules Approval Order 1978 and shall come into operation on 20th October 1978.

2. The Insurance Brokers Registration Council (Registration and Enrolment) Rules 1978 made by the Insurance Brokers Registration Council in exercise of their powers under section 8(2), (3) and (4) of the Insurance Brokers (Registration) Act 1977 are hereby approved as set out in the Schedule to this Order.

SCHEDULE

THE INSURANCE BROKERS REGISTRATION COUNCIL (REGISTRATION AND ENROLMENT) RULES 1978

The Insurance Brokers Registration Council, in exercise of their powers under section 8(2), (3) and (4) of the Insurance Brokers (Registration) Act 1977 hereby make the following Rules:

1. These Rules may be cited as the Insurance Brokers Registration Council (Registration and Enrolment) Rules 1978.

2.—(1) In these Rules, unless the context otherwise requires:

'the Act' means the Insurance Brokers (Registration) Act 1977;

'the alteration fee' has the meaning assigned to it by rule 15(2);

'the appropriate form' and 'the appropriate supplementary form' means an application form issued by the Council for the type of application in question and a requirement that an application shall be made on the appropriate form shall imply that the Council are entitled to require the completion of the form;

'the enrolment retention fee' has the meaning assigned to it by rule 11(1);

'approved qualifications' means qualifications approved by the Council for the purposes of paragraph (*a*) of section 3(1) of the Act;

'recognised qualifications' means qualifications recognised by the Council for the purposes of paragraphs (*b*), (*d*), (*f*) or (*h*) of section 3(1) of the Act;

'the registered address' means the address entered in the register or list in respect of the registered insurance broker or enrolled body corporate;

'the registration retention fee' has the meaning assigned to it by rule 9(1):

'the supplementary fee' has the meaning assigned to it by rule 7(2);

'the supplementary retention fee' has the meaning assigned to it by rule 10(1).

(2) The Interpretation Act 1889 shall apply for the interpretation of these Rules as it applies for the interpretation of an Act of Parliament.

3. . . . .[repealed].

The register

4. In relation to the registration of an insurance broker, the particulars to be entered in the register shall be:

(1) his surname, forenames, approved or recognised qualifications, date of birth and the address at which he ordinarily resides, and

(2) in respect of an insurance broker who is carrying on business as an insurance broker the address of his principal place of business instead of the address at which he ordinarily resides and any business names under which he carries on business as an insurance broker.

The list

5. In relation to the enrolment of a body corporate carrying on business as an insurance broker, the particulars to be entered in the list shall be its name, the address of its principal place of business and any business names under which it carries on business as an insurance broker.

Application for registration

6.—(1) Any application for registration as an insurance broker shall be accompanied by a fee of £40. An insurance broker who is carrying on business shall be further subject to the requirements of rule 7 hereof.

(2) The Registrar may require any person applying for registration to supply evidence sufficient to show that the requirements for registration are satisfied.

(3) Every application shall be made upon the appropriate form available from the Registrar upon request.

(4) The Council may require any person applying for registration to cause a public advertisement to be issued announcing that the application has been made and inviting comment thereon. The Council may require the person to provide evidence sufficient to establish compliance with this rule.

(5) The Registrar shall not enter in the register the name of an insurance broker until the fee specified in paragraph (1) of this rule has been paid.

7.—(1) An application for registration submitted by an insurance broker who is carrying on business shall be made upon the form referred to in rule 6(3) hereof and the appropriate supplementary form available from the Registrar upon request.

(2) The application forms referred to in paragraph (1) of this rule shall in addition to the fee of £40 payable under rule 6(1) hereof be accompanied by a further fee ('the supplementary fee') of £130.

(3) Except in respect of the application form referred to in rule 6(3) hereof when two or more persons are carrying on business together in a partnership one appropriate supplementary form referred to in paragraph (1) of this rule may be submitted and one supplementary fee may be paid on behalf of all such persons.

(4) The Registrar shall not enter in the register the name of an insurance broker until the fees specified in paragraph (2) of this rule have been paid.

Application for enrolment

8.—(1) Any application by a body corporate for enrolment in the list shall be accompanied by a fee of £130.

(2) The Registrar may require any body corporate applying for enrolment to supply evidence of its suitability to be enrolled.

(3) Every application shall be made upon the appropriate form available from the Registrar upon request.

(4) The Registrar shall not enter in the list the name of a body corporate until the fee specified in paragraph (1) of this rule has been paid.

Retention of name in the register or list and non-payment of fees

9.—(1) Subject to rule 10 hereof any person registered as an insurance broker shall pay on 1st January in each year a fee of £30 ('the registration retention fee') in respect of the retention of his name on the register for the ensuing calendar year.

(2) Where a registration retention fee is not received on or before the beginning of the year to which it relates the Registrar shall send to the person concerned at the registered address a Notice requiring payment of the said fee to be made within fourteen days. If payment is not made before the expiry of that period, the Registrar shall send a further Notice by recorded delivery to the person at the registered address warning him that failure to pay the fee within a further fourteen days will occasion the erasure of his name from the register on the expiry of such period and if the fee is not paid after such further Notices, the Registrar shall erase from the register the name of that person.

(3) The name of the person erased from the register under this rule may only be restored to the register upon receipt of an application made upon the appropriate form available from the Registrar on request accompanied by the registration retention fee of £30 and an additional fee of £10.

(4) The Registrar shall not restore to the register the name of an insurance broker until the fees specified in paragraph (3) of this rule have been paid.

10.—(1) In addition to the registration retention fee required by rule 9 hereof any practising insurance broker shall pay on 1st January in each year a fee of £130 ('the supplementary retention fee') in respect of the retention of his name in the register for the ensuing calendar year.

(2) Where a supplementary retention fee is not received on or before the beginning of the year to which it relates the Registrar shall send to the person concerned at the registered address a Notice requiring payment of the said fee to be made within fourteen days. If payment is not made before the expiry of that period, the Registrar shall send a further Notice by recorded delivery to the person at the registered address warning him that failure to pay the fee within a further fourteen days will occasion the erasure of his name from the register on the expiry of such period and if the fee is not paid after such further Notice, the Registrar shall erase from the register the name of that person.

(3) The name of the person erased from the register under this rule may only be restored to the register upon receipt of an application made upon the appropriate form available from the Registrar on request accompanied by the supplementary retention fee of £130 which shall be in addition to any fee required by rule 9(3) hereof.

(4) In satisfaction of the fee required by paragraphs (1) or (3) of this rule, two or more practising insurance brokers carrying on business together in a partnership may pay one supplementary retention fee on behalf of all such persons in the partnership who apply for retention or submit application forms.

(5) The Registrar shall not restore to the register the name of a practising insurance broker until the fee specified in paragraph (3) of this rule has been paid.

11.—(1) Any enrolled body corporate shall pay on 1st May in each year a fee of £130 ('the enrolment retention fee') in respect of the retention of its name on the list for the ensuing calendar year.

(2) Where an enrolment retention fee is not received on or before the beginning of the year to which it relates the Registrar shall send to the body corporate at the registered address a Notice requiring payment of the said fee to be made within fourteen days. If payment is not made before the expiry of that period, the Registrar shall send a further Notice by recorded delivery to the body corporate at the registered address warning the body corporate that failure to pay the fee within a further fourteen days will occasion the erasure of the name of the body corporate from the list on the expiry of such period and if

the fee is not paid after such further Notice, the Registrar shall erase from the list the name of that body corporate.

(3) The name of the body corporate erased from the list under this rule may only be restored to the list upon receipt of an application made upon the appropriate form available from the Registrar on request accompanied by the enrolment retention fee of £130 and an additional fee of £10.

(4) The Registrar shall not restore to the list the name of a body corporate until the fees specified in paragraph (3) of this rule have been paid.

12.—(1) The Registrar shall be entitled at any time to require a registered insurance broker or an enrolled body corporate to supply such information as may be required by the Registrar with a view to ensuring that the particulars entered in the register or list in respect of that registered insurance broker or enrolled body corporate are correct.

(2) In requiring the supply of information under paragraph (1) of this rule the Registrar may require such information to be supplied within such period, not being less than fourteen days, as he may specify. If information required by the Registrar has not been supplied to his satisfaction within such specified period, the Registrar shall send a Notice by recorded delivery to the registered insurance broker or enrolled body corporate, as the case may be, at the registered address warning that failure to supply such information within a further period of fourteen days will occasion the erasure of the name of the registered insurance broker or the enrolled body corporate from the register or list on the expiry of such period; and if the information is not supplied after such further Notice, the Registrar shall erase from the register or list the name of the registered insurance broker or enrolled body corporate.

13. Where a registered insurance broker or enrolled body corporate is subject to disciplinary proceedings under section 13 or 14 of the Act, the Registrar shall not erase from the register or list the name of that insurance broker or body corporate for failure to pay the appropriate fee or fees under rules 9, 10 and 11 or for failure to supply the information required under rule 12 above until he is satisfied that such disciplinary proceedings have been finally determined.

Alteration or removal of entries in the register or list

14. When the Registrar receives information that an entry in the register or list has become incorrect or application is made by or on behalf of a registered insurance broker or enrolled body corporate for an entry in the register or list to be altered, he shall make the required correction or alteration. Subject to the provisions of rule 15 hereof, no charge shall be made for a correction or alteration under this rule.

15.—(1) Where a registered insurance broker commences business as an insurance broker after registration he shall forthwith make application for the alteration of the particulars entered in respect of him in the register upon the appropriate form available from the Registrar upon request.

(2) The form referred to in paragraph (1) of this rule shall be accompanied by a fee ('the alteration fee') of £130.

(3) When two or more registered insurance brokers commence business together in a partnership, one appropriate form referred to in paragraph (1) of this rule and one alteration fee may be paid on behalf of all such persons.

(4) The Registrar shall not alter in the register the particulars of a practising insurance broker until the fee specified in paragraph (2) of this rule has been paid.

16.—(1) The Registrar shall remove from the register or the list particulars of any person who has died, and of any body corporate which has entered into liquidation (whether voluntarily or compulsorily) or has been struck off the Register of Companies.

(2) The Registrar may remove from the register or the list the name of any registered insurance broker or enrolled body corporate upon receipt of a written application by or

on behalf of the registered insurance broker or enrolled body corporate stating the grounds on which the application is made and accompanied by a statutory declaration that the applicant is not aware of any reason which might lead to the erasure of the name under section 15 or 17 of the Act.

INSURANCE BROKERS REGISTRATION COUNCIL (CONSTITUTION OF THE INVESTIGATING COMMITTEE) RULES APPROVAL ORDER 1978

(SI 1978/1456)

1. This Order may be cited as the Insurance Brokers Registration Council (Constitution of the Investigating Committee) Rules Approval Order 1978 and shall come into operation on 31st October 1978.

2. The Insurance Brokers Registration Council (Constitution of the Investigating Committee) Rules 1978 made by the Insurance Brokers Registration Council in exercise of their powers under section 13(3) of the Insurance Brokers (Registration) Act 1977 are hereby approved as set out in the Schedule to this Order.

SCHEDULE

THE INSURANCE BROKERS REGISTRATION COUNCIL (CONSTITUTION OF THE INVESTIGATING COMMITTEE) RULES 1978

The Insurance Brokers Registration Council, in exercise of their powers under section 13(3) of the Insurance Brokers (Registration) Act 1977, hereby make the following Rules:

1. These Rules may be cited as the Insurance Brokers Registration Council (Constitution of the Investigating Committee) Rules 1978.

2. (*a*) In these Rules:
'the Act' means the Insurance Brokers (Registration) Act 1977;
'the Committee' means the Investigating Committee set up by the Council in pursuance of section 13 of the Act for the preliminary investigation of disciplinary cases.
(*b*) The Interpretation Act 1889 shall apply for the interpretation of these Rules as it applies for the interpretation of an Act of Parliament.

3. The Council shall appoint the Chairman of the Council to be a member of the Committee and shall in addition from time to time appoint not more than fourteen individuals to be the members of the Committee provided that at least two-thirds of the members of the Committee shall be members of the Council. In making such appointments the Council shall ensure that at all times there are at least three members of the Committee who are not insurance brokers.

4. Each member of the Committee other than the Chairman of the Council shall retire on the 31st day of December next following his appointment unless the Council shall have resolved before such date to renew his appointment for a further year.

5. A member of the Committee may at any time, by notice in writing addressed to the Registrar, resign his office.

6. The appointment of any member of the Committee other than the Chairman of the Council may be revoked at any time by a resolution of the Council passed at a meeting of the Council by a majority of not less than three-quarters of the members of the Council present at such meeting.

7. A member of the Committee who at the time of his appointment was a member of the Council shall, upon ceasing to be a member of the Council, also cease to be a member of the Committee.

8. The Chairman of the Council shall cease to be a member of the Committee upon ceasing to be Chairman of the Council.

9. A member of the Committee who ceases to be a member for any reason shall be eligible for re-appointment to the Committee at any time.

10. The Chairman of the Council shall be Chairman of the Committee.

INSURANCE BROKERS REGISTRATION COUNCIL (CONSTITUTION OF THE INVESTIGATING COMMITTEE) RULES APPROVAL ORDER 1978

(SI 1978/1456)

1. This Order may be cited as the Insurance Brokers Registration Council (Constitution of the Disciplinary Committee) Rules Approval Order 1978 and shall come into operation on 31st October 1978.

2. The Insurance Brokers Registration Council (Constitution of the Disciplinary Committee) Rules 1978 made by the Insurance Brokers Registration Council in exercise of their powers under section 14(2) and (3) of the Insurance Brokers (Registration) Act 1977 are hereby approved as set out in the Schedule to this Order.

SCHEDULE

THE INSURANCE BROKERS REGISTRATION COUNCIL (CONSTITUTION OF THE DISCIPLINARY COMMITTEE) RULES 1978

The Insurance Brokers Registration Council, in exercise of their powers under section 14(2) and (3) of the Insurance Brokers (Registration) Act 1977, hereby make the following Rules:

1. These Rules may be cited as the Insurance Brokers Registration Council (Constitution of the Disciplinary Committee) Rules 1978.

2. (*a*) In these Rules:—

'the Act' means the Insurance Brokers (Registration) Act 1977;

'case' means any disciplinary case or other case of which the Committee has cognizance under section 16 or 17 of the Act and any matters ancillary or appertaining thereto;

'the Committee' means the Disciplinary Committee set up under section 14(1) of the Act and constituted under rule 3 of these Rules;

'disciplinary case' means a disciplinary case within the meaning of section 13(1) of the Act which has been referred to the Disciplinary Committee pursuant to section 13(3) of the Act;

'the Investigating Committee' means the Investigating Committee set up under section 13 of the Act.

(*b*) The Interpretation Act 1889 shall apply for the interpretation of these Rules as it applies for the interpretation of an Act of Parliament.

3. The Committee shall consist of not more than eleven members of whom (subject to the provisions of rule 5 of these Rules) five shall from time to time be appointed by the Council and not more than six may from time to time be co-opted by the Committee to serve for such period as the Committee shall determine. The Council shall ensure that at all times there is at least one member of the Committee who is not an insurance broker.

4. Subject to the provisions of rule 5 of these Rules the Committee shall be entitled to act notwithstanding that it may be composed of less than eleven individuals at any time.

5. The Committee may include persons who are not members of the Council, but at least two-thirds of the members of the Committee shall be members of the Council.

6. The appointment of any member of the Committee may be revoked at any time, other than during the hearing of any case in relation to which he is not disqualified from acting as a member of the Committee, by resolution of the Council passed at a meeting of

the Council by a majority of not less than three-quarters of the members of the Council present at such meeting.

7. The Council shall appoint one of the persons appointed under rule 3 to be a member of the Committee to be Chairman of the Committee.

8. At any meeting of the Committee the Chairman of the Committee, or in his absence such member of the Committee who is also a member of the Council as the Committee may choose, shall be Chairman.

9. The quorum of the Committee shall be three members provided that at least two-thirds of the members present at any meeting shall also be members of the Council. If in the course of hearing any case a casual vacancy shall occur in the members acting in that case the remaining members if not less than two in number may continue to act notwithstanding that they do not constitute a quorum.

10. Subject to anything contained in these Rules any member of the Committee shall automatically cease to be a member thereof if:—

(i) he resigns his office by notice in writing addressed to the Registrar; or

(ii) he becomes bankrupt or makes any arrangement or composition with his creditors generally; or

(iii) in the opinion of the Council he becomes incapable by reason of mental disorder of discharging his duty as a Committee member; or

(iv) he has been convicted of a criminal offence under the laws of the United Kingdom which in the opinion of the Council shall merit disqualification from membership of the Committee; or

(v) at the time of his appointment under rule 3 of these Rules he was a member of the Council, upon his ceasing to be a member thereof.

11. Other than the Chairman of the Council an individual who has acted in relation to any disciplinary case as a member of the Investigating Committee shall not act in relation to that case as a member of the Committee.

12. If any member of the Committee is or becomes directly or indirectly interested in any contract with or directly or indirectly connected with any registered insurance broker or enrolled body corporate who or which is the subject of a case, the member shall be disqualified from acting in relation to that case as a member of the Committee.

13. The Committee shall meet as often as may be necessary for the expeditious despatch of their business.

14. The Committee shall meet at the offices of the Council unless the Chairman of the Committee directs that a meeting shall be held elsewhere in the United Kingdom, on the grounds that this would be for the convenience of the members of the Committee or of parties and witnesses in a case to be heard at the meeting, or would be desirable in the special circumstances of any such case.

15. Before the date fixed for any meeting of the Committee, the Registrar shall inform every member of the Committee of the date, time and place of the meeting, and shall send to every such member a programme of business for that meeting which shall include particulars of every case to be considered at that meeting.

INSURANCE BROKERS REGISTRATION COUNCIL (PROCEDURE OF THE DISCIPLINARY COMMITTEE) RULES APPROVAL ORDER 1978

(SI 1978/1458)

1. This Order may be cited as the Insurance Brokers Registration Council (Procedure of the Disciplinary Committee) Rules Approval Order 1978 and shall come into operation on 31st October 1978.

2. The Insurance Brokers Registration Council (Procedure of the Disciplinary Committee) Rules 1978 made by the Insurance Brokers Registration Council in exercise of their powers under section 19(4) of the Insurance Brokers (Registration) Act 1977 are hereby approved as set out in the Schedule to this Order.

SCHEDULE

The Insurance Brokers Registration Council (Procedure of the Disciplinary Committee) Rules 1978

The Insurance Brokers Registration Council, having complied with the provisions of section 19(5) of the Insurance Brokers (Registration) Act 1977, in exercise of their powers under section 19(4) of the Act, hereby make the following Rules:—

Part I

Citation and Interpretation

1.—(1) These Rules may be cited as the Insurance Brokers Registration Council (Procedure of the Disciplinary Committee) Rules 1978.

(2) In these Rules, unless the context otherwise requires—

'the Act' means the Insurance Brokers (Registration) Act 1977;

'case' means any disciplinary case or other case to which these Rules apply;

'the Chairman' means the Chairman or the Acting Chairman of the Committee;

'the Committee' means the Disciplinary Committee set up by the Council in pursuance of section 14(1) of the Act;

'the complainant' means a person or body by whom a complaint has been made to the Council in a case to which these Rules apply; a complainant shall not be deemed to appear in any proceedings if he takes part therein only as a witness;

'conviction' means a conviction within the meaning of section 15(1)(*a*) of the Act;

'disciplinary case' means a disciplinary case within the meaning of section 13(1) of the Act which has been referred to the Disciplinary Committee pursuant to section 13(2) of the Act;

'inquiry' means the proceedings at which the Committee consider and determine any case;

'the Investigating Committee' means the Committee set up by the Council in pursuance of section 13(1) of the Act for the preliminary consideration of disciplinary cases;

'the Legal Assessor' means an assessor appointed by the Council or the Committee for the purposes of section 20 of the Act;

'party to the inquiry' means the complainant (if any), the Solicitor and any person on whom a notice of inquiry has been served in accordance with these Rules: provided that if the complainant does not appear at the inquiry he shall not thereafter be included in the said phrase;

'the respondent' means any person or body corporate whose name has been entered in the register or list under the provisions of the Act and in respect of whom a case to which these Rules apply has been referred to the Committee for inquiry;

'the Solicitor' means a solicitor nominated by the Council to act as their solicitor for the purposes of these Rules, and in relation to an inquiry includes counsel instructed by the Solicitor to act on his behalf.

(3) The Interpretation Act 1889 shall apply for the interpretation of these Rules as it applies for the interpretation of an Act of Parliament.

Part II

Preliminary Proceedings

Notice of inquiry

2.—(1) The Solicitor shall, as soon as may be after a disciplinary case has been referred to the Committee, serve upon the respondent a notice of inquiry as nearly as may be in the form set out in the Appendix to these Rules stating the substance of the allegation or complaint (set out as a charge or charges) and specifying the facts relied on in relation to each allegation or complaint and the provision of section 15 of the Act which the Committee considers relevant, and stating also the day, time and place at which the Committee will hold an inquiry into these matters, and enclosing a copy of these Rules and of the Act. The said notice and copies shall be sent by post in a registered or recorded delivery letter addressed to the respondent.

(2) If there is a complainant the Solicitor shall send him a copy of the notice of inquiry and a copy of these Rules.

(3) The Committee shall not hold an inquiry unless a notice of inquiry has been served upon the respondent in accordance with the foregoing provisions of this rule.

(4) Except with the agreement of the respondent the inquiry shall not be held within twenty-eight days after the date of posting the notice of inquiry in accordance with paragraph (1) of this rule.

Postponement or cancellation of inquiry

3.—(1) The Chairman, of his own motion or upon the application of any party thereto, may postpone the hearing of an inquiry, or may refer a disciplinary case to the Investigating Committee for further consideration as to whether an inquiry should be held.

(2) Where before the inquiry opens it appears to the Chairman, or at any stage of the proceedings it appears to the Committee, that a notice of inquiry is defective, he or they shall cause the notice to be amended, unless it appears to him or them that the required amendment cannot be made without injustice, or, if he or they consider that the circumstances in which an amendment is made require it, he or they may direct that the amended notice shall be served on the respondent and that the inquiry shall be postponed.

(3) The Solicitor shall, as soon as may be, give to all parties to whom a notice of inquiry has been sent notification of any decision to postpone or not to hold an inquiry, and inform them of any date fixed for the hearing of a postponed inquiry.

Access to documents

4. Upon application by any party to the inquiry the Solicitor shall send to that party a copy of any statutory declaration, complaint, answer, admission, explanation or other similar document received by the Council from any party to the inquiry.

Part III

Disciplinary Cases

The reading of the charge or charges

5.—(1) The charge or charges shall be read in the presence of the respondent, and of the complainant if one appears:

Provided that if the respondent does not appear at the inquiry but the Committee nevertheless decide that the inquiry shall proceed the charge or charges shall be read in his absence.

(2) As soon as the charge or charges have been read the respondent may, if he so desires, object to the charge or charges, or to any part thereof, in point of law, and any other party may reply to any such objection; and, if any such objection is upheld, no further proceedings shall be taken on a charge or on a part of a charge to which the objection relates.

Proof of the facts alleged

6.—(1) If the respondent has appeared at the inquiry the Chairman shall ask if all or any of the facts alleged in the charge or charges are admitted.

(2) The complainant or, if no complainant appears, the Solicitor shall then open the case and may call witnesses and adduce evidence of any facts not admitted by the respondent and of any matter connected with the facts alleged which may be relevant. The respondent may cross-examine any such witness and the witness may thereafter be re-examined.

(3) The respondent may then submit that the evidence adduced by the complainant or the Solicitor does not establish the charge alleged or does not justify the erasure of his name from the register or list. The Committee shall consider and determine any such submission, and the Chairman shall thereupon announce their determination.

(4) If no such submission is made, or if any such submission is not upheld, the respondent may then call witnesses and adduce evidence; such witnesses may be cross-examined and re-examined, and the respondent may address the Committee either before or after such evidence but not more than once save with the leave of the Committee. The complainant or, if no complainant appears, the Solicitor may address the Committee on any point of law raised by the respondent.

(5) Where the respondent adduces evidence the complainant or, if no complainant appears, the Solicitor may address the Committee thereon and may call witnesses and adduce evidence in rebuttal and such witnesses may be cross-examined and re-examined. The respondent shall have the right to address the Committee upon such address or evidence in rebuttal.

(6) The Committee shall then deliberate, and decide in relation to each charge which remains outstanding whether the facts alleged in such charge have been proved and in relation to any facts found by the Committee to have been proved whether they are such as to substantiate such charge, and the Chairman shall announce the Committee's findings:

Provided that if the Committee find that any charge under section 15 of the Act is not proved a finding to that effect shall be recorded and in cases where it is alleged that the respondent is guilty of unprofessional conduct its finding shall specifically record that the respondent is not guilty of such conduct in respect of the matters to which the allegation relates and in cases where it is alleged that the respondent was liable to have his or its name erased from the register or list under section 15(2) of the Act its finding shall specifically record that the respondent is not guilty of the matters alleged. A copy of any finding so recorded shall be sent, in the manner provided for the service of notices under rule 2, to the respondent and such other persons, being persons likely to be affected by the finding as the Chairman may direct.

7.—(1) Where the Committee find that a charge is proved the Chairman shall invite the complainant or, if no complainant appears, the Solicitor to adduce evidence of the circumstances leading up to the facts found proved and as to the character and antecedents of the respondent.

(2) The respondent may then address the Committee in mitigation and adduce any relevant evidence.

(3) The Committee shall then deliberate and decide whether they can properly reach a decision forthwith not to erase the name of the respondent from the register or list.

(4) If the Committee decide the question under the last foregoing paragraph in the negative they shall then decide whether to postpone judgement or forthwith to direct the Registrar to erase the name of the respondent from the register or list.

(5) If the Committee decide under the last foregoing paragraph to postpone judgement, they shall specify either a period for which judgement is postponed, or a further meeting of the Committee at which they will further consider the judgement.

(6) Any decision of the Committee under this rule shall be announced by the Chairman in such terms as the Committee may approve and a copy of the decision shall be sent, in the manner provided for the service of notices under rule 2 hereof, to the respondent and such other persons, being persons likely to be affected by the finding, as the Chairman may direct.

Procedure upon postponement of judgement

8.—(1) Where under the foregoing provisions of these Rules the judgement of the Committee in any case stands postponed, the procedure shall be as follows—

(*a*) The Solicitor shall, not less than six weeks before the day fixed for the resumption of proceedings, send to the respondent a notice which shall—

(i) specify the day, time and place at which the proceedings are to be resumed and invite him to appear thereat,

(ii) unless the Chairman otherwise directs, invite the respondent to furnish the Registrar with the names and addresses of persons to whom reference may be made confidentially or otherwise concerning his character and conduct, and

(iii) invite the respondent to send to the Solicitor, not less than three weeks before the day fixed for the resumption of proceedings, a copy of any statement or statutory declaration, whether made by the respondent or not, relating to his conduct or setting out any material facts which have arisen since that hearing.

(*b*) A copy of the notice and of any statement or statutory declaration sent in accordance with the provisions of the last foregoing sub-paragraph shall be sent to the complainant, if any, if he is then a party to the inquiry and he may in turn, if he so desires, send to the Solicitor a statement or statutory declaration, whether made by himself or not, as to the matters mentioned in that sub-paragraph, or as to any other material facts which have arisen since the hearing. A copy of any such statement or statutory declaration shall thereupon be supplied to the respondent.

(*c*) At the meeting at which the proceedings are resumed the Chairman shall first invite the Solicitor to recall for the information of the Committee, the position in which the case stands, and the Committee may then receive further oral or documentary evidence as to the conduct of the respondent or any material facts which may have arisen since the hearing, and shall hear any party to the inquiry who desires to be heard.

(*d*) The Committee shall then consider their decision, and paragraphs (3) to (6) of rule 7 shall apply to their procedure.

(2) At any resumed proceedings any new charge alleged against the respondent in accordance with these Rules shall first be dealt with in accordance with such of the provisions of rules 5 to 7 as may be applicable, and the Committee may apply paragraphs (3) to (6) of rule 7 simultaneously to the new charge and to the charge in respect of which they had postponed judgement.

(3) Nothing in the last foregoing paragraph shall prevent the Committee from receiving evidence at any resumed proceedings of any conviction recorded against the respondent which has not been made the subject of a charge under these Rules.

(4) Subject to the provisions of the Act, the validity of any resumed proceedings shall not be called into question by reason only that members of the Committee who were present at any former meeting were not present at the resumed meeting or that members present at the resumed meeting were not present at any former meeting.

(5) The Chairman, of his own motion or upon the application of any party thereto, may postpone the resumption of proceedings, and in that case the Solicitor shall so soon as may be inform all parties to whom notice of the resumption of proceedings has been given of the postponement and of any date now fixed for the resumption of proceedings.

Part IV

Removal of Name of Body Corporate from the List Under Section 15(3) of the Act

9.—(1) This Part of these Rules applies to proceedings brought for the purpose of removing the name of a body corporate from the list, under Section 15(3) of the Act.

(2) Where—

(i) the name of a director of an enrolled body corporate is erased from the register under section 15 of the Act, or

(ii) a director of an enrolled body corporate is convicted of an offence under the Act, or

(iii) the name of a registered insurance broker employed by an enrolled body corporate is erased from the register (unless the Committee have stated that they are satisfied that the act or omission constituting the ground on which it was erased was not instigated or connived at by a director of the body corporate or, if the act of omission was a continuing act or omission, that a director of the body had not nor was reasonably required to have had knowledge of the continuance thereof),

and the period within which proceedings might be brought by way of appeal under section 18 of the Act has expired, or any such appeal has been dismissed, withdrawn or struck out, the provisions or rule 10 shall apply.

10.—(1) The Solicitor shall send to the respondent body corporate and to the complainant (if any) a notice of inquiry in accordance with rule 2, the charges and facts to be specified being the circumstances falling under rule 9 which are relevant to the case.

(2) A copy of the notice shall be sent to every director of or registered insurance broker employed by the respondent who is named therein. The Chairman may direct that a copy of the notice shall also be sent to any other person or body.

(3) Any other person or body may with the leave of the Chairman or of the Committee appear at the inquiry as an additional respondent.

(4) Any erasure from the register shall be proved by a certificate to that effect signed by the Registrar.

(5) Subject to the provisions of this rule the provisions of Parts II (except as regards reference to the Investigating Committee) and III of these Rules shall apply to any proceedings to which this rule applies.

Part V

Cases under Section 17 of the Act Relating to Fraudulent or Incorrect Entries in Register or List

11.—(1) Where any question whether an entry in the register or list has been fraudulently or incorrectly made has been referred to the Committee, the Solicitor shall send to the respondent (being the person or body corporate in relation to whom the entry was made) a notice of inquiry specifying the nature of the fraud or mistake alleged, stating the day, time and place at which the Committee will hold an inquiry into the question, inviting his attendance thereat, and containing such further information as the nature of the case may require.

(2) Subject to the provisions of this rule, the provisions of Part II of these Rules (except as regards reference to the Investigating Committee) shall apply to any proceedings to which this rule applies.

(3) Where the question is whether the entry in the register or list has been fraudulently made, a copy of the notice shall be sent to any person who is alleged to have been a party to the fraud and to any other person (if any) as the Chairman may direct. Any such person may with the leave of the Chairman or of the Committee appear at the inquiry as an individual party thereto.

(4) The inquiry shall proceed as though the question were a charge contained in a notice of inquiry in a disciplinary case and the provisions of rule 6 shall accordingly apply thereto so far as may be.

(5) If the Committee determine that the entry has been proved to their satisfaction to

have been fraudulently or incorrectly made, they shall make an order in writing, signed by the Chairman, that the entry having been proved to the satisfaction of the Committee to have been fraudulently or incorrectly made (as the case may be) shall be erased from the register or list, and the Chairman shall announce the determination in terms indicating whether in the view of the Committee the entry was made fraudulently or was made incorrectly but not fraudulently.

(6) Where an inquiry relates to two or more entries, the Committee may proceed under the foregoing provisions of this rule to consider the allegations in respect of those entries either separately or taken together, as the Committee may think fit; and where an inquiry relates to an entry specifying two or more particulars, the Committee may proceed thereunder in respect of so much of the entry as specifies each of those particulars as if it were a separate entry.

Part VI

Restoration of Names after Erasure

12. Where an application is made—

(*a*) in accordance with section 16 of the Act by a person or body whose name has been erased from the register or list in pursuance of a direction made under section 15 of the Act; or

(*b*) in accordance with section 17(2) of the Act by a person or body whose name has been erased from the register or list on the ground of fraud in pursuance of a direction by the Committee under section 17(1);

the following provisions shall have effect—

(i) the Committee shall afford the applicant an opportunity of being heard by the Committee and of adducing evidence;

(ii) the Committee may require such evidence as they think necessary concerning the identity or character of the applicant, or his conduct since his name was erased from the register or list, and for this purpose may receive written or oral evidence;

(iii) the application shall otherwise be disposed of as nearly as may be in accordance with the procedure provided by these Rules.

Part VII

General

Hearing and adjournment

13.—(1) Subject to the provisions of section 20(3) of the Act, and of any Rules made thereunder, the Committee may deliberate in camera (with or without the Legal Assessor) at any time and for any purpose during or after the hearing of any proceedings.

(2) Save as aforesaid all proceedings before the Committee shall take place in the presence of all parties thereto who appear therein and shall be held in public except as provided by the next following paragraph of this rule.

(3) Where in the interests of justice it appears to the Committee that the public should be excluded from any proceedings or part thereof, the Committee may direct that the public shall be so excluded; but a direction under this paragraph shall not apply to the announcement in pursuance of any of these Rules of a determination of the Committee.

(4) The Committee may adjourn their proceedings from time to time as they think fit.

Evidence

14.—(1) Where a respondent or an applicant under rule 12 has supplied to the Committee or to the Registrar on their behalf the name of any person to whom reference may be made confidentially as to his character or conduct, the Committee may consider any information received from such person in consequence of such reference without disclosing the same to the respondent or applicant.

(2) The Committee may receive oral, documentary or other evidence of any fact which appears to them relevant to the inquiry into the case before them—

Provided that, where a fact which it is sought to prove, or the form in which any evidence is tendered, is such that it would not be admissible in criminal proceedings in a court of law the Committee shall not receive evidence of the fact or in that form, unless after consultation with the Legal Assessor they are satisfied that it is desirable in the interests of justice to receive it having regard to the difficulty and expense of obtaining evidence which would be so admissible.

(3) The Committee may cause any person to be called as a witness in any proceedings before them whether or not the parties consent thereto. Questions may be put to any witness by the Committee through the Chairman or by the Legal Assessor with the leave of the Chairman.

Voting

15.—(1) Any question put to the vote shall be put in the form of a motion by the Chairman. The Chairman shall call upon members present to vote for or against the motion and shall declare that the motion appears to him to have been carried or not carried as the case may be.

(2) Where the result so declared is challenged by any member, the Chairman shall call upon the Registrar to read the roll, and as his name is read every member present including the Chairman (who shall be called last) shall say 'For' or 'Against' according to whether his vote is given for or against the motion. The Chairman shall thereupon declare the number of members who have voted for the motion and the number who have voted against the motion, and whether the motion has been carried or not carried.

(3) Where on any question the votes are equal, the question shall be deemed to have been resolved in favour of the respondent or of the applicant under rule 12, as the case may be.

Procedure where there is more than one respondent

16. Nothing in this Part of these Rules shall prevent one inquiry being held into charges against two or more respondents, and where such an inquiry is held the foregoing Rules shall apply with the necessary adaptations and subject to any directions given by the Committee as to the order in which proceedings shall be taken under any of these Rules by or in relation to the several respondents; so however that any of the rights of a respondent under these Rules shall be exercised separately by each of the respondents who desires to invoke that right.

Supplementary

17.—(1) Any party being an individual may appear either in person or by counsel or solicitor, or if the party so elects by any officer or member of any organisation of which he is a member, or by any member of his family.

(2) Any party being a body corporate or an unincorporated body of persons may appear by their secretary or other officer duly appointed for the purpose or by counsel or solicitor.

18. A shorthand-writer shall be appointed by the Committee to take shorthand notes of proceedings before them (except that the Committee may dispense with a shorthand-writer in proceedings under Part VI of these rules) and any party to an inquiry shall, on application to the Solicitor and on payment of the proper charge on a scale fixed by the Council, be furnished by the Solicitor with a transcript of the shorthand notes of any part of the inquiry at which the party was entitled to be present.

INSURANCE BROKERS REGISTRATION COUNCIL (DISCIPLINARY COMMITTEE) LEGAL ASSESSOR RULES 1978

(SI 1978/1503)

1. These Rules may be cited as the Insurance Brokers Registration Council (Disciplinary Committee) Legal Assessor Rules 1978 and shall come into operation on 10th November 1978.

2. (1) In these Rules—

'the Act' means the Insurance Brokers (Registration) Act 1977;

'the Committee' means the Disciplinary Committee constituted under the provisions of section 14 of the Act; and

'Legal Assessor' means an assessor appointed under the provisions of section 20 of the Act.

(2) The Interpretation Act 1889 shall apply to the interpretation of these Rules as it applies to the interpretation of an Act of Parliament.

3. It shall be the duty of the Legal Assessor to be present at all proceedings before the Committee and to advise the Committee on any questions of law arising in the proceedings which they may refer to him.

4. It shall be the duty of the Legal Assessor to inform the Committee forthwith of any irregularity in the conduct of proceedings before them which may come to his knowledge and to advise them of his own motion where it appears to him that, but for such advice, there is a possibility of a mistake of law being made.

5. The advice of the Legal Assessor shall be tendered to the Committee in the presence of every party, or person representing a party, to the proceedings who appears thereat:

Provided that if, in the case of any question referred by the Committee to the Legal Assessor while they are deliberating in private, the Committee consider that it would be prejudicial to the discharge of their duties for the advice to be tendered in the presence of the said parties or their representatives, it may be tendered in their absence, but the Legal Assessor shall, as soon as may be, personally inform them of the question which has been put to him by the Committee and of his advice thereon, and his advice shall subsequently be put in writing and a copy thereof shall be given to every such party or representative.

6. If on any occasion the Committee do not accept the advice of the Legal Assessor, a record shall be made of the question referred to him, of the advice given and of the refusal to accept it (together with the reasons for such refusal), and a copy of the record shall be given to every party, or person representing a party, to the proceedings who appears thereat.

7. Copies of written advice, made for the purposes of either of the last two foregoing Rules, shall be available on application to every party to the proceedings who does not appear thereat.

INSURANCE BROKERS REGISTRATION COUNCIL (CONSTITUTION OF THE DISCIPLINARY COMMITTEE) RULES APPROVAL ORDER 1978

(SI 1978/1457)

1. This Order may be cited as the Insurance Brokers Registration Council (Indemnity Insurance and Grants Scheme) Rules Approval Order 1979 and shall come into operation on 1st July 1979.

2. The Insurance Brokers Registration Council (Indemnity Insurance and Grants Scheme) Rules 1979 made by the Insurance Brokers Registration Council in exercise of their powers under section 12 of the Insurance Brokers (Registration) Act 1977 are hereby approved as set out in the Schedule to this Order.

SCHEDULE

THE INSURANCE BROKERS REGISTRATION COUNCIL (INDEMNITY INSURANCE AND GRANTS SCHEME) RULES 1979

The Insurance Brokers Registration Council, in exercise of their powers under section 12 of the Insurance Brokers (Registration) Act 1977, hereby make the following Rules:

PART I—PRELIMINARY

1. These Rules may be cited as the Insurance Brokers Registration Council (Indemnity Insurance and Grants Scheme) Rules 1979.

2.—(1) In these Rules, unless the context otherwise requires:

'the Act' means the Insurance Brokers (Registration) Act 1977;

'the applicant' has the meaning assigned to it by rule 7(1);

'brokerage' means any remuneration originating from insurance broking business;

'business' means an insurance broking business or any business which includes an insurance broking business;

'a grant' and 'the Grants Scheme' have the meanings assigned to them by rule 6;

'the grantee' has the meaning assigned to it by rule 14(4);

'the Grants Fund' has the meaning assigned to it by rule 15(1);

'the insured', 'the insurer' and 'the policy' have, for the purposes of Part II of these Rules, the meanings assigned to them by rule 3(1);

'a levy' and 'the levy date' have the meanings assigned to them by rule 9;

'the maximum levy' has the meaning assigned to it by rule 11(1);

'partner' includes any person held out as a partner and 'former partner' shall be construed accordingly;

'the registered address' means the address entered in the register or list in respect of the practising insurance broker or enrolled body corporate;

'the total actual levy' and 'the total maximum levy' have the meanings assigned to them by rule 11(2).

(2) For the purposes of these Rules, unless the context otherwise requires, every business carried on by a partnership shall be deemed to be carried on jointly and severally by all the partners thereof and employees or former employees of a partnership shall be deemed to be employees or former employees of all the partners thereof jointly and severally.

PART II—PROFESSIONAL INDEMNITY INSURANCE

3.—(1) Practising insurance brokers and enrolled bodies corporate shall, in respect of each business which they carry on, take out and maintain in accordance with the provisions of this rule a policy or policies of insurance ('the policy') with an authorised insurer ('the insurer') which shall indemnify the practising insurance broker or the enrolled body corporate, or where the business is or was carried on in partnership the practising insurance broker or enrolled body corporate and any former partner who, as a practising insurance broker or enrolled body corporate, carried on such business in partnership (in each case 'the insured') against losses arising from claims in respect of any description of civil liability incurred by them or by employees or former employees of theirs, in connection with such business.

(2) The policy shall comply with the following requirements:

(i) without prejudice to the generality of the foregoing provisions of this rule the policy shall indemnify the insured:

(*a*) against losses arising from claims made against the insured:

(A) for breach of duty in connection with the business by reason of any negligent act, error, or omission or by reason of any dishonest or fraudulent act or omission; and

(B) in respect of libel or slander or in Scotland defamation, committed in the conduct of the business by the insured, any employee or former employee of the insured, and where the business is or was carried on in partnership any partner or former partner of the insured; and

(*b*) against claims arising in connection with the business in respect of:

(A) any loss of money or other property whatsoever belonging to the insured or for which the insured is legally liable in consequence of any dishonest or fraudulent act or omission of any employee or former employee of the insured, and where the business is or was carried on in partnership any partner or former partner of the insured; and

(B) legal liability incurred by reason of loss of documents and costs and expenses incurred in replacing or restoring such documents.

PROVIDED THAT the policy shall not be required to afford indemnity to any person committing, making or condoning any dishonest or fraudulent act or omission.

(ii) Subject as provided in paragraph (2)(iii) of this rule the policy shall at inception and at each renewal date, which shall not be more than twelve months from inception or the last renewal date, provide a minimum limit of indemnity in either:

(*a*) a sum of £250,000; or

(*b*) a sum equal to three times the brokerage of the business for the last accounting period ending prior to inception or renewal of the policy,

whichever sum shall be the greater provided that in no case shall the minimum limit of indemnity be required to exceed £7,500,000.

(iii) Notwithstanding the provisions of paragraph (2)(ii) of this rule if the minimum limit of indemnity as provided by such paragraph shall be £500,000 or less then such minimum limit shall apply at all times to each and every claim or series of claims arising out of the same occurrence and if the minimum limit of indemnity required by paragraph (2)(ii) of this rule shall be greater than £500,000 then not less than the initial £500,000 of such minimum limit shall apply at all times to each and every claim or series of claims arising out of the same occurrence.

(iv) No policy shall without the previous consent in writing of the Council being obtained have an excess or deductible applying to the insurance in an amount which exceeds one-half per cent of the minimum limit of indemnity required by paragraph (2)(ii) of this rule.

(v) The policy shall cover the insured for the full indemnity required by paragraph (2)(i), (ii), (iii) and (iv) of this rule in respect of all claims first made and reported during the period of insurance regardless of the time at which the error, omission, act, event or occurrence which gives rise to any such claim may have occurred.

(vi) The policy shall indemnify the insured in respect of claims made against the insured, or losses incurred by the insured, and arising in respect of all business which the insured carried on either alone or in partnership when registered or enrolled.

(vii) The policy shall specifically provide that 'This Policy of Insurance is taken out pursuant to the Insurance Brokers Registration Council (Indemnity Insurance and Grants Scheme) Rules 1979'.

(3) (i) For the purposes of sub-paragraph (*b*) of paragraph (2)(ii) of this rule:

(*a*) 'the brokerage of the business for the last accounting period ending prior to inception or renewal of the policy' shall mean any brokerage disclosed or contained in the last accounts of the business which have been prepared and submitted to the Council in accordance with rules made under section 11 of the Act or where no such accounts have been prepared and submitted since registration or enrolment any brokerage disclosed or contained in the most recent accounts of the business submitted to the Council with or at the time of any application leading to registration or enrolment; and

(*b*) if the period covered by any such accounts shall be greater or less than twelve months then the figure for the brokerage disclosed or contained in such accounts shall be amended pro rata to give an equivalent figure for a twelve month period.

(ii) For the purposes of paragraph (2)(v) of this rule 'claims first made and reported during the period of insurance' shall include claims subsequently made and reported if the circumstances or occurrence which give rise to any such claim have been notified to the insurer during the period of insurance.

(4) Practising insurance brokers and enrolled bodies corporate shall:

(*a*) forthwith inform the Council in writing if;

(i) during the currency of a policy the insurer has avoided or cancelled the policy or has notified his intention of doing so;

(ii) the policy has not been renewed or has been cancelled and another policy complying with the provisions of these Rules has not been taken out from the date on which the previous policy lapsed or was cancelled;

(iii) during the currency of a policy the terms or conditions are altered in any way so that the policy no longer complies with the provisions of these Rules;

(iv) the insurer has intimated that he intends to decline to indemnify the insured in respect of a claim under the policy;

(v) the insurer has given notice that the policy will not be renewed or will not be renewed in a form which will enable the policy to comply with the provisions of these Rules;

(vi) during the currency of a policy the risks covered by the policy, or the conditions or terms relating thereto, are altered in any way;

(*b*) forthwith inform the insurer in writing:

(i) of a claim by or against the insured; and

(ii) of all circumstances or occurrences of which the insured is aware which may subsequently give rise to a claim by or against the insured; and

(*c*) comply at all times with the terms and conditions of the policy.

(5) The insurer shall be entitled at any time to disclose to the Council the following information relating to the policy:

(i) any particulars of the policy relating to the requirements of this rule;

(ii) any other information relating to the policy whether or not the policy is in force or may have been avoided or cancelled or has lapsed;

(iii) whether the policy has lapsed or not been renewed or whether the insurer has avoided or cancelled the policy for any reason or intends to do so;

(iv) that he has intimated that he intends to decline to indemnify the insured in respect of a claim under the policy;

(v) whether in the opinion of the insurer the policy complies with the requirements of these Rules.

(6) For the purposes of this rule 'the insured' shall include:

(*a*) the estate or personal representatives or trustee, or assignee, in bankruptcy of such person; and

(*b*) in Scotland the partnership in addition to the members thereof.

4.—(1) For the purposes of demonstrating to the satisfaction of the Council that the provisions of rule 3 of these Rules are being complied with practising insurance brokers and enrolled bodies corporate shall, in respect of each business which they carry on:

(*a*) within fourteen days of being registered or enrolled or commencing business; and

(*b*) within fourteen days of the date on which the policy is renewed or inception of a new policy,

submit to the Council the policy, or renewal receipt as the case may be, or a cover note, or such other written evidence as the Council may require to establish compliance with these Rules.

(2) At any time and from time to time a practising insurance broker or enrolled body corporate shall within fourteen days of being required in writing to do so produce to the Council written evidence satisfactory to the Council that a policy which in all respects complies with the provisions of these Rules is in full force and effect in respect of each of the businesses of the practising insurance broker or of the enrolled body corporate.

(3) Notwithstanding the provisions of paragraphs (1) and (2) of this rule the submission of a cover note, renewal receipt or other written evidence signed or issued by a practising insurance broker or an enrolled body corporate in respect of a policy, which relates to his or its business must be accompanied by a receipt for payment of the premium under the policy from the insurer or a Lloyd's broker.

5. The Council shall have powers, from time to time and in their absolute discretion, for the purposes of ascertaining whether or not the provisions of Part II of these Rules are being complied with, to require practising insurance brokers or enrolled bodies corporate to:

(1) supply other or additional information;

(2) instruct the insurer to supply other or additional information;

(3) produce, at a time during ordinary business hours and at a place to be fixed by the Council, their accounting records, the policy and all or any documentation in any way connected therewith, and any other necessary documents for the inspection of any person appointed by the Council and to supply to such person any necessary information and explanations.

PART III—THE GRANTS SCHEME

6. There shall be a scheme to be known as 'the Grants Scheme' which shall be maintained and administered by the Council for the purpose of making grants or other payments ('a grant') to relieve or mitigate losses suffered by persons as hereinafter defined in consequence of negligence or fraud or other dishonesty on the part of practising insurance brokers or enrolled bodies corporate, or of employees of theirs, in connection with their businesses or the failure on the part of practising insurance brokers or enrolled bodies corporate to account for money received by them in connection with their businesses,

PROVIDED THAT no grant or application for a grant shall be made under the Grants Scheme in respect of losses resulting from any negligence arising, or fraud or other dishonesty committed, or failure to account for money occurring, before the earlier of 1st December 1980 or the date of the coming into operation of section 22 of the Act.

7.—(1) The person who shall be entitled to apply to the Council for a grant under the Grants Scheme ('the applicant') shall be individuals or partnerships or other unincorporated bodies of persons all the members of which are individuals, who are or have been insured under a United Kingdom policy of insurance but excluding a policy of reinsurance or reassurance and who have suffered loss in consequence of the negligence or fraud or other dishonesty on the part of practising insurance brokers or enrolled bodies corporate, or of employees of theirs, in connection with such United Kingdom policy of insurance or through failure on the part of practising insurance brokers or enrolled bodies corporate to account for money received by them in connection with such United Kingdom policy of insurance.

(2) References to persons who are or have been insured under a United Kingdom policy of insurance shall include persons who had sought advice or given instructions in contemplation of becoming an insured under a United Kingdom policy of insurance.

(3) A policy of insurance is a United Kingdom policy for the purposes of this rule at any time when the performance by the insurance company of any of its obligations under the contract evidenced by the policy would constitute the carrying on by the insurance company of insurance business of any class in the United Kingdom.

(4) For the purposes of this rule the expressions 'insured' and 'insurance' shall include 'assured' and 'assurance'.

8. Notwithstanding the provisions of rule 7 of these Rules the Council shall in their absolute discretion be entitled to make a grant or grants under the Grants Scheme to such other person or persons as they may decide in all the circumstances.

9. Where the Council so resolve under the provisions of rule 17(2) of these Rules or where they have made a grant or propose to make a grant they shall, subject to the provisions of rule 11 of these Rules, be entitled to impose a levy ('a levy') upon all practising insurance brokers and enrolled bodies corporate who are or were on the register or list on a day to be specified by the Council ('the levy date').

10.—(1) A levy to be imposed by the Council in accordance with the provisions of rule 9 of these Rules shall be based:

(i) (*a*) in the case of an enrolled body corporate upon the aggregate number of individuals engaged in the business of, or employed by, the enrolled body corporate in the United Kingdom; or

(*b*) in the case of each business of a practising insurance broker who is a sole proprietor, upon the aggregate of the practising insurance broker and the number of individuals engaged in the business of, or employed by, the practising insurance broker in the United Kingdom; or

(*c*) in the case of each business which is being carried on by a practising insurance broker or an enrolled body corporate in partnership, upon the aggregate of the number of practising insurance brokers and enrolled bodies corporate carrying on business in partnership and the number of individuals engaged in the business of, or employed by, such partnership in the United Kingdom so that only one levy shall be payable in respect of each business by all practising insurance brokers and enrolled bodies corporate carrying on such business in partnership,

PROVIDED THAT the liability of each such practising insurance broker or enrolled body corporate to pay a levy shall be a joint and several liability to the Council;

AND

(ii) upon the latest information supplied to the Council by the practising insurance broker or the enrolled body corporate under the provisions of rule 13(5) of these Rules.

(2) For the purposes of this rule individuals who are engaged in the business of, or employed by, the practising insurance broker or enrolled body corporate for less than twenty hours per week shall be regarded as engaged or employed part-time, so that two individuals so engaged or employed shall make up one full-time individual and so that any part numbers shall be ignored.

11.—(1) The Council shall not be entitled to levy in each calendar year commencing on 1st January an amount in respect of each practising insurance broker or enrolled body corporate which will exceed an amount in respect of each business ('the maximum levy') calculated as follows:

Number of persons ascertained in accordance with rule 10	*Calculation of the maximum levy*
1–50 inclusive	£25 per person, subject to a minimum of £100
51–200 inclusive	The aggregate of: (*a*) £25 per person for the first 50 persons (£1,250); and (*b*) £20 per person for the remainder
201–1000 inclusive	The aggregate of: (*a*) £25 per person for the first 50 persons (£1,250); (*b*) £20 per person for the next 150 persons (£3,000); and (*c*) £15 per person for the remainder
1001–2000 inclusive	The aggregate of: (*a*) £25 per person for the first 50 persons (£1,250); (*b*) £20 per person for the next 150 persons (£3,000); (*c*) £15 per person for the next 800 persons (£12,000); and (*d*) £10 per person for the remainder
Over 2000	The aggregate of: (*a*) £25 per person for the first 50 persons £1,250); (*b*) £20 per person for the next 150 persons (£3,000); (*c*) £15 per person for the next 800 persons (£12,000); (*d*) £10 per person for the next 1000 persons (£10,000); and (*e*) £5 per person for the remainder.

(2) When the Council have resolved to impose a levy under rule 9 of these Rules they shall calculate the maximum amount which could be levied on all practising insurance brokers and enrolled bodies corporate who are subject to a levy and on the register or list on the levy date ('the total maximum levy') such amount being calculated in accordance with paragraph (1) of this rule. The Council shall then levy on each practising insurance broker or enrolled body corporate who is subject to a levy an amount which is to be calculated in respect of each business in accordance with the following fraction:

$$\frac{\text{the total actual levy}}{\text{the total maximum levy}} \times \text{the maximum levy}$$

where 'the total actual levy' means the aggregate amount to be levied on all practising insurance brokers and enrolled bodies corporate who are subject to a levy.

12. (1)(i) Enrolled bodies corporate which are related companies for the purposes of these Rules may agree and if so notify the Council in writing from time to

time of such agreement that for the purposes of rules 10 and 11 of these Rules the levy shall be based upon the aggregate number of individuals engaged in the business of, or employed by, all such related companies in the United Kingdom but so that the liability of each such related company to pay the levy so calculated shall be a joint and several liability to the Council.

(ii) In the events referred to in paragraph (1)(i) of this rule one statement shall be completed and submitted to the Council under the provisions of rule 13(5) of these Rules in respect of all the related companies who have agreed and notified their agreement to the Council under the provisions of paragraph (1)(i) of this rule provided that the obligation to complete and submit such a statement shall be a joint and several obligation on each of the related companies.

(iii) The provisions of paragraph (1)(i) and (ii) of this rule shall not apply in respect of businesses carried on in partnership.

(2) (i) A practising insurance broker who carries on more than one business as a sole proprietor may for the purposes of rules 10 and 11 of these Rules notify the Council in writing that the levy to be paid by him shall be based upon the aggregate of the practising insurance broker and the number of individuals engaged in, or employed by him, in all such businesses.

(ii) In the events referred to in paragraph 2(i) of this rule one statement shall be completed and submitted to the Council under the provisions of rule 13(5) of these Rules in respect of all such businesses.

(3) Practising insurance brokers and enrolled bodies corporate who carry on business in two or more partnerships in which not less than one half of the partners in each such partnership are the same persons may agree and if so notify the Council in writing from time to time of such agreement for the purposes of rules 10 and 11 of these Rules that they shall be deemed to be related companies and that the provisions of paragraph (1) of this rule shall apply mutatis mutandis to all such practising insurance brokers and enrolled bodies corporate.

(4) The expression 'related company' in this rule shall mean any subsidiary or holding company or any subsidiary of a holding company of the enrolled body corporate where 'subsidiary' and 'holding company' shall be construed in accordance with the provisions of section 154 of the Companies Act 1948 or section 148 of the Companies Act (Northern Ireland) 1960 as the case may be.

13.—(1) On imposing a levy under the provisions of these Rules the Council shall send to every practising insurance broker and enrolled body corporate to whom a levy applies a written notice in accordance with the provisions of these Rules.

(2) A notice under paragraph (1) of this rule shall indicate:

(i) the circumstances in which a levy is being imposed;

(ii) the amount of the total levy; and

(iii) the amount of the levy payable in respect of each of the businesses of the practising insurance broker or enrolled body corporate.

(3) The practising insurance broker or enrolled body corporate to whom notice of a levy is sent under paragraph (1) of this rule shall pay to the Council within one month from the date of service of the notice the amount specified in the notice provided that if the said amount is not paid within such month the Council may, without prejudice to any remedy or action they may be entitled to take, charge interest on any unpaid amounts at a rate of 4 per centum per annum over the Bank of England's prevailing minimum lending rate from the expiry of the said month until the date of payment.

(4) Any sum due to the Council in respect of a levy imposed under the provisions of these Rules shall be recoverable in any court of competent jurisdiction.

(5) For the purpose of providing the Council with evidence for the calculation of any levy practising insurance brokers and enrolled bodies corporate shall at the same time as

any fee is paid under rules made under section 8 of the Act complete and submit a statement upon the appropriate form available from the Registrar.

(6) A notice under the provisions of these Rules imposing a levy may be sent by post, and a letter containing such a notice shall be deemed to be properly addressed if it is addressed to the practising insurance broker or enrolled body corporate at the registered address in respect of such practising insurance broker or enrolled body corporate.

14.—(1)(i) Every applicant shall complete, sign and deliver to the Council a Notice in the form set out in the Appendix to these Rules.

(ii) Every such Notice shall be delivered within six months after the loss or likelihood of loss, or failure to account, as the case may be, first came to the knowledge of the applicant.

(2) The Council may require an application to be supported by a statutory declaration made by the applicant and by the production to the Council of any relevant documents and may cause such enquiries to be made in relation to the application as they see fit.

(3) The Council may, before deciding whether or not to make a grant, require the pursuit of any civil remedy which in their opinion is still available in respect of the loss to the applicant or that criminal proceedings shall have been instituted in respect of any dishonesty leading to the loss.

(4) Where the Council make or intend to make a grant under the Scheme the Council shall be subrogated, to the extent specified in the following paragraph of this rule, to any rights and remedies of the applicant to whom the grant is made ('the grantee') in relation to the act or default in respect of which it is made, and shall be entitled, upon giving him a sufficient indemnity against costs, to require him, whether before or after payment of the grant, to sue in his own name but on behalf of the Council for the purpose of giving effect to the Council's rights, and to permit the Council to have the conduct of the proceedings.

(5) The extent to which the Council is subrogated under the provisions of paragraph (4) of this rule is the amount of any grant made to the grantee.

(6) A grantee shall be required by the Council upon receiving a sufficient indemnity against costs to sign an undertaking to prove or rank, if required, in the bankruptcy or liquidation of the practising insurance broker or enrolled body corporate or partnership as the case may be together with a further undertaking to comply with all proper requirements of the Council in exercise of subrogated rights under the provisions of paragraph (4) of this rule.

(7) The Council may entertain an application for a supplementary grant by way of a sum in lieu of interest on a principal grant in respect of the period from the date of the loss to the date of the authorisation of the principal grant and the Council may also entertain an application for a further grant for the amount of the applicant's solicitor's costs incurred wholly and exclusively in connection with the preparation, submission and proof of the application for a principal or supplementary grant.

(8) A grant under the provisions of these Rules may be made by way of a loan upon such terms and conditions including terms and conditions as to the time and manner of repayment, the payment of interest and the giving of security for repayment as the Council may determine and the Council may at any time or times, upon such terms and conditions, if any, as the Council shall decide, waive or refrain from enforcing the repayment of the whole or any part of the loan, the payment of any interest on the loan or any of its terms and conditions.

(9) For the purposes of these Rules 'a grant by way of loan' shall be deemed to be a grant for all other purposes of these Rules.

(10) If the Council refuse to make a grant for either the whole or part of the amount applied for then the Council shall cause the applicant to be informed in writing of the reason for their decision.

(11) In these Rules, where the context so admits, references to the applicant or

grantee shall include, in the event of his death, insolvency or other disability, reference to his personal representatives or to his trustee, or assignee, in bankruptcy or other representative as the case may be.

15.—(1) All levies received by the Council under the provisions of these Rules shall be paid into a fund to be maintained and administered by the Council on trust for the purposes provided in these Rules, such fund to be known as 'the Grants Fund'.

(2) All grants to be made by the Council shall be made out of the Grants Fund.

(3) The Council may invest in securities in which trustees are authorised by law to invest trust funds in their hands, any money which forms part of the Grants Fund.

(4) Subject to the provisions of section 1 of the Borrowing (Control and Guarantees) Act 1946 and of any order under that section for the time being in force, the Council may borrow for the purposes of the Grants Fund from any lender and may charge any investments of the Grants Fund by way of security for any such loan.

(5) There shall be carried to the credit of the Grants Fund:

(i) all levies paid to the Council in pursuance of these Rules;
(ii) all interest, dividends and other income and accretions of capital arising from the investment of the Grants Fund or any part of it;
(iii) the proceeds of any realisation of any investments of the Grants Fund;
(iv) all money borrowed for the purposes of the Grants Fund;
(v) all sums received by the Council under the provisions of rules 14, 17 and 18 of these Rules;
(vi) all other money which may belong or accrue to the Grants Fund or be received by the Council in respect of the Grants Fund;
(vii) all tax recovered by the Council in respect of the Grants Fund.

(6) All money from time to time forming part of the Grants Fund and all investments of the Grants Fund shall be applicable:

(i) for payment of any grants which the Council may make under the provisions of these Rules;
(ii) for payment of any costs, charges and expenses of establishing, maintaining, administering and applying the Grants Fund;
(iii) for payment of any premiums on insurances effected by the Council under the provisions of rule 17 of these Rules;
(iv) for repayment of any money borrowed by the Council for the purposes of the Grants Fund and for payment of interest on any money so borrowed;
(v) for payment of all costs, charges and expenses incurred by the Council by virtue of rules 14 and 18 of these Rules;
(vi) for payment of any other sums properly payable out of the Grants Fund by virtue of the provisions of these Rules;
(vii) for payment of any tax assessable in respect of the Grants Fund.

16. The Council shall have power from time to time and in their absolute discretion, for the purpose of Part III of these Rules to require practising insurance brokers or enrolled bodies corporate to:

(1) supply other and additional information; and

(2) produce, at a time during ordinary business hours and at a place to be fixed by the Council, their accounting records, files, other records and all or any documentation as may relate to matters covered by these Rules for the inspection of any person appointed by the Council and to supply to such person any necessary information and explanations.

Part IV—Miscellaneous

17.—(1) The Council may effect a policy or policies of insurance with authorised insurers, in such amounts without limit as the Council shall decide, to provide:

(i) all or any of the Council, practising insurance brokers or former practising insurance brokers or enrolled bodies corporate or former enrolled bodies corporate with indemnity against claims arising from all or any matters referred to in rule 3(1) and (2) of these Rules; and

(ii) the Council with indemnity in respect of payments made under the Grants Scheme referred to in these Rules.

(2) If the Council so resolve the premium or premiums payable under any policy or policies taken out under the provisions of paragraph (1) of this rule may be recovered by the Council by way of levy under the provisions of rule 9 of these Rules.

18.—(1) In the event that a practising insurance broker or enrolled body corporate has failed to comply with the provisions of these Rules either in whole or in part and in consequence of such failure a grant has been made under Part III of these Rules or a claim made under any policy or policies taken out under the provisions of rule 17 of these Rules the Council or the insurer under such policy or policies shall be entitled to be indemnified by him or it in respect of the full amount of the grant or claim and to recover such amount and all costs, charges and expenses incurred by the Council or insurer in respect thereof.

(2) Where a grant has been made by the Council under the provisions of these Rules in consequence of the act or omission of a practising insurance broker or enrolled body corporate then the Council or, if the insurer under a policy taken out under the provisions of rule 17 of these Rules shall have indemnified the Council in respect of the whole or part of such grant, the insurer with the consent of the Council may take proceedings against him or it in respect of the sum so paid by way of grant or indemnity and all costs, charges and expenses incurred in connection therewith.

19. A practising insurance broker or enrolled body corporate shall be exempt from complying with the requirements of Part II of these Rules in respect of any business, whether carried on alone or in partnership, which is accepted by the Committee of Lloyd's as a Lloyd's broking business provided that on any such business ceasing to be accepted as a Lloyd's broking business by the Committee of Lloyd's a practising insurance broker or enrolled body corporate carrying on such business shall forthwith be required to ensure that the requirements of the said Part II of these Rules are complied with in respect of such business.

APPENDIX

GRANTS SCHEME

Form of Application for Grant

Name(s) of insurance broker(s)
in respect of whom this Notice is
delivered.................................

....

....

Address....................................

I/We..

....

....

(full name(s) in block capitals)

of..

....

(full address in block capitals)

hereby give Notice that I (we) have sustained a loss of (or approximately of) ....

which I (we) believe to be in consequence of the negligence or fraud or dishonesty of the insurance broker(s) named above or employees of his (theirs), or which I (we) allege to be through failure on the part of the insurance broker(s) named above to account to me (us) for money received by him (them) or employees of his (theirs).

I (we) apply to the Insurance Brokers Registration Council that in the exercise of the discretion conferred upon them by the Insurance Brokers Registration Council (Indemnity Insurance and Grants Scheme) Rules 1979 they make a grant to me (us) in respect of my (our) loss of any sum which they may think proper out of the Grants Scheme for the purpose of relieving or mitigating the loss which I (we) have suffered in consequence of the negligence, fraud or dishonesty of or failure to account by the insurance broker(s).

Full details relative to this claim are set out in the Schedule of Particulars attached to this application.

Signed ....

....

Date ....

(Note: The Council reserve the right in their absolute discretion to require the applicant to make a statutory declaration in support of this application).

To: The Registrar,

Insurance Brokers Registration Council,

15 St Helen's Place,

London EC3A 6DS.

Schedule of Particulars

This should contain the following information which should be given in numbered paragraphs:

1. The circumstances in which and the date or dates upon which the money in respect of which the loss has been sustained came into possession of the insurance broker(s) or his (their) employee(s).
2. Full particulars of the money.
3. The facts relied upon in support of the allegation of negligence or fraud or dishonesty or failure to account.
4. The circumstances in and date upon which the loss first came to the knowledge of the applicant.
5. Particulars of any relevant documents which can be produced in support of this application.
6. Whether it is known that any other application is likely to be made in respect of the facts set out in this Schedule.
7. Whether any civil, criminal or disciplinary proceedings have been or will be taken in respect of the facts set out in this application. If proceedings have already been taken give the result.
8. The name and address of any solicitor instructed on behalf of the applicant.

9. Whether there are any sums due to the insurance broker(s) relating to the transaction(s) giving rise to the loss or relating to any other transaction in which the insurance broker(s) acted for the applicant.

INSURANCE BROKERS REGISTRATION COUNCIL (ACCOUNTS AND BUSINESS REQUIREMENTS) RULES APPROVAL ORDER 1979

(SI 1979/489)

1. This Order may be cited as the Insurance Brokers Registration Council (Accounts and Business Requirements) Rules Approval Order 1979 and shall come into operation on 1st July 1979.

2. The Insurance Brokers Registration Council (Accounts and Business Requirements) Rules 1979 made by the Insurance Brokers Registration Council in exercise of their powers under section 11(1), (2), (3) and (7) of the Insurance Brokers (Registration) Act 1977 are hereby approved as set out in the Schedule to this Order.

SCHEDULE

THE INSURANCE BROKERS REGISTRATION COUNCIL (ACCOUNTS AND BUSINESS REQUIREMENTS) RULES 1979

The Insurance Brokers Registration Council, in exercise of their powers under section 11(1), (2), (3) and (7) of the Insurance Brokers (Registration) Act 1977, hereby make the following Rules:

PART I—PRELIMINARY

1. These Rules may be cited as the Insurance Brokers Registration Council (Accounts and Business Requirements) Rules 1979.

2.—(1) In these Rules, unless the context otherwise requires:

'the Act' means the Insurance Brokers (Registration) Act 1977;

'brokerage' means any remuneration originating from insurance broking business;

'business' means an insurance broking business or any business which includes an insurance broking business.

(2) For the purposes of these Rules, unless the context otherwise requires, every business carried on by a partnership shall be deemed to be carried on jointly and severally by all the partners thereof.

PART II

REQUIREMENTS AS TO WORKING CAPITAL, ASSETS AND INDEPENDENCE (PURSUANT TO SECTION 11(1) OF THE ACT)

3.—(1) Practising insurance brokers and enrolled bodies corporate shall ensure that at all times they have working capital of not less than £1,000 in each of their businesses.

(2) For the purposes of this rule:

(i) practising insurance brokers and enrolled bodies corporate carrying on a business in partnership shall ensure that at all times there is working capital of not less than £1,000 in such business but so that the liability of each such partner to ensure compliance with this rule shall be a joint and several obligation on each of the partners; and

(ii) 'working capital' shall mean the aggregate of the current assets of the business, being the figure to be shown in Total K in paragraph 2 of Part I of the Statement of Particulars set out in the Appendix to these Rules calculated in accordance with the provisions of such Appendix, less the aggregate of the current liabilities of the business, being the figure to be shown in Total X in paragraph 2 of Part I of the said Statement of Particulars calculated in accordance with the provisions of such Appendix.

4.—(1) Practising insurance brokers and enrolled bodies corporate shall ensure that at all times the value of the assets of each of their businesses exceeds the amount of the liabilities of that business by not less than £1,000.

(2) For the purposes of this rule:

(i) practising insurance brokers and enrolled bodies corporate carrying on a business in partnership shall ensure that at all times the value of the assets of such business exceeds the amount of the liabilities of that business by not less than £1,000 but so that the liability of each such partner to ensure compliance with this rule shall be a joint and several obligation on each of the partners;

(ii) 'the value of the assets' shall mean the aggregate of the value of the assets of the business being the figure to be shown in Total M in paragraph 2 of Part I of the Statement of Particulars set out in the Appendix to these Rules calculated in accordance with the provisions of such Appendix; and

(iii) 'the amount of the liabilities' shall mean the aggregate amount of the liabilities of the business being the figure to be shown in Total Z in paragraph 2 of Part I of the Statement of Particulars set out in the Appendix to these Rules calculated in accordance with the provisions of such Appendix.

5.—(1) Practising insurance brokers and enrolled bodies corporate shall ensure that the number of insurance companies with which each of their businesses place insurance business, and the amount of insurance business which each of their businesses place with each insurance company, is such as to prevent each such business from becoming unduly dependent on any particular insurance company.

(2) For the purposes of demonstrating to the satisfaction of the Council that the provisions of paragraph (1) of this rule are being complied with practising insurance brokers and enrolled bodies corporate shall at the same time as they submit any accounts or statement to the Council in respect of a business in accordance with the provisions of rule 8 of these Rules complete and submit the Questionnaire in Part II of the Statement of Particulars set out in the Appendix to these Rules in respect of such business.

Part III

Requirements as to Accounts and Accounting Records (Pursuant to Section 11(2) of the Act)

6.—(1) For the purposes set out in this rule one or more separate bank accounts shall be maintained with approved banks by each practising insurance broker and enrolled body corporate for each separate insurance broking business which they carry on. Each such account shall contain in its title the name of the practising insurance broker or enrolled body corporate or the names of the partners or the name of the partnership if the practising insurance broker or enrolled body corporate carries on the business in partnership. Each such account shall be designated and is hereinafter called an 'Insurance Broking Account', and money standing to the credit of such an Insurance Broking Account shall be used solely for the purposes set out in this rule.

(2) A practising insurance broker or enrolled body corporate opening an Insurance Broking Account with an approved bank shall inform such bank in writing and forthwith obtain a written acknowledgement therefrom:

(i) that the account shall be designated 'Insurance Broking Account' and that the title of the account shall contain the name of the practising insurance broker or enrolled body corporate or the names of the partners or the name of the partnership if the practising insurance broker or enrolled body corporate carries on the business in partnership;

(ii) that the Insurance Broking Account is being opened to comply with the provisions of these Rules; and

(iii) that the bank is not to be entitled to any charge, encumbrance, lien, right of set-off, compensation or retention against money standing to the credit of the Insurance Broking Account or any approved short term assets held for the Insurance Broking Account of the practising insurance broker, enrolled body corporate or partnership except in the circumstances set out in paragraph (7) of this rule.

(3) Practising insurance brokers and enrolled bodies corporate shall without delay pay or cause to be paid into the Insurance Broking Account and into no other account all monies paid to or received by them from all sources and which relate to insurance transactions of any kind in connection with their insurance broking business, including brokerage.

(4) Practising insurance brokers and enrolled bodies corporate shall use the Insurance Broking Account and no other account for payment to an insured or an insurance company of all monies due under insurance transactions of any kind in connection with their insurance broking business.

(5) In addition to the purposes set out in paragraphs (3) and (4) of this rule and always subject to there being no breach of paragraph (8) of this rule at the time the Insurance Broking Account is used, the Insurance Broking Account shall be used for the following purposes and for none other:

(i) for all transactions relating to approved short term assets as provided for in paragraph (6) of this rule;

(ii) for the withdrawal of brokerage;

(iii) for the withdrawal of any money paid into the Insurance Broking Account in error;

(iv) for the receipt of funds necessary for the operation of the account;

(v) for the withdrawal of any surpluses arising on the Insurance Broking Account.

(6) (i) Subject to the provisions of sub-paragraph (v) of this paragraph practising insurance brokers and enrolled bodies corporate are permitted to hold monies standing to the credit of the Insurance Broking Account in, or to purchase out of such monies, any approved short term assets. Such approved short term assets shall be:

EITHER

(*a*) registered in their name or the partnership name if appropriate and designated 'Insurance Broking Account';

OR

(*b*) so far as the approved short term assets defined in paragraph (9)(ii), (vii) or (viii) of this rule are concerned, held for the Insurance Broking Account of the practising insurance broker, enrolled body corporate or partnership if appropriate at the approved bank at which such Insurance Broking Account is held.

(ii) Approved short term assets must be readily realisable, that is to say, within a period of not more than one month, they can be readily and easily converted into or sold or realised for cash which can be immediately credited to or is immediately eligible for credit to an Insurance Broking Account.

(iii) Monies, other than interest, arising from approved short term assets or their realisation, sale or disposal shall be paid into an Insurance Broking Account and no other account.

(iv) For the purpose of this rule, unless the context otherwise requires, the expression 'Insurance Broking Account' shall include all approved short term assets so designated or held for such Insurance Broking Account in accordance with the provisions of this paragraph (6).

(v) No money standing to the credit of the Insurance Broking Account shall be held in any approved short term assets defined in paragraph (9)(i) of this rule until the practising insurance broker or enrolled body corporate shall have informed in writing the approved bank or licensed institution with whom the deposit account is to be opened or from whom the deposit receipt is to be obtained and forthwith obtained a written acknowledgement therefrom:—

(*a*) that the deposit account and deposit receipt shall be designated 'Insurance Broking Account' and that the title of the account shall contain the name of the practising insurance broker or enrolled body corporate or the names of the partners or the name of the partnership if the practising insurance broker or enrolled body corporate carries on the business in partnership; and

(*b*) that the approved bank or licensed institution is not to be entitled to any charge, encumbrance, lien, right of set-off, compensation or retention against money standing to the credit of the deposit account or represented by the deposit receipt except in the circumstances set out in paragraph (7) of this rule.

(7) (i) (*a*) No advance, whether by way of loan, overdraft or otherwise, may be obtained by a practising insurance broker or an enrolled body corporate for any purpose relating to the Insurance Broking Account except on a bank account with an approved bank in circumstances which do not give rise to a breach of the requirements of paragraph (8) of this rule.

(*b*) Any advance obtained shall be of a temporary nature and repaid as soon as reasonably practicable and the bank account itself shall be designated 'Insurance Broking Account' and be used only for the purposes set out in paragraph (4) of this rule and the withdrawal of brokerage but not for the withdrawal of any surpluses on the Insurance Broking Account.

(*c*) Subject to the provisions of paragraph (7)(ii) of this rule approved short term assets may only be charged to or deposited with an approved bank to secure an advance by way of loan, overdraft or otherwise on a bank account obtained in accordance with the provisions of this rule but not otherwise.

(*d*) An approved bank making an advance by way of loan, overdraft or otherwise on an Insurance Broking Account in accordance with the provisions of these Rules shall be entitled to any lien, right of set-off, compensation or retention in respect of such advance to which that bank is otherwise entitled at law over or against monies standing to the credit of another Insurance Broking Account of the same business held with that bank.

(ii) Approved short term assets may be charged to or deposited with an approved bank to secure the issue of a letter of credit by an approved bank PROVIDED THAT such letter of credit shall only be obtained in circumstances which do not give rise to a breach of the requirements of paragraph (8) of this rule and shall be used only for the purposes set out in paragraph (4) of this rule but not for the withdrawal of brokerage or surpluses on the Insurance Broking Account.

(iii) Nothing in these Rules shall be construed as requiring an approved bank making an advance or issuing a letter of credit in accordance with the provisions of this rule to make any inquiry or satisfy itself that the provisions of these Rules are or will be complied with by the practising insurance broker or enrolled body corporate to whom or to whose partnership such an advance is to be made or for whom or for whose partnership such letter of credit is being issued.

(8) (i) Practising insurance brokers and enrolled bodies corporate shall ensure that at all times the value of the insurance transactions assets of each of their businesses is not less than the amount of the insurance transactions liabilities of that business.

(ii) For the purposes of paragraph (8)(i) of this rule:

'insurance transactions assets' shall mean the aggregate of balances on banking accounts designated 'Insurance Broking Account', approved short term assets designated 'Insurance Broking Account' or held for the Insurance Broking Account of the practising insurance broker, enrolled body corporate or partnership at an approved bank at which such Insurance Broking Account is held and debtors in respect of insurance transactions being the figure to be shown in Total H in paragraph 2 of Part I of the Statement of Particulars set out in the Appendix to these Rules and calculated in accordance with the provisions of such Appendix; and

'insurance transactions liabilities' shall mean the aggregate of creditors in respect of insurance transactions and bank advances designated 'Insurance Broking Account' being the figure to be shown in Total V in paragraph 2 of Part I of the Statement of Particulars set out in the Appendix to these Rules and calculated in accordance with the provisions of such Appendix.

(9) For the purposes of this rule 'approved short term assets' shall be those assets purchased with or provided from monies drawn from an Insurance Broking Account and which fall into one of the following categories:

(i) deposit accounts and deposit receipts with approved banks and licensed institutions;

(ii) certificates of deposit of approved banks and licensed institutions;

(iii) deposits with a building society which has been designated for the purpose of section 1 of the House Purchase and Housing Act 1959;

(iv) loans to and deposits with any local authority in the United Kingdom;

(v) fixed or floating rate interest marketable securities which will mature for repayment within five years from the date of purchase and (*a*) are issued or guaranteed by Her Majesty's Government in the United Kingdom; or (*b*) are issued in the United Kingdom by any local authority or public authority or nationalised undertaking in the United Kingdom; or (*c*) are issued by any water authority or statutory water company in the United Kingdom; or (*d*) are issued by the International Bank for Reconstruction and Development being securities registered in the United Kingdom;

(vi) British Savings Bonds;

(vii) British Treasury Bills and Northern Ireland Treasury Bills;

(viii) Bills accepted by any public or local authority or nationalised undertaking in the United Kingdom or bank acceptances eligible for rediscount at the Bank of England.

(10) Except as provided by these Rules, practising insurance brokers or enrolled bodies corporate shall not by their own act or omission create, nor so far as they are legally able shall they permit to arise, any charge or encumbrance upon an Insurance Broking Account, or upon any approved short term assets, or upon debtors in respect of insurance transactions, nor shall they create or permit to arise by their own act or omission, nor so far as they are able shall they by their own act or omission permit to arise as a matter of law, any lien, right of set-off, compensation or retention in favour of any other person over or against money standing to the credit of an Insurance Broking Account, or any approved short term assets, or upon debtors in respect of insurance transactions.

(11) For the purposes of this rule:

(i) 'approved bank' means:

(*a*) a recognised bank within the meaning of the Banking Act 1979; and (*b*) a trustee savings bank as defined by section 3 of the Trustee Savings Bank Act 1969; and

(*c*) the National Girobank being the name under which the Post Office provides its banking services;

(ii) 'insurance' includes assurance, reinsurance or reassurance and 'insured' shall be construed accordingly;

(iii) 'insured' and 'insurance company' include agents of an insured or insurance company, and any other person to whom payments are due under, or in connection with, a contract of insurance;

(iv) 'monies which relate to insurance transactions' and 'monies due under insurance transactions' include the following individual items or balances representing the same:

(*a*) premiums, additional premiums and return premiums of all kinds;

(*b*) claims and other monies due under contracts of insurance;

(*c*) refunds and salvages;

(*d*) fees, charges, taxes and similar fiscal levies relating to contracts of insurance;

(*e*) all forms of reserves under contracts of insurance and any adjustment of them;

(*f*) discounts and brokerage.

(v) 'licensed institution' means a licensed institution within the meaning of the Banking Act 1979.

7. Practising insurance brokers and enrolled bodies corporate shall ensure that accounting records are kept in respect of each of their businesses in accordance with the following requirements:

(i) the accounting records shall be sufficient to show and explain the transactions of the business;

(ii) the accounting records shall be such as to:

(*a*) disclose with reasonable accuracy, at any time, the financial position of the business at that time; and

(*b*) ensure that any balance sheet, profit and loss account or other statement of the financial position of the business prepared is capable of giving a true and fair view of the state of affairs of the business as at the date to which the balance sheet is drawn up and of the profit or loss for the accounting period then ended;

(iii) the accounting records shall in particular contain:

(*a*) entries from day to day of all sums of money received and expended in the course of the business and the matters in respect of which the receipt and expenditure takes place; and

(*b*) a record of the assets and liabilities of the business;

(iv) the accounting records shall be such as to enable compliance with the relevant provisions of these Rules to be demonstrated at any time.

(v) the accounting records shall be preserved for at least three years from the date of the last entry made therein.

8.—(1) Practising insurance brokers and enrolled bodies corporate shall prepare and draw up accounts in respect of each of their businesses:

(i) if the business has not been carried on for twelve consecutive months at the date of, or at the date of amendment to, registration or enrolment for a period beginning with the day of commencement of business and not exceeding twelve months; and

(ii) if the business has been carried on for more than twelve consecutive months at the date of, or at the date of amendment to, registration or enrolment for a period beginning with the day following the accounting date referred to in the appropriate form submitted to the Council in connection with an application for, or amendment to, registration or enrolment and not exceeding twelve months

and thereafter shall similarly draw up and prepare accounts for periods not exceeding twelve months and beginning with the day following the expiry of the period for which the previous accounts were prepared and drawn up.

(2) The accounts required by this rule and the statement required by rule 9(2)(iii) of these Rules shall be submitted to the Council within six months of the expiry of the accounting period to which they relate.

(3) In any case where a practising insurance broker or enrolled body corporate makes a written application to the Council before the expiry of the period in which any accounts would otherwise have been required to be submitted in accordance with the provisions of this rule the Council, if they think fit, may by notice in writing to the practising insurance broker or enrolled body corporate extend by such further period as may be specified in the notice the period of twelve months referred to in paragraph (1) of this rule but so that the said period as so extended may not exceed eighteen months. In the event of the Council giving such notice they may lay down such other requirements as they consider necessary in all the circumstances.

9.—(1)(i) Accounts to be prepared and drawn up in respect of the business of practising insurance brokers and partnerships in accordance with paragraph (1) of rule 8 of these Rules shall comprise a balance sheet, a profit and loss account and notes to the accounts such as to show a true and fair view of the state of affairs of the business as at the date to which the balance sheet is drawn up and of the profit or loss for the accounting period then ended and attached thereto shall be an auditor's report in compliance with the requirements of rule 11 of these Rules.

(ii) The profit and loss account referred to in paragraph (1)(i) of this rule shall:

(*a*) show the total revenue of the business, dividing such revenue between that directly derived from insurance broking business and all other revenue;

(*b*) classify expenditure grouped under appropriate headings; and

(*c*) show or disclose by way of note to the account the total brokerage contained in the account.

(iii) Where the profit and loss account referred to in paragraph (1)(i) of this rule includes revenue derived from any business other than insurance broking business the nature of each such business shall be disclosed by way of note annexed to the account.

(2) (i) Accounts to be prepared and drawn up by enrolled bodies corporate in accordance with paragraph (1) of rule 8 of these Rules shall comply in all respects with the Companies Act 1948 and the Companies Act 1967 or, in the case of Northern Ireland, the Companies Acts (Northern Ireland) 1960 and 1978 and shall include such documents as are or would be required to be comprised in the accounts if they were to be laid before the enrolled body corporate in general meeting in accordance with the Companies Act 1948, the Companies Act 1967 and the Companies Act 1976 or, in the case of Northern Ireland, the Companies Acts (Northern Ireland) 1960 and 1978.

(ii) Accounts to be prepared and drawn up by a holding company in respect of its own business in accordance with paragraph (1) of rule 8 of these Rules may be group accounts provided that such accounts shall comply in all respects with the provisions of paragraph (2)(i) of this rule and provided further that a profit and loss account shall also be prepared and drawn up in respect of its own business. Such profit and loss account shall comply in all respects with the Companies Act 1948 and the Companies Act 1967 or, in the case of Northern Ireland, the Companies Acts (Northern Ireland) 1960 and 1978, as if it had been a profit and loss account to which the provisions of such Acts applied.

(iii) The profit and loss account of an enrolled body corporate's own business shall be supplemented by a statement:

(*a*) showing the total revenue of the business dividing such revenue between that directly derived from insurance broking business and all other revenue;

(*b*) classifying expenditure grouped under appropriate headings; and

(*c*) showing the total brokerage contained in the account unless specifically disclosed therein.

(iv) Where the profit and loss account of an enrolled body corporate's own business comprising part of the accounts referred to in paragraph (2)(i) or (2)(ii) of this rule includes revenue derived from any business other than insurance broking business the nature of each such business shall be disclosed in the statement referred to in paragraph (2)(iii) of this rule.

(v) For the purposes of this rule the expression 'holding company' shall be construed in accordance with the provisions of section 154 of the Companies Act 1948 or, in the case of Northern Ireland, section 148 of the Companies Act (Northern Ireland) 1960.

PART IV—SUPPLEMENTARY

10. Practising insurance brokers and enrolled bodies corporate shall at the same time as they submit any accounts or statement to the Council in respect of a business in accordance with the provisions of rule 8 of these Rules complete and submit a Statement of Particulars in the form set out in the Appendix to these Rules in respect of such business and the balance sheet of their own business forming part of the accounts prepared and drawn up in accordance with the provisions of rule 9 of these Rules shall also be analysed and set out in the form of Part I of the Statement of Particulars set out in the Appendix to these Rules and in accordance with the definitions and instructions contained therein.

11.—(1) The accounts required to be prepared and drawn up and submitted to the Council by practising insurance brokers and enrolled bodies corporate in accordance with the provisions of rules 8 and 9 of these Rules shall in the case of the business of:

(i) enrolled bodies corporate be audited in accordance with the provisions of the Companies Act 1948 and the Companies Act 1967 or, in the case of Northern Ireland, the Companies Acts (Northern Ireland) 1960 and 1978, and the enrolled body corporate shall ensure that a report shall be made by the auditor to comply in all respects with the provisions of section 14 of the Companies Act 1967 or, in the case of Northern Ireland, the corresponding provisions of the Companies Acts (Northern Ireland) 1960 and 1978; and

(ii) practising insurance brokers and partnerships be audited and each practising insurance broker or partner shall ensure that the auditor shall make a report to the practising insurance broker or the partners stating whether in the auditor's opinion a true and fair view is given, in the case of the balance sheet, of the state of the affairs of the business at the end of the period covered by the accounts, and, in the case of the profit and loss account, of the profit or loss of the business for that period.

(2) (i) A practising insurance broker or an enrolled body corporate shall ensure that the auditor in preparing his report in accordance with the provisions hereof shall carry out such investigations as will enable him to form an opinion as to the following matters, that is to say:

(*a*) whether proper accounting records have been kept in accordance with the provisions of rule 7 of these Rules and proper returns adequate for the audit have been received from branches not visited; and

(*b*) whether the balance sheet and profit and loss account are in accordance with the accounting records and returns and if the auditor is of the opinion that proper accounting records have not been kept in accordance with the provisions of rule 7 of these Rules or that proper returns adequate for the audit have not been received from branches not visited or if the balance sheet and profit and loss account are not in agreement with the accounting records and returns, the practising insurance broker or the enrolled body corporate shall ensure that the auditor shall state that fact in his report.

(ii) If the auditor fails to obtain all the information and explanations which, to the best of his knowledge and belief, are necessary for the purposes of the audit, the practising insurance broker or the enrolled body corporate shall ensure that he shall state that fact in his report.

(3) The Statement of Particulars in the form set out in the Appendix to these Rules shall contain an accountant's report in the form set out in Part IV of such Appendix.

(4) Practising insurance brokers and enrolled bodies corporate shall allow the auditor or accountant signing the report for the purposes of carrying out his duties in accordance with these Rules full right of access at all times to the books, vouchers and accounting records and the said auditor or accountant shall be entitled to require from practising insurance brokers or the officers of enrolled bodies corporate such information and explanations as he may think necessary for the performance of his duties as auditor or accountant under these Rules.

12. Any auditor's report submitted to the Council in compliance with these Rules shall only be given by an accountant qualified in accordance with subsections (4), (5) and (6) of section 11 of the Act.

13. The Council shall have powers, from time to time and in their absolute discretion, for the purposes of ascertaining whether or not the provisions of these Rules are being complied with, to require practising insurance brokers or enrolled bodies corporate to:

(i) supply other or additional information, explanations or reports;

(ii) instruct the auditor or accountant signing a report to supply other or additional information, explanations or reports; and

(iii) produce, at a time during usual business hours and at a place to be fixed by the Council, the accounting records, bank passbooks, looseleaf bank statements, statements of account, vouchers and any other necessary documents for the inspection of any person appointed by the Council and to supply to such person any necessary information and explanations.

Part V—Exemptions

14. A practising insurance broker or enrolled body corporate shall be exempt from complying with the requirements of these Rules in respect of any business, whether carried on alone or in partnership, which is accepted by the Committee of Lloyd's as a Lloyd's broking business provided that on any such business ceasing to be accepted as a Lloyd's broking business by the Committee of Lloyd's a practising insurance broker or enrolled body corporate carrying on such business shall forthwith be required to ensure that the requirements of these Rules are complied with in respect of such business.

APPENDIX

NOTE: Paragraph 2 of Part I of this statement of Particulars may be completed to demonstrate compliance with rules 3, 4 or 6 of the Rules and paragraph 2 of Part I when completed with the remainder of the Statement of Particulars will enable the provisions of rules 5(2) and 10 of the Rules to be complied with.

Statement of Particulars

to the Insurance Brokers Registration Council as required by the Insurance Brokers

Registration Council (Accounts and Business Requirements) Rules 1979 ('the Rules') submitted in connection with the following business:

A. NAME:.. (referred to herein as 'the insurance broker')
(Show (*a*) the forenames and surname in the case of a sole proprietor; or
(*b*) the partnership name under which the business is carried on; or
(*c*) the name of the body corporate carrying on the business)

B. PRINCIPAL PLACE OF BUSINESS:...

C. TRADING AS: ....
(Show trading or business name(s) used in addition to that in paragraph A above.)

D. Where the business is carried on in partnership or by a body corporate the names of *all* the partners OR the names of *all* the directors are shown below or on the attached schedule:

Full name including all forenames	*Registration record number* (where applicable)
....	....
....	....
....	....
....	....
....	....

(If one (or more) of the partners in the partnership is a body corporate the number shown above should be the enrolment record number and not the particulars of the directors of the body corporate.)

PART I

1. Attached are the insurance broker's latest audited accounts submitted to the Council as required by rule 8 of the rules including a balance sheet as at .... 19...... ('the accounting date'*) and a profit and loss account for the period from .... 19...... to that date, together with notes to the said accounts and an auditor's report thereon and where appropriate a statement as required by rule 9(2)(iii) of the Rules.

2. (i) The figures shown below in column 1 are based on and extracted from the accounting records as at .... 19...... ('the accounting date'*) and they have, in accordance with the definitions and instructions set out below, been analysed in the said column 1.

(ii) Where this Statement of Particulars is submitted in compliance with rule 10 of the Rules the figures shown in the audited balance sheet of the insurance broker's own business referred to in paragraph 1 above, have, in accordance with the definitions and instructions set out below, been analysed in column 1.

(iii) Where an amount appears in column 1 that amount has been restated in column 2 *but* amended where necessary to comply with the requirements of the said definitions and instructions.

*NOTE: For the purposes of the definitions and instructions set out below 'the accounting date' shall mean where this Statement of Particulars is submitted in compliance with rule 10 of the Rules the date as at which the balance sheet referred to in paragraph 1 was drawn up and in all other circumstances the date as at which the figures were extracted from the accounting records. When this Statement of Particulars is submitted in compliance with rule 10 of the Rules paragraph (i) above will not apply.

ASSETS

	Column 1	Reference numbers of the definitions and instructions	Column 2
Banking accounts designated 'Insurance Broking Account' and approved short term assets	£	1	£
Debtors in respect of insurance transactions:			
Related companies	£	2 and 20	£
Others	£	2	£
Total A	£	Total H	£
Cash and bank current account balances	£	3	£
Deposits and bills—short term	£	4	£
Other debtors—current:			
Related companies	£	5 and 20	£
Others	£	5	£
Listed investments	£	6	£
Fixed assets—office furniture and equipment and motor vehicles	£	7	£
Total B	£	Total J	£
Total A+B=Total C	£	Total H+J=Total K	£
Fixed assets—others	£	7	£
Other debtors—non-current:			
Related companies	£	5 and 20	£
Others	£	5	£
Deposits and bills—long term	£	8	£
Unlisted investments:			
Related companies	£	9 and 20	£
Others	£	9	£
Total D	£	Total L	£
Total A+B+D=Total E	£	Total H+J+L=Total M	£
All assets other than those specified above	£	10	N/A*
.. ..	£	.. .. ..	N/A*
.. ..	£	.. .. ..	N/A*
.. ..	£	.. .. ..	N/A*
Total F	£		
Total A+B+D+F=G	£		

(***Not applicable*)

NOTES OF EXPLANATION

(i) The total H in column 2 represents the aggregate of the insurance transactions assets referred to in rule 6(8)(ii) of the Rules.
(ii) The total K in column 2 represents the aggregate of the current assets referred to in rule 3(2)(ii) of the Rules.
(iii) The total M in column 2 represents the value of the assets referred to in rule 4(2)(ii) of the Rules.

LIABILITIES

	Column 1	*Reference numbers of the definitions and instructions*	*Column 2*
Creditors in respect of insurance transactions:			
Related companies.. ..	£	11 and 20	£
Others	£	11	£
Bank advances designated 'Insurance Broking Account' ..	£	12	£
Total N	£	Total V	£
Bank advances	£	13	£
Other current liabilities:			
Related companies.. ..	£	14 and 20	£
Others	£	14	£
Total P	£	Total W	£
Total N+P=Total Q	£	Total V+W=Total X	£
Deferred taxation payable within three years	£	15	£
Contingent liabilities	N/A*	16	£
Total R	£	Total Y	£
Total N+P+R=Total S	£	Total V+W+Y=Total Z	£
Long term liabilities	£	17	N/A*
Deferred taxation—long term	£	15	N/A*
Share capital and reserves (applicable only to bodies corporate)	£	18	N/A*
Proprietors' capital, reserves and undrawn profits (applicable only to partnerships and sole proprietors)	£	19	N/A*
Total T	£		
Total N+P+R+T=Total U	£		

(**Not applicable*)

NOTES OF EXPLANATION

(i) The total V in column 2 represents the aggregate of the insurance transactions liabilities referred to in rule 6(8)(ii) of the Rules.
(ii) The total X in column 2 represents the aggregate of the current liabilities referred to in rule 3(2)(ii) of the Rules.
(iii) The total Z in column 2 represents the amount of the liabilities referred to in rule 4(2)(iii) of the Rules.

3. The following assets included in the amounts in column 2 of paragraph 2 above are subject to a fixed charge, lien or encumbrance to the extent shown below or there is a 'floating charge' against the business to the extent shown below:

Description of asset	*The value of the asset included in the amount shown in the said column 2*	*Extent of charge*
....	£......................................	£......................................
....	£......................................	£......................................
....	£......................................	£......................................
....	£......................................	£......................................

If none state 'NONE'

Further charges, liens or encumbrances should be shown on a separate sheet.

4. Where *debtors in respect of insurance transactions* have been included in column 2 of paragraph 2 above and such debtors have been outstanding at the accounting date referred to in paragraph 1 above for more than nine months from the date as at which the entry is made in the insurance broker's accounting records, the total of such debtors is shown below:

£.................... If none state 'NONE'

5. During the period referred to in paragraph 1 above the following advances by way of loan, overdraft or otherwise were obtained from approved banks on an Insurance Broking Account in accordance with the provisions of rule 6(7) of the Rules for the undermentioned periods:

Periods: From	*To*	*Nature (Loan, overdraft, etc.) and purpose of the advance*	*Maximum amount of advance* £	*Details of any security given*
....	....	....	....	....

If none state 'NONE'

Further particulars should be shown on a separate sheet.

Definitions and Instructions Applying to Paragraph 2 of Part I

Note 1: Under the individual definitions and instructions *illustrations* are given of the assets or liabilities to be included. These are intended to be *illustrations* only and are not definitive of the assets or liabilities to be included under the individual headings.

Note 2: Where any asset is subject to a charge the asset shall be shown under the heading of Assets in paragraph 2 of Part I of the Appendix without any deduction for the liabilities secured by the charge. The liability shall be shown under the appropriate heading of Liabilities in paragraph 2 of Part I of the Appendix in accordance with the following definitions and instructions.

Reference number

1. *Banking accounts designated 'Insurance Broking Account' and approved short term assets* shall be those assets which satisfy rule 6 of the Rules. Such approved short term assets shall be restated in column 2 at their realisable value which in the case of marketable securities shall be deemed to be their mid-market value.
2. *Debtors in respect of insurance transactions* shall mean amounts owing by ALL debtors in respect of insurance transactions of any kind in connection with the insurance broking business as shown in the insurance broker's accounting records and shall in the case of bodies corporate (but not partnerships) be sub-divided between those due from related companies (see No. 20 below) and all other persons. These debts shall be restated in column 2 after making proper provision for any bad or doubtful debts, any discounts, rebates or other allowances requiring to be deducted therefrom. No amount shall be included in column 2 which has been outstanding at the accounting date for more than NINE months from the date as at which the entry was made in the insurance broker's accounting records unless the insurance broker is satisfied that such amount will be recovered. Where such debtors have been included there shall be disclosed the total of such debtors as required in paragraph 4 of Part I hereof.
3. *Cash and bank current account balances* shall mean such amounts as are shown by the insurance broker's accounting records and shall include cash in hand and bank current accounts where not overdrawn and which are NOT designated 'Insurance Broking Account'.
4. *Deposits and bills—short term* shall mean those deposits and bills having a realisation date on or within TWELVE months from the accounting date which are NOT designated 'Insurance Broking Account' and include bank deposit accounts, bank deposit receipts, certificates of deposit, bills, loans to and deposits with a local authority in the United Kingdom and deposits and accounts with a building society. The realisable value thereof as at the accounting date shall be restated in column 2.
5. *Other debtors* shall mean any other amounts owed to the insurance broker as shown in the insurance broker's accounting records including prepayments *(after excluding all debts due in connection with insurance transactions which debts shall be included under the heading 'Debtors in respect of insurance transactions')* and shall in the case of bodies corporate (but not partnerships) be sub-divided between those due from related companies (see No. 20 below) and all other persons. Such debtors shall also be sub-divided between those due for payment within TWELVE months of the accounting date (which shall be termed 'current') and all other amounts (which shall be termed 'non-current'). These amounts shall be restated in column 2 after making adequate provision for bad or doubtful debts.
6. *Listed investments* shall mean any investment listed on a recognised Stock Exchange which is NOT designated 'Insurance Broking Account'. The mid-market value thereof as at the accounting date shall be restated in column 2.
7. *Fixed assets—office furniture and equipment and motor vehicles* shall mean only such assets; and
   Fixed assets—others shall mean all other fixed assets, provided that in neither case shall they include any intangible assets.
   All such fixed assets shall be restated in column 2 at the option of the insurance broker, either:
   (*a*) at the value shown in column 1 provided that such value is not greater than the value calculated in accordance with (*b*) below, or

(*b*) at their estimated realisable value after due provision for any costs of realisation.

If the value as restated in column 2 were to be realised and a taxation liability would arise thereon such liability shall be included within contingent liabilities where not otherwise provided (see No. 16 below).

8. *Deposits and bills—long term* shall mean those deposits and bills having a realisation date more than TWELVE months from the accounting date which are NOT designated 'Insurance Broking Account' and include bank deposit accounts, bank deposit receipts, certificates of deposit, bills, loans to and deposits with a local authority in the United Kingdom and deposits and accounts with a building society. The realisable value thereof as at the accounting date shall be restated in column 2.

9. *Unlisted investments* shall in the case of bodies corporate (but not partnerships) be sub-divided between those in related companies (see No. 20 below) and all others. They shall be restated in column 2 at directors' or partners' or proprietor's valuation as at the accounting date. *(Amounts due from or to related companies (see No. 20 below) in respect of insurance transactions and other amounts due from or to related companies shall be shown under the appropriate headings.)*

10. *All assets other than those specified above* shall mean all assets of whatever nature not otherwise shown or included above, shall be specified separately, and shall include goodwill, formation expenses not written off and other intangible assets. No entries shall be made in column 2 in respect thereof.

11. *Creditors in respect of insurance transactions* shall mean amounts owing to ALL creditors in respect of insurance transactions of any kind in connection with the insurance broker's accounting records irrespective of when such amounts fall due for payment and shall in the case of bodies corporate (but not partnerships) be sub-divided between those due to related companies (see No. 20 below) and all other persons.

12. *Bank advances designated 'Insurance Broking Account'* shall mean such amounts as are shown by the insurance broker's accounting records to be owed to bankers on such accounts.

13. *Bank advances* shall mean such amounts as are shown by the insurance broker's accounting records to be owed to bankers on bank accounts, including bank loans, which are NOT designated 'Insurance Broking Account' and which are due for repayment on or within THIRTY-SIX months from the accounting date. *(Bank loans due for repayment after thirty-six months from the accounting date shall be included under the heading 'Long term liabilities'.)*

14. *Other current liabilities* shall mean any amount due by the insurance broker as shown in the insurance broker's accounting records including accrued expenditure, taxation and dividends *(but excluding any amounts due in respect of insurance transactions which liabilities shall be included under the heading 'Creditors in respect of insurance transactions')* which shall fall due for payment on or within THIRTY-SIX months from the accounting date and shall in the case of bodies corporate (but not partnerships) be sub-divided between those due to related companies (see No. 20 below) and all other persons.

In respect of sole proprietors and partnerships *other current liabilities* shall be restated in column 2 to include provision for partners' or proprietor's taxation for an amount whichever is the greater of:

(*a*) the total amount of the income tax at the basic rate and at the higher rates (or a fair estimate thereof) outstanding in respect of all years of assessment ended on or before the accounting date and, where applicable, the accrued proportion for the year of assessment in which the accounting date falls,

OR

(*b*) the total amount of the income tax at the basic rate and at the higher rates (or a fair estimate thereof) which would be payable if the insurance broker had ceased business at the accounting date.

15. *Deferred taxation payable within three years.* There shall be included under this heading that part of the amount which has been provided for in the insurance broker's accounting records and which it is anticipated will fall due for payment on or within THIRTY-SIX months from the accounting date. *All other deferred taxation so provided shall be included under the heading 'Deferred taxation—long term'.*
16. *Contingent liabilities.* There shall be included as contingent liabilities under column 2 (where not otherwise provided) the appropriate aggregate amount of such liabilities which shall have been quantified by the insurance broker after considering all the relevant facts and circumstances. Such appropriate aggregate amount shall be sufficient as at the accounting date to cover, for example, capital expenditure in respect of intangible assets for which the insurance broker is contracted but which is not provided for, dilapidations under leases, liabilities under contracts or guarantees, brokerage repayable to insurance companies where brokerage has been received on indemnity terms, brokerage which is repayable under the direction of the Policyholders Protection Board established by the Policyholders Protection Act 1975 and the aggregate of any contingent taxation liability that would arise from the realisation of any asset at the value included in column 2. No entry shall be made in column 1 in respect thereof.
17. *Long term liabilities* shall mean any amount due by the insurance broker as shown in the insurance broker's accounting records *(but excluding any amounts due in respect of insurance transactions which liabilities shall be included under the heading 'Creditors in respect of insurance transactions')* falling due for payment after THIRTY-SIX months from the accounting date. No entry shall be made in column 2 in respect thereof.
18. *Share capital and reserves* (applicable only to bodies corporate) shall not be required to be shown in column 2.
19. *Proprietors' capital, reserves and undrawn profits* (applicable only to partnerships and sole proprietors) shall not be required to be shown in column 2. Provision for taxation shall be included as required under No. 14 above.
20. In these definitions and instructions the expression *'related companies'* (applicable only to bodies corporate) shall mean any subsidiary or holding company or any subsidiary of a holding company of the enrolled body corporate where 'subsidiary' and 'holding company' shall be construed in accordance with the provisions of section 154 of the Companies Act 1948, or in the case of Northern Ireland, section 148 of the Companies Act (Northern Ireland) 1960, and shall also include companies which are under the control of connected persons where 'control' and 'connected' shall be construed in accordance with section 302 and 533 respectively of the Income and Corporation Taxes Act 1970.

PART II

QUESTIONNAIRE

This Part is to be completed by the insurance broker in compliance with rule 5(2) of the Rules.

1. With how many insurance companies has insurance business been placed in the last accounting period? (If over ten, write 'over ten')..................
2. What is the largest percentage of the brokerage in the last accounting period derived from such business placed with a single insurance company? (If under 15%, write 'under 15%')..................
3. If the answer to question 1 is four or less, or if the answer to question 2 is 35% or more, state below (or on a separate sheet) why it is considered that the business is not unduly

dependent on any of the insurance companies with whom such business has been placed.

....

....

NOTE OF INSTRUCTION

For the purposes of questions 1 and 2 'the last accounting period' shall mean the period covered by the accounts which have been prepared in accordance with the Insurance Brokers Registration Council (Accounts and Business Requirements) Rules 1979 and are attached to the Statement of Particulars of which this questionnaire forms part; the brokerage referred to in question 2 is the brokerage of the insurance broker's own business disclosed or contained in those accounts. 'Brokerage' means any remuneration originating from insurance broking business.

PART III

CERTIFICATE BY OR ON BEHALF OF THE INSURANCE BROKER

When this Statement of Particulars is submitted in compliance with rule 10 of the Rules the insurance broker shall certify in the following terms:

*for sole proprietors — *I, ... being the insurance broker, hereby certify to the best of my knowledge and belief that:

OR

*For partnerships — *I, ... being one of the persons carrying on the business of the insurance broker in partnership and being duly authorised on behalf of all such persons hereby certify to the best of the knowledge and belief of, and on behalf of, all such persons that:

OR

*For bodies corporate — *I, ... being a registered broker and a director of the insurance broker and being duly authorised hereby certify, on behalf of the insurance broker, to the best of my knowledge and belief that:

(i) the information contained in this Statement of Particulars is correct;

(ii) except as disclosed to the Council in writing, the provisions of rules 3, 4, 5, 6 and 7 of the Insurance Brokers Registration Council (Accounts and Business Requirements) Rules 1979 were satisfied at all times during the period referred to in paragraph 1 of Part I of this Statement of Particulars other than in respect of any period prior to registration or enrolment.

*(*delete whichever is not applicable)*

When this Statement of Particulars is submitted in circumstances other than in compliance with rule 10 of the Rules the insurance broker shall certify in the following terms:

*For sole proprietors — *I, ... being the insurance broker, hereby certify to the best of my knowledge and belief that:

OR

*For partnerships — *I, ... being one of the persons carrying on the business of the insurance broker in partnership and being duly authorised on behalf of all such persons hereby certify to the best of the knowledge and belief of, and on behalf of, all such persons that:

OR

*For bodies corporate

*I, ... being a registered insurance broker and a director of the insurance broker and being duly authorised hereby certify, on behalf of the insurance broker, to the best of my knowledge and belief that:

(i) the information contained in this Statement of Particulars is correct;

(ii) except as disclosed to the Council in writing, the provisions of rules 3, 4, 5, 6 and 7 of the Insurance Brokers Registration Council (Accounts and Business Requirements) Rules 1979 were satisfied as at the accounting date referred to in paragraph 2(i) of Part I of this Statement of Particulars and at all times up to such date since the later of registration or enrolment or the date as at which the last accounts submitted to the Council under rule 8 of the said Rules were drawn up.

*(*delete whichever is not applicable)*

Date.................. Signature..............................

PART IV

ACCOUNTANT'S REPORT

to the Insurance Brokers Registration Council in respect of this Statement of Particulars.

This report must be given by an accountant qualified in accordance with the provisions of sub-sections (4), (5) and (6) of section 11 of the Insurance Brokers (Registration) Act 1977.

When this Statement of Particulars is submitted in compliance with rule 10 of the Insurance Brokers Registration Council (Accounts and Business Requirements) Rules 1979 the accountant shall report in the following terms (setting out any qualifications or reservations in a separate letter to be attached):

1. I/We have examined the accounting records of .... for the period ended .... 19...... being the period referred to in paragraph 1 of Part I of this Statement of Particulars.

2. In my/our opinion:
   (*a*) there were no material breaches of rules 6 and 7 of the Insurance Brokers Registration Council (Accounts and Business Requirements) Rules 1979 during the period referred to in paragraph 1 of this report;
   (*b*) the amounts shown in column 1 of paragraph 2 of Part I of this Statement of Particulars have been extracted from the audited balance sheet and have been analysed in accordance with the definitions and instructions applying to the said paragraph 2 of Part I;
   (*c*) the amounts shown in column 2 of the said paragraph 2 of Part I have been stated in accordance with the said definitions and instructions;
   (*d*) the information set out in paragraph 3, 4 and 5 of Part I and paragraphs 1 and 2 of Part II of this Statement of Particulars has been fairly stated.

3. I/We have inspected, in respect of each Insurance Broking Account maintained at any time during the period referred to in paragraph 1 of this report, a written acknowledgment from bankers in accordance with the provisions of paragraph (2) of rule 6 of the Insurance Brokers Registration Council (Accounts and Business Requirements) Rules 1979 and have received confirmation from such bankers that the terms of such acknowledgment were in force during the period referred to in paragraph 1 of this report.

When this Statement of Particulars is submitted in circumstances other than in compliance with rule 10 of the Insurance Brokers Registration Council (Accounts and Business Requirements) Rules 1979 the accountant shall report in the following terms (setting out any qualifications or reservations in a separate letter to be attached):

1. I/We have examined the financial statement as at .... 19...... of .... (referred to herein as 'the insurance broker') set out in paragraph 2 of Part I of this Statement of Particulars.

2. In my/our opinion the amounts shown in column 1 of the said paragraph 2 of Part I have been extracted from the accounting records of the insurance broker as at that date and analysed and restated in column 2 in accordance with the definitions and instructions applying to the said paragraph 2 of Part I. No audit of the financial statement has been carried out.

3. I/We have verified by appropriate procedures, the cash, bank balances, investments and fixed assets shown in column 2 of the said paragraph 2 of Part I. I/We have reviewed the amounts shown therein as debtors without conducting an audit.

4. I/We have discussed with the insurance broker the amounts of assets not verified and of liabilities included in columns 1 and 2 of the said paragraph 2 of Part I and, after appropriate enquiry, am/are of the opinion that the figures in the said paragraph 2 of Part I are consistent with the information and explanations given to me/us.

Signed.............................Date......................

Name and address of practice (in block letters):...

....

Note: It is the Council's policy to issue an acknowledgment of the Statement of Particulars to the accountant signing the above.

INSURANCE BROKERS REGISTRATION COUNCIL ELECTION SCHEME APPROVAL ORDER 1980

(SI 1980/62)

1. This Order may be cited as the Insurance Brokers Registration Council Election Scheme Approval Order 1980 and shall come into operation on 1st March 1980.

2. The Insurance Brokers Registration Council Election Scheme 1979, as made by the Insurance Brokers Registration Council in exercise of their powers under paragraph 2(2)(*a*) of the Schedule to the Insurance Brokers (Registration) Act 1977 and as set out in the Schedule to this Order, is hereby approved.

SCHEDULE

THE INSURANCE BROKERS REGISTRATION COUNCIL ELECTION SCHEME 1979

The Insurance Brokers Registration Council, in exercise of their powers under paragraph 2(2)(*a*) of the Schedule to the Insurance Brokers (Registration) Act 1977, hereby make the following Scheme:

PART I

Preliminary

1. This Scheme may be cited as the Insurance Brokers Registration Council Election Scheme 1979.

2.—(1) In this Scheme, unless the context otherwise requires:—

'the Act' means the Insurance Brokers (Registration) Act 1977;

'county' and 'Greater London' have the meanings respectively assigned to them by the Local Government Act 1972 and the London Government Act 1963;

'the registered address' means the address entered in the register in respect of a registered insurance broker or such other address as may be notified from time to time to the Registrar in accordance with paragraph 9 of this Scheme.

(2) A document is published in accordance with the requirements of this Scheme, and information is published for the purposes of paragraphs 8, 15 and 24 of this Scheme, if a copy of such document or a notice containing such information:—

- (*a*) is sent to at least two organisations representing the interests of registered insurance brokers and to at least two newspapers or periodicals which give special attention to insurance matters;
- (*b*) is made available for inspection at the address specified under paragraph 8(2) of this Scheme; and
- (*c*) is sent to any person on request.

(3) Any notice or other document authorised or required to be given or sent to a registered insurance broker under this Scheme shall be sent to his address entered in the register.

3. The requirements in paragraphs 10, 13, 20, 26 and 28 of this Scheme that documents conveying respectively nominations, withdrawals of candidates, votes, returns and protests shall be received by days fixed under any of those paragraphs mean that such documents shall be valid only if delivered to or received by post at the address specified under paragraph 8(2) of this Scheme not later than 5.00 p.m. on the day fixed for the purpose:

Provided that the Returning Officer shall accept as valid any such document sent through the post and received at the appropriate address after 5.00 p.m. on the day fixed for the purpose, or by first post on the following day, if he is satisfied by examination of the post-mark, or otherwise, that it was posted on a day preceding the day fixed for the purpose, at such time that it would normally have been received not later than that day.

PART II

National Members and Constituency Members

4. For the purpose of choosing twelve persons to be members of the Council representing registered insurance brokers:—

- (*a*) one person shall be elected in accordance with this Scheme for each of the six constituencies listed in paragraph 5 of this Scheme to represent all registered insurance brokers whose registered addresses are within that constituency (each such member being referred to in this Scheme as 'a constituency member'); and
- (*b*) six persons shall be elected in accordance with this Scheme to represent all registered insurance brokers (each such member being referred to in this Scheme as 'a national member').

5. For the purposes of the election of the constituency members the six constituencies shall be:—

- (*a*) 'Central Constituency' consisting of Northern Ireland; together with the counties of Clwyd, Gwynedd, Powys, Cheshire, Greater Manchester, Hereford and Worcester, Lancashire, Merseyside, Salop, Staffordshire, Warwickshire and West Midlands.
- (*b*) 'Eastern Constituency' consisting of the counties of Bedfordshire, Cambridgeshire, Derbyshire, Leicestershire, Lincolnshire, Norfolk, Northamptonshire, Nottinghamshire and Suffolk.

(*c*) 'Metropolitan Constituency' consisting of Greater London and all parts of the world outside the United Kingdom.

(*d*) 'Northern Constituency' consisting of Scotland; together with the counties of Cleveland, Cumbria, Durham, Humberside, Northumberland, Tyne and Wear, North Yorkshire and West Yorkshire.

(*e*) 'South Eastern Constituency' consisting of the counties of Berkshire, Buckinghamshire, Essex, Hertfordshire, Kent and Surrey.

(*f*) 'South Western Constituency' consisting of the counties of Dyfed, Mid Glamorgan, South Glamorgan, West Glamorgan, Gwent, Avon, Cornwall, Devon, Dorset, Gloucestershire, Hampshire, Isle of Wight, Oxfordshire, Somerset, East Sussex, West Sussex and Wiltshire.

6.—(1) The persons chosen in the first instance to represent registered insurance brokers pursuant to paragraph 2(1) of the Schedule to the Act shall retire with effect on and from 30th November 1981.

(2) (*a*) Prior to 30th November 1981 the Council shall cause elections to be held in accordance with this Scheme for the election of six constituency members and six national members to hold office subject to paragraph 32 of this Schedule on and from 1st December 1981.

(*b*) Thereafter the Council shall cause elections to be held from time to time in accordance with this Scheme for the election of constituency members or national members (as appropriate) to fill vacancies arising in the membership of the Council.

(3) A member of the Council elected under this Scheme shall forthwith cease to hold office or shall forthwith be disqualified from taking up office after election if, as the case may be:—

(*a*) he ceases to be a registered insurance broker; or

(*b*) he abstains without the consent of the Council from attending the meetings of the Council for a period of 90 consecutive days, from the date of the first meeting of the Council which he has failed to attend; or

(*c*) he is adjudged bankrupt or makes any arrangement or composition with his creditors; or

(*d*) he is a person to whom apply the powers and provisions of Part VIII of the Mental Health Act 1959, relating to management and administration or any statutory modification or amendment thereof.

(4) Subject as aforesaid and to the provisions of sub-paragraph (5) of this paragraph the term of office of all national members and constituency members shall be four years provided that the national members elected on and from the 1st December 1981 shall retire on and from the 30th November 1983.

(5) In the event of a casual vacancy occurring amongst the members of the Council elected in accordance with this Scheme at a date earlier than twelve months from the due date of retirement from the Council of the member in question a separate election in accordance with this Scheme (as if the vacancy fell within paragraph 24 hereof) shall be held forthwith to elect a person to fill that vacancy such person to hold office during the remainder of the term of office of the person whose vacancy he has filled.

PART III

Returning Officer

7.—(1) Not less than six months before the date on which all or any of the members of the Council for the time being chosen to represent registered insurance brokers are due to retire the Council shall appoint a Returning Officer for the election of persons to represent registered insurance brokers in succession to such members and a Deputy

Returning Officer entitled to carry out the functions of the Returning Officer at such times as he is absent or unable to act.

(2) The Council shall also similarly forthwith appoint a Returning Officer and Deputy Returning Officer for an election of any person to fill a casual vacancy arising under the provisions of paragraph 6(5) of this Scheme.

(3) Any person (including the Registrar) except a member of the Council shall be eligible to be appointed as Returning Officer or Deputy Returning Officer.

(4) A Returning Officer or Deputy Returning Officer appointed under this Scheme shall cease to hold office when the election for which he is appointed (including any further election held under paragraph 24 of this Scheme) has been completed, and if either of them should previously resign his office or die or be unable to act the Council may appoint another person in his place.

8.—(1) Not less than five months before the date on which all or any of the members of the Council for the time being chosen to represent registered insurance brokers are due to retire the Returning Officer shall fix a nomination day and shall publish the date he has fixed for this purpose.

(2) Not less than 21 days before the nomination date thus fixed and published the Returning Officer shall send in the case of an election of constituency members to all registered insurance brokers whose registered addresses are in the constituency and in the case of an election of national members to all registered insurance brokers a notice as appropriate in the form set out in either Appendix A or Appendix B to this Scheme, specifying the address to which all nomination forms are to be returned, and the date of the nomination day, accompanied by a nomination paper as appropriate in the form set out in Appendix C or Appendix D to this Scheme.

9.—(1) Whenever a fee is paid to the Council under rules made under Section 8 of the Act any person, other than a practising insurance broker, shall be entitled for the purposes of this Scheme to notify the Registrar, or to revoke such notification or give a further notification, on the appropriate form of the address in the United Kingdom which is that person's principal place of business in relation to insurance broking.

(2) On such notification being received by the Registrar that person shall for the purposes of nominating candidates for an election, standing as a candidate at an election and voting in an election be deemed to have a registered address within the constituency in which the address so notified is situate and none other.

(3) No notification or revocation given under the provisions of this paragraph after a nomination day has been fixed and published under paragraph 8(1) of this Scheme and during the period of an election under this Scheme shall take effect until after the completion of such election.

PART IV

Nominations

10.—(1) (*a*) A candidate for election as a constituency member shall be nominated specifically for one of the constituencies specified in paragraph 5 of this Scheme.

(*b*) Such a candidate shall be nominated in writing by not less than six registered insurance brokers whose registered addresses are in the constituency for which the candidate is nominated.

(2) A candidate for election as a national member shall be nominated in writing by not less than six registered insurance brokers.

(3) A nomination shall be valid only if received by the nomination day and made on the appropriate form set out in Appendix C or Appendix D to this Scheme and signed by the person or persons nominating the candidate.

(4) The nominations may be comprised in more than one form but every form shall

include a statement signed by the candidate identifying himself and confirming his willingness and qualification to stand as a candidate.

11.—(1) A registered insurance broker may nominate only one candidate for election as the constituency member for the constituency in which his registered address is situate but may nominate howsoever many candidates for election as national members as there are national members to be elected at the election in question.

(2) If a registered insurance broker purports to nominate more candidates than he is entitled to do his signature shall be valid only on the form first received by the Returning Officer or, if he is entitled to nominate more than one candidate on the first forms (and the first completed nomination on such forms) containing such number of nominations as he is entitled to make which are so received. When two or more forms are received simultaneously at the address specified by the Returning Officer under paragraph 8(2) of this Scheme they shall be deemed for the purposes of this sub-paragraph to have been received by the Returning Officer in the order in which he in fact sees them.

12. A person may only be nominated as a candidate for election as a person to represent registered insurance brokers if he is himself a registered insurance broker and has not within a period of 5 years ending on the nomination day fixed and published under paragraph 8(1) of this Scheme been adjudged bankrupt or made any arrangement or composition with his creditors:

Provided that a candidate for election as a constituency member may be nominated only for the constituency in which his registered address is situate.

13. A candidate may withdraw his candidature by notice in writing signed by him and received by the Returning Officer by the nomination day, and in that event the nomination of that candidate shall be disregarded for the purposes of Parts V to IX of this Scheme.

PART V

Elections

14. If after the expiration of the time allowed under this Scheme for nominations of candidates:—

(*a*) no more candidates have been nominated than there are vacancies to be filled, the Returning Officer shall forthwith declare the candidates so nominated to have been elected to fill those vacancies;

(*b*) two or more candidates have been nominated in relation to any constituency, or more candidates have been nominated in relation to the election of national members than there are such vacancies, the Returning Officer shall cause a poll to be held.

15.—(1) When a poll is necessary the Returning Officer shall fix a polling day and shall publish:—

(*a*) the date thereof, which shall be not less than 21 days later than the date of such publication and shall be a date preceding the day on which the relevant members of the Council are due to retire;

(*b*) the names, and in the case of constituency elections the registered addresses (and the addresses contained in the register if different), of all candidates;

(*c*) subject as provided in the next following sub-paragraph, the names and, in the case of constituency elections the registered addresses (and the addresses contained in the register if different), of registered insurance brokers nominating each candidate; and

(*d*) in respect of each candidate and each person nominating such candidate:—

(i) the names of all enrolled bodies corporate of which they are directors;

(ii) all business names under which they or a partnership of which they are members carry on business as insurance brokers;

(iii) the names of all enrolled bodies corporate by which they are employed or in whose businesses they are engaged;

(iv) if they are employed or engaged as an insurance broker by a registered insurance broker or a partnership of which a registered insurance broker or an enrolled body corporate is a member the name of the registered insurance broker or the partnership and any other business name under which such business is carried on.

(2) If the Returning Officer receives more than six nominations in relation to any one candidate, he shall invite the candidate to state which six nominations should be published in connection with the candidature.

(3) If the Returning Officer cannot obtain within four days such a statement from the candidate, he shall publish in connection with the candidature the six nominations earliest received, or where several nominations are on one form, those first mentioned therein.

(4) For the purposes of the foregoing sub-paragraph the provisions of paragraph 11(2) of this Scheme shall apply where necessary for determining the order of time in which nominations shall be deemed to have been received by the Returning Officer.

(5) The Returning Officer shall send a copy of this Scheme to each person nominated as a candidate, and shall draw attention to paragraphs 17, 25, 26 and 27 of this Scheme, which relate respectively to the publicity available to the Returning Officer, the restrictions on expenditure, the statutory declaration which candidates are required to make and the restrictions on electioneering.

16.—(1) On a poll to elect a constituency member every registered insurance broker whose registered address is in that constituency shall be entitled to vote only for one candidate.

(2) On a poll to elect a person or persons as a national member or national members every registered insurance broker shall be entitled to vote for that number of candidates as there are vacancies to be filled.

PART VI

Conduct of Polls

17.—(1) Where a poll is to be held the Returning Officer shall as soon as may be after nomination day invite each candidate to supply within seven days particulars of his age, qualifications and career and an election address in a statement of not more than three hundred words in all.

(2) Subject to the provisions of this paragraph such statement shall be printed at the cost of the Council and sent along with the voting papers issued under paragraph 19 of this Scheme to all registered insurance brokers eligible to vote for the candidate.

(3) Nothing in this paragraph shall require the Returning Officer to issue a statement of a length greater than that specified in this paragraph or to issue anything which in his opinion is or may be libellous or scandalous or untrue on matters of fact.

(4) Every candidate who supplies such a statement shall be deemed to have agreed:—

(*a*) that the decision of the Returning Officer not to issue the same or any part thereof shall be final; and

(*b*) to indemnify the Returning Officer, the Deputy Returning Officer and the Council against any liability to any third party which they may incur by reason of issuing the same or any part thereof.

18.—(1) Where a poll is to be held the Returning Officer shall prepare voting papers and lists of candidates and nominators and Declarations of Identity together with inner and outer envelopes for them.

(2) The outer envelopes shall be addressed to the Returning Officer at the address specified under paragraph 8(2) of this Scheme.

(3) The Declarations of Identity shall be in the appropriate form set out in Appendix E to this Scheme.

(4) Where a poll is for the election of constituency members voting papers shall be in the form set out in Appendix F and lists of candidates and nominators shall be in the form set out in Appendix G to this Scheme; and where the poll is for the election of national members the voting papers shall be in the form set out in Appendix H and the lists of candidates and nominators shall be in the form set out in Appendix I to this Scheme.

19.—(1) The Returning Officer shall at least eight days before the polling day send to each registered insurance broker entitled to vote in the poll (but not to any registered insurance broker who has informed him in writing that on grounds of conscience he does not wish to be so entitled) a voting paper, a list of candidates and nominators, an inner envelope, an outer envelope and an appropriate form of Declaration of Identity prepared in accordance with the provisions of this Scheme along with any statements which he is required to issue under paragraph 17 of this Scheme.

(2) Each registered insurance broker entitled to vote in the poll shall be entitled to receive one voting paper, one inner envelope and one outer envelope, and no more, and votes shall not be valid unless made upon a voting paper received from the Returning Officer and in accordance with the requirements of this Scheme:

Provided that the Returning Officer may replace a voting paper or an envelope inadvertently spoiled if application is made to him for this purpose on or before the polling day.

20. Votes shall be cast as follows:—

(*a*) The voter shall record his vote or votes on the voting paper in accordance with the instructions thereon.

(*b*) The voter shall enclose the voting paper in the inner envelope, seal such envelope without making any distinguishing mark, complete the Declaration of Identity and enclose in the outer envelope the Declaration of Identity and the inner envelope containing the voting paper.

(*c*) The voter shall return the outer envelope and its contents to the address given on the envelope so that it is received there by polling day.

21.—(1) Immediately after the polling day the Returning Officer shall:—

(*a*) ascertain the validity of the votes by examination of the Declarations of Identity in the outer envelopes;

(*b*) when the Declarations are in order withdraw the inner envelopes from the outer envelopes and, without opening or marking them, collect them in some place away from the outer envelopes;

(*c*) withdraw the voting papers from the inner envelopes; and

(*d*) count the votes validly cast for each candidate.

(2) For the purposes of this paragraph a vote shall be deemed to have been validly cast if, but only if, it has been cast in accordance with paragraph 20 of this Scheme.

22. If in any poll the same number of votes is cast for each of two or more candidates, the Returning Officer shall, where necessary to decide the result of the election, determine by lot which of the candidates shall be deemed to have obtained the highest or the next highest number of votes for the purposes of this Scheme.

PART VII

Declaration of Election

23.—(1) When the Returning Officer declares the result of an election, he shall certify in writing:—

(*a*) the name of each person elected to be a national member or constituency member (as appropriate) and, in the case of a constituency member, the constituency in respect of which he was elected;

(*b*) if a poll has been held, the names of all other candidates, and the number of votes cast respectively for the persons elected and for every other candidate.

(2) The Returning Officer shall publish his certificate and shall forthwith send a copy of the same to all candidates named therein and to all members of the Council, and shall submit the certificate to the Council at their next meeting.

24.—(1) If:—

(*a*) after the nomination day a candidate dies or becomes disqualified from being a candidate before an election has taken place in respect of the vacancy for which he has been nominated;

(*b*) a candidate who has been elected dies, resigns or becomes disqualified from taking up office as a member of the Council before the date upon which the members for the time being chosen to represent registered insurance brokers shall have retired; or

(*c*) after an election has taken place in accordance with the foregoing provisions of this Scheme there remains any vacancy unfilled due to an insufficiency of nominations or the withdrawal of candidates or any other cause;

the Returning Officer shall in respect only of the vacancy for which the deceased or resigning or disqualified candidate was nominated or which remains unfilled as a result of such death or other cause (as the case may be) cause a further election to be held as soon as practicable and for that purpose shall forthwith fix another nomination date and publish the date thereof, and thereafter if necessary fix another polling day and publish the date thereof, and shall proceed with the further election in accordance with the foregoing provisions of this Scheme with such modifications only as the circumstances may require:

Provided that the death, resignation or disqualification of a candidate shall not affect the validity of the nomination of another candidate and any such nomination duly made in respect of the first election shall, (subject to the provisions of paragraph 30 of this Scheme) be deemed to be a valid nomination for a further election for the same vacancy held pursuant to this paragraph.

(2) For the purpose of this Scheme a candidate shall forthwith become disqualified from being a candidate if:—

(*a*) he ceases to be a registered insurance broker; or

(*b*) he is adjudged bankrupt or makes any arrangement or composition with his creditors; or

(*c*) he is a person to whom apply the powers and provisions of Part VIII of the Mental Health Act 1959, relating to management and administration or any statutory modification or amendment thereof.

PART VIII

Expenses of Candidates

25.—(1) Other than expenditure incurred on his behalf by the Council under paragraph 17(2) of this Scheme no sum shall be paid and no expenditure shall be incurred by or on behalf of a candidate either before, during or after an election, on account of or in respect of the conduct or management of, or in connection with, the election.

(2) No expenditure shall, with a view to promoting or procuring the election of a candidate at an election, be incurred by any other person, whether before, during or after an election.

26. Not later than the fourteenth day after declaration of the result of an election, every candidate declared to have been elected shall furnish to the Returning Officer a statutory declaration in the form specified in Appendix J to this Scheme.

27.—(1) No person shall by word, message, writing or in any other manner, endeavour to persuade any person to give, or dissuade any person from giving, his vote for a particular candidate at an election.

(2) No person shall, for the purpose of affecting the return of any candidate at an election, make or publish any statement or fact in relation to a candidate or nominator.

(3) No person shall, with intent to influence persons to give or refrain from giving their votes for a particular candidate, use, or aid, abet, counsel or procure the use of, any television or other wireless transmitting station for the transmission of any matter having reference to the election.

(4) No person shall make a payment, or enter into a contract for a payment, for the purpose of promoting or procuring the election of a candidate at an election on account of the exhibition of, or the use of any house, land, building or premises for the exhibition of, any address, bill or notice.

(5) No person shall for the purpose of promoting or procuring the election of a candidate:—

- (*a*) print, publish or distribute, or cause to be printed, published or distributed, any bill, placard, poster or document having reference to an election; or
- (*b*) post, or cause to be posted, any such bill, placard, poster or document as aforesaid.

(6) No person shall hold, or procure to be held, a public or private meeting for the purpose of promoting or procuring the election of any candidate.

(7) No person shall canvass the support of any other person for the purpose of promoting or procuring the election of any candidate.

PART IX

Validity of Election

28. The certificate of the Returning Officer published under paragraph 23 of this Scheme shall be conclusive evidence of the facts stated therein unless in respect of the election of any person a written notice of protest signed by not less than twenty-five registered insurance brokers eligible to vote in the election of the person in question is received by the Returning Officer not later than the twenty-eighth day after the publication of the certificate. Such protest may be made on one or more of the following grounds:—

- (*a*) that the election of that person was not in accordance with the requirements of this Scheme;
- (*b*) that there was a breach of any of the provisions of paragraphs 25(2) or 27 of this Scheme in connection with the election;
- (*c*) that the election of that person was furthered by conduct which in the case of an election regulated by the Representation of the People Act 1949 would be a corrupt practice by way of bribery, treating or undue influence under Sections 99, 100 and 101 of that Act (which are reproduced as Appendix K to this Scheme);
- (*d*) that the person elected, or a person acting on his behalf, contravened the requirements of paragraph 25(1) of this Scheme, or did not comply with the requirements of paragraph 26 of this Scheme.

29. If any candidate declared to have been elected fails to submit a statutory declaration in accordance with the requirements of paragraph 26 of this Scheme the Returning Officer shall forthwith make a report on the matter to the Council and shall send a copy thereof to every person entitled to receive a copy of his certificate under paragraph 23 of this Scheme.

30.—(1) Any protest under paragraph 28 of this Scheme, or any report by the Returning Officer under paragraph 29 of this Scheme, shall be considered by the Council at their next meeting.

(2) The Council shall afford the person concerned an opportunity of making a reply in writing to the protest or the report, and may if they think fit hear oral statements from representatives of the persons signing the protest, from the Returning Officer and from any other persons concerned.

(3) If the Council are satisfied:

(*a*) that the election of the person concerned was furthered by such conduct as is described in paragraph 28(*c*) of this Scheme; or

(*b*) that expenditure was incurred by him or on his behalf in the conduct or management of the election; or

(*c*) that his election was in some other respect not in accordance with the requirements of this Scheme; or

(*d*) that he has failed to furnish a statutory declaration as required by paragraph 26 of this Scheme; or

(*e*) that there was a breach of any of the provisions of paragraphs 25(2) or 27 of this Scheme;

then (unless, in the case of (*c*), it appears to the Council that the election was conducted substantially in accordance with the requirements of this Scheme and that non-compliance with those requirements did not affect the result or unless, in the case of (*e*), it appears to the Council that the breach of any of the provisions of the said paragraphs 25(2) or 27 did not affect the result) the Council may declare that person's election invalid, and in that event the resulting vacancy shall be filled by a further election as provided by paragraph 24 of this Scheme.

(4) If the Council declare the election of any person invalid they shall forthwith proceed to consider whether in the circumstances of the case they should also declare that person or any other person to be disqualified from being nominated as a candidate in such further election, and if they declare him or any such person so disqualified any nomination of that person shall be rejected as invalid by the Returning Officer.

31. Any declaration made by the Council under paragraph 30(4) of this Scheme shall be published and shall be binding upon all persons.

32. A person elected under this Scheme shall notwithstanding paragraph 6 hereof not come into office immediately after the expiration of the term of office of the members previously chosen to represent registered insurance brokers if that person is the subject of any protest made under paragraph 28 of this Scheme or of any report made under paragraph 29 of this Scheme and such persons shall not come into office unless and until such protest or report shall have been considered and disposed of by the Council.

APPENDICES

APPENDIX A

(See paragraph 8(2))

THE INSURANCE BROKERS REGISTRATION COUNCIL ELECTION SCHEME 1979

Form of the Notice of Election required under paragraph 8 of the Election Scheme.

..............CONSTITUENCY

(Central, Eastern, Metropolitan, Northern, South Eastern or South Western, as the case may be.)

1. Notice is hereby given that an election is about to be held of one member of the Insurance Brokers Registration Council to represent registered insurance brokers whose registered addresses* are within the above constituency.

2. Candidates for election as constituency members must be nominated by 6 registered insurance brokers whose registered addresses* are within the constituency for which they are seeking to nominate. All nominations must be made in a nomination paper in the form enclosed herewith. The form states the full requirements of the Election Scheme with regard to nominations. I will supply further forms on request.
3. A candidate for election as a constituency member must have his registered address* in the constituency for which he is standing.
4. If a poll is necessary it will be held in the month of .... A registered insurance broker will be entitled to vote only for one candidate for election as a member for the constituency in which his registered address* is situated.
5. Nominations must reach me at: ....

.... by ....

Dated............................

............................Returning Officer

*Note: 'the registered address' means the address entered in the register in respect of the registered insurance broker or, until such notification is revoked, such other address as may be notified from time to time to the Registrar in accordance with paragraph 9 of the Election Scheme.

APPENDIX B

(See paragraph 8(2))

THE INSURANCE BROKERS REGISTRATION COUNCIL ELECTION SCHEME 1979

Form of the Notice of Election required under paragraph 8 of the Election Scheme.

1. Notice is hereby given that an election is about to be held of [a] member(s) of the Insurance Brokers Registration Council to represent registered insurance brokers.
2. Candidates for election as national members must be nominated by 6 registered insurance brokers. All nominations must be made in a nomination paper in the form enclosed herewith. The form states the full requirements of the Election Scheme with regard to nominations. I will supply further forms on request.
3. If a poll is necessary it will be held in the month of .... A registered insurance broker will be entitled to vote for [a] candidate(s) being the number of vacancies amongst the national members as set out in paragraph 1.
4. Nominations must reach me at: ....

.... by............................

Dated..........................

.... Returning Officer

[a] Insert number of vacancies.

APPENDIX C

(See paragraph 8(2))

THE INSURANCE BROKERS REGISTRATION COUNCIL ELECTION SCHEME 1979

Form of Nomination Paper for Candidates for election as constituency members.

.... CONSTITUENCY

(Central, Eastern, Metropolitan, Northern, South Eastern or South Western, as the case may be.)

PART I

WE, the undersigned, being registered insurance brokers whose registered addresses (see Note 1) are in the constituency mentioned above, hereby nominate............................ .... for election to the Insurance Brokers Registration Council to represent registered insurance brokers in the said constituency.

Name of Nominator	No. in register	Registered Address (see Note 1)	Particulars of directorships, businesses and employment (see Note 2)	Signature of Nominator

Six signatures are required and the candidate must sign each form on which signatures are submitted.

PART II

I hereby declare that I am the person nominated in this form, that I consent to be so nominated and that I will accept office if I am duly elected; and that I am a registered insurance broker qualified to be a candidate for membership of the Council and my registered address (see Note 1) is in the constituency mentioned above.

Signature of Nominated Candidate	No. in register	Registered Address (see Note 1)	Particulars of directorships, businesses and employment (see Note 2)

NOTES:—

1. 'the registered address' means the address entered in the register in respect of the registered insurance broker or, until such notification is revoked, such other address as may be notified from time to time to the Registrar in accordance with paragraph 9 of the Election Scheme.

2. The following information is required to be given in respect of each candidate and each person nominating such candidate:

(i) the names of all enrolled bodies corporate of which they are directors;

(ii) all business names under which they or a partnership of which they are members carry on business as insurance brokers;

(iii) the names of all enrolled bodies corporate by which they are employed or in whose businesses they are engaged;

(iv) if they are employed or engaged as an insurance broker by a registered insurance broker or a partnership of which a registered insurance broker or an enrolled body corporate is a member the name of the registered insurance broker or the partnership and any other business name under which such business is carried on.

PLEASE USE SEPARATE SHEETS IF NECESSARY

3. A person may only be nominated if he is a registered insurance broker having a registered address (see Note 1) in the constituency and has not within a period of five years ending on the nomination day fixed and published under paragraph 8(1) of this Scheme been adjudged bankrupt or made any arrangement or composition with his creditors.

4. Nominations are valid only if made in this form and if received at .... by 5.00 p.m. on .... except where the Returning Officer is satisfied that a nomination paper received by post not later than the first post on .... was posted on a day at such a time that it would normally have been received not later than ....

5. A registered insurance broker may only nominate one candidate in respect of the constituency in which his registered address is situated. His signature will therefore only be valid on the nomination paper first received.

6. The constituencies consist of the following areas:—

(*a*) 'Central Constituency' consisting of Northern Ireland; together with the counties of Clywd, Gwynedd, Powys, Cheshire, Greater Manchester, Hereford and Worcester, Lancashire, Merseyside, Salop, Staffordshire, Warwickshire and West Midlands.

(*b*) 'Eastern Constituency' consisting of the counties of Bedfordshire, Cambridgeshire, Derbyshire, Leicestershire, Lincolnshire, Norfolk, Northamptonshire, Nottinghamshire and Suffolk.

(*c*) 'Metropolitan Constituency' consisting of Greater London and all parts of the world outside the United Kingdom.

(*d*) 'Northern Constituency' consisting of Scotland; together with the counties of Cleveland, Cumbria, Durham, Humberside, Northumberland, Tyne and Wear, North Yorkshire and West Yorkshire.

(*e*) 'South Eastern Constituency' consisting of the counties of Berkshire, Buckinghamshire, Essex, Hertfordshire, Kent and Surrey.

(*f*) 'South Western Constituency' consisting of the counties of Dyfedd, Mid Glamorgan, South Glamorgan, West Glamorgan, Gwent, Avon, Cornwall, Devon, Dorset, Gloucestershire, Hampshire, Isle of Wight, Oxfordshire, Somerset, East Sussex, West Sussex and Wiltshire.

APPENDIX D

(See paragraph 8(2))

THE INSURANCE BROKERS REGISTRATION COUNCIL ELECTION SCHEME 1979

Form of Nomination Paper for Candidates for election as national members.

PART I

We, the undersigned, being registered insurance brokers hereby nominate .... for election to the Insurance Brokers Registration Council to represent registered insurance brokers.

Name of Nominator	No. in register	Particulars of directorships, businesses and employment (see Note 1)	Signature of Nominator

Six signatures are required, and the candidate must sign each form on which signatures are submitted.

PART II

I hereby declare that I am the person nominated in this form, that I consent to be so nominated, that I will accept office if I am duly elected and that I am a registered insurance broker qualified to be a candidate for membership of the Council.

Signature of Nominated Candidate	No. in register	Particulars of directorships, businesses and employment (See Note 1)

NOTES:—

1. The following information is required to be given in respect of each candidate and each person nominating such candidate:—

   (i) the names of all enrolled bodies corporate of which they are directors;

(ii) all business names under which they or a partnership of which they are members carry on business as insurance brokers;

(iii) the names of all enrolled bodies corporate by which they are employed or in whose businesses they are engaged;

(iv) if they are employed or engaged as an insurance broker by a registered insurance broker or a partnership of which a registered insurance broker or an enrolled body corporate is a member the name of the registered insurance broker or the partnership and any other business name under which such business is carried on.

PLEASE USE SEPARATE SHEETS IF NECESSARY

2. A person may only be nominated if he is a registered insurance broker and has not within a period of five years ending on the nomination day fixed and published under paragraph 8(1) of this Scheme been adjudged bankrupt or made any arrangement or composition with his creditors.

3. Nominations are valid only if made in this form and if received at .... by 5.00 p.m. on .... except where the Returning Officer is satisfied that a nomination paper received by post not later than the first post on .... was posted on a day at such a time that it would normally have been received not later than ....

4. A registered insurance broker may join in nominating not more candidates than there are vacancies to be filled at the election. His signature will therefore only be valid on the first such number of nomination papers received.

APPENDIX E

(See paragraph 18(3))

Forms of Declaration of Identity under Part VI of the Scheme

1. In the case of a poll for the election of constituency members.
   '..............................Constituency (Central, Eastern, Metropolitan, Northern, South Eastern or South Western, as the case may be.)
   My name, ... (here insert *full* name in block capitals) is in the register and my registered address is in the above constituency.
   Signed............................. No. in register.............................'

2. In the case of a poll for the election of national members.
   'My name, ... (here insert *full* name in block capitals) is in the register.
   Signed.............................. No. in register.............................'

APPENDIX F

(See paragraph 18(4))

THE INSURANCE BROKERS REGISTRATION COUNCIL ELECTION SCHEME 1979

Form of Voting Paper for election of constituency member.

.... CONSTITUENCY

(Central, Eastern, Metropolitan, Northern, South Eastern or South Western, as the case may be.)

Instructions to Voters

1. Registered insurance brokers whose registered addresses (see Note) are in the constituency mentioned above are entitled to vote only for one candidate.

2. The voter must record his vote by putting a mark thus X against the name of one only of the candidates mentioned in this voting paper.

3. The voter must then put this voting paper in the envelope marked 'inner envelope', seal this envelope without making on it any distinguishing mark, complete the Declaration of Identity, put the 'inner envelope' and the Declaration in the 'outer envelope', seal this latter and take or send it with its contents to ....

4. If the 'outer envelope' and its contents is sent by post it must be stamped. It must reach .... by 5.00 p.m. on .... except where the Returning Officer is satisfied that a vote received by post not later than the first post on .... was posted on a day .... at such a time that it would normally have been received not later than.............................

5. Persons now elected hold office for 4 years from 1st December next.

Voting Paper

Names of candidates	Column for the voter's mark X

Note: 'the registered address' means the address entered in the register in respect of the registered insurance broker or, until such notification is revoked, such other address as may be notified from time to time to the Registrar in accordance with paragraph 9 of the Election Scheme.

APPENDIX G

(See paragraph 18(4))

Form of List of Candidates for election as constituency members and their nominators.

THE INSURANCE BROKERS REGISTRATION COUNCIL ELECTION SCHEME 1979

Election of constituency member in the .... Constituency (Central, Eastern, Metropolitan, Northern, South Eastern or South Western, as the case may be.)

List of Candidates and Nominators

Names and *registered addresses (and address in register if different) of candidates	Particulars of directorships, businesses and employment of candidates	Names and *registered addresses (and address in register if different) of nominators	Particulars of directorships, businesses and employment of nominators

*Note: 'the registered address' means the address entered in the register in respect of the registered insurance broker or, until such notification is revoked, such other address as may be notified from time to time to the Registrar in accordance with paragraph 9 of the Election Scheme.

APPENDIX H

(See paragraph 18(4))

Form of voting paper for election of national members.

THE INSURANCE BROKERS REGISTRATION COUNCIL ELECTION SCHEME 1979

Instructions to Voters

1. Registered insurance brokers are entitled to vote only for .... candidate(s).

[Insert the same number as there are vacancies to be filled at the election.]

2. The voter must record his vote by putting a mark thus X against the names of the number of candidates up to the maximum pursuant to paragraph 1 above given in the voting paper.

3. The voter must then put this voting paper in the envelope marked 'inner envelope', seal this envelope without making on it any distinguishing mark, complete the Declaration of Identity, put the 'inner envelope' and the Declaration in the 'outer envelope', seal this latter, and take or send it with its contents to ....

4. If the 'outer envelope' and its contents is sent by post it must be stamped. It must reach .... by 5.00 p.m. on .... except where the Returning Officer is satisfied that a vote received by post not later than the first post on .... was posted on a day at such a time that it would normally have been received not later than ....

5. Persons now elected hold office for four years (a) from 1st December next.

Voting Paper

Names of candidates	Column for the voter's mark X

(a) in the case of the first election of national members insert 'two years'.

APPENDIX I

(See paragraph 18(4))

Form of List of Candidates for election as national members and their nominators.

THE INSURANCE BROKERS REGISTRATION COUNCIL ELECTION SCHEME 1979

Election of national members.

List of Candidates and Nominators

Names of Candidates	Particulars of directorships, businesses and employment of candidate	Names of Nominators	Particulars of directorships, businesses and employment of nominators

APPENDIX J

(See paragraph 26)

Form of Statutory Declaration.

I, A.B., do solemnly and sincerely declare that I have paid no sum and incurred no expenditure either before, during or after the election, on account of or in respect of the conduct or management of, or in connection with, the election and, to the best of my knowledge and belief, no expenditure has, with a view to promoting or procuring my election as a candidate at the election, been incurred by any other person whether before, during or after the election; and to the best of my knowledge and belief no breach of the provisions of paragraph 27 of the Insurance Brokers Registration Council Election Scheme 1979 has been committed by me or any other person; and that I have not been a party to any bribery, treating or undue influence within the meaning of sections 99, 100 and 101 of the Representation of the People Act 1949; and I make this solemn declaration conscientiously believing the same to be true, and by virtue of the Statutory Declarations Act 1835.

APPENDIX K

(See paragraph 28)

Sections 99, 100 and 101 of the Representation of the People Act 1949.

Bribery, treating and undue influence

Section 99: Bribery

(1) A person shall be guilty of a corrupt practice if he is guilty of bribery.

(2) A person shall be guilty of bribery if he, directly or indirectly, by himself or by any other person on his behalf—

(*a*) gives any money or procures any office to or for any voter or to or for any other person on behalf of any voter or to or for any other person in order to induce any voter to vote or refrain from voting; or

(*b*) corruptly does any such act as aforesaid on account of any voter having voted or refrained from voting; or

(*c*) makes any such gift or procurement as aforesaid to or for any person in order to induce that person to procure, or endeavour to procure, the return of any person at an election or the vote of any voter;

or if upon or in consequence of any such gift or procurement as aforesaid he procures or engages, promises or endeavours to procure the return of any person at an election or the vote of any voter.

For the purposes of this subsection—

(i) references to giving money shall include references to giving, lending, agreeing to give or lend, offering, promising, or promising to procure or endeavour to procure any money or valuable consideration; and

(ii) references to procuring any office shall include references to giving, procuring, agreeing to give or procure, offering, promising, or promising to procure or to endeavour to procure any office, place or employment.

(3) A person shall be guilty of bribery if he advances or pays or causes to be paid any money to or to the use of any other person with the intent that that money or any part thereof shall be expended in bribery at any election or knowingly pays or causes to be paid any money to any person in discharge or repayment of any money wholly or in part expended in bribery at any election.

(4) The foregoing provisions of this section shall not extend or be construed to extend to any money paid or agreed to be paid for or on account of any legal expenses incurred in good faith at or concerning an election.

(5) A voter shall be guilty of bribery if before or during an election he directly or indirectly by himself or by any other person on his behalf receives, agrees, or contracts for any money, gift, loan or valuable consideration, office, place or employment for himself or for any other person for voting or agreeing to vote or for refraining or agreeing to refrain from voting.

(6) A person shall be guilty of bribery if after an election he directly or indirectly by himself or by any other person on his behalf, receives any money or valuable consideration on account of any person having voted or refrained from voting or having induced any other person to vote or refrain from voting.

(7) In this section the expression includes any person who has or claims to have a right to vote.

Section 100: Treating

(1) A person shall be guilty of a corrupt practice if he is guilty of treating.

(2) A person shall be guilty of treating if he corruptly, by himself or by any other person, either before, during or after an election, directly or indirectly gives or provides, or pays wholly or in part the expense of giving or providing, any meat, drink, entertainment or provision to or for any person—

(*a*) for the purpose of corruptly influencing that person or any other person to vote or refrain from voting; or

(*b*) on account of that person or any other person having voted or refrained from voting or being about to vote or refrain from voting.

(3) Every elector or proxy for an elector who corruptly accepts or takes any such meat, drink, entertainment or provision shall also be guilty of treating.

Section 101: Undue Influence

(1) A person shall be guilty of a corrupt practice if he is guilty of undue influence.

(2) A person shall be guilty of undue influence—

(*a*) if he, directly or indirectly, by himself or by any other person on his behalf, makes use of or threatens to make use of any force, violence or restraint, or inflicts or threatens to inflict, by himself or by any other person, any temporal or spiritual injury, damage, harm or loss upon or against any person in order to induce or compel that person to vote or refrain from voting; or on account of that person having voted or refrained from voting; or

(*b*) if, by abduction, duress of any fraudulent device or contrivance, he impedes or prevents the free exercise of the franchise of an elector or proxy for an elector, or thereby compels, induces or prevails upon an elector or proxy for an elector either to vote or to refrain from voting.

Index